Global Marketing

FIFTH EDITION

Warren J. Keegan

Lubin Graduate School of Business
Pace University—New York City and Westchester, New York

Mark C. Green

Department of Accounting, Economics, Management, and Marketing
Simpson College—Indianola, Iowa

PEARSON

Prentice Hall

Pearson Education International

Editor-in-Chief: David Parker
Product Development Manager: Ashley Santora
Project Manager, Editorial: Melissa Pellerano
Editorial Assistant: Christine Ietto
Assistant Editor, Media: Denise Vaughn
Media Project Manager: Lisa Rinaldi
Marketing Manager: Anne Howard
Marketing Assistant: Susan Osterlitz
Senior Managing Editor: Judy Leale
Project Manager, Production: Kelly Warsak
Manager, Rights & Permissions: Charles Morris
Senior Operations Supervisor: Arnold Vila
Art Director: Steve Frim
Interior Design: Michael Fruhbeis
Cover Design: Steve Firm
Cover Photo Brazil: Antonio Scorza/AFP/Getty Images
Cover Photo Russia: Alexander Nemenov/AFP/Getty Images, Inc.
Cover Photo India: Steve Raymer/Corbis
Cover Photo China: Linda Whitwam/Dorling Kindersley
Illustration (Interior): Integra Software Services
Director, Image Resource Center: Melinda Patelli
Manager, Rights and Permissions: Zina Arabia
Manager, Visual Research: Beth Brenzel
Manager, Cover Visual Research & Permissions: Karen Sanatar
Image Permission Coordinator: Ang'John Ferreri
Photo Researcher: Teri Stratford
Composition: Integra Software Services
Full-Service Project Management: Jennifer Welsch/BookMasters, Inc.
Printer/Binder: Courier/Kendallville
Cover Printer: Phoenix Color Corp.
Typeface: 10/12 Palatino

Credits and acknowledgments borrowed from other sources and reproduced, with permission, in this textbook appear on appropriate page within text or on pages 613–616.

If you purchased this book within the United States or Canada you should be aware that it has been wrongfully imported without the approval of the Publisher or the Author.

Pearson Education Ltd., London
Pearson Education Singapore, Pte. Ltd
Pearson Education, Canada, Ltd
Pearson Education–Japan
Pearson Education Australia PTY, Limited

Pearson Education North Asia Ltd
Pearson Educación de Mexico, S.A. de C.V.
Pearson Education Malaysia, Pte. Ltd.
Pearson Education, Upper Saddle River,
   New Jersey

10 9 8 7 6 5 4 3 2
ISBN-13: 978-0-13-813386-3
ISBN-10:   0-13-813386-7

To Bergin, Hunter, Cian, and Hanna
—WJK

To Lauren, Tommy, and Jonny
—MCG

BRIEF CONTENTS

CONTENTS

PART 3   APPROACHING GLOBAL MARKETS   184

PREFACE

Global Marketing, Fifth Edition, builds on the worldwide success of the previous editions of *Principles of Global Marketing* and *Global Marketing*. Those books took an environmental and strategic approach by outlining the major dimensions of the global business environment. We also provided a set of conceptual and analytical tools that would prepare students to successfully apply the four Ps to global marketing. We have approached all five editions with the same goal: to write a book that is authoritative in content yet relaxed and assured in style and tone. The following student comments suggest that we accomplished our goal: "the textbook is very clear and easy to understand," "an excellent textbook with many real-life examples," "the authors use simple language and clearly state the important points," "this is the best textbook that I am using this term," "the authors have done an excellent job of writing a text than can be read easily." When *Principles of Global Marketing* first appeared in 1996, we invited students to "look ahead" to such developments as the ending of America's trade embargo with Vietnam, Europe's new currency, Daimler-Benz's Smart car project, and Whirlpool's expansion into emerging markets. Those topics represented "big stories" in the global marketing arena and continue to receive press coverage on a regular basis.

As was the case with the first four editions, we wrote *Global Marketing*, Fifth Edition, with today's students and instructors in mind. Guided by our experience using the text in undergraduate and graduate classrooms and in corporate training seminars, we have revised, updated, and expanded *Global Marketing*, Fifth Edition. We have benefited tremendously from adopter feedback and input; we also continue to draw on our direct experience in the Americas, Asia, Europe, Africa, and the Middle East. The result is a text that addresses the needs of students and instructors in every part of the world. *Global Marketing* has been adopted at scores of colleges and universities in the United States; international adoptions of the English-language edition include Australia, Canada, China, Ireland, Japan, Malaysia, South Korea, and Sri Lanka. The text is also available in Chinese (simplified and traditional), Portuguese, and Spanish editions.

WHAT'S NEW

If there is a single unifying theme in the fifth edition, it is the growing impact of emerging nations on the global scene. Brazil, Russia, India, and China—the BRIC nations—figure prominently in the text. A new sidebar feature, "BRIC Briefing Book," includes timely information and marketing insights drawn from practitioner experience in these key markets. More broadly, the book examines emerging markets as a whole; it is safe to say that Indonesia, Mexico, and Turkey and a handful of other emerging nations are rapidly approaching the "tipping point" in terms of both competitive vigor and marketing opportunity. We can also expect that global companies such as Embraer (Brazil), Lukoil (Russia), Cemex (Mexico), Lenovo (China), and India's Big Three—Wipro, Infosys, and Tata—will becoming increasingly visible on the global stage. That these companies are likely to stand alongside established global giants such as Coca-Cola, Nestlé, and Toyota is one measure of how, as Thomas L. Friedman has noted, the world has flattened.

The fifth edition also includes new material on newsworthy and relevant topics such as the expanded European Union, the impact of religion on global marketing activities, and the global music industry's ongoing efforts to combat music piracy. Current research findings have been incorporated into each of the chapters. For example, Shaoming Zou and S. Tamer Cavusgil's work on global marketing strategy (from *Journal of Marketing*, October 2002) is an important addition to Chapter 1 "Introduction to Global Marketing." Similarly, our thinking about global market segmentation and targeting has been influenced by David Arnold's recent book, *The Mirage of Global Markets*. We have added scores of current examples of global marketing practice as well as quotations from global marketing practitioners and industry experts. Throughout the text, organizational Web sites are referenced for further student study and exploration. A Companion Website (**www.prenhall.com/keegan**) is integrated with the text as well.

Each chapter contains several illustrations, photos, and ads that bring global marketing to life. Chapter-opening vignettes introduce a company, a country, a product, or a global marketing issue that directly relates to chapter themes and content. More than half the opening vignettes in the fifth edition are new, including: Microsoft's antitrust woes in Europe (Chapter 5), EU tariffs on shoe imports from China (Chapter 8), Pernod Ricard and Chivas Regal (Chapter 10), and Lenovo (Chapter 14). In addition, every chapter contains one or more sidebars on various themes including global marketing in action, strategic decisions, a look behind the scenes of global marketing, issues that are "open to discussion," and the cultural differences that challenge the global marketer. A new sidebar, "Global Marketing Q&A," features interview excerpts with top executives of well-known global companies.

CASES

The case set in *Global Marketing*, Fifth Edition, strikes a balance between revisions of earlier cases (e.g., Case 1-1 "McDonald's Expands Globally While Adjusting Its Local Recipe" and Case 16-1 "Boeing Versus Airbus: A Battle for the Skies") and entirely new cases (e.g., Case 3-1 "The Free Trade Area of the Americas," Case 9-1 "Ford Bets Billions on Jaguar," Case 16-2 "Boeing Versus Airbus: A Battle for the Skies," and Case 17-1 "eBay in Asia"). The cases vary in length from a few hundred words to more than 2,600 words, yet they are all short enough to be covered in an efficient manner. The cases were written with the same objectives in mind: to raise issues that will encourage student interest and learning, to stimulate class discussion, and to enhance the classroom experience for students and instructors alike. Every chapter and case has been classroom tested. Supplements include an instructor's resource manual, a video collection, PowerPoint slides, and a test bank prepared by the authors. Special consideration was given to the test bank, with considerable effort devoted to minimizing the number of simplistic, superficial multiple-choice questions with "all of the above"-type answers.

SUPPLEMENTS

We're pleased to offer an Instructor's Manual, Video, a PowerPoint Set, a Test Item File, and TestGen to accompany *Global Marketing*, Fifth Edition.

All these resources can be accessed on our password-protected Instructor's Resource Center online at www.prenhall.com/keegan. Many of these resources are included on the Instructor's Resource CD as well, while the Video is available on DVD. One of the challenges facing your author team is the rate of change in the global business environment. Yesterday's impossibility becomes today's reality; new companies explode onto the scene; company leadership changes abruptly. In short, any book can be quickly outdated by events. Even so, we set out to create a compelling narrative that captures the unfolding drama that is inherent in marketing in the globalization era. The authors are passionate about the subject of global marketing; if our readers detect a note of enthusiasm in our writing, then we have been successful. We believe that adopters will find *Global Marketing*, Fifth Edition, to be the most engaging, up-to-date, relevant, useful text of its kind.

ACKNOWLEDGMENTS

We are grateful to the reviewers of this book for their many insights and helpful suggestions.

Ajay S. Sukhdial, Oklahoma State University
Lizzie Ngwenya-Scoburgh, The University of Northwestern Ohio
Concha Neeley, University of North Texas
Jaebeom Suh, Kansas State University
Julie Stanton, Saint Joseph's University
Paul Callahan, Cincinnati State Technical and Community College
Scott R Davidson, University at Albany
Paul Wellen, Roosevelt University
Barbara Ross Wooldridge, The University of Tampa
Roberto Sanchez, Oregon State University

This book reflects the contributions, labor, and insights of many persons.

I would like to thank my students, colleagues, associates, and clients for sharing their insights and understanding of global marketing theory and practice. It is impossible to single out everyone who has contributed to this edition, but I would especially like to thank Stephen Blank, Jean Boddewyn, Lawrence G. Bridwell, Steve Burgess, Arthur Centonze, J. Hugh Davidson, Bertrand de Frondeville, John Dory, Bob Fulmer, Pradeep Gopalakrisna, Doug Jebb, Steve Kobrin, Susan Douglas, Donald Gibson, Jim Gould, David Heenan, Robert Isaak, Hermawan Kartajaya, Suren Kaushik, Hermann Kopp, Raymond Lopez, Malcolm McDonald, Bodo B. Schlegelmilch, Barbara Stöttinger, Oleg Smirnoff, John Stopford, Jim Stoner, Martin Topol, Robert Vambery, , Kathy Winsted, Dominique Xardel, Michael Szenberg, and Alan Zimmerman.

I also wish to acknowledge the many contributions of the students in my doctoral seminar on global strategic marketing. The Pace doctoral students are a remarkable group of experienced executives who have decided to pursue a doctoral degree while working full time. Michael Friedman, CEO of Purdue Pharma and a Pace DPS graduate of the class of 2006, has been particularly supportive and helpful in sharing his experience and insight with me and my M.B.A. and doctoral students while at the same time providing exceptional leadership to Purdue Pharma.

My associates at Keegan & Company, Eli Seggev, Mark Keegan, and Anthony Donato, are outstanding expert consultants. Their collective backgrounds include doctoral degrees in marketing and law, and a masters degree in public administration. The cross-fertilization of their training and experience and challenging client assignments addressing contemporary marketing issues is a continuing source of new ideas and insights on global strategic marketing.

My research assistants, Nitin Singula, Ashish Agarwal, and Kandarp Shah, provided invaluable research assistance in many areas, including the very difficult task of creating the global income and population data that appears in this edition. My office managers, Gail Pietrangolare Weldon and my secretary Mary O'Connor at the Pace Graduate Center, Dianna Powell Ward and Nicola Simpson at the Center for Applied Research at the Pace NYC campus, and Sally Basso at Keegan & Company have provided support above and beyond the call of duty.

Special thanks are due to the superb librarians at Pace University: Michelle Lang, head, Graduate Center Library, and Anne B. Campbell, reference librarian, have a remarkable ability to find anything. Like the Canadian Mounties who always get their man, Michelle and Anne always get the document. My admiration for their talent and appreciation for their effort is unbounded.

Elyse Arno Brill, my co-author of *Offensive Marketing* (Butterworth Heinemann), has provided invaluable assistance in research, writing, and teaching. Her energy and creativity are unbounded. I am in awe of her ability to juggle a large and growing family, community service, and a working farm with our joint projects. She is an original and creative thinker with an impressive ability to identify important new directions and insights in marketing.

Jeff Shelstad, editor-in-chief, and Katie Stevens, acquisitions editor, marketing, at Prentice Hall, were quick to endorse and support this great fifth edition as was Melissa Pellerano, our project manager. David Parker, our new editor-in-chief, has also been very supportive. We are grateful for the continuity of the support at Prentice Hall.

Finally, I wish to thank my partner, Dr. Cynthia MacKay, who is a constant source of inspiration, support, and delight, as well as my companion in global market field research trips (many by motorcycle).

Warren J. Keegan
March 2007

I am indebted to the many colleagues and friends who carefully read and critiqued individual manuscript sections and chapters. Their comments improved the clarity and readability of the text. In particular, I would like to thank Hunter Clark, Frank Colella, Dave Collins, Wendy Foughty, Mark Freyberg, Alexandre Gilfanov, Carl Halgren, Kathy Hill, Mark Juffernbruch, Peter Kvetko, Keith Miller, Gayle Moberg, James Palmieri, and Alexandre Plokhov.

Several individuals were instrumental in helping us secure permissions, and I want to acknowledge everyone who "went the extra mile" in supporting this revision. I would especially like to thank Kirk Edmondson, Lexus Advanced Business Development; Adam Huening, *Greensburg (Ind.) Daily News*; Lou Ireland, Pioneer Hi-Bred International; Daniel McDonnell, Forrester Research; Pat McFadden, Nucor; Morgan Molinoff, Edelman; Peter VanVaalen, *Greensburg (Ind.) Daily News*; and Jeff Wilson, Firestone Agricultural Tire.

Colleagues at several institutions contributed material to this revision. The authors are indebted to Keith Miller, Ellis and Nelle Levitt Distinguished Professor of Law at Drake University Law School, for contributing a timely new case on Internet gambling. Thanks also to Alexandra Kennedy-Scott, David Henderson, and Michel Phan of the ESSEC Business School for permission to include a revised version of "Barbie: Growing Pains as the American Girl Goes Global" in this edition's case set. Yong Tae Bang of the College of Business Administration at Paichai University kindly offered feedback and suggestions that improved our discussion of South Korea.

I would also like to thank the many present and former students at Simpson College and the University of Iowa who have offered feedback on previous editions of *Global Marketing* and suggested improvements. Simpson alumna Beth Dorrell graciously offered her expertise on export documentation. Mikkel Jakobsen wrote about his first job in global marketing for a Chapter 8 "Day in the Life" sidebar; Mikkel also provided source material on Denmark for the opening vignette in Chapter 4. Thanks also to Alanah Davis for her work on Case 1-2 "Acer Inc." and to Caleb Hegna for supplying important data about the white goods market in Germany. I have relied heavily on Jing Hao (Simpson College) and Chao-Hsiang Cheng (University of Iowa) for useful insights about China; they also contributed English-to-Chinese and Chinese-to-English translations to this edition. My conversations with Benedikt Schwoll helped shaped the text discussion of marketing practices in Germany.

It was a great pleasure working with the Prentice Hall team that supervised production of this edition. My thanks to Melissa Pellerano and Kelly Warsak. Jennifer Welsch at BookMasters rounded out our virtual team; she deserves much credit for keeping the production process on track and on schedule. Kudos also to our photo researcher, Teri Stratford, for demonstrating once again that "every picture tells a story," and to Melinda Alexander for permissions research on ads and other illustrations. Thanks also to Anne Howard for her great work on marketing support materials and to the entire PH sales team for helping promote the book in the field. Daniel Wells, the PH sales representative for the Midwest, also gets a heartfelt "thank you" for his support and encouragement. I also want to acknowledge the contributions of Tony L. Henthorne at University of Southern Mississippi for his fine work on the Instructor's Manual, Jill Solomon at the University of South Florida for preparing a new set of PowerPoint slides, and Mahmood A. Khan at Virginia Tech for preparing the Test Item File. As was the case with previous editions, administration and faculty colleagues at Simpson College were very supportive of my research and writing endeavors.

Last, but not least, my love and appreciation to Lauren, Tommy, and Jonny for understanding and supporting what dad is trying to do during those long hours he spends in the office.

Mark C. Green
March 2007

ABOUT THE AUTHORS

Dr. Warren J. Keegan

Warren J. Keegan is Distinguished Professor of Marketing and International Business and Director of the Institute for Global Business Strategy at the Lubin School of Business, Pace University, New York City and Westchester. He is the founder of Warren Keegan Associates, Inc., a consulting consortium of experts in global strategic management and marketing, and Keegan & Company LLP, a firm specializing in litigation support.

Dr. Keegan is the author of many books. His text, *Global Marketing Management*, Seventh Edition (Prentice Hall, 2002), is recognized as the leading global marketing text for M.B.A. courses around the world. His other books include *Global Marketing*, Fourth Edition (Prentice Hall, 2005); *Offensive Marketing: An Action Guide to Gaining the Offensive in Business* (with Hugh Davidson) (Elsevier, Butterworth Heinemann, 2004); *Marketing Plans That Work*, Second Edition (with Malcolm McDonald) (Butterworth-Heinemann, 2002); *Marketing*, Second Edition, (Prentice Hall, 1995); *Marketing Sans Frontieres* (InterEditions, 1994); *Advertising Worldwide* (Prentice Hall, 1991); and *Judgments, Choices and Decisions* (Wiley, 1984). He has published in the leading business journals including the *Harvard Business Review, Journal of Marketing, Journal of International Business Studies, Administrative Science Quarterly* and the *Columbia Journal of World Business*.

He is a former MIT Fellow in Africa where he served as Assistant Secretary, Ministry of Development Planning, and Secretary of the Economic Development Commission for the Government of Tanzania. He was a consultant with Boston Consulting Group and Arthur D. Little, and chairman of Douglas A. Edwards, a New York corporate real estate firm.

Dr. Keegan holds an M.B.A. and doctorate from the Harvard Business School. He has been a visiting professor at New York University, INSEAD (France), IMD (Switzerland), the Stockholm School of Economics, Emmanuel College of Cambridge University, and the University of Hawaii. He is a former faculty member of Columbia Business School, Baruch College, and the School of Government and Business Administration of The George Washington University.

He is a Lifetime Fellow of the Academy of International Business, Individual Eminent Person (IEP) Appointed by Asian Global Business Leaders Society (other awardees include: Noel Tichy, Rosabeth Moss Kanter, and Gary Wendt). His biography is listed in *Who's Who in America* (A. N. Marquis). He is a member of the International Advisory Board of École des Hautes Études Commerciales (HEC), Montreal; the Editorial Advisory Board, Cranfield School of Management and *Financial Times* Management Monograph Series; and is a current or former director of The S.M. Stoller Company, Inc.; The Cooper Companies, Inc. (NYSE); Inter-Ad, Inc.; American Thermal Corporation, Inc.; Halfway Houses of Westchester, Inc.; Wainwright House; and The Rye Arts Center.

He is an enthusiastic global traveler and enjoys teaching and learning, motorcycle touring, tennis, reading, theatre, movies, museums, swimming and rowing, loafing and working, home improvements, and life.

Dr. Mark C. Green

Dr. Green is Professor of Management and Marketing at Simpson College in Indianola, Iowa, where he teaches courses in management, marketing, advertising, international marketing, and entrepreneurship and innovation. He is also a

Visiting Professor at the University of Iowa's Tippie College of Business. Dr. Green earned his B.A. degree in Russian literature from Lawrence University, M.A. and Ph.D. degrees in Russian linguistics from Cornell University, and an M.B.A. degree in marketing management from Syracuse University.

In addition to co-authoring *Global Marketing*, Fifth Edition with Warren Keegan, Dr. Green has also contributed case studies and chapter materials to several other textbooks published by Prentice Hall. These include: *Advertising Principles and Practices*, Fourth Edition, by William Wells, John Burnett, and Sandra Moriarty (1997); *Behavior in Organizations*, Sixth Edition, by Jerald Greenberg and Robert Baron (1996); *Business*, Fourth Edition, by Ricky Griffin and Ronald Ebert (1995); and *Principles of Marketing* by Warren Keegan, Sandra Moriarty, and Thomas Duncan (1992). Dr. Green has also written essays on technology and global business that have appeared in the *Des Moines Register* and other newspapers.

Dr. Green has traveled to the former Soviet Union on numerous occasions. In 1995 and 1996, he participated in a grant project funded by the U.S. Agency for International Development (USAID) and presented marketing seminars to audiences in Nizhny Novgorod. In addition, Dr. Green has served as a consultant to several Iowa organizations that have business and cultural ties with Russia and other former Soviet republics. Dr. Green has lectured in Russia and Ukraine on topics relating to emerging market economies. His 1992 monograph, *Developing the Russian Market*, received an award from the Iowa-based International Network on Trade.

In 1997, Dr. Green was the recipient of Simpson College's Distinguished Research and Writing Award. Dr. Green also received the 1995 Distinguished Teaching Award for senior faculty. In 1990, he was the recipient of Simpson's Excellence in Teaching Award for junior faculty. He also received the 1988 Outstanding Faculty of the Year awarded by the Alpha Sigma Lambda adult student honorary at Simpson College.

Dr. Green enjoys playing bass and guitar with the Sonny Humbucker Band; the members include Simpson colleagues David Wolf (associate professor of English) and Mark Juffernbruch (associate professor of accounting). Rounding out the lineup are David Kochel, a political consultant with JDK Marketing & Public Affairs, and Thom Wright, an architect with RDG Planning & Design. Dr. Green also manages tenor saxophone jazz great Dave Tofani, who records for the SoloWinds label.

IN MEMORIAM

Since the publication of the fourth edition of *Global Marketing*, two of the major contributors to the field of global marketing have died. We are in their debt for their contributions to the field and to this book.

Theodore Levitt (1925–2006) died at the age of 81 and was one of the most recognized and influential marketing thinkers of all time. His article "Marketing Myopia" was one of the most popular *Harvard Business Review* articles of all time. In this article, he argued that industries decline because managers think too narrowly about markets. Professor Levitt used the unforgettable example of the railroad industry; it went into decline, he argued, because managers and executives failed to recognize that they were in the transportation business, not in the railroad business.

In his 1983 *Harvard Business Review* article "The Globalization of Markets," Professor Levitt argued that the future belonged not to the multinational corporation but to the global corporation. The difference between the two was the global corporation's deeper understanding of what customers in markets wanted: value and an organizational ability to deliver that value. The article is as relevant today as it was the day it was written.

Professor Levitt was born in Germany and moved with his family to Ohio to escape the Nazis. He was drafted into the U.S. Army and served in Europe during WWII. His first job upon returning to the United States after the war was as a sports writer. He had a doctorate in economics from Ohio State University and began teaching at the University of North Dakota. After a stint as a consultant, he joined the Harvard Business School faculty where he was a popular teacher and prolific author.

Sumantra Ghoshal (1948–2004) died at the age of 55. He was one of the most influential academics in the field of international business. With Professor Chris Bartlett, his mentor at Harvard Business School, he coined the phrase "transnational corporation" and developed the important five stage model of development of the transnational corporation, which distinguishes between the domestic, international, multinational, global, and transnational. He, like Ted Levitt, had a sharp mind and an intense and charming style that held the attention of generations of students and executives. He was appointed the first dean of the Indian School of Business in Hyderabad. He quit six months before the school opened, explaining that he was not cut out for daily management.

Ghoshal was born in Calcutta. He graduated in physics at Delhi University and joined Indian Oil before moving to the United States on a Fulbright Fellowship in 1981. In the United States, he earned doctoral degrees at MIT's Sloan School of Management and at Harvard Business School. He was appointed to INSEAD in France in 1985, becoming a full professor in record time and producing a stream of influential books and articles on multinational enterprise; he joined the London Business School in 1994.

I had the privilege of knowing both of these great scholars. They will be missed, but their contributions and insights live on in this fifth edition.

Warren J. Keegan
March 2007

Global Marketing

1

Introduction to Global Marketing

Consider the following proposition: *We live in a global marketplace.* McDonald's restaurants, Sony digital TVs, LEGO toys, Swatch watches, Burberry trench coats, and Caterpillar earthmoving equipment are found practically everywhere on the planet. Global companies are fierce rivals in key markets. For example, American auto industry giants General Motors and Ford are locked in a competitive struggle with Toyota, Hyundai, and other global Asian rivals as well as European companies such as Volkswagen. U.S.-based Intel, the world's largest chip maker, competes with South Korea's Samsung. In the global cell phone market, Nokia (Finland), Ericsson (Sweden), Motorola (United States), and Samsung are key players. Appliances from Whirlpool and Electrolux compete for precious retail space with products manufactured and marketed by China's Haier Group and LG of South Korea.

Now consider a second proposition: *We live in a world in which markets are local.* In China, for example, Yum Brands' new East Dawning fast-food chain competes with local restaurants such as New Asia Snack.[1] France's domestic film industry generates about 40 percent of local motion picture box office receipts; U.S.-made movies account for about 50 percent. In Turkey, local artists such as Sertab Erener account for more than 80 percent of recorded music sales. *Kiki*, a Japanese magazine for teenage girls, competes for newsstand sales with *Vogue Girl*, *Cosmo Girl*, and other titles from Western publishers. In Germany, children's television powerhouse Nickelodeon competes with local broadcaster Super RTL. In Brazil, many consumers are partial to Antarctica and other local soft drink brands made from guaraná, a berry that grows in the Amazon region.

The global marketplace versus local markets paradox lies at the heart of this textbook. In later chapters, we will investigate the nature of local markets in more detail. For now, however, we will focus on the first part of the paradox. Think for a moment about brands and products that are found throughout the world. Ask the average consumer where this global "horn of plenty" comes from, and you'll likely hear a variety of answers. It's certainly true that some brands—McDonald's, Corona Extra, Swatch, Waterford, Benetton, and Burberry, for instance—are strongly identified with a particular country. In much of the world, McDonald's is the quintessential American fast-food restaurant, just as Burberry is synonymous with British country life. However, for many other products, brands, and companies, the sense of identity with a particular country is becoming blurred. Which brands are Japanese? American? Korean? German? Where is Nokia headquartered? When is a German car *not* a German car? Can a car be both German *and* American? Consider:

- A 2005 American-built Ford Mustang has 65 percent American and Canadian content; a 2005 American-built Toyota Sienna XLE minivan has 90 percent American and Canadian content.[2]

---

[1]   Janet Adamy, "East Eats West: One U.S. Chain's Unlikely Goal: Pitching Chinese Food in China," *The Wall Street Journal*, October 20, 2006, pp. A1, A8.

[2]   Jathon Sapsford and Norihiko Shirouzu, "Mom, Apple Pie and . . . Toyota?" *The Wall Street Journal*, May 11, 2006, p. B1.

England's Burberry Group celebrated its 150th anniversary in 2006. Burberry's trademark is registered in more than 90 countries. The company's signature plaid pattern—often referred to as "the check"—is incorporated into a wide range of apparel items and accessories. The Burberry brand is enjoying renewed popularity throughout the world; sales in Asia are particularly strong. New CEO Angela Ahrendts wants to broaden the brand's appeal. To do this, she intends to introduce two new logos: an equestrian knight and the cursive signature of company founder Thomas Burberry.

- China's Nanjing Automobile Group has purchased the rights to the MG, the legendary two-seat British sports car. Nanjing plans to manufacture MGs in a new factory in Oklahoma.
- German carmaker BMW exports the X5 sport utility vehicle that it builds in Spartanville, South Carolina, to more than 100 countries.

INTRODUCTION AND OVERVIEW

As the preceding examples illustrate, the global marketplace finds expression in many ways. Some are quite subtle, others are not. While shopping, you may have noticed more multilanguage labeling on your favorite products and brands. Your local filling station may have changed its name from Getty to Lukoil, reflecting the Russian energy giant's expanding global reach. Wal-Mart buys about $10 billion worth of goods from China each year. When you shop at your local gourmet coffee store, you may have noticed that some beans are labeled "Fair Trade Certified." Your toll-free telephone call to a software technical support service or an airline customer service center may be answered in Mumbai. Quentin Tarantino's movie *Kill Bill* was filmed on soundstages in China, and Chinese films such as *Hero* and *House of Flying Daggers* have been international hits. Possibly you heard or read recent news accounts of antiglobalization protesters disrupting meetings of the World Trade Organization in Cancún, London, or some other major city.

The growing importance of global marketing is the one aspect of a sweeping transformation that has profoundly affected the people and industries of many nations during the past 160 years. International trade has existed for centuries; beginning in 200 BC, for example, the legendary Silk Road connected the East with the West. Even so, prior to 1840, students sitting at their desks would not have had any item in their possession that was manufactured more than a few miles from where they lived—with the possible exception of the books they were reading. From the mid-1800s to the early 1920s, with Great Britain the dominant economic power in the world, international trade flourished. A series of global upheavals, including World War I, the Bolshevik Revolution, and the Great Depression, brought that era to an end. Then, following World War II, a new era began. Unparalleled expansion into global markets by companies that previously served only customers located in their home country characterizes this new global era.

Three decades ago, the phrase *global marketing* did not even exist. Today, savvy businesspeople utilize global marketing for the realization of their companies' full commercial potential. That is why, no matter whether you live in Asia, Europe, North America, or South America, you may be familiar with the brands mentioned in the opening paragraphs. However, there is another, even more critical reason why companies need to take global marketing seriously: survival. A management team that fails to understand the importance of global marketing risks losing its domestic business to competitors with lower costs, more experience, and better products.

But what is global marketing? How does it differ from "regular" marketing? **Marketing** is an organizational function and a set of processes for creating, communicating, and delivering value to customers and for managing customer relationships in ways that benefit the organization and its stakeholders.[3] Marketing activities center on an organization's efforts to satisfy customer wants and needs with products and services that offer competitive value. The marketing mix (product, price, place, and promotion) comprises a contemporary marketer's primary tools. Marketing is a universal discipline, as applicable in Argentina as it is in Zimbabwe.

This book is about *global marketing.* An organization that engages in **global marketing** focuses its resources and competencies on global market opportunities and threats. A fundamental difference between "regular" marketing and "global" marketing is the scope of activities. A company that engages in global marketing conducts important business activities outside the home-country market. The scope issue can be conceptualized in terms of the familiar product or market matrix of growth strategies (see Table 1-1). Some companies pursue a *market development strategy*; this involves seeking new customers by introducing existing products or services into new geographical markets. For example, as Wal-Mart expands into Guatemala and other Central America countries, it is implementing a market development strategy. Global marketing may also take the form of a *diversification strategy* in which a company creates new products or services and introduces them into new geographical markets. This is the strategy that South Korea's LG Electronics has used to target the American home appliance market. LG's product offerings include a stylish, high-tech refrigerator priced at $3,000; the unit features a built-in flat-panel LCD television. LG's commitment to innovative products prompted Home Depot to start carrying the LG appliance line.[4] When successfully formulated and implemented, these globally oriented growth strategies can result in increased revenues for a company.

Companies that engage in global marketing frequently encounter unique or peculiar features in specific countries or regions of the world. In China, for example, product piracy is rampant. Companies doing business there must take extra care to protect their intellectual property and deal with "knockoffs." In some regions of the world, bribery and corruption are deeply entrenched. A successful global marketer understands specific concepts and has a broad and deep understanding of the world's varied business environments. He or she also must understand the strategies that, skillfully implemented in conjunction with universal marketing fundamentals,

Table 1-1

Product/Market Growth Matrix

		Product Orientation	
		Existing Products	New Products
Market Orientation	Existing markets	1. Market penetration strategy	2. Product development strategy
	New markets	3. Market development strategy	4. Diversification strategy

---

3 American Marketing Association.
4 Cheryl Lu-Lien Tan, "The New Asian Import: Your Oven," *The Wall Street Journal,* June 22, 2005, pp. D1, D4.

increase the likelihood of market success. This book concentrates on the major dimensions of global marketing. A brief overview of marketing is presented next, although the authors assume that the reader has completed an introductory marketing course or has equivalent experience.

PRINCIPLES OF MARKETING: A REVIEW

As defined in the previous section, marketing is one of the functional areas of a business, distinct from finance and operations. Marketing can also be thought of as a set of activities and processes that, along with product design, manufacturing, and transportation logistics, comprise a firm's **value chain**. Decisions at every stage, from idea conception to support after the sale, should be assessed in terms of their ability to create value for customers.

For any organization operating anywhere in the world, the essence of marketing is to surpass the competition at the task of creating perceived value (i.e., a superior value proposition) for customers. The **value equation** is a guide to this task:

Value = Benefits/Price (money, time, effort, etc.)

The marketing mix is integral to the equation because benefits are a combination of the product, promotion, and distribution. As a general rule, value, as the customer perceives, can be increased in two basic ways. Markets can offer customers an improved bundle of benefits or lower prices (or both). Marketers may strive to improve the product itself, to design new channels of distribution, to create better communications strategies, or a combination of all three. Marketers may also seek to increase value by finding ways to cut costs and prices. Nonmonetary costs are also a factor, and marketers may be able to decrease the time and effort that customers must expend to learn about or seek out the product.[5] Companies that use price as a competitive weapon may scour the globe to ensure an ample supply of low-wage labor or access to cheap raw materials. Companies can also reduce prices if costs are low because of process efficiencies in manufacturing or because of economies of scale associated with high production volumes.

Recall the definition of a market: *people or organizations that are both able* and *willing to buy*. In order to achieve market success, a product or brand must measure up to a threshold of acceptable quality and be consistent with buyer behavior, expectations, and preferences. If a company is able to offer a combination of superior product, distribution, or promotion benefits *and* lower prices than the competition, it should enjoy an extremely advantageous position. Toyota, Nissan, and other Japanese automakers made significant gains in the American market in the 1980s by creating a superior value proposition: They offered cars with higher quality and lower prices than those made by General Motors, Ford, and Chrysler.

However, some of Japan's initial auto exports were market failures. In the late 1960s, for example, Subaru of America began importing the Subaru 360 automobile and selling it for $1,297. After *Consumer Reports* judged the 360 "not acceptable," sales ground to a halt. Similarly, the Yugo automobile achieved a modest level of U.S. sales in the 1980s (despite a "don't buy" rating from a consumer magazine) because its sticker price of $3,999 made it the cheapest new car available. Low quality was the primary reason for the market failure of both the Subaru 360 and the Yugo.[6] Wal-Mart's departure from the German market was due in part to the fact that Germans could find lower prices at stores known as "hard discounters." In addition, many German consumers prefer to go to several small shops rather than seek out the convenience of a single "all-in-one" store.

---

[5] With certain categories of differentiated goods, including designer clothing and other luxury products, higher price is often associated with increased value.

[6] The history of the Subaru 360 is documented in Randall Rothman, *Where the Suckers Moon: The Life and Death of an Advertising Campaign* (New York: Vintage Books, 1994), Chapter 4.

Competitive Advantage, Globalization, and Global Industries

When a company succeeds in creating more value for customers than its competitors, that company is said to enjoy **competitive advantage** in an industry.[7] Competitive advantage is measured relative to rivals in a given industry. For example, your local Laundromat is in a local industry; its competitors are local. In a national industry, competitors are national. In a global industry—consumer electronics, apparel, automobiles, steel, pharmaceuticals, furniture, and dozens of other sectors—the competition is, likewise, global (and, in many industries, local as well). Global marketing is essential if a company competes in a global industry or one that is globalizing.

The transformation of formerly local or national industries into global ones is part of a broader process of *globalization*, which Thomas L. Friedman defines as follows:

> Globalization is the inexorable integration of markets, nation-states and technologies to a degree never witnessed before—in a way that is enabling individuals, corporations and nation-states to reach around the world farther, faster, deeper and cheaper than ever before, and in a way that is enabling the world to reach into individuals, corporations and nation-states farther, faster, deeper, and cheaper than ever before.[8]

From a marketing point of view, globalization presents companies with tantalizing opportunities—and challenges—as executives decide whether or not to offer their products and services everywhere. At the same time, globalization presents companies with unprecedented opportunities to reconfigure themselves; as John Micklethwait and Adrian Wooldridge put it, "the same global bazaar that allows consumers to buy the best that the world can offer also allows producers to find the best partners."[9]

National Football League (NFL) Europe and Major League Soccer (MLS) are dedicated to promoting, respectively, American football globally and soccer in the United States. The NFL is focusing on a handful of key markets: Canada, Germany, Japan, Mexico, the United Kingdom, and China. Placekicker Gao Wei hopes to be in the lineup when the Seattle Seahawks and the New England Patriots play an exhibition game in Beijing's Workers Stadium in 2008.

Soccer United Marketing, an MLS offshoot, has purchased English-language TV rights for several World Cup championships. As MLS's Don Garber notes, "In the global culture the universal language is soccer. That's the sweet spot. If it weren't for the shrinking world caused by globalization, we wouldn't have the opportunity we have today."[10]

7 Jay Barney notes that "a firm is said to have a competitive advantage when it is implementing a value-creating strategy not simultaneously being implemented by any current or potential competitors." See Barney, "Firm Resources and Sustained Competitive Advantage," *Journal of Management* 17, no. 1 (1991), p. 102.
8 Thomas L. Friedman, *The Lexus and the Olive Tree* (New York: Anchor Books, 2000), p. 9.
9 John Micklethwait and Adrian Wooldridge, *A Future Perfect: The Challenge and Hidden Promise of Globalization* (New York: Crown Publishers, 2000), p. xxvii.
10 Grant Wahl, "Football vs. Fútbol," *Sports Illustrated*, July 5, 2004, pp. 68–72.

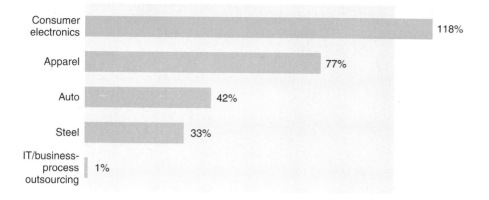

Figure 1-1

Degree of Industry Globalization

Source: Diana Farrell, "Assessing Your Company's Global Potential," Harvard Business Review 82, no. 12 (December 2004), p. 85.

Is there more to a global industry than simply global competition? Definitely. As defined by management guru Michael Porter, a **global industry** is one in which competitive advantage can be achieved by integrating and leveraging operations on a worldwide scale. Put another way, an industry is global to the extent that a company's industry position in one country is interdependent with its industry position in other countries. Indicators of globalization include the ratio of cross-border trade to total worldwide production, the ratio of cross-border investment to total capital investment, and the proportion of industry revenue generated by companies that compete in all key world regions.[11] Figure 1-1 ranks several industries in terms of degree of globalization. The figure was created by calculating the ratio of the annual value of global trade in the sector—including components shipped to various countries during the production process—to the annual value of industry sales.

Achieving competitive advantage in a global industry requires executives and managers to maintain a well-defined strategic focus. **Focus** is simply the concentration of attention on a core business or competence. The importance of focus for a global company is evident in the following comment by Helmut Maucher, former chairman of Nestlé SA:

> Nestlé is focused: We are food and beverages. We are not running bicycle shops. Even in food we are not in all fields. There are certain areas we do not touch. For the time being we have no biscuits [cookies] in Europe and the United States for competitive reasons, and no margarine. We have no soft drinks because I have said we either buy Coca-Cola or we leave it alone. This is focus.[12]

However, company management may choose to initiate a change in focus as part of an overall strategy shift. Even Coca-Cola has been forced to sharpen its focus on its core beverage brands. Following sluggish sales in 2000 and 2001, former Chairman and CEO Douglas Daft formed a new alliance with Nestlé that jointly developed and marketed coffees and teas. Daft also tried to transform Coca-Cola's Minute Maid unit into a global division that marketed juice brands worldwide. As Daft explained:

> We're a network of brands and businesses. You don't just want to be a total beverage company. Each brand has a different return on investment, is sold differently, drunk for different reasons, and has different managing structures. If you mix them all together, you lose the focus.[13]

---

[11] Vijay Govindarajan and Anil Gupta, "Setting a Course for the New Global Landscape," *Financial Times—Mastering Global Business,* part I (1998), p. 3.

[12] Elizabeth Ashcroft, "Nestlé and the Twenty-First Century," *Harvard Business School Case* 9–595–074, 1995. See also Ernest Beck, "Nestlé Feels Little Pressure to Make Big Acquisitions," *The Wall Street Journal,* June 22, 2000, p. B4.

[13] Betsy McKay, "Coke's 'Think Local' Strategy Has Yet to Prove Itself," *The Wall Street Journal,* March 1, 2001, p. B6.

In 2006, Honda Motor announced plans to build a new $550 million auto assembly plant in the Midwest. Michigan, Ohio, and other job-hungry states were under consideration as potential sites. To encourage Honda to build the plant in their town, 200 residents of Greensburg, Indiana posed for this photo while standing in the shape of Honda's "H" logo. Jordan Fischer, a photographer for the Greensburg Daily News, captured this image from the roof of a nearby building. Honda eventually did choose Greensburg as the site for its plant, which will produce 200,000 fuel-efficient cars each year and employ 2,000 people.

Examples abound of corporate executives addressing the issue of focus, often in response to changes in the global business environment. In recent years Fiat, Volvo, Electrolux, Toshiba, Colgate, Royal Philips Electronics, Henkel, Bertelsmann, and many other companies have stepped up efforts to sharpen their strategic focus on core businesses. Specific actions can take a number of different

LESSONS
from the global marketplace

Managing Global Growth

The beginning of the twenty-first century has challenged deal-making top executives at several global companies. In 1998, Edgar Bronfman, Jr., the CEO of Montreal-based Seagram Company, paid $1 billion for music giant PolyGram NV and sold Seagram's Tropicana orange juice unit to PepsiCo. Bronfman then sold Chivas Regal, several other major spirits brands, and Seagram's wine business to Diageo PLC and Pernod Ricard SA. Collectively, these transactions shifted Seagram's focus from beverages to entertainment; the combination of PolyGram with Seagram's MCA record unit created a global music powerhouse. In 2000, Bronfman agreed to a $32 billion takeover by France's Vivendi. The resulting company, Vivendi Universal, was tightly focused in two industry sectors: environmental services and communications. The strategic plan for the communications businesses called for distributing Universal's entertainment content via an Internet portal that PCs, wireless phones, and other electronic devices could access. However, Vivendi Universal had taken on too much debt, and Chairman Jean-Marie Messier was forced to resign in 2002. In 2003, the theme park, movie, and television businesses were sold to GE. Today, the company is known simply as Vivendi.

ABB Inc., the Swiss and Swedish electrical and engineering firm that was once comprised of 1,300 companies in 140 countries, is another global giant that has been forced to restructure. During the 1990s, ABB was frequently cited as a textbook example of a successful transnational company. Former Chief Executive Percy Barnevik was legendary in business circles for his charismatic and visionary leadership. However, one of his acquisitions, Combustion Engineering, an American producer of power-plant boilers, proved disastrous because of asbestos-related liability claims. Although his decentralized management structure helped the company grow, it also resulted in conflict and breakdowns in communication between far-flung management units. Between 1997 and 2003, two chief executives—Göran Lindahl and Jörgen Centerman—came and went in quick succession. The company lost nearly $700 million in 2001; also in 2001, Barnevik, who had remained with the company as a nonexecutive chairman, was forced to resign after a scandal involving pension benefits. The following year, losses totaled nearly $800 million. ABB's next chief executive, Jürgen Dormann, sold the finance unit and other non-core assects in an effort to reduce debt; the slimmed-down company's two core businesses are focused around automation and power technologies. Commenting on Barnevik's legacy, Dormann noted "We had a lack of focus as Percy went on an acquisition spree . . . The company wasn't disciplined enough."

Sources: Bruce Orwall, "Universal Script: Vivendi-Seagram Deal Has the Former MCA Playing Familiar Role," The Wall Street Journal, June 20, 2000, pp. A1, A8; John Carreyrou and Martin Peers, "Damage Control: How Messier Kept Cash Crisis at Vivendi Hidden for Months," The Wall Street Journal, October 31, 2002, pp. A1, A15; Dan Bilefsky and Anita Raghavan, "Blown Fuse: How 'Europe's GE' and Its Star CEO Tumbled to Earth," The Wall Street Journal, January 23, 2003, pp. A1, A8.

STRATEGIC DECISION-MAKING *in global marketing*

IBM

IBM originally succeeded in the data-processing industry by focusing on customer needs and wants better than Univac. After decades of success, however, IBM remained focused on mainframe computers, despite customers who were increasingly turning to PCs. IBM was a key player in the early days of the PC revolution, but its corporate culture was still oriented toward mainframes. "Big Blue" faltered in the early 1990s—it lost more than $8 billion in 1993—in part because competitors specializing in PCs had become even *more* clearly focused on

what PC customers needed and wanted; namely, low prices and increased speed. Within a few years, however, then-CEO Lou Gerstner succeeded in refocusing the company's PC business and broadening its scope to higher-margin products such as servers for electronic commerce. Gerstner and e-business marketing chief Abby Kohnstamm also leveraged IBM's reputation for providing expertise-based solutions for its customers; in 2006, global services accounted for 53 percent of revenues and 37 percent of profits. In 2006, IBM became even more tightly focused with the sale of its personal computer business to China's Lenovo.

forms besides alliances, including mergers, acquisitions, divestitures, and folding some businesses into other company divisions.[14]

Value, competitive advantage, and the focus required to achieve them are universal in their relevance and they should guide marketing efforts in any part of the world. Global marketing requires attention to these issues on a worldwide basis and utilization of an information system capable of monitoring the globe for opportunities and threats. A fundamental premise of this book can be stated as follows: Companies that understand and engage in global marketing can offer more overall value to customers than companies that do not have that understanding. There are many who share this conviction. In the mid-1990s, for example, C. Samuel Craig and Susan P. Douglas noted:

> Globalization is no longer an abstraction but a stark reality. . . . Choosing not to participate in global markets is no longer an option. All firms, regardless of their size, have to craft strategies in the broader context of world markets to anticipate, respond, and adapt to the changing configuration of these markets.[16]

Evidence is mounting that companies in a range of industries are getting the message. For example, three Italian furniture companies have joined together to increase sales outside of Italy and ward off increased competition from Asia. Luxury goods purveyors such as LVMH and Prada Group provided the model for the new business entity, which unites Poltrona Frau, Cassina, and Cappellini.[17] Hong Kong's Tai Ping Carpets International is also globalizing. Top managers have been dispersed to different parts of the world; while the finance and technology functions are still in Hong Kong, the marketing chief is based in New York City and the head of operations is in Singapore. As company director John Ying noted, "We're trying to create a minimultinational."[18]

"We believe a company can only think in one set of terms. If you are premium, you have to focus on it."

Helmut Panke, Chairman Bayerische Motoren Werke AG[15]

---

[14] Robert A. Guth, "How Japan's Toshiba Got Its Focus Back," *The Wall Street Journal,* December 12, 2000, p. A6.

[15] Scott Miller, "BMW Bucks Diversification to Focus on Luxury Models," *The Wall Street Journal,* March 20, 2002, p. B4.

[16] C. Samuel Craig and Susan P. Douglas, "Responding to the Challenges of Global Markets: Change, Complexity, Competition, and Conscience," *Columbia Journal of World Business* 31, no. 4 (Winter 1996), pp. 6–18.

[17] Gabriel Kahn, "Three Italian Furniture Makers Hope to Create a Global Luxury Powerhouse," *The Wall Street Journal,* October 31, 2006, p. B1.

[18] Phred Dvorak, "Big Changes Drive Small Carpet Firm," *The Wall Street Journal,* October 30, 2006, p. B3.

GLOBAL MARKETING: WHAT IT IS AND WHAT IT ISN'T

The discipline of marketing is universal. It is natural, however, that marketing practices will vary from country to country, for the simple reason that the countries and peoples of the world are different. These differences mean that a marketing approach that has proven successful in one country will not *necessarily* succeed in another country. Customer preferences, competitors, channels of distribution, and communication media may differ. An important task in global marketing is learning to recognize the extent to which marketing plans and programs can extend worldwide, as well as the extent to which they must adapt.

The way a company addresses this task is a reflection of its **global marketing strategy (GMS)**. Recall that in single country marketing, strategy development addresses two fundamental issues: choosing a target market and developing a marketing mix. The same two issues are at the heart of a firm's GMS, although they are viewed from a somewhat different perspective (see Table 1-2). *Global market participation* is the extent to which a company has operations in major world markets. *Standardization versus adaptation* is the extent to which each marketing mix element can be standardized (i.e., executed the same way) or adapted (i.e., executed in different ways) in various country markets. GMS has three additional dimensions that pertain to marketing management. First, *concentration of marketing activities* is the extent to which activities related to the marketing mix (e.g., promotional campaigns or pricing decisions) are performed in one or a few country locations. *Coordination of marketing activities* refers to the extent to which marketing activities related to the marketing mix are planned and executed interdependently around the globe. Finally, *integration of competitive moves* is the extent to which a firm's competitive marketing tactics in different parts of the world are interdependent. The GMS should enhance the firm's performance on a worldwide basis.[19]

Some brands are found in virtually every country; Coke is a case in point. Coke is the best-known, strongest brand in the world; its enviable global position has resulted in part from the Coca-Cola Company's willingness and ability to back its flagship brand with a network of local bottlers and a strong local marketing effort. However, companies that engage in global marketing do not necessarily conduct business in every one of the world's 200-plus country markets. For example, in the $30 billion market for recorded music, 12 countries—including the United States, Japan, the United Kingdom, and France—account for 70 percent of sales. Global marketing *does* mean widening business horizons to encompass the world in scanning for opportunities and threats. The decision to enter one or more particular markets outside the home country depends on a company's resources,

	Single-Country Marketing Strategy	Global Marketing Strategy

Table 1-2
 	
Comparison of Single-Country Marketing Strategy and Global Marketing Strategy
	Target Market Strategy
	Marketing Mix Development
	  Product
	  Price
	  Promotion
	  Place
		Global Market Participation
		Marketing Mix Development
		  Product adaptation or standardization
		  Price adaptation or standardization
		  Promotion adaptation or standardization
		  Place adaptation or standardization
		Concentration of Marketing Activities
		Coordination of Marketing Activities
		Integration of Competitive Moves

---

[19] Shaoming Zou and S. Tamer Cavusgil, "The GMS: A Broad Conceptualization of Global Marketing Strategy and Its Effect on Performance," *Journal of Marketing* 66, no. 4 (October 2002), pp. 40–56.

its managerial mind-set, and the nature of opportunities and threats. Today, most observers agree that Brazil, Russia, India, and China—four emerging markets known collectively as BRIC—represent significant growth opportunities. Throughout this text, marketing issues and opportunities in these countries are highlighted in "BRIC Briefing Book" sidebars.

The issue of standardization versus adaptation has been at the center of a long-standing controversy among both academicians and business practitioners. Much of the controversy dates back to Professor Theodore Levitt's 1983 article in the *Harvard Business Review*, "The Globalization of Markets." Levitt argued that marketers were confronted with a "homogeneous global village." He advised organizations to develop standardized, high-quality world products and market them around the globe by using standardized advertising, pricing, and distribution. Some well-publicized failures by Parker Pen and other companies that tried to follow Levitt's advice brought his proposals into question. The business press frequently quoted industry observers who disputed Levitt's views. As Carl Spielvogel, chairman and CEO of the Backer Spielvogel Bates Worldwide advertising agency, told the *Wall Street Journal* in the late 1980s, "Theodore Levitt's comment about the world becoming homogenized is bunk. There are about two products that lend themselves to global marketing—and one of them is Coca-Cola."[20]

Global marketing made Coke a worldwide success. However, that success was *not* based on a total standardization of marketing mix elements. For example, Coca-Cola achieved success in Japan by spending a great deal of time and money to become an insider; that is, the company built a complete local infrastructure with its sales force and vending machine operations. Coke's success in Japan is a function of its ability to achieve "global localization," being as much of an insider as a local company but still reaping the benefits that result from world-scale operations.[21] Similarly, in India, the company's local Thums Up cola brand competes with—and even outsells—the flagship cola.[22]

What does the phrase *global localization* really mean? In a nutshell, it means that a successful global marketer must have the ability to "think globally and act locally." As we will see many times in this book, *global* marketing may include a combination of standard (e.g., the actual product itself) and nonstandard (e.g., distribution or packaging) approaches. A global product may be the same product everywhere and yet different. Global marketing requires marketers to behave in a way that is both global *and* local at the same time by responding to similarities and differences in world markets. Kenichi Ohmae summed up this paradox as follows:

> The essence of being a global company is to maintain a kind of tension within the organization without being undone by it. Some companies say the new world requires homogeneous products—"one size fits all"—everywhere. Others say the world requires endless customization—special products for every region. The best global companies understand it's neither and it's both. They keep the two perspectives in mind simultaneously.[23]

As the Coca-Cola Company has convincingly demonstrated, the ability to think globally and act locally can be a source of competitive advantage. Because the company is adept at adapting sales promotion, distribution, and customer service efforts to local needs, Coke has become a billion-dollar-plus brand in six

[20] Joanne Lipman, "Ad Fad: Marketers Turn Sour on Global Sales Pitch Harvard Guru Makes," *The Wall Street Journal*, May 12, 1988, p. 1.

[21] Kenichi Ohmae, *The Borderless World: Power and Strategy* (New York: Harper Perennial, 1991), pp. 26–27.

[22] Nikhil Deogun and Jonathan Karp, "For Coke in India, Thums Up Is the Real Thing," *The Wall Street Journal*, April 29, 1998, pp. B1, B2.

[23] William C. Taylor and Alan M. Webber, *Going Global: Four Entrepreneurs Map the New World Marketplace* (New York: Penguin Books USA, 1996), pp. 48–49.

markets outside the United States: Brazil, Germany, Great Britain, Japan, Mexico, and Spain. This type of success does not happen overnight. For example, Coca-Cola managers initially did not understand the Japanese distribution system. However, with considerable investment of time and money, they succeeded in establishing a sales force that was as effective in Japan as it was in the United States. The Japanese unit has also created numerous new beverage products expressly for the Japanese market; these include Georgia-brand canned coffee and Qoo, a noncarbonated juice drink. Although the company has experienced a recent sales decline in Japan, it remains a key market that accounts for about 20 percent of the Coca-Cola Company's total worldwide operating revenues.[24]

The Coca-Cola Company supports its Coke, Fanta, and Powerade brands with marketing mix elements that are both global and local. Dozens of other companies also have successfully pursued global marketing by creating strong global brands. This has been accomplished in various ways. The Altria Group for example, made Marlboro the world's number one cigarette by identifying the brand with a cowboy. By creating distinctive, user-friendly handset designs, Nokia has become the world's leading cell phone brand. In automobiles, Daimler AG's Mercedes enjoys global recognition thanks to Germany's reputation for excellence in automotive engineering. Virtually all Nokia phones are manufactured in Finland; by contrast, some Mercedes models are manufactured outside Germany. Gillette uses the same packaging for its flagship Mach3 razor everywhere in the world. Italy's Benetton utilizes a sophisticated distribution system to quickly deliver the latest fashions to its worldwide network of stores.

HSBC Holdings is the largest banking firm in the United Kingdom. The company has more than 1,000 offices in 80 countries, including HSBC USA, HSBC Bank Canada, and HSBC Bank Middle East. HSBC takes pride in being "The world's local bank." The company's current marketing campaign extends that notion by asking the question, "Isn't it better to be open to other people's points of view?" The campaign is integrated with a Web site, www.yourpointofview.com; visitors to the site can view all of HSBC's ads and also write blog-entries on weekly topics of general interest.

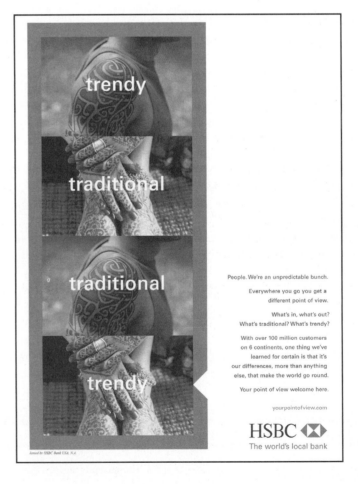

24 Chad Terhune, "Coke Tries to Pop Back in Vital Japan Market," *The Wall Street Journal*, July 11, 2006, pp. C1, C3.

The backbone of Caterpillar's global success is a network of dealers who support a promise of "24-hour parts and service" anywhere in the world. As these examples indicate, there are many different paths to success in global markets. In this book, we do *not* propose that global marketing is a knee-jerk attempt to impose a totally standardized approach to marketing around the world. A central issue in global marketing is how to tailor the global marketing concept to fit particular products, businesses, and markets.[25]

As shown in Table 1-3, McDonald's global marketing strategy is based on a combination of global and local marketing mix elements. For example, a vital element in McDonald's business model is a restaurant system that can be set up virtually anywhere in the world. McDonald's offers core menu items—hamburgers, French fries, and soft drinks—in most countries, and the company also customizes menu offerings in accordance with local eating customs. The average price of a Big Mac in the United States is $3.10. By contrast, in China, Big Macs sell for the equivalent of $1.31. In absolute terms, Chinese Big Macs are cheaper than American ones. But is it a fair comparison? Real estate costs vary from country to country, as do per capita incomes. McDonald's prices can be understood in terms of the length of time a person must work to earn enough money to buy a Big Mac. Each year UBS, a Swiss bank, publishes a study of purchasing power based on a weighted average of hourly wages across 13 occupations. For example, in Los Angeles and Tokyo, earnings from 10 minutes of work can buy a Big Mac; by contrast, in Bogotá and Nairobi, the corresponding figures are, respectively, 97 minutes and 91 minutes.[26]

Some of Coke's many faces around the world. Although the basic design of the label is the same (white letters against a red background), the Coca-Cola name is frequently translated into local languages. In the left-hand column, the Arabic label (second from top) is read from right to left; the Chinese label's (fourth from the top) translation is "delicious/happiness."

[25] John A. Quelch and Edward J. Hoff, "Customizing Global Marketing," *Harvard Business Review* 64, no. 3 (May–June 1986), p. 59.
[26] "Working Time Required to Buy . . . ," *Prices and Earnings,* 2006 Edition (UBS), p. 11.

Table 1-3	Marketing Mix Element	Standardized	Localized
Examples of Effective Global Marketing—McDonald's	Product	Big Mac	McAloo Tikka potato burger (India)
	Promotion	Brand name	Slang nicknames, for example, Macca's (Australia), MakDo (Philippines), McDoo" (Germany)
		Advertising slogan "i'm loving it"	*McJoy* magazine "Hawaii Surfing Hula" promotion (Japan)
	Place	Free-standing restaurants in high-traffic public areas	McDonald's Switzerland operates themed dining cars on Swiss national rail system; McDonald's served on Stena Line ferry from Helsinki to Oslo; home delivery (India)
	Price	Average price of a Big Mac is $3.10 (United States); same in Turkey	$5.21 (Switzerland); $1.31 (China)

The particular approach to global marketing that a company adopts will depend on industry conditions and its source or sources of competitive advantage. For example:

- Harley-Davidson's motorcycles are perceived around the world as *the* all-American bike. Should Harley-Davidson start manufacturing motorcycles in a low-wage country such as Mexico?
- The success of Honda and Toyota in world markets was initially based on exporting cars from factories in Japan. Now, both companies have invested in manufacturing and assembly facilities in the Americas, Asia, and Europe. From these sites, the automakers supply customers in the local market and also export to the rest of the world. For example, each year Honda exports tens of thousands of Accords and Civics from U.S. plants to Japan and dozens of other countries. Will European consumers continue to buy Honda vehicles exported from America? Will American consumers continue to snap up American-built Toyotas?
- As of 2007, Gap operated 2,692 stores in the United States and more than 450 stores internationally. The company sources most of its clothing from apparel factories in Honduras, the Philippines, India, and other low-wage countries. Should Gap open more stores in Asia?

The answer to these questions is: It all depends. Because Harley's competitive advantage is based in part on its "Made in the USA" positioning, shifting production outside the United States is not advisable. The company has opened a new production facility in Kansas and taken a majority stake in Buell Motorcycle, a manufacturer of "American street bikes." Toyota's success in the United States is partly attributable to its ability to transfer world-class manufacturing skills to America while using advertising to stress that American workers build the Camry with many components purchased from American suppliers. As noted, several hundred Gap stores are located outside the United States; key country markets include Canada, the United Kingdom, Japan, and France. Japan may present an opportunity for Gap to increase revenues and profits in a major non-U.S. market. A recent annual report noted that, in terms of sales revenues, the apparel market outside the United States is twice as large as that within the United States. Also, "American style" is in high demand in Japan and other parts of the world. Gap's management team has responded to this situation by selectively targeting key country markets—especially areas with high population densities—while

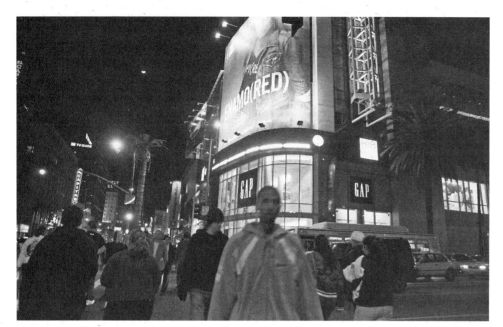

continuing to concentrate on trends in the U.S. fashion marketplace. However, recent operating difficulties in the core U.S. market led to the departure of several executives; CEO Paul Pressler left Gap early in 2007 after five years at the helm. This situation suggests that management's top priority at this time should be the domestic market.[27]

THE IMPORTANCE OF GLOBAL MARKETING

The largest single market in the world in terms of national income is the United States representing roughly 25 percent of the total world market for all products and services. U.S. companies that wish to achieve maximum growth potential must "go global" because 70 percent of world market potential is outside their home country. Management at Coca-Cola clearly understands this; it generates about 75 percent of the company's operating income and two-thirds of its operating revenue outside North America. Non-U.S. companies have an even greater motivation to seek market opportunities beyond their own borders; their opportunities include the 300 million people in the United States. For example, even though the dollar value of the home market for Japanese companies is the second largest in the world (after the United States), the market *outside* Japan is almost 90 percent of the world potential for Japanese companies. For European countries, the picture is even more dramatic. Even though Germany is the largest single country market in Europe, about 94 percent of the world market potential for German companies is outside Germany.

Many companies have recognized the importance of conducting business activities outside their home country. Industries that were essentially national in scope only a few years ago are dominated today by a handful of global companies. The rise of the global corporation closely parallels the rise of the national corporation, which emerged from the local and regional corporation in the 1880s

---

[27] Gap's transformation into a global brand is chronicled in Nina Munk, "Gap Gets It," *Fortune*, August 3, 1998, pp. 68–74+; see also Jayne O'Donnell and Mindy Fetterman, "Can Gap Be Saved?" *USA Today*, January 24, 2007, pp. 1B, 2B.

and 1890s in the United States. The auto industry provides a dramatic example: In the early twentieth century, there were thousands of auto companies scattered around the globe. The United States alone was home to more than 500 automakers. Today, fewer than 20 major companies remain worldwide. A dramatic illustration of the ongoing consolidation in the auto industry is Daimler-Benz's $36 billion takeover of Chrysler in 1998. In most industries, the companies that will survive and prosper in the twenty-first century will be global enterprises. Some companies that fail to formulate adequate responses to the challenges and opportunities of globalization will be absorbed by more dynamic, visionary enterprises. Others—ABB, for example—will undergo wrenching transformations and, if the effort succeeds, will emerge from the process greatly transformed. There is a third, grimmer, scenario as well: Some companies will simply disappear. Table 1-4 lists the top 25 of *Fortune* magazine's 2006 ranking of the 500 largest service and manufacturing companies by revenues. Market capitalization figures are listed in the third column.

Four of the companies in the top 10 are giants in the global auto industry: GM, Ford, Daimler AG, and Toyota. Note too that, measured by market capitalization, Toyota (ranked eighth in revenue) is the world's most valuable car company. Today, Toyota sells more cars worldwide than Ford; its market capitalization (roughly $200 billion) is nearly equal to the *combined* valuations of the eight leading Western automakers! Clearly, Toyota is doing something right. Oil companies occupy half of the spots in the top 10 rankings by revenues; ExxonMobil also ranked first in profitability in the *Fortune* Global 500. This showing is not surprising given the recent surge in oil prices. Wal-Mart, the world's top retailer, rounds

O P E N *to* discussion

Are We Ready for One World?

William Greider believes that the globalization of industries and markets will have some unintended, possibly dire, consequences in the coming years. In his book *One World, Ready or Not*, Greider describes how the logic of commerce and capital in the closing years of the twentieth century created an economic revolution and launched great social transformations. As Greider sees it, the message of globalization contains good news and bad news. The good news is that modern technology and global marketing are enabling people and nations throughout the world to leap into the modern era. The bad news, Greider warns, is that modern technology tends to be more individualistic and antiegalitarian than the mass assembly technology that revolutionized production in the first part of the twentieth century. As a result, disregard for basic human rights and the exploitation of the weak in developing nations may result in great social upheavals and, eventually, a breakdown in the global system.

One issue that concerns Greider is the fact that productivity and revenues at many global corporations have risen dramatically, while overall worldwide employment has not. Meanwhile, a dispersal of productive wealth is underway as global corporations establish operations in key developing countries like Brazil and China. Many economists agree that this dispersal will narrow the gap between poor and rich nations. Back in the industrialized nations, however, there is an increasing sense of social distress as workers see their plants close and jobs shipped out of the country. One by-product of globalization, Greider observes, is that it pits the interests of the older, more prosperous

workers against the interests of newly recruited, lower-paid workers. Greider warns that deeper political instability lies ahead for the United States, Germany, France, and Britain as workers take up the fight to save their jobs.

In addition, the globalization of industries such as steel, automobiles, and consumer electronics has created surplus production capacity on a massive scale. Greider notes that the U.S. economy serves as a sort of safety valve for the global system. Because the U.S. market places relatively few restrictions on imports, this "benevolent openness" means that the United States serves as a "buyer of last resort" by absorbing much of the world's excess production. As a result of the chronic imbalance in the trading system, the United States continues to post massive trade deficits that defy conventional economic analysis.

What can, or should, be done? Greider argues that U.S.-based global companies that create jobs overseas at the expense of domestic jobs should not be permitted to finance export deals by borrowing from tax-supported agencies such as the Export-Import Bank. At the same time, Greider says that American public interest would be better served if government policy shifted away from supporting and underwriting the interests of global companies and focused instead on jobs and wages. Finally, Greider advocates the use of emergency tariffs to reduce the trade deficit if American policy makers are unable to gain more access in foreign markets to U.S. export.

Sources: William Greider, One World, Ready or Not: The Manic Logic of Global Capitalism (Upper Saddle River, NJ: Simon & Schuster, 1997); William Greider, "Who Governs Globalism?" American Prospect, no. 30 (January–February 1997), pp. 73–80.

Table 1-4

The Fortune *Global 500: Largest Corporations by Revenues*

Company	Revenues (US$ millions)	Market Capitalization (US$ millions)
1. ExxonMobil (USA)	339,938	435,162
2. Wal-Mart Stores (USA)	315,654	193,401
3. Royal Dutch/Shell Group (UK/NL)	306,731	NA
4. BP (Britain)	267,600	224,066
5. General Motors (USA)	192,604	19,536
6. Chevron (USA)	189,481	153,034
7. Daimler AG (Germany)	186,106	60,072
8. Toyota Motor (Japan)	185,805	196,921
9. Ford Motor (USA)	177,210	16,139
10. ConocoPhillips (USA)	166,683	103,831
11. General Electric (USA)	157,153	362,535
12. Total (France)	152,360	163,434
13. ING Group (Netherlands)	138,253	95,586
14. Citigroup (USA)	131,045	248,799
15. AXA (France)	129,839	75,706
16. Allianz (Germany)	121,406	83,451
17. Volkswagen (Germany)	118,376	NA
18. Fortis (Belgium/Netherlands)	112,351	NA
19. Crédit Agricole (France)	110,764	NA
20. AIG (USA)	108,905	187,933
21. Assicurazioni Generali (Italy)	101,403	NA
22. Siemens (Germany)	100,098	86,952
23. Sinopec (China)	98,784	3,607
24. NTT (Japan)	94,869	68,960
25. Carrefour (France)	94,454	NA

Source: Adapted from "The *Fortune* Global 500," *Fortune,* July 24, 2006, p. 113. Figures cited from the most recent fiscal year.

out the top 10 ranks. Wal-Mart currently generates only about one-third of its revenues outside the United States. However, global expansion is the key to the company's growth strategy over the next few years.

Examining the size of individual product markets, measured in terms of annual sales, provides another perspective on global marketing's importance. Many of the companies identified in Table 1-4 are key players in the global marketplace. Annual sales in select global industry sectors markets are shown in Table 1-5. Table 1-6 shows annual sales in individual countries for select product categories.

MANAGEMENT ORIENTATIONS

The form and substance of a company's response to global market opportunities depend greatly on management's assumptions or beliefs—both conscious and unconscious—about the nature of the world. The world view of a company's personnel can be described as ethnocentric, polycentric, regiocentric, and geocentric.[28] Management at a company with a prevailing ethnocentric orientation may consciously make a decision to move in the direction of geocentricism. The orientations are collectively known as the **EPRG framework**.

---

[28] Adapted from Howard Perlmutter, "The Tortuous Evolution of the Multinational Corporation," *Columbia Journal of World Business* (January–February 1969).

Table 1-5

How Big Is the Market I? Product Category

Product or Service	Size of Market	Key Players and Brands
Textiles and clothing	$350 billion	Bangladesh, Macau, Cambodia, Pakistan, El Salvador, China, India
Cigarettes	$295 billion	Altria Group (USA); British American Tobacco (UK); Japan Tobacco (Japan)
Cosmetics	$200 billion	L'Oréal SA (France); Estée Lauder (USA); Shiseido (Japan)
Personal computers	$175 billion	Hewlett-Packard (USA); Dell (USA)
Bottled water	$100 billion	Nestlé (Switzerland); Groupe Danone (France); Coca-Cola (USA); PepsiCo (USA)
White goods (major appliances)	$85 billion	Whirlpool (USA); Electrolux (Sweden); Bosch-Siemens (Germany)
Construction equipment	$70 billion	Caterpillar (USA); Komatsu (Japan); Volvo (Sweden)
Cell phones	$60 billion	Nokia (Finland); Motorola (USA); Samsung (South Korea)
Luxury goods	$55 billion	LVMH Group (France); Richemont (Switzerland); PPR (France)
LCD and plasma flat-screen TVs	$54 billion	Samsung (South Korea); Sony (Japan)
Recorded music	$32 billion	Sony BMG (Japan/Germany); Warner Music (USA); EMI (UK); Universal Music Group (France)
Crop seeds	$30 billion	Monsanto (USA); DuPont (USA)
DRAM chips	$26 billion	Samsung (South Korea); Infineon Technologies AG (Germany); Hynix Semiconductor (South Korea)
Customer relationship management (CRM) services	$6 billion	Oracle (USA); SAP (Germany)
Regional jet aircraft	$5.9 billion	Bombardier (Canada); Embraer (Brazil)

Source: Compiled by the authors.

Country	Category	Annual Sales
United States	Online retail	$172 billion
	Wood furniture	$23 billion
	Video game consoles and games	$10 billion
	Toothpaste	$1.5 billion
	Ringtones	$600 million
Japan	Pharmaceuticals	$50 billion
	Luxury goods	$10.5 billion
India	Total retail	$300 billion
	Soft drinks	$2.3 billion
	Chocolate	$157 million
Europe	Online retail	$48 billion
	Cigarettes	$18 billion
	Home appliances (wholesale)	€20 billion
China	Consumer electronics	$85 billion
	Home appliances	$38 billion
	Cosmetics and toiletries	$10.3 billion
	Auto parts	$19 billion
	Pharmaceuticals	$11.7 billion

Source: Compiled by the authors.

Country or Region	Category	Annual Sales
Latin America	Automobiles	4 million vehicles
European Union	Shoes	2.5 billion pairs
Worldwide	Flat-panel TVs	50 million units

Table 1-7

*How Big Is the Market III?—
Individual Country/Regional
Markets by Product Category
and Units Sold*

Ethnocentric Orientation

A person who assumes that his or her home country is superior to the rest of the world is said to have an **ethnocentric orientation**. Ethnocentrism is sometimes associated with attitudes of national arrogance or assumptions of national superiority. Company personnel with an ethnocentric orientation see only similarities in markets, and *assume* that products and practices that succeed in the home country will be successful anywhere. At some companies, the ethnocentric orientation means that opportunities outside the home country are largely ignored. Such companies are sometimes called *domestic companies*. Ethnocentric companies that conduct business outside the home country can be described as *international companies*; they adhere to the notion that the products that succeed in the home country are superior. This point of view leads to a **standardized** or **extension approach** to marketing based on the premise that products can be sold everywhere without adaptation.

In the ethnocentric international company, foreign operations or markets are typically viewed as being secondary or subordinate to domestic ones. (We are using the term *domestic* to mean the country in which a company is headquartered). An ethnocentric company operates under the assumption that "tried and true" headquarters knowledge and organizational capabilities can be applied in other parts of the world. Although this can sometimes work to a company's advantage, valuable managerial knowledge and experience in local markets may go unnoticed. For a manufacturing firm, ethnocentrism may mean foreign markets are viewed as a dumping ground for surplus domestic production. Plans for overseas markets are developed utilizing policies and procedures modeled on those employed at home. Little or no systematic marketing research is conducted outside the home country, and no major modifications are made to products. Even if customer needs or wants differ from those in the home country, those differences are ignored at headquarters.

Nissan's ethnocentric orientation was quite apparent during its first few years of exporting cars and trucks to America. Designed for mild Japanese winters, the vehicles were difficult to start in many parts of the United States during the cold winter months. In northern Japan, many car owners would put blankets over the hoods of their cars. Nissan's assumption—which turned out to be false—was that Americans would do the same thing. As a Nissan spokesman said, "We tried for a long time to design cars in Japan and shove them down the American consumer's throat. That didn't work very well."[29] Until the 1980s, Eli Lilly and Company operated as an ethnocentric company: Activity outside the United States was tightly controlled by headquarters and the focus was on selling products originally developed for the U.S. market.[30] Similarly, executives at California's Robert Mondavi Corporation operated the company for many years as an ethnocentric international entity. As former CEO Michael Mondavi explains:

> Robert Mondavi was a local winery that thought locally, grew locally, produced locally, and sold globally. . . . To be a truly global company, I believe it's imperative

---

[29] Norihiko Shirouzu, "Tailoring World's Cars to U.S. Tastes," *The Wall Street Journal,* January 1, 2001, pp. B1, B6.
[30] T. W. Malnight, "Globalization of an Ethnocentric Firm: An Evolutionary Perspective," *Strategic Management Journal* 16, no. 2 (February 1995), p. 125.

the rest of the story

The Global Marketplace

Now that we've got you thinking about global marketing, it's time to test your knowledge of global current events. Some well-known companies and brands are listed in the left-hand column. The question is in what country is the parent corporation located? Possible answers are shown in the right-hand column. Write the letter corresponding to the country of your choice in the space provided; each country can be used more than once. Answers are provided at the bottom of the box.

_____ 1. Firestone Tire & Rubber   a. Germany

_____ 2. Ray Ban   b. France

_____ 3. Rolls-Royce   c. Japan

_____ 4. RCA televisions   d. Great Britain

_____ 5. Dr Pepper   e. United States

_____ 6. Ben & Jerry's Homemade   f. Switzerland

_____ 7. Gerber   g. Italy

_____ 8. Miller Beer   h. Sweden

_____ 9. Rollerblade   i. Finland

_____ 10. Case New Holland   j. China

_____ 11. Weed Eater

_____ 12. Holiday Inn

_____ 13. Wild Turkey bourbon

_____ 14. Thinkpad

_____ 15. Wilson Sporting Goods

_____ 16. Right Guard

Answers: 1. Japan (Bridgestone) 2. Italy (Luxottica SpA) 3. Germany (Volkswagen) 4. China (TTE) 5. Great Britain (Cadbury Schweppes PLC) 6. Great Britain/Netherlands (Unilever) 7. Switzerland (Nestlé) 8. Great Britain (SABMiller) 9. Italy (Benetton) 10. Italy (Fiat) 11. Sweden (AB Electrolux) 12. Great Britain 13. France (Groupe Pernod Ricard) 14. China (Lenovo) 15. Finland (Amer Group) 16. Germany (Henkel)

to grow and produce great wines in the world in the best wine-growing regions of the world, regardless of the country or the borders.[31]

Sixty years ago, most business enterprises—and especially those located in a large country like the United States—could operate quite successfully with an ethnocentric orientation. Today, however, as Mondavi's words make clear, ethnocentrism is one of the major internal weaknesses that must be overcome if a company is to transform itself into an effective global competitor.

Polycentric Orientation

The **polycentric orientation** is the opposite of ethnocentrism. The term *polycentric* describes management's belief or assumption that each country in which a company does business is unique. This assumption lays the groundwork for each

---

[31] Robert Mondavi, *Harvests of Joy: My Passion for Excellence* (New York: Harcourt Brace & Company, 1998), p. 333.

subsidiary to develop its own unique business and marketing strategies in order to succeed; the term *multinational company* is often used to describe such a structure. This point of view leads to a **localized** or **adaptation approach** that assumes products must be adapted in response to different market conditions. Until the mid-1990s, Citicorp's financial services around the world operated on a polycentric basis. James Bailey, a Citicorp executive, offered this description of the company: "We were like a medieval state. There was the king and his court and they were in charge, right? No. It was the land barons who were in charge. The king and his court might declare this or that, but the land barons went and did their thing."[32] Realizing that the financial services industry was globalizing, then-CEO John Reed attempted to achieve a higher degree of integration between Citicorp's operating units. Like Jack Welch at GE, Reed sought to instill a geocentric orientation throughout his company.

"What unites us through our brands, markets, and businesses is the group's identity, which we refer to as "a worldwide business with local presence." Everywhere we operate, our priority is to create or develop a strong brand that reflects consumer needs in that market as closely as possible."[33]

Franck Riboud, Chairman and CEO
Groupe Danone

Regiocentric Orientation

In a company with a **regiocentric orientation**, a region becomes the relevant geographic unit; management's goal is to develop an integrated regional strategy. For example, a U.S. company that focuses on the countries included in the North American Free Trade Agreement (NAFTA)—namely, the United States, Canada, and Mexico—has a regiocentric orientation. Similarly, a European company that focuses its attention on Europe is regiocentric. Some companies serve markets throughout the world, but do so on a regional basis. Such a company could be viewed as a variant of the multinational model discussed previously. For decades, a regiocentric orientation prevailed at General Motors: Executives in different parts of the world—Asia-Pacific and Europe, for example—were given considerable autonomy when designing vehicles for their respective regions. Company engineers in Australia, for example, developed models for sale in the local market. One result of this approach: A total of 270 different types of radios were being installed in GM vehicles around the world. As GM Vice Chairman Robert Lutz told an interviewer in 2004, "GM's global product plan used to be four regional plans stapled together."[34]

---

[32] Saul Hansell, "Uniting the Feudal Lords at Citicorp," *The New York Times,* January 16, 1994, Section 3, p. 1.
[33] Franck Riboud, "Think Global, Act Local," *Outlook* no. 3 (2003), p. 8.
[34] Lee Hawkins, Jr., "New Driver: Reversing 80 Years of History, GM Is Reining in Global Fiefs," *The Wall Street Journal,* October 6, 2004, pp. A1, A14.

Geocentric Orientation

A company with a **geocentric orientation** views the entire world as a potential market and strives to develop integrated global strategies. A company whose management has adopted a geocentric orientation is sometimes known as a *global* or *transnational company*.[35] During the past several years, longstanding regiocentric policies at GM such as those discussed previously have been replaced by a geocentric approach. Among other changes, the new policy calls for engineering jobs to be assigned on a worldwide basis; a global council based in Detroit determines the allocation of the company's $7 billion annual product development budget. One goal of the geocentric approach: Save 40 percent in radio costs by using only 50 different radios.

It is a positive sign that, at many companies, management realizes the need to adopt a geocentric orientation. However, the transition to new structures and organizational forms can take time to bear fruit. As new global competitors emerge on the scene, management at long-established industry giants such as GM must face up to the challenge of organizational transformation. A decade ago, Louis R. Hughes, a GM executive, said, "We are on our way to becoming a transnational corporation." Basil Drossos, former president of GM de Argentina, echoed his colleague's words, noting, "We are talking about becoming a global corporation as opposed to a multinational company; that implies that the centers of expertise may reside anywhere they best reside."[36] For the moment, GM is still the world's number one automaker in terms of revenue. However, as Table 1-8 makes clear, Toyota has surpassed GM in terms of profitability and market value. And, in the first quarter of 2007, Toyota sold more vehicles worldwide than GM!

A global company can be further described as one that pursues either a strategy of serving world markets from a single country, or one that sources globally for the purposes of focusing on select country markets. In addition, global companies tend to retain their association with a particular headquarters country. Harley-Davidson and Waterford serve world markets from the United States and Ireland, respectively. By contrast, Gap sources its apparel from low-wage

Table 1-8

GM and Toyota Compared (2006)

	General Motors	Toyota
Revenue	$205 billion	$185 billion
Profit or <Loss>	<$11.3 billion>	$12.6 billion
Market value*	$17.5 billion	$197 billion
Worldwide car production	9.2 million	8.3 million
Percentage of worldwide workforce in the United States	45	11
Percentage of U.S. light-vehicle sales	24.8	15

*Share price × number of outstanding shares.

---

[35] Although the definitions provided here are important, to avoid confusion we will use the term *global marketing* when describing the general activities of global companies. Another note of caution is in order: Usage of the terms *international, multinational,* and *global* varies widely. Alert readers of the business press are likely to recognize inconsistencies; usage does not always reflect the definitions provided here. In particular, companies that are (in the view of the authors as well as numerous other academics) global, are often described as *multinational enterprises* (abbreviated MNE) or *multinational corporations* (abbreviated MNC). The United Nations prefers the term *transnational company* rather than *global company*. When we refer to an "international company" or a "multinational," we will do so in a way that maintains the distinctions described in the text.

[36] Rebecca Blumenstein, "Global Strategy: GM Is Building Plants in Developing Nations to Woo New Markets," *The Wall Street Journal*, August 4, 1997, p. A4.

countries in all parts of the world; a sophisticated supply chain ensures timely delivery to its network of stores. Although Gap is a global brand, it focuses primarily on the key U.S. market. Harley-Davidson, Waterford, and Gap all may be thought of as global companies.

Transnational companies both serve global markets and utilize global supply chains; in addition, there is often a blurring of national identity. A true transnational would be characterized as "stateless." Toyota is a good example of a company that is coming close to fulfilling the criteria of transnationality. At global and transnational companies, management uses a combination of standardized (extension) and localized (adaptation) elements in the marketing program. A key factor that distinguishes global and transnational companies from international or multinational companies is *mind-set*: at global and transnational companies, decisions regarding extension and adaptation are not based on assumptions. Rather, such decisions are made on the basis of ongoing research into market needs and wants.

"These days everyone in the Midwest is begging Honda to come into their hometown. It is no longer viewed as a "Japanese" company, but a 'pro-American-worker corporation' flush with jobs, jobs, jobs."[37]

Douglas Brinkley, Professor of History Tulane University

One way to assess a company's "degree of transnationality" is to compute an average of three figures: sales outside the home country to total sales; assets outside the home country to total assets; and employees outside the home country to total employees. Viewed in terms of these metrics, Nestlé, Unilever, Nortel Networks, Royal Philips Electronics, GlaxoSmithKline, and the News Corporation are all transnational companies. Each is headquartered in a relatively small home country market, a fact of life that has compelled management to adopt regiocentric or geocentric orientations to achieve revenue and profit growth.

The geocentric orientation represents a synthesis of ethnocentrism and polycentrism; it is a "world view" that sees similarities and differences in markets and countries and seeks to create a global strategy that is fully responsive to local needs and wants. A regiocentric manager might be said to have a world view on a regional scale; the world outside the region of interest will be viewed with an ethnocentric or a polycentric orientation, or a combination of the two. However, research suggests that many companies are seeking to strengthen their regional competitiveness rather than moving directly to develop global responses to changes in the competitive environment.[38]

The ethnocentric company is centralized in its marketing management, the polycentric company is decentralized, and the regiocentric and geocentric companies are integrated on a regional and global scale, respectively. A crucial difference between the orientations is the underlying assumption for each. The ethnocentric orientation is based on a belief in home-country superiority. The underlying assumption of the polycentric approach is that there are so many differences in cultural, economic, and marketing conditions in the world that it is futile to attempt to transfer experience across national boundaries. A key challenge facing organizational leaders today is managing a company's evolution beyond an ethnocentric, polycentric, or regiocentric orientation to a geocentric one. As noted in one highly regarded book on global business, "The multinational solution encounters problems by ignoring a number of organizational impediments to the implementation of a global strategy and underestimating the impact of global competition."[39]

[37] Douglas Brinkley, "Hoosier Honda," *The Wall Street Journal*, July 18, 2006, p. A14.
[38] Allan J. Morrison, David A. Ricks, and Kendall Roth, "Globalization Versus Regionalization: Which Way for the Multinational?" *Organizational Dynamics* (Winter 1991), p. 18.
[39] Michael A. Yoshino and U. Srinivasa Rangan, *Strategic Alliances: An Entrepreneurial Approach to Globalization* (Boston: Harvard Business School Press, 1995), p. 64.

BRIC Briefing Book

FORCES AFFECTING GLOBAL INTEGRATION AND GLOBAL MARKETING

The remarkable growth of the global economy over the past 60 years has been shaped by the dynamic interplay of various driving and restraining forces. During most of those decades, companies from different parts of the world in different industries achieved great success by pursuing international, multinational, or global strategies. During the 1990s, changes in the business environment have presented a number of challenges to established ways of doing business. Today, the growing importance of global marketing stems from the fact that driving forces have more momentum than restraining forces. The forces affecting global integration are shown in Figure 1-2.

Regional economic agreements, converging market needs and wants, technology advances, pressure to cut costs, pressure to improve quality, improvements in communication and transportation technology, global economic growth, and opportunities for leverage all represent important driving forces; any industry subject to these forces is a candidate for globalization.

Multilateral Trade Agreements

A number of multilateral trade agreements have accelerated the pace of global integration. NAFTA is already expanding trade among the United States, Canada, and Mexico. The General Agreement on Tariffs and Trade (GATT), which was ratified by more than 120 nations in 1994, has created the World Trade Organization (WTO) to promote and protect free trade. In Europe, the expanding membership of the European Union is lowering boundaries to trade within the region. The creation of a single currency zone and the introduction of the euro are also expected to expand dramatically European trade in the twenty-first century.

Figure 1-2

Driving and Restraining Forces Affecting Global Integration

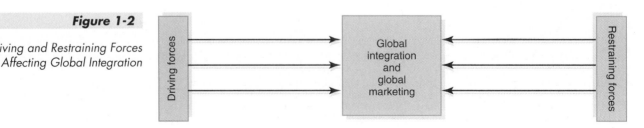

Philips Electronics: How Global Companies Win

Royal Philips Electronics is a giant $35 billion consumer electronics company headquartered in the Netherlands. Philips manufactures a vast array of products. For example, Philips Lighting is the largest manufacturer of lightbulbs in the world; in Western Europe alone, the Philips brand commands more than one-third share of the lightbulb market. Other divisions include domestic appliances, consumer electronics, industrial electronics, semiconductors, and medical systems.

Philips is a company that has changed with the times. For example, to meet the challenge of Japanese consumer electronics manufacturers such as Sony and Matsushita, Philips executives abandoned its polycentric, multinational approach and adopted a more geocentric orientation. A first step in this direction was to create industry groups in the Netherlands responsible for developing global strategies for research and development (R&D), marketing, and manufacturing. The change has paid off in Europe, where today Philips is the number one selling color television brand.

Despite such successes, the company lost $3.4 billion in 2002. Part of the problem is the fact that the company's U.S. consumer electronics division has been losing money for years. Even though Philips was a pioneer in developing new product categories, such as CD players, the company was mostly known for Philips-Magnavox, a low-end brand of television. Philips is stepping up its marketing efforts in the key North American market, which accounts for about 26 percent of overall consumer electronics sales. In 2001, Larry Blanford, formerly president of Maytag Corporation's appliance division, was assigned the task of revitalizing Philips' U.S. business. The stakes are high: Soon after Blanford took the job, the word was passed along from headquarters that if the U.S. unit didn't show a profit for 2004, it would be shut down.

Blanford mapped out a strategy designed to position Philips as a premium, high-tech brand and to boost sales of high-margin, must-have digital products such as wide-screen flat-panel HDTV monitors, DVD recorders, and portable MP3 music players. The U.S. sales team was quadrupled in size to 50 people; Blanford also instituted a policy requiring salespeople to visit at least two retail stores each week. Even as Philips works to improve relations with specialty electronics retailers, it has spent millions of dollars on consumer brand awareness advertising campaigns keyed to the themes "Getting Better" and "Sense and Simplicity." Some industry observers warned that Blanford had his work cut out for him. As a Dutch consumer electronics analyst noted, "In the U.S., Philips has been seen as a clunky brand, not at all sexy. They have a long road ahead to change people's minds."

Sources: Dan Bilefsky, "Lost in Translation: A European Electronics Giant Races to Undo Mistakes in U.S.," The Wall Street Journal, January 7, 2004, pp. A1, A10; Gregory Crouch, "Philips Electronics Reports Best Profit in Three Years," The New York Times, October 15, 2003, p. W1; Gregory Crouch, "Philips Electronics Lost $3.4 Billion Last Year," The New York Times, February 12, 2003, p. W1; Dan Bilefsky, "Famed Philips Tries to Raise U.S. Profile," The Wall Street Journal, October 3, 2002, p. B4; Dave Pringle and Dan Bilefsky, "Philips Plans to Unveil Digital Videodisc Recorder," The Wall Street Journal, August 24, 2001, p. B7.

Converging Market Needs and Wants and the Information Revolution

A person studying markets around the world will discover cultural universals as well as differences. The common elements in human nature provide an underlying basis for the opportunity to create and serve global markets. The word *create* is deliberate. Most global markets do not exist in nature; marketing efforts must create them. For example, no one *needs* soft drinks, and yet today in some countries per capita soft drink consumption *exceeds* the consumption of water. Marketing has driven this change in behavior, and today, the soft drink industry is a truly global one. Evidence is mounting that consumer needs and wants around the world are converging today as never before. This creates an opportunity for global marketing. Multinational companies pursuing strategies of product adaptation run the risk of falling victim to global competitors that have recognized opportunities to serve global customers.

The information revolution—what Thomas L. Friedman refers to as the *democratization of information*—is one reason for the trend toward convergence. Thanks to satellite dishes and globe-spanning TV networks, such as CNN and MTV, people in even the remotest corners of the globe can compare their own lifestyles and standards of living with those in other countries. In regional markets, such as Europe and Asia, the increasing overlap of advertising across national boundaries and the mobility of consumers have created opportunities for marketers to pursue pan-regional product positionings. The Internet is an even stronger driving force: When a company establishes a site on the Internet, it automatically becomes global. In addition, the Internet allows people everywhere in the world to reach out, buying and selling a virtually unlimited assortment of products and services.

Transportation and Communication Improvements

The time and cost barriers associated with distance have fallen tremendously over the past 100 years. The jet airplane revolutionized communication by making it possible for people to travel around the world in less than 48 hours. Tourism enables people from many countries to see and experience the newest products sold abroad. In 1970, 75 million passengers traveled internationally; according to figures compiled by the International Air Transport Association, that figure increased to nearly 540 million passengers in 2003. One essential characteristic of the effective global business is face-to-face communication among employees and between the company and its customers. Modern jet travel made such communication feasible. Today's information technology allows airline alliance partners such as United and Lufthansa to sell seats on each other's flights, thereby making it easier for travelers to get from point to point. Meanwhile, the cost of international telephone calls has fallen dramatically over the past several decades. That fact, plus the advent of new communication technologies such as e-mail, fax, video teleconferencing, Wi-Fi, and broadband Internet means that managers, executives, and customers can link up electronically from virtually any part of the world without traveling at all.

A similar revolution has occurred in transportation technology. The costs associated with physical distribution, both in terms of money and time, have been greatly reduced as well. The per-unit cost of shipping automobiles from Japan and Korea to the United States by specially designed auto-transport ships is less than the cost of overland shipping from Detroit to either U.S. coast. Another key innovation has been increased utilization of 20- and 40-foot metal containers that can be transferred from trucks to railroad cars to ships.

Product Development Costs

The pressure for globalization is intense when new products require major investments and long periods of development time. The pharmaceutical industry provides a striking illustration of this driving force. According to the Pharmaceutical Research and Manufacturers Association, the cost of developing a new drug in 1976 was $54 million. Today, the process of developing a new drug and securing regulatory approval to market it can take 14 years; the average total cost of bringing a new drug to market is estimated to exceed $400 million.[40] Such costs must be recovered in the global marketplace because no single national market is likely to be large enough to support investments of this size. Thus, Pfizer, Merck, GlaxoSmithKline, Novartis, Bristol-Myers Squibb, Sanofi-Aventis, and other leading pharmaceutical companies have little choice but to engage in global marketing. As noted earlier, however, global marketing does not necessarily mean operating everywhere; in the pharmaceutical industry, for example, seven countries account for 75 percent of sales. As shown in Figure 1-3, demand for pharmaceuticals in China and India is expected to triple over the next decade. In an effort to tap that market and to reduce development costs, Novartis and its rivals are establishing research and development centers in China.[41]

---

[40] Joseph A. DiMasi, Ronald W. Hansen, and Henry G. Grabowski, "The Price of Innovation: New Estimates of Drug Development Costs," *Journal of Health Economics* 22, no. 2 (March 2003), p. 151.
[41] Nicholas Zamiska, "Novartis to Establish Drug R&D Center in China," *The Wall Street Journal*, November 11, 2006, p. A3.

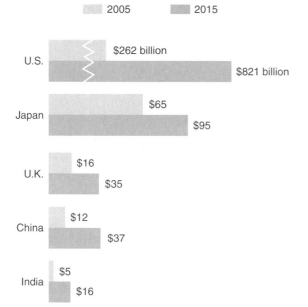

U.S.
$262 billion
$821 billion

Japan
$65
$95

U.K.
$16
$35

China
$12
$37

India
$5
$16

Figure 1-3

Estimated Spending on Prescription Drugs, Projections to 2015

Source: IMS Health.

Global marketing strategies can generate greater revenue and greater operating margins which, in turn, support design and manufacturing quality. A global and a domestic company may each spend 5 percent of sales on R&D, but the global company may have many times the total revenue of the domestic because it serves the world market. It is easy to understand how Nissan, Matsushita, Caterpillar, and other global companies have achieved world-class quality. Global companies "raise the bar" for all competitors in an industry. When a global company establishes a benchmark in quality, competitors must quickly make their own improvements and come up to par. For example, the U.S. auto manufacturers have seen their market share erode over the past four decades as Japanese manufacturers built reputations for quality and durability. Recently Detroit has faced

Caterpillar, the world's largest manufacturer of construction and mining equipment, diesel and natural gas engines, and industrial gas turbines, is also the technology leader in construction, transportation, mining, forestry, energy, logistics and electric power generation. In countries around the world Caterpillar turns on the lights, builds the roads, and brings the financing, the technology, and the experience to create lasting change. Caterpillar's goal is "to make sure the world will be better tomorrow, because of the work we're doing today." This ad highlights Caterpillar's role in making progress possible in China by converting toxic methane gas into clean electric power.

new threats: For example, when Ford rolled out its new F-150 pickup truck in January 2003, Toyota, Nissan, and other Japanese automakers were introducing their own full-sized truck models in the U.S. market for the first time. More recently, the Japanese have invested heavily in hybrid vehicles that are increasingly popular with eco-conscious drivers. The Toyota Prius is a case in point.

World Economic Trends

Economic growth has been a driving force in the expansion of the international economy and the growth of global marketing for three reasons: First, economic growth in key developing countries has created market opportunities that provide a major incentive for companies to expand globally. At the same time, slow growth in industrialized countries has compelled management to look abroad for opportunities in nations or regions with high rates of growth.

Second, economic growth has reduced resistance that might otherwise have developed in response to the entry of foreign firms into domestic economies. When a country such as China is experiencing rapid economic growth, policy makers are likely to look more favorably on outsiders. A growing country means growing markets; there is often plenty of opportunity for everyone. It is possible for a "foreign" company to enter a domestic economy and establish itself without threatening the existence of local firms. The latter can ultimately be strengthened by the new competitive environment. Without economic growth, however, global enterprises may take business away from domestic ones. Domestic businesses are more likely to seek governmental intervention to protect their local position if markets are not growing. Predictably, the worldwide recession of the early 1990s created pressure in most countries to limit foreign access to domestic markets.

The worldwide movement toward free markets, deregulation, and privatization is a third driving force. The trend toward privatization is opening up formerly closed markets; tremendous opportunities are being created as a result. In a recent book, Daniel Yergin and Joseph Stanislaw described these trends as follows:

> It is the greatest sale in the history of the world. Governments are getting out of businesses by disposing of what amounts to trillions of dollars of assets. Everything is going—from steel plants and phone companies and electric utilities to airlines and railroads to hotels, restaurants, and nightclubs. It is happening not only in the former Soviet Union, Eastern Europe, and China but also in Western Europe, Asia, Latin America, and Africa—and in the United States.[42]

For example, when a nation's telephone company is a state monopoly, it is much easier to require it to buy only from national companies. An independent, private company will be more inclined to look for the best offer, regardless of the nationality of the supplier. Privatization of telephone systems around the world is creating huge opportunities for companies such as Lucent Technologies and Northern Telcom.

Leverage

A global company possesses the unique opportunity to develop leverage. In the context of global marketing, **leverage** means some type of advantage that a company enjoys by virtue of the fact that it has experience in more than one country. Leverage allows a company to conserve resources when pursuing opportunities in new geographical markets. In other words, leverage enables a company to

---

[42] Daniel Yergin and Joseph Stanislaw, *The Commanding Heights* (New York: Simon & Schuster, 1998), p. 13.

expend less time, less effort, or less money. Four important types of leverage are experience transfers, scale economies, resource utilization, and global strategy.

Experience Transfers

A global company can leverage its experience in any market in the world. It can draw upon management practices, strategies, products, advertising appeals, or sales or promotional ideas that have been market-tested in one country or region and apply them in other comparable markets. For example, Whirlpool has considerable experience in the United States dealing with powerful retail buyers such as Sears and Circuit City. The majority of European appliance retailers have plans to establish their own cross-border "power" retailing systems; as former Whirlpool CEO David Whitwam explained, "When power retailers take hold in Europe, we will be ready for it. The skills we've developed here are directly transferable."[43]

Chevron is another example of a global company that gains leverage through experience transfers. As H. F. Iskander, general manager of Chevron's Kuwait office, explains:

> Chevron is pumping oil in different locations all over the world. There is no problem we have not confronted and solved somewhere. There isn't a rock we haven't drilled through. We centralize all that knowledge at our headquarters, analyze it, sort it out, and that enables us to solve any oil-drilling problem anywhere. As a developing country you may have a national oil company that has been pumping your own oil for twenty years. But we tell them, "Look, you have twenty years of experience, but there's no diversity. It is just one year of knowledge twenty times over." When you are operating in a multitude of countries, like Chevron, you see a multitude of different problems and you have to come up with a multitude of solutions. You have to, or you won't be in business. All those solutions are then stored in Chevron's corporate memory. The key to our business now is to tap that memory, and bring out the solution that we used to solve a problem in Nigeria in order to solve the same problem in China or Kuwait.[44]

Scale Economies

The global company can take advantage of its greater manufacturing volume to obtain traditional scale advantages within a single factory. Also, finished products can be manufactured by combining components manufactured in scale-efficient plants in different countries. Japan's giant Matsushita Electric Company is a classic example of global marketing in action; it achieved scale economies by exporting VCRs, televisions, and other consumer electronics products throughout the world from world-scale factories in Japan. The importance of manufacturing scale has diminished somewhat as companies implement flexible manufacturing techniques and invest in factories outside the home country. However, scale economies were a cornerstone of Japanese success in the 1970s and 1980s.

Leverage from scale economies is not limited to manufacturing. Just as a domestic company can achieve economies in staffing by eliminating duplicate positions after an acquisition, a global company can achieve the same economies on a global scale by centralizing functional activities. The larger scale of the global company also creates opportunities to improve corporate staff competence and quality.

---

[43] William C. Taylor and Alan M. Webber, *Going Global: Four Entrepreneurs Map the New World Marketplace* (New York: Penguin USA, 1996), p. 18.
[44] Friedman, pp. 221–222.

Resource Utilization

A major strength of the global company is its ability to scan the entire world to identify people, money, and raw materials that will enable it to compete most effectively in world markets. For a global company, it is not problematic if the value of the "home" currency rises or falls dramatically because for this company there really is no such thing as a home currency. The world is full of currencies, and a global company seeks financial resources on the best available terms. In turn, it uses them where there is the greatest opportunity to serve a need at a profit.

Global Strategy

The global company's greatest single advantage can be its global strategy. A global strategy is built on an information system that scans the world business environment to identify opportunities, trends, threats, and resources. When opportunities are identified, the global company adheres to the three principles identified earlier: It leverages its skills and focuses its resources to create superior perceived value for customers and achieve competitive advantage. *The global strategy is a design to create a winning offering on a global scale.* This takes great discipline, much creativity, and constant effort. The reward is not just success, it's survival. For example, French automaker Renault operated for many years as a regional company. During that time, its primary struggle was a two-way race with Peugeot Citroën for dominance in the French auto industry. However, in an industry dominated by Toyota and other global competitors, Chairman Louis Schweitzer had no choice but to formulate global strategy. Initiatives include acquiring a majority stake in Nissan Motor and Romania's Dacia. Schweitzer has also invested $1 billion in a plant in Brazil and is spending hundreds of millions of dollars in South Korea.[45]

A note of caution is in order: A global strategy is no guarantee of ongoing organizational success. The severe downturn in the business environment in the early years of the twenty-first century has wreaked havoc with strategic plans. As noted earlier in the chapter, ABB and Vivendi Universal struggled as their chief executives' ambitious global visions came to grief and expensive strategic bets did not pay off. Although both companies survived, they are smaller, more focused entities than they were in the mid-1990s. Companies that cannot formulate or successfully implement a coherent global strategy may lose their independence, as evidenced by the fortunes of Gerber, Helene Curtis, and others. Some strategic bets do not yield the expected results, as seen in the deals that created DaimlerChrysler and AOL Time Warner.

Restraining Forces

Despite the impact of the driving forces identified previously, several restraining forces may slow a company's efforts to engage in global marketing. In addition to the market differences discussed earlier, important restraining forces include management myopia, organizational culture, national controls, and opposition to globalization. As we have noted, however, in today's world the driving forces predominate over the restraining forces. That is why the importance of global marketing is steadily growing.

---

[45] John Tagliabue, "Renault Pins Its Survival on a Global Gamble," *The New York Times,* July 2, 2000, Section 3, pp. 1, 6; Don Kirk and Peter S. Green, "Renault Rolls the Dice on Two Auto Projects Abroad," *The New York Times,* August 29, 2002, pp. W1, W7.

Management Myopia and Organizational Culture

In many cases, management simply ignores opportunities to pursue global marketing. A company that is "nearsighted" and ethnocentric will not expand geographically. Myopia is also a recipe for market disaster if headquarters attempts to dictate when it should listen. Global marketing does not work without a strong local team that can provide information about local market conditions. Executives at Parker Pen once attempted to implement a top-down marketing strategy that ignored experience gained by local market representatives. Costly market failures resulted in Parker's buyout by managers of the former U.K. subsidiary. Eventually, the Gillette Company acquired Parker.

In companies where subsidiary management "knows it all," there is no room for vision from the top. In companies where headquarters management is all-knowing, there is no room for local initiative or an in-depth knowledge of local needs and conditions. Executives and managers at successful global companies have learned how to integrate global vision and perspective with local market initiative and input. A striking theme emerged during interviews conducted by one of the authors with executives of successful global companies. That theme was the respect for local initiative and input by headquarters executives, and the corresponding respect for headquarters' vision by local executives.

Opposition to Globalization

To many people around the world, globalization and global marketing represent a threat. The term *globaphobia* is sometimes used to describe an attitude of hostility toward trade agreements, global brands, or company policies that appear to result in hardship for some individuals or countries while benefiting others. Globaphobia manifests itself in various ways, including protests or violence directed at policy makers or well-known global companies. Opponents of globalization include labor unions, college and university students, nongovernmental organizations (NGOs), and others. In the United States, for example, some people believe that globalization has depressed the wages of American workers and resulted in the loss of both blue-collar and white-collar

Concerns about surging Chinese imports and possible loss of jobs have fueled antiglobalization sentiment in America. Some products that are "Made in China" have come under even closer scrutiny following revelations about tainted pet food, toothpaste that may contain chemical toxins, and toys contaminated with lead paint.

jobs even as companies post record profits. In many developing countries, there is a growing suspicion that the world's advanced countries—starting with the United States—are reaping most of the rewards of free trade. As an unemployed miner in Bolivia put it, "Globalization is just another name for submission and domination. We've had to live with that here for 500 years and now we want to be our own masters."[46]

National Controls

Every country protects the commercial interests of local enterprises by maintaining control over market access and entry in both low- and high-tech industries. Such control ranges from a monopoly controlling access to tobacco markets to national government control of broadcast, equipment, and data transmission markets. Today, tariff barriers have been largely removed in the high-income countries, thanks to the WTO, GATT, NAFTA, and other economic agreements. However, **nontariff barriers (NTBs)** such as "Buy Local" campaigns, food safety rules, and other bureaucratic obstacles still make it difficult for companies to gain access to some individual country and regional markets.

OUTLINE OF THIS BOOK

This book has been written for students and businesspersons interested in global marketing. Throughout the book, we present and discuss important concepts and tools specifically applicable to global marketing.

The book is divided into five parts. Part I consists of Chapter 1, an overview of global marketing and the basic theory of global marketing. Chapters 2 through 5 comprise Part II, in which we cover the environments of global marketing. Chapters 2 and 3 cover economic and regional market characteristics, including the location of income and population, patterns of trade and investment, and stages of market development. In Chapter 4, we examine social and cultural elements; and in Chapter 5, we present the legal, political, and regulatory dimensions.

We devote Part III to topics that must be considered when approaching global markets. We cover marketing information systems and research in Chapter 6. Chapter 7 discusses market segmentation, targeting, and positioning. Chapter 8 covers the basics of importing, exporting, and sourcing. We devote Chapter 9 to various aspects of global strategy, including strategy alternatives for market entry and expansion.

We devote Part IV to global considerations pertaining to the marketing mix. Chapters 10 through 14 cover in detail the application of product, price, channel, and marketing communications decisions in response to global market opportunity and threat.

The three chapters in Part V address issues of corporate strategy, leadership, and the impact of the digital revolution on global marketing. Chapter 15 includes an overview of strategy and competitive advantage. Chapter 16 addresses some of the leadership challenges facing the chief executives of global companies. In addition, the chapter covers the organization and control of global marketing programs and the importance of corporate social responsibility and ethical business practices. The final chapter explores the ways that the Internet, e-commerce, and other aspects of the digital revolution are creating new opportunities and challenges for global marketers.

---

[46] Larry Rohter, "Bolivia's Poor Proclaim Abiding Distrust of Globalization," *The New York Times,* October 17, 2003, p. A3.

A company that engages in **global marketing** focuses its resources on global market opportunities and threats. Successful global marketers such as Nestlé, Coca-Cola, and Honda use familiar **marketing mix** elements—the four Ps—to create global marketing programs. Marketing, R&D, manufacturing, and other activities comprise a firm's **value chain**; firms configure these activities to create superior customer **value** on a global basis. Global companies also maintain strategic **focus** while relentlessly pursuing **competitive advantage**. The marketing mix, value chain, competitive advantage, and focus are universal in their applicability, irrespective of whether a company does business only in the home country or has a presence in many markets around the world. However, in a **global industry**, companies that fail to pursue global opportunities risk being pushed aside by stronger global competitors.

A firm's **global marketing strategy (GMS)** can enhance its worldwide performance. The GMS addresses several issues. First is the nature of the marketing program in terms of the balance between a **standardization (extension) approach** to the marketing mix elements and a **localization (adaptation) approach** that is responsive to country or regional differences. Second, is the **concentration of marketing activities** in a few countries or the dispersal of such activities across many countries. Companies that engage in global marketing can also engage in **coordination of marketing activities**. Finally, a firm's GMS will address the issue of **global market participation**.

The importance of global marketing today can be seen in the company rankings compiled by the *Wall Street Journal, Fortune, Financial Times*, and other publications. Whether ranked by revenues, market capitalization, or some other measure, most of the world's major corporations are active regionally or globally. The size of global markets for individual industries or product categories helps explain why companies "go global." Global markets for some product categories represent hundreds of billions of dollars in annual sales; other markets are much smaller. Whatever the size of the opportunity, successful industry competitors find that increasing revenues and profits means seeking markets outside the home country.

Company management can be classified in terms of its orientation toward the world: **ethnocentric**, **polycentric**, **regiocentric**, or **geocentric**. The terms reflect progressive levels of development or evolution. An ethnocentric orientation characterizes *domestic* and *international companies*; international companies pursue marketing opportunities outside the home market by extending various elements of the marketing mix. A polycentric worldview predominates at a *multinational company*, where country managers operating autonomously adapt the marketing mix. When management moves to integrate and coordinate activities on a regional basis, the decision reflects a regiocentric orientation. Managers at *global* and *transnational companies* are geocentric in their orientation and pursue both extension and adaptation strategies in global markets.

The dynamic interplay of several driving and restraining forces shapes the importance of global marketing. Driving forces include market needs and wants, technology, transportation and communication improvements, product costs, quality, world economic trends, and a recognition of opportunities to develop **leverage** by operating globally. Restraining forces include market differences, management myopia, organizational culture, and national controls.

1. What are the basic goals of marketing? Are these goals relevant to global marketing?

2. What is meant by "global localization"? Is Coca-Cola a global product? Explain.

3. Describe some of the global marketing strategies available to companies. Give examples of companies that use the different strategies.

4. How do the global marketing strategies of Harley-Davidson and Toyota differ?

5. Describe the difference between ethnocentric, polycentric, regiocentric, and geocentric management orientations.

6. Identify and briefly describe some of the forces that have resulted in increased global integration and the growing importance of global marketing.

7. Define *leverage* and explain the different types of leverage available to companies with global operations.

Virtually every company mentioned in this chapter is using the Internet as a communications tool. You can learn a great deal about a company's geographic scope and marketing activities by visiting its Web site. Many companies also post their annual reports online; you can read and print them if your computer is equipped with Adobe's Acrobat software. A company's universal resource locator (URL) is often based on its name (e.g., **www.caterpillar.com**) or initials (e.g., **www.ibm.com**). If, after a couple of tries, you are unable to locate a company's home page, consult Hoover's (**www.hoovers.com**). You may already be familiar with the company's printed reference book, *Hoover's Handbook*. Hoover's Web site offers free company capsules that contain basic information including names of top executives, headquarters address, annual sales, and links to other corporate Web sites.

1. Each August, *Fortune* magazine publishes its survey of the Global 500. The top 25 companies for 2005 are shown in Table 1-4. Browse through the list and choose any company that interests you. Compare its 2005 ranking with the most recent ranking (which you can find either by referring to the print version of *Fortune* or by visiting ww. fortune. com). How has the company's ranking changed? Consult additional sources (e.g., magazine articles, annual reports, the company's Web site) to enhance your understanding of the factors and forces that contributed to the company's move up or down in the rankings.

2. The following is a list of countries from various regions of the world. What category of goods do you think is the number one export from each? Possible answers are shown in the right-hand column. Write the letter corresponding to the product or product category of your choice in the space provided; each product answer can be used more than once. The answers follow.

_____	1. Brazil	a. cocoa
_____	2. Finland	b. gold
_____	3. Ghana	c. telecommunication and technology products
_____	4. Saudi Arabia	d. aircraft equipment and parts
_____	5. Nigeria	e. petroleum
_____	6. Australia	f. metal ores and extractive minerals
_____	7. Russia	g. electronics
_____	8. Singapore	h. motor vehicles
_____	9. Germany	i. coffee beans
_____	10. Peru	

Answers: 1. d 2. c 3. a 4. e 5. e 6. f 7. e 8. g 9. h 10. b

There's a saying in the business world that "nothing fails like success." In this chapter, you read about some of Gap's recent problems. How can a fashion retailer that was once *the* source for wardrobe staples such as chinos and white T-shirts suddenly lose its marketing edge? Motorola is another company that has fallen victim to its own success. The company's Razr model was a huge hit with customers, but Motorola has struggled to leverage that success. Also, Starbucks CEO Howard Shultz has recently warned that his company and brand risk becoming commoditized. Conduct some exploratory research to learn more about these companies. What lessons can be learned from their recent market performance?

For readers who want to better understand China, we recommend the following:

James McGregor, *One Billion Customers: Lessons from the Front Lines of Doing Business with China* (New York: Free Press, 2005).

James Kynge, *China Shakes the World* (New York: Houghton Mifflin, 2006).

Case 1-1

McDonald's Expands Globally While Adjusting Its Local Recipe

McDonald's Corporation is a fast-food legend whose famous golden arches can be found in 118 different countries. The company is the undisputed leader in the quick service restaurant (QSR) segment of the hospitality industry, with more than twice the systemwide revenues of Burger King. McDonald's built its reputation by promising and delivering three things to customers: inexpensive food with consistent taste regardless of location; quick service; and a clean, familiar environment. The company was also a pioneer in the development of convenience-oriented features such as drive-through windows and indoor playgrounds for children. Today, thanks to memorable advertising and intensive promotion efforts, McDonald's is one of the world's most valuable brands. The golden arches are said to be the second most recognized symbol in the world, behind the Olympic rings. In the United States alone, McDonald's typically spends about twice as much on advertising as Burger King and Wendy's.

Today, however, the company faces competitive attacks from several directions. During the 1990s, a wide range of upscale food and beverage purveyors arrived on the scene. For example, consumers are flocking to Starbucks coffee bars where they spend freely on lattes and other coffee-based specialty drinks. The "fast-casual" segment of the industry that includes companies such as Panera Bread, Cosi, and Baja Fresh is attracting customers seeking higher-quality menu items in more comfortable surroundings. Meanwhile, Subway overtook McDonald's as the restaurant chain with the most outlets in the United States. Some industry observers suggested that, in terms of both food offerings and marketing, McDonald's was losing touch with modern American lifestyles.

Table 1 McDonald's Sales by Region: Increase (Decrease)

	United States	Europe	APMEA	Latin America	Canada	Total
2005	4.4%	2.6%	4.0%	11.6%	0.3%	3.9%
2004	9.6%	2.4%	5.6%	13.0%	5.4%	6.9%
2003	6.4%	(0.9)%	(4.2)%	2.3%	0.0%	2.4%

Until recently, the picture appeared brighter outside the United States. Thanks to changing lifestyles around the globe, more people are embracing the notion of fast food. McDonald's responded to the opportunities by stepping up its rate of new unit openings. As shown in Tables 1 and 2, McDonald's International is organized into four geographic regions: (1) Europe; (2) Asia/Pacific, Middle East, and Africa (APMEA); (3) Latin America; and (4) Canada. In 2005, the offices of the country heads for Europe and Asia were moved from headquarters to their respective regions; now, for example, the head of APMEA manages his business from Hong Kong. Commenting on the change, Ken Koziol, vice president of worldwide restaurant innovation, explained, "McDonald's was built on a strong foundation of a core menu that we took around the world but we need to make sure we are more locally relevant. Taste profiles and desires are changing."

Asia-Pacific

The Indian market appears to hold huge potential for McDonald's. In fall 1996, the company opened its first restaurants in New Delhi and Mumbai. In Delhi, the golden arches competes with Nirula's, a quick-service restaurant chain with about two dozen outlets; in addition, there are hundreds of smaller regional chains throughout India. The U.S.-based Subway chain opened its first Indian location in 2001; Pizza Hut, KFC, and Domino's Pizza are also setting up shop. The Pizza Hut on Juhu Road in Mumbai is housed in a three-story-tall building with large plate glass windows and central air conditioning; on most nights, a long line of customers forms outside. Indian demand for meals from the major fast-food chains is growing at an estimated rate of 40 percent annually; analysts forecast that the market would grow to $1.3 billion by 2005. Management identifies strategic locations in areas with a great deal of pedestrian traffic such as the shopping street in Bandra in the Mumbai suburbs. Other restaurant locations include a site near a college in Vile Parle and another opposite the Andheri train station. Prices are lower than in other countries; most sandwiches cost about 40 rupees (less than $1). Drinks cost 15 rupees, and a packet of French fries is 25 rupees. A complete meal costs the equivalent of about $2.

Table 2 Total Number of Systemwide Restaurants

	United States	Europe	APMEA	Latin America	Canada	Other	Total
2005	13,727	6,352	7,692	1,617	1,378	1,120	31,886
2004	13,673	6,287	7,567	1,607	1,362	1,065	31,561
2003	13,609	6,186	7,475	1,578	1,339	942	31,129

Source: McDonald's corporate Web site; accessed December 28, 2005.

Because the Hindu religion prohibits eating beef, McDonald's developed the lamb-based Maharaja Mac specifically for India. Despite protests from several Hindu nationalist groups, the first McDonald's attracted huge crowds to its site near the Victoria railway terminal; customers included many tourists from across India and from abroad as well as locals commuting to and from work. In short order, however, Hindu activists renewed their protests, this time accusing the company of using beef tallow in its cooking. Management responded by posting signs reading "No beef or beef products sold here," but the doubts raised by the controversy kept many potential customers away. In an effort to bring back the crowds, McDonald's has worked steadily to prove that it is sensitive to Indian tastes and traditions. As is the case throughout the world, McDonald's emphasizes that most of the food ingredients it uses—as much as 95 percent—are produced locally. In addition, to accommodate vegetarians, each restaurant has two separate food preparation areas. The "green" kitchen is devoted to vegetarian fare such as the spicy McAloo Tikka potato burger, Pizza McPuff, and Paneer Salsa McWrap. Meat items are prepared on the red side. Even the mayonnaise is made without eggs. Some of the new menu items developed for India are being introduced in Europe and the United States.

> " he tastes of the urban, upwardly mobile Indian are evolving, and more Indians are looking to eat out and experiment. The potential Indian customer base for a McDonald's or a Subway is larger than the size of entire developed countries."
>
> Sapna Nayak, food analyst at Raobank India

China is currently home to the world's largest McDonald's. The first Chinese location opened in mid-1992 in central Beijing, a few blocks from Tiananmen Square. Despite having a 20-year lease for its first store, McDonald's found itself in the middle of a dispute between the central government and Beijing's city government. City officials decided to build a new $1.2 billion commercial complex in the city center and demanded that McDonald's vacate the site. However, central government officials had not approved the city's plans. McDonald's was forced to abandon the location; despite the turbulent start, McDonald's now has more than 800 restaurants in China. The restaurants purchase 95 percent of their supplies, including lettuce, from local sources.

In Asia and elsewhere, McDonald's protects itself from currency fluctuations by purchasing as much as possible from local suppliers. For example, the company's Singapore locations now buy chicken patties from Thailand rather than from the United States. However, French fries must still be imported from Australia or the United States. To help offset higher costs, McDonald's offers customers the choice of rice as a side dish at a lower price.

Western Europe

The golden arches are a familiar sight in Europe, particularly in England, France, and Germany; there is even a four-star Golden Arch hotel in Zurich. Overall, Europe contributes 25 percent of sales and 45 percent of operating income, making it a key world region. However, from 1999 to 2000, Europe posted a 3 percent decline in sales, due in large part to consumer concerns about mad cow disease. The chain's British business was hit especially hard; the public health scare about mad cow disease that began in 1996 resulted in bans on British beef exports to continental Europe. Responding to public concerns, McDonald's immediately substituted imported beef at its British restaurants. By mid-1997, convinced that British beef was safe, McDonald's put it back on the menu. Ironically, no sooner had the beef furor subsided than Burger King brought its aptly named Big King sandwich ("20 percent more beef than a Big Mac") to England. In 2000 and 2001, concerns over the safety of the meat supply surfaced again amid an outbreak of hoof-and-mouth disease and ongoing media reports about mad cow disease. The public's reduced appetite for beef was reflected in decreases in systemwide sales, revenues, and operating income for McDonald's European division in 2000.

France's tradition of culinary excellence makes it a special case in Europe; dining options range from legendary three-star Michelin restaurants to humble neighborhood bistros. From the time McDonald's opened its first French outlet in 1972, policy makers and media commentators have voiced concerns about the impact of fast food on French culture. Even so, with nearly 1,000 outlets, France today represents McDonald's third-largest market in Europe. However, controversy has kept the company in the public eye. For example, some French citizens objected when McDonald's became the official food of the World Cup finals that were held in France in 1998.

In August 1999, a sheep farmer named Jose Bové led a protest against construction of the 851st French McDonald's near the village of Millau. The group used construction tools to dismantle the partially finished structure. Bové told the press that the group had singled out McDonald's because, in his words, it is a symbol of America, "the place where they not only promote globalization and industrially produced food but also unfairly penalize our peasants." In 2002, executives at McDonald's France even ran an ad in *Femme Actuelle* magazine suggesting that children should eat only one meal at McDonald's per week.

McDonald's French franchisees experience some of the same competitive pressures facing the U.S. units; there are also key differences. On the plus side, for example, Burger King closed its last restaurant in France in 1998. However, local bistros operators have enjoyed great success selling fresh-baked baguettes filled with ham and brie, effectively neutralizing McDonald's advantage of fast service and low prices. In response, executives hired an architecture firm to develop new restaurant designs specifically for the French market.

A total of eight different themes were developed; many of the redesigned stores have hardwood floors and exposed brick walls. Signs are in muted colors rather than the chain's signature red and yellow, and the golden arches are displayed more subtly. Overall, the restaurants don't look like McDonald's elsewhere. The first redesigned store is located on the Champs Elysées on a site previously occupied by a Burger King; called "Music," the restaurant provides diners with the opportunity to listen to music on iPods and watch music videos on TV monitors. In some locations, lime green Danish designer armchairs have replaced plastic seats. As McDonald's locations in France underwent style makeovers, some franchisees reported sales increases of 10 percent to

20 percent. Impressed by these results, some American franchisees began undertaking similar renovations.

Central and Eastern Europe

On January 31, 1990, after 14 years of negotiation and preparation, the first Bolshoi Mac went on sale in what was then the Soviet Union; by the end of the decade, there were more than two dozen McDonald's restaurants in Russia. The first Moscow McDonald's was built on Pushkin Square, near a major metro station just a few blocks from the Kremlin. It has 700 indoor seats and another 200 outside. It boasts 800 employees and features a 70-foot counter with 27 cash registers, equivalent to 20 ordinary McDonald's rolled into one. At present, there are more than 70 McDonald's locations in Russia, but the original Pushkin Square store enjoys the distinction of being the busiest McDonald's in the world. To ensure a steady supply of high-quality raw materials, the company built McComplex, a huge $45 million processing facility on the outskirts of Moscow. McDonald's also worked closely with local farmers to boost yields and quality; today, the company sources 75 percent of its ingredients from a network of 100 in-country suppliers.

From the outset, George Cohon, the Canadian who is senior chairman of McDonald's Russia, decreed that the restaurants would accept rubles, which was the only currency ordinary Russian citizens were allowed to possess. It was a gutsy decision because the ruble was not convertible; in other words, rubles were worthless outside Russia. Among the handful of other Western eateries in Moscow at the time, some required that customers pay in dollars or other "hard" (i.e., convertible) currencies; by contrast, Pizza Hut's Moscow restaurant offered separate service lines for ruble patrons and those paying in hard currency. Although McDonald's Russia could not initially send any profits out of the country, there was another alternative: reinvesting rubles in choice Moscow real estate and opening additional restaurants.

The turmoil stemming from the dissolution of the Soviet Union and Russia's sometimes tortuous journey toward a market economy during the 1990s has presented the management of McDonald's Russia with a number of challenges. Although massive public demonstrations followed a failed coup attempt in August 1991, the protesters did not target McDonald's. Perhaps management's biggest challenge to date was the currency crisis that began in the summer of 1998 when the Russian government devalued the ruble and defaulted on its foreign debt. Many companies immediately raised prices to compensate for the precipitous drop in the ruble's value, and customers stopped buying.

Ukraine and Belarus are among the other members of the Commonwealth of Independent States with newly opened restaurants. The first Ukrainian McDonald's opened in Kiev in 1997; the company envisions 100 locations by 2007 for a total investment of $120 million. McDonald's has also set its sights on Central Europe, where plans call for hundreds of new restaurants to be opened in Croatia, Slovakia, Romania, and other countries.

Refocusing on the U.S. Market

By the late 1990s, McDonald's strategy of growing its U.S. business by opening new restaurants was not yielding the desired results. In 1998, McDonald's struggles led to a management shake up: Chairman and CEO Michael R. Quinlan relinquished the top position to Jack M. Greenberg, who had headed McDonald's USA. Greenberg immediately launched a range of new growth-oriented initiatives, including the company's first forays outside the core business. For example, McDonald's acquired a majority stake in the Chipotle Mexican Grill chain. The move signaled McDonald's recognition both of the increasing popularity of ethnic foods and of heightened interest among consumers in healthy eating. McDonald's also acquired Aroma, a coffeehouse chain in London. The acquisition trend continued as McDonald's snapped up Donatos Pizza and Boston Market, a floundering chain featuring home-style cooking. As Greenberg conceded, "There are pieces of the business we can't do under the arches. When you're out with friends on a Saturday night for pizza and wine, you don't go to McDonald's." Greenberg envisioned that these partner brands would add at least 2 percent to McDonald's growth rate within a few years. In addition, McCafé, a gourmet coffee shop modeled on a successful Australian concept, was tested in downtown Chicago, and a McTreat ice cream parlor had a trial run in Houston.

"McDonald's comes off as uncool. If you want to be chic, you eat sushi. Indian food is even more cutting edge. McDonald's is like white bread."

Daniel, a 26-year-old architectural draftsman in San Francisco

In 2002, Greenberg resigned and Jim Cantalupo became CEO. Cantalupo was a retired vice chairman whose 28-year career at McDonald's included considerable international experience. He pledged to review all his predecessor's initiatives, including the noncore acquisitions. He also vowed to get the company back on track by focusing on the basics, namely customer service, clean restaurants, and reliable food. Unhappy with the company's recent "Smile" advertising theme, Cantalupo took the extraordinary step of calling a summit meeting of senior creative personnel from 14 advertising agencies representing McDonald's 10 largest international markets. Foremost among them was New York-based DDB Worldwide, the lead agency on the McDonald's account that handles advertising in 34 countries including Australia, the United States, and Germany. In addition, Leo Burnett is responsible for ads targeting children. McDonald's marketing and advertising managers from key countries were also summoned to the meeting at company headquarters in Oakbrook, Illinois.

As Larry Light, former global chief marketing officer for McDonald's, noted:

> Creative talent is a rare talent, and creative people don't belong to geographies, to Brazil or France or Australia. We're going to challenge our agencies to be more open-minded about sharing between geographies.

Charlie Bell, a former executive at McDonald's Europe who was promoted to chief operating officer, didn't mince words about the company's advertising. "For one of the world's best brands, we have missed the mark," he said before the summit meeting. In June, the company announced that it had picked the phrase "i'm lovin' it" as its new global marketing theme; the idea was proposed by Heye & Partner, a DDB Worldwide unit located in Germany. Tragically, within a few months, both

Cantalupo and Bell died unexpectedly. Jim Skinner, the company's current chief executive officer, instituted a "Plan to Win" initiative to increase McDonald's momentum.

Even as McDonald's executives attempted to come to grips with the problems facing their company, various business experts offered advice of their own. In the mid-1990s, one market analyst said, "McDonald's is similar to Coca-Cola ten years ago. It's on the verge of becoming an international giant, with the United States as a major market, but overseas as the driving force." Adrian J. Slywotzky, author of *Value Migration*, noted, "McDonald's needs to move the question from 'How can we sell more hamburgers?' to 'What does our brand allow us to consider selling to our customers?'" Mark DiMassimo, chief executive of a New York-based company that specializes in brand advertising, calls McDonald's "a large lost organization that is searching for a strategy." In his view, "The company must focus, focus, focus, and stand for one thing."

There is evidence that, several years on, the "Plan to Win" strategy is gaining traction. *Consumer Reports* magazine lauded the company's efforts to upgrade its coffee program. Consumers have embraced "better-for-you" menu items such as salads and sandwiches. The company is also seeking ways to be more environmentally conscious by using less plastic packaging and recycling more. Denis Hennequin, the executive in charge of European operations, is pleased with the results of his plan to redefine McDonald's image. He said, "I'm changing the story. We've got to be loyal to our roots, we have to be affordable, we have to be convenient . . . but we have to add new dimensions." In 2007, bolstered in part by strong sales growth in Europe, McDonald's stock price reached its highest level in years.

Discussion Questions

1. Identify the key elements in McDonald's global marketing strategy. In particular, how does McDonald's approach the issue of standardization?

2. Do you think government officials in developing countries such as Russia, China, and India welcome McDonald's? Do consumers in these countries welcome McDonald's? Why or why not?

3. At the end of 2003, McDonald's announced it was selling the Donatos Pizza unit. Then, in 2006, the Chipotle chain was spun off. In light of these strategic actions, assess McDonald's prospects for success beyond the burger-and-fries model.

4. Is it realistic to expect that McDonald's—or any well-known company—can expand globally without occasionally making mistakes or generating controversy? Why do antiglobalization protesters around the world frequently target McDonald's?

Visit the Web site

www. mcdonalds. com *includes a directory to country-specific sites*

Sources: Jenny Wiggins, "Burger, Fries, and a Shake-Up," *Financial Times* (January 27, 2007), p. 7; Steven Gray, "Beyond Burgers: McDonald's Menu Upgrade Boosts Meal Prices and Results," *The Wall Street Journal*, February 18–19, 2006, pp. A1, A7; Jeremy Grant, "Golden Arches Bridge Local Tastes," *Financial Times*, February 9, 2006, p. 10; Saritha Rai, "Tastes of India in U.S. Wrappers," *The New York Times*, April 29, 2003, pp. W1, W7; Bruce Horovitz, "It's Back to Basics for McDonald's," *USA Today*, May 21, 2003, pp. 1B, 2B; Sherri Day, "After Years at Top, McDonald's Strives to Regain Ground," *The New York Times*, March 3, 2003, pp. A1, A19; Sherri Day and Stuart Elliot, "At McDonald's, an Effort to Restore Lost Luster," *The New York Times*, April 8, 2003, pp. B1, B4; Shirley Leung and Suzanne Vranica, "Happy Meals Are No Longer Bringing Smiles at McDonald's," *The Wall Street Journal*, January 31, 2003, p. B1; Shirley Leung and Ron Lieber, "The New Menu Option at McDonald's: Plastic," *The Wall Street Journal*, November 26, 2002, pp. D1, D2; Shirley Leung, "McHaute Cuisine: Armchairs, TVs and Espresso—Is It McDonald's?" *The Wall Street Journal*, August 30, 2002, pp. A1, A6; Bruce Horovitz, "McDonald's Tries a New Recipe to Revive Sales," *USA Today*, July 10, 2001, pp. 1A, 2A; Geoff Winestock and Yaroslav Trofimov, "McDonald's Reassures Italians About Beef," *The Wall Street Journal*, January 16, 2001, pp. A3, A6; Kevin Helliker and Richard Gibson, "The New Chief Is Ordering Up Changes at McDonald's," *The Wall Street Journal*, August 24, 1998, pp. B1, B4; Bethan Hutton, "Fast-Food Group Blows a McBubble in Slow Economy," *Financial Times*, May 8, 1998, p. 24; Bruce Horovitz, "'My Job Is Always on the Line,'" *USA Today*, March 16, 1998, p. 8B; David Leonhardt, "McDonald's: Can It Regain Its Golden Touch?" *Business Week*, March 9, 1998, pp. 70–74+; Richard Tomkins, "When the Chips Are Down," *Financial Times*, August 16, 1997, p. 13; Yumiko Ono, "Japan Warms to McDonald's Doting Dad Ads," *The Wall Street Journal*, May 8, 1997, pp. B1, B12.

Case 2-1

Acer Inc.

Acer Inc. is a leading marketer of notebook and desktop PCs. The company, which posted sales of $9.6 billion in 2005, also produces other products such as flat-screen monitors and personal digital assistants. As Taiwan gained a reputation as the "tech workshop of the world," Acer was able to become Taiwan's number one exporter by manufacturing and marketing computers sold under its own brand name. Acer also produced equipment on an original equipment manufacturer (OEM) basis for well-known global companies such as IBM, Dell, and Hitachi. Company founder, Chairman, and CEO Stan Shih built Acer into one of Taiwan's most successful companies.

Despite Acer's success, the company had trouble breaking into the American market. Between 1995 and 1997,

Acer's U.S. market share dropped from 15 percent to 5 percent. In the late 1990s, Shih noted, "In the United States and Europe, we are relatively weak. The local players there are very strong. The problem is that we don't have good experience in marketing in those regions. It's a people issue, not a product issue." Shih has discovered that building brands in the business-to-business market is easier than building brands in the business-to-consumer market. "Business-to-consumer brands have more value but also face more challenges. People involved in business-to-business are usually rational, but consumers in business-to-consumer are usually emotional in choosing their brands," he says.

In 2000, in a major restructuring, Acer spun off its manufacturing operations. The reason: Shih wanted to transform Acer from a top 10 global PC manufacturer into a "marketing and services powerhouse." Shih also refocused Acer's distribution and marketing on the vast, fast-growing China market. Acer and other key players in Taiwan's high-tech industry stand to benefit from closer economic ties with the mainland giant, which joined the WTO in 2001. WTO rules require that both China and Taiwan eliminate limitations on foreign investment. As a result, the Taiwan-based producers from which Acer now sources its products have most of their factories in China.

Shih envisions building a solid market base in greater China (mainland China, Taiwan, and Hong Kong) and expanding from there to the rest of the world. "The market in China is very critical for Taiwanese companies to become global companies," Shih says. "Innovation is not necessarily related to whether you are smart or not. The reality is that if you don't have a big market it's not easy to innovate because the return on investment is too low. The potential of China is not just big markets and low-cost labor. Actually, it's also for highly educated engineers or professionals." Shih believes that, if greater China becomes the company's "home" market (as opposed to just Taiwan), Acer will capture critical economies of scale that will allow it to develop innovative new products that will succeed in China as well as the rest of the world.

Shih understands that it is crucial for Acer to develop a strong brand image in China. "The challenge for this region is really the poor image that is often associated with products here," says Shih. Shih believes that it is necessary for all companies to be stable and secure in the local market before pursuing regional, then global markets. He continues, "Another important feature is also the government and the general public. They have to understand the role of supporting activities for local brands. If they do not support or use the locally made products, there will be no improvement in this area."

Ronald Chwang, Acer's chief technology officer, anticipates that Acer's knowledge of China's market will help the company achieve its growth and market share objectives; as he puts it, "Now we have a market where we understand the culture and the people's needs. That should enable Acer to move a lot of hardware." J. T. Wang, Acer's president, points out, "China and Taiwan share not just the same language and culture, but a lot of our Taiwanese suppliers are already there. We can take our brand global by building a strong home market."

Still, Acer faces tough competition in China. Lenovo, a local mainland brand, dominates with about one-third of the market. Wang believes Acer is well positioned to overtake local mainland firms such as Lenovo to become the leader in PC sales in China. Shih believes Acer will have an advantage compared to local PC makers because Acer is "more global." At the same time, Shih is convinced his company will be able to compete with better-known global companies that are entering China because Acer is more "local" than they are. Acer's international identity gives the company access to advanced business practices, technology, and economies of scale that companies like Lenovo do not have. "We have more technology. . . . We have more global exposure. . . . We have more international know-how. . . . We can gradually gain more market share," Shih says.

Shih admits that sales of Acer's desktop PCs in China have developed more slowly than he expected. He attributes this to Acer's poor brand recognition in the mainland. However, Shih made a strategic bet that the company's notebook computers would help Acer establish a quality name and high-end image. Meanwhile, Lenovo acquired IBM's Thinkpad notebook business in a move that catapulted the company into third place among the world's computer makers.

Shih had promised his wife he would retire at the end of 2004 when he turned 60 years old. He kept his promise, stepping down in December of that year. Why? "This way the company can have new blood," he said. "Acer is solid and stable, but a little bit old-fashioned. Sometimes we are not aggressive enough among the middle and high level managers." The move is paying off: Acer is currently the top notebook brand in Europe, and its low prices are a crucial selling point in key emerging markets, such as India and Eastern Europe. By all indications, Acer is on track to surpass Lenovo and become the world's third largest PC marketer by the end of 2007. Will the new leadership team headed by J. T. Wang be able to replicate Acer's European success in the United States and Asia?

Discussion Questions

1. Acer's strategy has been described as "divide and conquer." Explain.
2. How did the "global markets–local markets" paradox figure into Shih's strategy for China?
3. Can Acer become the world's third largest PC company, behind Dell and Hewlett-Packard?
4. Growth in the U.S. PC market has started to slow down. Despite strong competition from Dell and Hewlett-Packard, Acer's U.S. market share increased from 1 percent in 2004 to 3.3 percent by the end of 2006. What are Acer's prospects for gaining further share in the United States?

This case was prepared by Research Assistant Alanah Davis under the supervision of Professor Mark Green.

Sources: Jane Spencer, "Taiwan's Acer May Take Bronze," *The Wall Street Journal*, November 16, 2006, p. B6; Jason Dean, "PC Underdog Raises Its Sights," *The Wall Street Journal*, September 20, 2005, p. C6; "Special Report—Stars of Asia—Managers," *Business Week*, July 12 2004; Bruce Einhorn, Amy Reinhardt, and Maureen Kline, "Acer: How Far Can It Ride This Hot Streak?" *Business Week*, May 17, 2004, p. 52; Hiawatha Bray, "Acer Embodies Taiwanese Climb up Manufacturing Food Chain," *Boston Globe*, June 24, 2002; Simon Burns and Kathy Wilhelm, "Acer Who?" *Far Eastern Economic Review* (May 24, 2001), pp. 47; Wai-Chan Chan, Martin Hirt, and Stephen M. Shaw, "The Greater China High-Tech Highway," *The McKinsey Quarterly* no. 4 (October 11, 2002); Charles S. Lee, "Acer's Last Stand?" *Fortune*, June 10, 2002; Yu Wui Wui, "Marketing Asian Brands," *New Straits Times—Management Times*, October 4, 2000.

2
The Global Economic Environment

n August 1998, the Russian economy imploded. The ruble plunged in value, and the government defaulted on its foreign debt obligations. Many Russians faced wage cuts and layoffs; savings were wiped out as banks collapsed. The meltdown sent shock waves through global financial markets. Russia was down, but it was not out; in the years since the crisis, Russia's economy has experienced substantial growth. By 2006, a country that had teetered on the brink of bankruptcy had posted four consecutive years of 6 percent economic growth and had amassed $250 billion in foreign currency reserves. The dramatic economic recovery can be attributed in part to record world prices for oil and gas; the energy sector is Russian's most important source of export revenue. A second explanation for the rebounding economy was politics. In 2000, Vladimir Putin succeeded Boris Yeltsin as president. Putin initiated a reform program that included a new tax code, streamlined customs regulations, slashed subsidies to state-owned enterprises, and made other improvements in the business climate. A third factor in Russia's economic rebound was the fact that price increases for imports caused by the ruble's devaluation stimulated local production of a wide range of goods. As one economist noted, "The crash of '98 really cleaned out the macroeconomy." Putin confidently predicted that national income in Russia would double by 2010.

The collapse of Russia's economy in 1998 and its subsequent rebound in the first years of the new millennium vividly illustrate the dynamic nature of today's economic environment. Recall the basic definition of a **market**: people or organizations with needs and wants and both the willingness and ability to buy or sell. As noted in Chapter 1, many companies engage in global marketing in an effort to reach new customers outside the home country and thereby increase sales, profits, and market share. Today, Russia represents a major growth opportunity for global companies. Russia, along with Brazil, India, and China, are collectively referred to as **BRIC**—four fast-growing markets that represent important opportunities.[1] This chapter will identify the most salient characteristics of the world economic environment, starting with an overview of the world economy, a survey of economic system types, a discussion of stages of market development, and a review of the balance of payments. The final section of the chapter discusses foreign exchange.

> "As the saying goes, if you are not manufacturing in China or selling in India, you are as good as finished."[2]
>
> Dipankar Halder,
> Associate Director
> KSA Technopak, India

[1] The "BRIC" designation first appeared in a 2001 report published by Goldman Sachs, the New York-based investment bank, hedge fund, and private equity firm.
[2] Saritha Rai, "Tastes of India in U.S. Wrappers," *The New York Times*, April 29, 2003, p. W7.

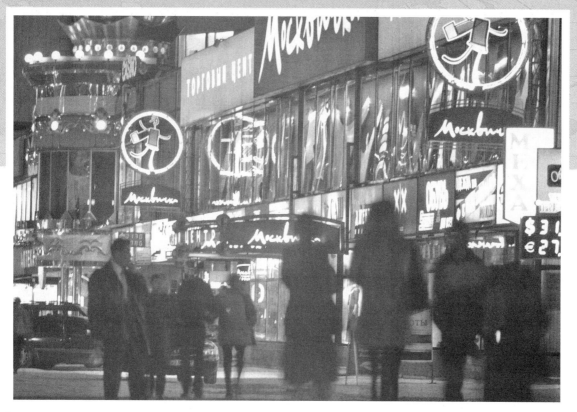

Russia is a nation that is being transformed by economic change. In Moscow, for example, affluent Russians can shop at boutiques that offer Versace, Burberry, Bulgari, and other exclusive brands. Although per capita gross national income (GNI) in Russia is only $3,400, Russian shoppers spend an estimated $4 billion each year on luxury goods. Flush with dollars from oil exports, in 2006 the Russian government lifted all currency controls, making the ruble freely convertible in world markets. As one observer noted, "Russia has now graduated to being a normal, if not developed, at least upwardly developing, country."

THE WORLD ECONOMY: AN OVERVIEW

The world economy has changed profoundly since World War II.[3] Perhaps the most fundamental change is the emergence of global markets; responding to new opportunities, global competitors have steadily displaced or absorbed local ones. Concurrently, the integration of the world economy has increased significantly. Economic integration stood at 10 percent at the beginning of the twentieth century; today, it is approximately 50 percent. Integration is particularly striking in the European Union (EU) and the North American Free Trade Area.

Just 60 years ago, the world was far less integrated than it is today. As evidence of the changes that have taken place, consider the automobile. Cars with European nameplates such as Renault, Citroen, Peugeot, Morris, Volvo, and others were radically different from the American Chevrolet, Ford, or Plymouth, or Japanese models from Toyota or Nissan. These were local cars built by local companies, mostly destined for local or regional markets. Even today, global and regional auto companies make cars for their home-country car buyers that are not marketed abroad. However, it is also true that the world car is a reality for Toyota, Nissan, Honda, and Ford. Product changes reflect organizational changes as well: The world's largest automakers have, for the most part, evolved into global companies.

During the past two decades, the world economic environment has become increasingly dynamic; change has been dramatic and far-reaching. To achieve success, executives and marketers must take into account the following new realities:[4]

- Capital movements have replaced trade as the driving force of the world economy.
- Production has become "uncoupled" from employment.

---

[3] Numerous books and articles survey this subject; see, for example, Lowell Bryan et al., *Race for the World: Strategies to Build a Great Global Firm* (Boston: Harvard Business School Press, 1999).

[4] William Greider offers a thought-provoking analysis of these new realities in *One World, Ready or Not: The Manic Logic of Global Capitalism* (New York: Simon & Schuster, 1997).

- The world economy dominates the scene; individual country economies play a subordinate role.
- The struggle between capitalism and socialism that began in 1917 is largely over.
- The growth of e-commerce diminishes the importance of national barriers and forces companies to reevaluate their business models.

The first change is the increased volume of capital movements. The dollar value of world trade is running at roughly $11 trillion per year. However, the London foreign exchange market turns over $450 billion each working day; overall, foreign exchange transactions worth approximately $1.5 trillion are booked every day—far surpassing the dollar volume of world trade in goods and services.[5] There is an inescapable conclusion in these data: Global capital movements far exceed the dollar volume of global trade. This explains the paradoxical combination of U.S. trade deficits and a strong dollar during the first half of the 1980s and again in the early twenty-first century. According to orthodox economic theory, when a country runs a deficit on its trade accounts, its currency should depreciate in value. Today, it is capital movements and trade that determine currency value.

The second change concerns the relationship between productivity and employment. **Gross domestic product (GDP)** is the total market value of final goods and services produced within a nation's borders; it is a measure of economic output. Another economic indicator, **gross national income (GNI)**, is comprised of GDP plus income generated from nonresident sources. Economic growth, as measured by GDP, reflects increases in a nation's productivity. Although employment in manufacturing remains steady or has declined, productivity continues to grow. The pattern is especially clear in American agriculture, where fewer farm employees produce more output. In the United States, manufacturing's share of GDP has declined from 19.2 percent in 1989 to 13 percent in 2004.[6] In 2001, about 13 percent of U.S. workers were employed by factories; in 1971, the figure was 26 percent. During that 30-year period, productivity has increased dramatically. Similar trends can be found in many other major industrial economies as well. One recent study of 20 large economies found that, between 1995 and 2002, more than 22 million factory jobs have been eliminated. Manufacturing is not in decline—it is *employment* in manufacturing that is in decline.[7]

The third major change is the emergence of the world economy as the dominant economic unit. Company executives and national leaders who recognize this have the greatest chance of success. For example, the real secret of the economic success of Germany and Japan is the fact that business leaders and policy makers focus on world markets and their respective countries' competitive positions in the world economy. This change has brought two questions to the fore: How does the global economy work, and who is in charge? Unfortunately, the answers to these questions are not clear-cut.

---

[5] Alan C. Shapiro, *Multinational Financial Management*, 7th ed. (Hoboken, NJ: John Wiley & Sons, 2003), p. 137. A Eurodollar is a U.S. dollar held outside the United States. U.S. dollars are subject to U.S. banking regulations; Eurodollars are not.

[6] A third economic indicator, gross national product (GNP), the total value of final goods and services produced in a country by its citizens and domestic business enterprises, plus the value of output produced by citizens working abroad, plus income generated by capital held abroad, minus transfers of net earnings by global companies operating in the country. GDP also measures economic activity; however, GDP includes all income produced within a country's borders by its residents and domestic enterprises as well as foreign-owned enterprises. Income earned by citizens working abroad is not included. For example, Ireland has attracted a great deal of foreign investment, and foreign-owned firms account for nearly 90 percent of Ireland's exports. This helps explain the fact that, in 2005, Ireland's GDP and GNP totaled €161 billion and €135 billion, respectively. However, as a practical matter, GNP, GDP, and GNI figures for many countries will be roughly the same.

[7] Jon E. Hilsenrath and Rebecca Buckman, "Factory Employment Is Falling World-Wide," *The Wall Street Journal*, October 20, 2003, p. A2. Some companies have cut employment by outsourcing or subcontracting nonmanufacturing activities such as data processing, accounting, and customer service.

The fourth change is the end of the Cold War. The demise of communism as an economic and political system can be explained in a straightforward manner: Communism is not an effective economic system. The overwhelmingly superior performance of the world's market economies has given leaders in socialist countries little choice but to renounce their ideology. A key policy change in such countries has been the abandonment of futile attempts to manage national economies with a single central plan. This policy change frequently goes hand in hand with governmental efforts to foster increased public participation in matters of state by introducing democratic reforms.[8]

Finally, the personal computer revolution and the advent of the Internet era have in some ways diminished the importance of national boundaries.

the rest of the story

Russia's Economic Rebound

Will President Putin be able to realize his vision for economic growth in Russia? Can the current recovery be sustained? Some indicators are positive; for example, foreign investment topped $13 billion in 2005, more than three times the 2002 level. Negotiations are ongoing to gain Russia admittance to the WTO. From the American perspective, issues such as market access for U.S. financial services companies and intellectual property protection are top priorities. Software, music, and video piracy are well-entrenched; annual losses from illegal software alone are estimated to be about $1.5 billion. Resolving those issues would pave the way for a lifting of U.S. economic restrictions known as the Jackson-Vanik amendments and the granting of permanent normal trade relations with Russia.

Putin hosted the 2006 Group of Eight Summit in St. Petersburg, further enhancing Russia's status on the world stage. Despite the positive publicity, however, other recent events have raised concerns in the world community. There is concern in Washington that Putin is suppressing the growth of democratic institutions. The phrase *managed democracy* describes what some call the arbitrary exercise of state power. Russia plans to limit foreign investment in strategic industries such as oil; the term *renationalization* has been applied to the process by which state-owned enterprises are acquiring rivals. *Kleptocracy* refers to rampant corruption and bribery.

Russia is so dependent on revenues from the fuel and energy sectors that a major decline in world oil prices would likely have a destabilizing effect. A related problem is the fact that Russia's energy industry is dominated by a handful of huge conglomerates. The men who run these companies are known as oligarchs; at one time, Yukos Oil's Mikhail Khodorkovsky, Sibneft's Roman Abramovich, and their peers are among Russia's ultra-rich elite. However, there is widespread resentment among the Russian citizenry about the manner in which the oligarchs gained control of their respective companies. In July 2003, the Putin government sent a message to the oligarchs by arresting billionaire businessman Platon Lebedev on charges of paying too little for a fertilizer plant that he acquired in 1994. Khodorkovsky was also arrested and his Yukos empire was forced into bankruptcy.

There are other problems as well. Putin's tax reform program was relatively easy to implement; however, further reforms may face more opposition. Russia's entrenched bureaucracy is a barrier to increased economic freedom. The banking system remains fragile and in need of reform. Tragically, in the fall of 2006, Andrei Kozlov, Russia's top banking regulator, was shot to death on the streets of Moscow. Yevgeny Yasin, a former economy minister and an advocate of liberal reforms, noted recently, "The Russian economy is constrained by bureaucratic shackles. If the economy is to grow, these chains must be dropped. If we can overcome this feudal system of using power, we will create a stimulus for strong and sustainable economic growth and improve the standards of living."

A number of Western companies have taken note of Russia's improved economic climate. For example, IKEA, the global furniture retailer, is opening dozens of new stores across Russia. France's Auchan and German retail chains Rewe and Metro are targeting the grocery market. By contrast, Wal-Mart, Carrefour, and U.K.-based Tesco do not yet have a market presence; management at these companies believes the risks and difficulties of doing business in Russia are too great.

Ultimately, Putin must ensure that the needs of ordinary Russians are satisfied and, at the same time, reign in the oligarchs, embark on governance reforms, and maintain the rule of law. If he succeeds, Putin may well be credited with creating a sustained economic miracle in Russia.

Sources: Neil Buckley, "From Shock Therapy to Retail Therapy: Russia's Middle Class Starts Spending," Financial Times, October 31, 2006, p. 13; David Lynch, "Russia Brings Revitalized Economy to the Table," USA Today, July 13, 2006, pp. 1B, 2B; Guy Chazan, "Kremlin Capitalism: Russian Car Maker Comes under Sway of Old Pal of Putin," The Wall Street Journal, May 19, 2006, pp. A1, A7; Greg Hitt and Gregory L. White, "Hurdles Grow as Russia, U.S. Near Trade Deal," The Wall Street Journal, April 12, 2006, p. A4; Chazan, "Russia is Flush—For Now," The Wall Street Journal, November 17, 2004, p. A14; Peter Weinberg, "Russia Merits a Welcome Into the Trade Fold," Financial Times, October 27, 2003, p. 13; Mark Medish, "Russia's Economic Strength Begins at Home," Financial Times, September 22, 2003, p. 15; Andrew Jack and Stefan Wagstyl, "In 1998, Russia Was Nearly Bankrupt. Today It Has Reserves of $60 Bn. But Its Economic Future Remains Insecure," Financial Times, August 18, 2003, p. 9; Gregory L. White and Jeanne Whalen, "Why Russian Oil Is a Sticky Business," The Wall Street Journal, August 1, 2003, p. A7; Marshall Goldman, "Russia Will Pay Twice for the Fortunes of Its Oligarchs," Financial Times, July 26/27, 2003, p. 10.

---

[8] Marcus W. Brauchli, "Poll Vaults: More Nations Embrace Democracy—and Find It Can Often Be Messy," *The Wall Street Journal*, June 25, 1996, pp. A1, A6.

Worldwide, an estimated one billion people use PCs. In the so-called information age, barriers of time and place have been subverted by a transnational cyberworld that functions "24–7." Amazon.com, eBay, Google, MySpace, and YouTube are just a few of the online pioneers that are pushing the envelope in this brave new world.

ECONOMIC SYSTEMS

Traditionally, economists identified four main types of economic systems: market capitalism, centrally planned socialism, centrally planned capitalism, and market socialism. As shown in Figure 2-1 this classification was based on the dominant method of resource allocation (market versus command) and the dominant form of resource ownership (private versus state). Thanks to globalization, however, economic systems are harder to categorize within the confines of a four-cell matrix. Alternatively, more robust descriptive criteria include the following:[9]

- *Type of economy.* Is the nation an advanced industrial state, an emerging economy, a transition economy, or a developing nation?
- *Type of government.* Is the nation ruled by a monarchy, dictatorship, or tyrant? Is there an autocratic one-party system? Is the nation dominated by another state, or is it a democracy with a multi-party system? Is it an unstable or terrorist nation?
- *Trade and capital flows.* Is the nation characterized by almost completely free trade, incomplete free trade and part of a trading bloc? Is there a currency board or exchange controls? Is there no trade, or does the government dominated trade possibilities?
- *The commanding heights* (e.g., the transportation, communications, and energy sectors). Are these sectors state owned and operated? Is there a mix of state and private ownership? Are they all private, with or without controlled prices?
- *Services provided by the state and funded through taxes.* Are pensions, health care, and education provided? Pensions and education but not health care? Do privatized systems dominate?
- *Institutions.* Is the nation characterized by transparency, standards, the absence of corruption, and the presence of a free press and strong courts? Or is corruption a fact of life and the press dominated by the government? Are standards ignored and the court system compromised?

Figure 2-1

Economic Systems

Resource Allocation

		Market	Command
Resource Ownership	Private	Market capitalism	Centrally planned capitalism
	State	Market socialism	Centrally planned socialism

[9] The authors are indebted to Professor Francis J. Colella, Department of Business Administration and Economics, Simpson College, for suggesting these criteria.

- *Markets.* Does the nation have a free market system characterized by high risk/high reward entrepreneurial dynamism? Is it a free market that is dominated by monopolies, cartels, and concentrated industries? Is it a socialized market with cooperation between business, government, and labor but with little entrepreneurial support? Or is planning, including price and wage controls, dominated by the center?

Market Capitalism

Market capitalism is an economic system in which individuals and firms allocate resources and production resources are privately owned. Simply put, consumers decide what goods they desire and firms determine what and how much to produce; the role of the state in market capitalism is to promote competition among firms and ensure consumer protection. Today, market capitalism is practiced widely around the world, most notably in North America and Western Europe (see Table 2-1).

It would be a gross oversimplification, however, to assume that all market-oriented economies function in an identical manner. Economist Paul Krugman has remarked that the United States is distinguished by its competitive, "wild free-for-all" and decentralized initiative. By contrast, outsiders sometimes refer to Japan as "Japan Inc." The label can be interpreted in different ways, but it basically refers to a tightly run, highly regulated economic system that is also market oriented.

Centrally Planned Socialism

At the opposite end of the spectrum from market capitalism is **centrally planned socialism**. In this type of economic system, the state has broad powers to serve the public interest as it sees fit. State planners make "top-down" decisions about what goods and services are produced and in what quantities; consumers can spend their money on what is available. Government ownership of entire industries as well as individual enterprises is characteristic of centrally planned socialism. Because demand typically exceeds supply, the elements of the marketing mix are not used as strategic variables.[10] Little reliance is placed on product differentiation, advertising, or promotion; to eliminate "exploitation" by intermediaries, the government also controls distribution.

The clear superiority of market capitalism in delivering the goods and services that people need and want has led to its adoption in many formerly socialist

Type of System	Key Characteristics	Countries
Anglo-Saxon Model	Private ownership; free enterprise economy; capitalism; minimal social safety net; highly flexible employment policies	United States, Canada, Great Britain
Social Market Economy Model	Private ownership; "social partners" orientation that includes employer groups, unions, and banks; inflexible employment policies	Germany, France, Italy
Nordic Model	Mix of state ownership and private ownership; high taxes, some market regulation, generous social safety net	Sweden, Norway

Table 2-1

Western Market Systems

---

10 Peggy A. Golden, Patricia M. Doney, Denise M. Johnson, and Jerald R. Smith, "The Dynamics of a Marketing Orientation in Transition Economies: A Study of Russian Firms," *Journal of International Marketing* 3, no. 2 (1995), pp. 29–49.

countries. An ideology developed in the nineteenth century by Marx and perpetuated in the twentieth century by Lenin and others has been resoundingly refuted. As William Greider writes:

> Marxism is utterly vanquished, if not yet entirely extinct, as an alternative economic system. Capitalism is triumphant. The ideological conflict first joined in the mid-nineteenth century in response to the rise of industrial capitalism, the deep argument that has preoccupied political imagination for 150 years, is ended.[11]

For decades, the economies of China, the former Soviet Union, and India functioned according to the tenets of centrally planned socialism. All three countries are now engaged in economic reforms characterized, in varying proportions, by increased reliance on market allocation and private ownership. Even as China's leaders attempt to maintain control over society, they acknowledge the importance of economic reform. At a recent plenum, the Communist Party said that reform "is an inevitable road for invigorating the country's economy and promoting social progress, and a great pioneering undertaking without parallel in history."

Centrally Planned Capitalism and Market Socialism

In reality, market capitalism and centrally planned socialism do not exist in "pure" form. In most countries, to a greater or lesser degree, command and market resource allocation are practiced simultaneously, as are private and state resource ownership. The role of government in modern market economies varies widely. An economic system in which command resource allocation is utilized extensively in an overall environment of private resource ownership can be called **centrally planned capitalism**. A fourth variant, **market socialism**, is also possible. In such a system, market allocation policies are permitted within an overall environment of state ownership.

In Sweden, for example, where the government controls two-thirds of all expenditures, resource allocation is more "command" oriented than "market" oriented.

In 2003, the Rolling Stones' 40 Licks CD went on sale in China. However, some of the band's most famous hits—"Brown Sugar," "Beast of Burden," "Honky Tonk Women," and "Let's Spend the Night Together"— were left off because officials viewed them as promoting social permissiveness. The Stones were scheduled to bring their fortieth anniversary tour to Beijing and Shanghai in 2003. However, the concerts were postponed due to the SARS outbreak. When Mick, Keith and company finally did perform in China in 2006, government officials ordered the band to omit five songs from its set list.

---

[11] William Greider, *One World, Ready or Not: The Manic Logic of Global Capitalism* (New York: Simon & Schuster, 1997), p. 37.

Company	Industry Sector	State Ownership %
TellaSonera	Telecom	45
SAS	Airline	21
Nordea	Banking	20
OMX	Stock exchange	7
Vin & Spirit	Alcohol	100

Table 2-2

Examples of Government Resource Ownership in Sweden

Also, as indicated in Table 2-1, the Swedish government has significant holdings in key business sectors. Thus, Sweden's so-called "welfare state" has a hybrid economic system that incorporates elements of both centrally planned socialism and capitalism. The Swedish government is embarking on a privatization plan that calls for selling its stakes in some of the businesses in Table 2-2.[12]

As noted previously, China is an example of centrally planned socialism. However, China's Communist leadership has given considerable freedom to businesses and individuals in the Guangdong Province to operate within a market system. Today, China's private sector accounts for more than 75 percent of national output. Even so, state enterprises still receive more than two-thirds of the credit available from the country's banks.

Market reforms and nascent capitalism in many parts of the world are creating opportunities for large-scale investments by global companies. Coca-Cola returned to India in 1994, two decades after being forced out by the government. A new law allowing 100 percent foreign ownership of enterprises helped pave the way. By contrast, Cuba stands as one of the last bastions of the command

"Countries with planned economies have never been part of economic globalization. China's economy must become a market economy."[13]

Long Yongtu, Chief WTO negotiator for China

O P E N ^{to} discussion

Which Operating System Do You Use?

Author Thomas L. Friedman compares and contrasts various types of economic systems by drawing an analogy with the main elements of a computer system. First is the "hardware," the basic shell around a country's economy. In the Cold War era, there were three basic types of hardware: free-market capitalism, communism, and hybrid. Second is the "operating system," which Friedman compares to a country's broad economic policies. Utilizing a pun on the title of Marx's classic work *Das Kapital*, Friedman categorizes these operating systems in a continuum ranging from DOScapital 0.0 through DOScapital 6.0. The basic "economic operating system" in communist countries, as noted previously, was central planning, which is version 0.0. The liberalized economies of the United States, Hong Kong, Taiwan, and the United Kingdom appear at the other end of the continuum. Various combinations of socialism, free markets, and crony capitalism characterize the hybrid states.

For example, Friedman classifies Hungary as DOScapital 1.0, and China is running version 1.0 in rural provinces but 4.0

in Shanghai. Thailand and Indonesia are both DOScapital 3.0, and Korea is 4.0. To get the most out of its hardware and operating system, a computer needs software. In Friedman's analysis, a country's "software" is comprised of the basic institutions of a free society. These include a functioning judicial system, a free press, free speech, economic reform, civic institutions, and multiple political parties. In short, a country's software is a reflection of how well developed its legal and regulatory systems are and the degree to which laws are understood, embraced, and made workable.

As Friedman asserts, with the end of the Cold War, virtually every country in the world is using the same basic hardware: free-market capitalism. Even so, some countries have yet to find the optimum balance between software and hardware; for example, Friedman views Russia and Venezuela as "illiberal democracies" because their governments currently emphasize hardware more than software.

Sources: Thomas L. Friedman, "Needed: Iraqi Software," The New York Times, May 7, 2003, p. A29; Friedman, The Lexus and the Olive Tree (New York: Anchor Books, 2000), pp. 151–152.

---

12 Joel Sherwood and Terence Roth, "Defeat of Sweden's Ruling Party Clears Way for Sales of State Assets," *The Wall Street Journal*, September 19, 2006, p. A8.

13 Nicholas R. Lardy, *Integrating China into the Global Economy* (Washington, D.C.: The Brookings Institution, 2003), p. 21.

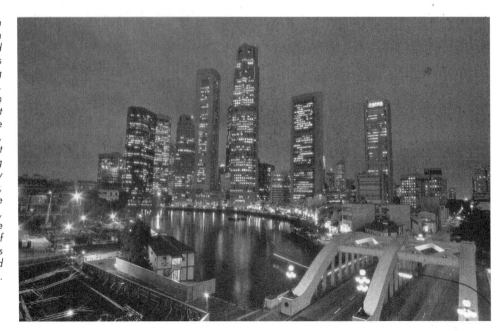

For decades, Singapore has been an important trade hub in Asia. Although efficiency, economic stability, and cleanliness have been the city-state's hallmarks, Singapore is now being remade as a cultural destination. Leaders have embarked upon an ambitious real estate development program designed to keep Singapore up-to-date and competitive with Doha, Dubai, and other popular tourist centers in the region. A striking symbol of this trend is the new Esplanade—Theaters on the Bay, adjacent to the Singapore cityscape pictured here. Another development, a mixed-use, integrated resort on the edge of the city, features thousands of apartments and villas, as well as hotels, a casino complex, and numerous retail shops.

allocation approach. Daniel Yergin and Joseph Stanislaw sum up the situation in the following way:

> Socialists are embracing capitalism, governments are selling off companies they had nationalized, and countries are seeking to entice multinational corporations expelled just two decades earlier. Today, politicians on the left admit that their governments can no longer afford the expansive welfare state. . . . The decamping of the state from the "commanding heights" marks a great divide between the 20th and 21st centuries. It is opening the doors of many formerly closed countries to trade and investment, and vastly increasing the global market.[14]

The Washington, D.C.-based Heritage Foundation, a conservative think tank, takes a more conventional approach classifying economies: It compiles a survey of more than 150 countries ranked by degree of economic freedom (Table 2-3). A number of key economic variables are considered: trade policy, taxation policy, government consumption of economic output, monetary policy, capital flows and foreign investment, banking policy, wage and price controls, property rights, regulations, and the black market. The rankings form a continuum from "free" to "repressed," with "mostly free" and "mostly unfree" in between. Hong Kong and Singapore are ranked first and second in terms of economic freedom; Burma, Iran, and North Korea are ranked lowest.

There is a high correlation between the degree of economic freedom and the extent to which a nation's mixed economy is heavily market oriented. However, the validity of the ranking has been subject to some debate. For example, author William Greider has observed that the authoritarian state capitalism practiced in Singapore deprives the nation's citizens of free speech, a free press, and free assembly. For example, in 1992, Singapore banned the import, manufacture, and sale of chewing gum because discarded wads of gum were making a mess on sidewalks, and in buildings, buses, and subway trains. Today, gum is available at pharmacies; before buying a pack, however, consumers must register their names and addresses. Greider notes, "Singaporeans are comfortably provided for by a harshly autocratic government that administers paranoid control over press and politics and an

---

[14] Daniel Yergin and Joseph Stanislaw, "Sale of the Century," *Financial Times Weekend*, January 24–25, 1998, p. I.

Table 2-3

*Index of Economic Freedom—
2006 Rankings*

Free

1. Hong Kong
2. Singapore
3. Ireland
4. Luxembourg
5. Iceland
   United Kingdom
7. Estonia
8. Denmark
9. Australia
   New Zealand
   United States
12. Canada
    Finland
14. Chile
15. Switzerland
16. Cyprus
    Netherlands
18. Austria
19. Germany
    Sweden

Mostly Free

21. Czech Republic
22. Belgium
23. Lithuania
24. Malta
25. Bahrain
26. Barbados
27. Armenia
    Bahamas
    Japan
30. Botswana
    Norway
    Portugal
33. Spain
34. El Salvador
    Slovak Republic
36. Israel
37. Taiwan
38. Slovenia
39. Latvia
40. Hungary
41. Poland
42. Italy
    Trinidad and Tobago
44. France
45. South Korea
46. Cape Verde
    Costa Rica
    Uruguay
49. Panama
50. Kuwait
    South Africa
52. Albania
    Madagascar
54. Jamaica
55. Belize
    Croatia

57. Greece
    Jordan
    Macedonia
60. Mexico
    Mongolia
62. Saudi Arabia
63. Peru
64. Bulgaria
65. United Arab Emirates
66. Uganda
67. Bolivia
68. Cambodia
    Georgia
    Malaysia
71. Kyrgyz Republic
    Thailand

Mostly Unfree

73. Lebanon
74. Bosnia and
    Herzegovina
    Guatemala
    Oman
77. Mauritius
78. Qatar
    Swaziland
80. Nicaragua
81. Brazil
    Mauritania
83. Moldova
    Senegal
85. Guyana
    Namibia
    Turkey
88. Ivory Coast
    Mali
90. Fiji
91. Colombia
92. Romania
    Sri Lanka
94. Djibouti
    Kenya
    Tanzania
97. Morocco
98. Philippines
99. Lesotho
    Tunisia
    Ukraine
102. Burkina Faso
103. Gabon
     Honduras
105. Chad
     Ghana
107. Argentina
     Ecuador
109. Paraguay
110. Pakistan
111. China
     Zambia

113. Kazakhstan
     Mozambique
115. Niger
116. Dominican Republic
117. Benin
118. Central African
     Republic
119. Algeria
     Cameroon
121. India
122. Russia
123. Azerbaijan
     Gambia
125. Nepal
     Rwanda
127. Guinea
128. Egypt
129. Surinam
130. Malawi
131. Guinea-Bissau
132. Burundi
133. Ethiopia
134. Indonesia
     Toga
136. Equatorial Guinea
137. Sierra Leone
     Tajikistan
139. Angola
     Yemen
141. Bangladesh
142. Vietnam
143. Congo, Rep.
144. Uzbekistan
145. Syria

Repressed

146. Nigeria
147. Haiti
148. Turkmenistan
149. Laos
150. Cuba
151. Belarus
152. Libya
     Venezuela
154. Zimbabwe
155. Burma
156. Iran
157. North Korea

Unrated

Congo (Dem. Rep.)
Iraq
Serbia and
Montenegro
Sudan

Source: The Wall Street Journal (Eastern Edition) by Mary Anastasia O'Grady. Copyright 2006 by Dow Jones & Company, Inc..
Reproduced with permission of Dow Jones & Company, Inc. in the format Textbook via Copyright Clearance Center.

effective welfare state that keeps everyone well housed and fed, but not free."[15] As Greider's observation makes clear, some aspects of "free economies" bear more than a passing resemblance to command-style economic systems.

STAGES OF MARKET DEVELOPMENT

At any point in time, individual country markets are at different stages of economic development. The World Bank has developed a four-category classification system that uses per capita GNI as a base. Although the income definition for each of the stages is arbitrary, countries within a given category generally have a number of characteristics in common. Thus, the stages provide a useful basis for global market segmentation and target marketing. Table 2-4 shows the categories.

A decade ago, a number of countries in Central Europe, Latin America, and Asia were expected to experience rapid economic growth. Known as *big emerging markets* (BEMs), the list included China, India, Indonesia, South Korea, Brazil, Mexico, Argentina, South Africa, Poland, and Turkey.[16] Today, much attention is focused on opportunities in Brazil, India, and China, plus, for reasons discussed in the chapter opening, Russia. As noted, these four countries are collectively known as BRIC. Experts predict that the BRIC nations will be key players in global trade even as their track records on human rights, environmental protection, and other issues come under closer scrutiny by their trading partners. The BRIC government leaders will also come under pressure at home as their developing market economies create greater income disparity. For each of the stages of economic development discussed here, special attention is given to the BRIC countries.

Low-Income Countries

Low-income countries have a GNI per capita of less than $825. The general characteristics shared by countries at this income level are:

1. Limited industrialization and a high percentage of the population engaged in agriculture and subsistence farming
2. High birth rates
3. Low literacy rates
4. Heavy reliance on foreign aid
5. Political instability and unrest
6. Concentration in Africa south of the Sahara

Table 2-4

Stages of Market Development

Income Group by Per Capita GNI	2004 GNI ($ millions)	2004 GNI Per Capita ($)	% of World GNI	2004 Population (millions)
High-income countries GNI per capita >$10,066	32,245,297	32,112	80.05	1,004
Upper-middle-income countries GNI per capita >$3,256 but ≤$10,065	2,748,229	4,769	6.82	576
Lower-middle-income countries GNP per capita ≥$826 but ≤$3,255	4,116,012	1,686	10.22	2,442·
Low-income countries GNP per capita <$825	1,187,702	507	2.95	2,343

[15] Greider, pp. 36–37. See also Steve Glain, "Political Grudges? For South Korean Firms, Speaking Too Freely May Carry Steep Price," *The Wall Street Journal,* August 18, 1995, pp. A1, A10.

[16] For an excellent discussion of BEMs, see Jeffrey E. Garten, *The Big Ten: The Big Emerging Markets and How They Will Change Our Lives* (New York: Basic Books, 1997).

Although about 40 percent of the world's population is included in this economic category, many low-income countries represent limited markets for products. Still, there are exceptions; for example, in Bangladesh, where per capita GNI is approximately $380, the garment industry has enjoyed burgeoning exports. Finished clothing exports to the United States alone amounted to $2.4 billion in 2002; an estimated 1.8 million Bangladeshis—mostly women—work in the industry for an average monthly wage of about $35. Bangladesh received preferential treatment under the Multifiber Arrangement (MFA), an international pact dating back to the mid-1970s that established import quotas to regulate the global trade in garments. The MFA expired at the end of 2004; some observers expected that a shakeout in the garment industry would lead to widespread unemployment and social and political unrest. However, this has not happened. The garment sector continues to thrive, due in part to Bangladesh's extremely low labor costs and new limits on Chinese textile exports to the United States.[17]

Many low-income countries have such serious economic, social, and political problems that they represent extremely limited opportunities for investment and operations. Some are low-income, no-growth countries such as Burundi and Rwanda that are beset by one disaster after another. Others were once growing, relatively stable countries that have become divided by political struggles. The result is a tinderbox or flash point environment characterized by civil strife, declining income, and, often, considerable danger to residents. Haiti is a case in point. Countries embroiled in civil wars are dangerous areas; most companies find it prudent to avoid them.

The newly independent countries of the former Soviet Union present an interesting situation: Income is declining, and there is considerable economic hardship. The potential for disruption is certainly high. Are they problem cases, or are they attractive opportunities with good potential for moving out of the low-income category? These countries present an interesting risk-reward trade-off; many companies have taken the plunge, but many others are still assessing whether to take the risk. Table 2-3 rates two low-income former Soviet republics—Turkmenistan and Belarus—as "repressed" in terms of economic freedom. This is one indication of a risky business environment. Russia itself, whose economy is at the lower end of the upper-middle income category, is below the middle of the ranking (number 122). As evidenced by the events of 1998 and as well as actions by the Putin administration to cut off supplies of natural gas to some former Soviet republics, economic and political instability are present here as well.

With 2004 per capita GNI of $620, India is the sole low-income country in the BRIC grouping. In 2007, India commemorated the sixtieth anniversary of its independence from Great Britain. For many decades, economic growth was weak. As the 1990s began, India was in the throes of economic crisis: Inflation was high, and foreign exchange reserves were low. Country leaders opened India's economy to trade and investment and dramatically improved market opportunities. Monmohan Singh was placed in charge of India's economy. Singh, former governor of the Indian central bank and finance minister, noted, "For years, India has been taking the wrong road." Accordingly, he set about dismantling the planned economy by eliminating import licensing requirements for many products, reducing tariffs, easing restrictions on foreign investment, and liberalizing the rupee. The results were impressive: Foreign exchange reserves jumped to $13 billion in 1993 from $1 billion in 1991. Singh became prime minister in 2004. Yashwant Sinha, the country's former finance minister, declared that the twenty-first century will be "the century of India."

"It may feel like the temperature has only risen a couple of degrees so far, but this heralds the end of India's economic Ice Age."[18]

Vivek Paul, Vice Chairman, Wipro

---

[17] Mahtab Haider, "Defying Predictions, Bangladesh's Garment Factories Thrive," *The Christian Science Monitor*, February 7, 2006, p. 4. See also Peter Fritsch, "Looming Trouble: As End of a Quota System Nears, Bangladesh Fears for Its Jobs," *The Wall Street Journal*, November 20, 2003, pp. A1, A12.

[18] Manjeet Kirpalani, "The Factories are Humming," *Business Week*, October 18, 2004, pp. 54–55.

Lower-Middle-Income Countries

The United Nations designates fifty countries in the bottom ranks of the low-income category as **least-developed countries (LDCs)**; the term is sometimes used to indicate a contrast with **developing** (i.e., upper ranks of low-income plus lower-middle and upper-middle-income) **countries** and **developed** (high-income) **countries**. **Lower-middle-income countries** are those with a GNI per capita between $826 and $3,255. Consumer markets in these countries are expanding rapidly. Countries such as China, Indonesia, and Thailand represent an increasing competitive threat as they mobilize their relatively cheap—and often highly motivated—labor forces to serve target markets in the rest of the world. The developing countries in the lower-middle-income category have a major competitive advantage in mature, standardized, labor-intensive industries, such as making toys and textiles.

China and Brazil are the BRIC nations in the lower-middle-income category. China represents the largest single destination for foreign investment in the developing world. Attracted by the country's vast size and market potential, companies in Asia, Europe, and the United States are making China a key country in their global strategies. Despite ongoing market reforms, Chinese society does not have democratic foundations. Although China has joined the WTO, trading partners are still concerned about human rights, protection of intellectual property rights, and other issues. The country's leaders must deal with China's sprawling bureaucracy while reforming the state enterprise sector. Avon, the Coca-Cola Company, Dell, Ford, General Motors, Honda, McDonald's, Motorola, Procter & Gamble, Samsung, Siemens AG, Volkswagen, and many other global companies are actively pursuing opportunities in China.

Brazil is the largest country in South America in terms of the size of its economy, population, and geographic territory. Brazil also boasts the richest reserves of natural resources in the hemisphere. Brazil has tamed hyperinflation, and liberalized trade is replacing tariff protection and an import quota system. Global companies doing business in Brazil include Electrolux, Fiat, Ford, General Motors, Nestlé, Nokia, Raytheon, Toyota, Unilever, and Whirlpool. Typical of countries at this stage of development, Brazil is a study in contrasts. Grocery distribution companies use logistics software to route their trucks; meanwhile, horse-drawn carts are still a common sight on many roads. To help them keep pace with the volatile financial environment, many local retailers have invested in modern computer and communications systems. They utilize sophisticated inventory management software to maintain financial control. Former French president Chirac underscored Brazil's importance on the world trade scene when he noted, "Geographically, Brazil is part of America. But it's European because of its culture and global because of its interests."[19]

Upper-Middle-Income Countries

Upper-middle-income countries, also known as industrializing or developing countries, are those with GNI per capita ranging from $3,256 to $10,065. In these countries, the percentage of population engaged in agriculture drops sharply as people move to the industrial sector and the degree of urbanization increases. Malaysia, Chile, Hungary, and many other countries in this stage are rapidly industrializing. They have rising wages and high rates of literacy and advanced education but significantly lower wage costs than the advanced countries. Innovative local companies can become formidable competitors and help

---

[19] Matt Moffett and Helene Cooper, "Silent Invasion: In Backyard of the U.S., Europe Gains Ground in Trade, Diplomacy," *The Wall Street Journal,* September 18, 1997, pp. A1, A8.

With per capita GNI of $4,030, Venezuela is considered an upper-middle-income country. Venezuela is one of the world's top oil-producing countries, and an important source of U.S. oil imports. A state-owned company, Petróleos de Venezuela S.A. (PDVSA), has operations in many different countries. For example, its CITGO Petroleum subsidiary operates 13,000 filling stations in the United States.

contribute to their nations' rapid, export-driven economic growth. Russia, with per capita GNI of $3,400, is currently the only BRIC nation in the upper-middle-income category.

Upper-middle-income countries that achieve the highest rates of economic growth are sometimes referred to collectively as **newly industrializing economies (NIEs)**. In Hungary and other upper-middle-income countries, scores of manufacturing companies have received ISO-9000 certification for documenting compliance with recognized quality standards. The influx of technology, particularly the computer revolution, creates startling juxtapositions of the old and the new in these countries.

Marketing Opportunities in LDCs and Developing Countries

Despite many problems in LDCs and developing countries, it is possible to nurture long-term market opportunities. Today, Nike produces and sells only a small portion of its output in China, but when the firm refers to China as a "two-billion-foot

Blessed with a location near the equator, Ecuador's cut-flower industry generates $345 million in sales each year. About 70 percent of Ecuador's flower harvest is exported to the United States; in all, about one-fourth of the cut roses sold in the United States come from Ecuador. For years, thanks to the Andean Trade Promotion and Drug Eradication Act, flowers from Ecuador, Colombia, Bolivia, and Peru were imported into the United States duty-free. The U.S. Congress passed the act to encourage Latin American farmers to cultivate ornamental flowers rather than plants that are part of the illegal drug trade. However, the act expired at the end of 2006; the flower trade with Peru and Colombia is covered by bilateral trade agreements. Although Ecuador's duty-free status was extended, new president Rafael Correa is opposed to free-trade talks with the United States.

market," it clearly has the future in mind. C. K. Prahalad and Allen Hammond have identified several assumptions and misconceptions about the "bottom of the pyramid" (BOP) that need to be corrected:[20]

- Mistaken assumption #1: *The poor have no money.* The aggregate buying power of poor communities can be substantial. In rural Bangladesh, for example, villagers spend considerable sums to use village phones operated by local entrepreneurs.
- Mistaken assumption #2: *The poor are too concerned with fulfilling basic needs to "waste" money on nonessential goods.* Consumers who are too poor to purchase a house do buy "luxury" items, such as television sets and gas stoves, to improve their lives.
- Mistaken assumption #3: *The goods sold in developing markets are so inexpensive that there is no room for a new market entrant to make a profit.* Because the poor often pay higher prices for many goods, there is an opportunity for efficient competitors to realize attractive margins by offering quality and low prices.
- Mistaken assumption #4: *People in BOP markets cannot use advanced technology.* Residents of rural areas can and do quickly learn to use cell phones, PCs, and similar devices.
- Mistaken assumption #5: *Global companies that target BOP markets will be criticized for exploiting the poor.* The informal economies in many poor countries are highly exploitative. A global company offering basic goods and services that improve a country's standard of living can earn a reasonable return while benefiting society.

Despite the difficult economic conditions in parts of Southeast Asia, Latin America, Africa, and Eastern Europe, many nations in these regions will evolve into attractive markets. One of marketing's roles in developing countries is to focus resources on the task of creating and delivering products that are best suited to local needs and incomes. Appropriate marketing communications techniques can also be applied to accelerate acceptance of these products. Marketing can

---

[20] C. K. Prahalad and Allen Hammond, "Serving the World's Poor, Profitably," *Harvard Business Review* 80, no. 9 (September 2002), pp. 48–57.

be the link that relates resources to opportunity and facilitates need satisfaction on the consumer's terms.

An interesting debate in marketing is whether it has any relevance to the process of economic development. Some people believe that marketing is relevant only in affluent, industrialized countries, where the major problem is directing society's resources into ever-changing output or production to satisfy a dynamic marketplace. In the less-developed country, the argument goes, the major problem is the allocation of scarce resources toward obvious production needs. Efforts should focus on production and how to increase output, not on customer needs and wants.

Conversely, it can be argued that the process of focusing an organization's resources on environmental opportunities is a process of universal relevance. The role of marketing—to identify people's needs and wants and to focus individual and organizational efforts to respond to these needs and wants—is the same in all countries, irrespective of the level of economic development. When global marketers respond to the needs of rural residents in emerging markets, such as China and India, they are also more likely to gain all-important government support and approval.

For example, pursuing alternative sources of energy, such as wind and solar power, is important for two reasons: the lack of coal reserves in many countries and concerns that heavy reliance on fossil fuels contributes to global warming. Similarly, people everywhere need affordable, safe drinking water. Recognizing this fact, Nestlé launched Pure Life bottled water in Pakistan. The price was set at about $0.35 a bottle, and advertising promised "Pure safety. Pure trust. The ideal water." Pure Life quickly captured 50 percent of the bottled water market in Pakistan; the brand has been rolled out in dozens of other low-income countries.[21] The Coca-Cola Company recently began to address dietary and health needs in low-income countries by developing Vitango, a beverage product that can help fight anemia, blindness, and other ailments related to malnutrition.

There is also an opportunity to help developing countries join the Internet economy. Intel chairman Craig Barrett has been visiting villages in China and India and launching programs to provide Internet access and computer training. One aspect of Intel's World Ahead initiative is the development of a $550 computer that is powered by a car battery. Similarly, Hewlett-Packard engineers are working to develop solar-powered communication devices that can link remote areas to the Internet.[22] Meanwhile, at the Massachusetts Institute of Technology's Media Lab, a project called One Laptop Per Child has the goal of developing a laptop computer that governments in developing countries can buy for $100.[23]

Global companies can also contribute to economic development by finding creative ways to preserve old-growth forests and other resources while creating economic opportunities for local inhabitants. In Brazil, for example, DaimlerChrysler works with a cooperative of farmers who transform coconut husks into natural rubber to be used in auto seats, headrests, and sun visors. French luxury-goods marketer Hermès has created a line of handbags called "Amazonia" made of latex extracted by traditional rubber tappers. Both DaimlerChrysler and Hermès are responding to the opportunity to promote

> "Sustainable energy pioneers who focus on the base of the pyramid could set the stage for one of the biggest bonanzas in the history of commerce, since extensive adoption and experience in developing markets would almost certainly lead to dramatic improvements in cost and quality."
>
> Stuart L. Hart and Clayton M. Christensen[24]

21 Ernest Beck, "Populist Perrier? Nestlé Pitches Bottled Water to World's Poor," *Asian The Wall Street Journal*, June 18, 1999, p. B1.
22 Jason Dean and Peter Wonacott, "Tech Firms Woo 'Next Billion' Users," *The Wall Street Journal*, November 3, 2006, p. A2. See also David Kirkpatrick, "Looking for Profits in Poverty," *Fortune*, February 5, 2001, pp. 174–176.
23 Steve Stecklow, "The $100 Laptop Moves Closer to Reality," *The Wall Street Journal*, November 14, 2005, pp. B1, B2.
24 Stuart L. Hart and Clayton M. Christensen, "The Great Leap: Driving Innovation from the Base of the Pyramid," *MIT Sloan Management Review* 44, no. 1 (Fall 2002), p. 56.

The One Laptop Per Child initiative was started by Nicholas Negroponte, the former director of MIT's Media Lab. Negroponte recently reached an agreement with the government of Libya to supply all 1.2 million Libyan school children with wireless laptop computers by 2008. The total purchase price is $250 million, and includes one server per school and technical support. Negroponte also has tentative agreements with Brazil, Argentina, Nigeria, and Thailand. One Laptop Per Child was recently featured on the CBS news magazine 60 Minutes; the DVD of the segment is must-see viewing for students of global marketing.

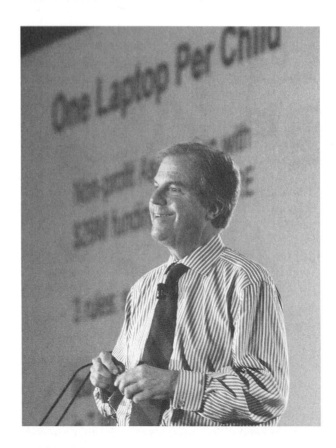

themselves as environmentally conscious while appealing to "green"-oriented consumers. As Isabela Fortes, director of a company in Rio de Janeiro that retrains forest workers, notes, "You can only prevent forest people from destroying the jungle by giving them viable economic alternatives."[25]

India's Suzlon Energy has become a major player in the wind-turbine industry. Historically, India's power distribution system has been inefficient and inconsistent; users pay high prices for electricity but still must endure blackouts on a regular basis. Moreover, burning coal to generate electricity can have serious environmental consequences. For these reasons, industrial users in India seeking alternative sources of energy are Suzlon's primary customers. Suzlon is also thinking globally: The company has opened a turbine-blade factory in Minnesota, where it also operates a wind farm.[26]

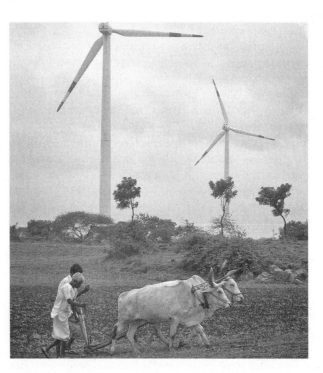

[25] Miriam Jordan, "From the Amazon to Your Armrest," *The Wall Street Journal*, May 1, 2001, pp. B1, B4.
[26] Keith Bradsher, "The Ascent of Wind Power," *The New York Times*, September 28, 2006, pp. C1, C4.

According to the World Bank, approximately 25 percent of the world's population lives on less than $2 per day. In Brazil, Latin America's largest market, low-income consumers comprise 87 percent of the population and account for 512 billion reals—$240 billion—in annual income. The balance of Brazil's population accounts for 454 billion reals. Nestlé's competitors in Brazil include both local and global brands. Sales of Nestlé's Bono brand cookies increased 40 percent in Brazil after both the serving size and the price were decreased.

High-Income Countries

High-income countries, also known as advanced, developed, industrialized, or postindustrial countries, are those with GNI per capita of $10,066 or higher. With the exception of a few oil-rich nations, the countries in this category reached their present income level through a process of sustained economic growth.

The phrase *postindustrial countries* was first used by Daniel Bell of Harvard to describe the United States, Sweden, Japan, and other advanced, high-income societies. Bell suggests that there is a difference between the industrial and the postindustrial societies that goes beyond mere measures of income. Bell's thesis is that the sources of innovation in postindustrial societies are derived increasingly from the codification of theoretical knowledge rather than from "random" inventions. Other characteristics are the importance of the service sector (more than 50 percent of GNI); the crucial importance of information processing and exchange; and the ascendancy of knowledge over capital as the key strategic resource, of intellectual technology over machine technology, of scientists and professionals over engineers and semiskilled workers. Other aspects of the postindustrial society are an orientation toward the future and the importance of interpersonal relationships in the functioning of society.

Product and market opportunities in a postindustrial society are more heavily dependent upon new products and innovations than in industrial societies. Ownership levels for basic products are extremely high in most households. Organizations seeking to grow often face a difficult task if they attempt to expand their share of existing markets. Alternatively, they can endeavor to create new markets. Today, for example, global companies in a range of communication-related industries are seeking to create new e-commerce markets for interactive forms of electronic communication. A case in point is Barry Diller's IAC/InterActiveCorp, which includes Ask.com, Expedia.com, Hotels.com, and other Internet businesses.

South Korea occupies a unique position among the high-income countries in that it is the only one classified as an emerging market by influential stock market indexes. South Korea is home to Samsung Electronics, LG Group, Kia Motors Corporation, Daewoo Corporation, Hyundai Corporation, and other well-known

When Russian president Vladimir Putin hosted the Group of Eight Summit in Saint Petersburg in 2006, he took advantage of the opportunity to show his country to the world in a positive light. The PR effort included a two-hour television broadcast during which Putin answered questions submitted from around the world via the Internet. Despite Putin's public efforts, some observers fear that, behind the scenes, the Kremlin is attempting to reassert state control over Russia's energy sector and other strategic assets. The figure on Putin's laptop depicts the Bronze Horseman, a statue near St. Isaac's Cathedral that faces the Neva River. The monument was commissioned by Catherine the Great in tribute to Peter the Great, who founded Saint Petersburg as Russia's "Window on the West."

global enterprises. In place of substantial barriers to free trade, South Korea has initiated major reforms in its political and economic system in response to the "Asian flu." Even so, investors note the political risk posed by North Korea. Another concern is inconsistent treatment of foreign investors by the government. For example, authorities recently raided the local offices of French retailer Carrefour. If the indexes do eventually reclassify South Korea as a "developed" market, the change would trigger a wave of investment inflows.[27]

Seven high-income countries—the United States, Japan, Germany, France, Britain, Canada, and Italy—comprise the **Group of Seven (G-7)**. Finance ministers, central bankers, and heads of state from the seven nations have worked together for a quarter of a century in an effort to steer the global economy in the direction of prosperity and to ensure monetary stability. Whenever a global crisis looms—be it the Latin American debt crisis of the 1980s or Russia's struggle to transform its economy in the 1990s—representatives from the G-7 nations gather and try to coordinate policy. Starting in the mid-1990s, Russia began attending the G-7 summit meetings. In 1998, Russia became a full participant, giving rise to the **Group of Eight (G-8)**.

Another institution comprised of high-income countries is the **Organization for Economic Cooperation and Development** (**OECD**; www.oecd.org). The 30 nations that belong to the OECD believe in market-allocation economic systems and pluralistic democracy. The organization has been variously described as an "economic think tank" and a "rich-man's club"; in any event, the OECD's fundamental task is to "enable its members to achieve the highest sustainable economic growth and improve the economic and social well-being of their populations." Today's organization is based in Paris and evolved from a group of European nations that worked together after World War II to rebuild the region's economy. Canada and the United States have been members since 1961; Japan joined in 1964. Evidence of the increasing importance of the BRIC group is the fact that Brazil, Russia, India, and China have all formally announced their intention to join the OECD. Applicants must demonstrate progress toward economic reform.

Representatives from OECD member nations work together in committees to review economic and social policies that affect world trade. The secretary-general

---

[27] Ian McDonald and Karen Richardson, "For South Korea, 'Emerging' Label Can Be a Burden," *The Wall Street Journal,* July 12, 2006, p. C1.

presides over a council that meets regularly and has decision-making power. Committees comprised of specialists from member countries provide a forum for discussion of trade and other issues. Consultation, peer pressure, and diplomacy are the keys to helping member nations candidly assess their own economic policies and actions. The OECD publishes country surveys and an annual economic outlook. Recently, the OECD has become more focused on global issues, social policy, and labor market deregulation. For example, the OECD tackled the vexing problem of bribery; the goal is to establish a treaty aimed at outlawing bribery of foreign officials.[28]

O P E N *to* discussion

Is Ireland Truly a "Celtic Tiger"?

The term *tiger* has frequently been used to describe fast-growing economies in Asia. For years, Hong Kong, Singapore, Taiwan, and South Korea were considered tigers because they posted double-digit rates of economic growth. As the decade of the 1990s came to an end, however, the Asian "economic miracle" had given way to hard times. Concurrently, some observers began calling Ireland the "Celtic Tiger." Riding the wave of the technology boom of the late 1990s, Ireland's economy grew at an annual rate of 9.6 percent. Lured by low corporate tax rates and a skilled workforce, companies from the United States, the United Kingdom, Germany, and Japan established subsidiaries in Ireland. The country best known for exports such as Waterford crystal, Guinness stout, *Riverdance*, and U2 had been transformed into a preferred location for high-tech manufacturing. More than 500 U.S. companies created tens of thousands of jobs as Intel, Motorola, and Gateway built factories to keep pace with burgeoning global demand for personal computers and other high-tech products. Before long, however, there were signs that Ireland's economic bubble might burst. The country's infrastructure was showing signs of stress, labor was in short supply, and inflation soared. By mid-2000, the pot of gold at the end of the rainbow gave way to gray and gloom. As the U.S. economy slowed down and the technology sector slumped, the impact on Ireland was immediate. Exports fell as foreign companies severely curtailed operations in Ireland or even closed down altogether.

A potential bright spot for Ireland is Media Lab Europe, which opened in July 2000 in Dublin in a building that once was the site of a Guinness brewery. Media Lab Europe is an offshoot of the original Media Lab that was established at the Massachusetts Institute of Technology (MIT) more than 20 years ago. The Media Lab is a research facility; in exchange for sponsorship contributions of $5 million or more, global companies such as BT, Intel, the LEGO Group, and Swatch AG get a first look at the lab's innovations in such areas as robotic design, speech synthesis, and holographic imaging. Total corporate funding for the original lab has passed the $500 million mark, and 50 new companies have been spun off after being incubated at the lab.

The Irish government allocated nearly $50 million in funding to establish Media Lab Europe, including a $10 million payment to MIT for the right to use the Media Lab name. Government officials believe the investment will pay off by strengthening the country's position in advanced information-technology research. By the end of 2001, several organizational sponsors had signed on and pledged an additional $7.5 million in support. However, there were problems. For one thing, some researchers at MIT have been reluctant to move their work to Ireland. By mid-2001, only six researchers and about two dozen research associates, assistants, and graduate students were working in a facility designed to accommodate 250 people.

"We're transitioning the nation from being a supplier and producer of other people's ideas to a place where you can actually do that development."

Enda Connolly, Industrial Development Agency of Ireland

Some Irish academics are offended by the notion that Ireland needs outside help; critics also question whether the lab will contribute to economic growth to the extent envisioned by the government. To placate such critics, the government has increased funding for local research efforts. Science Foundation Ireland (SFI) is an initiative funded by the Irish government to create an economic base in information technology, telecommunications, and biotechnology. Currently, more than 100 scientists from around the globe are conducting research at Irish universities; a typical SFI research grant provides €1 million in annual support for five years. The Irish government hopes that, attracted by the skills and talent of students graduating from local universities, global companies currently operating in Ireland will increase their level of investment. Ultimately, the government hopes to create its own world-class companies.

Visit the Web site

www.medialabeurope.org

Sources: Glenn R. Simpson, "Wearing of the Green: Irish Subsidiary Lets Microsoft Slash Taxes in U.S. and Europe," The Wall Street Journal November 11, 2005, pp. A1, 10; John Murray Brown, "Ireland Extends Its Hospitality to Top Scientists," Financial Times, November 8, 2003, p. 12; Alana Cowell, "Ireland, Once a Celtic Tiger, Slackens Its Stride," The New York Times, February 19, 2003, pp. C1, C4; Saritha Rai, "Rift in India Leads M.I.T. to Abandon a Media Lab," The New York Times, May 8, 2003, p. C4; David Armstrong, "Many Irish Eyes Aren't Smiling on MIT Import," The Wall Street Journal, July 5, 2001, pp. B1, B4; Jeffrey R. Young, "MIT's Media Lab, a Media Darling, Seeks Global Role and New Missions," The Chronicle of Higher Education (October 12, 2001), pp. A41-A43; Christopher Rhoads, "U.S. Slowdown Muffles the Volume of Ireland's Boom," The Wall Street Journal, March 6, 2001, p. A18; Mike Burns, "High-Tech Shudders for the Celtic Tiger," Europe, no. 406 (May 2001), pp. 14–15; Stewart Brand, The Media Lab: Inventing the Future at M.I.T. (New York: Viking Penguin, 1988).

---

[28] Michael Hershman, "A Blow Against Bribery," *Financial Times*, February 28, 1998, p. 14.

When he's not fronting the world's greatest rock band, U2's Bono promotes debt cancellation for developing countries as a means of fostering sound economic policies. Bono is a key figure in several advocacy organizations. DATA (debt, AIDS, trade, Africa) is a lobbying group that helped influence the G-8's decision to provide an additional $25 billion in aid to sub-Saharan Africa by 2010. ONE (The Campaign to Make Poverty History) is a constellation of several nongovernmental organizations united in an effort to generate grassroots interest in policy issues via alternative media such as YouTube and MySpace. EDUN Apparel's goal is to "make ethical fashion sexy"; garments sold under the EDUN label are designed in New York City, sewn in developing countries, and distributed through upscale retailers such as Anthropologie and Harvey Nichols. Finally, Bono was instrumental in launching Project (Red), a marketing initiative with Apple, American Express, GAP, and other corporate partners. A percentage of profits from sales of RED-branded product is donated to the Global Fund to Fight AIDS.

The Triad

The ascendancy of the global economy has been noted by many observers in recent years. One of the most astute is Kenichi Ohmae, former chairman of McKinsey & Company Japan. His 1985 book *Triad Power* represented one of the first attempts to develop a coherent conceptualization of the new emerging order. Ohmae argued that successful global companies had to be equally strong in Japan, Western Europe, and the United States. These three regions, which Ohmae collectively called the **Triad**, represented the dominant economic centers of the world. Today, about two-thirds of world income as measured by GNI is located in the Triad. Ohmae has recently revised his view of the world; in the **expanded Triad**, the Japanese leg encompasses the entire Pacific region; the American leg includes Canada and Mexico; and the boundary in Europe is moving eastward. Coca-Cola is a perfect illustration of a company with a balanced revenue stream. Approximately one-quarter of the company's revenues are generated in Asia; another 25 percent come from Europe, Eurasia, and the Middle East. North America accounts for about 40 percent.

Marketing Implications of the Stages of Development

The stages of economic development described previously can serve as a guide to marketers in evaluating **product saturation levels**, or the percentage of potential

Currency Crisis in Mexico

On December 20, 1994, the Bank of Mexico embarked on a course of action that sent shock waves around the world. A combination of circumstances, including a $28 billion current-account deficit, dwindling reserves, the murder of presidential candidate Donaldo Colosio, and eroding investor confidence, forced the Bank of Mexico to devalue the peso. The Clinton administration quickly arranged $20 billion in loans and loan guarantees, secured in part by some of Mexico's $7 billion in annual oil export revenues. Opponents of NAFTA—notably Ross Perot—seized the opportunity to denounce both the loans and the trade agreement. The devalued peso, critics predicted, would make U.S. exports to Mexico more expensive and reduce the $2 billion trade surplus that the United States enjoys with Mexico. NAFTA opponents also noted that increased imports of Mexican goods into the United States would constitute a new threat to U.S. jobs.

The Bank of Mexico's decision to devalue the peso meant that the Mexican currency declined nearly 40 percent relative to key currencies such as the dollar, the mark, and the yen. One immediate effect of the devaluation was a sharp decline in Mexican purchases of U.S. imports. For example, Westinghouse and Lennox had been aggressively selling air conditioners after NAFTA reduced tariffs; sales quickly slowed down after the devaluation. McDonald's, KFC, Dunkin' Donuts, and other U.S. restaurant chains were also hard hit as they were forced to raise prices. Many franchisors had contracted to pay rent for their facilities in dollars; after the devaluation, franchisors who couldn't pay the rent were forced to shut down. Simply put, the purchasing power of Mexican consumers was cut nearly in half. To reduce the risk of inflation, the Mexican government pledged to cut spending and allow interest rates to rise. Meanwhile, investors who had poured money into Mexico since the late 1980s, lured by the promise of low inflation and a stable currency, faced huge declines in the value of their holdings.

For many manufacturing companies, the weaker peso wreaked havoc with 1995 sales forecasts. GM, for example,

had hoped to export 15,000 vehicles to Mexico in 1995, a goal rendered unattainable by the financial crisis. Ford raised vehicle prices in Mexico; the increases applied to vehicles built in Mexico as well as those imported from Canada and the United States. Shares of Avon Products, whose Mexican sales comprise 11 percent of the company's $4 billion in annual revenue, declined sharply on Wall Street. Hoping to calm investors' fears, company executives predicted that a decline in Mexican sales would be offset in 1995 by gains in other countries.

Supporters and opponents of NAFTA debated the long-term effects of the devaluation. Harley Shaiken, a labor professor at the University of California and NAFTA critic, noted, "It will have a dual impact: It will diminish the market for U.S. goods in Mexico, but the more sizable impact will be the transfer of production to Mexico. It's going to make Mexico less desirable as a place to sell things and far more desirable as a place to make things." Persons holding opposing views acknowledged that the devaluation cut Mexican wages in dollar terms. However, NAFTA supporters have pointed out that labor's percentage of total cost in autos and auto parts, which constitute Mexico's largest export sector, is relatively low. Despite the devaluation, NAFTA supporters denied that there would be a "giant sucking sound" caused by an exodus of U.S. jobs south of the border. In 2004, the tenth anniversary of NAFTA, policy makers and the general public were still divided. Perhaps the best assessment came from a recent report by the Carnegie Endowment of International Peace which noted, "NAFTA has been neither the disaster its opponents predicted nor the savior hailed by its supporters."

Sources: James Cox, "10 Years Ago, NAFTA Was Born," USA Today, December 31, 2003, p. 3B; Craig Torres, "Headed South: Mexico's Devaluation Stuns Latin America—and U.S. Investors," The Wall Street Journal, December 22, 1994, pp. A1, A12; "Ford Lifts Prices, Avon Tries to Calm Holders, Dina Estimates Loss as Peso Fallout Continues," The Wall Street Journal, January 13, 1995; Michael Clements and Bill Montague, "Will Peso's Fall Prove Perot Right?" USA Today, January 17, 1995, pp. B1, B2.

buyers or households who own a particular product. In countries with low per capita income, product saturation levels for many products are low. For example, India's teledensity—a measure of ownership of private telephones—is only about 20 percent of the population. In China, saturation levels of private motor vehicles and personal computers are quite low; there is only one car or light truck for every 43,000 Chinese, and only one PC for every 6,000 people. In Poland in 2001, there were 21 cars per 100 compared with 49 in the 15-nation European Union; in 2002, Poland had 11 PCs per 100 people. In the EU, the ratio was 34 PCs per 100 people.[29]

BALANCE OF PAYMENTS

The **balance of payments** is a record of all economic transactions between the residents of a country and the rest of the world. Table 2-5 shows the U.S. balance of payments statistics for the period 2002 to 2006. International trade data for the United

---

[29] Stefan Wagstyl, "The Next Investment Wave: Companies in East and West Prepare for the Risks and Opportunities of an Enlarged EU," *Financial Times,* April 27, 2004, p. 13.

Table 2-5

U.S. Balance of Payments,
2002-2006 (US$ billions)

	2002	2003	2004	2005	2006
A. Current Account	**-472,466**	**-527,514**	**-665,286**	**-791,508**	**-811,477**
1. Goods exports (BoP basis)	682,422	713,415	807,516	894,631	1,023,109
2. Goods imports (BoP basis)	-1,164,720	-1,260,717	-1,472,926	-1,677,371	-1,861,380
3. Balance on goods	-482,298	-547,302	-665,410	-782,740	-838,271
4. Services: Credit	292,299	302,681	344,426	380,614	422,594
5. Services: Debit	-231,069	-250,276	-290,312	-314,604	-342,845
6. Balance on services	61,230	52,405	54,114	66,011	79,749
7. Balance on goods and services	-421,068	-494,897	-611,296	-716,730	-758,522
B. Capital Account					

Source: www.bea.gov.

States is available from the U.S. Bureau of Economic Analysis (www.bea.gov); the bureau's interactive Web site enables users to generate customized reports. The International Monetary Fund's *Balance of Payments Statistics Yearbook* provides trade statistics and summaries of economic activity for all countries in the world.[30]

The balance of payments is divided into the current and capital accounts. The **current account** is a broad measure that includes **merchandise trade** (i.e., manufactured goods) and **services trade** (i.e., intangible, experience-based economic output) plus certain categories of financial transfers such as humanitarian aid. A country with a negative current account balance has a **trade deficit**; that is, the outflow of money to pay for imports exceeds the inflow of money for sales of exports. Conversely, a country with a positive current account balance has a **trade surplus**. The **capital account** is a record of all long-term direct investment, portfolio investment, and other short- and long-term capital flows. The minus signs signify outflows of cash; for example, in Table 2-6, line 2 shows an outflow of $1.86 trillion in 2006 that represents payment for U.S. merchandise imports. (Other entries not shown in Table 2-5 represent changes in net errors and omissions, foreign liabilities, and reserves.) These are the entries that make the balance of payments balance. In general, a country accumulates reserves when the net of its current and capital account transactions shows a surplus; it gives up reserves when the net shows a deficit. The important fact to recognize about the overall balance of payments is that it is always in balance. Imbalances occur in subsets of the overall balance. For example, a commonly reported balance is the trade balance on goods (line 3 in Table 2-5).

A close examination of Table 2-5 reveals that the United States regularly posts deficits in both the current account and the trade balance in goods. The United States' growing trade deficit reflects a number of factors, including increased imports from China, a seemingly insatiable consumer demand for imported goods, and the enormous cost of military operations in the Middle East. Table 2-6

Table 2-6

U.S. Goods and Services Trade
with Brazil, India, and China
2005 (US$ billions)

	China	India	Brazil
1. U.S. goods exports to	41,799	7,972	15,174
2. Goods imports from	-243,472	-18,803	-24,434
3. Balance on goods	-201,673	-10,831	-9,260
4. U.S. services exports to	9,105	5,152	5,871
5. Services imports from	-6,537	-3,571	-2,097
6. U.S. balance on services	2,568	1,581	3,774
7. U.S. balance on goods and services	-199,105	-9,250	-5,486

Source: www.bea.gov.

---

[30] Balance of payments data are available from a number of different sources, each of which may show slightly different figures for a given line item.

shows a record of goods and services trade between the United States and Brazil, India, and China for 2005. A comparison of lines 4 and 5 in the two tables shows a bright spot from the U.S. perspective: The United States has maintained services trade surplus with the rest of the world. Overall, however, the United States posts balance of payments deficits while important trading partners, such as China, have surpluses. China offsets its trade surpluses with an outflow of capital, while the United States offsets its trade deficit with an inflow of capital. As trading partners, U.S. consumers and businesses own an increasing quantity of foreign products, while foreign investors own more U.S. land, real estate, and government securities. Foreign-owned U.S. assets total $2.5 trillion; in 2005, the United States borrowed 6 percent of its output in goods and services from foreign countries.[31] Some policy makers in Washington are becoming alarmed about the U.S. trade deficit with China, which reached $200 billion in 2005.

TRADE IN MERCHANDISE AND SERVICES

Thanks in part to the achievements of GATT and the WTO, world merchandise trade has grown at a faster rate than world production since the end of World War II. Put differently, import and export growth has outpaced the rate of increase in GNP. According to figures compiled by the WTO, the dollar value of world trade in 2004 totaled $11 trillion. In 2004, GNP increased at an average rate of 3.7 percent; by contrast, the volume of merchandise exports increased by about 9 percent. The top exporting and importing countries are shown in Table 2-7. In 2003, Germany surpassed the United States as the world's top merchandise exporter. German manufacturers of all sizes have benefited from global economic growth because they provide the motors, machines, vehicles, and other capital goods that are required to build factories and country infrastructures; worldwide, machinery and transport equipment constitute approximately one-third of global exports. Today, exports generate 40 percent of Germany's GDP, and 9 million jobs are export related. In addition, annual sales by the foreign subsidiaries of German-based companies are $1.5 billion.[32]

China's third place in the export rankings underscores its role as an export powerhouse. Even in the face of Asia's economic downturn in the late 1990s and the SARS outbreak, China demonstrated continued economic strength by achieving double-digit export growth. Chinese exports to the United States have surged since

Leading Exporters	2004	Leading Importers	2004
1. Germany	912	1. United States	1,526
2. United States	819	2. Germany	717
3. China	593	3. China	561
4. Japan	566	4. France	466
5. France	449	5. Great Britain	464
6. Netherlands	358	6. Japan	455
7. Italy	349	7. Italy	351
8. Great Britain	347	8. Netherlands	319
9. Canada	317	9. Belgium	286
10. Belgium	307	10. Canada	280

Table 2-7

Top Exporters and Importers in World Merchandise Trade, 2004 (US$ billions)

Source: WTO Publications.

---

[31] David Wessel, "Counting on a Miracle with U.S. Debt," *The Wall Street Journal*, September 29, 2005, p. A2.

[32] Bertrand Benoit and Richard Milne, "Germany's Best-Kept Secret: How Its Exporters Are Beating the World," *Financial Times*, May 19, 2006, p. 11.

Table 2-8

*Top Exporters and Importers in
World Merchandise Trade, 2004
(percentage of total)*

Leading Exporters	2004	Leading Importers	2004
1. European Union	18.1	1. United States	21.8
2. United States	12.3	2. European Union	18.3
3. China	8.9	3. China	8.0
4. Japan	8.5	4. Japan	6.9
5. Canada	4.8	5. Canada	4.0
6. South Korea	3.8	6. South Korea	3.2
7. Mexico	2.8	7. Mexico	3.0
8. Russia	2.8	8. Taiwan	2.4
9. Taiwan	2.7	9. Switzerland	1.6
10. Malaysia	1.9	10. Australia	1.6

Source: WTO Publications.

China joined the WTO in 2001; in fact, policy makers in Washington are pressuring Beijing to boost the value of the yuan in an effort to stem the tide of imports.

Table 2-8 provides a different perspective on global trade. The EU is treated as a single entity with imports and exports that exclude intraregional trade among the 25 nations that were EU members at the end of 2006. South Korea, Mexico, and Russia appear in the top 10 exporter rankings; South Korea and Mexico also rank in the top 10 importers table. Figures are cited as a percentage of the world total.

The fastest-growing sector of world trade is trade in services. Services include travel and entertainment; education; business services such as engineering, accounting, and legal services; and payments of royalties and license fees. One of the major issues in trade relations between the high- and lower-income countries is trade in services. As a group, low-, lower-middle, and even upper-middle-income countries are lax in enforcing international copyrights and protecting intellectual property and patent laws. As a result, countries that export service products such as computer software, music, and video entertainment suffer a loss of income. According to a recent Global Software Piracy Study conducted by the Business Software Association, annual worldwide losses due to software piracy amount to approximately $29 billion. In China alone, software piracy cost the industry an estimated $3.6 billion in lost sales in 2005.

The United States is a major service trader. As shown in Figure 2-2, U.S. services exports in 2006 totaled $422 billion. This represents more than one-quarter of total U.S. exports. The U.S. services surplus (service exports minus imports) stood at $80 billion. This surplus partially offset the U.S. merchandise trade deficit,

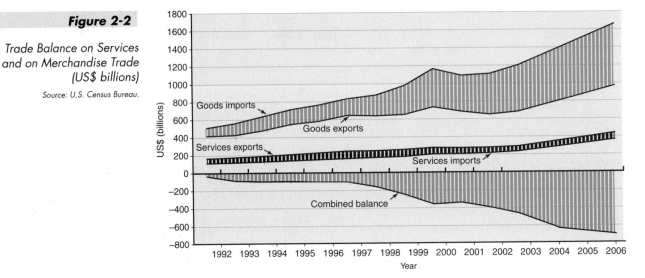

which reached $658 billion in 2006. American Express, Walt Disney, IBM, and Microsoft are a few of the U.S. companies currently enjoying rapid growth in demand for their services around the world.

OVERVIEW OF INTERNATIONAL FINANCE

Foreign exchange makes it possible for a company in one country to conduct business in other countries with different currencies. However, foreign exchange is an aspect of global marketing that involves certain financial risks, decisions, and activities that are completely different than those facing a domestic marketer. Moreover, those risks can be even higher in developing markets such as Thailand, Malaysia, and South Korea. When a company conducts business within a single country or region with customers and suppliers paying in the same currency, there is no exchange risk. All prices, payments, receipts, assets, and liabilities are in the given currency. However, when conducting business across boundaries in countries with different currencies, a company is thrust into the turbulent world of exchange risk.

The foreign exchange market consists literally of a buyer's and a seller's market where currencies are traded for both spot and future delivery on a continuous basis. The *spot* market is for immediate delivery; the market for future delivery is called the *forward* market. This is a true market where prices are based on the combined forces of supply and demand that come into play at the moment of any transaction. Who are the participants in this market? First, a country's central bank can buy and sell currencies in the foreign exchange market and government securities in an effort to influence exchange rates. For example, in the five-year period between 2001 and 2006, China bought more than $250 billion in U.S. Treasury bonds. Such purchases help ensure that China's currency is relatively weak compared to the U.S. dollar.[33] Second, some of the trading in the foreign exchange market takes the form of transactions needed to settle accounts for the global trade in goods and services. For example, because Porsche is a German company, the dollars spent on Porsche automobiles by American car buyers must be converted to euros. Finally, currency speculators also participate in the foreign exchange market.

Devaluation can result from government action that decrees a reduction in the value of the local currency against other currencies. In 1994, for example, the Chinese devalued the yuan (also known as *renminbhi* or "people's money"). The immediate result was to ensure the low-cost position of Chinese exporters. However, the action also set the stage for the 1997 devaluations of the Thai baht, Malaysian ringgit, and Indonesian rupiah; the expression "beggar thy neighbor" is sometimes used to describe devaluations designed to increase export competitiveness.

To the extent that a country sells more goods and services abroad than it buys, there will be a greater demand for its currency and a tendency for it to appreciate in value—unless government policy makers do not allow the currency to fluctuate. In 2005, the Chinese government responded to pressure from its trading partners by adopting a policy of **revaluation** to strengthen the yuan against the dollar and other currencies. A stronger yuan would make China's exports to the United States more expensive while making U.S. exports to China less expensive. The net result would be a reduction in China's trade surplus with the United States. The initial 2.1 percent increase in the yuan's value was not expected to have much impact on prices; some experts believe the yuan is undervalued by 20 percent or more (see Case 2-2).[34]

Table 2-9 shows how fluctuating currency values can affect financial risk, depending on the terms of payment specified in the contract. Suppose, at the time

---

[33] Mark Whitehouse, "U.S. Foreign Debt Shows Its Teeth as Rates Climb," *The Wall Street Journal*, September 25, 2006, p. A9.

[34] Sue Kirchhoff, "First Step: China Will Stop Pegging Yuan to Dollar," *USA Today*, July 22, 2005, pp. 1b, 2B.

Table 2-9

Exchange Risks and Gains in Foreign Transactions

Foreign Exchange Rates	$1,000,000 Contract		€1,100,000 Contract	
	U.S. Seller Receives	European Buyer Pays	U.S. Seller Receives	European Buyer Pays
€1.25 = $1.00	$1,000,000	€1,250,000	$880,000	€1,100,000
€1.10 = $1.00	$1,000,000	€1,100,000	$1,000,000	€1,100,000
€1.00 = $1.00	$1,000,000	€1,000,000	$1,100,000	€1,100,000
€0.85 = $1.00	$1,000,000	€850,000	$1,294,118	€1,100,000

a deal is made, the exchange rate is €1.10 equals $1.00. How is a U.S. exporter affected if the dollar strengthens against the euro (e.g., trades at €1.25 equals $1.00) and the contract specifies payment in dollars? What happens if the dollar weakens (e.g., €0.85 equals $1.00)? Conversely, what if the European buyer contracts to pay in euros rather than dollars?

Purchasing Power Parity

Given that currencies fluctuate in value, a reasonable question to ask is whether a given currency is over- or undervalued compared with another. Recall from the previous discussion that the currency's value could reflect government policy (as in the case of China) or market forces. One way to answer the question is to compare world prices for a single well-known product: McDonald's Big Mac hamburger. The so-called Big Mac Index is a "quick and dirty" way of determining which of the world's currencies are too weak or strong. The underlying assumption is that the price of a Big Mac in any world currency should, after being converted to dollars, equal the price of a Big Mac in the United States. (Similar indexes have been proposed based on the price of Starbucks coffee and IKEA furniture). A country's currency would be overvalued if the Big Mac price (converted to dollars) is higher than the U.S. price. Conversely, a country's currency would be undervalued if the converted Big Mac price is lower than the U.S. price. Economists use the concept of **purchasing power parity (PPP)** when adjusting national income data to improve comparability. Table 2-10 shows the Big Mac Index for selected countries in 2006. The first column of figures shows the price of a Big Mac converted from the local currency to dollars at the prevailing exchange rate on May 22, 2006. Thus, we can see that the Chinese yuan is undervalued against the dollar by about 58 percent. In other words, based on the U.S price for a Big Mac, the yuan/dollar exchange rate ought to be ¥3.39/$1.00 rather than ¥8.03 to $1.00.[35] India is not included in the index. Can you explain why?

Table 2-10

The 2006 Big Mac Index

Country	Big Mac Price Converted to $	Official Exchange Rate	Over- or Undervaluation of Local Currency (%)
Switzerland	5.21	1.21/$1.00	+68
Euro zone	3.77	1.28/$1.00	+22
United States	3.10	—	—
Brazil	2.78	2.30/$1.00	−10
Japan	2.23	112.00/$1.00	−28
Russia	1.77	27.10/$1.00	−43
China	1.31	8.03/$1.00	−58

Source: Adapted from "McCurrencies," *Economist*, May 27, 2006.

---

[35] The authors acknowledge that the PPP theory-based-Big Mac Index is simplistic; as noted in this section, exchange rates are also affected by interest rate differentials and monetary and fiscal policies—not just prices.

Economic Exposure

Economic exposure refers to the impact of currency fluctuations on the present value of a company's expected future cash flows. Economic exposure can occur when a company's transactions result in sales or purchases denominated in foreign currencies. Diageo, for example, faces transaction exposure to the extent that it accepts payment for exports of Scotch whiskey at one exchange rate but actually settles its accounts at a different rate of exchange.[36] Economic exposure is directly proportional to the amount of business a company conducts outside the home market. Obviously, currency exposure is a critical issue for Nestlé, with 98 percent of annual sales taking place outside Switzerland. Among countries in the euro zone, GlaxoSmithKline, DaimlerChrysler, BP, Sanofi-Aventis, Royal Dutch Shell, Astra Zeneca, and SABMiller all generate more than one-third of total sales in the U.S. market. Given the current weakness of the dollar relative to the euro, all of these companies face potential economic exposure. By comparison, GE generates about 50 percent of its revenues in the domestic United States market, so the relative extent of GE's exposure is less than that of Nestlé. Even so, as noted in its annual report, GE does face economic exposure:

> When countries or regions experience currency and/or economic stress, we often have increased exposure to certain risks, but also often have new profit opportunities. Potential increased risks include, among other things, high receivable delinquencies and bad debts, delays or cancellations of sales and orders principally related to power and aircraft equipment, higher local currency financing costs and slowdown in established financial services activities.[37]

In dealing with the economic exposure introduced by currency fluctuations, a key issue is whether the company can use price as a strategic tool for maintaining its profit margins. Can the company adjust prices in response to a rise or fall of foreign exchange rates in various markets? That depends on the price elasticity of demand. The less price sensitive the demand, the greater the flexibility a company has in responding to exchange rate changes. In the late 1980s, for example, Porsche raised prices in the United States three times in response to the weak dollar. The result: Porsche's U.S. sales dropped precipitously, from 30,000 vehicles in 1986 to 4,500 vehicles in 1992. Clearly, U.S. luxury car buyers were exhibiting elastic demand curves for pricey German sports cars!

Managing Exchange Rate Exposure

It should be clear from this discussion that the difficulty of accurately forecasting exchange rate movements is a major challenge to global marketers. Over the years, the search for ways of managing cash flows to eliminate or reduce exchange rate risks has resulted in the development of numerous techniques and financial strategies. For example, it may be desirable to sell products in the company's home country currency. When this is not possible, techniques are available to reduce both transaction and operating exposure.

Hedging exchange rate exposure involves establishing an offsetting currency position such that the loss or gain of one currency position is offset by a corresponding gain or loss in some other currency. The practice is common among global companies that sell products and maintain operations in different countries. Today, for example, Porsche relies on currency hedging rather than price increases to boost pretax profits on sales of its automobiles. Porsche manufactures all its cars in Europe but generates about 45 percent of its sales in the United

---

[36] John Willman, "Currency Squeeze on Guinness," *Financial Times–Weekend Money* (September 27–28, 1997), p. 5.
[37] *General Electric 2004 Annual Report*, p. 58.

States. Thus, Porsche faces economic exposure stemming from the relative value of the dollar to the euro. Porsche is *fully hedged*; that is, it takes currency positions to protect all earnings from foreign-exchange movements.[38]

If company forecasts indicate that the value of the foreign currency will weaken against the home currency, it can hedge to protect against potential transaction losses. Conversely, for predictions that the foreign currency will appreciate (strengthen) against the home currency, then a gain, rather than a loss, can be expected on foreign transactions when revenues are converted into the home currency. Given this expectation, the best decision may be not to hedge at all. (The operative word is *may*; many companies hedge anyway unless management is convinced the foreign currency will strengthen.) Porsche has profited by (correctly) betting on a weak dollar.

External hedging methods for managing both transaction and translation exposure require companies to participate in the foreign currency market. Specific hedging tools include forward contracts and currency options. *Internal hedging methods* include price adjustment clauses and intracorporate borrowing or lending in foreign currencies.

The **forward market** is a mechanism for buying and selling currencies at a preset price for future delivery. If it is known that a certain amount of foreign currency is going to be paid out or received at some future date, a company can insure itself against exchange loss by buying or selling forward. With a forward contract, the company can lock in a specific fixed exchange rate for a future date and immunize itself from the loss (or gain) caused by the exchange rate fluctuation. By consulting sources such as *Financial Times*, *The Wall Street Journal*, or www.ozforex.com, it is possible to determine exchange rates on any given day. In addition to spot prices, 30-, 60-, and 180-day forward prices are quoted for dozens of world currencies.

Companies use the forward market when the currency exposure is known in advance (e.g., when a firm contract of sale exists). In some situations, however, companies are not certain about the future foreign currency cash inflow or outflow. Consider the risk exposure of a U.S. company that bids for a foreign project but won't know if the project will be granted until sometime later. The company needs to protect the dollar value of the contract by hedging the *potential* foreign currency cash inflow that will be generated if the company turns out to be the winning bidder. In such an instance, forward contracts are not the appropriate hedging tool.

A foreign currency **option** is best for such situations. A **put option** gives the buyer the right, not the obligation, to sell a specified number of foreign currency units at a fixed price, up to the option's expiration date. (Conversely, a **call option** is the right, but not the obligation, to buy the foreign currency.) In the example of bidding on the foreign project, the company can take out a put option to sell the foreign currency for dollars at a set price in the future. In other words, the U.S. company locks in the value of the contract in dollars. Thus, if the project is granted, the future foreign currency cash inflow has been hedged by means of the put option. If the project is *not* granted, the company can trade the put option in the options market without exercising it; remember, options are rights, not obligations. The only money the company stands to lose is the difference between what it paid for the option and what it receives upon selling it.

Financial officers of global firms can avoid economic exposure altogether by demanding a particular currency as the payment for its foreign sales. As noted, a U.S.-based company might demand U.S. dollars as the payment currency for its foreign sales. This, however, does not eliminate currency risk; it simply shifts that risk to the customers. In common practice, companies typically attempt to invoice exports (receivables) in strong currencies and imports (payables) in weak currencies. However, in today's highly competitive world market, such practice may reduce a company's competitive edge.

---

[38] Stephen Power, "Porsche Powers Profit with Currency Play," *The Wall Street Journal*, December 8, 2004, p. C3.

The economic environment is a major determinant of global market potential and opportunity. In today's global economy, capital movements are the key driving force, production has become uncoupled from employment, and capitalism has vanquished communism. Based on patterns of resource allocation and ownership, the world's national economies can be categorized as **market capitalism**, **centrally planned capitalism**, **centrally planned socialism**, and **market socialism**. The final years of the twentieth century were marked by a transition toward market capitalism in many countries that had been centrally controlled. However, there still exists a great disparity among the nations of the world in terms of economic freedom.

Countries can be categorized in terms of their stage of economic development: **low income, lower-middle income, upper-middle income,** and **high income. Gross domestic product (GDP)** and **gross national income (GNI)** are commonly used measures of economic development. The fifty poorest countries in the low-income category are sometimes referred to as **least-developed countries** (LDCs). Upper-middle-income countries with high growth rates are often called **newly industrializing economies** (NIEs). Several of the world's economies are notable for their fast growth; the **BRIC** nations include Brazil (lower-middle income), Russia (upper-middle income), India (low income), and China (lower-middle income).

The **Group of Seven (G-7), Group of Eight (G-8),** and **Organization for Economic Cooperation and Development (OECD)** represent efforts by high-income nations to promote democratic ideals and free-market policies throughout the rest of the world. Most of the world's income is located in the **Triad**, which is comprised of Japan, the United States, and Western Europe. Companies with global aspirations generally have operations in all three areas. Market potential for a product can be evaluated by determining **product saturation levels** in light of income levels.

A country's **balance of payments** is a record of its economic transactions with the rest of the world; this record shows whether a country has a **trade surplus** (value of exports exceeds value of imports) or a **trade deficit** (value of imports exceeds value of exports). Trade figures can be further divided into **merchandise trade** and **services trade** accounts; a country can run a surplus in both accounts, a deficit in both accounts, or a combination of the two. The U.S. merchandise trade deficit was $780 billion in 2005. However, the United States enjoys an annual service trade surplus. Overall, the United States is a debtor; Japan enjoys an overall trade surplus and serves as a creditor nation.

Foreign exchange provides a means for settling accounts across borders. The dynamics of international finance can have a significant impact on a nation's economy as well as the fortunes of individual companies. Currencies can be subject to **devaluation** or **revaluation** as a result of actions taken by a country's central bank. Currency trading by international speculators can also lead to devaluation. When currency values fluctuate, global firms face various types of economic exposure. Firms can manage exchange rate exposure by **hedging**.

1. Explain the difference between **market capitalism, centrally planned capitalism, centrally planned socialism,** and **market socialism**. Give an example of a country that illustrates each type of system.

2. Why are Brazil, Russia, India, and China (BRIC) highlighted in this chapter? Identify the current stage of economic development for each BRIC nation.

3. Turn to the Index of Economic Freedom (Table 2-3) and identify where the BRIC nations are ranked.

What does the result tell you in terms of the relevance of the index to global marketers?

4. A manufacturer of satellite dishes is assessing the world market potential for his products. He asks you if he should consider developing countries as potential markets. How would you advise him?

5. A friend is distressed to learn that America's merchandise trade deficit hit a record $780 billion in 2005. You want to cheer your friend up by demonstrating that the trade picture is not as bleak as it sounds. What do you say?

1. The BRIC countries (Brazil, Russia, India, and China) discussed in this chapter are frequently in the news. Choose one of the countries to study during the semester; keep a current events journal with notes or pasted-up articles from the press. What economic issues identified in the chapter continue to affect trade prospects in your country? What new issues, if any, have developed?

2. The seven criteria for describing a nation's economy introduced at the beginning of this chapter can be combined in a number of different ways. For example, the United States can be characterized as follows:

- *Type of economy:* Advanced industrial state
- *Type of government:* Democracy with a multi-party system

- *Trade and capital flows:* Incomplete free trade and part of trading bloc
- *The commanding heights:* Mix of state and private ownership
- *Services provided by the state and funded through taxes:* Pensions and education but not health care
- *Institutions:* Transparency, standards, corruption is absent, a free press and strong courts
- *Markets:* Free market system characterized by high risk/high reward entrepreneurial dynamism

   Use the seven criteria found on pp. 44–45 to develop a profile of one of the BRIC nations, or any other country that interests you. How does this profile impact marketing opportunities in the country?

1. The Heritage Foundation's *Index of Economic Freedom* is not the only ranking that assesses countries in terms of successful economic policies. For example, the World Economic Forum (WEF; www.weforum.org) publishes an annual *Global Competitiveness Report*; in the 2006–2007 report, the United States ranks in sixth place according to the

WEF's metrics. By contrast, Sweden is in third place. According to the *Index of Economic Freedom*'s rankings, the United States and Sweden are in tenth place and nineteenth place, respectively. Why are the rankings so different? What criteria does each index consider?

Economist magazine's Web site offers briefings on more than 60 countries representing all stages of development at:

www.economist.com/countries

The U.S. Census Bureau compiles data on U.S. trade and makes it available on the Web. You can find this data under the headings "FT900" and "Supplement" at:

www.census.gov/foreign-trade/www

The United States Bureau of Economic Analysis posts a great deal of information about the U.S. economy. You can access the database at:

www.bea.doc.gov

C. K. Prahalad, *The Fortune at the Bottom of the Pyramid: Eradicating Poverty Through Profits* (Philadelphia: Wharton Press, 2006). The book

includes a 35 minute video CD with case studies from India, Brazil, and other emerging markets.

Case 2-1

From Communism to Capitalism: Vietnam's Economic Transformation

In October 2001, U.S. President George Bush signed an agreement that created a U.S.-Vietnam free trade area. The signing marked yet another milestone along Vietnam's path toward a more open market, the timeline for which includes the following:

● In February 1994, U.S. President Bill Clinton ended America's 19-year economic embargo of Vietnam and opened the door for U.S. companies to target the world's twelfth most populous country.

● In July 1995, President Clinton reestablished diplomatic relations with Vietnam. In the absence of diplomatic relations, many Vietnamese manufactured exports to the United States faced prohibitive tariffs.

● In 1995, Vietnam joined the Association of Southeast Asian Nations (ASEAN).

● In 1998, the White House announced that it would exempt Vietnam from the Jackson-Vanik amendment. The exemption meant that, pending congressional approval, American companies investing in Vietnam could apply for financial assistance from the Overseas Private Investment Corporation (OPIC) and the Export-Import Bank.

● In July 2000, U.S. President Bill Clinton signed a trade pact with Vietnam.

● The Asia-Pacific Economic Cooperation (APEC) Summit was held in Hanoi in November 2006.

● Vietnam joined the WTO in 2007.

After being ratified by Congress, President Clinton's actions in the mid-1990s established normal trading relations (NTR) between the two countries. In particular, Vietnam benefited from an immediate lowering of duties on a number of goods produced by its light industry sector (see Figure 1). Vietnamese tariffs and quotas on imports from the United States would be lowered more gradually. A number of U.S. companies immediately seized the opportunity. As Brian Watson, a Hong Kong-based deputy regional director for the McCann-Erickson advertising agency, said in the mid-1990s, "Vietnam is the next great frontier. There is an enormous amount of interest among clients. Every meeting starts with a question about going into Vietnam."

While the U.S. business community hailed the U.S. government's initiatives, many American firms found themselves playing catch up; by the early 1990s, many non-U.S. global companies had preceded the Americans into Vietnam. For example, South Korean industrial giant Daewoo was a key investor; other companies with major commitments included Sony, Toshiba, Honda, Peugeot, and British Petroleum. Carrier was among the first U.S. companies to legally market in Vietnam in 1994; the company's window air conditioners appeared in stores in Hanoi and

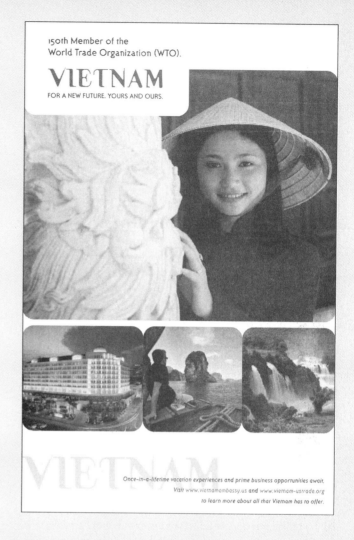

150th Member of the World Trade Organization (WTO).

VIETNAM
FOR A NEW FUTURE. YOURS AND OURS.

VIETNAM

Once-in-a-lifetime vacation experiences and prime business opportunities await. Visit www.vietnamembassy.us and www.vietnam-ustrade.org to learn more about all that Vietnam has to offer.

Figure 1

Duty Rates Vietnamese Exports to the United States with and Without NTR

Source: Vietnam Economic Times.

Figure 2

Foreign Direct Invesment in Vietnam, 1992–2002

$3.1 billion in 1997 after rising steadily since the early 1990s (see Figure 2). After falling to about $2.1 billion in 1999, investment rebounded to $2.3 billion in 2002. As encouraging as those figures are, however, investment levels in China are much higher.

There are still many challenges for companies seeking to invest in Vietnam. The population is very poor, with a 2004 annual per capita GNI of only about $540. However, urbanites with savings estimated at $1 billion to $2 billion comprise one quarter of the population. The infrastructure is undeveloped: Only 10 percent of roads are paved, electricity sources are unreliable, there is less than one telephone per 100 people, and the banking system is undeveloped. The Communist Party of Vietnam (CPV) is struggling to adapt to the principles of a market economy, and the layers of bureaucracy built up over decades of communist rule slow the pace of change. A key agency is the State Committee for Cooperation and Investment (SCCI); as Vu Tien Phuc, a deputy director of the agency, explained, "Every authority would like to have the last say. We have to improve the investment climate." William Ratliff, an analyst with the Hoover Institute, points out that the question for Vietnam is "whether it's possible to carry on free-market reforms and maintain absolute political power."

Yvonne Gupwell, a business consultant who was born in Vietnam, believes that "The biggest mistake companies make is they think because the Vietnamese are so polite, they're a little bit dim. The Vietnamese are poor, but they are not mentally poor at all." Statistics support this view; for example, adult literacy is nearly 90 percent. An emerging entrepreneurial class has developed a taste for expensive products such as Nikon cameras and Ray Ban sunglasses, both of which are available in stores. Notes Do Duc Dinh of the Institute on the World Economy, "There is a huge unofficial economy. For most people, we can live only 5 days or 10 days a month on our salary. But people build houses. Where does the money come from? Even in government ministries, there are two sets of books—one for the official money and one for unofficial."

"In 1996, you were told where to invest, and you also had to build the road, the school, the hospital. You said, 'Thank you very much; my new address is Malaysia.'"

A foreign businessman in Vietnam

Ho Chi Minh City. Gillette began shipping razor blades and disposable razors, and AT&T began selling home and office telephone products through a distributor in Taiwan. ExxonMobil began exploring for oil, Caterpillar set up equipment-leasing operations, and the Otis Elevator division of United Technologies joined in the construction boom. J.Walter Thompson, Ogilvy & Mather, and Backer Spielvogel Bates Worldwide became the first Western ad agencies to open liaison offices in Vietnam.

In view of the fact that 60 percent of Vietnam's population is under the age of 25, it is no surprise that PepsiCo and the Coca-Cola Company were also quick to make moves in Vietnam. At the time of the official announcement about ending the embargo, McCann-Erickson had already produced a TV commercial for Coca-Cola that included the global slogan "Always"; likewise, Ogilvy & Mather had a Pepsi ad ready for TV. Coca-Cola is building a $20 million bottling plant outside of Hanoi, but was denied permission to build in Ho Chi Minh City (formerly Saigon). Pepsi's joint venture with a Vietnamese firm in Ho Chi Minh City is bottling Pepsi; local production began within hours of President Clinton's 1994 announcement. To supply the market in the south, Coca-Cola imported canned soda from Singapore. As a result, a can of Coke costs twice as much as a bottle of Pepsi.

Experts agree that the Vietnamese market holds tremendous potential over the long term. It may be two decades before Vietnam reaches the level of economic development found in Thailand today. Meanwhile, the country's location in the heart of Asia and the presence of an ample low-wage workforce are powerful magnets for foreign companies. By the end of 1999, France ranked first in foreign investment while Japan was the top trading partner. Overall foreign direct investment peaked at about

Euphoria over Vietnam's potential showed signs of waning at the end of the 1990s. Part of the problem was the "currency contagion" that struck Asia in mid-1997; Asian countries that had been major investors were forced to scale back their activities in Vietnam. More generally, many companies were finding it difficult to make a profit. Cross-border smuggling from Thailand depressed legitimate sales of products produced locally by Procter & Gamble, Unilever, American Standard, and other companies. Foreign companies were also frustrated by the shallow pool of qualified local managers. It was also clear that China was attracting a great deal of foreign investment away from other countries in the region.

Today, many companies are discovering that Vietnam is an excellent source of low-cost labor. Burgeoning apparel and textile exports to the United States led to an agreement on export quotas in 2003. The fledgling tech sector also appears to hold great promise. Vietnam's universities turn out graduates who are highly trained in information technology. One company, Glass Egg Digital Media, provides software-writing services to leading global video game developers such as France's Infogames and U.S.-based Electronic Arts. Glass Egg founder Phil Tran pays programmers annual salaries of about $4,000, tens of thousands less than programmers in the United States are paid.

Although still strongly influenced by Communist hardliners, the bureaucrats in Hanoi have demonstrated an increased willingness to adopt much-needed reforms to foreign investment laws. In January 2000, for example, the regulatory environment improved with the enactment of an enterprise law that streamlined the process of market entry and setting up a business; a stock market was also opened. Increasingly, decisions about foreign investment are being made at the provincial level, and local officials are offering incentives and issuing import licenses more quickly. Investors in many industry sectors are now able to set up wholly foreign-owned firms; previously, the government rarely approved such arrangements. Instead, foreign companies were encouraged to form joint ventures with state-owned enterprises. The improved investment climate helps explain why a number of foreign automakers, including Ford, GM, Toyota, and DaimlerChrysler, have established operations in Vietnam. Noted one local businessman approvingly, "In the past, it was absolutely horrendous to set up a private company. Now, 99 percent of the difficulties are gone."

> "The reform is definitely irreversible. Any attempt to come back to a centrally planned economy, to overplay the state sector, is economically irrational, inefficient and, psychologically, is counterproductive."
>
> Le Dang Doanh, advisor to the Vietnam government

Vietnam's free trade area agreement with the United States entered into force in December 2001. The effect was immediate: The value of U.S. imports from Vietnam more than doubled in 2002, to nearly $2.4 billion. At the end of 2003,

the two nations signed an air services agreement that will make it easy for travelers to book flights to Vietnam. The agreement comes as Vietnam's government is marketing the country as an attractive vacation destination. Despite such positive news, however, many problems remain. For example, Vietnam's legal system is still bewildering, and regulations can change on a moment's notice. Relations between the new trading partners have shown some signs of strain, as evidenced by U.S. charges that Vietnam has been dumping catfish in the U.S. market at artificially low prices.

Visit the Web site
www.vietnam-ustrade.org

Discussion Questions

1. Assess the market opportunities in Vietnam for both consumer-products companies and industrial-products companies. What is the nature of the opportunity?

2. Nike and several other well-known American companies are sourcing some of their production in Vietnam, thereby taking advantage of a labor force that is paid the equivalent of $2 per day or less. Are goods labeled "Made in Vietnam" likely to find widespread acceptance among American consumers?

3. Some critics have argued that Cuba is more deserving of diplomatic and trade relations with the United States than Vietnam. What are some of the factors behind this argument?

An excellent video overview is found in "Visions of a New Vietnam." The progam was originally aired on the Nightly Business Report; we recommend viewing the DVD in conjunction with the case discussion.

Sources: Keith Bradsher, "Vietnam's Roaring Economy Is Set for World Stage," *The New York Times,* October 25, 2006, pp. A1, C4; Joseph Erlich, "Vietnam's Trade-War Wounds," *The Wall Street Journal,* August 26, 2005, p. A10; Dan Reed, "Ex-Enemies Make a Deal," *USA Today,* December 9, 2003, p. 5B; Reginald Chua and Margot Cohen, "Vietnamese Tiger Growls Again; Investors Want a Change of Stripes," *The Wall Street Journal,* March 13, 2003, p. A10; Margot Cohen, "Foreign Investors Take New Look at Vietnam and Like What They See," *The Wall Street Journal,* January 28, 2003, pp. A14; Amy Kamzin, "Vietnam's Change of Heart," *Financial Times,* August 28, 2002, p. 13; Bruce Knecht, "Vietnam Taps Videogame Talent," *The New York Times,* October 21, 2001, p. B5; Frederik Balfour, "Back on the Radar Screen," *Business Week,* November 20, 2000, pp. 56–57; Wayne Arnold, "Clearing the Decks for a Trade Pact's Riches," *The New York Times,* August 27, 2000, Section 3, pp. 1, 12; Samantha Marshall, "Vietnam Pullout: This Time, Investors Pack Up Gear, Stymied by Bureaucracy, Lack of Reforms," *The Wall Street Journal,* June 30, 1998, p. A15; Marshall, "P&G Squabbles with Vietnamese Partner," *The Wall Street Journal,* February 27, 1998, p. A10; Reginald Chua, "Vietnam Frustrate Foreign Investors as Leaders Waffle on Market Economy," *The Wall Street Journal,* November 25, 1996, p. A10; "Vietnam," *Economist,* July 8, 1995, pp. 1–18 (survey); William J. Ardrey, Anthony Pecotich, and Clifford J. Schultz, "American Involvement in Vietnam, Part II: Prospects for U.S. Business in a New Era, "*Business Horizons* 38 (March/April 1995), pp. 21–27; Edward A. Gargan, "For U.S. Business, a Hard Road to Vietnam," *The New York Times*, July 14, 1995, p. C1; Marilyn Greene, "Very Soon, Vietnam Will Be Very Good," *USA Today*, April 1, 1994, p. 8A; Robert Keatley, "Vietnam, Despite Promise, Faces Climb," *The Wall Street Journal*, August 18, 1994, p. A8; Philip Shenon, "Vietnam: Behind a Red-Tape Curtain," *The*

New York Times, November 13, 1994, Section 3, p. 6; James Cox, "Vietnamese Look Forward to Trade, Jobs," *USA Today*, July 12, 1995, pp. 1A, 2A; Kevin Goldman, "Agencies Get Ready for Vietnam Business," *The Wall Street Journal*, February 7, 1994, p. B10.

Case 2-2

Is China's Currency Too Strong?

In July 2005, the Peoples Bank of China announced the end of a 10-year effort to peg the value of the Chinese currency, the yuan, to the value of the U.S. dollar. Instead, the yuan would be linked to a basket of several foreign currencies. The announcement signaled Beijing's decision to abandon a policy of fixed exchange rates, according to which 8.28 yuan equaled $1, and adopt a policy of flexible rates. In short, by ending the peg, China's central bank was finally allowing the yuan to float.

The United States and other key trading partners had been urging such an action for years. *The New York Times* called the Chinese central bank's decision "the most hotly anticipated event for the foreign-exchange world in years." Many economists believed that the yuan had been undervalued relative to the dollar and other currencies by as much as 40 percent, and this weakness was cited as one of the factors contributing to growing trade deficits with China. For example, the U.S. trade deficit with China was more than $200 billion in 2006. This had occurred, it was argued, because the Chinese government had deliberately manipulated its currency to give Chinese exports a price advantage compared to goods from the United States and other countries.

Some observers favored a quick change in the yuan's value; others argued for a go-slow, gradualist approach. The immediate result of the revaluation was a 2.1 percent increase in the yuan's value, to 8.11 yuan equals $1. The stronger yuan was expected to have a ripple effect on the economies of China's top trading partners. For one thing, it was likely to result in increased prices for Chinese exports to the United States and elsewhere. This would be good news to some of the 12,000 members of the National Association of Manufacturers (N.A.M.). Many small factory owners in the United States are worried about competing with low-priced Chinese goods. However, a stronger yuan could be bad news for Wal-Mart and other retailers that buy billions of dollars worth of goods from China each year. Likewise, American-based global companies such as Whirlpool that source manufactured goods in China might be forced to raise prices.

By mid-2007, the yuan had appreciated about 8.5 percent against the dollar. However, that was not enough to satisfy some policymakers. Impatient with the slow pace of the revaluation, some members of the U.S. Congress introduced legislation designed to punish China for its currency policy. One bill, co-sponsored by Senate Finance Chairman Max Baucus, a democrat, and Charles Grassley, the

Republican Senator from Iowa, was contingent on the U.S. Treasury Department determining that a "currency misalignment" had occurred. Following such a finding, the United States would impose fines in the form of antidumping penalties and the Chinese government would have six months to make the required currency adjustments. If China didn't take action, the U.S. trade representative would request dispute settlement at the WTO. A final ruling would be issued in 2010.

The introduction of the Congressional bill raised several questions. For example, it was unclear whether a dispute involving currency issues was a legitimate trade issue that the WTO would agree to hear. Another issue was whether it was possible to determine exactly how much the yuan would have to appreciate for it to be fairly aligned with the dollar.

Some observers warned that the Baucus-Grassley bill and others like it could undermine the trade relationship between the United States and China and actually harm U.S. companies that do business with China. Since joining the WTO in 2001, China has become America's fourth-largest export market. According to a study by the American Chamber of Commerce in China, American companies sold $61 billion worth of goods to China in 2005. Chamber chairman James Zimmerman noted, "A revalued yuan will not force the Chinese to buy American goods and services." Others warned that Chinese companies could diversify their export base by expanding trade with other countries. A trade war was another possibility. Scott Miller, director of trade policy for Procter & Gamble, said, "You can't rule out a backlash. That ought to be part of the calculus that lawmakers should consider." Some observers raised concerns that, in retaliation for trade sanctions, China might restrict market access for American goods.

Discussion Questions

1. Consumer goods, including shoes and electronics, represent about 80 percent of U.S. imports from China. American consumers have saved an estimated $600 billion over the past 10 years by buying inexpensive Chinese goods. If the Chinese government revalues the yuan by 20 percent or more and American consumers pay higher prices, is this a desirable outcome?

2. Protectionist sentiments in the United States are fueled by the argument that China is to blame for the flood of imports, the giant U.S. current account deficit, and downward pressure on wages in some industries. Do you agree?

3. Do you think an aggressive legislative posture with respect to China's currency is the best approach for any trade partner to take?

Sources: John McCary and Andrew Batson, "Punishing China: Will It Fly?" *The Wall Street Journal*, June 23–24, 2007, p. A4; Wu Yi, "It's Win-Win on U.S. China Trade," *The Wall Street Journal*, May 17, 2007, p. A21; Martin Wolf, "How China Has Managed to Keep the Renminbi Pinned Down," *Financial Times*, October 11, 2006, p. 13; E. S. Browning, "Yuan Move Might Stir Big Ripples," *The Wall Street Journal*, July 25, 2005, pp. C1, C4; Sue Kirchhoff, "First Step: China Will Stop Pegging Yuan to Dollar," *USA Today*, July 22, 2005, pp. 1B, 2B; Keith Bradsher, "A Chinese Revaluation May Not Help U.S.," *The New York Times*, January 4, 2005, pp. C1, C5.

Regional Market Characteristics and Preferential Trade Agreements

Have you heard of the "Doha Round?" It is the latest in a series of multilateral trade negotiations among members of the WTO. The current round was launched in 2001 in Doha, Qatar. The talks are aimed at promoting economic growth in developing countries by reducing agricultural subsidies and tariffs on agricultural products in the developed world. During the past several years, trade meetings have taken place in Cancun, London, Hong Kong, and other cities. On one side of the negotiating table are two separate groups. One is comprised of leading agricultural importing nations that are not EU members, including Switzerland and Japan. Policy makers from this group do not want to make major cuts in tariffs that protect their farm sectors. The EU has broken ranks with these nations by offering to cut farm tariffs by an average of 38 percent. On the other side of the negotiating table, Brazil, India, and other developing nations are pushing for tariff reductions of 54 percent. Until that goal is met, they are refusing to cut tariffs on imports of manufactured goods. When trade ministers from 149 countries met in Hong Kong in December 2005, the most intractable issue was agriculture. Negotiations covered such topics as export subsidies, trade-distorting subsidies, and market access. In addition, several West African nations were pressing the United States on the issue of cotton subsidies. The ministers meeting in Hong Kong also took up the cause of eliminating duties on exports from the world's poorest nations.

Since World War II, there has been a tremendous interest among nations in furthering the cause of economic cooperation. As the Doha Round illustrates, trade negotiations can be quite broad in scope. Alternatively, negotiations can be limited to as few as two nations and result in bilateral arrangements such as the new free agreement between the United States and Chile. The regional nature of the Free Trade Area of the Americas represents a third type of agreement that is narrower in scope than a global arrangement but broader than a bilateral one (see Case 3-1).

Our survey of the world trade environment begins at the global level with the WTO and its predecessor, the GATT. Next, the four main types of regional preferential trade agreements are identified and described. An introduction to individual countries in the world's major market regions follows; each section also includes a detailed discussion of the specific preferential trade agreements in which those countries participate. Important marketing issues in each region are also discussed. Several important emerging country markets were described in Chapter 2; in this chapter, special attention will be given to individual country markets that were not previously discussed.

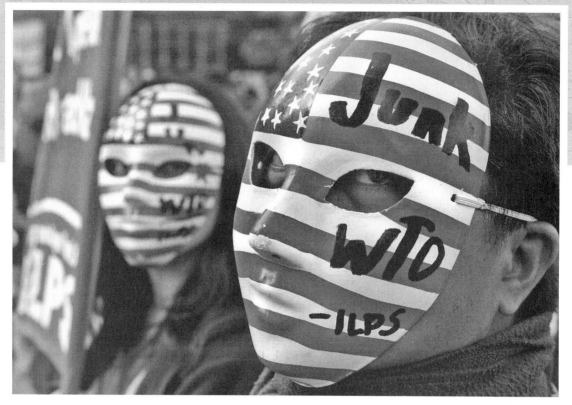

Anti-WTO protests have become increasingly common as the International League of Peoples' Struggles (ILPS) and other groups opposed to globalization attempt to disrupt the multilateral trade negotiations.

THE WTO AND GATT

The year 2007 marked the sixtieth anniversary of the General Agreement on Tariffs and Trade (GATT), a treaty among nations whose governments agree, at least in principle, to promote trade among members. GATT was intended to be a multilateral, global initiative, and GATT negotiators did succeed in liberalizing world merchandise trade. GATT was also an organization that handled 300 trade disputes—many involving food—during its half century of existence. GATT itself had no enforcement power (the losing party in a dispute was entitled to ignore the ruling), and the process of dealing with disputes sometimes stretched on for years. Little wonder, then, that some critics referred to GATT as the "General Agreement to Talk and Talk."

The successor to GATT, the World Trade Organization (WTO), came into existence on January 1, 1995. From its base in Geneva, the WTO provides a forum for trade-related negotiations among its 150 members. The WTO's staff of neutral trade experts also serve as mediators in global trade disputes. The WTO has a Dispute Settlement Body (DSB) that mediates complaints concerning unfair trade barriers and other issues between the WTO's member countries. During a 60-day consultation period, parties to a complaint are expected to engage in good-faith negotiations and reach an amicable resolution. If that fails, the complainant can ask the DSB to appoint a three-member panel of trade experts to hear the case behind closed doors. After convening, the panel has nine months within which to issue its ruling.[1] The DSB acts on the panel's recommendations. The losing party has the option of turning to a seven-member appellate body. If, after due process, a country's trade policies are found to violate WTO rules, it is expected to change those policies. If changes are not forthcoming, the WTO can authorize trade sanctions against the loser. Table 3-1 lists some recent cases that have been brought to the WTO.

Trade ministers representing the WTO member nations meet annually to work on improving world trade. It remains to be seen whether the WTO will live up to expectations when it comes to additional major policy initiatives on such vexing issues as foreign investment and agricultural subsidies. As noted in the chapter opening, the current round of WTO negotiations began in 2001; the talks collapsed in 2005, and attempts to revive them in 2006 were not successful.

---

[1] Scott Miller, "Global Dogfight: Airplane Battle Spotlights Power of a Quirky Court," *The Wall Street Journal,* June 1, 2005, pp. A1, A14.

Table 3-1

Recent WTO Cases

Countries Involved in Dispute	Nature of Dispute and Outcome
United States, European Union, Canada versus China	In 2006, the complainants asked the DSB to consider Chinese tariffs on imported auto parts. The complainants argue that their auto manufacturers are at a disadvantage when importing auto parts into China.
United States versus Brazil	In 2003, Brazil filed a complaint against the United States charging that cotton subsidies depressed prices and disadvantaged producers in emerging markets. In 2004, the DSB, in its first-ever ruling on agricultural subsidies, agreed that cotton subsidies violate international trade rules.
Antigua and Barbuda versus the United States	In 2003, Antigua filed suit charging that, by prohibiting Internet gambling, the United States was violating global trade agreements. In 2004, the WTO ruled in favor of Antigua.
United States versus European Union	In 2002, U.S. President Bush imposed 30 percent tariffs on a range of steel imports for a period of 3 years. The EU lodged a protest, and in 2003, the WTO ruled that the tariffs were illegal. President Bush responded by lifting the tariffs.
European Union versus Philippines and Thailand	In 2002, the EU imposed 24 percent tariffs on canned tuna imports from the Philippines and Thailand but granted imports from former Africa, Caribbean, and Pacific (ACP) colonies duty-free status. Dispute was resolved in 2003 when Philippines and Thailand agreed to minimum access volumes of tuna exports to EU.
United States versus European Union, Canada, and Japan	In 2000, the U.S. Congress passed the so-called Byrd Amendment, which allows companies that have been harmed by dumping to receive revenues from anti-dumping tariffs. The WTO ruled against the law and allowed the plaintiffs to impose retaliatory tariffs. Canada imposed duties on live hogs, cigarettes, and seafood imports from the United States. Japan imposed 15 percent tariffs on imports of ball bearing.
United States versus European Union	In 1999, the United States imposed tariffs on select imports from the EU in retaliation for the EU's policy of giving preference to bananas imported from ACP countries. WTO ruled in favor of the United States; in 2001, the EU agreed to revise its import scheme, and the United States lifted the tariffs.

PREFERENTIAL TRADE AGREEMENTS

> *"For the WTO process to work, countries have to start liberalizing policies in politically sensitive sectors."[2]*
>
> Daniel Griswold, Center for Trade Policy Studies, Cato Institute

The GATT treaty promotes free trade on a global basis; in addition, countries in each of the world's regions are seeking to liberalize trade within their regions. A **preferential trade agreement** is a mechanism that confers special treatment on select trading partners. By favoring certain countries, such agreements frequently discriminate against others. For that reason, it is customary for countries to notify the WTO when they enter into preference agreements. In recent years, more than

---

[2] Scott Miller, "Trade Talks Twist in the Wind," *The Wall Street Journal*, November 8, 2005, p. A14.

150 preferential trade agreements have notified the WTO. Few fully conform to WTO requirements; none, however, has been disallowed.

Free Trade Area

A **free trade area (FTA)** is formed when two or more countries agree to eliminate tariffs and other barriers that restrict trade. When trading partners successfully negotiate a **free trade agreement** (also abbreviated FTA), the ultimate goal of which is to have zero duties on goods that cross borders between the partners, it creates a free trade area. In some instances, duties are eliminated on the day the agreement takes effect; in other cases, duties are phased out over a set period of time. Countries that belong to an FTA can maintain independent trade policies with respect to third countries. **Rules of origin** discourage the importation of goods into the member country with the lowest external tariff for transshipment to one or more FTA members with higher external tariffs; customs inspectors police the borders between members. For example, because Chile and Canada established an FTA in 1997, a Canadian-built Caterpillar grader tractor imported into Chile would not be subject to duty. If the same piece of equipment was imported from a factory in the United States, the importer would pay about $13,000 in duties. Could Caterpillar send the U.S.-built tractor to Chile by way of Canada, thereby allowing the importer to avoid paying the duty? No, because the tractor would bear a "Made in the U.S.A." certificate of origin indicating it was subject to the duty. Little wonder, then, that the U.S. government negotiated its own bilateral free trade agreement with Chile in 2003.

To date, dozens of free trade agreements, many of them bilateral, have been successfully negotiated; for example, Mexico has free trade agreements with 31 countries. Table 3-2 lists free trade agreements that the United States and Chile have, respectively, negotiated with other countries. Additional examples of FTAs include the European Economic Area, a free trade area that includes the 27-nation EU plus Norway, Liechtenstein, and Iceland; the Group of Three (G3), an FTA encompassing Colombia, Mexico, and Venezuela; and the Closer Economic Partnership Agreement, a free trade agreement between China and Hong Kong.

Customs Union

A **customs union** represents the logical evolution of a free trade area. In addition to eliminating internal barriers to trade, members of a customs union agree to the establishment of **common external tariffs (CETs)**. In 1996, for example, the EU

United States	Chile	**Table 3-2**
Canada and Mexico (North American Free Trade Agreement or NAFTA)	Canada (1997)	*Free Trade Agreements*
Jordan	Mexico	
Israel	European Union	
Singapore	South Korea	
Chile	United States	
El Salvador, Guatemala, Honduras, Nicaragua (Central American Free Trade Agreement or CAFTA)	Bolivia	
Morocco		
South Africa, Botswana, Lesotho, Namibia, and Swaziland (Southern Africa Free Trade and Development Agreement or SAFTDA)		
Australia		
Vietnam		
Bahrain		
Peru		
Colombia		

and Turkey initiated a customs union in an effort to boost two-way trade above the average annual level of $20 billion. The arrangement called for the elimination of tariffs averaging 14 percent that added $1.5 billion each year to the cost of European goods imported by Turkey. Other customs unions discussed in this chapter are the Andean Community, the Central American Integration System (SICA), Mercosur, and CARICOM.

Common Market

A **common market** is the next level of economic integration. In addition to the removal of internal barriers to trade and the establishment of common external tariffs, the common market allows for free movement of factors of production, including labor and capital. The Andean Community, the SICA, and CARICOM, which currently function as customs unions, may ultimately evolve into true common markets.

Economic Union

An **economic union** builds upon the elimination of the internal tariff barriers, the establishment of common external barriers, and the free flow of factors. It seeks to coordinate and harmonize economic and social policy within the union to facilitate the free flow of capital, labor, and goods and services from country to country. An economic union is a common marketplace not only for goods but also for services and capital. For example, if professionals are going to be able to work anywhere in the EU, the members must harmonize their practice licensing so that a doctor or lawyer qualified in one country may practice in any other. The full evolution of an economic union would involve the creation of a unified central bank, the use of a single currency, and common policies on agriculture, social services and welfare, regional development, transport, taxation, competition, and mergers. A true economic union requires extensive political unity, which makes it similar to a nation. The further integration of nations that were members of fully developed economic unions would be the formation of a central government that would bring together independent political states into a single political framework. The EU is approaching its target of completing most of the steps required to become a full economic union. Table 3-3 compares the various forms of regional economic integration.

NORTH AMERICA

North America, which includes Canada, the United States, and Mexico, comprises a distinctive regional market. The United States combines great wealth, a large population, vast space, and plentiful natural resources in a single national economic and political environment and presents unique marketing characteristics. High product-ownership levels are associated with high income and relatively high receptivity to innovations and new ideas both in consumer and industrial products. The United

Table 3-3 *Forms of Regional Economic Integration*	Stage of Integration	Elimination of Tariffs and Quotas Among Members	Common External Tariff (CET) and Quota System	Elimination of Restrictions on Factor Movements	Harmonization and Unification of Economic and Social Policies and Institutions
	Free Trade Area	Yes	No	No	No
	Customs Union	Yes	Yes	No	No
	Common Market	Yes	Yes	Yes	No
	Economic Union	Yes	Yes	Yes	Yes

the rest of the story

Sixty Years of Trade Negotiation

Between 1947 and 1994, the member countries of GATT completed eight rounds of multilateral trade negotiations. Tariffs have been reduced from an average of 40 percent in 1945 to 5 percent today. The result has been a tremendous growth in trade: In the three decades from 1945 to 1975, the volume of world trade expanded by roughly 500 percent. The seventh round of negotiations was launched in Tokyo and ran from 1973 to 1979. These talks succeeded in cutting duties on industrial products valued at $150 billion by another 30 percent so that the remaining tariffs averaged about 6 percent. In terms of agricultural trade, there was a standoff between the United States, Europe, and Japan. The confrontation pitted the interests of the American farm lobby against the equally politically powerful farmers of Europe and Japan. Deep-rooted differences resulted in little change in the agricultural area during the Tokyo round. The most notable feature of the Tokyo round was not the duty cuts, but rather a series of nine new agreements on nontariff trade barriers.

GATT officials also devoted considerable attention to the services industry, addressing market-entry barriers in banking, insurance, telecommunications, and other sectors. The services issue was so volatile that the opening of the Uruguay round was delayed from 1982 until 1986. In addition to trade in services, these negotiations focused on the aforementioned nontariff measures that restrict or distort trade, including agricultural trade policy, intellectual property protection, and restrictions on foreign investment.

Agricultural subsidies and quotas that developed outside the multilateral framework remain a divisive issue. Critics argue that trade patterns are distorted when affluent countries protect and subsidize farm production. While home-market consumers pay higher prices, surplus output is sold abroad at artificially low prices. According to the Organization for Economic Cooperation and Development, in the mid-1990s, the total cost of these subsidies to rich-country taxpayers and consumers was more than $200 billion a year. Critics also believe that subsidies deny poor countries a natural path out of poverty, namely food exports. For example, in a 2002 report, Oxfam International estimated that U.S. cotton subsidies cost cotton farmers in Africa $300 million in lost exports each year.

The Uruguay negotiations were suspended in December 1990 after 30,000 French farmers took to the streets of Brussels to protest a proposed 30 percent cut in agricultural export subsidies. Negotiations resumed a few months later against the background of the united Western war effort in the Persian Gulf War. Negotiators finally succeeded in reaching an agreement by the December 15, 1993, deadline. A stalemate over agricultural subsidies was broken, with France and the EU nations agreeing to reductions. The U.S. Congress voted in favor of GATT at the end of 1994.

Competitive companies will benefit as tariffs are cut or eliminated entirely. The Triad nations agreed to end tariffs in pharmaceuticals, construction and agricultural equipment, scotch whiskey, furniture, paper, steel, and medical equipment. Also, U.S. restrictions on textile and apparel imports from developing countries were phased out over a 10-year period. Major issues remain unresolved in the entertainment industry; France has insisted on preferences and subsidies for French producers of television programming and motion pictures in order to limit what they feel is "cultural imperialism." Efforts to reduce European broadcast restrictions on U.S.-produced movies and television programming were unsuccessful.

Efforts to break the deadlock over agriculture have met with some success. For one thing, today's CAP is distinctly different than it was a decade ago. In 1999, EU governments agreed on Agenda 2000 reforms that have resulted in price support reductions and increased attention to environmental issues. In 2003, the EU undertook further reform of CAP by decoupling agricultural income support from production. In 2004, Brazil successfully challenged the EU sugar regime at the WTO. In 2005, the EU proposed cutting subsidies for agricultural exports; it also agreed to cut sugar subsidies by 36 percent over a 4-year period. Industry trade groups such as the Committee of Professional Agriculture Organizations and the General Confederation of Agricultural Cooperatives (COPA-COGECA) in the EU are steadfast in their efforts to serve the interests of farmers and provide input to policymakers; COPA-COGECA also is an advocate for sustainable development and related issues.

For its part, the U.S. government has proposed capping subsidies at a maximum of $250,000 per farmer per year. In 2005, the WTO ruled in favor of Brazil's challenge to U.S. cotton subsidies; meanwhile, a grassroots anti-subsidy movement is gaining traction. As Jerry Moran, a Republican congressman from Kansas, told *The Wall Street Journal*, "There are a growing number of people who want to weigh in on farm policy. They care about Africa. They care about the environment. They care about nutrition."

Sources: Alan Beattie, "Weight of Expectation Buries Deal," Financial Times, July 25, 2006, p. 2; Scott Killman and Roger Thurow, "Pork Chops: In Fight Against Farm Subsidies, Even Farmers are Joining Foes," The Wall Street Journal (March 14, 2006), pp. A1, A16; Keith Bradsher, "Trade Talks Now Expected to Focus on Exports of Poorest Nations," The New York Times December 12, 2005, pp. C1, C3; Noelle Knox, "French Rally Around Farmers at WTO Talks," USA Today (November 30, 2005), p. 5B; Scott Miller, "Trade Talks Twist in the Wind," The Wall Street Journal, November 8, 2005, pp. A14, A15; Shailagh Murray, "Subsidies Shackle EU Competitiveness," The Wall Street Journal, October 28, 1996, p. A13; "GATT's Last Gasp," Economist, December 1, 1990, p. 16; Joseph A. McKinney, "How Multilateral Trade Talks Affect the U.S.," Baylor Business Review (Fall 1991), pp. 24–25; Bob Davis, "Squeaky Wheels: GATT Talks Resume, with France and India Calling Many of the Shots," The Wall Street Journal, January 31, 1992, pp. A1, A13; "Free Trade's Fading Champion," Economist, April 11, 1992, p. 65; Davis and Lawrence Ingrassia, "Trade Acceptance: After Years of Talks, GATT Is at Last Ready to Sign Off on a Pact," The Wall Street Journal, December 15, 1993, pp. A1, A7.

States is home to more global industry leaders than any other nation in the world. For example, U.S. companies are the dominant producers in the computer, software, aerospace, entertainment, medical equipment, and jet engine industry sectors.

In 1988, the United States and Canada signed a free trade agreement (U.S.-Canada Free Trade Agreement, or CFTA); the Canada-U.S. Free Trade Area formally came into existence in 1989. This helps explain the fact that more than $400 billion per year in goods and services flows between Canada and the United States, the biggest trading relationship between any two single nations. Canada takes 20 percent of U.S. exports, and the United States buys approximately 85 percent of Canada's exports. Figure 3-1 illustrates the economic integration of North America: Canada is the number one trading partner of the United States, Mexico is second, and China ranks third. American companies have more invested in Canada than in any other country. Many U.S. manufacturers, including GE and IBM, use their Canadian operations as major global suppliers for some product lines. By participating in the Canadian auto market, U.S. automakers gain greater economies of scale. The CFTA, which was fully implemented when all duties were eliminated effective January 1998, is creating a true continental market for most other products.

Figure 3-1

U.S. Trade Partners 2005

Source: U.S. Bureau of the Census, www.census.gov.

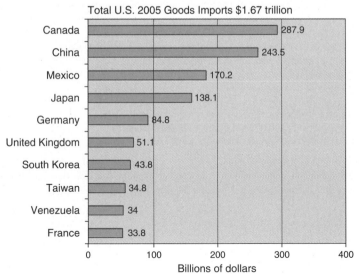

	2004 GNI (in millions)	2004 Population (in thousands)	2004 GNI Per Capita
United States	$12,168,482	293,655	$41,440
Canada	905,042	31,974	28,310
Mexico	704,906	103,795	6,790
Total/Mean GNP per capita	**$13,778,430**	429,424	$32,086*

*Indicates mean.
Source: Reprinted by permission of Warren Keegan Associates, Inc.

Table 3-4

NAFTA Income and Population

In 1992, representatives from the United States, Canada, and Mexico concluded negotiations for the **North American Free Trade Agreement (NAFTA)**. The agreement was approved by both houses of the U.S. Congress and became effective on January 1, 1994. The result is a free trade area with a combined population of roughly 430 million and a total GNI of almost $14 trillion (see Table 3-4 and Figure 3-2).

Why does NAFTA create a free trade area as opposed to a customs union or a common market? The governments of all three nations pledge to promote economic growth through tariff elimination and expanded trade and investment. At present, however, there are no common external tariffs nor have restrictions on labor and other factor movements been eliminated. The issue of illegal immigration from Mexico into the United States remains a contentious one. The benefits of continental free trade will enable all three countries to meet the economic challenges of the decades to come. The gradual elimination of barriers to the flow of goods, services, and investment, coupled with strong protection of intellectual property rights (patents, trademarks, and copyrights), will further benefit businesses, workers, farmers, and consumers.

The agreement does leave the door open for discretionary protectionism, however. For example, California avocado growers want government protection for a

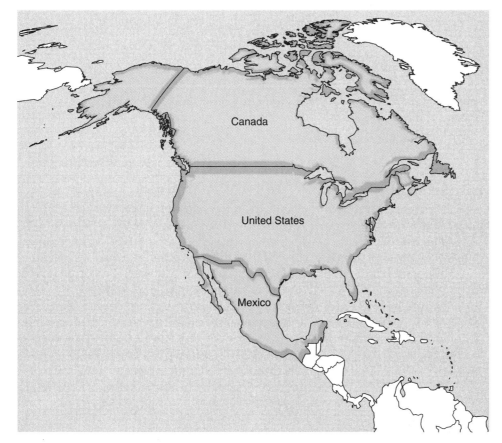

Figure 3-2

Map of NAFTA Countries

market worth $250 million; Mexican avocado growers can only ship their fruit to the United States during the winter months, and only to states in the northeast. Moreover, Mexican avocados are subject to quotas so only $30 million worth of avocados reach the United States each year. Mexican farmer Ricardo Salgado complained, "The California growers want to control all of the supply—that way they get the best prices. We'd love to have a bigger selling season, but right now we have to wait for the U.S. Congress to give us permission."[3] Mexico engages in some protectionism of its own; for example, in 2003, a 98.8 percent tariff was imposed on chicken leg quarters beyond the first 50,000 metric tons imported. In addition, Mexico imposed a 46.6 percent tariff on red and golden delicious apples.

LATIN AMERICA: SICA, ANDEAN COMMUNITY, MERCOSUR, CARICOM

Latin America includes the Caribbean and Central and South America (because of NAFTA, Mexico is grouped with North America). The allure of the Latin American market has been its considerable size and huge resource base. After a decade of no growth, crippling inflation, increasing foreign debt, protectionism, and bloated government payrolls, the countries of Latin America have begun the process of economic transformation. Balanced budgets are a priority and privatization is underway. Free markets, open economies, and deregulation have begun to replace the policies of the past. In many countries, tariffs that sometimes reached as much as 100 percent or more have been lowered to 10 percent to 20 percent. With the exception of Cuba, most elected governments throughout Latin America are democratic. However, there is widespread skepticism about the benefits of participating fully in the global economy. As left-leaning politicians such as Venezuela's President Hugo Chávez become more popular, concern is growing that free-market forces may lose momentum in the region. Global corporations are watching developments closely. They are encouraged by import liberalization, the prospects for lower tariffs within subregional trading groups, and the potential for establishing more efficient regional production. Many observers envision a free trade area throughout the hemisphere. The four most important preferential trading arrangements in Latin America are the SICA, the Andean Community, the Common Market of the South (Mercosur), and the Caribbean Community and Common Market (CARICOM).

Central American Integration System

Central America is trying to revive its common market, which was set up in the early 1960s. The five original members—El Salvador, Honduras, Guatemala, Nicaragua, and Costa Rica—decided in July 1991 to reestablish the Central American Common Market (CACM) by 1994. Efforts to improve regional integration gained momentum with the granting of observer status to Panama. Between 1994 and 1996, the volume of intraregional trade grew from $1.1 billion to $1.6 billion. In 1997, with Panama as a member, the group's name was changed to the Central American Integration System (Sistema de la Integración Centroamericana or SICA).

The Secretariat for Central American Economic Integration, headquartered in Guatemala City, helps to coordinate the movement toward a Central

---

[3] Joel Millman, "Bitter Fruit: Spats Persist Despite NAFTA," *The Wall Street Journal*, June 19, 2000, p. A23.

American common market. Common rules of origin were also adopted, allowing for freer movement of goods among current SICA countries. SICA countries agreed to conform to a common external tariff (CET) of 5 percent to 20 percent for most goods by the mid-1990s; many tariffs had previously exceeded 100 percent. For example, the Costa Rican government had previously benefited from the revenues generated by triple-digit tariffs on automobiles imported from Japan and elsewhere. As a practical matter, there was considerable variation in tariff rates until the end of the 1990s. Starting in 2000, import duties charged by the five SICA members converged to a range of 0 to 15 percent. Still, the region's attempts to achieve integration have been described as uncoordinated, inefficient, and costly. There are still tariffs on imports of products—sugar, coffee, and alcoholic beverages, for example— that are also produced in the importing country. As one Guatemalan analyst remarked, "Only when I see Salvadoran beer on sale in Guatemala and Guatemalan beer on sale in El Salvador will I believe that trade liberalization and integration is a reality."[4] Figure 3-3 shows the SICA group; Table 3-5 shows the income and population data.

Figure 3-3

Map of SICA Countries

	2004 GNI (in millions)	2004 Population (in thousands)	2004 GNI Per Capita
Costa Rica	$19,003	4,253	$4,470
El Salvador	15,701	6,762	2,320
Guatemala	26,945	12,295	2,190
Honduras	7,321	7,048	1,040
Nicaragua	4,481	5,376	830
Panama	13,377	3,175	4,210
Total/Mean GNP per capita	**$86,828**	**38,909**	**$2,232***

Table 3-5

SICA Income and Population

*Indicates mean.
Source: Reprinted by permission of Warren Keegan Associates, Inc.

---

[4] Johanna Tuckman, "Central Americans Start to Act Together," *Financial Times*, July 9, 1997, p. 4.

Andean Community

The Andean Community (Comunidad Andina de Naciones or CAN; see Figure 3-4 and Table 3-6) was formed in 1969 to accelerate the development of member states Bolivia, Colombia, Ecuador, Peru, and Venezuela through economic and social integration. Members agreed to lower tariffs on intragroup trade and work together to decide what products each country should produce. At the same time, foreign goods and companies were kept out as much as possible. One Bolivian described the unfortunate result of this lack of competition in the following way: "We had agreed, 'You buy our overpriced goods and we'll buy yours.' "[5]

In 1988, the group members decided to get a fresh start. Beginning in 1992, the Andean Pact signatories agreed to form Latin America's first operating subregional free trade area. The pact, which abolished all foreign exchange, financial and fiscal incentives, and export subsidies at the end of 1992, would affect more than 100 million consumers. Common external tariffs were established, marking the transition to a true customs union. The new approach yielded some successes; for example, Peru now boasts one of the fastest-growing economies in the region. Ecuador, meanwhile, has experienced years of economic and political instability. In 2000, in an attempt to bring rampant inflation under control, the government adopted the U.S. dollar as Ecuador's official currency. Overall, rural residents and the urban poor in the region have become frustrated and impatient with the lack of progress. As one Andean scholar put it, "After 10 or 15 years of operating with free-market policies, paradise hasn't come. People start wondering if the gospel was as good as advertised."[6]

Figure 3-4

Map of Andean Community and Mercosur

[5] "NAFTA Is Not Alone," *Economist*, June 18, 1994, pp. 47–48.
[6] Marc Lifsher, "The Andean Arc of Instability," *The Wall Street Journal*, February 24, 2003, p. A13.

Table 3-6

Andean Community Income
and Population

	2004 GNI (in millions)	2004 Population (in thousands)	2004 GNI Per Capita
Bolivia	$8,640	9,009	$960
Colombia	90,895	44,915	2,020
Ecuador	28,863	13,040	2,210
Peru	65,048	27,562	2,360
Venezuela	105,327	26,127	4,030
Total/Mean GNP per capita	**$298,773**	**120,653**	**$2,476***

*Indicates mean.
Source: Reprinted by permission of Warren Keegan Associates, Inc.

Common Market of the South (Mercosur)

March 2006 marked the fifteenth anniversary of the signing of the Asunción Treaty. The treaty signified the agreement by the governments of Argentina, Brazil, Paraguay, and Uruguay to form the Common Market of the South (Mercado Común del Sur or Mercosur; see Figure 3-4 and Table 3-7). The four countries agreed to begin phasing in tariff reform on January 1, 1995. Internal tariffs were eliminated, and CETs of up to 20 percent were established. In theory, goods, services, and factors of production will ultimately move freely throughout the member countries; until this goal is achieved, however, Mercosur will actually operate as a customs union rather than a true common market. Today, about 90 percent of goods are traded freely; however, individual members of Mercosur can change both internal and external tariffs when it suits the respective government.

Much depends on the successful outcome of this experiment in regional cooperation. The early signs were positive, as trade between the four full member nations grew dramatically during the 1990s. The region has weathered a series of financial crises; for example, Brazil's currency was devalued in 1995 and again in 1999. In 2002, Argentina's economy minister announced emergency measures that included a 29 percent currency devaluation for exports and capital transactions. Argentina was allowed to break from the CET and raise duties on consumer goods in response to its financial crisis. Now, trade is on the rebound; Venezuela became a full Mercosur member in 2006. Flush with revenues from oil exports, Venezuela is expected to have a positive impact on regional integration.

In 1996, Chile became an associate member of Mercosur. Policy makers opted against full membership because Chile already had lower external tariffs than the rest of Mercosur; ironically, full membership would have required raising them. (In other words, Chile participates in the free-trade-area aspect of Mercosur, not the

Table 3-7

Mercosur Income and Population

	2004 GNI (in millions)	2004 Population (in thousands)	2004 GNI Per Capita
Argentina	$137,326	38,372	$3,580
Bolivia*	8,640	9,009	960
Brazil	551,650	183,913	3,000
Chile*	84,160	16,124	5,220
Paraguay	6,866	6,017	1,140
Uruguay	13,424	3,439	3,900
Venezuela	105,327	26,127	4,030
Total/Mean GNP per capita	**$907,393**	**283,001**	**$3,206****

*Associate members that participate in free trade area only.
**Indicates mean.
Source: Reprinted by permission of Warren Keegan Associates, Inc.

BRIC Briefing Book

Brazil

As the figures in Table 3-7 clearly show, Brazil is an economic powerhouse in South America. Brazil has the largest geographical territory and the largest population in the region. Between 1994 and 2004, Brazil's exports grew at an annual rate of 8.78 percent; this rapid economic growth has given Brazil's policy makers, including President Lúiz Inácio Lula da Silva, a greater presence on the global stage and more clout at global trade talks.

One symbol of Brazil's new role in the global economy: Embraer, a jet aircraft manufacturer. Specializing in regional jets that seat fewer than 100 passengers, Embraer has won orders from JetBlue, Air Canada, Saudi Arabian Airlines, and other carriers. Embraer shared the cost of developing new models such as the E-170/175 with more than one dozen partners, including General Electric and Honeywell. In order to sell more regional jets to China, Embraer has also established a $50 million joint venture with China Aviation Industry Corporation.

Brazil's agricultural sector is also a leading exporter. Brazil is the world's number one exporter of beef, coffee, orange juice (check the label on your orange juice carton), and sugar. Brazil is rapidly gaining a reputation as a producer of sugar-based ethanol, which can serve as a sustainable substitute for expensive gasoline. Industry observers expect Brazil to double its sugar cane processing capacity by 2010. As Ermor Zambello, manager of the Grupo Farias sugar mill, notes, "Globalization has made us think more about foreign markets. Now, we have more of a global outlook, and we are concerned about global production."

As noted in the chapter introduction, the central issue in the Doha Round is agriculture. Brazil and India are taking the lead of a so-called Group of 20 developing nations calling for agricultural sector reform. For example, the average tariff on Brazil's exports to the 30 OECD nations is 27 percent. Government subsidies are also a key issue. In the EU, government spending accounts for about one-third of gross farm receipts; in the United States, the government provides about one-quarter of gross farm receipts. By contrast, Brazil's spending on farm support amounts to only about 3 percent of farm receipts.

Moving forward, Brazil faces a number of other challenges. Steady appreciation of Brazil's currency, the real, may require exporters to raise prices. Embraer faces tough competition from Canada's Bombardier. Brazil's infrastructure remains woefully underdeveloped; significant investment is required to improve highways, railroads, and ports. Business people speak of "the Brazil cost," a phrase that refers to such issues delays related to excessive red tape and a shortage of customs agents. Trade with China is presenting both opportunities and threats. From 1995 to 2005, Brazil's total two-way trade with China increased from $2.2 billion to $12.2 billion. China's explosive economic growth has created great demand for iron ore and other Brazilian commodity exports. However, Brazilian manufacturers in light-industry sectors such as toys, eyeglasses, and footwear are facing increased competition from low-priced Chinese imports.

Embraer is the world's fourth-largest aircraft manufacturer; however, in the regional aircraft sector, Embraer is second only to Canada's Bombardier.

Sources: David J. Lynch, "Brazil Hopes to Build On Its Ethanol Success," March 29, 2006, pp. 1B, 2B "China's Growing Pull Puts Brazil in a Bind," USA Today, March 21, 2006, pp. 1B, 2B; Lynch, "Comeback Kid Embraer Has Hot New Jet, and Fiery CEO to Match," USA Today, March 7, 2006, pp. 1B, 2B; David J. Lynch, "Brazil's Agricultural Exports Cast Long Shadow," USA Today, March 10, 2006, pp. 1B, 2B.

customs union.) Chile's export-driven success makes it a role model for the rest of Latin America as well as Central and Eastern Europe. Colombia, Ecuador, Peru, and Bolivia have become associate members of Mercosur. In 2004, Mercosur signed a cooperation agreement with the Andean Community. The EU is Mercosur's number one trading partner; Mercosur signed an agreement with the EU to establish a free trade area by 2005. Germany and France are opposed to such an agreement on the grounds that low-cost agricultural exports will harm farmers in Europe.

Caribbean Community and Common Market (CARICOM)

CARICOM was formed in 1973 as a movement toward unity in the Caribbean. It replaced the Caribbean Free Trade Association (CARIFTA) founded in 1965. The members are Antigua and Barbuda, Bahamas, Barbados, Belize, Dominica, Grenada, Guyana, Haiti, Jamaica, Montserrat, St. Kitts and Nevis, St. Lucia, St. Vincent and the Grenadines, and Trinidad and Tobago. The population of the entire 15-member CARICOM is about 15 million; disparate levels of economic development can be seen by comparing GNI per capita in Dominic and Grenada with that of Haiti (see Table 3-8).

To date, CARICOM's main objective has been to achieve a deepening of economic integration by means of a Caribbean common market. However, CARICOM was largely stagnant during its first two decades of existence. At its annual meeting in July 1991, member countries agreed to speed integration; a customs union was established with common external tariffs. At the 1998 summit meeting, leaders from the 15 countries agreed to move quickly to establish an economic union with a common currency. A recent study of the issue has suggested, however, that the limited extent of intraregional trade would limit the potential gains from lower transaction costs.[7]

	2004 GNI (in millions)	2004 Population (in thousands)	2004 GNI Per Capita
Antigua and Barbuda	$759	80	$9,480
Bahamas	4,684+	319	15,100+
Barbados	na	269	na
Belize	1,115	283	3,940
Dominica	262	71	3,670
Grenada	397	106	3,750
Guyana	765	750	1,020
Haiti	3,316+	8,407	400+
Jamaica	8,720	2,645	3,300
Montserrat	na	na	na
St. Kitts and Nevis	326+	47	6,980+
St. Lucia	684	164	4,180
St. Vincent and Grenadines	403	118	3,400
Suriname	997	446	2,230
Trinidad and Tobago	11,360	1,301	8,730
Total/Mean GNP per capita	**$33,788**	**15,006**	**$2,293*,a**

Table 3-8

CARICOM Income and Population

*Indicates mean.
aExcluding Montserrat.
Source: Reprinted by permission of Warren Keegan Associates, Inc.

---

[7] Myrvin L. Anthony and Andrew Hughes Hallett, "Is the Case for Economic and Monetary Union in the Caribbean Realistic?" *World Economy* 23, no. 1 (January 2000), pp. 119–144.

If the original 1973 treaty were revised, CARICOM nations could qualify for membership in the proposed Free Trade Area of the Americas (FTAA). As Owen Arthur, prime minister of Barbados explained, "The old treaty limited the movement of capital, skills, and business in the region. The treaty has to be changed so that regional trade policy can be widened to deal with the FTAA and the EU, and such matters as bilateral investments treaties, intellectual property rights, and trade in services."[8]

The English-speaking CARICOM members in the eastern Caribbean are also concerned with defending their privileged trading position with the United States. That status dates to the Caribbean Basin Initiative (CBI) of 1984, which promoted export production of certain products by providing duty-free U.S. market access to 20 countries, including members of CARICOM. Recently, CBI members requested that the CBI be expanded. The Caribbean Basin Trade Partnership Act, which went into effect on October 1, 2000, exempts textile and apparel exports from the Caribbean to the United States from duties and tariffs. Figure 3-5 shows CARICOM.

Current Trade-Related Issues

One of the biggest issues pertaining to trade in the Western Hemisphere is the FTAA (see Case 3-1). As noted earlier, leaders in many Latin American countries—Brazil in particular—are frustrated by what they perceive as America's failure to follow through on its promises in the region. As a result, Brazil and its Mercosur partners are advocating a slower, three-stage approach to negotiations. The first stage would include discussions on business facilitation issues such as standardized customs forms and industry deregulation; the second would focus on dispute settlement and rules of origin; and the third would focus on tariffs. Meanwhile, Mercosur, CARICOM, SICA, and the Andean Community intend to pursue further integration among themselves as well as with Europe.

Figure 3-5

CARICOM

---

8   Canute James, "Caribbean Community Grapples with Challenge of Creating a Single Market," *Financial Times*, July 10, 1998, p. 7.

Asia-Pacific: The Association of Southeast Asian Nations (ASEAN)

The Association of Southeast Asian Nations (ASEAN) was established in 1967 as an organization for economic, political, social, and cultural cooperation among its member countries. Brunei, Indonesia, Malaysia, the Philippines, Singapore, and Thailand were the original six members. Vietnam became the first Communist nation in the group when it was admitted to ASEAN in July 1995. Cambodia and Laos were admitted at the organization's thirtieth anniversary meeting in July 1997 Burma (known as Myanmar by the ruling military junta) joined in 1998, following delays related to the country's internal politics and human rights record (see Figure 3-6 and Table 3-9).

Individually and collectively, ASEAN countries are active in regional and global trade. ASEAN's top trading partners include the United States ($154 billion in total 2005 trade), Japan ($153.8 billion in total 2005 trade), the EU ($140 billion in total 2005 trade), and China ($113 billion in total 2005 trade). A few years ago, ASEAN officials realized that broad common goals were not enough to keep the association alive. A constant problem was the strict need for consensus among all members before proceeding with any form of cooperative effort. Although the ASEAN member countries are geographically close, they have historically been divided in many respects. In 1994, economic ministers from the member nations agreed to implement an ASEAN Free Trade Area (AFTA) by 2003, five years earlier than previously discussed.

Recently, Japan, China, and Korea were informally added to the member roster; some observers called this configuration "ASEAN plus three." When the roster expanded again to include Australia, New Zealand, and India, it was dubbed "ASEAN plus six." The latter is working to establish an East Asian Community, with the first step being the establishment of an East Asian Free Trade Area.[9] Although China's participation has met with some opposition, China's dynamic growth and increasing power in the region required a response. As ASEAN Secretary General Rodolfo Severino noted, "You can either close yourself off from China and crouch in fear or engage more closely. Although some industries will get hurt, the overall impact on both China and ASEAN would be beneficial."[10]

	2004 GNI (in millions)	2004 Population (in thousands)	2004 GNI Per Capita
Brunei	na	366	na
Cambodia	$4,808	13,798	$350
Indonesia	248,007	217,588	1,140
Laos	2,279	5,792	390
Malaysia	112,580	24,894	4,520
Myanmar	na	50,004	na
Philippines	95,085	81,617	1,170
Singapore	104,994	4,240	24,760
Thailand	158,372	63,694	2,490
Vietnam	44,631	82,162	540
Total/Mean GNP per capita	$770,756[a]	544,155	$1,561 *,a

Table 3-9

ASEAN Income and Population

[a]Excluding Brunei and Myanmar.

*Indicates mean.

Source: Reprinted by permission of Warren Keegan Associates, Inc.

---

9 Bernard Gordon, "The FTA Fetish," *The Wall Street Journal*, November 17, 2005, p. A16.

10 Amy Kazmin, "ASEAN and China Sign Deal for Free Trade Area," *Financial Times*, November 5, 2002, p. 6.

Figure 3-6

Map of ASEAN

Singapore represents a special case among the ASEAN nations. In fewer than three decades, Singapore transformed itself from a British colony to a vibrant, 240-square-mile industrial power. Singapore has an extremely efficient infrastructure—the Port of Singapore is the world's second-largest container port (Hong Kong's ranks first) and a standard of living second in the region only to Japan's. Singapore's 4.2 million citizens have played a critical role in the country's economic achievements by readily accepting the notion that "the country with the most knowledge will win" in global competition. Excellent training programs and a 93 percent literacy rate help explain why Singapore has more engineers per capita than the United States. Singapore's Economic Development Board has also actively recruited business interest in the nation. The manufacturing companies that have been attracted to Singapore read like a who's who of global marketing and include Hewlett-Packard, IBM, Philips, and Apple; in all, more than 3,000 companies have operations or investments in Singapore.

Singapore alone accounts for more than one-third of U.S. trading activities with ASEAN countries; U.S. exports to Singapore in 2003 totaled $16.5 billion, while imports totaled $15.1 billion. Singapore is closely tied with its neighbors; more than one-third of imports are reexported to other Asian countries. Singapore's efforts to fashion a civil society have gained the country some notoriety; crime is nearly nonexistent, thanks to the long-ruling People's Action Party's severe treatment of criminals.

Marketing Issues in the Asia-Pacific Region

Mastering the Japanese market takes flexibility, ambition, and a long-term commitment. Japan has changed from being a closed market to one that's just tough. There are barriers in Japan in terms of attitudes as well as laws. Any organization wishing to compete in Japan must be committed to providing top-quality products and services. In many cases, products and marketing must be tailored to local tastes. Countless visits and socializing with distributors are necessary to build trust. Marketers must also master the *keiretsu* system of tightly knit corporate alliances. All these factors served as a backdrop to the trade dispute between Japan and the United States that escalated in mid-1995. In an effort to pry open Japan's market for auto parts, the U.S. government threatened to impose stiff tariffs on Japanese luxury car imports.

India's huge population base also presents attractive opportunities. Several automakers—including Ford, General Motors, Hyundai, Mercedes, and Suzuki—are present in the market. Other companies currently investing in India are Benetton, Coca-Cola, DuPont, Fujitsu, IBM, L'Oréal, MTV, and Unilever. However, the political climate remains unpredictable. The nationalistic Bharatiya Janata Party (BJP) has been a vocal and powerful opponent of reform; in 2004, the BJP was ousted in national elections, and the left-leaning Congress party came to power. Manmohan Singh, India's former finance minister and the architect of the country's economic reforms, is the new prime minister. Financial markets reacted negatively to uncertainty over India's future direction; as one analyst put it, "This feels like the Asia crisis and the Mexico crisis times again."[11]

WESTERN, CENTRAL, AND EASTERN EUROPE

The countries of Western Europe are among the most prosperous in the world. Despite the fact that there are significant differences in income between the north and the south and obvious differences in language and culture, the once-varied societies of Western Europe have grown remarkably alike. Still, enough differences remain that many observers view Western Europe in terms of three tiers. Many Britons view themselves as somewhat apart from the rest of the continent; Euro-skepticism is widespread, and the country still has problems seeing eye-to-eye with historic rivals Germany and France. Meanwhile, across the English Channel, Portugal, Italy, Greece, and Spain have struggled mightily to overcome the stigma of being called "Club Med" nations and other derogatory nicknames by their northern neighbors.[12] Still, as they enter the first decade of the twenty-first century, the governments of Western Europe are achieving hitherto unprecedented levels of economic integration.

The European Union (EU)

The origins of the European Union (EU) can be traced back to the 1958 Treaty of Rome. The six original members of the European Community (EC), as the group was called then, were Belgium, France, Holland, Italy, Luxembourg, and West Germany. In 1973, Great Britain, Denmark, and Ireland were admitted, followed by Greece in 1981, and Spain and Portugal in 1986. Beginning in 1987, the 12 countries that were EC members set about the difficult task of creating a genuine single market in goods, services, and capital; in other words, an economic union. Adopting the Single European Act by the end of 1992 was a major EC achievement; the Council of Ministers adopted more than 200 pieces of legislation and regulations to make the single market a reality.

[11] Sara Calian, "In India, Plunges and Protest," *The Wall Street Journal*, May 18, 2004, p. C16.
[12] Thomas Kamm, "Snobbery: The Latest Hitch in Unifying Europe," *The Wall Street Journal*, November 6, 1996, p. A17; Kyle Pope, "More Than Water Divides U.K., Europe," *The Wall Street Journal*, June 30, 1995, p. A12.

The objective of the EU member countries is to harmonize national laws and regulations so that goods, services, people, and eventually money can flow freely across national boundaries. December 31, 1992, marked the dawn of the new economic era in Europe. Finland, Sweden, and Austria officially joined on January 1, 1995. (In November 1994, voters in Norway rejected a membership proposal.) Evidence that this is more than a free trade area, customs union, or common market is the fact that citizens of member countries are now able to freely cross borders within the union. The EU is encouraging the development of a communitywide labor pool; it is also attempting to shake up Europe's cartel mentality by handing down rules of competition patterned after U.S. antitrust law. Improvements to highway and rail networks are now being coordinated as well. Further EU enlargement is the big story in this region today. Cyprus, the Czech Republic, Estonia, Hungary, Poland, Latvia, Lithuania, Malta, the Slovak Republic, and Slovenia became full EU members on May 1, 2004. Bulgaria and Romania joined on January 1, 2007. Today, the 27 nations of the EU represent 480 million people and a combined GNI of $11.8 trillion (see Table 3-10). The map in Figure 3-7 shows EU member nations.

During the two decades between 1979 and 1999, the European Monetary System (EMS) was an important foundation of Western European commerce. The EMS was based on the European Currency Unit (ECU), a unit of account comprised of a hypothetical basket of "weighted" currencies. The ECU did not take the form of an actual currency; it existed physically in the form of checks and electronically in computers. Some companies priced their raw materials and

Table 3-10

The 27 Nations of the EU— Income and Population

	2004 GNI (in millions)	2004 Population (in thousands)	2004 GNI Per Capita
Austria	$263,867	8,173	$32,280
Belgium	325,976	10,502	31,280
Bulgaria	21,397	7,761	2,760
Cyprus	13,633	826	16,510
Czech Republic	93,289	10,216	9,130
Denmark	220,218	5,404	40,750
Estonia	9,548	1,349	7,080
Finland	171,942	5,228	32,880
France	1,888,407	60,380	30,370
Germany	2,532,281	82,516	30,690
Greece	184,973	11,057	16,730
Hungary	84,567	10,107	8,370
Ireland	139,567	4,086	34,310
Italy	1,513,111	57,573	26,280
Latvia	12,901	2,313	5,580
Lithuania	19,727	3,436	5,740
Luxembourg	25,559	453	56,380
Malta	4,834	401	12,050
Netherlands	523,108	16,282	32,130
Poland	232,931	38,182	6,100
Portugal	149,305	10,502	14,220
Romania	63,979	21,684	2,950
Slovak Republic	34,898	5,382	6,480
Slovenia	29,494	1,997	14,770
Spain	919,094	42,690	21,530
Sweden	322,255	8,992	35,840
United Kingdom	2,013,363	59,867	33,630
Total/Mean GNP per capita*	**$11,814,224**	**487,359**	**$20,993**

*Indicates mean.
Source: Reprinted by permission of Warren Keegan Associates, Inc.

Figure 3-7

Map of EU

Twelve newest members

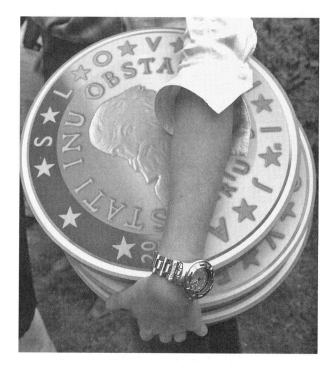

Tiny Slovenia (population 2 million) is the only one of the EU's newest members to meet criteria for joining the euro zone. Slovenia was able to join on January 1, 2007, because the government has kept inflation low and the budget deficit below 3 percent of GDP. Lithuania, Estonia, and others hope to adopt the euro within a few years.

products in ECU, thereby saving the time and cost of exchange transactions. The 1991 **Maastricht Treaty** set the stage for the transition from the EMS to an economic and monetary union (EMU) that includes a European central bank and a single European currency known as the **euro**. In May 1998, Austria, Belgium, Finland, Ireland, the Netherlands, France, Germany, Italy, Luxembourg, Portugal, and Spain were chosen as the 11 charter members of the **euro zone**. The single currency era, which officially began on January 1, 1999, is expected to bring many benefits to companies in the euro zone, such as eliminating costs associated with currency conversion and exchange rate uncertainty. The euro existed as a unit of account until 2002, when actual coins and paper money were issued and national currencies such as the French franc were withdrawn from circulation. Greece joined in 2001; Slovenia became the thirteenth member on January 1, 2007.

The European Free Trade Area (EFTA) and European Economic Area (EEA)

Since 1990, the EU has concluded more than 20 trade pacts with other nations. For example, in October 1991, the then-EC and the seven-nation European Free Trade Association (EFTA) reached agreement on the creation of the European Economic Area (EEA) beginning January 1993. The ultimate goal is to achieve the free movement of goods, services, capital, and labor between the two groups, but the EEA is a free trade area, not a customs union with common external tariffs. With Austria, Finland, and Sweden now members of the EU, Norway, Iceland, and Liechtenstein are the only remaining EFTA countries that are not EU members (Switzerland voted not to be part of the EEA). The three non-EU members of the new EEA are expected to adopt all the EU's single-market legislation. Meanwhile, the four members of EFTA (Norway, Iceland, Liechtenstein, and Switzerland) maintain free trade agreements with Israel and Turkey as well as nations in Central and Eastern Europe. EFTA also has cooperation agreements with Morocco, Tunisia, and Egypt.

Marketing Issues in the EU

The European Commission establishes directives and sets deadlines for their implementation by legislation in individual nations. The business environment in Europe has undergone considerable transformation since 1992, with significant implications for all elements of the marketing mix. Table 3-11 summarizes some of the marketing mix issues that must be addressed in Europe's single market. For example, content and other product standards that varied among nations have been harmonized. As a result, companies may have an opportunity to reap economies by cutting back on the number of product adaptations. Case Europe, for example, manufactures and markets farm machinery. When it introduced the Magnum tractor in Europe in 1988, it offered 17 different versions because of country regulations regarding placement of lights and brakes. Thanks to harmonization, Case offers the current model, the Magnum MX, in one version. However, because different types of implements and trailers are used in different countries, the MX is available with different kinds of hitches.[13] The advent of the euro on January 1, 1999, brought about more changes. Direct comparability of prices in the euro zone will force companies to review pricing policies. The marketing challenge is to develop strategies to take advantage of opportunities in

---

[13] George Russel, "Marketing in the 'Old Country': The Diversity of Europe Presents Unique Challenges," *Agri Marketing* 37, no. 1 (January 1999), p. 38.

Table 3-11

Marketing Strategies in the European Union

	Changes Affecting Strategies	Threats to Marketers' Planning	Management's Strategic Options
Product Strategies	Harmonization in product standards, testing, and certification process Common patenting and branding Harmonization in packaging, labeling, and processing requirements	Incorporating changes mandated by EC directives Complying with rules of origin Local content rules Differences in marketing research	Consolidate production Seek marketing economies Shift from brand to benefit segmentation Standardize packaging and labeling where possible
Pricing Strategies	More competitive environment Lifting of restrictions on foreign products Antimonopoly measures Opening up of the public procurement market	Parallel importing Different taxation of goods Less freedom in setting transfer prices	Exploit different excise and value-added taxes Understand price elasticity of consumer demand Emphasize high-margin products Introduce low-cost brand
Promotion Strategies	Common guidelines on TV broadcasting Deregulation of national broadcasting monopolies Uniform standards for TV commercials	Restrictions on alcohol and tobacco advertising Limits on foreign TV production Differences in permissible promotional techniques	Coordinate components of promotional mix via integrated marketing communications (IMC) Exploit advantage of pan-European media Position products according to local market preferences
Distribution Strategies	Simplification of transit documents and procedures Elimination of customs formalities	Increase in distributors' margins Lack of direct marketing infrastructure Restrictions in the use of computer databases	Consolidate manufacturing facilities Centralize distribution Develop nontraditional channels (direct marketing, telemarketing)

Source: Reprinted from *Long Range Planning*, Vol 5, G. Guido, "Implementing a pan-European Marketing Strategy," p. 32,1991, with permission from Elsevier.

one of the largest, wealthiest, most stable markets in the world. Corporations must assess the extent to which they can treat the region as one entity and how to change organizational policies and structures to adapt to and take advantage of a unified Europe.

The music industry is a case in point; long before online music distribution and MP3 file swapping had become issues, the major record companies faced a number of challenges. The single market meant that, for the first time, music retailers in Europe were allowed to buy CDs and tapes from distributors throughout the EU. This practice, known as transshipment, had not been permitted prior to the single market. Now, for example, a music retailer in Germany is no longer tied to a local supplier in Germany if better prices are available elsewhere. The change means that Sony, Warner, Bertelsmann, EMI, and the other major record companies have been forced to adopt more uniform pricing policies across Europe. This, in turn, has required them to find ways to cut costs without compromising the need to respond quickly to consumer demand. One solution has been to realign distribution via joint ventures or other arrangements; previously, each company had maintained its own distribution system. In 1998, however, Warner and Sony merged their distribution facilities in the United Kingdom.[14]

---

[14] Jeff Clark-Meads, "The Year in Europe: Union Members Confront Parallel Imports and Universes," *Billboard* 107 (December 23, 1995), p. YE14; Alice Rawsthorn, "Music's 'Big Five' Dip Toes in Common Distribution Pool," *Financial Times* (August 14, 1998), p. 60.

The enlargement of the EU will further impact marketing strategies. For example, food safety laws in the EU are different from those in some Central European countries. As a result, Coca-Cola had to delay launching its Powerade sports drink and other beverage products. Specifically, Polish and EU food law require the use of different ingredients. In addition to the harmonization of laws, the very size of the expanded EU offers opportunities. For example, Procter & Gamble executives foresee that, in the event of shortages in a particular country, they will be able to shift products from one market to another. A 27-nation EU also allows for more flexibility in the placement of factories. There will also be challenges. For example, South American banana growers now face 75 percent tariffs on exports to the new EU countries; previously, tariffs on bananas were virtually nonexistent. Also, because tariffs and quotas protect sugar production in the EU, both consumers and food producers, such as Kraft, will face rising costs.[15]

The Lomé Convention and the Cotonou Agreement

The EU maintains an accord with 71 countries in Africa, the Caribbean, and the Pacific (ACP). The Lomé Convention (named for the capital city of the West African nation of Togo) took effect in 1975. It was designed to promote trade and provide poor countries with financial assistance from a European Development Fund. The ACP signatories generally considered the treaty to be a success, as it allowed for preferential access to the EU for such commodities as sugar, bananas, rum, and rice. However, the WTO has ruled that some of the banana preferences are unfair. Recently, budget pressures at home have prompted some EU nations to push for cuts in Lomé aid. The convention expired in 2000; in June 2000, the EU and ACP nations signed a new 20-year pact known as the Cotonou Agreement. The new convention will be headquartered in the capital of Fiji. Government officials in Cuba have expressed a desire to become part of a post-Lomé arrangement in order to get better prices for sugar exports; Cuba is also interested in joining CARICOM.

Central European Free Trade Association (CEFTA)

In the early 1990s, the extraordinary political and economic reforms that swept through Central and Eastern Europe focused attention on a new 430-million-person market. The transition in the region from command to market economies—a process that is ongoing today—has toppled a number of entrenched institutions, including the Council for Mutual Economic Assistance. COMECON (or CMEA, as it was also known) was a group of Communist bloc countries allied with the Soviet Union. In the years since COMECON's demise in 1992, a number of proposals for multilateral cooperation have been advanced. In December 1992, Hungary, Poland, the Czech Republic, and Slovakia signed an agreement creating the Central European Free Trade Association (CEFTA). Slovenia, which declared its autonomy from the Yugoslav federation in 1992, is also a member. The signatories pledged cooperation in a number of areas, including infrastructure and telecommunications; an overriding common goal was to join the EU as a group. As noted previously, this goal has now been accomplished. Meanwhile, within the Commonwealth of

---

[15] Scott Miller, "Trading Partners Meet New EU," *The Wall Street Journal* (May 4, 2004), p. A17.

Independent States, formal economic integration between the former Soviet republics is proceeding slowly. In May 1995, the governments of Russia and Belarus agreed to form a customs union and remove border posts between their two countries. Hoping to capitalize on the opportunity to export to Russia without incurring prohibitive tariffs, Ford opened a $10 million vehicle assembly plant outside Minsk.

Because they are in transition, the markets of Central and Eastern Europe present interesting opportunities and challenges. Global companies view the region as an important new source of growth, and the first company to penetrate a country market often emerges as the industry leader. Exporting has been favored as a market entry mode, but direct investment in the region is on the rise; with wage rates much lower than those in Spain, Portugal, and Greece, the region offers attractive locations for low-cost manufacturing. For consumer products, distribution is a critical marketing mix element because availability is the key to sales.

One study examined the approaches utilized by 3M International, McDonald's, Philips Electronics, Henkel, Südzucker AG, and several other companies operating in Central Europe. Consumers and businesses in the region are eagerly embracing well-known global brands that were once available only to government elites and others in privileged positions. The study found a high degree of standardization of marketing program elements; in particular, the core product and brand elements were largely unchanged from those used in Western Europe. Consumer companies generally target high-end segments of the market and focus on brand image and product quality; industrial marketers concentrate on opportunities to do business with the largest firms in a given country.[16]

THE MIDDLE EAST

The Middle East includes 16 countries: Afghanistan, Bahrain, Cyprus, Egypt, Iran, Iraq, Israel, Jordan, Kuwait, Lebanon, Oman, Qatar, Saudi Arabia, Syria, the United Arab Emirates, and the reunited Yemen. The majority of the population is Arab, a large percentage is Persian, and a small percentage is Jewish. Persians and most Arabs share the same religion, beliefs, and Islamic traditions, making the population 95 percent Muslim and 5 percent Christian and Jewish.

Despite this apparent homogeneity, many differences exist. Middle Eastern countries fall into all categories of the index of economic freedom discussed in Chapter 2, including "mostly free" (e.g., Bahrain, Kuwait, Saudi Arabia, United Arab Emirates), "mostly unfree" (e.g., Qatar), and "repressed" (Iran and, until the 2003 regime change, Iraq). Moreover, the Middle East does not have a single societal type with a typical belief, behavior, and tradition. Each capital and major city in the Middle East has a variety of social groups that can be differentiated on the basis of religion, social class, education, and degree of wealth.

The price of oil drives business in the Middle East. Seven of the countries have high oil revenues: Bahrain, Iraq, Iran, Kuwait, Oman, Qatar, and Saudi Arabia hold significant world oil reserves. Oil revenues have widened the gap between poor and rich nations in the Middle East, and the disparities contribute to political

---

[16] Arnold Shuh, "Global Standardization as a Success Formula for Marketing in Central Eastern Europe," *Journal of World Business* 35, no. 2 (Summer 2000), pp. 133–148.

Dubai is one of the seven emirates that make up the United Arab Emirates (UAE). Although Dubai originally prospered by exporting oil, today its economy is more diversified. It is an important business hub for the manufacturing, IT, and finance sectors; Dubai has also become a popular tourism destination in the region. The Burj Dubai in the background is currently under construction. When work on the tower is completed, it will be the tallest building in the world.

and social instability in the area. Saudi Arabia, a monarchy with 22 million people and 25 percent of the world's known oil reserves, remains the most important market in this region.

In the past, pan-Arabism, a form of nationalism and loyalty that transcended borders and amounted to anti-Western dogma, characterized the region. During the Persian Gulf War in the early 1990s, this pan-Arabism weakened somewhat. To defeat Iraq, the Gulf Arabs and their allies broke many of their unwritten rules, including the acceptance of help from the United States, a traditional ally of Israel. However, anti-Americanism was ignited in 2003 following President George W. Bush's decision to invade Iraq and remove Saddam Hussein from power. The repercussions of America's military action continue to be felt throughout the region. The world community is watching to see whether political and social reform can take root in Iraq.

Cooperation Council for the Arab States of the Gulf

The key regional organization is the Gulf Cooperation Council (GCC), which was established in 1981 by Bahrain, Kuwait, Oman, Qatar, Saudi Arabia, and the United Arab Emirates (Table 3-12 and Figure 3-8). These six countries hold

Table 3-12

GCC Income and Population

	2004 GNI (in millions)	2004 Population (in thousands)	2004 GNI Per Capita
Bahrain	$10,288	716	$14,370
Kuwait	55,255	2,460	22,470
Oman	22,994	2,534	9,070
Qatar	na	777	na
Saudi Arabia	242,939	23,950	10,140
United Arab Emirates	102,693	4,320	23,770
Total/Mean GNP per capita	**$434,169[a]**	**34,757**	**$12,777*,[a]**

[a]Excluding Qatar.
*Indicates mean.
Source: Reprinted by permission of Warren Keegan Associates, Inc.

Figure 3-8

Map of GCC Countries

about 45 percent of the world's known oil reserves, but production is only about 18 percent of world oil output. Ironically, Saudi Arabia and several other Middle Eastern countries post current-account deficits, largely because they must import most of the goods and services that their citizens consume. The countries are heavily dependent on oil revenues to pay for their imports; efforts toward economic diversification are underway. For example, Saudi Arabia has developed new businesses in the petrochemical, cement, and iron industries; Bahrain is expanding its banking and insurance sectors, and the United Arab Emirates is focusing on information technology, media, and telecommunications.[17]

The organization provides a means of realizing coordination, integration, and cooperation in all economic, social, and cultural affairs. Gulf finance ministers drew up an economic cooperation agreement covering investment, petroleum, the abolition of customs duties, harmonization of banking regulations, and financial and monetary coordination. GCC committees coordinate trade development in the region, industrial strategy, agricultural policy, and uniform petroleum policies and prices. Current goals include establishing an Arab common market and increasing trade ties with Asia.

The GCC is one of three newer regional organizations. In 1989, two other organizations were established. Morocco, Algeria, Mauritania, Tunisia, and Libya banded together in the Arab Maghreb Union (AMU); Egypt, Iraq, Jordan, and North Yemen created the Arab Cooperation Council (ACC). Many Arabs see their new regional groups—the GCC, ACC, and AMU—as embryonic economic communities that will foster the development of inter-Arab trade and investment. The newer organizations are more promising than the Arab League,

---

[17] Moin A. Siddiqi, "GCC: A Force to Be Reckoned With," *Middle East* (December 2003).

which consists of 21 member states and has a constitution that requires unanimous decisions.

Marketing Issues in the Middle East

Connection is a key word in conducting business in the Middle East. Those who take the time to develop relationships with key business and government figures are more likely to cut through red tape than those who do not. A predilection for bargaining is culturally ingrained, and the visiting businessperson must be prepared for some old-fashioned haggling. Establishing personal rapport, mutual trust, and respect are essentially the most important factors leading to a successful business relationship. Decisions are usually not made by correspondence or telephone. The Arab businessperson does business with the individual, not with the company. Most social customs are based on the Arab male-dominated society. Women are usually not part of the business or entertainment scene for traditional Muslim Arabs.

AFRICA

The African continent is an enormous landmass with a territory of 11.7 million square miles; the United States would fit into Africa about three and a half times. It is not really possible to treat Africa as a single economic unit. The 54 nations on the continent can be divided into three distinct areas: the Republic of South Africa, North Africa, and sub-Saharan or Black Africa, located between the Sahara in the north and the Zambezi River in the south. With 1.3 percent of the world's wealth and 11.5 percent of its population, Africa is a developing region with an average per capita income of less than $600. Many African nations are former colonies of Europe, and the EU remains the continent's most important trading partner.

The Arabs living in North Africa are differentiated politically and economically. The six northern nations are richer and more developed, and several—notably Libya, Algeria, and Egypt—benefit from large oil resources. The Middle East and North Africa are sometimes viewed as a regional entity known as "Mena"; as oil prices have soared, the IMF is encouraging Mena policy makers to invest the petrodollar windfall in infrastructure improvements as a way of sustaining economic growth.[18] Most governments in the area are working to reduce their reliance on oil revenues and their public aid levels. The economies of non-oil, "emerging Mena" countries, which include Jordan, Lebanon, Morocco, and Tunisia, have also performed well in recent years.

Economic Community of West African States (ECOWAS)

The Treaty of Lagos establishing the Economic Community of West African States (ECOWAS) was signed in May 1975 by 16 states with the object of promoting trade, cooperation, and self-reliance in West Africa. The members are Benin, Burkina Faso, Cape Verde, The Gambia, Ghana, Guinea, Guinea-Bissau, Ivory Coast, Liberia, Mali, Mauritania, Niger, Nigeria, Senegal, Sierra Leone, and Togo (see Table 3-13 and Figure 3-9). In 1980, the member countries agreed to establish a free trade area for unprocessed agricultural products and handicrafts. Tariffs on

---

[18] Victoria Robson, "Window of Opportunity," *Middle East Economic Digest* 49, no. 18 (May 6, 2005), p. 6.

OPEN ^{to} discussion

An American Trade Bill with Africa

In March 1998, U.S. President Bill Clinton toured six African nations in an effort to promote the region's political and economic accomplishments to the American people. The tour came just days after the U.S. House of Representatives passed the African Growth and Opportunities Act (AGOA). Keyed to a theme of "Trade, not Aid," the bill's sponsors intended to support nations that had made significant progress toward economic liberalization. The bill would make it easier for African nations to gain access to financing from the U.S. Export-Import Bank; it also represented a formal step toward a U.S.-Africa free trade area. One of the bill's key provisions granted textile and apparel manufacturers in Kenya and Mauritius free access to the American market on up to $3.5 billion in exports each year. As Benjamin Kipkorir, Kenya's ambassador to the United States, observed, "Every country that has industrialized, starting from England in the eighteenth century, began with textiles. We'd like to do the same thing."

Under the Agreement on Textiles and Clothing negotiated during the Uruguay Round of GATT negotiations, global textile quotas were eliminated in 2005. Nevertheless, the textile provision in the bill is proving to be controversial. The United States imports about $50 billion in textiles and apparel each year, much of it from Asia, Latin America, and Africa. Wary legislators from textile-producing U.S. states fear job losses among their constituents. The bill's opponents pointed out that, by the mid-1990s, dozens of Asian companies had established operations in Kenya to take advantage of quota-free exports to the United States. Kenya's flourishing textile export industry eventually caught the attention of U.S. officials, who imposed import restrictions. As a result, dozens of companies shut down and 10,000 Kenyans lost their jobs.

More generally, there was concern that the act would not "create a transition path from development assistance to economic self-reliance." One especially harsh critic was representative Jesse Jackson Jr., who voted against the act. In a letter to *The Wall Street Journal*, he wrote:

> In my view, this bill will not benefit the common people of Africa or America, black or white. It will benefit multinational corporations operating in the global economy, but not African-American or American workers. Protection of African workers' rights, assurance of safe working conditions, prohibition of child labor or sweatshop conditions, and protection of the African environment are markedly absent. . . .The bill will force 48 sub-Saharan African nations into a straitjacket of economic austerity and deepening poverty in order to benefit transnational financial institutions, wealthy investors, and large corporations.

Beyond the ethical concerns expressed by Representative Jackson, other questions were raised about general prospects for improved trade with Africa. Communications are unreliable, the overall infrastructure remains underdeveloped, and basic legal protections for businesses are lacking. Exporters and importers quickly learn that the cost of moving freight, including port charges and air transport rates, are much higher than in Asia. Import barriers remain high in many nations. While some observers believe that Africa is poised for an era of growth similar to that in Asia, others feel that such comparisons are not justified. Despite such concerns, AGOA was signed into law in May 2000.

Visit the Web site
www.agoa.gov

Sources: Robert Block and Michael K. Frisby, "Clinton Tour Aims to Sell New Image of Africa," The Wall Street Journal, March 20, 1998, p. A13; Tony Hawkins and Michael Holman, "Clinton Talks Up Africa's Prospects for Investment," Financial Times, March 31, 1998, p. A10; Michael M. Phillips, "Some Blacks Are Torn by Africa Trade Bill," The Wall Street Journal, March 11, 1998, pp. A2, A8; Nicholas D. Kristof, "Why Africa Can Thrive Like Asia," The New York Times, May 25, 1997, Section 4, pp. 1, 4; Phillips, "U.S. Is Seeking to Build Its Trade with Africa," The Wall Street Journal, June 2, 1996, p. A1; Phillips, "U.S. Rethinks Trade Policy with Africa," The Wall Street Journal, July 15, 1996, p. A2.

	2004 GNI (in millions)	2004 Population (in thousands)	2004 GNI Per Capita
Benin	$3,667	8,177	$450
Burkina Faso	4,436	12,822	350
Cape Verde	852	495	1,720
Cote d'Ivoire	na	na	na
The Gambia	414	1,478	280
Ghana	8,272	21,664	380
Guinea	3,811	9,202	410
Guinea-Bissau	250	1,540	160
Liberia	374	3,214	120
Mali	4,335	13,124	330
Mauritania	1,573	2,980	530
Niger	2,836	13,499	210
Nigeria	55,326	128,709	430
Senegal	7,186	11,386	630
Sierra Leone	1,113	5,336	210
Togo	1,868	5,988	310
Total/Mean GNP per capita	$96,313^a	239,614	$402*,^{a}

Table 3-13

ECOWAS Income and Population

^{a}Excludes Cote d'Ivoire.
*Indicates mean.
Source: Reprinted by permission of Warren Keegan Associates, Inc.

Table 3-14

SADC Income and Population

	2004 GNI (in millions)	2004 Population (in thousands)	2004 GNI Per Capita
Angola	$14,408	15,490	$930
Botswana	7,714	1,769	4,360
DR of Congo	6,389	55,853	110
Lesotho	1,319	1,798	730
Malawi	2,036	12,608	160
Mauritius	5,724	1,234	4,640
Mozambique	5,279	19,424	270
Namibia	4,787	2,009	2,380
Seychelles	685	84	8,190
South Africa	165,326	45,509	3,630
Swaziland	1,856	1,120	1,660
Tanzania	11,560	37,627	320
Zambia	4,625	11,479	400
Zimbabwe	8,016	12,936	620
Total/Mean GNP per capita	**$239,724**	**218,940**	**$1,095***

*Indicates mean.

Source: Reprinted by permission of Warren Keegan Associates, Inc.

industrial goods were also to be abolished; however, there were implementation delays. By January 1990, tariffs on 25 items manufactured in ECOWAS member states had been eliminated. The organization installed a computer system to process customs and trade statistics and to calculate the loss of revenue resulting from the liberalization of intercommunity trade. In June 1990, ECOWAS adopted measures that would create a single monetary zone in the region by 1994. Despite

Figure 3-9

Map of ECOWAS and SADC Countries

such achievements, economic development has occurred unevenly in the region. In recent years, the economies of Benin, Ivory Coast, and Ghana have performed impressively, while Liberia and Sierra Leone are still experiencing political conflict and economic decline.

East African Cooperation

In 1996, the presidents of Kenya, Uganda, and Tanzania established a formal mechanism to promote free trade and economic integration. Tariff issues will be resolved and prospects for a customs union are being explored. Efforts are also underway to develop regional ties in tourism and coordinate energy projects. Although Kenya is the most developed of the three nations, Francis Muthaura, the executive secretary of the secretariat of the Commission of East African Cooperation, expressed optimism that all three will benefit: "A free market is going to generate competition and already we are seeing a lot of cross-border investment. If you have free movement of capital and goods and labor, imbalances will be sorted out in the long term."[19]

Southern African Development Community (SADC)

In 1992, the Southern African Development Community (SADC) superseded the South African Development Coordination Council as a mechanism by which the region's black-ruled states could promote trade, cooperation, and economic integration. The members are Angola, Botswana, Democratic Republic of Congo (formerly Zaire), Lesotho, Malawi, Mauritius, Mozambique, Namibia, South Africa, Seychelles, Swaziland, Tanzania, Zambia, and Zimbabwe (see Figure 3-9 and Table 3-14). South Africa joined the community in 1994; it represents about 75 percent of the income in the region and 86 percent of intraregional exports. The SADC's ultimate goal is a fully developed customs union; in 2000, an 11-nation free trade area was finally established (Angola, the DRC, and Seychelles are not participants). South Africa has been in discussions with the EU about the formation of a free trade area; other SADC members are concerned that such an arrangement would provide European global companies with a base from which to dominate the continent. South Africa, Botswana, Lesotho, Namibia, and Swaziland also belong to the Southern African Customs Union (SACU). Another concern is war in the Congo, which threatens to have a severe impact on economic growth in the region.[20]

---

[19] Michael Holman, "Learning from the Past," *Financial Times Survey*, November 5, 1996, p. 1.
[20] Tony Hawkins and Michael Holman, "Trade Tensions Send Southern Africa Regional Link-Up Reeling," *Financial Times*, September 2, 1998, p. 4.

This chapter examines the environment for world trade, focusing on the institutions and regional cooperation agreements that affect trade patterns. The multilateral **World Trade Organization (WTO)**, created in 1995 as the successor to the **General Agreement on Tariffs and Trade (GATT)**, provides a forum for settling disputes among member nations and tries to set policy for world trade. The world trade environment is also characterized by **preferential trade agreements** among smaller numbers of countries on a regional and subregional basis. These agreements can be conceptualized on a continuum of increasing economic integration. **Free trade areas (FTAs)** such as the one created by the **North American Free Trade Agreement (NAFTA)** represent the lowest level of economic integration. The purpose of a **free trade agreement** is to eliminate tariffs and quotas. **Rules of**

origin are used to verify the country from which goods are shipped. A **customs union** (e.g., Mercosur) represents a further degree of integration in the form of **common external tariffs (CETs)**. In a **common market** such as Central American Integration System (SICA), restrictions on the movement of labor and capital are eased in an effort to further increase integration. An **economic union**, such as the EU, the highest level of economic integration, is achieved by unification of economic policies and institutions. Other important cooperation arrangements include the Association of Southeast Asian Nations (ASEAN), the Cooperation Council for the Arab States of the Gulf (GCC). In Africa, the two main cooperation agreements are the Economic Community of West African States (ECOWAS) and the South African Development Community (SADC).

1. Explain the role of the WTO.

2. Describe the similarities and differences between a free trade area, a customs union, a common market, and an economic union. Give an example of each.

3. Identify a regional economic organization or agreement in each of the following areas: Latin America, Asia/Pacific, Western Europe, Central Europe, the Middle East, and Africa.

4. Several key dates mentioned in the chapter are listed here. Can you identify the event associated with each? (The answers follow.)

December 31, 1992
January 1, 1994
January 1, 1995
January 1, 1999
January 1, 2002
May 1, 2004
January 1, 2007

Answers: December 31, 1992—Single Market Act goes into effect; January 1, 1994—NAFTA becomes effective; January 1, 1995—GATT is renamed the WTO; January 1, 1999—introduction of the euro as a unit of account; January 1, 2002—euro currency goes into circulation; May 1, 2004—EU enlargement to 25 members; January 1, 2007—EU enlargement to 27 members

1. As this edition went to press, efforts were underway to restart the Doha round of trade talks. Over the course of the semester, monitor various media reports on the negotiations. What statements have been issued by the office of the United States Trade Representative. Have any key issues—for example, agricultural subsidies—been resolved?

2. More than one decade after NAFTA entered into force, there is lingering controversy over whether it has been a success or a failure. Using a variety of sources, familiarize yourself with the arguments on each side. What specific issues figure into the controversy? Can they be reduced to differences between "protectionists" and "free traders?"

3. The Middle East is experiencing a surge in economic development. What are some of the companies driving this trend in Egypt? In Israel? In Oman?

4. Tata Group is India's largest industrial group; its units include Tata Steel, Tata Motors, and Tata Tea. Wipro Limited is a leading provider of outsourcing services. A third Indian company, Infosys Technologies Limited, is a technology consulting firm. All three firms are expanding their global reach. Research one or more of the companies and familiarize yourself with the factors that have led to their success.

Updated trade statistics are available on the Internet. For example, ASEAN's Web site is **www.aseansec.org.**

For more information on the FTAA, visit:

www.ftaa-alca.org

The American Enterprise Institute, the Institute of International Economics, the Council on Hemispheric Affairs, the Cato Institute, and a number of other think tanks offer analysis and position papers on the FTAA and other trade-related topics.

www.corpwatch.org

www.iie.org

www.aei.org

www.coha.org

www.cato.org

The Secretariat of CARICOM maintains a Web site offering information, publications, and membership information.

www.caricom.org

Case 3-1

The Free Trade Area of the Americas

In the fall of 2005, leaders from 34 North, Central, and South American nations convened for the seventh Summit of the Americas in Mar Del Plata, Argentina, to discuss plans for a proposed Free Trade Area of the Americas (FTAA). If and when the trade talks come to fruition, the FTAA will stretch from Alaska to Tierra del Fuego, Argentina; the area will account for $11 trillion in annual economic output (approximately one-third of the world total) and encompass 800 million people. However, the meeting in Argentina did not turn out the way U.S. President George W. Bush had hoped. Hugo Chávez, the leftist president of Venezuela, condemned the U.S. proposals and called for closer trade ties among Latin American nations. His sentiments were seconded by Brazil and three other South American nations that form the Mercosur customs union. Opinion polls in Latin America indicate growing opposition to closer trade ties with the United States. The prospect of improved access to one of the world's most attractive consumer market holds considerable allure for some Latin American nations, particularly Costa Rica and Colombia. However, in other parts of the region, there is a widespread disillusionment and the perception that a trade deal would be most beneficial to the United States.

In Spanish and Portuguese, FTAA is abbreviated ALCA; the full Spanish translation is "Area de Libre Comercio de las Américas." (The Portuguese translation is "Area de Livre Comércio das Américas.") Here, protesters in Brazil take to the streets to voice concerns that they will not benefit from closer trade ties with the United States.

Former U.S. President Bill Clinton first formally proposed the idea for a hemispheric free trade area in 1994 during a summit of heads of state in Miami. Meeting in Brazil in May 1997, trade ministers from the 34 participating countries agreed to create "preparatory committees" in anticipation of formal talks that would begin in 1998. The Clinton administration was keen to open the region's fast-growing, big emerging markets to U.S. companies. In particular, the president wanted talks to focus immediately on tariffs and "early harvest" agreements on individual industry sectors such as information technology. The FTAA was formally launched in April 1998 during the second Summit of the Americas in Santiago, Chile.

After President George W. Bush took office, he viewed FTAA as one aspect of a multilevel approach to trade issues. Bush also hoped to pursue bilateral agreements between the United States and individual nations as well as global negotiations within the framework of the WTO. Prospects for the latter had been dimmed somewhat by the disastrous global trade talks in Seattle in the fall of 1999; protesters succeeded in disrupting the event.

The Canadian government went to unprecedented lengths to ensure security during the 2001 Summit of the Americas meeting in Quebec City, spending about $100 million on the effort. The meeting venue was enclosed by a 2.3 mile concrete and chain-link fence that demonstrators called the "Wall of Shame." As thousands of labor and environmental activists gathered behind barricades, Mexican president Vicente Fox, Brazilian president Henrique Cardoso, and their colleagues hoped for a clear signal from President George W. Bush that the United States was serious about free trade. One positive sign: the U.S. Congress granted the president trade promotion authority (TPA). TPA enables the president to negotiate trade agreements, which Congress then has to vote on without making any changes or amendments.

Opposition to the FTAA has been strongest in Brazil, despite the fact that its textile industry stands to benefit greatly if U.S. import quotas are lifted. By contrast, Brazil's paper and chemical industries could be severely hurt by strong American competitors. Executives in these and other industries have pleaded with the Brazilian government for more time to improve productivity and marketing. In some circles, a preference has been expressed for a trade pact with the EU.

The 2003 summit ended with the United States and Brazil agreeing to a draft declaration. Celso Amorim, Brazil's foreign minister, noted, "Things are moving in the right direction." Representatives of American companies disagreed. The declaration reduced the scope of the trade deal so that minimum common rights and obligations would be agreed on while giving individual nations leeway about whether or not to make additional commitments. A representative for the National Association of Manufacturers said that a "low quality" agreement was not worth having.

There has been considerable grassroots opposition to the FTAA. For a sampling, visit:

www.globalexchange.org
wtoaction.org/ftaa

Discussion Questions

1. A bipartisan coalition of U.S. policymakers favors the inclusion of labor and other non-trade-related requirements in trade treaties such as the FTAA. Labor law enforcement was included in the texts of the free trade agreements that the United States signed with Jordan and Morocco. However, Brazilian President Luiz Icácio Lula da Silva and other Latin American leaders are opposed to including labor standards in the FTAA. Whose stance do you support? Why?

2. Who would benefit the most from the FTAA? Established global corporations? Companies in emerging markets? Residents of emerging markets?

3. Opponents argue that passage of the FTAA will accelerate the loss of sovereign control over policy instruments that are critical for economic development in Latin America. Discuss.

Sources: Matt Moffett and John D. McKinnon, "Failed Summit Casts Shadow on Global Trade Talks," *The Wall Street Journal,* November 7, 2005, pp. A3, A17; David Luhnow, "Latin America Looks Hard at U.S.," *The Wall Street Journal,* November 28, 2003, p. A15; Guy de Jonquières, "U.S. Business Lobby Groups Unhappy at 'Low-Quality' FTAA Compromise," *Financial Times,* November 20, 2003, p. 6; "All in the Familia," *Economist,* April 21, 2001, pp. 19–21; "Breaking Barriers in the Americas," *Economist,* April 21, 2001, p. 14; Jonathan Karp, "Brazil to Be Vocal in Americas Trade Talks," *The Wall Street Journal,* April 19, 2001, p. A13; Helene Cooper, "New Trade Representative Faces an Old Obstacle: Fast-Track Fight," *The Wall Street Journal,* April 6, 2001, p. A16; Kenneth Maxwell, "Brazil's Free Traders Are in Dire Need of a U.S. Boost," *The Wall Street Journal,* April 6, 2001, p. A15.

Social and Cultural Environments

In 2005, while writing a children's book on the life of the prophet Mohammed, Danish author Kåre Bluitgen searched unsuccessfully for an illustrator. The problem: To many of the world's Muslims, it is blasphemy to depict images of the prophet. Denmark's conservative *Jyllands-Posten* newspaper picked up the story; concerned that this was a case of self-censorship, the paper's cultural editor challenged dozens of well-known illustrators to "draw Mohammed the way that they see him." In September, *Jyllands-Posten* printed submissions from 12 illustrators in conjunction with articles on freedom of speech; one of the images depicted Mohammed with a bomb in his turban. A few months later, the cartoons were reprinted in newspapers in France, Germany, Switzerland, and elsewhere. Reaction was swift: Protests erupted in Indonesia and other countries with large Muslim populations. The Danish and Norwegian missions in Damascus were set on fire. Some Arab governments supported boycotts of Danish goods and withdrew their ambassadors from Copenhagen. Meanwhile, the Danish government called *its* ambassadors back to Copenhagen, and Danish export marketers, such as Arla Foods and the LEGO Group, sought to deal with a growing consumer backlash in the Middle East. In the words of one employee at Saudi Arabia's airport, "Anything to do with Denmark is now history in the [Saudi] kingdom. Shops, businesses, imports. It's over." As Finn Hansen, head of international operations at Arla, noted, "This can happen to anyone, anywhere, at anytime if you don't understand other people's cultures."

The controversy that began in Denmark is an example of the way that differences in the social and cultural environments—in this case, religious differences—impact marketing opportunities and dynamics around the globe. This chapter focuses on the social and cultural forces that shape and affect individual, group, and corporate behavior in the marketplace. We start with a general discussion of the basic aspects of culture and society and the emergence of a twenty-first century global consumer culture. Next, several useful conceptual frameworks for understanding culture are presented. These include Hall's high- and low-context culture concept, Maslow's hierarchy, Hofstede's cultural typology, the self-reference criterion, and diffusion theory. The chapter includes specific examples of the impact of culture and society on the marketing of both consumer and industrial products.

SOCIETY, CULTURE, AND GLOBAL CONSUMER CULTURE

Both differences and similarities characterize the world's cultures, meaning that the task of the global marketer is twofold. First, marketers must study and understand the country cultures in which they will be doing business. Second, they must incorporate this understanding into the marketing planning process. In some instances, strategies and marketing programs will have to be adapted; however, marketers should also take advantage of shared cultural characteristics and avoid unneeded and costly adaptations of the marketing mix. Deep cultural understanding can actually be a source of competitive advantage for global companies. The aggressive expansion of Spain's Telefónica in Latin America provides a case in point. As Juan Villalonga, former chairman

In 2006, protesters across the Muslim world demonstrated against the publication of cartoon images of Mohammed in a Danish newspaper. Many supermarkets in Cairo, the largest city in the Arab world, removed Danish products from their shelves.

of Telefónica, noted, "It is not just speaking a common language. It is sharing a culture and understanding friendships in the same way."[1]

Any systematic study of a new geographic market requires a combination of tough-mindedness and generosity. While marketers should be secure in their own convictions and traditions, generosity is required to appreciate the integrity and value of other ways of life and points of view. People must, in other words, overcome the prejudices that are a natural result of the human tendency toward ethnocentricity. Although "culture shock" is a normal human reaction to the new and unknown, successful global marketers strive to comprehend human experience from the local point of view. One reason cultural factors challenge global marketers is that many of them are hidden from view. Because culture is a learned behavior passed on from generation to generation, it can be difficult for the inexperienced or untrained outsider to fathom. As they endeavor to understand cultural factors, outsiders gradually become insiders and develop cultural empathy. There are many different paths to the same goals in life. The global marketer understands this and rejoices in life's rich diversity.

Anthropologists and sociologists have offered scores of different definitions of culture. As a starting point, **culture** can be defined as "ways of living, built up by a group of human beings, that are transmitted from one generation to another." A culture acts out its ways of living in the context of *social institutions*, including family, educational, religious, governmental, and business institutions. Those institutions, in turn, function to reinforce cultural norms. Culture includes both conscious and unconscious values, ideas, attitudes, and symbols that shape human behavior *and that are transmitted from one generation to the next*. Organizational anthropologist Geert Hofstede defines *culture* as "the collective programming of the mind that distinguishes the members of one category of people from those of another."[2] A particular "category of people" may constitute a nation, an ethnic group, a gender group, an organization, a family, or some other unit.

Some anthropologists and sociologists divide cultural elements into two broad categories: material culture and nonmaterial culture. The former is sometimes referred to as the *physical component* or *physical culture* and includes physical objects and artifacts created by humans such as clothing and tools.

[1] Tom Burns, "Spanish Telecoms Visionary Beholds a Brave New World," *Financial Times*, May 2, 1998, p. 24.
[2] Geert Hofstede and Michael Harris Bond, "The Confucius Connection: From Cultural Roots to Economic Growth," *Organizational Dynamics* (Spring 1988), p. 5.

Nonmaterial culture (also known as *subjective* or *abstract culture*) includes intangibles such as religion, perceptions, attitudes, beliefs, and values. There is general agreement that the material and nonmaterial elements of culture are interrelated and interactive. Cultural anthropologist George P. Murdock studied material and nonmaterial culture and identified dozens of "cultural universals," including athletic sports, body adornment, cooking, courtship, dancing, decorative art, education, ethics, etiquette, family feasting, food taboos, language, marriage, mealtime, medicine, mourning, music, property rights, religious rituals, residence rules, status differentiation, and trade.[3]

It is against this background of traditional definitions that global marketers should understand a worldwide sociocultural phenomenon of the early twenty-first century.[4] It has been argued that consumption has become the hallmark of postmodern society. As cultural information and imagery flow freely across borders via satellite TV, the Internet, and similar communication channels, new global consumer cultures are emerging. Persons who identify with these cultures share meaningful sets of consumption-related symbols. Some of these cultures are associated with specific product categories; marketers speak of "fast-food culture," "credit card culture," "pub culture," "coffee culture," and so on. This cosmopolitan culture, which is comprised of various segments, owes its existence in large part to a wired world in which there is increasing interconnectedness of various local cultures. It can be exploited by **global consumer culture positioning (GCCP)**, a marketing tool that will be explained in more detail in Chapter 7. In particular, marketers can use advertising to communicate the notion that people everywhere consume a particular brand or to appeal to human universals.

Attitudes, Beliefs, and Values

If we accept Hofstede's notion of culture as "the collective programming of the mind," then it makes sense to learn about culture by studying the attitudes, beliefs, and values shared by a specific group of people. An **attitude** is a learned tendency to respond in a consistent way to a given object or entity. Attitudes are clusters of interrelated beliefs. A **belief** is an organized pattern of knowledge that an individual holds to be true about the world. Attitudes and beliefs, in turn, are closely related to values. A **value** can be defined as an enduring belief or feeling that a specific mode of conduct is personally or socially preferable to another mode of conduct.[5] In the view of Hofstede and others, values represent the deepest level of a culture and are present in the majority of the members of a particular culture.

Some specific examples will allow us to illustrate these definitions by comparing and contrasting attitudes, beliefs, and values. The Japanese, for example, strive to achieve cooperation, consensus, self-denial, and harmony. Because these all represent feelings about modes of conduct, they are *values*. Japan's monocultural society reflects the *belief* among the Japanese that they are unique in the world. Many Japanese, especially young people, also believe that the West is the source of important fashion trends. As a result, many Japanese share a favorable *attitude* toward American brands. Within any large, dominant cultural group, there are likely to be **subcultures**; that is, smaller groups of people with their own shared subset of attitudes, beliefs, and values. Values, attitudes, and beliefs can also be surveyed at the level of any "category of people" that is embedded within a broad culture. For example, if you are a vegetarian, then eating meat represents a mode of conduct that you and others who share your views avoid. Subcultures often represent attractive niche marketing opportunities.

---

[3] George P. Murdock, "The Common Denominator of Culture," in *The Science of Man in the World Crisis*, Ralph Linton, ed. (New York: Columbia University Press, 1945), p. 145.

[4] The following discussion is adapted from Dana L. Alden, Jan-Benedict Steenkamp, and Rajeev Batra, "Brand Positioning through Advertising in Asia, North America, and Europe: The Role of Global Consumer Culture," *Journal of Marketing* 63, no. 1 (January 1999), pp. 75–87.

[5] Milton Rokeach, *Beliefs, Attitudes, and Values* (San Francisco: Jossey-Bass, 1968), p. 160.

Religion

Religion is one important source of a society's beliefs, attitudes, and values. The world's major religions include Buddhism, Hinduism, Islam, Judaism, and Christianity; the latter is comprised of Roman Catholicism and numerous Protestant denominations. Examples abound of religious tenets, practices, holidays, and history directly impacting the way people of different faiths react to global marketing activities. For example, Hindus do not eat beef, which means that McDonald's does not serve hamburgers in India (see Case 1-1). Issues related to Jewish history and the Holocaust were raised in the wake of the 1998 merger of Germany's Daimler-Benz and the American Chrysler Corporation. For example, several Jewish organizations in the United States objected to DaimlerChrysler's 2002 corporate advertising campaign that used references to scientists Wernher Von Braun and Albert Einstein to promote the quality of Chrysler's cars. For one thing, critics noted, Von Braun was the leader of the Nazi rocket program. A second issue was the fact that Einstein was actually a Swiss citizen who fled Germany in 1933 and settled in the United States.[6]

In the aftermath of the September 2001 terror attacks in New York and Washington, D.C., and the subsequent American military actions in the Middle East, some Muslims have tapped into anti-American sentiment by urging a boycott of American brands. One entrepreneur, Tunisian-born Tawfik Mathlouthi, launched a soft drink brand, Mecca-Cola, as an alternative to Coca-Cola for Muslims living in the United Kingdom and France. The brand's name is both an intentional reference to the holy city of Islam as well as an ironic swipe at Coca-Cola, which Mathlouthi calls "the Mecca of capitalism." London's *Sunday Times* called Mecca-Cola "the drink now seen as politically preferable to Pepsi or Coke."[7] In 2003, Qibla Cola (the name comes from an Arabic word for "direction") was launched in the United Kingdom. Founder Zahida Parveen hopes to reach a broader market than Mecca-Cola by positioning the brand "for any consumer with a conscience, irrespective of ethnicity or religion."[8]

Religious issues have also been at the heart of a dispute about whether references to God and Christianity should be included in a new European constitution that will be adopted now that the EU has expanded its membership from 15 to 27 countries. On one side of the dispute are Europe's Catholic countries, including Ireland, Spain, Italy, and Poland. As Italy's deputy prime minister said, "The Italian government believes that [Europe's] common religious heritage should be explicitly referred to with the values of Judeo-Christian tradition." By contrast, the official position in France and Belgium is one of church-state separation. According to this view, religion has no place in the founding documents of the enlarged EU. In addition, Muslims constitute a politically active minority in France and other countries; Turkey is predominately Muslim. Representatives of Europe's Muslim population are resisting any reference to Christianity in the new constitution.[9]

---

[6] Joseph B. White, "Jewish Groups Say DaimlerChrysler Ads 'Whitewash' History," *The Wall Street Journal*, July 11, 2002, p. B1. See also Arch G. Woodside and Jean-Charles Chebat, "Updating Heider's Balance Theory in Consumer Behavior: A Jewish Couple Buys a German Car and Additional Buying-Consuming Transformation Stories," *Psychology & Marketing* 18, no. 5 (May 2001), pp. 475–495.

[7] Bill Britt, "Upstart Cola Taps Anti-War Vibe," *Advertising Age* (February 24, 2003), p. 1. See also Digby Lidstone, "Pop Idols," *Middle East Economic Digest* (August 22, 2003), p. 4.

[8] Meg Carter, "New Colas Wage Battle for Hearts and Minds," *The Financial Times*, January 8, 2004, p. 9.

[9] Richard Bernstein, "Continent Wrings Its Hands over Proclaiming Its Faith, "*The New York Times*, November 12, 2003, p. A4. See also Brandon Mitchener, "Birth of a Nation? As Europe Unites, Religion, Defense Still Stand in Way," *The Wall Street Journal*, July 11, 2003, pp. A1, A6.

Some global companies have successfully capitalized on the love-hate relationship between Muslims and the United States. In the Islamic world, Ramadan is a month of fasting that begins at the end of October. In Indonesia, home to the world's largest Muslim population, KFC uses Ramadan-themed outdoor advertising to encourage Indonesians to come to the restaurants at buka puasa, the end of each day's fast. Business at KFC Indonesia's 200 units is up as much as 20 percent during Ramadan.

Aesthetics

Within every culture, there is an overall sense of what is beautiful and what is not beautiful, what represents good taste as opposed to tastelessness or even obscenity, and so on. Such considerations are matters of **aesthetics**. Global marketers must understand the importance of *visual aesthetics* embodied in the color or shape of a product, label, or package. Likewise, different parts of the world perceive *aesthetic styles*—various degrees of complexity, for example—differently. Aesthetic elements that are attractive, appealing, and in good taste in one country may be perceived differently in another. In some cases, a standardized color can be used in all countries; examples include the distinctive yellow color on Caterpillar's earth-moving equipment and its licensed outdoor gear and the red chevron on a pack of Marlboro cigarettes. A number of companies seem to be experiencing a

Qibla Cola was launched in 2003; company executives hope to position Qibla as an alternative to mainstream American brands. As one executive noted, "We want to show that you can develop a brand that is global, ethical, quality, and commercially viable. We are not trying to do so by being anti-American but by being anti-injustice." By 2005, Qibla Cola was available in Canada, Libya, Malaysia, the Netherlands, Norway, Pakistan, and the United Kingdom.

case of the "blues," as evidenced by names such as Bluetooth, Blue Moon, and JetBlue Airways; likewise, Skyy vodka is packaged in a distinctive blue bottle.[10] However, because color perceptions can vary among cultures, adaptation to local preferences may be required. Such perceptions should be taken into account when making decisions about product packaging and other brand-related communications. In highly competitive markets, inappropriate or unattractive product packaging may put a company or brand at a disadvantage. New color schemes may also be mandated by a changing competitive environment. For example, after Wal-Mart entered the German market in the 1990s, local retailer Metro AG added blue, white, and yellow to the logo of its Real hypermarket stores.

There is nothing inherently "good" or "bad" about any color of the spectrum; all associations and perceptions regarding color arise from culture. Red is a popular color in most parts of the world; besides being the color of blood, in many countries red also is tied to centuries-old traditions of viticulture and winemaking. One recent study of perceptions in eight countries found that red is associated with "active," "hot," and "vibrant"; in most countries studied, it also conveys meanings such as "emotional" and "sharp."[11] As such, red has positive connotations in many societies. However, red is poorly received in some African countries. Blue, because of its associations with sky and water, has an elemental connotation with undertones of dependability, constancy, and eternity. White connotes purity and cleanliness in the West, but it is associated with death in parts of Asia. In the Middle East, purple is associated with death. Another research team concluded that gray connotes inexpensive in China and Japan, while it is associated with high quality and expensive in the United States. The researchers also found that the Chinese associated brown with soft drink labels and associated the color with good tasting; South Korean and Japanese consumers associated yellow with soft drinks and good tasting. For Americans, the color red has those associations.[12]

It has been said that upscale Tiffany & Company is in the "blue box business" rather than the jewelry business. When GM was vying for the right to build a sedan in China, company executives gave Chinese officials gifts from Tiffany's in the jeweler's signature blue box. However, the Americans replaced Tiffany's white ribbons with red ones because red is considered a lucky color in China and white has negative connotations. GM ultimately won government approval of its proposal.

10 Susan Carey, "More U.S. Companies Are Blue, and It's Not Just the Stock Market," *The Wall Street Journal*, August 30, 2001, pp. A1, A2.
11 Thomas J. Madden, Kelly Hewett, and Martin S. Roth, "Managing Images in Different Cultures: A Cross-National Study of Color Meanings and Preferences," *Journal of International Marketing* 8, no. 4 (2000), p. 98.
12 Laurence E. Jacobs, Charles Keown, Reginald Worthley, and Kyung-I Ghymn, "Cross-Cultural Colour Comparisons: Global Marketers Beware!" *International Marketing Review* 8, no. 3 (1991), pp. 21–30.

Music is an aesthetic component of all cultures, accepted as a form of artistic expression and source of entertainment. In one sense, music represents a "transculture" that is not identified with any particular nation. For example, rhythm, or movement through time, is a universal aspect of music. However, music is also characterized by considerable stylistic variation with regional or country specific associations. For example, bossa nova rhythms are associated with Argentina, samba with Brazil, salsa with Cuba, reggae with Jamaica, merengue with the Dominican Republic, and blues, driving rock rhythms, hip hop, and rap with the United States. Sociologists have noted that national identity derives in part from a country's indigenous or popular music; a unique music style can "represent the uniqueness of the cultural entity and of the community."[13]

Music provides an interesting example of the "think global, act local" theme of this book. Musicians in different countries draw from, absorb, adapt, and synthesize transcultural music influences as well as country-specific ones, as they create hybrid styles such as Polish reggae or Italian hip hop. Motti Regev describes this paradox as follows:

> Producers of and listeners to these types of music feel, at one and the same time, participants in a specific contemporary, global-universal form of expression *and* innovators of local, national, ethnic, and other identities. A cultural form associated with American culture and with the powerful commercial interests of the international music industry is being used in order to construct a sense of local difference and authenticity.[14]

global MARKETING Q&A

Wall Street Journal: "Are there instances where marketing in developing markets inspired marketing in developed ones?"

James Stengel, Global Marketing Officer, Procter & Gamble: "I would point to two that are just remarkable. One is a campaign from Rejoice, our shampoo in the Philippines. Filipinos are really into dance and music: They're tremendous entertainers. We ended up writing a song for a very popular group about a dance you would do for hair that's wonderful. It might seem corny, but it swept the country. It became the top song on radio stations, the top download on ringtones—when you talk about cell phone marketing, that's an authentic way of doing it. They associated a dance with it, a little bit like the Macarena. Our business, our share, our brand equity went up, and it made us think about the role of music in other brands and in other cultures.

A South African campaign for the Always feminine-hygiene brand benefited from that learning. It was a similar target consumer . . . and we wanted to associate with a positive value for girls in that market. It's still a very difficult market, just 12 years after apartheid, and it's still a struggle for a lot of people in that country. We held dance contests in many cities throughout the country, and branded it the Always Keep Movin' program. "Keep movin'" in South Africa has very positive overtones; the phrase means 'stay in school, don't get pregnant.' We held these programs in different cities and were overwhelmed by the response. It was associated with the brand in an honest way, and the brand became more relevant, more interesting, more hip, and the [volume] share went way up. Again it was music, but done in a way that's right for South Africa."

Source: The Wall Street Journal (Eastern Edition) by Ellen Byron. Copyright 2006 by Dow Jones & Company, Inc. Reproduced with permission of Dow Jones & Company, Inc. in the format Textbook via Copyright Clearance Center.

---

[13] Martin Stokes, *Ethnicity, Identity, and Music: The Musical Construction of Place* (Oxford: Berg, 1994).
[14] Motti Regev, "Rock Aesthetics and Musics of the World," *Theory, Culture & Society* 14, no. 3 (August 1997), pp. 125–142.

The March 2006 inaugural issue of Rolling Stone's *Chinese* edition featured local rocker Cui Jian on the cover. Mr. Cui was one of the first Chinese musicians to incorporate Western rock stylings into his music; he is also famous for a song titled "Nothing to My Name" that was an anthem to Chinese students participating in the 1989 Tiananmen Square democracy protests.

However, Chinese authorities had other concerns about the first issue; for one thing, they objected to the large Rolling Stone *masthead* on the magazine's cover. Regulators also disapproved of the U.S. magazine's choice of Audiovisual World as its local partner.

A few months later, Rolling Stone reappeared with a new look and a new publishing partner: for the October 2006 issue, the Rolling Stone *masthead* was scaled down and the magazine itself was incorporated into a separate publication titled Pop Times.

Because music plays an important role in advertising, marketers must understand what style is appropriate in a given national market. Although background music can be used effectively in broadcast commercials, the type of music appropriate for a commercial in one part of the world may not be acceptable or effective in another part.

Dietary Preferences

Cultural influences are also quite apparent in food preparation and consumption patterns and habits. Need proof? Consider the following:

- Domino's Pizza, the world's largest pizza-delivery company, pulled out of Italy because Italians perceived its product to be "too American." In particular, the tomato sauce was too bold and the toppings were too heavy.
- To successfully launch the Subway chain in India, it was necessary to educate consumers about the benefits of the company's sandwiches. Why? Because Indians do not normally consume bread.[15]

These examples underscore the fact that a solid understanding of food-related cultural preferences is important for any company that markets food or beverage products globally. Titoo Ahluwalia, chairman of a market research firm in Bombay, points out that local companies can also leverage superior cultural understanding to compete effectively with large foreign firms. He says, "Indian companies have an advantage when they are drawing from tradition. When it comes to food, drink, and medicine, you have to be culturally sensitive."[16] Companies that lack such sensitivity are bound to make marketing mistakes. When Subway expanded into India, the company chose two U.S.-educated Indian brothers to help open stores and supervise operations.

---

[15] Richard Gibson, "Foreign Flavors," *The Wall Street Journal*, September 25, 2006, p. R8.
[16] Fara Warner, "Savvy Indian Marketers Hold Their Ground," *The Wall Street Journal Asia*, December 1, 1997, p. 8.

While some food preferences remain deeply embedded in culture, there is plenty of evidence that global dietary preferences are converging. For example, "fast food" is gaining increased acceptance around the world. There are several explanations. Heads of families in many countries are pressed for time and are disinclined to prepare home-cooked meals. Also, young people are experimenting with different foods, and the global tourism boom has exposed travelers to pizza, pasta, and other ethnic foods. Shorter lunch hours and tighter budgets are forcing workers to find a place to grab a quick, cheap bite before returning to work.[17] As cultural differences become less relevant, such convenience products will be purchased in any country when consumer disposable income is high enough.

As we have seen, such processes can provoke a nationalist backlash. To counteract the exposure of its young citizens to *le Big Mac* and other American-style fast foods, the French National Council of Culinary Arts designed a course on French cuisine and "good taste" for elementary school students. The director of the council, Alexandre Lazareff, recently published *The French Culinary Exception*. Lazareff warns that France's vaunted *haute cuisine* is under attack by the globalization of taste. More generally, Lazareff is speaking out against perceived challenges to France's culinary identity and way of life. His concerns are real enough; while McDonald's continues to open new restaurants in France (there are currently about 1,000), the number of traditional bistros has declined from 55,000 to 25,000 over the past decade.[18] Meanwhile, the French have coined a new buzzword, *le fooding*, to express the notion that the nation's passion for food goes beyond mere gastronomy:

> To eat with feeling in France is to eat with your head and your spirit, with your nose, your eyes, and your ears, not simply your palate. *Le fooding* seeks to give witness to the modernity and new reality of drinking and eating in the 21st century . . . Everything is *fooding* so long as audacity, sense, and the senses mix.[19]

Language and Communication

The diversity of cultures around the world is also reflected in language. A person can learn a great deal about another culture without leaving home by studying its language and literature; such study is the next best thing to actually living in another country. Linguists have divided the study of *spoken* or *verbal* language into four main areas: syntax (rules of sentence formation), semantics (system of meaning), phonology (system of sound patterns), and morphology (word formation). *Unspoken* or *nonverbal* communication includes gestures, touching, and other forms of body language that supplement spoken communication. (Nonverbal communication is sometimes called the silent language.) Both the spoken and unspoken aspects of language are included in the broader linguistic field of *semiotics*, which is the study of signs and their meanings.

In global marketing, language is a crucial tool for communicating with customers, channel intermediaries, and others. The marketing literature is full of anecdotal references to costly blunders caused by incorrect or inept translations of product names and advertising copy. American English and British English

[17] John Willman, "'Fast Food' Spreads as Lifestyles Change," *Financial Times*, March 27, 1998, p. 7.
[18] Marlow Hood, "The Holy Terror," *Financial Times Weekend*, July 4–5, 1998, p. I.
[19] Jacqueline Friedrich, "All the Rage in Paris? Le Fooding," *The Wall Street Journal*, February 9, 2001, p. W11.

書 傘 鐘

book   umbrella   clock

provide examples of how linguistic differences can characterize the "same" language in different countries.

For example, when British retail-development firm BAA McArthurGlen set up a U.S.-style factory outlet mall in Austria, local officials wanted to know, "Where's the factory?" To win approval for the project, McArthurGlen was forced to call its development a "designer outlet center."[20] Anheuser-Busch and Miller Brewing both experienced market failures in the United Kingdom; the problem was the phrase "light beer," which was understood as meaning reduced alcohol levels rather than fewer calories. Now Miller Lite is marketed in Europe as "Miller Pilsner."[21]

Before Hearst Corporation launched *Good Housekeeping* magazine in Japan, managers experimented with Japanese translations. The closest word in Japanese, *kaji*, means "domestic duties." However, that word can be interpreted as tasks performed by servants. In the end, the American title was retained, with the word *Good* in much larger type on the front cover than the word *Housekeeping*. Inside the magazine, some of the editorial content has also been adapted to appeal to Japanese women; for example, the famous Seal of Approval was eliminated because the concept confused readers. Editor-in-chief Ellen

blitz
突袭:猛撞
(四分卫)一种
防守技术

sack `擒杀' (term) or
成功地擒抱四
分卫 sack (translation)

onside kick
赌博踢

play action
假跑真传

gambling kickoff
短开球

Hail Mary pass
长传到达阵区

punt
凌空踢球

touchdown
持球触地

20 Ernest Beck, "American-Style Outlet Malls in Europe Make Headway Despite Local Resistance," *The Wall Street Journal,* September 17, 1998, p. A17.
21 Dan Bilefsky and Christopher Lawton, "In Europe, Marketing Beer as 'American' May Not Be a Plus," *The Wall Street Journal* (July 21, 2004), p. B1.

Over the past three decades, advertising for Absolut vodka has achieved near-mythic status in the marketing world. Print campaigns often feature the distinctive high-shouldered bottle and a brief headline that incorporates the word "Absolut" in a clever way that ties in with a particular magazine, cultural trend, or geographic market. Sweden's V&S Vin & Spirit, the brand's owner, is moving swiftly to capitalize on opportunities in China. In 2005, in conjunction with Chinese New Year, the campaign focused on the Chinese character "fu," which can be translated as "blessing" or "fortune." When the character is turned upside down, the meaning changes to "fortune."

Levine said, "We have no interest in trying to export our product exactly as it is. That would be cultural suicide."[22] In China, Dell had to find a meaningful interpretation of "direct sales," the phrase that describes the company's powerful business model. A literal translation results in *zhi xiao*, which is the Chinese term for illegal pyramid marketing schemes. To counteract the negative connotation, Dell's sales representatives began using the phrase *zhi xiao ding gou*, which translates as "direct orders."[23]

Phonology can also come into play; Colgate discovered that, in Spanish, *colgate* is a command that means "go hang yourself." Whirlpool spent considerable sums of money on brand advertising in Europe only to discover that consumers in Italy, France, and Germany had trouble pronouncing the company's name.[24] Conversely, Renzo Rosso deliberately chose "Diesel" for a new jeans brand because, as he once noted, "It's one of the few words pronounced the same in every language." Rosso has built Diesel into a successful global youth brand and one of Italy's most successful fashion stories; sales revenues in 2004 totaled $1.2 billion.[25]

[22] Yumiko Ono, "Will Good Housekeeping Translate into Japanese?" *The Wall Street Journal* (December 30, 1997), p. B1.
[23] Evan Ramstad and Gary McWilliams, "Computer Savvy: For Dell, Success in China Tells Tale of Maturing Market," *The Wall Street Journal* (July 5, 2005), pp. A1, A8.
[24] Greg Steinmetz and Carl Quintanilla, "Tough Target: Whirlpool Expected Easy Going in Europe, and It Got a Big Shock," *The Wall Street Journal* (April 10, 1998), pp. A1, A6.
[25] Alice Rawsthorn, "A Hipster on Jean Therapy," *Financial Times* (August 20, 1998), p. 8.

Technology is providing interesting new opportunities for exploiting linguistics in the name of marketing. For example, young people throughout the world are using mobile phones to send text messages; it turns out that certain number combinations have meaning in particular languages. For example, in Korean, the phonetic pronunciation of the numerical sequence 8282, "Pal Yi Pal Yi," means "hurry up," and 7179 ("Chil Han Chil Gu") sounds like "close friend." Also, as many digital-savvy young people in South Korea can attest,, 4 5683 968 can be interpreted as "I love you."[26] Korean marketers are using these and other numerical sequences in their advertising. After eBay boosted its presence in China by acquiring the EachNet auction site in 2003, it used rebates and other promotions to attract users. For example, EachNet offered credits of 68 yuan on purchases of 168 yuan or more. The figures were chosen for their linguistic properties: In Chinese, the word *six* is a homophone (has the same pronunciation) for the word *safe*, and *eight* is pronounced the same as *prosperity*.[27]

One impact of globalization on culture is the diffusion of the English language around the globe. Today there are more people who speak English as a foreign language than there are people whose native language is English. Nearly 85 percent of the teenagers in the EU are studying English. Despite the fact that Sony is headquartered in Japan, the company makes it clear to job applicants in any part of the world that it does not consider English to be a "foreign language." The same is true for Finland's Nokia. Matsushita recently introduced a policy that requires all managers to pass an English language-competency test before being considered for promotion. Top management at Matsushita concluded that a staid corporate culture that was exclusively Japanese was eroding the company's competitiveness in the global market. The

Renzo Rosso is the founder and owner of Only The Brave, a holding company whose fashion divisions include Diesel, Martin Margiela, and Dsquared. When Rosso first launched his Diesel brand jeans, they featured "vintage" denim with cutting-edge fabrics and detailing. The price: $100 per pair. Today, to keep its finger on the cultural pulse—and protect its image as a hip brand— Diesel sponsors the annual U-Music Awards, a competition for unsigned rock bands from around the world. Winning bands in various categories can qualify for thousands of dollars in cash prizes as well as free legal and public relations services (www.diesel-u-music.com).

---

[26] The authors are indebted to Professor Yong Tae Bang, Department of International Trade, College of Business Administration, Paichai University, South Korea, for his comments on this section. See also Meeyoung Song, "How to Sell in Korea? Marketers Count the Ways," *The Wall Street Journal*, August 24, 2001, p. A6.

[27] Mylene Mangalindan, "Hot Bidding: In a Challenging Market, Ebay Confronts a Big New Rival," *The Wall Street Journal*, August 12, 2005, p. A1.

English-language requirement is a potent symbol that a Japanese company is globalizing.[28]

The challenges presented by nonverbal communication are perhaps even more formidable. For example, Westerners doing business in the Middle East must be careful not to reveal the soles of their shoes to hosts or pass documents with the left hand. In Japan, bowing is an important form of nonverbal communication that has many nuances. People who grow up in the West tend to be verbal; those from Asia exhibit behavior that places more weight on nonverbal aspects of interpersonal communication. There is a greater expectation in the East that people will pick up nonverbal cues and understand intuitively without being told.[29] Westerners must pay close attention not only to what they hear but also to what they see when conducting business in such cultures.

Several important communication issues may emerge. One is *sequencing*, which concerns whether the discussion goes directly from point A to point B or seems to go off on tangents. Another is *phasing*, which pertains to whether certain important agenda items are discussed immediately or after the parties have taken some time to establish rapport. According to two experts on international negotiations, there are 10 distinctly American tactics that frequently emerge during negotiations. These tactics are often effective with other Americans, but may require modification for people from other cultural backgrounds. In any communication situation, speakers offer a variety of verbal cues that can help astute observers understand the speaker's mind-set and mental programming. Table 4-1 summarizes some typical American English cues, the underlying culture-influenced attitudes and behaviors they signify, and suggested adaptations.

Marketing's Impact on Culture

Universal aspects of the cultural environment represent opportunities for global marketers to standardize some or all elements of a marketing program. The astute global marketer often discovers that much of the apparent cultural diversity in the world turns out to be different ways of accomplishing the same thing. Widespread shared preference for convenience foods, disposable products, popular music, and movies in the United States, Europe, and Asia suggests that many consumer products have broad, even universal, appeal. Increasing travel and improving communications have contributed to a convergence of tastes and preferences in a number of product categories. The cultural change and the globalization of culture have been capitalized upon, and even significantly accelerated, by companies that have seized opportunities to find customers around the world. However, as noted at the beginning of this chapter, the impact of marketing and, more generally, of global capitalism on culture can be controversial. For example, sociologist George Ritzer and others lament the so-called "McDonaldization of culture" that, they say, occurs when global companies break down cultural

---

[28] Kevin Voigt, "At Matsushita, It's a New Word Order," *Asian The Wall Street Journal Weekly*, June 18–24, 2001, p. 1

[29] See Anthony C. Di Benedetto, Miriko Tamate, and Rajan Chandran, "Developing Strategy for the Japanese Marketplace," *Journal of Advertising Research* (January–February 1992), pp. 39–48.

[30] Robert Frank and Thomas M. Burton, "Side Effects: Cross-Border Merger Results in Headaches for a Drug Company," *The Wall Street Journal*, February 4, 1997, p. A1.

Verbal Cues	Underlying Reality	Adaptation Required	
1. "I can go it alone."	Americans are typically outnumbered in negotiations. Reflects culture of individualism.	Greater reliance on teamwork and division of negotiating labor, especially in collectivist culture.	**Table 4-1** *American Communication Styles: Verbal Cues, Underlying Realities, and Suggested Adaptations*
2. "Just call me 'John.'"	Americans place a high value on informality and equality of participants in negotiations. This may conflict with the customs and class structures of foreign cultures.	Respect the customs, hierarchies, and class structure of other cultures. Learn more via self study; ask country nationals to explain local attitudes and values.	
3. "Do you speak English?"	Americans are culturally monolingual. (Old joke: Q: What do you call someone who speaks two languages? A: Bilingual. Q: What do you call someone who speaks one language? A: American!)	Ignore the conventional wisdom about how difficult it is to learn a foreign language; if you have ongoing business in a country, make the effort to study the language. At a minimum, develop a good working relationship with a skilled interpreter.	
4. "Get to the point."	Americans' short-term orientation manifests itself as a tendency to be blunt and impatient.	Understand that people from other cultures need to develop a sense of connection and personal trust in order to feel comfortable about doing business. This takes time.	
5. "Lay your cards on the table."	Americans like to state the case up front, and are not accustomed to "feeling out" prospective partners.	Slow down, and recognize the need to rephrase the question, several times if necessary. Prepare to spend double the time you think is needed to get the information you seek.	
6. "Why doesn't somebody say something?"	Americans are uncomfortable with silence during negotiations and often deal with their discomfort by continuing to speak.	Recognize that silence is golden in many cultures. It can be detrimental to keep up a constant stream of chatter. If there is silence, let it be. Reflect. Take in nonverbal information. *Value* the silence. Take advantage of it.	
7. "Don't take no for an answer."	Tenacity and the hard sell are highly valued in the United States.	If the answer is no, stop selling and find out why. Respond to the reasons for the answer no.	
8. "One thing at a time."	Many Americans favor a linear, organized, "left brain" negotiation style. "Point One, Point Two"-style sequencing is not a universal approach.	Recognize your own right-brain capability. Embrace a more holistic approach toward negotiations. Be patient if the discussion seems to proceed in loops and spirals.	
9. "A deal is a deal."	Expectations and perceptions may not be shared by all parties. Have you agreed on all the points in the contract, or have you agreed to work together?	Accept a more gradual, supplemental view of negotiations and joint effort.	
10. "I am what I am."	Americans have a tendency to see things in black-and-white terms.	Adopt a more flexible standpoint. Be willing to change your mind and manner and to adapt to your opposite.	

Source: Adapted from John L. Graham and Roy A. Heberger Jr., "Negotiators Abroad—Don't Shoot from the Hip," *Harvard Business Review* 61, no. 4 (July–August 1983), pp. 160–168.

Spain's Telefónica is a leading provider of both fixed-line and wireless communication sevices in Spain and Latin America. In Brazil, Telefónica's joint venture with Portugal Telecom commands one-third of the market. Now Telefónica is moving aggressively to provide "triple play" services that include high-speed Internet and video on demand in addition to regular voice communication. The company's U.K. subsidiary recently launched Look at Me, a service that lets cellphone subscribers create videos with their phones that they can upload and share with others.

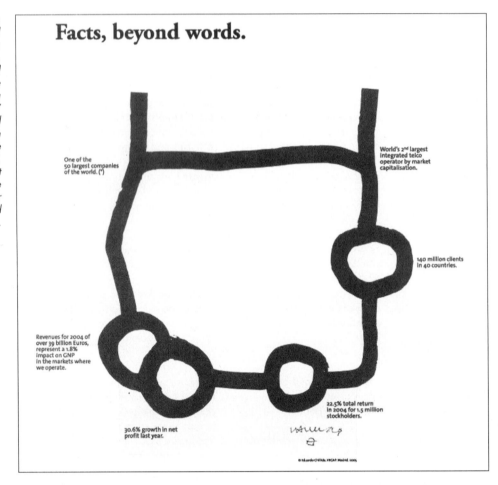

barriers while expanding into new markets with their products. As Ritzer noted in a recent book:

> Eating is at the heart of most cultures and for many it is something on which much time, attention and money are lavished. In attempting to alter the way people eat, McDonaldization poses a profound threat to the entire cultural complex of many societies.[31]

Fabien Ouaki is living proof that persons outside of academe and government have also joined the battle against McDonaldization. Ouaki is the managing director of Tati, a discount retailer based in France. Ouaki is opening new stores in select countries, including the United States. Ouaki claims that "personal revenge" is one motivation for entering the U.S. market. "As a Frenchman, it makes me sick to see kids crying to go see *Titanic*, eat at McDonald's, or drink Coke. I want to see New Yorkers crying to have a Tati wedding dress," he said.[32] Similarly, the international Slow Food movement boasts 70,000 members in 35 countries. Slow Food grew out of a 1986 protest over the opening of a McDonald's on a popular plaza in Rome; every two years,

---

[31] George Ritzer, *The McDonaldizNation Thesis* (London: Sage Publications, 1998), p. 8.
[32] Amy Barrett, "French Discounter Takes Cheap Chic World-Wide," *The Wall Street Journal*, May 27, 1998, p. B8.

Slow Food stages a Salone del Gusto in Italy that showcases traditional food preparation. As a spokesperson said, "Slow Food is about the idea that things should not taste the same everywhere."[33]

HIGH- AND LOW-CONTEXT CULTURES

Edward T. Hall has suggested the concept of high and low context as a way of understanding different cultural orientations.[34] In a **low-context culture**, messages are explicit and specific; words carry most of the communication power. In a **high-context culture**, less information is contained in the verbal part of a message. Much more information resides in the context of communication, including the background, associations, and basic values of the communicators. In general, high-context cultures function with much less legal paperwork than is deemed essential in low-context cultures. Japan, Saudi Arabia, and other high-context cultures place a great deal of emphasis on a person's values and position or place in society. In such cultures, a business loan is more likely to be based on "who you are" than on formal analysis of pro forma financial documents. In a low-context culture, such as the United States, Switzerland, or Germany, deals are made with much less information about the character, background, and values of the participants. Much more reliance is placed upon the words and numbers in the loan application. Similarly, Japanese companies, such as Sony, traditionally paid a great deal of attention to the university background of a new hire; preference would be given to graduates of Tokyo University. Specific elements on a résumé were less important.

In a high-context culture, a person's word is his or her bond. There is less need to anticipate contingencies and provide for external legal sanctions because the culture emphasizes obligations and trust as important values. In these cultures, shared feelings of obligation and honor take the place of impersonal legal sanctions. This helps explain the importance of long and protracted negotiations that never seem to get to the point. Part of the purpose of negotiating, for a person from a high-context culture, is to get to know the potential partner.

For example, insisting on competitive bidding can cause complications in low-context cultures. In a high-context culture, the job is given to the person who will do the best work and whom you can trust and control. In a low-context culture, one tries to make the specifications so precise that the threat of legal sanction forces a builder to do a good job. As Hall has noted, a builder in Japan is likely to say, "What has that piece of paper got to do with the situation? If we can't trust each other enough to go ahead without it, why bother?"

Although countries can be classified as high- or low-context in their overall tendency, there are exceptions to the general tendency. These exceptions are found in subcultures. The United States is a low-context culture with subcultures that operate in the high-context mode. The world of the central banker, for example, is a "gentleman's" world; that is, a high-context culture. Even during the most hectic day of trading in the foreign exchange markets, a central banker's word is sufficient for him or her to borrow millions of dollars. In a high-context culture, there is trust, a sense of fair play, and a widespread acceptance of the rules of the game as it is played. Table 4-2 summarizes some of the ways in which high- and low-context cultures differ.

---

[33] Jerry Shriver, "At Slow Food Fest, Taste Trumps Time," *USA Today*, November 9, 1998, p. 1D. See also Alexander Stille, "Slow Food's Pleasure Principles," *Utne Reader* (May–June 2002), pp. 56–58.

[34] Edward T. Hall, "How Cultures Collide," *Psychology Today* (July 1976), pp. 66–97.

Table 4-2

High- and Low-Context Cultures

Factors or Dimensions	High Context	Low Context
Lawyers	Less important	Very important
A person's word	Is his or her bond	Is not to be relied upon; "get it in writing"
Responsibility for organizational error	Taken by highest level	Pushed to lowest level
Space	People breathe on each other	People maintain a bubble of private space and resent intrusions
Time	Polychronic—everything in life must be dealt with in terms of its own time	Monochronic—time is money Linear—one thing at a time
Negotiations	Are lengthy—a major purpose is to allow the parties to get to know each other	Proceed quickly
Competitive bidding	Infrequent	Common
Country or regional examples	Japan, Middle East	United States, Northern Europe

HOFSTEDE'S CULTURAL TYPOLOGY

Organizational anthropologist Geert Hofstede was introduced earlier in this chapter in a discussion of his widely quoted definition of culture. Hofstede is also well known for research studies of social values suggesting that the cultures of different nations can be compared in terms of five dimensions.[35] Hofstede notes that three of the dimensions refer to expected social behavior, the fourth dimension is concerned with "man's search for Truth," and a fifth

Folk medicine is popular in many cultures. Street vendor stalls and open air markets selling health remedies and other products are a common sight in India. This stall sells an elixir made from purified cow urine. While such products are viewed with scepticism by some doctors, their medicinal properties are said to provide relief from a variety of ailments.

---

[35] Geert Hofstede and Michael Harris Bond, "The Confucius Connection: From Cultural Roots to Economic Growth," *Organizational Dynamics* (Spring 1988), p. 5.

reflects the importance of time. Table 4-3 shows a summary of Triad country rankings, plus Hong Kong and Taiwan (for more information, visit www.geert-hofstede.com).

The first dimension, **power distance**, is the extent to which the less powerful members of a society accept—even expect—power to be distributed unequally. To paraphrase Orwell, all societies are unequal, but some are more unequal than others. Hong Kong and France are both high power-distance cultures; low power distance characterizes Germany, Austria, the Netherlands, and Scandinavia.

The second dimension is a reflection of the degree to which individuals in a society are integrated into groups. In **individualist cultures**, each member of society is primarily concerned with his or her own interest and those of the immediate family. In **collectivist cultures**, all society's members are integrated into cohesive in-groups. High individualism is a general aspect of culture in the United States and Europe; low individualism is characteristic of Japanese and other Asian culture patterns.

Masculinity, the third dimension, describes a society in which men are expected to be assertive, competitive, and concerned with material success, and women fulfill the role of nurturer and are concerned with issues such as the welfare of children. **Femininity**, by contrast, describes a society in which the social roles of men and women overlap, with neither gender exhibiting overly ambitious or competitive behavior. Japan and Austria ranked highest in masculinity; Spain, Taiwan, the Netherlands, and the Scandinavian countries were among the lowest.

Uncertainty avoidance is the extent to which the members of a society are uncomfortable with unclear, ambiguous, or unstructured situations. Members of uncertainty avoiding cultures may resort to aggressive, emotional, intolerant

Table 4-3

Hofstede's Cultural Dimension Rankings: Triad

Country	Power Distance (PDI)		Individualism		Masculinity		Uncertainty Avoidance		Long-Term Orientation (LTO)	
	Index	Rank	Index	Rank	Index	Rank	Index	Rank	Index	Rank
Austria	11	53	55	18	79	**2**	70	24–25	31	22–24
Belgium	65	20	75	8	54	22	94	5–6	38	18
Denmark	18	51	74	9	16	50	23	51	46	10
Finland	33	46	63	17	26	47	59	31–32	41	14
France	68	**15–16**	71	10–11	43	35–36	86	10–15	39	17
Germany	35	42–44	67	15	66	9–10	65	29	31	22–24
Greece	60	27–28	35	30	57	18–19	112	**1**	—	—
Ireland	28	49	70	12	68	7–8	35	47–48	43	13
Italy	50	34	76	7	70	4–5	75	23	34	19
Netherlands	38	40	80	4–5	14	51	53	35	44	11–12
Portugal	63	24–25	69	13	31	45	104	2	30	25–26
Spain	57	31	51	20	42	37–38	86	10–15	19	31–32
Sweden	31	47–48	71	10–11	5	52	29	49–50	33	20
United Kingdom	65	42–44	89	3	66	9–10	35	47–48	25	28–29
United States	40	38	91	**1**	62	15	41	43	29	27
Japan	54	33	46	22–23	95	**1**	92	7	80	4
Hong Kong	68	**15–16**	25	37	57	18–19	29	49–50	96	**2**
Taiwan	58	29–30	17	44	45	32–33	69	26	87	3

Source: Geert Hofstede, *Culture's Consequences* (Thousand Oaks, CA: Sage, 2001), p. 500, © 2001 by Sage Publications, Reprinted by Permission of Sage Publications, Inc.

behavior; they are characterized by a belief in absolute truth. Members of uncertainty accepting cultures (e.g., Denmark, Sweden, Ireland, and the United States) are more tolerant of persons whose opinions differ from their own.

Greece and Portugal outrank the others in Table 4-3 in uncertainty avoidance; other Mediterranean countries and much of Latin America ranks high in uncertainty avoidance as well. Acceptance of uncertainty generally manifests itself in behavior that is more contemplative, relativistic, and tolerant; these values are evident in Southeast Asia and India.

Hofstede's research convinced him that, although these four dimensions yielded interesting and useful interpretations, they did not provide sufficient insight into possible cultural bases for economic growth. Hofstede was also disturbed by the fact that Western social scientists had developed the surveys used in the research. Because many economists had failed to predict the explosive economic development of Japan and the Asian tigers (i.e., South Korea, Taiwan, Hong Kong, and Singapore), Hofstede surmised that some cultural dimensions in Asia were eluding the researchers. This methodological problem was remedied by a Chinese Value Survey (CVS) developed by Chinese social scientists in Hong Kong and Taiwan. The CVS data supported the first three "social behavior" dimensions of culture: power distance, individualism/collectivism, and masculinity/femininity. Uncertainty avoidance, however, did not show up in the CVS. Instead, the CVS revealed a dimension, **long-term orientation (LTO)** versus **short-term orientation**, that had eluded Western researchers.[36] Hofstede interpreted this dimension as concerning "a society's search for virtue," rather than a search for truth. It assesses the sense of immediacy within a culture, whether gratification should be immediate or deferred.

Long-term values include *persistence* (perseverance), defined as a general tenacity in the pursuit of a goal. *Ordering relationships* by status reflects the presence of societal hierarchies, and *observing this order* indicates the acceptance of complementary relations. *Thrift* manifests itself in high savings rates. Finally, *a sense of shame* leads to sensitivity in social contacts. Hofstede notes that these values are widely held within high-performing Asian countries, such as Hong Kong, Taiwan, and Japan, but that the presence of these values by themselves is not sufficient to lead to economic growth. Two other conditions are necessary: the existence of a market and a supportive political context. Although Hofstede determined that India ranked quite high on the LTO dimension, market restrictions and political forces have, until recently, held back that nation's economic growth.

By studying Hofstede's work, marketers gain insights that can guide them in a range of activities, including product development, interacting with joint venture partners, and conducting sales meetings. For example, understanding the time orientation of one's native culture compared to others' is crucial (see Table 4-2). In Japan, Brazil, and India, building a relationship with a potential business partner takes precedence over transacting the deal. People from cultures that emphasize the short term must adapt to the slower pace of business in some countries. As noted earlier, language can offer some insights into cultural differences. For example, the phrase "in a New York minute" captures the urgent pace of American urban life.

Conversely, the Japanese notion of *gaman* ("persistence") provides insight into the willingness of Japanese corporations to pursue R&D projects for which the odds of short-term success appear low. When Sony licensed the newly invented transistor from Bell Laboratories in the mid-1950s, for example,

---

[36] In some articles, Hofstede refers to this dimension as "Confucian Dynamism" because it is highest in Japan, Hong Kong, and Taiwan.

the limited high-frequency yield (sound output) of the device suggested to American engineers that the most appropriate application would be for a hearing aid. However, *gaman* meant that Sony engineers were not deterred by the slow progress of their efforts to increase the yield. As Sony cofounder Masaru Ibuka recalled, "To challenge the yield is a very interesting point for us. At that time no one recognized the importance of it." Sony's persistence was rewarded when company engineers eventually made the yield breakthrough that resulted in a wildly successful global product—the pocket-sized transistor radio.[37]

By understanding the dimension of uncertainty avoidance, global marketers are better equipped to assess the amount of risk with which buyers are comfortable. In Japan and other Asian cultures characterized by a low tolerance for ambiguity, buyers will be conscious of brand names and are likely to exhibit high brand loyalty. Advertising copy in countries with high levels of uncertainty avoidance should provide reassurance by stressing warranties, money-back guarantees, and other risk-reducing features. Hong Kong has an even higher tolerance for ambiguity than the United States; Japan, however, ranks quite high in uncertainty avoidance, as do France and Spain.

The power distance dimension reflects the degree of trust among members of society. The higher the power distance (PDI), the lower the level of trust. Organizationally, high PDI finds expression in tall, hierarchical designs, a preference for centralization, and relatively more supervisory personnel. The PDI dimension also provides insights into the dynamics between superiors and subordinates. In cultures where respect for hierarchy is high, subordinates may have to navigate through several layers of assistants to get to the boss. If so, the latter is likely to be isolated in an office with the door closed. In such cultures, superiors may easily intimidate lower-level employees. Recent research has suggested that, when evaluating alternatives for entering global markets, companies in high PDI cultures prefer sole ownership of subsidiaries because it provides them with more control. Conversely, companies in low PDI cultures are more apt to use joint ventures.[38] Of the Triad countries in Table 4-3, France has the highest PDI. Other countries with high PDI scores are Mexico, India, and Hong Kong.

The masculinity-femininity dimension is likely to manifest itself in the relative importance of achievement and possessions (masculine values) compared with a spirit of helpfulness and social support (feminine values). Overall, an aggressive, achievement-oriented salesperson is better matched to the culture of Austria, Japan, or Mexico than that of Denmark. (Such a salesperson would also have to bear in mind that both Japan and Mexico rank high in LTO, a dimension that can be at odds with transaction-oriented assertiveness.) Similarly, a Western woman who is sent to make a presentation to a Japanese company will undoubtedly find that her audience consists of men. The Japanese managers may react negatively to a woman, especially if she is younger than they are.

The collective-individual orientation deserves special comment because there is wide agreement that it is an important component of culture. Knowing which cultures value the collective and which value the individual can help marketers in various ways. In Japan, for example, the team orientation and desire for *wa* ("harmony") means that singling out one person for distinction and praise in front of peers can be awkward for those involved. Again, language provides important

---

[37] James Lardner, *Fast Forward: Hollywood, the Japanese, and the VCR Wars* (New York: NAL Penguin, 1987), p. 45.

[38] Scott A. Shane, "The Effect of Cultural Differences in Perceptions of Transactions Costs on National Differences in the Preference for International Joint Ventures," *Asia Pacific Journal of Management* 10, no. 1 (1993), pp. 57–69.

the rest of the story

The cultural confrontation between Denmark and the Middle East cast a spotlight on the small European country. What is Denmark really like? The following profile captures Denmark in terms of Hofstede's cultural values framework.

Future Orientation

The extent to which a society encourages and rewards future-oriented behaviors such as planning, investing in the future, and delaying gratification. Denmark scores high.

In the Danish business environment, it is normal to prepare and discuss five-year budgets and business plans that are then adjusted yearly. Also, the Danish population is aware of the importance of saving up for retirement. Minister of Economic Affairs Bendt Bendtsen hopes to establish a world-class innovation center in Denmark. The center would focus on predicting consumer needs and elevate Denmark to the top ranks of countries with consumer-driven innovation. The key areas of study would be economics, anthropology, engineering, design, and psychology.

Gender Differentiation

The extent to which a society maximizes gender role differences. Denmark scores low.

In Denmark, gender role differences are insignificant. Danish women are strong and believe they can do anything that a man can. Because of this, it is very uncommon for men to open doors for women or give them flowers. A few years ago, it was very popular for women to attend "know your car" seminars. Denmark's maternity leave policy provides for a total of 12 months that both the mother and father can use. As is true in the United States, there are great differences between families in Denmark. Generally though, Danish women are very focused on equality both in the home and at work. It is very common for fathers to take equal part in cleaning and other duties around the house.

Uncertainty Avoidance

The extent to which the members of a society are accepting of ambiguous situations or comfortable with unfamiliar situations. Denmark scores low; in other words, it is an uncertainty accepting society.

Danes generally are not afraid of taking chances; they are comfortable doing things that are not carefully thought out or planned. The Danish social system provides a close-knit safety system to fall back on. In other words, making a mistake may not be very costly so people are less afraid of taking chances. Society relies on and supports a system that is costly but provides a constant sense of security. Health care is free for all Danish citizens, so a person doesn't have to worry about losing benefits if he or she changes jobs.

Power Distance

The degree to which members of a society expect power to be unequally shared. Denmark scores low.

This is an area where the countries of Europe differ to the extreme. Denmark scores very low on power distance, which results in very flat and informal organizational structures and the wide use of various matrix models. CEOs and other leaders are directly accessible to the average worker and it is common that leaders are satirized in sketches at company parties. In the Danish workplace, it is normal to be paid in accordance to qualifications instead of in accordance to position. *Janteloven* or "the law of Jante" deeply affects how Scandinavian people act and are expected to act. The term originated with writer Aksel Sandemose who wrote a novel about Jante, a village where one is not supposed to believe he or she is better or smarter than anyone else. Humility is important, and this limits power distance. It is not unusual for the Danish Queen Margrethe II to visit stores in Copenhagen without any visible protection. Also, Prince Felix, son of Prince Joachim and Princess Alexandra, attends a public school in his hometown of Møgeltønder.

Individualism/Collectivism

The degree to which societal institutions encourage individuals to integrate into groups within organizations and society. Denmark scores low.

Due to the high rates of taxes in Denmark schooling is free for everyone at all levels of education. The system is completely based on merit and does not favor people who are well off financially.

In-group Collectivism

Extent to which members of a society take pride in membership in small groups, such as their family and circle of close friends and the organizations in which they are employed. Denmark scores low.

Denmark's divorce rate is one of the highest in the world. It is difficult to find exact numbers to compare because of the many different ways of calculating it. High uncertainty acceptance may be a factor.

Sources: Mikkel Jakobsen, personal communication; David Ibison, "We Have to Think Differently," Financial Times, October 2, 2006, p. 7; Lydia Polgreen, "Nigeria Counts 100 Deaths over Danish Caricatures," The New York Times, February 24, 2006, p. A8; Andres Higgins, "Danish Businesses Struggle with Big Dilemma," The Wall Street Journal, February 10, 2006, p. A4; "The Cartoons That Shook the World," The Wall Street Journal, February 11–12, 2006, p. A7; Michael Kimmelman, "A Startling New Lesson in the Power of Imagery," The New York Times, February 8, 2006, p. B1; Bertrand Benoit, "Muslim Anger Spreads Round the World," Financial Times, February 4–5, 2006, p. 2.

cues about these cultural dimensions; as the saying goes in Japan, "The nail that sticks up gets hammered down." Throughout much of Asia, the collectivist orientation is dominant. In the highly individualist U.S. culture, however, a person whose individual accomplishments are publicly acknowledged is likely to be pleased by the recognition.[39]

Several teams of researchers have attempted to determine whether cross-national collective-individual differences are reflected in print and television advertisements. In theory, a global company's communication efforts should be adapted in accordance with a particular country's orientation. For example, in cultures where individualism is highly valued, ads would typically feature one person; in countries where individualism is less highly valued, ads would feature groups. Although one team[40] claimed to have found a strong correlation, the findings were not confirmed by a later study.[41] However, Cutler argues that print advertising is, by its very nature, designed to communicate to an individual reader. This suggests that the individualism-collectivism distinction may be a moot issue in print advertising.

In highly collectivist cultures, however, products or services that enjoy an early word-of-mouth buzz among influential consumer groups can quickly achieve phenomenon status that then spreads to other countries. The Tamagotchi craze of the late 1990s is a perfect example. The virtual pets were test marketed in central Tokyo in a shopping area frequented by teenage girls. *Kuchikomi* ("word of mouth") was so strong among schoolgirls that toymaker Bandai was hard-pressed to keep up with demand. By the time Tamagotchis reached New York toy retailer FAO Schwartz, the prerelease buzz ensured that the initial 10,000-unit shipment sold out immediately. Although Japanese teens also pay attention to print and television advertising, it is clear that marketers can reach this segment by providing selected youngsters with product samples.[42]

Other recent research suggests that Hofstede's framework can provide useful insights for global marketers hoping to create culturally appropriate consumer brand images. For example, researcher Martin Ross described three types of brand images: functional, social, and sensory. A product with a *functional brand image* is oriented toward problem solving and problem prevention; products with a *social brand image* fulfill consumers' needs for group membership and affiliation; a product with *sensory appeal* provides novelty, variety, and sensory gratification. In the United States, for example, the Crest, Ultra Brite, and Aim toothpaste brands respectively embody these images. Ross surveyed marketing managers at U.S. companies that market jeans and athletic shoes. His research suggests that in countries where power distance is high, social brand images enhance brand performance. Conversely, by limiting the use of social and sensory images and emphasizing functional benefits, marketers can enhance brand performance in countries or regions with low power distance. Ross also found strong evidence that sensory brand images would perform well in countries where high individualism is a dominant cultural pattern and that social brand image strategies would be effective in countries characterized by low individualism.[43]

---

[39] Adapted from Anne Macquin and Dominique Rouziès, "Selling across the Culture Gap," *Financial Times—Mastering Global Business, Part Seven*, 1998, pp. 10–11.

[40] Katherine Toland Frith and Subir Sengupta, "Individualism: A Cross-Cultural Analysis of Print Advertisements from the U.S. and India," paper presented at 1991 Annual Conference of Advertising Division of Association for Education in Journalism and Mass Communication, Boston, MA.

[41] Bob D. Cutler, S. Altan Erdem, and Rajshekhar G. Javalgi, "Advertisers' Relative Reliance on Collectivism-Individualism Appeals," *Journal of International Consumer Marketing* 9, no. 3 (1997), pp. 43–55.

[42] Bethan Hutton, "Winning Word-of-Mouth Approval," *Financial Times*, September 8, 1997, p. 10.

[43] Martin S. Roth, "The Effects of Culture and Socioeconomics on the Performance of Global Brand Image Strategies," *Journal of Marketing Research* 32 (May 1995), pp. 163–175.

THE SELF-REFERENCE CRITERION AND PERCEPTION

As we have shown, a person's perception of market needs is framed by his or her own cultural experience. A framework for systematically reducing perceptual blockage and distortion was developed by James Lee and published in *Harvard Business Review* in 1966. Lee termed the unconscious reference to one's own cultural values the **self-reference criterion (SRC)**. To address this problem and eliminate or reduce cultural myopia, he proposed a systematic four-step framework:

1. Define the problem or goal in terms of home-country cultural traits, habits, and norms.
2. Define the problem or goal in terms of host-country cultural traits, habits, and norms. Make no value judgments.
3. Isolate the SRC influence and examine it carefully to see how it complicates the problem.
4. Redefine the problem without the SRC influence and solve for the host-country market situation.[44]

The Walt Disney Company's decision to build a theme park in France provides an excellent vehicle for understanding SRC. As they planned their entry into the French market, how might Disney executives have done things differently had they used the steps of SRC?

Step 1. Disney executives believe there is virtually unlimited demand for American cultural exports around the world. Evidence includes the success of McDonald's, Coca-Cola, Hollywood movies, and American rock music. Disney has a stellar track record in exporting its American management system and business style. Tokyo Disneyland, a virtual carbon copy of the park in Anaheim, California, has been a runaway success. Disney policies prohibit sale or consumption of alcohol inside its theme parks.

Step 2. Europeans in general and the French in particular are sensitive about American cultural imperialism. Consuming wine with the midday meal is a long-established custom. Europeans have their own real castles, and many popular Disney characters come from European folk tales.

Step 3. The significant differences revealed by comparing the findings in Steps 1 and 2 suggest strongly that the needs upon which the American and Japanese Disney theme parks were based did not exist in France. A modification of this design was needed for European success.

Step 4. This would require the design of a theme park that is more in keeping with French and European cultural norms. Allow the French to put their own identity on the park.

The lesson that the SRC teaches is that a vital, critical skill of the global marketer is unbiased perception, the ability to understand a culture. Although this skill is as valuable at home as it is abroad, it is critical to the global marketer because of the widespread tendency toward ethnocentrism and use of the self-reference criterion. The SRC can be a powerful negative force in global business, and forgetting to check for it can lead to misunderstanding and failure. While planning Euro Disney, former Chairman Michael Eisner and other company

"Disney has learned that they can't impose the American will—or Disney's version of it—on another continent. They've bent over backward to make Hong Kong Disneyland blend in with the surroundings."[45]

Dennis McAlpine, media and entertainment research specialist

"We have been U.S.-centric forever. We realize that if we're going to be a global network, then we need to solicit material from around the world."[46]

Gary Marsh, Disney Channel Worldwide, commenting on Disney's new programming divisions in the United Kingdom and Japan.

44 James A. Lee, "Cultural Analysis in Overseas Operations," *Harvard Business Review* (March–April 1966), pp. 106–114.
45 Michael Schuman, "Disney's Great Leap into China," *Time*, July 18, 2005, p. 34.
46 Matthew Garrahan, "Disney Ventures into Famous Five Territory," *Financial Times*, December 4, 2006, p. 15.

GLOBAL *marketing in action*

Global Marketing in Action

The globalization of food tastes is one sign of broader cultural shifts that are taking place in many countries. Changing lifestyles as well as global retailing and food processing trends are driving changes in eating habits. Many Europeans, for example, are eating bigger breakfasts because lunch breaks have been shortened. Options for breakfast foods, in turn, have multiplied because supermarkets are popping up in neighborhoods in competition with small mom-and-pop stores. Supermarkets can stock a broader selection of food items and are more likely to offer new products to their customers. Global companies, such as Kellogg's and Cereal Partners Worldwide, are competing fiercely with each other and with smaller, local firms for a share of palates and pocketbooks.

Europeans are also developing a taste for salty snacks like tortilla chips. As with breakfast cereal, consumption of tortilla chips in Europe has historically been much lower than in the United States. However, the Tex-Mex concept is gaining momentum. Although Frito-Lay introduced its Doritos brand in Europe in 1994, Europeans viewed the chips as a snack for special occasions, and sales were below expectations. In 1998, Frito-Lay relaunched Doritos in the United Kingdom, France, Spain, Portugal, Belgium, the Netherlands, and Luxembourg. A $20 million advertising campaign, identical across the seven countries except for the individual languages, intended to raise European consumption of the snack chips. Following the recommendations of a brand consultant, Frito-Lay made two significant changes to the packaging. First, it dropped the America-style "see-through window" in favor of the type of sealed foil package that is used for potato chips in Europe. Second, the dominant color of the package was changed from white to black.

In another global food trend that some have likened to "taking coals to Newcastle," food items are being introduced in some countries from unlikely sources. American versions of cheddar cheese are being exported to southwest England, where cheddar was first produced. German imports of American wine increased sevenfold between 1991 and 1996. A Hong Kong noodle maker has achieved great success exporting to China. Grass-fed beef from Argentina is becoming popular in the United States.

Despite these trends, some local food preferences are likely to remain entrenched—at least for a while. For example, many Japanese prefer a traditional breakfast of *okayu* ("rice porridge") with *umeboshi* ("pickled plums"). In Vietnam, street venders offer *pho* (pronounced *fuh*) for breakfast, lunch, dinner, or as a snack. It consists of a broth made of oxtail, beef, and shrimp paste, seasoned with spices and served over rice noodles. One sign of the times: *Pho* is now sold from street carts in New York, Chicago, and Los Angeles.

Sources: Ernest Beck and Rekha Balu, "Europe Is Deaf to Snap! Crackle! Pop!" The Wall Street Journal, June 28, 1998, pp. B1, B8; Helene Cooper and Scott Kilman, "Exotic Tastes: Trade Wars Aside, U.S. and Europe Buy More of Each Other's Foods," The Wall Street Journal, June 28, 1998, pp. A1, A8; Anna Wilde Mathews, "Modern Menus Star Flown-in Fish, Game," The Wall Street Journal, July 7, 1998, pp. B1, B2; John Willman, "Salty Snack Attack on Europe," Financial Times, February 2, 1998, p. 11.

executives were blinded by a potent combination of their own prior success and ethnocentrism. Avoiding the SRC requires a person to suspend assumptions based on prior experience and success and be prepared to acquire new knowledge about human behavior and motivation.

Hong Kong Disneyland opened its gates for the first time on September 12, 2005. Donald Tsang, Hong Kong Special Administrative Region, Zeng Qinghong, Vice President of People's Republic of China, Michael D. Eisner, Chief Executive Officer of the Walt Disney Company and Robert A. Iger, Disney's President, Chief Operating Officer and CEO-Elect, were on hand for the opening ceremonies.

First-year attendance figures fell short of the target figure of 5.6 million people, prompting company executives to step up efforts to educate the Chinese about Mickey Mouse, Donald Duck, and other Disney characters. As Bill Ernest, managing director, told the Financial Times, "If you haven't grown up with the brand, the stories, or the theme, you are not quite sure what you are walking into."

DIFFUSION THEORY[47]

Hundreds of studies have described the process by which an individual adopts a new idea. Sociologist Everett Rogers reviewed these studies and discovered a pattern of remarkably similar findings. In *Diffusion of Innovations*, Rogers distilled the research into three concepts that are extremely useful to global marketers: the adoption process, characteristics of innovations, and adopter categories.

An innovation is something new. When applied to a product, *new* can mean different things. In an absolute sense, once a product has been introduced anywhere in the world, it is no longer an innovation because it is no longer new to the world. Relatively speaking, however, a product already introduced in one market may be an innovation elsewhere because it is new and different for the targeted market. Global marketing often entails just such product introductions. Managers find themselves marketing products that may be, simultaneously, innovations in some markets and mature or declining products in other markets.

The Adoption Process

One of the basic elements of Rogers's diffusion theory is the concept of an **adoption process**—the mental stages through which an individual passes from the time of his or her first knowledge of an innovation to the time of product adoption or purchase. Rogers suggests that an individual passes through five different stages in proceeding from first knowledge of a product to the final adoption or purchase of that product: awareness, interest, evaluation, trial, and adoption.

1. *Awareness.* In the first stage, the customer becomes aware for the first time of the product or innovation. Studies have shown that at this stage impersonal sources of information, such as mass media advertising, are most important. An important early communication objective in global marketing is to create awareness of a new product through general exposure to advertising messages.
2. *Interest.* During this stage, the customer is interested enough to learn more. The customer has focused his or her attention on communications relating to the product and will engage in research activities and seek out additional information.
3. *Evaluation.* In this stage, the individual mentally assesses the product's benefits in relation to present and anticipated future needs and, based on this judgment, decides whether or not to try it.
4. *Trial.* Most customers will not purchase expensive products without the "hands-on" experience marketers call "trial." A good example of a product trial that does not involve purchase is the automobile test drive. For healthcare products and other inexpensive consumer packaged goods, trial often involves actual purchase. Marketers frequently induce trial by distributing free samples. For inexpensive products, an initial single purchase is defined as trial.
5. *Adoption.* At this point, the individual either makes an initial purchase (in the case of the more expensive product) or continues to purchase—adopts and exhibits brand loyalty to—the less expensive product. Studies show that, as a person moves from the evaluation through trial to adoption, personal sources of information are more important than impersonal sources. It is during these stages that sales representatives and word of mouth become major persuasive forces affecting the decision to buy.

---

[47] This section draws from Everett M. Rogers, *Diffusion of Innovations* (New York: Free Press, 1962).

Characteristics of Innovations

In addition to describing the product adoption process, Rogers also identifies five **characteristics of innovations** that affect the rate at which innovations are ,adopted: relative advantage, compatibility, complexity, divisibility, and communicability.

1. *Relative advantage.* How a new product compares with existing products or methods in the eyes of customers. The perceived relative advantage of a new product versus existing products is a major influence on the rate of adoption. If a product has a substantial relative advantage vis-à-vis the competition, it is likely to gain quick acceptance. When compact disc players were first introduced in the early 1980s, industry observers predicted that only audiophiles would care enough about digital sound—and have the money—to purchase them. However, the sonic advantages of CDs compared to LPs were obvious to the mass market; as prices for CD players plummeted, the 12-inch black vinyl LP was rendered virtually extinct in less than a decade.

2. *Compatibility.* The extent to which a product is consistent with existing values and past experiences of adopters. The history of innovations in international marketing is replete with failures caused by the lack of compatibility of new products in the target market. For example, the first consumer VCR, the Sony Betamax, ultimately failed because it could only record for one hour. Most buyers wanted to record movies and sports events; they shunned the Betamax in favor of VHS-format VCRs that could record four hours of programming.

3. *Complexity.* The degree to which an innovation or new product is difficult to understand and use. Product complexity is a factor that can slow down the rate of adoption, particularly in developing country markets with low rates of literacy. In the 1990s, dozens of global companies are developing new interactive multimedia consumer electronics products. Complexity is a key design issue; it is a standing joke that in most households, VCR clocks flash 12:00 because users don't know how to set them. To achieve mass success, new products will have to be as simple to use as slipping a prerecorded videocassette into a VCR.

4. *Divisibility.* The ability of a product to be tried and used on a limited basis without great expense. Wide discrepancies in income levels around the globe result in major differences in preferred purchase quantities, serving sizes, and product portions. CPC International's Hellmann's mayonnaise was simply not selling in U.S.-size jars in Latin America. Sales took off after the company placed the mayonnaise in small plastic packets. The plastic packets were within the food budgets of local consumers, and they required no refrigeration—another plus.

5. *Communicability.* The degree to which benefits of an innovation or the value of a product may be communicated to a potential market. A new digital cassette recorder from Philips was a market failure, in part because advertisements did not clearly communicate the fact that the product could make CD-quality recordings using new cassette technology while still playing older analog tapes.

Adopter Categories

Adopter categories are classifications of individuals within a market on the basis of their innovativeness. Hundreds of studies of the diffusion of innovation demonstrate that, at least in the West, adoption is a social phenomenon that is characterized by a normal distribution curve, as shown in Figure 4-1.

Figure 4-1

Adopter Categories

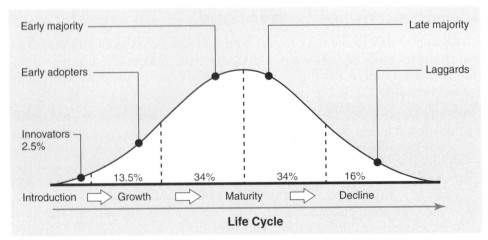

Five categories have been assigned to the segments of this normal distribution. The first 2.5 percent of people to purchase a product are defined as innovators. The next 13.5 percent are early adopters, the next 34 percent are the early majority, the next 34 percent are the late majority, and the final 16 percent are laggards. Studies show that innovators tend to be venturesome, more cosmopolitan in their social relationships, and wealthier than those who adopt later. Early adopters are the most influential people in their communities, even more than the innovators. Thus, the early adopters are a critical group in the adoption process, and they have great influence on the early and late majority, who comprise the bulk of the adopters of any product. Several characteristics of early adopters stand out. First, they tend to be younger, with higher social status, and in a more favorable financial position than later adopters. They must be responsive to mass media information sources and must learn about innovations from these sources because they cannot simply copy the behavior of early adopters.

One of the major reasons for the normal distribution of adopter categories is the *interaction effect*; that is, the process through which individuals who have adopted an innovation influence others. Adoption of a new idea or product is the result of human interaction in a social system. If the first adopter of an innovation or new product discusses it with two other people, and each of these two adopters passes the new idea along to two other people, and so on, the resulting distribution yields a normal bell shape when plotted.[48]

Diffusion of Innovations in Pacific Rim Countries

In a recent cross-national comparison of the United States, Japan, South Korea, and Taiwan, Takada and Jain present evidence that different country characteristics—in particular, culture and communication patterns—affect diffusion processes for room air conditioners, washing machines, and calculators. Proceeding from the observation that Japan, South Korea, and Taiwan are high-context cultures with relatively homogeneous populations, and the United States is a low-context, heterogeneous culture, Takada and Jain surmised that Asia would show faster rates of diffusion than the United States. A second hypothesis supported by the research was that adoption would proceed more quickly in markets where innovations were introduced relatively late. Presumably, the lag time

---

[48] For an excellent application and discussion of adopter categories, see Malcolm Gladwell, *The Tipping Point* (New York: Little, Brown, and Company, 2000), Chapter 6.

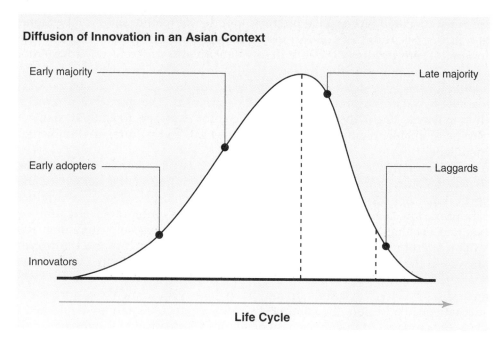

Diffusion of Innovation in an Asian Context

Early majority

Late majority

Early adopters

Laggards

Innovators

Life Cycle

Figure 4-2

Adopter Categories in Asia

Source: Hellmut Schütte, "Asian Culture and the Global Consumer," *Financial Times—Mastering Marketing* (September 21, 1998), p. 2.

would give potential consumers more opportunity to assess the relative advantages, compatibility, and other product attributes. Takada and Jain's research has important marketing implications. They note:

> If a marketing manager plans to enter the newly industrializing countries (NICs) or other Asia markets with a product that has proved to be successful in the home market, the product's diffusion processes are likely to be much faster than in the home market.[49]

Figure 4-2 shows how the curve of Asian adopter categories would differ from the curve associated with Western consumer behavior. As noted before, there are likely to be fewer innovators in Japan and other Asian countries, where risk avoidance is high. However, as the Tamagotchi story illustrated, once consumers become aware that others have tried the product, they follow suit quickly so as not to be left behind. Hence the left tail in Figure 4-2 is longer, reflecting hesitancy to try a new product; moreover, the curve is steeper and less symmetrical, reflecting the speed with which early adopters and early majority try the product.[50]

MARKETING IMPLICATIONS OF SOCIAL AND CULTURAL ENVIRONMENTS

The various cultural factors described earlier can exert important influences on consumer and industrial products marketing around the globe. These factors must be recognized in formulating a global marketing plan. **Environmental sensitivity** reflects the extent to which products must be adapted to the culture-specific needs of different national markets. A useful approach is to view products on a continuum of environmental sensitivity. At one end of the continuum

---

49 Hirokazu Takada and Dipak Jain, "Cross-National Analysis of Diffusion of Consumer Durable Goods in Pacific Rim Countries," *Journal of Marketing* 55 (April 1991), pp. 48–53.
50 Helmitt Schütte, "Asian Culture and the Global Consumer," *Financial Times—Mastering Marketing, Part Two,* September 21, 1998, p. 2

are environmentally insensitive products that do not require significant adaptation to the environments of various world markets. At the other end of the continuum are products that are highly sensitive to different environmental factors. A company with environmentally insensitive products will spend relatively less time determining the specific and unique conditions of local markets because the product is basically universal. The greater a product's environmental sensitivity, the greater the need for managers to address country-specific economic, regulatory, technological, social, and cultural environmental conditions.

The sensitivity of products can be represented on a two-dimensional scale as shown in Figure 4-3. The horizontal axis shows environmental sensitivity, the vertical axis shows the degree for product adaptation needed. Any product exhibiting low levels of environmental sensitivity—integrated circuits, for example—belongs in the lower left of the figure. Intel has sold more than 100 million microprocessors because a chip is a chip anywhere around the world. Moving to the right on the horizontal axis, the level of sensitivity increases, as does the amount of adaptation. Computers exhibit moderate levels of environmental sensitivity; variations in country voltage requirements require some adaptation. In addition, the computer's software documentation should be in the local language. At the upper right of Figure 4-3 are products with high environmental sensitivity. Food sometimes falls into this category because it is sensitive to climate and culture. As we saw in the McDonald's case at the end of Chapter 1, the fast-food giant has achieved great success outside the United States by adapting its menu items to local tastes. GE's turbine generating equipment may also appear on the high-sensitivity end of the continuum; in many countries, local equipment manufacturers receive preferential treatment when bidding on national projects.

Research studies show that, independent of social class and income, culture is a significant influence on consumption behavior and durable goods ownership.[51] Consumer products are probably more sensitive to cultural difference than are industrial products. Hunger is a basic physiological need in Maslow's

Figure 4-3

Environmental Sensitivity

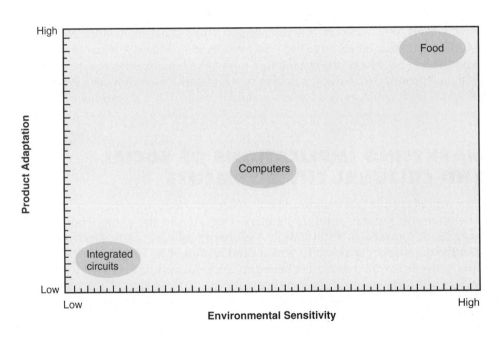

[51] Charles M. Schaninger, Jacques C. Bourgeois, and Christian W. Buss, "French-English Canadian Subcultural Consumption Differences," *Journal of Marketing* 49 (Spring 1985), pp. 82–92.

In countries where water from the tap or well may be contaminated, bottled water is a convenient alternative. The fastest growth in the industry is occurring in developing countries; in the past five years, bottled water consumption has tripled in India and more than doubled in China. Many consumers also choose bottled water as an alternative to other beverage choices. However, the Earth Policy Institute and other groups view bottled water as an overpriced, wasteful extravagance. The International Bottled Water Association disagrees with that view. A spokesman said, "We're an on-the-go society demanding convenient packaging and consistent quality, and that's what bottled water provides."

hierarchy; everyone needs to eat, but what we want to eat can be strongly influenced by culture. Evidence from the front lines of the marketing wars suggests that food is probably the most sensitive category of consumer products. CPC International failed to win popularity for Knorr dehydrated soups among Americans. The U.S. soup market was dominated by Campbell Soup Company; 90 percent of the soup consumed by households was canned. Knorr was a Swiss company acquired by CPC that had a major share of the European prepared food market, where bouillon and dehydrated soups account for 80 percent of consumer soup sales. Despite CPC's failure to change the soup-eating habits of Americans, the company (now called Bestfoods and a unit of Unilever) is a successful global marketer with operations in more than 60 countries and sales in 110 countries.

Thirst also shows how needs differ from wants. Hydration is a universal physiological need. As is the case with food and cooking, however, the particular liquids people *want* to drink can be strongly influenced by culture. Coffee is a beverage category that illustrates the point. On the European continent, coffee has been consumed for centuries. By contrast, Britain has historically been a nation of tea drinkers, and the notion of afternoon tea is firmly entrenched in British culture. In the 1970s, tea outsold coffee by a ratio of 4 to 1. Brits who did drink coffee tended to buy it in instant form because the preparation of instant is similar to that of tea. By the 1990s, however, Britain was experiencing an economic boom and an explosion of new nightclubs and restaurants. Trendy Londoners looking for a non-pub "third place" found it in the form of Seattle Coffee Company cafés. An instant success after the first store was opened by coffee-starved Americans in 1995, by 1998 Seattle Coffee had 55 locations around London. Starbucks bought the business from its founders for $84 million. By 2005, Starbucks had overcome the challenge of high real estate prices and had 466 locations in the United Kingdom.[52]

---

[52] Deborah Ball, "Lattes Lure Brits to Coffee," *The Wall Street Journal,* October 20, 2005, pp. B1, B6. See also Marco R. della Cava, "Brewing a British Coup," *USA Today,* September 16, 1998, pp. D1, D2.

Culture, a society's "programming of the mind," has both a pervasive and changing influence on each national market environment. Global marketers must recognize the influence of culture and be prepared to either respond to it or change it. Human behavior is a function of a person's own unique personality and that person's interaction with the collective forces of the particular society and culture in which he or she has lived. In particular, **attitudes**, **values**, and **beliefs** can vary significantly from country to country. Also, differences pertaining to **religion**, **aesthetics**, dietary customs, and language and communication can affect local reaction to a company's brands or products as well as the ability of company personnel to function effectively in different cultures. A number of concepts and theoretical frameworks provide insights into these and other cultural issues.

Cultures can be classified as **high-** or **low-context**; communication and negotiation styles can differ from country to country. Hofstede's **social values typology** helps marketers understand culture in terms of **power distance**, **individualism** versus **collectivism**, **masculinity** versus **femininity**, **uncertainty avoidance**, and **long-term** versus **short-term orientation**. By understanding the **self-reference criterion (SRC)**, global marketers can overcome the unconscious tendency for perceptual blockage and distortion. Rogers's classic study on the diffusion of innovations helps explain the product **adoption process** and the way products are adopted over time by different **adopter categories**. Rogers's findings concerning the **characteristics of innovations** can also help marketers successfully launch new products in global markets. Recent research has suggested that Asian adopter categories differ from the Western model. An awareness of **environmental sensitivity** can help marketers determine whether consumer and industry products must be adapted to the needs of different markets.

1. What are some of the elements that make up culture? How are these expressed in your native culture?

2. What is the difference between a low-context culture and a high-context culture? Give an example of a country that is an example of each type and provide evidence for your answer.

3. How can Hofstede's cultural typologies help Western marketers better understand Asian culture?

4. Explain the self-reference criterion. Find examples of product failures that might have been avoided through the application of the SRC.

5. Briefly explain the social research of Everett Rogers regarding the product adoption process, characteristics of innovations, and adopter categories. How does the adoption process in Asia differ from the traditional Western model?

6. Compare and contrast the United States and Japan in terms of traditions and organizational behavior and norms.

To better understand Hofstede's social values framework, interview a fellow student from another country. Develop a country cultural profile similar to the one for Denmark in this chapter.

John J. Miller and Mark Molesky, *Our Oldest Enemy* (New York: Doubleday, 2004).

What happens when the world's biggest brand collides with the world's largest religion?

Cola Wars: Message in a Bottle (Films for the Humanities & Sciences, 2004).

A 150-pound bag of coffee bans might earn a farmer in Latin America $50; the "street value" of that same bag—10,000 cups of coffee—is approximately $20,000.

Cappuccino Trail: The Global Economy in a Cup (Films for the Humanities & Sciences, 2002).

Case 4-1

Fair Trade Coffee: Ethics, Religion, and Sustainable Production

It's a basic law of economics: When supply goes up, price goes down. That is the situation facing the coffee industry today, as a glut of coffee beans led to sharply lower prices on world commodities markets. Historically, coffee has been one of the most lucrative exports in many developing nations. Green, unroasted coffee beans are traded on the London and New York futures markets; Volcafe and Neumann Gruppe are large coffee traders that buy about 25 percent of the world's coffee supply. Other major players include Procter & Gamble (P&G), Kraft, and Nestlé; all three are key suppliers to the grocery industry, where the greatest percentage of coffee is purchased. For example, P&G sells about $1 billion worth of Folgers coffee each year. Specialty coffees, such as those marketed by Starbucks, are regarded as niche products that account for only about 2 percent of the world's supply of coffee beans.

In 1999, the wholesale price for coffee was about $1.40 per pound; in 2001, the price dropped to $0.42. By the end of 2003, prices had recovered to about $0.50 per pound; however, the cost of producing and processing green coffee beans is between $0.80 and $0.90 per pound. Oversupply is another problem. Between 1990 and 2000, Vietnam's production soared from 84,000 tons to 950,000 tons; Vietnam produces mostly robusta beans, which are cheaper and have a harsher taste than arabica beans. According to the International Coffee Organization,

environmental and working conditions in developing countries. It was a pioneer in certifying lumber sourced from forests in the tropics. It certifies about $12.5 billion worth of coffee beans each year. The Fairtrade Labeling Organization International (FLO; www.fairtrade.net) is a certification authority based in Bonn, Germany, that licenses its trademark to organizations such as the U.K.'s Fairtrade Foundation (www.fairtrade.org.uk). The Fairtrade label on a bag or can of coffee indicates that growers were paid a fair price for their crops. TransFair USA is a fair-trade certification organization in the United States (www.transfairusa.org).

Coffee bearing the Fairtrade label is often marketed with the help of charitable organizations; for example, Oxfam, a private charity in Britain, joined with Equal Exchange, a fair trade distribution company, Traidcraft, and Twin, to create a new coffee brand called Cafédirect (www.cafedirect.co.uk). In addition to providing price supports, such organizations also sponsor training and development programs to help growers become more knowledgeable about market prices and learn ways to reach export markets. Catholic Relief Services (CRS) recently launched an effort to encourage America's 65 million Catholics to buy fair trade coffee (www. catholicrelief.org/coffee/trade). The CRS Coffee Project is part of a larger organization, the Interfaith Coffee Program of Equal Exchange; the latter includes participants from Lutheran, Presbyterian, and Methodist groups. The bottom line: Wholesale coffee buyers that participate in the fair trade program agree to pay farmers $1.26 per pound for regular coffee beans and $1.41 for higher quality, organic beans.

the 2001–2002 harvest yielded 115 million sacks of coffee. However, worldwide consumption only absorbed 105 million bags. Low prices and excess supply all add up to bad news for 25 million coffee farmers in Latin American and Africa.

Since the mid-1990s, Starbucks has pursued a policy of improving working conditions at its suppliers; however, Starbucks' annual coffee purchases amount to only about $180 million. A number of different nongovernmental organizations have begun to address the situation faced by farmers who supply the broader coffee market. For example, the Rainforest Alliance works with big corporations to monitor

The Fairtrade coffee movement is gaining momentum among socially conscious consumers. For example, in 2002, the interfaith partnership in the United States sold nearly $1.7 million of fair trade coffee at 7,500 houses of worship; sales in 2003 reached $2.7 million. Although impressive, that figure is a mere drop in the bucket; annually, Americans spend about $19 billion on coffee. However, as Paul Rice, President and CEO of Transfair, noted, "If we could get every Catholic in the country to drink fair-trade coffee, that would be a huge market right there." He added, "But it's the ripple effect— getting all those people kind of up to speed on what fair trade is all about and getting them to ask for it at their local stores—that's going to have a much broader effect on the market."

"We've been in this business for 100 years and want to be in it for another 100. . . . This is not philanthropy. This is about incorporating sustainable coffee into our mainstream brands as a way to have a more efficient and competitive way of doing business"

Annemieke Wijm, Senior Director for Commodity Sustainability Programs, Kraft Foods

Kraft recently signed an accord with the Rainforest Alliance; Kraft, which buys about 10 percent of the world's coffee crop, agreed to buy beans that are certified as produced with sustainable agricultural practices and blend them into their mass-market brands. The purchases will amount to about $3.1 billion annually and will benefit farmers in Brazil, Colombia, Mexico, and Central America. Tensie Whelen, executive director for the Rainforest Alliance, hailed the accord, noting, "This step by Kraft marks the beginning of transforming the coffee industry. You have a company capable of shaping markets commit to buying a significant amount of coffee and to mainstreaming across their brands and not 'ghettoising' it in one brand."

Meanwhile, industry experts disagree about ways to reduce the supply of low-quality beans. A recent Oxfam report recommended government financing to destroy 5 million bags of robusta beans currently being stored in warehouses in developing countries. Others would prefer not to ask for government intervention. Peter A. Reiling, president and chief executive of Technoserve, a nonprofit organization that promotes socially responsible entrepreneurship in developing countries, noted, "It's an emotional issue and everyone seems to have a different solution. I'd say there's no one silver bullet, but there are market solutions."

Discussion Questions

1. Is it important for coffee marketers, such as Starbucks, Kraft, and Nestlé, to create "ethical supply chains"? Why?

2. A recent study by the U.K.'s Institute of Grocery Distribution determined that the majority of consumers do not buy fair-trade products. The report noted, "Self-interest is at the center of food choice for most consumers. Few consumers consider the impact of their purchase decisions on anyone or anything but themselves and their family." Do you agree with this finding?

3. What recommendations would you make to help cure the ills of the coffee market?

Sources: Elizabeth Weise, "Fair Trade Sweetens Pot," *USA Today*, February 9, 2005, p. 6D; Mary Beth Marklein, "Goodness—To the Last Drop," *USA Today*, February 16, 2004, pp. 1D, 2D; Tony Smith, "Difficult Times for the Coffee Industry," *The New York Times*, November 25, 2003, p. W1; Sara Silver, "Kraft Blends Ethics with Coffee Beans," *Financial Times*, October 7, 2003, p. 10; Tim Harford, "Fairtrade Tries a Commercial Blend for Coffee," *Financial Times*, September 12, 2003, p. 10; In-Sung Yoo, "Faith Organizations Throw Weight Behind 'Fair Trade' Coffee Movement," *USA Today*, December 2, 2003, p. 7D; Peter Fritsche, "Bitter Brew: An Oversupply of Coffee Beans Deepens Latin America's Woes," *The Wall Street Journal*, July 8, 2002, pp. A1, A10.

Case 4-2

Barbie: Growing Pains as the American Girl Goes Global

In 1976, a time capsule was buried to commemorate the U.S. bicentennial. The capsule contained items that captured the essence of America and included a Barbie doll, described as the "quintessential American." Thirty years later, Barbie has become much more cosmopolitan. Although Mattel generates about 60 percent of its annual revenue in the U.S. market, millions of girls around the world have adopted Barbie as a favorite toy; Barbie is sold in more than 150 countries. Overall, Barbie is the best-selling toy brand in the world, and Mattel is the world's largest toy maker. However, as Barbie approaches her fiftieth birthday, the fashion doll's popularity is declining at home and abroad. For example, Bratz, a competing doll line featuring racing fashions, has exploded in popularity. By contrast, in the Middle East, the hottest-selling doll line, Fulla, is associated with Islamic values such as modesty and respect. Also, young girls are gravitating towards electronics devices such as digital music players. These and other trends spell trouble for Mattel, which depends on Barbie for about 20 percent of its annual sales.

What was the secret to Barbie's first several decades of success? Ruth Handler, Barbie's creator, believed that all children needed to play with mature dolls to effectively project their fantasies of growing up (Handler's children were named Barbie and Ken). Though Mattel's executives initially believed that a doll with a womanly bosom was improper and would never sell, Barbie became an instant success with American children.

Over time, Barbie's look has changed to reflect changing fashion and cultural trends. In 1968, for example, the first black Barbie was introduced to cater to the growing African-American market. Hispanic and Asian American Barbies have also been created in response to the growth of America's other ethnic markets. It was a natural step for the Mattel to target untapped groups of children in other parts of the world. A strategy dubbed "Mattel 2000" focused on the company's direction during the decade of the 1990s. As former CEO John Amerman noted,

"There are twice as many children in Europe as in the U.S. . . . three times as many in South America and fifteen times as many in Asia . . . the potential market for products like Barbie . . . is mind boggling." However, although Barbie has been successfully adapted to cultural differences in the United States, the opportunities for international growth come with formidable challenges. Even so, according to current CEO Robert Eckert, Mattel is "dedicated to becoming a truly global company."

Europe

Mattel adopted a pan-European, regiocentric approach to the Western European market. Barbie is a huge success in Europe; children in Italy, France, and Germany average five Barbie dolls in their toy collections. In the early 1990s, Mattel developed a new "Friendship Barbie" to sell in Central and Eastern Europe. The new doll was less elaborate than its Western European counterpart, which sports designer clothes and accessories. By contrast, Friendship Barbie reflects the more basic lifestyle children had experienced under communism. However, although Mattel has experimented with multicultural dolls, the company discovered that little girls in Europe prefer the well-known American Barbie to the local versions.

The Middle East

Since being introduced in the Middle East, Barbie has faced opposition on political, religious, and social grounds. Parents and religious leaders alike object to the cultural values that Barbie and Ken portray. Writing in the *Cairo Journal*, Douglas Jehl noted, "To put it plainly, the plastic icon of Western girlhood is seen in the Middle East, where modesty matters, as something of a tramp."

In Egypt and Iran, Barbie faces competition from several new doll brands aimed at providing an Islamic alternative to Barbie. As one Arab toy seller noted, "I think that Barbie is more harmful than an American missile." Barbie's challengers include demure-looking dolls such as Laila, who was designed according to recommendations of participants at the Arab League children's celebrations in 1998. Laila wears simple contemporary clothes such as a short-sleeve blouse and skirt and traditional Arab costumes. Abala Ibrahim, director of the Arab League's Department of Childhood, believes "there is a cultural gap when an Arab girl plays with a doll like Barbie . . . the average Arab girl's reality is different from Barbie's with her swimming pool, Cadillac, blond hair and boyfriend Ken."

Despite the cultural differences and a price equal to seven times the average monthly salary, Barbie has been highly successful in Iran. It remains to be seen whether Barbie, who is "forbidden by Islam," will struggle against new local competitors Sara and Dara, which have been created expressly to compete against Barbie. The dolls feature traditional clothing and headscarves and are available with family members, thus, reinforcing the importance of family for Iranian children. The dolls were launched in 2002 at prices about one-third of Barbie's.

Neither Laila nor Sara has achieved the popularity of Fulla, a doll named after the fragrance of the jasmine plant. Syria-based NewBoy Design Studio introduced Fulla in 2003. Packaged in a shiny pink box, Fulla dolls are clothed in modest "outdoor fashions." These include the hajib, or traditional headscarf, and a long gown known as an abaya; a pink prayer rug is included with each doll. As Fawaz Abidin, Fulla brand manager for NewBoy, explained, "This isn't just about putting the hijab on a Barbie doll. You have to create a character that parents and children will want to relate to. Our advertising is full of positive messages about Fulla's character. She's honest, loving, and caring, and she respects her father and mother."

Latin America

In Brazil, Barbie faces stiff competition from a cheaper local rival. Latin America was one of the first non-U.S. markets Barbie entered. Brazil is an important market for Mattel because dolls account for 37 percent of the country's annual $430 million in toy sales. However, Barbie has been losing market share to the Susi doll manufactured by Estrela, the company once licensed to distribute Barbie in Brazil. Due to Susi's overwhelming popularity, Estrela introduced Susi in Chile, Argentina, Paraguay, and Uruguay in 2000. Susi's success can be attributed to both a lower price and the inclusion of realistic Brazilian touches allowing Brazilian children to identify with Susi. Susi is a blond with a small chest and waist but wide thighs and dark skin, similar to Brazilian girls. Susi represents the philosophy that "young girls want dolls that show them as they are, not as they want to be."

Asia/Japan

Mattel has learned that, to be successful within a foreign culture, Barbie does not need a total overhaul but instead can be very profitable with minor cosmetic changes. For example, Barbie was successfully launched in India in 1995 and, while the core product remains unchanged, Indian dolls are painted with a head spot and dressed in a sari.

Mattel has had more difficulty conquering the world's second-largest toy market, Japan. The Japanese toy market is worth $8 billion in annual sales and is vital if Mattel is to achieve its goal of becoming more global. The Japanese market is notoriously difficult to penetrate as Mattel has found during 20 years of doing business in the country. Companies entering Japan must contend with complex distribution systems and intense competition from Japanese brands. Furthermore, dolls have a strong tradition in the Japanese culture with a heritage of over 800 years and ceremonial importance.

Mattel's initial attempts to market Barbie in Japan met with limited success. Management presumed that Barbie's success in other markets would be replicated in Japan. As John Amerman, CEO of Mattel in the mid-1990s, noted, "They didn't know what that product was, and it didn't work." To boost sales, Mattel enlisted the services of Takara, a Japanese toy specialist. Through focus groups, Mattel learned that Barbie's legs were too long and her chest too large—in short, Japanese girls didn't relate to Barbie's physical attributes. Also, Barbie's eyes were changed from blue to brown, and the doll ultimately took on a look that was appealing to the Japanese children's sense of aesthetics. The Takara Barbie was born.

Although sales improved, a licensing disagreement prompted Mattel to terminate the relationship with Takara and search for a new partner in Japan. Takara continued selling the doll as Jenny, which, ironically, became a competitor to the new Japanese Barbie. In 1986, Mattel joined forces with Bandai, Japan's largest toy company. Bandai produced Maba Barbies

("Ma" for Mattel and "ba" for Bandai) with wide brown eyes. Due to its similarities to the Jenny doll, however, Maba Barbie was withdrawn from the market before it achieved success. Maba was replaced by Bandai Barbies, which were again similar to Jenny, possessing the wide-eye look but wearing mainly ball gowns and unimaginative clothing.

Once again, market success eluded Mattel. Mattel was committed to neither Japanese style nor an American style and competed poorly against dolls whose identity was well defined. However, Mattel realized that its competitive advantage lay with its American culture. Though Mattel had attempted to adapt to the Japanese culture, Mattel discovered once again that girls prefer the well-known Barbie to the local versions. In 1991, Mattel ended its relationship with Bandai and opened its own marketing and sales office in Tokyo. Mattel introduced its American Barbie to Japan and experienced success with "Long Hair Star Barbie," which became one of the top-selling dolls in Japan. Although financial losses mounted until 1993, in 1994 Barbie made a profit in Japan with sales almost doubling since its reintroduction.

In 1999, Mattel refocused its Japanese efforts. Then-CEO Jill Barad promised to double Mattel's international sales within 5 years. To this end, a Japanese native named Sam Sugiyama was placed in charge of Mattel's Japanese operations; previously, American expatriates had held the position. Sugiyama stated that Mattel was "very anxious to do something quickly," understandable considering its past problems in the market. After almost 20 years of perseverance in Japan, it was imperative that Mattel improve its position. Therefore, the company joined forces once again with Bandai to form a marketing, sales, and product development alliance in an effort to tackle the complex Japanese distribution system. At the end of 2001, new CEO Robert Eckert reported that Mattel's strategic partnership with Bandai had "eliminated chronic operating losses" in Japan.

Mattel's Twenty-First-Century Challenge: Breathing New Life into Barbie

Writing in Mattel's 1999 *Annual Report*, acting CEO Ronald Loeb promised that the company "will proactively adapt its products to local tastes, economic conditions, and pricing, rather than viewing the rest of the world as an extension of our U.S. strategy." At the same time, Richard Dickson, senior vice president of Mattel's girl's consumer products worldwide, believed Barbie's global strategy must originate from a perspective of worldwide cohesion. He noted, "If I go on a plane from France to Japan to the United States and there's a Barbie billboard, you're going to sense that it's the same Barbie [in all three countries]." To facilitate its global approach, Mattel has given the U.S. president of Barbie the full responsibility for the brand around the world.

Even as Mattel executives tweaked the company's global strategy, a new competitive threat appeared on the home front. In 2001, MGA Entertainment—whose chief executive, ironically, is a native of Iran—introduced Bratz, a line of fashion dolls with oversized heads and a "street" attitude. In both the United States and Europe, they are most popular with girls 8 to 12 years old, a segment known as tweens. Within three years, global sales of Bratz dolls—in edgy black and purple

boxes—and merchandise totaled $2.5 billion. In 2003, alarmed that Barbie's share of the fashion doll market had dropped from 85 percent to 70 percent—a decline attributed largely to the success of Bratz—Mattel responded by rolling out its own line of trendy dolls for tweens called Flavas.

Mattel's management team was also faced with another critical decision. To rekindle Barbie's appeal to American girls under the age of 8, should they radically overhaul Barbie, and risk alienating young girls and their moms? Could such a proposal be embraced by Mattel's corporate culture? As one marketing consultant put it, "There's a depth that's missing from the Barbie brand. Mattel needs to build a foundation for this age and time. They need to ask 'What's my story? What is Barbie's new direction for the long term?'" Adds brand consultant Ken Markman, a former Mattel executive, "It's not a function of saving Barbie, it's a matter of recognizing what made her powerful to begin with and making that relevant today."

Discussion Questions

1. Describe Mattel's global marketing strategy for Barbie and assess its success. Does management demonstrate that it understands and embraces the need to "think global and act local"?

2. Approximately 90 percent of the world's children live in developing countries. Despite recent negative sales trends, Barbie remains the most popular toy in the world. What must Mattel do to capitalize on the strategic strength of the Barbie brand and take advantage of market opportunities around the globe?

3. How important is culture in dictating children's toy preferences? Will cultural differences result in failure for Mattel as the company faces new competitors in the Middle East?

4. Industry observers often refer to Barbie as an "icon." What does this mean? What should Mattel executives do to turn around sales of Barbie in the United States?

This is a revised and updated version of a case written by Alexandra Kennedy-Scott, David Henderson, and Michel Phan, ESSEC Business School. Used by permission. *Sources:* Edward Iwata, "How Barbie Is Making Business a Little Better," *USA Today*, March 27, 2006, pp. 1b, 2B; Michael Barbaro, "Breaking Up Was Hard to Do," *The New York Times*, February 9, 2006, pp. C1, C6; Souheila Al-Jadda, "Move over, Barbie," *USA Today*, December 14, 2005, p. 23A; T. L. Stanley, "Barbie Hits the Skids," *Advertising Age*, October 31, 2005, pp. 1, 33; Katherine Zoepf, "This Doll Has an Accessory Barbie Lacks: A Prayer Mat," *The New York Times*, September 22, 2005, p. A4; Queena Sook Kim and Ichiko Fuyuno, "Barbie's New Clothes," *The Wall Street Journal*, January 30, 2004, pp. B1, B3; Maureen Tkacik, "Dolled Up: To Lure Older Girls, Mattel Brings in Hip-Hop Crowd," *The Wall Street Journal*, July 18, 2003, pp. A1, A6; Richard Dickson, "Marketers of the Next Generation: Richard Dickson," *Brandweek*, April 8, 2002, p. 30; David Finnigan, "Mattel Dolls Up Barbie 'Nutcracker' with a Little Help from McD, CBS," *Brandweek*, July 16, 2001, p. 6; Jan Golab, "King Barbie: How I Gussied Up America's Favorite Toy and Turned My Struggling Company into a Megatoyopoly," *Los Angeles Magazine*, August 1, 1994, p. 66; Lawrence B. Chonko, "Case Study: Alliance Formation with Direct Selling Companies: Avon and Mattel," *Journal of Personal Selling & Sales Management* 19, no. 1 (Winter 1999), p. 6; "Big Game Hunting," *Economist*, April 17, 1999, p. 68; Mattel Inc. *Annual Report* (various years).

5

The Political, Legal, and Regulatory Environments of Global Marketing

n 1998, Sun Microsystems filed a lawsuit in U.S. Federal court alleging that Microsoft was restricting the ability of servers marketed by Sun and other companies to interface with PCs running the Windows operating system. More than 90 percent of the world's PCs run Windows as well as other Microsoft software; some of Microsoft's rivals believe the company uses unfair business practices to dominate the global software market. Although Microsoft settled the U.S. case in 2001, the European Commission had also begun to investigate Sun's complaint; the Commission also launched a separate investigation to determine whether Microsoft was creating a monopoly in digital music downloads and other new market segments by bundling Windows with its Media Player program. The Commission finally issued a ruling in spring 2004 that Microsoft had violated antitrust laws. Three penalties were imposed. First, Microsoft must allow computer makers to market Windows-equipped PCs equipped with alternative brands of media software for playing music and videos. Second, Microsoft must provide competitors with more information about Windows codes and protocols—spurring innovation in new software products. Finally, Microsoft was ordered to pay a record fine of $602 million.

The Microsoft case illustrates the impact that the political, legal, and regulatory environments can have on international trade and global marketing activities. Each of the world's national governments regulates trade and commerce with other countries and attempts to control the access of outside enterprises to national resources. Every country has its own unique legal and regulatory system that affects the operations and activities of the global enterprise, including the global marketer's ability to address market opportunities and threats. Laws and regulations constrain the cross-border movement of products, services, people, money, and know-how. The global marketer must attempt to comply with each set of national—and, in some instances, regional—constraints. The fact that laws and regulations are frequently ambiguous and continually changing hamper these efforts.

In this chapter, we consider the basic elements of the political, legal, and regulatory environments of global marketing, including the most pressing current issues and some suggested approaches for dealing with those issues. Some specific topics, such as rules for exporting and importing industrial and consumer products, standards for health and safety, and regulations regarding packaging, labeling, advertising, and promotion, are covered in later chapters devoted to individual marketing mix elements.

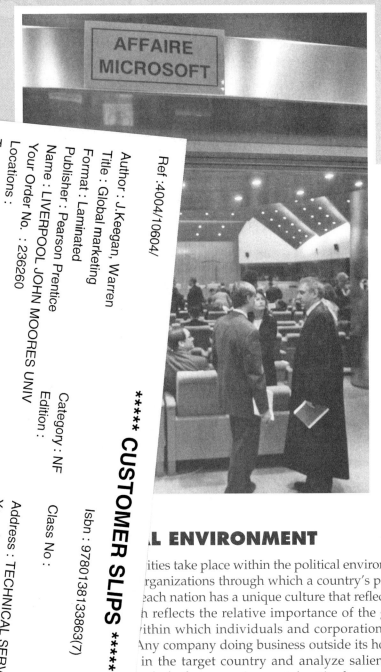

Following an antitrust ruling in 2004, Microsoft created Windows XP Edition N, an "unbundled" operating system for the European market that does not include the company's Media Player. In spring 2006, attorneys for Microsoft and the European Commission appeared before a 13-judge panel at the European Court of First Instance in Luxembourg. Microsoft's lawyers argued that negligible sales of Edition N constitute evidence that the 2004 ruling was a failure. In September 2007, the Court of First Instance upheld the European Commission's case against the software giant. Microsoft now has the option of appealing the case to the European Court of Justice.

AL ENVIRONMENT

...ities take place within the political environment of governmental institutions,
...rganizations through which a country's people and rulers exercise power. As
...each nation has a unique culture that reflects its society. Each nation also has a
...h reflects the relative importance of the government and legal system and
...ithin which individuals and corporations understand their relationship to
...Any company doing business outside its home country should carefully study
...in the target country and analyze salient issues arising from the political
...include the governing party's attitude toward sovereignty, political risk, taxes,
...ilution, and expropriation.

es and Sovereignty

...e defined as supreme and independent political authority. A century ago, U.S.
...hief Justice Melville Fuller said, "Every sovereign state is bound to respect the
...very other sovereign state, and the courts in one country will not sit in judgment
...ernment of another done within its territory." More recently, Richard Stanley,
...tanley Foundation, offered the following concise description:

...ate was considered free and independent. It regulated trade, managed the flow of
...d out of its boundaries, and exercised undivided jurisdiction over all persons and
...n its territory. It had the right, authority, and ability to conduct its domestic affairs
...e interference and to use its international power and influence with full discretion.[1]

---

[1] See *Changing Concepts of Sovereignty: Can the United Nations Keep Pace?* (Muscatine, IA: The Stanley Foundation, 1992), p. 7.

Government actions taken in the name of sovereignty occur in the context of two important criteria: a country's stage of development and the political and economic system in place in the country.

As outlined in Chapter 2, the economies of individual nations may be classified as industrialized, newly industrializing, or developing. Many governments in developing countries exercise control over their nations' economic development by passing protectionist laws and regulations. Their objective is to encourage economic development by protecting emerging or strategic industries. Government leaders can also engage in cronyism and provide favors for family members or "good friends." For example, former Indonesian president Suharto established a national car program that granted tax breaks and tariff privileges to a company established in South Korea by his youngest son. The United States, EU, and Japan responded by taking the matter to the WTO. Conversely, when many nations reach advanced stages of economic development, their governments declare that (in theory, at least) any practice or policy that restrains free trade is illegal. Antitrust laws and regulations are established to promote fair competition. Advanced country laws often define and preserve a nation's social order; laws may extend to political, cultural, and even intellectual activities and social conduct. In France, for example, laws forbid the use of foreign words such as *le weekend* or *le marketing* in official documents. Also, a French law passed in 1996 requires that at least 40 percent of the songs played by popular radio stations must be French.

We also noted in Chapter 2 that most of the world's economies combine elements of market and nonmarket systems. The sovereign political power of a government in a predominantly nonmarket economy reaches quite far into the economic life of a country. By contrast, in a capitalist, market-oriented democracy, that power tends to be much more constrained. A current global phenomenon in both nonmarket and market structures is the trend toward privatization, which reduces direct governmental involvement as a supplier of goods and services in a given economy. In essence, each act of privatization moves a nation's economy further in the free-market direction. The trend is clearly evident in Mexico, where, at one time, the government controlled over 1,000 "parastatals." By the early 1990s, most had been sold, as President Carlos Salinas de Gortari presided over the sale of full or partial stakes in enterprises worth $23 billion, including the two Mexican airlines, mines, and banks. Privatization in Mexico and elsewhere is evidence that national governments are changing *how* they exercise sovereign power.

Some observers believe global market integration is eroding national economic sovereignty. Economic consultant Neal Soss notes, "The ultimate resource of a government is power, and we've seen repeatedly that the willpower of governments can be overcome by persistent attacks from the marketplace."[2] Is this a disturbing trend? If the issue is framed in terms of marketing, the concept of the exchange comes to the fore: Nations may be willing to give up sovereignty in return for something of value. If countries can increase their share of world trade and increase national income, perhaps they will be willing to cede some sovereignty. In Europe, the individual EU countries are giving up the right to have their own currencies, ceding the right to set their own product standards, and are making other sacrifices in exchange for improved market access.

Political Risk

Political risk is the possibility of a change in a country's political environment or government policy that would adversely affect a company's ability to

---

[2] Cited in Karen Pennar, "Is the Nation-State Obsolete in a Global Economy?" *Business Week,* July 17, 1995, p. 80.

Mobil, AIG, and many other companies use corporate advertising to advocate their official position on trade-related issues. In the mid-1990s, Mobil mounted an ad campaign that addressed a number of topics of public interest, including trade issues, clean air, alternative fuels, and health care reform. This ad urges the U.S. Congress to approve GATT.

operate effectively and profitably. As Ethan Kapstein, a professor at INSEAD, has noted:

> Perhaps the greatest threats to the operations of global corporations, and those that are most difficult to manage, arise out of the political environment in which they conduct their business. One day, a foreign company is a welcome member of the local community; the next day, opportunistic politicians vilify it.[3]

Political risk can deter a company from investing abroad; to put it another way, when a high level of uncertainty characterizes a country's political environment, that country may have difficulty in attracting foreign investment. However, as Professor Kapstein points out, executives often fail to conceptualize political risk because they have not studied political science. For this reason, they have not been exposed to the issues that students of politics ask about the activities of global companies. (A strong argument for a liberal arts education!) Current events must be part of the information agenda; for example, businesspeople need to stay apprised of the formation and evolution of political parties. Valuable sources of information include *The Economist*, *Financial Times*, and other business periodicals.

---

[3] Ethan Kapstein, "Avoiding Unrest in a Volatile Environment," *Financial Times—Mastering Uncertainty, Part I*, March 17, 2006, p. 5.

The Economist Intelligence Unit (EIU; www.eiu.com), the Geneva-based Business Environment Risk Intelligence (BERI SA; www.beri.com), and the PRS Group (www.prsgroup.com) publish up-to-date political risk reports on individual country markets. These commercial sources vary somewhat in the criteria that constitute political risk. For example, BERI focuses on societal and system attributes, whereas PRS Group focuses more directly on government actions and economic functions (see Table 5-1).

For example, the political maneuverings of former president Boris Yeltsin's government in Russia created a high level of political risk. Vladimir Putin, Yeltsin's successor, is implementing reforms in an effort to pave the way for Russia's membership in the WTO and to attract foreign investment. The government has a number of bills pending that, if adopted, will strengthen intellectual property and contract law. Medium-term prospects for the transformation of the Russian market appear good. However, as Roland Nash, a Moscow-based investment banker, recently noted, "Political risk is still perceived as being very high here. As an investor in Russia, you have to believe in Putin. You still really can't believe in the rule of law."[4] The current political climate in the rest of Central and Eastern Europe is still characterized by varying degrees of uncertainty. Hungary, Latvia, and Albania represent three different levels of risk. Hungary and Latvia have already achieved upper-middle-income status, although Latvia is projected to grow more slowly. In Albania, the transition to a market economy has been hampered by an ongoing feud between the country's socialist prime minister and the leader of the opposition Democratic party.[5] Diligent attention to risk

Table 5-1 *Categories of Political Risk*	EIU	Business Environment Risk Intelligence (BERI)	PRS Group World Political Risk Forecasts
	War	Fractionalization of the political spectrum	Political turmoil probability
	Social unrest	Fractionalization by language, ethnic, and/or religious groups	Equity restrictions
	Orderly political transfer	Restrictive/coercive measures required to retain power	Local operations restrictions
	Politically motivated violence	Mentality (xenophobia, nationalism, corruption, nepotism)	Taxation discrimination
	International disputes	Social conditions (including population density and wealth distribution)	Repatriation restrictions
	Change in government/pro-business orientation	Organization and strength of forces for a radical government	Exchange controls
	Institutional effectiveness	Dependence on and/or importance to a major hostile power	Tariff barriers
	Bureaucracy	Negative influences of regional political forces	Other barriers
	Transparency or fairness	Societal conflict involving demonstrations, strikes, and street violence	Payment delays
	Corruption	Instability as perceived by assassinations and guerilla war	Fiscal or monetary expansion
	Crime		Labor costs
			Foreign debt

Source: Adapted from Llewellyn D. Howell, *The Handbook of Country and Political Risk Analysis*, 2nd ed. (Syracuse, NY: PRS Group, 1998).

[4] David Lynch, "Russia Brings Revitalized Economy to the Table," *USA Today*, July 13, 2006, p. 2B.
[5] Leyla Boulton, "Political Discord Slows EU March," *Financial Times—Albania: Special Report*, May 18, 2004, p. 22.

the rest of the story

Microsoft had taken the offensive by paying $3 billion to Sun, Novell, and RealNetworks to drop their charges in both the United States and the EU. Meanwhile, some regulators suggested that Microsoft was intentionally delaying compliance with the commission's orders. A key task was to produce an instruction manual that would help rival companies write Windows-compatible software. Microsoft took the position that doing so amounted to revealing intellectual property. The manual would be especially helpful to companies that service the low-cost, open-source operating system known as Linux. Microsoft views Linux as a threat to its business model, since Microsoft generates revenues by charging licensing fees. Both copyright and patent law protect Windows' source code.

Taking the legal notion of "disclosure" to an extreme, Microsoft sent the regulators boxes containing thousands of pages of documents pertaining to the manual. After the EU complained, Microsoft sent a lawyer to help sift through the documents. When engineers from Sun, Oracle, Novell, and IBM went to Microsoft headquarters to view the 12,000-page manual, security was tight. The visitors concluded that the manual was disorganized and of no use. The commission ordered Microsoft to improve the manual.

Meanwhile, Neelie Kroes, a former Dutch cabinet minister, became the European commissioner for competition. She met with Microsoft CEO Steve Ballmer to try to settle the matter, but to no avail. After an outside technical consultant determined that the manual was still inadequate, the commissioner formally charged Microsoft with disregarding orders. Microsoft countered that the commission had not made clear exactly what kind of documentation was to be produced.

In July 2006, the commission fined Microsoft an additional €280.5 million for failing to comply with the 2004 antitrust ruling. Kroes also indicated that the precedents in the case would be applied to Vista, Microsoft's forthcoming replacement for Windows. In particular, the concern is that Vista will be bundled with Internet search software that would be an alternative to Google as well as a fixed document reader similar to Adobe Acrobat.

Sources: Tobias Buck, "Microsoft Closer to European Truce," Financial Times, July 13, 2006, p. 14; Mary Jacoby, "EU Hits Microsoft with $358.3 Million Penalty," The Wall Street Journal, July 13, 2006, p. A3; Mary Jacoby, "Second Front: Why Microsoft Battles Europe Years After Settling with U.S.," The Wall Street Journal, May 5, 2006, pp. p. A1, A12; Adam Cohen, "Microsoft Faces Threat of More Fines in Europe," The Wall Street Journal, February 15, 2006, p. B2; Brandon Mitchener, "EU Backs Plans to Punish Microsoft," The Wall Street Journal, March 6, 2004, p. B3; Mitchener, James Kanter, and Don Clark, "Regulatory Jolt: EU Warns Microsoft Is Abusing Its Control of Certain Software," The Wall Street Journal, August 7, 2003, pp. A1, A2.

assessment throughout the region should be ongoing to determine when the risk has decreased to levels acceptable to management.

Companies can purchase insurance to offset potential risks arising from the political environment. In Japan, Germany, France, Britain, the United States, and other industrialized nations, various agencies offer investment insurance to corporations doing business abroad. The OPIC (www.opic.gov) provides various types of political risk insurance to U.S. companies; in Canada, the Export Development Corporation performs a similar function. OPIC's activities came under scrutiny in 1997 when the Clinton administration proposed reauthorizing it, along with the Ex-Im Bank. Some legislators wanted to dismantle both agencies as part of an effort to reduce government involvement in business. These legislators criticized the agencies for providing unnecessary subsidies to large corporations.[6]

Taxes

Governments rely on tax revenues to generate funds necessary for social services, the military, and other expenditures. Unfortunately, government taxation policies on the sale of goods and services frequently motivate companies and individuals to profit by *not* paying taxes. In China, import duties have dropped since the country joined the WTO. Even so, many goods are still subject to double-digit duties plus a 17 percent value-added tax. As a result, significant quantities of oil, cigarettes, photographic film, personal computers, and other products are smuggled into China. In some instances, customs documents are

---

[6]   Nancy Dunne, "Ex-Im Bank and Opic Face Survival Test in U.S." *Financial Times*, May 8, 1997, p. 8.

BRIC Briefing Book

falsified to undercount goods in a shipment; the Chinese military has allegedly escorted goods into the country as well. Ironically, global companies can still profit from the practice; it has been estimated, for example, that 90 percent of the foreign cigarettes sold in China are smuggled in. For Philip Morris, this means annual sales of $100 million to distributors in Hong Kong, who then smuggle the smokes across the border.[7] High excise and VAT taxes can also encourage legal cross-border shopping as consumers go abroad in search of good values. In Great Britain, for example, the Wine and Spirit Association estimates that, on average, cars returning from France are loaded with 80 bottles of wine.

Corporate taxation is another issue. The high level of political risk currently evident in Russia can be attributed in part to excessively high taxes on business operations. High taxes encourage many enterprises to engage in cash or barter transactions that are off the books and sheltered from the eyes of tax authorities. This, in turn, has created a liquidity squeeze that prevents companies from paying wages to employees; unpaid, disgruntled workers can contribute to political instability. Meanwhile, the Putin government is pursuing a tough new tax policy in an effort to shrink Russia's budget deficit and qualify for IMF loans. However, such policies should not have the effect of deterring foreign investment. As Bruce Bean, head of the American Chamber of Commerce in Moscow, summed up the situation:

> Change the name of the country, change the flag, change the border. Yes, this was done overnight. But build a market economy, introduce a meaningful tax system, create new accounting rules, accept the concept that companies which cannot compete should go bankrupt and the workers there lose their jobs? These things take time.[8]

Meanwhile, global companies are being caught up in the chaos. In July 1998, tax collectors seized dozens of automobiles belonging to Johnson & Johnson's (J&J) Russian division and froze the group's assets. The authorities claimed J&J owed $19 million in back taxes.

The diverse geographical activity of the global corporation also requires special attention to tax laws. Many companies make efforts to minimize their tax liability by shifting the location of income. For example, it has been estimated that tax minimization by foreign companies doing business in the United States costs the U.S. government $3 billion each year in lost revenue. In one approach, called "earnings stripping," foreign companies reduce earnings by making loans to U.S. affiliates rather than using direct investment to finance U.S. activities. The U.S. subsidiary can deduct the interest it pays on such loans and thereby reduce its tax burden.

---

[7] Craig S. Smith and Wayne Arnold, "China's Antismuggling Drive to Hurt U.S. Exporters That Support Crackdown," *The Wall Street Journal*, August 5, 1998, p. A12.

[8] Andrew Higgins, "Go Figure: At Russian Companies, Hard Numbers Often Hard to Come By," *The Wall Street Journal*, August 20, 1998, p. A9.

Seizure of Assets

The ultimate threat a government can pose toward a company is seizing assets. **Expropriation** refers to governmental action to dispossess a foreign company or investor. Compensation is generally provided, although not often in the "prompt, effective, and adequate" manner provided for by international standard. If no compensation is provided, the action is referred to as **confiscation**.[9] International law is generally interpreted as prohibiting any act by a government to take foreign property without compensation. **Nationalization** is generally broader in scope than expropriation; it occurs when the government takes control of some or all of the enterprises in a particular industry. International law recognizes nationalization as a legitimate exercise of government power, as long as the act satisfies a "public purpose" and is accompanied by "adequate payment" (i.e., one that reflects fair market value of the property). In 1959, for example, the newly empowered Castro government nationalized property belonging to American sugar producers in retaliation for new American import quotas on sugar. Cuban-owned production sources were not nationalized. Castro offered compensation in the form of Cuban government bonds, which was adequate under Cuban law. The U.S. State Department viewed the particular act of nationalization as discriminatory and the compensation offered as inadequate.[10] More recently, South Korea nationalized Kia, the nation's number three automaker, in the wake of the Asian currency crisis. Some industry observers believe that a much-needed reform of Japan's banking system will require nationalization.

Short of outright expropriation or nationalization, the phrase *creeping expropriation* has been applied to limitations on economic activities of foreign firms in particular countries. These have included limitations on repatriation of profits, dividends, royalties, and technical assistance fees from local investments or technology arrangements. Other issues are increased local content requirements, quotas for hiring local nationals, price controls, and other restrictions affecting return on investment. Global companies have also suffered discriminatory tariffs and nontariff barriers that limit market entry of certain industrial and consumer goods, as well as discriminatory laws on patents and trademarks. Intellectual property restrictions have had the practical effect of eliminating or drastically reducing protection of pharmaceutical products.

In April 1997, for example, the Canadian government banned a gasoline additive known as MMT. The U.S.-based Ethyl Corporation is the world's sole manufacturer of MMT. Ethyl sued the Canadian government for $231 million, citing the "expropriation and compensation" rule in the NAFTA agreement. In essence, Ethyl claimed that the Canadian government's ban had the effect of restricting Ethyl's ability to make a profit and, thus, constituted an expropriation of assets.

In the mid-1970s, J&J and other foreign investors in India had to submit to a host of government regulations to retain majority equity positions in companies already established. Many of these rules were later copied in whole or in part by Malaysia, Indonesia, the Philippines, Nigeria, and Brazil. By the late 1980s, after a "lost decade" in Latin America characterized by debt crises and low GNP growth, lawmakers reversed many of these restrictive and discriminatory laws. The goal was to again attract foreign direct investment and badly needed Western technology. The end of the Cold War and restructuring of political allegiances contributed significantly to these changes.

---

[9] Franklin R. Root, *Entry Strategies for International Markets* (New York: Lexington Books, 1994), p. 154.

[10] William R. Slomanson, *Fundamental Perspectives on International Law* (St. Paul, MN: West Publishing, 1990), p. 356.

When governments expropriate foreign property, there are impediments to action to reclaim that property. For example, according to the U.S. Act of State Doctrine, if the government of a foreign state is involved in a specific act, the U.S. court will not get involved. Representatives of expropriated companies may seek recourse through arbitration at the World Bank Investment Dispute Settlement Center. It is also possible to buy expropriation insurance from either a private company or a government agency such as OPIC. The expropriation of copper companies operating in Chile in 1970 to 1971 shows the impact that companies can have on their own fate. Companies that strenuously resisted government efforts to introduce home-country nationals into the company management were expropriated outright; other companies that made genuine efforts to follow Chilean guidelines were allowed to remain under joint Chilean-U.S. management.

INTERNATIONAL LAW

International law may be defined as the rules and principles that nation-states consider binding upon themselves. International law pertains to property, trade, immigration, and other areas that have traditionally been under the jurisdiction of individual nations. International law applies only to the extent that countries are willing to assume all rights and obligations in these areas. The roots of modern international law can be traced back to the seventeenth century Peace of Westphalia. Early international law was concerned with waging war, establishing peace, and other political issues such as diplomatic recognition of new national entities and governments. Although elaborate international rules gradually emerged—covering, for example, the status of neutral nations—the creation of laws governing commerce proceeded on a state-by-state basis in the nineteenth century. International law still has the function of upholding order, although in a broader sense than dealing with problems arising from war. At first, international law was essentially an amalgam of treaties, covenants, codes, and agreements. As trade grew among nations, order in commercial affairs assumed increasing importance. The law had originally dealt only with nations as entities, but a growing body of law rejected the idea that only nations can be subject to international law.

Paralleling the expanding body of international case law in the twentieth century, new international judiciary organizations have contributed to the creation of an established rule of international law: The Permanent Court of International Justice (1920–1945); the International Court of Justice (ICJ; www.icj-cij.org), the judicial arm of the United Nations, founded in 1946; and the International Law Commission, established by the United States in 1947. Disputes arising between nations are issues of **public international law**, and they may be taken before the ICJ or the World Court, located in The Hague. As described in the supplemental documents to the United Nations Charter, article 38 of the ICJ Statute concerns international law:

> The Court, whose function is to decide in accordance with international law such disputes as are submitted to it, shall apply:
>
> a. international conventions, whether general or particular, establishing rules expressly recognized by the contesting states;
> b. international custom, as evidence of a general practice accepted as law;
> c. the general principles of law recognized by civilized nations;
> d. subject to the provisions of Article 59, judicial decisions and the teachings of the most highly qualified publicists of the various nations, as subsidiary means for the determination of rules of law.

Other sources of modern international law include treaties, international customs, judicial case decisions in the courts of law of various nations, and scholarly writings. What happens if a nation has allowed a case against it to be brought before the ICJ and then refuses to accept a judgment against it? The plaintiff nation can seek recourse through the United Nations Security Council, which can use its full range of powers to enforce the judgment.

Common Law Versus Civil Law

Private international law is the body of law that applies to disputes arising from commercial transactions between companies of different nations. As noted, laws governing commerce emerged gradually, leading to a major split in legal systems between various countries.[11] The story of law in the Western world can be traced to two sources: Rome, from which the continental European civil law tradition originated, and English common law, from which the U.S. legal system originated.

A **civil-law country** is one in which the legal system reflects the structural concepts and principles of the Roman Empire in the sixth century.

> For complex historical reasons, Roman law was received differently and at vastly different times in various regions of Europe, and in the nineteenth century each European country made a new start and adopted its own set of national private-law codes, for which the *Code Napoleon* of 1804 was the prototype. But the new national codes drew largely on Roman law in conceptual structure and substantive content. In civil-law countries, the codes in which private law is cast are formulated in broad general terms and are thought of as completely comprehensive, that, is, as the all-inclusive source of authority by reference to which every disputed case must be referred for decision.[12]

In a **common-law country**, many disputes are decided by reliance on the authority of past judicial decisions (cases). Although much of contemporary American

---

[11] Much of the material in this section is adapted from Randall Kelso and Charles D. Kelso, *Studying Law: An Introduction* (St. Paul, MN: West Publishing, 1984).
[12] Harry Jones, "Our Uncommon Common Law," *Tennessee Law Review* 30 (1975), p. 447.

and English law is legislative in origin, the law inferred from past judicial decisions is equal in importance to the law set down in codes. Common-law countries often rely on codification in certain areas—the U.S. Uniform Commercial Code is one example—but these codes are not the all-inclusive, systematic statements found in civil-law countries.

The Uniform Commercial Code (UCC), fully adopted by 49 U.S. states, codifies a body of specifically designed rules covering commercial conduct. (Louisiana has adopted parts of the UCC, but its laws are still heavily influenced by the French civil code.) The host country's legal system—that is, common or civil law—directly affects the form a legal business entity will take. In common-law countries, companies are legally incorporated by state authority. In civil-law countries, a contract between two or more parties, who are fully liable for the actions of the company forms companies.

The United States, 9 of Canada's 10 provinces, and other former colonies with an Anglo-Saxon history, founded their systems on common law. Historically, much of continental Europe was influenced by Roman law and, later, the Napoleonic Code. Asian countries are split: India, Pakistan, Malaysia, Singapore, and Hong Kong are common-law jurisdictions. Japan, Korea, Thailand, Indochina, Taiwan, Indonesia, and China are civil-law jurisdictions. The legal systems in Scandinavia are mixed, displaying some civil-law attributes and some common-law attributes. Today, the majority of countries have legal systems based on civil-law traditions.

As various countries in Eastern and Central Europe wrestle with establishing legal systems in the post-Communist era, a struggle of sorts has broken out; consultants representing both common-law and civil-law countries are trying to influence the process. In much of Central Europe, including Poland, Hungary, and the Czech Republic, the German civil-law tradition prevails. As a result, banks not only take deposits and make loans but also engage in the buying and selling of securities. In Eastern Europe, particularly Russia, the United States has had greater influence. Germany has accused the United States of promoting a system so complex that it requires legions of lawyers. The U.S. response is that the German system is outdated.[13] In any event, the constant stream of laws and decrees issued by the Russian government creates an unpredictable, evolving legal environment. Specialized publications such as *The Russian and Commonwealth Business Law Report* are important resources for anyone doing business in Russia or the CIS.

Islamic Law

The legal system in many Middle Eastern countries is identified with the laws of Islam, which are associated with "the one and only one God, the Almighty."[14] In **Islamic law**, the *sharia* is a comprehensive code governing Muslim conduct in all areas of life, including business. The code is derived from two sources. First is the Koran, the Holy Book written in Arabic that is a record of the revelations made to the Prophet Mohammed by Allah. The second source is the Hadith, which is based on the life, sayings, and practices of Muhammad. In particular, the Hadith spells out the products and practices that are *haram* ("forbidden"). The orders and instructions found in the Koran are analogous to code laws; the guidelines of the Hadith correspond to common law. Any Westerner doing business in Malaysia in the Middle East should have, at minimum, a rudimentary

---

[13] Mark M. Nelson, "Two Styles of Business Vie in East Europe," *The Wall Street Journal*, April 3, 1995, p. A14.
[14] This section is adapted from Mushtaq Luqmani, Ugur Yavas, and Zahir Quraeshi, "Advertising in Saudi Arabia: Content and Regulation," *International Marketing Review* 6, no. 1 (1989), pp. 61–63.

understanding of Islamic law and its implications for commercial activities. Brewers, for example, must refrain from advertising beer on billboards or in local-language newspapers.

SIDESTEPPING LEGAL PROBLEMS: IMPORTANT BUSINESS ISSUES

Clearly, the global legal environment is very dynamic and complex. Therefore, the best course to follow is to get expert legal help. However, the astute, proactive marketer can do a great deal to prevent conflicts from arising in the first place, especially concerning issues such as jurisdiction, patents and trademarks, antitrust, licensing and trade secrets, bribery, and advertising and other promotion tools. Chapters 13 and 14 discuss regulation of specific promotion activities.

Jurisdiction

Company personnel working abroad should understand the extent to which they are subject to the jurisdiction of host-country courts. **Jurisdiction** pertains to global marketing insofar as it concerns a court's authority to rule on particular types of issues arising outside of a nation's borders or to exercise power over individuals or entities from different countries. Employees of foreign companies working in the United States must understand that courts have jurisdiction to the extent that the company can be demonstrated to be doing business in the state in which the court sits. The court may examine whether the foreign company maintains an office, solicits business, maintains bank accounts or other property, or has agents or other employees in the state in question. In a recent case, Revlon sued United Overseas Limited (UOL) in U.S. District Court for the Southern District of New York. Revlon charged the British company with breach of contract, contending that UOL had failed to purchase some specialty shampoos as agreed. Claiming lack of jurisdiction, UOL asked the court to dismiss the complaint. Revlon countered with the argument that UOL was, in fact, subject to the court's jurisdiction; Revlon cited the presence of a UOL sign above the entrance to the offices of a New York company in which UOL had a 50 percent ownership interest. The court denied UOL's motion to dismiss.[15]

Jurisdiction played an important role in two recent trade-related disputes. One pitted Volkswagen AG against General Motors. After GM's worldwide head of purchasing, José Ignacio López de Arriortúa, was hired by Volkswagen in 1992, his former employer accused him of taking trade secrets. Volkswagen accepted U.S. court jurisdiction in the dispute, although the company's lawyers requested that the U.S. District Court in Detroit transfer the case to Germany. Jurisdiction was also an issue in a trade dispute that pitted Eastman Kodak against Fuji Photo Film. Kodak alleged that the Japanese government helped Fuji in Japan by blocking the distribution of Kodak film. The U.S. government turned the case over to the WTO, despite the opinion expressed by many experts that the WTO lacks jurisdiction in complaints over trade and competition policy.

Intellectual Property: Patents, Trademarks, and Copyrights

Patents and trademarks that are protected in one country are not necessarily protected in another, so global marketers must ensure that patents and trademarks are registered in each country where business is conducted. A **patent** is a formal legal document that gives an inventor the exclusive right to make, use, and sell an invention for a specified period of time. Typically, the invention represents an "inventive leap" that is "novel" or "nonobvious." A **trademark** is defined as a distinctive mark, motto, device, or emblem that a manufacturer affixes to a particular product or package to distinguish it from goods produced by other manufacturers.

challenges in the global marketplace

Copyright Infringement

Tom Waits is an American music original: His distinctive vocal style—a gravelly growl—and songs about losers and dreams have endeared him to his fans. Within the music industry, Waits is distinctive for another reason: Unlike a growing number of musicians, he refuses to license his songs to marketers for use in broadcast commercials. In addition, he aggressively pursues lawsuits against marketers who use "ringers"—soundalikes—in their advertising.

Twenty years ago, Waits sued Frito-Lay for using a soundalike in a Doritos ad; he was awarded $2.5 million. Recently, the singer has pursued global marketers. For example, he sued Volkswagen's Audi division for a TV commercial that aired in Spain; Waits claimed that the music ripped off his song "Innocent When You Dream" and that the vocalist imitated his vocal style. An appeals court in Barcelona awarded Waits $43,000 for copyright infringement and $36,000 for violation of his "moral rights as an artist."

Waits says he does not mind it when another singer imitates him as a form of artistic expression. As Waits explains, "I make a distinction between people who use the voice as a creative item and people who are selling cigarettes and underwear. It's a big difference. We all know the difference. And it's stealing. They get a lot out of standing next to me, and I just get big legal bills."

Source: Ben Sisario, "Still Fighting for the Right to His Voice," The New York Times, January 20, 2006, p. B3. Copyright © 2006 by The New York Times Co. Reprinted with permission.

---

[15] Joseph Ortego and Josh Kardisch, "Foreign Companies Can Limit the Risk of Being Subject to U.S. Courts," *National Law Journal* 17, no. 3 (September 19, 1994), p. C2.

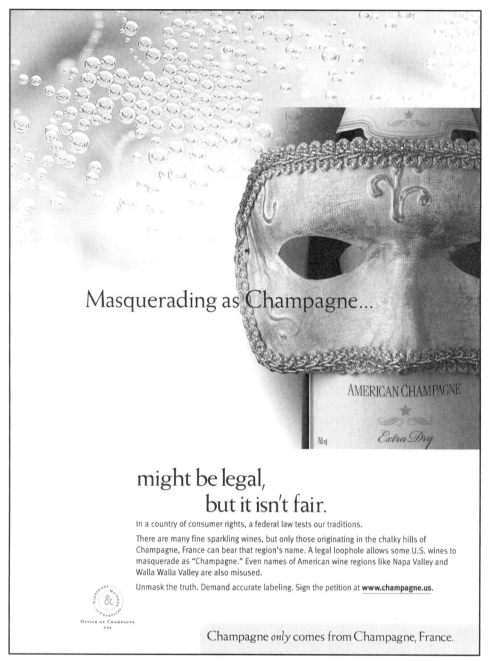

Masquerading as Champagne...

AMERICAN CHAMPAGNE

Extra Dry

might be legal,
    but it isn't fair.

In a country of consumer rights, a federal law tests our traditions.

There are many fine sparkling wines, but only those originating in the chalky hills of Champagne, France can bear that region's name. A legal loophole allows some U.S. wines to masquerade as "Champagne." Even names of American wine regions like Napa Valley and Walla Walla Valley are also misused.

Unmask the truth. Demand accurate labeling. Sign the petition at **www.champagne.us**.

Champagne *only* comes from Champagne, France.

Champagne is a region in France that is world famous for producing sparking wines. However, the word "Champagne" sometimes appears on labels of sparkling wines from the United States and other countries. The European Union recently asked the World Trade Organization for permission to restrict the use of "Champagne" and certain other words associated with traditional European products. Such "geographic indicators" would assure consumers about the origin and authenticity of the products they buy; in other words, a wine labeled "Champagne" would be from Champagne, France.

In 2005, representatives from several wine regions in the United States and the EU signed a Joint Declaration to Protect Wine Place & Origin. In addition, a Wine Accord signed by the United States and EU bans the misuse of 16 place names by marketers of wine products that do not originate in those places.

A **copyright** establishes ownership of a written, recorded, performed, or filmed creative work.

Infringement of intellectual property can take a variety of forms. **Counterfeiting** is the unauthorized copying and production of a product. An *associative counterfeit*, or *imitation*, uses a product name that differs slightly from a well-known brand but is close enough that consumers will associate it with the genuine product. A third type of counterfeiting is *piracy,* the unauthorized publication or reproduction of copyrighted work. Counterfeiting and piracy are particularly important in industries such as motion pictures, recorded music, computer software, and textbook publishing. Companies in these industries produce products that can be easily duplicated and distributed on a mass basis. The United States in particular has a vested interest in intellectual property protection around the globe because it is home to many companies in the industries just mentioned.

Headquartered in Geneva, Switzerland, the World Intellectual Property Organization (WIPO) is one of 16 specialized subunits of the United Nations. WIPO's mission is to promote and protect intellectual property throughout the world. WIPO views intellectual property as a critical element in economic development; it has created illustrated booklets that explain trademarks, copyright, and other intellectual property issues in a straightforward, easy-to-understand manner. Local agencies can access and print the booklets directly from WIPO's Internet site.

However, the United States faces significant challenges in countries such as China. As one expert has noted:

> Current attempts to establish intellectual property law, particularly on the Chinese mainland, have been deeply flawed in their failure to address the difficulties of reconciling legal values, institutions, and forms generated in the West with the legacy of China's past and the constraints imposed by its present circumstances.[16]

Case 5-1 at the end of this chapter describes some of the problems companies encounter as they try to enforce trademarks around the world.

In the United States, where patents, trademarks, and copyrights are registered with the Federal Patent Office, the patent holder retains all rights for the life of the patent even if the product is not produced or sold. The Trademark Act of 1946, also known as the Lanham Act, covers trademarks in the United States. President Reagan signed the Trademark Law Revision Act into law in November 1988. The law makes it easier for companies to register new trademarks. Patent and trademark protection in the United States is very good, and U.S. law relies on the precedent of previously decided court cases for guidance. To register a patent in Europe, a company has the option of filing on a country-by-country basis or applying to the European Patent Office in Munich for patent registration in a specific number of countries. A third option will soon be available: The Community Patent Convention will make it possible for an inventor to file for a patent that is effective in the 25 signatory nations. Currently, patent procedures in Europe are quite expensive, in part because of the cost of translating technical documents into

---

16 William P. Alford, *To Steal a Book is an Elegant Offense: Intellectual Property Law in Chinese Civilization* (Stanford, California: Stanford University Press, 1995), p. 2.

Budweiser is a registered trademark of St. Louis-based Anheuser-Busch (A-B), the world's largest brewing company. At the present time, however, A-B can't use the Budweiser brand name on a global basis. That's because, in 1895, the Budejovicky Budvar brewery was established in Budweis, Bohemia, and its beer was officially named Budweiser, "the beer of kings." A-B is now suing on a country-by-country basis to win the rights to the Budweiser name. It has won cases in Ireland, Portugal, Sweden, and other countries. Currently, more than two dozen cases are pending in various parts of the world.

all the languages of the EU countries; as of mid-2004, the translation issue remained unresolved.[17] In July 1997, in response to complaints, the European Patent Office instituted a 19 percent reduction in the average cost of an eight-country patent registration. The United States recently joined WIPO; governed by the Madrid agreement of 1891 and the more flexible 1996 **Madrid Protocol**, the system allows trademark owners to seek protection in as many as 74 countries with a single application and fee.

Companies sometimes find ways to exploit loopholes or other unique opportunities offered by patent and trademark laws in individual nations. Sometimes, individuals register trademarks in local country markets before the actual corporate entity files for trademark protection. For example, Starbucks filed for trademark protection in 1997 in Russia but did not open any cafés there. Sergei Zuykov, an attorney in Moscow, filed a petition in court in 2002 to cancel Starbucks' claim to the brand name because it had not been used in commerce. Technically, Zuykov is merely taking advantage of provisions in Russia's civil code; even though he has been denounced as a "trademark squatter," he is not violating the law. Zuykov has offered to sell Seattle-based Starbucks its name back for $600,000![19]

International concern about intellectual property issues in the nineteenth century resulted in two important agreements. The first is the International Convention for the Protection of Industrial Property. Also known as the Paris Union or Paris Convention, the convention dates to 1883 and is now honored by nearly 100 countries. This treaty facilitates multicountry patent registrations by ensuring that, once a company files in a signatory country, it will be afforded a "right of priority" in other countries for one year from the date of the original filing. A U.S. company wishing to obtain foreign patent rights must apply to the Paris Union within one year of filing in the United States or risk a permanent

"We have confidence in international law. When you invent something, it is necessary immediately to defend your creativity with intellectual patents. Italy has one of the poorest records in Europe with regard to patents. We need to educate businessmen about this."[18]

Mario Moretti Polegato, Chairman, Geox (Italy's biggest shoe company)

"There are two ways to fight piracy in China. The first is the Coca-Cola method. You make your product so well and you distribute it so cheaply that there's no money left for the counterfeiters. The second is the Budweiser approach: Budweiser beer cans in China have fluted edges that are difficult to manufacture. Chinese companies can brew beer and call it Budweiser, but they can't yet put it in a can that looks real. If you don't have an intellectual property rights plan as part of your business plan, you're in trouble."[20]

Thomas Boam, a commercial attaché for the United States Embassy, Beijing

---

[17] Frances Williams, "Call for Stronger EU Patent Laws," *Financial Times,* May 22, 1997.
[18] Tony Barber, "'Patents are Key' to Taking on China," *Financial Times,* July 25, 2006, p. 2.
[19] Andrew Kramer, "He Doesn't Make Coffee, but He Controls 'Starbucks' in Russia," *The New York Times,* October 12, 2005, pp. C1, C4.
[20] Robyn Meredith, "The Counterfeit Economy," *Forbes,* February 17, 2003, p. 82.

Luxury goods marketer Louis Vuitton recently sued Carrefour, the French hypermarket operator, in China. Attorneys for Louis Vuitton alleged that a Shanghai Carrefour store sold counterfeit copies of Vuitton's handbags for 50 yuan, the equivalent of about $6. Genuine Louis Vuitton handbags sell for about $1,000 in China. China is experiencing an increase in lawsuits involving patents, trade secrets, and counterfeit goods.

loss of patent rights abroad.[21] In 1886, the International Union for the Protection of Literary and Artistic Property was formed. Also known as the Berne Convention, this was a landmark agreement on copyright protection.

Two other treaties deserve mention. The Patent Cooperation Treaty (PCT) has more than 100 contracting states, including Australia, Brazil, France, Germany, Japan, North Korea, South Korea, the Netherlands, Switzerland, the Russian Federation and other former Soviet republics, and the United States. The members constitute a union that provides certain technical services and cooperates in the filing, searching, and examination of patent applications in all member countries. The European Patent Office administers applications for the European Patent Convention, which is effective in the EU and Switzerland. An applicant can file a single patent application covering all the convention states; the advantage is that the application will be subject to only one procedure of grant. Although national patent laws remain effective under this system, approved patents are effective in all member countries for a period of 20 years from the filing date.

In recent years, the U.S. government has devoted considerable diplomatic effort to improving the worldwide environment for intellectual property protection. For example, China agreed to accede to the Berne Convention in 1992; on January 1, 1994, China became an official signatory of the PCT. After years of discussion, the United States and Japan have agreed to make changes in their respective patent systems; Japan has promised to speed up patent examinations, eliminate challenges to patent submissions, and allow patent applications to be filed in English. Effective June 7, 1995, in accordance with GATT, new U.S. patents are granted for a period of 20 years from the filing date. Previously, patents had been valid for a 17-year term effective after being granted. Thus, U.S. patent laws now harmonize with those in the EU as well as Japan. Even with the changes, however, patents in Japan are narrower than those in the United States. As a result, companies, such as Caterpillar, have been unable to protect critical innovations in Japan because products very

---

21 Franklin R. Root, *Entry Strategies for International Markets* (New York: Lexington Books, 1994), p. 113.

Company	No. of Patents
1. IBM	2,941
2. Hitachi	1,918
3. Canon Kabushiki Kaisha	1,875
4. Matsushita Electric Industrial	1,813
5. Hewlett-Packard	1,808
6. Samsung Electronics	1,641
7. Micron Technology	1,561
8. Intel	1,549
9. Siemens	1,345
10. Toshiba	1,338

Table 5-2

Companies Receiving the Most U.S. Patents, 2005

Source: U.S. Patent and Trademark Office.

similar to those made by U.S. companies can be patented without fear of infringement.[22]

Another key issue is global patent protection for software. Although copyright laws protect the computer code, it does not apply to the idea embodied in the software. Beginning in 1981, the U.S. Patent and Trademark Office extended patent protection to software; Microsoft has more than 500 software patents. In Europe, software patents were not allowed under the Munich Convention; in June 1997, however, the EU indicated it was ready to revise patent laws so they cover software.[23]

Table 5-2 ranks the 10 companies that received the most U.S. patents in 2005. IBM, which has topped the rankings every year since 1993, generates more than $1 billion in revenues by licensing patents and other forms of intellectual property; Hewlett-Packard has more than 16,000 patents worldwide.

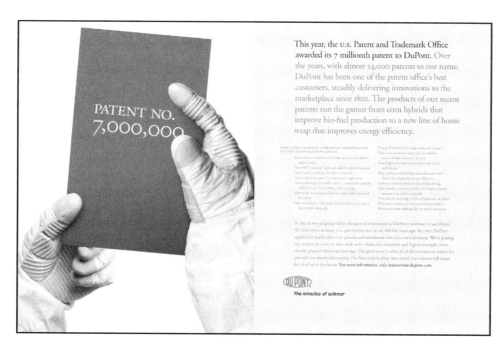

New products and innovaton are the lifeblood of E.I. du Pont de Nemours and Company, better known simply as DuPont. The company's business units include Safety & Protection, Coatings & Color Technologies, and Agriculture & Nutrition. One subsidiary, Pioneer Hi-Bred International, is a biotechnology company headquartered in Iowa. Pioneer develops hybrid seeds that enable farmers in all parts of the world to raise crop yields.

[22] John Carey, "Inching toward a Borderless Patent," *Business Week*, September 5, 1994, p. 35.
[23] Richard Pynder, "Intellectual Property in Need of Protection," *Financial Times*, July 7, 1998, p. 22.

Antitrust

Antitrust laws in the United States and other countries are designed to combat restrictive business practices and to encourage competition. Agencies such as the U.S. Federal Trade Commission, Japan's Fair Trade Commission, and the European Commission enforce antirust laws. Some legal experts believe that the pressures of global competition have resulted in an increased incidence of price-fixing and collusion among companies. As then-FTC chairman Robert Pitofsky said, "For years, tariffs and trade barriers blocked global trade. Now those are falling, and we are forced to confront the private anticompetitive behavior that often remains."[24]

A recent rash of antitrust actions brought in the United States against foreign companies has raised concerns that the United States is violating international law as well as the sovereignty of other nations. The U.S. antitrust laws are a legacy of the nineteenth century trust-busting era and are intended to maintain free competition by limiting the concentration of economic power. The Sherman Act of 1890 prohibits certain restrictive business practices, including fixing prices, limiting production, allocating markets, or any other scheme designed to limit or avoid competition. The law applies to the activities of U.S. companies outside U.S. boundaries, as well as to foreign companies conducting business in the United States. In a precedent-setting case, Nippon Paper Industries was found guilty in a U.S. court of conspiring with other Japanese companies to raise fax paper prices in the United States. The Japanese government denounced the U.S. indictment of Nippon Paper in December 1995 as a violation of international law and Japan's sovereignty. The meetings at which pricing strategies were allegedly discussed took place outside the United States; a U.S. federal judge struck down the indictment, ruling that the Sherman Act does not apply to foreign conduct. However, a federal appeals court in Boston reversed the decision. In his opinion, U.S. Circuit Judge Bruce Selya wrote, "We live in an age of international commerce, where decisions reached in one corner of the world can reverberate around the globe."[25]

BRIC Briefing Book

Antitrust in Brazil

Although antitrust laws are on the books in many countries, they are often weak or loosely enforced. Meanwhile, antitrust is taking on increasing importance in emerging country markets. For example, Colgate-Palmolive's 1995 acquisition of Brazil's Kolynos oral care company for $1 billion was subject to review by that country's Administrative Council of Economic Defense (CADE). Rival Procter & Gamble instigated the review by complaining that the acquisition would give Colgate a 79 percent share of the market. CADE ruled that Colgate must either license the trademark to another company for 20 years or halt sales of Kolynos brand toothpaste in Brazil for 4 years; Colgate agreed to the latter. The Miller Brewing unit of Philip Morris also ran into antitrust problems in Brazil following its 1995 investment of $50 million in a 50–50 joint venture with Cia. Cervejaria Brahma SA. CADE ruled that the venture, which produced and distributed Miller Genuine Draft beer, deprived consumers of head-to-head competition between the two brewing companies. CADE also criticized Miller for choosing a market entry strategy that required a relatively low level of investment. Nelio Weiss, a consultant at Coopers & Lybrand's Sao Paulo office, noted, "The message is that foreign companies shouldn't assume that antitrust authorities will be passive."

Source: Yumiko Ono, "Colgate Purchase Gets Brazil's Blessing but with Restrictions on Brand Name," The Wall Street Journal, September 20, 1996, p. A11; Matt Moffett, "Miller Brewing Is Ordered to Sell Its Stake in Brazilian Joint Venture," The Wall Street Journal, June 13, 1997, p. A15.

[24] John R. Wilke, "Hunting Cartels: U.S. Trust-Busters Increasingly Target International Business," The Wall Street Journal, February 5, 1997, p. A10.
[25] John R. Wilke, "U.S. Court Rules Antitrust Laws Apply to Foreigners," The Wall Street Journal, March 19, 1997, p. B5.

For the past four decades, the competition authority of the European Commission has had the power to prohibit agreements and practices that prevent, restrict, and distort competition. The commission has jurisdiction over European-based companies as well as non-European ones, such as Microsoft, that generate significant revenues in Europe. For example, the commission can block a proposed merger or joint venture, approve it with only minor modifications, or demand substantial concessions before granting approval. The commission begins with a preliminary study of a proposed deal; serious concerns can lead to an in-depth investigation lasting several months. Beginning in the mid-1990s, the commission has taken an increasingly activist approach. Mario Monti, an Italian with an economics background, was Europe's antitrust chief during this period. Nicknamed "Super Mario" by the European press, Monti blocked the proposed merger of WorldCom and Sprint in 2000. He also demanded major concessions before allowing America Online to acquire Time Warner.[26] Neelie Kroes recently took over the job from Monti. There have been calls for the EU to revamp its approach to antitrust issues and reduce its caseload. Any proposed changes will pit modernists against traditionalists. As one European attorney complained, "The commission is putting resources into regulating cases that don't actually restrict competition, which means that the cases that do need to be looked at are not being resolved efficiently."[27] Table 5-3 summarizes some recent joint ventures, mergers, and other global business deals that have been subject to review by antitrust authorities on both sides of the Atlantic.

Table 5-3

Antitrust Investigations

Companies Involved	Antitrust Review in the EU	Antitrust Review in the United States
Merger of Sony Music (Japan) and BMG (Germany), 2004	Approved	Approved
Acquisition of Honeywell (United States) by GE (United States), 2001, $40 billion	Deal was vetoed on grounds that merged firm would be stronger than competitors in aviation equipment.	Deal was on track for approval, subject to conditions.
Joint venture between music businesses of EMI Group PLC (Great Britain) and Time Warner (United States), 2000, $20 billion	Regulators expressed concern that the new EMI-Time Warner would dominate growing market for digital music distribution.	Deal was scrapped in October 2000 before regulatory review began.
Merger of WorldCom (United States) and MCI (United States), 1998, $37 billion	MCI ordered to divest all Internet-related assets.	U.S. concerns were incorporated into review by EU, which occurred first; EU's terms were acceptable to Federal Communications Commission and Department of Justice.
Strategic alliance between British Airways (United Kingdom) and American Airlines (United States), 1998	Commission required the two carriers to give up 267 weekly slots at London's Heathrow Airport.	Washington has demanded an "open skies" agreement with the UK allowing U.S. carriers other than United and American to fly into Heathrow.

26 Anita Raghavan and Brandon Mitchener, "'Super Mario': EU's Antitrust Czar Isn't Afraid to Say No; Just Ask Time Warner," *The Wall Street Journal*, October 2, 2000, pp. A1, A10.
27 Emma Tucker, "Europe's Paper Mountain," *Financial Times*, February 11, 1998, p. 21.

The interstate trade clause of the Treaty of Rome applies to trade with third countries, so that a company must be aware of the conduct of its affiliates. The commission also exempts certain cartels from Articles 85 and 86 of the treaty in an effort to encourage the growth of important businesses. The intent is to allow European companies to compete on an equal footing with Japan and the United States. In some instances, individual country laws in Europe apply to specific marketing mix elements. For example, some countries permit selective or exclusive product distribution. However, European Community law can take precedence.

In one case, Consten, a French company, had exclusive French rights to import and distribute consumer electronics products from the German Grundig company. Consten sued another French firm, charging the latter with bringing "parallel imports" into France illegally. That is, Consten charged that the competitor bought Grundig products from various foreign suppliers without Consten's knowledge and was selling them in France. Although Consten's complaint was upheld by two French courts, the Paris Court of Appeals suspended the judgment, pending a ruling by the European Commission on whether the Grundig-Consten arrangement violated Articles 85 and 86 of the Treaty of Rome. The commission ruled against Consten on the grounds that "territorial protection proved to be particularly damaging to the realization of the Common Market."[28]

In some instances, companies or entire industries have been able to secure exemption from antitrust rules. In the airline industry, for example, KLM and Northwest won an exemption from the U.S. government and now share-computer codes and set prices jointly. Similarly, the European Commission permitted United International Pictures (UIP), a joint venture between Paramount, Universal, and MGM/UA, to cut costs by collaborating on motion picture distribution in Europe. In 1998, the commission reversed itself and notified the three studios that they must distribute their films independently in

Neelie Kroes is the European Union's competition commissioner. Kroes intends to use the European Commission's March 2004 antitrust ruling to force Microsoft to change the way it markets operating systems, including Vista.

28 Detlev Vagts, *Transnational Business Problems* (Mineola, NY: The Foundation Press, 1986), pp. 285–291.

Europe.[29] A **cartel** is a group of separate companies that collectively set prices, control output, or take other actions to maximize profits. For example, the group of oil-producing countries known as OPEC is a cartel. In the United States, most cartels are illegal. One notable exception, however, has a direct impact on global marketing. A number of the world's major shipping lines, including the U.S.-based Sea-Land Service and Denmark's A. P. Moller/Maersk line, have enjoyed exemption from antitrust laws since the passage of the Shipping Act of 1916. The law was originally enacted to ensure reliability; today, it has been estimated that the cartel results in shipping prices that are 18 percent higher than they would be if shippers set prices independently. Attempts in recent years to change the law have not been successful.[30]

Licensing and Trade Secrets

Licensing is a contractual agreement in which a licensor allows a licensee to use patents, trademarks, trade secrets, technology, or other intangible assets in return for royalty payments or other forms of compensation. U.S. laws do not regulate the licensing process per se as do technology transfer laws in the EU, Australia, Japan, and many developing countries. The duration of the licensing agreement and the amount of royalties a company can receive are considered a matter of commercial negotiation between licensor and licensee, and there are no government restrictions on remittances of royalties abroad. Important considerations in licensing include analysis of what assets a firm may offer for license, how to price the assets, and whether to grant only the right to "make" the product or to grant the rights to "use" and to "sell" the product as well. The right to sublicense is another important issue. As with distribution agreements, decisions must also be made regarding exclusive or nonexclusive arrangements and the size of the licensee's territory.

To prevent the licensee from using the licensed technology to compete directly with the licensor, the latter may try to limit the licensee to selling only in its home country. The licensor may also seek to contractually bind the licensee to discontinue use of the technology after the contract has expired. In practice, host-government laws and even U.S. antitrust laws may make such agreements impossible to obtain. Licensing is a potentially dangerous action: It may be instrumental in creating a competitor. Therefore, licensors should be careful to ensure that their own competitive position remains advantageous. This requires constant innovation.

As noted, licensing agreements can come under antitrust scrutiny. In one recent case, Bayer AG granted an exclusive patent license for a new household insecticide to S. C. Johnson & Sons. The German firm's decision to license was based in part on the time required for EPA approval, which had stretched to three years. Bayer decided it made better business sense to let the U.S. firm deal with regulatory authorities in return for a 5 percent royalty on sales. However, a class action suit filed against the companies alleged that the licensing deal would allow Johnson to monopolize the $450 million home insecticide market. Then the U.S. Justice Department stepped in, calling the licensing agreement anticompetitive. In a statement, Anne Bingaman, then head of the justice department's antitrust unit, said, "The cozy arrangement that Bayer and Johnson maintained is unacceptable in a highly concentrated market." Bayer agreed to offer licenses to any interested company on better terms than the original contract with Johnson.

---

[29] Alice Rawsthorn and Emma Tucker, "Movie Studios May Have to Scrap Joint Distributor," *Financial Times*, February 6, 1998, p. 1.
[30] Anna Wilde Mathews, "Making Waves: As U.S. Trade Grows, Shipping Cartels Get a Bit More Scrutiny," *The Wall Street Journal*, October 7, 1997, pp. A1, A8.

Advanced Micro Devices (AMD) is the world's second largest supplier of microprocessors for PCs and servers. With its Athlon and Opteron chips, AMD has made significant inroads against Intel. On several occasions, AMD has filed lawsuits against Intel, claiming that Intel has has used its supplier power to stifle competition and engage engage in anticompetitive behavior in various markets, including the United States and Japan.

Johnson agreed to notify the U.S. government of any future pending exclusive licensing agreements for household insecticides. If Bayer is party to any such agreements, the justice department has the right to veto them. The reaction from the legal community was negative. One Washington lawyer who specializes in intellectual property law noted that the case "really attacks traditional licensing practices." As Melvin Jager, president of the Licensing Executives Society, explained, "An exclusive license is a very valuable tool to promote intellectual property and get it out into the marketplace."[31]

What happens if a licensee gains knowledge of the licensor's trade secrets? *Trade secrets* are confidential information or knowledge that has commercial value and is not in the public domain, and for which steps have been taken to keep it secret. Trade secrets include manufacturing processes, formulas, designs, and customer lists. To prevent disclosure, the licensing of unpatented trade secrets should be linked to confidentiality contracts with each employee who has access to the protected information. In the United States, trade secrets are protected by state law rather than federal statute; most states have adopted the Uniform Trade Secrets Act (UTSA). The U.S. law provides trade secret liability against third parties that obtain confidential information through an intermediary. Remedies include damages and other forms of relief.

The 1990s have seen widespread improvements in laws pertaining to trade secrets. Several countries have adopted trade secret statutes for the first time. Mexico's first statute protecting trade secrets became effective on June 28, 1991; China's first trade secret law took effect on December 1, 1993. In both countries, the new laws were part of broader revisions of intellectual property laws. Japan and South Korea have also recently amended their intellectual property laws to include trade secrets. Many countries in Central and Eastern Europe have also enacted laws to protect trade secrets. When NAFTA became effective on January 1, 1994, it marked the first international trade agreement with provisions for protecting trade secrets. This milestone was quickly followed by the Agreement on Trade-Related Aspects of Intellectual Property Rights (TRIPs) that resulted from the Uruguay Round of GATT negotiations. The TRIPs agreement requires signatory countries to protect against acquisition, disclosure, or use of trade secrets "in a manner contrary to honest commercial practices."[32] Despite these formal legal developments, in practice, enforcement is the key issue. Companies transferring trade secrets across borders should apprise themselves not only of the existence of legal protection but also of the risks associated with lax enforcement.

Bribery and Corruption: Legal and Ethical Issues

History does not record a burst of international outrage when Charles M. Schwab, head of Bethlehem Steel at the beginning of the twentieth century, presented a $200,000 diamond and pearl necklace to the mistress of Czar Alexander III's nephew.[33] In return for that consideration, Bethlehem Steel won the contract to supply the rails for the Trans-Siberian railroad. Today, in the post-Soviet era, Western companies are again being lured by emerging opportunities in Central and Eastern Europe. Here, as in the Middle East and other parts of the world, they are finding that bribery is a way of life, and that corruption is widespread. **Bribery** is the corrupt

---

[31] Brigid McMenamin, "Eroding Patent Rights," *Forbes,* October 24, 1994, p. 92.

[32] Salem M. Katsh and Michael P. Dierks. "Globally, Trade Secrets Laws Are All Over the Map," *The National Law Journal* 17, no. 36 (May 8, 1995), p. C12.

[33] Much of the material in this section is adapted from Daniel Pines, "Amending the Foreign Corrupt Practices Act to Include a Private Right of Action," *California Law Review* (January 1994), pp. 185–229.

Table 5-4

2006 Corruption Rankings

Rank/Country	2006 CPI Score	Rank/Country	2006 CPI Score
1. Finland	9.6	156. Chad	2.0
Iceland	9.6	Dem. Rep. of Congo	2.0
New Zealand	9.6	Sudan	2.0
4. Denmark	9.5	160. Guinea	1.9
5. Singapore	9.4	Iraq	1.9
6. Sweden	9.2	Burma	1.9
7. Switzerland	9.1	163. Haiti	1.8
8. Norway	8.8		
9. Australia	8.7		
Netherlands	8.7		

Source: Reprinted from Transparency International's Corruption Perceptions Index 2006, http://www.transparency.org/policy_research/surveys_indices/cpi/2006, *Transparency International: The Global Coalition Against Corruption.* Used with permission. For more information, visit http://www.transparency.org.

business practice of demanding or offering some type of consideration—typically cash payment—when negotiating a cross-border deal. U.S. companies in particular are constrained in their responses to such a situation by U.S. government policies of the post-Watergate age. Transparency International (www.transparency.org) compiles an annual report ranking countries in terms of a Corruption Perceptions Index (CPI). The "cleanest" score is 10. The 2006 ranking of the highest and lowest countries is shown in Table 5-4.

In the United States, the **Foreign Corrupt Practices Act (FCPA)** is a legacy of the Watergate scandal during Richard Nixon's presidency. In the course of his investigation, the Watergate special prosecutor discovered that more than 300 American companies had made undisclosed payments to foreign officials totaling hundreds of millions of dollars. Congress unanimously passed the act, and President Jimmy Carter signed the act into law on December 17, 1977. Administered by the Department of Justice and the Securities and Exchange Commission, the act was concerned with disclosure and prohibition. The disclosure part of the act required publicly held companies to institute internal accounting controls that would record all transactions. The prohibition part made it a crime for U.S. corporations to bribe an official of a foreign government or political party to obtain or retain business. Payments to third parties were also prohibited when the company had reason to believe that part or all of the money would be channeled to foreign officials.

The U.S. business community immediately began lobbying for changes to the act, complaining that the statute was too vague and so broad in scope that it threatened to severely curtail U.S. business activities abroad. President Ronald Reagan signed amendments to the statutes into law in 1988 as part of the Omnibus Trade and Competitiveness Act. Among the changes were exclusions for "grease" payments to low-level officials to cut red tape and expedite "routine governmental actions" such as clearing shipments through customs, securing permits, or getting airport passport clearance to leave a country.

Although several well-known U.S. companies have pleaded guilty to violations of the antibribery provisions, enforcement of the act has generally been lax. A total of 23 cases were filed between 1977 and 1988. In one such case, a business executive was convicted of giving money and honeymoon airplane tickets to a Nigerian government official in the hopes of securing a contract.[34] There are stiff penalties for violating the law: Convictions carry severe jail sentences (in excess of one to five years) and heavy fines (in excess of $1 million). A company cannot pay or reimburse fines, under the theory that individuals commit such crimes. It has

---

[34] Katherine Albright and Grace Won, "Foreign Corrupt Practices Act," *American Criminal Law Review* (Spring 1993), p. 787.

also been made clear that the law will not let a person do indirectly (e.g., through an agent, joint venture partner, or other third party) what it prohibits directly.

Some critics of the FCPA decry it as a regrettable display of moral imperialism. At issue is the extraterritorial sovereignty of U.S. law. It is wrong, according to these critics, to impose U.S. laws, standards, values, and mores on American companies and citizens worldwide. As one legal expert points out, however, this criticism has one fundamental flaw: There is no nation in which the letter of the law condones bribery of government officials. Thus, the standard set by the FCPA is shared, in principle at least, by other nations.[35]

A second criticism of the FCPA is that it puts U.S. companies in a difficult position vis-à-vis foreign competitors, especially those in Japan and Europe. Several opinion polls and surveys of the business community have revealed the widespread perception that the act adversely affects U.S. businesses overseas. Some academic researchers have concluded that the FCPA has not negatively affected the export performance of U.S. industry. However, a U.S. Commerce Department report prepared with the help of U.S. intelligence services indicated that in 1994 alone, bribes offered by non-U.S. companies were a factor in 100 business deals valued at $45 billion. Foreign companies prevailed in 80 percent of those deals.[36] Although accurate statistics are hard to come by, the rankings shown in Table 5-4 highlight some areas of the world where bribery is still rampant.

The existence of bribery as a fact of life in world markets will not change because the U.S. Congress condemns it. Bribery payments are considered a deductible business expense in many European countries. According to one estimate, the annual price tag for illegal payments by German firms alone is more than $5 billion. Still, increasing numbers of global companies are adopting codes of conduct designed to reduce illegal activities. Moreover, in May 1997, the OECD

"Corruption is probably the most immediate threat and difficulty that any business faces in Russia—and the trend is increasing.[37]

Carlo Gallo, business risk consultant

Anna Politkovskaya, a reporter for Russia's Novaya Gazeta ("New Paper"), often filed stories critical of President Vladimir Putin. On October 7, 2006, Politkovskaya was gunned down by assailants as she returned from a trip to the store. Since 2000, more than one dozen journalists have been murdered in Russia. Observers note that Russia's independent press has suffered as the Kremlin tightens control in anticipation of the 2008 presidential election.

---

[35] Daniel Pines, "Amending the Foreign Corrupt Practices Act to Include a Private Right of Action," *California Law Review* (January 1994), p. 205.

[36] Amy Borrus, "Inside the World of Greased Palms," *Business Week*, November 6, 1995, pp. 36–38.

[37] Rebecca Bream and Neil Buckley, "Investors Still Drawn to Russia Despite Pitfalls," *Financial Times*, December 1, 2006, p. 21.

adopted a formal standard against bribery by drafting a binding international convention that makes it a crime for a company bidding on a contract to bribe foreign officials. The OECD's antibribery convention (officially known as the Convention on Combating Bribery of Foreign Public Officials in International Business Transactions) went into effect in 1999. The OECD is also working on a smaller scale to create so-called islands of integrity. The goal is to achieve transparency at the level of an individual deal, with all the players pledging not to bribe.[38]

Despite the progress made to date on the new agreement, industry observers have expressed several concerns about the proposed treaty. First, it is unclear whether the new law will be enforced with equal rigor everywhere, and, if not, what sanctions will be imposed. Second, the treaty contains legal loopholes, such as the provision that business contracts can be linked to public aid projects such as building hospitals. Third, there is disagreement on what constitutes a "normal" versus an "abnormal" payment. Finally, it will be necessary to arrive at a workable definition of what constitutes a "public official."[39]

When companies operate abroad in the absence of home-country legal constraints, they face a continuum of choices concerning company ethics. At one extreme, they can maintain home-country ethics worldwide with absolutely no adjustment or adaptation to local practice. At the other extreme, they can abandon any attempt to maintain company ethics and adapt entirely to local conditions and circumstances as they are perceived by company managers in each local environment. Between these extremes, one approach that companies may select is to utilize varying degrees of extension of home-country ethics. Alternatively, they may adapt in varying degrees to local customs and practices.

What should a U.S. company do if competitors are willing to offer a bribe? Two alternative courses of action are possible. One is to ignore bribery and act as if it does not exist. The other is to recognize the existence of bribery and evaluate

global MARKETING Q&A

Wall Street Journal: "How do you deal with developing countries that have oil, but where there are governments and people with their hands out to you?"

Lord John Brown, chairman, BP PLC: "I think that the first thing you have to recognize is that in the vast majority of the world, corruption, whether it's dormant or active, lies very close below the surface. So, unless it is carefully policed, it becomes a monster that eats everybody. The first thing you must do is to look to the boundaries of the company and make sure that the payments we make are for services rendered, of a legal nature, and equal to the services obtained. We cannot be a nation's keeper. But we can influence. If corruption is around, it sort of says to people, well, maybe we can get away with something. So it will be very clear that we must always be reinforcing what we do and take swift and speedy action if someone does something bad."

Wall Street Journal: "Have you ever had to deal with someone with his hand out?"

Lord Browne: "Oh, yes. Not recently. It's very easy to say 'goodbye.'"

Source: Bhushan Bahree, "Beyond BP's Catchphrase," *The Wall Street Journal,* November 25, 2003, p. B11.

---

[38] José Ángel Gurría, "Rich Must Set the Example of Bribery," *Financial Times,* September 13, 2006, p. 5.

[39] John Mason and Guy de Jonquières, "Goodbye Mr. 10%," *Financial Times,* July 22, 1997, p. 13.

its effect on the customer's purchase decision as if it were just another element of the marketing mix. The overall value of a company's offer must be as good as, or better than, the competitor's overall offering, bribe included. It may be possible to offer a lower price, a better product, better distribution, or better advertising to offset the value added by the bribe. The best line of defense is to have a product that is clearly superior to that of the competition. In such a case, a bribe should not sway the purchase decision. Alternatively, clear superiority in service and in local representation may tip the scales.

CONFLICT RESOLUTION, DISPUTE SETTLEMENT, AND LITIGATION

The degree of legal cooperation and harmony in the EU is unique and stems in part from the existence of code law as a common bond. Other regional organizations have made far less progress toward harmonization. Countries vary in their approach toward conflict resolution. Table 5-5 shows the number of practicing lawyers per 100,000 in population in selected countries. The United States has more lawyers than any other country in the world and is arguably the most litigious nation on earth. In part, this is a reflection of the low-context nature of American culture and the spirit of confrontational competitiveness. Other factors can contribute to differing attitudes toward litigation. For example, in many European nations, class action lawsuits are not allowed. Also, European lawyers cannot undertake cases on a contingency fee basis. However, change is in the air, as Europe experiences a broad political shift away from the welfare state.[40]

Conflicts inevitably arise in business anywhere, especially when different cultures come together to buy, sell, establish joint ventures, compete, and cooperate in global markets. For American companies, the dispute with a foreign party is frequently in the home-country jurisdiction. The issue can be litigated in the United States, where the company and its attorneys might be said to enjoy "home court" advantage. Litigation in foreign courts, however, becomes vastly more complex, partly because of differences in language, legal systems, currencies, and traditional business customs and patterns. In addition, problems arise from differences in procedures relating to discovery. In essence, *discovery* is the process of obtaining evidence to prove claims and determining which evidence may be admissible in which countries under which conditions. A further complication is

Country	Lawyers per 100,000 People
United States	290
Australia	242
United Kingdom	141
France	80
Germany	79
Hungary	79
Japan	11
Korea	3

Table 5-5

Lawyers: An International Comparison

Source: Adapted from Frank B. Cross, "Lawyers, the Economy, and Society," *American Business Law Journal* (Summer 1998), pp. 477+.

[40] Charles Fleming, "Europe Learns Litigious Ways," *The Wall Street Journal*, February 24, 2004, p. A17.

the fact that judgments handed down in courts in another country may not be enforceable in the home country. For all these reasons, many companies prefer to pursue arbitration before proceeding to litigate.

Alternatives to Litigation for Dispute Settlement[41]

In 1995, the Cuban government abruptly cancelled contracts with Endesa, a Spanish utility company. Rather than seek restitution in a Cuban court, Endesa turned to the International Arbitration Tribunal in Paris, seeking damages of $12 million. Endesa's actions illustrate how alternative dispute resolution (ADR) methods allow parties to resolve international commercial disputes without resorting to the court system. Formal arbitration is one means of settling international business disputes outside the courtroom. **Arbitration** is a negotiation process that the two parties have, by prior agreement, committed themselves to using. It is a fair process in the sense that the parties using it have created it themselves. Generally, arbitration involves a hearing of the parties before a three-member panel; each party selects one panel member, and those two panel members, in turn, select the third member. The panel renders a judgment that the parties agree to abide by in advance.

The most important treaty regarding international arbitration is the 1958 United Nations Convention on the Recognition and Enforcement of Foreign Arbitral Awards. Also known as the New York Convention, the treaty has more than 110 signatory countries, including China. Brazil became a signatory to the New York Convention in 2002, as did the Dominican Republic, Iceland, Jamaica, and Zambia. The framework created by the New York Convention is important for several reasons. First, when parties enter into agreements that provide for international arbitration, the signatory countries can hold the parties to their pledge to use arbitration. Second, after arbitration has taken place and the arbitrators have made an award, the signatories recognize and can enforce the judgment. Third, the signatories agree that there are limited grounds for challenging arbitration decisions. The grounds that are recognized are different than the typical appeals that are permitted in a court of law.

Some firms and lawyers inexperienced in the practice of international commercial arbitration approach the arbitration clauses in a contract as "just another clause." The terms of every contract are different and, therefore, no two arbitration clauses should be the same. Consider, for example, the case of a contract between an American firm and a Japanese one. If the parties resort to arbitration, where will it take place? The American side will be reluctant to go to Japan; conversely, the Japanese side will not want to arbitrate in the United States. An alternative, "neutral" location—Singapore or London, for example—must be considered and specified in the arbitration clause. In what language will the proceedings be conducted? If no language is specified in the arbitration clause, the arbitrators themselves will choose.

In addition to location and language, other issues must be addressed as well. For example, if the parties to a patent-licensing arrangement agree in the arbitration clause that the validity of the patent cannot be contested, such a provision may not be enforceable in some countries. Which country's laws will be used as the standard for invalidity? Pursuing such an issue on a country-by-country basis would be inordinately time-consuming. In addition, there is the issue of acceptance: By law, U.S. courts must accept an arbitrator's decision in patent disputes; in other countries, however, there is no general rule of

---

[41] The authors are indebted to Louis B. Kimmelman of O'Melveny & Meyers LLP, New York City, New York, for his contributions to this section.

acceptance. To reduce delays relating to such issues, one expert suggests drafting arbitration clauses with as much specificity as possible. To the extent possible, for example, patent policies in various countries should be addressed; arbitration clauses may also include a provision that all foreign patent issues will be judged according to the standard of home-country law. Another provision could forbid the parties from commencing separate legal actions in other countries. The goal is to help the arbitration tribunal zero in on the express intentions of the parties.[42]

For decades, business arbitration has also been promoted through the International Court of Arbitration at the Paris-based International Chamber of Commerce (ICC; www.iccwbo.org). The ICC recently modernized some of its older rules. However, because it is such a well-known organization, it has an extensive backlog of cases. Overall, the ICC has gained a reputation for being slower, more expensive, and more cumbersome than some alternatives. As U.S. involvement in global commerce grew dramatically during the post-World War II period, the American Arbitration Association (AAA) also became recognized as an effective institution within which to resolve disputes. In 1992, the AAA signed a cooperation agreement with China's Beijing Conciliation Center. Each year, the AAA uses mediation to help resolve thousands of disputes. The AAA has entered into cooperation agreements with the ICC and other global organizations to promote the use of ADR methods; it serves as the agent to administer arbitrations in the United States under ICC auspices. In one recent case, Toys "R" Us was the losing party in a dispute brought to the AAA. The dispute's origins date back to a 1982 licensing agreement between the toy retailer and Alghanin & Sons regarding toy stores in the Middle East. The AAA ruled that Toys "R" Us was to pay a $55 million arbitration award.

Another agency for settling disputes is the Swedish Arbitration Institute of the Stockholm Chamber of Commerce. This agency frequently administered disputes between Western and Eastern European countries and has gained credibility for its evenhanded administration. However, a favorable ruling from the arbitration tribunal is one thing; enforcement is another. For example, Canada's IMP Group took its case against a Russian hotel development partner to Stockholm and was awarded $9.4 million. When payment was not forthcoming, IMP's representatives took matters into their own hands: They commandeered an Aeroflot jet in Canada and released it only after the Russians paid up![43] Other alternatives have proliferated in recent years. In addition to those mentioned, active centers for arbitration exist in Vancouver, Hong Kong, Cairo, Kuala Lumpur, Singapore, Buenos Aires, Bogotá, and Mexico City. A World Arbitration Institute was established in New York; in the United Kingdom, Advisory, Conciliation and Arbitration Service (ACAS) has achieved great success at handling industrial disputes. An International Council for Commercial Arbitration (ICCA) was established to coordinate the far-flung activities of arbitration organizations. The ICCA meets in different locations around the world every four years.

The United Nations Conference on International Trade Law (UNCITRAL; www.uncitral.org) has also been a significant force in the area of arbitration. Its rules have become more or less standard, as many of the organizations just named have adopted them with some modifications. Many developing countries, for example, long held prejudices against the ICC, AAA, and other developed-country

---

42 Bruce Londa, "An Agreement to Arbitrate Disputes Isn't the Same in Every Language," *Brandweek,* September 26, 1994, p. 18. See also John M. Allen, Jr., and Bruce G. Merritt, "Drafters of Arbitration Clauses Face a Variety of Unforeseen Perils," *National Law Journal* 17, no. 33 (April 17, 1995), pp. C6–C7.
43 Dorothee J. Feils and Florin M. Sabac, "The Impact of Political Risk on the Foreign Direct Investment Decision: A Capital Budgeting Analysis," *Engineering* 45, no. 2 (2000), p. 129.

organizations. Representatives of developing nations assumed that such organizations would be biased in favor of multinational corporations. Developing nations insisted on settlement in national courts, which was unacceptable to the multinational firms. This was especially true in Latin America, where the Calvo Doctrine required disputes arising with foreign investors be resolved in national courts under national laws. The growing influence of the ICCA and UNCITRAL rules, coupled with the proliferation of regional arbitration centers, have contributed to changing attitudes in developing countries and resulted in the increased use of arbitration around the world.

THE REGULATORY ENVIRONMENT

The regulatory environment of global marketing consists of a variety of governmental and nongovernmental agencies that enforce laws or set guidelines for conducting business. These regulatory agencies address a wide range of marketing issues, including price control, valuation of imports and exports, trade practices, labeling, food and drug regulations, employment conditions, collective bargaining, advertising content, and competitive practices. As noted in *The Wall Street Journal*:

> Each nation's regulations reflect and reinforce its brand of capitalism—predatory in the U.S., paternal in Germany, and protected in Japan—and its social values. It's easier to open a business in the U.S. than in Germany because Germans value social consensus above risk-taking, but it's harder to hire people because Americans worry more about discrimination lawsuits. It's easier to import children's clothes in the U.S. than Japan because Japanese bureaucrats defend a jumble of import restrictions, but it's harder to open bank branches across the U.S. because Americans strongly defend state prerogatives.[44]

In most countries, the influence of regulatory agencies is pervasive, and an understanding of how they operate is essential to protect business interests and advance new programs. Executives at many global companies are realizing the need to hire lobbyists to represent their interests and to influence the direction of the regulatory process. For example, in the early 1990s, McDonald's, Nike, and Toyota didn't have a single representative in Brussels. Today, each of the companies has several people representing its interests to the European Commission. U.S. law firms and consulting firms also have sharply increased their presence in Brussels; in an effort to gain insight into EU politics and access to its policy makers, some have hired EU officials. In all, there are currently approximately 15,000 lobbyists in Brussels representing about 1,400 companies and nonprofit organizations from around the world.[45]

Regional Economic Organizations: The EU Example

The overall importance of regional organizations such as the WTO and the EU was discussed in Chapter 3. The legal dimensions are important, however, and will be briefly mentioned here. The Treaty of Rome established the EC, the

---

44 Bob Davis, "Red-Tape Traumas: To All U.S. Managers Upset by Regulations: Try Germany or Japan," *The Wall Street Journal*, December 14, 1995, p. A1.
45 Raphael Minder, "The Lobbyists Take Brussels by Storm," *Financial Times*, January 26, 2006, p. 7. See also Brandon Mitchener, "Standard Bearers: Increasingly, Rules of Global Economy Are Set in Brussels," *The Wall Street Journal*, April 23, 2002, p. A1.

precursor to the EU. The treaty created an institutional framework in which a council (the Council of Ministers) serves as the main decision-making body, with each country member having direct representation. The other three main institutions of the community are: the European Commission, the EU's executive arm; the European Parliament, the legislative body; and the European Court of Justice.

The 1987 Single European Act amended the Treaty of Rome and provided strong impetus for the creation of a single market beginning January 1, 1993. Although technically the target was not completely met, approximately 85 percent of the new recommendations were implemented into national law by most member states by the target date, resulting in substantial harmonization. A relatively new body known as the European Council (a distinct entity from the Council of Ministers) was formally incorporated into the EC institutional structure by Article 2 of the 1987 act. Comprised of heads of member states plus the president of the commission, the European Council's role is to define general political guidelines for the union and provide direction on integration-related issues such as monetary union.[46] Governments in Central and Eastern European countries that hope to join are currently getting their laws in line with those of the EU.

The Treaty of Rome contains hundreds of articles, several of which are directly applicable to global companies and global marketers. Articles 30 through 36 establish the general policy referred to as "Free Flow of Goods, People, Capital and Technology" among the member states. Articles 85 through 86 contain competition rules, as amended by various directives of the 20-member EU Commission. The commission is the administrative arm of the EU; from its base in Brussels, the commission proposes laws and policies, monitors the observance of EU laws, administers and implements EU legislation, and represents the EU to international organizations.[47] Commission members represent the union rather than their respective nations. The laws, regulations, directives, and policies that originate in the commission must be submitted to the parliament for an opinion and then passed along to the council for a final decision. Once the council approves a prospective law, it becomes union law, which is somewhat analogous to U.S. federal law. Regulations automatically become law throughout the union; directives include a time frame for implementation by legislation in each member state. For example, in 1994 the commission issued a directive regarding use of trademarks in comparative advertising. Individual member nations of the EU have been working to implement the directive; in the United Kingdom, the 1994 Trade Marks Act gave companies the right to apply for trademark protection of smells, sounds, and images and also provides improved protection against trademark counterfeiting.

The Single Market era is one in which many industries face new regulatory environments. The European Court of Justice, based in Luxembourg, is the EU's highest legal authority. It is responsible for ensuring that EU laws and treaties are upheld throughout the union. Based in Luxembourg, it consists of two separate tribunals. The senior body is known as the Court of Justice; a separate entity, the Court of First Instance, hears cases involving commerce and competition (see Table 5-6). Although the European Court of Justice plays a role similar to that of the U.S. Supreme Court, there are important differences. The European court cannot decide which cases it will hear, and it does not issue dissenting opinions. The court exercises jurisdiction over a range of civil matters involving trade, individual rights, and environmental law. For example, the

---

[46] Klaus-Dieter Borchardt, *European Integration: The Origins and Growth of the European Union.* (Luxembourg: Office for Official Publications of the European Communities, 1995), p. 30.
[47] Klaus-Dieter Borchardt, *The ABC of Community Law* (Luxembourg: Office for Official Publications of the European Communities, 1994), p. 25.

Table 5-6

Recent and Pending Actions by the European Court of Justice

Country/Plaintiffs Involved	Issue
EU/Microsoft	The Court of First Instance will make a preliminary ruling on antitrust sanctions imposed by the European Commission on Microsoft (e.g., the separation of Windows Media from Windows OS).
United Kingdom/Airtours	In 1999, the European Commission blocked a takeover by U.K.-based Airtours of rival travel company First Choice. In 2002, the Court ruled that Airtours could appeal. The court's action marked the first time it overturned an antitrust ruling by the European Commission.
Italy/Monsanto, Syngenta, Pioneer Hi-Bred International	In 2000, fearing risk to human health, Italy banned foods containing four strains of genetically modified corn. The Italian court hearing the plaintiffs' appeal asked for ECJ intervention; in 2003, the ECJ ruled that the ban was not justified. The case was returned to Italy for a final ruling. The Italian court ruled that the government was not entitled to impose the ban.

court can assess damages against countries that fail to introduce directives by the date set. The court also hears disputes that arise among the 27 EU member nations on trade issues such as mergers, monopolies, trade barriers and regulations, and exports. The court is also empowered to resolve conflicts between national law and EU law. In most cases, the latter supersedes national laws of individual European countries.

Marketers must be aware, however, that national laws should always be consulted. National laws may be *stricter* than community law, especially in such areas as competition and antitrust. To the extent possible, community law is intended to harmonize national laws to promote the purposes defined in Articles 30 through 36. The goal is to bring the lax laws of some member states up to designated minimum standards. However, more restrictive positions may still exist in some national laws. Conversely, national laws may be *less* restrictive than community law. Germany, for example, had traditionally placed few restrictions on banana imports (Germany is Europe's top banana-consuming country). When a German court decreed that German companies could import bananas without complying with the EU's 1993 banana regime regulations, the Court of Justice ruled that national courts could not grant interim judicial relief.[48]

---

[48] Rikke Thagesen and Alan Matthews, "The EU's Common Banana Regime: An Initial Evaluation," *Journal of Common Market Studies* 35, no. 4 (December 1997), p. 623.

The **political environment** of global marketing is the set of governmental institutions, political parties, and organizations that are the expression of the people in the nations of the world. In particular, anyone engaged in global marketing should have an overall understanding of the importance of **sovereignty** to national governments. The political environment varies from country to country, and **political risk** assessment is crucial. It is also important to understand a particular government's actions with respect to taxes and seizure of assets. Historically, the latter have taken the form of **expropriation, confiscation,** and **nationalization.**

The **legal environment** consists of laws, courts, attorneys, legal customs, and practices. **International law** is comprised of the rules and principles that nation-states consider binding upon themselves. The countries of the world can be broadly categorized as having either **common-law** legal systems or **civil code-law legal systems.** The United States and Canada and many former British colonies are common-law countries; most other countries use code law. A third system, **Islamic law,** predominates

in the Middle East. Some of the most important legal issues pertain to **jurisdiction, antitrust,** and **licensing.** In addition, **bribery** is pervasive in many parts of the world; the **Foreign Corrupt Practices Act (FCPA)** applies to American companies operating abroad. **Intellectual property protection** is another critical issue. **Counterfeiting** is a major problem in global marketing; it often involves infringement of a company's **copyright, trademark, or patent.** When legal conflicts arise, companies can pursue the matter in court or use **arbitration.**

The **regulatory environment** consists of agencies, both governmental and nongovernmental, that enforce laws or set guidelines for conducting business. Global marketing activities can be affected by a number of international or regional economic organizations; in Europe, for example, the EU makes laws governing member states. The WTO will have a broad impact on global marketing activities in the years to come. Although all three environments are complex, astute marketers plan ahead to avoid situations that might result in conflict, misunderstanding, or outright violation of national laws.

1. What is sovereignty? Why is it an important consideration in the political environment of global marketing?

2. Describe some of the sources of political risk. Specifically, what forms can political risk take?

3. Briefly describe some of the differences between the legal environment of a country that embraces common law and one that observes civil law.

4. Global marketers can avoid legal conflicts by understanding the reasons conflicts arise in the first place. Identify and describe several legal issues that relate to global commerce.

5. You are an American traveling on business in the Middle East. As you are leaving country X, the passport control officer at the airport tells you there will be a passport "processing" delay of 12 hours. You explain that your plane leaves in 30 minutes, and the official suggests that a contribution of $50 would probably speed things up. If you comply with the suggestion, have you violated U.S. law? Explain.

6. "See you in court" is one way to respond when legal issues arise. Why can that approach backfire when the issue concerns global marketing?

Case 5-1

America's Cuban Conundrum

On March 12, 1996, President Clinton signed the Cuban Liberty and Democratic Solidarity Act, also known as the Helms-Burton Act. The president's actions came after Cuban MiGs shot down two U.S. civilian airplanes, killing the four Cuban-Americans who were on board. The act has two key provisions. First, it denies entry into the United States to corporate officers of companies from other countries doing business on U.S. property in Cuba that was confiscated by the Cuban government. Second, it allows U.S. companies and citizens to sue foreign firms and investors doing business on U.S. property confiscated in Cuba. However, in July 1996, the president ordered a six-month moratorium on lawsuits. Washington pledged to keep the embargo in place until Cuban President Fidel Castro held free elections and released political prisoners.

Despite the fact that the United States is currently engaged in limited trading with Castro's Cuba, Fidel Castro remains unrepentant and appears determined to cling to his economic policies. In denouncing "neo-liberal globalization," Castro said, "The more contact we have with capitalism, the more repugnance I feel."

Cuba-U.S. Relations Prior to 1996

Cuba is a communist outpost in the Caribbean where "socialism or death" is the national motto. After Fidel Castro came to power in 1959, his government took control of most private companies without providing compensation to the owners. American assets owned by both consumer and industrial companies worth approximately $1.8 billion were among those expropriated; today, those assets are worth about $6 billion (see Table 1). President Kennedy responded by imposing a trade embargo on the island nation. Four decades later, Fidel Castro was still in power, despite the fact that his politics had fallen from fashion in many parts of the world. In 1990, Cuba opened its economy to foreign investment; by the mid-1990s, foreign commitments to invest in Cuba totaled more than half a billion dollars.

In 1993, Castro decreed that the U.S. dollar was legal tender although the peso would still be Cuba's official currency. As a result, hundreds of millions of dollars are injected into Cuba's economy each year; Cuban exiles living in the United States send much of the money. Cubans can spend their dollars in special stores that stock imported foods and other hard-to-find products. In a country where doctors are among the highest paid workers with salaries equal to about $20 per month, the cash infusions can significantly improve a family's standard of living. In 1994, mercados agropecuarios ("farmers markets") were created as a mechanism to enable farmers to earn more money.

Cuba desperately needs investment and U.S. dollars, in part to compensate for the end of subsidies following the demise of the Soviet Union. Oil companies from Europe and Canada were among the first to seek potential opportunities in Cuba. Many American executives are concerned that lucrative opportunities will be lost as Spain, Mexico, Italy, Canada, and other countries move aggressively into Cuba. Anticipating a softening in the U.S. government's stance, representatives from scores of U.S. companies visit Cuba regularly to meet with officials from state enterprises.

Table 1 American Companies Seeking Restitution from Cuba

Company	Amount of Claim (millions)
American Brands	$10.6
Coca-Cola	$27.5
General Dynamics	$10.4
ITT	$47.6
Lone Star Cement	$24.9
Standard Oil	$71.6
Texaco	$50.1

Source: U.S. Justice Department.

Those U.S. companies that are found guilty of violating trade embargoes, including the one on Cuba, are subject to fines of up to $1 million. Cuba remained officially off-limits to all but a handful of U.S. companies. Some telecommunications and financial services were allowed; AT&T, Sprint, and other companies have offered direct-dial service between the United States and Cuba since 1994. Also, a limited number of charter flights were available each day between Miami and Havana. Sale of medicines was also permitted under the embargo. At a state department briefing for business executives, former Assistant Secretary of State for Inter-American Affairs Alexander Watson told his audience, "The Europeans and the Asians are knocking on the door in Latin America. The game is on and we can compete effectively, but it will be a big mistake if we leave the game to others." Secretary Watson was asked whether his comments on free trade applied to Cuba. "No, no. That simply can't be, not for now," Watson replied. "Cuba is a special case. This administration will maintain the embargo until major democratic changes take place in Cuba."

Within the United States, the government's stance toward Cuba has both supporters and opponents. Senator

Jesse Helms pushed for a tougher embargo and sponsored a bill in Congress that would penalize foreign countries and companies for doing business with Cuba. The Cuban-American National Foundation actively engaged in anti-Cuba and anti-Castro lobbying. Companies that have openly spoken out against the embargo include Carlson Companies, owner of the Radisson Hotel chain; grain-processing giant Archer Daniels Midland; and the Otis Elevator division of United Technologies. A spokesperson for Carlson noted, "We see Cuba as an exciting new opportunity—the forbidden fruit of the Caribbean." A number of executives, including Ron Perelman, whose corporate holdings include Revlon and Consolidated Cigar Corporation, are optimistic that the embargo will be lifted within a few years.

Meanwhile, opinion was divided on the question of whether the embargo was costing U.S. companies once-in-a-lifetime opportunities. Some observers argued that many European and Latin American investments in Cuba were short-term, high-risk propositions that would not create barriers to U.S. companies. The opponents of the embargo, however, pointed to evidence that some investments were substantial. Three thousand new hotel rooms have been added by Spain's Grupo Sol Melia and Germany's LTI International Hotels. Both companies were taking advantage of the Cuban government's goal to increase tourism. Moreover, Italian and Mexican companies were snapping up contracts to overhaul the country's telecommunications infrastructure. Wayne Andreas, chairman of Archer Daniels Midland, summed up the views of many American executives when he said, "Our embargo has been a total failure for 30 years. We ought to have all the Americans in Cuba doing all the business they can. It's time for a change."

The Helms-Burton Era

The Helms-Burton Act brought change, but not the type advocated by ADM's Andreas. The toughened U.S. stance signaled by Helms-Burton greatly concerned key trading partners, even though Washington insisted that the act was consistent with international law. In particular, supporters noted, the "effects doctrine" of international law permits a nation to take "reasonable" measures to protect its interests when an act outside its boundaries produces a direct effect inside its boundaries. Unmoved by such rationalizations, the European Commission responded in mid-1996 by proposing legislation barring European companies from complying with Helms-Burton. Although such a "blocking statute" was permitted under Article 235 of the EU treaty, Denmark threatened to veto the action on the grounds that doing so exceeded the European Commission's authority; its concerns were accommodated, and the legislation was adopted. Similarly, the Canadian government enacted legislation that would allow Canadian companies to retaliate against U.S. court orders regarding sanctions. Also, Canadian companies that complied with the U.S. sanctions could be fined $1 million for doing so.

Meanwhile, executives at Canada's Sherritt International and Mexico's Grupo Domos received letters from the U.S. government informing them that they would be barred from entering the United States because of their business ties with Cuba. Sherritt operated a Cuban nickel mine, and Grupo Domos owned a 37 percent stake in Cuba's national telephone company. Both assets had been confiscated from U.S. companies. Canada and Mexico initiated arbitration proceedings as provided for under NAFTA. Meanwhile, in the fall of 1996, Canada registered its defiance of Helms-Burton by hosting Cuba's vice president for a four-day visit.

In August 1996, President Clinton signed another piece of legislation designed to put economic pressure on foreign governments. The Iran and Libya Sanctions Act stipulated that foreign governments and companies that invest $40 million or more in the oil or gas industry sectors in Iran or Libya would be subject to U.S. sanctions. Expert opinion was divided as to whether such sanctions would be effective.

In the fall of 1996, the WTO agreed to a request by the EU to convene a three-person trade panel that would determine whether Helms-Burton violated international trade rules. The official U.S. position was that Helms-Burton was a foreign policy measure designed to promote the transition to democracy in Cuba. The United States also hinted that, if necessary, it could legitimize Helms-Burton by invoking the WTO's national security exemption. That exemption, in turn, hinged on whether the United States faced "an emergency in international relations."

Meanwhile, efforts were underway to resolve the issue on a diplomatic basis. Sir Leon Brittan, trade commissioner for the EU, visited the United States in early November with an invitation for the United States and EU to put aside misunderstandings and join forces in promoting democracy and human rights in Cuba. He noted:

> By opposing Helms-Burton, Europe is challenging one country's presumed right to impose its foreign policy on others by using the threat of trade sanctions. This has nothing whatever to do with human rights. We are merely attacking a precedent which the U.S. would oppose in many other circumstances, with the full support of the EU.

In December, senior EU officials approved a resolution sponsored by Spain that formally clarified the EU's intention to step up pressure on Castro. The U.S. State Department hailed the move as "a breakthrough in U.S.-EU relations." The EU insisted that the policy statement did not represent a change in its position or a concession to the United States. Even so, Spain's move surprised Havana because Spain is Cuba's biggest foreign investor. However, Spain's newly elected conservative government was taking a harder line. Spain's prime minister and Castro even engaged in a bit of public name-calling.

In January 1997, President Clinton extended the moratorium on lawsuits against foreign investors in Cuba. In the months since the Helms-Burton Act had been in effect, a dozen companies had ceased operating on confiscated U.S. property in Cuba. Stet, the Italian telecommunications company, agreed to pay ITT for confiscated assets thereby exempting itself from possible sanctions. However, in some parts of the world, reaction to the president's action was lukewarm. The EU issued a statement noting that the action "falls short of the European Commission's hopes for a more comprehensive resolution of this difficult issue in trans-Atlantic relations." The EU also reiterated its intention of pursuing the case at the WTO. Art Eggleton, Canada's international trade minister responded with a less guarded tone: "It continues to be unacceptable behavior by the United States in foisting its foreign policy onto Canada, and other countries, and threatening Canadian business and anybody who wants to do business legally with Cuba."

Meanwhile, there was evidence that the U.S. sanctions, combined with other factors, were hurting Cuba. Sherritt and other foreign investors found the going slower than they expected. A number of legal reforms had still not been implemented. Also, the 1997 sugar crop, critical to Cuba's export earnings, was lower than anticipated. Another interesting twist occurred in Canada, where Wal-Mart temporarily removed Cuban-made pajamas from its 136 retail outlets. The issue was whether Wal-Mart was in violation of the Cuban Democracy Act, which makes U.S. global firms responsible for any boycott violations committed by foreign subsidiaries. After spending two weeks studying the matter and consulting with legal experts, Wal-Mart executives ordered the Cuban goods to be returned to the shelves.

In February, the WTO appointed the panel that would consider the dispute. However, Washington declared that it would boycott the panel proceedings on the grounds that the panel's members weren't competent to review U.S. foreign policy interests. Stuart Eizenstat, undersecretary for international trade at the U.S. Commerce Department, said, "The WTO was not created to decide foreign-policy and national-security issues." One expert on international trade law cautioned that the United States was jeopardizing the future of the WTO. Professor John Jackson of the University of Michigan School of Law said, "If the U.S. takes these kinds of unilateral stonewalling tactics, then it may find itself against other countries doing the same thing in the future."

The parties averted a confrontation at the WTO when the EU suspended its complaint in April, following President Clinton's pledge to seek congressional amendments to Helms-Burton. In particular, the president agreed to seek a waiver of the provision denying U.S. visas to employees of companies using expropriated property. A few days later, the EU and the United States announced plans to develop an agreement on property claims in Cuba with "common disciplines" designed to deter and inhibit investment in confiscated property. Washington hoped such a bilateral agreement could be introduced into the negotiations at the OECD pertaining to the Multilateral Agreement on Investment. However, the agreement spelled out the EU's right to resume the trade panel or launch new proceedings if the United States took action against any European companies. The EU had one year to reactivate its complaint; it chose not to, however, and the panel was allowed to lapse in April 1998.

The U.S. stance was seen in a new perspective following the pope's visit to Cuba in January 1998. Many observers were heartened by Cuban authorities' decision to release nearly 300 political prisoners in February. Opinion within the Cuban-American community in Miami, which had historically supported the embargo, now appeared to be divided. In the fall of 1998, several former U.S. secretaries of state called upon President Clinton to create a National Bipartisan Commission on Cuba to review U.S. policy. In the fall of 2000, President Clinton signed a law that permits Cuba to buy unlimited amounts of food and medicine from the United States. The slight liberalization of trade represented a victory for the U.S. farm lobby, although all purchases must be made in cash. In 2002, several pieces of legislation were introduced in the U.S. Congress that would effectively undercut the embargo. One bill prohibited funding that would be used to enforce sanctions on private sales of medicine and agricultural products. Another proposal would have the effect of withholding budget money earmarked for enforcing both the ban on U.S. travel to Cuba and limits on monthly dollar remittances. Also in 2002, Castro began to clamp down on the growing democracy movement; about 70 writers and activists were jailed. President George W. Bush responded by phasing out cultural travel exchanges between the United States and Cuba.

Discussion Questions

1. What was the key issue that prompted the EU to take the Helms-Burton dispute to the WTO?

2. Who benefits the most from an embargo of this type? Who suffers?

3. Assess attempts by some U.S. policy makers to limit or end *enforcement* of the embargo rather than the embargo itself. Do you agree with this approach?

Sources: Jerry Perkins, "Making American Dollar Legal Tenderizes Tough Cuban Economy," *Des Moines Register,* April 6, 2003, pp. 1D, 5D; Mary Anastasia O'Grady, "Threshing Out a Deal Between the Farmers and Fidel," *The Wall Street Journal,* September 20, 2002, p. A11; Pascal Fletcher, "Cuba Sees Itself as Shining Example Amid Global Troubles," *Financial Times,* September 19–20, 1998, p. 3; Carl Gershman, "Thanks to the Pope, Civil Society Stirs in Cuba," *The Wall Street Journal,* September 18, 1998, p. A11; Stuart E. Eizenstat, "A Multilateral Approach to Property Rights," *The Wall Street Journal,* April 11, 1997, p. A18; Therese Raphael, "U.S. and Europe Clash over Cuba," *The Wall Street Journal,* March 31, 1997, p. A14; Robert Greenberger, "Washington Will Boycott WTO Panel," *The Wall Street Journal,* February 21, 1997, p. A2; Robert Greenberger, "U.S. Holds Up Cuba Suits, Pleasing Few," *The Wall Street Journal,* January 6, 1997, p. A7; Brian Coleman, "EU to Push for Human Rights in Cuba," *The Wall Street Journal,* December 2, 1996, p. A12; Guy de Jonquières, "Brittan Calls for End to Cuba Row," *Financial Times,* November 7, 1996, p. 10; Julie Wolf and Brian Coleman, "EU Challenges U.S. Plan to Penalize Foreign Firms That Trade with Cuba," *The Wall Street Journal,* July 31, 1996, p. A1; Gail DeGeorge, "U.S. Business Isn't Afraid to Shout *Cuba Si!*" *Business Week,* November 6, 1995, p. 39; Jose De Cordoba, "Cuba's Business Law Puts Off Foreigners," *The Wall Street Journal,* October 10, 1995, p. A14; Sam Dillon, "Companies Press Clinton to Lift Embargo on Cuba," *The New York Times,* August 27, 1995, pp. 1, 4; Thomas T. Vogel, Jr., "Havana Headaches: Investors Find Cuba Tantalizing yet Murky in Financial Matters," *The Wall Street Journal,* August 7, 1995, pp. A1, A4.

Case 5-2
Gambling Goes Global on the Internet

Mankind has engaged in gambling for many centuries. Archeologists have unearthed six-sided dice dating from around 3000 B.C. Ancient Egyptians played a game resembling backgammon. On the Indian subcontinent more than 3,500 years ago, there were public and private gambling houses, dice games, and betting on fights between animals. Farther east, Asian cultures also have a rich and long tradition of gambling. As cultural artifacts, playing cards had their primitive origins in Asia.

When Europeans arrived in North America, they found that the native peoples had been gambling in a variety of ways for centuries. Of course, the European settlers and colonists were no strangers to gambling themselves. They brought with them a penchant for gambling in various forms, including card-playing, dice games, and lotteries. Even the Puritan settlers played cards.

Much of America's Revolutionary War was funded from lottery proceeds. Likewise, several of the young nation's new universities, including Columbia, Yale, and Princeton, were founded with substantial financial assistance from lotteries. America's connection to gambling has continued throughout its Civil War, two World Wars, and the emergence of Nevada as the icon of "Las Vegas-style" gambling.

Today, gambling has gone global. This seems logical, given gambling's prevalence through time around the world. The Internet Age is creating new opportunities for gamblers as well as challenges for those wanting to limit the spread of gambling and access to it. No longer is it necessary to physically travel to a casino or horse track to place bets on blackjack, sporting events, and horse racing. "Virtual" casinos have sprung up to engage the gambler in online gaming opportunities. In the 1990s, online casinos proliferated as Internet entrepreneurs sought to satisfy the worldwide demand for online gaming. These companies were based outside the United States because of questions about the legality of such activity under state and federal law. Many of these companies, including Gibraltar-based PartyGaming Plc and 888 Holdings Plc, are publicly traded corporations.

Despite its long history of gambling, the United States has also engaged in strict regulation of the industry. The surge in Internet gaming triggered efforts to ban such activity, and to prosecute those who are the principals of the so-called offshore online casinos. This regulatory action has angered governments in various countries, especially smaller countries where the online casinos are based. One country, Antigua and Barbuda (Antigua), filed a claim with the WTO in 2004 arguing that United States laws and policies pertaining to online gambling violate the terms of a fair trade agreement known as the General Agreement on Trade in Services (GATS).

Antigua claimed that the United States discriminated against foreign suppliers of "recreational services," including Internet gaming. The claim was based on the following argument: Even as it maintains a number of federal laws that prohibit offshore Internet gaming, the United States exempts off-track betting on horse races over the Internet from these same federal laws. According to the suit, this situation benefits domestic interests at the expense of offshore casinos.

In 2005, a WTO compliance panel ruled that the United States had, in fact, discriminated between foreign and domestic suppliers of gambling services. But the panel gave the United States an opportunity to show that the prevention of offshore betting was necessary as a means of protecting "public order and public morals." In 2006, U.S. authorities arrested David Caruthers, a British citizen who is the chief executive of Costa Rica-based BetonSports, while he was in the Dallas/Fort Worth airport en route from London to Costa Rica. In a 26-page indictment, the U.S. Department of Justice charged Caruthers and others with 22 counts of racketeering, conspiracy, and fraud.

The debate is far from over. Additional efforts are underway to make Internet gambling in the United States illegal, or at least difficult. In the fall of 2006, U.S. President George W. Bush signed into law the SAFE Port Act, which included the Unlawful Internet Gaming Enforcement Act. This measure prohibits United States banks, credit card companies, and other financial intermediaries from sending or receiving money to offshore casinos. Thus, the law makes it difficult for gamblers to fund their offshore accounts. Commenting on the signing of the measure, Michael Bolcerek, president of the Poker Players Alliance (PPA), said, "Today is a dark day for the great American game of poker. Twenty-three million Americans who play the game online will effectively be denied the ability to enjoy this popular form of entertainment, even in the privacy of their own homes."

In March 2007, the WTO ruled again. It found that the continuing exemption for online gambling on horseracing in the United States unfairly discriminated against foreign casinos. The ruling stated that the United States can restrict online gambling only so long as its laws are equally applied to American operators as well as foreign operators. The WTO ruling allows Antigua to seek trade sanctions against the United States. While Antigua may not have the economic muscle to force U.S. lawmakers to overturn the ban, it is possible that other countries affected by the United States ban, including Great Britain, may also petition the WTO for relief.

Discussion Questions

1. Do you think that the Unlawful Internet Gaming Enforcement Act unfairly discriminates against offshore gaming companies?

2. How likely is it that legislative efforts to prevent people who want to gamble from gambling will be successful?

3. The United States is devoting substantial time and money to curtail offshore Internet gambling. Is this a good use of government resources?

The *60 Minutes* segment on Internet gambling titled "Illegal and Thriving" makes an excellent companion to this case. It is available on DVD.

This case was prepared by Keith Miller, Ellis and Nelle Levitt Distinguished Professor of Law, Drake University Law School. Additional sources: Roger Blitz, "The Unlucky Gambler," *Financial Times*, July 23/23, 2006, p. 7; Blitz and Tom Braithwaite, "Online Operators Weigh Up the Odds," *Financial Times*, July 19, 2006, p. 21; Scott Miller and Christina Binkley, "Trade Body Rules Against U.S. Ban On Web Gambling," *The Wall Street Journal*, March 25, 2004, p. A2.

6

Global Information Systems and Market Research

For years, Coach was known as a purveyor of sturdy, long-lasting leather goods. Although many professional women appreciated the conservative styling of the signature Coach bag, they did not necessarily regard Coach's accessories as must-have fashion items. Today, the Coach brand is viewed as cutting-edge, and in key countries such as Japan, Coach's share of the luxury fashion accessories market has doubled and tripled. The company has become particularly adept at creating and marketing new types of handbags for various occasions. In an industry dominated by Prada, Gucci, Chanel, and other luxury brands whose bags can sell for hundreds of dollars, Coach pioneered the concept of "accessible luxury." How has Coach CEO Lew Frankfort accomplished this transformation? For one thing, the company's varied distribution channels and network of factories in more than one dozen countries means that its products cost an average of 40 percent less than those of competitors. But price is only part of the story; marketing information systems and extensive consumer research are equally important. Company executives rely on daily feedback from department stores, the company's stand-alone boutiques, the Coach Web site, and factory outlet stores. In addition, new designs are test-marketed with an obsessive focus on "the numbers." As Reed Krakoff, Coach's head designer for handbags and accessories, explains, "When something doesn't sell, I never say, 'Well, people didn't understand it.' If people don't understand it, it doesn't belong in the store."

Coach's resurgence in the competitive fashion goods business shows how information about buyer behavior and the overall business environment is vital to effective managerial decision making. When researching any market, marketers must know where to go to obtain information, what subject areas to investigate and information to look for, the different ways to acquire information, and the various analysis approaches that will yield important insights and understanding. However, similar challenges are likely to present themselves wherever the marketer goes. It is the marketer's good fortune that a veritable cornucopia of market information is available on the Internet. A few keystrokes can yield literally hundreds of articles, research findings, and Web sites that offer a wealth of information about particular country markets. Even so, marketers must do their homework if they are to make the most of modern information technology. First, they need to understand the importance of information technology and marketing information systems as strategic assets. Second, they should have a general understanding of the formal market research process. Finally, they should know how to manage the marketing information collection system and the marketing research effort. These topics are the focus of this chapter.

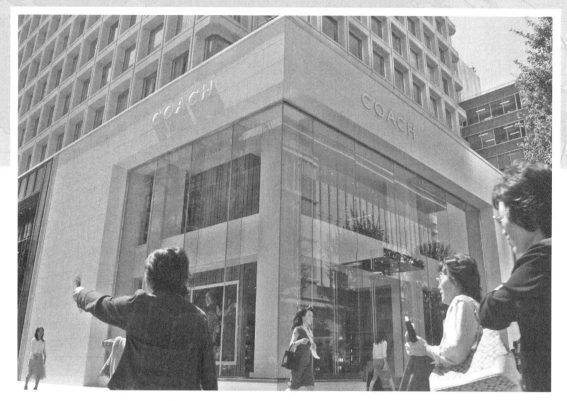

Japan is Coach's second-largest market, representing about 20 percent of global sales. The company's $500 handbags are especially popular with young Japanese women. Now Coach chairman and chief executive Lew Frankfort wants to elevate the brand's image among its core customers. To accomplish this, Coach has launched a new upscale line, Legacy, in Japan; Legacy stores have been created inside existing Coach retail locations, including the largest Tokyo store.

INFORMATION TECHNOLOGY FOR GLOBAL MARKETING

The phrase **information technology (IT)** refers to an organization's processes for creating, storing, exchanging, using, and managing information. For example, a **management information system (MIS)** provides managers and other decision makers with a continuous flow of information about company operations. MIS is a general term that can be used in reference to a system of hardware and software that a company uses to manage information. (The term can also be used to describe an IT department; in this case, it refers to people, hardware, and software.) An MIS should provide a means for gathering, analyzing, classifying, storing, retrieving, and reporting relevant data. The MIS should also cover important aspects of a company's external environment, including customers and competitors. Global competition intensifies the need for an effective MIS that is accessible throughout the company. As Jean-Pierre Corniou, chief information officer (CIO) at Renault, noted:

> My vision is to design, build, sell, and maintain cars. Everything I do is directly linked to this, to the urgent need to increase turnover, margins, and brand image. Every single investment and expense in the IT field has to be driven by this vision of the automotive business.[1]

Caterpillar, GE, Boeing, Federal Express, Diageo, Ford, and Texas Instruments, and many other companies with global operations have made significant investments in IT in recent years.

Such investment is typically directed at upgrading a company's computer hardware and software. Microsoft, Sun Microsystems, SAP, Oracle, and IBM are some of the beneficiaries of this trend. All are global enterprises, and many of their customers are global as well. Vendors of complex software systems can find it difficult to achieve 100 percent customer satisfaction. Thomas Siebel, founder of Siebel Systems, explains how his company met this challenge:

> Siebel Systems is a global company, not a multinational company. I believe the notion of the multinational company—where a division is free to follow its own set of business rules—is obsolete, though

[1] Jean-Pierre Corniu, "Bringing Business Technology out into the Open," *Financial Times—Information Technology Review,* September 17, 2003, p. 2.

there are still plenty around. Our customers—global companies like IBM, Zurich Financial Services, and Citicorp—expect the same high level of service and quality, and the same licensing policies, no matter where we do business with them around the world. Our human resources and legal departments help us create policies that respect local cultures and requirements worldwide, while at the same time maintaining the highest standards. We have one brand, one image, one set of corporate colors, one set of messages, across every place on the planet.[2]

In 2006, Siebel merged with Oracle.

Unlike the public Internet, an **intranet** is a private network that allows authorized company personnel or outsiders to share information electronically in a secure fashion without generating mountains of paper. Intranets allow a company's information system to serve as a 24-hour nerve center, enabling Amazon.com, Dell, and other companies to operate as *real time enterprises* (RTEs). The RTE model is expected to grow in popularity as wireless Internet access becomes more widely available.

An **electronic data interchange (EDI)** system allows a company's business units to submit orders, issue invoices, and conduct business electronically with other company units as well as outside companies. One of the key features of EDI is that its transaction formats are universal. This allows computer systems at different companies to speak the same language. Wal-Mart is legendary for its sophisticated EDI system; for years, vendors received orders from the retailer on personal computers using dial-up modems connected to third-party transmission networks. In 2002, Wal-Mart informed vendors it was switching to an Internet-based EDI system. The switch saves both time and money; the modem-based system was susceptible to transmission interruptions, and the cost was between $0.10 and $0.20 per thousand characters transmitted. Any vendor that wishes to do business with Wal-Mart in the future must purchase and install the necessary computer software.[3]

Poor operating results can often be traced to insufficient data and information about events both inside and outside the company. For example, when a new management team was installed at the U.S. unit of Adidas AG, the German athletic shoe maker, data were not even available on normal inventory turnover rates. A new reporting system revealed that archrivals Reebok and Nike turned inventories five times a year, compared with twice a year at Adidas. This information was used to tighten the marketing focus on the best-selling Adidas products. Benetton SpA's use of MIS as a strategic competitive tool is described later. In Japan, 7-Eleven's computerized distribution system also provides it with a competitive advantage in the convenience store industry. Every 7-Eleven store is linked with each other and with distribution centers. As one retail analyst noted:

> With the system they have established, whatever time you go, the shelves are never empty. If people come in at 4 AM and the stores don't have what they want, that will have a big impact on what people think of the store.[4]

Globalization puts increased pressure on companies to achieve as many economies as possible. IT provides a number of helpful tools. As noted previously, EDI links with vendors to enable retailers to improve inventory management and restock hot-selling products in a timely, cost-effective manner. In addition to EDI, retailers are increasingly using a technique known as **efficient consumer**

---

2 Bronwyn Fryer, "High-Tech the Old-Fashioned Way: An Interview with Tom Siebel of Siebel Systems," *Harvard Business Review*, March 2001, pp. 118–125.

3 Ann Zimmerman, "To Sell Goods to Wal-Mart, Get on the Net," *The Wall Street Journal*, November 21, 2003, pp. B1, B6.

4 Bethan Hutton, "Japan's 7-Eleven Sets Store by Computer Links," *Financial Times*, March 17, 1998, p. 26.

response (ECR) in an effort to work more closely with vendors on stock replenishment. ECR can be defined as a joint initiative by members of a supply chain to work towards improving and optimizing aspects of the supply chain to benefit customers. ECR systems utilize **electronic point of sale (EPOS)** data gathered by checkout scanners to help retailers identify product sales patterns and how consumer preferences vary with geography. Although currently most popular in the United States, the ECR movement is also gaining traction in Europe. Companies such as Carrefour, Metro, Coca-Cola, and Henkel have all embraced ECR. Supply chain innovations, such as radio frequency identification tags (RFID), are likely to provide increased momentum for ECR (see Case 12-2).

EPOS, ECR, and other IT tools are also helping businesses improve their ability to target consumers and increase loyalty. The trend among retailers is to develop customer-focused strategies that will personalize and differentiate the business. In addition to point-of-sale scanner data, loyalty programs that use electronic smart cards will provide retailers with important information about shopping habits. A new business model that helps companies collect, store, and analyze customer data is called **customer relationship management (CRM)**. Although industry experts offer varying descriptions and definitions of CRM, the prevailing view is that CRM is a philosophy that values two-way communication between company and customer. Every point of contact ("touchpoint" in CRM-speak) a company has with a consumer or business customer—through a Web site, a warranty card or sweepstakes entry, payment on credit card account, or inquiry to a call center—is an opportunity to collect data. CRM tools allow companies such as Credit Suisse, AT&T, and Hewlett-Packard to determine which customers are most valuable and to react in a timely manner with customized product and service offerings that closely match customer needs. If implemented correctly, CRM can make employees more productive and enhance corporate profitability; it also benefits customers by providing value-added products and services.

A company's use of CRM can manifest itself in various ways. Some are visible to consumers, others are not; some make extensive use of leading-edge information technology, others do not. In the hotel industry, for example, CRM can take the form of front desk staff who monitor, respond to, and anticipate the needs of repeat customers. A visitor to Amazon.com who buys *The Red Hot Chili Peppers Greatest Hits* CD encounters CRM when he or she gets the message "Customers who bought this title also bought *In Time: The Very Best of REM 1988–2003*." CRM can also be based on the click path that a Web site visitor follows. In this case, however, Internet users may be unaware that a company is tracking their behavior and interests.

One challenge is to integrate data into a complete picture of the customer and his or her relationship to the company and its products or services. This is sometimes referred to as a "360-degree view of the customer." The challenge is compounded for global marketers. Subsidiaries in different parts of the world may use different customer data formats, and commercial CRM products may not support all the target languages. In view of such issues, industry experts recommend implementing global CRM programs in phases. The first could focus on a specific task such as **sales force automation (SFA)**; the term refers to a software system that automates routine aspects of sales and marketing functions such as lead assignment, contact follow-up, and opportunity reporting. An SFA system can also analyze the cost of sales and the effectiveness of marketing campaigns. Some SFA software can assist with quote preparation and management of other aspects of a sales campaign, such as mass mailings and conference or convention attendee follow-up.

For example, an important first step in implementing a CRM system could be to utilize SFA software from a company such as Oracle or Onyx Software. The objective at this stage of the CRM effort would be to provide sales representatives

"The major thing is, 'One size fits all' is not true. CRM is designed to support the sales process, and if I develop a system that works in the U.S., it might not work in Europe."

Jim Dickie, Insight Technology Group

in all country locations with access via an Internet portal to sales activities throughout the organization. To simplify the implementation, the company could require that all sales activities be recorded in English. Subsequently, marketing, customer service, and other functions could be added to the system.[5]

Privacy issues also vary widely from country to country. In the EU, for example, a Directive on Data Collection has been in effect since 1998. Companies that use CRM to collect data about individual consumers must satisfy the regulations in each of the EU's 27 member countries. There are also restrictions about sharing such information across national borders. In 2000, the U.S. Department of Commerce and the EU concluded a Safe Harbor agreement that establishes principles for privacy protection for companies that wish to transfer data to the United States from Europe. The principles, which are posted in detail at www.export. gov/safeharbor, include:

- The purposes for which information is collected and used and the means by which individuals can direct inquiries to the company
- An "opt out" option to prevent the disclosure of personal information to third parties
- An agreement that information can only be transferred to third parties that are in compliance with Safe Harbor Principles
- Individuals must have access to information collected about them and must be able to correct or delete inaccurate information

Databases called **data warehouses** are frequently an integral part of a company's CRM system. Data warehouses can serve other purposes as well. For example, they can help retailers with multiple store locations fine-tune product assortments. Company personnel, including persons who are not computer specialists, can access data warehouses via standard Web browsers. Behind the familiar interfaces, however, is specialized software capable of performing multidimensional analysis by using sophisticated techniques such as linear programming and regression analysis. This enhances the ability of managers to respond to changing business conditions by adjusting marketing mix elements. MicroStrategy, an information services company in the United Kingdom, is one of several companies creating data warehouses for clients. As former vice president Stewart Holness explains, "Many corporations have a vast amount of information which they have spent money accumulating, but they have not been able to distribute it. The Web is the perfect vehicle for it."[6]

As Holness's comment makes clear, the Internet is revolutionizing corporate information processing (see Chapter 17). Companies slow to recognize the revolution risk falling behind competitors. For example, Germany is home to the *Mittelstand*, a group of 3 million small and mid-size manufacturers that have traditionally been focused and successful global marketers. The *Mittelstand* are often cited as an illustration of how small companies can help propel economic growth and sustain prosperity. As Dietmar Hopp, chief executive of Germany's largest software firm, noted in the mid-1990s:

> With globalization there is no difference now between the *Mittelstand* and big companies—the business processes are comparable. It is only a matter of time before foreign competitors use the Internet to strengthen their foothold in Germany. German companies should follow their example and build up their U.S. and Asian activities through electronic marketing and commerce.[7]

[5]   Gina Fraone, "Facing Up to Global CRM," *eWeek*, July 30, 2001, pp. 37–41.
[6]   Vanessa Houlder, "Warehouse Parties," *Financial Times*, October 23, 1996, p. 8. See also John W. Verity, "Coaxing Meaning out of Raw Data," *Business Week*, February 3, 1997, pp. 134+.
[7]   Graham Bowley, "In the Information Technology Slow Lane," *Financial Times*, November 11, 1997, p. 14.

There is evidence that *Mittelstand* companies have gotten the message. According to a recent study conducted by IBM Germany and *Impulse,* a German magazine for entrepreneurs, most *Mittelstand* companies now have Web home pages. Approximately one-third use the Web for e-business activities such as ordering and cross-linking with suppliers.[8]

These examples show just some of the ways that IT is affecting global marketing. However, EDI, ECR, EPOS, SFA, CRM, and other aspects of IT do not simply represent marketing issues; they are organizational imperatives. The tasks of designing, organizing, and implementing information systems must be coordinated in a coherent manner that contributes to the overall strategic direction of the organization. Modern IT tools provide the means for a company's marketing information system and research functions to provide relevant information in a timely, cost-efficient, and actionable manner.

the rest of the story

The Transformation of Coach

In 2004, Coach spent $3 million on research. Each year, the company conducts personal interviews with more than 10,000 consumers. It supplements this research with a variety of other techniques, including focus groups, e-mails, and questionnaires. Questions range from Coach's brand image to the strap length on its bags; Coach gathers data about fashion collections already in stores as well as items that are in the planning stages. As Peter Emmerson, president of global business development, explains, when the company entered Japan, research had provided managers with an understanding of the need for a window in the bag that could hold a train pass. Likewise, bags designed for the Japanese market had to be scaled down in size. The typical Japanese consumer "likes smaller, cute things, and the American tends to bigger sizes with lots of compartments," Emmerson says.

> "While consumers are enormously brand-centric in Japan, they are not as brand loyal as they are in America. American women tend to carry two to three brands on a regular basis, while her Japanese counterpart tends to carry as many as five."
>
> Lew Frankfort, Coach CEO

The value of Coach's research effort was evident in the successful introduction of the "Signature" collection; launched in 2001, the bags were made from leather and fabric and were covered with the letter C. The collection represented a radical departure from traditional Coach designs. The collection tested so well that, prior to the launch, Frankfort doubled the number of units ordered from suppliers. That same year, Coach executives discovered that the company's cosmetics cases were enjoying surprisingly strong sales. It turned out that women were putting the smaller cases inside the larger Coach bag so they could find cell phones and other important items without rummaging. Management recognized that the unexpected success of the cosmetics case represented an opportunity to innovate; as David Duplantis, vice president of retail merchandising, put it, "We

recognized an opportunity to accessorize the accessory." The design team created a 4-inch by 6-inch zippered bag with a wrist strap and a clip. Called a "wristlet," the new bag represented a bracelet-wallet hybrid for the wrist.

The new product was a huge hit, especially with young women who had not previously been Coach customers. The success of the Signature collection suggested, and subsequent marketing surveys confirmed, that women want bags that feature materials other than leather. The surveys also indicated that Coach was still perceived as a "serious" brand. Armed with this knowledge, Krakoff and Frankfort hit on the idea of a "Hampton Weekend" line of less expensive bags that were suited to weekend leisure pursuits. The line was intended as an impulse purchase; the bags range in price from about $100 to about $200—less than a typical Coach bag.

In 2002, Lexus launched a car model with a leather trim package that was co-branded with Coach. As brand strategy consultant Troy Nottingham noted, "What's happened here is that Lexus is a hallmark for luxury in the auto industry, and Coach has certainly been one of the top names in leather. It's one more crown for Lexus, and it takes Coach into a whole new category."

In 2003, Coach opened a small boutique inside the Harvey Nichols department store in London's fashionable Knightsbridge area. Emmerson hopes that, after gaining a foothold in Great Britain, the Coach brand will gain popularity as tourists from France, Germany, and Italy return home with their bags. Says Emmerson, "The UK will give us some sense as to what the opportunity size in Europe might be."

Sources: Deborah L. Vence, "Product Enhancement," Marketing News, May 1, 2005, p. 19; Ginny Parker, "A Yen for Coach," The Wall Street Journal, March 11, 2005, pp. B1, B4; Ellen Byron, "Case by Case: How Coach Won a Rich Purse by Inventing New Uses for Bags," The Wall Street Journal, November 17, 2004, pp. A1, A13; Lauren Foster, "How Coach Pulled into Luxury's Fast Lane," Financial Times, June 30, 2004, p. 8; Vanessa Friedman, "Handbag Invasion," Financial Times, August 2–3, 2003, p. W9; Erin White, "How Stodgy Turned Stylish," The Wall Street Journal, May 3, 2002, pp. B1, B3.

---

[8] "E-Business in the *Mittelstand,*" www.impulse.de (January 23, 2002).

Overall, then, the global organization has the following needs:

- An efficient, effective system that will scan and digest published sources and technical journals in the headquarters country as well as all countries in which the company has operations or customers.
- Daily scanning, translating, digesting, abstracting, and electronic input of information into a market intelligence system. Today, thanks to advances in IT, full-text versions of many sources are available online as PDF files. Print documentary material can be easily scanned, digitized, and added to a company's information system.
- Expanding information coverage to other regions of the world.

SOURCES OF MARKET INFORMATION

Although environmental scanning is a vital source of information, research has shown that headquarters executives of global companies obtain as much as two-thirds of the information they need from *personal sources*. A great deal of external information comes from executives based abroad in company subsidiaries, affiliates, and branches. These executives are likely to have established communication with distributors, consumers, customers, suppliers, and government officials. A striking feature of the global corporation—and a major source of competitive strength—is the role that executives abroad play in acquiring and disseminating information about the world environment. Headquarters executives generally acknowledge that company executives overseas are the people who know best what is going on in their areas. The following is a typical comment of headquarters executives:

> Our principal sources are internal. We have a very well-informed and able overseas establishment. The local people have a double advantage. They know the local scene and they know our business. Therefore, they are an excellent source. They know what we are interested in learning, and because of their local knowledge they are able to effectively cover available information from all sources.

The information issue exposes one of the key weaknesses of a domestic company: Although more attractive opportunities may be present outside existing areas of operation, they are likely to go unnoticed by inside sources in a domestic company because the scanning horizon tends to end at the home-country border. Similarly, a company with only limited geographical operations may be at risk because internal sources abroad tend to scan only information about their own countries or regions.

behind the scenes

Nestlé Customers Call In

Nestlé is an excellent case study in using the telephone as a low-cost tool to supplement traditional research and focus groups. The company receives hundreds of thousands of calls on its toll-free numbers each year; in an effort to get closer to customers, managers return some of those calls. After callers complained that the standard 8-ounce Coffee-mate jar was too small, the company changed its standard jar size to 15 ounces; sales increased significantly. Likewise, when callers complained that pastel colors on Coffee-mate labels made it hard to differentiate different varieties, Nestlé responded by brightening the colors. However, only about 20 percent of the incoming calls are complaints; many callers offer suggestions. Telephone research also revealed that most people start drinking coffee when they get their first job. Armed with this information, Nestlé began distributing samples of Coffee-mate to college students returning to campus in the fall.

Source: The Wall Street Journal (Eastern Edition) by Deborah Ball. Copyright 2004 by Dow Jones & Company, Inc.. Reproduced with permission of Dow Jones & Company, Inc. in the format Other book via Copyright Clearance Center.

Direct sensory perception provides a vital background for the information that comes from human and documentary sources. Direct perception gets all the senses involved. It means seeing, feeling, hearing, smelling, or tasting for oneself to find out what is going on in a particular country, rather than getting second-hand information by hearing or reading about a particular issue. Some information is easily available from other sources but requires sensory experience to sink in. Often, the background information or context one gets from observing a situation can help fill in the big picture. For example, Wal-Mart's first stores in China stocked a number of products—extension ladders and giant bottles of soy sauce, for example—that were inappropriate for local customers. Joe Hatfield, Wal-Mart's top executive for Asia, began roaming the streets of Shenzhen in search of ideas. His observations paid off; when Wal-Mart's giant store in Dalian opened in April 2000, a million shoppers passed through its doors in the first week. They snapped up products ranging from lunch boxes to pizza topped with corn and pineapple.[9] Jim Stengel, global marketing officer at Procter & Gamble, is moving his managers away from a preoccupation with research data to a wider view based on direct perception. As Stengel noted:

> We often find consumers can't articulate it. That's why we need to have a culture where we are understanding. There can't be detachment. You can't just live away from the consumer and the brand and hope to gain your insights from data or reading or talking to academics. You have to be experiential. And some of our best ideas are coming from people getting out there and experiencing and listening.[10]

Direct perception can also be important when a global player dominates a company's domestic market. Such was the case with Microsoft and its Xbox video game system, which was launched in a market dominated by Sony. Cindy Spodek-Dickey, group manager for national consumer promotions and sponsorships, took Xbox "on the road" with various promotional partners such as the Association of Volleyball Professionals (AVP). At AVP tournaments in different

global MARKETING Q&A

Wall Street Journal: "How do you keep the people who manage the brands fresh and focused on consumer needs?"

Niall FitzGerald, Co-Chairman, Unilever: "To be a successful marketer you have to be prepared to fail and to live with failure. If you try to make a decision without having 40 percent of what you need, you're in trouble. And if you wait until after you've got 70 percent, it's too late. So be brave enough to make your decisions in the 40 percent to 70 percent zone.

Wall Street Journal: "What do you do personally to get this message across?"

Niall FitzGerald: "I visit consumer homes. It sends a message flashing through the organization. It says, 'Good God, if he's going to do that, I'd better get out there before him!' One time I visited a family in Rio de Janeiro. We asked a woman to bring her clothes and she hand washed them with a powder. It looked as if the clothes were already clean. She actually washed the clothes in a stream with stones and only used the powder for a final brightening-up. I asked what the most important thing was for her. It was the fragrance. At the time, we weren't putting enough attention into fragrance. We are now."

Source: Deborah Ball, "Stocking a Global Pantry," *The Wall Street Journal*, May 24, 2004, pp. B1, B3.

9   Peter Wonacott, "Wal-Mart Finds Market Footing in China," *The Wall Street Journal*, July 17, 2000, p. A31.
10 Gary Silverman, "How May I Help You?" *Financial Times*, February 4–5, 2006, p. W2.

Joe Hatfield, chief executive of Wal-Mart Asia, is responsible for the retailer's 66 Chinese stores. Hatfield works 17-hour days in his quest to help Wal-Mart edge past Carrefour as China's largest hypermarket operator. Wal-Mart's China strategy includes building a nationwide distribution network; to accomplish this, the company has spent tens of millions of dollars in Kengzi and Shanghai. Industry observers forecast that, by 2015, 200 million Chinese households will have annual incomes equal to $3,200.

"China and India are very interesting because they are large, fast-growing economics. Indeed, I have a full-time analyst researching the Chinese market for potential acquisitions—on top of a regular market intelligence team that flies in and out of the country as needed. Right now we have terabytes of information on China."[12]

Lorenzo Zambrano, CEO, Cemex

cities, spectators (and potential customers) had the opportunity to visit the Xbox hospitality tent to try out the new machine. At one tournament event, Spodek-Dickey explained the importance of informal market research:

What are the other sponsors doing? What's the crowd into? What brands are they wearing? How are they interacting with our property? I'll stop them as they come out of the tent and say: 'What do you think? What do you like about Xbox? What do you think of your PlayStation?' It's mother-in-law research. I wouldn't want to stake a $10 million ad campaign on it, but I think it keeps you credible and real. When you start to hear the same feedback, three, four, five times, you'd better be paying attention. . . . I believe it is part of any good marketer's job to be in touch with their audience and their product. There's no substitute for face-to-face, eye-to-eye, hand-to-hand.[11]

FORMAL MARKET RESEARCH

Information is a critical ingredient in formulating and implementing a successful marketing strategy. As described earlier, a marketing information system should produce a continuous flow of information. **Market research**, by contrast, is the project-specific, systematic gathering of data. The American Marketing Association defines *marketing research* as "the activity that links the consumer, customer and public to the marketer through information."[13] In **global market research**, this activity is carried out on a global scale. The challenge of global marketing research is to recognize and respond to the important national differences that influence the way information can be obtained. These include cultural, linguistic, economic, political, religious, historical, and market differences.

Michael Czinkota and Illka Ronkainen note that the objectives of international market research are the same as the objectives of domestic research. However, they

11 Kenneth Hein, "We Know What Guys Want," *Brandweek*, November 14, 2002, p. M48.
12 John Lyons, "Cemex Prowls for Deals in Both China and India," *The Wall Street Journal*, January 27, 2006, p. C4.
13 Peter D. Bennett, ed., *Dictionary of Marketing Terms*, 2d ed. (Chicago: American Marketing Association, 1995), p. 169.

have identified four specific environmental factors that may require international research efforts to be conducted differently than domestic research. First, researchers must be prepared for new parameters of doing business. Not only will there be different requirements, but the ways in which rules are applied may differ as well. Second, "cultural megashock" may occur as company personnel come to grips with a new set of culture-based assumptions about conducting business. Third, a company entering more than one new geographic market faces a burgeoning network of interacting factors; research may help prevent psychological overload. Fourth, company researchers may have to broaden the definition of competitors in international markets to include competitive pressures that would not be present in the domestic market.[14]

There are two basic ways to conduct marketing research. One is to design and implement a study with in-house staff. The other is to use an outside firm specializing in marketing research. In global marketing, a combination of in-house and outside research efforts is often advisable. Many outside firms have considerable international expertise; some specialize in particular industry segments. According to figures compiled by *Marketing News*, global market research revenues for the top 25 research companies totaled $13.3 billion in 2004.[15] VNU is the world's largest market research organization; its Nielsen Media Research unit is the source of the well-known Nielsen TV ratings. In July 2005, VNU announced that it would acquire IMS for $7 billion.[16] The top global marketing research companies are shown in Table 6-1.

The process of collecting data and converting it into useful information can be quite detailed, as shown in Figure 6-1. In the discussion that follows, we will focus on eight basic steps: information requirement, problem definition, choosing unit of analysis, examining data availability, assessing the value of research, research design, data analysis, and presenting the research findings.

Company (Home Country)	2004 Research-only Revenues ($ billions)	Competitive Focus
1. VNU NV (United States and the Netherlands)	$3.4	Units include ACNielsen, Nielsen Media Research, Claritas, and Spectra. Focus on media monitoring and business information.
2. Taylor Nelson Sofres PLC (United Kingdom)	$1.7	Custom business research; polling and social research; syndicated services.
3. IMS Health Inc. (United States)	$1.6	Provides market information to pharmaceutical and health-care industries.
4. The Kantar Group (United States; unit of WPP Group)	$1.1	Units include Millward Brown and Research International. Focus on brand awareness and media analysis.
5. GfK Group (Germany)	$.835	Five business units offer custom research and consumer tracking services, plus research on retail and technology, media, and health-care sectors.

Table 6-1

Leading Global Market Research Companies

Source: Adapted from Anne Ryman, "Top 25 Global Research," *Marketing News*, August 15, 2005.

---

[14] Michael R. Czinkota and Ilkka A. Ronkainen, "Market Research for Your Export Operations: Part I—Using Secondary Sources of Research," *International Trade Forum* 30, no. 3 (1994), pp. 22–33.

[15] Datamonitor, "Global Market Research—Industry Profile," November 2003, p. 6.

[16] Jason Singer and Dennis K. Berman, "VNU Weighs Big Moves to Get Its Prize," *The Wall Street Journal*, September 29, 2005, p. A3.

Figure 6-1

The International Marketing Research Process

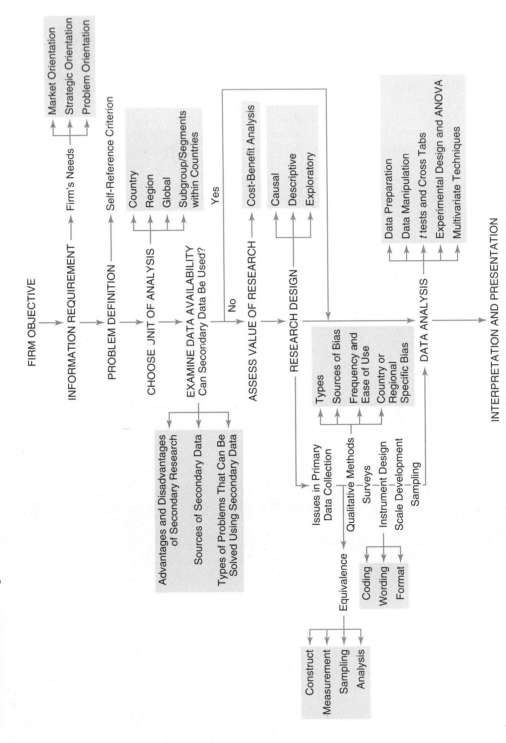

Source: Kumar, V., *International Marketing Research*, 1st Edition, © 2000. Reprinted by permission of Pearson Education, Inc. Upper Saddle River, NJ.

Step 1: Identify the Information Requirement

The following story illustrates the first step in the formal marketing research process:

> The vice presidents of finance and marketing of a shoe company were traveling around the world to estimate the market potential for their products. They arrived in a very poor country and both immediately noticed that none of the local citizens wore shoes. The vice president of finance said, "We might as well get back on the plane. There is no market for shoes in this country." The vice president of marketing replied, "What an opportunity! Everyone in this country is a potential customer!"

The potential market for shoes was enormous in the eyes of the marketing executive. To formally confirm his instinct, some research would be required. As this story shows, research is often undertaken after a problem or opportunity has presented itself. Perhaps a competitor is making inroads in one or more important markets around the world. Maybe research on local taste preferences is required to determine if a food product must be adapted. Or, as in this story, a company may wish to determine whether a particular country or regional market offers good growth potential. What is the likelihood that potential customers can be converted into *actual* customers? It is a truism of market research that a problem well defined is a problem half solved. Thus, regardless of what situation sets the research effort in motion, the first two questions a marketer should ask are "What information do I need?" and "Why do I need this information?" Table 6-2 lists various subject categories that may require research.

Step 2: Problem Definition

As noted in Chapter 4, when a person's home-country values and beliefs influence the assessment of a foreign culture or country, the self-reference criterion (SRC) is at work. The SRC tendency underscores the importance of understanding the cultural environments of global markets, as the following examples illustrate:

- When Mattel first introduced Barbie in Japan, managers assumed that Japanese girls would find the doll's design just as appealing as American girls did. They didn't.
- When the Walt Disney Company opened Disneyland Paris, park employees were expected to comply with a detailed written code regarding personal appearance. The goal was to ensure that guests receive the kind of experience associated with the Disney name. However, the French considered the code to be an insult to French culture, individualism, and privacy.

Category	Coverage
1. Market potential	Demand estimates, consumer behavior, review of products, channels, communication media
2. Competitor information	Corporate, business, and functional strategies; resources and intentions; capabilities
3. Foreign exchange	Balance of payments, interest rates, attractiveness of country currency, expectations of analysts
4. Prescriptive information	Laws, regulations, rulings concerning taxes, earnings, dividends in both host and home countries
5. Resource information	Availability of human, financial, physical, and information resources
6. General conditions	Overall review of sociocultural, political, technological environments

Table 6-2

Subject Agenda Categories for a Global Marketing Information System

As these examples show, assumptions that companies make based on home-country marketing success can turn out to be wrong when applied globally. It may also be the case that marketers assume that a marketing program that is successful in one country market can be applied to other country markets in the region. Consider the case of Disney's theme park business again. Although Disneyland Japan was a huge success from opening day, the $3.2 billion Hong Kong Disneyland that opened in 2005 has been less successful. This is due in part to the fact that mainland Chinese have little familiarity with traditional Disney "face characters" such as Snow White. As Jay Rasulo, president of Disney's park and resort division, noted, "People from the mainland don't show up with the embedded 'Disney software' like at other parks."[17]

When approaching global markets, it is best to have "eyes wide open." In other words, marketers must be aware of the impact that SRC and other cross-cultural assumptions can have. Such awareness can have several positive effects. First, it can enhance management's willingness to conduct market research in the first place. Second, an awareness of SRC can help ensure that the research effort is designed with minimal home-country or second-country bias. Third, it can enhance management's receptiveness to accepting research findings—even if they contradict "tried and true" marketing experience in other markets.

Step 3: Choose Unit of Analysis

The next step involves the need to identify in what part(s) of the world the company should be doing business and finding out as much as possible about the business environment in the area(s) identified. These issues are reflected in the subject agenda categories in Table 6-2. The unit of analysis may be a single country; it may also be a region such as Europe or South America. In some instances, the marketer is interested in a segment that is global. Countrywide data are not required for all market entry decisions. Rather, a specific city, state, or province may be the relevant unit of analysis. For example, a company that is considering entering China may focus initially on Shanghai. Located in the Jiangsu province, Shanghai is China's largest city and main seaport. Because Shanghai is a manufacturing center, has a well-developed infrastructure, and is home to a population with relatively high per capita income, it is the logical focus of a market research effort.

Step 4: Examine Data Availability

The first task at this stage is to answer several questions regarding the availability of data. What type of data should be gathered? Are data available in company files, a library, industry or trade journals, or online? Can secondary data be used? When does management need the information in order to make a decision regarding market entry? Marketers must address these issues before proceeding to the next step of the research process. Using data that are readily available saves both money and time. A formal market study can cost hundreds of thousands of dollars and take many months to complete.

A low-cost approach to market research and data collection begins with desk research. In other words, "the key to creating a cost-effective way of surveying foreign markets is to climb on the shoulders of those who have gone before."[18] Suppose a marketer wants to assess the basic market potential for a particular product. To find the answer, secondary sources are a good place to start. Personal files, company or public libraries, online databases, government census records,

---

17 Merissa Marr and Geoffrey A. Fowler, "Chinese Lessons for Disney," *The Wall Street Journal,* June 12, 2006, p. B1.
18 Michael R. Czinkota and Ilkka A. Ronkainen, "Market Research for Your Export Operations: Part I—Using Secondary Sources of Research," *International Trade Forum* 30, no. 3 (1994), p. 22.

and trade associations are just a few of the data sources that can be tapped with minimal effort and cost. Data from these sources already exist. Such data are known as *secondary data* because they were not gathered for the specific project at hand. *Statistical Abstract of the United States* is just one of the annual publications issued by the U.S. government that contains myriad facts about international markets. The U.S. government's most comprehensive source of world trade data is the National Trade Data Base (NTDB), an online resource from the Department of Commerce. Another commerce department Web site, STAT-USA/Internet (www.stat-usa.gov), is an excellent online source for merchandise trade, gross domestic product, and other current and historical data. Most countries compile national accounts estimates of gross national product (GNP), gross domestic product (GDP), consumption, investment, government expenditures, and price levels. Demographic data indicating the population size, distribution of population by age category, and rates of population growth are also available. Market information is also available from export census documents compiled by the department of commerce on the basis of shipper's export declarations (known as "ex-decs" or SEDs, these must be filled out for any export valued at $1,500 or more). Another important source of market data is the Foreign Commercial Service. Many countries have set up Web sites to help small firms find opportunities in world markets. For example, the Canadian Trade Commissioner Service (www.infoexport.gc.ca) is a service of Canada's Department of Foreign Affairs and International Trade (DFAIT). The site is a computerized database containing the names of Canadian companies that export.

These do not exhaust the types of data available, however. A single source, *The Statistical Yearbook of the United Nations*, contains global data on agriculture, mining, manufacturing, construction, energy production and consumption, internal and external trade, railroad and air transport, wages and prices, health, housing, education, communication infrastructure, and availability of mass communication media. The U.S. Central Intelligence Agency publishes *World Factbook*, which is revised yearly. Other important sources are the World Bank, the International Monetary Fund, and Japan's Ministry of International Trade and Industry (MITI). *The Economist* and *Financial Times* regularly compile comprehensive surveys of regional and country markets and include them in their publications. Data from these sources are generally available in both print and electronic form.

How can such data be useful? Take industrial growth patterns as one example. Because they generally reveal consumption patterns, production patterns are helpful in assessing market opportunities. Additionally, trends in manufacturing production indicate potential markets for companies that supply manufacturing inputs. At the early stages of growth in a country, when per capita incomes are low, manufacturing centers on such necessities as food and beverages, textiles, and other forms of light industry. As incomes rise, the relative importance of these industries declines as heavy industry begins to develop.

A word of caution is in order at this point: Remember that data are compiled from various sources, some of which may not be reliable. Even when the sources are reliable, there is likely to be some variability from source to source. Anyone using data should be clear on exactly what the data are measuring. For example, studying income data requires understanding whether one is working with GNP or GDP figures. Also, anyone using the Internet as an information source should evaluate the credibility of the person(s) responsible for the Web site. Moreover, as Czinkota and Ronkainen note,[19] secondary data may support the decision to pursue a market opportunity outside the home country, but it is unlikely to shed light on specific questions: What is the market potential for our furniture in Indonesia? How much does the typical Nigerian consumer spend on soft drinks? If a packaging change is

[19] Michael R. Czinkota and Ilkka A. Ronkainen, "Market Research for Your Export Operations: Part II—Conducting Primary Marketing Research," *International Trade Forum* 31, no. 1 (1995), p. 16.

Table 6-3

*Global Market Research Reports
from MarketResearch.com*

Title of Study	Length in Pages	Price
World Pharmaceutical Chemicals	438	$4,500
Internet Commerce in Canada 2000–2006	22	$4,500
World Alcohol—Strategic Review	900	$3,950
Global Airport Retailing	185	$1,115
The Market for Travel and Tourism in Russia	73	$1,000
Pet Food and Pet Products in India	36	$1,000
Online Music in Japan	12	$995
The 2000–2005 World Ice Cream Outlook	110	$795
Automobiles and Automotive Parts in Brazil	170	$136

Source: The Information Catalog, 2nd Quarter 2002, MarketResearch.com. Marketing Research Association.

made to ensure compliance with Germany's Green Dot Ordinance, what effect, if any, will the change have on consumer purchasing behavior?

Syndicated studies published by private research companies are another source of secondary data and information (the word *syndicated* comes from the newspaper industry and refers to the practice of selling articles, cartoons, or guest columns to a number of different organizations). For example, MarketResearch.com (www.marketresearch.com) sells reports on a wide range of global business sectors; the company partners with 350 research firms to offer a comprehensive set of reports. A sampling of reports available from MarketResearch.com is shown in Table 6-3; while a single report can cost thousands of dollars, a company may be able to get the market information it needs without incurring the cost associated with primary research.

Step 5: Assess Value of Research

When data are not available through published statistics or studies, management may wish to conduct further study of the country market, region, or global segment. However, collecting information costs money. Thus, the plan should also spell out what this information is worth to the company in dollars (or euro, yen, etc.) compared with what it would cost to collect it. What will the company gain by collecting this data? What would be the cost of not getting the data that could be converted into useful information? Research requires an investment of both money and managerial time, and it is necessary to perform a cost-benefit analysis before proceeding further. In some instances, a company may pursue the same course of action no matter what the research reveals. Even when more information is needed to ensure a high-quality decision, a realistic estimate of a formal study may reveal that the cost to perform research is simply too high.

The small markets around the world pose a special problem for the researcher. The relatively low profit potential in smaller markets justifies only modest expenditures for marketing research. Therefore, the global researcher must devise techniques and methods that keep expenditures in line with the market's profit potential. In smaller markets, there is pressure on the researcher to discover economic and demographic relationships that permit estimates of demand based on a minimum of information. It may also be necessary to use inexpensive survey research that sacrifices some elegance or statistical rigor to achieve results within the constraints of the smaller market research budget.

Step 6: Research Design

As indicated in Figure 6-1, if secondary data can be used, the researcher can go directly to the data analysis step. Suppose, however, data are not available through published statistics or studies; in addition, suppose that the cost-benefit analysis indicated in Step 4 has been performed and that the decision has been made to carry on with the research effort. *Primary data* are gathered through original research pertaining to the particular problem identified in Step 1. At this point, it is time to establish a research design.

Global marketing guru David Arnold offers the following guidelines regarding data gathering:[20]

- Use multiple indicators rather than a single measure. This approach will decrease the level of uncertainty for decision makers. As the saying goes, "There are three sides to every story: your side, my side, and the truth." A land surveyor can pinpoint the location of a third object given the known location of two objects. This technique, known as *triangulation*, is equally useful in global market research.
- Individual companies should develop customized indicators specific to the industry, product market, or business model. Such indicators should leverage a company's previous experience in global markets. For example, in some developing markets, Mary Kay Cosmetics uses the average wage of a female secretary as a basis for estimating income potential for its beauty consultants.
- Always conduct comparative assessments in multiple markets. Do not assess a particular market in isolation. Comparative assessment enables management to develop a "portfolio" approach in which alternative priorities and scenarios can be developed. For example, to better understand Czech consumers in general, a company might also conduct research in nearby Poland and Hungary. By contrast, if a brewing company wished to learn more about beer consumption patterns in the Czech Republic, it might also conduct research in Ireland and Germany where per capita beer consumption is high.
- Observations of purchasing patterns and other behavior should be weighted more heavily than reports or opinions regarding purchase intention or price sensitivity. Particularly in developing markets, it is difficult to accurately survey consumer perceptions.

With these guidelines in mind, the marketer must address a new set of questions and issues in primary data collection. Should the research effort be geared toward quantitative, numerical data that can be subjected to statistical analysis or should qualitative techniques be used? In global marketing research, it is advisable for the plan to call for a mix of techniques. For consumer products, qualitative research is especially well suited to accomplish the following tasks:[21]

- To provide consumer understanding; to "get close" to the consumer
- To describe the social and cultural context of consumer behavior, including cultural, religious, and political factors that impact decision making
- Identify core brand equity and "get under the skin" of brands
- To "mine" the consumer and identify what people really feel

Issues in Data Collection

The research problem may be more narrowly focused on marketing issues, such as the need to adapt products and other mix elements to local tastes and assessing demand and profit potential. Demand and profit potential, in turn, depend in part on whether the market being studied can be classified as existing or potential. *Existing markets* are those in which customer needs are already being served by

---

[20] David Arnold, *The Mirage of Global Markets* (Upper Saddle River, NJ: Financial Times Prentice Hall, 2004), pp. 41–43.

[21] John Pawle, "Mining the International Consumer," *Journal of the Market Research Society* 41, no. 1 (1999), p. 20.

one or more companies. In many countries, data about the size of existing markets—in terms of monetary volume and unit sales—are readily available. In some countries, however, formal market research is a relatively new phenomenon and data are scarce. McKinsey & Company, Gartner Group Asia, and Grey China Advertising have been very active in China. For example, using focus groups and other techniques, Grey China gathers a wealth of information about attitudes and buying patterns that it publishes in its *Grey ChinaBase Annual Consumer Study*. Recent findings point to growing concerns about the future, Westernization of grocery purchases, growing market saturation, increasingly discerning customers, and a rise in consumer willingness to try new products. Even so, data gathered by different sources may be inconsistent. What is the level of soft-drink consumption in China? Euromonitor International estimates consumption at 23 billion liters, while Coca-Cola's in-house marketing research team places the figure at 39 billion liters. Likewise, CSM, a Chinese television-rating agency, estimates the TV-advertising market at $2.8 billion per year. According to Nielsen Media Research, the figure is closer to $7.5 billion.[22]

In such situations, and in countries where such data are not available, researchers must first estimate the market size, the level of demand, or the rate of product purchase or consumption. A second research objective in existing markets may be assessment of the company's overall competitiveness in terms of product appeal, price, distribution, and promotional coverage and effectiveness. Researchers may be able to pinpoint a weakness in the competitor's product or identify an under- or unserved market segment. The minivan and sport utility vehicle segments of the auto industry illustrate the opportunity an existing market can present. Chrysler dominates the U.S. minivan market, for which annual sales total about 1.2 million vehicles. Most global marketers compete in this segment. For example, Toyota introduced its Japanese-built Previa in the United States in 1991; critics mocked the teardrop styling and dismissed it as being underpowered. For the 1998 model year, the Previa was replaced with the American-built Sienna. To ensure that Sienna suited American tastes, Toyota designers and engineers studied Chrysler minivans and duplicated key features such as numerous cup holders and a sliding driver-side rear door.

In some instances, there is no existing market to research. Such *potential markets* can be further subdivided into latent and incipient markets. A **latent market** is, in essence, an undiscovered segment. It is a market in which demand would materialize *if* an appropriate product were made available. In a latent market, demand is zero before the product is offered. In the case of existing markets such as the one for minivans described previously, the main research challenge is to understand the extent to which competition fully meets customer needs. As J. Davis Illingworth, an executive at Toyota Motor Sales USA, explained, "I think the American public will look at Sienna as an American product that meets their needs."[23] With latent markets, initial success is not based on a company's competitiveness. Rather, it depends on the prime mover advantage—a company's ability to uncover the opportunity and launch a marketing program that taps the latent demand. This is precisely what Chrysler achieved by single-handedly creating the minivan market.

Sometimes, traditional marketing research is not an effective means for identifying latent markets. In a *The Wall Street Journal* article, Peter Drucker pointed out that the failure of American companies to successfully commercialize fax machines—an American innovation—can be traced to research that indicated no potential demand for such a product. The problem, in Drucker's view, stems from the typical survey question for a product targeted at a latent market. Suppose a researcher asks, "Would you buy a telephone accessory that costs upwards of $1,500 and enables you to send,

---

22 Gabriel Kahn, "Chinese Puzzle: Spotty Consumer Data," *The Wall Street Journal*, October 15, 2003, p. B1.
23 Kathleen Kerwin, "Can This Minivan Dent Detroit?" *Business Week*, February 3, 1997, p. 37.

for $1 a page, the same letter the post office delivers for $0.25?" On the basis of economics alone, the respondent most likely will answer, "No."

Drucker explained that Japanese companies are the leading sellers of fax machines today because their understanding of the market was not based on survey research. Instead, they reviewed the early days of mainframe computers, photocopy machines, cellular telephones, and other information and communications products. The Japanese realized that, judging only by the initial economics of buying and using these new products, the prospects of market acceptance were low. However, each of these products had become a huge success after people began to use them. This realization prompted the Japanese to focus on the market for the *benefits* provided by fax machines, rather than the market for the machines themselves. By looking at the success of courier services such as FedEx, the Japanese realized that, in essence, the fax machine market already existed.[24]

"At that time, Japanese women almost never used mascaras because, by nature, they have very straight, short and thin lashes. We designed a mascara that was able to lengthen and curl lashes. It was a huge success. We would never have seen that in a focus group."[25]

Jean-Paul Agon, CEO, L'Oréal, discussing the decision to relaunch the Maybelline makeup brand in Japan with mascara.

challenges in the global marketplace

Motorola spent more than a decade and billions of dollars developing Iridium, an ambitious new business that would offer satellite-global personal communications services to supplement ground-based wire and cellular telephone services. If it succeeded, Iridium would be a historic first: A business that was truly global from day one of operations. Iridium's first customers were expected to include globetrotting business executives who need to send and receive voice messages and data and who want a single telephone number that will work anywhere on the planet. In addition, the business concept was based on the fact that 90 percent of the world's population lacks access to telephones. Iridium could bring wireless telephone service to rural areas in South America, India, and Africa.

Motorola executives projected that Iridium would attract 5 million users by the year 2002. Each subscriber was expected to contribute $1,000 per year in net revenues to Iridium. In essence, Iridium was a huge bet that the varying technology standards of conventional cellular telephone systems would provide the key to Iridium's success. At the time, cellular phone standards were different in Europe and the United States so a European businessperson's cell phone unit is rendered inoperable across the Atlantic in the United States. Iridium's early customers would have to pay approximately $3,000 for new telephones. Usage fees for satellite telephone calls were set in a range from $1.75 to $7.00 per minute

Industry observers were skeptical. Some wondered whether Motorola could really recoup its investment. One consultant got to the heart of the matter when he asked, "The biggest single issue is, can they sell it? There is no good head count of international businessmen who need this." For their part, Iridium executives reasoned that some 40 million people travel from the United States each year. Even if a small percentage of them became Iridium users, the service would be a success.

Early in 1997, Iridium management announced a number of strategic changes. The company was now aiming to sign up 3 million businesspeople such as contractors, people employed in the oil and gas industries, maritime workers, and employees of heavy construction firms such as Schlumberger

and Bechtel. Such professional travelers, it was hoped, would account for about two-thirds of Iridium's revenues. As Dr. Edward Staiano, Iridium's vice chairman and chief executive, said, "The guy who's going to pay for this system is the guy who doesn't look at his phone bill." This change deemphasized the opportunity in emerging markets with undeveloped telephone systems.

A $140 million global print advertising campaign created by Ammirati Puris Lintas was launched in June 1998. Voice services began on November 1, with paging services available November 15. However, the required number of actual customers never materialized, and by 2000, it appeared that it was all over for Iridium except for the funeral. The apparent lesson: There was no latent market for a premium-priced global satellite telephone service.

However, in late 2000, a group of private investors bought Iridium's assets for the fire-sale price of $25 million. The new owners, doing business as Iridium Satellite LLC, secured a two-year contract with the Pentagon to provide satellite phones to embassy employees and other government agencies. Then Boeing signed an agreement to maintain the satellite network. "We do not see Iridium as a mass consumer service," said Dan Colussy, chairman of the Iridium Satellite LLC. "It is a communications service that addresses the very specific needs of the industrial markets and other specialized segments. Because of our significantly reduced cost structure and Iridium's unique system capabilities, we will be able to serve these markets more effectively than any other existing service." The satellite phone system has proved its worth in the aftermath of natural disasters such as the Asian tsunami in 2004 and Hurricane Katrina in 2005.

Sources: Sarmad Ali, "Reliable Connections Broaden Demand for Satellite Phones," The Wall Street Journal, November 3, 2005, p. B1; Paul Davidson, "Satellite Phones Provide Critical Link to Outside World," USA Today, September 6, 2005, p. 3B; Quentin Hardy, "Iridium Gets U.S. as First Big Customer of Wireless Communications System," The Wall Street Journal, January 26, 1998, p. B6; Sally Beatty, "Iridium Hopes to Ring Up Global Sales," The Wall Street Journal, June 22, 1998, p. B8; Quentin Hardy, "Iridium Creates New Plan for Global Cellular Service," The Wall Street Journal, August 18, 1997, p. B4.

---

[24] Peter F. Drucker, "Marketing 101 for a Fast-Changing Decade," *The Wall Street Journal,* November 20, 1990, p. A17.
[25] Adam Jones, "How to Make Up Demand," *Financial Times,* October 3, 2006, p. 8.

Today's Iridium satellite telephone system operates on a much smaller scale than when the service was launched in 1999. Meanwhile, hoping to recover several billion dollars from the failed investment, creditors are suing Motorola in bankruptcy court. Among other things, the plaintiffs allege that Iridium overpaid Motorola for the satellites that it built. In 2007, a U.S. bankruptcy judge dismissed most of the claims against Motorola.

"When we first started, we said there is no existing market for Red Bull, but Red Bull will create it. And this is what finally became true."[26]

Dietrich Mateschitz, creator of Red Bull energy drink, hired a market research firm to test Red Bull. The test indicated a negative reaction to the taste, the logo, and the brand name. Mateschitz ignored the research, and Red Bull is now a $2 billion brand.

An **incipient market** is a market that will emerge if a particular economic, demographic, political, or sociocultural trend continues. A company is not likely to achieve satisfactory results if it offers a product in an incipient market before the trends have taken root. After the trends have had a chance to unfold, the incipient market will become latent and, later, existing. The concept of incipient markets can also be illustrated by the impact of rising income on demand for automobiles and other expensive consumer durables. As per capita income rises in a country, the demand for automobiles will also rise. Therefore, if a company can predict a country's future rate of income growth, it can also predict the growth rate of its automobile market. For example, to capitalize on China's rapid economic growth, Volkswagen, Peugeot, Chrysler, and other global automakers have established in-country manufacturing operations. There is even incipient demand in China for imported exotic cars; in early 1994, Ferrari opened its first showroom in Beijing. Because of a 150 percent import tax, China's first Ferrari buyers were entrepreneurs who had profited from China's increasing openness to Western-style marketing and capitalism. By the end of the 1990s, demand for luxury cars had grown at a faster rate than anticipated. Today, there are 30 million cars and light trucks for China's 1.3 billion people. Clearly, China is a very attractive market opportunity for carmakers.

By contrast, some companies have concluded that China has limited potential at present. For example, in 1998, U.K.-based retailer Marks & Spencer closed its office in Shanghai and tabled plans to open a store in China. Commenting to the press, a company representative directly addressed the issue of whether or not China represented an incipient market:

> After three years of research, we have come to the conclusion that the timing is not right. The majority of our customers are from middle-income groups. But, our interest is in Shanghai, and the size of the middle-income group, although it is growing, is not yet at a level that would justify us opening a store there.[27]

26 Kerry A. Dolan, "The Soda with Buzz," *Forbes*, March 28, 2005, p. 126.
27 James Harding, "Foreign Investors Face New Curbs on Ownership of Stores," *Financial Times*, November 10, 1998, p. 7.

Research Methodologies

Survey research, interviews, consumer panels, observation, and focus groups are some of the tools used to collect primary market data. These are the same tools used by marketers whose activities are not global; however, some adaptations and special considerations for global marketing may be required.

Survey research utilizes questionnaires designed to elicit quantitative data ("How much would you buy?"), qualitative responses ("Why would you buy?"), or both. Survey research is often conducted by means of a questionnaire distributed through the mail, by telephone, or in person. Many good marketing research textbooks provide details on questionnaire design and administration.

In global marketing research, a number of survey design and administration issues may arise. When using the telephone as a research tool, it is important to remember that what is customary in one country may be impossible in others because of infrastructure differences, cultural barriers, or other reasons. For example, telephone directories or lists may not be available; also, important differences may exist between urban dwellers and people in rural areas. In China, for example, the Ministry of Information Industry reports that 77 percent of households in coastal areas have at least one fixed-line telephone; in rural areas, the number is only 40 percent.

At a deeper level, culture shapes attitudes and values in a way that will directly affect people's willingness to respond to interviewer questions. Open-ended questions may help the researcher identify a respondent's frame of reference. In some cultures, respondents may be unwilling to answer certain questions, or they may intentionally give inaccurate answers.

Recall that Step 2 of the global market research process calls for identifying possible sources of SRC bias. This issue is especially important in survey research: SRC bias can originate from the cultural backgrounds of those designing the questionnaire. For example, a survey designed and administered in the United States may be inappropriate in non-Western cultures, even if it is carefully translated. This is especially true if the person designing the questionnaire is not familiar with the SRC. A technique known as **back translation** can help increase comprehension and validity; the technique requires that, after a questionnaire or survey instrument is translated into a particular target language, it is translated once again into the original by a different translator. For even greater accuracy, **parallel translations**—that is, two versions by different translators—can be used as input to the back translation. The same techniques can ensure that advertising copy is accurately translated into different languages.

Personal interviews allow researchers to ask "why?" and then explore answers with the respondent on a face-to-face basis.

A **consumer panel** is a sample of respondents whose behavior is tracked over time. For example, a number of companies, including the Nielsen Media Research unit of Netherlands-based VNU, AGB, GfK, and TNS, conduct television audience measurement (TAM) by studying the viewing habits of household panels. Broadcasters use audience share data to set advertising rates; advertisers such as Procter & Gamble, Unilever, and Coca-Cola use the data to choose programs during which to advertise. In the United States, Nielsen has enjoyed a virtual monopoly on viewership research for half a century. For years, however, the four major U.S. television networks have complained that they lose advertising revenues because Nielsen's data collection methods undercount viewership. Nielsen has responded to these concerns by upgrading its survey methodology; the company now uses an electronic device known as a **peoplemeter** to collect national audience data. Peoplemeter systems are currently in use in dozens of countries around the world, including China; Nielsen is also rolling out peoplemeters to collect local audience viewership data in key metropolitan markets, such as New York City.

When **observation** is used as a data collection method, one or more trained observers (or a mechanical device such as a video camera) watch and record the

behind the scenes

behavior of actual or prospective buyers. The research results are used to guide marketing managers in their decision making. For example, after Volkswagen's U.S. sales began to slump a few years ago, the company launched "Moonraker," an 18-month effort designed to help its engineers, marketers, and design specialists better understand American consumers. Despite the presence of a design center in California, decision makers at headquarters in Wolfsburg, Germany, generally ignored feedback from U.S. customers. As Stefan Liske, director of product strategy at VW, acknowledged, "We needed a totally different approach. We asked ourselves, 'Do we really know everything about this market?'" The Moonraker team visited the Mall of America in Minneapolis and the Rock and Roll Hall of Fame in Cleveland; they also spent spring break in Florida observing college students. The experience was an eye-opener; as one designer explained, "In Germany, it's all about driving, but here, it's about everything *but* driving. People here want to use their time in other ways, like talk on their cell phone." Another member of the team, an engineer, shadowed a single mom as she took her kids to school and ran errands. The engineer noted that American drivers need a place to store a box of tissues and a place to put a bag of fast food picked up at a drive-through window. "I began thinking about what specific features her car needed. It was about living the customer's life and putting ourselves in their place," he said.[28]

A marketer of breakfast cereals might send researchers to preselected households at 6 AM to watch families go about their morning routines. The client could also assign a researcher to accompany family members to the grocery store to observe their behavior under actual shopping conditions. The client might wish to know about the shoppers' reactions to in-store promotions linked to an advertising campaign. The researcher could record comments using a cassette recorder or discretely take photographs with a small camera. Companies using observation as a research methodology must be sensitive to public concerns about privacy issues. A second problem with observation is **reactivity**, which is the tendency of research subjects to behave differently for the simple reason that they know they are under study. Additional examples include the following:

- Hoping to gain insights for product and package design improvements, Procter & Gamble (P&G) sent video crews into 80 households in the United Kingdom, Italy, Germany, and China. P&G's ultimate goal is to amass an in-house video library that can be directly accessed by key word searches. Stan Joosten, an IT manager, noted, "You could search for 'eating snacks'

---

[28] Gina Chon, "VW's American Road Trip," *The Wall Street Journal*, January 4, 2006, pp. B1, B9.

and find all clips from all over the world on that topic. Immediately, it gives you a global perspective on certain topics."[29]

- Michelle Arnau, a marketing manager for Nestlé's PowerBar brand, attended the 2004 New York City Marathon to see how runners were using single-serve packets of PowerGel, a concentrated, performance-boosting gel in a single-serving packet. Arnau observed that runners typically tore off the top with their teeth and attempted to consume the gel in a single squeeze without breaking their stride. Arnau was dismayed to see that the long neck of the packet sometimes prevented the gel from flowing out quickly. Designers at Nestlé created an improved package with an upside-down triangular-shaped top that is narrow enough to control the flow of the gel but also fits into the athlete's mouth.[30]

In **focus group** research, a trained moderator facilitates discussion of a product concept, a brand's image and personality, advertisement, social trend, or other topic with a group comprised of 6 to 10 people. Global marketers can use focus groups to arrive at important insights. For example:

- In the mid-1990s, Whirlpool launched a European advertising campaign that featured fantasy characters such as a drying diva and a washing-machine goddess. The campaign's success prompted management to adapt it for use in the United States and Latin America. First, however, the company conducted focus groups to gauge reaction to the ads. Nick Mote, Whirlpool's worldwide account director at France's Publicis advertising agency, said, "We've had some incredible research results. It was just like somebody switched the lights on."[31]
- In Singapore, focus groups comprised of young teens were used to help guide development of Coca-Cola's advertising program. As Karen Wong, Coke's country marketing director for Singapore, explained, "We tested everything from extreme to borderline boring: body-piercing all over, grungy kids in a car listening to rock music and head-banging all the way. Youth doing things that youth in America do." Some participants found much of

Country	Technological/ Informational Infrastructure	Geographic Issues	Recommended Data Gathering Methodology	Privacy Issues
Brazil	Minimal. Government census is poor source of population data; difficult to get representative sample. Expensive to design a national probability sample. Lack of telephone penetration.	Research is expensive when sampling beyond metropolitan centers.	Face-to-face interviews; when interviewing broad socioeconomic groups, demo of interviewers should match demo of respondent group. Use street or mall intercept techniques. Security issues require use of teams. Researchers may offer a gift rather than cash as an incentive.	Wealthy respondents unlikely to answer questions about personal finance. To ensure confidentiality, banks bring interviewers based in the United States. To gain trust, ask respondents to recommend others.

Table 6-4

Market Research in Latin America

Source: Adapted from Arundhati Parmar, "Tailor Techniques to Each Audience in Latin Market," *Marketing News*, February 3, 2003, pp. 4–6.

[29] Emily Nelson, "P&G Checks Out Real Life," *The Wall Street Journal*, May 17, 2001, pp. B1, B4.
[30] Deborah Ball, "The Perils of Packaging: Nestlé Aims for Easier Openings," *The Wall Street Journal*, November 17, 2005, p. B1.
[31] Katheryn Kranhold, "Whirlpool Conjures Up Appliance Divas," *The Wall Street Journal*, April 27, 2000, p. B1.

Coke's imagery—for example, a shirtless young man crowd surfing at a rock concert and careening down a store aisle on a grocery cart—too rebellious. As one young Singaporean remarked, "They look like they're on drugs. And if they're on drugs, then how can they be performing at school?" Armed with the focus group results, Coca-Cola's managers devised an ad campaign for Singapore that was well within the bounds of societal approval.[32]

- When Blockbuster Video was planning its entry into Japan, the world's number two video rental market, the company convened focus groups to learn more about Japanese preferences and perceptions of existing video rental outlets. In the mid-1990s, most video stores in Japan were tiny operations with limited display space. Video titles were piled up from the floor to the ceilings, making it difficult to find and retrieve individual titles. Acting on the information provided by the focus groups, Blockbuster designed its Japanese stores with 3,000 square feet of floor space and display shelves that were more accessible.[33]

A typical focus group meets at a facility equipped with recording equipment and a one-way mirror behind which representatives of the client company observe the proceedings. The moderator can utilize a number approaches to elicit reactions and responses, including projective techniques, visualization, and role plays. When using a **projective technique**, the researcher presents open-ended or ambiguous stimuli to a subject. Presumably, when verbalizing a response, the subject will "project"—that is, reveal—his or her unconscious attitudes and biases. By analyzing the responses, researchers are better able to understand how consumers perceive a particular product, brand, or company. For example, in a focus group convened to assess car-buying preferences among a Striver-type segment, the researcher might ask participants to describe a party where various automotive brands are present. What is Nissan wearing, eating, and drinking? What kind of sneakers does Honda have on? What are their personalities like? Who's shy? Who's loud? Who gets the girl (or guy)? Interaction among group members can result in synergies that yield important qualitative insights that are likely to differ from those based on data gathered through more direct questioning. Focus group research is a technique that has grown in popularity. However, some industry observers caution that the technique has been used so much that participants, especially those who are used on a regular basis, have become overly familiar with its workings.

Focus group research yields qualitative data that does not lend itself to statistical projection. Such data suggests rather than confirms hypotheses; also, qualitative data tends to be directional rather than conclusive. Such data is extremely valuable in the exploratory phase of a project and is typically used in conjunction with data gathered via observation and other methods.

Scale Development

Market research requires assigning some type of measure, ranking, or interval to a response. To take a simple example of measurement, a *nominal scale* is used to establish the identity of a survey element. For example, male respondents could be labeled "1" and female respondents could be labeled "2." Scaling can also entail placing each response in some kind of continuum; a common example is the Likert scale that asks respondents to indicate whether they "strongly agree" with a statement, "strongly disagree," or whether their attitude falls somewhere in the middle. In a multicountry research project, it is important to

---

[32] Cris Prystay, "Selling to Singapore's Teens Is Tricky," *The Wall Street Journal*, October 4, 2002, p. B4.
[33] Khanh T. L. Tran, "Blockbuster Finds Success in Japan That Eluded the Chain in Germany," *The Wall Street Journal*, August 28, 1998, p. A14.

have **scalar equivalence**, which means that two respondents in different countries with the same value for a given variable receive equivalent scores on the same survey item.

Even with standard data-gathering techniques, the application of a particular technique may differ from country to country. Matthew Draper, vice president at New Jersey-based Total Research Corporation, cites "scalar bias" as a major problem: "There are substantial differences in the way people use scales, and research data based on scales such as rating product usefulness on a scale of 1 to 10 is therefore frequently cluttered with biases disguising the truth." For example, while the typical American scale would equate a high number such as 10 with "most" or "best" and 1 with "least," Germans prefer scales in which 1 is "most/best." Also, while American survey items pertaining to spending provide a range of figures, Germans prefer the opportunity to provide an exact answer.[34]

Sampling

When collecting data, researchers generally cannot administer a survey to every possible person in the designated group. A sample is a selected subset of a population that is representative of the entire population. The two best-known types of samples are probability samples and nonprobability samples. A probability sample is generated by following statistical rules that ensure that each member of the population under study has an equal chance—or probability—of being included in the sample. The results of a probability sample can be projected to the entire population with statistical reliability reflecting sampling error, degree of confidence, and standard deviation.

The results of a nonprobability sample cannot be projected with statistical reliability. One form of nonprobability sample is a *convenience sample*. As the name implies, researchers select people who are easy to reach. For example, in one study that compared consumer shopping attitudes in the United States, Jordan, Singapore, and Turkey, data for the latter three countries were gathered from convenience samples recruited by an acquaintance of the researcher. Although data gathered in this way are not subject to statistical inference, they may be adequate to address the problem defined in Step 1. In this study, for example, the researchers were able to identify a clear trend toward cultural convergence in shopping attitudes and customs that cut across modern industrial countries, emerging industrial countries, and developing countries.[35]

To obtain a *quota sample*, the researcher divides the population under study into categories; a sample is taken from each category. The term *quota* refers to the need to make sure that enough people are chosen in each category to reflect the overall makeup of the population. For example, assume a country's population may be divided into six categories according to monthly income as follows:

Percent of population	10%	15%	25%	25%	15%	10%
Earnings per month	0–9	10–19	20–39	40–59	60–69	70–100

If it is assumed that income is the characteristic that adequately differentiates the population for study purposes, then a quota sample would include respondents of different income levels in the same proportion as they occurred in the population, that is, 15 percent with monthly earnings from 10 to 19, and so on.

---

[34] Jack Edmonston, "U.S., Overseas Differences Abound," *Business Marketing* (January 1998), p. 32.
[35] Eugene H. Fram and Riad Ajami, "Globalization of Markets and Shopping Stress: Cross-Country Comparisons," *Business Horizons* 37, no. 1 (January–February 1994), pp. 17–23.

Step 7: Analyzing Data[36]

The data collected up to this point must be subjected to some form of analysis if it to be useful to decision makers. Although a detailed discussion is beyond the scope of this text, a brief overview is in order. First, the data must be prepared—the term *cleaned* is sometimes used—before further analysis is possible. It must be logged and stored in a central location or database; when research has been conducted in various parts of the world, rounding up data can pose some difficulties. Are data comparable across samples so that multicountry analysis can be performed? Some amount of editing may be required; for example, some responses may be missing or difficult to interpret. Next, questionnaires must be coded. Simply put, coding involves identifying the respondents and the variables. Finally, some data adjustment may be required.

Data analysis continues with *tabulation*, that is, the arrangement of data in tabular form. Researchers may wish to determine various things: the mean, median, and mode; range and standard deviation; and the shape of the distribution (e.g., normal curve). For nominally scaled variables such as "male" and "female," a simple cross-tabulation may be performed. Suppose, for example, Nielsen Media Research surveyed video gamers to determine how they felt about products (e.g., soft drinks) and advertisements (e.g., a billboard for a cell phone) embedded in video games. Nielsen could use cross-tabulation to separately examine the responses of male and female subjects to see if their responses differed significantly. If females were equally or more positive in their responses than males, video game companies could use this information to persuade consumer products companies to pay to have select products targeted at women featured as integral parts of the game. Researchers can also use various relatively simple statistical techniques such as hypothesis testing and chi-square testing; advanced data analysis such as analysis of variance (ANOVA), correlation analysis, and regression analysis can also be used.

If the researcher is interested in the interaction between variables, *interdependence techniques* such as factor analysis, cluster analysis, and multidimensional scaling (MDS) can be used. **Factor analysis** can be used to transform large amounts of data into manageable units; specialized computer programs perform data reduction by "distilling out" a few meaningful factors that underlie attitudes and perceptions from a multitude of survey responses. Factor analysis is useful in psychographic segmentation studies; it can also be used to create perceptual maps. In this form of analysis, variables are not classified as dependent or independent. Subjects are asked to rate specific product benefits on five-point scales; Table 6-5 shows a hypothetical scale that Nokia might use to assess

Table 6-5

Hypothetical Scales for Obtaining Consumer Perceptions of Nokia Music Phone

Instructions: Please rate this product on the following product characteristics or benefits.

Variables (Product Characteristic/Benefit)	Rating				
	Low 1	2	3	4	High 5
1. Long battery life	____	____	____	____	____
2. Many games available	____	____	____	____	____
3. Wireless Internet access	____	____	____	____	____
4. Thin case	____	____	____	____	____
5. Attractive styling	____	____	____	____	____
6. Music file storage capacity	____	____	____	____	____
7. Bright display screen	____	____	____	____	____
8. Fits hand comfortably	____	____	____	____	____
9. Works anywhere in the world	____	____	____	____	____
10. Custom face plates available	____	____	____	____	____

---

[36] Parts of this section are adapted from Glen L. Urban, John R. Hauser, and Nikhilesh Dholakia, *Essentials of New Product Management* (Upper Saddle River, NJ: Prentice Hall, 1987), Chapters 6 and 7.

Figure 6-2

How Factor Analysis Works

| Large number of variables (e.g., "bright display screen" and other key product attributes)—how do they interact? | → | Computer generates *factor loadings* for each variable so that a smaller number of factors (e.g., "easy to use") can be inferred by the researcher. | → | Computer generates *factor scores* for each respondent, which are used to create perceptual maps. |

consumer perceptions of a new combination cell phone/digital music player. Although the scale shown in Table 6-5 lists ten characteristics/benefits, factor analysis will generate *factor loadings* that enable the researcher to determine two or three factors that underlie the benefits. That is why it is said that factor analysis results in date reduction. For the N-Gage, the researcher might label the factors "easy to use" and "stylish." The computer will also output *factor scores* for each respondent; respondent 1 might have a factor score of .35 "easy to use"; respondent 2 might have .42, and so on. When all respondents' factor scores are averaged, the position of Nokia's music phone position on a perceptual map can be determined. Similar determinations can be made for other cell phone brands.

Cluster analysis allows the researcher to group variables into clusters that maximize within-group similarities and between-group differences. Cluster analysis shares some characteristics of factor analysis: It does not classify variables as dependent or independent, and it can be used in psychographic segmentation. Cluster analysis is well suited to global marketing research because similarities and differences can be established between local, national, and regional markets of the world. Cluster analysis can also be used to perform benefit segmentation and identify new product opportunities.

MDS is another technique for creating perceptual maps. When the researcher is using MDS, the respondent is given the task of comparing products or brands, one pair at a time, and judging them in terms of similarity. The researcher then infers the dimensions that underlie the judgments. MDS is particularly useful when there are many alternatives from which to choose—soft drink, toothpaste, or automotive brands, for instance—and when consumers may have difficulty verbalizing their perceptions. To create a well-defined spatial map, a minimum of eight products or brands should be used.

Suppose, for example, that a consumer uses an underlying perceptual dimension of "distinct image" in assessing the similarity of pairs of crossover SUVs. Table 6-6 shows a five-point similarity judgment scale for eight current

	Very Similar				Very Different
	1	2	3	4	5
Acura MDX/ Volvo XC90	___	___	___	___	___
Acura MDX/Infiniti FX45	___	___	___	___	___
Acura MDX/Lexus RX330	___	___	___	___	___
Acura MDX/Honda Pilot	___	___	___	___	___
Acura MDX/Nissan Murano	___	___	___	___	___
Acura MDX/Buick Rendezvous	___	___	___	___	___
Acura MDX/Toyota Highlander	___	___	___	___	___
Volvo XC90/Infiniti FX45	___	___	___	___	___
Volvo XC90/Lexus RX330	___	___	___	___	___
Volvo XC90/Honda Pilot	___	___	___	___	___
Volvo XC90/Nissan Murano	___	___	___	___	___
Volvo XC90/Buick Rendezvous	___	___	___	___	___
Volvo XC90/Toyota Highlander	___	___	___	___	___

Table 6-6

MDS Study Inputs: Similarity Judgment Scales for Pairs of Crossover SUVs

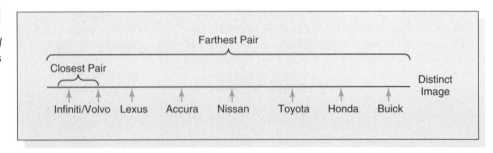

Figure 6-3

Hypothetical One-Dimensional Illustration of Similarity Judgments

crossover SUV models. Figure 6-3 shows the position of the eight SUV brands on the "distinct image" dimension for a hypothetical respondent. The figure shows that Infiniti and Volvo are the most similar while Infiniti and Buick are the farthest apart. The responses help marketers understand which brands in a particular category—crossover SUV brands in this example—are in direct competition with each other and which are not. The responses are input into a computer running an MDS program; the output is a perceptual map such as that shown in Figure 6-4. Once the computer has generated the map, the marketer examines the positions of different SUV models and infers the dimensions, which in this case are "comfort" and "distinct image." Such a map would have been helpful to, say Kia when management was designing its second-generation Sportage crossover SUV.

Dependence techniques assess the interdependence of two or more dependent variables with one or more independent variables. Conjoint analysis is an example of a dependence technique that is useful in both single market and global market research. To continue with the SUV example, suppose Kia's new product team has selected an ideal position on Figure 6-4; now the task is to select specific product features that will deliver that positioning. The researchers want to determine the relative importance of a product's *salient attributes* in consumer decision making; that is, the relevance or importance that consumers attach to a product's qualities or properties. If the target position is "smooth, car-like ride while protecting your family," the team must determine relevant physical product characteristics (e.g., 6-cylinder engine, rollover sensors, side-curtain airbags, and onboard global

Figure 6-4

Hypothetical MDS-based Perceptual Map for Crossover SUVs

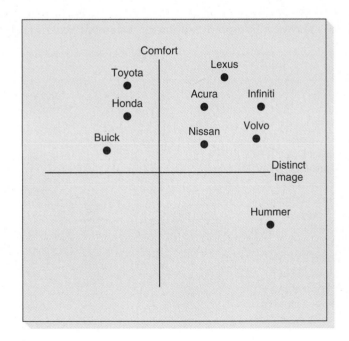

	Engine Size	Side-Curtain Airbags	Warranty	Price
Level 1	—	Side-curtain airbags for front-seat passengers only	—	$22,500
Level 2	6 cylinder	Side-curtain airbags for front-seat and middle passengers	5 years	$27,500
Level 3	8 cylinder	Side-curtain airbags for front-seat, middle, and third-row passengers	10 years	$32,500

Table 6-7

Product Feature Combinations for Crossover SUV

positioning system). The team must also determine other characteristics (e.g., price, mileage, warranty, etc.) that consumers most prefer. Each attribute should be available in different levels (e.g., 5-year or 10-year warranty). **Conjoint analysis** is a tool that researchers can use to gain insights into the combination of features that will be most attractive to consumers; it is assumed that features affect both perception and preferences. Table 6-7 shows a listing of possible features; a total of 36 combinations are possible. In a full-profile approach, each of these combinations (e.g., 6 cylinder, side-curtain airbags for three rows, 5-year warranty, $27,500) is printed on an index card, and consumers are asked to rank them in order by preference. Conjoint analysis then determines the values or *utilities* of the various levels of product features and plots them graphically. Because the number of combinations can overwhelm subjects and lead to fatigue, it is sometimes preferable to use a pair-wise approach that allows them to consider two attributes at a time.

Better marketing research might have helped Nokia in its struggle to maintain leadership in the highly competitive global cellular phone market. Nokia focused on the functionality and features of its phones, even as consumer tastes and preferences were shifting to trendy styling and features such as cameras and large color screens. For years, Nokia only manufactured so-called "candy bar" phones; because executives believed that the shape was a signature of the Nokia brand, the company did not offer flip (clamshell), slide, or swivel styles. Meanwhile, Sony, LG, Samsung, and Motorola were offering sleek new designs. In Europe, Nokia's market share fell from 51 percent in 2002 to about 33 percent in 2004. "Nokia didn't have the coolness factor," says industry consultant Jack Gold. "They didn't really do flip phones; they were a little late with cameras, and they didn't push them. Coolness in the consumer space is a big deal, and they were stodgy." Ansii Vanjoki, Nokia's head of multimedia, acknowledges, "We read the signs in the marketplace a bit wrong. The competition was emphasizing factors such as color richness and screen size. That's attractive at the point of sale. We missed that one."[37]

Comparative Analysis and Market Estimation by Analogy

One of the unique opportunities in global marketing analysis is to conduct comparisons of market potential and marketing performance in different country or regional markets at the same point in time. A common form of comparative analysis is the intracompany cross-national comparison. For example, general market conditions in two or more countries (as measured by income, stage of industrialization, or some other indicator) may be similar. If there is a significant discrepancy between per capita sales of a given product in the countries, the marketer might reasonably wonder about it and determine what actions need to be taken.

- Soon after George Fisher became CEO of Kodak, he asked for a review of market share in color film on a country-by-country basis. Fisher was shocked to learn that Kodak's market share in Japan was only 7 percent,

[37] Nelson D. Schwartz and Joan M. Levinstein, "Has Nokia Lost It?" *Fortune*, January 24, 2005, pp. 98–106.

compared with 40 percent in most other countries. The situation prompted Fisher to lodge a petition with the U.S. trade representative seeking removal of alleged anticompetitive barriers in Japan. The WTO ultimately ruled against Kodak.

- Campbell's commands nearly 80 percent of the U.S. canned soup market. However, former CEO Dale Morrison set aggressive growth goals for Campbell based on figures showing that Campbell's has just 10 percent market share throughout the rest of the world.[38]
- Catalog sales in the United States represent about 3 percent of overall retail sales. By comparison, catalog sales in Germany account for 5.8 percent of overall sales. This suggests that there is a catalog marketing opportunity in Germany.[39]

In these examples, data are, for the most part, available. However, global marketers may find that certain types of desired data are unavailable for a particular country market. This is especially true in developing country markets. If this is the case, it is sometimes possible to estimate market size or potential demand by analogy. Drawing an *analogy* is simply stating a partial resemblance. For example, the advertising and computer industries in the United States both have geographic nicknames. The advertising industry is often referred to as "Madison Avenue," while the phrase "Silicon Valley" is synonymous with California's high-tech industry center. Suppose someone is familiar with the Silicon Valley but has never heard of Madison Avenue. One way to explain it is to say that Silicon Valley is to the computer industry as Madison Avenue is to the advertising industry. Statements such as this are analogies. Analogy reduces the unknown by highlighting the "commonness" of two different things.[40]

David Arnold notes that there are four possible approaches to forecasting by analogy:[41]

- Data is available on a comparable product in the same country.
- Data is available on the same product in a comparable country.
- Data is available on the same product from an independent distributor in a neighboring country.
- Data is available about a comparable company in the same country.

Time-series displacement is an analogy technique based on the assumption that an analogy between markets exists in different time periods. Displacing time is a useful form of market analysis when data are available for two markets at different levels of development. The time displacement method requires a marketer to estimate when two markets are at similar stages of development. For example, the market for Polaroid instant cameras in Russia at the present time is comparable to the instant camera market in the United States in the mid-1960s. By obtaining data on the factors associated with demand for instant cameras in the United States in 1964 and in Russia today, as well as actual U.S. demand in 1964, one could estimate current potential in Russia.

---

[38] Amy Barrett, "Souping Up Campbell's," *Business Week,* November 3, 1997, p. 70.
[39] Cecilie Rohwedder, "U.S. Mail-Order Firms Shake Up Europe," *The Wall Street Journal,* January 6, 1998, p. A15.
[40] Ikujiro Nonaka and Hirotaka Takeuchi, *The Knowledge-Creating Company* (Cambridge, MA: Harvard Business School Press, 1995), p. 67. As Nonaka and Takeuchi explain, "Metaphor and analogy are often confused. Association of two things through metaphor is driven mostly by intuition and holistic imagery and does not aim to find differences between them. On the other hand, association through analogy is carried out by rational thinking and focuses on structural/ functional similarities between two things . . . Thus analogy helps us understand the unknown through the known. . . ."
[41] David Arnold, *The Mirage of Global Markets* (Upper Saddle River, NJ: Financial Times Prentice Hall, 2004), pp. 41–43.

Step 8: Presenting the Findings

The report based on the market research must be useful to managers as input to the decision-making process. Whether the report is presented in written form, orally, or electronically via videotape, it must relate clearly to the problem or opportunity identified in Step 1. Generally, it is advisable for major findings to be summarized concisely in a memo that indicates the answer or answers to the problem first proposed in Step 1. Many managers are uncomfortable with research jargon and complex quantitative analysis. Results should be clearly stated and provide a basis for managerial action. Otherwise, the report may end up on the shelf, where it will gather dust and serve as a reminder of wasted time and money. As the data provided by a corporate information system and market research become increasingly available on a worldwide basis, it becomes possible to analyze marketing expenditure effectiveness across national boundaries. Managers can then decide where they are achieving the greatest marginal effectiveness for their marketing expenditures and can adjust expenditures accordingly.

HEADQUARTERS CONTROL OF MARKETING RESEARCH

An important issue for the global company is where to locate control of the organization's research capability. The difference between a multinational, polycentric company and a global, geocentric company on this issue is significant. In the multinational company, responsibility for research is delegated to the operating subsidiary. The global company delegates responsibility for research to operating subsidiaries but retains overall responsibility and control of research as a headquarters' function. A key difference between single-country market research and global market research is the importance of comparability. In practice, this means that the global company must ensure that research is designed and executed so as to yield comparable data.

Simply put, **comparability** means that the results can be used to make valid comparisons between the countries covered by the research.[42] To achieve this, the company must inject a level of control and review of marketing research at the global level. The director of worldwide marketing research must respond to local conditions as he or she develops a research program that can be implemented on a global basis. The research director must pay particular attention to whether data gathered is based on emic analysis or etic analysis. These terms, which come from anthropology, refer to the perspective taken in the study of another culture. **Emic analysis** is similar to ethnography in that it attempts to study a culture from within, using its own system of meanings and values. **Etic analysis** is "from the outside"; in other words, it is a more detached perspective that is often used in comparative or multicountry studies. In a particular research study, an etic scale would entail using the same set of items across all countries. This approach enhances comparability but some precision is lost. By contrast, an emic study would be tailored to fit a particular country; inferences about cross-cultural similarities based on emic research have to be made subjectively. A good compromise is to use a survey instrument that incorporates elements of both types of analysis. It is likely that the marketing director will end up with a number of marketing programs tailored to clusters of countries that exhibit within-group similarities. The agenda of a coordinated worldwide research program might look like the one in Table 6-8.

---

[42] V. Kumar, *International Marketing Research* (Upper Saddle River, NJ: Prentice Hall, 1999), p. 15.

Table 6-8

*Worldwide Marketing
Research Plan*

Research Objective	Country Cluster A	Country Cluster B	Country Cluster C
Identify market potential			X
Appraise competitive intentions		X	X
Evaluate product appeal	X	X	X
Study market response to price	X		
Appraise distribution channels	X	X	X

The director of worldwide research should not simply direct the efforts of country research managers. His or her job is to ensure that the corporation achieves maximum results worldwide from the total allocation of its research resources. Achieving this requires that personnel in each country are aware of research being carried out in the rest of the world and are involved in influencing the design of their own in-country research as well as the overall research program. Ultimately, the director of worldwide research must be responsible for the overall research design and program. It is his or her job to take inputs from the entire world and produce a coordinated research strategy that generates the information needed to achieve global sales and profit objectives.

The Marketing Information System as a Strategic Asset

The advent of the transnational enterprise means that boundaries between the firm and the outside world are dissolving. Marketing has historically been responsible for managing many of the relationships across that boundary. The boundary between marketing and other functions is also dissolving, and the traditional notion of marketing as a distinct functional area within the firm may be giving way to a new model. The process of marketing decision making is also changing, largely because of the changing role of information from a support tool to a wealth-generating, strategic asset.

Many global firms are creating flattened organizations, with less hierarchical, less centralized decision-making structures. Such organizations facilitate the exchange and flow of information between otherwise noncommunicative departments. The more information intensive the firm, the greater the degree to which marketing is involved in activities traditionally associated with other functional areas. In such firms there is parallel processing of information.

Information intensity in the firm has an impact on perceptions of market attractiveness, competitive position, and organizational structure. The greater a company's information intensity, the more the traditional product and market boundaries shift. In essence, companies increasingly face new sources of competition from other firms in historically noncompetitive industries, particularly if those firms are also information intensive. One example is the emergence of the "superindustry," combining telecommunications, computers, financial services, and retailing into what is essentially an information industry. Such diverse firms as AT&T, IBM, Merrill Lynch, Citicorp, and Sears now find themselves in direct competition with each other. They offer essentially the same products, although not as a result of diversification. Rather, the new competition reflects a natural extension and redefinition of traditional product lines and marketing activities. Today, when a company speaks of "value added," it is less likely to be referring to unique product features. Rather, the emphasis is on the information exchanged as part of customer transactions, much of which cuts across traditional product lines.

Information is one of the most basic ingredients of a successful marketing strategy. A company's **management information system (MIS) and intranet** provide decision makers with a continuous flow of information. **Information technology (IT)** is profoundly affecting global marketing activities by allowing managers to access and manipulate data to assist in decision making. **Electronic data interchange (EDI), electronic point of sale (EPOS)** data, **efficient consumer response (ECR), customer relationship management (CRM),** and **data warehouses** are some of the new tools and techniques available. The global marketer must scan the world for information about opportunities and threats and make information available via a management information system.

Formal **market research**—the project-specific, systematic gathering of data—is often required before marketers make key decisions. **Global market research** links customers and marketers through information gathered on a global scale. The research process begins when marketers define the problem and set research objectives; this step may entail assessing whether a particular market should be classified as **latent** or **incipient**. A research plan specifies the relative amounts of **qualitative** and **quantitative** information desired. Information is collected using either **primary** or **secondary data**

sources. In today's wired world, the Internet has taken its place alongside more traditional channels as an important secondary information source. In some instances, the cost of collecting primary data may outweigh the potential benefits. Secondary sources are especially useful for researching a market that is too small to justify a large commitment of time and money.

If collection of primary data can be justified on a cost-benefit basis, research can be conducted via **surveys, personal interviews, consumer panels, observation,** and **focus groups**. Before collecting data, researchers must determine whether a probability sample is required. In global marketing, careful attention must be paid to issues such as eliminating cultural bias in research, accurately translating surveys, and ensuring data **comparability** in different markets. A number of techniques are available for analyzing survey data, including **factor analysis, cluster analysis, multidimensional scaling (MDS),** and **conjoint analysis**. Researchers must present findings and recommendations clearly. A final issue is how much control headquarters will have over research and the overall management of the organization's information system. To ensure comparability of data, the researcher should utilize both **emic** and **etic** approaches.

summary

1. Explain how information technology puts powerful tools in the hands of global marketers.

2. Assume that you have been asked by the president of your organization to devise a systematic approach to scanning. The president does not want to be surprised by major market or competitive developments. What would you recommend?

3. Outline the basic steps of the market research process.

4. How can the SRC affect the global market research process?

5. What is the difference between existing, latent, and incipient demand? How might these differences affect the design of a marketing research project?

6. Describe some of the analytical techniques used by global marketers. When is it appropriate to use each technique?

discussion questions

1. Coach, the company introduced in the opening vignette, has been described as "a textbook lesson on how to revitalize a brand." The same could be said for Burberry, the British fashion goods company discussed in Chapter 1. Locate some

articles about Burberry and read about the decisions its management has made and the formula it used to polish the brand. Are the approaches evident at the two companies similar? Are they competitors?

integrate your global marketing skills

www.imf.org

www.jetro.org

www.unsystem.org

www.worldbank.org

www.odci.gov/cia/publications/factbook

www.miti.go.jp

www.euromonitor.com

www.ft.com

www.MarketResearch.com

www.euromonitor.com

Focus group moderators are also known as *qualitative researchers*. Many belong to the Qualitative Research Consultants Association. The QRCA Web site includes the Association's code of ethics and links to other research-oriented sites. The Web site for the U.K.-based Association of Qualitative Research (AQR) includes a concise history of qualitative research.

www.qrca.org

www.aqr.co.uk

Case 6-1

Research Helps Whirlpool Act Local in the Global Market

Whirlpool Corporation, headquartered in Benton Harbor, Michigan, is the number one appliance company in the United States and number two worldwide. The company sells more than $18 billion worth of "white goods" each year; this category includes refrigerators, stoves, washing machines, and microwave ovens. Whirlpool's success has been achieved in part by offering products in three different price ranges: top-of-the-line Kitchen Aid appliances, the medium-priced Whirlpool and Sears Kenmore lines, and Roper and Estate at the low end. In part, the impetus for overseas expansion comes from a mature domestic market that is only growing 2 percent or 3 percent annually. However, Whirlpool is not new to foreign markets; the company has been in Latin America since 1957. Today, it is the market share leader in that region.

At the beginning of 1993, David Whitwam, who was chairman and CEO of Whirlpool Corporation, told an interviewer, "Five years ago we were essentially a domestic company. Today about 40 percent of our revenues are overseas, and by the latter part of this decade, a majority will be." The CEO's comments came three years after he placed his first bet that the appliance industry is globalizing. By acquiring Philips Electronics' European appliance business for $1 billion, Whirlpool vaulted into the number three position in Europe. Whitwam pledged another $2 billion investment in Europe alone. As the decade of the 1990s drew to a close, however, Whitwam's ambitious plans for expanding beyond Europe into Japan and the developing nations in Asia and Latin America hadn't yet achieved the desired results. Noting that Whirlpool stock underperformed the bull market of the 1990s, analysts began questioning whether Whitwam's global vision was on target. As one analyst put it, "The strategy has been a failure. Whirlpool went big into global markets and investors have paid for it." Others fault the company on execution. Another analyst said, "I respect Whirlpool's strategy. They just missed on the blocking and tackling."

The challenge facing Whirlpool is rooted partially in the structure of the appliance industry. In Europe, for example, the presence of more than 200 brands and 170 factories makes the appliance industry highly fragmented and highly competitive. Electrolux, a Swedish company, ranks number one. European appliance sales have been flat for years, with sales volumes growing at a mere 1 percent or 2 percent; industry overcapacity is a major issue. Although analysts expect to see a surge in demand from Central and Eastern Europe within a few years, there will also be an influx of products from low-cost producers in those regions. To cut costs and bring margins up, the company has streamlined its European organization. Four regional sales offices replaced sales organizations in 17 separate countries. Hank Bowman, president of Whirlpool Europe BV, trimmed the number of warehouses from 30 to 16 and hopes eventually to have as few as 5 or 6. A global parts-sourcing strategy has helped reduce the number of suppliers by 40 percent. Over the course of several years, Whirlpool invested hundreds of millions of dollars in new-product development. It has already begun marketing a new clothes dryer designed to operate more efficiently and provide higher quality despite containing fewer parts.

Bowman believes that a global market segmentation approach is the key to success in Europe. Whirlpool relies heavily on market research to maintain its leadership in the United States; listening to consumers is important in Europe and Latin America as well. "Research tells us that the trends, preferences and biases of consumers, country by country, are reducing as opposed to increasing," Bowman said recently. He believes that European homemakers fall into distinct "Euro-segments"—traditionalists and aspirers, for example—allowing Whirlpool to duplicate the three-tiered approach to brands that has worked so well in the United States. The Bauknecht brand is positioned at the high end of the market, with Whirlpool in the middle, and Ignis at the lower end. For example, appliance shoppers in Germany visiting a department store such as Saturn can choose a Bauknecht Neptun 1400 priced at €699 or a Whirlpool for €369.

Research has also indicated that consumers in different countries prefer different types of features. Thus, Whirlpool has begun emphasizing product platforms as a means to produce localized versions of ovens, refrigerators, and other appliance lines more economically. A platform is essentially a technological core underneath the metal casing of an appliance. The platform—for example, the compressor and sealant system in a refrigerator—can be the same throughout the world. Country or region-specific capabilities can be added late in the production cycle. The goal was to cut 10 percent from Whirlpool's $200 million annual production development budget and achieve a 30 percent productivity increase among the company's 2,000 member product-development staff. Ultimately, the platform project team hopes to reduce the total number of platforms in the company from 135 to 65. Specific goals include reducing the number of dishwasher platforms from 6 to 3, and refrigerator platforms from 48 to 25.

Market research also drives the search for new products that address the specific needs of developing markets. In Brazil, for example, Whirlpool's market entry strategy included acquiring two local established appliance brands, Brastemp and Consul. However, with a basic washer priced at $300, even the low end of Whirlpool's product lines proved to be too expensive for many Brazilians. Economic data indicated that Brazil's 30 million low-income households, many with monthly incomes of about $220, account for about one-third of national consumption. Moreover, studies showed that these households ranked an automatic washer second only to a cell phone as an aspirational purchase. Whirlpool's researchers convened focus groups and made visits to representative low-income households. Marcele Rodrigues is director of laundry technology at Multibrás SA Eletrodomésticos, Whirlpool's Brazilian division. "It wasn't a matter of stripping down an existing model," he noted recently. "We had to innovate for the masses."

Whirlpool's response was to develop what it proudly calls the world's least expensive automatic washer. The company has a strong team of engineers and industrial designers in Brazil, as well as some of its most technologically advanced factories. Despite the fact that Brazil's economy was in turmoil, Whirlpool invested $30 million to develop the new washer, the Ideale, to meet the needs of a large class of consumers who still wash clothes by hand. One cost-saving design breakthrough was a patentable technology that allows the machine to switch from the wash cycle to the spin cycle without shifting gears. The design involves some performance compromises: Compared with more expensive models, the spin cycle takes longer and clothes come out damper. However, research indicated that these were not critical issues for most consumers.

Focus group research also indicated that consumers would find a smaller capacity washer acceptable because low-income families do laundry more often. Because Brazilian housewives like to wash floors underneath furniture, the Ideale sits high on four legs as opposed to resting on the floor as most conventional units do. Perhaps the most significant thing that the Ideale design team learned from its research was that form matters too. As Emerson Do Valle, vice president of Multibrás, explained, "We realized the washer should be aesthetically pleasing; it's a status symbol for these people." The team selected a rounded design with a yellow start button and blue lettering on the control panel. Because white is widely associated with cleanliness in Brazil, the Ideale is only available in white.

Although the Ideale incorporates many design features that appeal to consumers in Brazil, adaptations of the Ideale platform are also being manufactured and marketed in China and India. In India, the color options include green, blue, and white; the setting for delicate fabrics is labeled "sari." Also, the Indian units are mounted on casters so they can be moved easily.

In China, an appliance with a white exterior would be undesirable because of the prevailing belief that white shows dirt easily. For that reason, the Chinese Ideale is available in light blue and gray. In addition, the heavy-duty wash cycle in China is labeled "grease removal" for the simple reason that many Chinese use bicycles for daily transportation. Although the majority of Chinese washing machines have separate tubs for the wash and spin cycles, sales of single-drum washers such as the Ideale and a new frontloading model, the Sunrise, are growing. Overall, washer sales in China totaled 16.5 million units in 2005; Whirlpool expects that number to reach 22.2 million by 2011.

After a decade of losses, Whirlpool China finally posted a profit in 2006. The company first entered the market in the mid-1990s via joint ventures with local partners. Whirlpool called its strategy "T-4": offering refrigerators, washing machines, microwave ovens, and air conditioners, the four most-sought home appliances. Several of the ventures quickly went sour; as one executive recalls, "We quickly jumped into joint ventures without insights into Chinese consumers. We brought in North American know-how, but we also needed to distill local know-how." For one thing, Whirlpool underestimated the speed at which Haier and other local competitors are evolving into world-class manufacturers. Company executives note that, since China joined the World Trade Organization in 2001, it has been easier for Western companies to do business there.

In 2006, Jeff M. Fettig succeeded David Whitwam as Whirlpool's CEO and chairman. If emerging markets are to be drivers of global growth under Fettig's leadership, Whirlpool will have to build brand recognition in countries such as Brazil, India, and China. Also, consumers in emerging markets must be persuaded to move beyond washing machines to purchase some of the company's other appliances. That trend is already gaining traction: Middle-class Chinese consumers are splurging on high-end appliances such as a side-by-side Whirlpool refrigerator that costs the equivalent of $2,500. Many of the units find their way into living rooms. As Michael Todman, president of Whirlpool International, noted, "Appliances can be furniture, too. It's a source of pride to own one: 'Gee, look what I can own. I'm doing well.'"

Discussion Questions

1. Describe Whirlpool's global marketing strategy.
2. Summarize the role of market research in Whirlpool's globalization strategy. What different types of research methodologies does the company use? What are the advantages of each methodology described in the case?

3. Do you believe developing products for low-income consumers in emerging markets is the right strategy?

4. What are the key lessons to be learned from Whirlpool's experience in China?

Sources: Calum McCleod, "Whirlpool Spins China Challenge into Turnaround," *USA Today,* April 5, 2007, pp. 1B, 2B, Miriam Jordan and Jonathan Karp, "Machines for the Masses," *The Wall Street Journal,* December 9, 2003, pp. B1, B2; Katheryn Kranhold, "Whirlpool Conjures Up Appliance Divas," *The Wall Street Journal,* April 27, 2000, p. B1; Peter Marsh and Nikki Tait, "Whirlpool's Platform for Growth," *Financial Times,* March 26, 1998, p. 8; Peter Marsh and Nikki Tait, "Whirlpool Sticks to Its Global Guns," *Financial Times,* February 2, 1998, p. 4; Greg Steinmetz and Carl Quintanilla, "Tough Target: Whirlpool Expected Easy Going in Europe, and It Got a Big Shock," *The Wall Street Journal,* April 10, 1998, pp. A1, A6; Carl Quintanilla, "Despite Setbacks, Whirlpool Pursues Overseas Markets," *The Wall Street Journal,* December 9, 1997, p. B4; Peter Marsh, "Rough and Tumble Industry," *Financial Times,* July 2, 1997, p. 13; Bill Vlasic, "Did Whirlpool Spin Too Far Too Fast?" *Business Week,* June 24, 1996 pp. 134–136; Patrick Oster, "Call It Worldpool," *Business Week,* November 28, 1994, pp. 98–99; Robert L. Rose, "Whirlpool Is Expanding in Europe Despite the Slump," *The Wall Street Journal,* January 27, 1994, p. B4; Sally Solo, "Whirlpool: How to Listen to Consumers," *Fortune,* January 11, 1993, pp. 77, 79; Gregory E. David, "Spin Dry: Asia Is the Last Phase in Whirlpool's Global Wash Cycle," *Financial World,* October 26, 1993, pp. 30–31.

7

Segmentation, Targeting, and Positioning

he world's best-known cosmetics companies are setting their sights on a lucrative new market segment: the emerging middle classes in countries such as Brazil, Russia, India, and China. For example, the Chinese spent $10.3 billion on cosmetics and toiletries in 2005; that figure is expected to increase to $17 billion by 2010. Not surprisingly, marketers at L'Oréal, Procter & Gamble, Shiseido, and Estée Lauder Companies are moving quickly. William Lauder, president and CEO of Estée Lauder, calls China a "$100 billion opportunity." Noting that there is no "one-size-fits-all" ideal of beauty, cosmetics marketers pride themselves on sensitivity to local cultural preferences. As Jean-Paul Agon, chief executive of L'Oréal, explains, "We have different customers. Each customer is free to have her own aspirations. Our intention is just to respond as well as possible to each customer aspiration. Some want to be gorgeous, some want to be natural, and we just have to offer them the best quality and the best product to satisfy their wishes and their dreams." For example, many Asian women use whitening creams to lighten and brighten their complexions; in China, white skin is associated with wealth. L'Oréal responded by creating White Perfect; Shiseido offers Aupres White.

The global cosmetics giants' worldwide success is a convincing example of the power of skillful global market segmentation and targeting. **Market segmentation** represents an effort to identify and categorize groups of customers and countries according to common characteristics. **Targeting** is the process of evaluating the segments and focusing marketing efforts on a country, region, or group of people that has significant potential to respond. Such targeting reflects the reality that a company should identify those consumers it can reach most effectively, efficiently, and profitably. Finally, proper *positioning* is required to differentiate the product or brand in the minds of target customers.

Consider the following examples of market segmentation and targeting by global companies:

- The personal computer market can be divided into home users, corporate (also known as "enterprise") users, and educational users. Dell originally targeted corporate customers; even today, sales of products for home use only account for 20 percent of revenues. After focusing on the PC market only, Dell then branched out into other computer categories such as servers and storage hardware. In 2003, Dell dropped the word *Computer* from its corporate name as it ramped up sales of new categories of consumer electronics products including PDAs, flat-panel TVs, and digital cameras.
- In 2003, after convening worldwide employee conferences to study women's shaving preferences, Schick-Wilkinson Sword introduced Intuition—a shaving system for women that features a replaceable blade cartridge. The system incorporates a "skin-conditioning solid" that allows a woman to lather and shave her legs simultaneously. Intuition is a premium product targeted directly at users of Venus, Gillette's three-blade razor system for women.[1]

---

[1]   Charles Forelle, "Schick Puts a Nick in Gillette's Razor Cycle," *The Wall Street Journal*, October 3, 2003, p. B7.

L'Oréal is expanding distribution in China. After successful market tests at Wal-Mart and Carrefour stores, L'Oréal Paris, Maybelline, Garnier, and other brands are now available in retail stores as well as Chinese supermarkets. In 2006, L'Oréal China launched a new advertising campaign for the Mininurse Professional UV cosmetics line targeting women 18 years of age to 25 years of age. The ads communicate the brand's core benefits: UV protection, daytime skin whitening action, and nighttime hydrating action.

- Cosmed, a division of Germany's Beiersdorf AG, markets a line of skin care products for women under the NIVEA brand. Recently, the company launched a new brand, NIVEA for Men.

As these examples show, global markets can be segmented according to buyer category (e.g., consumer or enterprise), gender, age, and a number of other criteria. These examples also illustrate the fact that market segmentation and targeting are two separate but closely related activities. These activities serve as the link between market needs and wants and specific decisions on the part of company management to develop products that meet the specific needs of one or more segments. We examine segmentation, targeting, and positioning in this chapter.

GLOBAL MARKET SEGMENTATION

Global market segmentation has been defined as the process of identifying specific segments—whether they be country groups or individual consumer groups—of potential customers with homogeneous attributes who are likely to exhibit similar responses to a company's marketing mix.[2] Marketing practitioners and academics have been interested in global market segmentation for several decades. In the late 1960s, one observer suggested that the European market could be divided into three broad categories—international sophisticate, semisophisticate, and provincial—solely on the basis of consumers' presumed receptivity to a common advertising approach.[3] Another writer suggested that some themes—for example, the desire to be beautiful, the desire to be healthy and free of pain, the love of mother and child—were universal and could be used in advertising around the globe.[4]

---

2   Salah S. Hassan and Lea Prevel Katsanis, "Identification of Global Consumer Segments: A Behavioral Framework," *Journal of International Consumer Marketing* 3, no. 2 (1991), p. 17.
3   John K. Ryans, Jr., "Is It Too Soon to Put a Tiger in Every Tank?" *Columbia Journal of World Business* (March–April 1969), p. 73.
4   Arther C. Fatt, "The Danger of 'Local' International Advertising," *Journal of Marketing* 31, no. 1 (January 1967), pp. 60–62.

As noted in earlier chapters, a quarter century ago, Professor Theodore Levitt advanced the thesis that consumers in different countries increasingly seek variety, and that the same new segments are likely to show up in multiple national markets. Thus, ethnic or regional foods such as sushi, falafel, or pizza might be in demand anywhere in the world. Levitt suggested that this trend, known variously as the *pluralization of consumption* and *segment simultaneity*, provides an opportunity for marketers to pursue one or more segments on a global scale. Frank Brown, president of MTV Networks Asia, acknowledged this trend in explaining MTV's success in Asia despite the recent economic turmoil in the region. "When marketing budgets are tight, advertisers look for a more effective buy, and we can deliver a niche audience with truly panregional reach," he said.[5] Authors John Micklethwait and Adrian Wooldridge sum up the situation this way:

> The audience for a new recording of a Michael Tippett symphony or for a nature documentary about the mating habits of flamingos may be minuscule in any one country, but round up all the Tippett and flamingo fanatics around the world, and you have attractive commercial propositions. The cheap distribution offered by the Internet will probably make these niches even more attractive financially.[6]

Global market segmentation is based on the premise that companies should attempt to identify consumers in different countries who share similar needs and desires. However, the fact that significant numbers of pizza-loving consumers are found in many countries does not mean they are eating the exact same thing. In France, for example, Domino's serves pizza with goat cheese and strips of pork fat known as *lardoons*. In Taiwan, toppings include squid, crab, shrimp, and pineapple; Brazilians can order their pies with mashed bananas and cinnamon. As J. Patrick Doyle, executive vice president of Domino's international division, explains, "Pizza is beautifully adaptable to consumer needs around the world, simply by changing the toppings."[7]

A. Coskun Samli has developed a useful approach to global market segmentation that compares and contrasts "conventional" versus "unconventional" wisdom (see Table 7-1). For example, conventional wisdom might assume that consumers in Europe and Latin America are interested in World Cup soccer while those in America are not. Unconventional wisdom would note that the "global jock" segment exists in many countries, including the United States.[8] Similarly, conventional

Table 7-1

Contrasting Views of Global Segmentation

Conventional Wisdom	Unconventional Wisdom
1. Assumes heterogeneity between countries.	1. Assumes the emergence of segments that transcend national boundaries.
2. Assumes homogeneity within any given country.	2. Acknowledges the existence of within-country differences.
3. Focuses heavily on cultural differences at a macro level.	3. Emphasizes differences and commonalities in microlevel values, consumption patterns, etc.
4. Segmentation relies heavily on clustering of national markets.	4. Segmentation relies on grouping micromarkets within a country or between countries.
5. Within-country microsegments are assigned secondary priority.	5. Microsegments based on consumer behavior are assigned high priority.

Source: Adapted from A. Coskun Samli, *International Consumer Behavior* (Westport, CT: Quorum, 1995), p. 130.

---

5 Magz Osborne, "Second Chance in Japan," *Ad Age Global* 1, no. 9 (May 2001), p. 28.
6 John Micklethwait and Adrian Wooldridge. *A Future Perfect: The Challenge and Hidden Promise of Globalization* (New York: Crown Publishers, 2000), p. 198.
7 Neil Buckley, "Domino's Returns to Fast Food's Fast Lane," *Financial Times* (November 26, 2003), p. 10.
8 Robert Frank, "When World Cup Soccer Starts, World-Wide Productivity Stalls," *The Wall Street Journal*, June 12, 1998, pp. B1, B2; Daniela Deane, "Their Cup Runneth Over: Ethnic Americans Going Soccer Crazy," *USA Today*, July 2, 1998, p. 13A.

wisdom might assume that, because per capita income in India is about $490, all Indians have low incomes. Unconventional wisdom would note the presence of a higher-income, middle-class segment. As Sapna Nayak, a food analyst at Raobank India, noted, "The potential Indian customer base for a McDonald's or a Subway is larger than the size of entire developed countries."[9] The same is true of China; the average annual income of people living in eastern China is approximately $1,200. This is the equivalent to a lower-middle-income country market with 470 million people, larger than every other single country market except India.[10]

Today, global companies (and the research and advertising agencies that serve them) use market segmentation to identify, define, understand, and respond to customer wants and needs on a worldwide, rather than strictly local, basis. As we have noted many times in this book, global marketers must determine whether a standardized or adapted marketing mix best serves those wants and needs. By

the rest of the story

Cosmetics Giants Segment the Global Cosmetics Market

Market research is critical to understanding women's preferences in different parts of the world. According to Eric Bone, head of L'Oréal's Tokyo Research Center, "Japanese women prefer to use a compact foundation rather than a liquid. Humidity here is much higher and the emphasis is on long-lasting coverage." Armed with this knowledge, L'Oréal devotes more development time to compacts rather than liquids. The researchers have also learned that the typical Japanese woman cleanses her face twice.

In China, L'Oréal and its competitors have an opportunity to educate women about cosmetics, which were banned prior to 1982. Each year, L'Oréal observes and films 6,000 Chinese women applying and removing makeup. Alice Laurent, L'Oréal's skincare development manager in Shanghai, says, "In China, the number of products used in the morning and the evening is 2.2" At its Shanghai Innovation Centre, L'Oréal is also studying how to incorporate traditional Chinese medicine into new product lines.

L'Oréal and Procter & Gamble offer a wide range of products in China, including both mass market and premium brands. By contrast, Estée Lauder Company's focus is expensive prestige brands such as Estée Lauder, Clinique, and MAC that are sold through upmarket department stores. One research analyst cautions that Estée Lauder's targeting and positioning may be too narrow for China. According to Access Asia, Estée Lauder "is in danger of becoming too exclusively placed at the top end of the market and it may have to reposition itself more in the mass market to compete for a larger part of the Chinese market." Estée Lauder's Carol Shen views her company's brands as aspirational. "Chinese consumers are price sensitive but at the same time are willing to invest in products that are relatively expensive versus their income levels because they are so confident about the future," she says.

In India, L'Oréal has recently shifted from a low-price, mass-market strategy to a premium price, upscale strategy. Competitor Hindustan Lever rings up nearly $1 billion in annual sales by targeting the hundreds of millions of people who must live on the equivalent of $2 per day. This means body lotion priced at $0.70 and $0.90 bottles of perfume. Upon first entering India in 1991, L'Oréal used a similar strategy. However, its low-priced Garnier Ultra Doux shampoo failed to catch on with consumers. Offering no particular advantage relative to local brands, it was, in the words of Alain Evrard, L'Oréal's managing director for Africa, Orient, and the Pacific, "an absolute flop." Some shopkeepers were stuck with unsold inventories.

In the mid-1990s, Evrard was determined to gain a better understanding of the Indian market. He noted several different trends. The number of working women was increasing dramatically, and consumer attitudes were shifting. Thanks to cable television, CNN and MTV were finding large viewing audiences. To learn more about women's preferences, Evrard spoke with advertising executives and fashion magazine editors as well as L'Oréal's local employees. In doing so, Evrard arrived at a keen insight: Women in their 20s concerned about gray hair were not satisfied with existing do-it-yourself hair color products. Evrard responded by launching L'Oréal Excellence Crème in India. An innovative but expensive product popular in Europe, Excellence Crème was priced at $9 and positioned as a luxury purchase. To gain support among shopkeepers, a local L'Oréal staffer named Dinesh Dayal mounted a retailer education campaign and personally promoted the product at local shops. Today Excellence Crème is widely available in India. In 2004, after more than a decade of losses, L'Oréal's Indian operations became profitable.

Sources: Christina Passariello, "Beauty Fix: Behind L'Oreal's Makeover in India: Going Upscale," The Wall Street Journal, July 13, 2007, pp. A1, A14; Beatrice Adams, "Big Brands Are Watching You," Financial Times, November 4–November 5, 2006, p. W18; Adam Jones, "How to Make Up Demand," Financial Times, October 3, 2006, p. 8; Lauren Foster and Andrew Yeh, "Estée Lauder Puts on a New Face," Financial Times, March 23, 2006, p. 7; Rebecca Rose, "Global Diversity Gets All Cosmetic," Financial Times, April 11–12, 2004, p. W11.

---

[9] Saritha Rai, "Tastes of India in U.S. Wrappers," *The New York Times*, April 29, 2003, p. W7.

[10] Joseph Kahn, "Made in China, Bought in China," *The New York Times*, January 5, 2003, Section 3, p. 10.

performing market segmentation, marketers can generate the insights needed to devise the most effective approach.

The process of global market segmentation begins with the choice of one or more variables to use as a basis for grouping customers. Common variables include demographics (including national income and size of population), psychographics (values, attitudes, and lifestyles), behavioral characteristics, and benefits sought. It is also possible to cluster different national markets in terms of their environments (e.g., the presence or absence of government regulation in a particular industry) to establish groupings.

Demographic Segmentation

Demographic segmentation is based on measurable characteristics of populations such as income, population, age distribution, gender, education, and occupation. A number of global demographic trends—fewer married couples, smaller family size, changing roles of women, higher incomes and living standards, for example— have contributed to the emergence of global market segments. Here are several key demographic facts and trends from around the world:

- A widening age gap exists between the older populations in the West and the large working-age populations in developing countries.
- In the EU, the number of consumers 16 years old and younger is rapidly approaching the number of consumers 60 years old and older.
- Asia is home to 500 million consumers 16 years old and younger.
- Half of Japan's population will be 50 years old or older by 2025.
- America's three main ethnic groups—African/Black Americans, Hispanic Americans, and Asian Americans—represent a combined annual buying power of $1 trillion.
- The United States is home to 28.4 million foreign-born residents with a combined income of $233 billion.
- By 2030, 20 percent of the U.S. population—70 million Americans—will be 65 years old or older versus 13 percent (36 million) today.
- India has the youngest demographic profile among the world's large nations: More than half its population is younger than 25 years old.

Statistics such as these can provide valuable insights to marketers who are scanning the globe for opportunities. Managers at global companies must be alert to the possibility that marketing strategies will have to be adjusted in response to the aging of the population and other demographic trends. For example, consumer products companies will need to convene focus groups consisting of people over 50 years old who are nearing retirement. These same companies will also have to target developing country markets such as Vietnam, Brazil, and Mexico to achieve growth objectives in the years to come.

Demographic changes can create opportunities for marketing innovation. In France, for example, two entrepreneurs began rewriting the rules of retailing years before Sam Walton founded the Wal-Mart chain. Marcel Fournier and Louis Defforey opened the first Carrefour ("crossroads") hypermarket in 1963. At the time, France had a fragmented shop system that consisted of small, specialized stores with only about 5,000 square feet of floor space such as the *boulangerie* and *charcuterie*. The shop system was part of France's national heritage, and shoppers developed personal relationships with a shop's proprietor. However, time pressed, dual-parent working families had less time to stop at several stores for daily shopping. The same trend was occurring in other countries. By 1993, Carrefour SA was a global chain with $21 billion in sales and a market capitalization of $10 billion. By 2006, sales had reached $102 billion; today, Carrefour operates 12,000 stores in 30 countries. As Adrian Slywotzky has noted, it was a demographic shift that provided the opportunity for Fournier and Defforey to create a novel, customer-matched, cost-effective business design.[11]

Segmenting Global Markets by Income and Population

When a company charts a plan for global market expansion, it often finds that income is a valuable segmentation variable. After all, a market consists of those who are willing and *able* to buy. For cigarettes, soft drinks, photographic film, candy, and other consumer products that have a low per-unit cost, population is often a more valuable segmentation variable than income. Nevertheless, for a vast range of industrial and consumer products offered in global markets today, income is a valuable and important macro indicator of market potential. About two-thirds of world GNI is generated in the Triad; however, only about 12 percent of the world's population is located in Triad countries. The concentration of wealth in a handful of industrialized countries has significant implications for global marketers. After segmenting in terms of a single demographic variable—income—a company can reach the most affluent markets by targeting fewer than 20 nations: half the EU, North America, and Japan. By doing so, however, the marketers are *not* reaching almost 90 percent of the world's population! A word of caution is in order here. Data about income (and population) have the advantage of being widely available and inexpensive to access. However, management may unconsciously "read too much" into such data. In other words, while providing some measure of market potential, such macrolevel demographic data should not necessarily be used as the sole indicator of presence (or absence) of a market opportunity. This is especially true when an emerging country market or region is being investigated.

Ideally, GNI and other measures of national income converted to U.S. dollars should be calculated on the basis of purchasing power parities (i.e., what the currency will buy in the country of issue) or through direct comparisons of actual prices for a given product. This would provide an actual comparison of the standards of living in the countries of the world. Table 7-2 ranks the top 10 countries in terms of 2004 per capita income followed by a ranking adjusted for purchasing power parity. Although the United States ranks fourth in per capita income, only Luxembourg surpasses its standard of living—as measured by what money can buy.[12] By most measures, the U.S. market is enormous: About $12 trillion in national income and a population that passed the 300 million milestone in 2006. Little

2004 Per Capita Income		2004 Income Adjusted for Purchasing Power	
1. Luxembourg	$56,380	1. Luxembourg	$61,610
2. Norway	$51,810	2. United States	$39,820
3. Switzerland	$49,600	3. Norway	$38,680
4. United States	$41,440	4. Switzerland	$35,660
5. Denmark	$40,750	5. Ireland	$32,930
6. Iceland	$37,920	6. Iceland	$32,370
7. Japan	$37,050	7. Austria	$31,800
8. Sweden	$35,840	8. Denmark	$31,770
9. Ireland	$34,310	9. Hong Kong	$31,560
10. United Kingdom	$33,630	10. Belgium	$31,530

Table 7-2

Per Capita Income, 2004

Source: 2006 World Development Indicators. Reprinted by permission of Warren Keegan Associates, Inc.

[11]   Adrian Slywotzky, *Value Migration* (Cambridge, MA: Harvard Business School Press, 1996), p. 37.
[12]   For a more detailed discussion, see Malcolm Gillis et al., *Economics of Development* (New York: Norton, 1996), pp. 37–40.

wonder, then, that so many non-U.S. companies target and cater to American consumers and organizational buyers! A case in point is Mitsubishi Motors, which had begun redesigning its Montero Sport SUV with the goal of creating a "global vehicle" that could be sold worldwide with little adaptation. Then the design program changed course; the new goal was to make the vehicle more "American" by providing more interior space and more horsepower. Hiroshi Yajima, a Mitsubishi executive in North America, attributed the change to the vibrancy and sheer size of the American auto market. "We wouldn't care if the vehicle didn't sell outside the U.S.," he said.[13]

Despite having comparable per capita incomes, other industrialized countries are nevertheless quite small in terms of *total* annual income. In Sweden, for example, per capita GNI is $35,840; however, Sweden's smaller population—9 million—means that annual national income is only about $322 billion. This helps explain why Ericsson, IKEA, Saab, and other companies based in Sweden have looked beyond their borders for significant growth opportunities.

While Table 7-2 highlights differences between straightforward income statistics and standard of living in the world's most affluent nations, such differences can be even more pronounced in less-developed countries. A visit to a mud house in Tanzania will reveal many of the things that money can buy: an iron bed frame, a corrugated metal roof, beer and soft drinks, bicycles, shoes, photographs, radios, and even televisions. What Tanzania's per capita GNI of $320 does not reflect is the fact that instead of utility bills, Tanzanians have the local well and the sun. Instead of nursing homes, tradition and custom ensure that families will take care of the elderly at home. Instead of expensive doctors and hospitals, villagers may utilize the services of witch doctors and healers.

In industrialized countries, a significant portion of national income is the value of goods and services that would be free in a poor country. Thus, the standard of living in low- and lower-middle income countries is often higher than income data might suggest; in other words, the *actual* purchasing power of the local currency may be much higher than that implied by exchange values. For example, the per capita income average for China of $1,500 equals 12,165 Chinese Renminbi (at an exchange rate of 8.11 Renminbi = US$1.00), but 12,165 Renminbi will buy much more in China than $1,500 will buy in the United States. Adjusted for purchasing power parity, per capita income in China is estimated to be $5,890; this amount is nearly four times higher than the unadjusted figure suggests. Similarly, calculated in terms of purchasing power, per capita income in Tanzania is approximately $670. A visit to the capital city of Dar Es Salaam reveals that

Table 7-3

Top 10 Nations Ranked by GNI, 2004

Country	GNI (in millions)
United States	12,168,482
Japan	4,734,255
Germany	2,532,281
United Kingdom	2,013,363
China	1,937,965
France	1,888,407
Italy	1,513,111
Spain	919,094
Canada	905,042
Brazil	704,906

Source: Reprinted by permission of Warren Keegan Associates, Inc.

---

13 Norihiko Shirouzu, "Tailoring World's Cars to U.S. Tastes," *The Wall Street Journal*, January 1, 2001, p. B1.

Country	GNI* (in millions)
1. United States	13,626,144
2. Japan	5,078,401
3. Germany	2,886,668
4. China	2,709,427
5. United Kingdom	2,369,060
6. France	2,243,490
7. Italy	1,752,603
8. Spain	1,167,132
9. Canada	1,107,281
10. India	894,399

Table 7-4

Top 10 Nations Ranked by GNI, 2007 Projections

*Data forecast by author based on extrapolation of 2004 actual GNI data using World Bank average growth rates for GDP for 2000 to 2004.

Source: 2006 World Development Indicators. Reprinted by permission of Warren Keegan Associates, Inc.

stores are stocked with televisions and CD players, and businesspeople can be seen negotiating deals using their cell phones.[14]

No one knows with certainty what the future will bring, but using 2004 GNI data as a baseline (Table 7-3) and extrapolating current economic growth trends to 2007 produces interesting results (Table 7-4). The United States, Japan, and Germany retain their rankings in the first three positions; China moves up to fourth place. These extrapolation results suggest that China, with its combination of high real income growth and relatively low population growth, is a strong candidate to become a leading world economic power. Even if this forecast turns out to be overly optimistic, China is expected to fare better than other Asian countries.

In 2004, the 10 most populous countries in the world accounted for 52 percent of world income; the 5 most populous accounted for 39 percent (see Table 7-5). Although population is not as concentrated as income, there is, in terms of size of nations, a pattern of considerable concentration. The 10 most populous countries in the world account for roughly 60 percent of the world's population today. The concentration of income in the high-income and large-population countries means that a company can be "global" by targeting buyers in 10 or fewer countries. World population is now approximately 6.4 billion; at the present rate of growth, it will reach 12 billion by the

Table 7-5

The 10 Most Populous Countries, 2004 and 2007 Projections

Global Income and Population	2004 Population (thousands)	Percent of World Population	Projected Population 2007*	2004 GNI (millions)	Per Capita GNI	Percent of World GNI
WORLD TOTAL	6,364,981	100.00%	6,580,194	40,282,301	6,329	100.0%
1. China	1,296,157	20.36%	1,320,201	1,937,965	1,500	4.81%
2. India	1,079,721	16.96%	1,123,227	673,205	620	1.67%
3. United States	293,655	4.61%	301,858	12,168,482	41,440	30.21%
4. Indonesia	217,588	3.42%	224,991	248,007	1,140	0.62%
5. Brazil	183,913	2.89%	190,528	551,650	3,000	1.37%
6. Pakistan	152,061	2.39%	162,383	90,663	600	0.23%
7. Russian Federation	143,850	2.26%	141,723	488,501	3,400	1.21%
8. Bangladesh	139,215	2.19%	146,397	61,324	440	0.15%
9. Nigeria	128,709	2.02%	136,575	55,326	430	0.14%
10. Japan	127,764	2.01%	127,700	4,734,255	37,050	11.75%

*Data forecast by author based on extrapolation of 2004 actual population data using World Bank average growth rates for population for 2004 to 2020.
Source: 2006 World Development Indicators. Reprinted by permission of Warren Keegan Associates, Inc.

---

[14] Robert S. Greenberger, "Africa Ascendant: New Leaders Replace Yesteryear's 'Big Men,' and Tanzania Benefits," *The Wall Street Journal*, December 10, 1996, pp. A1, A6.

middle of the century. Simply put, global population will probably double during the lifetime of many students using this textbook.

As noted previously, for products whose price is low enough, population is a more important variable than income in determining market potential. As former Kodak CEO George Fisher commented more than a decade ago, "Half the people in the world have yet to take their first picture. The opportunity is huge, and it's nothing fancy. We just have to sell yellow boxes of film."[15] Thus, China and India, with respective populations of 1.3 billion and 1 billion, represent attractive target markets. In a country like China, one segmentation approach would call for serving the existing mass market for inexpensive consumer products. L'Oréal, Kao, Johnson & Johnson, Procter & Gamble, Unilever, and other packaged goods companies are targeting and developing the China market, lured in part by the presence of hundreds of millions of Chinese customers who are willing and able to spend a few cents for a single-use pouch of shampoo and other personal care products. As noted in the chapter introduction, L'Oréal is targeting India's burgeoning middle class. GM's original strategy for entering China was based on its success in reaching the segment comprised of government and company officials who are entitled to a large sedan-style automobile. Today, GM's lineup for China includes the Buick Century, targeted at the country's middle class, and the $10,000 Buick Sail.

McDonald's global expansion illustrates the significance of both income and population on marketing activities. On the one hand, as noted in Case 1-1, McDonald's operates in more than 120 countries. What this figure conceals, however, is that 80 percent of McDonald's restaurants are located in nine country markets: Australia, Brazil, Canada, China, France, Germany, Japan, the United Kingdom, and the United States. These nine countries generate about 75 percent of the company's total revenues. Seven of these countries appear in the top 10 GNI ranking shown in Table 7-4; however, only four appear in the Table 7-5 population rankings. At present, the restaurants in the company's approximately 100 nonmajor country markets contribute less than 20 percent to operating income. McDonald's is counting on an expanded presence in China

global MARKETING Q&A

USA Today: "You've said that you don't feel that the increase in elevator sales, particularly in China, is part of an elevator 'bubble.' If China's growth is not sustainable, will elevator sales start to come down and affect your growth?"

George David, Chief Executive Officer, United Technologies: "China's growth is sustainable, so I don't go along with your 'if' qualification. We measure elevator populations in countries as units installed per thousand people. And in China, the number today is about one-half an elevator per thousand people. In most countries of the world outside of the U.S., people live in elevator- and storied apartment houses. It's true all over Europe, all over Asia, South America, certainly true in China. And in a mature market like Europe, the installed population is about six elevators per thousand people. And so we're on our way to some portion of six, and that's why it is so far away from saturation. The United Nations says 250 million more people will urbanize in the next several years. The Chinese population is today only 32 percent urban. That compares with 70 percent urban in the U.S. and Europe. It's not a bubble."

Source: Ron Insana, "United Tech Outperforms Peers Year After Year," USA Today, April 4, 2005, p. 3B.

---

[15] Mark Maremont, "Kodak's New Focus," *Business Week*, January 30, 1995, p. 63.

and other high-population country markets to drive corporate growth in the twenty-first century.

As noted earlier, marketers must be careful not to be overly optimistic when using income, population, and other macro-level data to segment markets. It is also possible to underestimate a market's potential. Marketers should keep in mind, for example, that national income figures, such as those cited for China and India, are averages. Large, fast-growing, higher-income segments are present in both of these countries. More than 100 million Indians can be classified as "upper-middle-class," with average incomes of more than $1,400. Pinning down a demographic segment may require additional information; according to some estimates, India's middle class totals 300 million people. However, if middle class is defined more narrowly as "households that own cars, computers, and washing machines," the figure would be much lower. According to one Indian expert, India's population can be further segmented to include a "bike" segment of 25 million households in which telephones and motorbikes are present. However, the vast majority of India's population comprises a "bullock cart" segment whose households lack most comforts but typically own a television.[16] The lesson is to guard from being blinded by averages; as Samli has suggested, do not *assume* homogeneity.

"Urban India is getting saturated. In the cities, everyone who can afford a television has one. If you want to maintain high growth, you have to penetrate into rural India."[17]

K. Ramachandran, Chief Executive, Philips Electronics India

Age Segmentation

Age is another useful demographic variable in global marketing. One global segment based on demographics is **global teens**, young people between the ages of 12 and 19. Teens, by virtue of their shared interest in fashion, music, and a youthful lifestyle, exhibit consumption behavior that is remarkably consistent across borders. As Renzo Rosso, creator of the Diesel designer jeans brand, explains, "A group of teenagers randomly chosen from different parts of the world will share many of the same tastes."[18] Young consumers may not yet have conformed to cultural norms; indeed, they may be rebelling against them. This fact, combined with shared universal wants, needs, desires, and fantasies (for name brands, novelty, entertainment, trendy, and image-oriented products), make it possible to reach the global teen segment with a unified marketing program. This segment is attractive both in terms of its size (about 1.3 billion) and its multi-billion-dollar purchasing power. Coca-Cola, Benetton, Swatch, and Sony are some of the companies pursuing the global teenage segment. The global telecommunications revolution is a critical driving force behind the emergence of this segment. Global media such as MTV and the Internet are perfect vehicles for reaching this segment. Satellites such as AsiaSatI are beaming Western programming and commercials to millions of viewers in China, India, and other countries.

Another global segment is the so-called **global elite**—affluent consumers who are well traveled and have the money to spend on prestigious products with an image of exclusivity. Although this segment is often associated with older individuals who have accumulated wealth over the course of a long career, it also includes movie stars, musicians, elite athletes, entrepreneurs, and others who have achieved great financial success at a relatively young age. This segment's needs and wants are spread over various product categories: durable goods (luxury automobiles such as Mercedes Benz), nondurables (upscale beverages such as Perrier mineral water or Grey Goose vodka), and financial services (American Express Gold and Platinum cards).

---

[16] Sundeep Waslekar, "India Can Get Ahead if It Gets on a Bike," *Financial Times*, November 12, 2002, p. 15.
[17] Chris Prystay, "Companies Market to India's Have-Littles," *The Wall Street Journal*, June 5, 2003, p. B1.
[18] Alice Rawsthorn, "A Hipster on Jean Therapy," *Financial Times*, August 20, 1998, p. 8.

Rolls-Royce, the automaker whose name is synonymous with exclusive luxury, only sells 800 vehicles each year. Prices start at $400,000; the company's customers are typically members of the global elite, with more than $30 million in liquid assets. Rolls-Royce buyers often order customized vehicles; in China, one of the fastest-growing markets for luxury cars, a customer recently paid $2.2 million for a stretch version of the Phantom. In December 2006, Rolls-Royce announced that the Peninsula Hotel in Hong Kong had bought 14 Phantoms.

Gender Segmentation

For obvious reasons, segmenting markets by gender is an approach that makes sense for many companies. Less obvious, however, is the need to ensure that opportunities for sharpening the focus on the needs and wants of one gender or the other do not go unnoticed. Although some companies—fashion designers and cosmetics companies, for example—market primarily or exclusively to women, other companies offer different lines of products to both genders. For example, in 2000, Nike generated $1.4 billion in global sales of women's shoes and apparel, a figure representing 16 percent of total Nike sales. Nike executives believe its global women's business is poised for big growth. To make it happen, Nike is opening concept shops inside department stores and creating free-standing retail stores devoted exclusively to women.[19] In Europe, Levi Strauss is taking a similar approach. In 2003, the company opened its first boutique for young women, Levi's for Girls, in Paris. As Suzanne Gallacher, associate brand manager for Levi's in Europe, the Middle East, and Africa, noted, "In Europe, denim is for girls."[20] The move is part of a broader strategy to boost Levi Strauss' performance in the face of strong competition from Calvin Klein and Gap in the United States and Diesel in Europe. Gallacher predicts that, if Levi's for Girls is a success in France, similar stores will be opened in other European countries.

Psychographic Segmentation

Psychographic segmentation involves grouping people in terms of their attitudes, values, and lifestyles. Data are obtained from questionnaires that require respondents to indicate the extent to which they agree or disagree with a series of statements. Psychographics is primarily associated with SRI International, a market research organization whose original VALS and updated VALS 2 analyses of consumers are widely known. Finland's Nokia relies heavily on psychographic segmentation of mobile phone users; its most important segments are "poseurs,"

---

19 Paula Stepanowsky, "Nike Tones Up Its Marketing to Women with Concept Shops, New Apparel Lines," *The Wall Street Journal*, September 5, 2001, p. B19.
20 John Tagliabue, "2 Sexes Separated by a Common Levi's," *The New York Times*, September 30, 2003, p. W1.

"trendsetters," "social contact seekers," and "highfliers." By carefully studying these segments and tailoring products to each, Nokia has captured 40 percent of the world's market for mobile communication devices.[21]

Porsche AG, the German sports car maker, turned to psychographics after experiencing a worldwide sales decline from 50,000 units in 1986 to about 14,000 in 1993. Its U.S. subsidiary, Porsche Cars North America, already had a clear demographic profile of its typical customer: a 40-plus-year-old male college graduate whose annual income exceeded $200,000. A psychographic study showed that, demographics aside, Porsche buyers could be divided into several distinct categories Top Guns, for example, buy Porsches and expect to be noticed; for Proud Patrons and Fantasists, on the other hand, such conspicuous consumption is irrelevant. Porsche used the profiles to develop advertising tailored to each type. As Richard Ford, Porsche vice president of sales and marketing, noted: "We were selling to people whose profiles were diametrically opposed. You wouldn't want to tell an elitist how good he looks in the car or how fast he could go." The results were impressive; Porsche's U.S. sales improved nearly 50 percent after a new advertising campaign was launched.[22]

Honda's recent experience in Europe demonstrates the potential value of using psychographic segmentation to supplement the use of more traditional variables such as demographics. When Honda executives were developing a communication strategy to support the European launch of the company's new HR-V sport utility vehicle in the late 1990s, they brought together a panel of experts from the United Kingdom, Germany, France, and Italy. The goal was to develop a pan-European advertising campaign targeted squarely at a relatively young demographic. The researchers agreed that, irrespective of nationality, European youth exhibit more similarities than differences: They listen to the same music, enjoy the same films, and pursue the same recreational activities. The resulting ad campaign, dubbed "Joy Machine," was targeted at 25- to 35-year-olds. However, the HR-V proved to be popular with Europeans of *all* ages; one out of six buyers was a grandparent! Reflecting on this turn of events, Chris Brown, an advertising executive at Honda Motor Europe, noted, "The decision within advertising should be about attitudes, not ages. I was recently reminded that [former British prime minister] John Major and Mick Jagger of the Rolling Stones are the same age."[23] Brown's statement underscores the insight that people of the same age don't necessarily have the same attitudes, just as people in one age bracket sometimes share attitudes with those in other age brackets. Sometimes it is preferable to market to a mind-set rather than a particular age group; in such an instance, psychographic studies can help marketers arrive at a deeper understanding of consumer behavior than is possible with traditional segmentation variables such as demographics.

However, such understanding does come at a price. Psychographic market profiles are available from a number of different sources; companies may pay thousands of dollars to use these studies. SRI International has recently created psychographic profiles of the Japanese market; broader-scope studies have been undertaken by several global advertising agencies. For example, a research team at D'arcy Massius Benton & Bowles (DMBB) focused on Europe and produced a 15-country study entitled *The Euroconsumer: Marketing Myth or Cultural Certainty?*[24] The researchers identified four lifestyle groups: Successful Idealists, Affluent Materialists, Comfortable Belongers, and Disaffected

[21] John Micklethwait and Adrian Wooldridge, *Future Perfect: The Challenge and Hidden Promise of Globalization* (New York: Crown Business, 2000), p. 131.
[22] Alex Taylor III, "Porsche Slices Up Its Buyers," *Fortune*, January 16, 1995, p. 24.
[23] Ian Morton, "Target Advertising Is Not an Exact Science," *Automotive News Europe*, June 19, 2000, p. 28.
[24] The following discussion is adapted from Rebecca Piirto, *Beyond Mind Games: The Marketing Power of Psychographics* (Ithaca, NY: American Demographics Books, 1991).

Survivors. The first two groups represent the elite, the latter two, mainstream European consumers:

Successful Idealists Comprising from 5 percent to 20 percent of the population, this segment consists of persons who have achieved professional and material success while maintaining commitment to abstract or socially responsible ideals.

Affluent Materialists These status-conscious "up-and-comers"—many of whom are business professionals—use conspicuous consumption to communicate their success to others.

Comfortable Belongers Comprising one-fourth to one-half of a country's population, this group, like Global Scan's Adapters and Traditionals, is conservative and most comfortable with the familiar. Belongers are content with the comfort of home, family, friends, and community.

Disaffected Survivors Lacking power and affluence, this segment harbors little hope for upward mobility and tends to be either resentful or resigned. This segment is concentrated in high-crime urban inner city-type neighborhoods. Despite Disaffecteds' lack of societal status, their attitudes nevertheless tend to affect the rest of society.

The segmentation and targeting approach used by a company can vary from country to country. In Europe, Levi Strauss is relying heavily on gender segmentation. By contrast, former CEO Phil Marineau believed that a psychographic segmentation strategy is the key to revitalizing the venerable jeans brand in its home market. Marineau's team identified several different segments, including "fashionistas," trendy teens, middle-aged men, and budget shoppers. The goal was to create different styles of jeans at different price points for each segment and to make them available at stores ranging from Wal-Mart to Neiman Marcus.[25] Likewise, Sony Electronics, a unit of Sony Corp. of America, recently undertook a reorganization of its marketing function. Traditionally, Sony had approached marketing from a product category point of view. In the future, a new unit, the Consumer Segment Marketing Division, will be responsible for getting closer to consumers in the United States (see Table 7-6).[26] What variables did Sony use to develop these categories?

Behavior Segmentation

Behavior segmentation focuses on whether or not people buy and use a product, as well as how often, and how much they use or consume. Consumers can be categorized in terms of **usage rates**: for example, heavy, medium, light, and

Table 7-6

Sony's U.S. Consumer Segments

Segment	Description
Affluent	High-income consumers
CE Alphas	Early adopters of high-tech consumer electronics products, irrespective of age
Zoomers	55 years old or older
SoHo	Small office home office
Families	35 to 54 years old
Young Professionals/D.I.N.K.S.	Dual income no kids, 25 to 34 years old
Gen Y	Younger than 25 years old (includes tweens, teens, college students)

25 Sally Beatty, "At Levi Strauss, Trouble Comes from All Angles," *The Wall Street Journal*, October 13, 2003, pp. B1, B3.
26 Tobi Elkin, "Sony Marketing Aims at Lifestyle Segments," *Advertising Age*, March 18, 2002, pp. 1, 72.

BRIC Briefing Book

Psychographic and Behavioral Segmentation in Russia

DMBB has also created a psychographic profile of the Russian market. The study divides Russians into five categories, based on their outlook, behavior, and openness to Western products. The categories include *kuptsy*, Cossacks, students, business executives, and Russian Souls. Members of the largest group, the *kuptsy* (the label comes from the Russian word for "merchant"), theoretically prefer Russian products but look down on mass-produced goods of inferior quality. *Kuptsy* are most likely to admire automobiles and stereo equipment from countries with good reputations for engineering, such as Germany and Scandinavia. Nigel Clarke, the author of the study, notes that segmentation and targeting are appropriate in Russia, despite the fact that its broad consumer market is still in its infancy. "If you're dealing with a market as different as Russia is, even if you want to go 'broad,' it's best to think: 'Which group would go most for my brand? Where is my natural center of gravity?'"

The study's marketing implications became clearer in the late 1990s. Market share growth for many Western brands began to slow; the trend accelerated after the economic crisis of 1998. As Sergei Platinin, director of a Russian company that markets fruit juices, noted, "People used to want only to buy things that looked foreign. Now they want Russian." In the world of fashion, expensive blue jeans from designer Valentin Yudashkin are supplanting Armani as *the* hip jeans. At the other end of the price spectrum, McDonald's has begun offering *pirozhki*—meat and cheese pies. The local Nestlé subsidiary has revived several brands of Russian chocolate candies. According to a survey conducted by Comcon 2, nearly two-thirds of upper-income Russians prefer to buy domestic chocolates, even though they can afford to buy imported brands.

As for behavioral segmentation, Diageo PLC, V&S Vin & Spirit AB, Seagram, and other marketers of distilled spirits know that Russians consume a great deal of vodka. (The word *vodka* is derived from the Russian word for "water," and Russians believe vodka originated in their country in the fourteenth century.) Estimated 2002 vodka consumption in Russia was 4 billion liters—about 14.4 liters per capita, the highest in the world. However, as noted previously, Russian consumers have recently shown an increased preference for domestic brands. Production of homemade vodka, known as *samogon*, and illegal bootleg vodka surpasses official production by a ratio of 2 to 1 (see Figure 7-1) and the Russian government loses an estimated $1.9 billion in annual tax revenues. As a result of high duties, as well as the marketing goal of retaining a premium image, imports such as Smirnoff and Absolut are priced significantly higher than local brands. To date, imported vodka brands have only captured about 1 percent of the Russian market.

At a time when economic uncertainty is high and workers can go months without being paid, price is a significant factor for the average Russian. An entrepreneur named Vladimir Dovgan has prospered by launching several different brands of vodka priced between $5 and $10 per bottle. The label features Dovgan's picture, and he also appears in print and television ads. Meanwhile, in the late 1990s, Diageo PLC began producing Smirnoff in St. Petersburg. Ironically, Smirnoff's heritage is truly Russian, although for decades the brand was produced only in the West. As a company executive noted, "This should make Smirnoff seem more Russian. We want Russians to realize that Smirnoff came to Russia to produce for Russians."

Even as marketers of distilled spirits adjust their strategies, market preferences are changing; young Russians are turning to beer, with demand up 25 percent in the five-year period between 1995 and 2000. In 2002, expenditures on beer surpassed vodka for the first time. Local brands are favored, as the weak ruble priced imports out of the reach of the average consumer. Some observers attribute the change to the influence of healthier, Western lifestyles. Also, vodka is associated with heavy drinking during Russia's tumultuous transition to a market economy in the 1990s.

Sources: Stuart Elliot, "Figuring Out the Russian Consumer," The New York Times, April 1, 1992, pp. C1, C19; Betsy McKay, "In Russia, West No Longer Means Best; Consumers Shift to Home-Grown Goods," The Wall Street Journal, December 9, 1996, p. A9; John Varoli, "Bored by Vodka, Russians Find More Style in Beer," The New York Times, December 19, 1999, sec. 3, p. 7; Nick Paton Walsh, "Russia Lite: Nyet to Vodka, Da to Beer," Observer, October 20, 2002.

nonuser. Consumers can also be segmented according to **user status**: potential users, nonusers, ex-users, regulars, first-timers, and users of competitors' products. Marketers sometimes refer to the **80/20 rule** when assessing usage rates. This rule, (also known as the *law of disproportionality* or Pareto's Law), suggests that 80 percent of a company's revenues or profits are accounted for by 20 percent of a firm's products or customers. As noted earlier, nine country markets generate about 80 percent of McDonald's revenues. This situation presents McDonald's executives with strategy alternatives: Should the company pursue growth in the handful of countries where it is already well known and popular? Or, should it focus on expansion and growth opportunities in the scores of countries that, as yet, contribute little to revenues and profits?

Benefit Segmentation

Global **benefit segmentation** focuses on the numerator of the value equation: the B in $V = B/P$. This approach is based on marketers' superior understanding of the problem a product solves, the benefit it offers, or the issue it addresses, regardless of geography. Food marketers are finding success creating products that can help parents create nutritious family meals with a minimal investment of time. Campbell Soup is making significant inroads into Japan's $500 million soup market as time-pressed homemakers place a premium on convenience. Marketers of health and beauty aids also use benefit segmentation. Many toothpaste brands are straightforward cavity fighters, and as such they reach a very broad market. However, as consumers become more concerned about whitening, sensitive teeth, gum disease, and other oral care issues, marketers are developing new toothpaste brands suited to the different sets of perceived needs.

The European pet food market represents $30 billion in annual sales. Nestlé discovered that cat owners' attitudes toward feeding their pets are the same everywhere. In response, a pan-European campaign was created for Friskies Dry Cat Food. The appeal was that dry cat food better suits a cat's universally recognized independent nature. Likewise, many Europeans are concerned with

OPEN ^{to} discussion

Segmenting Europe's Single Market

It may be a single market, but the demographics of twenty-first century Europe still offer ample opportunities for market segmentation. One approach known as "3G" addresses issues pertaining to three distinct segments: people born between 1980 and 2000 (Generation Y), adults 60 years old and older (the Golden Grays), and transnational corporations ("Globerations").

The following trends and traits associated with each have major implications for marketing strategy in the years 2008 and beyond.

Generation Y

- Share few family activities
- Display less reverence toward established authorities
- Approach leisure time as "pay-per-play"
- Maintain a heavy diet that is heavily weighted toward "convenience food"
- Are tech savvy
- Are deluged with passive information

Golden Grays

- Consider it important to mix fun and work
- Are relatively affluent, meaning more out-of-home activities
- Enjoy high-tech gaming

- Expect home-health-care devices and biotechnology to extend life expectancy
- Are deluged with passive information

Globerations

- Employees will be less inclined to leave their companies as nations gradually reduce the benefits associated with the "social safety net"
- Knowledge workers will be challenged finding work-life balance
- Customers will want build-to-order solutions
- Online auctions will be a significant sales channel
- A few, powerful consumer-to-business buying groups will emerge

Given these trends, which industries will be the winners and which will be the losers? Likely losers in the leisure sector will include general interest consumer magazines and national newspapers; winners will include interactive services, audio books, and social sports such as golf and tennis. Business services losers will likely be newspaper publishers, grocery coupon distributors, and mass market retailers. Winning services offerings will likely be corporate concierges, personalized telecom networks, and domestic services. Marketers are particularly advised to take the Golden Grays seriously and market brands that provide happiness, convenience, and time savings.

Source: Allyson L. Stewart-Allen, "EU's Future Consumers: Three Groups to Watch," Marketing News 35, no. 12 (June 4, 2001), pp. 9–10.

Worldwide, only about 100 million women use tampons; the total market potential is estimated to be 1.7 billion women. In the mid-1990s, Tambrands, marketers of Tampax brand tampons, approached market segmentation in terms of how resistant women are to using tampons. Cluster 1 (the United States, the United Kingdom, and Australia) is comprised of women who use tampons and believe themselves to be well informed about them. Tampon use in Cluster 2 (France, Israel, and South Africa) is limited to about 50 percent of women; some women in this cluster are concerned that tampon use may result in a loss of virginity. Advertising to women in Cluster 2 focused on endorsements by gynecologists.

Cluster 3, which includes Brazil, China, and Russia, presents the biggest challenge. In these markets, Tambrands must deal with two issues: virginity concerns and the fact that most women in the cluster have little or no experience using tampons. Despite the fact that advertising messages will vary by cluster, each ad will end with the slogan "Tampax. Women Know." Tambrands allocated $65 million for an advertising campaign targeted at the three clusters in 27 countries. One risk: The campaign's frank language would offend women. Commenting on Tambrands' plans, Jeffrey Hill of Meridian Consulting Group commented, "The greatest challenge in the global expansion of tampons is to address the religious and cultural mores that suggest that vaginal insertion is fundamentally prohibited by culture."

Sources: Emily Nelson and Miriam Jordan, "Sensitive Export: Seeking New Markets for Tampons, P&G Faces Cultural Barriers," The Wall Street Journal, December 8, 2000, pp. A1, A8; Yumiko Ono, "Tambrands Ads Aim to Overcome Cultural and Religious Obstacles," The Wall Street Journal, March 17, 1997, p. B8; Dyan Machan, "Will the Chinese Use Tampons?" Forbes, January 16, 1995, pp. 86–87.

improving the health and longevity of their pets. Accordingly, Procter & Gamble is marketing its Iams brand premium pet food as a way to improve pets' health.[27]

Ethnic Segmentation

In many countries, the population includes ethnic groups of significant size. In the United States, for example, there are three major ethnic segments: African/Black Americans, Asian Americans, and Hispanic Americans. Each segment shows

Home brew vodka made from grain or beets is a long-standing tradition in Russia. Consider the following excerpt from Vladimir Voinovich's satirical novel The Life and Extraordinary Adventures of Private Ivan Chonkin:

"They clinked glasses. Ivan downed the contents of his glass and nearly fell of his chair. He instantly lost his breath, just as if he'd been punched in the stomach . . .

Gladishev, who had downed his own glass without any difficulty, looked over at Ivan with a sly grin. 'Well, Ivan, how's the home brew?'

'First rate stuff,' praised Chonkin, wiping the tears from his eyes with the palm of his hand. 'Takes your breath away.'"

---

[27] Sarah Ellison and Emily Nelson, "Pet-Food Companies Compete to Be the Pick of the Litter," *The Wall Street Journal*, July 31, 2001, p. B11.

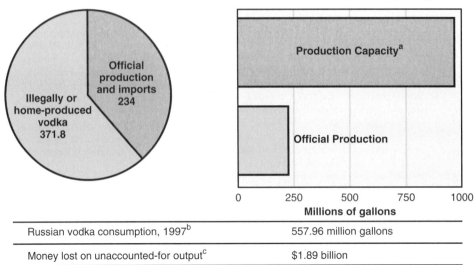

Figure 7-1

Russia's Vodka Industry

Official vs. Total Production . . .   **. . . And vs. Total Capacity**

Official production and imports 234

Illegally or home-produced vodka 371.8

Production Capacity[a]

Official Production

0   250   500   750   1000

Millions of gallons

Russian vodka consumption, 1997[b]	557.96 million gallons
Money lost on unaccounted-for output[c]	$1.89 billion

[a]For 800 enterprises licensed to produce hard, or 128-proof, liquor
[b]Consumption level is believed to be much higher
[c]Converted to U.S. dollars from rubles at current rate

great diversity and can be further subdivided. For example, Asian Americans include Thai Americans, Vietnamese Americans, and Chinese Americans, each of whom speak a different language. By contrast, America's Hispanic population includes Mexican Americans, Puerto-Rican Americans, Cuban Americans, and others who share a common language. The Hispanic American segment is comprised of more than 40 million people, representing about 14 percent of the population and $560 billion in annual buying power. As a group, Hispanic Americans are hard working and exhibit a strong family and religious orientation. In addition, consider the following statistics:

- Mexican households in California have after-tax income of $100 billion, half the total of all Mexican Americans.
- The number of Hispanic teens is projected to swell from 12 percent of the U.S. teen population to 18 percent in the next decade.

From a marketing point of view, these groups offer great opportunity. Companies in a variety of industry sectors, including food and beverages, consumer durables, and leisure and financial services are recognizing the need to include these segments when preparing marketing programs for the United States. For example, companies based in Mexico are zeroing in on opportunities to the north. Three Mexican retailers—Famso, Grupo Gigant SA, and Grupo Comercial Chedraui SA—have opened stores in the United States. As Famsa president Humberto Garza Valdez explained at the grand opening of a store in San Fernando, California, "We're not coming to the U.S. to face big companies like Circuit City or Best Buy. Our focus is the Hispanic market."[28]

From 1999 through 2000, new-vehicle registrations by Hispanics in the United States grew 20 percent, twice the overall national growth rate. Honda, Toyota, and other Japanese automakers have been courting U.S. Hispanics for years and have

---

[28] Joel Millman, "Mexican Retailers Enter U.S. to Capture Latino Dollars," *The Wall Street Journal*, February 8, 2001, p. A18.

built up a great deal of brand loyalty. Ford and GM are playing catch up, with mixed results; despite large increases in advertising targeting Hispanics, GM's market share is slipping.[29] Sales of Corona Extra beer in the United States have grown dramatically, thanks in part to savvy marketing to the Hispanic segment. In lower-income neighborhoods, imported premium beer brands represent "affordable luxuries." Although a six-pack of Corona typically costs at least a dollar more than Budweiser at a local bodega, it is usually priced lower than Heineken. Marketers must understand, though, that many Hispanic Americans live in two worlds; while they identify strongly with the United States, there is also a sense of pride associated with brands that connect to their heritage.[30]

ASSESSING MARKET POTENTIAL AND CHOOSING TARGET MARKETS OR SEGMENTS[31]

After segmenting the market by one or more of the criteria just discussed, the next step is to assess the attractiveness of the identified segments. This part of the process is especially important when sizing up emerging country markets as potential targets. It is at this stage that global marketers should be mindful of several potential pitfalls associated with the market segmentation process. First, there is a tendency to overstate the size and short-term attractiveness of individual country markets, especially when estimates are based primarily on demographic data such as income and population. For example, while China, India, Brazil, and other emerging markets undoubtedly offer potential in the long run, management must realize that short-term profit and revenue growth objectives may be hard to achieve. During the 1990s, Procter & Gamble and other consumer packaged-goods companies learned this lesson in Latin America. By contrast, the success of McDonald's Russia during the same period is a case study in the rewards of persistence and long-term outlook. A second trap that global marketers can set for themselves is to target a country because shareholders or competitors exert pressure on management not to "miss out" on a strategic opportunity. Recall from Chapter 2, for example, the statement by India's finance minister that the twenty-first century will be "the century of India." Such pronouncements can create the impression that management must "act now" to take advantage of a limited window of opportunity. Third, there is a danger that management's network of contacts will emerge as a primary criterion for targeting. The result can be market entry based on convenience rather than rigorous market analysis. For example, a company may enter into a distribution agreement with a non-national employee who wants to represent the company after returning to his or her home country. The issue of choosing the right foreign distributor will be discussed in detail in Chapter 12.

With these pitfalls in mind, marketers can utilize three basic criteria for assessing opportunity in global target markets: current size of the segment and anticipated growth potential, competition, and compatibility with the company's overall objectives and the feasibility of successfully reaching a designated target.

---

[29] Eduardo Porter, "Ford, Other Auto Makers Target Hispanic Community," *The Wall Street Journal*, November 9, 2000, p. B4.

[30] Suein L. Hwang, "Corona Ads Target Hispanics in Effort to Hop to Head of U.S. Beer Market," *The Wall Street Journal Europe*, November 21–22, 1997, p. 9; Michael Barone, "How Hispanics Are Americanizing," *The Wall Street Journal*, February 6, 1998, p. A22.

[31] Parts of the following discussion are adapted from David Arnold, *The Mirage of Global Markets* (Upper Saddle River, NJ: Pearson Education, 2004), Chapter 2.

Current Segment Size and Growth Potential

Is the market segment currently large enough to present a company with the opportunity to make a profit? If the answer is not today, does it have significant growth potential to make it attractive in terms of a company's long-term strategy? Consider the following:

- India is the world's fastest growing cell phone market. The industry is expanding at a rate of 50 percent annually, with 5 million new subscribers added every month. Even so, barriers originating in the political and regulatory environments have shackled private-sector growth.[32]
- In India, 60 million middle class men and women earn more than $275 per month. The segment is growing rapidly and is expected to increase to 73 million by 2010. Young, brand-conscious consumers are buying $100 Tommy Hilfiger jeans and $700 Louis Vuitton handbags. Mohan Murjani owns the rights to sell Tommy Hilfiger in India. Commenting on the country's decade-long economic boom, he notes, "Aspirationally, things changed dramatically. What we were seeing was huge growth in terms of consumers' assets, in terms of their incomes and in terms of their spending power through credit."[33]

As noted earlier, one of the advantages of targeting a market segment globally is that, while the segment in a single-country market might be small, even a narrow segment can be served profitably if the segment exists in several countries. The billion-plus members of the global MTV Generation is a case in point. Moreover, by virtue of its size and purchasing power, the global teen segment is extremely attractive to consumer goods companies. In the case of a huge country market such as India or China, segment size and growth potential may be assessed in a different manner. From the perspective of a consumer packaged-goods company, for example, low incomes and the absence of a distribution infrastructure offset the fact that 75 percent of India's population lives in rural areas. The appropriate decision may be to target urban areas only, even though they are home to only 25 percent of the population. Visa's strategy in China perfectly illustrates this criterion as it relates to demographics: Visa is targeting persons with a monthly salary equivalent to $300 or more. The company estimates that currently 60 million people fit that description; by 2010, the number could include as many as 200 million people.

Thanks to a combination of favorable demographics and lifestyle-related needs, the United States has been a very attractive market for foreign automakers. For example, demand for sports utility vehicles exploded during the 1990s. From 1990 to 2000, SUV sales tripled, growing from nearly 1 million units in 1990 to 2 million units in 1996 and passing 3 million units sold in 2000. Why are these vehicles so popular? Primarily it is the security of four-wheel drive and the higher clearance for extra traction in adverse driving conditions. They also typically have more space for hauling cargo. Reacting to high demand for the Jeep Cherokee, Ford Explorer, and Chevy Blazer, manufacturers from outside the United States introduced models of their own at a variety of price points (see Table 7-7) AutoPacific consultancy predicted that by 2006, at least 79 SUV models would be available as Toyota, Nissan, Rover, BMW, Mercedes, Volkswagen, and other global automakers target American buyers. Even as growth slows in the United States, SUVs are growing in popularity in many other countries. In China, for example,

---

[32] Eric Bellman, "India's Cellphone Boom May Lose Charge," *The Wall Street Journal*, August 25, 2006, p. A6.

[33] Eric Bellman, "As Economy Grows, India Goes for Designer Goods," *The Wall Street Journal*, March 27, 2007, pp. A1, A17. See also Christina Passariello, "Beauty Fix: Behind L'Oréal's Makeover in India: Going Upscale," *The Wall Street Journal*, July 13, 2007, pp. A1, A14.

In China, only about 1 percent of the population currently owns a credit card. That means roughly 13 million cards for 1.3 billion people. Albert Shiung, China vice president for Visa International Asia Pacific, predicts that 50 million credit cards will be in circulation by 2010. Bank of China offers Visa credit cards bearing the Chinese Olympic symbol: a dancing figure based on the Chinese character jing that means "capital/Beijing." Visitors to the Beijing Olympics in 2008 will expect to use their plastic. The Chinese government wants 60 percent of stores with annual sales of 1 million yuan to accept credit cards by the time the games begin.

SUVs represent the fastest-growing sector in the auto industry; SUVs account for about 40 percent of auto imports. Officials at GM's Cadillac division are considering exporting the company's popular $50,000-plus Escalade model to China.[34]

Potential Competition

A market segment or country market characterized by strong competition may be a segment to avoid. However, if the competition is vulnerable in terms of price or quality disadvantages, it is possible for a market newcomer to make significant inroads. Over the past several decades, for example, Japanese companies in a variety of industries targeted the U.S. market despite the presence of entrenched domestic market leaders. Some of the newcomers proved to be extremely adept at segmenting and targeting; as a result, they made significant inroads. In the motorcycle industry, for example, Honda first created the market for small-displacement dirt bikes. The company then moved upmarket with bigger bikes targeted at casual riders whose psychographic profiles were quite different than those of the hardcore Harley-Davidson riders. In document imaging, Canon outflanked Xerox

Table 7-7

Global Automakers Targeting the U.S. Market with SUVs

Automaker	Current SUV model	Current Price* (or range)	Country of Assembly or Manufacture	Year Introduced
Porsche	Cayenne	$42,000–$100,000	Germany	2003
Volkswagen	Touareg	$35,000–$54,000	Slovakia	2004
Honda	CR-V	$21,000	Japan	1995
Toyota	RAV-4	$19,000–$25,000	Japan	1994
Kia	Sorento	$20,500–$29,000	South Korea	2003
BMW	X5	$40,000–$70,000	United States	2000
Mercedes-Benz	ML 350	$42,000–$50,000	United States	2003

* Price variations due to engine, drive train, trim, and other options.

---

[34] Peter Wonacott and Lee Hawkins Jr., "Saying 'Beamer' in Chinese," *The Wall Street Journal*, November 6, 2003, p. B1. See also Joseph B. White, "Rollback: America's Love Affair with Sport Utilities Is Now Cooling Off," *The Wall Street Journal*, May 30, 2001, pp. A1, A8.

by offering compact desktop copiers and targeting department managers and secretaries. Similar case studies can be found in earth-moving equipment (Komatsu versus Caterpillar), photography (Fuji versus Kodak), and numerous other industries. By contrast, there are also many examples of companies whose efforts to develop a position in the United States ended in failure. For example, in the computer industry, Acer failed to make headway in a U.S. market dominated by such strong brand names such as Dell (see Case 1-2).

Feasibility and Compatibility

If a market segment is judged to be large enough, and if strong competitors are either absent or deemed to be vulnerable, then the final consideration is whether a company can and should target that market. The feasibility of targeting a particular segment can be negatively impacted by various factors. For example, significant regulatory hurdles may be present that limit market access. This issue is especially important in China today. The company may also encounter cultural barriers, as was the case with Tambrands' efforts to build its feminine-hygiene market. Other marketing-specific issues can arise; in India, for example, three to five years are required to build an effective distribution system for many consumer products. This fact may serve as a deterrent to foreign companies that might otherwise be attracted by the apparent potential of India's large population.[35]

Managers must decide how well a company's product fits the country market in question—or, as noted, if the company does not currently offer a suitable product, can it develop one? To make this decision, a marketer must consider several criteria:

- Will adaptation be required? If so, is this economically justifiable in terms of the expected sales volume?
- Will import restrictions, high tariffs, or a strong home-country currency drive up the price of the product in the target market currency and effectively dampen demand?
- Is it advisable to source locally? In many cases, reaching global market segments requires considerable expenditures for distribution and travel by company personnel. Would it make sense to source products in the country for export elsewhere in the region?

Finally, it is important to address the question of whether targeting a particular segment is compatible with the company's overall goals, its brand image, or established sources of competitive advantage. For example, BMW is one of the world's premium auto brands. Should BMW add a minivan to its product lineup? As BMW CEO Helmut Panke explained recently, "There is a segment in the market which BMW is not catering to and that is the minivan or MPV segment. We don't have a van because a van as it is in the market today does not fulfill any of the BMW group brand values. We all as a team said 'no'."[36]

A Framework for Selecting Target Markets

As one can infer from this discussion, it would be extremely useful to have formal tools or frameworks available when assessing emerging country markets. Table 7-8 presents a market selection framework that incorporates some of the

---

[35] Khozem Merchant, "Sweet Rivals Find Love in a Warm Climate," *Financial Times*, July 24, 2003, p. 9.
[36] Neal E. Boudette, "BMW's CEO Just Says 'No' to Protect Brand," *The Wall Street Journal*, November 26, 2003, p. B1.

Market	Market Size	Competitive Advantage		Market Potential	Terms of Access	Market Potential
China (1.3 billion)	100	.07	=	7	.50	3.5
Russia (150 million)	50	.10	=	5	.60	3.0
Mexico (94 million)	20	.20	=	4	.90	3.6

Table 7-8

Market Selection Framework

elements just discussed. Suppose an American company has identified China, Russia, and Mexico as potential country target markets. The table shows the countries arranged in declining rank by market size. At first glance, China might appear to hold the greatest potential simply on the basis of size. However, the competitive advantage of our hypothetical firm is 0.07 in China, 0.10 in Russia, and 0.20 in Mexico. Multiplying the market size and competitive advantage index yields a market potential of 7 in China, 5 in Russia, and 4 in Mexico.

The next stage in the analysis requires an assessment of the various market access considerations. In Table 7-8, all these conditions or terms are reduced to an index number of terms of access, which is 0.50 for China, 0.60 for Russia and 0.90 Mexico. In other words, the "market access considerations" are more favorable in Mexico than in Russia, perhaps in this instance due to NAFTA. Multiplying the market potential by the terms of access index suggests that Mexico, despite its small size, holds greater export potential than China or Russia.

Although the framework in Table 7-8 should prove useful as a preliminary screening tool for intercountry comparisons, it does not go far enough in terms of assessing actual market potential. Global marketing expert David Arnold has developed a framework that goes beyond demographic data and considers other, marketing-oriented assessments of market size and growth potential. Instead of a "top-down" segmentation analysis beginning with, for example, income or population data from a particular country, Arnold's framework is based on a "bottom-up" analysis that begins at the product-market level. The term **product-market** refers to a market defined by a product category; in the automotive industry, for example, phrases such as "luxury car market," "SUV market," and "minivan market" refer to specific product-markets. By contrast, phrases such as "the Russian market" or "the Indian market" refer to country markets.

As shown in Figure 7-2, Arnold's framework incorporates two core concepts: marketing model drivers and enabling conditions. **Marketing model drivers** are key elements or factors required for a business to take root and grow in a particular country market environment. The drivers may differ depending on whether a company serves consumer or industrial markets. Does success hinge on establishing or leveraging a brand name? Or, is distribution or a tech-savvy sales staff the key element? Marketing executives seeking an opportunity must arrive at insights into the true driving force(s) that will affect success for their particular product-market. **Enabling conditions** are structural market characteristics whose presence or absence can determine whether the marketing model can succeed. For example, in India, refrigeration is not widely available in shops and market food stalls. This creates challenges for Nestlé and Cadbury Schweppes as they attempt to capitalize on Indians' increasing appetite for chocolate confections. Although Nestlé's KitKat and Cadbury's Dairy Milk bars have been reformulated to better withstand heat, the absence or rudimentary nature of refrigeration hampers the companies' efforts to ensure their products are in saleable condition.

Figure 7-2

Screening Criteria for Market Segments

Source: Arnold, David, *Mirage of Global Markets, The: How Globalizing Companies Can Succeed As Markets Localize,* 1st Edition, © 2004. Reprinted by permission of Pearson Education, Inc., Upper Saddle River, NJ.

What are the key drivers of this marketing model?

Are enabling conditions in place for this marketing model?

What is the cost of entry?
What is the cost of waiting?

Is the risk/control trade-off appropriate?

After marketing-model drivers and enabling conditions have been identified, the third step is for management to weigh the estimated costs associated with entering and serving the market with potential short- and long-term revenue streams. Does this segment or country market merit entry now? Or, would it be better to wait until specific enabling conditions are established? The issue of timing is often framed in terms of the quest for **first-mover advantage**. The conventional wisdom is that the first company to enter a market has the best chance of becoming the market leader. Examples from the history of global marketing that appear to support this notion include the Coca-Cola Company, which established itself globally during World War II. However, there are also first-mover *disadvantages*. The first company to enter a market often makes substantial investments in marketing only to find that a late-arriving competitor reaps some of the benefits. There is ample evidence that late entrants into global markets can also achieve success. One way they do this is by benchmarking established companies and then outmaneuvering them, first locally and then globally. Jollibee, the Philippines-based fast-food chain, is a case in point.

Late movers can also succeed by developing innovative business models. This approach was used by Stephen Millar, chief executive of Australian wine producer BRL Hardy. Millar's insight was that no leading global brand had emerged in the wine business; in other words, there was no equivalent to Coca-Cola. During the 1990s, Hardy established itself as a leading global brand. It accomplished this by moving on several fronts. First, it took control of the sales function. Second, the company made sure its wines were crafted to appeal to a broader demographic than "wine snobs" who tend to favor bottles from France and Italy. Third, it supplemented its line of Australian brands with select brands from other countries. In 2002, Hardy sold 20 million cases of wine worldwide. Today, Hardy is one of the world's top 10 wine companies.[37]

One way to determine the marketing model drivers and enabling conditions is to create a product-market profile. The profile should address some or all of the following basic questions:

1. Who buys our product or brand?
2. Who does not buy our product or brand?
3. What need or function does our product serve? Does our product or brand address that need?

---

[37] Christopher A. Bartlett and Sumantra Ghoshal, "Going Global: Lessons from the Late Movers," *Harvard Business Review* 78, no. 2 (March–April 2000), pp. 138–140. See also Christopher Lawton, "Aussie Wines Star at Spirits Marketer Constellation Brands," *The Wall Street Journal*, January 16, 2004, pp. B1, B4.

4. Is there a market need that is not being met by current product, or brand, offerings?
5. What problem does our product solve?
6. What are customers currently buying to satisfy the need or solve the problem that our product targets?
7. What price are they paying for the product they are currently buying?
8. When is our product purchased?
9. Where is our product purchased?

PRODUCT-MARKET DECISIONS

The next step is in assessing market segments is a company review of current and potential product offerings in terms of their suitability for the country market or segment. This assessment can be performed by creating a product-market grid that maps markets as horizontal rows on a spreadsheet and products as vertical columns. Each cell represents the possible intersection of a product and a market segment. In the case of the candy companies just discussed, both Nestlé and Cadbury determined that a liquid chocolate confection would be one way to address the issue of India's hot weather. The companies are also working to improve the enabling conditions for selling traditional chocolate treats by supplying coolers to merchants.

Table 7-9 shows a product-market grid for Lexus. Toyota launched the Lexus brand in 1989 with two sedan models. In market segmentation terms, the luxury car buyer Lexus hoped to attract is associated with an upper-income demographic. In 1996, Lexus launched its first sport utility vehicle. The decision to enter the SUV product-market represented management's desire to reach upper-income consumers whose lifestyles required something other than a luxury sedan. In 2007, Lexus offered a total of nine different models in the United States; these include the top-of-the line LX470 luxury utility vehicle, the LS430 luxury sedan and, at the entry level, the IS series. Lexus vehicles are marketed in more than 60 countries; the United States is the number one market. Ironically, in Japan the vehicles were sold for years under the Toyota nameplate; the line was relaunched under the Lexus brand in 2005.[38]

Lexus sold about 50,700 vehicles in Europe in 2006, with the United Kingdom accounting for about 30 percent of those sales. Management intends to build Lexus into a global luxury brand; the goal is to sell 65,000 cars in Europe by the end of the decade. That, in turn, means that the company has to target Germany, the largest market in Europe where 4 in 10 vehicles bought are luxury models. Approximately 15 million cars are sold in Europe each year; Germany accounts for nearly one-quarter of the total. In 2003, Lexus sold about 2,500 cars in Germany; by comparison, Mercedes and BMW sold a combined total of more than 500,000 vehicles. Can Lexus succeed on the home turf of two of the world's leading luxury carmakers? To appeal to Germany's nationalistic car buyers, Lexus vehicles are undergoing significant adaptation. For example, because Germans want the option of buying vehicles with diesel engines, Lexus developed new diesel models for 2006 as well as a gas-electric hybrid engine for the RX330 SUV. Note that, in Europe, Lexus offers the top-of-the-line LX470 in only one country: Russia. Can you explain this situation? How do the model offerings vary among the BRIC countries?

---

[38] Jathon Sapsford, "Toyota Introduces a New Luxury Brand in Japan: Lexus," *The Wall Street Journal,* August 3, 2005, pp. B1, B5.

Table 7-9

Product-Market Grid for Lexus, Select Country Markets, 2006

Country Segment	Vehicle Model								
	ES	GS	GX	IS	LS	LX	RX	RX HV	SC
Asia									
Hong Kong	X	X		X	X		X	X	X
China	X	X		X	X	X	X		X
Taiwan	X	X		X	X	X	X	X	X
India					X				
North America									
Canada	X	X	X	X	X	X	X	X	X
USA	X	X	X	X	X	X	X	X	X
Mexico									
South America									
Brazil									
Europe									
Austria		X		X	X		X	X	X
Belgium		X		X	X		X	X	X
Czech Rep.		X		X	X		X	X	X
Denmark		X		X	X		X	X	X
Finland		X		X	X		X	X	X
France		X		X	X		X	X	X
Germany		X		X	X		X	X	X
Gr. Britain		X		X	X		X	X	X
Greece		X		X	X		X	X	X
Ireland		X		X	X		X	X	X
Netherlands		X		X	X		X	X	X
Portugal		X		X	X		X	X	X
Russia		X		X	X	X	X	X	X
Sweden		X		X	X		X	X	X
Switzerland		X		X	X		X	X	X
Middle East									
Israel		X		X	X				
Kuwait	X	X		X	X	X	X		X
Saudi Arabia	X	X		X	X	X	X		X

Source: Lexus Marketing.

TARGET MARKET STRATEGY OPTIONS

After evaluating the identified segments in terms of the three criteria presented, a decision is made whether to pursue a particular opportunity or not. If the decision is made to proceed, an appropriate targeting strategy must be developed. There are three basic categories of target marketing strategies: standardized marketing, concentrated marketing, and differentiated marketing.

Standardized Global Marketing

Standardized global marketing is analogous to mass marketing in a single country. It involves creating the same marketing mix for a broad mass market of potential buyers. Standardized global marketing, also known as *undifferentiated target marketing*, is based on the premise that a mass market exists around the world. In addition, that mass market is served with a marketing mix of standardized elements. Product adaptation is minimized, and a strategy of intensive distribution ensures that

Targeting Adventure Seekers with an American Classic

In 2003, Harley-Davidson (H-D) celebrated its one-hundredth anniversary. The company grew impressively during its first 100 years of operation; as the twenty-first century began, H-D had sales of $2.1 billion, 8,000 employees worldwide, and a network of 1,300 dealerships in 48 countries. Savvy export marketing enabled H-D to dramatically increase worldwide sales of its heavyweight motorcycles. From Australia to Germany to Mexico City, H-D enthusiasts are paying the equivalent of up to $25,000 to own an American-built classic. In many countries, dealers must put would-be buyers on a six-month waiting list because of high demand.

H-D's international success came after years of neglecting overseas markets. The company was also slow to react to a growing threat from Japanese manufacturers. Early on, the company used an export-selling approach, symbolized by its underdeveloped dealer network. Moreover, print advertising simply used word-for-word translations of the U.S. ads. By the late 1980s, after recruiting dealers in the important Japanese and European markets, company executives discovered a basic principle of global marketing. "As the saying goes, we needed to think global but act local," said Jerry G. Wilke, vice president for worldwide marketing during that time. Managers began to adapt the company's international marketing to make it more responsive to local conditions.

In Japan, for example, H-D's rugged image and high quality helped make it the best-selling imported motorcycle. Still, Toshifumi Okui, president of H-D's Japanese division, was not satisfied. He worried that the tag line from the U.S. ads, "One steady constant in an increasingly screwed-up world," didn't connect with Japanese riders. Okui finally convinced Milwaukee to allow him to launch a Japan-only advertising campaign juxtaposing images from both Japan and the United States, such as American cyclists passing a rickshaw carrying a geisha. After learning that riders in Tokyo consider fashion and customized bikes to be essential, H-D opened two stores specializing in clothes and bike accessories.

In Europe, H-D discovered that an "evening out" means something different than it does in America. The company sponsored a rally in France, where beer and live rock music were available until midnight. Recalls Wilke, "People asked us why we were ending the rally just as the evening was starting. So I had to go persuade the band to keep playing and reopen the bar until 3 or 4 am." Still, rallies are less common in Europe than in the United States so H-D encourages its dealers to hold open houses at their dealerships. While biking through Europe, Wilke also learned that German bikers often travel at speeds exceeding 100 miles per hour. The company made design changes to create a smoother ride at Autobahn speeds. H-D's German marketing effort began focusing on accessories to increase rider protection. Today, the company has a clear picture of its core European customers; as Klaus Stobel, European affairs director for Harley-Davidson Europe, explained, "The people who buy Harleys in Europe are like the people who buy BMWs in the U.S. They are dentists and lawyers." Even so, in 2002, Europe accounted for just 8 percent of 2002 global revenues.

> *"Everyone thinks we produce big, showy, custom motorcycles. We actually have a broad range of bikes that well suit European riding habits. We have a perception problem around Harley which is an issue we need to tackle."*
>
> John Russell, Managing Director, Harley-Davidson Europe

Despite high demand from brand-loyal enthusiasts, the company intentionally limits production increases to keep quality high and to keep the product supply limited in relation to demand. The company's total motorcycle production recently passed the 250,000 mark. Even so, there are not enough bikes to go around, a situation that seems to suit company executives just fine. As former H-D president James H. Paterson once commented, "Enough motorcycles is too many motorcycles."

Sources: Jeremy Grant and Harald Ehren, "Harley-Davidson Eyes Europe," Financial Times, July 28, 2003, p. 17; Kevin Kelly and Karen Lowry Miller, "The Rumble Heard Round the World: Harleys," Business Week, May 24, 1993, pp. 58, 60; Robert L. Rose, "Vrooming Back: After Nearly Stalling, Harley-Davidson Finds New Crowd of Riders," The Wall Street Journal, August 31, 1990, pp. A1, A6; John Holusha, "How Harley Outfoxed Japan with Exports," The New York Times, August 12, 1990, p. F5; Robert C. Reid, "How Harley Beat Back the Japanese," Fortune, September 25, 1989, pp. 155+.

the product is available in the maximum number of retail outlets. The appeal of standardized global marketing is clear: lower production costs. The same is true of standardized global communications.

CONCENTRATED GLOBAL MARKETING

The second global targeting strategy, concentrated target marketing, involves devising a marketing mix to reach a **niche**. A niche is simply a single segment of the global market. In cosmetics, the House of Lauder, Chanel, and other cosmetics marketers have used this approach successfully to target the upscale, prestige segment of the market. Similarly, Body Shop International PLC caters to consumers in many countries who wish to purchase "natural" beauty aids and cosmetics that have not been tested on animals. Concentrated targeting is also the strategy

As Harley-Davidson continues to expand internationally, it is diversifying its customer base by targeting female riders in key markets such as Japan. Recently, H-D has posted double-digit sales increases outside the United States. According to chief executive Jim Ziemer, this is evidence that the company's long-term strategy is working. H-D has replaced many dealers in Europe, acquired its Australian distributor, and is establishing full-service dealerships in China and Thailand.

"There is a significant difference between the 'mass market' and the premium segment. In the mass market, customers are looking for a good deal. In the premium segment, they are searching for a vehicle that fulfills their expectations and their emotions."[40]

Helmut Panke, Chairman BMW

employed by the hidden champions of global marketing: Companies unknown to most people that have succeeded by serving a niche market that exists in many countries. These companies define their markets narrowly and strive for global depth rather than national breadth. For example, Germany's Winterhalter is a hidden champion in the dishwasher market, but the company has never sold a dishwasher to a consumer, hospital, or school. Instead, it focuses exclusively on dishwashers and water conditioners for hotels and restaurants. As Jürgen Winterhalter noted recently, "The narrowing of our market definition was the most important strategic decision we ever made. It is the very foundation of our success in the past decade."[39]

Differentiated Global Marketing

The third target marketing strategy, **differentiated global marketing**, represents a more ambitious approach than concentrated target marketing. Also known as **multisegment targeting**, this approach entails targeting two or more distinct market segments with multiple marketing mix offerings. This strategy allows a company to achieve wider market coverage. For example, in the sport utility vehicle segment described previously, Rover has a $68,000 Range Rover at the high end of the market. A scaled-down version, the Land Rover Discovery, competes directly with the Jeep Grand Cherokee. Rover's newest vehicle, the Freelander, has been on sale in Europe for several years. Freelander was introduced in the U.S. market in December 2001 with prices starting at $25,000. Likewise, Stolichnaya produces three brands of Russian vodka, each targeted at a different market segment: superpremium Stolichnaya Cristal, the premium "base" brand Stolichnaya, and low-priced Privet (the name means "greetings" in Russian).

---

[39] Hermann Simon, *Hidden Champions: Lessons from 500 of the World's Best Unknown Companies* (Boston: Harvard Business School Press, 1996), p. 54.
[40] Helmut Panke and Alex Taylor III, "BMW Turns More American Than Ever," *Fortune*, February 2004, p. 130.

In the cosmetics industry, Unilever pursues differentiated global marketing strategies by targeting both ends of the perfume market. Unilever targets the luxury market with Calvin Klein and Elizabeth Taylor's Passion; Wind Song and Brut are its mass-market brands. Mass marketer Procter & Gamble, known for its Old Spice and Incognito brands, also embarked upon this strategy with its 1991 acquisition of Revlon's EuroCos, marketer of Hugo Boss for men and Laura Biagiotti's Roma perfume. In the mid-1990s, P&G launched a new prestige fragrance, Venezia, in the United States and several European countries. Currently, P&G also markets Envy, Rush, and other Gucci fragrances as a licensee of the Italian fashion house. Conversely, in 1997 Estée Lauder acquired Sassaby, owner of the mass-market Jane brand. This action marked the first move by Lauder outside the prestige segment.[41]

POSITIONING

The term *positioning* is attributed to marketing gurus Al Ries and Jack Trout, who first introduced it in a 1969 article published in *Industrial Marketing* magazine. **Positioning** refers to the act of differentiating a brand in customers' minds in relation to competitors in terms of attributes and benefits that the brand does and does not offer. Put differently, positioning is the process of developing strategies for "staking out turf" or "filling a slot" in the mind of target customers.[42] Positioning is frequently used in conjunction with the segmentation variables and targeting strategies discussed previously. For example, Unilever and other consumer goods companies often engage in differentiated target marketing, offering a full range of brands within a given product category. Unilever's 10 detergent brands include All, Wisk, Surf, and Persil; each is positioned slightly differently. In some instances, extensions of a popular brand can be positioned in different ways. For example, Colgate's Total toothpaste is positioned as the brand that addresses a full range of oral health issues, including gum disease. In most parts of the world Total is available in several formulations, including Total Advanced Clean, Total Clean Mint Paste, and Total Whitening Paste. Effective positioning differentiates each variety from the others.

In the decades since Ries and Trout first focused attention on the importance of the concept, marketers have utilized a number of general positioning strategies. These include positioning by attribute or benefit, quality and price, use or user,

global MARKETING Q&A

Outlook: "You have a number of brands that are somewhat similar. Isn't there a risk of cannibalization among them?"

Franck Riboud, Chairman and CEO, Groupe Danone: "Our brands have different positionings within the same market. With our bottled waters, for example, Evian is strongly associated with health and beauty—a promise of youthful looks through drinking water—while Volvic promotes the same message but associates it with energy through replenishing the body during sports activities. They don't cannibalize each other, because they're marketed as promoting different qualities."

Source: "Think Global, Act Local," Outlook no. 3 (2003), p. 9.

---

41 Tara Parker-Pope, "Estée Lauder Buys Jane Brand's Owner for Its First Venture into Mass Market," *The Wall Street Journal*, September 27, 1997, p. B8.
42 Al Ries and Jack Trout, *Positioning: The Battle for Your Mind* (New York: Warner Books, 1982), p. 44.

and competitor.[43] Recent research has identified three additional positioning strategies that are particularly useful in global marketing: global consumer culture positioning, local consumer culture positioning, and foreign consumer culture positioning.

Attribute or Benefit

A frequently used positioning strategy exploits a particular product attribute, benefit, or feature. Economy, reliability, and durability are frequently used attribute/benefit positions. Volvo automobiles are known for solid construction that offers safety in the event of a crash. By contrast, BMW is positioned as "the ultimate driving machine," a reference that signifies performance. In the ongoing credit card wars, Visa's advertising theme "It's Everywhere You Want to Be" draws attention to the benefit of worldwide merchant acceptance. In global marketing, it may be deemed important to communicate the fact that a brand is imported. This approach is known as *foreign consumer culture positioning* (FCCP).

Quality and Price

This strategy can be thought of in terms of a continuum from high fashion/quality and high price to good value (rather than "low quality") at a reasonable price. A legendary print ad campaign for Belgium's Stella Artois beer juxtaposes a cap pried off a bottle of Stella with images of prized possessions such as a Steinway piano. The tagline "Reassuring expensive" is the only copy; upon close inspection of the Steinway, the reader can see that one of the keys is broken because it was used to open the bottle! InBev, the world's biggest brewer in terms of volume, markets the Stella Artois brand. InBev was formed in 2004 by the merger of Belgium's Interbrew and AmBev, Brazil's leading brewer. While Stella is regarded as an "everyday" beer in its local market of Belgium, the marketing team at InBev has repositioned it as a premium global brand.[44]

At the high end of the distilled spirits industry, marketers of imported vodkas such as Belvedere and Stolichnaya Gold have successfully positioned their brands as superpremium entities selling for twice the price of premium ("ordinary") vodka. Ads for several export vodka brands emphasize their national origins, demonstrating how FCCP can reinforce quality and price positioning. Marketers sometimes use the phrase "transformation advertising" to describe advertising that seeks to change the experience of buying and using a product—in other words, the product benefit—to justify a higher price/quality position. Presumably, buying and drinking Grey Goose (from France), Belvedere (Poland), Ketel One (the Netherlands), or Stolichnaya Gold (Russia) is a more gratifying consumption experience than that of buying and drinking a "bar brand" such as Popov (who knows where it is made?).

Use or User

Another positioning strategy represents how a product is used or associates the brand with a user or class of users. For example, to capitalize on the global success and high visibility of the *Lord of the Rings* trilogy, Gillette's Duracell battery unit ran print and TV ads proclaiming that, on location in remote areas of New Zealand, *Rings* director Peter Jackson and his crew used Duracell exclusively. Likewise, Max Factor makeup is positioned as "the makeup that makeup artists use."

---

[43] David A. Aaker and J. Gary Shansby, "Positioning Your Product," *Business Horizons* 25, no. 2 (May–June 1982), pp. 56–62.
[44] "Head to Head," *Economist*, October 29, 2005, pp. 66–69.

From SEIKO WATCH CORPORATION
pulsarwatches.com

Addicted
to reality TV.
Hates coriander.
Believes in ghosts.
Has two pet Chihuahuas.
Likes 8os music, 7os décor.
Champion sandcastle builder.
Reading Dostoevsky. Loves stripes.
Former vegan.
Wears a Pulsar

it's all in the details

alarm chronograph • dual time capability • stainless steel case
and bracelet • 3 bar water resistant • Prestige Collection

RRP €160

PULSAR

Competition

Implicit or explicit reference to competitors can provide the basis for an effective positioning strategy. For example, when Anita Roddick started Body Shop International in the 1970s, she emphasized the difference between the principles pursued by "mainstream" health and beauty brands and those of her company. The Body Shop brand stands for natural ingredients, no animal testing, and recyclable containers. Moreover, Roddick abandoned the conventional industry approach of promising miracles; instead, women were given realistic expectations of what health and beauty aids can accomplish. More recently, Dove's "Campaign for Real Beauty" broke new ground by positioning the brand around a new definition of beauty. The campaign is based on research commissioned by Silvia Lagnado, Dove's global brand director. The research

The Dove Campaign for Real Beauty supports the mission of the Dove® brand to widen the definition of beauty. The Campaign supports the Dove Self-Esteem Fund by developing workshops and education tools that help foster positive self-esteem in both girls and young women. The Campaign for Real Beauty has generated a significant amount of favorable publicity worldwide.

indicated that, worldwide, only 2 percent of women consider themselves beautiful. Armed with this insight, Ogilvy & Mather Worldwide's office in Dusseldorf developed the concept that is the basis of the "Campaign for Real Beauty."

Global, Foreign, and Local Consumer Culture Positioning[45]

As noted in Chapter 4 and discussed briefly in this chapter, global consumer culture positioning is a strategy that can be used to target various segments associated with the emerging global consumer culture. **Global consumer culture positioning (GCCP)** is defined as a strategy that identifies the brand as a symbol of a particular global culture or segment. It has proven to be an effective strategy for communicating with global teens, cosmopolitan elites, globe-trotting laptop warriors who consider themselves members of a "transnational commerce culture," and other groups. For example, Sony's brightly colored "My First Sony" line is positioned as *the* electronics brand for youngsters around the globe with discerning parents. Philips' current global corporate image campaign is keyed to the theme "Sense and Simplicity." Benetton uses the slogan "United Colors of Benetton" to position itself as a brand concerned with the unity of humankind. Heineken's strong brand equity around the globe can be attributed in good measure to a GCCP strategy that reinforces consumers' cosmopolitan self-image.

Certain categories of products lend themselves especially well to GCCP. High-tech and high-touch products are both associated with high levels of customer involvement and by a shared "language" among users.[46] *High-tech products* are

---

[45] The following discussion is adapted from Dana L. Alden, Jan-Benedict Steenkamp, and Rajeev Batra, "Brand Positioning Through Advertising in Asia, North America, and Europe: The Role of Global Consumer Culture," *Journal of Marketing* 63, no. 1 (January 1999), pp. 75–87.

[46] Teresa J. Domzal and Lynette Unger, "Emerging Positioning Strategies in Global Marketing," *Journal of Consumer Marketing* 4, no. 4 (Fall 1987), pp. 26–27.

sophisticated, technologically complex, and/or difficult to explain or understand. When shopping for them, consumers often have specialized needs or interests and rational buying motives. High-tech brands and products are frequently evaluated in terms of their performance against established objective standards. Portable MP3 players, cellular phones, personal computers, home theater audio/video components, luxury automobiles, and financial services are some of the high-tech product categories for which companies have established strong global positions. Buyers typically already possess—or wish to acquire—considerable technical information. Generally speaking, for example, computer buyers in all parts of the world are equally knowledgeable about Pentium microprocessors, 120-gigabyte hard drives, software RAM requirements, and flat-panel displays. High-tech global consumer positioning also works well for special interest products associated with leisure or recreation. Fuji bicycles, Adidas sports equipment, and Canon cameras are examples of successful global special-interest products. Because most people who buy and use high-tech products "speak the same language" and share the same mindset, marketing communications should be informative and emphasize performance-related attributes and features to establish the desired GCCP.

By contrast, when shopping for *high-touch products*, consumers are generally energized by emotional motives rather than rational ones. Consumers may feel an emotional or spiritual connection with high-touch products, the performance of which is evaluated in subjective, aesthetic terms rather than objective, technical terms. Consumption of high-touch products may represent an act of personal indulgence, reflect the user's actual or ideal self-image, or reinforce interpersonal relationships between the user and family members or friends. High-touch products appeal to the senses more than the intellect; if a product comes with a detailed user's manual, it's probably high tech; by contrast, the consumption experience associated with a high-touch product probably does not entail referring to an instruction manual. Luxury perfume, designer fashions, and fine champagne are all examples of high-touch products that lend themselves to GCCP. Some high-touch products are linked with the joy or pleasure found in "life's little moments." Ads that show friends chatting over a cup of coffee in a café or someone's kitchen put the product at the center of everyday life. As Nestlé has convincingly

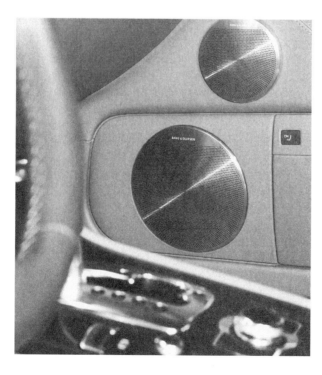

B&O recently unveiled a $7,000, 14-speaker sound system for the Audi A8. Even when played at maximum volume, persons outside the vehicle can't hear anything.

demonstrated with its Nescafé brand, this type of high-touch, emotional appeal is understood worldwide.

A brand's GCCP can be reinforced by the careful selection of the thematic, verbal, or visual components that are incorporated into advertising and other communications. For marketers seeking to establish a high-touch GCCP, leisure, romance, and materialism are three themes that cross borders well. By contrast, professionalism and experience are advertising themes that work well for high-tech products such as global financial services. Several years ago, for example, Chase Manhattan bank launched a $75 million global advertising campaign geared to the theme "Profit from Experience." According to Aubrey Hawes, a vice president and corporate director of marketing for the bank, Chase's business and private banking clients "span the globe and travel the globe. They can only know one Chase in their minds, so why should we try to confuse them?"[47] Presumably, Chase's target audience is sophisticated enough to appreciate the subtlety of the copywriter's craft—"profit" can be interpreted as either a noun ("monetary gain") or a verb ("reap an advantage").

In some instances, products may be positioned globally in a "bipolar" fashion as both high tech and high touch. This approach can be used when products satisfy buyers' rational criteria while evoking an emotional response. For example, audio-video components from Denmark's Bang & Olufsen, by virtue of their performance and elegant styling, are perceived as both high tech ("advanced engineering and sonically superior") and high touch ("sleek modern design blends in nicely with the rest of the décor"). As CEO Torben Ballegaard Sørensen explains, "Our brand is about feeling good at home, or where you feel at home—in a car or in a hotel. When daily life is cluttered, you can come home to a system that works and is tranquil. It cocoons you."[48] Nokia has become the world's leading cellular phone brand because the company combines state-of-the-art technical performance with a fashion orientation that allows users to view their phones as extensions of themselves. Likewise, Apple Inc. positions its products on the basis of both performance ("64-bit Intel Core 2 Duo processor") and design (the hard drive and other components are integrated with the iMac's flat-screen display).

Writing in the Financial Times, *Jonathan Margolis describes Apple's iPod music player as "an all-time design classic." Similarly, in his review in the* Far Eastern Economic Review, *Charles Bickers praised the Titanium G4 laptop for its "stunning" looks and noted that the laptop "oozes understated corporate power." eWeek's reviewer asserted that the G4's tough, sleek titanium shell "redefines how a notebook computer should appear and feel." High-touch products are intended to evoke these types of responses. Style is not the only story, however; the technical features of Apple products, including the iPhone, iPod Touch, and new iMac computer models pictured here, also satisfy users' requirements for performance and functionality.*

47 Gary Levin, "Ads Going Global," *Advertising Age,* July 22, 1991 p. 42.
48 John Gapper, "When High Fidelity Becomes High Fashion," *Financial Times,* December 20, 2005, p. 8.

To the extent that English is the primary language of international business, mass media, and the Internet, one can make the case that English signifies modernism and a cosmopolitan outlook. Therefore, the use of English in advertising and labeling throughout the world is another way to achieve GCCP. Benetton's tag line "United Colors of Benetton" appears in English in all the company's advertising. The implication is that fashion-minded consumers everywhere in the world shop at Benetton. Recall the Chapter 4 discussion of the use of English as a marketing tool in Japan. Even though a native English speaker would doubtless find the syntax to be muddled, it is the symbolism associated with the use of English that counts rather than specific meanings that the words might (or might not) convey. A third way to reinforce a GCCP is to use brand symbols that cannot be interpreted as associated with a specific country culture. Examples include Nestlé's "little nest" logo with an adult bird feeding its babies, the Nike swoosh, and the Mercedes-Benz star.

A second option is **foreign consumer culture positioning (FCCP)**, which associates the brand's users, use occasions, or production origins with a foreign country or culture. Foster's Brewing Group's U.S. advertising proudly trumpets the brand's national origin; print ads feature the tag line "Foster's. Australian for Beer" while TV and radio spots are keyed to the theme "How to Speak Australian." Needless to say, these ads are not used in Australia itself. Advertising for Grupo Modelo's Corona Extra brand is identified more generally with Latin America. The "American-ness" of Levi jeans, Marlboro cigarettes, and Harley-Davidson motorcycles—sometimes conveyed with subtlety, sometimes not—enhances their appeal to cosmopolitans around the world and offers opportunities for FCCP. FCCP is sometimes used in automobile advertising; in the early 1990s, for example, Volkswagen ran an advertising campaign featuring a German word, *Fahrvergnügen*, that was meant to signify both the cars' German origins and a European joy of driving. Sometimes, brand names suggest an FCCP even though a product is of local origin. For example, the name "Häagen-Dazs" was made up to imply Scandinavian origin even though the ice cream was launched by an American company. Conversely, a popular chewing gum in Italy marketed by Perfetti bears the brand name "Brooklyn."

Marketers can also utilize **local consumer culture positioning (LCCP)**, a strategy that associates the brand with local cultural meanings, reflects the local culture's norms, portrays the brand as consumed by local people in the national culture, or depicts the product as locally produced for local consumers. An LCCP approach can be seen in Budweiser's U.S. advertising; ads featuring the Clydesdale horses, for example, associate the brand with small-town American culture. Researchers studying television advertising in seven countries found that LCCP predominated, particularly in ads for food, personal nondurables, and household nondurables.

The global environment must be analyzed before a company pursues expansion into new geographic markets. Through **global market segmentation**, a company can identify and group customers or countries according to common needs and wants. **Demographic segmentation** can be based on country income and population, age, ethnic heritage, or other variables. **Psychographic segmentation** groups people according to attitudes, interests, opinions, and lifestyles. **Behavioral segmentation** utilizes **user status** and **usage rate** as segmentation variables. Segmentation can also be based on the **benefits** buyers seek. **Global teens** and **global elites** are two examples of global market segments.

After marketers have identified segments, the next step is **targeting**: The identified groups are evaluated and compared, and one or more segments with the greatest potential is selected from them. The groups are evaluated on the basis of several factors, including segment size and growth potential, competition, and compatibility and

feasibility. Target market assessment also entails a thorough understanding of the **product-market** in question and determining **marketing model drivers** and **enabling conditions** in the countries under study. The timing of market entry should take into account whether a **first-mover advantage** is likely to be gained. After evaluating the identified segments, marketers must decide on an appropriate targeting strategy. The three basic categories of global target marketing strategies are **standardized marketing, concentrated (niche) marketing**, and **differentiated (multisegment) marketing**.

Positioning a product or brand to differentiate it in the minds of target customers can be accomplished in various ways: positioning by attribute or benefit, positioning by quality/price, positioning by use or user, and positioning by competition. In global marketing **global consumer culture positioning (GCCP), foreign consumer culture positioning (FCCP),** and **local consumer culture positioning (LCCP)** are additional strategic options.

1. Identify the five basic segmentation strategies. Give an example of a company that has used each one.

2. Explain the difference between segmenting and targeting.

3. Compare and contrast standardized, concentrated, and differentiated global marketing. Illustrate each strategy with an example from a global company.

4. American Izuzu Motors recently introduced the AXIOM SUV in the United States with a base sticker price of $25,985. The base price for a Honda CRV is $18,750; prices for Toyota's RAV4

start at $16,365. Assess Isuzu's decision to target the U.S. market for sport utility vehicles.

5. What is positioning? Identify the different positioning strategies presented in the chapter and give examples of companies or products that illustrate each.

6. What is global consumer culture positioning (GCCP)? What other strategic positioning choices do global marketers have?

7. What is a high-touch product? Explain the difference between high-tech product positioning and high-touch product positioning. Can some products be positioned using both strategies? Explain.

Case 7-1

Carmakers Target Gen Y

The world's automakers have Generation Y (Gen Y) in their sights. Gen Y is the cohort of 71 million Americans born between 1977 and 1994. As their customer base ages, the automakers want to build brand loyalty among the nation's youth. For example, the average Toyota buyer is 47 years old; for Honda, the figure is 44 years old (Table 1). Moreover, at home in Japan, not only is the population rapidly aging, it is expected to stop growing entirely by 2007. In a reversal of the orthodox notion in some parts of the world that "globalization = Americanization," young American car buyers are equating Japanese-designed cars with coolness.

The trend began in California; the letters *JDM* ("Japanese Domestic Market") are shorthand for car accessories that, due to different regulations, are only available in Japan. Using the Internet, car buffs—many of whom favor the Honda Civic—order turbo chargers and other parts and customize their vehicles. The West coast "tuner" trend gained nationwide traction with the release of the movie *The Fast and the Furious* in 2002.

Honda is targeting Gen Y consumers with the Element, a compact SUV that features dramatic exterior styling, a dash-mounted shifter, and waterproof seat fabric. Launched in 2003, the Element is available in both 2-wheel and 4-wheel drive models. First-year sales exceeded the target of 50,000 units; half the people who bought Elements have never owned a Honda before.

Betting that Gen Y car buyers are ready to try something new, Toyota, Honda, and other companies are using a variety of product strategies. In spring 2003, Honda launched the

Table 1 *Average Buyer Age for Select Auto Brands*

Brand	Average Age of Buyer
Toyota	47
Chevrolet	45
Ford	45
Honda	44
Pontiac	44
Mitsubishi	41
Volkswagen	41
Toyota Scion	39

Element, a boxy sport utility vehicle that is manufactured in the United States. With a base price of $18,300, the vehicle is targeted at 24-year-old males. Toyota responded by launching the Scion xB miniwagon in the United States; the vehicle was already available in Japan, where it is known as a youthmobile.

> "Somehow the idea got propagated that young people like really weird automobiles and that'll attract young people because they wear their baseball caps backwards and trousers that look like they're about to slip off their butts. Well, they don't. If you go to university campuses in the U.S., I dare say that if you look at the parking lot you'll see a very heavy proportion of BMW 3-series. Now, they're not new 3-series . . . but the aspirational vehicle for them is the BMW 3-series. To sort of give them some goofy-looking contraption and say 'look, we designed this just for you,' that's the kiss of death. My answer is: sell them a three-or four-year-old used car. That's the way it's always been."
>
> Bob Lutz, Vice Chairman, General Motors

Other automakers are sizing up the potential and attractiveness of the Gen Y segment. Hyundai fields Hyundai Investigative Teams (HIT) in an effort to better understand the needs, wants, and preferences of young car buyers. For example, early in 2004, an HIT unit comprised of eight teens, 16 years old to 18 years old, visited the Chicago Motor Show. They spent a day looking at vehicles and provided feedback. Hyundai does not currently target the youth market. However, the company is using HIT to assess the strength of rivals' product offerings. After viewing the Scion xB, one female HIT member described it as, "A clown bus. I laughed when I saw it. *That's* what everyone thinks we'd like?"

> "Scion's initial positioning ignored the fact that they were part of Toyota. Toyota now has just about every hold in the market covered."
>
> George Peterson, CEO, AutoPacific

Despite such reactions, the Scion has turned out to be hugely popular with young people. In 2006, Scion easily exceeded its sales goal of 150,000 vehicles; 80 percent of buyers had never purchased a Toyota before. That success prompted management to cap sales at the 150,000 mark in future model years. Executives were also discussing whether to abandon Scion's limited television advertising schedule in favor of event marketing and so-called branded entertainment. Already, the Scion brand has been extended to a music label for emerging artists and a clothing line. In addition, Scion's online presence has been moved from MySpace.com to Second Life. As Mark Templin, vice president of Scion, explained, "Because we no longer have to focus on brand awareness, we can be even more edgy and more risky."

Discussion Questions

1. Why are Japanese automakers targeting Gen Y?
2. Do you think Honda and Toyota are using the right strategy by creating new vehicles such as the Element and the Scion?
3. Do you agree with Toyota's decision to limit the number of Scion vehicles available for sale?

Sources: Bernard Simon, "Scion Brand Greases the Wheels for Toyota," *Financial Times,* April 26, 2006, p. 11; Gina Chon, "A Way Cool Strategy: Toyota's Scion Plans to Sell Fewer Cars," *The Wall Street Journal,* November 10, 2006, pp. B1, B2; Chris Woodyard, "Outside-the-Box Scion Scores with Young Drivers," *USA Today,* May 2, 2005, pp. 1B, 2B; Jeremy Grant, "Carmakers Try to Fathom the Teenage Taste," *Financial Times,* February 10, 2004, p. 10; Jeremy Grant, "In the Driving Seat of a Car Giant: Bob Lutz," *Financial Times,* January 3–4, 2004, p. W3; Sholnn Freeman and Norihiko Shirouzu, "Toyota's Gen Y Gamble," *The Wall Street Journal,* July 30, 2003, p. B1; Micheline Maynard, "Carmakers Design for Generation Y," *The New York Times,* January 16, 2003, pp. C1, C16; Norihiko Shirouzu and Todd Zaun, "Big Wheels: Japan Auto Makers Train Their Sights on the U.S. Again," *The Wall Street Journal,* January 3, 2003, pp. A1, A6; Sholnn Freeman, "New Wheels for Generation Y," *The Wall Street Journal,* January 14, 2002, pp. B1, B3.

Case 7-2

The Youth of the World Proclaim, "We Want Our MTV!"

Janet Jackson's "wardrobe malfunction" during the halftime show of the 2004 Super Bowl caused a worldwide sensation. For better or for worse, MTV, which produced the show, demonstrated that it still had the ability to shake things up. Worldwide, musical tastes and trends have changed significantly since MTV first went on the air in 1981. Few current viewers are likely to remember the Buggles, the British duo whose song "Video Killed the Radio Star" was featured in the first clip aired. In some ways, MTV looks the same in the twenty-first century as it did in the 1980s. Today, however, MTV's reach extends far beyond the United States; Viacom's MTV Networks unit, which also includes VH1, Comedy Central, and Nickelodeon, it comprises the world's largest network with nearly 1 billion viewers in 160 countries.

However, MTV has not prospered by offering the same sights and sounds in every market. Rather, it owes much of its success to the realization that viewer sensibilities and tastes vary on a regional and country-by-country basis. MTV carefully researches those sensibilities and tastes, and then caters to them. MTV is especially popular with persons 15 years old to 34 years old, with 15 year olds to 24 year olds—a pure youth audience, as executives proudly note—as the core consumer. MTV executives are quick to point out that the channel's programming is extremely audience driven; shows like *Total Request Live* (*TRL*) allow the channel to stay close to its viewing audience.

Within six years of its launch, MTV had penetrated some 50 million U.S. households, virtually the entire domestic cable audience at the time. Having conquered America, and with support from youth-oriented advertisers such as Coca-Cola, Levi's, and Nike, MTV Europe was launched in Rotterdam in 1987. Today, MTV has 16 local feeds in Europe with coverage stretching from Ireland to Russia. The local feeds are important because as much as 70 percent of revenues come from advertisers in local markets. One driver of local ad revenues is MTV's commitment to introducing its viewers to local music groups. Despite its sensitivity to local preferences, however, executives and producers still seek economies. As Bill Roedy, president of MTV Networks International, told *Billboard* magazine in 2000, "MTV looks for format opportunities to make content from one area travel to another with a local look and feel."

The blend of global and local elements in proportions that reflect local preferences is especially clear in Asia. When MTV first entered Japan in 1992, it was met with limited success because a licensing agreement with several electronics manufacturers restricted the control that channel executives had over content; the result was an overemphasis on international pop music that was out of sync with viewers. MTV Japan was relaunched with an emphasis on extensive audience research and a new focus on local music and artists.

Today, MTV Asia reaches 125 million households and is comprised of seven channels: Japan, Taiwan, Hong Kong, China, Korea, MTV India, and MTV Southeast Asia (with English-language local feeds for Singapore, Indonesia, Malaysia, Thailand, and the Philippines). In India, the channel presents itself as zany, colorful, and light-hearted. For example, comedian Cyrus Barocha hosts a show called *MTV Bakra* that plays hidden camera pranks on unsuspecting victims. Programming in Taiwan, by contrast, is similar to that in the United States: edgy and in your face. Overall, MTV Mandarin's playlist contains about 80 percent local music, while MTV Philippines features predominantly international artists.

In 2003, Roedy unveiled a new "gain market scale" strategy. As he noted, "We've built up a big infrastructure. It's now time to leverage our resources and develop programming that can cross borders, regions, and even go global." New programming can cost between $200,000 and $350,000 per 30-minute episode; Roedy hopes to

Nigerian singer Tuface performed in Johannesburg for the launch of MTV Base. MTV executive Bill Roedy expects that some local artists featured on the channel will achieve broader global recognition. Roedy said, "We are looking to Africa to be a huge contributor. It is going to enrich our channels around the world. We work very hard to develop local artists. It is something we passionately believe in."

develop shows that will have appeal no matter where the viewers live.

Meanwhile, the global media landscape was rapidly changing. New media forms, including MySpace, YouTube, Facebook, and numerous other Web sites featuring user-generated content, had burst onto the scene. The youth market was fragmenting as consumers downloaded and shared videos and other content using computers, cell phones, and portable music players. In 2005, News Corporation paid $580 million MySpace; Google acquired YouTube for $1.65 billion. Thanks to new corporate owners with deep pockets, the upstarts were going global in a hurry. For example, MySpace rolled out customized sites in the United Kingdom, Ireland, Australia, Germany, France, and Japan.

In 2006, Viacom Executive Chairman Sumner Redstone fired CEO and president Tom Freston; Redstone believed Freston had not done moved aggressively enough to acquire MySpace or a similar hot new media property. Now, as MTV retrenches, Mika Salmi, president of global media at MTV Networks, is confident that his company can reinvent itself. He says, "We have an incredible reach across multiple platforms. We want to go deeper, people want more targeted programming."

Despite such pronouncements, some industry observers question whether MTV can create its own must-have digital content. As media analyst Kaan Yigit put it, "The analogy is the Gap. Both are really Gen X brands with their heyday behind them. . . . They are iconic, well-known, well-liked and respected for their past significance but not central to our culture anymore."

Discussion Questions

1. Describe MTV's global marketing strategy.
2. What are some of the pitfalls of targeting the global youth segment?
3. MTV's original success was based on its reputation as a trendsetting in music and video. How can the company reposition itself in today's new media environment?
4. How can MTV develop a digital strategy that will maintain viewer loyalty and ensure a strong brand presence on the Internet?

Sources: Tim Burt, "Veteran Leads MTV's Attack," *Financial Times*, August 12, 2003, p. 6; Charles Goldsmith, "MTV Seeks Global Appeal," *The Wall Street Journal*, January 21, 2003, pp. B1, B3; Anne-Marie Crawford, "MTV: Out of Its Teens," *Ad Age Global* 1, no. 9 (May 2001), pp. 25–26; Magz Osborne, "Second Chance in Japan," *Ad Age Global* 1, no. 9 (May 2001), pp. 26, 28; Claudia Penteado, "MTV Brazil Wins Success with Local Programming, " *Ad Age Global* 1, no. 9 (May 2001), p. 29; Mimi Turner, "A Q&A with Bill Roedy," *Billboard* 112 no. 36 (September 2, 2000), pp. 48, 54; Owen Hughes, "MTV Asia's Five Branches," *Billboard* 112, no. 36 (September 2, 2000), pp. 48, 54; Sally Beatty and Carol Hymowitz, "How MTV Stays Tuned In to Teens," *The Wall Street Journal*, March 21, 2000, pp. B1, B4.

Europe is famous as a source for fine leather goods such as handbags and shoes. Each year, consumers in Europe buy 2.5 billion pairs of shoes. Shoes from China currently account for about one-third of the market; since 2001, when China joined the WTO, Chinese imports have increased tenfold. Imports from Vietnam have doubled in the same period. The flood of shoe imports from China and Vietnam has been a boon for European retailers and value-conscious consumers. However, faced with a threat to their business, manufacturers in Italy, Spain, and France sought protection. In an effort to curb the tide of imports, the European Commission imposed tariffs for a period of two years: 16.5 percent on shoes from China and 10 percent on shoes from Vietnam. Overall, the tariffs will affect 11 percent of the shoes sold in Europe. The vote by representatives of the EU member nations was close: 13 to 12. The narrow margin of victory for the tariffs reflects divergent views in Europe about how to deal with low-cost Asian goods. Countries that advocate free trade, including the United Kingdom, Ireland, and Sweden, oppose the tariffs. A trade group, the European Branded Footwear Coalition, also objected, noting that the tariffs would increase the price of a pair of women's boots by €6.50—more than $8.

The success of Chinese and Vietnamese exporters—and the EU's subsequent imposition of tariffs— serves as a reminder of the impact exporting and importing can have on national and regional economies. This chapter provides an overview of import-export basics. We begin by explaining the difference between export selling and export marketing. Next is a survey of organizational export activities. An examination of national policies that support exports and/or discourage imports follows. After a discussion of tariff systems, we introduce key export participants. The next section provides an overview of organizational design issues as they pertain to exporting. This is followed by a section devoted to material that can be extremely useful to undergraduates who are majoring in international business: export financing and payment methods. For many students, that all-important first job may be in the import-export department. A familiarity with documentary credits, Incoterms, and other payment-related terminology can help you make a good impression during a job interview and, perhaps, help you land a job as an export/import coordinator or administrator. The chapter ends with a discussion of outsourcing, a topic that is becoming increasingly important as companies in many parts of the world cut costs by shifting both blue-collar and white-collar work to nations with low-wage workforces.

Vietnam is home to dozens of state-run textile and apparel manufacturers that export $1 billion in clothing and footwear each year. The country's garment sector produces merchandise for Nike, Zara, The Limited, and other popular brands. Recently, Vietnam's National Textile-Garment Group (Vinatex) began working with Western consultants to transform the structure and culture of its affiliated companies.

EXPORT SELLING AND EXPORT MARKETING: A COMPARISON

To better understand importing and exporting, it is important to distinguish between **export selling** and **export marketing**. Export selling does not involve tailoring the product, the price, or the promotional material to suit the requirements of global markets. The only marketing mix element that differs is the "place"; that is, the country where the product is sold. This selling approach may work for some products or services; for unique products with little or no international competition, such an approach is possible. Similarly, companies new to exporting may initially experience success with selling. Even today, the managerial mind-set in many companies still favors export selling. However, as companies mature in the global marketplace or as new competitors enter the picture, export *marketing* becomes necessary.

Export marketing targets the customer in the context of the total market environment. The export marketer does not simply take the domestic product "as is" and sells it to international customers. To the export marketer, the product offered in the home market represents a starting point. It is modified as needed to meet the preferences of international target markets; this is the approach the Chinese have adopted in the U.S. furniture market. Similarly, the export marketer sets prices to fit the marketing strategy and does not merely extend home-country pricing to the target market. Charges incurred in export preparation, transportation, and financing must be taken into account in determining prices. Finally, the export marketer also adjusts strategies and plans for communications and distribution to fit the market. In other words, effective communication about product features or uses to buyers in export markets may require creating brochures with different copy, photographs, or artwork. As the vice president of sales and marketing of one manufacturer noted, "We have to approach the international market with *marketing* literature as opposed to *sales* literature."

Export marketing is the integrated marketing of goods and services that are destined for customers in international markets. Export marketing requires:

1. An understanding of the target market environment
2. The use of marketing research and identification of market potential

3. Decisions concerning product design, pricing, distribution and channels, advertising, and communications—the marketing mix

After the research effort has zeroed in on potential markets, there is no substitute for a personal visit to size up the market firsthand and begin the development of an actual export marketing program. A market visit should do several things. First, it should confirm (or contradict) assumptions regarding market potential. A second major purpose is to gather the additional data necessary to reach the final go or no-go decision regarding an export marketing program. Certain kinds of information simply cannot be obtained from secondary sources. For example, an export manager or international marketing manager may have a list of potential distributors provided by the U.S. Department of Commerce. He or she may have corresponded with distributors on the list and formed some tentative idea of whether they meet the company's international criteria. It is difficult, however, to negotiate a suitable arrangement with international distributors without actually meeting face-to-face to allow each side of the contract to appraise the capabilities and character of the other party. A third reason for a visit to the export market is to develop a marketing plan in cooperation with the local agent or distributor. Agreement should be reached on necessary product modifications, pricing, advertising and promotion expenditures, and a distribution plan. If the plan calls for investment, agreement on the allocation of costs must also be reached.

One way to visit a potential market is through a **trade show** or a state- or federally sponsored **trade mission**. Each year hundreds of trade fairs, usually organized around a product category or industry, are held in major markets. By attending trade shows and missions, company representatives can conduct market assessment, develop or expand markets, find distributors or agents, or locate potential end users. Perhaps most important, attending a trade show enables company representatives to learn a great deal about competitors' technology, pricing, and depth of market penetration. For example, exhibits often offer product literature with strategically useful technological information. Overall, company managers or sales personnel should be able to get a good general impression of competitors in the marketplace as they try to sell their own company's product.

ORGANIZATIONAL EXPORT ACTIVITIES

Exporting is becoming increasingly important as companies in all parts of the world step up their efforts to supply and service markets outside their national boundaries.[1] Research has shown that exporting is essentially a developmental process that can be divided into the following distinct stages:

1. The firm is unwilling to export; it will not even fill an unsolicited export order. This may be due to perceived lack of time ("too busy to fill the order") or to apathy or ignorance.
2. The firm fills unsolicited export orders but does not pursue unsolicited orders. Such a firm is an export seller.
3. The firm explores the feasibility of exporting (this stage may bypass Stage 2).
4. The firm exports to one or more markets on a trial basis.
5. The firm is an experienced exporter to one or more markets.
6. After this success, the firm pursues country- or region-focused marketing based on certain criteria (e.g., all countries where English is spoken or all countries where it is not necessary to transport by water).

---

[1] This section relies heavily on Warren J. Bilkey, "Attempted Integration of the Literature on the Export Behavior of Firms," *Journal of International Business Studies* 8, no. 1 (1978) pp. 33–46. The stages are based on Rogers' adoption process. See Everett M. Rogers, *Diffusion of Innovations* (New York: Free Press, 1995).

Table 8-1

Potential Export Problems

Logistics	Servicing Exports
Arranging transportation	Providing parts availability
Transport rate determination	Providing repair service
Handling documentation	Providing technical advice
Obtaining financial information	Providing warehousing
Distribution coordination	**Sales Promotion**
Packaging	Advertising
Obtaining insurance	Sales effort
Legal Procedure	Marketing information
Government red tape	**Foreign Market Intelligence**
Product liability	Locating markets
Licensing	Trade restrictions
Customs and duty	Competition overseas
Contract	
Agent-Distributor Agreements	

7. The firm evaluates global market potential before screening for the "best" target markets to include in its marketing strategy and plan. *All* markets—domestic and international—are regarded as equally worthy of consideration.

The probability that a firm will advance from one stage to the next depends on different factors. Moving from Stage 2 to Stage 3 depends on management's attitude toward the attractiveness of exporting and their confidence in the firm's ability to compete internationally. However, *commitment* is the most important aspect of a company's international orientation. Before a firm can reach Stage 4, it must receive and respond to unsolicited export orders. The quality and dynamism of management are important factors that can lead to such orders. Success in Stage 4 can lead a firm to Stages 5 and 6. A company that reaches Stage 7 is a mature, geocentric enterprise that is relating global resources to global opportunity. To reach this stage requires management with vision and commitment.

One recent study noted that export procedural expertise and sufficient corporate resources are required for successful exporting. An interesting finding was that even the most experienced exporters express lack of confidence in their knowledge about shipping arrangements, payment procedures, and regulations. The study also showed that, although profitability is an important expected benefit of exporting, other advantages include increased flexibility and resiliency and improved ability to deal with sales fluctuations in the home market. Although research generally supports the proposition that the probability of being an exporter increases with firm size, it is less clear that export intensity—the ratio of export sales to total sales—is positively correlated with firm size. Table 8-1 lists some of the export-related problems that a company typically faces.[2]

NATIONAL POLICIES GOVERNING EXPORTS AND IMPORTS

It is hard to overstate the impact of exporting and importing on the world's national economies. In 1997, for example, total imports of goods and services by the United States passed the $1 trillion mark for the first time; in 2005, the

---

[2] Masaaki Kotabe and Michael R. Czinkota, "State Government Promotion of Manufacturing Exports: A Gap Analysis," *Journal of International Business Studies* 23, no. 4 (Fourth Quarter 1992), pp. 637–658.

Chinese and Vietnamese Imports

Officially, the EU tariffs on Chinese and Vietnamese shoe imports are known as antidumping duties. In general, such tariffs reflect a finding that products are being sold in export markets for less than the selling price in the exporter's home country. In other words, as explained in detail later in the chapter, they are being "dumped." In economic terms, China and Vietnam—both ruled by Communist governments—are considered "nonmarket economies." From the EU's point of view, this means that the two countries' domestic prices are artificial. In such countries, where many enterprises are state-owned, profitability in the Western sense is less of a priority than job creation. To prove dumping, investigators have only to compare the cost of the imported shoes with prices of shoes produced in true market economies where the laws of supply and demand determine costs and prices. In such a comparison, the Chinese and Vietnamese appear to have a significant price advantage.

The *Financial Times* noted that the tariffs reflect a triumph of the interests of a small number of EU producers at the expense of the region's 450 million consumers. As an editorial in the *Financial Times* observed, antidumping duties are usually used in large-scale, capital intensive industries such as steel. The editorial noted that, "Shoemaking is not a strategic industry with gigantic economics of call where predatory export pricing could deliver an exploitable competitive advantage. [Shoemaking] is an open global market where fierce competition will soon erode large profit margins." The editors continued, "If subsidized shoes are

indeed being shipped halfway around the world to be sold off cheaply, more fool their producers. If Beijing and Hanoi want to subsidize European consumers to build their shoe collections, let them."

Shoes are not the only European industry sector protected by antidumping duties. In 2005, prompted by a complaint by the European Bicycle Manufacturers Association, the European Commission raised tariffs on Chinese bicycles from 30.6 percent to 48.5 percent and imposed a 34.5 percent tariff on bicycles from Vietnam. Some observers believed it was unfair to combine Vietnamese and Chinese bike imports in the same trade suit. They attempted to draw a distinction between the two nations by noting that Chinese bicycles are sold in supermarkets and department stores. By contrast, Vietnamese consumers buy bikes in small shops. According to this line of argument, bicycles from the two countries don't compete with each other in export markets and should, therefore, not be investigated in the same antidumping suit. However, the European Commission concluded that Vietnam and China produce the same type of bicycles and distribute them through similar channels.

Sources: John W. Miller, "EU Levies Tariffs on China, Vietnam," *The Wall Street Journal,* October 5, 2006, p. A8; John W. Miller, "EU Proposes Duties on Chinese, Vietnamese Shoes," *The Wall Street Journal,* August 31, 2006, p. A4; Juliane von Reppert-Bismarck, "EU Shoe Duty Trips Up Retailers," *The Wall Street Journal,* April 24, 2006, p. A6; "Soft Shoe Shuffle," *Financial Times,* February 27, 2006, p. 12; Raphael Minder, "Mandelson to Defy Shoe Import Furor," *Financial Times,* February 23, 2006, p. 3; Joseph Erlich, "Vietnam's Trade-War Wounds, "*The Wall Street Journal,* August 26, 2005, p. A10.

combined total was $1.9 trillion. Trends in both exports and imports reflect China's pace-setting economic growth in the Asia-Pacific region. Exports from China have grown significantly; as the chapter introduction makes clear, they are growing even faster now that China has joined the WTO. As shown in Table 8-2, Chinese apparel exports to the United States command more than a 13 percent share of the overall apparel market. Historically, China protected its own producers by imposing double-digit import tariffs. These will gradually be reduced as China complies with WTO regulations. Representatives of the furniture, textile, and apparel industries in the United States are deeply concerned about the impact increased trade with China will have on these sectors. As this example suggests, one word can summarize national policies toward exports and imports: contradictory. For centuries, nations have combined two opposing policy

Table 8-2

Market Share of Top 10 Apparel Exporting Countries to the United States, 2004 (percent)

China	13.1
Mexico	10.2
Honduras	6.0
Bangladesh	4.5
El Salvador	4.5
Hong Kong	4.1
Dominican Republic	3.9
Vietnam	3.7
Indonesia	3.4
Korea	3.2

Source: United States Census Bureau.

attitudes toward the movement of goods across national boundaries. On the one hand, nations directly encourage exports; the flow of imports, on the other hand, is generally restricted.

Government Programs that Support Exports

To see the tremendous results that can come from a government-encouraged export strategy, consider Japan, Singapore, South Korea and the so-called greater-China or "China triangle" market, which includes Taiwan, Hong Kong, and the People's Republic of China. Japan totally recovered from the destruction of World War II and became an economic superpower as a direct result of export strategies devised by the Ministry for International Trade and Industry (MITI). The four tigers—Singapore, South Korea, Taiwan, and Hong Kong—learned from the Japanese experience and built strong export-based economies of their own. Although Asia's "economic bubble" burst in 1997 as a result of uncontrolled growth, Japan and the tigers are moving forward in the twenty-first century at a more moderate rate. China, an economy unto itself, has attracted increased foreign investment from DaimlerChrysler, Hewlett-Packard, GM, and other companies that are setting up production facilities to support local sales, as well as exports to world markets.

Any government concerned with trade deficits or economic development should focus on educating firms about the potential gains from exporting. This is true at the national, regional, and local government levels. Governments commonly use four activities to support and encourage firms that engage in exporting. These are tax incentives, subsidies, export assistance, and free trade zones.

First, *tax incentives* treat earnings from export activities preferentially either by applying a lower rate to earnings from these activities or by refunding taxes already paid on income associated with exporting. The tax benefits offered by export-conscious governments include varying degrees of tax exemption or tax deferral on export income, accelerated depreciation of export-related assets, and generous tax treatment of overseas market development activities.

From 1985 until 2000, the major tax incentive under U.S. law was the **foreign sales corporation (FSC)**, through which American exporters could obtain a 15 percent exclusion on earnings from international sales. Big exporters benefited the most from the arrangement; Boeing, for example, saved about $100 million per year, and Eastman Kodak saved about $40 million annually. However, in 2000, the WTO ruled that any tax break that was contingent on exports amounted to an illegal subsidy. Accordingly, the U.S. Congress has set about the task of overhauling the FSC system; failure to do so would entitle the EU to impose up to $4 billion in retaliatory tariffs. So far, congressional efforts have been hampered by the fact that potential winners and losers from a change in the FSC law are lobbying furiously. One proposed version of a new law would benefit GM, Procter & Gamble, Wal-Mart, and other U.S. companies with extensive manufacturing or retail operations overseas. By contrast, Boeing would no longer benefit. As Rudy de Leon, a Boeing executive in charge of government affairs, noted, "As we look at the bill, the export of U.S. commercial aircraft would become considerably more expensive."[3]

Governments also support export performance by providing outright **subsidies**, which are direct or indirect financial contributions or incentives that benefit producers. Subsidies can severely distort trade patterns when less competitive but subsidized producers displace competitive producers in world markets (see Case 8-2). OECD members spend nearly $400 billion annually on farm subsidies; currently, total

---

[3] Edmund L. Andrews, "A Civil War Within a Trade Dispute," *The New York Times*, September 20, 2002, pp. C1, C2.

annual farm support in the EU is estimated at $100 billion. With about $40 billion in annual support, the United States has the highest subsidies of any single nation. Agricultural subsidies are particularly controversial because, although they protect the interests of farmers in developed countries, they work to the detriment of farmers in developing areas such as Africa and India. The EU has undertaken an overhaul of its **Common Agricultural Policy (CAP)**, which critics have called "as egregious a system of protection as any" and "the single most harmful piece of protectionism in the world."[4] In May 2002, much to Europe's dismay, President George W. Bush signed a $118 billion farm bill that actually *increased* subsidies to American farmers over a six-year period. The Bush administration takes the position that, despite the increases, overall U.S. subsidies are still lower than those in Europe and Japan. Congress recently voted to extend the farm bill for another five years.

The third support area is *governmental assistance* to exporters. Companies can avail themselves of a great deal of government information concerning the location of markets and credit risks. Assistance may also be oriented toward export

BRIC Briefing Book

Furniture Exports from China

Furniture imports are flooding into the United States from China. Until recently, a Chinese-made wooden table might have suffered from obvious flaws such as a warped top or loose legs. Today, however, the situation is quite different: Chinese manufacturers are improving quality and offering designs that appeal to traditional American tastes in décor. The improvements have coincided with historically low mortgage rates in the United States; as a result, a record number of Americans are buying new homes or moving into bigger existing ones. To be sure, there are drawbacks to buying something made halfway around the world. For one thing, oceangoing container ships can encounter delays, and replacement parts can be hard to obtain if a piece breaks. In the case of leather furniture, low prices may be due in part to lower quality leather or a narrower range of color choices. However, China's low labor rates—a typical worker in a furniture factory earns monthly wages equivalent to about $100—translate into reasonable prices that are attractive to budget-conscious American furniture shoppers. For example, some leather sofas from China are priced below $1,000, hundreds less than pieces made in America or Europe. Likewise, an eight-piece dining room set sells for $2,500 to $3,500; a comparable American set would cost twice as much.

The furniture industry has become one of the fastest-growing sectors of China's economy. China currently accounts for about 10 percent of global furniture exports, and some industry experts believe exports could increase 30 percent annually through the end of the decade. However, such forecasts are subject to unexpected changes in the business environment. Once such change was the Asian SARS crisis. New furniture orders fell precipitously as foreign buyers stayed away from Chinese factories and fewer Chinese traveled abroad. At the retail level, many American furniture stores began stocking pieces from non-Asian sources. Some American furniture shoppers were reluctant to buy Chinese-made goods for fear that the disease could somehow be transmitted to humans via inanimate objects. As Lynn Chipperfield, senior vice president at Furniture Brands International, the biggest furniture importer in the United States, noted, "Importing is a constant challenge even under normal circumstances. This doesn't help."

Although the SARS crisis quickly passed, China's export success has caught the attention of American manufacturers and policy makers. American furniture companies, many of which are located in North Carolina and Virginia, have been laying off employees and closing plants. A recent study by an economist at the University of California–Santa Cruz found 500,000 furniture workers lost their jobs between 1979 and 1999; 38 percent were unable to find new jobs. In response, a coalition group called the American Furniture Manufacturers Committee for Legal Trade has petitioned U.S. trade officials. The group is asking investigators to examine whether Chinese furniture prices violate U.S. antidumping statutes.

Sources: Dan Morse and Katy McLaughlin, "China's Latest Export: Your Living Room," The Wall Street Journal, January 17, 2003, p. D1; Karby Leggett and Peter Wonacott, "The World's Economy: Surge in Exports from China Jolts Global Industry," The Wall Street Journal, October 10, 2002, pp. A1, A8; Jon E. Hilsenrath and Peter Wonacott, "Imports Hammer Furniture Makers," The Wall Street Journal, September 20, 2002, p. A2.

---

4   John Micklethwait and Adrian Wooldridge, *A Future Perfect: The Challenge and Hidden Promise of Globalization* (New York: Crown Publishers, 2000), p. 261.

Lecong, a city in Guangdong Province, can boast that it is the "furniture capital of the world": approximately 6,000 production facilities are located nearby in the Pearl River delta. The Chinese are adept at carving and other special woodworking skills, and monthly wages are as low as $100. In 2003, China's furniture exports to the United States totaled nearly $14 billion. In mid-2004, the U.S. government imposed antidumping duties on wooden bedroom furniture imports to provide some relief for American producers. Meanwhile, Ethan Allen Interiors, Furniture Brands International, Howard Miller Company, and other U.S. manufacturers have little choice but to source at least some of their production in China.

promotion. Government agencies at various levels often take the lead in setting up trade fairs and trade missions designed to promote sales to foreign customers.

The export or import process can entail red tape and bureaucratic delays. This is especially true in emerging markets, such as China and India. In an effort to facilitate exports, countries are designating certain areas as **free trade zones (FTZ)** or **special economic zones (SEZ)**. These are geographic entities that offer manufacturers simplified customs procedures, operational flexibility, and a general environment of relaxed regulations.

Governmental Actions to Discourage Imports and Block Market Access

Measures such as tariffs, import controls, and a host of nontariff barriers are designed to limit the inward flow of goods. **Tariffs** can be thought of as the "three R's" of global business: rules, rate schedules (duties), and regulations of individual countries. Duties on individual products or services are listed in the schedule of rates (see Table 8-3). One expert on global trade defines **duties** as "taxes that punish individuals for making choices of which their governments disapprove."[5]

As noted in earlier chapters, a major U.S. objective in the Uruguay round of GATT negotiations was to improve market access for U.S. companies with major U.S. trading partners. When the round ended in December 1993, the United States had secured

Country or Region	Tariff Barriers	NTBs
European Union	16.5% antidumping tariff on shoes from China, 10% on shoes from Vietnam	Quotas on Chinese textiles
China	Tariffs as high as 28% on foreign-made auto parts	

Table 8-3

Examples of Trade Barriers

---

[5] Edward L. Hudgins, "Mercosur Gets a 'Not Guilty' on Trade Diversion," *The Wall Street Journal,* March 21, 1997, p. A19.

reductions or total elimination of tariffs on 11 categories of U.S. goods exported to the EU, Japan, five of the EFTA nations (Austria, Switzerland, Sweden, Finland, and Norway), New Zealand, South Korea, Hong Kong, and Singapore. The categories affected included equipment for the construction, agricultural, medical, and scientific industry sectors, as well as steel, beer, brown distilled spirits, pharmaceuticals, paper, pulp and printed matter, furniture, and toys. Most of the remaining tariffs were phased out over a five-year period. A key goal of the recent Doha round of trade talks is the reduction in agricultural tariffs, which currently average 12 percent in the United States, 31 percent in the EU, and 51 percent in Japan.

Developed under the auspices of the Customs Cooperation Council (now the World Customs Organization), the **Harmonized Tariff System (HTS)** went into effect in January 1989 and has since been adopted by the majority of trading nations. Under this system, importers and exporters have to determine the correct classification number for a given product or service that will cross borders. With the Harmonized Tariff Schedule B, the export classification number for any exported item is the same as the import classification number. Also, exporters must include the Harmonized Tariff Schedule B number on their export documents to facilitate customs clearance. Accuracy, especially in the eyes of customs officials, is essential. The U.S. Census Bureau compiles trade statistics from the HTS system. Any HTS with a value of less than $2,500 is not counted as a U.S. export. However, *all* imports, regardless of value, are counted.

In spite of the progress made in simplifying tariff procedures, administering a tariff is an enormous problem. People who work with imports and exports must familiarize themselves with the different classifications and use them accurately. Even a tariff schedule of several thousand items cannot clearly describe every product traded globally. The introduction of new products and new materials used in manufacturing processes creates new problems. Often, determining the duty rate on a particular article requires assessing how the item is used or determining its main component material. Two or more alternative classifications may have to be considered. A product's classification can make a substantial difference in the duty applied. For example, is a Chinese-made X-Men action figure a doll or a toy? For many years, dolls were subject to a 12 percent duty when imported into the United States; the rate was 6.8 percent for toys. Moreover, action figures that represent non-human creatures such as monsters or robots were categorized as toys and qualified for lower duties than human figures that the Customs Service classifies as dolls.

Ed Kostenski, president of Nationwide Equipment in Jacksonville, Florida, walks in front of some of his refurbished Caterpillar equipment. The U.S. Commerce Department encourages small and medium-sized businesses like Nationwide to export more. In 2004, Kostenski struck a deal to sell $1.37 million in construction equipment to west Africa. But the U.S. Export-Import Bank canceled Kostenski's deal, leaving him with an unsold excavator, grader, loader, vibrating compactor and two bulldozers. For the second time in four years, the U.S. Congress is trying to change the agency's small-business financing operations.

OPEN to discussion

Duties on both categories have been eliminated; however, the Toy Biz subsidiary of Marvel Enterprises spent nearly six years on an action in the U.S. Court of International Trade to prove that its X-Men action figures do not represent humans. Although the move appalled many fans of the mutant super heroes, Toy Biz hoped to be reimbursed for overpayment of past duties made when the U.S. Customs Service had classified imports of Wolverine and his fellow figures as dolls.[6]

A **nontariff barrier (NTB)** is any measure other than a tariff that is a deterrent or obstacle to the sale of products in a foreign market. Also known as *hidden trade barriers*, NTBs include quotas, discriminatory procurement policies, restrictive customs procedures, arbitrary monetary policies, and restrictive regulations.

A **quota** is a government-imposed limit or restriction on the number of units or the total value of a particular product or product category that can be imported. Generally, the quotas are designed to protect domestic producers. In 2005, for example, textile producers in Italy and other European countries were granted quotas on 10 categories of textile imports from China. The quotas, which are scheduled to run through the end of 2007, are designed to give European producers an opportunity to prepare for increased competition.[7]

Discriminatory procurement policies can take the form of government rules and administrative regulations specifying that local vendors or suppliers receive priority consideration. For example, the Buy American Act of 1933 stipulates that

---

[6] Neil King Jr., "Is Wolverine Human? A Judge Answers 'No'; Fans Howl in Protest," *The Wall Street Journal*, January 20, 2003, p. A1.

[7] Juliane von Reppert-Bismarck and Michael Carolan, "Quotas Squeeze European Boutiques," *The Wall Street Journal*, October 22, 2005, p. A9.

GLOBAL *marketing in action*

A Day in the Life of an Export Coordinator

Mikkel Jakobsen works as an export coordinator with Shipco Transport, a subsidiary of Scan-Group, a major European transportation company. Shipco Transport has offices all over the world, including 12 branches in North America. Shipco has an extensive network of independent agents in most areas of the world. Shipco's core business is Less than a Container Load (LCL) ocean freight, but also offers Full Container Load (FCL) ocean freight services, as well as airfreight. Mikkel and four other coworkers constitute the company's FCL Chicago branch export team. As a Non-Vessel Operating Common Carrier (NVOCC), Shipco Transport operates similarly to shipping companies such as Maersk Sealand, Mediterranean Shipping Company, and others, with one key difference: Shipco has no vessels of its own. Instead, Shipco relies on favorable contracts with over 40 carriers, enabling them to offer competitive rates on routings to destinations around the world. Most of Shipco's customers are freight forwarders, but the company also deals directly with exporting companies, and on occasion, private individuals. Because of its Midwest location, a significant number of containers come through Chicago on a daily basis and are railed to ports around the country.

In 2006, Mikkel earned a BA degree in international management and economics from a small liberal arts college in the Midwest. He is a citizen of Denmark, and currently works in the United States on a J-1 work visa, sponsored by Shipco Transport. How did he get his first job after graduating? Mikkel explains, "In the spring of 2006, I contacted 15 different companies operating in the United States that had a connection to Denmark. I was offered a position in Shipco Transport's Chicago branch."

Mikkel's day begins at 8:30 AM, and usually ends at 5:30 PM, depending on the workload. Most customers are located in the Midwest, but overnight, he receives e-mails from overseas that he processes in the morning hours. Mikkel says, "In general, my job consists of quoting out shipping costs to customers, placing bookings with steamship lines, preparing export documentation, and dealing with problems that arise during the container's journey from shipper to consignee."

"A customer contacts me with a rate request on a certain routing," Mikkel continues. "He may wish to ship one 20-foot container with auto parts from Indianola, to the port of Ningbo, China. Based on our carrier contracts, I work up a quote including drayage from Indianola, Iowa to an appropriate rail hub, rail transportation from hub to port, and ocean freight from U.S port to port of discharge Ningbo. Several things must be considered including what carrier is cheapest on the routing, differences in transit times, if the commodity is covered in the contract, and what profit level is appropriate. If the customer accepts the quote, the booking is placed with the steamship line, and a dispatch is sent to the chosen trucking company. Certain situations need additional attention. If the commodity is hazardous, the hazardous declaration must be approved by the steamship line. Also, certain goods, such as automobiles, must be cleared by customs before leaving the United States to avoid U.S customs demanding the return of the container for inspection, at the expense of the party at fault.

"Although quoting and setting up bookings takes up a lot of my work day, the majority is spent addressing various problems and issues that arise. Problems such as carriers running out of equipment at their depots, loadings taking longer than expected, or rail delays, are common and dealt with regularly. More serious issues are derailments, problems securing payment, and container abandonment. As an example, disposing of scrap materials in the United States can be expensive, and in the past, some have overcome the problem by loading it in a container, and sending it to places like India as a collect shipment with a nonexistent consignee. This can become an extremely costly situation as demurrage (storage charges), unloading and disposal charges may apply.

"In ocean freight, we work with ETD's (Estimated Time of Departure) and ETA's (Estimated Time of Arrival), because vessels crossing oceans tend to deviate from their schedule. Although this is a fact, customers sometimes have a difficult time understanding the concept. In the world of shipping, vessels running late, expected early, or even on time can be a problem. If so, I am contacted by my customer who either needs an explanation or appropriate action taken. As a middleman, I will contact the specific carrier with the same request. Most of the time, the problem is that the container hasn't reached its destination according to the ETA.

"Interestingly, sometimes a shipper is interested in a delay, and wants the container held up on its journey. This could be because more time is needed to secure payment, or it could represent an attempt to avoid a holiday in the destination country."

How did Mikkel's college studies prepare him for the job? "Incoterms, Letter of Credit, SED (Shippers Export Declaration), and B/L (Bill of Lading) are just some of the industry jargon used on a daily basis. Working with customers, familiarity is expected. The documentation part of export shipping is important, and demands attention to detail. As an NVOCC, Shipco produces both a House B/L and a Line B/L that holds information on the shipper and consignee, and on the products shipped. Most of our containers are released on an express release basis, but some require the use of original bills of lading. In these instances, the original B/L must be presented before a container is released. Although I do not get directly involved in the intricacies of L/C (Letter of Credit) shipments, special attention must be given to the accuracy of B/L information because small deviations can be troublesome. When doing business internationally it is essential to recognize the differences in how business is conducted around the world. South America and Russia in particular are destinations where we rely heavily on our overseas offices and agents and their knowledge of local customs and regulations."

Summing up, Mikkel says, "I enjoy operating on an international level on a daily basis, while doing my part to alleviate the current American trade deficit. Working in the transportation industry, I am sometimes surprised by how many different and obscure items are exported around the world. Although the process may seem overwhelming, with the help of a company such as Shipco that specializes in shipping, any company anywhere can view the entire world as a potential market."

U.S. federal agencies must buy articles produced in the United States unless domestically produced goods are not available, the cost is unreasonable, or purchasing U.S. materials would be inconsistent with the public interest. Similarly, the Fly American Act states that employees of the U.S. government must fly on domestic carriers whenever possible. Formal or informal company policies can also discriminate against foreign suppliers. In the automotive industry, the relatively low level of Japanese imports of U.S.-made auto parts is a contentious issue that centers on procurement policies.

Customs procedures are considered restrictive if they are administered in a way that makes compliance difficult and expensive. For example, the U.S. Department of Commerce might classify a product under a certain harmonized number; Canadian customs may disagree. The U.S. exporter may have to attend a hearing with Canadian customs officials to reach an agreement. Such delays cost time and money for both the importer and exporter.

Discriminatory exchange rate policies distort trade in much the same way as selective import duties and export subsidies. As noted earlier, some Western policy makers have argued that China is pursuing policies that ensure an artificially weak currency. Such a policy has the effect of giving Chinese goods a competitive price edge in world markets.

Finally, **restrictive administrative and technical regulations** also can create barriers to trade. These may take the form of antidumping regulations, product size regulations, and safety and health regulations. Some of these regulations are intended to keep out foreign goods; others are directed toward legitimate domestic objectives. For example, the safety and pollution regulations being developed in the United States for automobiles are motivated almost entirely by legitimate concerns about highway safety and pollution. However, an effect of these regulations has been to make it so expensive to comply with U.S. safety requirements that some automakers have withdrawn certain models from the market. Volkswagen, for example, was forced to stop selling diesel automobiles in the United States for several years.

As discussed in earlier chapters, there is a growing trend to remove all such restrictive trade barriers on a regional basis. The largest single effort was undertaken by the EU and resulted in creation of a single market starting January 1, 1993. The intent was to have one standard for all of Europe's industry sectors, including automobile safety, drug testing and certification, and food and product quality controls. The introduction of the euro has also facilitated trade and commerce.

Chennai (formerly Madras) is both the capital of Tamil Nadu and the automotive capital of India. These Hyundai autos are awaiting export from Chennai; Daewoo, Fiat, Ford, GM, Honda, Mitsubishi, and Peugeot are among the global auto makers that also have operations in India. India's Automotive Mission Plan calls for sales in the sector to grow 16 percent annually. The Ministry of Heavy Industry expects vehicle sales will quadruple over the next decade, reaching $145 billion. By that time, the automotive industry will employ as many as 25 million people.

TARIFF SYSTEMS

Tariff systems provide either a single rate of duty for each item applicable to all countries or two or more rates, applicable to different countries or groups of countries. Tariffs are usually grouped into two classifications.

The **single-column tariff** is the simplest type of tariff; a schedule of duties in which the rate applies to imports from all countries on the same basis. Under the **two-column tariff** (Table 8-4), Column 1 includes "general" duties plus "special" duties indicating reduced rates determined by tariff negotiations with other countries. Rates agreed upon by "convention" are extended to all countries that qualify for **normal trade relations (NTR**; formerly most-favored nation or MFN) status within the framework of the WTO. Under the WTO, nations agree to apply their most favorable tariff or lowest tariff rate to all nations—subject to some exceptions—that are signatories to the WTO. Column 2 shows rates for countries that do not enjoy NTR status.

Table 8-5 shows a detailed entry from Chapter 89 of the HTS pertaining to "Ships, Boats, and Floating Structures" (for explanatory purposes, each column has been identified with an alphabet letter). Column A contains the heading level numbers that uniquely identify each product. For example, the product entry for heading level 8903 is "yachts and other vessels for pleasure or sports; row boats and canoes." Subheading level 8903.10 identifies "inflatable"; 8903.91 designates "sailboats with or without auxiliary motor." These six-digit numbers are used by more than 100 countries that have signed on to the HTS. Entries can extend to as many as 10 digits, with the last four used on a country-specific basis for each nation's individual tariff and data collection purposes. Taken together, E and F correspond to Column 1 as shown in Table 8-5, while G corresponds to Column 2.

The United States has given NTR status to some 180 countries around the world, so the name is really a misnomer. Only North Korea, Iran, Cuba, and Libya are excluded, showing that NTR is really a political tool more than an economic one. In the past, China had been threatened with the loss of NTR status because of alleged human rights violations. The landed prices of its products would have risen significantly, which would have priced many Chinese products out of the U.S. market. The U.S. Congress granted China permanent NTR as a precursor to its joining the WTO in 2001. Table 8-6 illustrates what a loss of NTR status would have meant to China.

A **preferential tariff** is a reduced tariff rate applied to imports from certain countries. GATT prohibits the use of preferential tariffs, with three major exceptions. First are historical preference arrangements such as the British Commonwealth preferences and similar arrangements that existed before GATT. Second, preference schemes that are part of a formal economic integration treaty, such as free trade areas or common markets, are excluded. Third, industrial countries are permitted to grant preferential market access to companies based in less-developed countries.

Table 8-4

Sample Rates of Duty for U.S. Imports

Column 1		Column 2
General	Special	Non-NTR
1.5%	Free (A, E, IL, J, MX)	30%
	0.4% (CA)	

A, Generalized System of Preferences
E, Caribbean Basin Initiative (CBI) Preference
IL, Israel Free Trade Agreement (FTA) Preference
J, Andean Agreement Preference
MX, NAFTA Canada Preference
CA, NAFTA Mexico Preference

Table 8-5

Chapter 89 of the Harmonized System

A	B	C	D	E	F	G
8903		Yachts and other vessels for pleasure or sports; row boats and canoes				
8903.10.00		Inflatable		2.4%	Free (A,E,IL,J,MX)[a] 0.4% (CA)	
		Valued over $500				
	15	With attached rigid hull .... No				
	45	Other... No				
	60	Other... No				
8903.91.00		Other: Sailboats, with or without auxiliary motors		1.5%	Free (A,E,IL,J,MX) 0.3% (CA)	

A, Generalized System of Preferences
E, Caribbean Basin Initiative (CBI) Preference
IL, Israel Free Trade Agreement (FTA) Preference
J, Andean Agreement Preference
MX, NAFTA Canada Preference
CA, NAFTA Mexico Preference

The United States is now a signatory to the GATT customs valuation code. U.S. customs value law was amended in 1980 to conform to the GATT valuation standards. Under the code, the primary basis of customs valuation is "transaction value." As the name implies, **transaction value** is defined as the actual individual transaction price paid by the buyer to the seller of the goods being valued. In instances where the buyer and seller are related parties (e.g., when Honda's U.S. manufacturing subsidiaries purchase parts from Japan), customs authorities have the right to scrutinize the transfer price to make sure it is a fair reflection of market value. If there is no established transaction value for the good, alternative methods that are used to compute the customs value sometimes result in increased values and, consequently, increased duties. In the late 1980s, the U.S. Treasury Department began a major investigation into the transfer prices charged by the Japanese automakers to their U.S. subsidiaries. It charged that the Japanese paid virtually no U.S. income taxes because of their "losses" on the millions of cars they import into the United States each year.

During the Uruguay round of GATT negotiations, the United States successfully sought a number of amendments to the Agreement on Customs Valuations. Most important, the United States wanted clarification of the rights and obligations of importing and exporting countries in cases where fraud was suspected. Two overall categories of products were frequently targeted for investigation. The first included exports of textiles, cosmetics, and consumer durables; the second included entertainment software such as videotapes, audiotapes, and compact

	NTR	Non-NTR
Gold jewelry, such as plated neck chains	6.5%	80%
Screws, lock washers, misc. iron/steel parts	5.8%	35%
Steel products	0–5%	66%
Rubber footwear	0	66%
Women's overcoats	19%	35%

Table 8-6

Tariff Rates for China, NTR Versus Non-NTR

Source: U.S. Customs Service

disks. Such amendments improve the ability of U.S. exporters to defend their interests if charged with fraudulent practices. The amendments were also designed to encourage nonsignatories, especially developing countries, to become parties to the agreement.

Customs Duties

Customs duties are divided into two categories. They may be calculated either as a percentage of the value of the goods (ad valorem duty), as a specific amount per unit (specific duty), or as a combination of both of these methods. Before World War II, specific duties were widely used, and the tariffs of many countries, particularly those in Europe and Latin America, were extremely complex. During the past half century, the trend has been toward the conversion to ad valorem duties.

An **ad valorem duty** is expressed as a percentage of the value of goods. The definition of customs value varies from country to country. An exporter is well advised to secure information about the valuation practices applied to his or her product in the country of destination. The reason is simple: to be price competitive with local producers. In countries adhering to GATT conventions on customs valuation, the customs value is landed cost, insurance, and freight (CIF) amount at the port of importation. This cost should reflect the arm's-length price of the goods at the time the duty becomes payable.

A **specific duty** is expressed as a specific amount of currency per unit of weight, volume, length, or other units of measurement; for example, "US$0.50 per pound," "US$1.00 per pair," or "US$0.25 per square yard." Specific duties are usually expressed in the currency of the importing country, but there are exceptions, particularly in countries that have experienced sustained inflation.

Both ad valorem and specific duties are occasionally set out in the custom tariff for a given product. Normally, the applicable rate is the one that yields the higher amount of duty, although there are cases where the lower is specified. Compound or mixed duties provide for specific, plus ad valorem, rates to be levied on the same articles.

Other Duties and Import Charges

Dumping, which is the sale of merchandise in export markets at unfair prices, is discussed in detail in Chapter 11. To offset the impact of dumping and to penalize guilty companies, most countries have introduced legislation providing for the imposition of **antidumping duties** if injury is caused to domestic producers. Such duties take the form of special additional import charges equal to the dumping margin. Antidumping duties are almost invariably applied to products that are also manufactured or grown in the importing country. In the United States, antidumping duties are assessed after the commerce department finds a foreign company guilty of dumping and the International Trade Commission rules that the dumped products injured American companies.

Countervailing duties (CVDs) are additional duties levied to offset subsidies granted in the exporting country. In the United States, countervailing duty legislation and procedures are very similar to those pertaining to dumping. The U.S. Commerce Department and the International Trade Commission jointly administer both the countervailing duty and antidumping laws under provisions of the Trade and Tariff Act of 1984. Subsidies and countervailing measures received a great deal of attention during the Uruguay GATT negotiations. In 2001, the ITC and commerce department imposed both countervailing and antidumping duties on Canadian lumber producers. The CVDs were intended to offset subsidies to Canadian sawmills in the form of low fees for cutting trees in forests owned by the Canadian government. The antidumping duties on imports of softwood lumber, flooring, and siding were in response to complaints by American producers that the Canadians were exporting lumber at prices below their production cost.

Several countries, including Sweden and some other members of the EU, apply a system of **variable import levies** to certain categories of imported agricultural products. If prices of imported products would undercut those of domestic products, the effect of these levies is to raise the price of imported products to the domestic price level. **Temporary surcharges** have been introduced from time to time by certain countries, such as the United Kingdom and the United States, to provide additional protection for local industry and, in particular, in response to balance-of-payments deficits.

KEY EXPORT PARTICIPANTS

Anyone with responsibilities for exporting should be familiar with some of the entities that can assist with various export-related tasks. Some of these entities, including purchasing agents, export brokers, and export merchants, have no assignment of responsibility from the client. Others, including export management companies, manufacturers' export representatives, export distributors, and freight forwarders, are assigned responsibilities by the exporter.

Foreign purchasing agents are variously referred to as *buyer for export*, *export commission house*, or *export confirming house*. They operate on behalf of, and are compensated by, an overseas customer known as a "principal." They generally seek out the manufacturer whose price and quality match the specifications of their principal. Foreign purchasing agents often represent governments, utilities, railroads, and other large users of materials. Foreign purchasing agents do not offer the manufacturer or exporter stable volume except when long-term supply contracts are agreed upon. Purchases may be completed as domestic transactions with the purchasing agent handling all export packing and shipping details, or the agent may rely on the manufacturer to handle the shipping arrangements.

The **export broker** receives a fee for bringing together the seller and the overseas buyer. The fee is usually paid by the seller, but sometimes the buyer pays it. The broker takes no title to the goods and assumes no financial responsibility. A broker usually specializes in a specific commodity, such as grain or cotton, and is less frequently involved in the export of manufactured goods.

Export merchants are sometimes referred to as *jobbers*. These are marketing intermediaries that identify market opportunities in one country or region and make purchases in other countries to fill these needs. An export merchant typically buys unbranded products directly from the producer or manufacturer. The export merchant then brands the goods and performs all other marketing activities, including distribution. For example, an export merchant might identify a good source of women's boots in a factory in China. The merchant then purchases a large quantity of the boots and markets them in, for example, the EU or the United States.

Export management company (EMC) is the term used to designate an independent marketing intermediary that acts as the export department for two or more manufacturers ("principals") whose product lines do not compete with each other. The EMC usually operates in the name of its principals for export markets, but it may operate in its own name. It may act as an independent distributor, purchasing and reselling goods at an established price or profit margin. Alternatively, it may act as a commission representative, taking no title and bearing no financial risks in the sale. According to one recent survey of U.S.-based EMCs, the most important activities for export success are gathering marketing information, communication with markets, setting prices, and ensuring parts availability. The same survey ranked export activities in terms of degree of difficulty; analyzing political risk, sales force management, setting pricing, and obtaining financial information were found to be the most difficult to accomplish. One of the study's conclusions was that the U.S. government should do a better job of helping EMCs and their clients analyze the political risk associated with foreign markets.[8]

Another type of intermediary is the **manufacturer's export agent (MEA)**. Much like an EMC, the MEA can act as an export distributor or as export commission representative. However, the MEA does not perform the functions of an export department and the scope of market activities is usually limited to a few countries. An **export distributor** assumes financial risk. The export distributor usually represents several manufacturers and is, therefore, sometimes known as a *combination export manager*. The firm usually has the exclusive right to sell a manufacturer's products in all or some markets outside the country of origin. The distributor pays for the goods and assumes all financial risks associated with the foreign sale; it handles all shipping details. The agent ordinarily sells at the manufacturer's list price abroad; compensation comes in the form of an agreed percentage of list price. The distributor may operate in its own name or in the manufacturer's.

The **export commission representative** assumes no financial risk. The manufacturer assigns all or some foreign markets to the commission representative. The manufacturer carries all accounts, although the representative often provides credit checks and arranges financing. Like the export distributor, the export commission representative handles several accounts and is also known as a combination export management company.

The **cooperative exporter**, sometimes called a *mother hen*, *piggyback exporter*, or *export vendor*, is an export organization of a manufacturing company retained by other independent manufacturers to sell their products foreign markets. Cooperative exporters usually operate as export distributors for other manufacturers, but in special cases they operate as export commission representatives. They are regarded as a form of export management company.

Freight forwarders are licensed specialists in traffic operations, customs clearance, and shipping tariffs and schedules; simply put, they can be thought of as travel agents for freight. Minnesota-based C.H. Robinson Worldwide is one such company. Freight forwarders seek out the best routing and the best prices for transporting freight and assist exporters in determining and paying fees and insurance charges. Forwarders may also do export packing, when necessary. They usually handle freight from port of export to overseas port of import. They may also move inland freight from factory to port of export and, through affiliates abroad, handle freight from port of import to customer. Freight forwarders also perform consolidation services for land, air, and ocean freight. Because they contract for large blocks of space on a ship or airplane, they can resell that space to various shippers at a rate lower than is generally available to individual shippers dealing directly with the export carrier.

A licensed forwarder receives brokerage fees or rebates from shipping companies for booked space. Some companies and manufacturers engage in freight forwarding or some phase of it on their own, but they may not, under law, receive brokerage from shipping lines.

---

[8] Donald G. Howard, "The Role of Export Management Companies in Global Marketing," *Journal of Global Marketing* 8, no. 1 (1994), pp. 95–110.

ORGANIZING FOR EXPORTING IN THE MANUFACTURER'S COUNTRY

Home-country issues involve deciding whether to assign export responsibility inside the company or to work with an external organization specializing in a product or geographic area. Most companies handle export operations within their own in-house export organization. Depending on the company's size, responsibilities may be incorporated into an employee's domestic job description. Alternatively, these responsibilities may be handled as part of a separate division or organizational structure.

The possible arrangements for handling exports include the following:

1. As a part-time activity performed by domestic employees.
2. Through an export partner affiliated with the domestic marketing structure that takes possession of the goods before they leave the country.
3. Through an export department that is independent of the domestic marketing structure.
4. Through an export department within an international division.
5. For multidivisional companies, each of the preceding options is available.

A company that assigns a sufficiently high priority to its export business will establish an in-house organization. It then faces the question of how to organize effectively. This depends on two things: the company's appraisal of the opportunities in export marketing and its strategy for allocating resources to markets on a global basis. It may be possible for a company to make export responsibility part of a domestic employee's job description. The advantage of this arrangement is obvious: It is a low-cost arrangement requiring no additional personnel. However, this approach can work under only two conditions: First, the domestic employee assigned to the task must be thoroughly competent in terms of product and customer knowledge; second, that competence must be applicable to the target international market(s). The key issue underlying the second condition is the extent to which the target export market is different from the domestic market. If customer circumstances and characteristics are similar, the requirements for specialized regional knowledge are reduced.

The company that chooses not to perform its own marketing and promotion in-house has numerous external export service providers from which to choose. As described previously, these include export trading companies (ETCs), EMCs, export merchants, export brokers, combination export managers, manufacturers' export representatives or commission agents, and export distributors. However, because these terms and labels may be used inconsistently, we urge the reader to check and confirm the services performed by a particular independent export organization.

ORGANIZING FOR EXPORTING IN THE MARKET COUNTRY

In addition to deciding whether to rely on in-house or external export specialists in the home country, a company must also make arrangements to distribute the product in the target market country. Every exporting organization faces one basic decision: To what extent do we rely on direct market representation as opposed to representation by independent intermediaries?

There are two major advantages to direct representation in a market: control and communications. Direct market representation allows decisions concerning program development, resource allocation, or price changes to be implemented unilaterally. Moreover, when a product is not yet established in a market, special efforts are necessary to achieve sales. The advantage of direct representation is that the marketer's investment ensures these special efforts. With indirect or independent representation, such efforts and investment are often not forthcoming; in many cases, there is simply not enough incentive for independents to invest significant time and money in representing a product. The other great advantage to direct representation is that the possibilities for feedback and information from the market are much greater. This information can vastly improve export marketing decisions concerning product, price, communications, and distribution.

Direct representation does not mean that the exporter is selling directly to the consumer or customer. In most cases, direct representation involves selling to wholesalers or retailers. For example, the major automobile exporters in Germany and Japan rely upon direct representation in the U.S. market in the form of their distributing agencies, which are owned and controlled by the manufacturing organization. The distributing agencies sell products to franchised dealers.

In smaller markets, it is usually not feasible to establish direct representation because the low sales volume does not justify the cost. Even in larger markets, a small manufacturer usually lacks adequate sales volume to justify the cost of direct representation. Whenever sales volume is small, use of an independent distributor is an effective method of sales distribution. Finding "good" distributors can be the key to export success.

EXPORT FINANCING AND METHODS OF PAYMENT

The appropriate method of payment for a given international sale is a basic credit decision. A number of factors must be considered, including currency availability in the buyer's country, creditworthiness of the buyer, and the seller's relationship to the buyer. Finance managers at companies that have never exported often express concern regarding payment. Many CFOs with international experience know that there are generally fewer collections problems on international sales than on domestic sales, provided the proper financial instruments are used. The reason is simple: A letter of credit can be used to guarantee payment for a product.

The export sale begins when the exporter-seller and the importer-buyer agree to do business. The agreement is formalized when the terms of the deal are set down in a pro forma invoice, contract, fax, or some other document. Among other things, the **pro forma invoice** spells out how much, and by what means, the exporter-seller wants to be paid.

Documentary Credit

Documentary credits (also known as letters of credit) are widely used as a payment method in international trade. A **letter of credit (L/C)** is essentially a document stating that a bank has substituted its creditworthiness for that of the importer-buyer. Next to cash in advance, an L/C offers the exporter the best assurance of being paid. That assurance arises from the fact that the payment obligation under an L/C lies with the buyer's bank and not with the buyer. The international standard by which L/Cs are interpreted is ICC Publication No. 500 of the Uniform Customs and Practice for Documentary Credits, also known as UCP 500.

The importer-buyer's bank is the "issuing" bank; the importer-buyer is, in essence, asking the issuing bank to extend credit. The importer-buyer is considered the applicant. The issuing bank may require that the importer-buyer deposit funds in the bank or use some other method to secure a line of credit. After agreeing to extend the credit, the issuing bank requests that the exporter-seller's bank advise or confirm the L/C. (A bank "confirms" an L/C by adding its name to the document.) The seller's bank becomes the "advising" or "confirming" bank. Whether it is advised or confirmed, the L/C represents a guarantee that assures payment contingent on the exporter-seller's (the beneficiary in the transaction) complying with the terms set forth in the L/C.

The actual payment process is set in motion when the exporter-seller physically ships the goods and submits the necessary documents as requested in the L/C. These could include a transportation bill of lading (which may represent title to the product), a commercial invoice, a packing list, a certificate of origin, or insurance certificates. For most of the world, a commercial invoice and bill of lading represent the minimum documentation required for customs clearance. If the pro forma invoice specifies a confirmed L/C as the method of payment, the exporter-seller receives payment at the time the correct shipping documents are presented to the confirming bank. The confirming bank, in turn, requests payment from the issuing bank. In the case of an irrevocable L/C, the exporter-seller receives payment only after the advising bank negotiates the documents and requests payment from the issuing bank in accordance with terms set forth in the L/C. Once the shipper sends the documents to the advising bank, the advising bank negotiates those documents and is referred to as the negotiating bank. Specifically, it takes each shipping document and closely compares it to the L/C. If there are no discrepancies, the negotiating or confirming bank transfers the money to the exporter-seller's account.

The fee for an irrevocable L/C—for example, "1/8 of 1 percent of the value of the credit, with an $80 minimum"—is lower than that for a confirmed L/C. The higher bank fees associated with confirmation can drive up the final cost of the sale; fees are also higher when the transaction involves a country with a high level of risk. Good communication between the exporter-seller and the advising or confirming bank regarding fees is important; the selling price indicated on the pro forma invoice should reflect these and other costs associated with exporting. The process described here is illustrated in Figures 8-1 and 8-2.

Figure 8-1

Flowchart of a Documentary Credit

Documentary Collections (Sight or Time Drafts)

After an exporter and an importer have established a good working relationship and the finance manager's level of confidence increases, it may be possible to move to a documentary collection or open-account method of payment. A documentary collection is a method of payment that uses a bill of exchange, also known as a *draft*. A **bill of exchange** is a negotiable instrument that is easily

Figure 8-2

Flowchart of Documentary Credit Documents

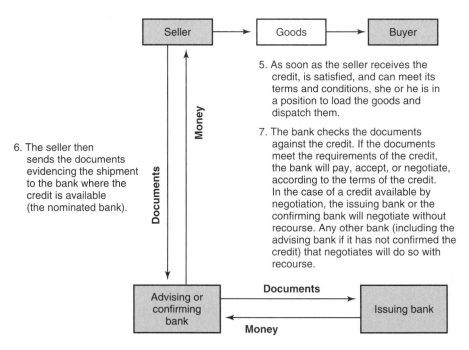

transferable from one party to another. In its simplest form, it is a written order from one party (the *drawer*) directing a second party (the *drawee*) to pay to the order of a third party (the *payee*). Drafts are distinctly different from L/Cs; a **draft** is a payment instrument that transfers all the risk of nonpayment onto the exporter-seller. Banks are involved as intermediaries but they do not bear financial risk. Because a draft is negotiable, however, a bank may be willing to buy the draft from the seller at a discount and assume the risk. Also, because bank fees for drafts are lower than those for L/Cs, drafts are frequently used when the monetary value of an export transaction is relatively low.

With a documentary draft, the exporter delivers documents such as the bill of lading, the commercial invoice, a certificate of origin, and an insurance certificate to a bank in the exporter's country. The shipper or bank prepares a collection letter (draft) and sends it via courier to a correspondent bank in the importer-buyer's country. The draft is presented to the importer; payment takes place in accordance with the terms specified in the draft. In the case of a *sight draft* (also known as *documents against payment* or D/P), the importer-buyer is required in principle to make payment when presented with both the draft and the shipping documents, even though the buyer may not have taken possession of the goods yet. *Time drafts* can take two forms. As the name implies, an *arrival draft* specifies that payment is due when the importer-buyer receives the goods; a *date draft* requires payment on a particular date, irrespective of whether the importer has the goods in hand.

Cash in Advance

A number of conditions may prompt the exporter to request cash payment—in whole or in part—in advance of shipment. Examples include times when credit risks abroad are high, when exchange restrictions within the country of destination may delay return of funds for an unreasonable period, or when, for any other reason, the exporter may be unwilling to sell on credit terms. Because of competition and restrictions against cash payment in many countries, the volume of business handled on a cash-in-advance basis is small. A company that manufactures a unique product for which there are no substitutes available can also use cash in advance. For example, Compressor Control Corporation is a Midwestern firm that manufactures special equipment for the oil industry. It can stipulate cash in advance because no other company offers a competing product.

Sales on Open Account

Goods that are sold on open account are paid for after delivery. Intracorporate sales to branches or subsidiaries of an exporter are frequently on open-account terms. Open-account terms also generally prevail in areas where exchange controls are minimal and exporters have had long-standing relations with good buyers in nearby or long-established markets. For example, Jimmy Fand is the owner of the Tile Connection in Tampa, Florida. He imports high-quality ceramic tile from Italy, Spain, Portugal, Colombia, Brazil, and other countries. Fand takes pride in the excellent credit rating that he has built up with his vendors. The manufacturers from whom he buys no longer require an L/C; Fand's philosophy is "pay in time," and he makes sure that his payables are sent electronically on the day they are due.

The main objection to open-account sales is the absence of a tangible obligation. Normally, if a time draft is drawn and then dishonored after acceptance, it can be used as a basis of legal action. By contrast, if an open-account transaction is dishonored, the legal procedure may be more complicated. Starting in 1995, the Export-Import Bank expanded insurance coverage on open-account transactions to limit the risk for exporters.

ADDITIONAL EXPORT AND IMPORT ISSUES

In the post-September 11 business environment in the United States, imports have come under increased scrutiny as an issue of national security. A number of initiatives have been launched to ensure that international cargo cannot be used for terrorism. On such initiative is the **Customs Trade Partnership Against Terrorism (C-TPAT)**. As noted on the U.S. Customs and Border Protection Web site:

> C-TPAT recognizes that U.S. Customs and Border Protection (CBP) can provide the highest level of cargo security only through close cooperation with the ultimate owners of the international supply chain such as importers, carriers, consolidators, licensed customs brokers, and manufacturers. Through this initiative, CBP is asking businesses to ensure the integrity of their security practices and communicate and verify the security guidelines of their business partners within the supply chain.

CBP is responsible for screening import cargo transactions; the goal of C-TPAT is to secure voluntary cooperation of supply chain participants in an effort to reduce inspection delays. Organizations that have achieved certified C-TPAT status are entitled to priority status for CBP inspections.

Another issue is **duty drawback**. This refers to refunds of duties paid on imports that are processed or incorporated into other goods and then reexported. Drawbacks have long been used in the United States to encourage exports. However, when NAFTA was negotiated, the United States Trade Representative agreed to restrict drawbacks on exports to Canada and Mexico. As the United States negotiates new trade agreements, some industry groups are lobbying in favor of keeping drawbacks.[9] Duty drawbacks are also common in protected economies and represent a policy instrument that aids exporters by reducing the price of imported production inputs. China was required to remove duty drawbacks as a condition for joining the WTO. As duty rates around the world fall, the drawback issue will become less important.

SOURCING

In global marketing, the issue of customer value is inextricably tied to the **sourcing decision**: whether a company makes or buys its products as well as where it makes or buys its products. **Outsourcing** means shifting production jobs or work assignments to another company to cut costs. When the outsourced work moves to another country, the terms *global outsourcing* or *offshoring* are sometimes used. In today's competitive marketplace, companies are under intense pressure to lower costs; one way to do this is to locate manufacturing and other activities in China, India, and other low-wage countries. And why not? Many consumers do not know where the products they buy—sneakers, for example—are manufactured. It is also true that, as the quiz in Chapter 1 indicated, people often can't match corporate and brand names with particular countries. In theory, this situation bestows great flexibility on companies. However, in the United States, the sourcing issue became highly politicized during the 2004 presidential campaign. Several Democratic candidates tapped into Americans' fears and concerns over a "jobless" economic recovery. The first wave of nonmanufacturing outsourcing primarily affected **call centers**. These are sophisticated telephone operations that provide customer support and other services to inbound callers from around the world. Call centers also perform outbound services such as telemarketing. Now, however, outsourcing is expanding and includes white-collar, high-tech service sector jobs. Workers in low-wage countries are performing a variety of tasks,

---

[9]   R. G. Edmonson, "Drawback Under Attack at USTR," *The Journal of Commerce*, August 11–17, 2003, p. 21.

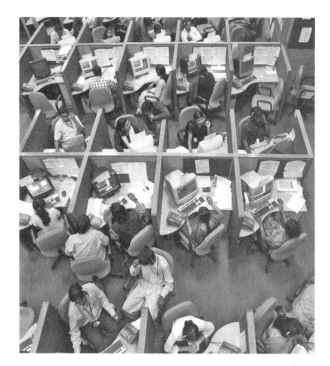

In Bangalore, India, and other locations, call centers such as this one specialize in "long-distance" or "arm's length" services. India's well-educated workforce and the growing availability of broadband Internet connections mean that more Western service jobs and industries are subject to global outsourcing. Among the tasks being outsourced to India are medical record transcription, tax return preparation, and technical writing. The book you are reading was typeset in Jawahar Nagar, Pondicherry, India.

including completing tax returns, performing research for financial services companies, reading medical CAT scans and X-rays, and drawing up architectural blueprints. American companies that transfer work abroad are finding themselves in the spotlight.

As this discussion suggests, the decision of where to locate key business activities depends on other factors besides cost. There are no simple rules to guide sourcing decisions, and, the sourcing decision is one of the most complex and important decisions faced by a global company. Several factors may figure in the

global MARKETING Q&A

USA Today: "Offshoring is a polarizing issue. One survey says 16 percent of Americans agree that it's good for the U.S. economy. If the masses are wrong, why?"

Uwe Doerken, Former Executive Chairman, DHL: "Offshoring first of all benefits the consumer. More efficient and less costly production leads to more affordable products and services and allows companies in higher-labor-cost economies like the USA or Europe to stay competitive and preserve their remaining jobs."

USA Today: "To many, it doesn't seem to be working. Good-paying technology jobs are moving to India. Exporting unskilled jobs was one thing. What about offshoring skilled jobs?"

Uwe Doerken: "Skilled and unskilled are not absolute. Economies move up the skill curve continuously, and what was a high-skill job yesterday may have become a medium skill today and low skill tomorrow. Sewing mass-market clothing was high-tech in England in the nineteenth century and a major industry in developed countries until the 1970s. It has migrated mostly to India, China, and other Asian economies. For the USA, it's about staying ahead of the game by always adapting and keeping the highest value-added jobs in the country."

Source: Ron Insana, "Executive Suite: 'Offshoring . . . Benefits the Consumer'" USA Today, January 17, 2005, p. 6B.

sourcing decision: management vision, factor costs and conditions, customer needs, public opinion, logistics, country infrastructure, political factors, and exchange rates.

Management Vision

Some chief executives are determined to retain some or all manufacturing in their home country. Nicolas Hayek, head of the Swatch Group, is one such executive. Hayek presided over the spectacular revitalization of the Swiss watch industry. The Swatch Group's portfolio of brands includes Blancpain, Omega, Breguet, Rado, and, the inexpensive Swatch brand. Hayek demonstrated that the fantasy and imagination of childhood and youth can be translated into breakthroughs that allow mass-market products to be manufactured in high-wage countries side-by-side with handcrafted luxury products. The Swatch story is a triumph of engineering, as well as a triumph of the imagination. Similarly, top management at Canon has chosen to maintain a strategic focus on high value-added products rather than manufacturing location. The company aims to keep 60 percent of its manufacturing at home in Japan. The company offers a full line of office equipment, including popular products such printers and copiers; it is also one of the top producers of digital cameras. Instead of increasing the level of automation in its Japanese factories, it has converted from assembly lines to so-called cell production.[10]

Factor Costs and Conditions

Factor costs are land, labor, and capital costs (remember Economics 101). Labor includes the cost of workers at every level: manufacturing and production, professional and technical, and management. Basic manufacturing direct labor costs today range from less than $1 per hour in the typical emerging country to $6 to $12 per hour in the typical developed country. In certain industries in the United States, direct labor costs in manufacturing exceed $20 per hour without benefits. German hourly compensation costs for production workers in manufacturing are 160 percent of those in the United States while

---

[10] Sebastian Moffett, "Canon Manufacturing Strategy Pays Off with Strong Earnings," *The Wall Street Journal*, January 4, 2004, p. B3.

those in Mexico are only 15 percent of those in the United States. For Volkswagen, the wage differential between Mexico and Germany, combined with the strength of the mark and, most recently, the euro, dictate a Mexican manufacturing facility that builds Golf and Jetta models destined for the United States. The company's new Touareg SUV is assembled in Bratislava, Slovakia. Do lower wage rates demand that a company relocate 100 percent of its manufacturing to low-wage countries? Not necessarily. During his tenure as chairman at VW, Ferdinand Piech improved his company's competitiveness by convincing unions to accept flexible work schedules. For example, during peak demand, employees work six-day weeks; when demand slows, factories produce cars only three days per week.

Labor costs in nonmanufacturing jobs are also dramatically lower in some parts of the world. For example, a software engineer in India may receive an annual salary of $12,000; by contrast, an American with the same educational credentials might earn $80,000.

The other factors of production are land, materials, and capital. The cost of these factors depends upon their availability and relative abundance. Often, the differences in factor costs will offset each other so that, on balance, companies have a level field in the competitive arena. For example, some countries have abundant land and Japan has abundant capital. These advantages partially offset each other. When this is the case, the critical factor is management, professional, and worker team effectiveness.

The application of advanced computer controls and other new manufacturing technologies has reduced the proportion of labor relative to capital for many businesses. In formulating a sourcing strategy, company managers and executives should also recognize the declining importance of direct manufacturing labor as a percentage of total product cost. It is certainly true that, for many companies in high-wage countries, the availability of cheap labor is a prime consideration when choosing manufacturing locations; this is why China has become "the world's workplace." However, it is also true that direct labor cost may be a relatively small percentage of the total production cost. As a result, it may not be worthwhile to incur the costs and risks of establishing a manufacturing activity in a distant location. For example, Greg Petsch, senior vice president of manufacturing at Compaq, had to decide whether to close plants in Houston and Scotland and contract out assembly work to the Far East. After determining that the human labor content in a PC is only about 15 minutes, he opted to run Compaq's existing Houston factory 24 hours a day. Another decision was whether to source motherboards from a vendor in Asia. Petsch calculated that Compaq could produce the boards—which account for 40 percent of the cost of a PC—for $25 less than suppliers in the Far East. Manufacturing in Houston also saved two weeks in shipping time, which translated into inventory savings.[11]

Customer Needs

Although outsourcing can help reduce costs, sometimes customers are seeking something besides the lowest possible price. Dell Computer recently rerouted some of its call center jobs back to the United States after complaints from key business customers that Indian tech support workers were offering scripted responses and having difficulty answering complex problems. In such instances, the need to keep customers satisfied justifies the higher cost of home-country support operations.

---

[11] Doron P. Levin, "Compaq Storms the PC Heights from Its Factory Floor," *The New York Times*, November 4, 1994, Section 3, p. 5.

Logistics

In general, the greater the distance between the product source and the target market, the greater the time delay for delivery and the higher the transportation cost. However, innovation and new transportation technologies are cutting both time and dollar costs. To facilitate global delivery, transportation companies such as CSX Corporation are forming alliances and becoming an important part of industry value systems. Manufacturers can take advantage of intermodal services that allow containers to be transferred among rail, boat, air, and truck carriers. In Europe, Latin America, and elsewhere, the trend toward regional economic integration means fewer border controls, which greatly speeds up delivery times and lowers costs.

Despite these overall trends, a number of specific issues pertaining to logistics can affect the sourcing decision. For example, in the wake of the 2001 terror attacks, importers are required to send electronic lists to the U.S. government prior to shipping. The goal is to help the U.S. Customs Service identify high-risk cargo that could be linked to the global terror network. In fall 2002, a 10-day strike on the West Coast shut down 29 docks and cost the U.S. economy an estimated $20 billion. Such incidents can delay shipments by weeks or even months.

> *"Supply Chain 101 says the most important thing is continuity of supply. When you establish a supply line that is 12,000 miles long, you have to weigh the costs of additional inventory and logistics costs versus what you can save in terms of lower costs per unit or labor costs."*[12]
>
> Norbert Ore, Institute for Supply Management

Country Infrastructure

In order to present an attractive setting for a manufacturing operation, it is important that the country's infrastructure be sufficiently developed to support a manufacturing operation. The required infrastructure will vary from company to company, but minimally, it will include power, transportation and roads, communications, service and component suppliers, a labor pool, civil order, and effective governance. In addition, a country must offer reliable access to foreign exchange for the purchase of necessary material and components from abroad as well as a physically secure setting where work can be done and product can be shipped to customers.

A country may have cheap labor, but does it have the necessary supporting services or infrastructure to support a manufacturing activity? Many countries offer these conditions, including Hong Kong, Taiwan, and Singapore. There are many other countries that do not, such as Lebanon, Uganda, and El Salvador. One of the challenges of doing business in the new Russian market is an infrastructure that is woefully inadequate to handle the increased volume of shipments. The Mexican government, anticipating much heavier trade volume because of NAFTA, has committed billions of dollars for infrastructure improvements.

Political Factors

As discussed in Chapter 5, political risk is a deterrent to investment in local sourcing. Conversely, the lower the level of political risk, the less likely it is that an investor will avoid a country or market. The difficulty of assessing political risk is inversely proportional to a country's stage of economic development: All other things being equal, the less developed a country, the more difficult it is to predict political risk. The political risk of the Triad countries, for example, is quite limited as compared to that of a less-developed country in Africa, Latin America, or Asia. The recent rapid changes in Central and Eastern Europe and the dissolution of the Soviet Union have clearly demonstrated the risks *and* opportunities resulting from political upheavals.

---

[12] Barbara Hagenbaugh, "Moving Work Abroad Tough for Some Firms," *USA Today*, December 3, 2003, p. 2B.

Other political factors may weigh on the sourcing decision. For example, with protectionist sentiment on the rise, for example, the U.S. Senate recently passed an amendment that would prohibit the U.S. Treasury and Department of Transportation from accepting bids from private companies that use offshore workers. In a highly publicized move, the state of New Jersey changed a call center contract that had shifted jobs offshore. About one dozen jobs were brought back instate—at a cost of about $900,000.

Market access is another type of political factor. If a country or a region limits market access because of local content laws, balance-of-payments problems, or any other reason, it may be necessary to establish a production facility within the country itself. The Japanese automobile companies invested in U.S. plant capacity because of concerns about market access. By producing cars in the United States, they have a source of supply that is not exposed to the threat of tariff or import quotas. Market access figured heavily in Boeing's decision to produce airplane components in China. China ordered 100 airplanes valued at $4.5 billion; in return, Boeing is making investments and transferring engineering and manufacturing expertise.[13]

Foreign Exchange Rates

In deciding where to source a product or locate a manufacturing activity, a manager must take into account foreign exchange rate trends in various parts of the world. Exchange rates are so volatile today that many companies pursue global sourcing strategies as a way of limiting exchange-related risk. At any point in time, what has been an attractive location for production may become much less attractive due to exchange rate fluctuation. For example, *endaka* is the Japanese term for a strong yen. In 2003, the exchange rate went from ¥122/$1 to ¥107/$1. For every one yen increase relative to the American dollar, Canon's

global MARKETING Q&A

USA Today: "[In 2003] you cut 2,000 U.S. jobs by closing a Wrangler factory. How should companies respond to criticism about moving jobs offshore?"

Mackey McDonald, Chief Executive Officer, VF Corp.: "The most important thing is to stay competitive. If you don't, all jobs will be lost. We stay competitive and increase some of the higher-paying jobs. The American consumer will buy the best product at the best price. That's the deciding factor, and you can't lose sight of it."

USA Today: "Are critics of offshoring naïve?"

Mackey McDonald: "What they say resonates with everyone. We want more jobs in this country. Without them, they can't buy apparel. We're all concerned. But those who are shouting aren't offering solutions, they're just shouting. This country has gone through transition for centuries. That's why we have the standard of living that we do. The solution is education and training, to keep our workforce moving into higher-paying jobs."

Source: Ron Insana, "Executive Suite: Do You Wear VF Clothes? Probably," USA Today, November 15, 2004, p. 3B.

---

[13] Jeff Cole, Marcus W. Brauchli, and Craig S. Smith, "Orient Express: Boeing Flies into Flap over Technology Shift in Dealings with China," *The Wall Street Journal*, October 13, 1995, pp. A1, A11. See also Joseph Kahn, "Clipped Wings: McDonnell Douglas' High Hopes for China Never Really Soared," *The Wall Street Journal*, May 22, 1996, pp. A1, A10.

operating income declines ¥6 billion! As noted earlier, Canon's management is counting on R&D investment to ensure that its products deliver superior margins that offset the strong yen.

The dramatic shifts in price levels of commodities and currencies are a major characteristic of the world economy today. Such volatility argues for a sourcing strategy that provides alternative country options for supplying markets. Thus, if the dollar, the yen, or the mark becomes seriously overvalued, a company with production capacity in other locations can achieve competitive advantage by shifting production among different sites.

A company's first business dealings outside the home country often take the form of **exporting** or **importing**. Companies should recognize the difference between **export marketing** and **export selling**. By attending **trade shows** and participating in **trade missions,** company personnel can learn a great deal about new markets.

Governments use a variety of programs to support exports, including tax incentives, subsidies, and export assistance. Governments also discourage imports with a combination of **tariffs** and **nontariff barriers**. Export-related policy issues include the status of **foreign sales corporations** (**FSC**) in the United States, Europe's **Common Agricultural Policy** (**CAP**), and **subsidies.**

The **Harmonized Tariff System** (**HTS**) has been adopted by most countries that are actively involved in export-import trade. **Single-column tariffs** are the simplest; **two-column tariffs** include special rates such as those available to countries with **normal trade relations** (**NTR**) status. Governments can also impose special types of duties. These include **antidumping duties** imposed on products whose prices government officials deem too low

and **countervailing duties** to offset government subsidies.

Key participants in the export-import process include **foreign purchasing agents**, **export brokers**, **export merchants**, **export management companies**, **manufacturers' export representatives**, **export distributors**, export commission representatives, cooperative exporters, and freight forwarders.

A number of export-import payment methods are available. A transaction begins with the issue of a **pro forma invoice** or some other formal document. A basic payment instrument is the **letter of credit** (**L/C**) that assures payment from the buyer's bank. Sales may also be made using a **bill of exchange** (**draft**), **cash in advance**, **sales on open account**, or a **consignment** agreement.

Exporting and importing is directly related to a management's decisions regarding **sourcing**. Concern is mounting in developed countries about job losses linked to **outsourcing** of jobs, both skilled, and unskilled, to low-wage countries. A number of factors determine whether a company makes or buys the products it markets as well as *where* it makes or buys.

summary

1. What is the difference between export marketing and export selling?

2. Why is exporting from the United States dominated by large companies? What, if anything, could be done to increase exports from smaller companies?

3. Describe the stages a company typically goes through as it learns about exporting.

4. Governments often pursue policies that promote exports while limiting imports. What are some of those policies?

5. What are the various types of duties that export marketers should be aware of?

6. What is the difference between an L/C and other forms of export-import financing? Why do sellers often require L/Cs in international transactions?

7. What criteria should company management consider when making sourcing decisions?

discussion questions

The U.S. Department of Commerce provides export support through its Market Access and Compliance Web site. Visit MAC Online at:

www.mac.doc.gov

The U.S. federal government provides information on the HTS at:

www.usitc.gov/tata/index.htm

The database maintained by the U.S. International Trade Commission can be accessed at:

http://dataweb.usitc.gov

web resources

Case 8-1

Concerns About Factory Safety and Worker Exploitation in Developing Countries

In April 1997, President Bill Clinton announced the creation of a code of conduct aimed at combating sweatshops on a worldwide basis. Representatives from Phillips-Van Heusen (PVH), Nike, Reebok, Liz Claiborne, and six other manufacturers had served on a task force that spent eight months studying the sweatshop issue. The code established a minimum age of 14 for apparel workers and a maximum work week of 60 hours. Companies were required to pay the prevailing minimum wage in the country where the factory was located. Michael Posner, executive director of the Lawyers Committee for Human Rights, hailed the code as a breakthrough agreement. "It establishes a framework that provides consumers with confidence that companies are making good-faith efforts to address sweatshop practices," he said. Despite such optimism, the manufacturers and human rights advocates that were task force members disagreed on several issues. One concern was countries in which the official minimum wage was not a true "living wage" sufficient to support a family. Another issue was monitoring labor practices; the manufacturers wanted the right to select accounting firms, while activists and labor groups wanted nonprofit groups to perform the task of monitoring.

Background to the Code of Conduct

In August 1995, federal agents raided a garment-manufacturing facility near Los Angeles. The agents discovered 60 people, all from Thailand, who worked as many as 22 hours per day for $1.60 an hour to repay expenses for travel to the United States. The U.S. Labor Department charged the six Thai nationals believed to be running the sweatshop operation with harboring illegal immigrants and smuggling immigrants. The labor department also alleged that May Department Stores, Sears, and other retailers were selling goods that originated in the Los Angeles factory. Under the Fair Labor Standards Act, the labor department was authorized to hold the various apparel manufacturers that bought goods from the sweatshop legally liable for $5 million in worker back pay.

A year later, the sweatshop issue stayed in the news thanks to Kathie Lee Gifford, who was best known to television viewers as the host of a popular talk show and as a celebrity endorser who appeared in ads for Carnival Cruise Lines and Ultra Slim-Fast. Many Wal-Mart shoppers also associated Kathie Lee's name with a line of moderately priced apparel. Some items in the Kathie Lee clothing line were produced under contract in factories in Honduras and other developing countries. Labor rights activist Charles Kernaghan charged that working conditions in many of those factories fit the definition of "sweatshop": long hours, low wages, and abusive supervisors. Moreover, many employees in the factories were alleged to be minors. Kernaghan accused Gifford and other endorsers of profiting from worker exploitation.

Sweatshops in the Spotlight

The sweatshop bust in Los Angeles and the revelations surrounding Kathie Lee Gifford finally focused the public's attention on an issue that had been gathering momentum for years. Catastrophic industrial fires in several countries have resulted in extensive loss of life. In Dongguan, China, 80 workers died in a fire at a raincoat factory in 1991. In 1993, 84 people were killed in a handicrafts factory fire in the Chinese city of Shenzhen. The most deadly industrial fire in history broke out on May 10, 1993, in a four-story toy factory near Bangkok, Thailand. Nearly 200 workers—most of whom were women and teenage girls—died in the blaze. The factory was owned by Kader Industrial Toy Company, which supplies toys to well-known U.S. companies such as Fisher-Price, Toys "R" Us, and Hasbro. One reason so many perished is that several emergency exit doors were locked.

Government support is just one reason that companies can rely on far-flung manufacturing; 900 million, about 15 percent, of the world's 6 billion people are unemployed. Thus, governments in many countries encourage foreign investment that will create jobs. Moreover, manufacturing companies account for nearly three-fourths of the dollar value of world trade. Improved communications technology allows company headquarters to closely monitor operations throughout the world. As John Cavanagh, a fellow at Washington's Institute for Policy Studies, explains, "Companies can coordinate production in plants scattered all over the world on a real-time, minute-to-minute basis."

Not surprisingly, many U.S. companies are scouring the globe for low-cost sources of labor. As wages have increased in South Korea, Taiwan, and Singapore, offshore assembly and manufacturing has moved to developing countries such as Indonesia, Thailand, India, Mexico, and China. For example, almost half of all the toys sold in the United States are produced in Asia; in 1992, Chinese factories turned out $3.3 billion worth of toys for the United States. The minimum wage in China is about $0.80 per day.

Disturbed by the trend, many U.S. observers had long characterized factories in developing countries as sweatshops where "semislave labor" was forced to work in inhumane, unsafe working conditions for extremely low wages. These critics suggest that profit-hungry American executives often turn a blind eye to working conditions outside the United States. For their part, executives and industry spokespersons point out that, in many cases, U.S. companies do not own the factories where goods are made. Labor movement representatives in the United States, concerned that U.S. companies are unwilling to support improved working conditions abroad, have even attempted to align with labor movements in developing countries.

Despite the terrible tragedies in Thailand and China, not everyone in the United States agrees with the view that workers in developing countries are being exploited. Although wages in some countries may seem low by U.S. standards, they are relatively high by Asian standards. Compared to an agriculture-based subsistence standard of living, these wages represent both an improvement and an important step forward in terms of economic development. As advocates of global production point out, wages in Japan, Taiwan, and South Korea were low in the years after World War II, but increased as those countries' economies developed. The first step toward a developed economy involved sweatshops. As economist Paul Krugman noted, "The overwhelming mainstream view among

economists is that the growth of this kind of employment is tremendous good news for the world's poor." Krugman has adopted a pragmatic viewpoint on the child labor issue. Noting that some impoverished parents sell their children to syndicates who force them to work as beggars, Krugman says, "If that is the alternative, it is not so easy to say that children should not be working in factories."

Still, some experts predict that business executives are starting to realize that it is simply good business to be concerned with factory conditions. Notes Professor Elliot Schrage of Columbia University, "Many companies are being forced to examine their labor practices around the world by consumer pressure or fear of consumer backlash." The U.S. government hoped that publicizing the names of retailers who bought from the Los Angeles manufacturers would encourage retailers to improve their social responsibility policies.

Nike and the Sneaker Controversy

The truth in Schrage's observation has been amply illustrated in the athletic shoe industry. Nike, Reebok, and other sneaker marketers source virtually 100 percent of their shoes in Asia, where contractors are responsible for the production of the shoes. For example, 80 million pairs of Nikes are manufactured each year in dozens of factories outside the United States. During the 1980s, most of Nike's manufacturing was located in South Korea and Taiwan. As workers there gained the right to organize and strike, wage rates increased. Nike responded by shifting production to China, Malaysia, Indonesia, and Thailand and leaving 20 closed factories in its wake. In Indonesia, where 50 factories make shoes for Nike, the nonunion workforce is made up mostly of young women paid wages starting at about $1.35 a day. Nike subcontractors employ an estimated 300,000 young Asian women.

Nike's practice of following cheap labor around the globe made it the target of criticism from the ranks of workers and scholars alike. For example, Solidarity magazine, published by the United Auto Workers, once urged union members to send their "dirty, smelly, worn-out" running shoes to Nike as a way of protesting overseas production. John Cavanagh and others have written numerous articles criticizing Nike for profiting at the expense of low-wage workers. Cavanagh has pointed out that, although 2.5 million people enter the Indonesian job market each year, employment options are so limited that most people can only find work making athletic shoes. Low wages permit only subsistence living in shanties without electricity or plumbing and also result in malnutrition. Nike pays superstar Michael Jordan $20 million annually in endorsement fees, an amount that has been estimated to exceed the total annual wages for Indonesian workers who make the sneakers.

For several years, Nike executives responded to inquiries about working conditions in contract factories by noting that the company focuses on marketing and design rather than manufacturing. Still, the company was coming under increased pressure from both human rights groups and the general public to address the sweatshop issue. In 1997, Nike commissioned former U.N. ambassador Andrew Young to visit some of the Asian factories and report his findings. After spending 15 days personally inspecting working conditions,

Young reported that he did not find abuse or mistreatment of workers. Critics took Nike to task for asking Young to focus only on working conditions and failing to investigate wage rates as well. However, in September 1997, Nike canceled contracts with four factories in Indonesia where pay was below minimum government levels. By 1998, the controversy began to affect Nike's bottom line. Nike's profits dropped as sneaker sales slumped. The sweatshop backlash was not the only cause, however; increasing numbers of consumers were turning to "brown shoes," snapping up casual wear from Hush Puppies, Timberland, and other makers.

Nike was not the only company caught up in the controversy. Allegations surfaced that a subcontractor for Adidas-Salomon AG employed Chinese political prisoners in labor camps near Shanghai to sew soccer balls that commemorated the 1998 World Cup. Adidas, like Nike, has adopted a code of conduct and closely monitors production to prevent such things from occurring. The allegations came as President Clinton was visiting China with an agenda that downplayed human rights issues. An estimated 230,000 Chinese are held in camps dedicated to "reeducation through labor." Soccer balls are hand sewn from 32 precut panels, a process that is so labor-intensive that the work is often done in rural "stitching centers" with the country's lowest labor costs. Adidas confirmed that the allegations were based in fact but that the prison labor had been utilized without the company's knowledge. Adidas announced that it would not source soccer balls in China until production was centralized in one location that excluded the possibility of using prison labor.

Visit the Web site

Read Nike's Revised Code of Conduct and learn more about the company's labor practices at:

www.nikebiz.com

Global Exchange, a human rights group, offers information on efforts to combat sweatshops:

www.globalexchange.org

Discussion Questions

1. Do you think toy company executives—in Japan, the United States, and elsewhere—should take steps to ensure the safety and welfare of factory workers in developing countries? Why or why not?

2. How have the low wages paid in developing country manufacturing operations affected the number of manufacturing jobs in the high-wage Triad countries?

3. If higher wages in toy factories led to higher prices in the United States for toys, how would it affect the toy industry?

4. Should international trade agreements include guidelines and requirements for working conditions?

5. Do you think companies are doing enough to act responsibly and ensure that human rights standards are upheld for workers both inside and outside their home countries?

Sources: Craig S. Smith and A. Craig Copetas, "For Adidas, China Could Prove Trouble," *The Wall Street Journal*, June 26, 1998, p. A13; Holman W. Jenkins, Jr. "The Rise and Stumble of Nike," *The Wall Street Journal*, June 3, 1998, p. A19; Steven Greenhouse, "Accord to Battle Sweatshop Labor Faces Obstacles," *The New York Times*, April 13, 1997, pp. 1, 13; Allen R. Myerson, "In Principle, a Case for More 'Sweatshops,'" *The New York Times*, June 22, 1997, p. 5; Asra Q. Nomani, "Labor Department Asks $5 Million for Alleged Worker Enslavement," *The Wall Street Journal*, August 16, 1995, p. B4; Lori Ioannou, "Capitalizing on Global Surplus Labor," *International Business* (April 1995), pp. 32–34+; G. Pascal Zachary, "Multinationals Can Aid Some Foreign Workers," *The Wall Street Journal*, April 24, 1995, p. A1; Bob Herbert, "Terror in Toyland," *The New York Times*, December 21, 1994, p. A27; "102 Dead in Thai Factory Fire; Higher Toll Seen," *The New York Times*, May 11, 1993, p. A3; "Thai Factory Fire's 200 Victims Were Locked Inside, Guards Say," *The New York Times*, May 12, 1993, p. A5; Jeffrey Ballinger, "The New Free-Trade Heel," *Harper's Magazine*, August 1992 pp. 46–47; Geraldine E. Willigan, "High-Performance Marketing: An Interview with Nike's Phil Knight," *Harvard Business Review* (July–August 1992) pp. 91–101; Richard J. Barnet and John Cavanagh, "Just Undo It: Nike's Exploited Workers," *The New York Times*, February 13, 1994, Section 3, p. 11.

Case 8-2

U.S. Sugar Subsidies: Too Sweet a Deal?

A turf war has broken out over one of the humblest commodities traded on world markets: sugar. On one side are small-scale farmers in some of the poorest regions of the world; desperate to increase their incomes and improve their living standards, these farmers seek increased exports of sugar cane. On the other side are farmers in some of the richest nations in the world who are equally intent on preserving a system of quotas and subsidies to support production of sugar cane and sugar beets. Caught in the middle are processed food and beverage companies that use sugar in baked goods, ice cream, jams and jellies, soft drinks, and a range of other products. There is also an impact on consumers: Sugar subsidies result in higher prices for popular food and beverage products.

The debate over agricultural policy is at the heart of the struggle. Worldwide, agricultural subsidies amount to approximately $300 billion each year. The subsidies issue has been central to the current round of global trade negotiations; it has also been debated at the World Summit on Sustainable Development. Brazil, Australia, and Thailand rank first, third, and fourth, respectively, among top sugar exporters; the EU ranks second. Collectively, Brazil, Australia, and Thailand have challenged the EU's sugar export policy at the WTO.

In Europe, protection of the agricultural sector was a response to the shortages and rationing that occurred during World War II. Thanks to an initiative known as the Common Agricultural Policy (CAP), European farmers supply virtually all Europe's food consumption needs. Ag producers also made gains in the 1960s in negotiations relating to the creation of the Common Market—the precursor to today's EU. The EU currently spends more than $90 billion each year to support domestic agriculture; ironically, the EU also spends $25 billion in development aid for low-income nations. Former French president Jacques Chirac was a particularly vocal advocate of EU farm policy, and farmers in France are well organized. The current EU farm bill expired in 2006.

Europe's agricultural policies have led to sugar beet production in Sweden and Finland—countries not renowned for favorable growing conditions—as well as France. The impact of the sugar regime is clear: European farmers operate with quotas that specify how much they can produce. The farmers are also guaranteed prices for their crops that are roughly three times higher than the world price. Furthermore, the EU produces much more sugar than it can use; as a result, about 6 tons of European sugar are dumped on the world market each year. Moreover, EU sugar supports benefit former colonies such as Mauritius and Fiji, which sell raw sugar to the EU at the higher, protected prices. However, these imports are offset by an equivalent amount of exports from the EU; the annual cost of this practice to EU taxpayers is estimated at $800 million.

In the United States, the current sugar regime can be traced back to the Sugar Act of 1934. The act was designed to stabilize prices; today, as in Europe, the U.S. price for raw sugar is about three times the world market price. The General Accounting Office estimates that the program costs Americans $2 billion annually in inflated sugar prices; it will cost an additional $2 billion to store surplus sugar over the course of 10 years. In contrast to Europe, however, the United States exports only a fraction of the 8 tons of sugar it produces each year; quotas limit sugar imports to about 15 percent of U.S. consumption. The U.S. government pays approximately $50 billion in farm aid each year; in May 2002, president George W. Bush signed a new farm bill that actually increased support to some farmers. Not surprisingly, the Europeans point to the bill as evidence that the United States is hypocritical on trade issues. U.S. sugarcane and sugar beet producers rank first in contributions to political campaigns, ahead of both tobacco farmers and dairy farmers. Florida, the key sugar producing state, is a crucial swing state in national elections. However, sugar beets are also grown in North Dakota and other states in the northern plains.

The Sugar Association heads the industry's lobbying effort in the United States. However, the industry flexes its political muscle in other ways. For example, the WHO and the Food and Agriculture Organization have identified sugar as a key contributor to obesity. A recent report titled *Diet, Nutrition and the Prevention of Chronic Diseases* recommended that no more than 10 percent of an individual's caloric intake should come from "added sugars." The Sugar Association assailed the "'dubious nature" of the report, and implied that more than $400 million in congressional funding to the World Health Organization (WHO) could be jeopardized. Andrew Briscoe, president of the association, said, "We are not opposed to a global strategy in the fight against obesity. No one, including the sugar industry, wants anybody to be obese and we want to be part of the solution. But we want that solution to be based on the preponderance of science."

President Bush's administration has actively pursued bilateral and regional trade agreements, a fact that also has the sugar industry up in arms. For example, as part of the newly-negotiated Central American Free Trade Agreement, the United States agreed to import 100,000 tons of sugar—about 1 percent of the U.S. market—from Guatemala and its neighbors. Industry reaction was swift. Robert Coker, senior vice president of Florida-based U.S. Sugar Corporation, "If the U.S. agrees in regional trade negotiations to open up the U.S. sugar market, American sugar producers, including our company, will be wiped out." The president of the American Sugarbeet Growers Association summed up the situation more succinctly. "If you go to free trade, Brazil wins and everybody else gets killed," he said. As noted earlier, Australia is the world's number three sugar exporter; however, when the United States and Australia completed negotiations on a free trade agreement in 2004, sugar was not included.

Discussion Questions

1. Why do Europe and the United States spend so much on agricultural subsidies?

2. Do individual consumers care where their sugar comes from? If not, should they?

3. Which poses the biggest threat to sugar producers in wealthy countries, the growing concern over obesity or increased imports from developing countries?

Sources: Tobias Buck, "EU to Consider Sugar Subsidy Reform," *Financial Times*, June 24, 2004, p. 7; Robert B. Zoellick, "Don't Get Bitter About Sugar," *The Wall Street Journal*, February 25, 2004, p. A14; Edward Alden and Neil Buckley, "Sweet Deals: 'Big Sugar' Fights Threats from Free Trade and a Global Drive to Limit Consumption," *Financial Times*, February 27, 2004, p. 11; Mary Anastasia O'Grady, "Clinton's Sugar Daddy Games Now Threaten NAFTA's Future," *The Wall Street Journal*, December 20, 2002, p. A15; Roger Thurow and Geoff Winestock, "Bittersweet: How an Addiction to Sugar Subsidies Hurts Development," *The Wall Street Journal*, September 16, 2002, pp. A1, A10.

rom modest beginnings in Seattle's Pike Street Market, Starbucks Corporation has become a global marketing phenomenon. Today, Starbucks is the world's leading specialty coffee retailer, with 2006 sales of $7.7 billion. Starbucks' founder and chairman, Howard Schultz, and his management team have used a variety of market entry approaches—including direct ownership as well as licensing and franchising—to create an empire of more than 12,000 coffee cafés in 35 countries. In addition, Schultz has licensed the Starbucks brand name to marketers of noncoffee products, such as ice cream. The company is also diversifying into movies and recorded music. However, coffee remains Starbucks' core business; to reach its ambitious goal of 40,000 shops worldwide, Starbucks is expanding aggressively in key countries. For example, at the end of 2006, Starbucks had 67 branches in 21 German cities; that number is expected to reach 100 by the end of 2007. Starbucks had set a higher growth target for Germany; those plans had to be revised, however, after a joint venture with retailer Karstadt-Quelle was dissolved. Now Starbucks intends to pursue further expansion independently. Despite competition from local chains such as Café Einstein, Cornelius Everke, the head of Starbucks' German operations, says, "We see the potential of several hundred coffee shops in Germany."

Starbucks' relentless pursuit of new market opportunities in Germany and other countries illustrates the fact that most firms face a broad range of strategy alternatives. In the last chapter, we examined exporting and importing as one way to exploit global market opportunities. However, for Starbucks and other companies whose business models include a service component or store experience, exporting (in the conventional sense) is not the best way to "go global." In this chapter, we go beyond exporting to discuss several additional entry mode options that form a continuum. As shown in Figure 9-1, the level of involvement, risk, and financial reward increases as a company moves from market entry strategies such as licensing to joint ventures and, ultimately, various forms of investment.

When a global company seeks to enter a developing country market, there is an additional strategy issue to address: Whether to replicate the strategy that served the company well in developed markets without significant adaptation. This is the issue that Starbucks is facing. To the extent that the objective of entering the market is to achieve penetration, executives at global companies are well advised to consider embracing a mass-market mind-set. This may well mandate an adaptation strategy.[1] Formulating a **market entry strategy** means that management must decide which option or options to use in pursuing opportunities outside the home country. The particular market entry strategy company executives choose will depend on their vision, attitude toward risk, how much investment capital is available, and how much control is sought.

---

1   David Arnold, *The Mirage of Global Markets: How Globalizing Companies Can Succeed as Markets Localize* (Upper Saddle River, NJ: Prentice Hall, 2004), pp. 78–79.

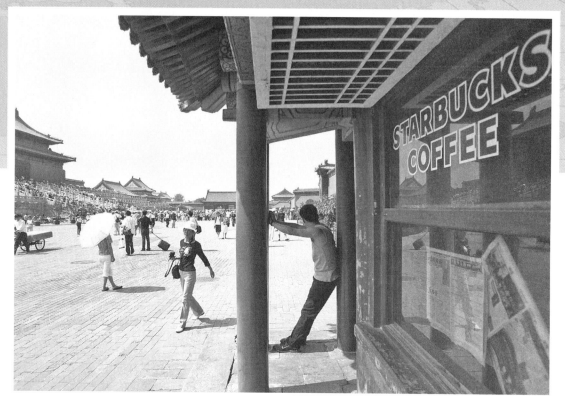

Starbucks opened a small coffee café in Beijing's Forbidden City in 2000. However, in 2007, bowing to criticism that the presence of a Western brand near the former imperial palace was disrespectful, Starbucks closed the shop. The company still has more than 540 other locations in China.

LICENSING

Licensing is a contractual arrangement whereby one company (the licensor) makes a legally protected asset available to another company (the licensee) in exchange for royalties, license fees, or some other form of compensation.[2] The licensed asset may be a brand name, company name, patent, trade secret, or product formulation. Licensing is widely used in the fashion industry. For example, the namesake companies associated with Bill Blass, Hugo Boss, and other global design icons typically generate

Figure 9-1

Involvement/Risk/Reward of Market Entry Strategies

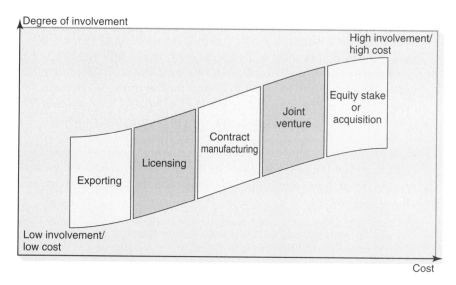

2   Franklin R. Root, *Entry Strategies for International Markets* (New York: Lexington Books, 1994), p. 107.

more revenue from licensing deals for jeans, fragrances, and watches than from their high-priced couture lines. Organizations as diverse as Disney, Caterpillar, the National Basketball Association, and Coca-Cola also make extensive use of licensing. None is an apparel manufacturer; however, licensing agreements allow them to leverage their brand names and generate substantial revenue streams. As these examples suggest, licensing is a global market entry and expansion strategy with considerable appeal. It can offer an attractive return on investment for the life of the agreement, provided that the necessary performance clauses are included in the contract. The only cost is signing the agreement and policing its implementation.

There are two key advantages associated with licensing as a market entry mode. First, because the licensee is typically a local business that will produce and market the goods on a local or regional basis, licensing enables companies to circumvent tariffs, quotas, or similar export barriers discussed in Chapter 8. Second, when appropriate, licensees are granted considerable autonomy and are free to adapt the licensed goods to local tastes. Disney's success with licensing is a case in point. Disney licenses trademarked cartoon characters, names and logos to producers of clothing, toys, and watches for sale throughout the world. Licensing allows Disney to create synergies based on its core theme park, motion picture, and television businesses. Its licensees are allowed considerable leeway to adapt colors, materials, or other design elements to local tastes. In China, licensed goods were practically unknown until a few years ago; by 2001, annual sales of all licensed goods totaled $600 million. Industry observers expect that figure to more than double by 2010. Similarly, yearly worldwide sales of licensed Caterpillar merchandise are running at $900 million as consumers make a fashion statement with boots, jeans, and handbags bearing the distinctive black-and-yellow Cat label. Stephen Palmer is the head of London-based Overland Ltd., which holds the worldwide license for Cat apparel. He notes, "Even if people here don't know the brand, they have a feeling that they know it. They have seen Caterpillar tractors from an early age. It's subliminal, and that's why it's working."[3]

Licensing is associated with several disadvantages and opportunity costs. First, licensing agreements offer limited market control. Because the licensor typically does not become involved in the licensee's marketing program, potential returns from marketing may be lost. The second disadvantage is that the

---

3   Cecilie Rohwedder and Joseph T. Hallinan, "In Europe, Hot New Fashion for Urban Hipsters Comes from Peoria," *The Wall Street Journal* (August 8, 2001), p. B1.

STRATEGIC DECISION-MAKING *in global marketing*

Sony and Apple

Perhaps the most famous example of the opportunity costs associated with licensing dates back to the mid-1950s, when Sony cofounder Masaru Ibuka obtained a licensing agreement for the transistor from AT&T's Bell Laboratories. Ibuka dreamed of using transistors to make small, battery-powered radios. However, the Bell engineers with whom he spoke insisted that it was impossible to manufacture transistors that could handle the high frequencies required for a radio; they advised him to try making hearing aids. Undeterred, Ibuka presented the challenge to his Japanese engineers who spent many months improving high-frequency output. Sony was not the first company to unveil a transistor radio; a U.S.-built product, the Regency, featured transistors from Texas Instruments and a colorful plastic case. However, it was Sony's high quality, distinctive approach to styling, and marketing savvy that ultimately translated into worldwide success.

Conversely, the *failure* to seize an opportunity to license can also lead to dire consequences. In the mid-1980s, Apple Computer chairman John Sculley decided against a broad licensing program for Apple's famed operating system (OS). Such a move would have allowed other computer manufacturers to produce Mac-compatible units. Meanwhile, Microsoft's growing world dominance in both OS and applications got a boost in 1985 from Windows, which featured a Mac-like graphic interface. Apple sued Microsoft for infringing on its intellectual property; however, attorneys for the software giant successfully argued in court that Apple had shared crucial aspects of its OS without limiting Microsoft's right to adapt and improve it. Belatedly, in the mid-1990s, Apple began licensing its operating system to other manufacturers. However, the global market share for machines running the Mac OS continues to hover in the low single digits.

The return of Steve Jobs and Apple's introduction of the new iMac in 1998 marked the start of a new era for Apple. More recently, the popularity of the company's iPod digital music players, iTunes Music Store, and the new iPhone have boosted its fortunes. However, Apple's failure to license its technology in the pre-Windows era arguably cost the company tens of billions of dollars. What's the basis for this assertion? Microsoft, the winner in the operating systems war, had a market capitalization of nearly $300 billion in 2006. By contrast, Apple's 2006 market cap was roughly $66 billion.

agreement may have a short life if the licensee develops its own know-how and begins to innovate in the licensed product or technology area. In a worst-case scenario (from the licensor's point of view), licensees—especially those working with process technologies—can develop into strong competitors in the local market and, eventually, into industry leaders. This is because licensing, by its very nature, enables a company to "borrow"—that is, leverage and exploit—another company's resources. A case in point is Pilkington, which has seen its leadership position in the glass industry erode as Glaverbel, Saint-Gobain, PPG, and other competitors have achieved higher levels of production efficiency and lower costs.[4]

Companies may find that the upfront easy money obtained from licensing turns out to be a very expensive source of revenue. To prevent a licensor-competitor from gaining unilateral benefit, licensing agreements should provide for a cross-technology exchange among all parties. At the absolute minimum, any company that plans to remain in business must ensure that its license agreements include a provision for full cross licensing (i.e., that the licensee shares its developments with the licensor). Overall, the licensing strategy must ensure ongoing competitive advantage. For example, license arrangements can create export market opportunities and open the door to low-risk manufacturing relationships. They can also speed diffusion of new products or technologies.

Special Licensing Arrangements

Contract manufacturing such as that discussed in Case 8-1 requires a global company—Nike, for example—to provide technical specifications to a subcontractor or local manufacturer. The subcontractor then oversees production. Such arrangements offer several advantages. The licensing firm can specialize in product design and marketing, while transferring responsibility for ownership of manufacturing facilities to contractors and subcontractors. Other advantages include limited commitment of financial and managerial resources and quick entry into

---

[4] Charis Gresser, "A Real Test of Endurance," *Financial Times—Weekend* (November 1–2, 1997), p. 5.

Table 9-1

Worldwide Franchise Activity

Company	Overseas Sites	Countries
7-Eleven	23,652	18
McDonald's	22,571	110
Yum Brands	14,057	100
Doctor's Associates (Subway)	5,962	85
Domino's Pizza	3,038	55
Jani-King International (commercial cleaning)	2,210	20

Source: The Wall Street Journal *(Western Edition) by* The Wall Street Journal. *Copyright 2006 by Dow Jones & Company, Inc. Reproduced with permission of Dow Jones & Company, Inc. in the format Other book via Copyright Clearance Center.*

target countries, especially when the target market is too small to justify significant investment.[5] One disadvantage, as already noted, is that companies may open themselves to public scrutiny and criticism if workers in contract factories are poorly paid or labor in inhumane circumstances. Timberland and other companies that source in low-wage countries are using image advertising to communicate their corporate policies on sustainable business practices.

Franchising is another variation of licensing strategy. A franchise is a contract between a parent company-franchiser and a franchisee that allows the franchisee to operate a business developed by the franchiser in return for a fee and adherence to franchise-wide policies and practices. Table 9-1 lists several U.S.-based franchisers with an extensive network of overseas locations.

Franchising has great appeal to local entrepreneurs anxious to learn and apply Western-style marketing techniques. Franchising consultant William Le Sante suggests that would-be franchisers ask the following questions before expanding overseas:

- Will local consumers buy your product?
- How tough is the local competition?
- Does the government respect trademark and franchiser rights?
- Can your profits be easily repatriated?
- Can you buy all the supplies you need locally?
- Is commercial space available and are rents affordable?
- Are your local partners financially sound and do they understand the basics of franchising?[6]

By addressing these issues, franchisers can gain a more realistic understanding of global opportunities. In China, for example, regulations require foreign franchisers to directly own two or more stores for a minimum of one year before franchisees can take over the business. Intellectual property protection is also a concern in China.[7]

The specialty retailing industry favors franchising as a market entry mode. For example, there are more than 1,800 Body Shop stores around the world; franchisees operate 90 percent of them. Franchising is also a cornerstone of global growth in the fast-food industry; McDonald's reliance on franchising to expand globally is a case in point. The fast-food giant has a well-known global brand name and a business system that can be easily replicated in multiple country markets. Crucially, McDonald's headquarters has learned the wisdom of leveraging local market knowledge by granting franchisees considerable leeway to tailor restaurant interior designs and menu offerings to suit country-specific preferences and tastes (see Case 1-1). Generally speaking, however, franchising is a market entry strategy that is typically executed with less localization than licensing.

When companies do decide to license, they should sign agreements that anticipate more extensive market participation in the future. Insofar as is possible, a

"One of the key things licensees bring to the business is their knowledge of the local marketplace, trends, and consumer preferences. As long as it's within the guidelines and standards, and it's not doing anything to compromise our brand, we're very willing to go along with it."[8]

Paul Leech, COO, Allied Domecq Quick Service Restaurants

---

5   Root, p. 138.
6   Eve Tahmincioglu, "It's Not Only the Giants with Franchises Abroad," *The New York Times* (February 12, 2004), p. C4.
7   Richard Gibson, "ForeNign Flavors," *The Wall Street Journal* (September 26, 2006), p. R8. Root, p. 138.
8   Sarah Murray, "Big Names Don Camouflage," *Financial Times* (February 5, 2004), p. 9.

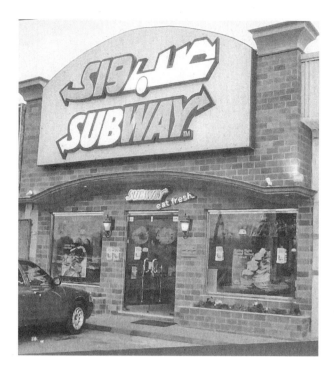

company should keep options and paths open for other forms of market participation. Many of these forms require investment and give the investing company more control than is possible with licensing.

INVESTMENT

After companies gain experience outside the home country via exporting or licensing, the time often comes when executives desire a more extensive form of participation. In particular, the desire to have partial or full ownership of operations outside the home country can drive the decision to invest. **Foreign direct investment (FDI)** figures reflect investment flows out of the home country as companies invest in or acquire plants, equipment, or other assets. Foreign direct investment allows companies to produce, sell, and compete locally in key markets. Examples of FDI abound: Honda is building a $550 million assembly plant in Greensburg, Indiana; IKEA has spent nearly $2 billion to open stores in Russia, and South Korea's LG Electronics purchased a 58 percent stake in Zenith Electronics. Each of these represents foreign direct investment.

The final years of the twentieth century were a boom time for cross-border mergers and acquisitions. At the end of 2000, cumulative foreign investment by U.S. companies totaled $1.2 trillion. The top three target countries for U.S. investment were the United Kingdom, Canada, and the Netherlands. Investment in the United States by foreign companies also totaled $1.2 trillion; the United Kingdom, Japan, and the Netherlands were the top three sources of investment.[9] Investment in developing nations also grew rapidly in the 1990s. For example, as noted in earlier chapters, investment interest in the BRIC nations is increasing, especially in the automobile industry and other sectors critical to the countries' economic development.

Foreign investments may take the form of minority or majority shares in joint ventures, minority or majority equity stakes in another company, or, as in the case of Sandoz and Gerber, outright acquisition. A company may choose to use a combination of these entry strategies by acquiring one company, buying an equity stake in another,

---

[9]   Maria Borga and Raymond J. Mataloni, Jr., "Direct Investment Positions for 2000: Country and Industry Detail," *Survey of Current Business* 81, no. 7 (July 2001), pp. 16–29.

"Drive your way" is the advertising slogan for Hyundai Motor Company, South Korea's leading automaker. In a press statement, Hyundai chairman Chung Mong Koo noted, "Our new brand strategy is designed to ensure that we reach industry-leading levels, not only in terms of size but also in terms of customer perception and overall brand value." To better serve the U.S. market, Hyundai recently invested $1 billion in an assembly plant in Montgomery, Alabama. The plant will produce two models, the popular Sonata sedan and the Santa Fe SUV.

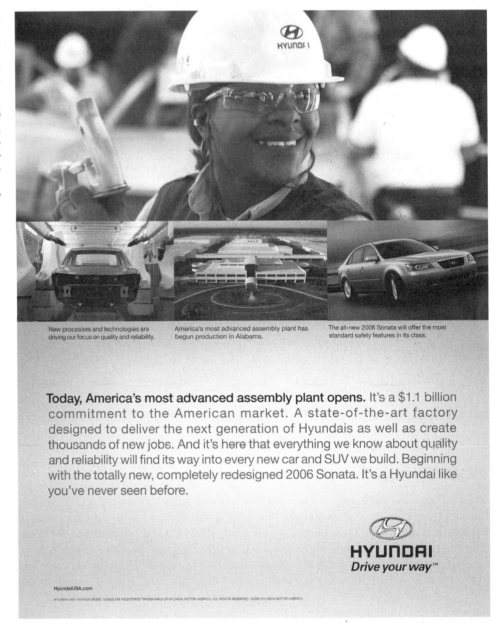

New processes and technologies are driving our focus on quality and reliability.

America's most advanced assembly plant has begun production in Alabama.

The all-new 2006 Sonata will offer the most standard safety features in its class.

Today, America's most advanced assembly plant opens. It's a $1.1 billion commitment to the American market. A state-of-the-art factory designed to deliver the next generation of Hyundais as well as create thousands of new jobs. And it's here that everything we know about quality and reliability will find its way into every new car and SUV we build. Beginning with the totally new, completely redesigned 2006 Sonata. It's a Hyundai like you've never seen before.

HYUNDAI
Drive your way™

HyundaiUSA.com

HYUNDAI AND HYUNDAI MODEL NAMES ARE REGISTERED TRADEMARKS OF HYUNDAI MOTOR AMERICA. ALL RIGHTS RESERVED. ©2005 HYUNDAI MOTOR AMERICA.

and operating a joint venture with a third. In recent years, for example, UPS has made more than 16 acquisitions in Europe and has also expanded its transportation hubs.

Joint Ventures

A joint venture with a local partner represents a more extensive form of participation in foreign markets than either exporting or licensing. Strictly speaking, a **joint venture** is an entry strategy for a single target country in which the partners share ownership of a newly created business entity.[10] This strategy is attractive for several reasons. First and foremost is the sharing of risk. By pursuing a joint venture entry strategy, a company can limit its financial risk as well as its exposure to political uncertainty. Second, a company can use the joint venture experience to learn about a new market environment. If it succeeds in becoming an insider, it may later increase the level of commitment and exposure. Third, joint ventures allow

---

[10] Root, p. 309.

Starbucks

Starbucks has also been successful in other European countries, including the United Kingdom and Ireland. This success comes despite competition from local rivals such as Ireland's Insomnia Coffee Company and Bewley's and the fact that per capita consumption of roasted coffee in the two countries is the lowest in Europe. In January 2004, Starbucks opened its first outlets in Paris. CEO Howard Schultz acknowledged that the decision to target France was a gutsy move; relations between the United States and France had been strained because of political differences regarding President Bush's Iraq policy. Moreover, café culture has long been an entrenched part of the city's heritage and identity. The French prefer dark espresso, and the conventional wisdom is that Americans don't know what good coffee is. As one Frenchman put it, "American coffee, it's only water. We call it *jus des chaussette*—'sock juice.'"

Greater China—including the mainland, Hong Kong, and Taiwan—represents another strategic growth market for Starbucks. Starting with one store in Beijing at the China World Trade Center that opening in 1999, Starbucks now has more than 400 locations. Starbucks has faced several different types of challenges in this part of the world. First of all, government regulations forced the company to partner with local firms. After the regulations were eased, Starbucks stepped up its rate of expansion, focusing on metropolises such as Beijing and Shanghai.

Another challenge comes from the traditional Chinese teahouse. One rival, Real Brewed Tea, aims to be "the Starbucks of tea." A related challenge is the perceptions and preferences of the Chinese, who do not care for coffee. Those who had tasted coffee were only familiar with the instant variety. Faced with one of global marketing's most fundamental questions—adapt offerings for local appeal or attempt to change local tastes—Starbucks hopes to educate the Chinese about coffee.

Chinese consumers exhibit different behavior patterns than in Starbucks' other locations. For one thing, most orders are consumed in the cafés; in the United States, by contrast, most patrons order drinks for carryout. (In the United States, Starbucks is opening hundreds of new outlets with drive-through service) Also, store traffic in China is heaviest in the afternoon. This behavior is consistent with Starbucks' research findings, which indicated that the number one reason the Chinese go to cafés is to have a place to gather.

Sources: Janet Adamy, "Different Brew: Eyeing a Billion Tea Drinkers, Starbucks Pours It on in China," The Wall Street Journal (November 29, 2006), pp. A1, A12; Gerhard Hegmann and Birgit Dengel, "Starbucks Looks to Step Up Openings in Germany," Financial Times (September 5, 2006), p. 23; Steven Gray, "'Fill 'Er Up—With Latte,'" The Wall Street Journal (January 6, 2006), pp. A9, A10; John Murray Brown and Jenny Wiggins, "Coffee Empire Expands Reach by Pressing Its Luck in Ireland," Financial Times (December 15, 2005), p. 21; Gray and Ethan Smith, "New Grind: At Starbucks, a Blend of Coffee and Music Creates a Potent Mix," The Wall Street Journal (July 19, 2005), pp. A1, A11; Noelle Knox, "Paris Starbucks Hopes to Prove U.S. Coffee Isn't 'Sock Juice'," USA Today (January 16, 2004), p. 3B.

partners to achieve synergy by combining different value chain strengths. One company might have in-depth knowledge of a local market, an extensive distribution system, or access to low-cost labor or raw materials. Such a company might link up with a foreign partner possessing well-known brands or cutting-edge technology, manufacturing know-how, or advanced process applications. A company that lacks sufficient capital resources might seek partners to jointly finance a project. Finally, a joint venture may be the only way to enter a country or region if government bid award practices routinely favor local companies, if import tariffs are high, or if laws prohibit foreign control but permit joint ventures.

Many companies have experienced difficulties when attempting to enter the Japanese market. Anheuser-Busch's experience in Japan illustrates both the interactions of the entry modes discussed so far and the advantages and disadvantages of the joint venture approach. Access to distribution is critical to success in the Japanese market; Anheuser-Busch first entered by means of a licensing agreement with Suntory, the smallest of Japan's four top brewers. Although Budweiser had become Japan's top-selling imported beer within a decade, Bud's market share in the early 1990s was still less than 2 percent. Anheuser-Busch then created a joint venture with Kirin Brewery, the market leader. Anheuser-Busch's 90 percent stake in the venture entitled it to market and distribute beer produced in a Los Angeles brewery through Kirin's channels. Anheuser-Busch also had the option to use some of Kirin's brewing capacity to brew Bud locally. For its part, Kirin was well positioned to learn more about the global market for beer from the world's largest brewer. By the end of the decade, however, Bud's market share hadn't increased and the venture was losing money. On January 1, 2000, Anheuser-Busch dissolved the joint venture and eliminated most of the associated job positions in Japan; it reverted instead to a licensing agreement with Kirin. The lesson for consumer products marketers

BRIC Briefing Book

Joint Ventures

Joint venture investment in the BRIC nations is growing rapidly. China is a case in point; for many companies, the price of market entry is the willingness to pursue a joint venture with a local partner. Procter & Gamble has several joint ventures in China. China Great Wall Computer Group is a joint venture factory in which IBM is the majority partner with a 51 percent stake. In automotive joint ventures, the Chinese government limits foreign companies to minority stakes. Despite this, Japan's Isuzu Motors has been a joint venture partner with Jiangling Motors for more than a decade. The venture produces 20,000 pickup trucks and one-ton trucks annually.

As indicated in Table 9-2, in 1995 General Motors pledged $1.1 billion for a joint venture with Shanghai Automotive Industry to build Buicks for government and business use. GM was selected after giving high-level Chinese officials a tour of GM's operations in Brazil and agreeing to the government's conditions regarding technology transfer and investment capital. In 1997, GM was chosen by the Chinese government as the sole Western partner in a joint venture in Guangzhou that will build smaller, less expensive cars for the general public. Other global carmakers competing with GM for the project were BMW, Mercedes-Benz, Honda Motor, and Hyundai Motor.

Russia represents a huge, barely tapped market for a number of industries. The number of joint ventures is increasing. In 1997, GM became the first Western automaker to begin assembling vehicles in Russia. To avoid hefty tariffs that pushed the street price of an imported Blazer over $65,000, GM invested in a 25–75 joint venture with the government of the autonomous Tatarstan republic. Elaz-GM assembled Blazer sport utility vehicles from imported components until the end of 2000. Young Russian professionals were expected to snap up the vehicles as long as the price was less than $30,000. However, after about 15,000 vehicles had been sold, market demand evaporated. At the end of 2001, GM terminated the joint venture.

GM executives are counting on better results with AvtoVAZ, the largest carmaker in the former Soviet Union. AvtoVAZ is home to Russia's top technical design center and also has access to low-cost Russian titanium and other materials. GM originally intended to assemble a stripped-down, reengineered car based on its Opel model. However, market research revealed that a "Made in Russia" car would only be acceptable if it sported a very low sticker price; GM had anticipated a price of approximately $15,000. The same research pointed GM toward an opportunity to put the Chevrolet nameplate on a redesigned domestic model, the Niva. With GM's financial aid, the Chevrolet Niva was launched in fall 2002; another model, the Viva, was launched in 2004. In addition to GM, several other automakers are joining with Russian partners. BMW Group AG has already begun the local manufacture of its 5-series sedans; Renault SA is producing Megane and Clio Symbol models at a plant near Moscow. Fiat SpA and Ford also anticipate starting production at joint venture plants. Some other recent joint venture alliances are outlined in Table 9-2.

Sources: Keith Naughton, "How GM Got the Inside Track in China," Business Week (November 6, 1995), pp. 56–57; Gregory L. White, "Off Road: How the Chevy Name Landed on SUV Using Russian Technology," The Wall Street Journal (February 20, 2001), pp. A1, A8.

considering market entry in Japan is clear. It may make more sense to give control to a local partner via a licensing agreement rather than making a major investment.[11]

The disadvantages of joint venturing can be significant. Joint venture partners must share rewards as well as risks. The main disadvantage associated with joint ventures is that a company incurs very significant costs associated with control and coordination issues that arise when working with a partner. (However, in some instances, country-specific restrictions limit the share of capital help by foreign companies.)

A second disadvantage is the potential for conflict between partners. These often arise out of cultural differences, as was the case in a failed $130 million joint venture between Corning Glass and Vitro, Mexico's largest industrial manufacturer. The venture's Mexican managers sometimes viewed the Americans as too direct and aggressive; the Americans believed their partners took too much time to make important decisions.[12] Such conflicts can multiply when there are several partners in the venture. Disagreements about third-country markets

---

[11] Yumiko Ono, "Beer Venture of Anheuser, Kirin Goes Down Drain on Tepid Sales," The Wall Street Journal (November 3, 1999), p. A23.
[12] Anthony DePalma, "It Takes More Than a Visa to Do Business in Mexico," The New York Times (June 26, 1994), sec. 3, p. 5.

where partners face each other as actual or potential competitors can lead to "divorce." To avoid this, it is essential to work out a plan for approaching third-country markets as part of the venture agreement.

A third issue, also noted in the discussion of licensing, is that a dynamic joint venture partner can evolve into a stronger competitor. Many developing countries are very forthright in this regard. Yuan Sutai, a member of China's Ministry of Electronics Industry, told *The Wall Street Journal*, "The purpose of any joint venture, or even a wholly-owned investment, is to allow Chinese companies to learn from foreign companies. We want them to bring their technology to the soil of the People's Republic of China."[13] GM and South Korea's Daewoo Group formed a joint venture in 1978 to produce cars for the Korean market. By the mid-1990s, GM had helped Daewoo improve its competitiveness as an auto producer, but Daewoo chairman Kim Woo-Choong terminated the venture because its provisions prevented the export of cars bearing the Daewoo name.[14]

As one global marketing expert warns, "In an alliance you have to learn skills of the partner, rather than just see it as a way to get a product to sell while avoiding a big investment." Yet, compared with U.S. and European firms, Japanese and Korean firms seem to excel in their ability to leverage new knowledge that comes out of a joint venture. For example, Toyota learned many new things from its partnership with GM—about U.S. supply and transportation and managing American workers—that have been subsequently applied at its Camry plant in Kentucky. However, some American managers involved in the venture complained that the manufacturing expertise they gained was not applied broadly throughout GM. To the extent that this complaint has validity, GM has missed opportunities to leverage new learning. Still, many companies have achieved great successes in joint ventures. Gillette, for example, has used this strategy to introduce its shaving products in the Middle East and Africa.

Investment via Ownership or Equity Stake

The most extensive form of participation in global markets is investment that results in either an equity stake or full ownership. An **equity stake** is simply an investment; if the investing company acquires fewer than 50 percent of the total

Companies Involved	Purpose of Joint Venture
GM (United States), Toyota (Japan)	NUMMI—a jointly operated plant in Freemont, California
GM (United States), Shanghai Automotive Industry (China)	50–50 joint venture to build assembly plant to produce 100,000 midsized sedans for Chinese market beginning in 1997 (total investment of $1 billion)
GM (United States), Hindustan Motors (India)	Joint venture to build up to 20,000 Opel Astras annually (GM's investment $100 million)
GM (United States), governments of Russia and Tatarstan	25–75 joint venture to assemble Blazers from imported parts and, by 1998, to build a full assembly line for 45,000 vehicles (total investment $250 million)
Ford (United States), Mazda (Japan)	Joint operation of a plant in Flat Rock, Michigan
Ford (United States), Mahindra & Mahindra Ltd. (India)	50–50 joint venture to build Ford Fiestas in Indian state of Tamil Nadu ($800 million)
Chrysler (United States), BMW (Germany)	50–50 joint venture to build a plant in South America to produce small-displacement 4-cylinder engines ($500 million)

Table 9-2

Market Entry and Expansion by Joint Venture

---

13 David P. Hamilton, "China, With Foreign Partners' Help, Becomes a Budding Technology Giant," *The Wall Street Journal* (December 7, 1995), p. A10.
14 "Mr. Kim's Big Picture," *Economist* (September 16, 1995), pp. 74–75.

shares, it is a minority stake; ownership of more than half the shares makes it a majority equity position. **Full ownership**, as the name implies, means the investor has 100 percent control. This may be achieved by a start-up of new operations, known as **greenfield operations** or **greenfield investment**, or by a merger or acquisition of an existing enterprise. According to Thomson Financial Securities Data, worldwide merger and acquisition (M&A) deals worth nearly $3 trillion were struck in 2000. Significantly, about one-third of these were cross-border transactions. M&A activity in Europe and Latin America grew at a faster rate than in the United States. In recent years, the media and telecommunications industry sectors have been among the busiest for M&A worldwide. Ownership requires the greatest commitment of capital and managerial effort and offers the fullest means of participating in a market. Companies may move from licensing or joint venture strategies to ownership in order to achieve faster expansion in a market, greater control, or higher profits. In 1991, for example, Ralston Purina ended a 20-year joint venture with a Japanese company to start its own pet food subsidiary. Monsanto and Bayer AG, the German pharmaceutical company, are two other companies that have also recently disbanded partnerships in favor of wholly owned subsidiaries in Japan.

If government restrictions prevent majority or 100 percent ownership by foreign companies, the investing company will have to settle for a minority equity stake. In Russia, for example, the government restricts foreign ownership in joint ventures to a 49 percent stake. A minority equity stake may also suit a company's business interests. For example, Samsung was content to purchase a 40 percent stake in computer maker AST. As Samsung manager Michael Yang noted, "We thought 100 percent would be very risky, because any time you have a switch of ownership, that creates a lot of uncertainty among the employees."[15] In other instances, the investing company may start with a minority stake and then increase its share. In 1991, Volkswagen AG made its first investment in the Czech auto industry by purchasing a 31 percent share in Skoda. By 1995, Volkswagen had increased its equity stake to 70 percent (the government of the Czech Republic owns the rest). Similarly, Ford purchased a

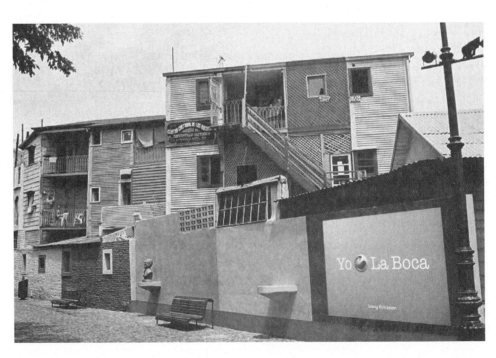

Sony Ericsson is a 50:50 joint venture between Sweden's Telefonaktiebolaget LM Ericsson, the world's leading manufacturer of wireless telecom equipment, and Japanese consumer electronics giant Sony Corporation. Sony Ericsson's logo is a green circular symbol that is used as a "verb" in print ads for a new line of Walkman phones. Headlines include "I [logo] music," "I [logo] my long commute," and "I [logo] it loud." The campaign can also be localized, as evident from this outdoor ad in Brazil.

15 Ross Kerber, "Chairman Predicts Samsung Deal Will Make AST a Giant," *Los Angeles Times* (March 2, 1995), p. D1.

Table 9-3

Investment in Equity Stake

Investing Company (Home Country)	Investment (Share, Amount, Date)
General Motors (United STates)	Suzuki Motor Co. (Japan, 3.5% stake, 1981; increased to 10%, 1998, increased to 20%, $490 million, 2000) Fuji Heavy Industries (Japan, 20% stake, $1.4 billion, 1999) Saab Automobiles AB (Sweden, 50% stake, $500 million, 1990; remaining 50%, 2000)
Volkswagen AG (Germany)	Skoda (Czech Republic, 31% stake, $6 billion, 1991; increased to 50.5%, 1994; currently owns 70% stake)
Ford (USA)	Mazda Motor Corp. (Japan, 25% stake, 1979; increased to 33.4%, $408 million, 1996)
DaimlerChrysler (Germany and United States)	Mitsubishi Motors Corp. (Japan, 34% stake, 2000)
Renault SA (France)	Nissan Motors (Japan, 35% stake, $5 billion, 2000)
Proton (Malaysia)	Lotus Cars (Great Britain, 80% stake, $100 million, 1996)

25 percent stake in Mazda in 1979; in 1996, Ford spent another $408 million to raise its stake to 33.4 percent.

Large-scale direct expansion by means of establishing new facilities can be expensive and require a major commitment of managerial time and energy. However, political or other environmental factors sometimes dictate this approach. For example, Japan's Fuji Photo Film Company invested hundreds of millions of dollars in the United States after the U.S. government ruled that Fuji was guilty of dumping (i.e., selling photographic paper at substantially lower prices than in Japan). As an alternative to greenfield investment in new facilities, acquisition is an instantaneous—and sometimes, less expensive—approach to market entry or expansion. Although full ownership can yield the additional advantage of avoiding communication and conflict of interest problems that may arise with a joint venture or coproduction partner, acquisitions still present the demanding and challenging task of integrating the acquired company into the worldwide organization and coordinating activities.

Tables 9-3, 9-4, and 9-5 provide a sense of how companies in the automotive industry utilize a variety of market entry options discussed previously, including equity stakes, investments to establish new operations, and acquisition. Table 9-3 shows that GM favors minority stakes in non-U.S. automakers; from 1998 through 2000, the company spent $4.7 billion on such deals. Ford spent twice as much on acquisitions. Despite the fact that GM losses from the deals resulted in substantial write-offs, the strategy reflects management's skepticism about making big mergers work. As GM chairman and CEO Rick Wagoner said, "We could have bought 100 percent of somebody, but that probably wouldn't have been a good use of capital." Meanwhile, the investments in minority stakes are finally paying off: The company enjoys scale-related savings in purchasing, it has gained access

Table 9-4

Investment to Establish New Operations

Investing Company (Home Country)	Investment (Location)
Bayerische Motoren Werke AG (Germany)	$400 million auto assembly plant (South Carolina, United States, 1995)
Mercedes-Benz AG (Germany)	$300 million auto assembly plant (South Carolina, United States)
Hyundai	$1.1 billion auto assembly and manufacturing facility producing Sonata and Santa Fe models (Georgia, United States, 2005)
Toyota (Japan)	$3.4 billion manufacturing plant producing Camry, Avalon, and minivan models (Kentucky, United States); $400 million engine plant (West Virginia, United States)

Table 9-5

Market Entry and Expansion by Acquisition

Acquiring Company	Target (Country, Date, Amount)
Daimler Benz (Germany)	Merger with Chrysler Corporation (United States, 1998, $40 billion)
Volkswagen AG (Germany)	Sociedad Española de Automoviles de Turisme (SEAT, Spain, $600 million, purchase completed in 1990)
BMW (Germany)	Rover (United Kingdom, $1.2 billion, 1994)
Ford Motor Company (United States)	Jaguar (United Kingdom, $2.6 billion, 1989)
	Volvo car unit (Sweden, $6.5 billion, 1999)
Paccar (United States)	DAF Trucks (Netherlands, $543 million, 1996)

to diesel technology, and Saab produced a new model in record time with the help of Subaru.[16]

What is the driving force behind many of these acquisitions? It is globalization. In cases like Gerber, management realizes that the path to globalization cannot be undertaken independently. Management at Helene Curtis Industries came to a similar realization and agreed to be acquired by Unilever. Ronald J. Gidwitz, president and CEO, said, "It was very clear to us that Helene Curtis did not have the capacity to project itself in emerging markets around the world. As markets get larger, that forces the smaller players to take action."[17] Still, management's decision to invest abroad sometimes clashes with investors' short-term profitability goals. Although this is an especially important issue for publicly held U.S. companies, there is an increasing trend toward foreign investment by U.S. companies. For example, cumulative U.S. direct investment in Canada between 1994 and 2003 totaled $228 billion.

Several of the advantages of joint ventures also apply to ownership, including access to markets and avoidance of tariff or quota barriers. Like joint ventures, ownership also permits important technology experience transfers and provides a company with access to new manufacturing techniques. For example, the Stanley Works, a tool maker with headquarters in New Britain, Connecticut, has acquired more than a dozen companies since 1986, among them is Taiwan's National Hand Tool/Chiro Company, a socket wrench manufacturer and developer of a "cold-forming" process that speeds up production and reduces waste. Stanley is now using that technology in the manufacture of other tools. Former chairman Richard H. Ayers presided over the acquisitions and envisioned such global cross-fertilization and "blended technology" as a key benefit of globalization.[18] In 1998, former GE executive John Trani succeeded Ayers as CEO; Trani brought considerable experience with international acquisitions, and his selection was widely viewed as evidence that Stanley intended to boost global sales even more.

The alternatives discussed here—licensing, joint ventures, minority or majority equity stake, and ownership—are points along a continuum of alternative strategies for global market entry and expansion. The overall design of a company's global strategy may call for combinations of exporting-importing, licensing, joint ventures, and ownership among different operating units. Avon Products uses both acquisition and joint ventures to enter developing markets. Similarly, Jamont, a European paper-products company, utilizes both joint ventures and acquisitions. A company's strategy preference may change over time. For example, Borden ended licensing and joint venture arrangements for branded food products in Japan and set up its own production, distribution,

---

[16] James Mackintosh, "GM Stands By Its Strategy for Expansion," *Financial Times* (February 2, 2004), p. 5.

[17] Richard Gibson and Sara Calian, "Unilever to Buy Helene Curtis for $770 Million," *The Wall Street Journal* (February 19, 1996), p. A3.

[18] Louis Uchitelle, "The Stanley Works Goes Global," *The New York Times* (July 23, 1989), sec. 3, pp. 1, 10.

While U.S. Commerce Secretary Carlos Gutierrez was in China for trade talks in 2006, Home Depot announced it would acquire the HomeWay do-it-yourself chain. China's home-improvement market generates an estimated $50 billion in annual sales and is growing at double-digit rates. Home Depot, which also has operations in Mexico and Canada, is experiencing a business slowdown in the U.S. market. According to Annette Verschuren, president of Home Depot's Asian operations, the company's China strategy will include further acquisitions to fuel revenue growth.

and marketing capabilities for dairy products. Meanwhile, in nonfood products, Borden has maintained joint venture relationships with Japanese partners in flexible packaging and foundry materials.

It can also be the case that competitors within a given industry pursue different strategies. For example, Cummins Engine and Caterpillar both face very high costs—in the $300 to $400 million range—for developing new diesel engines suited to new applications. However, the two companies vary in their strategic approaches to the world market for engines. Cummins management looks favorably on collaboration; also, the company's relatively modest $6 billion in annual revenues presents financial limitations. Thus, Cummins prefers joint ventures. The biggest joint venture between an American company and the Soviet Union linked Cummins with the KamAZ truck company in Tatarstan. The joint venture allowed the Russians to implement new manufacturing technologies while providing Cummins with access to the Russian

Cable

"OK, but just suppose China *did* make a takeover move on our B-school."

Gerber

Gerber Products is the undisputed leader in the U.S. baby food market. Despite a 70 percent market share, Gerber faces a mature market and stagnant growth at home. Because 9 out of 10 of the world's births take place outside the United States, Gerber executives hoped to make international sales a greater part of the company's $1.17 billion in annual revenues. Overall, Gerber's international sales increased 150 percent between 1989 and 1993, from $86.5 million to $216.1 million.

Still, a combination of changing market conditions, management inconsistency, and decisions that didn't pay off slowed Gerber's globalization effort for two decades. Gerber entered the Latin American market in the 1970s, but then it closed down operations in Venezuela in the wake of government-imposed price controls. Management's focus on the U.S. market resulted in a series of diversifications into nonfood categories that were not successful. Meanwhile, management was not willing to sacrifice short-term quarterly earnings growth to finance an international effort. As Michael A. Cipollaro, Gerber's former president of international operations, remarked, "If you are going to sow in the international arena today to reap tomorrow, you couldn't have that [earnings] growth on a regular basis." In the 1980s, Gerber pursued a strategy of licensing the manufacture and distribution of its baby food products to other companies. In France, for example, Gerber selected CPC International as a licensee.

Unfortunately, Gerber couldn't force its licensees to make baby food a priority business. In France, for example, baby food represented a meager 2 percent of CPC's European revenues. When CPC closed down its French plant, Gerber had to find another manufacturing source. It bought a stake in a Polish factory, but production was held up for months while quality improvements were made. The delay ended up costing Gerber its market position in France.

Belatedly, Gerber discovered that strong competitors already dominated many markets around the globe. Heinz has about one-third of the $1.5 billion baby food market outside the United States; Gerber's share of the global market is 17 percent.

Competitors with less global share than Gerber—including France's BSN Group (15 percent market share), and Switzerland's Nestlé SA (8 percent)—have been aggressively building brand loyalty. In France, for example, parents traveling with infants can get free baby food and diapers through Nestlé's system of roadside changing stations. Another barrier is that many European mothers think homemade baby food is healthier than food from a jar.

Meanwhile, Gerber's global efforts were interrupted by the resignations of several key executives. Cipollaro, the chief of international operations, left, as did the vice president for Europe and the international director of business development. Gerber's management team was forced to rethink its strategy: In May 1994, it agreed to an acquisition by Sandoz AG, a $10.3 billion Swiss pharmaceutical and chemical company. As market analyst David Adelman noted, "It was very expensive for Gerber to build business internationally. This was one of the driving reasons why Gerber wanted to team up with a larger company."

Some industry analysts expressed doubts about the logic behind the acquisition. London broker Peter Smith said, "I'm sorry: Baby food and anticancer drugs don't really come together." Nevertheless, the deal gave Gerber immediate access to a global marketing and distribution network that is particularly strong in developing countries such as China and India. Sandoz, which faces expiring patents for some of its most profitable drugs, instantly assumed a strong position in the U.S. nutrition market. In 2007, Nestlé acquired Gerber for $5.5 billion; plans call for increasing Gerber's market share both at home and abroad.

Sources: Jennifer Reingold, "The Pope of Basel," Financial World (July 18, 1995), pp. 36–38; Margaret Studer, "Sandoz AG Is Foraging for Additional Food Holdings," The Wall Street Journal (February 21, 1995), p. B4; Richard Gibson, "Growth Formula: Gerber Missed the Boat in Quest to Go Global, So It Turned to Sandoz," The Wall Street Journal (May 24, 1994), pp. A1, A7; Leah Rickard and Laurel Wentz, "Sandoz Opens World for Gerber," Advertising Age (May 30, 1994), p. 4; Margaret Studer and Ron Winslow, "Sandoz, Under Pressure, Looks to Gerber for Protection," The Wall Street Journal (May 25, 1994), p. B3.

market. Cummins also has joint ventures in Japan, Finland, and Italy. Management at Caterpillar, by contrast, prefers the higher degree of control that comes with full ownership. The company has spent more than $2 billion in recent years on purchases of Germany's MaK, British engine maker Perkins, and others. Management believes that it is often less expensive to buy existing firms than to develop new applications independently. Also, Caterpillar is concerned about safeguarding proprietary knowledge that is basic to manufacturing in its core construction equipment business.[19]

GLOBAL STRATEGIC PARTNERSHIPS

In Chapter 8 and the first half of Chapter 9, we surveyed the range of options—exporting, licensing, joint ventures, and ownership—traditionally used by companies wishing either to enter global markets for the first time or to expand their

---

[19] Peter Marsh, "Engine Makers Take Different Routes," *Financial Times* (July 14, 1998), p. 11.

activities beyond present levels. However, recent changes in the political, economic, sociocultural, and technological environments of the global firm have combined to change the relative importance of those strategies. Trade barriers have fallen, markets have globalized, consumer needs and wants have converged, product life cycles have shortened, and new communications technologies and trends have emerged. Although these developments provide unprecedented market opportunities, there are strong strategic implications for the global organization and new challenges for the global marketer. Such strategies will undoubtedly incorporate—or may even be structured around—a variety of collaborations. Once thought of only as joint ventures with the more dominant party reaping most of the benefits (or losses) of the partnership, cross-border alliances are taking on surprising new configurations and even more surprising players.

Why would any firm—global or otherwise—seek to collaborate with another firm, be it local or foreign? For example, despite its commanding 37 percent share of the global cellular handset market, Nokia recently announced that it would make the source code for its proprietary Series 60 software available to competing handset manufacturers such as Siemens AG. Why did Nokia's top executives decide to collaborate, thereby putting the company's competitive advantage with software development (and healthy profit margins) at risk? As noted, a "perfect storm" of converging environmental forces is rendering traditional competitive strategies obsolete. Today's competitive environment is characterized by unprecedented degrees of turbulence, dynamism, and unpredictability; global firms must respond and adapt quickly. To succeed in global markets, firms can no longer rely exclusively on the technological superiority or core competence that brought them past success. In the twenty-first century, firms must look toward new strategies that will enhance environmental responsiveness. In particular, they must pursue "entrepreneurial globalization" by developing flexible organizational capabilities, innovating continuously, and revising global strategies accordingly."[20] In the second half of this chapter, we will focus on global strategic partnerships. In addition, we will examine the Japanese *keiretsu* and various other types of cooperation strategies that global firms are using today.

THE NATURE OF GLOBAL STRATEGIC PARTNERSHIPS

The terminology used to describe the new forms of cooperation strategies varies widely. The phrases **collaborative agreements**, **strategic alliances**, **strategic international alliances**, and **global strategic partnerships (GSPs)** are frequently used to refer to linkages between companies from different countries to jointly pursue a common goal. This terminology can cover a broad spectrum of interfirm agreements, including joint ventures. However, the strategic alliances discussed here exhibit three characteristics (see Figure 9-2).[21]

1. The participants remain independent subsequent to the formation of the alliance.
2. The participants share the benefits of the alliance as well as control over the performance of assigned tasks.
3. The participants make ongoing contributions in technology, products, and other key strategic areas.

---

[20] Michael Y. Yoshino and U. Srinivasa Rangan, *Strategic Alliances: An Entrepreneurial Approach to Globalization* (Boston: Harvard Business School Press, 1995), p. 51.

[21] Yoshino and Rangan, p. 5. For an alternative description see Riad Ajami and Dara Khambata, "Global Strategic Alliances: The New Transnationals," *Journal of Global Marketing* 5, no. 1/2, (1991), pp. 55–59.

Figure 9-2

Three Characteristics of Strategic
Alliances

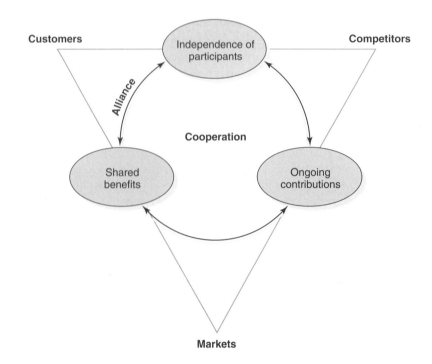

According to estimates, the number of strategic alliances has been growing at a rate of 20 percent to 30 percent since the mid-1980s. The upward trend for GSPs comes in part at the expense of traditional cross-border mergers and acquisitions. Since the mid-1990s, a key force driving partnership formation is the realization that globalization and the Internet will require new inter corporate configurations. Table 9-6 lists some of the GSPs that have been formed recently.

Roland Smith, chairman of British Aerospace, offers a straightforward reason why a firm would enter into a GSP: "A partnership is one of the quickest and cheapest ways to develop a global strategy."[22] Like traditional joint ventures, GSPs have some disadvantages. Partners share control over assigned tasks, a situation that creates management challenges. Also, there are potential risks associated with strengthening a competitor from another country.

Despite these drawbacks, GSPs are attractive for several reasons. First, high product development costs in the face of resource constraints may force a company to seek one or more partners; this was part of the rationale for Sony's partnership with Samsung to produce flat-panel TV screens. Second, the technology requirements of many contemporary products mean that an individual company

Table 9-6

Examples of Global Strategic
Partnerships

Name of Alliance or Product and Web Address	Major Participants	Purpose of Alliance
S-LCD	Sony Corp., Samsung Electronics Co.	Produce flat-panel LCD screens for high-definition televisions.
Beverage Partners Worldwide	Coca-Cola and Nestlé	Offer new coffee, tea, and herbal beverage products in "rejuvenation" category.
Star Alliance www.star-alliance.com	United Airlines, Air Canada, SAS, Lufthansa, Thai Airways International, and Varig Airlines	Create a global travel network by linking airlines and providing better service for international travelers.

---

[22] Main, p. 121.

The Star Alliance is a global network that brings together United Airlines and carriers in a number of different countries. Passengers booking a ticket on any Alliance member can easily connect with other carriers for smooth travel to more than 130 countries. A further benefit for travelers is the fact that frequent flyer miles earned can be redeemed on any Alliance member.

may lack the skills, capital, or know-how to go it alone.[23] Third, partnerships may be the best means of securing access to national and regional markets. Fourth, partnerships provide important learning opportunities; one expert regards GSPs as a "race to learn." Professor Gary Hamel of the London Business School has observed that the partner that proves to be the fastest learner can ultimately dominate the relationship.[24]

As noted earlier, GSPs differ significantly from the market entry modes discussed in the first half of the chapter. Because licensing agreements do not call for continuous transfer of technology or skills among partners, such agreements are not strategic alliances.[25] Traditional joint ventures are basically alliances focusing on a single national market or a specific problem. The Chinese joint venture described previously between GM and Shanghai Automotive fits this description; the basic goal is to make cars for the Chinese market. A true global strategic partnership is different; it is distinguished by five attributes.[26] S-LCD, Sony's strategic alliance with Samsung, offers a good illustration of each attribute.[27]

1. *Two or more companies develop a joint long-term strategy aimed at achieving world leadership by pursuing cost-leadership, differentiation, or a combination of the two.* Samsung and Sony are jockeying with each other for leadership in the global television market. One key to profitability in the flat-panel TV market is being the cost leader in panel production. S-LCD is a $2 billion joint venture to produce 60,000 panels per month.

---

[23] Kenichi Ohmae, "The Global Logic of Strategic Alliances," *Harvard Business Review* 67, no. 2 (March–April 1989), p. 145.

[24] Main, p. 122.

[25] Michael Y. Yoshino and U. Srinivasa Rangan, *Strategic Alliances: An Entrepreneurial Approach to Globalization* (Boston: Harvard Business School Press, 1995), p. 6.

[26] Howard V. Perlmutter and David A. Heenan, "Cooperate to Compete Globally," *Harvard Business Review* 64, no. 2 (March–April 1986), p. 137.

[27] Discussion is adapted from Phred Dvorak and Evan Ramstad, "TV Marriage: Behind Sony-Samsung Rivalry, An Unlikely Alliance Develops," *The Wall Street Journal* (January 3, 2006), pp. A1, A6.

2. *The relationship is reciprocal. Each partner possesses specific strengths that it shares with the other; learning must take place on both sides.* Samsung is a leader in the manufacturing technologies used to create flat-panel TVs. Sony excels at parlaying advanced technology into world-class consumer products; its engineers specialize in optimizing TV picture quality. Jang Insik, Samsung's chief executive, says, "If we learn from Sony, it will help us in advancing our technology."

3. *The partners' vision and efforts are truly global, extending beyond home countries and the home regions to the rest of the world.* Sony and Samsung are both global companies that market global brands throughout the world.

4. *The relationship is organized along horizontal, not vertical, lines. Continual transfer of resources laterally between partners is required, with technology sharing and resource pooling representing norms.* Jang and Sony's Hiroshi Murayama speak by telephone on a daily basis; they also meet face-to-face each month to discuss panel making.

5. When competing in markets excluded from the partnership, the participants retain their national and ideological identities.

SUCCESS FACTORS

Assuming that a proposed alliance meets these five prerequisites, it is necessary to consider six basic factors deemed to have significant impact on the success of GSPs: mission, strategy, governance, culture, organization, and management.[28]

1. *Mission.* Successful GSPs create win-win situations, where participants pursue objectives on the basis of mutual need or advantage.
2. *Strategy.* A company may establish separate GSPs with different partners; strategy must be thought out up front to avoid conflicts.
3. *Governance.* Discussion and consensus must be the norms. Partners must be viewed as equals.
4. *Culture.* Personal chemistry is important, as is the successful development of a shared set of values. The failure of a partnership between Great Britain's General Electric Company and Siemens AG was blamed in part on the fact that the former was run by finance-oriented executives, the latter by engineers.
5. *Organization.* Innovative structures and designs may be needed to offset the complexity of multicountry management.
6. *Management.* GSPs invariably involve a different type of decision making. Potentially divisive issues must be identified in advance and clear, unitary lines of authority established that will result in commitment by all partners.

Companies forming GSPs must keep these factors in mind. Moreover, the following four principles will guide successful collaborators. First, despite the fact that partners are pursuing mutual goals in some areas, partners must remember that they are competitors in others. Second, harmony is not the most important measure of success—some conflict is to be expected. Third, all employees, engineers, and managers must understand where cooperation ends and competitive compromise begins. Finally, as noted earlier, learning from partners is critically important.[29]

---

[28] Perlmutter and Heenan, p. 137.
[29] Gary Hamel, Yves L. Doz, and C. K. Prahalad, "Collaborate with Your Competitors—and Win," *Harvard Business Review* 67, no. 1 (January–February 1989), pp. 133–139.

The issue of learning deserves special attention. As one team of researchers notes,

> The challenge is to share enough skills to create advantage vis-à-vis companies outside the alliance while preventing a wholesale transfer of core skills to the partner. This is a very thin line to walk. Companies must carefully select what skills and technologies they pass to their partners. They must develop safeguards against unintended, informal transfers of information. The goal is to limit the transparency of their operations.[30]

Alliances with Asian Competitors

Western companies may find themselves at a disadvantage in GSPs with an Asian competitor, especially if the latter's manufacturing skills are the attractive quality. Unfortunately for Western companies, manufacturing excellence represents a multifaceted competence that is not easily transferred. Non-Asian managers and engineers must also learn to be more receptive and attentive—they must overcome the "not-invented-here" syndrome and begin to think of themselves as students, not teachers. At the same time, they must learn to be less eager to show off proprietary lab and engineering successes. To limit transparency, some companies involved in GSPs establish a "collaboration section." Much like a corporate communications department, this department is designed to serve as a gatekeeper through which requests for access to people and information must be channeled. Such gatekeeping serves an important control function that guards against unintended transfers.

A 1991 report by McKinsey and Company shed additional light on the specific problems of alliances between Western and Japanese firms.[31] Often, problems between partners had less to do with objective levels of performance than with a feeling of mutual disillusionment and missed opportunity. The study identified four common problem areas in alliances gone wrong. The first problem was that each partner had a "different dream"; the Japanese partner saw itself emerging from the alliance as a leader in its business or entering new sectors and building a new basis for the future; the Western partner sought relatively quick and risk-free financial returns. Said one Japanese manager, "Our partner came in looking for a return. They got it. Now they complain that they didn't build a business. But that isn't what they set out to create."

A second area of concern is the balance between partners. Each must contribute to the alliance and each must depend on the other to a degree that justifies participation in the alliance. The most attractive partner in the short run is likely to be a company that is already established and competent in the business with the need to master, say, some new technological skills. The best long-term partner, however, is likely to be a less competent player or even one from outside the industry.

Another common cause of problems is "frictional loss," caused by differences in management philosophy, expectations, and approaches. All functions within the alliance may be affected, and performance is likely to suffer as a consequence. Speaking of his Japanese counterpart, a Western businessperson said, "Our partner just wanted to go ahead and invest without considering whether there would be a return or not." The Japanese partner stated that "the foreign partner took so long to decide on obvious points that we were always too slow." Such differences often lead to frustration and time-consuming debates that stifle decision making.

---

[30] Hamel, Doz, Prahalad, p. 136.
[31] Kevin K. Jones and Walter E. Schill, "Allying for Advantage," *The McKinsey Quarterly* no. 3 (1991), pp. 73–101.

Last, the study found that short-term goals can result in the foreign partner limiting the number of people allocated to the joint venture. Those involved in the venture may perform only two- or three-year assignments. The result is "corporate amnesia," that is, little or no corporate memory is built up on how to compete in Japan. The original goals of the venture will be lost as each new group of managers takes their turn. When taken collectively, these four problems will almost ensure that the Japanese partner will be the only one in it for the long haul.

CFM International, GE, and SNECMA: A Success Story

Commercial Fan Moteur (CFM) International, a partnership between GE's jet engine division and Snecma, a government-owned French aerospace company, is a frequently cited example of a successful GSP. GE was motivated, in part, by the desire to gain access to the European market so it could sell engines to Airbus Industrie; also, the $800 million in development costs was more than GE could risk on its own. While GE focused on system design and high-tech work, the French side handled fans, boosters, and other components. In 2004, the French government sold a 35 percent stake in Snecma; in 2005, Sagem, an electronics maker, acquired Snecma. The combined companies are known as Safran. Today, the Snecma division has operations throughout the world and more than 300 commercial and military customers worldwide including Boeing, Airbus, and the United States Air Force. In 2006, Snecma generated sales of €3.4 billion.

The alliance got off to a strong start because of the personal chemistry between two top executives, GE's Gerhard Neumann and the late General René Ravaud of Snecma. The partnership thrives despite each side's differing views regarding governance, management, and organization. Brian Rowe, senior vice president of GE's engine group, has noted that the French like to bring in senior executives from outside the industry, whereas GE prefers to bring in experienced people from within the organization. Also, the French prefer to approach problem solving with copious amounts of data, and Americans may take a more intuitive approach. Still, senior executives from both sides of the partnership have been delegated substantial responsibility.

Boeing and Japan: A Controversy

In some circles, GSPs have been the target of criticism. Critics warn that employees of a company that becomes reliant on outside suppliers for critical components will lose expertise and experience erosion of their engineering skills. Such criticism is often directed at GSPs involving U.S. and Japanese firms. For example, a proposed alliance between Boeing and a Japanese consortium to build a new fuel-efficient airliner, the 7J7, generated a great deal of controversy. The project's $4 billion price tag was too high for Boeing to shoulder alone. The Japanese were to contribute between $1 billion and $2 billion; in return, they would get a chance to learn manufacturing and marketing techniques from Boeing. Although the 7J7 project was shelved in 1988, a new wide body aircraft, the 777, was developed with about 20 percent of the work subcontracted out to Mitsubishi, Fuji, and Kawasaki.[32]

---

[32] John Holusha, "Pushing the Envelope at Boeing," *The New York Times* (November 10, 1991), sec. 3, pp. 1, 6.

Critics envision a scenario in which the Japanese use what they learn to build their own aircraft and compete directly with Boeing in the future—a disturbing thought since Boeing is a major exporter to world markets. One team of researchers has developed a framework outlining the stages that a company can go through as it becomes increasingly dependent on partnerships:[33]

Stage One: Outsourcing of assembly for inexpensive labor

Stage Two: Outsourcing of low-value components to reduce product price

Stage Three: Growing levels of value-added components move abroad

Stage Four: Manufacturing skills, designs, and functionally related technologies move abroad

Stage Five: Disciplines related to quality, precision-manufacturing, testing, and future avenues of product derivatives move abroad

Stage Six: Core skills surrounding components, miniaturization, and complex systems integration move abroad

Stage Seven: Competitor learns the entire spectrum of skills related to the underlying core competence

Yoshino and Rangan have described the interaction and evolution of the various market entry strategies in terms of cross-market dependencies (Figure 9-2).[34] Many firms start with an export-based approach as described in Chapter 8. For example, the striking success of Japanese firms in the automobile and consumer electronics industries can be traced back to an export drive. Nissan, Toyota, and Honda initially concentrated production in Japan, thereby achieving economies of scale. Eventually, an export-driven strategy gives way to an affiliate-based one. The various types of investment strategies described previously—equity stake, investment to establish new operations, acquisitions, and joint ventures—create operational interdependence within the firm. By operating in different markets, firms have the opportunity to transfer production from place to place, depending on exchange rates, resource costs, or other considerations. Although at some companies, foreign

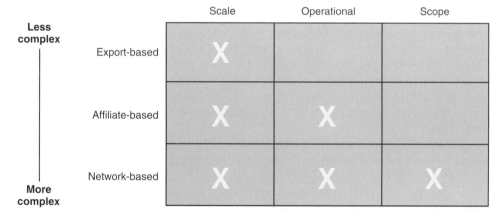

Figure 9-3

Evolution and Interaction of Entry Strategies

Source: Adapted from Michael Y. Yoshino and U. Srinivasa Rangan, Strategic Alliances: An Entrepreneurial Approach to Globalization (Boston: Harvard Business School Press, 1995), p. 51.

---

[33] David Lei and John W. Slocum Jr., "Global Strategy, Competence-Building and Strategic Alliances," *California Management Review* 35, no. 1 (Fall 1992), pp. 81–97.

[34] Michael A. Yoshino and U. Srinivasa Rangan, *Strategic Alliances: An Entrepreneurial Approach to Globalization* (Boston: Harvard Business School Press, 1995), pp. 56–59.

affiliates operate as autonomous fiefdoms (the prototypical multinational business with a polycentric orientation), other companies realize the benefits that operational flexibility can bring. The third and most complex stage in the evolution of a global strategy comes with management's realization that full integration and a network of shared knowledge from different country markets can greatly enhance the firm's overall competitive position. As implied by Figure 9-3, as company personnel opt to pursue increasingly complex strategies, they must simultaneously manage each new interdependency as well as preceding ones. The stages described here are reflected in the evolution of Taiwan's Acer Group as described in Case 1-2.

INTERNATIONAL PARTNERSHIPS IN DEVELOPING COUNTRIES

Central and Eastern Europe, Asia, India, and Mexico offer exciting opportunities for firms that seek to enter gigantic and largely untapped markets. An obvious strategic alternative for entering these markets is the strategic alliance. Like the early joint ventures between U.S. and Japanese firms, potential partners will trade market access for know-how. Other entry strategies are also possible, of course; in 1996, for example, Chrysler and BMW agreed to invest $500 million in a joint venture plant in Latin America capable of producing 400,000 small engines annually. While then-Chrysler chairman Robert Eaton was skeptical of strategic partnerships, he believed that limited forms of cooperation such as joint ventures make sense in some situations. Eaton said, "The majority of world vehicle sales are in vehicles with engines of less than 2.0 liters, outside of the United States. We have simply not been able to be competitive in those areas because of not having a smaller engine. In the international market, there's no question that in many cases such as this, the economies of scale suggest you really ought to have a partner."[35]

Assuming that risks can be minimized and problems overcome, joint ventures in the transition economies of Central and Eastern Europe could evolve at a more accelerated pace than past joint ventures with Asian partners. A number of factors combine to make Russia an excellent location for an alliance: There is a well-educated workforce, and quality is very important to Russian consumers. However, several problems are frequently cited in connection with joint ventures in Russia; these include organized crime, supply shortages, and outdated regulatory and legal systems in a constant state of flux. Despite the risks, the number of joint ventures in Russia is growing, particularly in the services and manufacturing sectors. In the early-post Soviet era, most of the manufacturing ventures were limited to assembly work, but higher value-added activities such as component manufacture are now being performed.

A Central European market with interesting potential is Hungary. Hungary already has the most liberal financial and commercial system in the region. It has also provided investment incentives to Westerners, especially in high-tech industries. Like Russia, this former communist economy has its share of problems. Digital's recent joint venture agreement with the Hungarian Research Institute for Physics and the state-supervised computer systems design firm Szamalk is a case in point. Although the venture was formed so Digital would

---

[35] Angelo B. Henderson, "Chrysler and BMW Team Up to Build Small-Engine Plant in South America," *The Wall Street Journal* (October 2, 1996), p. A4.

be able to sell and service its equipment in Hungary, the underlying importance of the venture was to stop the cloning of Digital's computers by Central European firms.

COOPERATIVE STRATEGIES IN JAPAN: *KEIRETSU*

Japan's *keiretsu* represents a special category of cooperative strategy. A **keiretsu** is an interbusiness alliance or enterprise group that, in the words of one observer, "resembles a fighting clan in which business families join together to vie for market share."[36] *Keiretsu* exist in a broad spectrum of markets, including the capital market, primary goods markets, and component parts markets.[37] *Keiretsu* relationships are often cemented by bank ownership of large blocks of stock and by cross-ownership of stock between a company and its buyers and nonfinancial suppliers. Further, *keiretsu* executives can legally sit on each other's boards, and share information, and coordinate prices in closed-door meetings of "presidents' councils." Thus, *keiretsu* are essentially cartels that have the government's blessing. While not a market entry strategy per se, *keiretsu* played an integral role in the international success of Japanese companies as they sought new markets.

Some observers have disputed charges that *keiretsu* have an impact on market relationships in Japan and claim instead that the groups primarily serve a social function. Others acknowledge the past significance of preferential trading patterns associated with *keiretsu* but assert that the latter's influence is now weakening. Although it is beyond the scope of this chapter to address these issues in detail, there can be no doubt that, for companies competing with the Japanese or wishing to enter the Japanese market, a general understanding of *keiretsu* is crucial. Imagine, for example, what it would mean in the United States if an automaker (e.g., GM), an electrical products company (e.g., GE), a steelmaker (e.g., USX), and a computer firm (e.g., IBM) were interconnected, rather than separate, firms. Global competition in the era of *keiretsu* means that competition exists not only among products, but between different systems of corporate governance and industrial organization.[38]

As the hypothetical example from the United States suggests, some of Japan's biggest and best-known companies are at the center of *keiretsu*. For example, several large companies with common ties to a bank are at the center of the Mitsui Group and Mitsubishi Group. These two, together with the Sumitomo, Fuyo, Sanwa, and DKB groups make up the "big six" *keiretsu* (in Japanese, *roku dai kigyo shudan* or six big industrial groups). The big six strive for a strong position in each major sector of the Japanese economy; because intragroup relationships often involve shared stockholdings and trading relations, the big six are sometimes known as *horizontal keiretsu*.[39] Annual revenues in each group are in the hundreds of billions of dollars. In absolute terms, *keiretsu* constitute a small percentage of all Japanese companies. However, these alliances can effectively block foreign suppliers from entering the market and result in higher prices to Japanese consumers, while at the same time resulting in corporate stability, risk sharing, and long-term

---

[36] Robert L. Cutts, "Capitalism in Japan: Cartels and Keiretsu," *Harvard Business Review* 70, no. 4 (July–August 1992), p. 49.

[37] Michael L. Gerlach, "Twilight of the *Kereitsu*? A Critical Assessment," *Journal of Japanese Studies* 18, no. 1 (Winter 1992), p. 79.

[38] Ronald J. Gilson and Mark J. Roe, "Understanding the Japanese Keiretsu: Overlaps Between Corporate Governance and Industrial Organization," *Yale Law Journal* 102, no. 4 (January 1993), p. 883.

[39] Kenichi Miyashita and David Russell, *Keiretsu: Inside the Hidden Japanese Conglomerates* (New York: McGraw-Hill, 1996), p. 9.

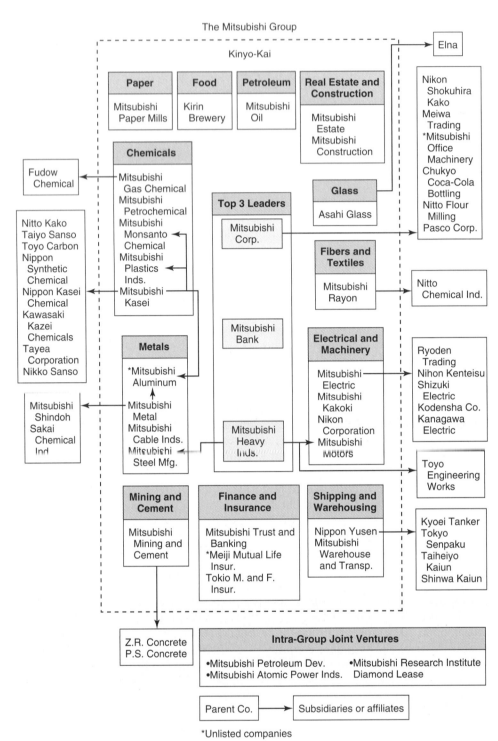

Figure 9-4

Mitsubishi Group's Keiretsu Structure

Source: Adapted from Collins and Doorley Teaming Up for the 90s. Deloitte & Touche, 1991.

The Mitsubishi Group

Kinyo-Kai

Paper
Mitsubishi Paper Mills

Food
Kirin Brewery

Petroleum
Mitsubishi Oil

Real Estate and Construction
Mitsubishi Estate
Mitsubishi Construction

Elna

Nikon
Shokuhira
Kako
Meiwa Trading
*Mitsubishi Office Machinery
Chukyo Coca-Cola Bottling
Nitto Flour Milling
Pasco Corp.

Chemicals
Mitsubishi Gas Chemical
Mitsubishi Petrochemical
Mitsubishi Monsanto Chemical
Mitsubishi Plastics Inds.
Mitsubishi Kasei

Fudow Chemical

Nitto Kako
Taiyo Sanso
Toyo Carbon
Nippon Synthetic Chemical
Nippon Kasei Chemical
Kawasaki Kazei Chemicals
Tayea Corporation
Nikko Sanso

Mitsubishi Shindoh
Sakai Chemical Ind

Glass
Asahi Glass

Top 3 Leaders
Mitsubishi Corp.

Mitsubishi Bank

Mitsubishi Heavy Inds.

Fibers and Textiles
Mitsubishi Rayon

Nitto Chemical Ind.

Metals
*Mitsubishi Aluminum
Mitsubishi Metal
Mitsubishi Cable Inds.
Mitsubishi Steel Mfg.

Electrical and Machinery
Mitsubishi Electric
Mitsubishi Kakoki
Nikon Corporation
Mitsubishi Motors

Ryoden Trading
Nihon Kenteisu
Shizuki Electric
Kodensha Co.
Kanagawa Electric

Toyo Engineering Works

Mining and Cement
Mitsubishi Mining and Cement

Finance and Insurance
Mitsubishi Trust and Banking
*Meiji Mutual Life Insur.
Tokio M. and F. Insur.

Shipping and Warehousing
Nippon Yusen
Mitsubishi Warehouse and Transp.

Kyoei Tanker
Tokyo Senpaku
Taiheiyo Kaiun
Shinwa Kaiun

Z.R. Concrete
P.S. Concrete

Intra-Group Joint Ventures
• Mitsubishi Petroleum Dev.   • Mitsubishi Research Institute
• Mitsubishi Atomic Power Inds.   Diamond Lease

Parent Co. → Subsidiaries or affiliates

*Unlisted companies

employment. The Mitsubishi Group's *keiretsu* structure is shown in detail in Figure 9-4.

In addition to the big six, several other *keiretsu* have formed, bringing new configurations to the basic forms described previously. *Vertical* (i.e., supply and distribution) *keiretsu* are hierarchical alliances between manufacturers and retailers. For example, Matsushita controls a chain of 25,000 National stores in Japan through which it sells its Panasonic, Technics, and Quasar brands. About half of Matsushita's domestic sales are generated through the National chain, 50 percent to 80 percent of whose inventory consists of Matsushita's brands. Japan's other major consumer electronics manufacturers, including Toshiba and Hitachi, have similar alliances. (Sony's chain of stores is much smaller and weaker by comparison.) All are fierce competitors in the Japanese market.[40]

Another type of manufacturing *keiretsu* consists of vertical hierarchical alliances between automakers and suppliers and component manufacturers. Intergroup operations and systems are closely integrated, with suppliers receiving long-term contracts. Toyota, for example, has a network of about 175 primary and 4,000 secondary suppliers. One supplier is Koito; Toyota owns about one-fifth of Koito's shares and buys about half of its production. The net result of this arrangement is that Toyota produces about 25 percent of the sales value of its cars, compared with 50 percent for GM. Manufacturing *keiretsu* show the gains that can result from an optimal balance of supplier and buyer power. Because Toyota buys a given component from several suppliers (some are in the *keiretsu*, some are independent), discipline is imposed down the network. Also, since Toyota's suppliers do not work exclusively for Toyota, they have an incentive to be flexible and adaptable.[41]

The *keiretsu* system ensured that high-quality parts were delivered on a just-in-time basis, a key factor in the high quality for which Japan's auto industry is well known. However, as U.S. and European automakers have closed the quality gap, larger Western parts makers are building economies of scale that enable them to operate at lower costs than small Japanese parts makers. Moreover, the stock holdings that Toyota, Nissan, and others have in their supplier network ties up capital that could be used for product development and other purposes. At Nissan, for example, a new management team from France recently began divesting some of the company's 1,300 *keiretsu* investments.[42]

Some observers have questioned whether *keiretsu* violate antitrust laws. As many observers have noted, the Japanese government frequently puts the interests of producers ahead of the interests of consumers. The *keiretsu* were formed in the early 1950s as regroupings of four large conglomerates—*zaibatsu*—that dominated the Japanese economy until 1945. *Zaibatsu* were dissolved after the occupational forces introduced antitrust as part of the reconstruction. Today, Japan's Fair Trade Commission appears to favor harmony rather than pursuing anticompetitive behavior. As a result, the U.S. Federal Trade Commission has launched several investigations of price fixing, price discrimination, and exclusive supply arrangements. Hitachi, Canon, and other Japanese companies have also been accused of restricting the availability of high-tech products in the U.S. market. The Justice Department has considered prosecuting the U.S. subsidiaries of Japanese companies if the parent company is found guilty of unfair trade practices in the Japanese market.[43]

How *Keiretsu* Affect American Business: Two Examples

Clyde Prestowitz provides the following example to show how *keiretsu* relationships have a potential impact on U.S. businesses. In the early 1980s, Nissan was in the market for a supercomputer to use in car design. Two vendors under consideration were Cray, the worldwide leader in supercomputers at the time, and Hitachi, which had no functional product to offer. When it appeared that

---

[40] The importance of the chain stores is eroding due to increasing sales at mass merchandisers not under the manufacturers' control.
[41] "Japanology, Inc. –Survey," *Economist* (March 6, 1993), p. 15.
[42] Norihiko Shirouzu, "U-Turn: A Revival at Nissan Shows There's Hope for Ailing Japan Inc.," *The Wall Street Journal* (November 16, 2000), pp. A1, A10.
[43] Rappoport, p. 84.

the purchase of a Cray computer was pending, Hitachi executives called for solidarity; both Nissan and Hitachi were members of the same big six *keiretsu*, the Fuyo group. Hitachi essentially mandated that Nissan show preference to Hitachi, a situation that rankled U.S. trade officials. Meanwhile, a coalition within Nissan was pushing for a Cray computer; ultimately, thanks to U.S. pressure on both Nissan and the Japanese government, the business went to Cray.

Prestowitz describes the Japanese attitude toward this type of business practice:[44]

> . . . It respects mutual obligation by providing a cushion against shocks. Today Nissan may buy a Hitachi computer. Tomorrow it may ask Hitachi to take some of its redundant workers. The slightly lesser performance it may get from the Hitachi computer is balanced against the broader considerations. Moreover, because the decision to buy Hitachi would be a favor, it would bind Hitachi closer and guarantee slavish service and future Hitachi loyalty to Nissan products. . . . This attitude of sticking together is what the Japanese mean by the long-term view; it is what enables them to withstand shocks and to survive over the long term.[45]

Because *keiretsu* relationships are crossing the Pacific and directly affecting the American market, U.S. companies have reason to be concerned with *keiretsu* outside the Japanese market as well. According to 1991 data compiled by Dodwell Marketing Consultants, in California alone *keiretsu* own more than half of the Japanese-affiliated manufacturing facilities. But the impact of *keiretsu* extends beyond the West Coast. Illinois-based Tenneco Automotive, a maker of shock absorbers and exhaust systems, does a great deal of worldwide business with the Toyota *keiretsu*. In 1990, however, Mazda dropped Tenneco as a supplier to its U.S. plant in Kentucky. Part of the business was shifted to Tokico Manufacturing, a Japanese transplant and a member of the Mazda *keiretsu*; a non-*keiretsu* Japanese company, KYB Industries, was also made a vendor. A Japanese auto executive explained the rationale behind the change: "First choice is a *keiretsu* company, second choice is a Japanese supplier, third is a local company."[46]

COOPERATIVE STRATEGIES IN SOUTH KOREA: *CHAEBOL*

South Korea has its own type of corporate alliance groups, known as *chaebol*. Like the Japanese *keiretsu*, **chaebol** are composed of dozens of companies, centered around a central bank or holding company, and dominated by a founding family. However, *chaebol* are a more recent phenomenon; in the early 1960s, Korea's military dictator granted government subsidies and export credits to a select group of companies. By the 1980s, Daewoo, Hyundai, LG, and Samsung had become leading producers of low-cost consumer electronics products. The *chaebol* were a driving force behind South Korea's economic miracle; GNP increased from $1.9 billion in 1960 to $238 billion in 1990. Since the economic crisis of 1997, however, South Korean President Kim Dae Jung has pressured *chaebol* leaders to

---

[44] For years, Prestowitz has argued that Japan's industry structure—*keiretsu* included—gives its companies unfair advantages. A more moderate view might be that any business decision must have an economic justification. Thus, a moderate would caution against overstating the effect of *keiretsu*.

[45] Clyde Prestowitz, *Trading Places: How We Are Giving Our Future to Japan and How to Reclaim It* (New York: Basic Books, 1989), pp. 299–300.

[46] Carla Rappoport, "Why Japan Keeps on Winning," *Fortune* (July 15, 1991), p. 84.

initiate reform. Prior to the crisis, the *chaebol* had become bloated and heavily leveraged; recently, some progress has been made in improving corporate governance, changing corporate cultures, and reducing debt levels.[47]

TWENTY-FIRST CENTURY COOPERATIVE STRATEGIES: TARGETING THE DIGITAL FUTURE

Increasing numbers of companies in all parts of the world are entering into alliances that resemble *keiretsu*. The phrase *digital keiretsu* is frequently used to describe alliances between companies in several industries—computers, communications, consumer electronics, and entertainment—that are undergoing transformation and convergence. These processes are the result of tremendous advances in the ability to transmit and manipulate vast quantities of audio, video, and data and the rapidly approaching era of a global electronic "superhighway" composed of fiber optic cable and digital switching equipment.

One U.S. technology alliance, Sematech, is unique in that it is the direct result of government industrial policy. The U.S. government, concerned that key companies in the domestic semiconductor industry were having difficulty competing with Japan, agreed to subsidize a consortium of 14 technology companies beginning in 1987. Sematech was originally comprised of 700 employees, some permanent and some on loan from IBM, AT&T, Advanced Micro Devices, Intel, and other companies. The task facing the consortium was to save the U.S. chipmaking equipment industry, whose manufacturers were rapidly losing market share in the face of intense competition from Japan. Although initially plagued by attitudinal and cultural differences between different factions, Sematech eventually helped chipmakers try new approaches with their equipment vendors. By 1991, the Sematech initiative, along with other factors such as the economic downturn in Japan, reversed the market share slide of the semiconductor equipment industry. Sematech's creation heralded a new era in cooperation among technology companies. As the company has expanded internationally, its membership roster has expanded to include Agere Systems, Conexant, Hewlett-Packard, Hynix, Infineon, Motorola, Philips, STMicroelectronics, and Taiwan Semiconductor. Companies in a variety of industries are pursuing similar types of alliances.

Beyond Strategic Alliances

The "relationship enterprise" is said to be the next stage of evolution of the strategic alliance. Groupings of firms in different industries and countries, they will be held together by common goals that encourage them to act almost as a single firm. Cyrus Freidheim, former vice chairman of the Booz Allen Hamilton consulting firm, outlined an alliance that, in his opinion, might be representative of an early relationship enterprise. He suggests that, within the next few decades, Boeing, British Airways, Siemens, TNT, and Snecma might jointly build several new airports in China. As part of the package, British Airways and TNT would be granted preferential routes and landing slots, the Chinese government would contract to buy all its aircraft from Boeing/Snecma, and Siemens would provide air traffic control systems for all 10 airports.[48]

More than the simple strategic alliances we know today, relationship enterprises will be super-alliances among global giants, with revenues approaching

---

[47] "The Chaebol Spurn Change," *Economist* (July 27, 2000), pp. 59–60.
[48] "The Global Firm: R.I.P." *Economist* (February 6, 1993), p. 69.

$1 trillion. They would be able to draw on extensive cash resources, circumvent antitrust barriers, and, with home bases in all major markets, enjoy the political advantage of being a "local" firm almost anywhere. This type of alliance is not driven simply by technological change but by the political necessity of having multiple home bases.

Another perspective on the future of cooperative strategies envisions the emergence of the "virtual corporation." As described in a *Business Week* cover story, the virtual corporation "will seem to be a single entity with vast capabilities but will really be the result of numerous collaborations assembled only when they're needed."[49] On a global level, the virtual corporation could combine the twin competencies of cost effectiveness and responsiveness; thus, it could pursue the "think globally, act locally" philosophy with ease. This reflects the trend toward "mass customization." The same forces that are driving the formation of the digital *keiretsu*—high-speed communication networks, for example—are embodied in the virtual corporation. As noted by William Davidow and Michael Malone in their book *The Virtual Corporation*, "The success of a virtual corporation will depend on its ability to gather and integrate a massive flow of information throughout its organizational components and intelligently act upon that information."[50]

Why has the virtual corporation suddenly burst onto the scene? Previously, firms lacked the technology to facilitate this type of data management. Today's distributed databases, networks, and open systems make possible the kinds of data flow required for the virtual corporation. In particular, these data flows permit superior supply chain management. Ford provides an interesting example of how technology is improving information flows among the far-flung operations of a single company. Ford's $6 billion "world car"—known as the Mercury Mystique and Ford Contour in the United States, the Mondeo in Europe—was developed using an international communications network linking computer workstations of designers and engineers on three continents.[51]

MARKET EXPANSION STRATEGIES

Companies must decide whether to expand by seeking new markets in existing countries or, alternatively, seeking new country markets for already identified and served market segments.[52] These two dimensions in combination produce four **market expansion strategy** options, as shown in Table 9-7. Strategy 1, **country and market concentration**, involves targeting a limited number of customer segments in a few countries. This is typically a starting point for most companies. It matches company resources and market investment needs. Unless a company is large and

Table 9-7			Market	
			Concentration	Diversification
Market Expansion Strategies	Country	Concentration	1. Narrow focus	2. Country focus
		Diversification	3. Country diversification	4. Global diversification

49 John Byrne, "The Virtual Corporation," *Business Week* (February 8, 1993), p. 103.
50 William Davidow and Michael Malone, *The Virtual Corporation: Structuring and Revitalizing the Corporation for the 21st Century* (New York: HarperBusiness, 1993), p. 59.
51 Julie Edelson Halpert "One Car, Worldwide, with Strings Pulled from Michigan," *The New York Times* (August 29, 1993), sec. 3, p. 7.
52 This section draws on I. Ayal and J. Zif, "Market Expansion Strategies in Multinational Marketing," *Journal of Marketing* 43 (Spring 1979), pp. 84–94; and "Competitive Market Choice Strategies in Multinational Marketing," *Columbia Journal of World Business* (Fall 1978), pp. 72–81.

endowed with ample resources, this strategy may be the only realistic way to begin.

In Strategy 2, **country concentration and market diversification**, a company serves many markets in a few countries. This strategy was implemented by many European companies that remained in Europe and sought growth by expanding into new markets. It is also the approach of the American companies that decide to diversify in the U.S. market as opposed to going international with existing products or creating new global products. According to the U.S. Department of Commerce, the majority of U.S. companies that export limit their sales to five or fewer markets. This means that U.S. companies typically pursue Strategies 1 or 2.

Strategy 3, **country diversification and market concentration**, is the classic global strategy whereby a company seeks out the world market for a product. The appeal of this strategy is that, by serving the world customer, a company can achieve a greater accumulated volume and lower costs than any competitor and, therefore, have an unassailable competitive advantage. This is the strategy of the well-managed business that serves a distinct need and customer category.

Strategy 4, **country and market diversification**, is the corporate strategy of a global, multibusiness company such as Matsushita. Overall, Matsushita is multicountry in scope and its various business units and groups serve multiple segments. Thus, at the level of corporate strategy, Matsushita may be said to be pursuing Strategy 4. At the operating business level, however, managers of individual units must focus on the needs of the world customer in their particular global market. In Table 9-7, this is Strategy 3—country diversification and market concentration. An increasing number of companies all over the world are beginning to see the importance of market share not only in the home or domestic market but also in the world market. Success in overseas markets can boost a company's total volume and lower its cost position.

Companies that wish to move beyond exporting and importing can avail themselves of a wide range of alternative **market entry strategies**. Each alternative has distinct advantages and disadvantages associated with it; the alternatives can be ranked on a continuum representing increasing levels of investment, commitment, and risk. **Licensing** can generate revenue flow with little new investment; it can be a good choice for a company that possesses advanced technology, a strong brand image, or valuable intellectual property. **Contract manufacturing** and **franchising** are two specialized forms of licensing that are widely used in global marketing.

A higher level of involvement outside the home country may involve **foreign direct investment (FDI)**. This can take many forms. **Joint ventures** offer two or more companies the opportunity to share risk and combine value chain strengths. Companies considering joint ventures must plan carefully and communicate with partners to avoid "divorce." Foreign direct investment can also be used to establish company operations outside the home country through **greenfield investment**, acquisition of a minority or majority **equity stake** in a foreign business, or taking **ownership** of an existing business entity through merger or outright acquisition.

Cooperative alliances known as **global strategic partnerships (GSPs)** represent an important market entry strategy in the twenty-first century. GSPs are ambitious, reciprocal, cross-border alliances that may involve business partners in a number of different country markets. GSPs are particularly well suited to emerging markets in Central and Eastern Europe, Asia, and Latin America. Western businesspeople should also be aware of two special forms of cooperation found in Asia, namely Japan's *keiretsu* and South Korea's *chaebol*.

To assist managers in thinking through the various alternatives, market expansion strategies can be represented in matrix form: **country and market concentration**, **country concentration and market diversification**, **country diversification and market concentration**, and **country and market diversification**. The preferred expansion strategy will be a reflection of a company's stage of development (i.e., whether it is international, multinational, global, or transnational). The Stage 5 transnational combines the strengths of these four stages into an integrated network to leverage worldwide learning.

1. What are the advantages and disadvantages of using licensing as a market entry tool? Give examples of companies from different countries that use licensing as a global marketing strategy.

2. The president of XYZ Manufacturing Company of Buffalo, New York, comes to you with a license offer from a company in Osaka. In return for sharing the company's patents and know-how, the Japanese company will pay a license fee of 5 percent of the ex-factory price of all products sold based on the U.S. company's license. The president wants your advice. What would you tell him?

3. What is foreign direct investment (FDI)? What forms can FDI take?

4. What is meant by the phrase *global strategic partnership*? In what ways does this form of market entry strategy differ from more traditional forms such as joint ventures?

5. What is *keiretsu*? How does this form of industrial structure affect companies that compete with Japan or that are trying to enter the Japanese market?

6. Which strategic options for market entry or expansion would a small company be likely to pursue? A large company?

Case 9-1

Ford Bets Billions on Jaguar

In 1989, the Ford Motor Company acquired Jaguar PLC of Coventry, England, for $2.6 billion. L. Lindsay Halstead, then chairman of Ford of Europe, said the acquisition fulfilled "a longtime strategic objective of entering the luxury car market in a significant way." Ford lacked a high-end luxury model for both the U.S. and European markets, and the company was betting it could leverage an exclusive nameplate by launching a new, less expensive line of Jaguars and selling it to more people. The challenge was to execute this strategy without diminishing Jaguar's reputation; as Daniel Jones, a professor at the University of Cardiff and an auto industry expert, noted, the Ford name is synonymous with "bread and butter" cars. Meanwhile, Ford's Japanese competitors, including Honda, Nissan, and Toyota, pursued a different strategy: They launched new nameplates and upgraded their dealer organizations. Status- and quality-conscious car buyers have embraced Lexus, Infiniti, and other new luxury sedans that offer high performance and outstanding dealer organizations.

In 2006, Jaguar launched the 420 hp XKR luxury sports car. The company, which is part of Ford Motor Company's Premier Automotive Group, faces strong competition in Europe from Toyota.

Ford also confronted other challenges. Despite Jaguar's classy image and distinguished racing heritage, the cars were also legendary for their unreliability. Gears sometimes wouldn't shift, headlights wouldn't light, and the brakes sometimes caught fire. Part of the problem could be traced to manufacturing: in 1990, there were 2,500 defects per 100 cars produced. By 1992, that number had been reduced to 500 defects per 100 cars. Even so, in the closely watched J.D. Power rankings, Jaguar's quality in 1992 was rated just a notch above that of the lowly Yugo. Ironically, die-hard Jaguar loyalists seemed to thrive on the misery associated with owning an unreliable car. Jaguar clubs in the United States bestowed "Cat Bite" awards on members with the best tales of woe.

Because Jaguar was arguably one of the world's worst auto-manufacturing operations, Ford invested heavily to update and upgrade Jaguar's plant facilities and improve productivity. As a benchmark, Ford's manufacturing experts knew that German luxury carmakers could build a vehicle in 80 hours; in Japan, the figure was 20 hours. If Jaguar were ever to achieve world-class status, Jaguar's assembly time of 110 hours per car had to be drastically reduced. Jaguar's chief executive, Sir Nicholas Scheele, attacked the quality problem on a number of different fronts. For example, line employees made telephone calls to Jaguar owners who were experiencing problems with their vehicles.

As the decade came to an end, Jaguar introduced three new vehicles. In 1997, amid industry estimates that Ford's total investment had reached $6 billion, Jaguar launched the XK8 coupe and roadster. With a base price of $64,900, styling cues clearly identified this model as the successor to Jaguar's legendary XK-E, or E-Type. In spring 1999, the S-Type sedan was introduced to widespread acclaim. The new model was based on the same platform as the parent company's Lincoln LS sport sedan. One observer called the S-Type a "handsome car, instantly recognizable as a Jaguar, yet totally contemporary." In 2001, the long-awaited "baby Jaguar," the $30,000 X-Type compact sport sedan, was unveiled. Company executives hoped to attract a new generation of drivers and capture a significant share of the entry-level luxury market dominated by the BMW 3-series and the

Jaguar's S-type represented the venerable automaker's bid to become a mainstream luxury nameplate and double its North American sales to 80,000 cars each year. In terms of styling, the $45,000 S-Type recalls the classic Jaguar designs of the 1950s and 1960s. Worldwide, Jaguar executives hoped to quadruple sales from 50,000 units to 200,000 units by 2003. Unfortunately, that goal proved to be unrealistic.

In 1988, its best sales year before the acquisition, Jaguar sold fewer than 50,000 cars worldwide. Ford set a production target of 150,000 cars by the end of the 1990s, two-thirds of which would be the lower-priced sporty sedan. Ford executives also expected Jaguar to show a positive cash flow by the end of 1992. Unfortunately, the Jaguar acquisition coincided with the global recession that hurt sales in Japan, Germany, and the United States. To make matters worse, a 10 percent luxury tax imposed in the United States was a deterrent to potential buyers. By 1991, Jaguar sales slipped to slightly more than 25,000 cars. In the face of losses totaling $431 million in 1990 and 1991, Ford scaled back its original end-of-decade volume target to 100,000 cars.

Mercedes C-Class. The X-Type was built on the same platform as the Ford Contour.

The early signs were positive. In 2000, Jaguar sold 90,000 cars worldwide; in 2002, first-year sales of the X-Type boosted Jaguar's worldwide sales by 29 percent, to 130,000 vehicles. Unfortunately, the company was not able to sustain the 2002 sales peak. A backlash began to develop. For example, critics of the X-Type derided it as a "warmed-over Ford." Critics also found fault with Ford for failing to move Jaguar's styling forward enough. As one long-time Jaguar owner explained, "They lost their way in what the public wanted. Instead of making Jaguar a niche player, where it should be, they tried to go the mass-production route. That may very well work for the Ford Fusion, but that's not Jaguar's forte." In 2005, bowing to pressures to move the venerable nameplate upmarket again, it was announced that the least expensive Jaguar model, the 2.5 liter X-Type, would be discontinued.

> *"We have to fix the Jaguar business. The cars are great. Quality has improved. It's not a product problem. It's a business problem."*
> William Ford, Jr., Chairman, Ford Motor Company

The decision came as Ford's corporate situation was worsening. The company lost $1.6 billion in the first half of 2006 alone; Jaguar's 2006 sales goal was a projected 90,000 vehicles. There was some good news: The $75,000 XK coupe wowed the automotive world, and initial sales have been strong. Ford's Premier Auto Group, which includes Jaguar, Volvo, Aston Martin, and Land Rover, was expected to show a profit in 2007. Despite the promising outlook, some industry observers suggest that Ford should sell the Jaguar business. Charles Lemonides, an institutional investor, said, "Ford doesn't necessarily get a halo effect from the brand, nor does it get a significant marketplace presence from the brand. It's not clear what Ford gains from having it. It will never be big enough to be important to Ford."

Discussion Questions

1. Do you agree with Ford's decision to acquire Jaguar 20 years ago? What was more valuable to Ford—the physical assets or the name?

2. Assess management's decision to introduce the X-Type to broaden Jaguar's appeal from niche player to major competitor in the luxury segment.

3. Ford recently announced it would sell Aston Martin. Should Ford sell the Jaguar business as well? If so, is the buyer likely to be American, European, or Asian?

Sources: Gordon Fairclough, "Bill Ford Jr.: For Auto Makers, China Is the New Frontier," *The Wall Street Journal* (October 27, 2006), p. B5; James Mackintosh, "Ford's Luxury Unit Hits Problems," *Financial Times* (October 24, 2006), p. 23; Sharon Silke Carty, "Will Ford Make the Big Leap?" *USAToday* (August 31, 2006), pp. 1B, 2B; James Macintosh, "Jaguar Still Aiming to Claw Back Market Share," *Financial Times* (July 20, 2006), p. 14; Reinventing a '60s Classic, *"The Wall Street Journal* (May 5, 2006), p. W9; James R. Healy, "Cheapest Jags Get Kicked to the Curb," *USA Today* (March 29, 2005), p. 1B; Danny Hakim, "Restoring the Heart of Ford," *The New York Times* (November 14, 2001), pp. C1, C6; Haig Simonian, "Jag's Faces for the Future," *Financial Times* (November 7–November 8, 1998), p. 12; Joann S. Lublin and Craig Forman, "Going Upscale: Ford Snares Jaguar, But $2.5 Billion Is High Price for Prestige," *The Wall Street Journal* (November 3, 1989), pp. A1, A4; Steven Prokesch, "Jaguar Battle at a Turning Point," *The New York Times* (October 29, 1990), p. C1; Prokesch, "Ford's Jaguar Bet: Payoff Isn't Close," *The New York Times* (April 21, 1992) p. C1; Robert Johnson, "Jaguar Owners Love Company and Sharing Their Horror Stories," *The Wall Street Journal* (September 28, 1993), p. A1.

Case 9-2
SABMiller in China

South African Breweries PLC had a problem. The company owned more than 100 breweries in 24 countries. South Africa, where the company had a commanding 98 percent share of the beer market, accounted for about 14 percent of annual revenues. However, South Africa's currency, the rand, was quite volatile. Moreover, most of the company's brands, which include Castle Lager, Pilsner Urquell, and Carling Black Label, were sold on a local or regional basis; none had the global status of Heineken, Amstel, or Guinness. Nor were the company's brands well known in the key U.S. market, where a growing number of the "echo boom"—the children of the nation's 75 million baby boomers—were reaching drinking age.

In 2002, a solution presented itself: South African Breweries had an opportunity to buy the Miller Brewing unit from Philip Morris. The $3.6 billion deal created SABMiller, a new company that ranks as the world's number three brewer in terms of production volume; InBev and Anheuser-Busch rank first and second, respectively. Miller operates nine breweries in the United States, where its flagship brand, Miller Lite, had been losing market share for a number of years. The challenge facing Graham McKay, SABMiller's CEO, was to revitalize the Miller Lite brand in the United States and then launch Miller in Europe as a premium brand.

A few years ago, South African Breweries was a local company that dominated its domestic market. Using joint ventures and acquisitions, the company expanded into the rest of Africa as well as key emerging markets such as China, India, and Central Europe. Today, following the acquisition of Miller, SABMiller is the world's second largest brewer with a strong presence in the U.S. market.

In 1998, South Africa Breweries shifted its stock listing from Johannesburg to the London Stock Exchange; the move meant the company was in a better position to raise equity capital. Recognizing the need for global scale, McKay immediately went on an acquisition drive in Europe, starting in Hungary. He noted, "All the growth to be had is outside the developed world." In the former communist countries of Central and Eastern Europe, the strategy took the form of buying privatized breweries, modernizing them, and using Western marketing techniques to build the brands locally. McKay also acquired several breweries in China, the world's second-largest beer market behind the United States.

As for the new Miller unit, Norman Adami was named CEO six months after the acquisition. Miller had less than 20 percent of the $67 billion U.S. market for domestic beer with brands such as Miller Lite, Miller Genuine Draft, and Miller High Life; archrival Anheuser-Busch had about 50 percent. New packaging was the first step in revitalizing the brand; the color of Miller's label was changed from silver to royal blue, and the typography was made bolder. In January 2003, Miller launched a controversial TV advertising campaign featuring two attractive women whose argument about whether Miller "tastes great" or is "less filling" escalates into a catfight. Some industry observers interpreted the ads as indicating that SABMiller was prepared to take greater creative risks than Miller's former corporate parent. Bob Garfield, the influential advertising critic for *Advertising Age* magazine, denounced the spots for their "*Maxim*-style neo-pinupism." Despite all the publicity surrounding the campaign, Miller continues to struggle. CEO Adami expects the U.S. sales picture to worsen before it improves. The brewery launched a corporate branding ad campaign designed to highlight the brand's history as an innovator.

SABMiller and its competitors are also making strategic investments in China, the world's largest beer market with $6 billion in annual sales. As Sylvia Mu Yin, an analyst with Euromonitor, notes, "Local brewers are keen to explore strategic alliances with large multinational companies. At the same time, foreign companies are eager to sell to the 1.3 billion Chinese, but lack local knowledge." SABMiller has partnerships with more than two dozen Chinese breweries. In 2003, SABMiller purchased a 29 percent equity share of Harbin Brewery Group, China's oldest and fourth-largest brewer. The brand is popular in northeast China, and SABMiller hoped to expand the brand in other regions. However, in 2004, Anheuser-Busch announced that it was also buying 29 percent of Harbin. That, in turn, triggered a bid by SABMiller to buy the rest of Harbin's shares. When the resulting bidding war was over, Anheuser-Busch emerged as the victor.

Meanwhile, some of SABMiller's local brands are being introduced in the United States. The company hopes to build Pilsner Urquell, the number one beer in the Czech Republic, into a national brand in the United States. If that effort succeeds, it can be the foundation for building Urquell into a global premium brand that rivals Heineken. SABMiller is also launching Tyskie, a popular Polish brand, in cities such as Chicago that are home to large Polish immigrant communities. The company hopes to successfully position Miller Genuine Draft as a premium global brand in Eastern Europe. Some industry observers predict it will be a hard sell. As one analyst noted, "American beer has a bad reputation in Eastern Europe, because beer drinkers think it tastes like water." Will all these efforts succeed? SABMiller's chief harbors no doubts; if the Miller acquisition does *not* pay off, he says, "I'll fall on my sword."

Discussion Questions

1. Describe SABMiller's global marketing strategy.
2. Assess the potential for repositioning Pilsner Urquell into a global brand.
3. Can Miller Genuine Draft—or any American beer—be positioned as a premium global brand?
4. Why are SABMiller, Anheuser-Busch, and InBev investing in China?

Sources: Maggie Urry and Adam Jones, "SABMiller Chief Preaches the Lite Fantastic," *Financial Times* (November 21, 2003), p. 22; Dan Bilefsky and Christopher Lawton, "SABMiller Has U.S. Hangover," *The Wall Street Journal* (November 20, 2003), p. B5; Christopher Lawton and Dan Bilefsky, "Miller Lite Now: Haste Great, Less Selling," *The Wall Street Journal* (October 4, 2002), pp. B1, B6; Nicol Deglil Innocenti, "Fearless Embracer of Challenge," *Financial Times* Special Report—Investing in South Africa (October 2, 2003), p. 6; David Pringle, "Miller Deal Brings Stability to SAB," *The Wall Street Journal* (May 31, 2002), p. B6; John Willman, "Time for Another Round," *Financial Times* (June 21, 1999), p. 15

10 Brand and Product Decisions in Global Marketing

"Thin is in." That is the verdict from consumers in all parts of the world who have made widescreen, flat-panel TV sets one of the hottest new consumer electronics products in years. The new digital sets represent a major improvement over the analog cathode-ray tube (CRT) technology that was an integral part of TV design for more than 50 years. Today's TVs incorporate innovative technologies such as liquid-crystal display (LCD) screens that previously were offered with personal computers. Television manufacturers are now offering a variety of screen technology options, including LCD, plasma, Digital Light Processing (DLP), and others. No matter which type of set they buy, consumers agree on one point: These TV sets are sleek, sexy, and cool. They also offer vastly improved performance compared to conventional TVs. Viewers are enthralled by the sharper, brighter image quality and multichannel sound of high-definition TV broadcasts; they also enjoy watching wide-screen DVD movies at home. In short, the consumer electronics industry has produced a much-needed new hit product.

The success of Samsung, Sharp, and other marketers of flat-panel HDTVs highlights the fact that products—and the brands associated with them—are arguably the most crucial element of a company's marketing program; they are integral to the company's value proposition. In Part III, we surveyed several topics that directly impact product strategy as a company approaches global markets. Input from a company's MIS and market research studies guides the product development process. The market must be segmented, one or more target markets selected, and a strong positioning established. Global marketers must also make decisions about exporting and sourcing; other market entry strategies, such as licensing and strategic alliances, may be considered as well. As we will see in Part IV, every aspect of a firm's marketing program, including pricing, distribution, and communication policies, must fit the product. This chapter examines the major dimensions of global product and brand decisions. First is a review of basic product and brand concepts, followed by a discussion of local, international, and global products and brands. Product design criteria are identified, and attitudes toward foreign products are explored. The next section outlines strategic alternatives available to global marketers. Finally, new product issues in global marketing are discussed.

The growing popularity of flat-panel HDTVs has propelled Sharp and Samsung Electronics to the front ranks of the world's consumer electronics companies. In 2007, Sharp unveiled a 108-inch LCD TV—the world's largest. As prices fall, global demand is growing rapidly. The Consumer Electronics Association estimates that 55 percent of U.S. households currently own at least one high-definition television.

BASIC PRODUCT CONCEPTS

The product "P" of the marketing mix is at the heart of the challenges and opportunities facing global companies today: Management must develop product and brand policies and strategies that are sensitive to market needs, competition, and company ambitions and resources on a global scale. Effective global marketing often entails finding a balance between the payoff from extensively adapting products and brands to local market preferences and the benefits that come from concentrating company resources on relatively standardized global products and brands.

A **product** is a good, service, or idea with both tangible and intangible attributes that collectively create value for a buyer or user. A product's *tangible* attributes can be assessed in physical terms such as weight, dimensions, or materials used. Consider, for example, a flat-panel TV with an LCD screen that measures 42 inches across. The unit weighs 100 pounds, is 4 inches deep, is equipped with two high-definition media interface (HDMI) connections, has a built-in tuner capable of receiving high-definition TV signals over the air, and delivers a screen resolution of 1080p. These tangible, physical features translate into benefits that enhance the enjoyment of watching HDTV broadcasts and DVD movies. Accessories such as wall mounts and floor stands enhance the value offering by enabling great flexibility in placing the set in a living room or home theater. *Intangible* product attributes, including status associated with product ownership, a manufacturer's service commitment, and a brand's overall reputation or mystique, are also important. When shopping for a new TV set, for example, many people want "the best": They want a TV loaded with features (tangible product elements), as well as one that is "cool" and makes a status statement (intangible product element).

Product Types

A frequently used framework for classifying products distinguishes between consumer and industrial goods. For example, Kodak offers products and services to both amateur and professional photographers worldwide. Consumer and industrial goods, in turn, can be further classified on the basis of criteria such as buyer orientation. Buyer orientation is a composite measure of the amount of effort a customer expends, the level of risk associated with a purchase, and buyer involvement in the purchase. The buyer orientation framework includes such categories as convenience, preference, shopping, and specialty goods. Although film is often a low-involvement purchase, many film buyers in the United States show a strong preference for Kodak film, and significant numbers of Japanese photographers prefer Fuji. Products can also be categorized in terms of their life span (durable, nondurable, and disposable). Kodak and other companies market both single-use (disposable) cameras as well as more expensive units that are meant to last for many years. As these examples from the photo industry suggest, traditional product classification frameworks are fully applicable to global marketing.

Brands

A **brand** is a complex bundle of images and experiences in the customer's mind. Brands perform two important functions. First, a brand represents a promise by a particular company about a particular product; it is a sort of quality certification. Second, brands enable customers to better organize their shopping experience by helping them seek out and find a particular product. Thus, an important brand function is to differentiate a particular company's offering from all others.

Customers integrate all their experiences of observing, using, or consuming a product with everything they hear and read about it. Information about products and brands comes from a variety of sources and cues, including advertising, publicity, word-of mouth, sales personnel, and packaging. Perceptions of service after the sale, price, and distribution are also taken into account (Figure 10-1). The sum

Figure 10-1

Components of a Brand Image

Wall Street Journal: "BMW is one of the top brands in any industry. For you, as CEO, are there special responsibilities you have in maintaining or building your brand image?"

Helmut Panke, Chief Executive Officer, BMW: "As provocative as it sounds, the biggest task is to be able to say, 'No.' Because in the end, authentic brand management boils down to understanding that a brand is a promise that has to be fulfilled everywhere, at any time. So when something doesn't fit, you must make sure that that is not done. The most important role of senior management, not just the CEO, is to understand that the brand is not just a label that you can put on and take off. BMW . . . settles for fewer compromises, which goes back to what the brand stands for."

Source: The Wall Street Journal (Eastern Edition) by Neal E. Boudette. Copyright 2003 by Dow Jones & Company, Inc. Reproduced with permission of Dow Jones & Company, Inc. in the format Textbook via Copyright Clearance Center.

of impressions is a **brand image**, a single—but often complex—mental image about both the product itself and the company that markets it.

Another important brand concept is **brand equity**, which represents the total value that accrues to a product as a result of a company's cumulative investments in the marketing of the brand. Just as a homeowner's equity grows as a mortgage is paid off over the years, brand equity grows as a company invests in the brand. Brand equity can also be thought of as an asset representing the value created by the relationship between the brand and customers over time. The stronger the relationship, the greater the equity. For example, the value of global megabrands such as Coca-Cola and Marlboro runs in the tens of *billions* of dollars.[1]

Warren Buffett, the legendary American investor who heads Berkshire Hathaway, asserts that the global power of brands such as Coca-Cola and Gillette permits the companies that own them to set up a protective moat around their economic castles. As Buffett once explained, "The average company, by contrast, does battle daily without any such means of protection."[2] That protection often yields added profit because the owners of powerful brand names can typically command higher prices for their products than can owners of lesser brands. In other words, the strongest global brands have tremendous brand equity.

Companies develop logos, distinctive packaging, and other communication devices to provide visual representations of their brands. A logo can take a variety of forms, starting with the brand name itself. For example, the Coca-Cola brand is expressed in part by a *word mark* consisting of the words *Coke* and *Coca-Cola* written in a distinctive white script. The "wave" that appears on red Coke cans and bottle labels is an example of a *nonword mark logo*, sometimes known as a *brand symbol*. Nonword marks such as the Nike swoosh, the three-pronged Mercedes star, and McDonald's golden arches have the great advantage of transcending language and are, therefore, especially valuable to global marketers. To protect the substantial investment of time and money required to build and sustain brands, companies register brand names, logos, and other brand elements as trademarks or service marks. As discussed in Chapter 5, safeguarding trademarks and other forms of intellectual property is a key issue in global marketing.

"We have to shift to high value-added products, and to do that we need to improve our brand."[3]

Noboru Fujimoto, President, Sharp Electronics Corporation

---

[1] For a complete discussion of brand equity, see Kevin Lane Keller, *Strategic Brand Management* (Upper Saddle River, NJ: Prentice Hall, 1998), Chapter 2.

[2] John Willman, "Labels That Say It All," *Financial Times—Weekend Money* (October 25–26, 1997), p. 1.

[3] Peter Landers, "Sharp Covets the Sony Model: A Sexy, High-end Image," *The Wall Street Journal* (March 11, 2002), p. A13.

the rest of the story

Wide Screen Flat-Panel TVs Rule

The explosive growth of HDTV sales has been a boon for the world's leading electronics marketers. In 2005, South Korea's LG Electronics was the world's number one TV set maker with sales of 18.2 million sets. Samsung was number two with sales of 16.3 million units. By contrast, Sony, long a world leader in TV manufacturing and a strong global brand name, ranked fifth in TV set market share. Although Sony is legendary for its spirit of innovation, it was a late entrant into the growing market for flat-panel displays. Sony focused on its Wega-brand TVs that offered flat screens in a conventional CRT format; company engineers insisted that Sony's Trinitron CRT technology was superior to flat-panel technology which, in any event, the company had no experience producing.

Sony is a good example of a company whose preference for its own technology has proven to be counterproductive. Innovation guru Henry Chesbrough notes that today, the technologies needed for products are so complex and with rivals so numerous that no company—even one as big and capable as Sony—can develop all it needs internally. A case in point is the cost of building an LCD production facility. The price tag is about $2.7 billion, too high a cost for Sony to bear alone. Sony's strong track record as an innovator and inventor of whole classes of technologies blinded it to the merits of using technologies from other companies. It was hard hit by shrinking profit margins in its electronics business; in 2003, Sony announced it would close 12 of 17 factories that made analog TVs. It also announced a joint venture with Samsung to manufacture LCD sets. Meanwhile, new competitors, including Dell and Hewlett-Packard, have entered the TV market. Despite these new entrants into the industry, Sony's goal is to have 30 percent share of the global flat-panel market.

Prices have been dropping as the manufacturers build new, state-of-the-art factories. Because the screen panel itself represents about 85 percent of the cost of an entire set, companies are innovating to bring the cost down. For example, Corning is a key supplier of glass products to the industry; the company recently found a way to ship 500 glass panel sheets in the space that would previously only accommodate 20 sheets. The result was a dramatic drop in shipping costs to Asian manufacturers. Likewise, Sharp and other manufacturers have found ways to reduce the amount of time required to insert the liquid-crystal substance between the glass panels. In 2001, five days were required to fabricate a finished screen; today, a 30-inch screen can be produced in just two hours. Some industry observers expect the price of a 42-inch LCD model to drop below $1,000 sometime in 2007.

There is some confusion in the marketplace, as consumers try to choose between the different technologies. Also, although an increasing amount of programming is available in the widescreen format, many shows are still broadcast in standard definition; ironically, the 480i standard definition images look worse on an expensive HDTV than on a conventional TV. Many viewers are not sure when they are watching an actual high-definition broadcast as opposed to a standard definition one. The manufacturers themselves are facing another challenge: How to keep revenues and profits strong as manufacturers slash prices to gain market share. Prices are expected to stabilize as the rate of new factory openings slows.

Sources: Evan Ramstad, "Flat-Panel TVs, Long Touted, Finally are Becoming the Norm," The Wall Street Journal (April 15/16, 2006), pp. A1, A2; Martin Fackler, "Running Away from the Pack In Japan," The New York Times (March 22, 2006), pp. C1, C5; Eric A. Taub, "Flat-Panel Sets to Enhance the Visibility of Samsung," The New York Times (January 8, 2004), pp. C1, C4; Andrew Ward, Kathrin Hille, Michiyo Nakamoto, Chris Nuttal, "Flat Out for Flat Screens: The Battle to Dominate the $29 bn Market Is Heating Up but the Risk of Glut Is Growing," Financial Times (December 24, 2003), p. 9; Evan Ramstad, "Rise of Flat-Screen TVs Reshapes Industry," The Wall Street Journal (November 20, 2003), p. B8; Phred Dvorak, "Facing a Slump, Sony to Revamp Product Lines," The New York Times (September 12, 2003), p. B1, B2; Michiyo Nakamoto, "Sony Discusses Screen Venture with Samsung," Financial Times (September 23, 2003), p. 19; Elliot Spagat, "Is It Finally Time to Get a Flat-Panel TV?" The Wall Street Journal (September 12, 2002), p. D1; Peter Landers, "Sharp Covets the Sony Model: A Sexy, High-End Image," The Wall Street Journal (March 11, 2002), p. A13.

Local Products and Brands

A **local product** or **local brand** is one that has achieved success in a single national market. Sometimes a global company creates local products and brands in an effort to cater to the needs and preferences of particular country markets. For example, Coca-Cola has developed several branded drink products for sale only in Japan, including a noncarbonated, ginseng-flavored beverage; a blended tea known as Sokenbicha; and Lactia-brand fermented milk drink. In India, Coca-Cola markets Kinely brand bottled water. The spirits industry often creates brand extensions to leverage popular brands without large marketing expenditures. For example, Diageo PLC markets Gordon's Edge, a gin-based ready-to-drink beverage in the United Kingdom. Allied Domecq created TG, a brand flavored with Teacher's Scotch and guaraná, in Brazil.[4]

"There is a strong local heritage in the brewing industry. People identify with their local brewery, which makes beer different from detergents or electronic products."[5]

Karel Vuursteen, Chairman, Heineken

---

4   Deborah Ball, "Liquor Makers Go Local," *The Wall Street Journal* (February 13, 2003), p. B3.
5   John Willman, "Time for Another Round," *Financial Times* (June 21, 1999), p. 15.

Local products and brands also represent the lifeblood of domestic companies. Entrenched local products and brands can represent significant competitive hurdles to global companies entering new country markets. In China, for example, a sporting goods company started by Olympic gold medalist Li Ning sells more sneakers than global powerhouse Nike. In developing countries, global brands are sometimes perceived as overpowering local ones. Growing national pride can result in a social backlash that favors local products and brands. In China, a local TV set manufacturer, Changhong Electric Appliances, has built its share of the Chinese market from 6 percent to more than 22 percent by cutting prices and using patriotic advertising themes such as "Let Changhong hold the great flag of revitalizing our national industries."

White-goods maker Haier Group has also successfully fought off foreign competition and now accounts for 40 percent of China's refrigerator sales. In addition, Haier enjoys a 30 percent share of both the washing machine and air conditioner markets. Slogans stenciled on office walls delineate the aspirations of company president Zhang Ruimin: "Haier–Tomorrow's Global Brand Name," and "Never Say 'No' to the Market."[6] In 2002, Haier Group announced a strategic alliance with Taiwan's Sampo Group. The deal, which is valued at $300 million, calls for each company to manufacture and sell the other's refrigerators and telecommunications products both globally and locally.

International Products and Brands

International products and **international brands** are offered in several markets in a particular region. For example, a number of "Euro products" and "Euro brands" such as DaimlerChrysler's two-seat Smart car are available in Europe but not the rest of the world (see Case 10-2). The experience of GM with its Corsa model in the early 1990s provides a case study in how an international product or brand can be taken global. The Opel Corsa was a new model originally introduced in Europe. GM then decided to build different versions of the Corsa in China, Mexico, and Brazil. As David Herman, chairman of Adam Opel AG, noted, "The original concept was not that we planned to sell this car from the tip of Tierra del Fuego to the outer regions of Siberia. But we see its possibilities are limitless." GM calls the Corsa its "accidental world car."[7] Honda had a similar experience with the Fit, a five-door hatchback built on the company's Global Small Car platform. Following Fit's successful Japanese launch in 2001, Honda rolled out the vehicle in Europe (where it is known as Jazz). Over the next few years, Fit was introduced in Australia, South America, South Africa, and China. The Fit made its North American market debut in 2006.

Global Products and Brands

The globalization of industry is putting pressure on companies to develop global products and to leverage brand equity on a worldwide basis. A **global product** meets the wants and needs of a global market. A true global product is offered in all world regions, including the Triad and in countries at every stage of development. A **global brand** has the same name and, in some instances, a similar image and positioning throughout the world. Some companies are well established as global brands. For example, when Nestlé asserts that it "Makes the very best," the quality promise is understood and accepted globally.

---

[6] John Ridding, "China's Own Brands Get Their Acts Together," *Financial Times* (December 30, 1996), p. 6; Kathy Chen, "Global Cooling: Would America Buy a Refrigerator Labeled 'Made in Quingdao'?" *The Wall Street Journal* (September 17, 1997), pp. A1, A14.

[7] Diana Kurylko, "The Accidental World Car," *Automotive News* (June 27, 1994), p. 4.

In French ("La perfection au masculin"), German ("Für das Beste im Mann"), Italian ("Il meglio di un uomo"), Portuguese ("O melhor para o homem"), or any other language, Gillette's trademarked brand promise is easy to understand—especially when superstar athlete David Beckham is featured in the ad.

The same is true for Gillette ("The best a man can get"), BMW ("The ultimate driving machine"), GE ("Imagination at work"), Harley-Davidson ("An American legend"), Visa International ("Life takes Visa"), and many other global companies.

Former Gillette CEO Alfred Zeien explained his company's approach as follows:

> A multinational has operations in different countries. A global company views the world as a single country. We know Argentina and France are different, but we treat them the same. We sell them the same products, we use the same production methods, we have the same corporate policies. We even use the same advertising—in a different language, of course.[8]

As this quote implies, companies such as Gillette enjoy several benefits and advantages that derive from creating global products and utilizing global branding. These include economies of scale associated with creating a single ad campaign for the world and the advantages of executing a single brand strategy. All global companies are trying to increase the visibility of their brands, especially in the key markets such as the United States and China. Examples include Philips with its "Sense and simplicity" global image advertising and Siemens' recent "Be inspired" campaign.

In the twenty-first century, global brands are becoming increasingly important. As one research team noted:

> People in different nations, often with conflicting viewpoints, participate in a shared conversation, drawing upon shared symbols. One of the key symbols in that conversation is the global brand. Like entertainment stars, sports celebrities, and politicians, global brands have become a lingua franca for consumers all over the world. People may love or hate transnational companies, but they can't ignore them.[9]

[8] Victoria Griffith, "As Close as a Group Can Get to Global," *Financial Times* (April 7, 1998), p. 21.
[9] Douglas B. Holt, John A. Quelch, and Earl L. Taylor, "How Global Brands Compete," *Harvard Business Review* 82, no. 9 (September 2004), p. 69.

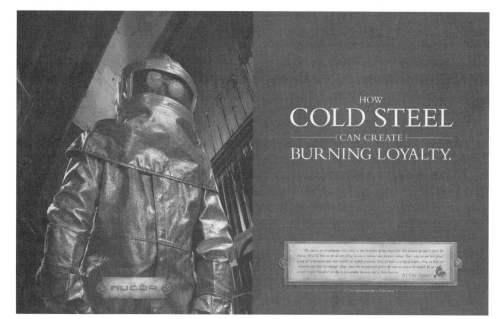

HOW
COLD STEEL
— CAN CREATE —
BURNING LOYALTY.

Nucor is a steel company best known for its pioneering use of the minimill. Minimills produce steel by melting scrap in electric arc furnaces. This process is much more efficient than that used by traditional integrated steel producers. Nucor uses print and online media for an integrated general branding campaign featuring the tagline "It's our nature." The campaign is designed to raise awareness about the company's stance on a variety of issues, including the environment, energy conservation, and the importance of creating a strong corporate culture.

These researchers note that brands that are marketed around the world are endowed with both an aura of excellence and a set of obligations. Worldwide, consumers, corporate buyers, governments, activists, and other groups associate global brands with three characteristics; consumers use these characteristics as a guide when making purchase decisions.

- *Quality signal.* Global brands compete fiercely with each other to provide world-class quality. A global brand name differentiates product offerings and allows marketers to charge premium prices.
- *Global myth.* Global brands are symbols of cultural ideals. As noted in Chapter 7, marketers can use global consumer culture positioning (GCCP) to communicate a brand's global identity and link that identity to aspirations in any part of the world.
- *Social responsibility.* Customers evaluate companies and brands in terms of how they address social problems and how they conduct business.

Note that a global brand is not the same thing as a global product. For example, personal stereos are a category of global product; Sony is a global brand. Many companies, including Sony, make personal stereos. However, Sony created the category more than 20 years ago when it introduced the Walkman in Japan. The Sony Walkman is an example of **combination** or **tiered branding**, whereby a corporate name (Sony) is combined with a product brand name (Walkman). By using combination branding, marketers can leverage a company's reputation while developing a distinctive brand identity for a line of products. The combination brand approach can be a powerful tool for introducing new products. Although Sony markets a number of local products, the company also has a stellar track record as a global corporate brand, a creator of global products, and a marketer of global brands. For example, using the Walkman brand name as a point of departure, Sony created the Discman portable CD player and the Watchman portable TV. Sony's recent global product-brand offerings include Bravia brand HDTV sets and the PlayStation family of video game consoles and portables (see Case 10-1).

Co-branding is a variation on combination branding in which two or more *different* company or product brands are featured prominently on product

STRATEGIC DECISION-MAKING *in global marketing*

"We believe strongly that there isn't a so-called global consumer, at least not when it comes to food and beverages. People have local tastes based on their unique cultures and traditions—a good candy bar in Brazil is not the same as a good candy bar in China. Therefore, decision-making needs to be pushed down as low as possible in the organization, out close to the markets. Otherwise, how can you make good brand decisions? A brand is a bundle of functional and emotional characteristics. We can't establish emotional links with consumers in Vietnam from our offices in Vevey."[10]

Peter Brabeck-Letmathe, Chairman and CEO, Nestlé

packaging or in advertising. Properly implemented, co-branding can engender customer loyalty and allow companies to achieve synergy. However, co-branding can also confuse consumers and dilute brand equity. The approach works most effectively when the products involved complement each other. Credit card companies were the pioneers, and today it is possible to use cards to earn frequent flyer miles and discounts on automobiles. Another well-known example of co-branding is the Intel Inside campaign promoting both the Intel Corporation and its Pentium-brand processors in conjunction with advertising for various brands of personal computers.

Global companies can also leverage strong brands by creating **brand extensions**. This strategy entails using an established brand name as an umbrella when entering new businesses or developing new product lines that represent new categories to the company. British entrepreneur Richard Branson is an acknowledged master of this approach: The Virgin brand has been attached to a wide range of businesses and products (www.virgin.com). Virgin is a global brand, and the company's businesses include an airline, a railroad franchise, retail stores, movie theaters, financial services, and soft drinks. Some of these businesses are global, and some are local. For example, Virgin Megastores are found in many parts of the world, while the operating scope of Virgin Rail Group is limited to the United Kingdom. The brand has been built on Branson's shrewd ability to exploit weaknesses in competitors' customer service skills, as well as a flair for self-promotion. Branson's business philosophy is that brands are built around reputation, quality, innovation, and price rather than image. Although Branson is intent on establishing Virgin as *the* British brand of the new millennium, some industry observers wonder if the brand has been spread too thin.

Table 10-1 shows the four combinations of local and global products and brands in matrix form. Each represents a different strategy; a global company can use one or more strategies as appropriate. As noted previously, some global companies pursue Strategy 1 by developing local products and brands for individual country or regional markets. Coca-Cola makes extensive use of this strategy; Georgia canned coffee in Japan is one example. Coca-Cola's flagship

---

10 Suzy Wetlaufer, "The Business Case Against Revolution," *Harvard Business Review* 79, no. 2 (February 2001), p. 116.

Table 10-1

Product/Brand Matrix for Global Marketing

Brand		Product	
		Local	Global
Brand	Local	1. Local product/local brand	2. Global product/local brand
	Global	3. Local product/global brand	4. Global product/global brand

Table 10-1

Product/Brand Matrix for Global Marketing

cola brand is an example of Strategy 4. In South Africa, Coca-Cola markets Valpre brand bottled water (Strategy 2). The global cosmetics industry makes extensive use of Strategy 3; the marketers of Chanel, Givenchy, Clarins, Guerlain and other leading cosmetics brands create different formulations for different regions of the world. However, the brand name and the packaging may be uniform everywhere.

Global Brand Development

Table 10-2 shows global brands ranked in terms of their economic value as determined by analysts at the Interbrand consultancy and Citigroup. To be included in the rankings, the brand had to generate about one-third of sales outside the home country; brands owned by privately held companies such as Mars are not included. Not surprisingly, Coca-Cola tops the list. However, one of the telling findings of the rankings is that strong brand management is now being practiced by companies in a wide range of industries, not just by consumer packaged-goods marketers.[11]

Rank	Value ($ billions)
1. Coca-Cola	67.0
2. Microsoft	56.9
3. IBM	56.2
4. GE	48.9
5. Intel	32.3
6. Nokia	30.1
7. Toyota	27.9
8. Disney	27.8
9. McDonald's	27.5
10. Mercedes-Benz	21.7
11. Citi	21.4
12. Marlboro	21.3
13. Hewlett-Packard	20.4
14. American Express	19.6
15. BMW	19.6
16. Gillette	19.5
17. Louis Vuitton	17.6
18. Cisco	17.5
19. Honda	17.0
20. Samsung	16.1
21. Merrill Lynch	13.0
22. Pepsi	12.9
23. Nescafé	12.5
24. Google	12.3
25. Dell	12.2

Table 10-2

The World's Most Valuable Brands

Source: Adapted from "The 100 Top Brands," *Business Week* (August 7, 2006), pp. 60–61.

---

[11] Gerry Khermouch, "The Best Global Brands," *Business Week* (August 6, 2001), pp. 50+.

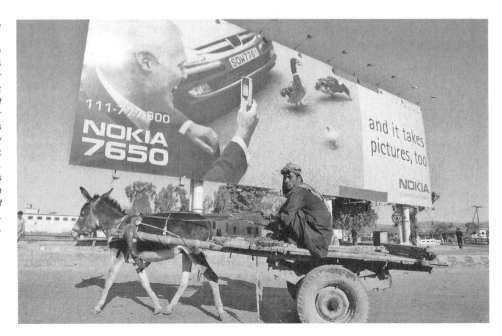

Annual global cellphone sales have passed the one billion unit mark. Now, faced with saturated markets in the West, Nokia and its competitors are turning to emerging markets for new customers. Robust economic growth and rising incomes mean that consumers in China, India, and other emerging markets can buy cellphones as status symbols. As indicated by this billboard on the Grand Trunk Highway outside of Islamabad, Pakistan, brand-conscious shoppers are upgrading to new handsets with fashionable designs and the latest features, including color screens, cameras, and digital music players.

Developing a global brand is not always an appropriate goal. As David Aaker and Erich Joachimsthaler noted in the *Harvard Business Review,* managers who seek to build global brands must first consider whether such a move fits well with their company or their markets. First, managers must realistically assess whether anticipated scale economies will actually materialize. Second, they must recognize the difficulty of building a successful global brand team. Finally, managers must be alert to instances in which a single brand cannot be imposed on all markets successfully. Aaker and Joachimsthaler recommend that companies place a priority on creating strong brands in *all* markets through **global brand leadership**:

> Global brand leadership means using organizational structures, processes, and cultures to allocate brand-building resources globally, to create global synergies, and to develop a global brand strategy that coordinates and leverages country brand strategies.[12]

The following six guidelines can assist marketing managers in their efforts to establish global brand leadership:[13]

- Create a compelling value proposition for customers in every market entered, beginning with the home-country market. A global brand begins with this foundation of value.
- Before taking a brand across borders, think about all elements of brand identity and select names, marks, and symbols that have the potential for globalization. Give special attention to the Triad and BRIC nations.
- Develop a company-wide communication system to share and leverage knowledge and information about marketing programs and customers in different countries.
- Develop a consistent planning process across markets and products. Make a process template available to all managers in all markets.

---

[12] David Aaker and Erich Joachimsthaler, "The Lure of Global Branding," *Harvard Business Review* 77, no. 6 (November–December 1999), pp. 137–144.

[13] Warren J. Keegan, "Global Brands: Issues and Strategies," Center for Global Business Strategy, Pace University, Working Paper Series, 2002.

STRATEGIC DECISION-MAKING *in global marketing*

Mars

Mars Inc. confronted the global brand issue with its chocolate-covered caramel bar that sold under a variety of national brand names such as Snickers in the United States and Marathon in the United Kingdom. Management decided to transform the candy bar—already a global product—into a global brand. This decision entailed some risk, such as the possibility that consumers in the United Kingdom would associate the name Snickers with knickers, the British slang for a woman's undergarment. Mars also changed the name of its successful European chocolate biscuit from Raider to Twix, the same name used in the United States. In both instances, a single brand name gives Mars the opportunity to leverage all of its product communications across national boundaries. Managers were

forced to think globally about the positioning of Snickers and Twix, something that they were not obliged to do when the candy products were marketed under different national brand names. The marketing team rose to the challenge; as Lord Saatchi described it:

> Mars decided there was a rich commercial prize at stake in ownership of a single human need: hunger satisfaction. From Hong Kong to Lima, people would know that Snickers was "a meal in a bar." Owning that emotion would not give them 100 percent of the global confectionery market but it would be enough. Its appeal would be wide enough to make Snickers the number one confectionery brand in the world, which it is today.

Source: Lord Saatchi, "Battle for Survival Favours the Simplest," Financial Times (January 5, 1998), p. 19.

- Assign specific responsibility for managing branding issues to ensure that local brand managers accept global best practices. This can take a variety of forms, ranging from a business management team or a brand champion (led by senior executives) to a global brand manager or brand management team (led by middle managers).
- Execute brand-building strategies that leverage global strengths and respond to relevant local differences.

Coke is arguably the quintessential global product and global brand. Coke relies on similar positioning and marketing in all countries; it projects a global image of fun, good times, and enjoyment. The product itself may vary to suit local tastes; for example, Coke increased the sweetness of its beverages in the Middle East where customers prefer a sweeter drink. Also, prices may vary to suit local competitive conditions, and the channels of distribution may differ. In 2006, Coke adopted the global advertising theme "The Coke Side of Life." The global campaign will be supplemented with ads created in local markets such as Russia and China.[14] However, the basic, underlying strategic principles that guide the management of the brand are the same worldwide. The issue is not exact uniformity but rather: Are we offering *essentially* the same product and brand promise? As discussed in the next few chapters, other elements of the marketing mix—for example, price, communications appeal and media strategy, and distribution channels—may also vary.

Local Versus Global Products and Brands: A Needs-Based Approach

Coca-Cola, McDonald's, Singapore Airlines, Mercedes-Benz, and Sony are a few of the companies that have transformed local products and brands into global ones. The essence of marketing is finding needs and filling them. **Maslow's needs hierarchy**, a staple of sociology and psychology courses, provides a useful framework for understanding how and why local products and brands can be extended beyond home country borders. Maslow proposed that people's desires can be arranged into a hierarchy of five needs.[15] As an individual fulfills needs at

---

[14] Chad Terhune, "Coke's New Ads Try to Conjure Up Old Magic," *The Wall Street Journal* (March 30, 2006), pp. B1, B2.

[15] A. H. Maslow, "A Theory of Human Motivation," in *Readings in Managerial Psychology*, eds. Harold J. Levitt and Louis R. Pondy (Chicago: University of Chicago Press, 1964), pp. 6–24.

BRIC Briefing Book

GM in China

General Motor's experience in China provides a good example of how a company's global brand strategy must be adapted to the needs of the market. In the Chapter 9 discussion of GM's joint venture in China it was noted that, in the mid-1990s, the American automaker was selected to produce Buick sedans for government and business. Why was the Buick nameplate chosen from among GM's various vehicle brands? In an interview with *Business Week*, GM CEO Rick Wagoneer related the following story:

> There is a straightforwardness to the way the Chinese negotiate things. What they are interested in becomes clear quickly. When we were ready to go into the China market, they said, "Okay, we will choose GM, and we want you to use Buick." We said, "It is not really one of our global brands. We'd probably rather use something else." They said, "We'd like you to use Buick." We said, "We'll use Buick." And it has worked great.

each level, he or she progresses to higher levels (Figure 10-2). At the most basic level of human existence, physiological and safety needs must be met. People need food, clothing, and shelter, and a product that meets these basic needs has potential for globalization.

However, the basic human need to consume food and drink is not the same thing as wanting or preferring a Big Mac or a Coke. Before the Coca-Cola Company and McDonald's conquered the world, they built their brands and business systems at home. Because their products fulfilled basic human needs and because both companies are masterful marketers, they were able to cross geographic boundaries and build global brand franchises. At the same time, Coca-Cola and McDonald's have learned from experience that some food and drink preferences—China is a case in point—remain deeply embedded in culture.[16] Responding to those differences has meant creating local products and brands for particular country markets. Sony has prospered for a similar reason. Audio and

Figure 10-2

Maslow's Hierarchy of Needs

Source: A. H. Maslow, "A Theory of Human Motivation," in Readings in Managerial Psychology, Harold J. Levitt and Louis R. Pondy, eds. (Chicago: University of Chicago Press, 1964), pp. 6–24. Original—Psychological Review 50 (1943).

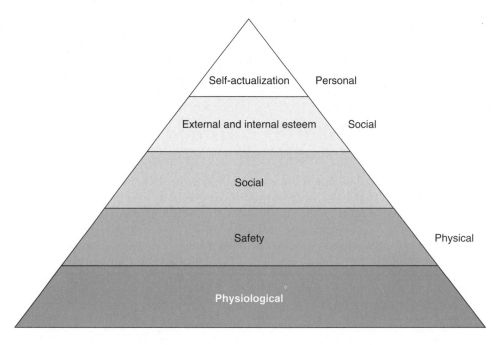

____
16 Jeremy Grant, "Golden Arches Bridge Local Tastes," *Financial Times* (February 9, 2006), p. 10.

video entertainment products fulfill important social functions. Throughout its history, Sony's corporate vision has called for developing new products such as the transistor radio and the Walkman personal stereo that fulfill the need for entertainment.

Mid-level needs in the hierarchy include self-respect, self-esteem, and the esteem of others. These social needs, which can create a powerful internal motivation driving demand for status-oriented products, cut across the various stages of country development. Gillette's Alfred Zeien understood this. Marketers in Gillette's Parker Pen subsidiary are confident that consumers in Malaysia and Singapore shopping for an upscale gift will buy the same Parker pen as Americans shopping at Neiman Marcus. "We are not going to come out with a special product for Malaysia," Zeien has said.[17] In Asia today, young women are taking up smoking as a status symbol—and showing a preference for Western brands such as Marlboro. However, as noted earlier, smokers' needs and wants may be tempered by economic circumstances. Recognizing this, companies such as BAT create local brands that allow individuals to indulge their desire or need to smoke at a price they can afford to pay.

Luxury goods marketers are especially skilled at catering to esteem needs on a global basis. Rolex, Louis Vuitton, and Dom Perignon are just a few of the global brands that consumers buy in an effort to satisfy esteem needs. Some consumers flaunt their wealth by buying expensive products and brands that others will notice. Such behavior is referred to as *conspicuous consumption* or *luxury badging*. Any company with a premium product or brand that has proven itself in a local market by fulfilling esteem needs should consider devising a strategy for taking the product global.

Products can fulfill different needs in different countries. Consider the refrigerator as used in industrialized, high-income countries. The *primary function* of the refrigerator in these countries is related to basic needs as fulfilled in that society. These include storing frozen foods for extended periods; keeping milk, meat, and other perishable foods fresh between car trips to the supermarket; and making ice cubes. In lower-income countries, by contrast, frozen foods are not widely available.

In India, Vietnam, and other emerging markets, many people cannot afford housing or automobiles. That means that amenities such as refrigerators and flush toilets are considered status symbols when a family welcomes visitors to their home. In public, cellphones serve a similar secondary purpose.

[17] Louis Uchitelle, "Gillette's World View: One Blade Fits All," *The New York Times* (January 3, 1994), p. C3.

Homemakers shop for food daily rather than weekly. People are reluctant to pay for unnecessary features such as icemakers. These are luxuries that require high-income levels to support. The function of the refrigerator in a lower-income country is to store small quantities of perishable food for one day and to store leftovers for slightly longer periods. Because the needs fulfilled by the refrigerator are limited in these countries, a relatively small refrigerator is quite adequate. In some developing countries, refrigerators have an important *secondary purpose* related to higher-order needs: They fulfill a need for prestige. In these countries, there is demand for the largest model available, which is prominently displayed in the living room rather than hidden in the kitchen.

Hellmut Schütte has proposed a modified hierarchy to explain the needs and wants of Asian consumers (Figure 10-3).[18] Although the two lower-level needs are the same as in the traditional hierarchy, the three highest levels emphasize social needs. *Affiliation needs* in Asia are satisfied when an individual has been accepted by a group. Conformity with group norms becomes a key force driving consumer behavior. For example, when a cool new cell phone hits the market, every teenager who wants to fit in buys one. Knowing this, managers at Japanese companies develop local products specifically designed to appeal to teens. The next level is *admiration*, a higher-level need that can be satisfied through acts that command respect within a group. At the top of the Asian hierarchy is *status*, the esteem of society as a whole. In part, attainment of high status is character driven. However, the quest for status also leads to luxury badging. Support for Schütte's contention that status is the highest-ranking need in the Asian hierarchy can be seen in the geographic breakdown of the $35 billion global luxury goods market. Fully 20 percent of industry sales are generated in Japan alone, with another 22 percent of sales occurring in the rest of the Asia-Pacific region. Nearly half of all sales revenues of Italy's Gucci Group are generated in Asia.

"For Asians, face is very important, so you have to show you are up to date with the latest available product."[19]

Alan Chang, View Sonic (Taiwan), explaining the popularity of flat-panel TVs in Japan

Figure 10-3

Maslow's Hierarchy: The Asian Equivalent

Source: Hellmut Schütte, "Maslow's Hierarchy: The Asian Equivalent," Consumer Behavior in Asia (New York: New York University Press, 1998), p. 93.

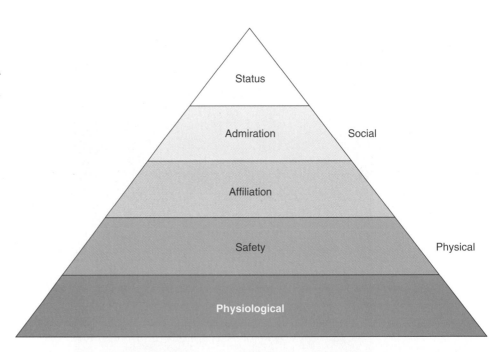

---

[18] Hellmut Schütte, "Asian Culture and the Global Consumer," *Financial Times–Mastering Marketing* (September 21, 1998), p. 2.

[19] Andrew Ward, Kathrin Hille, Michiyo Nakamoto, Chris Nuttal, "Flat Out for Flat Screens: The Battle to Dominate the $29 bn Market Is Heating Up but the Risk of Glut Is Growing," *Financial Times* (December 24, 2003), p. 9.

"COUNTRY OF ORIGIN" AS BRAND ELEMENT

One of the facts of life in global marketing is that perceptions about and attitudes towards particular countries often extend to products and brands known to originate in those countries. Such perceptions contribute to the **country-of-origin effect**; they become part of a brand's image and contribute to brand equity. This is particularly true for automobiles, electronics, fashion, beer, recorded music, and certain other product categories. Perceptions and attitudes about a product's origins can be positive or negative. On the positive side, as one marketing expert pointed out in the mid-1990s, "'German' is synonymous with quality engineering, 'Italian' is synonymous with style, and 'French' is synonymous with chic."[20] More than a decade later, those associations are still evident. Within a given country, consumers are likely to differ in terms of both the importance they ascribe to a product's country of origin and their perceptions of different countries. Moreover, as industries globalize, the origin issue is becoming more complex. Country-of-design, country-of-manufacture, and country sources for parts can all become relevant considerations.

The manufacturing reputation of a particular country can change over time. Studies conducted during the 1970s and 1980s indicated that the "made in the USA" image lost ground to the "made in Japan" image. Today, however, U.S. brands are finding renewed acceptance globally. Examples include Jeep Cherokee sports utility vehicles, Lands' End clothing, and Budweiser beer, all of which are being successfully marketed with strong "USA" themes. Korea's image has improved greatly in recent years, thanks to the reputations of global companies such as Hyundai, Daewoo, and Samsung. Industry observers expect other Asian corporate megabrands to emerge in the coming years.

Finland is home to Nokia, which rose in stature from a local brand to a global brand in little more than a decade. However, as brand strategy expert Simon Anholt points out, other Finnish companies need to move quickly to capitalize on Nokia's success if Finland is to become a valuable nation brand. For example, Raisio Oy has developed Benecol brand margarine that has been proven to lower cholesterol levels. If large numbers of health-conscious consumers around the world embrace so-called nutraceutical products, Raisio and Benecol may become well-known brands and further raise Finland's profile on the global scene. Anholt also notes that some countries are "launch brands" in the sense that they lack centuries of tradition and foreign interaction upon which to build their reputations:

> For a country like Slovenia to enhance its image abroad is a very different matter than for Scotland or China. Slovenia needs to be launched: Consumers around the world first must be taught where it is, what it makes, what it has to offer, and what it stands for. This in itself represents a powerful opportunity: The chance to build a modern country brand, untainted by centuries of possibly negative associations.[22]

Since the mid-1990s, the "made in Mexico" image has gained in stature as local companies and global manufacturers have established world-class manufacturing plants in Mexico to supply world demand. For example, General Motors, Volkswagen, DaimlerChrysler, Nissan, Ford, and other global automakers have established Mexican operations that produce nearly 2 million vehicles per year, three-fourths of which are exported.[23]

"China is complex and becoming more so. But 'Made in Germany' still carries great appeal here and if you prepare seriously, there are few limits to what you can achieve."[21]

Christian Sommer, German Centre for Industry and Trade

"Consider labels such as 'Made in Brazil' and 'Made in Thailand.' Someday they may be symbols of high quality and value, but today many consumers expect products from those countries to be inferior."[24]

Christopher A. Bartlett and Sumantra Ghoshal

---

[20] Dana Milbank, "Made in America Becomes a Boast in Europe," *The Wall Street Journal* (January 19, 1994), p. B1.

[21] Bertrand Benoit and Geoff Dyer, "The Mittelstand is Making Money in the Middle Kingdom," *Financial Times* (June 6, 2006), p. 13.

[22] Simon Anholt, "The Nation as Brand," *Across the Board* 37, no. 10 (November–December 2000), pp. 22–27.

[23] Elliot Blair Smith, "Early PT Cruiser Took a Bruisin'," *USA Today* (August 8, 2001), pp. 1B, 2B; see also Joel Millman, "Trade Wins: The World's New Tiger on the Export Scene Isn't Asian; It's Mexico," *The Wall Street Journal* (May 9, 2000), pp. A1, A10.

[24] Christopher A. Bartlett and Sumantra Ghoshal, "Going Global: Lessons from Late Movers," *Harvard Business Review* 78, no. 2 (March-April 2000), p. 133.

In some product categories, foreign products have a substantial advantage over their domestic counterparts simply because of their "foreign-ness." Global marketers have an opportunity to capitalize on the situation by charging premium prices. The import segment of the beer industry is a case in point. In one study of American attitudes about beer, subjects who were asked to taste beer with the labels concealed indicated a preference for domestic beers over imports. The same subjects were then asked to indicate preference ratings for beers in an open test with labels attached. In this test, the subjects preferred imported beer. Conclusion: The subjects' perceptions were positively influenced by the knowledge they were drinking an import. In 1997, thanks to a brilliant marketing campaign, Grupo Modelo's Corona Extra surpassed Heineken as the best-selling imported beer in America. With distribution in 150 countries, Corona is a textbook example of a local brand that has been built into a global powerhouse.

If a country's manufacturers produce high-quality products that are nonetheless *perceived* as being of lower quality than similar goods from other countries, there are two alternatives. One is to disguise the foreign origin of the product. Package, label, and product design can minimize evidence of foreign derivation. A brand policy of using local names will contribute to a domestic identity. The other alternative is to continue the foreign identification of the product and attempt to change buyer attitudes toward the product. Over time, as consumers experience higher quality, the perception will change and adjust. It is a fact of life that perceptions of quality often lag behind reality.

PACKAGING

In many instances, packaging is an integral element of product-related decisions. Packaging is an important consideration for products that are shipped to markets in far-flung corners of the world. Moreover, the phrase "consumer packaged goods" applies to a wide variety of products whose packaging is designed to protect or contain the product during shipping, at retail locations, and at the point of use or consumption. "Eco-packaging" is a key issue today, and package designers must address environmental issues such as recycling and biodegradability. In Germany, for example, product packaging must conform to Green Dot regulations. Packaging also serves important communication functions: Packages (and labels attached to them) offer communication cues that provide consumers with a basis for making a purchase decision. Today, many industry experts agree that packaging must engage the senses, make emotional connections, and enhance a consumer's brand experience. According to Bernd Schmitt, director of Columbia University's Center on Global Brand Leadership, "Packages are creating an experience for the customer that goes beyond the functional benefits of displaying and protecting the object."[25] Absolut vodka, Altoids breath mints, and Godiva chocolates are a few examples of brands whose value proposition includes "experiential packaging."

---

[25] Queena Sook Kim, "The Potion's Power Is in Its Packaging," *The Wall Street Journal* (December 21, 2000), p. B12.

Brewers, soft drink marketers, distillers, and other beverage firms typically devote considerable thought to ensuring that packages speak to consumers or provide some kind of benefit beyond simply holding liquid. For example, a critical element in the success of Corona Extra beer in export markets was management's decision to retain the traditional package design that consisted of a tall transparent bottle with "Made in Mexico" etched directly on the glass. At the time, the conventional wisdom in the brewing industry was that export beer bottles should be short, green or brown in color, with paper labels. In other words, the bottle should resemble Heineken's! The fact that consumers could see the beer inside the Corona Extra bottle made it seem more pure and natural. Today, Corona is the top-selling imported beer brand in the United States, Australia, Belgium, the Czech Republic, and several other countries.[26]

Coca-Cola's distinctive (and trademarked) contour bottle comes in both glass and plastic versions and helps consumers seek out the "real thing." The Coke example also illustrates the point that packaging strategies can vary by country and region. In North America, where large refrigerators are found in many households, Coca-Cola's latest packaging innovation is the Fridge Pack, a long, slender carton that holds the equivalent of 12 cans of soda. The Fridge Pack fits on a refrigerator's lower shelf and includes a tap for easy dispensing. In Latin America, by contrast, Coca-Cola executives intend to boost profitability by offering Coke in several different sized bottles. Until recently, for example, 75 percent of Coke's volume in Argentina was accounted for by 2 liter bottles priced at $0.45 each. Coke has introduced cold, individual-serving bottles priced at $0.33 that are stocked in stores near the front; unchilled, 1.25 liter returnable glass bottles priced at $0.28 are available on shelves further back in the store.[27] Other examples include:

- Grey Goose, the world's top-selling super premium vodka brand, is the brainchild of Sidney Frank. The owner of an importing business in New Rochelle, New York, Frank first devised the bottle design and name. Only then did he approach a distiller in Cognac, France, to create the actual vodka.[28]
- Nestlé has packaging teams throughout the world that are required to contribute packaging improvement suggestions on a quarterly basis. Implemented changes include a new plastic lid to make ice cream containers easier to open; slightly deeper indentations in the flat end of candy wrappers in Brazil that make them easier to rip open; and deeper notches on single-serve packets of Nescafé in China. Nestlé also asked suppliers to find a type of glue to make the clicking sound louder when consumers snap open a tube of Smarties brand chocolate candies.[29]

Labeling

One hallmark of the modern global marketplace is the abundance of multilanguage labeling that appears on many products. In today's self-service retail environments, product labels may be designed to attract attention, to support a product's positioning, and to help persuade consumers to buy. Labels can also provide consumers with various types of information. Care must be taken that all ingredient information and use and care instructions are properly translated. The content of product labels may also be dictated by country- or region-specific regulations. Regulations regarding

[26] Sara Silver, "Modelo Puts Corona in the Big Beer League," *Financial Times* (October 30, 2002), p. 26.
[27] Betsy McKay, "Coke's Heyer Finds Test in Latin America," *The Wall Street Journal* (October 15, 2002), p. B4.
[28] Christina Passariello, "France's Cognac Region Gives Vodka a Shot," *The Wall Street Journal* (October 20, 2004), p. B1.
[29] Deborah Ball, "The Perils of Packaging: Nestlé Aims for Easier Openings," *The Wall Street Journal* (November 17, 2005), p. B1.

mandatory label content vary in different parts of the world; for example, the EU now requires mandatory labeling for some foods containing genetically modified ingredients. Regulators in Australia, New Zealand, Japan, Russia, and several other countries have also proposed similar legislation. In the United States, the Nutrition Education and Labeling Act that went into effect in the early 1990s was intended to make food labels more informative and easier to understand. Today, virtually all food products sold in the United States must present information regarding nutrition (e.g., calories and fat content) and serving size in a standard format. The use of certain terms such as *light* and *natural* is also restricted. Other examples of labeling in global marketing include:

- Mandatory health warnings on tobacco products are required in most countries.
- The American Automobile Labeling Act clarifies the country of origin, the final assembly point, and percentages of the major sources of foreign content of every car, truck, and minivan sold in the United States (effective since October 1, 1994).
- Since mid-2004, the EU has required labels on all food products that include ingredients derived from genetically modified crops.
- Responding to pressure from consumer groups, in 2006 McDonald's began posting nutrition information on all food packaging and wrappers in approximately 20,000 restaurants in key markets worldwide. Executives indicated that issues pertaining to language and nutritional testing would delay labeling in 10,000 additional restaurants in smaller country markets.[30]
- Nestlé recently introduced Nan, an infant-formula brand that is popular in Latin America, in the American market. Targeted at Hispanic mothers, Nestlé Nan's instructions are printed in Spanish on the front of the can. Other brands have English-language labeling on the outside; Spanish-language instructions are printed on the reverse side.[31]

Aesthetics

In Chapter 4, the subject of aesthetics was introduced in a discussion of varying perceptions of color in different parts of the world. Global marketers must understand the importance of *visual aesthetics* embodied in the color or shape of a product, label, or package. Likewise, *aesthetic styles*, such as the degree of complexity found on a label, are perceived differently in different parts of the world. For example, it has been said that German wines would be more appealing in export markets if the labels were simplified. Aesthetic elements that are deemed appropriate, attractive, and appealing in one's home country may be perceived differently elsewhere. In some cases, a standardized color can be used in all countries; examples include the distinctive yellow color on Caterpillar's earth-moving equipment and its licensed outdoor gear and the red Marlboro chevron. In other instances, color choices should be changed in response to local perceptions. It was noted in Chapter 4 that white is associated with death and bad luck in some Asian countries; recall that when GM executives were negotiating with China for the opportunity to build cars there, they gave Chinese officials gifts from upscale Tiffany & Company in the jeweler's signature blue box. The Americans astutely replaced Tiffany's white ribbons with red ones because red is considered a lucky color in China and white has negative connotations.

---

[30] Steven L. Gray and Iian Brat, "Read It and Weep? Big Mac Wrapper to Show Fat, Calories," *The Wall Street Journal* (October 26, 2005), p. B1.
[31] Miriam Jordan, "Nestlé Markets Baby Formula to Hispanic Mothers in U.S.," *The Wall Street Journal* (March 4, 2004), p. B1.

Packaging aesthetics are particularly important to the Japanese. This point was driven home to the chief executive of a small U.S. company that manufactures an electronic device for controlling corrosion. After spending much time in Japan, the executive managed to secure several orders for the device. Following an initial burst of success, Japanese orders dropped off; for one thing, the executive was told, the packaging was too plain. "We couldn't understand why we needed a five-color label and a custom-made box for this device, which goes under the hood of a car or in the boiler room of a utility company," the executive said. While waiting for the bullet train in Japan one day, the executive's local distributor purchased a cheap watch at the station and had it elegantly wrapped. The distributor asked the American executive to guess the value of the watch based on the packaging. Despite all that he had heard and read about the Japanese obsession with quality, it was the first time the American understood that, in Japan, "a book is judged by its cover." As a result, the company revamped its packaging, seeing to such details as ensuring that strips of tape used to seal the boxes were cut to precisely the same length.[32]

PRODUCT WARRANTIES

A warranty can be an important element of a product's value proposition. An **express warranty** is a written guarantee that assures the buyer is getting what he or she has paid for or that provides recourse in case a product's performance falls short of expectations. In global marketing, warranties can be used as a competitive tool to position a company in a positive way. For example, in the late 1990s, Hyundai Motor America chief executive Finbarr O'Neill realized that many American car buyers perceived Korean cars as "cheap" and were skeptical about the Hyundai nameplate's reliability. The company had made significant improvements in the quality and reliability of its vehicles, but consumer perceptions of the brand had not kept pace with the changes. O'Neill instituted a 10-year, 100,000-mile warranty program that represents the most comprehensive coverage in the auto industry. Concurrently, Hyundai launched several new vehicles and increased expenditures for advertising. The results are impressive: Hyundai's U.S. sales jumped from about 90,000 vehicles in 1998 to nearly 400,000 vehicles in 2003.

EXTEND, ADAPT, CREATE: STRATEGIC ALTERNATIVES IN GLOBAL MARKETING

To capitalize on opportunities outside the home country, company managers must devise and implement appropriate marketing programs. Depending on organizational objectives and market needs, a particular program may consist of extension strategies, adaptation strategies, or a combination of the two. A company that has developed a successful local product or brand can implement an **extension strategy** that calls for offering a product virtually unchanged (i.e., "extending" it) in markets outside the home country. A second option is an **adaptation strategy**; this involves changing elements of design, function, or packaging in response to needs or conditions in particular country markets. These product strategies can be used in conjunction with extension or adaptation communication strategies. This is the type of strategic decision facing executives at a company such as Starbucks who build a brand and a product or service offering in the home country market before expanding into global markets. A third strategic option, **product invention**, entails developing new products "from the ground up" with the world market in mind.

---

[32] Nilly Landau, "Face to Face Marketing Is Best," *International Business* (June 1994), p. 64.

Laws and regulations in different countries frequently lead to obligatory product design adaptations. This may be seen most clearly in Europe, where one impetus for the creation of the single market was the desire to dismantle regulatory and legal barriers that prevented pan-European sales of standardized products. These were particularly prevalent in the areas of technical standards and health and safety standards. In the food industry, for example, there were 200 legal and regulatory barriers to cross-border trade within the EU in 10 food categories. Among these were prohibitions or taxes on products with certain ingredients and different packaging and labeling laws. As these barriers are dismantled there will be less need to adapt product designs and many companies will be able to create standardized "Euro-products."

Despite the trend toward convergence, many product standards that remain on the books have not been harmonized. This situation can create problems for companies not based in the EU. Dormont Manufacturing, appropriately based in Export, Pennsylvania, makes hoses that hook up to deep-fat fryers and similar appliances used in the food industry. Dormont's gas hose is made of stainless-steel helical tubing with no covering. British industry requirements call for galvanized metal annular tubing and a rubber covering; Italian regulations specify stainless steel annual tubing with no covering. The cost of complying with these regulations effectively shuts Dormont out of the European market.[33] Moreover, the European Commission continues to set product standards that force many non-EU companies to adapt product or service offerings that satisfy domestic market regulations. For example, consumer safety regulations mean that McDonald's cannot give away soft-plastic toys with its Happy Meals in Europe. Microsoft has been forced to modify contracts with European software makers and Internet service providers to ensure that consumers in the EU have access to a wide range of technologies. The commission has also set stringent guidelines on product content as it affects recyclability. As Maja Wessels, a Brussels-based lobbyist for United Technologies (UT), noted, "Twenty years ago, if you designed something to U.S. standards you could pretty much sell it all over the world. Now the shoe's on the other foot." Engineers at UT's Carrier division are redesigning the company's air conditioners to comply with pending European recycling rules, which are tougher than U.S. standards.[34]

As noted in Chapter 1, the extension/adaptation/creation decision is one of the most fundamental issues addressed by a company's global marketing strategy. Although it pertains to all elements of the marketing mix, extension/adaptation is of particular importance in product and communications decisions. Earlier in the chapter, Figure 10-1 displayed product and brand strategic options in matrix form. Figure 10-4 expands on those options: All aspects of communication—not just branding—are considered. Figure 10-4 shows four strategic alternatives available to Starbucks or any other company seeking to expand from its domestic base into new geographic markets. Companies in the international, global, and transnational stages of development all employ extension strategies. The critical difference is one of execution and mind-set. In an international company, for example, the extension strategy reflects an ethnocentric orientation and the *assumption* that all markets are alike. A global company such as Gillette does not fall victim to such assumptions; the company's geocentric orientation allows it to thoroughly understand its markets and consciously take advantage of similarities in world markets. Likewise, a multinational company utilizes the adaptation strategy because of its polycentric orientation and the assumption that all markets are different. By contrast, the geocentric orientation of managers and executives in a global company has sensitized them to actual, rather than assumed, differences between markets.

---

[33] Timothy Aeppel, "Europe's 'Unity' Undoes a U.S. Exporter, "*The Wall Street Journal* (April 1, 1996), p. B1.

[34] Brandon Mitchener, "Standard Bearers: Increasingly, Rules of Global Economy Are Set in Brussels," *The Wall Street Journal* (April 23, 2002), p. A1.

Figure 10-4

Global Product Planning:
Strategic Alternatives

Strategy 1: Product-Communication Extension (Dual Extension)

Many companies employ **product-communication extension** as a strategy for pursuing opportunities outside the home market. Under the right conditions, this is the easiest product marketing strategy; it can be the most profitable one as well. Companies pursuing this strategy sell the same product with virtually no adaptation, using the same advertising and promotional appeals used domestically, in two or more country markets or segments. For this strategy to be effective, the advertiser's message must be understood across different cultures. This issue can be especially important in developing country markets.

As a general rule, extension/standardization strategies are utilized more frequently with industrial (business-to-business) products than with consumer products. The reason is simple: Industrial products tend not to be as rooted in culture as consumer goods. Technology companies and manufacturers of industrial products should be especially alert to extension possibilities. For example, Germany's Henkel KGaA markets the Loctite glue brand globally. However, Henkel also markets 760 other glues, detergents and personal care products with different formulas and different brand names. Speaking about Loctite, Henkel CEO Ulrich Lehner explains, "There aren't many products like that. Usually, you have to adapt to local tastes. You have to balance between local insight and centralized economies of scale. It's a constant battle."[35] Among technology-oriented consumer marketers, Apple utilizes the dual-extension strategy for its iPod digital music player.

The product-communication extension strategy has an enormous appeal to global companies because of the cost savings associated with this approach. The most obvious sources of savings are design and manufacturing economies of scale, inventory savings, and elimination of duplicate product R&D costs. Also important are the substantial economies associated with standardization of marketing communications. For a company with worldwide operations, the cost of preparing separate print and TV ads for each market can be enormous. Although these cost savings are important, they should not distract executives from the more important objective of maximum profit performance, which may require the use of an adaptation or invention strategy. Product extension, in spite of its immediate cost savings, may result in market failure.

"I can think of very few truly global ads that work. Brands are often at different stages around the world, and that means there are different advertising jobs to do."[36]

Michael Conrad, Chief Creative Officer, Leo Burnett Worldwide

---

[35] Gerrit Wiesmann, "Brands That Stop at the Border," *Financial Times* (October 6, 2006), p. 10.
[36] Vanessa O'Connell, "Exxon 'Centralizes' New Global Campaign," *The Wall Street Journal* (July 11, 2001), p. B6.

Strategy 2: Product Extension/Communication Adaptation

When taking a product beyond the home-country market, management sometimes discovers that consumer perceptions about "quality" and "value" are different from those in the home country. It may also turn out that a product fills a different need, appeals to a different segment, or serves a different function. Whatever the reason, extending the product while adapting the marketing communications program may result in market success. The appeal of the **product extension-communication adaptation** strategy is its relatively low cost of implementation. Because the physical product is unchanged, expenditures for R&D, manufacturing setup, and inventory are avoided. The biggest costs associated with this approach are in researching the market and revising advertising, sales promotion efforts, point-of-sale material, and other communication elements as appropriate.

- In Hungary, Slovakia, and other Central European countries, SABMiller positions Miller Genuine Draft as an international lifestyle brand rather than an American brand. The communication adaptation strategy was adopted after focus group research showed that many Europeans have a low regard for American beer.[37]

- Before executives at Ben & Jerry's Homemade launched their ice cream in the United Kingdom, the company conducted extensive research to determine whether the package design effectively communicated the brand's "super premium" position. The research indicated that British consumers perceived the colors differently than U.S. consumers. The package design was changed, and Ben & Jerry's was launched successfully in the U.K. market.

- To promote its Centrino wireless chip, Intel launched a global ad campaign that features different combinations of celebrities. The celebrities—including comedian John Cleese, actress Lucy Liu, and skateboard king Tony Hawk—were chosen because they are widely recognized in key world markets. In print, TV, and online ads, one of the celebrities sits on the lap of a mobile computer user.[38]

Marketers of premium American bourbon brands such as Wild Turkey have found that images of Delta blues music, New Orleans, and Route 66 appeal to upscale drinkers outside the United States. However, images that stress bourbon's rustic, backwoods origins do not appeal to Americans. Likewise, Jägermeister schnapps is marketed differently in key country markets. Chief executive Hasso Kaempfe believes that a diversity of images has been a key element in the success of Jägermeister outside of Germany, where the brown herb-based concoction originated. In the United States, Jägermeister was "discovered" in the mid-1990s by bar patrons, particularly college students. Eschewing traditional media advertising, Kaempfe's marketing team has capitalized on the brand's cult status by hiring "Jägerettes" girls to pass out free samples; the company's popular T-shirts and orange banners are also distributed at rock concerts. By contrast, in Italy, the brand's second-largest export market, Jägermeister is considered an up-market digestive to be consumed after dinner. In Germany, Austria, and Switzerland, where beer culture predominates, Jägermeister and other brands of schnapps have more traditional associations as a remedy for coughs, stomachaches, or hangovers.[39]

[37] Dan Bilefsky and Christopher Lawton, "In Europe, Marketing Beer as 'American' May Not Be a Plus," *The Wall Street Journal* (July 21, 2004), p. B1.

[38] Geoffrey A. Fowler, "Intel's Game: Play It Local, but Make It Global," *The Wall Street Journal* (September 30, 2005), p. B4.

[39] Bettina Wassener, "Schnapps Goes to College," *Financial Times* (September 4, 2003), p. 9.

Jägermeister is an example of **product transformation**: The same physical product ends up serving a different function or use than that for which it was originally designed or created. In some cases a particular country or regional environment will allow local managers a greater degree of creativity and risk taking when approaching the communication task.

Strategy 3: Product Adaptation-Communication Extension

A third approach to global product planning is to extend, without change, the basic home-market communications strategy or brand name while adapting the product to local use or preference conditions. This third strategy option is known as **product adaptation-communication extension**. There are many examples of products that have been adapted to perform the same function around the globe under different market conditions. For example, managers of GM's Cadillac brand intend to achieve annual sales of 20,000 vehicles outside the United States by 2010. A new Cadillac model, the BLS, will be built in Sweden; it is 6 inches shorter than the current CTS and is available with an optional diesel engine. The BLS will only be sold in Europe; as James Taylor, general manager of GM's Cadillac division, noted, "There's no Cadillac guy in the U.S. who is going to buy a four-cylinder low-displacement engine."[41]

Strategy 4: Product-Communication Adaptation (Dual Adaptation)

Sometimes, when comparing a new geographic market to the home market, marketers discover that environmental conditions or consumer preferences differ; the same may be true of the function a product serves or consumer receptivity to advertising appeals. In essence, this is a combination of the market conditions associated with Strategies 2 and 3. In such a situation, a company will utilize the **product-communication adaptation (dual adaptation)** strategy. For example, marketers of home appliances and household cleaning products discovered that Italian women are not interested in labor-saving conveniences. In a country where women spend more than 20 hours each week cleaning, ironing, and other tasks, the final result—a really clean, shiny floor, for example—is more important than saving time. For the Italian market, Unilever reformulated its Cif brand spray cleaner to do a better job on grease; several different varieties were also rolled out, as were bigger bottles. Television commercials portray Cif as strong rather than convenient.[42]

As noted previously, the four alternatives are not mutually exclusive. In other words, a company can simultaneously utilize different product-communication strategies in different parts of the world. For example, Nike has built a global brand by marketing technologically advanced, premium-priced athletic shoes in conjunction with advertising that emphasizes U.S.-style in-your-face brashness and "Just Do It" attitude. In the huge and strategically important China market, however, this approach had several limitations. For one thing, Nike's "bad boy" image is at odds with ingrained Chinese values such as respect for authority and filial piety. As a general rule, advertisements in China do not show disruption of harmony; this is due in part to a government that discourages dissent. Price was

"Europeans hate Americans when they think of them as being the policemen of the world, but they love Americans when they think about blue jeans and bourbon and ranches."[40]

Gary Regan, Author, *The Book of Bourbon*

---

[40] Kimberly Palmer, "Rustic Bourbon: A Hit Overseas, Ho-Hum in the U.S." *The Wall Street Journal* (September 2, 2003), p. B1.
[41] Mark Landler, "Europe, Meet Cadillac and Dodge," *The Wall Street Journal* (March 2, 2005), p. B6.
[42] Deborah Ball, "Women in Italy Like to Clean but Shun the Quick and Easy," *The Wall Street Journal* (April 25, 2006), pp. A1, A12.

Table 10-3

Levi's 501 Red-Tab Jeans: Adaptation/Extension Grid—United States Versus Europe

Marketing Mix Element	Standardized	Localized
Product	"501" brand name; red tab on back pocket.	Fit, finish, and fabric are different in United States and Europe. "Premium" brand image in Europe versus mass or "work-a-day" in United States.
Promotion		Previous ad campaigns in Europe had "Americana" or traditional testimonial themes; new European print and TV campaign shares plot elements and dialogue with Shakespeare's *Midsummer Night's Dream*.
Place		The first "Levi for Girls" boutiques were opened in Europe in 2003.
Price		Higher prices in Europe: €85 (about $110) versus $30 in the United States.

Source: Adapted from Robert Guy Matthews, "Levi Strauss Brushes Up on Its Shakespeare," *The Wall Street Journal* (January 14, 2005), p. B3.

"You can't just import cosmetics here. Companies have to understand what beauty means to Chinese women and what they look for, and product offerings and communication have to be adjusted accordingly. It's a lot harder than selling shampoo or skin care."[44]

Daisy Ching, Regional Group Account Director, Procter & Gamble, Grey Global Group

another issue: A regular pair of Nike shoes cost the equivalent of $60 to $78 while average annual family income ranges from about $200 in rural areas to $500 in urban areas. In the mid-1990s, Nike responded by creating a shoe that could be assembled in China specifically for the Chinese market using less expensive material and sold for less than $40. After years of running ads designed for Western markets by longtime agency Wieden & Kennedy, Nike hired Chinese-speaking art directors and copywriters working in WPP Group's J. Walter Thompson ad agency in Shanghai to create new advertising featuring local athletes that would appeal to Chinese nationalistic sentiments.[43]

Strategy 5: Product Invention

Extension and adaptation strategies are effective approaches to many but not all global market opportunities. For example, they do not respond to markets where there is a need but not the purchasing power to buy either the existing or adapted product. This latter situation applies to the emerging markets of the world, which are home to roughly three-quarters of the world's population. When potential customers have limited purchasing power, a company may need to develop an entirely new product designed to address the market opportunity at a price point that is within the reach of the potential customer. The converse is also true: Companies in low-income countries that have achieved local success may have to go beyond mere adaptation by "raising the bar" and bringing product designs up to world-class standards if they are to succeed in high-income countries. **Innovation**, the process of endowing resources with a new capacity to create value, is a demanding but potentially rewarding product strategy for reaching mass markets in less developed countries as well as important market segments in industrialized countries.

Two entrepreneurs working independently recognized that millions of people around the globe need low-cost eyeglasses. Robert J. Morrison, an American optometrist, created Instant Eyeglasses. These glasses utilize conventional lenses, can be assembled in minutes, and sell for about $20 per pair. Joshua Silva, a physics professor at Oxford University, took a more high-tech approach: glasses with transparent membrane lenses filled with clear silicone fluid. Using two manual adjusters, users can increase or decrease the power of the lenses by regulating the amount of fluid in them. Professor Silva hopes to sell the glasses in developing

---

43 Sally Goll Beatty, "Bad-Boy Nike Is Playing the Diplomat in China," *The Wall Street Journal* (November 10, 1997), p. B1.
44 Laurel Wentz, "P&G Launches Cover Girl in China," *Advertising Age* (October 31, 2005), p. 22.

countries for about $10 per pair.[45] Another example of the innovation strategy is the South African company that licensed the British patent for a hand-cranked, battery-powered radio. The radio was designed by an English inventor responding to the need for radios in low-income countries. Consumers in these countries do not have electricity in their homes, and they cannot afford the cost of replacement batteries. His innovation is an obvious solution: a hand-cranked radio. It is ideal for the needs of low-income people in emerging markets. Users simply crank the radio, and it will play on the charge generated by a short cranking session for almost an hour.

Sometimes manufacturers in developing countries that intend to go global also utilize innovation strategies. For example, Thermax, an Indian company, had achieved great success in its domestic market with small industrial boilers. Engineers developed a new design for the Indian market that significantly reduced the size of the individual boiler unit. However, the new design was not likely to succeed outside India. In India, where labor costs are low, relatively elaborate installation requirements are not an issue. The situation is different in higher-wage countries where industrial customers demand sophisticated integrated systems that can be installed quickly. The managing director at Thermax instructed his engineers to design for the world market. The gamble paid off: Today, Thermax is one of the world's largest producers of small boilers.[46]

The winners in global competition are the companies that can develop products offering the most benefits, which in turn create the greatest value for buyers anywhere in the world. In some instances, value is not defined in terms of performance, but rather in terms of customer perception. Product quality is essential—it is frequently a given—but it is also necessary to support the product quality with imaginative, value-creating advertising and marketing communications. Most industry experts believe that a global appeal and a global advertising campaign are more effective in creating the perception of value than a series of separate national campaigns.

"Designing a Harley-Davidson motorcycle for international markets requires constant collaboration among design teams around the world. We use videoconferencing, phone calls, e-mail, and on-site meetings to enhance communications. We advise our engineers to stay close to the customers in the markets in which the customers are located so we can quickly react to changing customer desires and international regulations.[48]

Bruce Roberts, Mechanical Design Engineer, Harley-Davidson

STRATEGIC DECISION-MAKING *in global marketing*

Colgate

Colgate pursued the product innovation strategy in developing Total, a new toothpaste brand whose formulation, imagery, and ultimate consumer appeal were designed from the ground up to readily cross national boundaries. The product was tested in six countries, each of which had a different cultural profile: the Philippines, Australia, Colombia, Greece, Portugal, and the United Kingdom. Total is now available in more than 100 countries; thanks to line extensions such as Total Advanced Clean, Colgate now commands a leading share—about 37 percent—of the U.S. toothpaste market. The brand is also achieving share gains in key markets such as Brazil, Russia, India, and Mexico. According to John Steel,

senior vice president for global business development at Colgate, Total's success results from the application of a fundamental marketing principle: Consumers are the ones who make or break brands. "There ain't no consumers at 300 Park Avenue," he says, referring to company headquarters. Steel explains, "You get a lot more benefit and you can do a lot more with a global brand than you can a local brand. You can bring the best advertising talent from the world on to a problem. You can bring the best research brains, the best leverage of your organization onto something that is truly global. Then all your R&D pays off, the huge packaging costs pay off, the advertising pays off, and you can leverage the organization all at once."[47]

45 Amy Borrus, "Eyeglasses for the Masses," *Business Week* (November 20, 1995), pp. 104–105; Nicholas Thompson, "Self-Adjusted Glasses Could Be Boon to Africa," *The New York Times* (December 10, 2002), p. D6.
46 Christopher A. Bartlett and Sumantra Ghoshal, "Going Global: Lessons from Late Movers," *Harvard Business Review* 78, no. 2 (March–April 2000), p. 137.
47 Pam Weisz, "Border Crossings: Brands Unify Image to Counter Cult of Culture," *Brandweek* (October 31, 1994), p. 24.
48 Bruce Wiebusch, "Deere, Hogs, and International Design," *Design News* (November 18, 2002).

Table 10-4

*Product Markets Compared:
United States and EU Versus BRIC*

United States and EU	Brazil	Russia	India	China
Product Development and Intellectual Property Rights (IPR)				
Sophisticated product-design capabilities are available. Governments enforce IPR and protect trademarks so R&D investments yield competitive advantages.	Local design capability exists. IPR disputes have arisen in some sectors.	Russia possesses a strong local design capability but exhibits an ambivalent attitude about IPR. Sufficient regulatory authority exists, but enforcement is inconsistent.	Some local design capability is available. IPR problems with the United States exist in some industries. Regulatory bodies monitor product quality and fraud.	Imitation and piracy abound. Punishment for IPR theft varies across provinces and by level of corruption.
Brand Perceptions and Management				
Markets are mature and have strong local and global brands. The profusion of brands clutters consumer choice. Numerous ad agencies are available.	Consumers accept both local and global brands. Global as well as local ad agencies are present.	Consumers prefer global brands in automobiles and high tech. Local brands thrive in the food and beverage businesses. Some local and global ad agencies are available.	Consumers buy both local and global brands. Global ad agencies are present, but they have been less successful than local ad agencies.	Consumers prefer to buy products from American, European, and Japanese companies. Global ad agencies dominate the business.

Source: Adapted from Tarun Khanna, Krishna G. Palepu, and Jayant Sinha, "Strategies That Fit Emerging Markets," *Harvard Business Review* 83, no. 6 (June 2005), p. 69.

How to Choose a Strategy

Most companies seek product-communications strategies that optimize company profits over the long term. Which strategy for global markets best achieves this goal? There is no general answer to this question. For starters, the considerations noted before must be addressed. In addition, it is worth noting that managers run the risk of committing two types of errors regarding product and communication decisions. One error is to fall victim to the **"not invented here" (NIH) syndrome**, *ignoring* decisions made by subsidiary or affiliate managers. Managers who behave in this way are essentially abandoning any effort to leverage product-communication policies outside the home-country market. The other error has been to *impose* policies upon all affiliate companies on the assumption that what is right for customers in the home market must also be right for customers everywhere.

To sum up, the choice of product-communication strategy in global marketing is a function of three key factors: (1) the product itself, defined in terms of the function or need it serves; (2) the market, defined in terms of the conditions under which the product is used, the preferences of potential customers, and the ability and willingness to buy; and (3) adaptation and manufacture costs to the company considering these product-communication approaches. Only after analysis of the product-market fit and of company capabilities and costs can executives choose the most profitable strategy. Table 10-4 identifies important product and communication strategy issues in the United States and EU and compares and contrasts them with the BRIC countries.

NEW PRODUCTS IN GLOBAL MARKETING

The matrix shown in Figure 10-4 provides a framework for assessing whether extension or adaptation strategies can be effective. However, the four strategic options described in the matrix do not necessarily represent the best possible responses to global market opportunities. To win in global competition, marketers, designers, and engineers must think outside the box and create innovative new products that offer superior value worldwide. In today's dynamic, competitive market environment, many companies realize that continuous development and introduction of new products are keys to survival and growth. That is the point of Strategy 5, product innovation. Similarly, marketers should look for opportunities to create global advertising campaigns to support the new product or brand.

Identifying New-Product Ideas

What is a new product? A product's newness can be assessed in the context of its relation to those who buy or use it. Newness may also be organizational, as when a company acquires an already existing product with which it has no previous experience. Finally, an existing product that is not new to a company may be new to a particular market. The starting point for an effective worldwide new-product program is an information system that seeks new-product ideas from all potentially useful sources and channels these ideas to relevant screening and decision centers within the organization. Ideas can come from many sources, including customers, suppliers, competitors, company salespeople, distributors and agents, subsidiary executives, headquarters executives, documentary sources (e.g., information service reports and publications), and, finally, actual firsthand observation of the market environment.

The product may be an entirely new invention or innovation that requires a relatively large amount of learning on the part of users. When such products are successful, they create new markets and new consumption patterns that literally represent a break with the past; they are sometimes called **discontinuous innovations**.[49] For example, the VCR's revolutionary impact can be explained by the concept of time shifting: The device's initial appeal was that it freed TV viewers from the tyranny of network programming schedules. For the first time, it was possible to record television programming for viewing at a later time. The VCR's market growth and acceptance was also driven by the video rental industry, which sprang up to serve the needs of VCR owners. Likewise, the personal computer revolution that began two decades ago has resulted in the democratization of technology. When they were first introduced, PCs were a continuous innovation that dramatically transformed the way users live and work.

An intermediate category of newness is less disruptive and requires less learning on the part of consumers; such products are called **dynamically continuous innovations**. Products that embody this level of innovation share certain features with earlier generations while incorporating new features that offer added value such as a substantial improvement in performance or greater convenience. Such products cause relatively smaller disruptions of previously existing consumption patterns. The Sensor, SensorExcel, and Mach3 shaving systems represent Gillette's ongoing efforts to bring new technology to bear on wet shaving, an activity that is performed today pretty much as it has been for decades. The consumer electronics industry has been the source of many dynamically continuous innovations. Personal stereos such as Sony's Walkman provide music on the go, something that people had grown accustomed to since the transistor radio was introduced in the

---

[49] The terminology and framework described here are adapted from Thomas Robertson, "The Process of Innovation and the Diffusion of Innovation," *Journal of Marketing* 31, no. 1 (January 1967), pp. 14–19.

Figure 10-5

New Product Continuum

Continuous innovations	Dynamically continuous innovations	Discontinuous innovations
Least disrupting influence on established consumption patterns	Some disrupting influence on established consumption patterns	Requires new consumption patterns and the creation of previously unknown products

1950s; the innovation was a miniaturized cassette playback system. The advent of the compact disc in the early 1980s provided an improved music listening experience but didn't require significant behavioral changes. Similarly, much to the delight of couch potatoes everywhere, widescreen TV sets with flat-panel LCD and plasma displays offer viewers significantly improved performance without enabling or requiring new behaviors.

Most new products fall into a third category, **continuous innovation**. Such products are typically "new and improved" versions of existing ones and require less R&D expenditure to develop than dynamically continuous innovations. Continuous innovations cause minimal disruption of existing consumption patterns and require the least amount of learning on the part of buyers. As noted previously, newness can be evaluated relative to a buyer or user. When a current PC user seeking an upgrade buys a new model with a faster processor or more memory, the PC can be viewed as a continuous innovation. However, to a first-time user, the same computer represents a discontinuous innovation. Consumer packaged goods companies and food marketers rely heavily on continuous innovation when rolling out new products. These often take the form of **line extensions** such as new sizes, flavors, and low-fat versions. The three degrees of product newness can be represented in terms of a continuum as shown in Figure 10-5.

New-Product Development

A major driver for the development of global products is the cost of product R&D. As competition intensifies, companies discover they can reduce the cost of R&D for a product by developing a global product design. Often the goal is to create a single **platform**, or core product design element or component, that can be quickly and cheaply adapted to various country markets. As Christopher Sinclair noted during his tenure as president and CEO of PepsiCo Foods and Beverages International, "What you really want to do is look at the four or five platforms that can allow you to cut across countries, become a scale operator, and do the things that global marketers do."[50]

Even automobiles, which must meet national safety and pollution standards, are now designed with global markets in mind. With a global product platform, automakers can offer an adaptation of a global design as needed instead of creating unique designs for individual countries or geographic regions. The Ford Focus, launched in Europe at the end of 1998 and in the United States in 1999, is being marketed globally with a minimum of adaptation. The chief program engineer on the Focus project was from Great Britain, the chief technical officer was German, an Irishwoman managed the project, and an Anglo-Australian was chief designer. Under Ford 2000, about $1,000 per vehicle was cut out of the development cost.[51]

---

[50] "Fritos 'Round the World," *Brandweek* (March 27, 1995), pp. 32, 35.
[51] Robert L. Simison, "Ford Hopes Its New Focus Will Be a Global Bestseller," *The Wall Street Journal* (October 8, 1998), p. B10.

A standardized platform was also a paramount consideration when GM set about the task of redesigning its minivan. GM's globally minded board directed the design team to create a vehicle that would be popular in both the United States and Europe. Because roads in Europe are typically narrower and fuel is more expensive, the European engineers lobbied for a vehicle that was smaller than the typical minivan. In the end, interior designers were able to provide ample interior space in a slightly smaller body. By using lightweight metals such as magnesium for some components, vehicle weight was minimized, with a corresponding improvement in fuel economy. In the United States, the minivans are marketed as the Chevrolet Venture, Pontiac Transport, and Oldsmobile Silhouette. The Opel Sentra version will be exported to Germany; the right-hand-drive Vauxhall Sintra is destined for the British market.[52]

Other design-related costs, whether incurred by the manufacturer or the end user, must also be considered. *Durability* and *quality* are important product characteristics that must be appropriate for the proposed market. In the United States and Europe, car buyers do not wish to incur high service bills. Ironically, the new Ford Focus was designed to be less expensive to maintain and repair. For example, engine removal takes only about 1.5 hours, about half the time required to remove the engine in the discontinued Escort. In addition, body panels are bolted together rather than welded, and the rear signal lights are mounted higher so they are less likely to be broken in minor parking lot mishaps.

The International New Product Department

As noted previously, a high volume of information flow is required to scan adequately for new-product opportunities, and considerable effort is subsequently required to screen these opportunities to identify candidates for product development. The best organizational design for addressing these requirements is a new-product department. Managers in such a department engage in several activities. First, they ensure that all relevant information sources are continuously tapped for new-product ideas. Second, they screen these ideas to identify candidates for investigation. Third, they investigate and analyze selected new-product ideas. Finally, they ensure that the organization commits resources to the most likely new-product candidates and is continuously involved in an orderly program of new-product introduction and development on a worldwide basis.

With the enormous number of possible new products, most companies establish screening grids in order to focus on those ideas that are most appropriate for investigation. The following questions are relevant to this task:

1. How big is the market for this product at various prices?
2. What are the likely competitive moves in response to our activity with this product?
3. Can we market the product through our existing structure? If not, what changes will be required, and what costs will be incurred to make the changes?
4. Given estimates of potential demand for this product at specified prices with estimated levels of competition, can we source the product at a cost that will yield an adequate profit?
5. Does this product fit our strategic development plan? (a) Is the product consistent with our overall goals and objectives? (b) Is the product consistent with our available resources? (c) Is the product consistent with our management structure? (d) Does the product have adequate global potential?

---

[52] Rebecca Blumenstein, "While Going Global, GM Slips at Home," *The Wall Street Journal* (January 8, 1997), pp. B1, B4.

For example, the corporate development team at Virgin evaluates more than a dozen proposals each day from outside the company, as well as proposals from Virgin staff members. Brad Rosser, Virgin's former Group Corporate Development Director, headed the team for several years. When assessing new-product ideas, Rosser and his group looked for synergy with existing Virgin products, pricing, marketing opportunities, risk versus return on investment, and whether the idea "uses or abuses" the Virgin brand. Recent ventures that have been given the green light are Virgin Jeans, a denim clothing store chain; Virgin Bride, a wedding consulting service; and Virgin Net, an Internet service provider.[53]

Testing New Products

The major lesson of new-product introduction outside the home market has been that whenever a product interacts with human, mechanical, or chemical elements, there is the potential for a surprising and unexpected incompatibility. Because virtually *every* product matches this description, it is important to test a product under actual market conditions before proceeding with full-scale introduction. A test does not necessarily involve a full-scale test-marketing effort. It may be simply observing the actual use of the product in the target market.

Failure to assess actual use conditions can lead to big surprises, as Unilever learned when it rolled out a new detergent brand in Europe without sufficient testing. Unilever spent $150 million to develop the new detergent, which was formulated with a stain-fighting manganese complex molecule intended to clean fabrics faster at lower temperatures than competing products such as Procter & Gamble's Ariel. Backed by a $300 million marketing budget, the detergent was launched in April 1994 as Persil Power, Omo Power, and other brand names. After a restructuring, Unilever had cut the time required to roll out new products in Europe from 3 years to 16 months. In this particular instance, the increased efficiency combined with corporate enthusiasm for the new formula resulted in a marketing debacle. Consumers discovered that some clothing items were damaged after being washed with Power. P&G was quick to capitalize on the situation; P&G ran newspaper ads denouncing Power and commissioned lab tests to verify that the damage did, in fact, occur. Unilever chairman Sir Michael Perry called the Power fiasco, "the greatest marketing setback we've seen." Unilever reformulated Power, but it was too late to save the brand. The company lost the opportunity to gain share against P&G in Europe.[54] Ultimately, a reformulated version of the product was launched under the Persil Performance brand.

---

[53] Elena Bowes, "Virgin Flies in Face of Conventions," *Ad Age International* (January 1997), p. i4.
[54] Laurel Wentz, "Unilever's Power Failure a Wasteful Use of Haste," *Advertising Age* (May 6, 1995), p. 42.

The product is the most important element of a company's marketing program. Global marketers face the challenge of formulating coherent product and brand strategies on a worldwide basis. A **product** can be viewed as a collection of tangible and intangible attributes that collectively provide benefits to a buyer or user. A **brand** is a complex bundle of images and experiences in the mind of the customer. In most countries, **local brands** compete with **international brands** and **global brands**. A **global product** meets the wants and needs of a global market. A **global brand** has the same name and a similar image and positioning in most parts of the world. Many global companies leverage favorable **brand images** and high **brand equity** by employing **combination (tiered) branding**, **co-branding**, and **brand extension** strategies. Companies can create strong brands in all markets through **global brand leadership**. **Maslow's hierarchy** is a needs-based framework that offers a way of understanding opportunities to develop local and global products in different parts of the world. Some products and brands benefit from the **country-of-origin effect**. Product decisions must also address packaging issues such as **labeling** and **aesthetics**. Also, **warranty** policies must be appropriate for each country market.

Product and communications strategies can be viewed within a framework that allows for combinations of three strategies: **extension strategy**, **adaptation strategy**, and **innovation strategy**.

Five strategic alternatives are open to companies pursuing geographic expansion: **product-communication extension**, **product extension-communication adaptation**, **product adaptation-communication extension**, **product-communication adaptation**, and **innovation**. The strategic alternative(s) that a particular company chooses will depend on the product and the need it serves, customer preferences and purchasing power, and the costs of adaptation versus standardization. **Product transformation** occurs when a product that has been introduced into new country markets serves a different function or is used differently than originally intended. When choosing a strategy, management should consciously strive to avoid the **"not invented here" (NIH) syndrome**.

Global competition has put pressure on companies to excel at developing standardized product **platforms** that can serve as a foundation for cost-efficient adaptation. New products can be classified as **discontinuous, dynamically continuous,** or **continuous innovations**. A successful product launch requires an understanding of how markets develop: sequentially over time or simultaneously. Today, many new products are launched in multiple national markets as product development cycles shorten and product development costs soar.

1. What is the difference between a product and a brand?

2. How do local, international, and global products differ? Cite examples.

3. What are some of the elements that make up a brand? Are these elements tangible or intangible?

4. What criteria should global marketers consider when making product design decisions?

5. How can buyer attitudes about a product's country of origin affect marketing strategy?

6. Identify several global brands. What are some of the reasons for the global success of the brands you chose?

7. Briefly describe various combinations of product-communication strategies available to global marketers. When is it appropriate to use each?

8. Compare and contrast the three categories of innovation discussed in the chapter. Which type of innovation do flat-panel widescreen HDTVs represent?

1. Each August, *Business Week* magazine features a survey of global brands as a cover story. The top-ranked brands for 2006 are shown in Table 10-2. Browse through the list and choose any brand that interests you. Compare its 2006 ranking with the most recent ranking, which you can find either by referring to the print version of *Business Week* or by accessing the article online. How has the brand's ranking changed? Consult additional sources (e.g., articles from print media, annual reports, the company's Web site) to enhance your understanding of the factors and forces that contributed to the brand's move up or down in the rankings.

1. In Chapter 1, you were introduced to the notion of *leverage* as a driver of a company's global marketing effort. Here in Chapter 10, Colgate's John Steel talks about the importance of leverage in the launch of Total brand toothpaste. Review the discussion in Chapter 1 and relate it to the Colgate discussion in Chapter 10. This should deepen your understanding of the importance of leverage in global marketing strategy decisions.

Case 10-1

Now Underway in Your Living Room: The Video Game Console Wars

Every year, flat-panel HDTVs are big sellers during the holiday shopping season (see chapter opening). A wide variety of HDTVs are available from the world's leading electronics manufacturers. Just down the aisle at Wal-Mart, Best Buy, and similar retailers, Nintendo and Sony are waging a separate marketing battle for the hearts, minds, and dollars of consumers. In November 2006, after months of delays, Sony launched PlayStation 3 (PS3) in the United States. PS3's advanced graphics capability was provided by a built-in high-definition DVD player using a format known as Blu-ray. PS3 was initially available in two models—one with a 20 gigabyte hard drive and the other with 60 gigabytes—priced at $499 and $599. In December, Nintendo launched Wii, its latest video game console. Priced at $250, €249 (eurozone), and £179 (United Kingdom), the Wii features a wireless motion-sensitive controller that allows players to simulate such activities as fishing, golfing, and fencing. The new game consoles began arriving about one year after Microsoft's Xbox 360, worldwide, approximately 10 million units had been sold by the end of 2006.

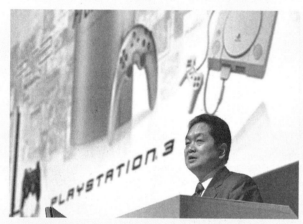

Sony Blu-ray / Mr. Kutaragi announcing launch

Industry observers noted that Nintendo and Sony's strategies for their respective game consoles entail major risks. Nintendo was defying orthodox wisdom in the industry, according to which each new generation of machines has to be faster and more powerful than the preceding generation. Nintendo's designers, whose previous consoles included the Nintendo 64 (1996) and GameCube (2001), deliberately chose a different path: They created a machine that is simpler to use and less costly to manufacture. The designers were also guided by the sense that many video games had gotten so complicated to learn that they appealed mainly to advanced gamers. As Satoru Iwata, president and director at Nintendo, noted, "Everyone thought that consumers would continue to buy new consoles as long as you could play more real and more impressive games. There were also people who would

quietly walk away because they got too complex." With the Wii, Nintendo hoped to appeal to veteran players addicted to games like *Mario Brothers* and *Zelda* as well as inexperienced or novice players.

Sony had enjoyed massive worldwide success with the PlayStation (1994) and PlayStation 2 (PS2) (2000), each of which had sold more than 100 million units. PS2 commanded an impressive 70 percent share of the console market. Sony's designers intended to "up the ante" with PS3. For one thing, the company spent nearly $2 billion on a new processing chip called Cell that packs as much speed as a supercomputer and offers superior graphics quality. Another component, a laser diode that plays next-generation high-definition DVDs, was intended to drive adoption of a new video format called Blu-ray that Sony had developed. However, the diode proved to be difficult to produce in mass quantities, contributing to product shortages at the U.S. holiday launch.

The PS3's Blu-ray capability represented a new battleground in the consumer electronic industry's drive to turn living rooms everywhere into digital entertainment hubs. As consumers upgrade to high-definition TVs, many also want to view DVD movies in high definition. Conventional DVDs can play movies in widescreen format; however, the picture is standard definition. Although this represents an improvement over VHS cassettes, conventional DVDs only offer 480 lines of resolution.

In spring 2006, Toshiba had launched dedicated next-generation digital video players with a format known as HD-DVD. Both HD-DVD and Blu-ray feature high-definition DVD playback; this means that home video buffs can enjoy 1080 lines of resolution—the highest-quality video playback possible—on their widescreen HDTV sets. However, Sony's Blu-ray technology is incompatible with Toshiba's; this means that a Blu-ray player such as Sony's BDP-S1 or PS3 is required to play a Blu-ray movie. Similarly, a player from Toshiba is required to view a movie in the HD-DVD format; alternatively, Xbox 360 owners can add an HD DVD Player to their game console for $199. In either format, stand-alone high-definition video players are expensive; the Sony BDP-S1 carries a list price of $999.99, while the S300 lists for $600.00. Toshiba's models range in price from $399.99 to $799.99.

In March 2007, PS3 finally went on sale in Europe. Some industry observers believe that the success or failure of the European launch will ultimately determine the outcome of the video console war. As Paul Jackson, an analyst with Forrester Research, explained, "I think Europe is viewed by Microsoft and Sony as the most important territory. Microsoft is almost certainly going to win in the United States and Sony is almost certainly going to win in Japan, eventually, depending on whether the Wii's appeal as a novelty item is going to peter out. Europeans, however, are pretty agnostic and tend to buy whatever has the coolest games."

Discussion Questions

1. Compare and contrast Nintendo's marketing strategy for the Wii with Sony's strategy for PS3.
2. What is the key to the Wii's popularity?

3. Do you agree with Sony's decision to incorporate a Blu-ray DVD player in the PS3?

4. Some industry observers have noted that the battle between HD-DVD and Blu-ray is reminiscent of the showdown between the Beta and VHS videocassette formats in the 1970s. What was the outcome?

Sources: Chris Nuttall, Maija Palmer, and Mariko Sanchanta, "Sony Console Hits Crucial European Market," *Financial Times* (March 23, 2007), p. 16; Josh Caffin and Paul Taylor, "Sony and Toshiba Could Be Left Behind in Format War," *Financial Times* (December 19, 2006), p. 14; Joseph Pereira and Nick Wingfield, "Wii! Wii! Wii! This Holiday Season Has Been a Wild Ride for Nintendo," *The Wall Street Journal* (December 12, 2006), p. b1; Chris Nuttal, "Console Makers Go for a Slam Dunk," *Financial Times* (November 17, 2006), p. 8; Michiyo Nakamoto and Leo Lewis, "Sony Prepares for Big Game Battle," *Financial Times* (November 10, 2006), p. 21; John Gapper, "Sony is Scoring Low at its Own Game," *Financial Times* (November 6, 2006), p. 8; Yukari Iwatani Kane and Nick Wingfield, "Out of the Box: Amid Videogame Arms Race, Nintendo Slows Things Down," *The Wall Street Journal* (November 2, 2006), pp. A1, A10; Paul Taylor, "Coming Soon: Films on File," *Financial Times* (May 31, 2006), p. 7; Robert Levine, "En Garde! Fight Foes Using a Controller Like a Sword," *The New York Times* (October 30, 2006), p. C5.

Case 10-2
The Smart Car

In the summer of 2006, DaimlerChrysler announced that the company's Smart car would be offered for sale in the United States the following year. Launched in Europe in 1998, the diminutive Smart had never turned a profit for its parent company. When Dieter Zetsche (who appeared in American TV ads for Chrysler as "Doctor Z") became DaimlerChrysler's CEO at the beginning of 2006, the Smart car issue was one of his top priorities.

At the time of the announcement, the Smart saga had been 15 years in the making. In 1991, Nicolas Hayek, chairman of Swatch, announced plans to develop a battery-powered "Swatch car" in conjunction with Volkswagen. At the time, Hayek said his goal was to build "an ecologically inoffensive, high-quality city car for two people" that would sell for about $6,400. The Swatchmobile concept was based on Hayek's conviction that consumers become emotionally attached to cars just as they do to watches. Like the Swatch, the Swatchmobile (officially named "Smart") was designed to be affordable, durable, and stylish. Early on, Hayek noted that safety would be another

Thanks to the success of the Smart car in Europe, several new models have been added to the Smart family. These include the convertible Smart Roadster and the Smart Forfour (a four-door model). An SUV—the Smart Formore—was introduced in 2006. The original model will be rechristened the Smart City Coupé. As one observer noted, "Buying a Smart is less like buying a small car and more like buying an iMac, a Blackberry PDA, or a box of take-out sushi".

key selling point, declaring, "This car will have the crash security of a Mercedes." Composite exterior panels mounted on a cage-like body frame would allow owners to change colors by switching panels. Further, Hayek envisioned a car that emitted almost no pollutants, thanks to its electric engine. The car would also offer gasoline-powered operation, using a highly efficient, miniaturized engine capable of achieving speeds of 80 miles per hour. Hayek predicted that worldwide sales would reach one million units, with the United States accounting for about half the market.

In 1993, the alliance with Volkswagen was dissolved. In the spring of 1994, Hayek announced that he had lined up a new joint venture partner. The Mercedes-Benz unit of Daimler-Benz AG would invest 750 million Deutsche marks in a new factory in Hambach-Saargemuend, France. In November 1998, after several months of production delays and repeated cost overruns, Hayek sold Swatch's remaining 19 percent stake in the venture, officially known as Micro Compact Car GmBH (MCC), to Mercedes. A spokesman indicated that Mercedes' refusal to pursue the hybrid gasoline-battery engine was the reason Swatch withdrew from the project.

The decision by Mercedes executives to take full control of the venture was consistent with its strategy for leveraging its engineering skills and broadening the company's appeal beyond the luxury segment of the automobile market. As Mercedes Chairman Helmut Werner said, "With the new car, Mercedes wants to combine ecology, emotion, and intellect." Approximately 80 percent of the Smart's parts are components and modules engineered by and sourced from outside suppliers and subcontractors known as "system partners." The decision to locate the assembly plant in France disappointed German labor unions, but Mercedes executives expected to save 500 marks per car. The reason: French workers are on the job 275 days per year, while German workers average only 242 days; also, overall labor costs are 40 percent lower in France than in Germany.

MCC claims that at Smart Ville, as the factory is known, only 7.5 hours are required to complete a vehicle—25 percent less time than required by the world's best automakers. The first 3 hours of the process are performed by systems partners. A Canadian company, Magna International, starts by welding the structural components, which are then painted by Eisenmann, a German company. Both operations are performed outside the central assembly hall; a conveyer then transports the body into the main hall. There VDO, another German company, installs the instrument panel. At this point, modules and parts manufactured by Krupp-Hoesch, Bosch, Dynamit Nobel, and Ymos are delivered for assembly by MCC employees. To encourage integration of MCC employees and system partners and to underscore the need for quality, both groups share a common dining room overlooking the main assembly hall.

The Smart City Coupé officially went on sale in Europe in October 1998. In an effort to create a distinct brand identity, a separate dealer network was established for Smart. In retrospect, this decision turned out to be an expensive one. Sales got off to a slow start amid concerns about the vehicle's stability. That problem was solved with a sophisticated electronic package that monitors wheel slippage. Late-night TV comedians gave the odd-looking car no respect and referred to it as "a motorized ski boot" and "a backpack on wheels." The sales picture was brightest in the United Kingdom; the brisk sales pace in Britain was especially noteworthy because MCC was only building left-hand drive models (the United Kingdom is the only country in Europe in which right-hand drive cars are the norm). Industry observers noted that Brits' affection for the Austin Mini, a tiny vehicle that first appeared in the 1960s, appeared to have been extended to the Smart. Despite this success, MCC reduced its annual sales target from 130,000 to 100,000. Robert Easton, joint chairman of DaimlerChrysler, went on record as being skeptical of the vehicle's future. In an interview with *Automotive News*, he said, "It's possible we'll conclude that it's a good idea but one whose time simply hasn't come."

In 2000, amid growing interest in the brand, the Smart exceeded its revised sales target. Wolf-Garten GmbH & Company, a German gardening equipment company, announced plans to convert the Smart to a lawn mower suitable for use on golf courses. Both convertible and diesel-engine editions have been added to the product line. In 2001, executives at DaimlerChrysler announced plans to research the U.S. market to determine prospects for the Smart. The announcement came as Americans were facing steep

increases in gasoline prices. Between 2001 and 2006, several other small cars in the $10,000 to $14,000 range were introduced in the U.S. market, including the Chevrolet Aveo (manufactured by Daewoo), the Toyota Yaris, and the Honda Fit. One challenge in bringing the Smart across the Atlantic is the euro's strength relative to the dollar.

Discussion Questions

1. What is Smart's competitive advantage?
2. Assess the U.S. market potential for the Smart. Do you think the car will be a success? Why or why not?
3. Identify other target markets into which you would introduce this car. What sequence of countries would you recommend for the introduction?

Integrate Your Global Marketing Skills

Review Case 7-1 on the Honda Element and Toyota Scion. Are these models targeting the same consumers as the Smart? In view of the Japanese carmakers' success with these brands, do you think the Smart's U.S. launch is too late?

Visit the Web Site
www.smart.com

Sources: Bernard Simon, "Daimler Weighs Smart's U.S. Appeal," *Financial Times* (March 28, 2006, p. 21; "Smart Shows Redesigned Fortwo," *The Wall Street Journal Online* (November 10, 2006); Neal E. Boudette and Stephen Power, "Will Chrysler's Move Be Smart?" *The Wall Street Journal* (June 24–25, 2006), p. A2; Dan McCosh, "Get Smart: Buyers Try to Jump the Queue," *The New York Times* (March 19, 2004), p. D1; Nicholas Foulkes "Smart Set Gets Even Smarter," *Financial Times* (February 14–15, 2004), p. W10; Will Pinkston and Scott Miller, "DaimlerChrysler Steers Toward 'Smart' Debut in U.S.," *The Wall Street Journal* (August 20, 2001), pp. B1, B4; Scott Miller, "Daimler May Roll Out Its Tiny Car Here," *The Wall Street Journal* (June 9, 2001), p. B1; Scott Miller, "DaimlerChrysler's Smart Car May Have a New Use," *The Wall Street Journal* (February 15, 2001), pp. B1, B4; Haig Simonian, "Carmakers' Smart Move," *Financial Times* (July 1, 1997), p. 12; William Taylor, "Message and Muscle: An Interview with Swatch Titan Nicolas Hayek," *Harvard Business Review* (March–April 1993), pp. 99–110; Kevin Helliker, "Swiss Movement: Can Wristwatch Whiz Switch Swatch Cachet to an Automobile?" *The Wall Street Journal* (March 4, 1994), pp. A1, A3; Ferdinand Protzman, "Off the Wrist, Onto the Road: A Swatch on Wheels," *The New York Times* (March 4, 1994), p. C1.

> *"The Smart brand is capable of sustainable profitability, and it will be profitable in 2007 and beyond. We are working on a cost basis that is almost 50% lower than it used to be. The production time at the Hambach plant in France and the assembly time for the new car are 20% shorter than with its predecessor."*
>
> Ulrich Walker, Chairman and CEO, DaimlerChrysler Northeast Asia Division, former President and CEO, Smart

11 Pricing Decisions

Twentieth Century Fox, the film entertainment unit of Rupert Murdoch's News Corporation, has a problem: Video pirates are siphoning off profits from the studio's hit movies. In many parts of the world, lax enforcement of intellectual property laws creates an opportunity for unscrupulous merchants to sell counterfeit DVDs at rock-bottom prices. In emerging markets, such as Mexico, Russia, and China, piracy costs Fox and rival movie studios hundreds of millions of dollars each year. These losses reflect both decreased ticket sales at movie theaters and decreased sales of legitimate DVD releases. It is not uncommon for counterfeit copies of Hollywood's latest blockbuster to hit the streets before the movie has even opened in local cinemas. The Motion Picture Association of America estimates that, in China alone, losses totaled $244 billion in 2005. In China and elsewhere, the movie studios take legal action against the counterfeiters. Despite such efforts, Chinese merchants do a brisk trade in DVDs that sell for as little as RMB10—the equivalent of about $1.20. Now Fox is adopting a new approach in China: charging less than RMB30 for new DVD releases. The studio is hoping that, at this price, Chinese movie lovers will be motivated to buy an official version rather than a counterfeit.

In general, two basic factors determine the boundaries within which prices should be set. The first is product cost, which establishes a *price floor*, or minimum price. Although pricing a product below the cost boundary is certainly possible, few firms can afford to do this over the long run. Moreover, as we saw in Chapter 8, low prices in export markets can invite dumping investigations. Second, prices for comparable substitute products create a *price ceiling*, or maximum price. In many instances, global competition puts pressure on the pricing policies and related cost structures of domestic companies. The imperative to cut costs—especially fixed costs—is one of the reasons for the growth of outsourcing. In some cases, local market conditions such as piracy force companies such as Fox to adopt innovative pricing tactics. Between the lower and upper boundary for every product there is an *optimum price*, which is a function of the demand for the product as determined by the willingness and ability of customers to buy. In this chapter, we will review basic pricing concepts and then discuss several pricing topics that pertain to global marketing. These include target costing, price escalation, and environmental considerations such as currency fluctuations and inflation. In the second half of the chapter, we will discuss gray market goods, dumping, price fixing, transfer pricing, and countertrade.

Home video piracy—including DVDs and VHS tapes—is rampant in many parts of the world. The Motion Picture Association of America claims that Hollywood loses $3.5 billion each year due to piracy; according to another estimate, the figure could exceed $6 billion.

BASIC PRICING CONCEPTS

Generally speaking, international trade results in lower prices for goods. Lower prices, in turn, help keep a country's rate of inflation in check. In a true global market, the **law of one price** would prevail: All customers in the market could get the best product available for the best price. As Lowell Bryan and his collaborators note in *Race for the World*, a global market exists for certain products such as integrated circuits, crude oil, and commercial aircraft: All other things being equal, a Boeing 777 costs the same worldwide. By contrast, beer, compact discs, and many other products that are available around the world are actually being offered in markets that are national rather than global in nature. That is, these are markets where national competition reflects differences in factors such as costs, regulation, and the intensity of the rivalry among industry members.[1] The beer market is extremely fragmented; for example, even though Budweiser is the leading global brand, it commands less than 4 percent of the total market. The nature of the beer market explains why; for example, a six-pack of Heineken varies in price by as much as 50 percent (adjusted for purchasing power parity, transportation, and other transaction costs) depending on where it is sold. In Japan, for example, the price is a function of the competition between Heineken, other imports, and five national producers—Kirin, Asahi, Sapporo, Suntory, and Orion—that collectively command 60 percent of the market.

Because of these differences in national markets, the global marketer must develop pricing systems and pricing policies that take into account price floors, price ceilings, and optimum prices. A firm's pricing system and policies must also be consistent with other uniquely global opportunities and constraints. For example, many companies that are active in the 13 nations of the euro zone are adjusting to the new cross-border transparency of prices. Similarly, the Internet has made price information for many products available around the globe. Companies must carefully consider how customers in one country or region will react if they discover they are paying significantly higher prices for the same product as customers in other parts of the world.

---

[1]   Lowell Bryan, *Race for the World: Strategies to Build a Great Global Firm* (Boston: Harvard Business School Press, 1999), pp. 40–41.

There is another important internal organizational consideration besides cost. Within the typical corporation, there are many interest groups and, frequently, conflicting price objectives. Divisional vice presidents, regional executives, and country managers are each concerned about profitability at their respective organizational levels. Similarly, the director of global marketing seeks competitive prices in world markets. The controller and financial vice president are concerned about profits. The manufacturing vice president seeks long production runs for maximum manufacturing efficiency. The tax manager is concerned about compliance with government transfer pricing legislation. Finally, company counsel is concerned about the antitrust implications of global pricing practices. Ultimately, price generally reflects the goals set by members or the sales staff, product managers, corporate division chiefs, and/or the company's chief executive.

GLOBAL PRICING OBJECTIVES AND STRATEGIES

Whether dealing with a single home country market or multiple country markets, marketing managers must develop pricing objectives as well as strategies for achieving those objectives. However, a number of pricing issues are unique to global marketing. The pricing strategy for a particular product may vary from country to country; a product may be positioned as a low-priced, mass-market product in some countries and a premium-priced, niche product in others. Stella Artois beer is a case in point. Pricing objectives may also vary depending on a product's life-cycle stage and the country-specific competitive situation. In making global pricing decisions, it is also necessary to factor in external considerations such as the added cost associated with shipping goods long distances across national boundaries. The issue of global pricing can also be fully integrated in the product-design process, an approach widely used by Japanese companies.

Market Skimming and Financial Objectives

Price can be used as a strategic variable to achieve specific financial goals, including return on investment, profit, and rapid recovery of product development costs. When financial criteria such as profit and maintenance of margins are the objectives, the product must be part of a superior value proposition for buyers; price is integral to the total positioning strategy. The **market skimming** pricing strategy is often part of a deliberate attempt to reach a market segment that is willing to pay a premium price for a particular brand or for a specialized or unique product. Companies that seek competitive advantage by pursuing differentiation strategies or positioning their products in the premium segment frequently use market skimming. LVMH and other luxury goods marketers that target the global elite market segment use skimming strategies. For years, Mercedes-Benz utilized a skimming strategy; however, this created an opportunity for Toyota to introduce its luxury Lexus line and undercut Mercedes.

The skimming pricing strategy is also appropriate in the introductory phase of the product life cycle when both production capacity and competition are limited. By setting a deliberately high price, demand is limited to innovators and early adopters who are willing and able to pay the price. When the product enters the growth stage of the life cycle and competition increases, manufacturers start to cut prices. This strategy has been used consistently in the consumer electronics industry; for example, when Sony introduced the first consumer VCRs in the 1970s, the retail price exceeded $1,000. The same was true when compact disc players were launched in the early 1980s. Within a few years, prices for these products dropped well below $500. Today, both products are considered commodities.

A similar pattern is evident with HDTVs; in the fall of 1998, HDTV sets went on sale in the United States with prices starting at about $7,000. This price maximized revenue on limited volume and matched demand to available supply. Already, prices for HDTV sets are dropping significantly as consumers become more familiar with HDTV and its advantages and as next-generation factories in Asia bring lower costs and increased production capacity. In 2005, Sony surprised the industry by launching a 40-inch HDTV for $3,500; by the end of 2006, comparable HDTVs were selling for about $2,000. The challenge facing manufacturers now is to hold the line on prices; if they do not succeed, HDTVs may also become commoditized.

Penetration Pricing and Nonfinancial Objectives

Some companies are pursuing nonfinancial objectives with their pricing strategy. Price can be used as a competitive weapon to gain or maintain market position. Market share or other sales-based objectives are frequently set by companies that enjoy cost-leadership positions in their industry. A **market penetration pricing strategy** calls for setting price levels that are low enough to quickly build market share. Historically, many companies that used this type of pricing were located in the Pacific Rim. Scale-efficient plants and low-cost labor allowed these companies to blitz the market.

It should be noted that a first-time exporter is unlikely to use penetration pricing. The reason is simple: Penetration pricing often means that the product may be sold at a loss for a certain length of time. Unlike Sony, many companies that are new to exporting cannot absorb such losses, nor are they likely to have the marketing

the rest of the story

Using Price to Combat Video Piracy

Pirated movies are found in other emerging country markets as well. In Russia, for example, customs duties and tariffs contribute to retail prices equivalent to $20 or $30 for an authentic DVD; pirated versions sell for about $4. Columbia TriStar has responded to the situation in Russia by cutting prices to the equivalent of $10; as Vyacheslav Dobychin, director of Columbia TriStar's licensee in Russia, explained, "The idea is to get Russian consumers used to buying licensed material, but at a price that most of the population can afford. We're changing distribution from the 'exclusive model' to the 'mass model' in Russia."

A similar situation exists in Mexico, where a movie ticket costs a day's pay and pirated DVDs sell for about $5.50. Videomax, Quality Films, and other Mexican distributors have responded by cutting retail prices for DVDs to about $4.50. As Carlos Cayon, vice president of Videomax, noted, "If we don't do something drastic, our business is finished." Another tactic is to bundle several older movie titles on individual DVDs that sell for $23 at Blockbuster, Sam's Club, and Wal-Mart stores in Mexico. Videomax is also experimenting with innovative

distribution channels such as street venders, many of whom previously sold pirated movies. These vendors set up stands in high-traffic areas such as public plazas and subway station entrances.

The video piracy problem isn't confined to emerging markets: In the United States, losses from piracy exceed $1 billion each year for the movie industry as a whole. In the United States, Europe, and Japan, DVDs of hit movies such as *X-Men: The Last Stand* sell for $20 to $24. For years, Hollywood studios have relied on a business model that calls for DVDs to be released several months after a movie's theatrical run; DVD sales generate substantial profits for the studios and can equal or exceed a movie's take at the box office.

Sources: Mure Dickie, "Fox in DVD Distribution Deal with China Partner," Financial Times (November 13, 2006), p. 23; Ross Johnson, "Good News in Hollywood. Shhh." The New York Times (January 31, 2005), pp. C1, C8; Erin Arvedlund, "To Combat Rampant DVD Piracy, U.S. Film Companies Cut Prices," The New York Times (April 7, 2004), p. E1; Ken Bensinger, "Film Companies Take to Mexico's Streets to Fight Piracy," The Wall Street Journal (December 17, 2003), p. B1.

STRATEGIC DECISION-MAKING *in global marketing*

Sony

When Sony was developing the Walkman in 1979, initial plans called for a retail price of ¥50,000 ($249) to achieve breakeven. However, it was felt that a price of ¥35,000 ($170) was necessary to attract the all-important youth market segment. After the engineering team conceded that they could trim costs to achieve breakeven volume at a price of ¥40,000, Chairman Akio Morita pushed them further and insisted on a retail price of ¥33,000 ($165) to commemorate Sony's thirty-third anniversary. At that price, even if the initial production run of 60,000 units sold out, the company would lose $35 per unit. The marketing department was convinced the product would fail: Who would want a tape recorder that couldn't record? Even Yasuo Kuroki, the project manager, hedged his bets: He ordered enough parts for 60,000 units but had only 30,000 actually produced. Although sales were slow immediately following the Walkman's launch in July 1979, they exploded in late summer. The rest, as the saying goes, is history.

Sony has used penetration strategies with numerous other product introductions. When the portable CD player was in development in the mid-1980s, the cost per unit at initial sales volumes was estimated to exceed $600. Realizing that this was a "no-go" price in the United States and other target markets, Chairman Morita instructed management to price the unit in the

$300 range to achieve penetration. Because Sony was a global marketer, the sales volume it expected to achieve in these markets led to scale economies and lower costs.

It is not unusual for a company to change its objectives as a product proceeds through its life cycle and as competitive conditions change. For example, in 2000, Sony rolled out its next-generation game console, the PlayStation 2 (PS2), for $299; competing systems from Microsoft (Xbox) and Nintendo (GameCube) were launched one year later. By March 2001, Sony had shipped 10 million units to Asia, Europe, and the United States. As of today, Sony has sold more than 100 million PS2 units worldwide; according to industry estimates, one out of three American households owns a PlayStation.

As noted in Case 10-1, Sony launched the PlayStation 3 (PS3) in November 2006; it is equipped with a chip that is capable of performing more than 200 billion calculations per second. The development cost of the chip alone was nearly $2 billion. Two different models are available, priced at $499 and at $599. Industry observers estimate that Sony will lose $100 on each PS3 unit sold.

Sources: P. Ranganath Nayak and John M. Ketteringham, Breakthroughs! How Leadership and Drive Create Commercial Innovations That Sweep the World (San Diego, CA: Pfeiffer, 1994), pp. 124–127; Lauren J. Flynn, "Deep Price Cuts Help Nintendo Climb to No. 2 in Game Sales," The New York Times (January 26, 2004), p. C3.

system in place (including transportation, distribution, and sales organizations) that allows global companies like Sony to make effective use of a penetration strategy. Many companies, especially those in the food industry, launch new products that are not innovative enough to qualify for patent protection. When this occurs, penetration pricing is recommended as a means of achieving market saturation before competitors copy the product.

Companion Products: "Razors and Blades" Pricing

One crucial element is missing from the discussion of video game console pricing in the previous section: the video games themselves. The biggest profits in the video industry come from sales of game software; even though Sony and Microsoft may actually lose money on each console, sales of hit video titles generate substantial revenues and profits. Sony, Microsoft, and Nintendo receive licensing fees from the companies that create the games. This illustrates the notion of *companion products*: a video game console has no value without software, a DVD player has no value without movies, a razor handle has no value without blades, a cellular phone has no value without a calling plan, and so on. As the saying goes, "If you make money on the blades, you can give away the razors." Thus, cellular phone companies heavily discount (or even give away) handsets to subscribers who sign long-term service contracts. Likewise, Gillette can sell a single Mach3 razor for less than $5; over a period of years, the company will make significant profits from selling packages of replacement blades. Moreover, a given household might own one or two consoles but dozens of games. Since launching the first

"Nobody buys a piece of hardware because they like hardware. They buy it to play movies or music content."[2]
Howard Stringer, CEO, Sony Corporation

---

[2]   Phred Dvorak and Merissa Marr, "Shock Treatment: Sony, Lagging Behind Rivals, Hands Reins to a Foreigner," *The Wall Street Journal* (March 7, 2005), p. A8.

PlayStation in 1994, Sony has sold more than 200 million game consoles worldwide. During the same time period, however, sales of PlayStation games have exceeded 880 million units.

Target Costing[3]

Japanese companies have traditionally approached cost issues in a way that results in substantial production savings and products that are competitively priced in the global marketplace. Toyota, Sony, Olympus, and Komatsu are some of the well-known Japanese companies that use target costing. The process, sometimes known as *design to cost*, can be described as follows:

> Target costing ensures that development teams will bring profitable products to market not only with the right level of quality and functionality but also with appropriate prices for the target customer segments. It is a discipline that harmonizes the labor of disparate participants in the development effort, from designers and manufacturing engineers to market researchers and suppliers . . . In effect, the company reasons backward from customers' needs and willingness to pay instead of following the flawed but common practice of cost-plus pricing.[4]

Western companies are beginning to adopt some of these money-saving ideas. For example, target costing was used in the development of Renault's Logan, a car that retails for less than $10,000 in Europe. According to Luc-Alexandre Ménard, chief of Renault's Dacia unit, the design approach prevented technical personnel from adding features that customers did not consider absolutely necessary. For example, the Logan's side windows have relatively flat glass; curved glass is more attractive but it adds to the cost. The Logan was originally targeted at consumers in Eastern Europe; to the company's surprise, it has also proven to be popular in Germany and France.[5]

As shown in Figure 11-1, the process begins with market mapping and product definition and positioning; this requires using concepts and techniques discussed in Chapters 6 and 7. The marketing team must do the following:

- Determine the segment(s) to be targeted, as well as the prices that customers in the segment will be willing to pay. Using market research techniques such as conjoint analysis, the team seeks to better understand how customers will perceive product features and functionalities.

Figure 11-1

The Target Costing Process

Source: Robin Cooper and W. Bruce Chew, "Control Tomorrow's Costs Through Today's Designs," Harvard Business Review 74, no. 1 (January–February 1996), p. 95.

---

[3] This section is adapted from Robin Cooper and W. Bruce Chew, "Control Tomorrow's Costs Through Today's Designs," *Harvard Business Review* 74, no. 1 (January–February 1996), pp. 88–97. See also Robin Cooper and Regine Slagmulder, "Develop Profitable New Products with Target Costing," *Sloan Management Review* 40, no. 4 (Summer 1999), pp. 23–33.

[4] Robin Cooper and W. Bruce Chew, "Control Tomorrow's Costs Through Today's Designs," *Harvard Business Review* 74, no. 1 (January–February 1996), pp. 88–97.

[5] Norihiko Shirouzu and Stephen Power, "Unthrilling but Inexpensive, the Logan Boosts Renault in Emerging Markets," *The Wall Street Journal* (October 14, 2006), pp. B1, B18.

- Compute overall target costs with the aim of ensuring the company's future profitability.
- Allocate the target costs to the product's various functions. Calculate the gap between the target cost and the estimated actual production cost. Think of debits and credits in accounting: Because the target cost is fixed, additional funds allocated to one subassembly team for improving a particular function must come from another subassembly team.
- Obey the cardinal rule: If the design team can't meet the targets, the product should not be launched.

Only at this point are design, engineering, and supplier pricing issues dealt with; extensive consultation between all value chain members is used to meet the target. Once the necessary negotiations and trade-offs have been settled, manufacturing begins, followed by continuous cost reduction. In the U.S. process, cost is typically determined after design, engineering, and marketing decisions have been made in sequential fashion; if the cost is too high, the process cycles back to square one—the design stage.

Calculating Prices: Cost-Plus Pricing and Export Price Escalation

The laptop computer exemplifies many characteristics of today's global marketplace: No matter what the brand—Acer, Apple, Dell, or Hewlett-Packard, for example—components are typically sourced in several different countries, and the computers themselves are assembled in China, Taiwan, or Japan (see Table 11-1). Within two days, the computers are sent via airfreight to the countries where they will be sold. As anyone who has studied managerial accounting knows, finished goods have a cost associated with the actual production. In global marketing, however, the total cost will depend on the ultimate market destination, the mode of transport, tariffs, and various fees, handling charges, and documentations costs. **Export price escalation** is the increase in the final selling price of goods traded across borders that reflects these factors. The following is a list of eight basic considerations for persons whose responsibility includes setting prices on goods that cross borders.[6]

1. Does the price reflect the product's quality?
2. Is the price competitive given local market conditions?
3. Should the firm pursue market penetration, market skimming, or some other pricing objective?
4. What type of discount (trade, cash, quantity) and allowance (advertising, trade-off) should the firm offer its international customers?
5. Should prices differ with market segment?
6. What pricing options are available if the firm's costs increase or decrease? Is demand in the international market elastic or inelastic?

Table 11-1

Sourcing a Laptop Computer

Component	Country of Manufacture
Hard-disk drive	Japan, China, Singapore, United States
Power supplies	China
Magnesium casings	China
Memory chips	South Korea, Taiwan, United States, Germany
Liquid-crystal displays	South Korea, Taiwan, Japan, China
Microprocessors	United States
Graphics processors	Designed in the United States, Canada; made in Taiwan

Source: Jason Dean and Pui-Wing Tam, "The Laptop Trail," *The Wall Street Journal* (June 9, 2005), p. B1.

6   Adapted from "Price, Quotations, and Terms of Sale are Key to Successful Exporting," *Business America* (October 4, 1993), p. 12.

USA Today: "The economy has become bifurcated. Some people will pay any price, while others want bargains. Do you think that will continue?"

Rich Gelfond, co-CEO, Imax: "I really do. We're seeing how much of an international trend it is. We have a theater in Moscow that's charging $11 for tickets, and on several movies, it's been among the top performers in the world. In India, people are paying triple the ticket price. In China, people are paying the equivalent of $10. So there's no question that as the demographic increases and you get an expanded upper-middle and wealthy class, there is more disposable income for entertainment."

Source: Adapted from Ron Insana, "Imax Chief Sees a Big Future in Big Screens," USA Today (December 5, 2005), p. 4B. Courtesy of NPN.

7. Are the firm's prices likely to be viewed by the host-country government as reasonable or exploitative?
8. Do the foreign country's dumping laws pose a problem?

Companies frequently use a method known as cost-plus pricing when selling goods outside their home-country markets. **Cost-based pricing** is based on an analysis of internal (e.g., materials, labor, testing) and external costs. As a starting point, firms that comply with Western cost accounting principles typically use the *full absorption cost method*; this defines per-unit product cost as the sum of all past or current direct and indirect manufacturing and overhead costs. However, when goods cross national borders, additional costs and expenses such as transportation, duties, and insurance are incurred. If the manufacturer is responsible for them, they too must be included. By adding the desired profit margin, managers can arrive at a final selling price; this process is known as *cost-plus pricing*. It is important to note that, in China and some other developing countries, many manufacturing enterprises are state run and state subsidized. This makes it difficult to calculate accurate cost figures and opens a country's exporters to charges that they are selling products for less than the "true" cost of producing them.

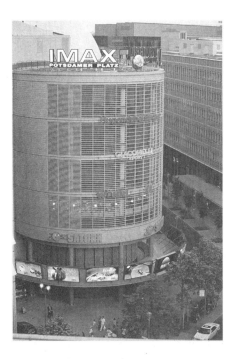

Canada's Imax Corporation is the world's premier provider of large-format motion picture projection technology. The company has identified nine hundred potential markets for new Imax theaters; two-thirds of those are global. Imax has developed a lower-cost projection system called Imax MPX that fits in existing movie theaters; by improving the economics for movie exhibitors, this innovation will expand the number of available market opportunities. In China, for example, 25 Imax theaters will be operating by 2008.

Companies using *rigid cost-plus pricing* set prices without regard to the eight considerations listed previously. They make no adjustments to reflect market conditions outside the home country. The obvious advantage of rigid cost-based pricing is its simplicity: Assuming that both internal and external cost figures are readily available, it is relatively easy to arrive at a quote. The disadvantage is that this approach ignores demand and competitive conditions in target markets; the risk is that prices will either be set too high or too low. If the rigid cost-based approach results in market success, it is only by chance. Rigid cost-plus pricing is attractive to inexperienced exporters, who are frequently less concerned with financial goals than with assessing market potential. Such exporters are typically responding to global market opportunities in a reactive manner, not proactively seeking them.

An alternative method, *flexible cost-plus pricing*, is used to ensure that prices are competitive in the context of the particular market environment. This approach is frequently used by experienced exporters and global marketers. They realize that the rigid cost-plus approach can result in severe price escalation, with the unintended result that exports are priced at levels above what customers can pay. Managers who utilize flexible cost-plus pricing are acknowledging the importance of the eight criteria listed earlier. Flexible cost plus sometimes incorporates the *estimated future cost method* to establish the future cost for all component elements. For example, the automobile industry uses palladium in catalytic converters. Because the market price of heavy metals is volatile and varies with supply and demand, component manufacturers might use the estimated future cost method to ensure that the selling price they set enables them to cover their costs.

Terms of the Sale

Every commercial transaction is based on a contract of sale, and the trade terms in that contract specify the exact point at which the ownership of merchandise is transferred from the seller to the buyer and which party in the transaction pays which costs. The following activities must be performed when goods cross international boundaries:

1. Obtaining an export license if required (in the United States, nonstrategic goods are exported under a general license that requires no specific permit)
2. Obtaining a currency permit if required
3. Packing the goods for export
4. Transporting the goods to the place of departure (this would normally involve transport by truck or rail to a seaport or airport)
5. Preparing a land bill of lading
6. Completing necessary customs export papers
7. Preparing customs or consular invoices as required by the country of destination
8. Arranging for ocean freight and preparation
9. Obtaining marine insurance and certificate of the policy

Who is responsible for performing these tasks? It depends on the terms of the sale. The internationally accepted terms of trade are known as **International Commercial Terms (Incoterms)**. Incoterms are classified into four categories. **Ex-works (EXW)**, the sole "E-Term" or "origin" term among Incoterms, refers to a transaction in which the buyer takes delivery at the premises of the seller; the buyer bears all risks and expenses from that point on. In principle, ex-works affords the buyer maximum control over the cost of transporting the goods. Ex-works can be contrasted with several "D-Terms" ("post-main-carriage" or "arrival" terms). For example, under **delivered duty paid (DDP)**, the seller has agreed to deliver the goods to the buyer at the place he or she names in the country of import, with all costs, including duties, paid. Under this contract, the seller is also responsible for obtaining the import license if one is required.

Another category of Incoterms is known as "F-Terms" or "pre-main-carriage terms." Because it is suited for all modes of transport, **free carrier (FCA)** is widely used in global sales. Under FCA, transfer from seller to buyer is effected when the goods are delivered to a specified carrier at a specified destination. Two additional F-terms apply to sea and inland waterway transportation only. **Free alongside ship (FAS) named port** is the Incoterm for a transaction in which the seller places the shipment alongside, or available to, the vessel upon which the goods will be transported out of the country. The seller pays all charges up to that point. The seller's legal responsibility ends once the goods have been cleared for export; the buyer pays the cost of actually loading the shipment. FAS is often used with *break bulk cargo*, which is noncontainerized, general cargo, such as iron, steel, or machinery (often stowed in the hold of a vessel rather than in containers on the deck). With **free on board (FOB) named port**, the responsibility and liability of the seller do not end until the goods—typically in containers—have cleared the ship's rail. As a practical matter, access to the terminal and harbor areas in many modern ports may be restricted; in such an instance, FCA should be used instead.

Several Incoterms are known as "C-Terms" or "main-carriage" terms. When goods are shipped **cost, insurance, freight (CIF) named port**, the risk of loss or damage to goods is transferred to the buyer once the goods have passed the ship's rail. In this sense, CIF is similar to FOB. However, with CIF, the seller has to pay the expense of transportation for the goods up to the port of destination, including the expense of insurance. If the terms of the sale are **cost and freight (CFR)**, the seller is not responsible for risk or loss at any point outside the factory.

Table 11-2 is a typical example of the kind of export price escalation that can occur when some of these costs are added to the per-unit cost of the product itself. In this example, a Kansas City-based distributor of agricultural equipment is shipping a container load of farm implements to Yokohama, Japan, through the port of Seattle. A shipment of product that costs ex-works $30,000 in Kansas City ends up with a

behind the scenes

Choosing the Terms of the Sale

Students of global marketing may feel a little overwhelmed by the various Incoterms discussed in this section. Mastering the nomenclature and understanding which term to choose takes a great deal of study and experience. As a practical matter, Beth Dorrell, an export coordinator at a U.S.-based company that markets industrial ink products, offers the following explanation:

We actually use different Incoterms as incentives for larger orders. Instead of offering a "price break" price, we offer a better Incoterm based upon the size of a customer's order. We adhere to some general guidelines: Any order less than 1 ton is sold on an ex-works basis. Anything 1 ton or more is sold CIF port. All air freight is ex-factory. We will, of course, go to great lengths to ensure that our customers are happy. So, even though a product is sold ex-works, we'll often arrange shipping to destination port (CIF) or airport (CIP), or to the domestic port (FOB) and simply tag the freight cost onto the invoice. We end up with an ex-factory price, but a CIF or FOB invoice total. Sounds complicated, doesn't it? It keeps me busy arranging shipping.

We also ship FCL (full container load). We usually do these "door-to-port." This means that we have the shipping line deliver the empty container to our warehouse dock where we load it. The shipping line then pulls away with the container and delivers it as far as the foreign port where the consignee (customer) must then arrange for local clearance and inland trucking. It's actually a ton of fun—as long as you load and secure the container properly!

When choosing among the various Incoterm options, remember that it all depends on how much work you want to do and how much responsibility you want to accept. From the seller's point of view, ex-works is easy, and FOB domestic port is fairly easy. The seller's responsibility increases with other Incoterms. For example, if I'm shipping CIF and the container ends up in a ditch on the way to the port because the truck driver fell asleep (it happened to us last week—what a mess!), then it's my responsibility and my problem. That's because we still own the freight, we have to deal with the insurance company, we have to replace the freight, and somehow we still have to get the freight there on time—which is almost impossible.

Item			Percentage of Ex-works Price
Ex-Works Kansas City		$30,000	100%
Container freight charges from Kansas City to Seattle	$1,475.00		
Terminal handling fee	350.00		
Ocean freight for 20-foot container	2,280.00		
Currency Adjustment Factor (CAF) (51% of ocean freight)	1,162.80		
Insurance (110% of CIF value)	35.27		
Forwarding fee	150.00		
Total shipping charges	5,453.07		18
Total CIF Yokohama value		35,453.07	
VAT (3% of CIF value)		1,063.69	3
		36,516.76	
Distributor markup (10%)		3,651.67	12
		40,168.43	
Dealer markup (25%)		10,042.10	33
Total retail price		$50,210.53	166%

*This was loaded at the manufacturer's door, shipped by stack train to Seattle, and then transferred via ocean freight to Yokohama. Total transit time from factory door to foreign port is about 28 days.

Source: The Wall Street Journal (Eastern Edition) by Mary Anastasia O'Grady. Copyright 2006 by Dow Jones & Company, Inc. Reproduced with permission of Dow Jones & Company, Inc. in the format Textbook via Copyright Clearance Center.

total retail price in excess of $50,000 in Yokohama. A line-by-line analysis of this shipment shows how price escalation occurs. First, there is the total shipping charge of $5,453.07, which is 18 percent of the ex-works Kansas City price. The principal component of this shipping charge is a combination of land and ocean freight totaling $5,267.80. A currency adjustment factor (CAF) is assessed to protect the seller from possible losses from disadvantageous shifts in the dollar-yen exchange rate. This figure will vary depending on the perceived volatility of exchange rates.

All import charges are assessed against the landed price of the shipment (CIF value). Note that there is no line item for duty in this example; no duties are charged on agricultural equipment sent to Japan.[7] Duties may be charged in other

Chrysler began exporting right-hand drive Jeeps to Japan in 1996. However, the country was in a deep recession at the time, forcing many American marketers—including Coca-Cola, J. Crew, Microsoft, and Jeep—to cut prices. Ten years later, Japan's economy has rebounded, and consumers are buying. Jeep is enjoying double-digit sales growth at the sixty-plus dealerships that sell Chrysler and Jeep vehicles.

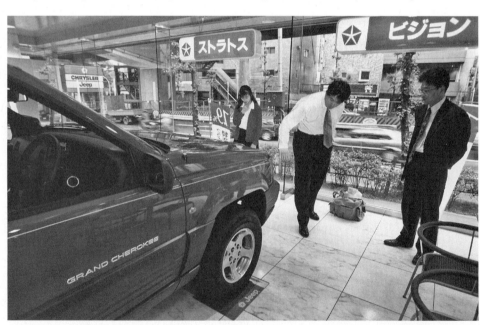

---
7   Since the Uruguay Round of GATT negotiations, Japan has lowered or eliminated duties on thousands of categories of imports. Japan's simple average duty rate for 2003 was 2.5 percent; approximately 60 percent of tariff lines (including most industrial products) were rated 5 percent or lower.

Item	Amount of Price Escalation	Total
Ex-works price	0	$30,000
Exchange rate adjustment	$2,100	$32,100
Shipping	$300	$32,400
Customs fees	$1,000	$33,400
Distributor margin	$3,700	$37,100
Inspection, accessories	$1,700	$38,800
Added options, prep	$3,000	$41,800
Final sticker price	$8,200	$50,000

Table 11-3

An American-Built Jeep Grand Cherokee Goes to Japan (Estimates)

countries. A nominal distributor markup of 10 percent ($3,652) actually represents 12 percent of the CIF Yokohama price because it is a markup not only on the ex-works price but on freight and VAT as well. (It is assumed here that the distributor's markup includes the cost of transportation from the port to Yokohama.) Finally, a dealer markup of 25 percent adds up to $10,042 (33 percent) of the CIF Yokohama price. Like distributor markups, dealer markup is based on the total landed cost.

The net effect of this add-on accumulating process is a total retail price in Yokohama of $50,210, or 166 percent of the ex-works Kansas City price. This is price escalation. The example provided here is by no means an extreme case. Longer distribution channels or channels that require a higher operating margin, as are typically found in export marketing, can contribute to price escalation. Because of the layered distribution system in Japan, the markups in Tokyo could easily result in a price that is 200 percent of the CIF value. An example of price escalation for a single product is shown in Table 11-3 A right-hand-drive Jeep Grand Cherokee equipped with a V8 engine ends up costing ¥5 million—roughly $50,000—by the time it reaches a dealer in Japan. The final price represents a 166 percent increase over the U.S. sticker price of $30,000.

These examples of cost-plus pricing show an approach that a beginning exporter might use to determine the CIF price. This approach could also be used for differentiated products such as the Jeep Cherokee for which buyers are willing to pay a premium. However, as noted earlier, experienced global marketers are likely to take a more flexible approach and view price as a strategic variable that can help achieve marketing and business objectives.

ENVIRONMENTAL INFLUENCES ON PRICING DECISIONS

Global marketers must deal with a number of environmental considerations when making pricing decisions. Among them are currency fluctuations, inflation, government controls and subsidies, and competitive behavior. Some of these factors work in conjunction with others; for example, inflation may be accompanied by government controls. Each is discussed in detail in the following paragraphs.

Currency Fluctuations

In global marketing, fluctuating exchange rates complicate the task of setting prices. As we noted in Chapter 2, currency fluctuations can create significant challenges and opportunities for any company that exports. Management faces different decision situations, depending on whether currencies in key markets have strengthened or weakened relative to the home-country currency. A weakening of the home country currency swings exchange rates in a favorable direction: A producer in a weak-currency country can choose to cut export prices to increase market share or maintain

Table 11-4

Value of U.S. Dollar Versus
Japanese Yen

	United States	Japan
January 2000	$1.00	¥101
April 2002	$1.00	¥130

its prices and reap healthier profit margins. Overseas sales can result in windfall revenues when translated into the home-country currency.

For example, as shown in Table 11-4, over a recent 16-month period the yen weakened approximately 29 percent relative to the dollar. The figures in the table should be interpreted in the following way: If the amount of yen (or other currency) per dollar increases in a given time period, it means the yen's value is decreasing. (Conversely, if the amount of yen per dollar had *decreased*, it would have indicated that the yen had strengthened relative to the dollar.) The currency shift indicated in Table 11-4 was a boon for Japanese companies such as Canon and Olympus Optical because each dollar in U.S. export sales was worth ¥130 in April 2002.

It is a different situation when a company's home currency strengthens; this is an unfavorable turn of events for the typical exporter because overseas revenues are reduced when translated into the home country currency. Fast forward one year from the situation shown in Table 11-4: By early 2003, as the Bush administration prepared for war, the dollar was down 11 percent from its 2002 peak against a weighted portfolio of foreign currencies. This was good news for American companies such as Boeing, Caterpillar, and GE but bad news for Canon and Olympus (and Americans shopping for cameras). Indeed, according to Teruhisa Tokunaka, chief financial officer of Sony, a 1 yen shift in the yen-dollar exchange rate can raise or lower the company's annual operating profit by 8 billion yen.[8] These examples underscore the point that "roller-coaster" or "yo-yo" style swings in currency values, which may move in a favorable direction for several quarters and then abruptly reverse, characterize today's business environment.

The degree of exposure varies among companies. For example, Harley-Davidson exports all of its motorcycles from the United States. In every export market, the company's pricing decisions must take currency fluctuations into account. Similarly, 100 percent of German automaker Porsche's production takes place at home; Germany serves as its export base. However, for exports within the euro zone, Porsche is insulated from currency fluctuations. The situation is more complicated for a transnational company such as Honda. The company is heavily dependent on the North American market, which accounts for more than half its operating income. How can Honda reduce the potential negative impact of currency fluctuations? About three-fourths of the cars Honda sells in America are produced in the United States. In late 2000, the dollar had fallen to ¥108 compared with ¥113 the previous year; the unfavorable shift had a direct negative impact on corporate profits.

The situation was even more complicated in Europe; Honda serves the entire European market from a single plant in the United Kingdom. The pound's strength relative to the euro in the first years of the decade resulted in a significant decline in Honda's European sales. At the same time, the euro weakened relative to the yen. So, not only did currency fluctuations negatively affect sales on the continent, but, translated into yen, the revenue that Honda realized from those sales was reduced as well![9]

In responding to currency fluctuations, global marketers can utilize other elements of the marketing mix besides price. Table 11-5 provides several guidelines. In

8 Robert A. Guth, Michael M. Phillips, and Charles Hutzler, "On the Decline: As the Yen Keeps Dropping, A New View of Japan Emerges," *The Wall Street Journal* (April 24, 2002), pp. A1, A8.
9 Todd Zaun, "Honda Takes Currency Hit in Europe," *The Wall Street Journal* (March 28, 2001), p. A16.

When Domestic Currency Is Weak	When Domestic Currency Is Strong
1. Stress price benefits.	1. Engage in nonprice competition by improving quality, delivery, and after-sale service.
2. Expand product line and add more costly features.	2. Improve productivity and engage in cost reduction.
3. Shift sourcing to domestic market.	3. Shift sourcing outside home country.
4. Exploit market opportunities in all markets.	4. Give priority to exports to countries with stronger currencies.
5. Use full-costing approach, but employ marginal-cost pricing to penetrate new or competitive markets.	5. Trim profit margins and use marginal-cost pricing.
6. Speed repatriation of foreign-earned income and collections.	6. Keep the foreign-earned income in host country; slow down collections.
7. Minimize expenditures in local (host-country) currency.	7. Maximize expenditures in local (host-country) currency.
8. Buy advertising, insurance, transportation, and other services in domestic market.	8. Buy needed services abroad and pay for them in local currencies.
9. Bill foreign customers in their own currency.	9. Bill foreign customers in the domestic currency.

Table 11-5

Global Pricing Strategies

Source: S. Tamer Cavusgil, "Pricing for Global Markets," *Columbia Journal of World Business* 31, no. 4 (Winter 1996), p. 69.

some instances, slight upward price adjustments due to the strengthening of a country's currency have little effect on export performance, especially if demand is relatively inelastic. The first two strategies in the right-hand column of Table 11-5 call for focusing attention on competitive issues besides price as well as productivity and cost reduction efforts. Companies in the strong-currency country can also choose to absorb the cost of maintaining international market prices at previous levels—at least for a while. Companies using the rigid cost-plus pricing method described earlier may be forced to change to the flexible approach. The use of the flexible cost-plus method to reduce prices in response to unfavorable currency swings is an example of a **market holding strategy** and is adopted by companies that do not want to lose market share. If, by contrast, large price increases are deemed unavoidable, managers may find their products can no longer compete.

As noted earlier, price discrepancies across the euro zone should gradually disappear because manufacturers will no longer be able to cite currency fluctuations as a justification for the discrepancies. **Price transparency** means that buyers will be

GLOBAL *marketing in action*

Pricing U.S. Exports to the Europe

In the three years immediately after the euro zone was established, the euro declined in value more than 25 percent relative to the dollar. This situation forced American companies, in particular small exporters, to choose from among the options associated with strong currencies listed in Table 11-5. The strategy chosen varies according to a company's particular circumstances. For example, Vermeer Manufacturing of Pella, Iowa, with annual sales of $650 million, prices its products in euros for the European market. As 2000 came to an end, Vermeer had been forced to raise its European prices four times since the euro's introduction. Its subsidiary in the Netherlands pays employees in euros and also buys materials locally, illustrating strategies number 7 and 8.

By contrast, Stern Pinball of Melrose Park, Illinois, prices its machines in dollars in export markets; this represents strong-currency strategy number 9. Company president Gary Stern's product strategy also reflects strong-currency strategy number 1 in Table 11-5: To offset the higher cost to European customers who must convert euros before paying in dollars, the company developed new features such as pinball machines that "speak" several European languages. It has also produced new products such as a soccer game themed to European interests as well as an Austin Powers game targeted at the United Kingdom. As Stern commented, "If I were bright enough to know which way the euro was going, I sure wouldn't be making pinball machines. I'd be trading currency."

Source: Christopher Cooper, "Euro's Drop Is Hardest for the Smallest," *The Wall Street Journal* (October 2, 2000), p. A21.

Table 11-6

Automobile Price Differences in the EU, 1998/2003

Small Segment		Medium Segment		Large Segment	
Opel Corsa	24.0%/13.6%	VW Golf	43.5%/28.0%	BMW 318I	12.0%/12.7%
Ford Fiesta	44.7%/23.1%	Opel Astra	26.0%/17.6%	Audi A4	13.0%/ 9.1%
Renault Clio	33.8%/17.3%	Ford Escort/Focus	33.8%/22.7%	Ford Mondeo	58.5%/21.0%
Peugeot 106/206	21.1%/24.6%	Renault Mégane	27.9%/19.6%	Opel Vectra	18.2%/16.0%
VW Polo	36.7%/19.3%	Peugeot 306/307	46.2%/16.9%	VW Passat	36.4%/39.0%

Source: Reprinted from the *Columbia Journal of World Business*, Vol. 31, S. Tamer Cavusgil, "Pricing for Global Markets," p. 4, Copyright © 2004, with permission from Elsevier.

> *"The car industry is going to be hurt. There will be greater price transparency. Prices are higher in northern Europe and once consumers there get wind of this there will be a move down in prices towards the southern countries."*[10]
>
> Marcie Krempel, AT Kearney

able to comparison shop easily because goods will be priced in euros as opposed to marks, francs, or lira. The European Commission publishes an annual report comparing automobile price differences in the EU. Table 11-6 shows prices from the late 1990s (pre-euro zone) and prices from November 2003. A comparison of the figures shows that, although price discrepancies for some models have narrowed, prices for a Volkswagen Passat are as much as 39 percent higher depending on the country of purchase. Not surprisingly, these differences encourage cross-border shopping.

Some automobile price differences in Europe are due to different standards for safety equipment and different tax levels. For example, Denmark and Sweden have a value-added tax (VAT) of 25 percent, the highest rates in the EU. Moreover, Denmark taxes luxury goods heavily. Taxes are also high in Finland, Belgium, Ireland, Austria, and Italy. Volkswagen has already begun to harmonize its wholesale prices for vehicles distributed in Europe.

Inflationary Environment

Inflation, or a persistent upward change in price levels, is a problem in many country markets. An increase in the money supply can cause inflation; as noted in the previous section, inflation is often reflected in the prices of imported goods for a country whose currency has been devalued. In 1998, for example, the Russian government defaulted on its foreign debt and devalued the ruble; prices for some goods in Russian stores rose as much as 300 percent. Likewise, in the Dominican Republic, the peso lost one-third of its value in 2002; suddenly, shoppers were faced with price increases of 40 percent to 50 percent. The situations in Russia and the Dominican Republic are extreme; overall, in 2000, the average rate of inflation in the world's advanced economies stood at a low 2.3 percent. In developing countries, inflation averaged about 6 percent. By comparison, inflation in 2000 was much higher in the transitional economies in Central and Eastern Europe with Russia experiencing inflation of 20 percent.

An essential requirement for pricing in an inflationary environment is the maintenance of operating profit margins. When present, inflation requires price adjustments, for a simple reason: Increased selling prices must cover rising costs. Regardless of cost accounting practices, if a company maintains its margins, it has effectively protected itself from the effects of inflation. This, in turn, requires manufacturers and retailers of all types to become more technologically adept. In Brazil, where the inflation rate was as high as 2,000 percent during the late 1980s, retailers sometimes changed prices several times each day. Shelf pricing, rather than individual unit pricing, became the norm throughout the retailing sector nearly 15 years before Wal-Mart arrived in the region. Because their warehouses contained goods that had been bought at different prices, local retailers were forced to invest in sophisticated computer and communications systems to help them keep pace with the volatile financial environment. They utilized sophisticated inventory

---

[10] Graham Bowley, "On the Road to Price Convergence," *Financial Times* (November 12, 1998), p. 29.

BRIC Briefing Book

Pricing Reeboks in India

When Reebok, the world's number two athletic shoe company, decided to enter India in 1995, it faced several basic marketing challenges. For one thing, Reebok was creating a market from scratch. Upscale sports shoes were virtually unknown, and the most expensive sneakers available at the time cost 1,000 rupees (about $23). Reebok officials also had to select a market entry mode. The decision was made to subcontract with four local suppliers, one of which, the Phoenix Group, became a joint venture partner. To reinforce Reebok's high-tech brand image, company officials decided to establish their own retail infrastructure. There were two other crucial pieces of the puzzle: product and price. Should Reebok create a line of mass-market shoes specifically for India and priced at Rs1,000? The alternative was to offer the same designs sold in other parts of the world and price them at Rs2,500 ($58), a figure that represents the equivalent of a month's salary for a junior civil servant.

In the end, Reebok decided to offer Indian consumers about 60 models chosen from the company's global offerings. The decision was based in part on a desire to sustain Reebok's brand image of high quality. Management realized that the decision could very well limit the size of the market; despite estimates that as many as 300 million Indians could be classified as "middle class," the number of people who could afford premium-priced products was estimated to be about 30 million.

Reebok's least expensive shoes were priced at about Rs2,000 per pair; for the same amount of money, a farmer could buy a dairy cow or a homeowner could buy a new refrigerator. Nevertheless, consumer response was very favorable, especially among middle-class youths. As Muktesh Pant, a former regional manager who became the first CEO of Reebok India, noted, "For Rs2,000 to Rs3,000, people feel they can really make a statement. It's cheaper than buying a new watch, for instance, if you want to make a splash at a party. And though our higher-priced shoes put us in competition with things like refrigerators and cows, the upside is that we're now being treated as a prestigious brand."

Sneakers represented just one aspect of the larger marketing of professional sports and sports culture to Indian youth. India's middle class households were spending more time in the living room watching cricket matches on TV, a trend that created an opportunity for sports sponsorships and sports-related ads. In the late 1990s, Reebok spent more than $1.5 million on event marketing and sponsoring teams such as the East Bengal Football Club.

Reebok quickly discovered that demand was strong outside of key metropolitan markets such as Delhi, Mumbai, and Chennai. The cost of living is lower in small towns so consumers have more disposable income to spend. Reebok appointed distributors in each of India's 26 states to distribute lower-priced shoe models in a network of about 1,500 multibrand footwear and apparel shops. One problem, however, is that knockoff versions of Reebok, Adidas, and Nike shoes were widely available. Reebok conducted several raids on outlets that were selling the counterfeit goods.

Reebok's agreement with the Phoenix Group called for the latter to create a 50-plus chain of stores. However, after the first 10 stores were opened, management at Phoenix decided to concentrate on marketing the company's own brands. Accordingly, Reebok began to identify individual partners to run stores in major cities; there are currently about 90 branded franchise stores in 50 cities. By establishing exclusive stores, promoting Reebok as a lifestyle brand, and offering a unique "sports fashion" shopping experience, Reebok was able to offer a taste of Western-style capitalist consumption for those so inclined. Between 1996 and 1999, Reebok's retail sales in India more than tripled, increasing from Rs250 million to Rs900 million.

Today, Reebok India exports hundreds of thousands of pairs of Indian-made shoes to Europe and the United States. CEO Pant was promoted to vice president of global brand marketing at Reebok International headquarters in Stoughton, Massachusetts. Reflecting on Reebok's Indian launch, he observed, "At first we were embarrassed about our pricing. But it has ended up serving us well."

Sources: Bernard D'Mello, "Reebok and the Global Footwear Sweatshop," Monthly Review 54, no. 9 (February 2003), pp. 26–41; Mark Nicholson, "Where a Pair of Trainers Costs As Much as a Cow," Financial Times (August 18, 1998), p. 10.

management software to help them maintain financial control. As Wal-Mart came to Brazil in the mid-1990s, it discovered that local competitors had the technological infrastructure that allowed them to match its aggressive pricing policies.[11]

Low inflation presents pricing challenges of a different type. With inflation in the United States in the low single digits in the late 1990s and strong demand forcing factories to run at or near capacity, companies should have been able to raise prices. However, the domestic economic situation was not the only consideration. In the mid-1990s, excess manufacturing capacity in many industries, high rates of

---

[11] Pete Hisey, "Wal-Mart's Global Vision," *Retail Merchandiser* 41, no. 4 (April 2001), pp. 21–49.

Reebok dominates the footwear market in India, where its cricket shoes are a top seller. In an effort to attract more foreign investment, India's leaders approved legislation in 2006 that will make it easier for Reebok and other global marketers to establish single-brand retail chains. Previously, market entry and expansion was done primarily through franchisees. Now, Reebok is stepping up its efforts to expand outside of large metropolitan areas such as Mumbai. Some three dozen Indian cities have populations exceeding one million people, including a rapidly growing base of middle class consumers.

unemployment in many European countries, and the lingering recession in Asia made it difficult for companies to increase prices. As John Ballard, CEO of a California-based engineering firm, noted in 1994, "We thought about price increases. But our research of competitors and what the market would bear told us it was not worth pursuing." By the end of the decade, globalization, the Internet, a flood of low-cost exports from China, and a new cost-consciousness among buyers were also significant constraining factors.[12]

Government Controls, Subsidies, and Regulations

Governmental policies and regulations that affect pricing decisions include dumping legislation, resale price maintenance legislation, price ceilings, and general reviews of price levels. Government action that limits management's ability to adjust prices can put pressure on margins. Under certain conditions, government action poses a threat to the profitability of a subsidiary operation. In a country that is undergoing severe financial difficulties and is in the midst of a financial crisis (for example, a foreign exchange shortage caused in part by runaway inflation), government officials are under pressure to take some type of action. This was true in Brazil for many years. In some cases, governments take expedient steps such as selective or broad price controls.

When selective controls are imposed, foreign companies are more vulnerable to control than local ones, particularly if the outsiders lack the political influence over government decision that local managers have. For example, Procter & Gamble encountered strict price controls in Venezuela in the late 1980s. Despite increases in the cost of raw materials, P&G was only granted about 50 percent of the price increases it requested; even then, months passed before permission to raise prices was forthcoming. As a result, by 1988, detergent prices in Venezuela were less than what they were in the United States.[13]

[12] Lucinda Harper and Fred R. Bleakley, "Like Old Times: An Era of Low Inflation Changes the Calculus for Buyers and Sellers," *The Wall Street Journal* (January 14, 1994), p. A1. See also Jacob M. Schlesinger and Yochi J. Dreazen, "Counting the Cost: Firms Start to Raise Prices, Stirring Fear in Inflation Fighters," *The Wall Street Journal* (May 16, 2000), pp. A1, A8.
[13] Alecia Swasy, "Foreign Formula: Procter & Gamble Fixes Aim on Tough Market: The Latin Americans," *The Wall Street Journal* (June 15, 1990), p. A7.

Government control can also take other forms. As discussed in Chapter 8, companies are sometimes required to deposit funds in a noninterest-bearing escrow account for a specified period of time if they wish to import products. For example, Cintec International, an engineering firm that specializes in restoring historic structures, spent eight years seeking the necessary approval from Egyptian authorities to import special tools to repair a mosque. In addition, the country's port authorities required a deposit of nearly $25,000 before allowing Cintec to import diamond-tipped drills and other special tools. Why would Cintec's management accept such conditions? Cairo is the largest city in the Muslim world, and there are hundreds of centuries-old historic structures in need of refurbishment. By responding to the Egyptian government's demands with patience and persistence, Cintec is positioning itself as a leading contender for more contract work.[14]

Cash deposit requirements such as the one described here clearly create an incentive for a company to minimize the stated value of the imported goods; lower prices mean smaller deposits. Other government requirements that affect the pricing decision are profit transfer rules that restrict the conditions under which profits can be transferred out of a country. Under such rules, a high transfer price paid for imported goods by an affiliated company can be interpreted as a device for transferring profits out of a country.

Also discussed in Chapter 8 were government subsidies. As noted earlier, the topic of agricultural subsidies is a sensitive one in the current round of global trade talks. Brazil and a bloc of more than 20 other nations are pressing Washington to end agricultural subsidies. For example, Washington spends between $2.5 billion and $3 billion per year on cotton subsidies (the EU spends about $700 million), a fact that has contributed to delays in completing the Doha round. Benin, Chad, Burkina Faso, and others complain that the subsidies keep U.S. cotton prices so low that it costs the African nations $250 to $300 million each year in lost exports.[15] Brazil recently won its WTO complaint against U.S. cotton subsidies.

Government regulations can affect prices in other ways. In Germany, for example, price competition was historically severely restricted in a number of industries. This was particularly true in the service sector. The German government's recent moves toward deregulation have improved the climate for market entry by foreign firms in a range of industries, including insurance, telecommunications, and air travel. Deregulation is also giving German companies their first experience with price competition in the domestic market. In some instances, deregulation represents a *quid pro quo* that will allow German companies wider access to other country markets. For example, the United States and Germany recently completed an open-skies agreement that will allow Lufthansa to fly more routes within the United States. At the same time, the German air market has been opened to competition. As a result, air travel costs between German cities have fallen significantly. Change is slowly coming to the retail sector as well. The Internet and globalization have forced policy makers to repeal two archaic laws. The first, the *Rabattgesetz* or Discount Law, limited discounts on products to 3 percent of the list price. The second, the *Zugabeverordnung* or Free Gift Act, banned companies from giving away free merchandise, such as shopping bags.[16]

---

[14] Scott Miller, "In Trade Talks, the Gloves Are Off," *The Wall Street Journal* (July 15, 2003), p. A12. See also James Drummond, "The Great Conservation Debate," *Financial Times Special Report— Egypt* (October 22, 2003), p. 6.

[15] Neil King, Jr. and Scott Miller, "Trade Talks Fail amid Big Divide over Farm Issues," *The Wall Street Journal* (September 15, 2003), pp. A1, A18.

[16] Greg Steinmetz, "Mark Down: German Consumers Are Seeing Prices Cut in Deregulation Push," *The Wall Street Journal* (August 15, 1997), pp. A1, A4; David Wessel, "German Shoppers Get Coupons," *The Wall Street Journal* (April 5, 2001), p. A1.

Competitive Behavior

Pricing decisions are bounded not only by cost and the nature of demand but also by competitive action. If competitors do not adjust their prices in response to rising costs, management—even if acutely aware of the effect of rising costs on operating margins—will be severely constrained in its ability to adjust prices accordingly. Conversely, if competitors are manufacturing or sourcing in a lower-cost country, it may be necessary to cut prices to stay competitive.

In the United States, Levi Strauss & Company is under price pressure from several directions. First, Levi faces stiff competition from the Wrangler and Lee brands marketed by VF Corporation. A pair of Wrangler jeans retails for about $20 at JCPenney's and other department stores, compared with about $30 for a pair of Levi 501s. Second, Levi's two primary retail customers, JCPenney and Sears, are aggressively marketing their own private label brands. Finally, designer jeans from Calvin Klein, Polo, and Diesel are enjoying renewed popularity. Exclusive fashion brands such as Seven and Lucky retail for more than $100 per pair. Outside the United States, thanks to the heritage of the Levi brand and less competition, Levi jeans command premium prices—$80 or more for one pair of 501s. To support the prestige image, Levi's are sold in boutiques. Levi's non-U.S. sales represent about one-third of revenues but more than 50 percent of profits. In an attempt to apply its global experience and enhance the brand in the United States, Levi has opened a number of Original Levi's Stores in select American cities. Despite such efforts, Levi rang up only $4.1 billion in sales in 2003 compared with $7.1 billion in 1996. In 2002, officials announced plans to close six plants and move most of the company's North American production offshore in an effort to cut costs.[17]

Using Sourcing as a Strategic Pricing Tool

The global marketer has several options for addressing the problem of price escalation or the environmental factors described in the last section. Product and market competition, in part, dictate the marketer's choices. Marketers of domestically manufactured finished products may be forced to switch to offshore sourcing of certain components to keep costs and prices competitive. In particular, China is quickly gaining a reputation as "the world's workshop." U.S. bicycle companies such as Huffy are relying more heavily on production sources in China and Taiwan.

Another option is a thorough audit of the distribution structure in the target markets. A rationalization of the distribution structure can substantially reduce the total markups required to achieve distribution in international markets. Rationalization may include selecting new intermediaries, assigning new responsibilities to old intermediaries, or establishing direct marketing operations. For example, Toys "R" Us successfully targets the Japanese toy market by bypassing layers of distribution and adopting a warehouse style of selling similar to its U.S. approach. Toys "R" Us was viewed as a test case of the ability of Western retailers—discounters in particular—to change the rules of distribution.

GLOBAL PRICING: THREE POLICY ALTERNATIVES

What pricing policy should a global company pursue? Viewed broadly, there are three alternative positions a company can take on worldwide pricing.

---

[17] Leslie Kaufman, "Levi Strauss to Close 6 U.S. Plants and Lay Off 3,300," *The New York Times* (April 9, 2002), p. C2.

Extension or Ethnocentric

The first can be called an *extension* or *ethnocentric* pricing policy. An **extension or ethnocentric pricing policy** calls for the per-unit price of an item to be the same no matter where in the world the buyer is located. In such instances, the importer must absorb freight and import duties. The extension approach has the advantage of extreme simplicity because it does not require information on competitive or market conditions for implementation. The disadvantage of the ethnocentric approach is that it does not respond to the competitive and market conditions of each national market and, therefore, does not maximize the company's profits in each national market or globally. When toymaker Mattel adapted U.S. products for overseas markets, for example, little consideration was given to price levels that resulted when U.S. prices were converted to local currency prices. As a result, Holiday Barbie and some other toys were overpriced in global markets.[18]

Similarly, Mercedes executives recently moved beyond an ethnocentric approach to pricing. As Dieter Zietsche, chairman of Daimler AG , noted, "We used to say that *we* know what the customer wants, and he will have to pay for it . . . we didn't realize the world had changed."[19] Mercedes got its wake-up call when Lexus began offering "Mercedes quality" for $20,000 less. After assuming the top position in 1993, Mercedes CEO Helmut Werner boosted employee productivity, increased the number of low-cost outside suppliers, and invested in production facilities in the United States and Spain in an effort to move toward more customer- and competition-oriented pricing. The company also rolled out new, lower-priced versions of its E Class and S Class sedans. *Advertising Age* immediately hailed management's new attitude for transforming Mercedes from "a staid and smug purveyor into an aggressive, market-driven company that will go bumper-to-bumper with its luxury car rivals—even on price."[20]

"In the past, Mercedes vehicles would be priced for the European market, and that price was translated into U.S. dollars. Surprise, surprise: You're 20 percent more expensive than the Lexus LS 400, and you don't sell too many cars."

Joe Eberhardt, Executive Vice President for Global Sales, Marketing and Service, Chrysler Group

Adaptation or Polycentric

The second policy, **adaptation** or **polycentric pricing**, permits subsidiary or affiliate managers or independent distributors to establish whatever price they feel is most appropriate in their market environment. There is no requirement that prices be coordinated from one country to the next. IKEA takes a polycentric approach to pricing: While it is company policy to have the lowest price on comparable products in every market, managers in each country set their own prices, which depend in part on local factors such as competition, wages, taxes, and advertising rates. Overall, IKEA's prices are lowest in the United States, where the company competes with large retailers. Prices are higher in Italy where local competitors tend to be smaller, more upscale furniture stores than those in the U.S. market. Generally, prices are higher in countries where the IKEA brand is strongest. When IKEA opened its first stores in mainland China, the young professional couples who are the company's primary target segment considered the store's offerings to be too expensive. Prices were promptly lowered; today, the average Chinese customer spends ¥300—about $36—per visit.[21]

One recent study of European industrial exporters found that companies utilizing independent distributors were the most likely to utilize polycentric pricing. Such an approach is sensitive to local market conditions; however, valuable

---

18 Lisa Bannon, "Mattel Plans to Double Sales Abroad," *The Wall Street Journal* (February 11, 1998), pp. A3, A11.
19 Alex Taylor III, "Speed! Power! Status!" *Fortune* (June 10, 1996), pp. 46–58.
20 Raymond Serafin, "Mercedes-Benz of the '90s Includes Price in Its Pitch," *Advertising Age* (November 1, 1993), p. 1.
21 Eric Sylvers, "IKEA Index Indicates the Euro Is Not a Price Equalizer Yet," *The New York Times* (October 23, 2003), p. W1. See also Paula M. Miller, "IKEA with Chinese Characteristics," *China Business Review* (July–August 2004), pp. 36–38.

knowledge and experience within the corporate system concerning effective pricing strategies are not brought to bear on each local pricing decision. Because the distributors or local managers are free to set prices as they see fit, they may ignore the opportunity to draw upon company experience. Arbitrage is also a potential problem with the polycentric approach; when disparities in prices between different country markets exceed the transportation and duty costs separating the markets, enterprising individuals can purchase goods in the lower-price country market and then transport them for sale in markets where higher prices prevail.

This is precisely what has happened in both the pharmaceutical and textbook publishing industries. Discounted drugs intended for AIDS patients in Africa have been smuggled into the EU and sold at a huge profit. Similarly, Pearson Education (which publishes this text), McGraw-Hill, Thomson, and other publishers typically set lower prices in Europe and Asia than in the United States. The reason is that the publishers use polycentric pricing: They establish prices on a regional or country-by-country basis using per capita income and economic conditions as a guide.

Geocentric

The third approach, geocentric pricing, is more dynamic and proactive than the other two. A company using **geocentric pricing** neither fixes a single price worldwide nor allows subsidiaries or local distributors to make independent pricing decisions. Instead, the geocentric approach represents an intermediate course of action. Geocentric pricing is based on the realization that unique local market factors should be recognized in arriving at pricing decisions. These factors include local costs, income levels, competition, and the local marketing strategy. Price must also be integrated with other elements of the marketing program. The geocentric approach recognizes that price coordination from headquarters is necessary in dealing with international accounts and . The geocentric approach also consciously and systematically seeks to ensure that accumulated national pricing experience is leveraged and applied wherever relevant.

Local costs plus a return on invested capital and personnel fix the price floor for the long term. In the short term, however, headquarters might decide to set a market penetration objective and price at less than the cost-plus return figure by using export sourcing to establish a market. This was the case described earlier with the Sony Walkman launch. Another short-term objective might be to arrive at an estimate of the market potential at a price that would be profitable given local sourcing and a certain scale of output. Instead of immediately investing in local manufacture, a decision might be made to supply the target market initially from existing higher-cost external supply sources. If the market accepts the price and product, the company can then build a local manufacturing facility to further develop the identified market opportunity in a profitable way. If the market opportunity does not materialize, the company can experiment with the product at other prices because it is not committed to a fixed sales volume by existing local manufacturing facilities.

For consumer products, local income levels are critical in the pricing decision. If the product is normally priced well above full manufacturing costs, the global marketer should consider accepting reduced margins and price below prevailing levels in low-income markets. *The important point here is that in global marketing there is no such thing as a "normal" margin.* Of the three methods described, the geocentric approach is best suited to global competitive strategy. A global competitor will take into account global markets and global competitors in establishing prices. Prices will support global strategy objectives rather than the objective of maximizing performance in a single country. Table 11-7 lists some comments by European exporters that provide insights into the real-world process of setting prices.

---

[22] Tamar Lewin, "Students Find $100 Textbooks Cost $50, Purchased Overseas," *The New York Times* (October 21, 2003), p. A16.

Statement by Management	Implication/Interpretation	Table 11-7
"We have the competitors' price list on our desk. I may speak frankly—who does not? We know exactly what our competitors charge for certain products, and we calculate accordingly."	When calculating prices for foreign markets, managers benchmark competitors' prices.	*How Managers Calculate Export Prices for Industrial Products*
"An interesting way of evaluating whether a product will fit requirements of the market has emerged. You give some machines to an auction house and set a very low price limit. Your products are then auctioned off. That way, you get a feel for the right price level as well as the potential demand for the product. It is a very easy and cost-effective method."	As a practical matter, some companies use innovative, trial-and-error approaches to determine price elasticity.	
"At trade shows, we go directly to our customers and try to find out what prices we can charge. We scan our price limits sensitively. This is how we get to a price list in the end."	Some companies take a methodical approach to determining price elasticity.	
"We differentiate simply because there are some countries where we can get a better price. Then there are countries where we can't."	Rationale for differentiating prices using either polycentric or geocentric approach.	
"I decided not to listen to people who advise me to differentiate prices. Wherever we are active, we want to have the image and the reputation of calculating our prices correctly and honestly."	Rationale for using standardized pricing.	

Source: Adapted from Barbara Stöttinger, "Strategic Export Pricing: A Long and Winding Road," *Journal of International Marketing* 9, no. 1 (2001), pp. 40–63.

GRAY MARKET GOODS

Gray market goods are trademarked products that are exported from one country to another where they are sold by unauthorized persons or organizations. Consider the following illustration:

> Suppose that a golf equipment manufacturer sells a golf club to its domestic distributors for $200; it sells the same club to its Thailand distributor for $100. The lower price may be due to differences in overseas demand or ability to pay. Or, the price difference may reflect the need to compensate the foreign distributor for advertising and marketing the club. The golf club, however, never makes it to Thailand. Instead, the Thailand distributor resells the club to a gray marketer in the United States for $150. The gray marketer can then undercut the prices charged by domestic distributors who paid $200 for the club. The manufacturer is forced to lower the domestic price or risk losing sales to gray marketers, driving down the manufacturer's profit margins. Additionally, gray marketers make liberal use of manufacturer's trademarks and often fail to provide warranties and other services that consumers expect from the manufacturer and its authorized distributors.[23]

This practice, known as **parallel importing**, occurs when companies employ a polycentric, multinational pricing policy that calls for setting different prices in different country markets. Gray markets can flourish when a product is in short supply, when producers employ skimming strategies in certain markets, or when the goods are subject to substantial markups. For example, in the European pharmaceuticals market, prices vary widely. In the United Kingdom and the Netherlands, for example, parallel imports account for as much as 10 percent of the sales of some pharmaceutical brands. The Internet is emerging as a powerful new tool that allows would-be gray marketers to access pricing information and reach customers.[24]

---

[23] Adapted from Perry J. Viscounty, Jeff C. Risher, and Collin G. Smyser, "Cyber Gray Market Is Manufacturers' Headache," *National Law Journal* (August 20, 2001), p. C3.

[24] Perry J. Viscounty, Jeff C. Risher, and Collin G. Smyser, "Cyber Gray Market Is Manufacturers' Headache," *National Law Journal* (August 20, 2001), p. C3.

Gray markets impose several costs or consequences on global marketers. These include:[25]

- *Dilution of exclusivity.* Authorized dealers are no longer the sole distributors. The product is often available from multiple sources, and margins are threatened.
- *Free riding.* If the manufacturer ignores complaints from authorized channel members, those members may engage in *free riding.* That is, they may opt to take various actions to offset downward pressure on margins. These options include cutting back on presale service, customer education, and salesperson training.
- *Damage to channel relationships.* Competition from gray market products can lead to channel conflict as authorized distributors attempt to cut costs, complain to manufacturers, and file lawsuits against the gray marketers.
- *Undermining segmented pricing schemes.* As noted earlier, gray markets can emerge because of price differentials that result from multinational pricing policies. However, a variety of forces—including falling trade barriers, the information explosion on the Internet, and modern distribution capabilities—hamper a company's ability to pursue local pricing strategies.
- *Reputation and legal liability.* Even though gray market goods carry the same trademarks as goods sold through authorized channels, they may differ in quality, ingredients, or some other way. Gray market products can compromise a manufacturer's reputation and dilute brand equity, as when prescription drugs are sold past their expiration dates or electronics equipment is sold in markets where they are not approved for use or where manufacturers do not honor warranties.

Sometimes, gray marketers bring a product produced in a single country—French champagne, for example—into export markets in competition with authorized importers. The gray marketers sell at prices that undercut those set by the legitimate importers. In another type of gray marketing, a company manufactures a product in the home-country market as well as in foreign markets. In this case, products manufactured abroad by the company's foreign affiliate for sales abroad are sometimes sold by a foreign distributor to gray marketers. The latter then bring the products into the producing company's home-country market, where they compete with domestically produced goods.

As these examples show, the marketing opportunity that presents itself requires gray market goods to be priced lower than goods sold by authorized distributors or domestically produced goods. Clearly, buyers gain from lower prices and increased choice. In the United Kingdom alone, for example, total annual retail sales of gray market goods are estimated to be as high as $1.6 billion. A recent case in Europe resulted in a ruling that strengthened the rights of brand owners. Silhouette, an Austrian manufacturer of upscale sunglasses, sued the Hartlauer discount chain after the retailer obtained thousands of pairs of sunglasses that Silhouette had intended for sale in Eastern Europe. The European Court of Justice found in favor of Silhouette. In clarifying a 1989 directive, the court ruled that stores cannot import branded goods from outside the EU and then sell them at discounted prices without permission of the brand owner. The *Financial Times* denounced the ruling as "bad for consumers, bad for competition, and bad for European economies."[26]

In the United States, gray market goods are subject to the Tariff Act of 1930. Section 526 of the act expressly forbids importation of goods of foreign

"The gray market is the biggest threat we have. You can't develop this market properly and make investments in retailing, merchandising, after-sales service and distribution without a legal market."[27]

Pankaj Mohindroo, President, Indian Cellular Association

[25] Kersi D. Antia, Mark Bergen, and Shantanu Dutta, "Competing with Gray Markets," *MIT Sloan Management Review* 46, no. 1 (Summer 2004), pp. 65–67.

[26] Peggy Hollinger and Neil Buckley, "Grey Market Ruling Delights Brand Owners," *Financial Times* (July 17, 1998), p. 8.

[27] Ray Marcelo, "Officials See Red Over Handset Sales," *Financial Times* (October 3, 2003), p. 16.

In the United States, drug makers set prices for that country that are the highest in the world. There is a reason for the high prices: The companies need to recover the high R&D costs associated with bringing a new drug to market. Elsewhere, governments set price ceilings that do not take R&D into account. For example, prices for Allegra, Lipitor, Viagra, Zocor, and other popular prescription drugs are as much as 85 percent lower in Canada than in the United States. High prices are one reason why, overall, the U.S. drug market rings up $200 billion in sales each year. High prices have also resulted in a thriving cross-border trade with Canada worth about $800 million per year. Many persons living near the Canadian border cross over by car or bus to shop. Americans who live farther from the border have several options: They can order drugs from Canadian pharmacies over the Internet or visit storefront operations such as RxDepot that fax prescriptions to Canada. Whichever option they choose, Americans who buy drugs in other countries are breaking the law.

manufacture without the permission of the trademark owner. However, because courts have considerable leeway in interpreting the act, one legal expert has argued that the U.S. Congress should repeal Section 526. In its place, a new law should require gray market goods to bear labels clearly explaining any differences between them and goods that come through authorized channels. Other experts believe that, instead of changing the laws, companies should develop proactive strategic responses to gray markets. One such strategy would be improved market segmentation and product differentiation to make gray market products less attractive; another would be to aggressively identify and terminate distributors that are involved in selling to gray marketers.

DUMPING

Dumping is an important global pricing strategy issue. GATT's 1979 antidumping code defined **dumping** as the sale of an imported product at a price lower than that normally charged in a domestic market or country of origin. In addition, many countries have their own policies and procedures for protecting national companies from dumping. For example, China has retaliated against years of Western antidumping rules by introducing rules of its own. China's State Council passed the Antidumping and Antisubsidy Regulations in March 1997. The Ministry of Foreign Trade and Economic Cooperation and the State Economic and Trade Commission have responsibility for antidumping matters.[28]

The U.S. Congress has defined *dumping* as an unfair trade practice that results in "injury, destruction, or prevention of the establishment of American industry." Under this definition, dumping occurs when imports sold in the U.S. market are priced either at levels that represent less than the cost of production plus an 8 percent profit margin or at levels below those prevailing in the producing country. The U.S. Commerce Department is responsible for determining whether products are being dumped in the United States; the International Trade Commission (ITC) then determines whether the dumping has resulted in injury to U.S. firms. Many of the dumping cases in the United States involve manufactured goods from Asia and frequently target a single or very narrowly defined group of products. U.S. companies that claim to be materially damaged by the low-priced imports often initiate such cases. In 2000, the U.S. Congress passed the so-called **Byrd Amendment**; this law calls for antidumping revenues to be paid to U.S. companies harmed by imported goods sold at below-market prices.[29]

---

[28] Lester Ross and Susan Ning, "Modern Protectionism: China's Own Antidumping Regulations," *China Business Review* (May–June 2000), pp. 30–33.

[29] Philip Brasher, "Clarinda Plant Takes Hit in Dispute over Imports," *Des Moines Register* (November 16, 2005), p. D1.

In Europe, the European Commission administers antidumping policy; a simple majority vote by the Council of Ministers is required before duties can be imposed on dumped goods. Six-month provisional duties can be imposed; more stringent measures include definitive, five-year duties. Low-cost imports from Asia have been the subject of dumping disputes in Europe. Another issue concerns $650 million in annual imports of unbleached cotton from China, Egypt, India, Indonesia, Pakistan, and Turkey. A dispute pitted an alliance of textile importers and wholesalers against Eurocoton, which represents textile weavers in France, Italy, and other EU countries. Eurocoton supports the duties as a means of protecting jobs from low-priced imports; the job issue is particularly sensitive in France. British textile importer Broome & Wellington maintains, however, that imposing duties would drive up prices and cost even more jobs in the textile finishing and garment industries.[30] In January 2005, the global system of textile quotas was abolished. Almost overnight, Chinese textile exports to the United States and Europe increased dramatically. Within a few months, the U.S. government had re-imposed quotas on several categories of textiles imports; in the EU, trade minister Peter Mandelson also imposed quotas for a period of two years.

Dumping was a major issue in the Uruguay round of GATT negotiations. Many countries took issue with the U.S. system of antidumping laws, in part because historically the U.S. Commerce Department almost always ruled in favor of the U.S. company that filed the complaint. For their part, U.S. negotiators were concerned that U.S. exporters were often targeted in antidumping investigations in countries with few formal rules for due process. The U.S. side sought to improve the ability of U.S. companies to defend their interests and understand the bases for rulings.

The result of the GATT negotiations was an agreement on interpretation of GATT Article VI. From the U.S. point of view, one of the most significant changes between the agreement and the 1979 code is the addition of a "standard of review" that will make it harder for GATT panels to dispute U.S. antidumping determinations. There are also a number of procedural and methodological changes. In some instances, these have the effect of bringing GATT regulations more in line with U.S. law. For example, in calculating "fair price" for a given product, any sales of the product at below-cost prices in the exporting country are not included in the calculations; inclusion of such sales would have the effect of exerting downward pressure on the fair price. The agreement also brought GATT standards in line with U.S. standards by prohibiting governments from penalizing differences between home market and export market prices of less than 2 percent.

For positive proof that dumping has occurred in the United States, both price discrimination and injury must be demonstrated. *Price discrimination* is the practice of setting different prices when selling the same quantity of "like-quality" goods to different buyers. The existence of either one without the other is an insufficient condition to constitute dumping. Companies concerned with running afoul of antidumping legislation have developed a number of approaches for avoiding the dumping laws. One approach is to differentiate the product sold from that in the home market so it does not represent "like quality." An example of this is an auto accessory that one company packaged with a wrench and an instruction book, thereby changing the "accessory" to a "tool." The duty rate in the export market happened to be lower on tools, and the company also acquired immunity from antidumping laws because the package was not comparable to competing goods in the target market. Another approach is to make nonprice competitive adjustments in arrangements with affiliates and distributors. For example, credit can be extended and essentially have the same effect as a price reduction.

[30] Neil Buckley, "Commission Faces Fight on Cotton 'Dumping,'" *Financial Times* (December 2, 1997), p. 5; Emma Tucker, "French Fury at Threat to Cotton Duties," *Financial Times* (May 19, 1997), p. 3.

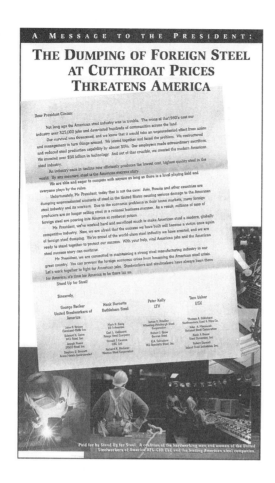

'Stand Up for Steel' Ad, sponsored by a coalition of the United Steelworkers of America and the major domestic steel companies: The Dumping of Foreign Steel At Cutthroat Prices Threatens America

Representatives of the U.S. steel industry sponsored this 1998 ad to urge President Clinton to get tough on unfairly-traded, government subsidized steel that was sold in the United States by producers in Western Europe, Asia, and Russia. In 2001, the International Trade Commission launched an investigation under the 'Section 201' provision of the U.S. Foreign Trade Act to determine whether steel imports were hurting American steel producers.

Based on the ITC's recommendation, in March 2002 President George W. Bush imposed sweeping tariffs of up to 30 percent on a wide range of steel imports for a three-year period. The European Union responded by drawing up a list of U.S. product imports that would be taxed in retaliation for the president's action. In 2003, President Bush dropped the tariffs.

PRICE FIXING

In most instances, it is illegal for representatives of two or more companies to secretly set similar prices for their products. This practice, known as **price fixing**, is generally held to be an anticompetitive act. Companies that collude in this manner are generally trying to ensure higher prices for their products than would generally be available if markets were functioning freely. In *horizontal price fixing*, competitors within an industry that make and market the same product conspire to keep prices high. For example, in the 1990s, Archer Daniels Midland (ADM) and several other companies were found guilty of colluding to prop up world prices for an enzyme used in animal feed. The term *horizontal* applies in this instance because ADM and its co-conspirators are all at the same supply-chain "level" (i.e., they are manufacturers). *Vertical price fixing* occurs when a manufacturer conspires with wholesalers or retailers (i.e., channel members at different "levels" from the manufacturer) to ensure certain retail prices are maintained. For example, the European Commission recently fined Nintendo nearly $150 million after it was determined that the video game company had colluded with European distributors to fix prices. During the 1990s, prices of Nintendo video game consoles varied widely across Europe. They were much more expensive in Spain than in Britain and other countries; however, distributors in countries with lower retail prices agreed not to sell to retailers in countries with high prices.[31] Another recent case of price fixing pits DeBeers SA, the South African diamond company, against the United States. The price fixing case involves industrial diamonds rather than gemstones; however, DeBeers is a well-known name in the United States thanks to a long-running advertising campaign

---

31 Paul Meller, "Europe Fines Nintendo $147 Million for Price Fixing," *The Wall Street Journal* (February 24, 2004), p. W1.

keyed to the tagline "A Diamond Is Forever." Because the company itself has no American retail presence, DeBeers diamonds are marketed in the United States by intermediaries. DeBeers executives have indicated a willingness to plead guilty and pay a fine in exchange for access to the United States. As a spokesperson said, "The U.S. is the biggest market for diamond jewelry—accounting for 50 percent of global retail jewelry sales—and we would really, really like to resolve these issues.[32]

TRANSFER PRICING

Transfer pricing refers to the pricing of goods, services, and intangible property bought and sold by operating units or divisions of the same company. In other words, transfer pricing concerns *intracorporate exchanges*, which are transactions between buyers and sellers that have the same corporate parent. For example, Toyota subsidiaries both sell to, and buy from, each other. Transfer pricing is an important topic in global marketing because goods crossing national borders represent a sale; therefore, their pricing is a matter of interest both to the tax authorities, who want to collect a fair share of income taxes, and to the customs service, which wants to collect an appropriate duty on the goods. Joseph Quinlan, chief marketing strategist at Bank of America, estimates that U.S. companies have 23,000 overseas affiliates; about 25 percent of U.S. exports represent shipments by American companies to affiliates and subsidiaries outside the United States.

In determining transfer prices to subsidiaries, global companies must address a number of issues, including taxes, duties and tariffs, country profit transfer rules, conflicting objectives of joint venture partners, and government regulations. Tax authorities, such as the Internal Revenue Service (IRS) in the United States, Inland Revenue in the United Kingdom, and Japan's National Tax Administration Agency, take a keen interest in transfer-pricing policies. Transfer pricing is proving to be a corporate key issue in Europe as the euro makes it easier for tax authorities to audit transfer-pricing policies.

Three major alternative approaches can be applied to transfer pricing decisions. The approach used will vary with the nature of the firm, products, markets, and historical circumstances of each case. A *market-based transfer price* is derived from the price required to be competitive in the global marketplace. In other words, it represents an approximation of an arm's-length transaction. *Cost-based transfer pricing* uses an internal cost as the starting point in determining price. Cost-based transfer pricing can take the same forms as the cost-based pricing methods discussed earlier in the chapter. The way costs are defined may have an impact on tariffs and duties of sales to affiliates and subsidiaries by global companies. A third alternative is to allow the organization's affiliates to determine *negotiated transfer prices* among themselves. This method may be employed when market prices are subject to frequent changes. Table 11-8 summarizes the results of recent studies comparing transfer-pricing methods by country. As shown in the table, market-based and cost-based transfer pricing are the two preferred methods in the United States, Canada, Japan, and the United Kingdom.

Tax Regulations and Transfer Prices

Because global companies conduct business in a world characterized by different corporate tax rates, there is an incentive to maximize system income in countries with the lowest tax rates and to minimize income in high-tax countries. Governmental regulatory agencies are well aware of this situation. In recent years, many governments have tried to maximize national tax revenues by examining

---

[32] John R. Wilke, "DeBeers Is in Talks to Settle Price-Fixing Charge," *The Wall Street Journal* (February 24, 2004), pp. A1, A14.

Methods	United States (%)	Canada (%)	Japan (%)	United Kingdom (%)
1. Market-based	35	37	37	31
2. Cost-based	43	33	41	38
3. Negotiated	14	26	22	20
4. Other	8	4	0	11
	100%	100%	100%	100%

Source: Adapted from Charles T. Horngren, Srikant M. Datar, and George Foster, Cost Accounting: A Managerial Emphasis (Upper Saddle River, NJ: Prentice Hall, 2003), p. 767.

Table 11-8

Transfer Pricing Methods Used in Selected Countries

company returns and mandating reallocation of income and expenses. Some companies recently involved in transfer-pricing cases include:

- Motorola may owe the IRS as much as $500 million in taxes from earnings from global operations that were booked incorrectly.
- The U.S. Labor Department filed a complaint against Swatch Group alleging that the Swiss watchmaker improperly used transfer pricing to evade millions of dollars in customs duties and taxes.[33]
- The U.S. government spent years attempting to recover $2.7 billion plus interest from pharmaceutical giant GlaxoSmithKline (GSK). The IRS charged that GSK did not pay enough tax on profits from Zantac, its hugely successful ulcer medication. Between 1989 and 1999, U.S. revenues from Zantac totaled $16 billion; the IRS charged that GSK's American unit overpaid royalties to the British parent company, thus, reducing taxable U.S. income. The case was scheduled for trial in 2007; however, in September 2006, GSK settled the case by agreeing to pay the IRS approximately $3.1 billion.[34]

Sales of Tangible and Intangible Property

Each country has its own set of laws and regulations for dealing with controlled intracompany transfers. Whatever the pricing rationale, executives and managers involved in global pricing policy decisions must familiarize themselves with the laws and regulations in the applicable countries. The pricing rationale must conform with the intention of these laws and regulations. Although the applicable laws and regulations often seem perplexingly inscrutable, ample evidence exists that most governments simply seek to prevent tax avoidance and to ensure fair distribution of income from the operations of companies doing business internationally.

Even companies that make a conscientious effort to comply with the applicable laws and regulations and that document this effort may find themselves in tax court. Should a tax auditor raise questions, executives should be able to make a strong case for their decisions. Fortunately, consulting services are available to help managers deal with the arcane world of transfer pricing. It is not unusual for large global companies to invest hundreds of thousands of dollars and hire international accounting firms to review transfer-pricing policies.

COUNTERTRADE

In recent years, many exporters have been forced to finance international transactions by taking full or partial payment in some form other than money.[35] A number of alternative finance methods, known as *countertrade*, are widely used.

---

[33] Leslie Lopez and John D. McKinnon, "Swatch Faces Complaint over Taxes," *The Wall Street Journal* (August 13, 2004), p. B2.

[34] Susannah Rodgers, "GlaxoSmithKline Gets Big Tax Bill," *The Wall Street Journal* (January 8, 2004), p. A8.

[35] Many of the examples in the following section are adapted from Matt Schaffer, *Winning the Countertrade War: New Export Strategies for America* (New York: John Wiley & Sons, 1989).

In a **countertrade** transaction, a sale results in product flowing in one direction to a buyer; a separate stream of products and services, often flowing in the opposite direction, is also created. Countertrade generally involves a seller from the West and a buyer in a developing country; for example, the countries in the former Soviet bloc have historically relied heavily on countertrade. This approach, which reached a peak in popularity in the mid-1980s, is now used in some 100 countries. Within the former Soviet Union, countertrade has flourished in the 1990s, following the collapse of the central planning system.

As one expert notes, countertrade flourishes when hard currency is scarce. Exchange controls may prevent a company from expatriating earnings; the company may be forced to spend money in-country for products that are then exported and sold in third-country markets. Historically, the single most important driving force behind the proliferation of countertrade was the decreasing ability of developing countries to finance imports through bank loans. This trend resulted in debt-ridden governments pushing for self-financed deals.[36] According to Pompiliu Verzariu, former director of the Financial Services and Countertrade Division of the International Trade Administration:

> In the 1990s, countertrade pressures abated in many parts of the world, notably Latin America, as a result of debt reduction induced by the Brady plan initiative, lower international interest rates, policies that liberalized trade regimes, and the emergence of economic blocs such as NAFTA and Mercosur, which integrate regional trade based on free-market principles.[37]

Today, several conditions affect the probability that importing nations will demand countertrade. First is the priority attached to the Western import. The higher the priority, the less likely it is that countertrade will be required. The second condition is the value of the transaction; the higher the value, the greater the likelihood that countertrade will be involved. Third, the availability of products from other suppliers can also be a factor. If a company is the sole supplier of a differentiated product, it can demand monetary payment. However, if competitors are willing to deal on a countertrade basis, a company may have little choice but to agree or risk losing the sale altogether. Overall, the advantages to nonmarket and developing economies are access to Western marketing expertise and technology in the short term, and creation of hard currency export markets in the long term. The U.S. government officially opposes government-mandated countertrade, which represents the type of bilateral trade agreement that violates the free trading system established by GATT.

Two categories of countertrade are discussed here. Barter falls into one category; the mixed forms of countertrade, including counterpurchase, offset, compensation trading, and switch trading belong in a separate category. They incorporate a real distinction from barter because the transaction involves money or credit.

Barter

The term **barter** describes the least complex and oldest form of bilateral, nonmonetized countertrade. Simple barter is a direct exchange of goods or services between two parties. Although no money is involved, both partners construct an approximate shadow price for products flowing in each direction. One contract formalizes simple barter transactions, which are generally for less than one year to avoid problems in price fluctuations. However, for some transactions, the exchange may span months or years, with contract provisions allowing adjustments in the exchange ratio to handle fluctuations in world prices.

---

[36] Pompiliu Verzariu, "Trends and Developments in International Countertrade," *Business America* (November 2, 1992), p. 2.

[37] Janet Aschkenasy, "Give and Take," *International Business* (September 1996), p. 11.

Companies sometimes seek outside help from barter specialists. For example, New York-based Atwood Richards engages in barter in all parts of the world. Generally, however, distribution is direct between trading partners, with no intermediary included. For example, during the Soviet era, General Electric sold a turbine generator to Romania. For payment, GE Trading Company accepted $150 million in chemicals, metals, nails, and other products that it then sold on the world market. One of the highest-profile companies involved in barter deals is PepsiCo, which has done business in the Soviet and post-Soviet market for decades. In the Soviet era, PepsiCo bartered soft-drink syrup concentrate for Stolichnaya vodka, which was, in turn, exported to the United States by the PepsiCo Wines & Spirits subsidiary and marketed by M. Henri Wines. In the post-Soviet market economy in the Commonwealth of Independent States, barter is not necessarily required. Today, Stolichnaya is imported into the United States and marketed by Carillon Importers, a unit of Diageo PLC.

Counterpurchase

This form of countertrade, also termed *parallel trading* or *parallel barter*, is distinguished from other forms in that each delivery in an exchange is paid for in cash. For example, Rockwell International sold a printing press to Zimbabwe for $8 million. The deal went through, however, only after Rockwell agreed to purchase $8 million in ferrochrome and nickel from Zimbabwe, which it subsequently sold on the world market.

The Rockwell-Zimbabwe deal illustrates several aspects of counterpurchase. Generally, products offered by the foreign principal are not related to the Western firm's exports and cannot be used directly by the firm. In most counterpurchase transactions, two separate contracts are signed. In one, the supplier agrees to sell products for a cash settlement (the original sales contract); in the other, the supplier agrees to purchase and market unrelated products from the buyer (a separate, parallel contract). The dollar value of the counterpurchase generally represents a set percentage—and sometimes the full value—of the products sold to the foreign principal. When the Western supplier sells these goods, the trading cycle is complete.

Offset

Offset is a reciprocal arrangement whereby the government in the importing country seeks to recover large sums of hard currency spent on expensive purchases such as military aircraft or telecommunications systems. In effect, the government is saying, "If you want us to spend government money on your exports, you must import products from our country." Offset arrangements may also involve cooperation in manufacturing, some form of technology transfer, placing subcontracts locally, or arranging local assembly or manufacturing equal to a certain percentage of the contract value.[38] In one deal involving offsets, Lockheed Martin Corp. sold F-16 fighters to the United Arab Emirates for $6.4 billion. In return, Lockheed agreed to invest $160 million in the petroleum-related UAE Offsets Group.[39]

Offset may be distinguished from counterpurchase because the latter is characterized by smaller deals over shorter periods of time.[40] Another major distinction between offset and other forms of countertrade is that the agreement is not contractual but reflects a memorandum of understanding that sets out the dollar value of products to be offset and the time period for completing the transaction. In

---

[38] The commitment to local assembly or manufacturing under the supplier's specifications is commonly termed a *coproduction agreement*, which is tied to the offset but does not, in itself, represent a type of countertrade.

[39] Daniel Pearl, "Arms Dealers Get Creative with 'Offsets,'" *The Wall Street Journal* (April 20, 2000), p. A18.

[40] Patricia Daily and S. M. Ghazanfar, "Countertrade: Help or Hindrance to Less-Developed Countries?" *Journal of Social, Political, and Economic Studies* 18, no. 1 (Spring 1993), p. 65.

addition, there is no penalty on the supplier for nonperformance. Typically, requests range from 20 percent to 50 percent of the value of the supplier's product. Some highly competitive sales have required offsets exceeding 100 percent of the valuation of the original sale.

Offsets have become a controversial facet of today's trade environment. To win sales in important markets such as China, global companies can face demands for offsets even when transactions do not involve military procurement. For example, the Chinese government requires Boeing to spend 20 percent to 30 percent of the price of each aircraft on purchases of Chinese goods. As Boeing executive Dean Thornton explained:

> "Offset" is a bad word, and it's against GATT and a whole bunch of other stuff, but it's a fact of life. It used to be twenty years ago in places like Canada or the UK, it was totally explicit, down to the decimal point. "You will buy 20 percent offset of your value." Or 21 percent or whatever. It still is that way in military stuff. [With sales of commercial aircraft], it's not legal so it becomes less explicit.[41]

Compensation Trading

Compensation trading, also called *buyback*, is a form of countertrade that involves two separate and parallel contracts. In one contract, the supplier agrees to build a plant or provide plant equipment, patents or licenses, or technical, managerial, or distribution expertise for a hard currency down payment at the time of delivery. In the other contract, the supplier company agrees to take payment in the form of the plant's output equal to its investment (minus interest) for a period of as many as 20 years.

Essentially, the success of compensation trading rests on the willingness of each firm to be both a buyer and a seller. The People's Republic of China has used compensation trading extensively. Egypt also used this approach to develop an aluminum plant. A Swiss company, Aluswiss, built the plant and also exports alumina (an oxide of aluminum found in bauxite and clay) to Egypt. Aluswiss takes back a percentage of the finished aluminum produced at the plant as partial payment for building the plant. As this example shows, compensation differs from counterpurchase in that the technology or capital supplied is related to the output produced.[42] In counterpurchase, as noted before, the goods taken by the supplier typically cannot be used directly in its business activities.

Switch Trading

Also called *triangular trade* and *swap*, **switch trading** is a mechanism that can be applied to barter or countertrade. In this arrangement, a third party steps into a simple barter or other countertrade arrangement when one of the parties is not willing to accept all the goods received in a transaction. The third party may be a professional switch trader, switch trading house, or a bank. The switching mechanism provides a "secondary market" for countertraded or bartered goods and reduces the inflexibility inherent in barter and countertrade. Fees charged by switch traders range from 5 percent of market value for commodities to 30 percent for high-technology items. Switch traders develop their own networks of firms and personal contacts and are generally headquartered in Vienna, Amsterdam, Hamburg, or London. If a party to the original transaction anticipates that the products received in a barter or countertrade deal will be sold eventually at a discount by the switch trader, the common practice is to price the original products higher, build in "special charges" for port storage or consulting, or require shipment by the national carrier.

---

41 William Greider, *One World, Ready or Not: The Manic Logic of Global Capitalism* (Upper Saddle River, NJ: Simon & Schuster, 1997), p. 130.
42 Patricia Daily and S. M. Ghazanfar, "Countertrade: Help or Hindrance to Less-Developed Countries?" *Journal of Social, Political, and Economic Studies* 18, no. 1 (Spring 1993), p. 66.

Pricing decisions are a critical element of the marketing mix that must reflect costs, competitive factors, and customer perceptions regarding value of the product. In a true global market, the **law of one price** would prevail. Pricing strategies include **market skimming**, **market penetration**, and **market holding**. Novice exporters frequently use **cost-plus pricing**. International terms of a sale such as **ex-works**, **DDP**, **FCA**, **FAS**, **FOB**, **CIF**, and **CFR** are known as **Incoterms** and specify which party to a transaction is responsible for covering various costs. These and other costs lead to **export price escalation**, the accumulation of costs that occurs when products are shipped from one country to another.

Expectations regarding currency fluctuations, inflation, government controls, and the competitive situation must also be factored into pricing decisions. The introduction of the euro has impacted price strategies in the EU because of improved **price transparency**. Global companies can maintain competitive prices in world markets by shifting production sources as business conditions change. Overall, a company's pricing policies can be categorized as **ethnocentric**, **polycentric**, or **geocentric**.

Several additional pricing issues are related to global marketing. The issue of **gray market goods** arises because price variations between different countries lead to **parallel imports**. **Dumping** is another contentious issue that can result in strained relations between trading partners. **Price fixing** among companies is anticompetitive and illegal. **Transfer pricing** is an issue because of the sheer monetary volume of intracorporate sales and because country governments are anxious to generate as much tax revenue as possible. Various forms of **countertrade** play an important role in today's global environment. **Barter**, **counterpurchase**, **offset**, **compensation trading**, and **switch trading** are the main countertrade options.

1. What are the basic factors that affect price in any market? What considerations enter into the pricing decision?

2. Define the various types of pricing strategies and objectives available to global marketers.

3. Identify some of the environmental constraints on global pricing decisions.

4. Why do price differences in world markets often lead to gray marketing?

5. What is dumping? Why was dumping such an important issue during the Uruguay Round of GATT negotiations?

6. What is a transfer price? Why is it an important issue for companies with foreign affiliates? Why did transfer pricing in Europe take on increased importance in 1999?

7. What is the difference between ethnocentric, polycentric, and geocentric pricing strategies? Which one would you recommend to a company that has global market aspirations?

8. If you were responsible for marketing CAT scanners worldwide (average price, $1,200,000), and your country of manufacture was experiencing a strong and appreciating currency against almost all other currencies, what options are available to you to maintain your competitive advantage in world markets?

9. Compare and contrast the different forms of countertrade.

Compare and contrast LVMH's pricing strategy (see Case 11-1) with that of Coach (Chapter 7).

Case 11-1
LVMH and Luxury Goods Marketing

Do you know anyone who spends $1,700 on a suit plus $600 for a matching handbag? When it comes to champagne and perfume, do your friends spend $100 or more for a single bottle? Welcome to the rarefied world of luxury goods marketing. In this world, affluent consumers eagerly seek out luxury brands such as Armani, Christian Dior, Gucci, Louis Vuitton, Prada, and Versace. They are willing and able to pay high prices for top-quality merchandise from fashion houses whose names are synonymous with status, good taste, and prestige. In France, *haute couture* traditionally meant that one outfit was meticulously crafted for members of the aristocracy, "old money" socialites, or celebrities. Today, however, the concept and meaning of *haute couture* are being transformed.

Although the *couture* image of the supermodel strutting down the catwalk is still a mainstay of the fashion world, some of the world's best-known fashion houses are redefining the notion of luxury by catering to the needs of a more diverse, *nouveau riche* clientele. Whereas in years past, fashion houses produced only clothing, today numerous licensing deals are generating more cash than the clothing itself. Countless items bearing the names of venerable *couture* houses are now available worldwide. Thanks to the stock market boom of the 1990s and rising prosperity levels in developing nations, a new class of affluent consumers has begun to develop a taste for luxury branded products, ranging from Gucci sunglasses to Dior pantyhose. Apparel goods constitute less than 20 percent of total sales volume by Hermés. As Lord Thurso, chief executive of a luxury health spa in Great Britain, noted, "The trick is not to sell real luxury to very rich people. It's to sell a *perception* of luxury to aspiring people."

One fashion house that is changing with the times is LVMH Moët Hennessy-Louis Vuitton SA, the largest marketer of luxury products and brands in the world. Chairman Bernard Arnault presides over a diverse empire of products and brands, sales of which totaled $16.5 billion €15.3 billion) in 2006 (see Figure 1). Arnault, whom some refer to as "the pope of high fashion," recently summed up the luxury business as follows: "We are here to sell dreams. When you see a couture show on TV around the world, you dream. When you enter a Dior boutique and buy your lipstick, you buy something affordable, but it has the dream in it." Sales of luggage and leather fashion goods, including the 100-year-old Louis Vuitton brand, account for 30 percent of revenues. The company's specialty group includes Duty Free Shoppers (DFS) and Sephora. DFS operates stores in international airports around the world; Sephora, which LVMH acquired in 1997, is Europe's second-largest chain of perfume and cosmetics stores. Driven by such well-known brands as Christian Dior, Givenchy, and Kenzo, perfumes and body products generate nearly 20 percent of LVMH's revenues. LVMH's wine and spirits

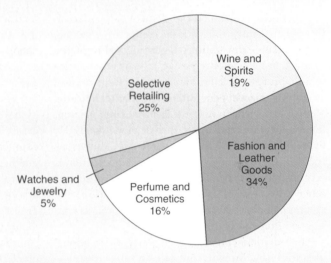

Figure 1
LVMH Operating Units by 2006 Net Sales

unit includes such prestigious such Champagne brands as Dom Perignon, Moët & Chandon, and Veuve Clicquot.

Despite the high expenses associated with operating elegant stores and purchasing advertising space in upscale magazines, the premium retail prices that luxury goods command translate into handsome profits. The Louis Vuitton brand alone accounts for about 60 percent of LVMH's operating profit. Unscrupulous operators have taken note of the high margins associated with Vuitton handbags, gun cases, and luggage displaying the distinctive beige-on-brown latticework LV monogram. Louis Vuitton SA spends $10 million annually battling counterfeiters in Turkey, Thailand, China, Morocco, South Korea, and Italy. Some of the money is spent on lobbyists who represent the company's interests in meetings with foreign government officials. Yves Carcelle, chairman of Louis Vuitton SA, recently explained, "Almost every month, we get a government somewhere in the world to destroy canvas, or finished products."

Another problem is a flourishing gray market. Givenchy and Christian Dior's Dune fragrance are just two of the luxury perfume brands that are sometimes diverted from authorized channels for sale at mass-market retail outlets. LVMH and other luxury goods marketers recently found a new way to combat gray market imports into the United States. In March 1995, the U.S. Supreme Court let stand an appeals court ruling prohibiting a discount drugstore chain from selling Givenchy perfume without permission. Parfums Givenchy USA had claimed that its distinctive packaging should be protected under U.S. copyright law. The ruling means that Costco, Wal-Mart, and other discounters will no longer be able to sell some imported fragrances without authorization.

Asia—particularly Japan—represents important markets for companies such as LVMH. The financial turmoil that began in July 1997 and the subsequent currency devaluations and weakening of the yen have translated into lower demand for luxury goods. Because price perceptions are a critical component of luxury goods' appeal, LMVH executives are making a number of adjustments in response to changing business conditions. For example, Patrick Choel, president of the perfume and cosmetics division, has raised wholesale prices in individual Asian markets. The goal is to discourage discount retailers from stocking up with designer products and then selling them to down-market consumers. Also, expenditures on perfume and cosmetics advertising have been reduced to maintain profitability in the face of a possible sales decline. Louis Vuitton chairman Yves Carcelle is also making adjustments. He canceled plans for a new store in Indonesia; group managers have raised prices to counteract the effect of currency devaluations. Because the DFS chain depends on Japanese tourists in Asia and Hawaii for 75 percent of sales, Louis Vuitton managers also work with tour operators to predict the flow of Japanese tourists. When tourism is at a peak, price increases from 10 percent to 22 percent help maximize profits on merchandise sales.

Arnault was confident that the Asian crisis would not severely affect his company's performance in the long term. As Arnault explained in the spring of 1998, "One has to distinguish between Japan, where most of our business is, and the rest of Asia. Japan is in a growth slump, but it isn't going to have the same difficulties as Korea or Indonesia. And our business in Japan is doing very well." Because the Louis Vuitton unit controls its own distribution, management has even been able to take advantage of the crisis by renegotiating store leases in key Asian cities. In some instances, the company has secured longer lease terms plus reductions in rates by as much as one-third. Arnault's optimism was well founded; with interest rates at record lows and a gloomy outlook for the stock market, Japanese consumers had few other spending options. In 2001, executives actually raised prices at Louis Vuitton's 45 Japanese stores.

"One friend of mine has 10 Louis Vuitton bags. In Japan, it's a status symbol. It's very important to have European luxury goods."

A 39-year-old flight attendant based in Tokyo

The United States is also a key market for LVMH. One particular marketing program focused on increasing awareness of Hennessy cognac. Thanks to a revival of "cocktail culture" in the United States, sales of hard spirits are up. To promote awareness and consumption among a younger demographic, in the mid-1990s Hennessy marketing managers recruited twentysomethings to go to upscale bars in major metropolitan markets and order drinks such as the "Hennessy martini" and "Hennessy sidecar" made with cognac. Although traditionalists consider the notion of mixing cognac heresy, it was essential to broadening the brand's appeal. If a bartender didn't know how to create a particular drink, the Hennessy agent helpfully explained the recipe while attracting the attention of other patrons. Hennessy also picked up the tab when their "secret agents" would buy rounds of cognac-based drinks for everyone at the bar. The promotion was designed to increase awareness among young adults and to communicate that cognac can be enjoyed by people other than "old fogies." The effort paid off in some unexpected ways: Urban hip-hop culture has embraced cognac, and cognac exports to the United States tripled over the past decade. LVMH's Hennessey is the brand of choice for many rap stars; the brand name has even popped up in more than 100 songs.

Such marketing tactics are a world away from the old days, when the companies that today make up LVMH were family-run enterprises focused more on prestige than on profit. They sold mainly to a small, very rich clientele. Even as he broadens the company's consumer base, Arnault has taken a number of steps to raise the level of professionalism of LVMH's management team. In 1997, Arnault implemented a corporate restructuring that groups the company's subsidiaries into divisions. Previously, the heads of individual subsidiaries reported directly to Arnault; now, division heads meet with him to discuss strategy. Notes Arnault, "It's much more efficient, because it allows us to put into practice all the synergies between the different brands in a coordinated way."

Arnault's choice of American designer Marc Jacobs to create the first-ever Louis Vuitton ready-to-wear line shows that times are changing. The line is priced quite high, and to preserve its exclusivity, it is currently available only through Louis Vuitton boutiques. There will be no markdowns on unsold merchandise. Any stocks that remain at the end of the season will be destroyed. Jacobs's first collection included a plain white cotton poplin raincoat that prompted one observer to ask, "Is this luxury?" Ironically, the signature LV is hard to spot on many pieces in the collection, such as a white-on-white patent leather bag.

In the late 1990s, Arnault sensed that cosmetics-buying habits were changing in key markets. He opened Sephora stores in New York, Chicago, and San Francisco in conjunction with a new Web site, Sephora.com. Today, there are more than 70 Sephora stores in the United States; plans call for expanding into Japan and Latin America as well. Customers who visit Sephora USA stores are encouraged to wander freely and sample products on an open floor without waiting for sales clerks to assist them. However, high start-up and promotion costs have reduced the financial contribution that Sephora makes to LVMH, and some analysts have asked when Sephora will be profitable.

Profitability is also an issue with another of Arnault's acquisitions, Donna Karan International Inc. In 2001, Arnault paid more than $600 million for the company and its trademarks. Arnault had tried without success to acquire Giorgio Armani; Donna Karan is LVMH's first American designer label. As Arnault noted, "What appealed to us is the fact that it is one of the best-known brand names in the world." After the deal was completed, however, company executives were surprised to learn that some items from the DKNY line could be found in discount stores such as T.J.Maxx. Arnault appointed Giuseppe Brusone, a former managing director of Armani, as Donna Karan's chief executive and instructed him to reshape the company. Brusone intends to improve quality, close company-owned outlet stores, and reduce shipments to department stores to keep the clothes from being marked down. He also intends to shift manufacturing out of New York; the move will both cut costs and lend the line the added prestige associated with garments that are "made in Italy."

All of these actions are designed to keep LVMH—and Arnault himself—at the forefront of the luxury goods business and one step ahead of an ever-changing business environment. Arnault is widely admired for his business instincts and acumen. However, some in the industry view his bold moves as emblematic of all that is wrong with luxury in the new millennium. An executive at a competitor noted disapprovingly, "They run this thing like Procter & Gamble."

Web Resources
www.lvmh.com
A complete PowerPoint presentation of the current year's financial results is available on the LVMH Web site.
www.sephora.com

Discussion Questions

1. Bernard Arnault has built LVMH into a luxury goods empire by making numerous acquisitions. What strategy is evident here?
2. How do LVMH executives adjust prices in response to changing economic conditions?
3. Do you think the high retail prices charged for luxury goods are worth paying?

Sources: Lisa Bannon and Alessandra Galloni, "Brand Manager Deluxe," *The Wall Street Journal* (October 10, 2003), p. B1; John Carreyrou and Christopher Lawton, "Napoleon's Nightcap Gets a Good Rap from Hip-Hop Set," *The Wall Street Journal* (July 14, 2003), pp. A1, A7; Teri Agins and Deborah Ball, "Changing Outfits: Did LVMH Commit a Fashion Faux Pas Buying Donna Karan?" *The Wall Street Journal* (March 21, 2002), pp. A1, A8; Deborah Ball, "Despite Downturn, Japanese Are Still Having Fits for Luxury Goods," *The Wall Street Journal* (April 24, 2001), pp. B1, B4; Bonnie Tsui, "Eye of the Beholder: Sephora's Finances," *Advertising Age* (March 19, 2001), p. 20; Lucia van der Post, "Life's Brittle Luxuries," *Financial Times* (July 18–19, 1998), p. I. Gail Edmondson, "LVMH: Life Isn't All Champagne and Caviar," *Business Week* (November 10, 1997), pp. 108+; Jennifer Steinhauer, "The King of Posh," *The New York Times* (August 17, 1997), sec. 3, pp. 1, 10–11; David Owen, "A Captain Used to Storms," *Financial Times* (June 21–22, 1997); Holly Brubach, "And Luxury for All," *The New York Times Magazine* (July 12, 1998), pp. 24–29+; Amy Barrett, "LVMH's Chairman Remains Calm Despite Turbulence," *The Wall Street Journal* (March 16, 1998), p. B4; Amy Barrett, "Gucci's Big Makeover Is Turning Heads," *The Wall Street Journal* (August 26, 1997), p. 12; Stewart Toy, "100 Years of Louis Vuitton," *Cigar Aficionado* (Autumn 1996), pp. 378–379+.

Appendix

Section 482 of the Internal Revenue Code

In any case of two or more organizations, trades, or businesses (whether or not incorporated, whether or not organized in the United States, and whether or not affiliated) owned or controlled directly or indirectly by the same interests, the Secretary may distribute, apportion, or allocate gross income, deductions, credits, or allowances between or among such organizations, trades, or businesses, if he determines that such distribution, apportionment, or allocation is necessary in order to prevent evasion of taxes or clearly to reflect the income of any of such organizations, trades, or businesses. In the case of any transfer (or license) of intangible property (within the meaning of section 936(h)(3)(B)), the income with respect to such transfer or license shall be commensurate with the income attributable to the intangible.

Source: The Wall Street Journal *(Western Edition) by* Internal Revenue Code. *Copyright 1987 by Dow Jones & Company, Inc. Reproduced with permission of Dow Jones & Company, Inc. in the format Other book via Copyright Clearance Center.*

12 Global Marketing Channels and Physical Distribution

Tesco is the largest supermarket chain in the United Kingdom. The company's slogan is "Every Little Helps"; it executes on that promise in various ways, including its Clubcard loyalty program and an online grocery retailing operation that fulfills more than 100,000 orders every week. Its supply chain—including relationships with suppliers and distributors—is one of the best in the industry. Despite these strengths, Tesco lags behind retailing giants Wal-Mart and Carrefour in terms of global presence. To address this weakness, Sir Terry Leahy, Tesco's chief executive, is implementing an expansion strategy. For example, his executives initiated negotiations with India's Bharti Enterprises about possible joint ventures. Sir Terry has also committed $435 million per year to open small stores in Los Angeles and Phoenix. The stores, which will have 15,000 square feet of floor space and bear the name "Tesco Fresh & Easy," will offer a focused selection of fresh foods, packaged goods, and prepared meals. Commenting on the $1 trillion U.S. grocery market, Sir Terry noted, "Demand for convenience shopping is very well developed there. There are lots of wealthy and busy people and it's multicultural. You've got to start somewhere and it's important to do it in bite-sized chunks."

Supermarkets and convenience stores comprise just two of the many elements that make up distribution channels around the globe. The American Marketing Association defines **channel of distribution** as "an organized network of agencies and institutions which, in combination, perform all the activities required to link producers with users to accomplish the marketing task."[1] **Physical distribution** is the movement of goods through channels; as suggested by the definition, channels are made up of a coordinated group of individuals or firms that perform functions that add utility to a product or service. Hypermarket operators such as Carrefour serve an important distribution function; when Western retailers set up shop in developing countries such as Poland and Indonesia, they provide customers with access to more products and lower prices than ever before. As Tadeusz Donocki, undersecretary of state at Poland's economics ministry, noted, "It's a way of bringing dreams closer to people, dreams which before they saw only in films."[2] In developed countries, the arrival of innovators such as Carrefour often serves as the catalyst for wrenching changes in long-established distribution traditions (see Case 12-1).

The appearance of hypermarkets around the world adds greater diversity to distribution channels, which already represent the most highly differentiated aspects of national marketing systems. On the opposite end of the spectrum from hypermarkets, for example, are small stores in Latin America called *pulperías*. The diversity of channels and the wide range of possible distribution strategies and market entry options can present challenges to managers responsible for designing global marketing programs. Smaller companies are often blocked by their inability to establish effective channel arrangements.

[1] Peter D. Bennett, *Dictionary of Marketing Terms* (Chicago: American Marketing Association, 1988), p. 29.
[2] Stefan Wagstyl, "Eastern Europe Takes a Shine to Hypermarket Shopping," *Financial Times* (January 20, 1999), p. 2.

Even as it prepares to challenge Wal-Mart on the U.S. retailing giant's home turf, Tesco is expanding in China. Tesco chief Sir Terry Leahy recently paid $350 million to increase his company's stake in the Hymall hypermarket chain from 50 percent to 90 percent.

In larger companies that operate via country subsidiaries, channel strategy is the element of the marketing mix that headquarters understands the least. It is important for managers responsible for world marketing programs to understand the nature of international distribution channels. Channels and physical distribution are crucial aspects of the total marketing program; without them, a great product at the right price and effective communications mean very little.

CHANNEL OBJECTIVES

Marketing channels exist to create utility for customers. The major categories of channel utility are **place utility** (the availability of a product or service in a location that is convenient to a potential customer), **time utility** (the availability of a product or service when desired by a customer), **form utility** (the availability of the product processed, prepared, in proper condition and/or ready to use), and **information utility** (the availability of answers to questions and general communication about useful product features and benefits). Because these utilities can be a basic source of competitive advantage and comprise an important element of the firm's overall value proposition, choosing a channel strategy is one of the key policy decisions management must make. For example, the Coca-Cola Company's leadership position in world markets is based in part on its ability to put Coke "within an arm's reach of desire"; in other words, to create place utility.

The starting point in selecting the most effective channel arrangement is a clear focus of the company's marketing effort on a target market and an assessment of the way(s) in which distribution can contribute to the firm's overall value proposition. Who are the target customers, and where are they located? What are their information requirements? What are their preferences for service? How sensitive are they to price? Customer preference must be carefully determined because there is as much danger to the success of a marketing program from creating too much utility as there is from creating too little utility. Moreover, each market must be analyzed to determine the cost of providing channel services. What is appropriate in one country may not be effective in another. Even marketers concerned with a single-country program can study channel arrangements in different parts of the world for valuable information and insight into possible new channel strategies and tactics. For example, retailers from Europe and Asia studied self-service discount retailing in the United States and then introduced the self-service concept in their own countries. Similarly, governments and business executives from many parts of the world have examined Japanese trading companies to learn from their success. Wal-Mart's formula has been closely studied and copied by competitors in the markets it has entered.

DISTRIBUTION CHANNELS: TERMINOLOGY AND STRUCTURE

As defined previously, distribution channels are systems that link manufacturers to customers. Although channels for consumer products and industrial products are similar, there are also some distinct differences. In **business-to-consumer marketing (b-to-c or B2C)**, consumer channels are designed to put products in the hands of people for their own use; as participants in a process known as **business-to-business marketing (b-to-b or B2B)**, industrial channels deliver products to manufacturers or other types of organizations that use them as inputs in the production process or in day-to-day operations. Distributors play important roles in both consumer and industrial channels; a **distributor** is a wholesale intermediary that typically carries product lines or brands on a selective basis. An **agent** is an intermediary who

the rest of the story

Tesco Expands in the United States

In its home market, Tesco operates more than 2,300 stores in four formats: supercenters, large stores with a limited range of nonfood items, regular supermarkets, and Tesco Express convenience stores. While the U.S. market entry will be limited to small neighborhood markets, Tesco has raised eyebrows with an ambitious plan to establish its own distribution network as well. Management expects prepared foods such as salads and chicken-based dishes to be big sellers. To execute, Tesco is bringing two suppliers across the Atlantic: Natures Way Foods, which specializes in salads, and 2 Sisters Food Group, a leading U.K. poultry purveyor.

Will Tesco succeed with its strategy for entering the U.S. market? Management is confident it has identified an opportunity. The small-store format makes it unlikely that Tesco will encounter the type of backlash that has been directed at Wal-Mart in some communities. Speaking about the U.S. retail environment, Tim Mason, director of marketing and property at Tesco, notes, "Generally, shopping either means the big-box model, where you get in your car once a week and drive out of town to do your shopping, or the convenience store at the end of the street. We found that the [U.S.] market for convenience stores at the end of your street is not very well served. There is more consumer opportunity and more retail opportunity."

The company does have an impressive track record outside the United Kingdom; Tesco has even penetrated markets that have proven to be difficult for Wal-Mart and Carrefour. For example, Tesco entered South Korea in 1999; today it is the number two retailer behind E-Mart, a local chain. Samsung Tesco, an 89-11 joint venture, operates Homeplus "value store" hypermarkets. Homeplus is known for more than just shopping: The stores also feature coffee shops and restaurants. As one analyst noted, the joint venture approach has served Tesco well. "Thanks to its local partner, Tesco has tailored its service well to local tastes, while Wal-Mart and Carrefour have struggled to win over consumers with their focus on prices," the analyst said.

Tesco has also been successful in Japan, although on a limited scale. Before entering the market, a team was dispatched to live with Japanese consumers, accompany them on shopping trips, and observe their food preparation customs. As David Reid, chairman and head of Tesco's international operations, explained, "In America you have big cars, you can drive several miles in five minutes, you can buy in bulk and store it in your double garage. Chalk and cheese compared to Japan. In Japan we learned that some housewives shop on bikes and shop daily. They visit six or seven shops looking for deals." Armed with these insights, Tesco acquired C-Two, a small discount convenience store chain with stores in Tokyo.

Sources: Cecilie Rohwedder, "Tesco Studies Hard for U.S. Debut," The Wall Street Journal (June 28, 2007), pp. B1, B2; Cecilie Rohwedder, "Stores of Knowledge: No. 1 Retailer in Britain Uses 'Clubcard' to Thwart Wal-Mart," The Wall Street Journal (June 6, 2006), pp. A1, A16; Jonathan Birchall, "Tesco Will Launch in LA and Phoenix," Financial Times (May 18, 2006) p. 17; Elizabeth Rigby, "Tesco Seeks to Gain Weight Abroad," Financial Times (May 2, 2006), p. 17; Song Jung-a, "One-Stop Model Gives Tesco Edge in Korea," Financial Times March 22, 2006), p. 17; Sophy Buckley and Jonathan Birchall, "Tesco Plans to Build Brand in US," Financial Times (February 10, 2006), p. 19; Cecilie Rohwedder, "Tesco Jumps the Pond," The Wall Street Journal (February 10, 2006), p. B2; Susanna Voyle, "Tesco's Tough Act: With Record Profits, Britain's Biggest Retailer Prepares for Further Challenges at Home and Abroad," Financial Times (April 20, 2004), p. 13; Alastair Ray, "Own-brand Broadcaster Tunes In," Financial Times (March 16, 2004), p. 10; Bayan Rahman, "Tesco's Japanese Shopping without The Hype," Financial Times (January 16, 2004), p. 20.

negotiates exchange transactions between two or more parties but does not take title to the goods being purchased or sold.

Consumer Products and Services

Figure 12-1 summarizes six channel structure alternatives for consumer products. The characteristics of both buyers and products have an important influence on channel design. The first alternative is to market directly to buyers via the Internet, mail order, various types of door-to-door selling, or manufacturer-owned retail outlets. The other options use retailers and various combinations of sales forces, agents or brokers, and wholesalers. The number of individual buyers and their geographic distribution, income, shopping habits, and reaction to different selling methods frequently vary from country to country and may require different channel approaches. Product characteristics such as degree of standardization, perishability, bulk, service requirements, and unit price have an impact as well. Generally speaking, channels tend to be longer (require more intermediaries) as the number of customers to be served increases and the price per unit decreases. Bulky products usually require channel arrangements that minimize the shipping distances and the number of times products change hands before they reach the ultimate customer.

The Internet and related forms of new media are dramatically altering the distribution landscape. EBay pioneered a form of online commerce known as *peer-to-peer* (**p-to-p**) marketing whereby individual consumers marketed products to other individuals. EBay's success was one reason that the Internet's potential was quickly recognized by traditional merchants. Now, eBay assists large companies such as Disney and IBM in setting up online "storefronts" to sell items for fixed prices in addition to conducting b-to-c auctions. "As we evolved from auction-style bidding to adding Buy It Now last year, the logical next step for us was to give sellers a place to showcase their listings," said Bill Cobb, eBay's senior vice president for global marketing.[3] Some observers predict that interactive television (ITV) will also become a viable direct distribution channel in the coming years as more households are wired with the necessary two-way technology. Time-pressed consumers in many countries are increasingly attracted to the time and place utility created by the Internet and similar communication technologies.

Low-cost, mass-market nondurable products and certain services can be sold door-to-door via a direct sales force. Door-to-door selling is a form of distribution that is mature in the United States; however, it is growing in popularity elsewhere. For example, by the mid-1990s, AIG had 5,000 agents selling insurance policies door-to-door in China. This innovative channel strategy was so successful that domestic Chinese companies such as People's Insurance and Ping An Insurance copied it. Noted one local insurance executive, "We have to adjust ourselves to the rising competition."[4] However, in April 1998, the state council imposed a blanket ban on all types of direct selling. Although the ban was aimed most directly at illegal pyramid schemes, Mary Kay, Tupperware, Avon, and Amway have been forced to adapt their business models. In the United States, for example, Mary Kay sales representatives are independent entrepreneurs who buy products from the company and then resell them. By contrast, to comply with the new government

---

[3] Nick Wingfield, "Ebay Allows Sellers to Set Up Storefronts Online in Bid to Expand Beyond Auctions," *The Wall Street Journal* (June 12, 2001), p. B8.
[4] Craig Smith, "AIG Reshapes China's Insurance Industry," *The Wall Street Journal* (February 9, 1996), p. A8.

Nestlé is using an innovative approach to distribution in Brazil with a program of door-to-door selling in low-income neighborhoods. Consumers in these areas often do not have access to supermarkets. Currently, 4,000 self-employed salespeople are selling Nestlé products door-to-door and allowing customers two weeks to pay. The salespeople increase volume by establishing relationships with their customers; as the proprietor of Vita N, a Nestlé distributor with a staff of 400, explains, "In the favelas, you have to be part of the community or you just don't get in." Nestlé now has more than two dozen factories in Brazil; the newest one, in Feira de Santana, produces products specifically targeted to low-income consumers.

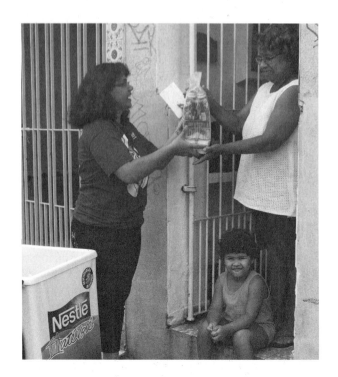

regulations, members of Mary Kay's Chinese sales force act as agents selling on behalf of the company.[5]

In Japan, the biggest barrier facing U.S. auto manufacturers isn't high tariffs; rather, it's the fact that half the cars that are sold each year are sold door-to-door. Toyota and its Japanese competitors maintain showrooms, but they also employ

Figure 12-1

Marketing Channel Alternatives: Consumer Products

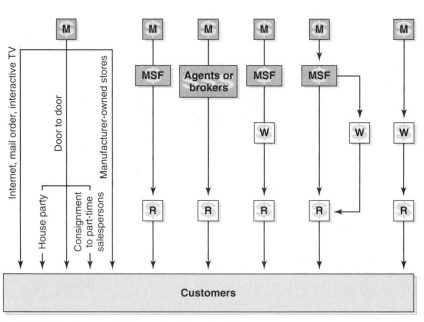

M = Manufacturer   MSF = Manufacturer's sales force
W = Wholesaler   R = Retailer

5 Ricky Y. K. Chan, "At the Crossroads of Distribution Reform: China's Recent Ban on Direct Selling," *Business Horizons* 42, no. 5 (September–October 1999), pp. 41–46. See also Virginia A. Hulme, "Mary Kay in China: More than Makeup," *China Business Review* 28, no. 1 (January–February 2001), pp. 42–46.

more than 100,000 car salespeople. Unlike their American counterparts, many Japanese car buyers never visit dealerships. The close, long-term relationships between auto salespersons and the Japanese people can be thought of as a consumer version of the *keiretsu* system discussed in Chapter 9. Japanese car buyers expect numerous face-to-face meetings with a sales representative, during which trust is established. The relationship continues after the deal is closed; sales reps send cards and continually seek to ensure the buyer's satisfaction. American rivals such as Ford, meanwhile, try to generate showroom traffic. Nobumasa Ogura manages a Ford dealership in Tokyo. "We need to come up with some ideas to sell more cars without door-to-door sales, but the reality is that we haven't come up with any," he said."[6]

Another direct selling alternative is the *manufacturer-owned store* or *independent franchise store*. One of the first successful U.S.-based international companies, Singer, established a worldwide chain of company-owned and company-operated outlets to sell and service sewing machines. More recently, the Walt Disney Company revised its strategy for the Disney Store chain of retail outlets in North America that offer apparel, videos, toys, and other merchandise featuring trade-marked Disney characters. The company had planned to spend $300 million to establish 600 new stores around the world.[7] However, in 2004, Disney sold its North American stores to the Children's Place Retail Stores organization. Disney's Japanese stores have been sold, and the future of the European stores is unclear. As noted in Chapter 9, Japanese consumer electronics companies integrate stores into their distribution groups. Nike, Levi Strauss, well-known fashion design houses, and other companies with strong brands sometimes establish one or a few

G L O B A L *marketing in action*

Selling Cosmetics Door-to-Door

Amway and Avon are two companies that have succeeded in extending their direct sales systems outside the United States. Amway currently has operations in 42 countries; in 1997, foreign markets accounted for about three-fourths of the company's $6.8 billion in revenues. Amway's foreign prices tend to be relatively high because all products are exported from the company's Michigan headquarters. In the Philippines, for example, most Amway products are subject to a 30 percent import charge; a 150-milliliter tube of Glister toothpaste sells for $6.54 versus $1.50 for a comparable tube of Colgate.

Avon has successfully used door-to-door sales in dozens of countries identified by company executives as having weak retail infrastructures. Also, it recognized that low discretionary income levels translate into modest expenditures on cosmetics and toiletries. Thus, the role of the sales force is to communicate the benefits of cosmetics and build demand. In such countries as Hungary, the Czech Republic, and Russia, in-home direct selling is the perfect channel strategy. Avon became the first company permitted to sell door-to-door in China. Since 1990, Avon has operated a joint venture with Guangzhou Cosmetics Factory in the province of Old Canton. However, after the Chinese government banned direct selling in 1998, Avon shifted its strategy and opened beauty boutiques. Today, the company has more than 5,700

boutiques across China. In 2006, Avon hired more than 100,000 sales representatives after the Ministry of Commerce and the State Administration for Industry and Commerce both gave their approval for Avon to resume direct selling.

Avon has recruited several thousand distributors in India, but its efforts to date have been surpassed by Sweden's Oriflame International. Oriflame's cosmetics are available throughout India, thanks to the company's success at recruiting nearly 100,000 sales representatives. The scale and scope of Oriflame's effort make it the most ambitious direct sales effort ever launched in India. Traditionally, India has had a bias against direct selling since it was associated with salesmen hawking goods of dubious quality. However, Avon and Oriflame have succeeded in part by targeting Indian women who are active socially and in part because India has a tradition of "kitty" parties where women sell each other saris and jewelry.

Sources: Lauren Foster, "Mistress of the Turnaround Answers Avon's Calling," Financial Times (November 6, 2003), p. 8; Emily Nelson and Ann Zimmerman, "Avon Goes Store to Store," The Wall Street Journal (September 18, 2000), pp. B1, B4; Erin White, "Ding-Dong, Avon Calling (on the Web, Not Your Door)," The Wall Street Journal (December 28, 1999), p. A1; Sumit Sharma, "Sell It Yourself: Direct Sales Help Makeup Brand Storm across India," Asian The Wall Street Journal (April 28, 1997), p. 10; Yumiko Ono, "On a Mission: Amway Grows Abroad, Sending 'Ambassadors' to Spread the Word," The Wall Street Journal (May 14, 1997), pp. A1, A6.

---

[6] Valerie Reitman, "Toyota Calling: In Japan's Car Market, Big Three Face Rivals Who Go Door-to-Door," *The Wall Street Journal* (September 28, 1994), pp. A1, A6.

[7] Bruce Orwall, "Disney's Magic Transformation," *The Wall Street Journal* (October 4, 2000), pp. B1, B4.

Apple operates more than 150 retail stores in the United States, Canada, Japan, and the United Kingdom. Each store features a "genius bar" where customers can seek one-on-one technical support with a knowledgeable employee. Many stores, including this one in London, feature a signature glass staircase that Apple co-founder and CEO Steve Jobs helped design.

flagship retail stores as product showcases or as a means of obtaining marketing intelligence. Such channels supplement, rather than replace, distribution through independent retail stores.

Other channel structure alternatives for consumer products include various combinations of a manufacturer's sales force and wholesalers calling on independent retail outlets, which in turn sell to customers (retailing is discussed in detail later in the chapter). For mass-market consumer products such as ice-cream novelties, cigarettes, and lightbulbs that are bought by millions of consumers, a channel that links the manufacturer to distributors and retailers is generally required to achieve market coverage. A channel structure that appears to have more intermediaries than necessary may actually reflect rational adjustment to costs and preferences in a market; it may also present an opportunity to the innovative marketer to pursue competitive advantage by introducing more effective channel arrangements. A cornerstone of Wal-Mart's phenomenal growth in the United States was its ability to achieve significant economies by buying huge volumes of goods directly from manufacturers. However, individual country customs vary. For example, Toys "R" Us faced considerable opposition from Japanese toy manufacturers that refused to engage in direct selling after the U.S. company opened its first stores in Japan.

Perishable products impose special form utility demands on channel members who must ensure that the merchandise is in satisfactory condition at the time of customer purchase. In developed countries, a company's own sales force or independent channel members handle the distribution of perishable food products; in either case, the distributor organization checks the stock to ensure that it is fresh. In less-developed countries, public marketplaces are important channels; they provide a convenient way for producers of vegetables, bread, and other food products to sell their goods directly. Sometimes, a relatively simple channel innovation in a developing country can significantly increase a company's overall value proposition. In the early 1990s, for example, the Moscow Bread Company (MBC) needed to improve its distribution system in the Russian capital. For Russians, bread is truly the staff of life, with consumers queuing up daily to buy fresh loaves at numerous shops and kiosks. Unfortunately, MBC's staff was burdened by excessive paperwork that resulted in the delivery of stale bread. Andersen Consulting found that as much as one-third of the bread the company produced was wasted. In developed countries, about 95 percent of food is sold packaged; the figure is much lower in the former Soviet Union. Whether a consumer bought bread at an open air market or in an enclosed store, it was displayed unwrapped. Therefore, it was imperative for the bread to get from MBC's ovens to the stores in the shortest possible time. Barring an improvement in delivery time, the bread's shelf life had to be extended. The consulting team devised a simple solution—plastic bags to keep the bread fresh. Russian consumers responded favorably to the change; not only did the bags guarantee freshness and extend the shelf life of the bread by 600 percent, but also the bags themselves created utility. In a country where such extras are virtually unknown, the bags constituted a reusable "gift."[8]

Piggyback marketing is another channel innovation that has grown in popularity. In this arrangement, one manufacturer obtains product distribution by utilizing another company's distribution channels. Both parties can benefit: The active distribution partner makes fuller use of its distribution system capacity and thereby increases the total revenue generated by the channel members. The manufacturer using the piggyback arrangement does so at a cost that is much lower than that required for any direct arrangement. Successful piggyback marketing requires that the combined product lines be complementary. They must appeal to the same customer, and they must not compete with each other. If these requirements are met, the piggyback arrangement can be an effective way of fully utilizing a global channel system to the advantage of both parties.

A case in point is Avon Products, which has a network of direct sales representatives in more than 100 countries. Dozens of companies have taken advantage of the opportunity to piggyback with Avon. Several of Mattel's toy lines are being marketed in China by local Avon representatives; in 1997, Mattel reaped more than $30 million in revenues from sales of Barbie dolls and cosmetics, Hot Wheel toys, and Sesame Street characters. As Andrea Jung, Avon's chairman and CEO, explained, "We knew we had a great thing in our hands. Our powerful distribution channel combined with their powerful brand is a huge opportunity." In Australia, New Zealand, Brazil, Canada, and France, Avon representatives offer *Reader's Digest* subscriptions along with Avon's health and beauty products. The agreement is reciprocal; Avon's direct response offers "ride along" in *Reader's Digest* product shipments and targeted mailings. In emerging markets, Avon offers a second catalog featuring products from Timex, Duracell, Time-Life, and others. The products are sold on consignment; piggyback products already account for 15 percent of sales in some emerging markets.[9]

Industrial Products

Figure 12-2 summarizes marketing channel alternatives for the industrial- or business- products company. As is true with consumer channels, product and customer characteristics have an impact on channel structure. Three basic elements are involved: the manufacturer's sales force, distributors or agents, and wholesalers. A manufacturer can reach customers with its own sales force, a sales force that calls on wholesalers who sell to customers, or a combination of these two arrangements. A manufacturer can sell directly to wholesalers without using a sales force, and wholesalers, in turn, can supply customers. Finally, a distributor or agent can call on wholesalers or customers for the manufacturer.

For vendors serving a relatively small customer base, a shorter channel design with relatively few (or no) intermediaries may be possible. For example, if there are only 10 customers for an industrial product in each national market, these 10 customers must be directly contacted by either the manufacturer or an agent.

---

8 "Case Study: Moscow Bread Company," Andersen Consulting, 1993.
9 Tara Parker-Pope and Lisa Bannon, "Avon's New Calling: Sell Barbie in China," *The Wall Street Journal* (May 1, 1997), pp. B1, B5; Clarence Murphy, "Scents and Sensibility," *Economist* (July 13, 1996), p. 57.

Figure 12-2

Marketing Channel Alternatives:
Industrial Products

M = Manufacturer   MSF = Manufacturer's sales force
W = Wholesaler   D or A = Distributor or agent

Channel innovation can be an essential element of a successful marketing strategy. Dell's rise to a leading position in the global PC industry was based on Michael Dell's decision to bypass conventional channels by selling direct and by building computers to customers' specifications. Dell began life as a b-to-b marketer; its business model proved so successful that the company then began marketing direct to the home PC market. Consider Boeing aircraft, for example; given the price, physical size, and complexity of a jet airliner, it is easy to understand why Boeing utilizes its own sales force. Other products sold in this way include mainframe computers and large photocopy systems; these are expensive, complicated products that require both explanation and applications analysis focused on the customer's needs. A company-trained salesperson, sales engineer, or sales team is well suited for the task of creating information utility for computer buyers.

Before deciding which structure to use and which wholesalers and agents to select, managers must study each country individually. In general, the larger the market, the more feasible it is for a manufacturer to use its own sales force. Kyocera Corporation of Kyoto, Japan, has successfully used its own sales force to achieve leadership in the billion-dollar global market for ceramic microchip covers. Company founder Kazuo Inamori went to great lengths to make sure the spiritual drive of Kyocera's unique corporate culture extended to all parts of the company, including the sales force. Kyocera successfully entered the U.S. market by custom-tailoring ceramic chip housings to each customer's needs. Kyocera also became legendary for its service among California's Silicon Valley chipmakers. Breaking with the norm in the electronics industry of using independent distributors, Kyocera relied on a salaried sales force. Early on, Kyocera earned a reputation for answering customer questions overnight, while domestic suppliers often took weeks to respond. Employees worked around the clock to satisfy customer requests for samples. Another hallmark: No company is too small for Kyocera to serve. Jerry Crowley of Gazelle Microcircuits in Santa Clara, California, reported, for example, that Kyocera salespeople began calling on him when he had only 11 employees. Gazelle has been buying custom chip packages from Kyocera ever since. Today, Kyocera has sales forces in the United States, Europe, and Japan that place unwavering emphasis on quality and customer service.

Dell rang up $56 billion in direct sales of made-to-order PC systems in 2006. The company has experienced phenomenal growth thanks in part to sales generated through the company's Web site. Now, company founder Michael Dell is moving beyond b-to-b marketing by targeting consumers. He also hopes to achieve success in Asia using the same direct-sales approach that has been effective in more than 100 countries.

ESTABLISHING CHANNELS AND WORKING WITH CHANNEL INTERMEDIARIES

A global company expanding across national boundaries must utilize existing distribution channels or build its own. Channel obstacles are often encountered when a company enters a competitive market where brands and supply relationships are already established. If management chooses *direct involvement*, the company establishes its own sales force or operates its own retail stores. As described earlier, Kyocera used this approach; Kodak adopted the direct approach in Japan, where Kodak Japan is a company-owned distributor. The other option is *indirect involvement*, which entails utilizing independent agents, distributors, and/or wholesalers. Channel strategy in a global marketing program must fit the company's competitive position and overall marketing objectives in each national market. Direct involvement in distribution in a new market can entail considerable expense. Sales representatives and sales management must be hired and trained. The sales organization will inevitably be a heavy loser in its early stage of operation in a new market because it will not have sufficient volume to cover its overhead costs. Therefore, any company contemplating establishing its own sales force should be prepared to underwrite losses for this sales force for a reasonable period of time. As noted previously, whichever strategy a company uses, the process of shaping international channels to fit overall company objectives is constrained by customer and product characteristics.

Channel decisions are important because of the number and nature of relationships that must be managed. Channel decisions typically involve long-term legal commitments and obligations to various intermediaries. Such commitments are often extremely expensive to terminate or change so it is imperative for companies to document the nature of the relationship with the foreign partner. As the saying goes, "The shortest pencil is better than the longest memory." At a minimum, the written agreement should include a definition of what constitutes "good cause" for termination. Also, as noted in Chapter 5, it is often preferable to settle business disputes through arbitration rather than in a local court. Thus, the distributor or agent agreement should also provide for arbitration in a neutral forum in a third country. In many instances, local laws protect agents and distributors; even in the absence of a formal written agreement, in a civil code country the law will be applied. In addition to written obligations, commitments must be backed by good faith and feelings of mutual obligation. In short, the selection of distributors and agents in a target market is critically important. A good agent or distributor can make the difference between zero performance and performance that is much better than expected.

Companies entering emerging markets for the first time must exercise particular care in choosing a channel intermediary. Typically, a local distributor is required because the market entrant lacks knowledge of local business practices and needs a partner with links to potential customers. In addition, newcomers to a particular market generally want to limit their risk and financial exposure. Although initial results may be satisfactory, with time the local distributor may come to be perceived as performing poorly. This is when managers from the global company often intervene and attempt to take control from the local distributor. Harvard professor David Arnold offers seven specific guidelines to help prevent such problems from arising.[10]

- *Select distributors. Don't let them select you.* A company may link up with a distributor by default after being approached by representatives at a trade fair. Such eager candidates may already be serving a company's competitors. Their objective may be to maintain control over the product category in a given market. A proactive market entrant can identify potential distributors by requesting a list from the U.S. Department of Commerce or its equivalent in other countries. The local chamber of commerce or trade association in a country can provide similar information.
- *Look for distributors capable of developing markets, rather than those with a few good customer contacts.* A distributor with good contacts may appear to be the "obvious" choice in terms of generating quick sales and revenues. However, a better choice is often a partner willing both to make the investment necessary to achieve success and draw upon the marketing experience of the global company. Such a partner may have no prior experience with a particular product category. In this case, the distributor may devote more effort and assign the new partner a higher priority simply because taking on the product line does not represent the status quo.

---

[10] The following discussion is adapted from David Arnold, "Seven Rules of International Distribution," *Harvard Business Review* 78, no. 6 (November–December 2000), pp. 131–137.

- *Treat local distributors as long-term partners, not temporary market-entry vehicles.* A contractual agreement that provides strong financial incentives for customer acquisition, new product sales, or other forms of business development is a signal to the distributor that the market entrant is taking a long-term perspective. Such development can be done with the input of managers from the global company.

- *Support market entry by committing money, managers, and proven marketing ideas.* In addition to providing sales personnel and technical support, management should consider demonstrating its commitment early on by investing in a minority equity stake in an independent distributor. The risks associated with such investment should be no greater than risks associated with independent distribution systems in the manufacturer's home country. The earlier such a commitment is made, the better the relationship that is likely to develop.

- *From the start, maintain control over marketing strategy.* To exploit the full potential of global marketing channels, the manufacturer should provide solid leadership for marketing in terms of which products the distributor should sell and how to position them. Again, it is necessary to have employees on site or to have country or regional managers monitor the distributor's performance. As one manager noted, "We used to give far too much autonomy to distributors, thinking that they knew their markets. But our value proposition is a tough one to execute, and time and again we saw distributors cut prices to compensate for failing to target the right customers or to sufficiently train salespeople." This is not to say that the intermediary should not be allowed to adapt the distribution strategy to suit local conditions. The point is for the manufacturer to take the lead.

- *Make sure distributors provide you with detailed market and financial performance data.* Distributor organizations are often a company's best source—maybe the only source—of market information. The contract between a manufacturer and distributor should include specific language to the effect that local market information and financial data will be transferred back to the manufacturer. One sign that a successful manufacturer-distributor relationship can be established is the latter's willingness to provide such information.

- *Build links among national distributors at the earliest opportunity.* A manufacturer should attempt to establish links between its networks of national distributors. This can be accomplished by setting up a regional corporate office or by establishing a distributor council. At any point in time, a company may have some excellent agents and distributors, others that are satisfactory, and a third group that is unsatisfactory. By creating opportunities for distributors to communicate, ideas for new product designs based on individual-market results can be leveraged, and overall distributor performance can be improved.

When devising a channel strategy, it is necessary to be realistic about the motives of the typical channel intermediary. On the one hand, it is the intermediary's responsibility to implement an important element of a company's marketing strategy. Left to their own devices, however, middlemen may seek to maximize their own profit rather than the manufacturer's. These agents sometimes engage in *cherry picking*, the practice of accepting orders only from manufacturers with established demand for products and brands. Cherry picking can also take the form of selecting only a few choice items from a vendor's product lines. This is a rational course of action for the middleman, but it can present a serious obstacle to a manufacturer who is attempting to break into a market with a new product. The cherry picker is not interested in developing a market for a new product, which is a problem for the expanding international company.

As noted previously, a manufacturer should provide leadership and invest resources to build the relationship with a desired distributor. A manufacturer with a new product or a product with a limited market share may find it more desirable to set up some arrangement for bypassing the cherry-picking channel member. In some cases, a manufacturer must incur the costs of direct involvement by setting up its own distribution organization to obtain a share of the market. When the company sales finally reach critical mass, management may decide to shift from direct involvement to a more cost-effective independent intermediary. The move does not mean that intermediaries are "better" than direct distribution. Such a move is simply a response by a manufacturer to cost considerations and the newly acquired attractiveness of the company's product to independent distributors.

An alternative method of dealing with the cherry-picking problem does not require setting up an expensive direct sales force. Rather, a company may decide to rely on a distributor's own sales force by subsidizing the cost of the sales representatives the distributor has assigned to the company's products. This approach has the advantage of holding down costs by tying in with the distributor's existing sales management team and physical distribution system. With this approach, it is possible to place managed direct selling support and distribution support behind a product at the expense of only one salesperson per selling area. The distributor's incentive for cooperating in this kind of arrangement is that he or she obtains a "free" sales representative for a new product with the potential to be a profitable addition to his or her line. This cooperative arrangement is ideally suited to getting a new export-sourced product into distribution in a market. A company may also decide to provide special incentives to independent channel agents; however, this approach can be expensive. The company might offer outright payments, either direct cash bonuses or contest awards, tied to sales performance. In competitive markets with sufficiently high prices, incentives could take the form of gross margin guarantees.

GLOBAL RETAILING

Global retailing is any retailing activity that crosses national boundaries. Since the mid-1970s, there has been growing interest among successful retailers in expanding globally. However, this is not a new phenomenon. For centuries, entrepreneurial merchants have ventured abroad both to obtain merchandise and ideas and to establish retail operations. During the nineteenth and early twentieth centuries, British, French, Dutch, Belgian, and German trading companies established retailing organizations in Africa and Asia. International trading and retail store operation were two of the economic pillars of the colonial system of that era. In the twentieth century, Dutch retailer C&A expanded across Europe, and Woolworths crossed the Atlantic from the United States to the United Kingdom. Great variety characterizes today's global retailing scene (Table 12-1 lists the top 25 companies by revenue). Before proceeding to a detailed discussion of global retailing issues, we will briefly survey some of the different forms retailing can take. Retail stores can be divided into categories according to the amount of square feet of floor space, the level of service offered, width and depth of product offerings, or other criteria. Each represents a strategic option for a retailer considering global expansion.

Department stores literally have several departments under one roof, each representing a distinct merchandise line and staffed with a limited number of

Table 12-1

Top 25 Global Retailers (2005 Sales; Millions)

Rank	Company	Country	Formats	Sales ($)
1	Wal-Mart Stores	United States	Discount store, Wholesale club	$285,222
2	Carrefour	France	Hypermarket	90,297
3	Home Depot	United States	Home improvement	73,094
4	Metro AG	Germany	Diversified	70,093
5	Royal Ahold NV	Netherlands	Supermarket/Hypermarket	64,615
6	Tesco PLC	United Kingdom	Supermarket/Hypermarket	62,284
7	Kroger	United States	Supermarket	56,434
8	Sears Holdings Corp	United States	Department store/General merchandise	55,800
9	Rewe Handelsgruppe	Germany	Diversified	50,698
10	Costco	United States	Food/General merchandise	48,107
11	ITM Entreprises (incl. Spar)	France	Diversified	47,218
12	Target Corp.	United States	Discount/Department store	45,682
13	Groupe Casino	France		45,155
14	Aldi Einkauf GmbJ & Co	Germany	Food/Discount	42,981
15	Schwarz Group (Lidi & Schwarz)	Germany	Discount department store and supermarket	42,571
16	Albertson's	United States	Supermarket	39,897
17	Edeka Gruppe	Germany	Diversified	39,227
18	Walgreen	United States	Drugstore	37,508
19	Groupe Auchan	France	Supermarkets, hypermarkets	37,335
20	Lowe's	United States	Home improvement	36,464
21	Safeway	United States	Supermarket	35,823
22	Aeon Co. Ltd.	Japan	Superstore and convenience store	35,307
23	Ito-Yokada (incl. 7-Eleven)	Japan	Diversified	33,547
24	E. Leclerc SA	France	Supermarket/Hypermarket	32,060
25	Tengelmann	Germany	Diversified	31,715

Source: Reprinted by permission from Chain Store Age (December 2005). Copyright Lebhar-Friedman, Inc. 425 Park Avenue, NY, NY 10022.

salespeople. Departments in a typical store might include men's, women's, children's, beauty aids, housewares, and toys. Table 12-2 lists major department stores that have expanded outside their home-country markets. However, in most instances, the expansion is limited to a few countries. As Maureen Hinton, a retail analyst with a London-based consultancy, notes, "It's quite difficult to transfer a department store brand abroad. You have to find a city with the right demographic for your offer. If you adapt your offer to the locality, you dilute your brand name." Marvin Traub, former chief executive of Bloomingdales, has

Table 12-2

Department Stores with Global Branches

Store	Original Store Location	Global Locations
Harvey Nichols	United Kingdom	Saudi Arabia, Hong Kong, Ireland, Dubai
Saks Fifth Avenue	United States	United Arab Emirates, Saudi Arabia
Barneys New York	United States	Japan
Lane Crawford	Hong Kong	China, Macao, Taiwan
Mitsukoshi	Japan	United States, Europe, Asia
H&M (Hennes & Mauritz)	Sweden	Austria, Germany, Kuwait, Slovakia, United States, 20 others

a different perspective. "Conceptually, department stores are global brands already because we live in a world with an enormous amount of travel between cities and continents," he says.[11]

Specialty retailers offer less variety than department stores. They are more narrowly focused and offer a relatively narrow merchandise mix aimed at a particular target market. Specialty stores offer a great deal of merchandise depth (e.g., many styles, colors, and sizes), high levels of service from knowledgeable staff persons, and a value proposition that is both clear and appealing to consumers. Laura Ashley, Body Shop, Victoria's Secret, Gap, Starbucks, and the Disney Store are examples of global retailers that have stores in many parts of the world. In some countries, local retailers operate the stores. In Japan, for example, the giant Aeon Group runs Laura Ashley and Body Shop stores and has a joint venture with Sports Authority.

Supermarkets are departmentalized, single-story retail establishments that offer a variety of food (e.g., produce, baked goods, meats) and nonfood items (e.g., paper products, health and beauty aids), mostly on a self-service basis. On average, supermarkets occupy between 50,000 square feet and 60,000 square feet of floor space. As noted in the chapter introduction, U.K.-based Tesco is one retailing group that is expanding globally. While home-country sales still account for slightly more than 80 percent of overall sales, the company has operations in more than a dozen foreign countries. Company officials typically study a country market for several years before choosing an entry strategy. Tesco's initial entry into Japan came via the acquisition of the C Two-Network, a chain of shops in Tokyo. As David Reid, head of international operations, explains, Tesco has succeeded globally because it does its homework and pays attention to details. Although Wal-Mart is generating headlines as it moves around the globe, American retailers lag behind the Europeans in moving outside their home countries. One reason is the sheer size of the domestic U.S. market.[12]

Wal-Mart's international division currently generates only 20 percent of company sales, but the world's biggest retail is staking its claim in China, India, and other emerging markets. By the end of 2006, Wal-Mart had 66 stores in China, including 61 Supercenters.

11 Cecilie Rohwedder, "Harvey Nichols's Foreign Affair," *The Wall Street Journal* (February 18, 2005), p. B3.
12 Michael Flagg, "In Asia, Going to the Grocery Increasingly Means Heading for a European Retail Chain," *The Wall Street Journal* (April 24, 2001), p. A21.

Convenience stores offer some of the same products as supermarkets, but the merchandise mix is limited to high-turnover convenience and impulse products. Prices for some products may be 15 percent to 20 percent higher than supermarket prices. In terms of square footage, these are the smallest retail stores discussed here. In the United States, for example, the typical 7-Eleven occupies 3,000 square feet. Typically, convenience stores are located in high-traffic locations and offer extended service hours to accommodate commuters, students, and other highly mobile consumers. 7-Eleven is the world's largest convenience store chain; it has a total of 26,000 locations, including franchisees, licensees, and stores the company operates itself. A trend in convenience store retailing is toward smaller stores placed inside malls, airports, office buildings, and in college and university buildings. As Jeff Lenard, spokesperson for the National Association of Convenience Stores, noted, "All the good street corners are gone, and the competition is so fierce for the ones that are left."[13]

Discount stores can be divided into several categories. The most general characteristic that they have in common is the emphasis on low prices. *Full-line discounters* typically offer a wide range of merchandise, including nonfood items and nonperishable food, in a limited-service format. As Table 12-1 clearly shows, Wal-Mart is the reigning king of the full-line discounters. Many stores cover 120,000 square feet (or more) of floor space; food accounts for about a third of floor space and sales. Wal-Mart stores typically offer middle-class customers a folksy atmosphere and value-priced brands.

When Wal-Mart expands into a new country market, local discounters must respond to the competitive threat. In Canada, for example, Hudson Bay's Zellers is the largest discount-store chain. After Wal-Mart bought a bankrupt Canadian chain, Zellers brightened its stores décor, widened aisles, and began catering to women with young children.[14] French discounter Tati is also going global; in addition to opening a store on New York's Fifth Avenue, Tati currently has stores in Lebanon, Turkey, Germany, Belgium, Switzerland, and the Côte d'Ivoire.

Wal-Mart is also a leader in the **warehouse club** segment of discount retailing; consumers "join" the club to take advantage of low prices on products displayed in their shipping boxes in a "no frills" atmosphere. Wal-Mart has taken its Sam's Club stores into Mexico and Brazil.

Hypermarkets, which were discussed in the chapter introduction, are a hybrid retailing format combining the discounter, supermarket, and warehouse club approaches under a single roof. Size-wise, hypermarkets are huge, covering 200,000 square feet to 300,000 square feet.

Supercenters offer a wide range of aggressively priced grocery items plus general merchandise in a space that occupies about half the size of a hypermarket. Supercenters are an important aspect of Wal-Mart's growth strategy, both at home and abroad. Wal-Mart opened its first supercenter in 1988; today, it operates more than 450 supercenters, including 75 stores in Mexico and units in Argentina and Brazil. Some prices at Wal-Mart's supercenters in Brazil are as much as 15 percent lower than competitors', and some observers wonder if the company has taken the discount approach too far. Company officials insist that profit margins are in the 20 percent to 22 percent range.[15]

Category killers is the label many in the retailing industry use when talking about stores such as Toys "R" Us, Home Depot, and IKEA. The name refers to the fact that such stores specialize in a particular product category such as toys or furniture, and offer a vast selection at low prices. In short, these stores represent

---

[13] Kortney Stringer, "Convenience Stores Turn a New Corner" *The Wall Street Journal* (June 1, 2004), p. B5.
[14] Elena Cherney and Ann Zimmerman, "Canada's Zellers Retools Itself in Bid to Battle Wal-Mart," *The Wall Street Journal* (December 10, 2001), p. B4.
[15] Matt Moffett and Jonathan Friedland, "Wal-Mart Won't Discount Its Prospects in Brazil, Though Its Losses Pile Up," *The Wall Street Journal* (June 4, 1996), p. A15; Wendy Zellner, "Wal-Mart Spoken Here," *Business Week* (June 23, 1997), pp. 138–139+.

retailing's "900 pound gorillas" that essentially demolish smaller, more traditional competitors and prompt department stores to scale down merchandise sections that are in direct competition.

Outlet stores are retail operations that allow companies with well-known consumer brands to dispose of excess inventory, out-of-date merchandise, or factory seconds. To attract large numbers of shoppers, outlet stores are often grouped together in **outlet malls**. The United States is home to 320 outlet malls such as the giant Woodbury Common mall in Central Valley, New York. Now, the concept is catching on in Europe and Asia as well. The acceptance reflects changing attitudes among consumers and retailers; in both Asia and Europe, brand-conscious consumers are eager to save money.

Currently, a number of environmental factors have combined to push retailers out of their home markets in search of opportunities around the globe. Saturation of the home country market, recession or other economic factors, strict regulation on store development, and high operating costs are some of the factors that prompt management to look abroad for growth opportunities. Wal-Mart is a case in point; its international expansion in the mid-1990s coincided with disappointing financial results in its home market.

Even as the domestic retailing environment grows more challenging for many companies, an ongoing environmental scanning effort is likely to turn up markets in other parts of the world that are underdeveloped or where competition is weak. In addition, high rates of economic growth, a growing middle class, a high proportion of young people in the population, and less stringent regulation combine to make some country markets very attractive.[16] Laura Ashley, Body Shop, Disney Stores, and other specialty retailers are being lured to Japan by developers who need established names to fill space in large, suburban, American-style shopping malls.[17] Such malls are being developed as some local and national restrictions on retail development are being eased and as consumers tire of the aggravations associated with shopping in congested urban areas.

However, the large number of unsuccessful cross-border retailing initiatives suggests that anyone contemplating a move into global retailing should do so with a great deal of caution. Among those that have scaled back expansion plans in the face of disappointment are France's Galeries Lafayette and Shanghai-based Yaohan Group. Galeries Lafayette opened a New York store on fashionable Fifth Avenue; however, the merchandise mix suffered in comparison with offerings at posh competitors such as Henri Bendel and Bonwit Teller. Yaohan has more than 400 stores in 13 countries, including the United States and China. However, Chinese expansion plans are on hold because consumers have reacted indifferently to the 10-story megastore in Shanghai. As one Chinese consumer remarked, "It's just so-so. I'm not really impressed."[18] Speaking of global opportunities for U.S.-based retailers, one industry analyst noted, "It's awfully hard to operate across the water. It's one thing to open up in Mexico and Canada, but the distribution hassles are just too big when it comes to exporting an entire store concept overseas."[19]

The critical question for the would-be global retailer is, "What advantages do we have relative to local competition?" The answer will often be, "Nothing," when competition, local laws governing retailing practice, distribution patterns, or other factors are taken into account. However, a company may possess competencies that can be the basis for competitive advantage in a particular retail market. A retailer has several

[16] Ross Davies and Megan Finney, "Retailers Rush to Capture New Markets," *Financial Times—Mastering Global Business*, Part VII, 1998, pp. 2–4.
[17] Norihiko Shirouzu, "Japanese Mall Mogul Dreams of American Stores," *The Wall Street Journal* (July 30, 1997), pp. B1, B10; Shirouzu, "Jusco Bets that U.S.-Style Retail Malls Will Revolutionize Shopping in Japan," *The Wall Street Journal* (April 21, 1997), p. A8.
[18] Norihiko Shirouzu and Fara Waner, "Asian Retailing Titan Hits a Great Wall," *The Wall Street Journal* (January 17, 1997), p. A10.
[19] Neil King, Jr., "Kmart's Czech Invasion Lurches Along," *The Wall Street Journal* (June 8, 1993), p. A11.

BRIC Briefing Book

India's Retail Sector

Global retailers that have set their sights on India face special challenges. The term *organized retailing* describes activity by large multistore chains such as Woolworths, Tesco, and Wal-Mart; such stores account for only about 3 percent of India's $200 billion to $250 billion annual retail sales. The vast majority of Indian retail activity is conducted in stalls approximately with about 50 square feet of floor space. There have been many calls for regulatory reform, and some observers believe organized retailing will grow at a rate of 30 percent to 35 percent in the next few years. For now, however, some members of the ruling Congress party are concerned about the impact of organized retailing on the millions of small-scale stores.

Modernization of the sector is inevitable, although it may be slow in coming. Global retailers are barred from participating directly in the Indian market; for that reason, Pizza Hut, Subway, and Benetton are present, with stores run by franchisees. In 2006, Bharti Enterprises, a large Indian business group, announced a partnership with Wal-Mart. However, because global retailers are barred from participating directly in the Indian market, Wal-Mart stores will be run as franchise operations.

Meanwhile, anticipating the arrival of the global retailers, local operators in India are investing for the future. For example, Pantaloon, India's largest retailer, operates department stores such as Central and Big Bazaar. The company has announced plans to expand and add more types of stores. Large business groups such as Reliance Industries and Birla Group are also planning to enter the retail sector. Meanwhile, Hindustan Lever, the Indian unit of packaged goods giant Unilever, has launched a consultancy service to help the "mom and pop" operators become more competitive.

Sources: Jo Johnson and Jonathan Birchall, "'Mom and Pop' Stores Braced for Challenge," Financial Times (November 28, 2006), p. 16; Joe Leahy, "Indian Regulation Hampers Retail Growth," Financial Times (October 26, 2006), p. 21; Anita Jain, "The 'Crown Jewel' Sector that's Ripe for Modernization," Financial Times Special Report: India and Globalization (January 26, 2006), p. 16.

things to offer consumers. Some are readily perceived by customers, such as selection, price, and the overall manner in which the goods are offered in the store setting. The last includes such things as store location, parking facilities, in-store atmosphere, and customer service. Competencies can also be found in less visible value chain activities such as distribution, logistics, and information technology.

For example, contrary to Japan's service-oriented reputation, Japanese retailers traditionally offered few extra services to their clientele. There were no special orders, no returns, and stock was chosen not according to consumer demand but, rather, according to purchasing preferences of the stores. Typically, a store would buy limited quantities from each of its favorite manufacturers and then, when the goods sold out, consumers had no recourse. Instead of trying to capitalize on the huge market, many retailers simply turned a deaf ear to customer needs. From the retailers' point of view, this came out fine in the end, however; most of their stock eventually sold because buyers were forced to purchase what was left over. They had no other choice. As Gap, Eddie Bauer, and other American retailers have entered Japan with liberal return policies, a willingness to take special orders, and a policy of replenishing stock, many Japanese consumers have switched loyalties. Also, thanks to economies of scale and modern distribution methods unknown to some Japanese department store operators, the American companies offer a greater variety of goods at lower prices. Although upscale foreign competition has hurt Japanese department store operators, Japan's depressed economy is another factor. Traditional retailers are also being squeezed from below as recession-pressed consumers flock to discounters such as the Y100 Shop chain.

JCPenney is expanding retailing operations internationally for a number of the reasons cited here. After touring several countries, JCPenney executives realized that retailers outside the United States often lack marketing sophistication when grouping and displaying products and locating aisles to optimize customer traffic. For example, a team visiting retailers in Istanbul in the early 1990s noted that one store featured lingerie next to plumbing equipment. As CEO William R. Howell noted at the time, JCPenney's advantage in such instances was its ability to develop an environment that invites the customer to shop. Although it struggled in Indonesia, the Philippines, and Chile, JCPenney has met with great success in Brazil. In 1999, the American retailer purchased a controlling stake in Renner, a regional chain with 21 stores. Crucially, JCPenney maintained the local name and local management team. Meanwhile, Renner, benefiting from JCPenney's expertise in logistics, distribution, and branding, has become Brazil's fastest-growing chain, with a total of 49 stores.[20]

Figure 12-3 shows a matrix-based scheme for classifying global retailers.[21] One axis represents private or own-label focus versus a manufacturer brands focus. The other axis differentiates between retailers specializing in relatively few product categories and retailers that offer a wide product assortment. IKEA, in quadrant A, is a good example of a global retailer with a niche focus (assemble-yourself furniture for the home) as well as an own-label focus (IKEA sells its own brand). IKEA and other retailers in quadrant A typically use extensive advertising and product innovation to build a strong brand image.

In quadrant B, the private-label focus is retained, but many more product categories are offered. This is the strategy of Marks & Spencer (M&S), the British-based department store company whose St. Michael private label is found on a broad range of clothing, food, home furnishings, jewelry, and other items. Private label retailers that attempt to expand internationally face a double-edged challenge: They must attract customers to both the store and the branded merchandise. M&S has succeeded by virtue of an entrepreneurial management style that has evolved over the last 100-plus years. M&S opened its first store outside the United Kingdom in 1974; it currently operates in 35 countries. In 1997, then-chairman Sir Richard Greenbury announced an ambitious plan to put M&S "well on its way to establishing a global business." It was his belief that consumer tastes are globalizing, at least with respect to fashion apparel. Food is a different story; because tastes are more localized, M&S executives anticipate that the proportion of revenues from food sales will be lower than they are in Great Britain.[22] The difficulty of today's retailing environment is underscored by M&S's recent financial woes. The company's profits and share price plunged in the late 1990s amid a sales slump and infighting between top executives; Sir Richard left the company in 1998. A turnaround strategy called for

Figure 12-3

Global Retailing Categories

Source: Adapted from Jacques Horovitz and Nirmalya Kumar, "Strategies for Retail Globalization," Financial Times—Mastering Global Business, Part VII, 1998, pp. 4–8.

20 Miriam Jordan, "Penney Blends Two Business Cultures," *The Wall Street Journal* (April 5, 2001), p. A15.
21 The discussion in this section is adapted from Jacques Horovitz and Nirmalya Kumar, "Strategies for Retail Globalization," *Financial Times—Mastering Global Business*, Part VII, 1998, pp. 4–8.
22 Rufus Olins, "M&S Sets Out Its Stall for World Domination," *Sunday Times* (November 9, 1997), p. 6. See also Andrew Davidson, "The Andrew Davidson Interview: Sir Richard Greenbury," *Management Today* (November 2001), pp. 62–67; and Judi Bevan, *The Rise and Fall of Marks & Spencer* (London: Profile Books, 2001).

disposing of non-core properties such as the Brooks Brothers and Kings Super Markets chains in the United States.

Retailers in the upper right quadrant offer many well-known brands in a relatively tightly defined merchandise range. Here, for example, we find Toys "R" Us, which specializes in toys and includes branded products from Mattel, Nintendo, and other marketers. Additional examples include such category killers as Blockbuster Video and Virgin Megastores. As noted earlier, this type of store tends to quickly dominate smaller established retailers by out-merchandising local competition and offering customers superior value by virtue of extensive inventories and low prices. Typically, the low prices are the result of buyer power and sourcing advantages that local retailers lack. The retailing environment in which Richard Branson built the Virgin Megastore chain illustrates once again the type of success that can be achieved through an entrepreneurial management style:

> It required little retailing expertise to see that the sleepy business practices of traditional record shops provided a tremendous opportunity. To rival the tiny neighborhood record shops, with their eclectic collections of records, a new kind of record store was coming into being. It was big; it was well-lit, and records were arranged clearly in alphabetical order by artist; it covered most tastes in pop music comprehensively; and it turned over its stock much faster than the smaller record retailer. . . . It was the musical equivalent of a supermarket.[23]

Starting with one megastore location on London's Oxford Street in 1975, Branson's Virgin Retail empire now extends throughout Europe, North America, Japan, Hong Kong, and Taiwan.

Carrefour, Promodès, Wal-Mart, and other retailers in the fourth quadrant offer the same type of merchandise available from established local retailers. What the newcomers bring to a market, however, is competence in distribution or some other value chain element. To date, Wal-Mart's international division has established more than 1,000 stores outside the United States; it is already the biggest retailer in Mexico and Canada. Other store locations include Argentina, Brazil, China, and, until recently, Germany. International revenues for the fiscal year ended January 31, 2004, totaled $47.5 billion.

Richard Branson, founder and chairman of the Virgin Group, at the opening of a megastore in New York's Time Square. The $15 million facility occupies 75,000 square feet of space on three levels and features more than 1,000 music listening stations. The charismatic Branson is so closely associated with his company that, in the minds of many observers, the man is the brand.

---

[23] Tim Jackson, *Virgin King: Inside Richard Branson's Business Empire* (London: HarperCollins, 1995), p. 277.

Figure 12-4

Global Retailing Market Entry Strategy Framework

Source: Adapted from Jacques Horovitz and Nirmalya Kumar, "Strategies for Retail Globalization," Financial Times—Mastering Global Business, Part VII, 1998, p. 5.

Four market entry expansion strategies are available to retailers that wish to cross borders. As shown in Figure 12-4, these strategies can be captured conceptually by a matrix that differentiates between (1) markets that are easy to enter versus those that are difficult to enter and (2) culturally close markets versus culturally distant ones. The upper half of the matrix encompasses quadrants A and D and represents markets in which shopping patterns and retail structures are similar to those in the home country. In the lower half of the matrix, quadrants C and B represent markets that are significantly different from the home country market in terms of one or more cultural characteristic. The right side of the matrix, in quadrants A and B, represents markets that are difficult to enter because of the presence of strong competitors, location restrictions, excessively high rent or real estate costs, or other factors. In quadrants C and D, any barriers that exist are relatively easy to overcome. The four entry strategies indicated by the matrix are organic, franchise, chain acquisition, and joint venture.

Organic growth occurs when a company uses its own resources to open a store on a greenfield site or to acquire one or more existing retail facilities from another company. In 1997, for example, M&S announced plans to expand from one store to four in Germany via the purchase of three stores operated by Cramer and Meerman. When Richard Branson set up the first Virgin Megastore in Paris, he did so by investing millions of pounds in a spectacular retail space on the Champs-Elysées. From the perspective of M&S and Virgin, the retail environments of Germany and France are both culturally close and easy to enter. The success of this strategy hinges on the availability of company resources to sustain the high cost of the initial investment.

Franchising, shown in quadrant C of Figure 12-4, is the appropriate entry strategy when barriers to entry are low yet the market is culturally distant in terms of consumer behavior or retailing structures. As defined in Chapter 9, franchising is a contractual relationship between two companies. The parent company-franchisor authorizes a franchisee to operate a business developed by the franchisor in return for a fee and adherence to franchise-wide policies and practices. The key to a successful franchise operation is the ability to transfer company know-how to new markets. Benetton, IKEA, and other focused, private-label retailers often use franchising as a market-entry strategy in combination with wholly owned stores that represent organic growth. IKEA has more than 100 company-owned stores across Europe and the United States; its stores in the Middle East and Hong Kong are franchise operations.

In global retailing, **acquisition** is a market-entry strategy that entails purchasing a company with multiple retail locations in a foreign country. This strategy can provide the buyer with quick growth as well as access to existing brand suppliers, distributors, and customers. M&S, for example, had no plans for organic growth in the United States; rather, it acquired the upscale private-label American retailer Brooks Brothers in 1988 for $750 million. Executives at Brooks Brothers spent most of the 1990s trying to expand the brand's customer base, and recent results have been promising. With hindsight, however, it is clear that M&S paid too much for the acquisition. As noted previously, M&S itself is currently in the midst of a financial retrenchment; at the end of 2001, it sold Brooks Brothers to Retail Brand Alliance, a private holding company.

Joint ventures, the final entry strategy, have been examined in detail in an earlier chapter. With regard to global retailing, a joint-venture strategy is advisable when culturally distant, difficult-to-enter markets are targeted. Many Western retailers are using joint ventures to enter China, Japan, and other Asian countries. The ownership split can be adjusted in proportion to perceived entry difficulty and previous experience. Virgin Group's retail expansion in Asia provides a case study in the appropriateness of the joint-venture approach. In Japan, commercial landlords typically require millions in up-front payments before they will lease retail space. Accordingly, in 1992, Virgin established a joint venture called Virgin Megastores Japan with Marui, a local retailer with a good track record of catering to the preferences of young people. The first megastore was set up in the basement of an existing Marui department store in Japan's Shinjuku district. That and subsequent stores have been wildly successful; Virgin has duplicated the joint-venture approach elsewhere in Asia, including Hong Kong, Taiwan, and South Korea. In each location, Virgin establishes a joint venture with a leading industrial group.[24]

Achieving retailing success outside the home-country market is not simply a matter of consulting a matrix and choosing the recommended entry strategy. Management must also be alert to the possibility that the merchandise mix, sourcing strategy, distribution, or other format elements will have to be adapted. Management at Crate & Barrel, for example, is hesitant to open stores in Japan. Part of the reason is research indicating that at least half the company's product line would have to be modified to accommodate local preferences. Another issue is the company's ability to transfer its expertise to new country markets.

LESSONS
from the global marketplace

Growing Pains When Retailers Expand Abroad

Retailers may have had a difficult time crossing borders if they fail to appreciate differences in retailing environments and consumer behavior and preferences. For example, when Galeries Lafayette opened a location in New York, the store was stocked with women's clothing that was too trendy to be practical. In addition, the clothing was proportioned for the French, rather than American, physique. In London, retailers typically locate their stores on "high streets," which are roughly equivalent to downtown in the United States. However, America is the land of the mall; there are no "high streets" in most American cities. Gap recently closed its 10 stores in Germany as price-conscious consumers shopped at H&M and other stores where prices are lower.

Other obstacles include breaking through to get the consumer's attention. In the United States, fresh product assortments and aggressive pricing drive retailing. Anita Roddick got her Body Shop off to a good start in the United States and then watched as Limited jumped into the category with Bath & Body Works, a division it launched in 1992. Bath & Body Works captured Body Shop's market by constantly changing products, entering as many malls as possible, and by keeping prices lower. Meanwhile, Body Shop did not even have a formal marketing department. Today, Bath & Body Works dominates the category that Body Shop created.

Until recently, the companies that avoided this trap were the exceptions to the rule. For example, Richard Branson, the

entrepreneurial leader of Virgin, has built the Virgin brand in the United States the American way—by adding more and more products and by being noisy and loud about the brand. There is some evidence, however, that increasing numbers of British retailers are changing with the times. Harrods, Harvey Nichols, and other top retailers are improving the décor in key stores and offering shoppers an entertainment experience. For example, visitors to Fifth Floor Harvey Nichols will find a posh restaurant, a wine shop, and a gourmet food hall.

Some of the biggest innovations have been at Selfridges, whose flagship store just off Oxford Street in London is home to Europe's largest cosmetics department. Window displays have featured buzz-building "performances" such as humans in animal costumes modeling lingerie. As Peter Williams, CEO of Selfridges, said," Our competitors are not just other department stores. Our competitors are restaurants, theaters, a weekend away, or other entertainment venues."

Sources: Cecilie Rohwedder, "Harvey Nichols's Foreign Affair," The Wall Street Journal (February 18, 2005), pp. B1, B3; Erin White, "Dress for Success: After Long Slump, U.S. Retailers Look to Britain for Fashion Tips," The Wall Street Journal (April 22, 2004), pp. A1, A8; Rohwedder, "Selling Selfridges," The Wall Street Journal (May 5, 2003), p. B1; Ernest Beck, "Marks & Spencer to Focus on Key Brands," The Wall Street Journal (July 15, 1999), p. B1; Jennifer Steinhauer, "The British Are Coming, and Going," The New York Times (September 22, 1998), pp. C1, C4.

---

[24] Tim Jackson, *Virgin King: Inside Richard Branson's Business Empire* (London: HarperCollins, 1995), pp. 289–291.

INNOVATION IN GLOBAL RETAILING

As noted at the beginning of this chapter, distribution channels around the world are highly differentiated. On the surface, it appears this differentiation can be explained only in terms of culture and the income level that exists in the market. However, the incidence and rate of retail innovation can be explained in terms of the following four observations:

1. Innovation takes place only in the most highly developed systems. In general, channel agents in less-developed systems will adapt developments already tried and tested in more highly developed systems.
2. The ability of a system to successfully adapt innovations is directly related to its level of economic development. Certain minimum levels of economic development are necessary to support anything beyond the most simple retailing methods.
3. Even when the economic environment is conducive to change, the process of adaptation may be either hindered or helped by local demographic factors, geographic factors, social mores, government action, and competitive pressures.
4. The process of adaptation can be greatly accelerated by the actions of aggressive individual firms.

Self-service is a major twentieth-century channel innovation. It provides an excellent illustration of the four points just outlined. Self-service retailing, which allows customers to handle and select merchandise themselves in a store with minimal assistance from sales personnel, originated in the United States. The spread of self-service to other countries supports the tendency of an economic system to support innovations only after a certain level of economic development has been achieved. Self-service was first introduced internationally into the most highly developed countries. It has spread to the countries at middle and lower stages of development but serves very small segments of the total market in these countries.

If a country market has reached a stage of economic development that will support a channel innovation, it is clear that the action of well-managed firms can contribute considerably to the diffusion of the channel innovation. The rapid growth of Benetton and McDonald's is a testament to the skill and competence of these firms as well as to the appeal of their product and service offerings. In some instances, retail innovations are improved, refined, and expanded outside the home country. For example, after the first 7-Eleven Japan franchise opened in 1973, the Asian stores quickly attracted customers seeking convenience. Today, with more than 11,300 stores, the company is Japan's largest convenience store operator; innovative merchandising includes *Shop America*, an in-store catalog that allows Japanese shoppers to order imported luxury products from companies like Tiffany's and Cartier. In 1991, 7-Eleven Japan acquired a 72.7 percent share in the U.S.-based parent company. Comparing the Japanese and American sides of the business that same year, a Japanese retailing analyst noted, "Their [U.S. management's] merchandising has been really backwards, and the gap between us is rather large. The biggest reason is that they kept their old style and did not improve their methods and adapt to consumers' changing tastes. They became really rigid."[25] The Americans got the message. Management at the U.S. affiliate started focusing on new merchandise and was more systematic about dropping slow-moving items. The company also launched an initiative called the "model market program" that allows individual store managers considerable autonomy

---

[25] James Sterngold, "New Japanese Lesson: Running a 7–11," *The New York Times* (May 9, 1991), p. C7. See also Bethan Hutton, "Japan's 7-Eleven Sets Store by Computer Links," *Financial Times* (March 17, 1998), p. 26.

Japanese shoppers can pay their household bills at their neighborhood 7-Eleven. Recent merchandising innovations include Shop America, a catalog service specializing in imported luxury goods such as Rolex watches.

in deciding the mix of products a particular store carries. Between 2003 and 2005, the value of 7-Eleven Inc.'s stock quadrupled; in 2005, 7-Eleven Japan acquired the remaining 27.3 percent of the company.[26]

PHYSICAL DISTRIBUTION, SUPPLY CHAINS, AND LOGISTICS MANAGEMENT

In Chapter 1, marketing was described as one of the activities in a firm's **value chain**. The distribution *P* of the marketing mix plays a central role in a given firm's value chain; after all, Coca-Cola, IKEA, Nokia, Toyota, and other global companies create value by making sure their products are available where and when customers want to buy them. As defined in this chapter, physical distribution consists of activities involved in moving finished goods from manufacturers to customers. However, the value chain concept is much broader, for two basic reasons. First, the value chain is a useful tool for assessing an organization's competence as it performs value-creating activities within a broader **supply chain** that includes *all* the firms that perform support activities by generating raw materials, converting them into components or finished products, and making them available to customers. Second, the particular industry in which a firm competes (for example, automobiles, pharmaceuticals, or consumer electronics) is characterized by a value chain. The specific activities an individual firm performs help define its position in the value chain. If a company is somewhat removed from the final customer, it is said to be *upstream* in the value chain. A company that is relatively close to customers—a retailer, for example—is said to be *downstream* in the value chain. **Logistics**, in turn, is the management process that integrates the activities of all companies—both upstream and downstream—to ensure an efficient flow of goods through the supply chain.

An industry's value chain can change over time. In pharmaceuticals, for example, research, testing, and delivery are the three steps that historically

"Strategy is to war what the plot is to the play. Tactics is represented by the role of the players; logistics furnishes the stage management, accessories, and maintenance. The audience, thrilled by the action of the play and the art of the performers, overlooks all of the cleverly hidden details of stage management."

Lt. Col. George C. Thorpe, *Pure Logistics* (1917)

---

[26] Kris Hudson, "Bid for 7-Eleven by Japan Called Inadequate," *The Wall Street Journal* (September 23, 2005), pp. C1, C4.

defined the industry from its beginnings in the early nineteenth century. Then, starting in the mid-1960s, after Crick and Watson published their groundbreaking work on DNA, two new upstream steps in the industry's value chain emerged: basic research into genes associated with specific diseases and identification of the proteins produced by those genes. More recently, with the mapping of the human genome largely complete, value in the pharmaceuticals industry is migrating downstream to identifying, testing, and producing molecules that operate on the proteins produced by genes.[27]

The value chain, logistics, and related concepts are extremely important as supply chains stretch around the globe. As export administrator Beth Dorrell notes, "A commodity raw material from Africa can be refined in Asia, then shipped to South America to be incorporated into a component of a final product that is produced in the Middle East and then sold around the world." Figure 12-5 illustrates some of these concepts and activities at IKEA, the global furniture marketer. IKEA purchases wood and other raw material inputs from a network of suppliers located in dozens of countries; these suppliers are upstream in the value chain, and the process by which wood is transported to the factories is known as *inbound logistics*. IKEA's factories add value to the inputs by transforming them into furniture kits that are then shipped on to IKEA's stores. The stores are

Table 12-3

United States and EU/BRIC Comparison

United States/EU	Brazil	Russia	India	China
Supplier Base and Infrastructure/Logistics				
Companies use national and international suppliers. Firms outsource and move manufacturing and services offshore instead of integrating vertically. A highly developed infrastructure is in place, but urban areas are saturated.	Suppliers are available in the Mercosur region. A good network of highways, airports, and ports exists but port congestion is a chronic problem. Customs clearance times can be lengthy. Overall freight costs are 20 percent higher than international average.	Companies can rely on local suppliers for simple components. The European region has adequate logistics networks, but trans-Ural Russia is not well developed.	Suppliers are available, but quality and dependability varies greatly. Roads are in poor condition. Ports and airports are under-developed.	Several suppliers have strong manufacturing capabilities, but few vendors have advanced technical abilities. The road network is well developed. Excellent port facilities. However, transportation/distribution costs are high. Lacks a network of refrigerated and containerized trucks and warehouses to connect farms with grocery retailers.

Source: Adapted from Tarun Khanna, Krishna G. Palepu, and Jayant Sinha, "Strategies That Fit Emerging Markets," *Harvard Business Review* 83, no. 6 (June 2005), p. 69.

---

[27] David Champion, "Mastering the Value Chain: An Interview with Mark Levin of Millennium Pharmaceuticals," *Harvard Business Review* 79, no. 6 (June 2001), pp. 108–115.

Figure 12-5

Supply Chain, Value Chain, and Logistics

downstream in IKEA's value chain; the activities associated with shipping furniture kits from factory to store are known as *outbound logistics*.[28]

Physical distribution and logistics are the means by which products are made available to customers when and where they want them. The most important distribution activities are order processing, warehousing, inventory management, and transportation.

Order Processing

Activities relating to order processing provide information inputs that are critical in fulfilling a customer's order. **Order processing** includes *order entry*, in which the order is actually entered into a company's information system; *order handling*, which involves locating, assembling, and moving products into distribution; and *order delivery*, the process by which products are made available to the customer.

In some instances the customer is a consumer, as is the case when you place an order with Amazon.com or Lands' End. In other instances, the customer is a channel member. Pepsi Bottling Group recently overhauled its supply chain in an effort to eliminate out-of-stock situations at retail. The company's handheld computers lacked wireless capability and required hookup to landline telephone service; by upgrading the technology, sales representatives can now enter orders wirelessly. Warehouse workers are equipped with bar-code scanners and headsets so they can do a better job of ensuring that each pallet of drink products contains exactly what retailers have ordered.[31]

Inventory Management

Proper inventory management ensures that a company neither runs out of manufacturing components or finished goods nor incurs the expense and risk of carrying excessive stocks of these items. Another issue is balancing order-processing costs against inventory-carrying costs. The more often a product is ordered, the higher the order-processing costs associated with unloading, stocking, and related activities. The less frequently a product is ordered, the higher the inventory-carrying costs, since more product must be kept in inventory to cover the longer period between orders. An important new tool for inventory management is radio frequency identification (RFID); RFID utilizes small tags that are attached to pallets, containers, or individual inventory items (see Case 12-2).

> "At IKEA, we went out into the forest to see which were the right trees to pick to optimize production and cost efficiency in the saw mills."[29]
>
> Anders Moberg, Former CEO, IKEA

> "We are trying to take advantage of the global factory. We are a global company; we should have a supply chain that reflects our customer base."[30]
>
> Keith Sherin, Finance Director, GE

---

[28] A detailed analysis of IKEA's approach to value creation is found in Richard Normann and Rafael Ramirez, "From Value Chain to Value Constellation: Designing Interactive Strategy," *Harvard Business Review* 71, no. 4 (July–August 1993), pp. 65–77.

[29] Ian Bickerton, "'It is All About the Value Chain,'" *Financial Times* (February 24, 2006), p. 10.

[30] Francesco Guerrera, "GE to Shift Output from U.S." *Financial Times* (July 27, 2006), p. 27.

[31] Chad Terhune, "Supply-Chain Fix for Pepsi," *The Wall Street Journal* (June 6, 2006), p. B3.

Warehousing

Warehouses are used to store goods until they are sold; another type of facility, the *distribution center*, is designed to efficiently receive goods from suppliers and then fill orders for individual stores or customers. Modern distribution and warehousing is such an automated, high-tech business today that many companies outsource this function. For example, ODW Logistics Inc. operates several warehouses on behalf of Deere & Company, Limited Brands, and other customers. Much of ODW's capacity is in Columbus, Ohio, a major U.S. port of entry for textiles. One of the driving forces behind the growth of third-party warehousing is the need to reduce fixed costs and speed up delivery times to customers. ODW adds additional utility by tracking shipments from the time they leave the factory in, say, China, until they reach Columbus. This enables the company to alert retailers of possible delays due to weather or port congestion. In addition, as manufacturers ramp up efforts to use RFID tags on shipments, ODW will split the cost of the new technology with its customers. As consultant John Boyd notes, "Right now, distribution warehousing is the next arena of corporate reengineering and corporate cost-cutting."[32]

Transportation

Finally, transportation decisions concern the method or *mode* a company should utilize when moving products through domestic and global channels. The word *mode* implies a choice, and the major transportation mode choices are rail, truck, air, water, pipeline, and the Internet. Each of these modes has its advantages and disadvantages, as summarized in Table 12-4. However, a particular mode may be unavailable in some countries because of an underdeveloped infrastructure or geographic barriers. Pipelines are highly specialized and used by companies transporting energy-related resources such as oil and natural gas.

Rail provides an extremely cost-effective means for moving large quantities of merchandise long distances. In the United States, carriers such as Burlington Northern Santa Fe (BNSF) account for about 42 percent of all cargo moved when measured by ton-miles; however, according to figures compiled by Eno Transportation Foundation, rail accounts for only about 10 percent of total U.S. freight transportation revenues. Rail's capability is second only to water in terms of the variety of products that can be transported. However, trains are less reliable than trucks. Poor track maintenance leads to derailments, and bottlenecks on heavily traveled lines can create delays.

Trucks are an excellent mode for both long-haul, transcontinental transport and local delivery of goods. In nations with well-developed highway systems, truck freight provides the highest level of accessibility of any mode. Thanks to modern information technology, truck shipments are also easily traced. According to the American Trucking Association, in the United States alone, the trucking industry

Table 12-4

Comparison of Major International Transportation Modes

Mode	Reliability	Cost	Speed	Accessibility	Capability	Ease of Tracing
Rail	average	average	average	high	high	low
Water	low	low	slow	low	high	low
Truck	high	varies	fast	high	high	high
Air	high	high	fast	low	moderate	high
Pipeline	high	low	slow	low	low	moderate
Internet	high	low	moderate to fast	moderate; increasing	low	high

Source: Containerization International.

32 Kris Maher, "Global Goods Jugglers," *The Wall Street Journal* (July 5, 2005), pp. A11, A12.

FedEx Express is a unit of Memphis-based FedEx Corporation. With operations in more than 220 countries, FedEx Express is the world's leading express delivery provider. China is the world's second-largest domestic air-cargo market, and FedEx forecasts that market growth there will average 10 percent annually over the next 15 years. FedEx recently spent $400 million to buy out its Chinese joint venture partner. In addition, FedEx is now offering the first guaranteed overnight express-delivery service in China, with deliveries to more than 100 cities.

handles nearly 70 percent of all freight tonnage; in 2003, the industry generated revenues of $610 billion. Thanks to government deregulation and a business trend toward focusing on core competencies, companies such as General Motors, Hewlett-Packard, and PPG Industries are turning to transportation companies for assistance.

challenges in the global marketplace

Foreign Management of U.S. Ports

In 2006, a controversy erupted in the United States after a British company, Peninsular & Oriental Steam Navigation (P&O) was acquired by Dubai Ports World (DP World) for $6.8 billion. P&O is a seaport operator with a strong global presence, including the United States. DP World was eager to expand in the U.S. market, and P&O was an attractive acquisition target. However, the deal meant that some container ports in six U.S. cities—New York, Elizabeth (New Jersey), Philadelphia, Baltimore, Miami, and New Orleans—would be operated by a unit of a Middle Eastern company.

The ensuing media scrutiny and popular backlash were part of a broader concern shared by many Americans that U.S. officials were not being sufficiently vigilant about globalization's potentially negative aspects. Dubai is one of seven semiautonomous regions that comprise the United Arab Emirates (UAE). The UAE has a history of possible links to terrorism; not surprisingly, the uproar in America stemmed from concerns about national security. Specifically, it was suggested that the Middle East connection would allow terror groups to gather information about U.S. port procedures and, perhaps, infiltrate the workforce.

However, some observers were quick to point out that companies based in China, Taiwan, Japan, Denmark, and other countries already manage some 30 percent of America's container ports. Many ports have multiple terminals, and each terminal can have a different foreign operator. The operators are often subsidiaries of foreign shipping companies; as one can see from examining Table 12-5, most of the major shipping companies are headquartered outside the United States. Peter Shaef is

managing director of a merchant bank specializing in the transportation industry. He says, "I don't think Americans have any realization of the global nature of the maritime industry."

Before the controversy became front-page news, DP World's proposed acquisition of P&O had already been approved by the Committee on Foreign Investment in the United States (CFIUS). Units of the U.S. Homeland Security Department would control security at the ports in questions, and DP World would be required to comply with all security policies and protocols. In early March 2006, a House panel voted overwhelming to block the deal. For his part, U.S. president George W. Bush vowed to veto any such attempt by Congress. However, as the controversy reached a peak, DP World announced that it would divest itself of holdings that were associated with U.S. ports. Although some claimed victory in this particular battle, others noted that the war had ended years ago. As George Washington University professor Prabir Bagchi noted, "For a long time in the United States, no one wanted stevedoring on their business card because it was not a glamorous job. Control of many of those low-paying jobs went east, and now look who's cheapest and best at providing customer service."

Sources: Youssef M. Ibrahim, "Ports Deal Collapse: A Lesson for the World," USA Today (March 15, 2006), p. 13A; Greg Hitt and Sarah Ellison, "Abandon Ship: Dubai Firm Bows to Public Outcry," The Wall Street Journal (March 10, 2006), pp. A1, A17; Laura Meckler and Daniel Machalaba, "Port Deal: Not a Foreign Idea," The Wall Street Journal (March 9, 2006), pp. B1, B5; Robert Wright, "A Steady Pilot in the Storm," Financial Times (February 25/26, 2006), p. 7; Simon Romero and Heather Timmons, "A Ship Already Sailed," The New York Times (February 24, 2006), pp. C1, C13; Bruce Stanley, "The Grab for Container Ports," The Wall Street Journal (January 1, 2006), p. B4.

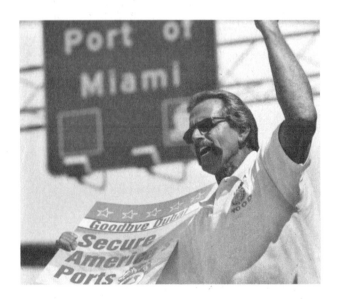

There are two main types of water transportation. *Inland water transportation* is an extremely low-cost mode generally used to move agricultural commodities, petroleum, fertilizers, and other goods that, by their nature, lend themselves to bulk shipping via barge. However, inland water transportation can be slow and subject to weather-related delays. Virtually any product can be shipped via *ocean transportation*. The world's deep-water ports can receive a variety of types of ocean-going vessels, such as container vessels, bulk and break-bulk vessels, and roll-on, roll-off (ro-ro) vessels. Although sailing times are not competitive with air transportation, it is generally more cost effective to ship large quantities of merchandise via ocean than by air. Denmark's Maersk Sealand is the world's largest shipping container line (see Table 12-5). Why is water rated "low" in reliability? In any given year, approximately 200 freighters sink due to bad weather or other factors. Compounding the tragic loss of human lives is the fact that the cargo ends up on the ocean floor. Cargo can sometimes be lost without a ship sinking. For example, in 1997, a huge wave rocked the freighter *Tokio Express* in the waters off Land's End, England. Several dozen shipping containers were tossed overboard, including one containing nearly 5 million LEGO pieces. The container was bound for Connecticut, where the LEGO pieces were to be assembled in kits. One year later, LEGO pieces began washing ashore in Florida!

Air is the fastest transport mode and the carrier of choice for perishable exports such as flowers or fresh fish, but it is also the most expensive. The size and the weight of an item may determine that it is more cost effective to ship via air

Table 12-5	Carrier	Number of Vessels	Capacity 20-Foot Units (thousands)
Leading Shipping Lines	Maersk Sealand (Denmark)	324	816
	Evergreen Marine (Taiwan)	209	493
	P&O Nedlloyd (United Kingdom)	155	414
	Hanjin Shipping (South Korea)	76	414
	American President Lines (United States)	78	260
	Cosco (China)	136	257
	CP Ships (United Kingdom)	85	193
	CMA-CGM (France)	74	191
	NYK Line (Japan)	61	189

Source: Containerization International.

than ocean. If a shipment's delivery is time sensitive, such as emergency parts replacement, air is also the logical mode.

Thanks to the digital revolution, the *Internet* is becoming an important transportation mode that is associated with several advantages and one major disadvantage. First, the bad news: the Internet's capability is low. As Nicolas Negroponte of MIT's Media Lab has famously observed, as long as something consists of atoms, it cannot be shipped via the Internet. However, anything that can be digitized—including text, voice, music, pictures, and video—can be sent via the Internet. Advantages include low cost and high reliability. Accessibility is increasing as global PC demand increases; today, it is estimated that more than 600 million households have Internet access. Accessibility is also growing thanks to telecommunications innovations that allow cell phones and other wireless digital devices to access the Internet. Speed depends on several factors, including bandwidth. As broadband technology becomes more widespread and compression technology improves, the speed at which large digital files such as full-length motion pictures can be downloaded will increase dramatically.

Channel strategy involves an analysis of each shipping mode to determine which mode, or combination of modes, will be both effective and efficient in a given situation. A number of firms specializing in third-party logistics are available to help companies with transportation logistics. For example, C.H. Robinson Worldwide matches shippers with trucking companies and other carriers in all parts of the world. An aspect of transportation technology that has revolutionized global trade is containerization—a concept that was first utilized in the United States starting in the mid-1950s. **Containerization** refers to the practice of loading ocean-going freight into steel boxes measuring 20 feet, 40 feet, or longer. Containerization offers many advantages, including flexibility in the product that can be shipped via container, as well as flexibility in shipping modes. **Intermodal transportation** of goods involves a combination of land and water shipping from producer to customer.[33] In the United States alone, railroads handle more than $150 billion in seaport goods, a statistic that is a testament to intermodal transportation's growing importance. Unfortunately, lack of investment in America's

Prior to 1985, the Port of New York was the busiest container port in the world. Then, New York went into decline as ports on the West coast and the South courted freight lines. Now, thanks to a high tide of imports from Asia, the Port of New York is experiencing a resurgence of traffic. Giant freighters leave China and travel through the Panama Canal.

Source: Keith Meyers/The New York Times.

---

[33] For an excellent case study of the evolution of intermodal technology in the United States, see Jon R. Katzenback and Douglas K. Smith, *The Wisdom of Teams: Creating the High-Performance Organization* (New York: HarperBusiness, 1994), chapter 2.

rail infrastructure has resulted in delays at seaports. As Bernard LaLonde, a professor of transportation and logistics, noted, "It's the Achilles' heel of global distribution. The ships keep getting bigger and faster. Trade keeps growing. But we don't have the rail links we need."[34]

Use of a particular mode of transportation may be dictated by a particular market situation, by the company's overall strategy, or by conditions at the port of importation. For example, every November, winemakers from France's Beaujolais region participate in a promotion celebrating the release of the current vintage. Although wine destined for European markets may travel by rail or truck, U.S.-bound wine is shipped via air freight. Normally, owing to weight and bulk considerations, French wine makes the transatlantic journey by water. Similarly, Acer Group ships motherboards and other high-tech components from Taiwan via air freight to ensure that the latest technology is incorporated into its computers. Bangladesh's primary port, Chittagong, is subject to frequent delays and strikes, which forces Gap and other clothing companies to ship via air. Every Christmas, supplies of the season's hottest-selling toys and electronics products are shipped via air from factories in Asia to ensure just-in-time delivery by Santa Claus. Sony's PS3 is a case in point; in the fall of 2006, the company shipped hundreds of thousands of units by air to the United States. Likewise, in 2007, the first shipments of Apple's highly anticipated iPhone arrived in the United States via air freight. An estimated $1 billion is added to U.S. shipping costs each year because companies are forced to compensate for railway delays by keeping more components or parts in inventory or by shipping via air.

Logistics Management: A Brief Case Study

The term **logistics management** describes the integration of activities necessary to ensure the efficient flow of raw materials, in-process inventory, and finished goods from producers to customers. JCPenney provides a case study in the changing face of logistics, physical distribution, and retail supply chains in the twenty-first century. Several years ago, JCPenney's management team made a key decision to outsource most elements of its private-label shirt supply chain to TAL Apparel Ltd. of Hong Kong. JCPenney's North American stores carry virtually no extra inventory of house-brand shirts; when an individual shirt is sold, EPOS scanner data is transmitted directly to Hong Kong. TAL's proprietary computer model then determines whether to replenish the store with the same size, color, and style. Replacement shirts are sent directly to stores without passing through JCPenney's warehouse system; sometimes the shirts are sent via air, sometimes by ship. This approach represents a dramatic departure from past practices; JCPenney typically carried six months' worth of inventory in its warehouses and three months' inventory in stores. By working more closely with TAL, JCPenney can lower its inventory costs, reduce the quantity of goods that have to be marked down, and respond more quickly to changing consumer tastes and fashion styles. As Wai-Chan Chan of McKinsey & Company Hong Kong noted, "You are giving away a pretty important function when you outsource your inventory management. That's something that not a lot of retailers want to part with."[35]

[34] Daniel Machalaba, "Cargo Hold: As U.S. Seaports Get Busier, Weak Point Is a Surprise: Railroads," *The Wall Street Journal* (September 19, 1996), p. A1.
[35] Alexandra Harney, "Technology Takes the Wrinkles Out of Textiles Manufacturing, " *Financial Times* (January 11, 2006), p.11. See also Gabriel Kahn, "Made to Measure: Invisible Supplier Has Penney's Shirts All Buttoned Up," *The Wall Street Journal* (September 11, 2003), pp. A1, A9.

A **channel of distribution** is the network of agencies and institutions that links producers with users. **Physical distribution** is the movement of goods through channels. **Business–to-consumer (b-to-c or B2C) marketing** uses consumer channels; **business-to-business (b-to-b or B2B) marketing** employs industrial channels to deliver products to manufacturers or other types of organizations. **Distributors** and **agents** are key intermediaries in both channel types Channel decisions are difficult to manage globally because of the variation in channel structures from country to country. Marketing channels can create **place utility**, **time utility**, **form utility**, and **information utility** for buyers. The characteristics of customers, products, middlemen, and environment all affect channel design and strategy.

Consumer channels may be relatively direct, utilizing direct mail or door-to-door selling, as well as manufacturer-owned stores. A combination of manufacturers' sales force, agents-brokers, and wholesalers may also be used. **Piggyback marketing** is a distribution innovation in which one manufacturer gains distribution in a particular country market by "riding along" with the products of another manufacturer. Channels for industrial products are less varied, with manufacturer's sales force, wholesalers, and dealers or agents used.

Global retailing is a growing trend as successful retailers expand around the world in support of growth objectives. **Retail distribution** takes many different forms, including **department stores**, **specialty retailers**, **supermarkets**, **convenience stores**, **discount stores**, **warehouse clubs**, **hypermarkets**, **supercenters**, **category killers**, and **outlet stores** and **outlet malls**. Selection, price, store location, and customer service are a few of the competencies that can be used strategically to enter a new market. It is possible to classify retailers in a matrix that distinguishes companies offering few product categories with an own-label focus; many categories-own-label focus; few categories-manufacturer-brand focus; and many categories-manufacturer-brand focus. Global retail expansion can be achieved via **organic growth**, **franchising**, **acquisition**, and **joint venture**.

Transportation and physical distribution issues are critically important in a company's value chain because of the geographical distances involved in sourcing products and serving customers in different parts of the world. A company's **supply chain** includes all the firms that perform support activities such as generating raw materials or fabricating components. **Logistics** and **logistics management** integrate the activities of all companies in a firm's value chain to ensure an efficient flow of goods through the supply chain. Important activities include **order processing**, **warehousing**, and **inventory management**. To cut costs and improve efficiency, many companies are reconfiguring their supply chains by outsourcing some or all of these activities. Six transportation modes—air, truck, water, rail, pipeline, and Internet—are widely used in global distribution. Distributing products around the globe is made easier by **containerization** and **intermodal transportation**.

summary

1. In what ways can channel intermediaries create utility for buyers?

2. What factors influence the channel structures and strategies available to global marketers?

3. What is *cherry picking*? What approaches can be used to deal with this problem?

4. Compare and contrast the typical channel structures for consumer products and industrial products.

5. Identify the different forms of retailing, and cite an example of each form. Identify retailers from as many different countries as you can.

6. Identify the four retail market expansion strategies discussed in the text. What factors determine the appropriate mode?

7. Briefly discuss the global issues associated with physical distribution and transportation logistics. Cite one example of a company that is making efficiency improvements in its channel or physical distribution arrangements.

8. What special distribution challenges exist in Japan? What is the best way for a non-Japanese company to deal with these challenges?

discussion questions

Each December, *Chain Store Age* magazine publishes its survey of the world's largest retailers. The top-ranked companies for 2005 are shown in Table 12-1. Browse through the list and choose any company that interests you. Compare its 2005 ranking with the most recent ranking (which you can find either by referring to the print version of *Chain Store Age* or by visiting www. chainstoreage. com). How have the industry rankings changed? Consult additional sources (e.g., magazine articles, annual reports, the company's Web site) to enhance your understanding of the factors and forces that contributed to the company's move up or down in the rankings. What do the current rankings tell you about changes in global retailing?

Charles Fishman, *The Wal-Mart Effect* (London: Penguin Press, 2005).

Is global retailing giant Wal-Mart a hero or a villain? Writing in *Financial Times*, a reviewer noted, "Wal-Mart isn't subject to market forces because it's creating them."

Marc Levinson, *The Box* (Princeton, New Jersey: Princeton University Press, 2005).

The story of entrepreneur Malcolm McClean's distribution revolution. As author Levinson points out, "McClean's big insight was that the customer doesn't care how you're shipping the goods. The customer wants to get it from here to there cheap and on time. The customer doesn't care if it goes by air or land or sea." A reviewer in the *Economist* noted, "Levinson makes a strong case that it was McClean's thinking that led to modern-day containcrization. Without the container, there would be no globalization."

Case 12-1
Carrefour Expands Abroad

Hypermarkets are giant stores as big as four or more football fields. Part supermarket and part department store, they feature a wide array of product categories—groceries, toys, furniture, fast food, and financial services—all beneath one roof. Hypermarkets have flourished in Europe for more than three decades. France's Carrefour SA opened the first hypermarket in 1963; with help from the French government, zoning laws ensured that competing stores would be kept from the vicinity. By 1973, the hypermarket concept had been introduced in Spain; today, Carrefour is the world's most global retailer with 10,000 stores in 30 countries. Most of the European stores were well established before competing retailing concepts such as shopping malls and discount stores made the Atlantic crossing from America. Now the hypermarket concept is being transplanted around the globe. Carrefour has established a strong presence in Asia; in December 2000, it became the first foreign retailer to open a hypermarket in Japan.

In the United States, retailing channels are quite diverse. In addition to long-entrenched shopping malls and discount stores, wholesale clubs such as Pace and Sam's offer rock-bottom prices, and Toys "R" Us, Circuit City, and other "category killers" offer tremendous depth in particular product categories. In February 1988, Carrefour ("Crossroads" in French) opened its first U.S. hypermarket, a gigantic store in Philadelphia with 330,000 square feet of floor space. Carrefour soon built a second American unit, but then shut down both stores in October 1993. The problem? Many shoppers simply found the stores too big and too overwhelming. Also, although the product assortment was very broad, there was little depth in some product categories. For many products, only one brand or one flavor was available.

"In the future, we will have local companies or global companies but not much in between. Globalization will lead those who are not in the first team, or who are national retailers, to make alliances."

Daniel Bernard, Former Chairman and Chief Executive, Carrefour

Despite problems in the United States, hypermarkets are thriving elsewhere. There are several reasons for this. First, in countries where shoppers must visit many smaller stores or markets to complete their shopping, the megastore concept is viewed as a welcome innovation, even though many customers feel loyalty to traditional family-owned stores. Also, hypermarket operators offer free parking in spacious lots, a lure to shoppers in countries where parking spaces are in short supply. A third reason is demographic: As more women enter the workforce, they have less time to shop. While U.S. shoppers can choose from many discount stores and supermarkets, consumers in other countries find that hypermarkets are the only convenient alternative to shopping store-to-store.

Venezuela's first hypermarket, Tiendas Exito, opened in May 2001. A French-Venezuelan-Colombian partnership opened the store despite Venezuela's relatively small population of 24 million people and an economy mired in recession. The partners reasoned that the soaring cost of living would motivate consumers to go bargain hunting.

Carrefour is still fine-tuning its global strategy. In November 1999, it acquired French rival Promodès; valued at $13.6 billion, the deal was the world's largest retail acquisition. In their quest to build a global brand, Carrefour executives changed the names of hundreds of Promodès' Pryca and Continent stores in Spain and France to Carrefour. Confused by the changes, some shoppers took their business elsewhere. Meanwhile a competitor, the Netherlands-based supermarket operator Royal Ahold NV, is retaining local store names as it expands around the globe. As the company's chief executive said, "Everything the customer sees, we localize. Everything they don't see, we globalize." Carrefour has pulled out of Japan, Mexico, and South Korea while establishing a presence in markets with stronger potential such as China and Brazil. Expansion plans unveiled in 2006 called for opening 100 new stores each year through 2008. Approximately one-fourth of the new stores will be in China.

"Carrefour has a proud history as the most international retailer, planting its flags in many countries. But I am not proud of putting my banner anywhere, at any price.

José Luis Duran, Chief Executive, Carrefour

Meanwhile, at home in France, Carrefour is facing intense competition from Aldi and other so-called "hard discounter" chains that feature private-label brands at lower prices. The French market is critical because it generates 60 percent of Carrefour's profits. After José Luis Duran became chief executive in 2005, one of his first priorities was "to get France right." Duran sent a message to his French store managers: henceforth, a major part of bonuses would be based on price competitiveness. Following Wal-Mart's strategy, Duran put an end to one-time discounts and implemented across-the-board low prices. Although Carrefour's financial results for 2005 were hurt by a profit decline in France, sales and market share increased.

Having addressed the price issue, Duran set about improving service in an effort to win customers from specialty stores. Stores that were understaffed have added more personnel. Duran is also taking a more flexible approach to store size and design; it is trying new formats such as "Mini-Hyper" and "Carrefour Express," a scaled-down supermarket.

Discussion Questions

1. What is the biggest competitive threat facing Carrefour as it expands in global markets?

2. Carrefour is currently the top global retailer in China. What must it do to maintain its leadership position as Wal-Mart expands operations there?

Sources: Cecilie, Rohwedder, "Market Mover: A New Chief Seeks to Make French Retailing Giant Nimbler," *The Wall Street Journal* (November 30, 2006), pp. A1, A14; Adam Jones and Elizabeth Rigby, "Carrefour Gets Competitive," *Financial Times* (March 10, 2006), p. 6; Robert Guy Matthews, "Problems in Carrefour's Home Market Sank CEO," *The Wall Street Journal* (February 4, 2005), pp. A1, A10; Sarah Ellison, "Carrefour and Ahold Find Shoppers Like to Think Local," *The Wall Street Journal* (August 31, 2001) p. A5; Marc Lifsher, "Will Venezuelans Shun Mom and Pop for the Hypermarket?" *The Wall Street Journal* (June 28, 2001) p. A13; Peggy Hollinger, "Carrefour's Revolutionary," *Financial Times* (December 4, 1998), p. 14; Laurie Underwood, "Consumers at a Crossroad," *Free China Review* (February 2, 1995), pp. 66–67; Laurie M. Grossman, "Hypermarkets: A Sure-Fire Hit Bombs," *The Wall Street Journal* (June 25, 1992), p. B1.

Case 12-2
The Future of RFID

Since the mid-1970s, shoppers in many parts of the world have been accustomed to laser scanners at checkout counters that scan bar codes on purchased items. Now, manufacturers and retailers are rolling out a new technology that could one day enable them to take a closer look at all the items in a person's grocery bag. RFID is a new technology employing tiny tags equipped with microchips and antennas. Developed at the Massachusetts Institute of Technology's Auto-ID Center, RFID has been used for such applications as security and access control and toll collection on roads and bridges. In October 2003, responsibility for commercializing RFID was turned over to EPCglobal, a joint venture created by the U.S.-based Uniform Code Council and Europe's EAN. Now, global companies are assessing the technology as a means of improving supply chain management. RFID tags can facilitate a company's efforts to track the location of components and parts as they move along an assembly line, or shipping containers as they move from global factories to retailers in various parts of the world. The tags currently cost about $0.25 each, and, thus, are too expensive to put on

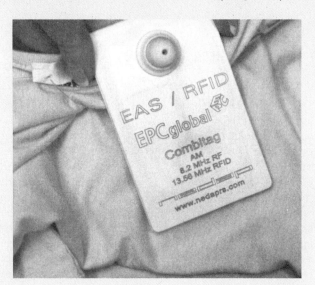

individual items. Even so, privacy advocates are already speaking out against the technology.

Katherine Albrecht is director of Citizens Against Supermarket Privacy Invasion and Numbering (Caspian), a consumer advocacy group that has previously targeted such common marketing techniques as shopper loyalty cards. Why all the fuss about an issue that is basically a matter of supply chain management? Albrecht, a doctoral student at Harvard University, is concerned that, if tags are embedded in clothing, companies—or government agencies—will be able to track the movements of the people wearing the clothes. She cautions, "Very few people grasp the enormity of this." Albrecht established a Web site (www.spychips.org) to help spread the word worldwide. Concerned about these activities, the Grocery Manufacturers Association began delving into Albrecht's personal background in an attempt to discredit or embarrass her. The ploy backfired when an internal GMA e-mail was inadvertently sent to Albrecht; the GMA subsequently issued an apology.

Benetton has already responded to the negative publicity surrounding the tags by reassuring consumers that it does not attach tags to any individual clothing items in its stores. In spring 2003, Wal-Mart canceled an experimental program that would have placed radio tags on razors and blades. During a trial program at the Tesco supermarket chain in Great Britain, consumers who bought tagged Gillette razors were photographed. In this test, the goal was to prevent shoplifting; each photo was deleted when the shopper paid for the razor at checkout. Europe's Metro Group supermarket chain went ahead with a two-month experiment that entailed setting up so-called smart shelves in German stores to track the presence of tagged items. After obtaining a Metro loyalty card, Albrecht discovered a hidden RFID chip in it. Metro could use the cards in conjunction with tagged grocery items to track all customer purchases. After Albrecht went public with the news, Metro recalled the cards and promised that it would no longer distribute tagged cards.

Despite the controversy, Wal-Mart is moving ahead with plans to integrate RFID into its supply chain. The company has told its top suppliers that, effective January 2005, they must attach RFIDs to each pallet and case of product. In typical Wal-Mart fashion, the retailer has stipulated that suppliers must absorb the cost of implementing the RFID program. Despite the cost involved and the controversy surrounding the privacy issue, RFID promises to benefit consumers and channel intermediaries alike. Even though Wal-Mart boasts the industry's most sophisticated inventory management system, one study found that, at any given moment, 7 percent of items that shoppers expect to find at Wal-Mart are temporarily out of stock. Because retailers will be able to pinpoint the exact location of a shipment, loss due to theft or simple error will be reduced. Stores can reduce the amount of excess inventory they carry, and consumers will be less likely to be disappointed by an out-of-stock situation.

The controversy gained new traction in fall 2005 when Albrecht published a book titled *Spychips: How Major Corporations and Government Plan to Track Your Every Move with RFID*. In its first week, *Spychips* was in the top 10 of Amazon.com's nonfiction best-seller list. Albrecht also began producing and distributing DVDs about the potential perils of RFID. Meanwhile, retailers and marketers proceeded with efforts to implement RFID-based inventory systems. Improved, second-generation tags were introduced in 2006. Dick Cantrell, who supervises Procter & Gamble's RFID program, is enthusiastic about the technology's potential. As he told the *Financial Times*, "Now we are establishing a new way of doing business and P&G is committed, and I know that Wal-Mart is committed at a high level."

Discussion Questions

1. Why do you think Katherine Albrecht is suspicious of the retail industry's motives for employing RFID?
2. What should the retail industry do in response to the mounting controversy over RFID?
3. Should retailers be forced to disclose when they are using RFID chips on products?

Sources: Jack Neff, "Surprising Bestseller Blasts P&G, Wal-Mart," *Advertising Age* (October 17, 2005), p. 6; Peter Sanders, "Casinos Bet on Radio-ID Gambling Chips," *The Wall Street Journal* (May 15, 2005), pp. B1, B7; Neff, "Privacy Activist Albrecht Tackles Marketers Head On," *Advertising Age* (April 19, 2004), p. 54; Barnaby J. Feder, "Wal-Mart Hits More Snags in Its Push to Use Radio Tags to Track Goods," *The New York Times* (March 29, 2004), p. C4; John Gapper, "Privacy Gets a Price-Tag When Bugs Go Shopping," *Financial Times* (March 2, 2004), p. 13; Kevin J. Delaney, "Inventory Tool to Launch in Germany," *The Wall Street Journal* (January 12, 2004), p. B5; Neff, "P&G Products to Wear Wire," *Advertising Age* (December 15, 2003), pp. 1, 32; Feder, "Wal-Mart Plan Could Cost Suppliers Millions," *The New York Times* (November 10, 2003), p. C2; Feder, "How to Find that Needle Hopelessly Lost in the Haystack," *The New York Times* (September 29, 2003), pp. C1, C4.

Scotch whiskey is a textbook example of a global product. Wealthy consumers with discerning palates do not hesitate to pay premium prices for top global brands such as Chivas Regal and Johnnie Walker. Moreover, Scotch drinkers everywhere associate the amber spirit with aspirational goals such as success and achievement. In the late 1990s, Diageo, the owner of the Johnnie Walker brand, launched a global advertising campaign featuring the tagline "Keep walking." The theme, which was developed by Britain's Bartle Bogle Hegarty (BBH) advertising agency, was keyed to the brand's logo: a red-coated, top-hatted gentleman in mid-stride. However, as BBH staffers working on the Johnnie Walker account understand, the things that constitute "achievement" can vary from culture to culture. In China, for example, the self-satisfaction that goes along with achieving a goal may not be enough; acknowledgment of the achievement by peers is also important. For this reason, BBH created a localized marketing campaign for China. One ad depicts two golfers hitting increasingly extreme shots that include teeing off from the roof of a golf cart and a ball that is hit from underneath a crocodile. The campaign coincided with rapid market growth; after China joined the WTO in 2001, tariffs on spirits imports were cut from 65 percent to 10 percent. According to the Scotch Whiskey Association, Scotch exports to China totaled £46 million in 2005, up from just £1.5 million in 2001. Today, Johnnie Walker has a 34 percent share of China's whiskey market.

Advertising and other forms of communication are critical tools in the marketing program. Marketing communications—the promotion *P* of the marketing mix—refers to all forms of communication used by organizations to inform, remind, explain, persuade, and influence the attitudes and buying behavior of customers and others. The primary purpose of marketing communications is to tell customers about the benefits and values that a company, product, or service offers. The elements of the promotion mix are advertising, public relations, personal selling, and sales promotion. Global marketing can use all these elements either alone or in varying combinations. The challenge facing the marketers of Johnnie Walker and other Scotch brands is developing and implementing promotional strategies that will resonate with consumers all over the world while speaking clearly to consumers in individual countries.

As Diageo's experience in China demonstrates, the environment in which marketing communications programs and strategies are implemented varies from country to country. The challenge of effectively communicating across borders is one reason that global companies and their advertising agencies are embracing a concept known as **integrated marketing communications (IMC)**. Adherents of an IMC approach explicitly recognize that the various elements of a company's

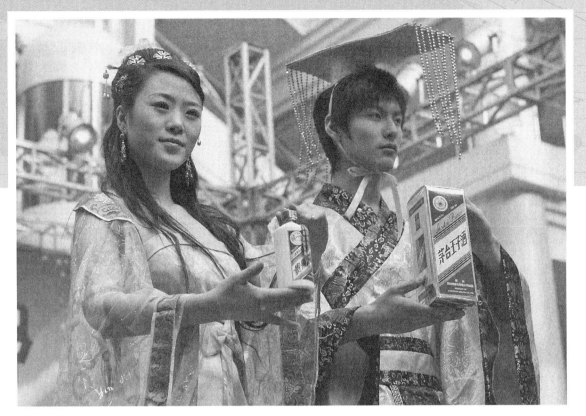

As noted throughout the text, global products and brands often compete with local ones. In China, Johnnie Walker Scotch competes with Maotai, a fragrant clear liquor that is associated with the southwestern province of Gui Zhou. Maotai is packaged in a fancy box with a glass bottle inside. Alcohol is "the" gift that the Chinese take when visiting friends. Depending on the quality, a single bottle of Maotai can cost anywhere from $25 to more than $1,000.

communication strategy must be carefully coordinated.[1] For example, Nike has embraced the IMC concept. Trevor Edwards is Nike's vice president for global brand and category management. He notes:

> We create demand for our brand by being flexible about how we tell the story. We do not rigidly stay with one approach . . . We have an integrated marketing model that involves all elements of the marketing mix from digital to sports marketing, from event marketing to advertising to entertainment, all sitting at the table driving ideas.[2]

This chapter examines advertising and public relations from the perspective of the global marketer. Chapter 14 covers sales promotion, personal selling, event marketing and sponsorships. As you study these chapters, keep Edwards's words in mind: All the communication tools described here should be used in a way that reinforces a consistent message about a product, brand, or company.

GLOBAL ADVERTISING

Advertising may be defined as any sponsored, paid message that is communicated in a nonpersonal way. Some advertising messages are designed to communicate with persons in a single country or market area. Regional or pan-regional advertising is created for audiences across several country

1 Thomas R. Duncan and Stephen E. Everett, "Client Perception of Integrated Marketing Communications," *Journal of Advertising Research* (May–June 1993), pp. 119–122; see also Stephen J. Gould, Dawn B. Lerman, and Andreas F. Grein, "Agency Perceptions and Practices on Global IMC," *Journal of Advertising Research* 39, no. 1 (January–February 1999), pp. 7–20.
2 Gavin O'Malley, "Who's Leading the Way in Web Marketing? It's Nike, Of Course," *Advertising Age* (October 26, 2006), p. D3.

markets, such as Europe or Latin America. **Global advertising** may be defined as messages whose art, copy, headlines, photographs, tag lines, and other elements have been developed expressly for their worldwide suitability. In addition to Diageo, other companies that have used global themes include McDonald's ("I'm lovin' it"), ("Solutions for a small planet"), De Beers ("A diamond is forever"), BP ("Beyond Petroleum"), and Vodafone ("Your voice"). In Chapter 10, we noted that some global companies simultaneously offer local, international, and global products and brands to buyers in different parts of the world. The same is true with advertising: A global company may use single-country advertising in addition to campaigns that are regional and global in scope.

A global company that has the ability to successfully transform a domestic campaign into a worldwide one, or to create a new global campaign from the ground up, possesses a critical marketing advantage. The search for a global advertising campaign should bring together everyone involved with the product to share information and leverage their experiences. Global campaigns with unified themes can help to build long-term product and brand identities and offer significant savings by reducing the cost associated with producing ads. Regional market areas such as Europe are experiencing an influx of standardized global brands as companies align themselves for a united region by making acquisitions and evaluating production plans and pricing policies. From a marketing point of view, there is a great deal of activity going on that will make brands truly pan-European in a short period of time. This phenomenon is accelerating the growth of global advertising.

The potential for effective global advertising also increases as companies recognize and embrace new concepts such as "product cultures." An example is the globalization of beer culture, which can be seen in the popularity of German-style beer halls in Japan and Irish-style pubs in the United States. Similarly, the globalization of coffee culture has created market opportunities for companies such as Starbucks. Companies also realize that some market segments can be defined on the basis of global demography—youth culture, for example—rather than ethnic or national culture. Athletic shoes and other clothing items, for instance, can be targeted to a worldwide segment of 18- to 25-year-old males. William Roedy, global chairman of MTV Networks, sees clear implications of such product cultures for advertising. MTV is just one of the media vehicles that enable people virtually anywhere to see how the rest of the world lives and to learn about products that are popular in other cultures.

According to data compiled by ZenithOptimedia, worldwide advertising expenditures in 2005 exceeded $400 billion. Because advertising is often designed to add psychological value to a product or brand, it plays a more important communications role in marketing consumer products than in marketing industrial products. Frequently purchased, low-cost products generally require heavy promotional support, which often takes the form of reminder advertising. Consumer products companies top the list of big global advertising spenders. P&G, Unilever, L'Oréal, and Nestlé are companies whose "globalness" can be inferred from the significant proportion of advertising expenditures outside the home-country markets. *Advertising Age*'s ranking of global marketers in terms of advertising expenditures is shown in Table 13-1. The top 100 advertisers spent nearly $100 billion in 2005; in addition, the top 100 spent $47.5 billion on U.S. advertising. A close examination of Table 13-1 provides clues to the extent of a company's globalization efforts. For example, packaged-goods giants P&G and Unilever spend significant amounts in all major world regions. By contrast, the table shows that the geographic scope of the United Kingdom's Vodafone is largely limited to Europe and Asia.

the rest of the story

Marketing Scotch Whiskey in China

BBH's Orlando Hooper-Greenhill explains the insights that were incorporated into the campaign. He says, "Johnnie Walker's marketing in China needed to reflect the importance of peer group and family perceptions of an individual's achievements, while also accommodating the fact that whiskey is a youthful drink." Hooper-Greenhill also notes that, in China, whiskey is consumed in a wider variety of settings than in the West. In Hooper-Greenhill's words, "Different messages were needed to reflect the different environments in which whiskey is consumed, and for more and less urbanized areas."

Market segmentation is an integral part of Diageo's approach to the Chinese market. As Kenneth MacPherson, managing director for Diageo China, notes, "The size of the market and the complex demographic composition leads to totally different consumption habits and patterns in different parts of China." The first segment, *guanxi* men, are status-driven business men aged 35 to 45 who spent a great deal of time networking and trying to set up business deals. The second segment is "strong independent women," also in the 35-to-45 age bracket. A third segment is comprised of upwardly mobile 25-to-35-year-old men and women who want to be seen as cutting edge. Finally, "the choice generation" consists of those in their twenties who seek out new experiences.

Although Johnnie Walker has achieved great success in China, the brand is in second place behind Chivas Regal, which commands a 50 percent market share. For decades, Chivas enjoyed a global reputation as *the* deluxe Scotch whiskey. As was the case with Johnnie Walker, the brand's promotional strategy also frequently called for global advertising campaigns. For example, in the early 1990s a print campaign was keyed to the slogan "There will always be a Chivas Regal." The campaign featured a series of universal images and was translated into 15 languages. Managers in each of 34 countries were authorized to choose individual ads from the campaign that they deemed appropriate for their markets.

In 2000, France's Pernod Ricard SA acquired the Chivas Regal brand from Seagram. Between 2000 and 2002, Chivas experienced a 10 percent overall decline in sales volume, while Johnnie Walker posted a 12 percent gain. Prior to the acquisition, Pernod Ricard was best known for Ricard, an anise-flavored beverage known as *pastis*. Some industry observers questioned whether a company that had focused on so-called "second tier" local brands had the marketing skills to reinvigorate a truly global brand such as Chivas. As one analyst put it, "Pernod Ricard was a very big French company that has joined the big time. Now they're taking on the big global brands, which requires different skills. The question is, do they have the skills that it takes?"

Ricard chairman Patrick Ricard is confident that the management team at Pernod Ricard does have the skills required to succeed in the global marketplace against giants such as Diageo. For one thing, the company's decentralized strategy is well matched to an industry sector characterized by local tastes. Unlike Diageo, Ricard passed over British advertising agencies in favor of TBWA Paris. *Impact*, an industry trade magazine, observed that "When you know," the enigmatic slogan developed for Seagram's final Chivas advertising campaign, was "utterly ineffective." As Martin Riley, international marketing director of Ricard's Chivas Brothers unit, explained, "When you get to a lot of countries that are not primarily English-speaking, like those in Asia or South America, they would like you to fill in the dots." A new slogan, "This is the Chivas life," was designed to appeal to the aspirations of Chivas drinkers throughout the world.

In China, the tagline "This is the Chivas Life" was replaced in 2005 by "This is the Chivas Party Experience." TEQUILA/China, the agency that developed the theme, wanted to target more cosmopolitan, affluent young adults. The agency's research indicated an aspiration for leisure and travel. The agency developed a communication program centered on a series of parties that were staged in Shanghai, Beijing, and other key cities. Each party had a distinct theme; one was dubbed "Chivas 2070 Futuristic Life," while another was called "Chivas Life 70s Psychedelic Disco Fever." Partygoers could sample Chivas cocktails, enjoy fashion makeovers, and listen to cutting-edge music.

Sources: Andrew Bolger, "Whiskey Finds New Lovers in New Markets," Financial Times (February 17–18, 2007), p. 9; Meg Carter, "Diageo Splashes Out on China's Whiskey Drinkers," Financial Times (November 14, 2006), p. 6; "Chivas Regal," Media Asia (October 21, 2005); R. W. Apple Jr., "A Rugged Drink for a Rugged Land," The New York Times (July 16, 2003), pp. D1, D7; Adam Jones, "Pernod Mulls Next Wave of Consolidation," Financial Times (March 9, 2004), p. 14; Deborah Ball, "Scotch on the Rocks? 'Single Malt' Diversifies," The Wall Street Journal (December 30, 2003), pp. B1, B4; Adam Jones, "Global Media Campaign Aims to Stress the Importance of Being Chivas," Financial Times—Scotch Whiskey Special Report (November 28, 2003), p. 10; Deborah Ball, "Pernod Acquisition Has Mixed Well," The Wall Street Journal (November 11, 2002), p. B3.

Global advertising also offers companies economies of scale in advertising as well as improved access to distribution channels. Where shelf space is at a premium, a company has to convince retailers to carry its products rather than those of competitors. A global brand supported by global advertising may be very attractive because, from the retailer's standpoint, a global brand is less likely to languish on the shelves. Landor Associates, a company specializing in brand identity and design, recently determined that Coke has the number one brand-awareness and esteem position in the United States, number two in Japan, and number six in Europe. However, standardization is not always required or even advised. Nestlé's Nescafé coffee is marketed as a global brand, even though advertising messages and product formulation vary to suit cultural differences.

Table 13-1

Top 25 Global Marketers, 2005 ($ millions)

Company/ Headquarters	Worldwide Ad Spending	U.S. Ad Spending	Asia Ad Spending*	Europe Ad Spending	Latin America Ad Spending
1. Procter & Gamble (U.S.)	8,190	3,410	1,743	2,553	216
2. Unilever (UK, Netherlands)	4,272	761	1,048	2,107	227
3. General Motors Corp. (U.S.)	4,173	3,004	138	800	92
4. Toyota Motor Corp. (Japan)	2,800	1,076	1,096	511	19
5. L'Oréal (France)	2,773	794	236	1,633	35
6. Ford Motor Co. (U.S.)	2,645	1,583	108	801	69
7. Time Warner (U.S.)	2,479	2,061	91	272	20
8. DaimlerChrysler (U.S., Germany)	2,104	1,590	46	375	32
9. Nestlé (Switzerland)	2,033	561	274	1,048	105
10. Johnson & Johnson (U.S.)	1,968	1,386	190	324	17
11. Honda Motor Co. (Japan)	1,854	861	781	159	13
12. Walt Disney Co. (U.S.)	1,813	1,413	117	245	1
13. Nissan Motor Co. (Japan)	1,778	1,023	488	173	30
14. Coca-Cola Co. (U.S.)	1,752	471	421	660	119
15. Altria Group (U.S.)	1,690	1,189	43	404	11
16. PepsiCo (U.S.)	1,644	1,129	150	210	91
17. GlaxoSmithKline (UK)	1,610	1,163	102	282	33
18. Sony Corp. (Japan)	1,607	996	259	275	11
19. McDonald's Corp (U.S.)	1,554	765	312	394	27
20. Volkswagen (Germany)	1,547	425	29	1,009	48
21. Reckitt Benckiser (UK)	1,408	256	140	948	24
22. Vodafone Group (UK)	1,329	0	538	774	0
23. Deutsche Telekom (Germany)	1,319	526	0	790	0
24. Danone Group (France)	1,291	80	10	1,123	56
25. General Electric Co. (U.S.)	1,282	1,131	17	98	0

*Asia includes Australia and New Zealand
Source: *Advertising Age* (November 20, 2006).

Global Advertising Content: The "Standardization" Versus "Adaptation" Debate

Communication experts generally agree that the overall requirements of effective communication and persuasion are fixed and do not vary from country to country. The same thing is true of the components of the communication process: The marketer is the source of the message; the message must be encoded, conveyed via the appropriate channel(s), and decoded by a member of the target audience. Communication takes place only when the intended meaning transfers from the source to the receiver. Four major difficulties can compromise an organization's attempt to communicate with customers in any location:

1. The message may not get through to the intended recipient. This problem may be the result of an advertiser's lack of knowledge about appropriate media for reaching certain types of audiences.
2. The message may reach the target audience but may not be understood or may even be misunderstood. This can be the result of an inadequate understanding of the target audience's level of sophistication or improper encoding.
3. The message may reach the target audience and may be understood but still may not compel the recipient to take action. This could result from a lack of cultural knowledge about a target audience.

4. The effectiveness of the message can be impaired by *noise*. Noise in this case is an external influence such as competitive advertising, other sales personnel, and confusion at the receiving end. These factors can detract from the ultimate effectiveness of the communication.

The key question for global marketers is whether the *specific* advertising message and media strategy must be changed from region to region or country to country because of environmental requirements. Proponents of the "one world, one voice" approach to global advertising believe that the era of the global village has arrived and that tastes and preferences are converging worldwide. According to the standardization argument, people everywhere want the same products for the same reasons. This means that companies can achieve significant economies of scale by unifying advertising around the globe. Advertisers who prefer the localized approach are skeptical of the global village argument. Instead, they assert that consumers still differ from country to country and must be reached by advertising tailored to their respective countries. Proponents of localization point out that most blunders occur because advertisers have failed to understand—and adapt to—foreign cultures. A decade ago, Nick Brien, managing director of Leo Burnett, explained the situation this way:

> As the potency of traditional media declines on a daily basis, brand building locally becomes more costly and international brand building becomes more cost effective. The challenge for advertisers and agencies is finding ads that work in different countries and cultures. At the same time as this global tendency, there is a growing local tendency. It's becoming increasingly important to understand the requirements of both.[3]

During the 1950s, the widespread opinion among advertising professionals was that effective international advertising required assigning responsibility for campaign preparation to a local agency. In the early 1960s, this idea of local delegation was repeatedly challenged. For example, Eric Elinder, head of a Swedish advertising agency, wrote: "Why should three artists in three different countries sit drawing the same electric iron and three copywriters write about what, after all, is largely the same copy for the same iron?"[4] Elinder argued that consumer differences between countries were diminishing and that he would more effectively serve a client's interest by putting top specialists to work devising a strong international campaign. The campaign would then be presented with insignificant modifications that mainly entailed translating the copy into language well suited for a particular country.

As the decade of the 1980s began, Pierre Liotard-Vogt, then-CEO of Nestlé, expressed similar views in an interview with *Advertising Age*.

Advertising Age: Are food tastes and preferences different in each of the countries in which you do business?

Liotard-Vogt: The two countries where we are selling perhaps the most instant coffee are England and Japan. Before the war they didn't drink coffee in those countries, and I heard people say that it wasn't any use to try to sell instant coffee to the English because they drink only tea and still less to the Japanese because they drink green tea and they're not interested in anything else.

---

3 Meg Carter, "Think Globally, Act Locally," *Financial Times* (June 30, 1997), p. 12.
4 Eric Elinder, "International Advertisers Must Devise Universal Ads, Dump Separate National Ones, Swedish Ad Man Avers," *Advertising Age* (November 27, 1961), p. 91.

When I was very young, I lived in England and at that time, if you spoke to an Englishman about eating spaghetti or pizza or anything like that, he would just look at you and think that the stuff was perhaps food for Italians. Now on the corner of every road in London you find pizzerias and spaghetti houses.

So I do not believe [preconceptions] about "national tastes." They are "habits," and they're not the same. If you bring the public a different food, even if it is unknown initially, when they get used to it, they will enjoy it too.

To a certain extent we know that in the north they like a coffee milder and a bit acid and less roasted; in the south, they like it very dark. So I can't say that taste differences don't exist. But to believe that those tastes are set and can't be changed is a mistake.[5]

The "standardized versus localized" debate picked up tremendous momentum after the 1983 publication, noted in earlier chapters, of Professor Ted Levitt's *Harvard Business Review* article, "The Globalization of Markets." Recently, global companies have embraced a technique known as **pattern advertising**. This is analogous to the concept of global product platforms discussed in Chapter 10. Representing a middle ground between 100 percent standardization and 100 percent adaptation, a pattern strategy calls for developing a basic pan-regional or global communication concept for which copy, artwork, or other elements can be adapted as required for individual country markets. For example, ads in a European print campaign for Boeing shared basic design elements, but the copy and the visual elements were localized on a country-by-country basis.

Much of the research on this issue has focused on the match between advertising messages and local culture. For example, Ali Kanso surveyed two different groups of advertising managers; those adopting localized approaches to advertising and those adopting standardized approaches. One finding was that managers who are attuned to cultural issues tended to prefer the localized approach, whereas managers less sensitive to cultural issues preferred a standardized approach.[6] Bruce Steinberg, ad sales director for MTV Europe, discovered that the people responsible for executing global campaigns locally can exhibit strong resistance to a global campaign. Steinberg reported that he sometimes had to visit as many as 20 marketing directors from the same company to get approval for a pan-European MTV ad.[7]

As Kanso correctly notes, the debate over advertising approaches will probably continue for years to come. Localized and standardized advertising both have their place and both will continue to be used. Kanso's conclusion: What is needed for successful international advertising is a global commitment to local vision. In the final analysis, the decision of whether to use a global or localized campaign depends on recognition by managers of the trade-offs involved. On the one hand, a global campaign will result in the substantial benefits of cost savings, increased control, and the potential creative leverage of a global appeal. On the other hand, localized campaigns focus on the most important attributes of a product or brand in each nation or culture. The question of *when* to use each approach depends on the product involved and a company's objectives in a particular market. Localized ads are less likely to be required for industrial products or for technology-oriented products sold to either consumers or business customers.

"I can think of very few truly global ads that work. Brands are often at different stages around the world, and that means there are different advertising jobs to do."[8]

Michael Conrad, Chief Creative Officer, Leo Burnett Worldwide

"If we could find one message on a global basis it could be effective, but so far there are different needs in different countries. We have been in Sweden for 60 years and in China for only four or five so our feeling is that retail is local. It is important to take advantage of local humor, and the things on people's minds."[9]

Nils Larsson, Manager, External Communications, IKEA

5   "A Conversation with Nestlé's Pierre Liotard-Vogt," *Advertising Age* (June 30, 1980), p. 31.
6   Ali Kanso, "International Advertising Strategies: Global Commitment to Local Vision," *Journal of Advertising Research* 32, no. 1 (January–February 1992), pp. 10–14.
7   Ken Wells, "Selling to the World: Global Ad Campaigns, After Many Missteps, Finally Pay Dividends," *The Wall Street Journal* (August 27, 1992), p. A1.
8   Vanessa O'Connell, "Exxon 'Centralizes' New Global Campaign," *The Wall Street Journal* (July 11, 2001), p. B6.
9   Emma Hall and Normandy Madden, "IKEA Courts Buyers with Offbeat Ideas," *Advertising Age* (April 12, 2004), p. 1.

By contrast, marketing and advertising managers at Pioneer Hi-Bred International frequently use both global and localized advertising executions. It is management's belief that some messages lend themselves to straight translation, while others need to be created in a way that is suited to the people, marketplace, and style of the particular country or region. Of the ads shown here, the top is for the United States, and the ad on the bottom was created for Québec.

"Eighteen-year olds in Paris have more in common with 18-year-olds in New York than with their own parents. They buy the same products, go to the same movies, listen to the same music, sip the same colas. Global advertising merely works on that premise."[10]

William Roedy, Global Chairman, MTV Networks

---

[10] Ken Wells, "Selling to the World: Global Ad Campaigns, after Many Missteps, Finally Pay Dividends," *The Wall Street Journal* (August 27, 1992), p. A1.

ADVERTISING AGENCIES: ORGANIZATIONS AND BRANDS

Advertising is a fast-paced business, and the ad agency world is fluid and dynamic. New agencies are formed, existing agencies are dismantled, and cross-border investment, spin-offs, joint ventures, and mergers and acquisitions are a fact of life. There is also a great deal of mobility in the industry as executives and top talent move from one agency to another. Table 13-2 shows the 20 largest global **advertising organizations** ranked by 2005 gross income. The key to understanding the table is the word *organization*; each firm identified in Table 13-2 is an umbrella corporation or holding company that includes one or more "core" advertising agencies, as well as units specializing in direct marketing, marketing services, public relations, or research. As shown in Figure 13-1, the family tree of Omnicom Group is quite complex. The group includes three core agencies: BBDO Worldwide, DDB Worldwide Communications, and TBWA Worldwide; each agency, in turn, has a global network. Omnicom also has one agency, Proximity, whose work is mostly outside the United States; Omnicom also owns several marketing services units, including Rapp Collins Worldwide, as well as Agency.com and other interactive agencies. Omnicom generates about 44 percent of annual revenues from advertising and media; public relations accounts for 10 percent, and CRM for 34.5 percent. Specialty services such as health care advertising account for the remaining 11.8 percent of revenues.

Table 13-3 presents the rankings of individual agencies (agency "brands") by 2005 worldwide income. Most of the agency brands identified in Table 13-3 are *full-service agencies*: In addition to creating advertising, they provide other services such as market research, media buying, and direct marketing. The agencies listed in Table 13-3 are all owned by larger holding companies; in addition to Omnicom Group, Interpublic, WPP, and Publicis are all represented by agency brands in the top 10 ranking.

Companies can create ads in-house, use an outside agency, or combine both strategies. For example, Chanel, Benetton, H&M, and Diesel rely on in-house marketing and advertising staffs for creative work; Coca-Cola has its own agency, Edge Creative, but also uses the services of outside agencies such as Leo Burnett. When one or more outside agencies are used, they can serve product accounts on a multicountry or even global basis. It is possible to select a local agency in each national market or an agency with both domestic and overseas offices. Like Coca-Cola, Levi Strauss and Polaroid also use local agencies. Today, however, there is a growing tendency for Western clients to designate global agencies for product accounts to support the integration of the marketing and advertising functions; Japan-based companies are less inclined to use this approach. For example, in 1995, Colgate-Palmolive consolidated its $500 million in global billings with Young & Rubicam. That same year, IBM consolidated its ad account with Ogilvy & Mather for the launch of the "Solutions for a small planet" global campaign. Similarly, Bayer AG consolidated most of its $300 million consumer products advertising with BBDO Worldwide; Bayer had previously relied on 50 agencies around the globe. Agencies are aware of this trend and are themselves pursuing international acquisitions and joint ventures to extend their geographic reach and their ability to serve clients on a global account basis. In an effort to remain competitive, many small independent agencies in Europe, Asia, and the United States belong to the Transworld Advertising Agency Network (TAAN). TAAN allows member agencies to tap into worldwide resources that would not otherwise be available to them.

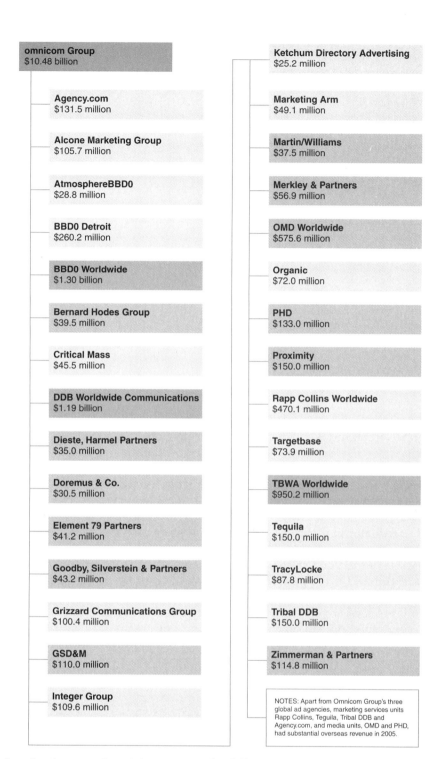

Figure 13-1

Omnicom Group "Family Tree"

omnicom Group $10.48 billion	**Ketchum Directory Advertising** $25.2 million
Agency.com $131.5 million	**Marketing Arm** $49.1 million
Alcone Marketing Group $105.7 million	**Martin/Williams** $37.5 million
AtmosphereBBD0 $28.8 million	**Merkley & Partners** $56.9 million
BBD0 Detroit $260.2 million	**OMD Worldwide** $575.6 million
BBD0 Worldwide $1.30 billion	**Organic** $72.0 million
Bernard Hodes Group $39.5 million	**PHD** $133.0 million
Critical Mass $45.5 million	**Proximity** $150.0 million
DDB Worldwide Communications $1.19 billion	**Rapp Collins Worldwide** $470.1 million
Dieste, Harmel Partners $35.0 million	**Targetbase** $73.9 million
Doremus & Co. $30.5 million	**TBWA Worldwide** $950.2 million
Element 79 Partners $41.2 million	**Tequila** $150.0 million
Goodby, Silverstein & Partners $43.2 million	**TracyLocke** $87.8 million
Grizzard Communications Group $100.4 million	**Tribal DDB** $150.0 million
GSD&M $110.0 million	**Zimmerman & Partners** $114.8 million
Integer Group $109.6 million	

NOTES: Apart from Omnicom Group's three global ad agencies, marketing services units Rapp Collins, Tequila, Tribal DDB and Agency.com, and media units, OMD and PHD, had substantial overseas revenue in 2005.

In selecting an advertising agency, the following issues should be considered:

Company organization. Companies that are decentralized may want to leave the choice to the local subsidiary.

National responsiveness. Is the global agency familiar with local culture and buying habits in a particular country or should a local selection be made?

Area coverage. Does the candidate agency cover all relevant markets?

Buyer perception. What kind of brand awareness does the company want to project? If the product needs a strong local identification, it would be best to select a national agency.

Table 13-2

Top 20 Global Advertising Organizations

Organization and Headquarters Location	Worldwide Revenue 2005 (millions)
1. Omnicom Group (New York)	$10,481.1
2. WPP Group (London)	10,032.2
3. Interpublic Group of Cos. (New York)	6,274.3
4. Publicis Group (Paris)	5,107.2
5. Dentsu (Tokyo)	2,887.8
6. Havas (Suresnes, France)	1,808.0
7. Aegis Group (London)	1,577.6
8. Hakuhodo DY Holdings (Tokyo)	1,364.0
9. Asatsu-DK (Tokyo)	444.8
10. MDC Partners (Toronto/New York)	443.5
11. Carlson Marketing Group (Minneapolis)	370.0
12. Sapient Corp. (Cambridge, MA)	358.4
13. Digitas (Boston)	340.5
14. aQuantive (Seattle)	258.4
15. Aspen Marketing Services (West Chicago, IL)	229.0
16. Media Square (London)	215.0
17. HealthSTAR Communications (Woodbridge, NJ)	213.0
18. Cheil Communications (Seoul)	210.7
19. George P. Johnson Co. (Auburn Hills, MI)	193.0
20. Epsilon (Wakefield, MA)	184.4

Source: "World's Top 25 Ad Organizations," *Advertising Age* (May 1, 2006), p. S-2.

Despite an unmistakable trend toward using global agencies to support global marketing efforts, companies with geocentric orientations will adapt to the global market requirements and select the best agency or agencies accordingly. Western agencies still find markets such as China and Japan very complex; similarly, Asian agencies find it just as difficult to establish local agency presence in Western markets.

As noted later in the chapter, advertising professionals face escalating pressure to achieve new heights of creativity. Some critics of advertising complain that agencies sometimes try to create advertising that will win awards and generate acclaim and prestige rather than advertising that serves clients' needs. The search for fresh answers to promotion challenges has prompted some client companies to look to new sources for creative ideas. For example, McDonald's historically relied on American agencies for basic creative direction. However, Larry Light, global marketing chief, staged a competition that included agencies from all over the world. A German agency devised the "i'm lovin' it"

Table 13-3

Top 10 Global Advertising Agency Brands

Agency	Estimated Worldwide Revenue 2005 (millions)
1. McCann-Erickson Worldwide (Interpublic)	$1,461.1
2. JWT (WPP)	1,313.5
3. BBDO Worldwide (Omnicom)	1,295.7
4. DDB Worldwide Communications (Omnicom)	1,190.6
5. Publicis (Publicis)	1,083.2
6. TBWA Worldwide (Omnicom)	950.2
7. Leo Burnett Worldwide (Publicis)	807.3
8. Ogilvy & Mather Worldwide (WPP)	801.4
9. Grey Worldwide (WPP)	629.1
10. Saatchi & Saatchi (Publicis)	551.8

Source: Adapted from "World's Top 10 Core Agency Brands," *Advertising Age* (May 1, 2006), p. S-2.

> **Wall Street Journal:** "As a global marketer, do you believe in using a single global ad agency to serve all your marketing and media needs?"
>
> **Peter Weedfald, Samsung Electronics, senior vice president of strategic marketing, North America:** "The responsibility of messaging for advertising, marketing and communications ought to come from inside the company. If you can find yourself a champion agency that can actually execute, that's magnificent. The problem for the agencies is that sometimes they come in and talk about advertising and maybe the client doesn't get it, or vice versa. We work with Interpublic Group's Foote Cone & Belding which we are very proud of, and our internal agency."
>
> Source: Ellen Byron, "Samsung Official Prepares for Consumer-Electronics Fight," The Wall Street Journal (December 24, 2003), p. B3.

tagline.[11] Leo Burnett China's ideas included a hand signal for McDonald's global campaign. As Light noted, "China just blew our minds. We didn't expect that kind of expression and joy. Our expectation was for more conservatism, much less individuality, and more caution."[12]

CREATING GLOBAL ADVERTISING

As suggested earlier in the discussion of the extension versus standardization debate, the *message* is at the heart of advertising. The particular message and the way it is presented will depend on the advertiser's objective. Is the ad designed to inform, entertain, remind, or persuade? Moreover, in a world characterized by information overload, ads must break through the clutter, grab the audience's attention, and linger in their minds. This requires developing an original and effective **creative strategy**, which is simply a statement or concept of what a particular message or campaign will say. Advertising agencies can be thought of as "idea factories"; in industry parlance, the Holy Grail in creative strategy development is something known as the **big idea**. Legendary ad man John O'Toole defined the *big idea* as "that flash of insight that synthesizes the purpose of the strategy, joins the product benefit with consumer desire in a fresh, involving way, brings the subject to life, and makes the reader or audience stop, look, and listen."[13] In his book about Subaru of America, Randall Rothenberg describes the big idea in the following way:

> The Big Idea is easier to illustrate than define, and easier to illustrate by what it is not than by what it is. It is not a "position" (although the place a product occupies in the consumer's mind may be a part of it). It is not an "execution" (although the writing or graphic style of an ad certainly contributes to it). It is not a slogan (although a tag line may encapsulate it).
>
> The Big Idea is the bridge between an advertising strategy, temporal and worldly, and an image, powerful and lasting. The theory of the Big Idea assumes that average consumers are at best bored and more likely irrational when it comes to deciding what to buy.[14]

Some of the world's most memorable advertising campaigns have achieved success because they originate from an idea that is so "big" that the campaign

---

[11] Erin White and Shirley Leung, "How Tiny German Shop Landed McDonald's," *The Wall Street Journal* (August 6, 2003), pp. B1, B3.
[12] Geoffrey A. Fowler, "Commercial Break: The Art of Selling," *Far Eastern Economic Review* (October 30, 2003), pp. 30–33.
[13] John O'Toole, *The Trouble with Advertising* (New York: Random House, 1985), p. 131.
[14] Randall Rothenberg, *Where the Suckers Moon* (New York: Vintage Books, 1995), pp. 112–113.

Regulation of Tobacco Advertising

China

In 1994, the Chinese government banned tobacco advertising from television and radio; the ban also extended to newspaper, magazine, and cinema ads. With a population of 1.3 billion people, including one-third of the world's smokers, China is a massive potential market for cigarette manufacturers at a time when Western markets are shrinking. The ban was part of China's first law of advertisements. The WHO has asked Chinese leaders to launch antismoking campaigns and impose tougher controls on cigarette smuggling and higher taxes on domestic cigarette producers. China recently agreed to ratify the UN's Framework Convention on Tobacco Control.

Central Europe

Tobacco companies face the prospect of tougher marketing regulations as countries in Central Europe work to meet requirements for entry into the EU. In the Czech Republic, the Association of Advertising Agencies (ARA) is battling a proposal to ban all cigarette advertising as of April 2001. Jiri Mikes, vice president of ARA, said his organization was not completely opposed to changes in the law, but questioned the government's implementation date since the EU's deadline for meeting tobacco advertising restrictions was not until 2006. In Lithuania, authorities began to enforce the country's three-year-old tobacco advertising ban on May 1, 2000; some newspapers printed blank pages in protest. Jurga Karmanoviene, media director for Saatchi & Saatchi Lithuania, interprets the enforcement as evidence that the government is sending a signal that it is beginning to meet EU requirements. Similar developments are occurring in Poland, Hungary, Bulgaria, and Romania.

Australia

In June 1994, the Philip Morris Company initiated legal action to overturn the Australian government's ban on cigarette advertising, contending that it infringed on the company's freedom of speech. Under legislation passed in 1992, tobacco advertising and sponsorship in Australia was phased out and banned entirely by 1996, except for international events such as Formula One racing. Philip Morris attempted to have the Commonwealth Tobacco Advertising Prohibition Act declared invalid on the grounds that the act went beyond preventing cigarette advertising and imposed a wide array of restrictions that infringe on basic rights. According to a company executive, "The Philip Morris Australian subsidiary says the anti-tobacco laws breach the Australian Constitution's implied guarantee of freedom of communication, breaches the states and is beyond the powers of the federal Government."

European Union

A union-wide tobacco ad ban proposal was introduced in mid-1991 with the aim of fulfilling single-market rules of the Maastricht Treaty. The directive would have prohibited tobacco advertising on billboards as of July 2001; newspaper and magazine advertising was slated to end by 2002, with sports sponsorship banned by 2003 (such "world level" sports as Formula One racing would be excluded until 2006). Tobacco companies and advertising associations opposed the proposed ban. The European Commission justified the directive on the grounds that various countries had or were considering restrictions on tobacco advertising and that there was a need for common rules on cross-border trade. Prior to the directive's implementation date, however, the German government took the issue to the European Court of Justice. The Germans argued that the directive was illegal because tobacco advertising is a health issue; thus, the directive could only be adopted if the member states agreed unanimously. The EU's advocate general concurred with the German government. On October 5, 2000, the court ruled that the directive prohibiting tobacco ads should be annulled. A revised directive concerning cross-border tobacco advertising was adopted in December 2002; it went into effect in August 2005. However, the German government challenged the new directive at the European Court of Justice on the grounds that it would restrict single-country print advertisements for local cigarette brands. Even so, by 2006 the German government was working on a bill to ban tobacco advertising.

For R.J. Reynolds International, Philip Morris International, B.A.T, and other tobacco marketers, the receding threat of a pan-European ban on tobacco ads comes as welcome news. The industry spends between $600 million and $1 billion on advertising in the EU annually. An EU ban would have hurt them most in the countries where they compete with entrenched state tobacco monopolies, namely, France, Italy, and Spain.

Sources: Geoffrey A. Fowler, "Treaty May Stub Out Cigarette Ads in China," The Wall Street Journal (December 2, 2003), pp. B1, B6; Joyce-Ann Gatsoulis, "EU Aspirants Shake Up Tobacco Marketing Scene," Advertising Age International (July 2000), p. 15; Tony Koenderman and Paul Meller, "EU Topples Tobacco Ad Rules," Advertising Age (October 9, 2000), pp. 4, 97; Juliana Koranteng, "EU Ad Ban on Tobacco Under Fire as Illegal," Advertising Age (July 10, 2000), pp. 4, 49; "Australia's Ad Ban Is Fought," The New York Times (June 7, 1994), p. 19; Marcus Brauchli, "China Passes Law in Move to Prohibit Ads for Tobacco," The Wall Street Journal, (October 31, 1994), p. B10; Lili Cui, "Mass Media Boycott Tobacco Ads," Beijing Review (June 6, 1994) p. 8; "Tobacco Adverts: Fuming," Economist (February 5, 1994), pp. 60–61.

offers opportunities for a variety of new executions. Such a campaign is said to have *legs* because it can be used for long periods of time. The print campaign for Absolut vodka is a perfect example: Over the course two decades, Absolut's agency has created hundreds of two-word puns on the brand name linked with various pictoral renderings of the distinctive bottle shape. Other campaigns based on Big Ideas include MSN ("Life's better with the butterfly") and MasterCard ("There are some things in life money can't buy"). In 2003, McDonald's executives launched a search for an idea "big" enough to be used in multiple country markets even as the company faces disapproval in some countries from consumers who link it to unpopular U.S. government policies (see Case 1-1).

The **advertising appeal** is the communications approach that relates to the motives of the target audience. For example, ads based on a **rational appeal** depend on logic and speak to the audience's intellect. Rational appeals are based on consumers' needs for information. Ads using an **emotional appeal** may tug at the heartstrings or tickle the funny bone of the intended audience and evoke a feeling response that will direct purchase behavior. The message elements in a particular ad will depend in part on which appeal is being employed. The **selling proposition** is the promise or claim that captures the reason for buying the product or the benefit that ownership confers. Because products are frequently at different stages in their life cycle in various national markets, and because of cultural, social, and economic differences that exist in those markets, the most effective appeal or selling proposition for a product may vary from market to market.

BRIC Briefing Book

Localizing Ad Executions in China

A creative challenge presented to Ogilvy & Mather in China illustrates the relationship between creative strategy, appeal, and execution. The client, Coca-Cola's Fanta, wanted a national TV ad that would communicate to consumers that Fanta is an antidote to everyday pressures on Chinese youth. This was the overall creative strategy; in other words, what the message should say. What type of appeal would be appropriate? Soft drinks lend themselves especially well to emotional appeals; that was the appeal Ogilvy & Mather preferred. The next step was to choose a specific execution. Soft drink marketers often utilize slice-of-life and fantasy executions, usually injected with an element of fun or humor. As Jeff Delkin, Ogilvy's regional business director in Shanghai, notes, for a U.S. ad, the creative strategy could be executed with a teen's fantasy or images of revenge on a mean teacher. However, in China, it is not acceptable to challenge or undermine the position of authority figures. The completed ad shows that drinking Fanta can create a fun experience in a classroom. When a student opens a can of Fanta, oranges begin to rain down. The teacher catches the oranges and juggles them—much to the delight of the students.

Another example is a Nike campaign created by Wieden & Kennedy in China. Nike's "Just Do It" ads typically showcase famous athletes and sports heroes and are legendary for their inspirational appeals. The selling proposition is universal—Nike is a "cool" brand. However, a localized execution of a Nike ad that featured Chinese superstar Wang Zhizhi did not connect with consumers; they prefer to draw inspiration from the world's best players rather than a national star who has yet to prove himself in the global arena. Nike tried a different execution with the theme "Chamber of Fear" featuring NBA star LeBron James defeating a kung fu master. This spot was banned after consumer complaints. In 2006, Nike launched a new campaign that featured Chinese youths who had overcome personal obstacles to excel at sports. Young people were encouraged to share their stories at Nike stores or at a Web site, www.nike.com.cn/justdoit. Visitors to the Web site can also view short, three- to four-minute films featuring Chinese youths playing sports in well-known locales. Shortened versions of the clips are used as TV ads. As Jesse Lin, Wieden's managing director in Shanghai, said, "China's younger generation is in the midst of forming its own style, mixing together Chinese elements and influences they've absorbed from the West, but they don't think they need to learn from the West. Nike realized this and wants to be a part of this new generation, rather than telling them what to do."

McDonald's also used a localized campaign for the Chinese launch of the Quarter Pounder sandwich; ironically, the campaign came as the fast-food giant removed menu items such as an Asian-style chicken or beef wrap with rice created to appeal to Chinese tastes. Beef is considered a luxury, upscale item in China; beef also is perceived to boost energy and heighten sex appeal. In Chinese, the word *beef* connotes manliness, strength, and skill. Television commercials for the Quarter Pounder have sex appeal: They include close-ups of a woman's neck and mouth juxtaposed with images of fireworks and spraying water. The voice-over says, "You can feel it. Thicker. You can taste it. Juicier." Print ads also conveyed sexual innuendo. One execution features a "beauty shot" of a Quarter Pounder with an extreme close up of a woman's mouth in the background. The copy reads, "Part of your body will be excited. You will feel 100 percent of the beef." As Jeffrey Schwartz, the head of McDonald's Chinese operations, explains, "Our customers are young, modern, and bilingual. If we're not edgy in communications, out front in technology, this consumer is going to blow right by us."

Sources: Gordon Fairclough and Janet Adamy, "Sex, Skin, Fireworks, Licked Fingers—It's a Quarter Pounder Ad in China," The Wall Street Journal (September 21, 2006), pp. B1, B2; Geoffrey A. Fowler, "Commercial Break: The Art of Selling," Far Eastern Economic Review (October 30, 2003), p. 32; Normandy Madden, "Nike Drops Its American Idols," Advertising Age (March 20, 2006), p. 12.

Effective global advertising may also require developing different presentations of the product's appeal or selling proposition. The way an appeal or proposition is presented is called the **creative execution**. In other words, there can be differences between *what* one says and *how* one says it. Agency personnel can choose from a variety of executions including straight sell, scientific evidence, demonstration, comparison, testimonial, slice of life, animation, fantasy, and dramatization. The responsibility for deciding on the appeal, the selling proposition, and the appropriate execution lies with **creatives**, a term that applies to art directors and copywriters.

Art Direction and Art Directors

The visual presentation of an advertisement—the "body language"—is a matter of **art direction**. The agency creative with general responsibility for the overall look of an ad is known as an art director. This individual chooses graphics, pictures, type styles, and other visual elements that appear in an ad. Some forms of visual presentation are universally understood. Revlon, for example, has used a French producer to develop television commercials in English and Spanish for use in international markets. These commercials are filmed in Parisian settings but communicate the universal appeals and specific benefits of Revlon products. By producing its ads in France, Revlon obtains effective television commercials at a much lower cost than it would have paid for commercials produced in the United States. PepsiCo has used four basic commercials to communicate its advertising themes. The basic setting of young people having fun at a party or on a beach has been adapted to reflect the general physical environment and racial characteristics of North America, South America, Europe, Africa, and Asia. The music in these commercials has also been adapted to suit regional tastes, ranging from rock and roll in North America to bossa nova in Latin America to high life in Africa.

The global advertiser must make sure that visual executions are not inappropriately extended into markets. In the mid-1990s, Benetton's United Colors of Benetton campaign generated considerable controversy. The campaign appeared in scores of countries, primarily in print and on billboards. The art direction focused on striking, provocative interracial juxtapositions—a white hand and a black hand handcuffed together, for example. Another version of the campaign, depicting a black woman nursing a white baby, won advertising awards in France and Italy. However, because the image evoked the history of slavery in the United States, that particular creative execution was not used in the U.S. market (see Case 13-1).

Copy and Copywriters

The words that are the spoken or written communication elements in advertisements are known as **copy**. **Copywriters** are language specialists who develop the headlines, subheads, and body copy used in print advertising and the scripts containing the words that are delivered by spokespeople, actors, or hired voice talents in broadcast ads. As a general rule, copy should be relatively short and avoid slang or idioms. Languages vary in terms of the number of words required to convey a given message; thus, the increased use of pictures and illustrations. Some global ads feature visual appeals that convey a specific message with minimal use of copy. Low literacy rates in many countries seriously compromise the use of print as a communications device and require greater creativity in the use of audio-oriented media.

---

[15] Elaine Sciolino, "Advertising: A Campaign to Shock the Bourgeoisie in France," *The Wall Street Journal* (January 21, 2003), p. C14.

OPEN *to* discussion

It is important to recognize overlap in the use of languages in many areas of the world (e.g., the EU, Latin America, and North America). Capitalizing on this, global advertisers can realize economies of scale by producing advertising copy with the same language and message for these markets. The success of this approach will depend in part on avoiding unintended ambiguity in the ad copy. Then again, in some situations, ad copy must be translated into the local language. Translating copy has been the subject of great debate in advertising circles. Advertising slogans often present the most difficult translation problems. The challenge of encoding and decoding slogans and tag lines in different national and cultural contexts can lead to unintentional errors. For example, the Asian version of Pepsi's "Come alive" copy line was rendered as a call to bring ancestors back from the grave.

Advertising executives may elect to prepare new copy for a foreign market in the language of the target country or to translate the original copy into the target language. A third option is to leave some (or all) copy elements in the original (home-country) language. In choosing from these alternatives, the advertiser must consider whether the intended foreign audience can receive and comprehend a translated message. Anyone with knowledge of two or more languages realizes that the ability to think in another language facilitates accurate communication. To be confident that a message will be understood correctly after it is received, one must understand the connotations of words, phrases, and sentence structures, as well as their translated meaning.

The same principle applies to advertising—perhaps to an even greater degree. A copywriter who can think in the target language and understands the consumers in the target country will be able to create the most effective appeals, organize the ideas, and craft the specific language, especially if colloquialisms, idioms, or humor are involved. For example, in southern China, McDonald's is careful not to advertise prices with multiple occurrences of the number four. The reason is simple: In Cantonese, the pronunciation of the word *four* is similar to that of the word *death*.[16] In its efforts to develop a global brand

---

[16] Jeanne Whalen, "McDonald's Cooks Worldwide Growth," *Advertising Age International* (July–August 1995), p. I4.

image, Citicorp discovered that translations of its slogan "Citi never sleeps" conveyed the meaning that Citibank had a sleeping disorder such as insomnia. Company executives decided to retain the slogan but use English throughout the world.[17]

Cultural Considerations

Knowledge of cultural diversity, especially the symbolism associated with cultural traits, is essential for creating advertising. Local country managers can share important information, such as when to use caution in advertising creativity. Use of colors and man-woman relationships can often be stumbling blocks. For example, in Japan, intimate scenes between men and women are in bad taste; they are outlawed in Saudi Arabia. Veteran adman John O'Toole offers the following insights to global advertisers:

> Transplanted American creative people always want to photograph European men kissing women's hands. But they seldom know that the nose must never touch the hand or that this rite is reserved solely for married women. And how do you know that the woman in the photograph is married? By the ring on her left hand, of course. Well, in Spain, Denmark, Holland, and Germany, Catholic women wear the wedding ring on the right hand.
>
> When photographing a couple entering a restaurant or theater, you show the woman preceding the man, correct? No. Not in Germany and France. And this would be laughable in Japan. Having someone in a commercial hold up his hand with the back of it to you, the viewer, and the fingers moving toward him should communicate "come here." In Italy it means "good-bye."[18]

Ads that strike viewers in some countries as humorous or irritating may not necessarily be perceived that way by viewers in other countries. American ads make frequent use of spokespeople and direct product comparisons; they use logical arguments to try to appeal to the reason of audiences. Japanese advertising is more image oriented and appeals to audience sentiment. In Japan, what is most important frequently is not what is stated explicitly but, rather, what is implied. Nike's U.S. advertising is legendary for its irreverent, "in your face" style and relies heavily on celebrity sports endorsers such as Michael Jordan. In other parts of the world, where soccer is the top sport, some Nike ads are considered to be in poor taste and its pitchmen have less relevance. Nike has responded by adjusting its approach; as Geoffrey Frost, former director of global advertising at Nike, noted a decade ago, "We have to root ourselves in the passions of other countries. It's part of our growing up."[19] Some American companies have canceled television ads created for the Latin American market portraying racial stereotypes that were offensive to persons of color. Nabisco, Goodyear, and other companies are also being more careful about the shows during which they buy airtime; some very popular Latin American programs feature content that exploits class, race, and ethnic differences.[20]

There are also widely varying standards for use of sexually explicit or provocative imagery. Partial nudity and same-sex couples are frequently seen in ads in Latin America and Europe. In the U.S. market, network television decency standards and

---

17   Stephen E. Frank, "Citicorp's Big Account Is at Stake as It Seeks a Global Brand Name," *The Wall Street Journal* (January 9, 1997), p. B6.
18   John O'Toole, *The Trouble with Advertising* (New York: Random House, 1985), pp. 209–210.
19   Roger Thurow, "Shtick Ball: In Global Drive, Nike Finds its Brash Ways Don't Always Pay Off," *The Wall Street Journal* (May 5, 1997), p. A10.
20   Leon E. Wynter, "Global Marketers Learn to Say 'No' to Bad Ads," *The Wall Street Journal* (April 1, 1998), p. B1.

Wall Street Journal: "For more than a decade, international marketers have focused on creating global marketing strategies. Why do you maintain the pendulum is swinging back to a more local approach?"

Sir Martin Sorrell, CEO, WPP Group: "What's happened is that companies are trying to run things in black and white ways, where one size fits all. And there's a very simple message: One size doesn't fit all. Consumers are more interesting for their differences rather than their similarities."

Wall Street Journal: "If one size doesn't fit all, should companies be marketing to certain consumer groups, such as Muslims, with specific messages?"

Sir Martin: "Yes, just as they'd market to Hispanics, Afro-Americans, or Asians. Muslims are 26 percent of the world's population today; by 2014, they will be 30 percent. That same year, two-thirds of the world's population will be Asian. Muslims are coming into sharp relief because of Iraq and Afghanistan. But the central theme is that nobody in the West has really spent enough time thinking about what differentiates the Muslim mind. We assume that if it works in New York it will work in Baghdad, but there are significant differences. There has to be more sensitivity to this issue."

Source: The Wall Street Journal (Western Edition) by Erin White and Jeffrey A. Trachtenberg. Copyright 2003 by Dow Jones & Company, Inc. Reproduced with permission of Dow Jones & Company, Inc. in the format Other book via Copyright Clearance Center.

the threat of boycotts by conservative consumer activists constrain advertisers. Some industry observers note a paradoxical situation in which the programs shown on U.S. TV are frequently racy, but the ads that air during those shows are not. As Marcio Moreira, worldwide chief creative officer at the McCann-Erickson agency, noted, "Americans want titillation in entertainment but when it comes to advertising they stop being viewers and become consumers and critics."[21] However, it is certainly not the case that anything goes outside the United States. Women in Monterrey, Mexico, recently complained about billboards for the Playtex unit of Sara Lee Corporation that featured supermodel Eva Herzegova wearing a Wonderbra. The campaign was created by a local agency, Perez Munoz Publicidad. Playtex responded by covering up the model on the billboards in some Mexican cities. French Connection UK made waves in the United States with print ads that prominently featured the British company's initials (i.e., FCUK). Public outcry prompted the company to tone down the ads by spelling out the name.

Food is the product category most likely to exhibit cultural sensitivity. Thus, marketers of food and food products must be alert to the need to localize their advertising. A good example of this is the effort by H. J. Heinz Company to develop the overseas market for ketchup. Heinz's strategy called for adapting both the product and advertising to target country tastes.[22] In Greece, for example, ads show ketchup pouring over pasta, eggs, and cuts of meat. In Japan, they instruct Japanese homemakers on using ketchup as an ingredient in Western-style food such as omelettes, sausages, and pasta. Barry Tilley, London-based general manager of Heinz's Western Hemisphere trading division, says Heinz uses focus groups to determine what foreign consumers want in the way of taste and image. Americans like a sweet ketchup, but Europeans prefer a spicier, more piquant variety. Significantly, Heinz's foreign marketing efforts are most successful when the company quickly adapts to local cultural

---

21 Melanie Wells and Dottie Enrico, "U.S. Admakers Cover It Up; Others Don't Give a Fig Leaf," *USA Today* (June 27, 1997), pp. B1, B2.
22 Gary Levin, "Ads Going Global," *Advertising Age* (July 22, 1991), pp. 4, 42.

preferences. In Sweden, the made-in-America theme is so muted in Heinz's ads that "Swedes don't realize Heinz is American. They think it is German because of the name," says Tilley. In contrast to this, American themes still work well in Germany. Kraft and Heinz are trying to outdo each other with ads featuring strong American images. In one of Heinz's TV ads, American football players in a restaurant become very angry when the 12 steaks they ordered arrive without ketchup. The ad ends happily, of course, with plenty of Heinz ketchup to go around.[23]

Much academic research has been devoted to the impact of culture on advertising. For example, Tamotsu Kishii identified seven characteristics that distinguish Japanese from American creative strategy:

1. Indirect rather than direct forms of expression are preferred in the messages. This avoidance of directness in expression is pervasive in all types of communication among the Japanese, including their advertising. Many television ads do not mention what is desirable about the brand in use and let the audience judge for themselves.
2. There is often little relationship between ad content and the advertised product.
3. Only brief dialogue or narration is used in television commercials, with minimal explanatory content. In the Japanese culture, the more one talks, the less others will perceive him or her trustworthy or self-confident. A 30-second advertisement for young menswear shows five models in varying and seasonal attire, ending with a brief statement from the narrator: "Our life is a fashion show!"
4. Humor is used to create a bond of mutual feelings. Rather than slapstick, humorous dramatizations involve family members, neighbors, and office colleagues.
5. Famous celebrities appear as close acquaintances or everyday people.
6. Priority is placed on company trust rather than product quality. Japanese tend to believe that if the firm is large and has a good image, the quality of its products should also be outstanding.
7. The product name is impressed on the viewer with short, 15-second commercials.[24]

Green, Cunningham, and Cunningham conducted a cross-cultural study to determine the extent to which consumers of different nationalities use the same criteria to evaluate soft drinks and toothpaste. Their subjects were college students from the United States, France, India, and Brazil. Compared to France and India, the U.S. respondents placed more emphasis on the subjective, as opposed to functional, product attributes. The Brazilian respondents appeared even more concerned with the subjective attributes than the Americans were. The authors concluded that advertising messages should not use the same appeal for these countries if the advertiser is concerned with communicating the most important attributes of its product in each market.[25]

23 Gabriella Stern, "Heinz Aims to Export Taste for Ketchup," *The Wall Street Journal* (November 20, 1992), p. B1.
24 C. Anthony Di Benedetto, Mariko Tamate, and Rajan Chandran, "Developing Creative Advertising Strategy for the Japanese Marketplace," *Journal of Advertising Research* (January–February 1992), pp. 39–48. A number of recent studies have been devoted to comparing ad content in different parts of the world, including Mary C. Gilly, "Sex Roles in Advertising: A Comparison of Television Advertisements in Australia, Mexico, and the United States," *Journal of Marketing* (April 1988), pp. 75–85; Marc G. Weinberger and Harlan E. Spotts, "A Situation View of Information Content in TV Advertising in the U.S. and U.K.," *Journal of Advertising* 53 (January 1989), pp. 89–94.
25 Robert T. Green, William H. Cunningham, and Isabella C. M. Cunningham, "The Effectiveness of Standardized Global Advertising," *Journal of Advertising* (Summer 1975), pp. 25–30.

In another study, Zandpour and Harich combined Hofstede's social values framework with a culture's perceptions of time (monochronic cultures focus on one thing at a time, while inhabitants of a polychronic culture do not display a preference for sequential schedules or presentation of information). Several relevant market factors were also studied, including advertising expenditures per capita, the presence or absence of U.S. advertising agencies or their affiliates, the availability of qualified advertising professionals, and the degree of government control over advertising. The researchers used these factors to group countries into "think" and "feel" clusters and predict whether rational or emotional appeals used in television advertising for food and beverage, personal care, and several other product categories would be most prevalent in a given country market.

The researchers divided rational appeals into *argument* (the ad relates facts or reasons why the purchase should be made) and *lecture* (ads are devoid of fictional characters or plot elements; rather, they include narration that directly addresses the audience and provides an explicit conclusion). Emotional appeals were classified as *dramatic* (narration, character, and plot are key message elements) and *psychological* (explicit statements of how the product will benefit the consumer; desire is created by appealing to a consumer's self-interest). The findings are summarized below in Figure 13-2 and Table 13-4. Figure 13-2 places the countries studied in a matrix classifying them in terms of the dimensions "think" and "feel." For example, the researchers rank Austria, Canada, Germany, Korea, and the United States high on both dimensions; consumers in these countries are presumed to be receptive to television advertising employing either rational or emotional appeals.[26] Table 13-4 is a guide to creating standardized appeals in terms of the clusters; for example, a standardized ad employing a rational/argument appeal could be translated as appropriate and used to good effect in Austria, Belgium, Italy, and the United States. Many German companies, for example, prefer ads that contain plenty of copy that presents a rational argument for a product's superiority. This is typical of ads for beer, automobiles, and food products. However, many creative campaigns are based on the understanding that sometimes the best approach is to disregard

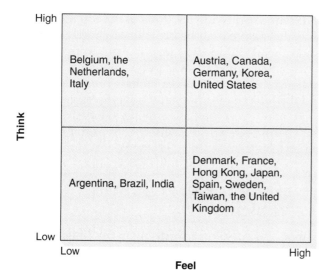

Figure 13-2

"Think" and "Feel" Country Clusters

[26] Fred Zandpour and Katrin R. Harich, "Think and Feel Country Clusters: A New Approach to International Advertising Standardization," *International Journal of Advertising* 15, no. 4 (1996), pp. 325–344.

Table 13-4

*Effective Advertising Appeal
Alternatives*

Type of Appeal	Cultural/Market Factors	Countries Where Appeal Is Appropriate
Rational/Argument	Monochronic cultures with low power distance; high uncertainty avoidance; and good supply of marketing professionals	Austria, Belgium, Germany, Italy, United States
Rational/Lecture	Collectivist cultures with high power distance and high uncertainty avoidance	Belgium, Italy, Mexico
Emotional/Psychological	Collectivist cultures with high power distance, high advertising expenditures, strict government control	Hong Kong, Taiwan, France, United States, South Korea, Spain
Emotional/Dramatic	High power distance; high advertising expenditures; limited supply of advertising professionals	Hong Kong, France, Japan

Source: Adapted from Fred Zandpour and Katrin R. Harich, "Think and Feel Country Clusters: A New Approach to International Advertising Standardization," *International Journal of Advertising* 15, no. 4 (1996), pp. 325–344.

guidelines and break some so-called rules. Recent German ads for the Mini Cooper are definitely offbeat when compared to mainstream auto ads.[27]

GLOBAL MEDIA DECISIONS

The next issue facing advertisers is which medium or media to use when communicating with target audiences. Media availability can vary from country to country. Some companies use virtually the entire spectrum of available media; Coca-Cola is a good example. Other companies prefer to utilize one or two media categories. In some instances, the agency that creates advertising also makes recommendations about media placement; however, many advertisers use the services of specialized media planning and buying organizations. Omnicom's OMD Worldwide, the Starcom Media Vest Group unit of Publicis, and WPP's MindShare Worldwide are three of the top media specialists.

The available alternatives can be broadly categorized as print media, electronic media, and other. Print media range in form from local daily and weekly newspapers to magazines and business publications with national, regional, or international audiences. Electronic media include broadcast television, cable television, radio, and the Internet. Additionally, advertisers may utilize various forms of outdoor, transit, and direct mail advertising. Globally, media decisions must take into account country-specific regulations. For example, France bans retailers from advertising on television.

Global Advertising Expenditures and Media Vehicles

Each year, more money is spent on advertising in the United States than anywhere else in the world. According to data compiled by TNS Media Intelligence, U.S. ad spending in 2005 totaled $143 billion. To put this figure in perspective, consider that 2005 ad spending in Japan, the number two advertising market, totaled ¥5.9 billion (approximately $50 billion). In addition, as one might expect, the largest per capita

---

[27] Erin White, "German Ads Get More Daring, but Some Firms Aren't Pleased," *The Wall Street Journal* (November 22, 2002), p. B6.

ad spending occurs in highly developed countries. However, much of the current growth in advertising expenditures—as much as one-third—is occurring in the BRIC countries. Russia alone represents a $5 billion advertising market; ad expenditures are growing at about 30 percent annually, compared with a rate of 4 percent or 5 percent in the United States and Europe. WPP Group recently announced an alliance with Video International, Russia's largest ad agency.[28]

Worldwide, television is the number one advertising medium, with estimated expenditures of $176 billion in 2008. However, media consumption patterns can vary from country to country. For example, television is the number one medium in both the United States and Japan. By contrast, newspapers are the leading medium in Germany; television ranks second. In Germany, outlays for newspaper advertising surpass those for television by a ratio of two to one. In real terms, television spending in the EU increased by 78 percent between 1990 and 2000, compared with 26 percent for newspapers and 11 percent for magazines during the same period. This trend is likely to continue as digital broadcasting gains acceptance in Europe.

Television is also important in the Latin American market. In Brazil, expenditures on television advertising are nearly three times higher than those for newspapers. The availability of media to advertisers and the conditions affecting media buys also vary greatly around the world. In Mexico, an advertiser that can pay for a full-page ad may get the front page, while in India, paper shortages may require booking an ad six months in advance. In some countries, especially those where the electronic media are government owned, television and radio stations can broadcast only a restricted number of advertising messages. In Saudi Arabia, no commercial television advertising was allowed prior to May 1986; currently, ad content and visual presentation are restricted.

As the figures show, worldwide, radio continues to be a less important advertising medium than print and television. However, in countries where advertising budgets are limited, radio's enormous reach can provide a cost-effective means of communicating with a large consumer market. Also, radio can be effective in countries where literacy rates are low. A clear trend is gaining traction throughout the world: Spending on CRM and Internet advertising is gaining ground at the expense of TV and print.

"The U.S. online advertising market is much bigger than Europe's, but it is a crowded market and the room for growth is shrinking. In Europe, online advertising is growing much faster and portals like Yahoo want to tap into that."[29]

Jupiter Research

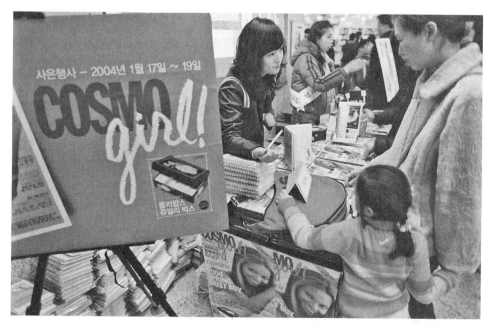

Two trends are driving the globalization of the magazine industry. First, marketers of global brands need a way to communicate with consumers in all parts of the world. Second, brand-conscious consumers are seeking out Western titles. For example, Hearst Corporation's Cosmopolitan is available in more than fifty foreign-language editions.

In South Korea, readers can choose from a wide variety magazines from local and global publishers. To encourage young women to purchase the Korean edition of Cosmo Girl, several free gifts were offered during this in-store promotion: a shoulder bag, a calendar, a makeup box, and a coupon that could be used at an online store.

Source: Otto Pohl/The New York Times.

28 Guy Chazan, "Moscow, City of Billboards," *The Wall Street Journal* (July 18, 2005), p. B1.
29 Dan Bilefsky, "Yahoo Tightens Control in Europe and Asia," *The New York Times* (November 8, 2005), p. C18.

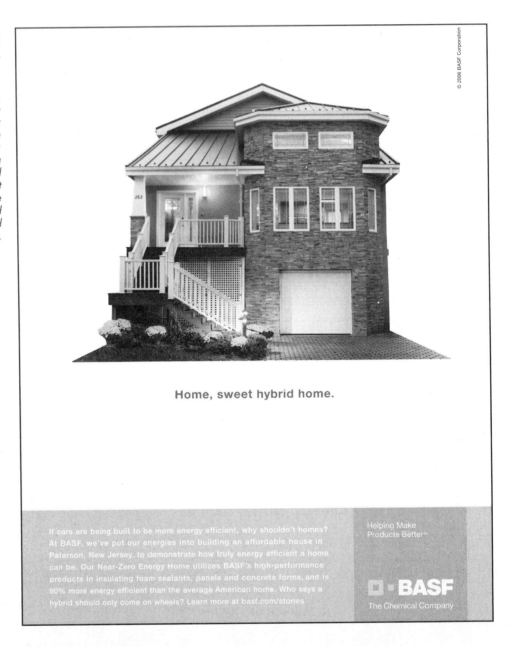

Home, sweet hybrid home.

If cars are being built to be more energy efficient, why shouldn't homes? At BASF, we've put our energies into building an affordable house in Paterson, New Jersey, to demonstrate how truly energy efficient a home can be. Our Near-Zero Energy Home utilizes BASF's high-performance products in insulating foam sealants, panels and concrete forms, and is 80% more energy efficient than the average American home. Who says a hybrid should only come on wheels? Learn more at basf.com/stories.

Helping Make Products Better™

□·BASF
The Chemical Company

Media Decisions

The availability of television, newspapers, and other forms of broadcast and print media varies around the world. Moreover, patterns of media consumption differ from country to country as well. In many developed countries, for example, newspapers are experiencing circulation and readership declines as consumers devote more time to new media options such as the Internet. In India, by contrast, print media are enjoying a revival as redesigned newspaper formats and glossy supplements lure a new generation of readers (see Figure 13-3). India is home to nearly 300 daily newspapers, including the *Times of India* and the *Hindustan Times*; the price per copy is only 5 rupees—about $0.10. Additional critical factors in India's media environment include the lack of penetration by cable television and the fact that only about 4 million Indians currently subscribe to an Internet service.[30] By contrast, billboards are the medium of choice in Moscow. As Thomas

---

[30] John Larkin, "Newspaper Nirvana? 300 Dailies Court India's Avid Readers," *The Wall Street Journal* (May 5, 2006), pp. B1, B3.

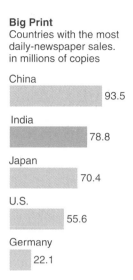

Big Print
Countries with the most
daily-newspaper sales.
in millions of copies

China
93.5

India
78.8

Japan
70.4

U.S.
55.6

Germany
22.1

Figure 13-3

Leading Countries for Daily Newspaper Sales (millions of copies)

Source: World Association of Newspapers.

L. Friedman has pointed out, Moscow is a city built for about 30,000 cars; during the past decade, the number of cars has grown from 300,000 to 3 million.[31] The result is massive traffic jams and commuting delays; affluent businessmen spend hours in traffic and have little time to read the newspaper or watch TV.

Even when media availability is high, its use as an advertising vehicle may be limited. For example, in Europe, television advertising is very limited in Denmark, Norway, and Sweden. Regulations concerning content of commercials vary; Sweden bans advertising to children younger than 12 years old. In 2001, when Sweden headed the EU, its policy makers tried to extend the ban to the rest of Europe. Although the effort failed, Sweden retained its domestic ban. This helps explain why annual spending on print media in Sweden is three times the annual spending for television.[32]

As noted earlier, cultural considerations often affect the presentation of the advertising message. One recent study comparing the content of magazine advertisements in the United States with those in the Arab world found the following:

- People are depicted less often in Arabic magazine ads. However, when people do appear, there is no difference in the extent to which women are depicted. Women appearing in ads in Arab magazines wear long dresses; their presence generally is relevant to the advertised product.
- U.S. ads tend to have more information content; by contrast, brevity is considered a virtue in the Arab world. Context plays a greater role in interpreting a message than in the United States.
- U.S. ads contain more price information, and are more likely to include comparative appeals than Arabic ads.[33]

PUBLIC RELATIONS AND PUBLICITY

Public relations (PR) is the department or function responsible for evaluating public opinion about, and attitudes toward, the organization and its products or brands. PR personnel also are responsible for fostering goodwill, understanding, and acceptance among a company's various constituents and publics. Like

---

[31] Thomas L. Friedman, "The Oil-Addicted Ayatollahs," *The New York Times* (February 2, 2007), p. A19.
[32] John Tylee, "EC Permits Sweden to Continue Child Ad Ban," *Advertising Age* (July 11, 2003), p. 6.
[33] Fahad S. Al-Olayan and Kiran Karande, "A Content Analysis of Magazine Advertisements from the United States and the Arab World," *Journal of Advertising* 29, no. 3 (Fall 2000), pp. 69–82. See also Mushtag Luqmani, Ugur Yavas, and Zahir Quraeshi, "Advertising in Saudi Arabia: Content and Regulation," *International Marketing Review* 6, no. 1 (1989), pp. 59–72.

advertising, PR is one of four variables in the promotion mix. One of the tasks of the PR practitioner is to generate favorable **publicity**. By definition, publicity is communication about a company or product for which the company does not pay. (In the PR world, publicity is sometimes referred to as "earned media," and advertising and promotions are known as "unearned media"). PR personnel also play a key role in responding to unflattering media reports or controversies that arise because of company activities in different parts of the globe. In such instances, PR's job is to make sure that the company responds promptly and gets its side of the story told. The basic tools of PR include news releases, newsletters, media kits, press conferences, tours of plants and other company facilities, articles in trade or professional journals, company publications and brochures, TV and radio talk show appearances by company personnel, special events, and home pages on the Internet. In addition to the examples discussed in the following pages, Table 13-5 summarizes several recent instances of global publicity involving well-known firms.

As noted earlier, a company exerts complete control over the content of its advertising and pays for message placement in the media. However, the media typically receive many more press releases and other PR materials than they can use. Generally speaking, a company has little control over when, or if, a news story runs; nor can the company directly control the spin, slant, or tone of the story. To compensate for this lack of control, many companies utilize **corporate advertising** which, despite the name, is generally considered part of the PR function. As with "regular" advertising, a company or organization identified in the ad pays for corporate advertising. However, unlike regular advertising, the objective of corporate advertising is not to generate demand by informing, persuading, entertaining, or reminding customers. In the context of IMC, corporate advertising is often used to call attention to the company's other communications efforts.

Table 13-5

Negative Publicity Affecting Global Marketers

Company or Brand (home country)	Nature of Publicity
Hyundai (South Korea)	Hyundai Motor Company Chairman Chung Mong Koo was convicted of embezzlement and fraud.
Samsung (South Korea)	Samsung officials allegedly bribed candidates in Korea's 1997 presidential election. It was also revealed that the children of Samsung chairman Lee Kun-Hee broke the law when purchasing securities of a Samsung affiliate.
Coca-Cola (United States) and **PepsiCo** (United States)	In India, allegations that soft drink products from both companies were contaminated with pesticide residue led to sharp sales drops in late summer 2003.
Halliburton (United States)	Allegations that the company overcharged the U.S. government for supplies and services rendered in Iraq.
Ford Motor Company (United States) and **Bridgestone/Firestone** (Japan/United States)	A rash of tire failures on Ford vehicles prompted a recall in 2000 of several tire models. Ultimately, Ford severed its decades-old relationship with Firestone.
Nike (United States)	Since the mid-1990s, Nike has been responding to the criticism that its subcontractors operate factories in which sweatshop conditions prevail. Filmmaker Michael Moore featured an interview with Nike CEO Phil Knight in the antiglobalization documentary *The Big One*.
McDonald's (United States)	Concerns about mad cow disease in Europe, a bitter legal battle in Great Britain, and extensive media reporting that links fast food to obesity have all presented PR challenges to the fast-food giant.

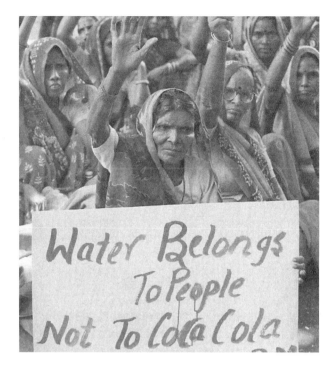

Because of its size and presence in more than 200 countries, the Coca-Cola Company is often the target of antiglobalization protests. The Indian villagers shown here were protesting the company's water consumption in areas severely affected by drought. Coca-Cola chairman and CEO E. Neville Isdell has responded to this type of negative publicity by guiding the company towards greater transparency in its global operations. Isdell also wants to make sure that the public perceives Coke as a global leader in corporate social responsibility. To do this, he is forging relationships and partnerships with non-governmental organizations (NGOs).

Image advertising enhances the public's perception of a company, creates goodwill, or announces a major change, such as a merger or acquisition. In 2004, for example, Interbrew and Ambev placed full-page ads in the business press to announce their new alliance. Global companies frequently use image advertising in an effort to present themselves as good corporate citizens in foreign countries. The Boeing ads that appear earlier in this chapter were part of a European print campaign launched in 1997 to enhance Boeing's image by raising awareness of the number of jobs the company created locally. BASF, the German chemical company, uses advertising to communicate its dedication to increasing energy efficiency in affordable housing construction in the United States. In **advocacy advertising**, a company presents its point of view on a particular issue. The ad in Chapter 11 with the headline "The Dumping of Foreign Steel at Cutthroat Prices Threatens America" is an example of advocacy advertising. Other examples of image and advocacy advertising by global marketers include the following:

- Nokia's purchase of full-page newspaper ads to congratulate the University of Florida Gators for winning the 1997 Sugar Bowl (which Nokia sponsored). The ads also mentioned the Nokia Sweepstakes, which featured a million-dollar prize if a contestant could throw a football through an inflated cellular phone at a distance of about 10 yards.
- Japan's Fuji Photo Film asked its advertising agency to develop an image campaign for the United States. At the time, Fuji was embroiled in a trade dispute with Kodak. Fuji had also invested more than $1 billion in U.S. production facilities and had won a long-term photofinishing contract with Wal-Mart. The campaign was designed to appeal both to Wal-Mart and to the giant retailer's customers; as a Wal-Mart spokesman said, "We've long said we buy American when we can. The more people understand how American Fuji is, the better."[34]
- In 1995, the American International Automobile Dealers Association (AIADA) hired Hill & Knowlton to create a PR campaign designed to convince then-President Bill Clinton, Congress, the media, and the general public that a

---

[34] Wendy Bounds, "Fuji Considers National Campaign to Develop All-American Image," *The Wall Street Journal* (October 1, 1996), p. B8.

proposed plan to impose 100 percent tariffs on 13 luxury cars was ill-advised. The campaign's central message was that foreign automakers account for many U.S. jobs that would be jeopardized if the sanctions were enacted. Nissan and other companies also sent position papers and information packets to dealers and the media. Interviews with representatives from auto dealers were carried by both print and electronic media. Within a few weeks, the Clinton administration announced that the United States and Japan had reached an agreement. No sanctions were imposed, and the AIADA was able to claim an important PR victory.

Senior executives at some companies relish the opportunity to generate publicity. For example, Benetton's striking print and outdoor ad campaigns keyed to the "United Colors of Benetton" generated both controversy and wide media attention. Richard Branson, the flamboyant founder of the Virgin Group, is a one-man publicity machine. His personal exploits as a hot-air balloon pilot have earned him and his company a great deal of free ink. The company does employ traditional media advertising; however, as Will Whitehorn, Virgin's head of brand development and corporate affairs, noted, "PR is the heart of the company. If we do things badly, it will reflect badly on the image of the brand more than most other companies." At Virgin, Whitehorn says, "advertising is a subset of PR, not the other way around."[35]

These examples notwithstanding, most global companies attempt to create an overall balance of promotion mix elements. PepsiCo made good use of IMC when it undertook an ambitious global program to revamp the packaging of its flagship cola. To raise awareness of its new blue can, Pepsi spent $500 million on advertising and PR; to generate publicity, Pepsi leased a Concorde jet and painted it in the new blue color. Pepsi also garnered free ink by spending $5 million to film an ad with two Russian cosmonauts holding a giant replica of the new can while orbiting the earth in the Mir space station. As Massimo d'Amore, PepsiCo's head of international marketing, told reporters, "Space is the ultimate frontier of global marketing. The cola wars have been fought all over the place, and it's time to take them to space."[36]

Sometimes a company generates publicity simply by going about the business of global marketing activities. As noted in Case 8-1, Nike and other marketers have received a great deal of negative publicity regarding alleged sweatshop conditions in factories run by subcontractors. Today, Nike's PR team

GLOBAL *marketing in action*

IBM Generates Publicity with "Deep Blue"

IBM spent about $5 million to stage a rematch of a 1996 chess game between a computer called Deep Blue and chess grandmaster and world champion Garry Kasparov. The match, which took place in New York City, was hailed as one of the best publicity stunts in recent years. To build visibility and interest, IBM purchased full-page newspaper ads, sent out numerous press releases, established an Internet site, and purchased bus posters in Manhattan. The effort was a textbook study in IMC; the match was widely covered by the world media. As Peter Harleman of Landor Associates, a corporate-identity firm, told *The Wall Street Journal,* "Money almost can't buy the advertising [IBM] is getting out of this." John Lister, of the Lister Butler brand identity consulting firm, agreed. "They're doing a tremendous job of

leveraging the brand in this. Not only do they have the IBM name attached to virtually every news report about, but they even branded their computer the corporate color, blue." Industry experts estimate that the match generated about $100 million in favorable earned media. IBM's Internet site provided live coverage and generated a million visits during a single match, a number that set a record for the World Wide Web. The publicity was especially gratifying to IBM officials because problems with its much-ballyhooed information system at the 1996 Olympics resulted in a great deal of negative news coverage. However, in the documentary film, *Game Over: Kasparov and the Machine,* director Vikram Jayanti raises the question of whether the IBM team unfairly provided "behind the scenes" input.

Source: The Wall Street Journal (Western Edition) by Bart Ziegler. Copyright 1997 by Dow Jones & Company, Inc. Reproduced with permission of Dow Jones & Company, Inc. in the format Other book via Copyright Clearance Center.

---

35 Elena Bowes, "Virgin Flies in Face of Conventions," *Ad Age International* (January 1997), p. i4.
36 Melanie Wells, "Pepsi, Coke Go into Orbit," *USA Today* (May 22, 1996), p. 1B.

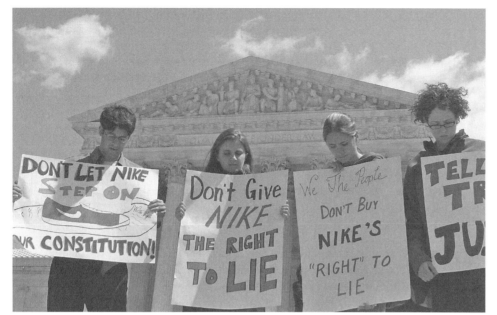

When making public appearances, Nike chairman Phil Knight and other executives frequently defend labor practices and policies in the Asian factories where the company's shoes are made. In the late 1990s, a protester filed a lawsuit against Nike alleging that the company's public assertions about working conditions constitute false advertising. Attorneys for Nike countered that statements made by executives are part of a public policy debate and therefore are protected by the First Amendment. After the California Supreme Court ruled against Nike, the company appealed. In 2003, the U.S. Supreme Court heard the case as protesters gathered outside. The Court later dismissed Nike's appeal, and the case was sent back to California.

is doing a batter job of counteracting the criticism by effectively communicating the positive economic impact Nike has had on the nations where it manufactures its sneakers.

Any company that is increasing its activities outside the home country can utilize PR personnel as boundary spanners between the company and employees, unions, stockholders, customers, the media, financial analysts, governments, or suppliers. Many companies have their own in-house PR staff. Companies may also choose to engage the services of an outside PR firm. During the past few years, some of the large advertising holding companies discussed previously have acquired PR agencies. For example, Omnicom Group bought Fleishman-Hillard, WPP Group acquired Canada's Hill & Knowlton, and Interpublic Group bought Golin/Harris International. Other PR firms, including the London-based Shandwick PLC and Edelman Public Relations Worldwide, are independent. Several independent PR firms in the United Kingdom, Germany, Italy, Spain, Austria, and the Netherlands have joined together in a network known as Globalink. The purpose of the network is to provide members with various forms of assistance such as press contacts, event planning, literature design, and suggestions for tailoring global campaigns to local needs in a particular country or region.[37]

The Growing Role of PR in Global Marketing Communications

PR professionals with international responsibility must go beyond media relations and serve as more than a company mouthpiece; they are called upon to simultaneously build consensus and understanding, create trust and harmony, articulate and influence public opinion, anticipate conflicts, and resolve disputes.[38] As companies become more involved in global marketing and the globalization of industries continues, company management must recognize the value of international PR. One recent study found that, internationally, PR expenditures are growing at an average of 20 percent annually. Fueled by soaring foreign

---

[37] Joe Mullich, "European Firms Seek Alliances for Global PR," *Business Marketing* 79 (August 1994), pp. 4, 31.

[38] Karl Nessman, "Public Relations in Europe: A Comparison with the United States," *Public Relations Journal* 21, no. 2 (Summer 1995), p. 154.

investment, industry privatization, and a boom in initial public offerings (IPOs), PR expenditures in India are reported to be growing by 200 percent annually.

The number of international PR associations is growing as well. The new Austrian Public Relations Association is a case in point; many European PR trade associations are part of the Confédération Européenne des Relations Publiques and the International Public Relations Association. Another factor fueling the growth of international PR is increased governmental relations between countries. Governments, organizations, and societies are dealing with broad-based issues of mutual concern such as the environment and world peace. Finally, the technology-driven communication revolution that has ushered in the information age makes PR a profession with truly global reach. Faxes, satellites, high-speed modems, and the Internet allow PR professionals to be in contact with media virtually anywhere in the world.

In spite of these technological advances, PR professionals must still build good personal working relationships with journalists and other media represen-tatives, as well as with leaders of other primary constituencies. Therefore, strong interpersonal skills are needed. One of the most basic concepts of the practice of PR is to know the audience. For the global PR practitioner, this means knowing the audiences in both the home country and the host country or countries. Specific skills needed include the ability to communicate in the language of the host country and familiarity with local customs. A PR professional who is unable to speak the language of the host country will be unable to communicate directly with a huge portion of an essential audience. Likewise, the PR profes-sional working outside the home country must be sensitive to nonverbal communication issues in order to maintain good working relationships with host-country nationals. Commenting on the complexity of the international PR professional's job, one expert notes that, in general, audiences are "increasingly more unfamiliar and more hostile, as well as more organized and powerful . . . more demanding, more skeptical and more diverse." International PR practi-tioners can play an important role as "bridges over the shrinking chasm of the global village."[39]

How PR Practices Differ Around the World

Cultural traditions, social and political contexts, and economic environments in specific countries can affect PR practices. As noted earlier in the chapter, the mass media and the written word are important vehicles for information dissemination in many industrialized countries. In developing countries, however, the best way to communicate might be through the gong man, the town crier, the market square, or the chief's courts. In Ghana, dance, songs, and storytelling are impor-tant communication channels. In India, where half of the population cannot read, writing press releases will not be the most effective way to communicate.[40] In Turkey, the practice of PR is thriving in spite of that country's reputation for harsh treatment of political prisoners. Although the Turkish government still asserts absolute control as it has for generations, corporate PR and journalism are allowed to flourish so that Turkish organizations can compete globally.

Even in industrialized countries, there are some important differences between PR practices. In the United States, the hometown news release comprises much of the news in a small, local newspaper. In Canada, on the other hand, large metropolitan population centers have combined with Canadian economic and climatic conditions to thwart the emergence of a local press. The dearth of small

[39] Larissa A. Grunig, "Strategic Public Relations Constituencies on a Global Scale," *Public Relations Review* 18, no. 2 (Summer 1992), pp. 127–136.

[40] Carl Botan, "International Public Relations: Critique and Reformulation," *Public Relations Review* 18, no. 2 (Summer 1992), pp. 150–151.

newspapers means that the practice of sending out hometown news releases is almost nonexistent.[41] In the United States, PR is increasingly viewed as a separate management function. In Europe that perspective has not been widely accepted; PR professionals are viewed as part of the marketing function rather than as distinct and separate specialists in a company. In Europe, fewer colleges and universities offer courses and degree programs in PR than in the United States. Also, European coursework in PR is more theoretical; in the United States, PR programs are often part of mass communication or journalism schools, and there is more emphasis on practical job skills.

A company that is ethnocentric in its approach to PR will extend home-country PR activities into host countries. The rationale behind this approach is that people everywhere are motivated and persuaded in much the same manner. This approach does not take cultural considerations into account. A company adopting a polycentric approach to PR gives the host-country practitioner more leeway to incorporate local customs and practices into the PR effort. Although such an approach has the advantage of local responsiveness, the lack of global communication and coordination can lead to a PR disaster.[42]

The ultimate test of an organization's understanding of the power and importance of public relations occurs during a time of environmental turbulence, especially a potential or actual crisis. When disaster strikes, a company or industry often finds itself thrust into the spotlight. A company's swift and effective handling of communications during such times can have significant implications. The best response is to be forthright and direct, reassure the public, and provide the media with accurate information.

China's ongoing trade-related friction with the United States highlights the need for a better PR effort on the part of the Chinese Foreign Ministry. Some sources of this friction have been discussed in earlier chapters, such as estimates that Chinese counterfeiting of copyrighted material alone costs U.S. companies $800 million annually or that 98 percent of the computer software used in China is pirated. Such revelations reflect poorly on China. Hong Kong businessman Barry C. Cheung notes, "China lacks skills in public relations generally and crisis management specifically, and that hurts them."[43] Part of the problem stems from the unwillingness of China's Communist leaders to publicly explain their views on these issues, to admit failure, and to accept advice from the West.

[41] Melvin L. Sharpe, "The Impact of Social and Cultural Conditioning on Global Public Relations," *Public Relations Review* 18, no. 2 (Summer 1992), pp. 103–107.
[42] Carl Botan, "International Public Relations: Critique and Reformulation," *Public Relations Review* 18, no. 2 (Summer 1992), p. 155.
[43] Marcus W. Brauchli, "A Change of Face: China Has Surly Image, but Part of the Reason Is Bad Public Relations," *The Wall Street Journal* (June 16, 1996), p. A1.

Marketing communications—the promotion P of the marketing mix—includes advertising, public relations, sales promotion, and personal selling. When a company embraces **integrated marketing communications (IMC)**, it recognizes that the various elements of a company's communication strategy must be carefully coordinated. **Advertising** is a sponsored, paid message that is communicated through nonpersonal channels. **Global advertising** uses the same advertising appeals, messages, artwork, and copy in campaigns around the world. The effort required to create a global campaign forces a company to determine whether or not a global market exists for its product. The trade-off between standardized and adapted advertising is often accomplished by means of pattern advertising, which can be used to create localized global advertising. Many advertising agencies are part of larger **advertising organizations**. Advertisers may place a single global agency in charge of worldwide advertising; it is also possible to use one or more agencies on a regional or local basis.

The starting point in ad development is the **creative strategy**, a statement of what the message will say. The people who create ads often seek a **big idea** that can serve as the basis for memorable, effective messages. The **advertising appeal** is the communication approach that best relates to buyer motives; **rational appeals** and **emotional appeals** are often used. The **selling proposition** is the promise that captures the reason for buying the product. The **creative execution** is the way an appeal or proposition is presented. **Art direction** and **copy** must be created with cultural considerations in mind. Perceptions of humor, male-female relationships, and sexual imagery vary in different parts of the world. Media availability also varies considerably from country to country. When selecting media, marketers are sometimes constrained by laws and regulations and by literacy rates.

A company utilizes **public relations (PR)** to foster goodwill and understanding among constituents both inside and outside the company. In particular, the PR department attempts to generate favorable **publicity** about the company and its products and brands. The PR department must also manage corporate communications when responding to negative publicity. The most important PR tools are press releases, media kits, interviews, and tours. Many global companies make use of various types of **corporate advertising**, including **image advertising** and **advocacy advertising**. PR is also responsible for providing accurate, timely information, especially in the event of a crisis.

1. In what ways can global brands and global advertising campaigns benefit a company?

2. How does the "standardized versus localized" debate apply to advertising?

3. What is the difference between an advertising appeal and creative execution?

4. When creating advertising for world markets, what are some of the issues that art directors and copywriters should take into account?

5. How do the media options available to advertisers vary in different parts of the world? What can advertisers do to cope with media limitations in certain countries?

6. How does PR differ from advertising? Why is PR especially important for global companies?

7. What are some of the ways PR practices vary in different parts of the world?

Each spring, *Advertising Age* magazine publishes its survey of the top 50 global advertising organizations. The top-ranked companies for 2005 were shown in Tables 13-2 and 13-3. Browse through either table and choose any agency organization or brand that interests you. Compare its 2005 ranking with the most recent ranking (which you can find either by referring to the print version of *Advertising Age* or by visiting www.adageglobal.com. How have the industry rankings changed? Consult additional sources (e.g., magazine articles, the company's Web site) to enhance your understanding of the factors and forces that contributed to the company's move up or down in the rankings. Has the agency been acquired by a large organization? Has it gained or lost an important account?

build your global marketing skills

1. Starting with Chapter 1, review the ads that appear in this text. Can you identify the ads that use emotional appeals? Rational appeals? What is the communication task of each ad? To inform? To persuade? To remind? To entertain?

integrate your global marketing skills

Case 13-1

Adidas AG

In February 1993, a group of investors headed by Robert Louis-Dreyfus, former CEO of Saatchi & Saatchi Advertising, bought a controlling interest in adidas AG. Optimistic about adidas' future, Dreyfus's group raised its stake to full ownership in 1995. Two years later, Dreyfus acquired Salomon, a French company. The move created adidas-Salomon AG, the second largest sports equipment company in the world after Nike. The move was short-lived; the Salomon unit was sold, and in 2006 adidas acquired Reebok. Today, the company markets sports shoes, athletic clothing, and equipment in nearly 200 countries.

Adidas has an illustrious history dating back many decades; when Jesse Owens won four gold medals at the 1936 Olympic games, he was wearing track shoes made by Adi Dassler. A few years later, Dassler founded adidas (Dassler's brother Rudolph started rival shoemaker Puma). Public triumphs such as Owens' Olympic wins helped make adidas the world leader in the sports shoe market; the company's Trefoil logo is iconic for the brand. By successfully leveraging its heritage, and bolstered by the Reebok acquisition, the company generated revenues of $13.3 billion in 2006.

This financial performance represents a sweet victory for the new owners. Years of financial controversy and changing ownership had diverted management's attention from the market and gradually eroded the company's fortunes. In Germany, adidas' share of sports shoe sales declined from 60 percent to 40 percent from the early 1980s to the early 1990s, including a 10-point slide in a two-year period. Sneaker sales doubled in Europe between 1985 and 1995, and Nike and Reebok's share of the market jumped to 50 percent from 5 percent despite extremely high import duties. The Americans' success was due in part to big spending on advertising. Nike and Reebok each spent about $100 million annually to promote their shoes in Europe; adidas' ad spending in Europe was considerably less. The popularity of American sneakers got an extra boost thanks to

the high visibility of the American Dream Team at the 1992 Olympics; NBA stars endorse both Reebok and Nike.

The American athletic shoe companies are skilled global marketers. In 2003, Nike rang up $10.6 billion in worldwide sales, while Reebok's sales totaled $3.1 billion in 2002. Reebok is the market leader in France, Spain, and England, and Nike is number one in many other European countries. Although advertising taglines such as "Just Do It" and "Planet Reebok" are presented in English, other parts of the message are adapted to reflect cultural differences. In France, for example, violence in ads is unacceptable so Reebok replaced boxing scenes with images of women running on a beach. Also, European participation in sports is lower than in America; accordingly, Europeans are less likely to visit sporting goods stores. In France, Reebok shoes are now sold in nearly 1,000 traditional shoe stores.

Even in the face of such tough and growing competition, adidas still enjoys high brand loyalty among older Europeans. The company recruits young people and pays them to wear adidas shoes in public; they are also paid to work at sporting goods stores and promote adidas products in other ways. Adidas also updated its image among younger European consumers by creating a new sport called Streetball. Ads airing on MTV Europe feature players outfitted in the company's new Streetball apparel line. Unlike its American rivals, adidas does not use a global ad campaign. For example, a 1995 campaign that ran outside the United States featured Emil Zatopke, a Czechoslovakian Olympic runner.

As the twenty-first century began, company executives realized the need for a new global strategy. The first step was unveiling a new brand position: "Forever Sport—from Competition to Lifestyle." As Erich Stamminger, global marketing chief, noted in 2001, "We want to mean more to more people. We want to expand our customer base and gain deeper market penetration in our existing markets." To achieve these goals, the company's three divisions were restructured along product lines: performance products, leisure products, and multifunctional products. In January 2002, the company dropped the advertising agency

This TV ad for adidas features two of the best-known athletes in the United States: New Orleans Saints running back Reggie Bush and Los Angeles Galaxy midfield extraordinaire David Beckham.

with which it had been affiliated for many years, London-based Leagas Delany. Adidas' new agency, Los Angeles-based TBWA, will work in conjunction with 180, a Dutch agency. Explaining the rationale for the change, Stamminger noted, "By appointing one global agency network, we are continuing our strategy of strengthening the adidas brand worldwide."

TBWA got right to work. Its Japanese unit developed a billboard featuring two people playing vertical soccer. The company received a boost at the 2003 World Athletic Championships in Paris, where a Caribbean sprinter named Kim Collins won the 100-meter final in a pair of retro-styled adidas track and field shoes. Adidas executives were looking forward to the 2004 Olympic Games in Athens, where the field included 18 teams sponsored by adidas. As Mike Riehl, head of global sports marketing, noted, "Athletics [track and field] goes

> *"Adidas has been in sports for four times as long as its competition, but the U.S. still doesn't appreciate the brand for what it is."*
>
> Lee Clow, Creative Director, 180/TBWA

back all the way for us—it is a fixed part of our philosophy to make products for all Olympic disciplines." Riehl asserted that the renewed focus on athletics was "all about brand positioning and our claim to be the Olympic brand."

Retro-style shoes are enjoying increased popularity in Europe, where track and field events are popular. However, the picture is not so clear in the United States, which is the world's largest market for athletic shoes. In spring 2003, Nike outmaneuvered its rivals by signing basketball phenomenon LeBron James to a sponsorship deal. Reebok was enjoying surging demand for new shoes endorsed by rappers Jay-Z and 50 Cent. Meanwhile, the integrity of athletics was coming under increased scrutiny after revelations that a new "designer steroid," tetrahydrogestrinon (THG), was being widely used. Dwain Chambers, a British sprinter who endorses adidas, had tested positive for THG. As 2003 came to a close, it was clear that the adidas strategy was not paying off. Orders in the key U.S. market were down; it remained to be seen whether U.S. interest in the Olympics would translate into greater sales. Nike was the clear industry leader, with nearly 40 percent share of the athletic shoe market. The adidas T-Mac shoe, endorsed by Tracy McGrady of the Orlando Magic, was the top-selling basketball shoe in the United States in 2001 and 2002. However, sales of a new T-Mac model launched in fall 2003 were below expectations.

To turn the situation around, Stamminger was dispatched to Portland, Oregon, and put in charge of the North American region. In spring 2004, adidas launched a $50 million global print and TV campaign keyed to the tagline "Nothing is impossible." Some of the ads feature boxing legend Muhammad Ali and tell a "past and present" story linking sports figures from earlier eras with modern-day stars. In May, Stamminger announced the fruits of a secret, three-year development effort: the $250 Adidas 1, a shoe with an onboard microchip that adjusts the cushioning level to an athlete's weight and performance needs. In a press release, Stamminger noted, "This is the world's first intelligent shoe. It senses, understands, and adapts."

In 2007, Adidas ramped up its efforts to unseat Nike as the leader in the U.S. sportswear market. Soccer superstar David Beckham, who had been a worldwide Adidas endorser for more than a decade, was at the center of the new promotional campaign. Following Beckham's highly publicized move from Real Madrid to Los Angeles Galaxy, he signed a five-year, $250 million contract. Beckham will be featured prominently in a variety of media, including billboards and prime-time television ads. Adidas executives expect Beckham's endorsement to lead to increased sales of a variety of branded merchandise. As Stephen Pierpoint, vice president for brand marketing at Adidas, said, "The U.S. market has a real opportunity to grow. Football has always been a core sport for Adidas. We hope David will be the catalyst for growth."

Discussion Questions

1. Do you think that ads proclaiming adidas' heritage will be effective in helping build the brand in the United States?

2. Assess the new "Nothing is impossible" advertising tagline. Do you think this phrase will become part of popular culture the way Nike's "Just do it" tagline has?

3. With an initial price tag of $250, the high-tech Adidas 1 is not targeted at a broad market. What role can the Adidas 1 play in the company's PR plan?

4. Assess adidas' acquisition of Reebok. What strategic purpose does the acquisition fulfill?

5. Adidas is Official Sportswear Partner for the 2008 Olympic Games in Beijing. What types of advertising and PR opportunities does this create?

Global Market Share

Reebok 9.6%
Adidas 15.4%
Other 41.8%
Nike 33.2%

Sources: Matthew Karnitschnig and Stephanie Kang, " Leap Forward: For Adidas, Reebok Deal Caps Push to Broaden urban Appeal," *The Wall Street Journal* (August 4, 2005), pp. A1, A6; Laura Petrecca and Theresa Howard, "Adidas-Reebok merger Lets Rivals Nip at Nike's Heels," *USA Today* (August 4, 2005), pp. 1B, 2B; Stephanie Kang, "Adidas Gets Artsy with its U.S. Ads," *The Wall Street Journal* (February 5, 2004), p. B3; Doug Cameron, "Adidas Puts Focus on US," *Financial Times* (December 11, 2003), p. 16; Uta Harnischfeger and Matthew Garrahan, "Adidas—Off the Pace and More Hurdles Ahead," *Financial Times* (November 10, 2003), p. 6; Geoffrey A. Fowler and Sebastian Moffett, "Adidas' Billboard Ads Give a Kick to Japanese Pedestrians," *The Wall Street Journal* (August 29, 2003), pp. B1, B4; J. Lacap, "Adidas Embraces New Global Strategy," *Sporting Goods Business* (November 2001), p. 8; Claire Cozens, "Adidas Drops Leagas Delaney," *MediaGuardian.co.uk* (January 9, 2002); Dagmar Mussey, "Adidas Strides on its Own Path," *Advertising Age* (February 13, 1995), p. 6; Kevin Goldman, "Adidas Tries to Fill its Rivals' Big Shoes," *The Wall Street Journal* (March 17, 1994), p. B5; Joseph Pereira, "Off and Running: Pushing U.S. Style, Nike and Reebok Sell Sneakers to Europe," *The Wall Street Journal* (July 22, 1993), pp. A1, A8; Stephen Barr, "Adidas on the Rebound," *CFO* (September 1991), pp. 48–56; Igor Reichlin, "Where Nike and Reebok Have Plenty of Running Room," *Business Week* (March) 11, 1991, pp. 56–60.

I n 2005, China's Lenovo Group acquired IBM's personal computer (PC) business for $1.25 billion. The acquisition vaulted China's top computer company into third place among the world's PC marketers, behind Dell and Hewlett-Packard. With annual revenues of $13 billion generated by sales in more than 60 countries, Lenovo now has almost 8 percent share of the world's PC market. The crown jewel in the acquisition was the popular ThinkPad, a laptop that features an exceptionally well-designed keyboard. President and CEO William J. Amelio is presiding over the gradual elimination of the IBM logo as Lenovo builds a global brand identity. Amelio and his marketing team decided to use the Olympics as a vehicle for building awareness about the corporate name and its products. Lenovo paid more than $60 million to become China's first Olympic sponsor; it provided several thousand PCs and servers at various competition venues during the 2006 Winter Olympics in Turin, Italy. The computers were clearly visible during television broadcasts of Olympic events and were used by Visa, Coca-Cola, and other sponsors. Lenovo also sponsored eleven athletes. As a sponsor, Lenovo was also entitled to invite preferred customers to the games to meet company executives, get hands-on time with some of the company's products, and, of course, view the sporting events. Lenovo is also the computer provider for the 2008 Beijing Summer Olympics. Speaking about the Olympics, CEO Amelio says, "It's a great opportunity. It's a coming-out party to say, 'Here's Lenovo, we're a global brand and we're here to stay.'"

Sponsorships have been a crucial marketing tool for Lenovo as it rebrands the ThinkPad. When developing IMC solutions and strategies, global companies and advertising agencies are giving sponsorship and other forms of promotion an increasingly prominent role; in the first decade of the twenty-first century, worldwide expenditures on sales promotion are growing at double-digit rates. Sales promotion, direct marketing, and specialized forms of marketing communication such as infomercials and the Internet are also growing in importance. Personal selling remains an important promotional tool as well. Worldwide expenditures on support media such as transit and billboard advertising are increasing. As noted, Lenovo and many other global companies sponsor high-profile events such as the Olympics and professional sports leagues and teams. Branded entertainment, in the form of product placement in television shows and movies is another popular promotional tool. Taken together, the communication elements discussed in this chapter and Chapter 13 can be used to create highly effective integrated promotional campaigns that support global brands.

In September 2005, with 150 days to go before the opening ceremonies of the 2006 Olympic Winter Games in Torino, Italy, Lenovo Chairman Yuanqing Yang and Philippe Davy, Vice President of Marketing, kick off the company's computing equipment sponsorship in New York City. Lenovo was the official computing equipment partner for the 2006 Olympic Winter Games; it is also the partner for the 2008 Olympic Games in Beijing.

SALES PROMOTION

Sales promotion refers to any paid consumer or trade communication program of limited duration that adds tangible value to a product or brand. In a *price promotion*, tangible value may take the form of a price reduction, coupon, or mail-in refund. *Nonprice promotions* may take the form of free samples, premiums, "buy one, get one free" offers, sweepstakes, and contests. **Consumer sales promotions** may be designed to make consumers aware of a new product, to stimulate nonusers to sample an existing product, or to increase overall consumer demand. **Trade sales promotions** are designed to increase product availability in distribution channels. At many companies, expenditures for sales promotion activities have surpassed expenditures for media advertising. At any level of expenditure, however, sales promotion is only one of several marketing communication tools. Sales promotion plans and programs should be integrated and coordinated with those for advertising, PR, and personal selling.

Worldwide, the increasing popularity of sales promotion as a marketing communication tool can be explained in terms of several strengths and advantages. Besides providing a tangible incentive to buyers, sales promotions also reduce the perceived risk buyers may associate with purchasing the product. From the point of view of the sponsoring company, sales promotion provides accountability; the manager in charge of the promotion can immediately track the results of the promotion. Overall, promotional spending is increasing at many companies as they shift advertising allocations away from traditional print and broadcast advertising. Several company-specific examples of sales promotion programs are shown in Table 14-1.

In addition, sweepstakes, rebates, and other forms of promotion require consumers to fill out a form and return it to the company, which can then build up information in its database for use when communicating with customers in the future. For example, Clicquot, a unit of LVMH Moët Hennessy-Louis Vuitton, markets Hine cognac and other fine wines and spirits. In an effort to build the company's in-house mailing list, managers offered cognac drinkers a gift for filling out a Hine Cognac crossword puzzle. Clicquot's marketers rented a list with the addresses of persons who had attended cigar "smoker" events in major cities.

Table 14-1

Sales Promotions by Global Marketers

Company/Country Market for Promotion	Promotion
Walt Disney Company/China	To fight counterfeiting, Disney Magical Journey promotion was keyed to mail-in hologram stickers on genuine Disney products. Participants can win Disney DVDs, TV sets, and trips to Hong Kong Disneyland.*
Mars/Global	Global Color Vote promotion invited consumers in 200 countries to vote whether a new M&M candy should be purple, aqua, or pink. Purple won.
Wm. Wrigley Co./United States	U.S. launch of European Orbit brand gum with "Orbit Institute" advertising tied to Orbit Institute Sampling Initiative that included "field research teams" who distributed 7 million gum samples while dressed like the characters in the ads.
Guinness/Malaysia, Singapore, Hong Kong	Promotion to select new bottle shape from four different design options for Guinness (e.g., "bullhorn" shape and guitar shape). Contest was advertised in magazines, billboards, and table tent cards.

*Geoffrey A. Fowler, "Disney Fires a Broadside at Pirates," *Wall Street Journal* (May 31, 2006), p. B3.

A global company can sometimes leverage experience gained in one country market and use it in another market. For example, PepsiCo experienced great success in Latin America with its Numeromania contest. When soft drink sales stalled in Poland in the mid-1990s, Pepsi rolled out Numeromania there; lured by the promise of big cash prizes, many economically squeezed Poles rushed out to buy Pepsi so they could enter the contest.[1] International managers can learn

Masterfoods USA, a unit of Mars, Inc., uses contests and other promotions to generate excitement about its M&M'S® brand chocolate candies. For example, on New Year's Eve 2003, Masterfoods launched the Great Candy Quest promotion. Black and white M&M'S® replaced the traditional colored versions, and consumers were invited to hunt for orange, brown, red, and other favorites. In March 2004, contest winners took part in a celebrity-filled ceremony in Los Angeles and M&M'S® were reintroduced with brighter colors, new packaging, and an updated, larger M logo on each piece of candy. Ads in a variety of media featuring the tagline "River of Chocolate" accompanied the relaunch. As senior marketing manager Doug Milne said, "We've made the brand transformation into a fun and interactive process, and by taking color away from M&M'S®, we've demonstrated just how important it is to have it back."

[1]   Roderick Oram, "Brand Experiences," *Financial Times* (October 30, 1996), FT Survey, p. III.

about American-style promotion strategies and tactics by attending seminars such as those offered by the Promotional Marketing Association of America (PMAA). Sometimes adaptation to country-specific conditions is required; for example, TV ads in France cannot have movie tie-ins. Ads must focus on the promotion rather than the movie. Such regulations would have an impact on Disney, for example.

As with other aspects of marketing communication, a key issue is whether headquarters should direct promotion efforts or leave them to local country managers. The authors of one study noted that Nestlé and other large companies that once had a polycentric approach to consumer and trade sales promotion have redesigned their efforts. Kashani and Quelch identify four factors that contribute to more headquarters involvement in the sales promotion effort: cost, complexity, global branding, and transnational trade:[2]

1. As sales promotions command ever-larger budget allocations, headquarters naturally takes a greater interest.
2. The formulation, implementation, and follow-up of a promotion program may require skills that local managers lack.
3. The increasing importance of global brands justifies headquarters involvement to maintain consistency from country to country and ensure that successful local promotion programs are leveraged in other markets.
4. As mergers and acquisitions lead to increased concentration in the retail industry and as the industry globalizes, retailers will seek coordinated promotional programs from their suppliers.

The level of headquarters involvement notwithstanding, in most cases, local managers in the market know the specific local situation. They should be consulted before a promotion is launched. A number of factors must be taken into account when determining the extent to which the promotion must be localized:

- In countries with low levels of economic development, low incomes limit the range of promotional tools available. In such countries, free samples and demonstrations are more likely to be used than coupons or on-pack premiums.
- Market maturity can also be different from country to country; consumer sampling and coupons are appropriate in growing markets, but mature markets might require trade allowances or loyalty programs.
- Local perceptions of a particular promotional tool or program can vary. Japanese consumers, for example, are reluctant to use coupons at the checkout counter. A particular premium can be seen as a waste of money.
- Local regulations may rule out use of a particular promotion in certain countries. Table 14-2 lists regulations governing coupon distribution in several countries.
- Trade structure in the retailing industry can affect the use of sales promotions. For example, in the United States and parts of Europe, the retail industry is highly concentrated (i.e., dominated by a few key players such as Wal-Mart). This situation requires significant promotional activity at both the trade and consumer level. By contrast, in countries where retailing is more fragmented—Japan is a case in point—there is less pressure to engage in promotional activities.

---

[2] Kamran Kashani and John A. Quelch, "Can Sales Promotion Go Global?" *Business Horizons* 33, no. 3 (May–June 1990), pp. 37–43.

Lenovo

Lenovo is also using other sports to raise its profile. For example, Lenovo has joined forces with the National Basketball Association (NBA) by becoming the "Official PC Partner of the NBA." The opportunity arose when Dell, which had a previous agreement with the NBA, chose not to renew it. Also, Brazilian soccer star Ronaldinho signed a one-year contract to serve as Lenovo's global brand ambassador.

Some observers have suggested that Lenovo is moving too quickly to distance itself from the IBM brand name. For example, University of Pennsylvania Professor David Reibstein says, "What Lenovo is trying to do is get itself established with credibility in this market, but it feels like a premature transition. Lenovo may be strong in China, but it is a non-name in the West." Deepak Advani, Lenovo's chief marketing officer, responds by noting, "The IBM brand is a double edged sword for us. It gives customers a sense of comfort and safety and provides some instant credibility. But the longer we hold on to a well-established brand like IBM, the more difficult it becomes for us to be known as Lenovo."

At least one industry analyst applauds the rebranding effort. Simon Yates, an analyst with technology consultancy Forrester Research, says, "The IBM brand says 'third place finisher, high-priced.' Lenovo needs to get rid of the IBM brand quickly because it came with a lot of baggage. It's not appealing to the market

they want to grab in the future: small business. The ThinkPad has a reputation for industrial strength and being I.T. friendly, but as an IBM product it was expensive. Now people can get it at close to Dell prices."

Today, Lenovo's headquarters are in the United States, although most of its employees are in China. While the rebranding effort is ongoing, Amelio faces additional challenges, such as bridging cultural differences among the company's far-flung employees and maintaining profitability despite a worldwide slowdown in PC sales. Amelio is in the midst of a $100 million restructuring program that will include a 5 percent workforce reduction. Substantial investment is also being made in sales and distribution channels. Will the result be market success? As one observer noted, "If you look at HP and Compaq, they took four or five years to integrate a Texas culture and a California culture. When you try to merge a U.S. company and a Chinese company, it is going to take a lot longer to make it successful."

Sources: Justine Lau and Mure Dickie, "Lenovo Shows how China Is Able to Take on the World," Financial Times (November 9, 2006), p. 19; Jane Spencer, "Lenovo Takes a Shot at Building Brand Awareness with NBA Deal," The Wall Street Journal (October 24, 2006), pl. B4; Evan Ramstad, "Lenovo Still Chewing on Its Byte of IBM," The Wall Street Journal (May 11, 2006), p. B4; Glenn Rifkin and Jenna Smith, "Quickly Erasing 'I' and 'B' and 'M,'" New York Times (April 12, 2006), p. C9; Steve Lohr, "Lenovo Evolves with Its IBM PC Unit in Tow," New York Times (August 30, 2005), p. C1.

Sampling

Sampling is a sales promotion technique that provides potential customers with the opportunity to try a product or service at no cost. As Marc Pritchard, vice president of global cosmetics and personal care at Procter & Gamble, noted, "The most fundamental thing that consumers want to do is try before they buy."[3] A typical sample is an individual portion of a consumer product, such as breakfast cereal, shampoo, cosmetics, or detergent, distributed through the mail, door-to-door, or at a retail location. For example:

- Kikkoman brand soy sauce was unknown in the United States until Yuzaburo Mogi, now Kikkoman's CEO, initiated a sampling program in American supermarkets. Mogi and his employees passed out free samples of food seasoned with Kikkoman; today, the U.S. market accounts for 85 percent of Kikkoman's profit from international operations.[4]
- When Unilever launched Axe deodorant body spray in the United States in 2002, the promotion strategy called for print ads and in-store sampling. Unilever hired attractive female models to offer samples to male shoppers at Wal-Mart and Costco stores. The successful U.S. launch helped propel Axe's global growth rate to 22 percent.[5]

The average cost per sample for such promotional programs can range from $0.10 to $0.50; 2 million to 3 million samples are distributed in a typical sampling

---

[3] Sarah Ellison, "Taking the 'Free' out of Free Samples," *The Wall Street Journal* (September 25, 2002), p. D1.
[4] Mariko Sanchanta, "Soy Sauce Seeps into the Culture," *Financial Times* (August 10, 2006), p. 6.
[5] Deborah Ball, "Consumer Goods Firms Duel for Shelf Space," *The Wall Street Journal* (October 22, 2004), p. B3.

program. Cost is one of the major disadvantages associated with sampling; another problem is that it is sometimes difficult for marketing managers to assess the contribution a sampling program makes to return on investment. Today, many companies utilize *event marketing* and *sponsorships* to distribute samples at concerts, sports events, or special events such as food and beverage festivals attended by large numbers of people. In the information age, sampling may also consist of a week's free viewing of a cable TV channel or a no-cost trial subscription to an online computer service; Internet users can also request free samples through a company's Web site.

Compared with other forms of marketing communication, sampling is more likely to result in actual trial of the product. To ensure trial, consumer products companies are increasingly using a technique known as "point-of-use" sampling. For example, Starbucks dispatches "chill patrols" in the summertime to pass out samples of ice-cold Frappucino to overheated commuters during rush hour in busy metropolitan areas. In an example of "point-of-dirt" sampling, Unilever recently hired a promotional marketing firm to pass out Lever2000 hand wipes in food courts and petting zoos. As Michael Murphy, director of home and personal-care promotions at Unilever, noted, "We're getting smarter. You must be much more precise in what, where, and how you deliver samples."[6] Sampling can be especially important if consumers are not persuaded by claims made in advertising or other channels. In China, for example, shoppers are reluctant to buy full-sized packages of imported consumer products that they haven't tried—especially because the price may be much higher than the price of local brands. Procter & Gamble's dominance in China's shampoo market can be attributed to the company's skillful use of market segmentation coupled with an aggressive sampling program. P&G offers four shampoo brands in China: Rejoice ("soft and beautiful hair"), Pantene ("nutrition"), Head & Shoulders (dandruff relief), and Vidal Sassoon (fashion).[7] P&G distributed millions of free samples of its shampoo products; after the no-risk trial, many consumers became adopters.

Couponing

A **coupon** is a printed certificate that entitles the bearer to a price reduction or some other special consideration for purchasing a particular product or service. In the United States and Great Britain, marketers rely heavily on newspapers to deliver coupons; nearly 90 percent of all coupons are distributed in a printed ride-along vehicle known as a *free-standing insert* (FSI). Sunday papers carry the vast majority of FSIs. *On-pack coupons* are attached to, or part of, the product package; they can frequently be redeemed immediately at checkout. *In-pack coupons* are placed inside the package. Coupons can also be handed out in stores, offered on a self-service basis from on-shelf dispensers, delivered to homes by mail, or distributed electronically at the checkout counter. Also, the number of coupons distributed via the Internet is growing. *Cross coupons* are distributed with one product but redeemable for a different product. For example, a toothpaste coupon might be distributed with a toothbrush. The United States leads the world in number of coupons issued, by a wide margin. NCH Marketing Services, which tracks coupon trends, reports that about 300 billion coupons are distributed in the United State each year; only about 1 percent are actually redeemed (see Figure 14-1). Online coupon distribution is growing at a rapid rate; Google is among the players experimenting with them.[8]

---

6 Geoffrey A. Fowler, "When Free Samples Become Saviors," *The Wall Street Journal* (August 14, 2001), p. B1.
7 "Winning the China FMCG Market," ATKearney, 2003.
8 Steve Lohr, "Clip and Save Holds Its Own Against Point and Click," *The New York Times* (August 30, 2006), p. C1.

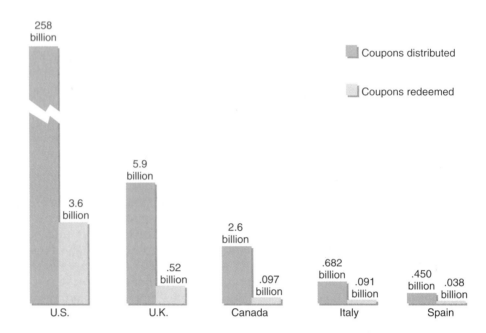

Figure 14-1

Coupon Distribution, United States Versus Select Country Markets

Source: NCH Marketing Services, Inc. Marketing Services 2004 Trend Report.

Coupons are a favorite promotion tool of consumer packaged goods companies such as Procter & Gamble and Unilever. The goal is to reward loyal users and stimulate product trial by nonusers. In the EU, couponing is widely used in the United Kingdom and Belgium. Couponing is not as prevalent in Asia where saving face is important. Although Asian consumers have a reputation for thriftiness, some are reluctant to use coupons because doing so might bring shame upon them or their families. According to Joseph Potacki, who teaches a "Basics of Promotion" seminar for the PMAA, couponing is the aspect of the promotion mix for which the practices in the United States differ the most from those in other countries. In the United States, couponing accounts for 70 percent of consumer promotion spending. Elsewhere, the percentage is much lower. According to Potacki, "It is far less—or nonexistent—in most other countries simply because the cultures don't accept couponing." Potacki notes that one reason couponing is gaining importance in countries such as the United Kingdom is because retailers are learning more about its advantages.[9] Table 14-2 gives an overview of regulations concerning coupon promotions in selected countries.

Sales Promotion: Issues and Problems

As noted earlier, many companies are being more strategic in targeting their sampling programs. In the case of coupons, retailers must bundle the redeemed coupons together and ship them to a processing point. Many times, coupons are not validated at the point of purchase; fraudulent redemption costs marketers hundreds of millions of dollars each year. Fraud can take other forms as well. For example, during the 2004 Super Bowl broadcast, PepsiCo launched a joint promotion with Apple Computer's iTunes Music Store. Apple planned to give away 100 million songs for free (regular price: $0.99); consumers could obtain a code from the caps of Pepsi bottles and enter the code online to quality for the download. The promotion was designed so that anyone purchasing a bottle of Pepsi had a one-in-three chance of being a winner. However, many people discovered that, by tilting the bottles to one side, they could tell whether the bottle was a winner. Moreover, they could read the code without having to pay for the Pepsi!

---

[9] Leslie Ryan, "Sales Promotion: Made in America," *Brandweek* (July 31, 1995), p. 28.

Companies must take extreme care when formulating and executing sales promotions. In some emerging markets, sales promotion efforts can raise eyebrows if companies appear to be exploiting regulatory loopholes and lack of consumer resistance to intrusion. Sales promotion in Europe is highly regulated. Sales promotions are popular in Scandinavia because of restrictions on broadcast advertising, but promotions in the Nordic countries are subject to regulations. If such regulations are relaxed as the single market develops in Europe and regulations are harmonized, companies may be able to roll out pan-European promotions.

A recent study examined coupon usage and attitudes toward both coupons and sweepstakes in Taiwan, Thailand, and Malaysia. The study has particular relevance to global companies that are targeting these and other developing nations in Asia where consumers have relatively little experience with coupons. The study utilized Hofstede's social values framework as a guide. All three countries in the studies are collectivist, and the researchers found that positive attitudes of family members and society as a whole influence an individual's positive attitude toward coupons and coupon usage. However, the three nations show some differences in value orientation. For example, Malaysia has a higher power distance and lower uncertainty avoidance than the others. For Malaysians, the fear of public embarrassment was a constraint on coupon usage. In all three countries, media consumption habits were also a factor; persons who were not

Country	Coupons by Mail	Home-Delivery Coupons	On-Pack Coupons	In-Pack Coupons
England	Legal	Legal	Legal	Legal
France	Legal for discount on same product. No cross coupons.	Legal for discount on same product. No cross coupons.	Legal for discount on same product. No cross coupons.	Legal for discount on same product. No cross coupons.
Germany	Legal for samples only. Price-off coupons not allowed.	Legal for samples only. Price-off coupons not allowed.	Price reduction cannot be made by retailer. Consumers mail on-pack code directly to manufacturer.	Prohibited in most cases.
Sweden	Legal to persons age 16 and older; illegal to send to persons younger than 16. Restrictions when sending to parents of new baby.	Legal to persons age 16 and older; illegal to send to persons younger than 16. Restrictions when sending to parents of new baby.	Legal	Legal
United States	Legal. Restrictions on alcohol, tobacco, and drugs.	Legal. Restrictions on alcohol, tobacco, and drugs.	Legal; all terms must be disclosed. Minimum 6-month redemption period required.	Legal; all terms must be disclosed. Minimum 6-month redemption period required.

Table 14-2

Coupon Promotion Regulation in Select Countries

Source: Adapted from *Promo* magazine.

regular readers of magazines or newspapers were less likely to be aware that coupons were available. Consumers in Taiwan and Thailand look more favorably upon coupons than sweepstakes. The impact of religion surprised the researchers. In Malaysia, where the population is primarily Muslim, the researchers assumed that consumers would avoid sweepstakes promotions. Sweepstakes can be compared to gambling, which is frowned on by Islam. However, Malaysians showed a preference for sweepstakes over coupons. In Taiwan, where Buddhism, Confucianism, and Taoism are all practiced, religion appeared to have little impact on attitudes toward promotions. One implication for marketing in developing countries is that, despite cultural differences, increased availability of promotions will result in higher levels of consumer utilization.[10]

PERSONAL SELLING

Personal selling is person-to-person communication between a company representative and a prospective buyer. The seller's communication effort is focused on informing and persuading the prospect, with the short-term goal of making a sale and with a longer-term goal of building a relationship with that buyer. The salesperson's job is to correctly understand the buyer's needs, match those needs to the company's product(s), and then persuade the customer to buy. Because selling provides a two-way communication channel, it is especially important in marketing industrial products that may be expensive and technologically complex. Sales personnel can often provide headquarters with important customer feedback that can be utilized in design and engineering decisions.

Effective personal selling in a salesperson's home country requires building a relationship with the customer; global marketing presents additional challenges because the buyer and seller may come from different national or cultural backgrounds. Despite such challenges, it is difficult to overstate the importance of a face-to-face, personal selling effort for industrial products in global markets. For example, when Spain's Iberia Airlines was modernizing its long-haul fleet, salespeople from Boeing and rival Airbus met numerous times with Enrique Dupuy de Lome, Iberia's chief financial officer. At stake was a 12-plane order worth about $2 billion. The aircraft under consideration were the Boeing 777–300ER ("Extended Range") and the Airbus A340–600. After each sales team presented initial bids, negotiations began; Toby Bright, Boeing's top salesperson for jets, faced off against John Leahy of Airbus. Iberia's demands included discounts off list prices and resale value guarantees for the aircraft. After months of meetings and revised proposals, Airbus was awarded the contract.[11]

Personal selling is also a popular marketing communication tool in countries with various restrictions on advertising. As noted in Chapter 13, it is difficult to obtain permission to present product comparisons in any type of advertising in Japan. In such an environment, selling is the best way to provide hard-hitting, side-by-side comparisons of competing products. Personal selling is also used frequently in countries where low wage rates allow large local sales forces to be hired. For example, Home Box Office built its core of subscribers in Hungary by selling door-to-door. The cost effectiveness of personal selling in certain parts of the world has been a key driver behind the decision at many U.S.-based firms to begin marketing products and services overseas. A company is more likely to test

---

[10] Lenard C. Huff and Dana L. Alden, "An Investigation of Consumer Response to Sales Promotions in Developing Markets: A Three Country Analysis," *Journal of Advertising Research* 38, no. 3 (May–June 1998), pp. 47–57.

[11] Daniel Michaels, "Dogfight: In the Secret World of Airplane Deals, One Battle Up Close," *The Wall Street Journal* (March 10, 2003), pp. A1, A9.

a new territory or product if the entry price is relatively low. For example, some high-tech firms have utilized lower-cost sales personnel in Latin America to introduce new product features to their customers. Only if the response is favorable do the firms commit major resources to a U.S. rollout.

The challenge to companies that wish to pursue low-cost personal selling overseas, however, is to establish and maintain acceptable quality among members of the sales team. The old saying, "You get what you pay for" has come to haunt more than one company that has undertaken global expansion. When MCI Communications first entered Latin America several decades ago, it was attracted in part by the prospect of achieving inexpensive market penetration for its large multinational client companies. Management's initial enthusiasm quickly gave way to an alarming realization that the quality of support in this part of the world was not on a level with what MCI's major accounts were used to in the United States. As a result, there was a period when both MCI and its competition chose the costlier sales approach of using U.S.-based personnel to provide remote, but higher quality, support to the Latin American sites of their respective global customer bases. However, MCI's upper management ultimately decided to invest more to create in-country sales and service teams whose output more closely mirrored that of their U.S. counterparts.

The risks inherent in establishing a personal selling structure overseas remain today. The crucial issue is not whether in-country sales and marketing people can provide more benefit than a remote force. Today, it's a given that, in the vast majority of scenarios, they can. The issue is whether the country team should consist of in-country nationals or **expatriates** (also known as expats); that is, employees who are sent from their home countries to work abroad. It should be noted that many of the environmental issues and challenges identified in earlier chapters often surface as a company completes the initial stages of implementing a personal selling strategy. These include:

- *Political risks.* Unstable or corrupt governments can completely change the rules for the sales team. Establishing new operations in a foreign country is especially tricky if a coup is imminent or if a dictator demands certain "considerations" (which has been the case in many developing countries). For example, Colombia offers great market potential and its government projects an image of openness. However, many companies have found the unspoken rules of the Cabal to be inordinately burdensome. In a country ruled by a dictatorship, the target audience and accompanying message of the sales effort tend to be far narrower and restricted because government planners mandate how business will be conducted. Firms selling in Hong Kong were concerned that China would impose its will and dramatically alter the selling environment after the transfer of power in 1997. In response to such concerns, British Telecom brought many members of its Hong Kong sales staff back to London prior to the changeover. However, to the great relief of Hong Kong's business community, Chinese officials ultimately recognized that a policy of minimal intervention would be the wisest approach.
- *Regulatory hurdles.* Governments sometimes set up quota systems or impose tariffs that affect entering foreign sales forces. In part, governments consider such actions to be an easy source of revenue, but, even more importantly, policy makers want to ensure that sales teams from local firms retain a competitive edge in terms of what they can offer and at what price. Regulations can also take the form of rules that disallow certain types of sales activities. In 1998, for example, the Chinese government banned door-to-door selling, effectively blocking Avon's business model. Avon responded by establishing a network of store representatives; today, China is Avon's fastest growing global market. Avon CEO Andrea Jung expects annual sales in China to reach $400 million by 2007.

- *Currency fluctuations.* There have been many instances where a company's sales effort has been derailed not by ineffectiveness or lack of market opportunity but by fluctuating currency values. In the mid-1980s, for example, Caterpillar's global market share declined when the dollar's strength allowed Komatsu to woo U.S. customers away. Then, while Caterpillar's management team was preoccupied with domestic issues, competitors chipped away at the firm's position in global markets.
- *Market unknowns.* When a company enters a new region of the world, its selling strategy may unravel because of a lack of knowledge of market conditions, the accepted way of doing business, or the positioning of its in-country competitors. When a game plan is finally crafted to counter the obstacles, it is sometimes too late for the company to succeed. However, if management devotes an inordinate amount of time to conducting market research prior to entry, it may discover that its window of opportunity has been lost to a fast-moving competitor that did not fall victim to the "analysis paralysis" syndrome. Thus, it is difficult to make generalizations about the optimal time to enter a new country.

If all these challenges can be overcome, or at least minimized, the personal selling endeavor can be implemented with the aid of a tool known as the Strategic/Consultative Selling Model.

The Strategic/Consultative Selling Model

Figure 14-2 shows the **Strategic/Consultative Selling Model**, which has gained wide acceptance in the United States. The model consists of five interdependent steps, each with three prescriptions that can serve as a checklist for sales personnel.[12] Many U.S. companies have begun developing global markets and have established face-to-face sales teams either directly, using their own personnel, or indirectly, through contracted sales agents. As a result, the Strategic/Consultative Selling Model is increasingly used on a worldwide basis. The key to ensuring that the model produces the desired outcome—building quality partnerships with customers—is to have it implemented and followed on a consistent basis. This is far more difficult to achieve with international sales teams than it is with U.S.-based units that are much more accessible to corporate headquarters.

First, a sales representative must develop a **personal selling philosophy**. This requires a commitment to the marketing concept and a willingness to adopt the role of problem solver or partner in helping customers. A sales professional must also be secure in the belief that selling is a valuable activity. The second step is to develop a **relationship strategy**, which is a game plan for establishing and maintaining high-quality relationships with prospects and customers. The relationship strategy provides a blueprint for creating the rapport and mutual trust that will serve as the basis of a lasting partnership. This step connects sales personnel directly to the concept of *relationship marketing*, an approach that stresses the importance of developing long-term partnerships with customers. Many U.S.-based companies have adopted the relationship marketing approach to selling in the American market; it is equally relevant—and perhaps even more so—to any company hoping to achieve success in global marketing.

In developing personal and relationship strategies on an international level, the representative is wise to take a step back and understand how these strategies will likely fit in the foreign environment. For example, an aggressive "I'll do

---

[12] This discussion of the Strategic/Consultative Selling Model is adapted from Gerald L. Manning and Barry L. Reece, *Selling Today: Creating Customer Value*, 9th ed. (Upper Saddle River, NJ: Prentice Hall, 2004), Chapter 1. The authors are also indebted to Larry Sirhall, a marketing consultant based in Bend, Oregon.

Figure 14-2

The Strategic/Consultative Selling Model

Source: Gerald L. Manning and Barry L. Reece,
Selling Today: Creating Customer Value, 10th ed.
© 2007, pp. 15, 18, 238. Reprinted/Adapted by
permission of Pearson Education, Inc., Upper
Saddle River, NJ.

Strategic/Consultative Selling Model

Strategic Step	Prescription
Develop a Personal Selling Philosophy	☐ Adopt Marketing Concept ☐ Value Personal Selling ☐ Become a Problem Solver/Partner
Develop a Relationship Strategy	☐ Adopt Win-Win Philosophy ☐ Project Professional Image ☐ Maintain High Ethical Standards
Develop a Product Strategy	☐ Become a Product Expert ☐ Sell Benefits ☐ Configure Value-Added Solutions
Develop a Customer Strategy	☐ Understand Buyer Behavior ☐ Discover Customer Needs ☐ Develop Prospect Base
Develop a Presentation Strategy	☐ Prepare Objectives ☐ Develop Presentation Plan ☐ Provide Outstanding Service

Strategic/consultative selling evolved in response to increased competition, more complex products increased emphasis on customer needs, and growing importance of long-term

Place	Promotion
Product	Price

whatever it takes to get your business" is the worst possible approach in some cultures, even though in many large U.S. cities it would be viewed as a standard, even preferred, practice. This is why it is prudent for a company's sales management and sales representative teams to invest the time and energy necessary to learn about the global market in which they will be selling. In many countries, people have only a rudimentary understanding of sales techniques; acceptance of those techniques may be low as well. A sophisticated sales campaign that excels in the United States may never hit the mark in other countries. In-country experts such as consultants or agents can be excellent sources of real-world intelligence that can help a sales representative create an effective international relationship strategy. Such people are especially helpful if the sales force will include many expatriates who will not have resident nationals as colleagues whom they can turn to for advice. Sales representatives must understand that patience and a willingness to assimilate host-country norms and customs are important attributes in developing relationships built on respect.

The third step, developing a **product strategy**, results in a plan that can assist the sales representative in selecting and positioning products that will satisfy customer needs. A sales professional must be an expert who possesses not only a deep understanding of the features and attributes of each product he or she represents but also an understanding of competitive offerings. That understanding is then used to position the product and communicate benefits that are relevant to the customer's wants and needs. As with the selling philosophy and relationship strategy, this step must include comprehension of the target market's characteristics and the fact that prevailing needs and wants may mandate products that are different than those offered in the home country.

Until recently, most American companies engaged in international selling have offered products rather than services. For example, John Deere did a marvelous job of increasing its global market share by supplying high-quality but relatively mundane farming equipment to countries where agriculture remains a mainstay of local economies. Today, however, with exploding worldwide demand for technology-related services, the picture is changing. For example, in 2006, IBM's two Global Services Segments—Global Technology Services and Global Business Services—together accounted for 53 percent of revenues and 37 percent of pretax profits.

Next comes a **customer strategy**, a plan that ensures that the sales professional will be maximally responsive to customer needs. Doing so requires a general understanding of consumer behavior; in addition, the salesperson must collect and analyze as much information as possible about the needs of each customer or prospect. The customer strategy step also includes building a prospect base, consisting of current customers as well as potential customers (or leads). A qualified lead is someone whose probability of wanting to buy the product is high. Many sales organizations diminish their own productivity by chasing after too many nonqualified leads. This issue can be extremely challenging for an international sales unit because customer cues or "buying signs" may not coincide with those that have been proven in the sales representative's home country.

The final step, the actual face-to-face selling situation, requires a **presentation strategy**. This consists of setting objectives for each sales call and establishing a presentation plan to meet those objectives. The presentation strategy must be based on the sales representative's commitment to provide outstanding service to customers. As shown in Figure 14-3, when these five strategies are integrated with an appropriate personal selling philosophy, the result is a high-quality partnership.

The **presentation plan** that is at the heart of the presentation strategy is typically divided into six stages: approach, presentation, demonstration, negotiation, closing, and servicing the sale (Figure 14-4). The relative importance of each stage can vary by country or region. As mentioned several times already, the global salesperson *must* understand cultural norms and proper protocol, from proper exchange of business

Figure 14-3

Building a High Quality Sales Partnership

Source: Gerald L. Manning and Barry L. Reece, Selling Today: Creating Customer Value, 10th ed. © 2007, pp. 15, 18, 238. Reprinted/Adapted by permission of Pearson Education, Inc., Upper Saddle River, NJ.

Figure 14-4

The Six-Step Presentation Plan

Source: Gerald L. Manning and Barry L. Reece,
Selling Today: Creating Customer Value, *10th ed.*
© 2007, pp. 15, 18, 238. Reprinted/Adapted
by permission of Pearson Education, Inc., Upper
Saddle River, NJ.

Step One: Approach	☐ Review Strategic/Consultative Selling Model ☐ Initiate customer contact
Step Two: Presentation	☐ Determine prospect needs ☐ Select product or service ☐ Initiate sales presentation
Step Three: Demonstration	☐ Decide what to demonstrate ☐ Select selling tools ☐ Initiate demonstration
Step Four: Negotiation	☐ Anticipate buyer concerns ☐ Plan negotiating methods ☐ Initiate win-win negotiations
Step Five: Close	☐ Plan appropriate closing methods ☐ Recognize closing clues ☐ Initiate closing methods
Step Six: Servicing the Sale	☐ Suggestion selling ☐ Follow through ☐ Follow-up calls

Service, retail, wholesale, and manufacturer selling

cards to the volume of one's voice during a discussion to the level of eye contact made with the decision maker. In some countries, the approach is drawn out, as the buyer gets to know or takes the measure of the salesperson on a personal level with no mention of the pending deal. In such instances, the presentation comes only after rapport has been firmly established. In some regions of Latin America and Asia, rapport development may take weeks, even months. The customer may place more importance on what occurs *following* work than on what is accomplished during the formal work hours of 8 AM to 5 PM.

In the six-step presentation plan, the first step, *approach*, is the sales representative's initial contact with the customer or prospect. The most crucial element of the step is to completely understand the decision-making process and the roles of each participant, such as decision maker, influencer, ally, or blocker. In some societies, it is difficult to identify the highest-ranking individual based on observable behavior during group meetings. This crucial bit of strategic information often is uncovered only after the representative has spent considerable time developing rapport and getting to know the overall customer organization from various perspectives and in various contexts.

In the *presentation* step, the prospect's needs are assessed and matched to the company's products. To communicate effectively with a foreign audience, the style and message of the presentation must be carefully thought out. In the United States, the presentation is typically designed to sell and persuade, whereas the intent of the international version should be to educate and inform. High-pressure tactics rarely succeed in global selling, despite the fact that they are natural components of many American sales pitches. The message is equally critical because what may be regarded as fully acceptable in U.S. discussions may either offend or confuse the overseas sales audience. A humorous example of this occurred during a session between representatives from Adolph Coors Company and a foreign prospect. The first slide in the presentation contained a translation of Coors' slogan "Turn It Loose," but within seconds of this slide being shown, the audience began to chuckle. As translated, the slogan described diarrhea—obviously something that the presenter had no desire to convey to this group!

Next comes the *sales demonstration*, during which the salesperson has the opportunity to tailor the communication effort to the customer and alternately tell and show how the product can meet the customer's needs. This step represents one of selling's important advantages as a promotional tool. The prospect's senses become involved, and he or she can actually see the product in action, touch it, taste it, or hear it, as the case may be.

During the presentation, the prospect may express concerns or objections about the product itself, the price, or some other aspect of the sale. Dealing with objections in an international setting is a learned art. In some cases, this is simply part of the sales ritual and the customer expects the representative to be prepared for a lively debate on the pros and cons of the product in question. In some instances, it is taboo to initiate an open discussion where any form of disagreement is apparent; such conversations are to be handled in a one-to-one situation or in a small group with a few key individuals present. A common theme in sales training is the concept of **active listening**; in global sales, verbal and nonverbal communication barriers of the type discussed in Chapter 4 present special challenges. When objections are successfully overcome, serious negotiations can begin.

Negotiation is required to ensure that both the customer and the salesperson come away from the presentation as winners. Experienced American sales representatives know that persistence during the negotiation stage is one tactic often needed to win an order in the United States. However, some foreign customers consider American-style persistence (inferring tenacity) or arm-twisting rude and offensive. This can end the negotiations quickly—or, in the worst case, such behavior can be taken as a display of self-perceived American superiority, which then must be countered aggressively or brought to an immediate end. Inappropriate application of American-style negotiation tactics has plagued some U.S. sales representatives attempting to assertively close deals with Canadian companies. Conversely, in other countries, persistence often means endurance, a willingness to patiently invest months or years before the effort results in an actual sale. For example, a company wishing to enter the Japanese market must be prepared for negotiations to take several years.

Having completed the negotiation step, the sales representative is able to move on to the *close* and, thus, asks for the order. Attitudes toward the degree of bluntness that is acceptable in making this request vary among countries. In Latin America, a bold closing statement is respected, whereas in Asia, it is something that must be done with more deference toward the decision maker. As with objection handling and negotiation, the close is a selling skill that comes with both knowledge and experience in global business and sales.

The final step is *servicing the sale*. A successful sale does not end when the order is written; to ensure customer satisfaction with the purchase, an implementation process (which may include delivery and installation) must be outlined and a customer service program established. Implementation can be complicated because of logistical and transportation issues as well as potential problems with the in-country resources to handle all the necessary steps. Transportation alternatives were discussed in Chapter 12. Decisions regarding resources for implementation and after-sale service are similar to decisions about the personal selling structure described in the following paragraphs. There are cost benefits to using in-country nationals for implementation, but quality control is more difficult to guarantee. Establishing expatriates for the primary function of implementation is costly and normally cannot be justified until international operations are more mature and profitable. But sending an implementation team to the host country creates a variety of expense and regulatory concerns. Even when implementation

This print advertisement for Bridgestone Firestone Brazil communicates the fact that the company's extensive dealer network is dedicated to top-notch customer service. Worldwide, the Firestone brand is associated with expert in-store service as well as quick in-field service. It is important for farmers to have the right tires on their equipment, and sales representatives at each dealership match the right tire to a particular application. In addition, dealers are able to replace damaged tires on-site to minimize downtime for the farmer. This ad campaign also incorporates "Leader in the Field," the corporate-wide slogan which is a very appropriate positioning for an agricultural company.

has been adequately addressed, the requirement for sold customer service raises all the same questions again: in-country nationals, expatriates, or third-country nationals?

Sales Force Nationality

As noted previously, a basic issue for companies that sell globally is the composition of the sales force in terms of nationality. It is possible to utilize expatriate salespersons, hire host country nationals, or utilize third-country sales personnel. The staffing decision is contingent on several factors, including management's orientation, the technological sophistication of the product, and the stage of economic development exhibited by the target country. Table 14-3 summarizes these decisions. A company with an ethnocentric orientation is likely to prefer expatriates and adopt a standardized approach without regard to technology or the level of economic development in the target country. Polycentric companies selling in developed countries should opt for expatriates to sell technologically sophisticated products; a host-country sales force

Table 14-3

Contingency Factors in Selecting Sales Force Nationality

| Technology Level | Management Orientation | | | | | |
| | Ethnocentric | | Polycentric | | Regiocentric | |
	Developed	Less Developed	Developed	Less Developed	Developed	Less Developed
High	Expatriates	Expatriates	Expatriates	Host-country nationals	Expatriates	Third-country nationals
Low	Expatriates	Expatriates	Host-country nationals	Host-country nationals (agents)	Third-country nationals	Third-country nationals (agents)

Source: Reprinted from *Industrial Marketing Management 24*, Earl D. Honeycutt Jr. and John B. Ford, "Guidelines for Managing an International Sales Force," p.139. © Copyright 1999–2003, with permission from Elsevier.

In global marketing, sales meetings and presentations typically involve people from various nationalities. A successful salesperson takes the time to adapt his or her personal selling philosophy, relationship strategy, and other elements of the strategic/consultative model to the specific selling situation. The various elements of the six-step presentation plan may also need to be adapted.

can be used when technological sophistication is lower. In less-developed countries, host-country nationals should be used for products in which technology is a factor; host-country agents should be used for low-tech products. The widest diversity of sales force nationality is found in a company in which a regiocentric orientation prevails. Except in the case of high-tech products in developed countries, third-country nationals are likely to be used in all situations.

In addition to the factors just cited, management must also weigh the advantages and disadvantages of each nationality type (Table 14-4). First, because they come from the home country, expatriates often possess a high

Table 14-4

Advantages and Disadvantages of Different Sales Types

Category	Advantages	Disadvantages
Expatriates	Superior product knowledge Demonstrated commitment to high customer service standards Train for promotion Greater HQ control	Highest cost High turnover Cost for language and cross-cultural training
Host country	Economical Superior market knowledge Language skills Superior cultural knowledge Implement actions sooner	Need product training May be held in low esteem Language skills may not be important Difficult to ensure loyalty
Third country	Cultural sensitivity Language skills Economical Regional sales coverage	Face identity problems Blocked promotions Income gaps Need product or company training Loyalty not assured

Source: Reprinted from *Industrial Marketing Management 24,* Earl D. Honeycutt Jr. and John B. Ford, "Guidelines for Managing an International Sales Force," p.139. © Copyright 1999–2003, with permission from Elsevier.

level of product knowledge and are likely to be thoroughly versed in their company's commitment to after-sales service. They come with corporate philosophies and culture well engrained. Also, they are better able to institute the acceptable practices and follow the policies of the home office and, generally, there is less potential for control or loyalty issues to arise. Finally, a foreign assignment can also provide employees with valuable experience that can enhance promotion prospects. There are also several disadvantages to utilizing expatriates. If the headquarters mind-set is *too* firmly ingrained, the expat may have a difficult time understanding the foreign environment and assimilating into it. This can eventually lead to significant losses; the sales effort may be poorly received in the market, or homesickness can lead to a costly reversal of the relocation process. Maintaining expat sales personnel is extremely expensive; the average annual cost to U.S. companies of posting employees and their families overseas exceeds $250,000. In addition to paying expat salaries, companies must pay moving expenses, cost-of-living adjustments, and host-country taxes. Despite the high investment, many expats fail to complete their assignments because of inadequate training and orientation prior to the cross-border transfer. In addition, studies have shown that one-quarter of U.S. expats leave their companies within a year of returning home.

An alternative is to build a sales force with host-country personnel. Locals offer several advantages, including intimate knowledge of the market and business environment, language skills, and superior knowledge of local culture. The last consideration can be especially important in Asia and Latin America. In addition, because in-country personnel are already in place in the target country, there is no need for expensive relocations. However, host-country nationals may possess work habits or selling styles that do not mesh with those of the parent company. Furthermore, the firms' corporate sales executives tend to have less control over an operation that is dominated by host-country nationals. Headquarters executives may also experience difficulty cultivating loyalty, and host-country nationals are likely to need hefty doses of training and education regarding both the company and its products.

A third option is to hire persons who are not natives of either the headquarters country or the host country; such persons are known as *third-country nationals*. For example, a U.S.-based company might hire someone from Thailand to represent it in China. This option has many advantages in common with the host-country national approach. In addition, if conflict, diplomatic tension, or some other form of disagreement has driven a wedge between the home country and the target sales country, a sales representative from a third country may be perceived as sufficiently neutral or at "arm's length" to enable the company to continue its sales effort. However, there are several disadvantages of the third-country option. For one thing, sales prospects may wonder why they have been approached by someone who is neither a local national nor a native of the headquarters country. Third-country nations may lack motivation if they are compensated less generously than expats or host-country sales personnel; also, they may find themselves passed over for promotions as coveted assignments go to others.

After much trial and error in creating sales forces, most companies today attempt to establish a hybrid sales force comprised of a balanced mix of expatriates and in-country nationals. The operative word for this approach is *balanced* because there always remains the potential for conflict between the two groups. It is also the most expensive proposition in terms of up-front costs because both relocation of expats and extensive training of in-country nationals are required. However, the short-term costs are usually deemed necessary in order to do business and conduct personal selling overseas.

After considering the options shown in Table 14-4, management may question the appropriateness of trying to create personal selling units made up of their own people. A fourth option is to utilize the services of **sales agents**. Agents work under contract rather than as full-time employees. In the United States, companies have used sales agents for many years, often with mixed results. From a global perspective, it often makes a great deal of sense to set up one or more agent entities to at least gain entry to a selected country or region. In some cases, because of the remoteness of the area or the lack of revenue opportunity (beyond servicing satellite operations of customers headquartered elsewhere), agents are retained on a fairly permanent level. To this day, the majority of U.S., Asian, and European companies with an Africa-based sales presence maintain agent groups to represent their interests.

Agents are much less expensive than full-time employees and possess the same advantage of understanding the market as a team of in-country nationals. Subsequently, if a certain degree of success is achieved, the role of agents can be diminished in favor of employee-based teams. Conversely, if the market does not prove to be financially viable, it is much less costly to pull out from an agent-oriented territory. However, the challenge of control that was discussed earlier is even greater due to the fact that agents frequently have other sources of income available to them. Thus, a company may find itself in a relatively weak bargaining position when coming to terms with agents. Additionally, because there are other job opportunities for agents (especially with the growing trend of firms in the same industry concurrently targeting the same overseas markets), the question of loyalty is significant. A company that employs foreign sales agents has to determine just what to provide in terms of product and strategic training because of the very real possibility that a competitor will lure those agents away with more attractive compensation packages. Agents have even used their remote locations as a shield to avoid detection as they accept assignments from competing firms, offering customers the best deal among the several options they represent. Situations such as this mean that companies must create some type of monitoring system within agent territories, either through an in-country manager or regular visits from the home office sales department.

Other international personal selling approaches that fall somewhere between sales agents and full-time employee teams include:

- *Exclusive license arrangements* in which a firm will pay commissions to an in-country company's sales force to conduct personal selling on its behalf. For example, when Canada's regulatory agency prevented U.S. telephone companies from entering the market on their own, AT&T, MCI, Sprint, and other firms crafted a series of exclusive license arrangements with Canadian telephone companies.
- *Contract manufacturing or production* with a degree of personal selling made available through warehouses or showrooms that are open to potential customers. Sears has employed this technique in various overseas markets, with the emphasis placed on the manufacturing and production but with the understanding that opportunities for some sales results do exist.
- *Management-only agreements* through which a corporation will manage a foreign sales force in a mode that is similar to franchising. Hilton Hotels has these types of agreements all over the world; not only for hotel operations but also for personal selling efforts aimed at securing conventions, business meetings, and large group events.
- *Joint ventures* with an in-country (or regional) partner. Because many countries place restrictions on foreign ownership within their borders, partnerships can serve as the best way for a company to obtain both a personal sales capability as well as an existing base of customers.

SPECIAL FORMS OF MARKETING COMMUNICATIONS: DIRECT MARKETING, SUPPORT MEDIA, EVENT SPONSORSHIP, AND PRODUCT PLACEMENT

The Direct Marketing Association defines **direct marketing** as any communication with a consumer or business recipient that is designed to generate a response in the form of an order, a request for further information, and/or a visit to a store or other place of business. Companies use direct mail, telemarketing, television, print, and other media to generate responses and build databases filled with purchase histories and other information about customers. By contrast, mass marketing communications are typically aimed at broad segments of consumers with certain demographic, psychographic, or behavioral characteristics in common. Table 14-5 shows other differences between direct marketing and "regular" marketing. Although direct marketing dates back decades, more sophisticated techniques and tools are being used today. For example, Don Peppers and Martha Rogers advocate an approach known as **one-to-one marketing**. Building on the notion of CRM, one-to-one marketing calls for treating different customers differently based on their previous purchase history or past interactions with the company. Peppers and Rogers describe the four steps in one-to-one marketing as follows[13]:

1. *Identify* customers and accumulate detailed information about them.
2. *Differentiate* customers and rank them in terms of their value to the company.
3. *Interact* with customers and develop more cost-efficient and effective forms of interaction
4. *Customize* the product or service offered to the customer (e.g., by personalizing direct mail offers).

Worldwide, the popularity of direct marketing has been steadily increasing in recent years. One reason is the availability of credit cards—widespread in some countries, growing in others—as a convenient payment mechanism for direct response purchases. (Visa, American Express, and MasterCard generate enormous

Direct Marketing	Mass Marketing	Table 14-5
Marketer adds value (creates place utility) by arranging for delivery of product to customer's door.	Product benefits do not typically include delivery to customer's door.	*Comparison of Direct Marketing and Mass Marketing*
Marketer controls the product all the way through to delivery.	Marketer typically loses control as product is turned over to distribution channel intermediaries.	
Direct response advertising is used to generate an immediate inquiry or order.	Advertising is used for cumulative effect over time to build image, awareness, loyalty, and benefit recall. Purchase action is deferred.	
Repetition is used within the ad/offer.	Repetition is used over a period of time.	
Customer perceives higher risk because product is bought unseen. Recourse may be viewed as distant or inconvenient.	Customer perceives less risk due to direct contact with product. Recourse is viewed as less distant.	

Source: Adapted from the Direct Marketing Association.

---

[13] Don Peppers, Martha Rogers, and Bob Dorf, "Is Your Company Ready for One-to-One Marketing?" *Harvard Business Review* 77, no. 1 (January–February 1999).

revenues by sending direct mail offers to their cardholders.) Another reason is societal: Whether in Japan, Germany, or the United States, dual-income families have money to spend but less time to shop outside the home. Technological advances have made it easier for companies to reach customers directly. Cable and satellite television allow advertisers to reach specific audiences on a global basis. As noted in Case 7-2, MTV reaches nearly 400 million households worldwide and attracts a young viewership. A company wishing to reach businesspeople can buy time on CNN, Fox News Network, or CNBC.

Direct marketing's popularity in Europe increased sharply during the 1990s. The European Commission expects investment in direct marketing to surpass expenditures for traditional advertising in the near future. One reason is that direct marketing programs can be readily made to conform to the "think global, act local" philosophy. As Tony Coad, managing director of a London-based direct marketing and database company, noted more than a decade ago, "Given the linguistic, cultural, and regional diversity of Europe, the celebrated idea of a Euro-consumer is Euro-baloney. Direct marketing's strength lies in addressing these differences and adapting to each consumer."[14] Obstacles still remain, however, including the European Commission's concerns about data protection and privacy, high postal rates in some countries, and the relatively limited development of the mailing list industry. Rainer Hengst of Deutsche Post offers the following guidelines for U.S.-based direct marketers that wish to go global:[15]

- The world is full of people who are not Americans. Be sure not to treat them like they are.
- Like politics, all marketing is local. Just because your direct mail campaign worked in Texas, do not assume it will work in Toronto.
- Although there may be a European Union, there is no such thing as a "European."
- Pick your target, focus on one country, and do your homework.
- You'll have a hard time finding customers in Paris, France, if your return address is Paris, Texas. Customers need to be able to return products locally or at least believe there are services available in their country.

Direct Mail

Direct mail uses the postal service as a vehicle for delivering a personally addressed offer to a prospect targeted by the marketer. Direct mail is popular with banks, insurance companies, and other financial services providers. As customers respond to direct mail offers, the marketer adds information to its database. That information, in turn, allows the marketer to refine subsequent offers and generate more precisely targeted lists. The United States is home to a well-developed mailing list industry. A company can rent a list to target virtually any type of buyer; naturally, the more selective and specialized the list, the more expensive it is. The availability of good lists and the sheer size of the market are important factors in explaining why Americans receive more direct mail than anyone else. However, on a per capita basis, German consumers are world-leader mail-order shoppers, buying more than $500 each in merchandise annually. Americans rank second, with annual per capita spending of $379.

Compared with the United States, list availability in Europe and Japan is much more limited. The lists that are available may be lower in quality and contain more errors and duplications than lists from the United States. Despite such problems, direct mail is growing in popularity in some parts of the world. In Europe, for example, regulators are concerned about the extent that children are

---

[14] Bruce Crumley, "European Market Continues to Soar," *Advertising Age* (February 21, 1994), p. 22.
[15] Rainer Hengst, "Plotting Your Global Strategy," *Direct Marketing* 63, no. 4 (August 2000), pp. 52–57.

GLOBAL *marketing in action*

exposed to, or even targeted by, traditional cigarette advertising. Faced with the threat of increased restrictions on it advertising practices, the tobacco industry is making a strategy shift toward direct mail. As David Robottom, development director at the Direct Marketing Association, noted, "Many of the promotions on cigarette packets are about collected data. [The tobacco companies] are working very hard at building up loyalty."

Following the economic crisis in Asia, a number of companies in that region have turned to direct mail in an effort to use their advertising budgets more effectively. Historically, the Asian direct marketing sector has lagged behind its counterparts in the United States and Europe. Grey Global Group established a Kuala Lumpur office of Grey Direct Interactive in 1997; OgilvyOne Worldwide is the Malaysian subsidiary of Ogilvy & Mather Group specializing in direct marketing. Companies in the banking and telecommunications sectors have been to the forefront of direct marketing initiatives in Asia, using their extensive databases to target individual consumers by mail or Internet.

Catalogs

A **catalog** is a magazine-style publication that features photographs, illustrations, and extensive information about a company's products. (The term "magalog" is sometimes used to describe this communication medium.) The global catalog retail sector generated revenues of nearly $380 billion in 2005.[16] Catalogs have a long and illustrious history as a direct marketing tool in both Europe and the United States. The European catalog market flourished after World War II as consumers sought convenience, bargain prices, and access to a wider range of goods. U.S.-based catalog marketers include JCPenney, Lands' End, L.L.Bean, The Sharper Image, and Victoria's Secret; in Europe, Otto GmbH & Co KG (Germany) is the leading catalog retailer. Catalogs are widely recognized as an important part of an IMC program, and many companies use catalogs in tandem with traditional retail distribution and e-commerce channels. The catalog retail sector in the United States represents about one-third of the total global market, accounting for about $112 billion in annual revenues.

Historically, catalogers in the United States benefited from the ability to ship goods from one coast to the other, crossing multiple state boundaries with relatively few regulatory hurdles. By contrast, prior to the advent of the single market, catalog sales in Europe were hindered by the fact that mail-order products passing through customs at national borders were subject to VAT. Because VAT drove up prices of goods that crossed borders, a particular catalog tended to be targeted at intracountry buyers. In other words, Germans bought from German catalogs, French consumers bought from French catalogs, and so on. Market-entry

---

[16] "Global Catalog Retail: Industry Profile," *Datamonitor* (April 2006), p. 7.

German supermodel Tatjana Patitz was featured on the cover of Otto's spring/summer 2007 catalog. Shoppers can choose from Pure Wear, Kind To Your Skin, and other eco-friendly fashion lines made from organic cotton. As Otto Group CEO Dr. Michael Otto explains, "Conscious buying and consumption behavior are an important contribution towards promoting environmentally friendly and socially compatible ways of manufacturing goods worldwide."

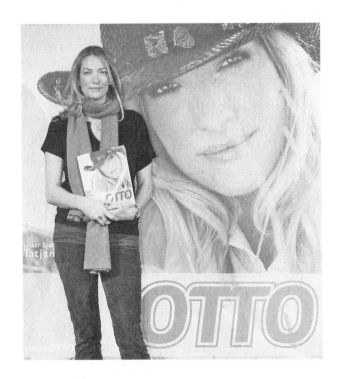

strategies were also affected by the customs regulations; catalogers grew by acquiring existing companies in various countries. For example, Otto GmbH & Co KG distributes hundreds of different catalogs in 20 countries.

Today, the single market means that mail-order goods can move freely throughout the EU without incurring VAT charges. Also, since January 1993, VAT exemptions have been extended to goods bound to the European Free Trade Area countries (Norway, Iceland, Switzerland, and Liechtenstein). Some predict robust growth in Europe's mail-order business, thanks to the increased size of the potential catalog market and the VAT-free environment. The single market is also attracting American catalogue retailers, who will be faced with higher costs for paper, printing, and shipping as well as the familiar issue of whether to adapt their offerings to local tastes. Stephen Miles, director of international development, Lands' End, said, "The most difficult thing is to know in which areas to be local. We're proud that we're an American sportswear company, but that doesn't mean your average German consumer wants to pick up the phone and speak English to someone."[17]

In Japan, the domestic catalog industry is well developed. Leading catalog companies include Cecile, with $1 billion in annual sales of women's apparel and lingerie; Kukutake Publishing, which sells educational materials; and Shaddy, a general merchandise company. As noted in Chapter 12, Japan's fragmented distribution system represents a formidable obstacle to market entry by outsiders. An increasing number of companies use direct marketing to circumvent the distribution bottleneck. Annual revenues for all forms of consumer and business direct response advertising in Japan passed the $1 trillion mark in the mid-1990s; they declined to $525 billion in 2000 as Japan's economic difficulties continued. Success can be achieved using different strategies. For example, Patagonia dramatically increased sales after publishing a Japanese-language catalog, whereas L.L.Bean offers a Japanese-language insert in its traditional catalog.

Even as they continue to develop the Japanese market, Western catalogers are now turning their attention to other Asian countries. In Hong Kong and Singapore,

---

[17] Cecilie Rohwedder, "U.S. Mail-Order Firms Shake Up Europe," *The Wall Street Journal* (January 6, 1998), p. A15.

efficient postal services, highly educated populations, wide use of credit cards, and high per capita income are attracting the attention of catalog marketers. Notes Michael Grasee, the former director of international business development at Lands' End, "We see our customer in Asia as pretty much the same customer we have everywhere. It's the time-starved, traveling, hardworking executive."[18] Catalogers are also targeting Asia's developing countries. Otto GmbH & Co KG, with 2006 revenues of $17 billion and about 6 percent of global mail-order sales, is planning to enter China, Korea, and Taiwan. Because these countries have few local mail-order companies that could be acquisition targets, executives at Otto have mapped out an entry strategy based on acquiring a majority stake in joint ventures with local retailers.

Infomercials, Teleshopping, and Interactive Television

An **infomercial** is a form of paid television programming in which a particular product is demonstrated, explained, and offered for sale to viewers who call a toll-free number shown on the screen. Thomas Burke, president of Saatchi & Saatchi's infomercial division, calls infomercials "the most powerful form of advertising ever created." The cost of producing a single infomercial can reach $3 million; advertisers then pay as much as $500,000 for time slots on U.S. cable and satellite systems and local TV channels. Because infomercials are typically 30 minutes in length and often feature studio audiences and celebrity announcers, many viewers believe they are watching regular talk show-type programming. Although originally associated with personal care, fitness, and household products, such as those from legendary direct-response pitchman Ron Popeil, infomercials have gone up-market in recent years. For example, Lexus generated more than 40,000 telephone inquiries after launching its used-car program with an infomercial; 2 percent of respondents ultimately purchased a Lexus automobile.

In Asia, infomercials generate several hundred million dollars in annual sales. Costs for a late-night time slot range from $100,000 in Japan to $20,000 in Singapore. Infomercials are also playing a part in the development of China's market sector. The government has given its blessing by allowing China Central Television, the state-run channel, to air infomercials and give Chinese consumers access to Western goods. Despite low per capita incomes, Chinese consumers are thought to achieve a savings rate as high as 40 percent because housing and health care are provided by the state. China Shop-A-Vision is in the vanguard, signing up 20,000 "TV shopping members" in its first year of airing infomercials. As these and other pioneers in Chinese direct-response television have learned, however, many obstacles remain, including the limited number of private telephones, low penetration of credit cards, and problems with delivery logistics in crowded cities such as Shanghai.[19]

With **teleshopping**, home-shopping channels such as QVC and the Home Shopping Network (HSN) take the infomercial concept one step further; the round-the-clock programming is *exclusively* dedicated to product demonstration and selling. Worldwide, home shopping is a multibillion-dollar industry. The leading home shopping channels are also leveraging the Internet. For example, in addition to operating home shopping channels in the United States, China, Germany and Japan, HSN also offers an online shopping experience at www.hsn.com.

Although home shopping giant QVC is staying out of China for now, QVC's agreement with Rupert Murdoch's British Sky Broadcasting (BSkyB) satellite company enables it to reach Germany and the United Kingdom. As QVC executive Francis Edwards explained, "European customers respond in different ways,

---

[18] James Cox, "Catalogers Expand in Asia," *USA Today* (October 18, 1996), p. 4B.
[19] Jon Hilsenrath, "In China, a Taste of Buy-Me TV," *The New York Times* (November 17, 1996), Sec. 3, pp. 1, 11.

though the basic premise and concept is the same. The type of jewelry is different. German consumers wouldn't buy 14-karat gold. They go for a higher karat. We can sell wine in Germany, but not in the U.S."[20] A number of local and regional teleshopping channels have sprung up in Europe. Germany's HOT (Home Order Television) is a joint venture with Quelle Schickedanz, a mail-order company. Sweden's TV-Shop is available in 15 European countries. Typically, Europeans are more discriminating than the average American teleshopping customer.

Industry observers expect the popularity of home shopping to increase during the next few years as **interactive television (ITV** or t-commerce) technology is introduced into more households. As the term implies, ITV allows television viewers to interact with the programming content that they are viewing. ITV has a greater presence in Europe than in the United States; in the United Kingdom alone, more than half of all pay-TV subscribers make use of ITV services. The remote control units provided by pay-TV service providers in the United Kingdom have a red button that viewers press to order products from home-shopping channels, choose different camera angles during sports broadcasts, vote during audience participation shows such as "Big Brother," or order free samples of advertised products. In 2005, Diageo tested an interactive ad for Smirnoff vodka; after the first 60 seconds, viewers must press the button two more times to see the ad in its entirety. Comparing traditional TV ads with the new format, James Pennefather, Smirnoff brand manager for the United Kingdom noted, "Interactive advertising is a lot more unproven and untested, and it is a calculated risk for us. We have to do this kind of thing to learn if it will be a success or not."[21]

Support Media

Traditional support media include transit and billboard advertising. In most parts of the world, outdoor advertising is growing at a faster rate than the overall

20 Michelle Pentz, "Teleshopping Gets a Tryout in Europe but Faces Cultural and Legal Barriers," *The Wall Street Journal* (September 9, 1996), p. A8.
21 Aaron O. Patrick, "Selling Vodka with an Interactive Twist," *The Wall Street Journal* (October 11, 2005), p. B3. See also "Europe Wants Its ITV," *Chain Store Age* 77, no. 7 (July 2001), pp. 76–78.
22 Kim Cleland, "Infomercial Audience Crosses over Cultures," *Advertising Age International* (January 15, 1996), p. i8.

Country	Percentage
France	11.7
United Kingdom	5.8
Spain	5.4
Italy	4.3
Canada	4.2
United States	4.0
Germany	4.0
Worldwide	5.9

Table 14-6

Expenditures for Outdoor Advertising as Percentage of Total Ad Spending

advertising market. As countries add mass transportation systems and build and improve their highway infrastructures, advertisers are utilizing more indoor and outdoor posters and billboards to reach the buying public. Japan's population relies heavily on public transportation; the average Tokyo resident spends 70 minutes commuting to work. Consequently, spending on outdoor and transit advertising in Japan is much higher than in most other countries; an estimated $4.4 billion annual expenditures on outdoor media amounts to as much as 12 percent of total ad spending.[23]

Worldwide spending on outdoor advertising amounts to about 6 percent of total ad spending; in Europe, 6.4 percent of advertising spending is allocated to outdoor, compared with 4 percent in the United States (see Table 14-6). The two largest players in the industry are Texas-based Clear Channel Outdoor Holdings, with more than 775,000 outdoor and transit displays worldwide, and France's JCDecaux. In 2006, citing planning rules that make it difficult to erect new billboards in the United States, JCDecaux announced its intention to buy Clear Channel Outdoor.

Sponsorship

Sponsorship is an increasingly popular form of marketing communications whereby a company pays a fee to have its name associated with a particular event,

The popularity of transit and billboard advertising is boosting the fortunes of JCDecaux, the outdoor advertising group. The market leader in Europe, the company operates in about 45 different countries. The outdoor advertising sector is exhibiting explosive growth in China, where JCDecaux competes with Tom Group, Clear Media, and thousands of other local companies. Much of the growth is occurring in large cities such as Beijing, Shanghai, and Guangzhou. The same trend is evident in Russia, especially in Moscow.

---

23 Geoffrey A. Fowler and Sebastian Moffett, "Adidas' Billboard Ads Give a Kick to Japanese Pedestrians," *The Wall Street Journal* (August 29, 2003), pp. B1, B4.

team or athletic association, or sports facility. Sponsorship combines elements of PR and sales promotion. From a PR perspective, sponsorship generally ensures that a corporate or brand name will be mentioned numerous times by on-air or public-address commentators. Large-scale events also draw considerable media attention that typically includes multiple mentions of the sponsoring company or brand in news reports or talk shows. Because event sponsorship typically provides numerous contact points with large numbers of people, it is a perfect vehicle for sampling and other sales promotion opportunities. An Olympic Games or World Cup soccer sponsorship can help a company reach a global audience;

sponsors are also drawn to events that reach national or regional audiences, such as professional team sports, car racing, hot air balloon competitions, rodeos, and music concerts.

Sony recently became an official U.S. sponsor of the NBA with the signing of a $10 million per year deal. One part of the deal calls for recordings by musicians on the Sony Music label—Aerosmith, Pearl Jam, and Mariah Carey, for example—to get priority consideration for air time during games. Hoping to achieve higher levels of brand awareness in the United States, Nokia sponsors the Sugar Bowl; Ericsson paid to have its name emblazoned on the stadium where the Carolina Panthers football team plays. In 1997, Fila and adidas engaged in a bidding war for sponsorship rights to the New York Yankees baseball team. Adidas eventually won a 10-year deal with a total value of $100 million; adidas recently announced that the sponsorship would be extended through the 2013 season. Although the adidas-Yankees deal set a record for sponsorship of an American sport, it was dwarfed by Nike's $200 million deal to sponsor the Brazilian national soccer team.

Sponsorship can be an effective component of an IMC program. It can be used in countries where regulations limit the extent to which a company can use advertising or other forms of marketing communication. In China, for example, where tobacco advertising is prohibited, B.A.T. and Philip Morris spent tens of millions of dollars sponsoring events such as a Hong Kong-Beijing car rally and China's national soccer tournament. However, in 2005, Chinese authorities ratified the WHO's Framework Convention on Tobacco Controls. This means that all forms of tobacco promotion and sponsorship will be phased out by 2010. Sponsorship was also popular in the United Kingdom, where Benson & Hedges paid £4 million for a five-year contract to sponsor cricket matches, and Rothman's spent £15 million annually to sponsor a Formula One racing team. However, to comply with the EU directive on tobacco advertising, tobacco sponsorship of all sports— including Formula One racing—was phased out by 2006.

Product Placement: Motion Pictures, Television Shows, and Public Figures

Companies can achieve a unique kind of exposure by using **product placement**: arranging for their products and brand names to appear in popular television programs, movies, and other types of performances. Marketers can also lend or donate products to celebrities or other public figures; the products get publicity when the celebrity appears in public using the product. This tactic is especially popular with auto manufacturers and fashion designers and is often used in conjunction with popular annual television events such as the Academy Awards and the Grammys that garner media attention. For example, Celeste Atkinson is a lifestyle and entertainment manager for Audi. Her job is to create buzz by ensuring that vehicles such as the Audi A8L, the 12-cylinder A8L, and the S8 sports sedan figure in paparazzi photos.[24] For the premiere of *Superman Returns* in 2006, Atkinson arranged for 35 Audis to chauffer Kevin Spacey and other stars to the event.

Worldwide audience figures for a blockbuster movie hit can equal tens of millions of people. In many instances, product placements generate considerable media interest and result in additional publicity. Placements can be arranged in several different ways. Sometimes companies pay a fee for the placement; alternatively, a show's producers will write the product into the script in exchange for marketing and promotion support of the new production. A brand's

---

[24] Chris Woodyard, "Audi Works the Ropes to Put Stars in Its Cars," *USA Today* (February 22, 2007), p. 3B.

Some global marketers are able to generate publicity for their brands from an unlikely source: Pope Benedict XVI. For example, in this photo taken during the pope's installment mass, His Holiness was wearing red shoes supplied by Italian shoemaker Geox. The pope also has been seen wearing Serengeti sunglasses, and he travels in a customized sport-utility vehicle with a bulletproof bubble that Mercedes-Benz donated to the Vatican. One global branding consultant notes that the pope's devoted following—one billion Catholics—makes a brand's association with him far more valuable than association with even an A-list celebrity.

owners can also strike a barter agreement whereby the company (Sony, for example) supplies the filmmakers with products that serve as props in exchange for licensing rights to the James Bond name in retail promotions. Product placement agencies such as Propaganda, Hero Product Placement, and Eon function like talent agencies for products. As such, the agencies fulfill several important functions such as obtaining legal clearances from a brand's owners, promoting their clients' products to producers, and arranging for products to be delivered to a soundstage.

In the case of television placement, the blurring of advertising and programming content comes as companies increasingly question the effectiveness of traditional advertising. There is research evidence suggesting that a prominent product placement in a television program leads to better recall than a traditional ad. Moreoever, many viewers use digital video records such as TiVo to "zap" commercials; consumers are, in effect, ignoring commercials. This trend forces advertisers to find new ways to expose viewers to their messages. Sometimes called *branded entertainment*, the effective integration of products and brands with entertainment can be seen on the monster TV hit *American Idol*. The branded entertainment trend is so important that *Advertising Age* magazine sponsors an annual "Madison + Vine" conference to bring together key players from the advertising and Hollywood entertainment industries.

In addition to the effectiveness issue, prop masters and set dressers facing budget pressures are compelled to obtain props for free whenever possible. Moreover, as the cost of marketing major feature films has increased—it is not unusual for a studio to spend $20 million to $30 million on marketing alone—studios are increasingly looking for partnerships to share the cost and attract the broadest possible viewing audience. Product placement raises an interesting issue for global marketers, especially consumer packaged-goods companies. This tactic virtually dictates a product standardization approach, because once footage of a scene is shot and incorporated into a movie or television

GLOBAL *marketing in action*

Products Star in Bond Films

The James Bond films are well known for integrating well-known brand names into the action. The 21 films featuring the suave British agent have grossed nearly $4 billion in worldwide ticket sales. However, the most recent films in the series, *Die Another Day* and *Casino Royale*, each cost nearly $100 million to produce. The series' popularity, plus the high cost of making the films, make Bond a perfect vehicle for showcasing products and brands.

Many companies are eager to be associated with a high-profile project like a Bond film. In 1996, when BMW introduced a sporty new Z3 convertible, it wanted to make a major global splash. BMW garnered extensive publicity by placing the Z3 in *Goldeneye*, the eighteenth James Bond film. In the film, gadget chief Q gives 007 a Z3 in place of his Aston-Martin; the Z car also figured prominently in movie previews and print ads. BMW dealers were provided with "BMW 007 kits" that allowed prospective buyers to learn more about both the movie and the car before either was available. As *Advertising Age* observed, "BMW has shaken, not just stirred, the auto industry with unprecedented media exposure and awareness for the Z3 and BMW in the U.S."

Tomorrow Never Dies, the follow up to *Goldeneye*, featured global brand promotional tie-ins worth an estimated $100 million. Ericsson, Heineken, Omega, Brioni, and Visa International all placed products in the film. Bond star Pierce Brosnan also appeared as Agent 007 in specially filmed television commercials. When *Die Another Day*, the twentieth installment in the series, was released at the end of 2002, BMW took a back seat to Ford. The U.S. automaker persuaded the producers to bring back the Aston-Martin (the nameplate was owned by Ford at the time); Jaguars and the new Thunderbird are also prominent in the film.

The latest Bond film, *Casino Royale*, features actor Daniel Craig in the role of 007. To avoid a backlash from fans and marketing executives, the film's producers deliberately limited the number of official global partners in the film to six: Sony Electronics, Sony Ericsson, Omega, Heineken, Ford, and Smirnoff. As Myles Romero, Ford's global brand entertainment director, noted, "It's great for brand awareness. The film takes us where we don't have marketing."

Sources: Emiko Terazono, "Brand New Bond has a License to Sell," Financial Times (November 14, 2006), p. 10; Tim Burt, "His Name's Bond, and He's Been Licensed to Sell," Financial Times (October 5–6, 2002), p. 22; Jon Rappoport, "BMW Z3," Advertising Age (June 24, 1996), p. S37.

---

program, the image of the product is "frozen" and will be seen without adaptation everywhere in the world.[25]

For better or for worse, product placements have even reached the world of live theater and opera: In fall 2002, a new Broadway production of Puccini's *La*

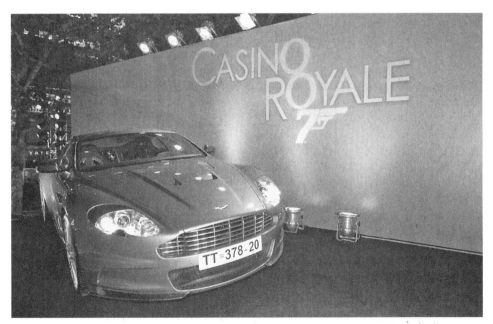

A legendary secret agent deserves a legendary car, so it is not surprising that the latest James Bond film pairs 007 with a new Aston Martin model, the DBS. Built by hand in England, Aston Martin cars offer "perfomance without compromise." The CoolBrands Council recently named Aston Martin "the UK's coolest brand."

---

[25] Stephen J. Gould, Pola B. Gupta, and Sonja Grabner-Krauter, "Product Placements in Movies: A Cross-Cultural Analysis of Austrian, French and American Consumers' Attitudes Toward This Emerging, International Promotional Medium," *Journal of Advertising* 29 no. 4 (Winter 2000) pp. 41–58.

It's only until tourism picks up.

Bohème was set in Paris circa 1957. The stage set included billboards for luxury pen maker Montblanc and Piper-Heidsieck champagne; during a crowd scene at Café Momus, Piper-Heidsieck was served. Some industry observers warn of a backlash. Ethical concerns are sometimes raised when controversial products such as cigarettes are featured prominently or glamorized. When advertising appears in conventional forms such as broadcast commercials, most consumers are aware of the fact that they are being exposed to an ad. This is not necessarily the case with product placement; in effect, viewers are being marketed to subliminally without their consent. What constitutes proper use of product placement? As Joe Uva, an executive of Omnicom's media planning group, noted, "It shouldn't be forced; it shouldn't be intrusive. If people say 'It's a sell out, it's product placement,' it didn't work." Eugene Secunda, a media studies professor at New York University, is skeptical. "I think it's a very dangerous plan. The more you get the audience to distrust the content of your programming, to look at it with suspicion in terms of your real agenda, the less likely they are to be responsive to the message because they're going to be looking at everything cynically and with resistance."[26]

---

[26] Richard Thomkins, "How Hollywood Brings Brands into Your Home," *Financial Times* (November 5, 2002), p. 15.

Sales promotion is any paid, short-term communication program that adds tangible value to a product or brand. **Consumer sales promotions** are targeted at ultimate consumers; **trade sales promotions** are used in business-to-business marketing. **Sampling** gives prospective customers a chance to try a product or service at no cost. A **coupon** is a certificate that entitles the bearer to a price reduction or other value-enhancing consideration when purchasing a product or service.

Personal selling is face-to-face communication between a prospective buyer and a company representative. The **Strategic/Consultative Selling Model** that is widely used in the United States is also being utilized worldwide. The model's five strategic steps call for developing a **personal selling philosophy**, a **relationship strategy**, a **product strategy**, a **customer strategy**, and a **presentation strategy**. The six steps in the presentation plan are: approach; presentation; demonstration; negotiation; close; and servicing the sale. Successful global selling may require adaptation of one or more steps in the presentation plan. An additional consideration in global selling is the composition of the sales force, which may include **expatriates**, host country natives, or sales agents.

Several other forms of communication can be used in global marketing. These include **direct marketing**, a measurable system that uses one or more media to start or complete a sale. **One-to-one marketing** is an updated approach to direct marketing that calls for treating each customer in a distinct way based on his or her previous purchase history or past interactions with the company. **Direct mail**, **catalogs**, **infomercials**, **teleshopping**, and **interactive television** are some of the direct marketing tools that have been successfully used on a global basis. Global marketers frequently try to place their products in blockbuster movies that will reach global audiences. **Sponsorships** and **product placement** are also becoming vital communication tools that can be used on a global basis.

1. Briefly review how the main tools of sales promotion (e.g., sampling and couponing) can be used in global markets. What issues and problems can arise in different country markets?

2. What potential environmental challenges must a company that uses personal selling as a promotional tool outside the home country take into account?

3. Identify the six steps in the Strategic/Consultative Selling Model and the outlined six-step presentation plan. Do these steps have global applicability or are they only used for selling in the home-country market? What special challenges face a sales representative outside his or her home country?

4. How does management's orientation (e.g., ethnocentric, polycentric, or regiocentric) correlate with decisions about sales force nationality? What other factors affect sales force composition?

5. What role does direct marketing have in a global company's promotion mix? Name three companies that have successfully used direct mail or other forms of direct-response advertising.

6. Why are infomercials, sponsorship, and product placement growing in importance for global marketers?

Located in the United Kingdom, the Direct Mail Information Service compiles statistics on direct mail trends in Europe. To review current statistics, log on to:

www.dmis.co.uk

American Brandstand tracks brand names that are mentioned in lyrics of hit songs on *Billboard* magazine's charts. Leading names in 2005 included Mercedes-Benz and Nike. Rapper 50 Cent topped the list of name-dropping artists. To learn more, log on to:

www.agendainc.com

Case 14-1

Marketing an Industrial Product in Latin America

Management at a large manufacturer located in the Mexican state of Nuevo León decided to improve productivity at one of its subsidiaries by investing several million dollars in state-of-the-art production equipment. As word circulated about the planned investment, vendors in Asia, Europe, and North America put together proposals. One such vendor was American company "Y," which had a global reputation for quality products and service. Management at the American firm reviewed the size of the order and decided to bypass its regular Latin American representative and send its international sales manager instead.

The sales manager arrived and checked into the leading hotel. He immediately had some difficulty pinning down just who was his business contact. After several days without results, he called the American Embassy where he found out that the commercial attaché had the necessary up-to-the-minute information. The commercial attaché listened to his story. The attaché realized the sales manager had already made a number of mistakes, but, figuring that the locals were used to American blundering, he reasoned that all was not lost. The attaché informed the sales manager that the Global Purchasing Manager was the key man and that whoever got the nod from him would get the contract. He also briefed the sales manager on methods of conducting business in Latin America and offered some pointers about dealing with the purchasing manager.

The attaché's advice ran somewhat as follows:

1. "You don't do business here the way you do in the States; it is necessary to spend much more time. You have to get to know your man and vice versa. Latin Americans like to do business with people they can trust. Many times it takes two or three lunch meetings before business is even discussed. And when the topic finally does come up, it is not uncommon for it to be discussed during the last few minutes of a two-hour lunch meeting."

2. "You must meet with him several times before you talk business. I will tell you at what point you can bring up the subject. Take your cues from me." (At this point, our American sales manager made a few observations to himself about "cookie pushers" and wondered how many payrolls the commercial attaché had met.)

3. "Take that price list and put it in your pocket. Don't get it out until I tell you to. Down here price is only one of the many things taken into account before closing a deal. In the United States, your past experience will prompt you to act according to a certain set of principles, but many of these principles will not work here. Every time you feel the urge to act or to say something, look at me. Suppress the urge and take your cues from me. This is very important."

4. "Down here people like to do business with men who are somebody. The person you are going to meet graduated from a prestigious university in Latin America. Titles are important here, and I recommend you use his title, especially when you are introduced to him. He is a *Licenciado*, which means he is a university graduate, and he will expect to be addressed using his title. (The sales manager thought to himself that it wasn't that big of a deal—everyone in the United States at this level has a university degree. He just didn't understand the importance of this in Latin America.)

5. "You will also note that the people here are very proud of their past and of their Spanish blood, but they are also exceedingly proud of their liberation from Spain and their independence. The fact that they are a democracy, that they are free, and also that they are no longer a colony is very, very important to them. They are warm and friendly and enthusiastic if they like you. If they don't, they are cold and withdrawn." The commercial attaché advised the sales manager not to talk about history, politics or religion unless the purchasing manager brought the topic up.

6. "And another thing, time down here means something different. It works in a different way. You know how it is back in the States when a certain type blurts out whatever is on his or her mind without waiting to see if the situation is right. Such a person is considered an impatient bore and somewhat egocentric. Well, down here you have to wait much, much longer, and I really mean much, *much* longer, before you can begin to talk about the reason for your visit." (By now the sales manager was becoming frustrated. Back at home, time is money, and he shouldn't have to spend so much time here to get the order—the purchasing manager should already know what he wants!)

7. "There is another point I want to caution you about. At home, the man who sells takes the initiative. Here, *they* tell you when they are ready to do business. But most of all, don't discuss price until you are asked and don't rush things."

The Presentation

The next day the commercial attaché introduced the sales manager to the purchasing manager. First, there was a long wait in the outer office while people went in and out. The sales manager looked at his watch, fidgeted, and finally asked whether the purchasing manager was really expecting him. The reply he received was scarcely reassuring, "Oh yes, he is expecting you but several things have come up that require his attention. Besides, one gets used to waiting down here." The sales manager irritably replied, "But doesn't he know I flew all the way down here from the United States to see him, and I have spent over a week already of my valuable time trying to find him?" "Yes, I know," was the answer, "but things just move much more slowly here."

At the end of about 30 minutes, the purchasing manager emerged from the office, greeted the commercial attaché with a double *abrazo*, throwing his arms around him and patting him on the back as though they were long-lost brothers. Now, turning and smiling, the purchasing manager extended his hand to the sales manager, who, by this time, was feeling rather miffed because he had been kept in the outer office so long. As the sales manager took a seat in the purchasing manager's office, the telephone rang. The purchasing manager took the call; as he was speaking, an administrative assistant walked in carrying several checks and other documents that needed the manager's signature. Then a second telephone call came in on another line; the purchasing manager quickly finished the first call and picked up the second call.

After what seemed to be an all-too-short chat, the purchasing manager rose, suggesting a well-known café where they might meet for dinner the next evening. The sales manager expected that, considering the nature of their business and the size of the order, he might be taken to the purchasing manager's home, not realizing that the Latin home is reserved for family and very close friends. To invite a stranger to his home becomes an act of great symbolism: the host is showing the real face of how he lives by sharing the intimacy of his family.

Until now, nothing at all had been said about the reason for the sales manager's visit, a fact that bothered him somewhat. The whole setup seemed wrong; additionally, he did not like the idea of wasting another day in town. He told the home office before he left that he would be gone for a week or 10 days at most, and made a mental note that he would clean this order up in 3 days and enjoy a few days in Puerto Vallarta or Mexico City. Now the week had already gone, and he would be lucky if he made it home in 10 days.

Voicing his misgivings to the commercial attaché, he wanted to know if the purchasing manager really meant business, and if he did, why could they not get together and talk about it? The commercial attaché by now was beginning to show the strain of constantly having to reassure the sales manager. Nevertheless, he tried again: "What you don't realize is that part of the time we were waiting, the purchasing manager was rearranging a very tight schedule so that he could spend tomorrow night with you. You see, down here they don't delegate responsibility the way we do in the States. They exercise much tighter control than we do. As a consequence, this man spends up to 15 hours a day at his desk. It may not look like it to you, but I assure you he really means business. He wants to give your company the order; if you play your cards right, you will get it."

The next evening was more of the same. Much conversation about food and music, about many of people the sales manager had never heard. They went to a nightclub, where the sales manager brightened up and began to think that perhaps he and the purchasing manager might have something in common after all. It bothered him, however, that the principal reason for his visit was not even alluded to

tangentially. But every time he started to talk about production equipment the commercial attaché would nudge him and proceed to change the subject.

The next meeting was to be held over morning coffee at a café. By now the sales manager was having difficulty hiding his impatience. To make matters worse, the purchasing manager had a mannerism that he did not like. When they talked, he was likely to put his hand on him; he would take hold of his arm and get so close that he nearly spit in his face. Consequently, the sales manager kept trying to dodge and put more distance between himself and the purchasing manager.

Following coffee, they walked in a nearby *zocalo* (downtown plaza). The purchasing manager expounded on the shrubs, the birds, and the beauties of nature, and at one spot he stopped to point at a statue and said: "There is a statue of the world's greatest hero, the liberator of mankind!" At this point, the worst happened. The sales manager asked who the statue was of and, when told the name of a famous Latin American patriot, said, "I never heard of him," and walked on. After this meeting, the American sales manager was never able to see the purchasing manager again. The order went to a Swedish concern.

Discussion Questions

1. What impression do you think the sales manager made on the purchasing manager?
2. How would you critique the quality of the communication among all parties in this case?
3. Is a high-context culture or a low-context culture at work in this case? Explain your answer.
4. When preparing to engage in personal selling outside the home country, how must a salesperson adapt the strategic/consultative selling model and the presentation plan?

The authors are indebted to Jeff Wilson, Strategic Business Planning Manager, Firestone Agricultural Tire, for his assistance in updating and revising this case. *Sources:* Edward T. Hall, "The Silent Language in Overseas Business," *Harvard Business Review* (May–June 1960), pp. 93–96; Alan Riding, *Distant Neighbors: A Portrait of the Mexicans* (New York: Vintage, 1989); Philip R. Harris and Robert T. Moran, "Doing Business with Latin Americans—Mexico, Central & South America," Chapter 14 *Managing Cultural Differences: High Performance Strategies for a New World of Business,* 3rd ed. (Houston: Gulf Publishing Company, 1991), Paul Leppert, *Doing Business with Mexico* (Fremont, CA: Jain Publishing Company, 1995); Lawrence Tuller, *Doing Business in Latin America and the Caribbean* (Chicago: Amacom, 1993).

15

Strategic Elements of Competitive Advantage

IKEA, the $22 billion global furniture powerhouse based in Sweden, faced a difficult business environment in the first few years of the twenty-first century. The euro's strength dampened financial results, as did an economic downturn in Central Europe. The company faces increasing competition from hypermarkets, "do-it-yourself" retailers such as Wal-Mart, and supermarkets that are expanding into home furnishings. Looking to the future, CEO Anders Dahlvig is stressing three areas for improvement: product assortment, customer service, and product availability. With stores in 34 countries, the company's success reflects founder Ingvar Kamprad's "social ambition" of selling a wide range of stylish, functional home furnishings at prices so low that the majority of people can afford to buy them. The store exteriors are painted bright blue and yellow: Sweden's national colors. Shoppers view furniture on the main floor in scores of realistic settings arranged throughout the cavernous showrooms. In a departure from standard industry practice, IKEA's furniture bears names such as "Ivar" and "Sten" instead of model numbers. At IKEA, shopping is a self-service activity; after browsing and writing down the names of desired items, shoppers can pick up their furniture on the lower level. There they find "flat packs" containing the furniture in kit form; one of the cornerstones of IKEA's strategy is having customers take their purchases home in their own vehicles and assemble the furniture themselves. The lower level of a typical IKEA store also contains a restaurant, a grocery store called the Swede Shop, a supervised play area for children, and a baby care room.

The essence of marketing strategy is successfully relating the strengths of an organization to its environment. As the horizons of marketers have expanded from domestic to regional and global, so too have the horizons of competitors. The reality in almost every industry today, including home furnishings, is global competition. This fact of life puts an organization under increasing pressure to master techniques for conducting industry analysis and competitor analysis, and understanding competitive advantage at both the industry and national levels. This chapter covers these topics in detail.

Global marketing experts cite IKEA as an illustration of several key strategic principles. IKEA exemplifies the concept of the flagship firm: The company has built a network of more than 2,000 suppliers in 50 countries. This arrangement has helped IKEA achieve and maintain a low-cost position in the global furniture industry. IKEA reaps further economies by minimizing transportation and delivery costs. Furniture is shipped to the stores in flat packaging; customers assemble the finished pieces themselves. In its quest for cost leadership, IKEA's management team is mindful of the need for ethical corporate citizenship. In 2000, IKEA launched an initiative in India designed to ensure that the companies that supply it with carpets do not use child labor. In part, the initiative helps poor women in India's "carpet belt" pay off their debts and achieve financial independence.

INDUSTRY ANALYSIS: FORCES INFLUENCING COMPETITION

A useful way of gaining insight into competitors is through industry analysis. As a working definition, an industry can be defined as a group of firms that produce products that are close substitutes for each other. In any industry, competition works to drive down the rate of return on invested capital toward the rate that would be earned in the economist's "perfectly competitive" industry. Rates of return that are greater than this so-called "competitive" rate will stimulate an inflow of capital either from new entrants or from existing competitors making additional investment. Rates of return below this competitive rate will result in withdrawal from the industry and a decline in the levels of activity and competition.

Harvard University's Michael E. Porter, a leading theorist of competitive strategy, developed a **five forces model** to explain competition in an industry: the threat of new entrants, the threat of substitute products or services, the bargaining power of buyers, the bargaining power of suppliers, and the competitive rivalry among current members of the industry. In industries such as soft drinks, pharmaceuticals, and cosmetics, the favorable nature of the five forces has resulted in attractive returns for competitors. However, pressure from any of the forces can limit profitability, as evidenced by the recent fortunes of some competitors in the PC and semiconductor industries. A discussion of each of the five forces follows.

Threat of New Entrants

New entrants to an industry bring new capacity, a desire to gain market share and position, and, quite often, new approaches to serving customer needs. The decision to become a new entrant in an industry is often accompanied by a major commitment of resources. New players mean prices will be pushed downward and margins squeezed, resulting in reduced industry profitability in the long run. Porter describes eight major sources of barriers to entry, the presence or absence of which determines the extent of threat of new industry entrants.[1]

The first barrier, *economies of scale*, refers to the decline in per-unit product costs as the absolute volume of production per period increases. Although the concept of scale economies is frequently associated with manufacturing, it is also applicable to R&D, general administration, marketing, and other business functions. Honda's efficiency at engine R&D, for example, results from the wide range of products it produces that feature gasoline-powered engines. When existing firms in an industry achieve significant economies of scale, it becomes difficult for potential new entrants to be competitive.

Product differentiation, the second major entry barrier, is the extent of a product's perceived uniqueness; in other words, whether or not it is a commodity. Differentiation can be achieved as a result of unique product attributes or effective marketing communications, or both. Product differentiation and brand loyalty "raise the bar" for would-be industry entrants who would be required to make substantial investments in R&D or advertising. For example, Intel achieved differentiation and erected a barrier in the microprocessor industry with its "Intel Inside" advertising campaign and logo that appear on many PC brands.

A third entry barrier relates to *capital requirements*. Capital is required not only for manufacturing facilities (fixed capital) but also for financing R&D, advertising, field sales and service, customer credit, and inventories (working capital). The enormous capital requirements in such industries as pharmaceuticals, mainframe computers, chemicals, and mineral extraction present formidable entry barriers.

A fourth barrier to entry are the one-time *switching costs* caused by the need to change suppliers and products. These might include retraining, ancillary equipment costs, the cost of evaluating a new source, and so on. The perceived cost to customers of switching to a new competitor's product may present an insurmountable obstacle preventing industry newcomers from achieving success. For example, Microsoft's huge installed base of PC operating systems and applications presents a formidable entry barrier.

A fifth barrier to entry is access to *distribution channels*. If channels are full, or unavailable, the cost of entry is substantially increased because a new entrant must invest time and money to gain access to existing channels or to establish new channels. Some Western companies have encountered this barrier in Japan.

Government policy is frequently a major entry barrier. In some cases, the government will restrict competitive entry. This is true in a number of industries, especially those outside the United States, that have been designated as "national" industries by their respective governments. Japan's postwar industrialization strategy was based on a policy of preserving and protecting national industries in their development and growth phases. The result was a market that proved difficult for non-Japanese competitors to enter, an issue that was targeted by the Clinton administration. American business executives in a wide range of industries urged adoption of a government policy that would reduce some of these barriers and open the Japanese market to more U.S. companies.

Established firms may also enjoy *cost advantages independent of scale economies* that present barriers to entry. Access to raw materials, a large pool of low-cost labor, favorable locations, and government subsidies are several examples.

---

[1] Michael E. Porter, *Competitive Strategy* (New York: Free Press, 1980), pp. 7–33.

Finally, expected *competitor response* can be a major entry barrier. If new entrants expect existing competitors to respond strongly to entry, their expectations about the rewards of entry will certainly be affected. A potential competitor's belief that entry into an industry or market will be an unpleasant experience may serve as a strong deterrent. Bruce Henderson, former president of the Boston Consulting Group, used the term *brinkmanship* to describe a recommended approach for deterring competitive entry. Brinkmanship occurs when industry leaders convince potential competitors that any market entry effort will be countered with vigorous and unpleasant responses. This is an approach that Microsoft has used many times to maintain its dominance in software operating systems and applications.

In the quarter century since Porter first described the five forces model, the digital revolution appears to have altered the entry barriers in many industries. First and foremost, technology has lowered the cost for new entrants. For example, Barnes & Noble watched an entrepreneurial upstart, Amazon.com, storm the barriers protecting traditional "brick-and-mortar" booksellers. Amazon.com founder Jeff Bezos identified and exploited a glaring inefficiency in book distribution: Bookstores ship unsold copies of books back to publishers to be shredded and turned into pulp. Amazon.com's centralized operations and increasingly personalized online service enable customers to select from millions of different titles at discount prices and have them delivered to their homes within days. For a growing number of book-buying consumers, Amazon.com eclipses the value proposition of local bookstores that offer "only" a few thousand titles and gourmet coffee bars. Since Bezos founded Amazon.com in 1995, sales have grown to $10.7 billion and the company has expanded into new product lines such as CDs and DVDs. The company serves tens of millions of customers in 160 countries. Barnes & Noble responded by entering the online book market itself even as it continues to be profitable in its traditional bricks-and-mortar business. In the meantime, Bezos has repositioned Amazon.com as an Internet superstore selling electronics and general merchandize. In 2003, the company earned a first-ever full-year profit of $35 million.

Threat of Substitute Products

A second force influencing competition in an industry is the threat of substitute products. The availability of substitute products places limits on the prices market leaders can charge in an industry; high prices may induce buyers to switch to the substitute. Once again, the digital revolution is dramatically altering industry structures. In addition to lowering entry barriers, the digital era means that certain types of products can be converted to bits and distributed in pure digital form. For example, the increased popularity of peer-to-peer (p-to-p) file swapping among music fans accompanied the development of the MP3 file format for music. Napster and other online music services offer a substitute to consumers who are tired of paying $15 or more for a CD. Although a U.S. court severely curtailed Napster's activities, other services—including several outside the United States—have sprung up in its place. Bertelsmann, Sony, and the top players in the music industry were taken by surprise, and even now are struggling to develop a coherent response to the threat to their core businesses (see Case 17-1).

Bargaining Power of Buyers

In Porter's model, "buyers" refers to manufacturers (e.g., GM) and retailers (e.g., Wal-Mart), rather than consumers. The ultimate aim of such buyers is to pay the lowest possible price to obtain the products or services that they require.

Usually, therefore, if they can, buyers drive down profitability in the supplier industry. To accomplish this, the buyers have to gain leverage over their vendors. One way they can do this is to purchase in such large quantities that supplier firms are highly dependent on the buyers' business. Second, when the suppliers' products are viewed as commodities—that is, as standard or undifferentiated—buyers are likely to bargain hard for low prices because many firms can meet their needs. Buyers will also bargain hard when the supplier industry's products or services represent a significant portion of the buying firm's costs. A fourth source of buyer power is the willingness and ability to achieve backward integration.

For example, because it purchases massive quantities of goods for resale, Wal-Mart is in a position to dictate terms to any vendor wishing to distribute its products at the retail giant's stores. The Coca-Cola Company and PepsiCo are two of the companies that cater to the retailer's demands, creating new products and altering delivery systems. Wal-Mart's influence also extends to the recorded music industry; Wal-Mart refuses to stock CDs bearing parental advisory stickers for explicit lyrics or violent imagery. Recording artists who want their recordings available at Wal-Mart have the option of altering lyrics and song titles or deleting offending tracks. Likewise, artists are sometimes asked to change album cover art if Wal-Mart deems it offensive. Recently, Wal-Mart launched Soundcheck, which consists of performances by up-and-coming bands that are broadcast every Friday night on the in-house television network found in each store. Exclusive tracks featuring special versions of songs by the Soundcheck sessions' artists are also available on walmart.com.[2]

"Wal-Mart is the 800-pound gorilla. You're going to want to do more things for a customer who is growing as fast as Wal-Mart is."[3]

Ted Taft, Meridian Consulting Group

Wal-Mart has become one of the biggest sellers of recorded music in the United States. Ten years, ago, "big-box retail" accounted for about 20 percent of recorded music sales; today, the figure is about 65 percent. Much of the discounter's growth in this area has come at the expense of specialty music stores. In 2006 alone, about 800 music stores—including those of the bankrupt Tower Records chain—closed. One way that Wal-Mart exercises its buying power is by refusing to stock CDs bearing "Parental Advisory" stickers warning of controversial or potentially offensive lyrics; many artists release edited versions so that Wal-Mart will carry them. However, some artists refuse to make such concessions. For example, Green Day's American Idiot and Mos Def's Black on Both Sides are not available in "clean" versions. As a result, shoppers won't find them at Wal-Mart.

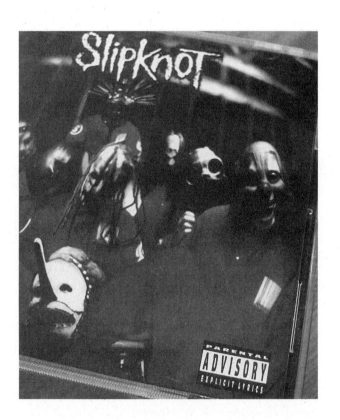

2   Jonathan Birchall, "Wal-Mart, the Record Label," *Financial Times* (January 31, 2006), p. 17.
3   Melanie Warner, "Its Wish, Their Command," *The New York Times* (March 3, 2006), p. C1.

Bargaining Power of Suppliers

Supplier power in an industry is the converse of buyer power. If suppliers have enough leverage over industry firms, they can raise prices high enough to significantly influence the profitability of their organizational customers. Several factors determine suppliers' ability to gain leverage over industry firms. Suppliers will have the advantage if they are large and relatively few in number. Second, when the suppliers' products or services are important inputs to user firms, are highly differentiated, or carry switching costs, the suppliers will have considerable leverage over buyers. Suppliers will also enjoy bargaining power if alternative products do not threaten their business. A fourth source of supplier power is the willingness and ability of suppliers to develop their own products and brand names if they are unable to get satisfactory terms from industry buyers. In the tech world, Microsoft and Intel are two excellent examples of companies with substantial supplier power. Because about 90 percent of the world's nearly 600 million PCs use Microsoft's operating systems and Intel's microprocessors, the two companies enjoy a great deal of leverage relative to Dell, Compaq, and other computer manufacturers. Because Microsoft became so powerful, the U.S. government and the EU launched separate antitrust investigations.

Rivalry Among Competitors

Rivalry among firms refers to all the actions taken by firms in the industry to improve their positions and gain advantage over each other. Rivalry manifests itself in price competition, advertising battles, product positioning, and attempts at differentiation. To the extent that rivalry among firms forces companies to rationalize costs, it is a positive force. To the extent that it drives down prices, and, therefore, profitability, and creates instability in the industry, it is a negative factor. Several factors can create intense rivalry. Once an industry becomes mature, firms focus on market share and how it can be gained at the expense of others. Second, industries characterized by high fixed costs are always under pressure to keep production at full capacity to cover the fixed costs. Once the industry accumulates excess capacity, the drive to fill capacity will push prices—and profitability—down. A third factor affecting rivalry is lack of differentiation or an absence of switching costs, which encourages buyers to treat the products or services as commodities and shop for the best prices. Again, there is downward pressure on prices and profitability. Fourth, firms with high strategic stakes in achieving success in an industry generally are destabilizing because they may be willing to accept below-average profit margins to establish themselves, hold position, or expand.

The PC industry is a case in point. For years, demand for PCs grew at an annual rate of 15 percent. Since the tech bubble burst in early 2000, however, firms have been dealing with a worldwide slowdown in demand; recent growth has been in the single digits. Dell has responded by aggressively cutting prices in a bid to boost share. With profit margins collapsing, competitors are struggling to adjust. The price war has claimed one victim already; in mid-2001, key rival Compaq agreed to an acquisition by Hewlett-Packard. Dell is legendary for its lean operating philosophy; just $0.115 of every sales dollar go to overhead, compared with $0.16 at Gateway, $0.21 at Compaq, and $0.225 at Hewlett-Packard. The company can assemble a complete PC in three minutes. With a build-to-order strategy at the heart of its business model, Dell's sales staff maintains close ties with customers. This approach gives Dell a great deal of flexibility when making pricing decisions.[4]

"Our goal is to shrink the profit pool and take the biggest slice."[5]

Kevin Rollins, President and COO, Dell

---

[4] Gary McWilliams, "Lean Machine: How Dell Fine-Tunes its PC Pricing to Gain Edge in a Slow Market," *The Wall Street Journal* (June 8, 2001), p. A1.

[5] Richard Waters, "Dell Aims to Stretch Its Way of Business," *Financial Times* (November 13, 2003), p. 8.

COMPETITIVE ADVANTAGE

Competitive advantage exists when there is a match between a firm's distinctive competencies and the factors critical for success within its industry. Any superior match between company competencies and customers' needs permits the firm to outperform competitors. There are two basic ways to achieve competitive advantage. First, a firm can pursue a low-cost strategy that enables it to offer products at lower prices than competitors. Competitive advantage may also be gained by a strategy of differentiating products so that customers perceive unique benefits, often accompanied by a premium price. Note that both strategies have the same effect: They both contribute to the firm's overall value proposition. Michael E. Porter explored these issues in two landmark books, *Competitive Strategy* (1985) and *Competitive Advantage* (1990); the latter is widely considered to be one of the most influential management books in recent years.

Ultimately, customer perception decides the quality of a firm's strategy. Operating results such as sales and profits are measures that depend on the level of psychological value created for customers: The greater the perceived consumer value, the better the strategy. A firm may market a better mousetrap, but the ultimate success of the product depends on customers deciding for themselves whether or not to buy it. Value is like beauty; it's in the eye of the beholder. In sum, creating more value than the competition achieves competitive advantage, and customer perception defines value.

Two different models of competitive advantage have received considerable attention. The first offers "generic strategies," four routes or paths that organizations choose to offer superior value and achieve competitive advantage. According to the second model, generic strategies alone did not account for the astonishing success of many Japanese companies in the 1980s and 1990s. The more recent model, based on the concept of "strategic intent," proposes four different sources of competitive advantage. The following paragraphs describe both models.

Generic Strategies for Creating Competitive Advantage

In addition to the "five forces" model of industry competition, Michael Porter has developed a framework of so-called generic business strategies based on the two types or sources of competitive advantage mentioned previously: *low-cost* and *differentiation*. The relationship of these two sources with the scope of the target market served (narrow or broad) or product mix width (narrow or wide) yields four **generic strategies**: *cost leadership*, *product differentiation*, *cost focus*, and *focused differentiation*.

Generic strategies aiming at the achievement of competitive advantage or superior marketing strategy demand that the firm make choices. The choices concern the *type* of competitive advantage it seeks to attain (based on cost or differentiation) and the *market scope* or *product mix width* within which competitive advantage will be attained.[7] The nature of the choice between types of advantage and market scope is a gamble, and it is the nature of every gamble that it entails *risk*: By choosing a given generic strategy, a firm always risks making the wrong choice.

Broad Market Strategies: Cost Leadership and Differentiation

Cost leadership is competitive advantage based on a firm's position as the industry's low-cost producer in broadly defined markets or across a wide mix of products. This strategy has gained widespread appeal in recent years as a result

---

[6] Regina Fazio Maruca, "The Right Way to Go Global: An Interview with Whirlpool CEO David Whitwam," *Harvard Business Review* 72, no. 2 (March–April 1994), p. 135.

[7] Michael E. Porter, *Competitive Advantage: Creating and Sustaining Superior Performance* (New York: Free Press, 1985), p. 12.

of the popularization of the experience curve concept. In general, a firm that bases its competitive strategy on overall cost leadership must construct the most efficient facilities (in terms of scale or technology) and obtain the largest share of market so that its cost per unit is the lowest in the industry. These advantages, in turn, give the producer a substantial lead in terms of experience with building the product. Experience then leads to more refinements of the entire process of production, delivery, and service, which leads to further cost reductions.

Whatever its source, cost leadership advantage can be the basis for offering lower prices (and more value) to customers in the late, more-competitive stages of the product life cycle. In Japan, companies in a range of industries—photography and imaging, consumer electronics and entertainment equipment, motorcycles, and automobiles—have achieved cost leadership on a worldwide basis.

Cost leadership, however, is a sustainable source of competitive advantage only if barriers exist that prevent competitors from achieving the same low costs. In an era of increasing technological improvements in manufacturing, manufacturers constantly leapfrog over one another in pursuit of lower costs. At one time, for example, IBM enjoyed the low-cost advantage in the production of computer printers. Then, the Japanese took the same technology and, after reducing production costs and improving product reliability, gained the low-cost advantage. IBM fought back with a highly automated printer plant in North Carolina, where the number of component parts was slashed by more than 50 percent and robots were used to snap many components into place. Despite these changes, IBM ultimately chose to exit the business; the plant was sold.

When a firm's product has an actual or perceived uniqueness in a broad market, it is said to have achieved competitive advantage by means of **differentiation**. This can be an extremely effective strategy for defending market position and obtaining above-average financial returns; unique products often command premium price. Examples of successful differentiation include Maytag in large home appliances, Caterpillar in construction equipment, and almost any successful branded consumer product. Maytag has been called "the Rolls-Royce of washers and dryers;" half the washers sold in the United States are priced at $399 or less, and Maytag does offer a model at that price point. However, Maytag also markets Neptune, a high-tech, water-saving machine; the Neptune line is priced substantially higher than "regular" washers. IBM traditionally has differentiated itself with a strong sales/service organization and the security of the IBM standard in a world of rapid obsolescence. Among athletic shoe manufacturers, Nike has positioned itself as the technological leader thanks to unique product features found in a wide array of shoes.

Narrow Target Strategies: Cost Focus and Focused Differentiation

The preceding discussion of cost leadership and differentiation considered only the impact on broad markets. By contrast, strategies to achieve a narrow focus advantage target a narrowly defined market or customer. This advantage is based on an ability to create more customer value for a narrowly targeted segment and results from a better understanding of customer needs and wants. A narrow-focus strategy can be combined with either cost- or differentiation-advantage strategies. In other words, while a *cost focus* means offering low prices to a narrow target market, a firm pursuing *focused differentiation* will position itself in terms of product uniqueness and premium prices that appeal to a tightly defined target market.

German's *Mittelstand* companies have been extremely successful pursuing **focused differentiation** strategies backed by a strong export effort. The world of "high-end" audio equipment offers another example of focused differentiation. A few hundred small companies design speakers, amplifiers, and related hi-fi gear that costs thousands of dollars per component. While audio components represent a $21 billion market worldwide, annual sales in the high-end segment are only

With annual revenues of $110 billion, Munich-based Siemens AG is a key global player in a variety of engineering sectors. Siemens pursues differentiation focus strategies by targeting key business-to-business segments with relevant marketing messages. Worldwide, public interest in energy-related issues has increased significantly. This advertisement for Siemens' U.S. unit underscores the company's commitment to innovation in power generation, transmission, and distribution to ensure that the nation's energy needs are met.

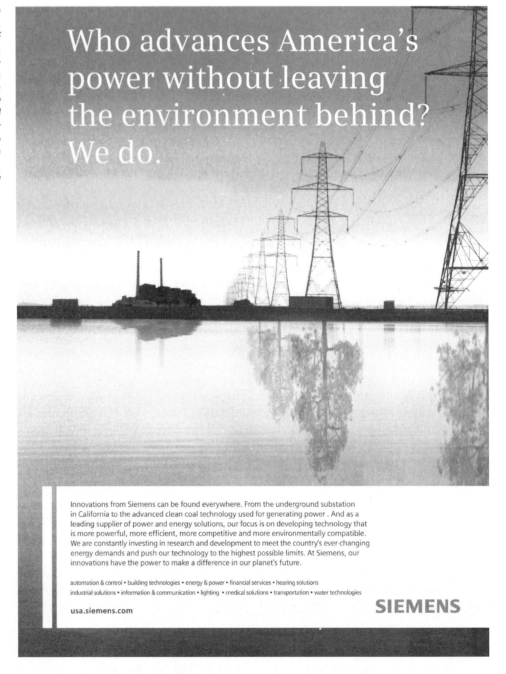

Who advances America's power without leaving the environment behind? We do.

Innovations from Siemens can be found everywhere. From the underground substation in California to the advanced clean coal technology used for generating power . And as a leading supplier of power and energy solutions, our focus is on developing technology that is more powerful, more efficient, more competitive and more environmentally compatible. We are constantly investing in research and development to meet the country's ever-changing energy demands and push our technology to the highest possible limits. At Siemens, our innovations have the power to make a difference in our planet's future.

automation & control • building technologies • energy & power • financial services • hearing solutions
industrial solutions • information & communication • lighting • medical solutions • transportation • water technologies

usa.siemens.com

SIEMENS

about $1.1 billion. American companies such as Audio Research, Conrad-Johnson, Krell, Mark Levinson, Martin-Logan, and Thiel dominate the segment, which also includes hundreds of smaller enterprises with annual sales of less than $10 million. The state-of-the-art equipment these companies offer is distinguished by superior craftsmanship and performance and is highly sought after by audiophiles in Asia (especially Japan and Hong Kong) and Europe. Industry growth is occurring as companies learn more about overseas customers and build relationships with distributors in other countries.[8]

---

8   Personal communication with Kerry Moyer, senior director, industry programs, Consumer Electronics Association, Arlington, Virginia.

In keeping with the design aesthetics or high-end audio gear, Aragon's seven-channel surround sound home theatre preamp and matching amplifier are the epitome of classic, minimalist design. The amplifier alone (bottom unit) retails for about $3,000.

The final strategy is **cost focus**, when a firm's lower cost position enables it to offer a narrow target market and lower prices than the competition. In the shipbuilding industry, for example, Polish and Chinese shipyards offer simple, standard vessel types at low prices that reflect low production costs.[9] Germany's Aldi, a no-frills "hard discounter" with operations in numerous countries, offers a very limited selection of household goods at extremely low prices. IKEA, the Swedish furniture company described in the chapter introduction, has grown into a successful global company by combining both the focused differentiation and cost focus strategies. As George Bradley, president of Levitz Furniture in Boca Raton, Florida, noted, "[IKEA] has really made a splash. They're going to capture their niche in every city

global MARKETING Q&A

Wall Street Journal: "Sixty percent of the operating profit of LVMH comes from Vuitton. Doesn't that worry you?"

Bernard Arnault, Chairman and Chief Executive Officer, LVMH Moët Hennessy-Louis Vuitton: "Not at all, because I think Vuitton is the brand that has the most growth potential and no direct, comparable competitor. There is a real economic reason people buy Vuitton. There's some fashion, but it's not really fashion. The real motivation is that it's the best value in leather goods. The price is high, but it's not crazy. Vuitton is like Microsoft. You cannot imitate the business model. It's impossible."

Wall Street Journal: "How concerned are you about Louis Vuitton counterfeits?"

Bernard Arnault: "Very concerned. On the other hand, this summer when I was on the beaches in Italy and France, all the counterfeit bags were Vuitton and Dior, so maybe it's a sign that the product is doing well—the price of success. We try to seize the counterfeits, but it's a constant struggle."

Source: The Wall Street Journal (Western Edition) by Lisa Bannon and Allesandra Galloni. Copyright 2003 by Dow Jones & Company, Inc. Reproduced with permission of Dow Jones & Company, Inc. in the format Textbook via Copyright Clearance Center.

[9] Michael E. Porter, *The Competitive Advantage of Nations* (New York: Free Press, 1990), p. 39.

they go into." Such a strategy can be risky. As Bradley explains, "Their market is finite because it is so narrow. If you don't want contemporary, knock-down furniture, it's not for you. So it takes a certain customer to buy it. And remember, fashions change."[10]

The issue of sustainability is central to this strategy concept. As noted, cost leadership is a sustainable source of competitive advantage only if barriers exist that prevent competitors from achieving the same low costs. Sustained differentiation depends on continued perceived value and the absence of imitation by competitors.[11] Several factors determine whether or not focus can be sustained as a source of competitive advantage. First, a cost focus is sustainable if a firm's competitors are defining their target markets more broadly. A focuser doesn't try to be all things to all people: Competitors may diminish their advantage by trying to satisfy the needs of a broader market segment—a strategy which, by definition, means a blunter focus. Second, a firm's differentiation focus advantage is only sustainable if competitors cannot define the segment even more narrowly. Also, focus can be sustained if competitors cannot overcome barriers that prevent imitation of the focus strategy, and if consumers in the target segment do not migrate to other segments that the focuser doesn't serve.

The Flagship Firm: The Business Network with Five Partners[12]

According to Professors Alan Rugman and Joseph D'Cruz, Porter's model is too simplistic given the complexity of today's global environment. Rugman and D'Cruz have developed an alternative framework based on business networks that they call the **flagship model** (Figure 15-1). Japanese vertical *keiretsu* and Korean *chaebol* have succeeded, Rugman and D'Cruz argue, by adopting strategies that are mutually reinforcing within a business system and by fostering a collective long-term outlook among partners in the system. Moreover, the authors note, "long-term competitiveness in global industries is less a matter of

Indian pharmaceutical companies such as Ranbaxy and Dr Reddy's Laboratories specialize in low-cost, generic versions of drugs to treat cancer, AIDS, and other diseases. Despite the fact that India passed new patent legislation in 2005 intended to limit the manufacture of generics, Western pharmaceutical companies are concerned about lack of clarity in the laws. Meanwhile, the Indian pharmaceutical sector is becoming more global; some industry experts expect Indian companies to have at least a 30 percent share of the worldwide generics market.

---

10 Jeffrey A. Trachtenberg, "Home Economics: IKEA Furniture Chain Pleases with Its Prices, Not with Its Service," *The Wall Street Journal* (September 17, 1991), pp. A1, A5.

11 Michael E. Porter, *Competitive Advantage: Creating and Sustaining Superior Performance* (New York: Free Press, 1985), p. 158.

12 The following discussion is adapted from Alan M. Rugman and Joseph R. D'Cruz. *Multinationals as Flagship Firms* (Oxford, England: Oxford University Press, 2000).

IKEA

IKEA's unconventional approach to the furniture business has enabled it to rack up impressive growth in a $30 billion industry in which overall sales have been flat. Sourcing furniture from a network of more than 1,600 suppliers in 55 countries helps the company maintain its low-cost, high-quality position. During the 1990s, IKEA expanded into Central and Eastern Europe. Because consumers in those regions have relatively low purchasing power, the stores offer a smaller selection of goods; some furniture was designed specifically for the cramped living styles typical in former Soviet bloc countries. Throughout Europe, IKEA benefits from the perception that Sweden is the source of high-quality products and efficient service. Currently, Germany and the United Kingdom are IKEA's top two markets. The United Kingdom represents the fastest-growing market in Europe; although Britons initially viewed the company's less-is-more approach as cold and "too Scandinavian," they were eventually won over. IKEA currently has 10 stores in the United Kingdom and plans to open 20 more in the next decade. As Allan Young, creative director of London's St. Luke's advertising agency, noted, "IKEA is anticonventional. It does what it shouldn't do. That's the overall theme for all IKEA ads: liberation from tradition."

In 2005, IKEA opened two stores near Tokyo; more stores are on the way as the company expands in Asia. IKEA's first attempt to develop the Japanese market in the mid-1970s resulted in failure. Why? As Tommy Kullberg, chief executive of IKEA Japan, explains, "In 1974, the Japanese market from a retail point of view was closed. Also, from the Japanese point of view, I do not think they were ready for IKEA, with our way of doing things, with flat packages and asking the consumers to put things together and so on." However, demographic and economic trends are much different today. After years of recession, consumers are seeking alternatives to paying high prices for quality goods. Also, IKEA's core customer segment—post-baby boomers in their thirties—will grow by nearly 10 percent between 2000 and 2010. In Japan, IKEA will offer home delivery and an assembly service option.

Industry observers predict that North America will eventually rise to the number one position in terms of IKEA's worldwide sales. The company opened its first U.S. store in Philadelphia in 1985;

> *"To succeed in Japan, I think we have to tell the whole story of why we can sell our products at affordable prices."*
>
> Tommy Kullberg, Chief Executive, IKEA Japan

as of 2003, IKEA operated 16 stores in the United States and 11 in Canada. Plans call for opening five U.S. stores each year over between now and 2015. As Goran Carstedt, president of IKEA North America, explains, "Our customers understand our philosophy, which calls for each of us to do a little in order to save a lot. They value our low prices. And almost all of them say they will come back again." As one industry observer noted, "IKEA is on the way to becoming the Wal-Mart Stores of the home-furnishing industry. If you're in this business, you'd better take a look."

Sources: Richard Tomkins, "How Ikea Has Managed to Treat Us Mean and Keep Us Keen," Financial Times (January 14–January 15, 2006), p. 7; Theresa Howard, "Ikea Builds on Furnishings Success," USA Today (December 29, 2004), p. 3B; Mariko Sanchanta, "Ikea's Second Try at Japan's Flat-Pack Fans," Financial Times (March 4, 2004), p. 11; Paula M. Miller, "IKEA with Chinese Characteristics," China Business Review (July–August 2004), pp. 36–38; Christopher Brown-Humes, "An Empire Built on a Flat Pack," Financial Times (November 24, 2003), p. 8; Brown-Humes, "Ikea Aims to Fill Up Homes One Catalogue at a Time," Financial Times (August 14, 2003), p. 14; Alan M. Rugman and Joseph R. D'Cruz, Multinationals as Flagship Firms (Oxford: Oxford University Press, 2000), Chapter. 3; Ernest Beck, "IKEA Sees Quirkiness as Selling Point in UK," The Wall Street Journal (January 4, 2001), pp. A1, A5; Loretta Roach, "IKEA: Furnishing the World," Discount Merchandiser (October 1994), pp. 46, 48; "Furnishing the World," Economist (November 19, 1994), pp. 79–80.

rivalry between firms and more a question of competition between business systems." A major difference between their model and Porter's is that Porter's is based on the notion of corporate individualism and individual business transactions. For example, as discussed previously, Microsoft's tremendous supplier power allows it to dictate to, and even prosper at the expense of, the computer manufacturers it supplies with operating systems and applications. The flagship model is evident in the strategies of Ford, Volkswagen, and other global automakers; Sweden's IKEA and Italy's Benetton are additional examples.

As shown in Figure 15-1, the flagship firm is at the center of a collection of five partners; together, they form a business system that consists of two types of relationships. The flagship firm provides the leadership, vision, and resources to "lead the network in a successful global strategy." *Key suppliers* are those that perform some value-creating activities, such as manufacturing of critical components, better than the flagship. The double-headed arrows that penetrate the flagship and key suppliers in Figure 15-1 indicate that this is a network relationship, with a sharing of strategies, resources, and responsibility for the success of the network. Other suppliers are kept at "arm's length"; these traditional commercial relationships are depicted diagrammatically by arrows that stop at the border of the flagship. Likewise, the flagship has network relationships with *key customers* and more traditional, arm's length commercial relationships with *key consumers*. In the case of Volkswagen, for example, dealers are its key customers while individual car buyers are key consumers; similarly,

Figure 15-1

The Flagship Model

Source: "The Flagship Model" (p.9) from "Multinationals as Flagship Firms" by Rugman, Alan M. and D'Cruz, Joseph R. (2003). By permission of Oxford University Press.

Benetton's key customers are its retail outlets while the individual clothes shopper is the key consumer. *Key competitors* are companies with which the flagship develops alliances such as those described at the end of Chapter 9. The fifth partner is the *nonbusiness infrastructure* (NBI), comprised of universities, governments, trade unions, and other entities that can supply the network with intangible inputs such as intellectual property and technology. In the flagship model, flagship firms often play a role in the development of a country's industrial policy.

Daewoo Group was once a typical Korean chaebol (family-run conglomerate). However, after the currency crisis of the 1990s, Daewoo underwent a dramatic restructuring. Daewoo Motors was acquired by GM, and India's Tata Motors bought Daewoo Commercial Vehicle. Today, the Korean government owns about 54 percent of Daewoo Shipbuilding & Marine Engineering (DSME); global investors hold the remaining shares. As an independent entity, DSME is prospering by pursuing a differentiation focus strategy. Its products include liquified-natural-gas tankers and offshore drilling platforms.

Benetton's success in the global fashion industry illustrates the flagship model. Benetton is the world's largest purchaser of wool, and its centralized buying enables the company to reap scale economies. The core activities of cutting and dyeing are retained in-house, and Benetton has made substantial investments in computer-assisted design and manufacturing. However, Benetton is linked to approximately 400 subcontractors that produce finished garments in exclusive supply relationships with the company. In turn, a network of 80 agents who find investors, train managers, and assist with merchandising, link the subcontractors to the 5,000 Benetton retail shops. As Rugman and D'Cruz note, "Benetton is organized to reward cooperation and relationship building and the company's structure has been created to capitalize on the benefits of long-term relationships."

Creating Competitive Advantage via Strategic Intent

An alternative framework for understanding competitive advantage focuses on competitiveness as a function of the pace at which a company implants new advantages deep within its organization. This framework identifies **strategic intent**, growing out of ambition and obsession with winning, as the means for achieving competitive advantage. Writing in the *Harvard Business Review*, Gary Hamel and C. K. Prahalad note:

> Few competitive advantages are long lasting. Keeping score of existing advantages is not the same as building new advantages. The essence of strategy lies in creating tomorrow's competitive advantages faster than competitors mimic the ones you possess today. An organization's capacity to improve existing skills and learn new ones is the most defensible competitive advantage of all.[13]

This approach is founded on the principles of W. E. Deming, who stressed that a company must commit itself to continuing improvement in order to be a winner in a competitive struggle. For years, Deming's message fell on deaf ears in the

---

[13] Gary Hamel and C.K. Prahalad, "Strategic Intent," *Harvard Business Review* 67, no. 3 (May–June 1989), pp. 63–76. See also Hamel and Prahalad, "The Core Competence of the Corporation," *Harvard Business Review* 68, no. 3 (May–June 1990), pp. 79–93.

United States, while the Japanese heeded his message and benefited tremendously. Japan's most prestigious business award is named after him. Finally, however, U.S. manufacturers are starting to respond.

The significance of Hamel and Prahalad's framework becomes evident when comparing Caterpillar and Komatsu. As noted earlier, Caterpillar is a classic example of differentiation: The company became the largest manufacturer of earthmoving equipment in the world because it was fanatical about quality and service. Caterpillar's success as a global marketer has enabled it to achieve a 35 percent share of the worldwide market for earthmoving equipment, more than half of which represents sales to developing countries. The differentiation advantage was achieved with product durability, global spare parts service (including guaranteed parts delivery anywhere in the world within 48 hours), and a strong network of loyal dealers.

Caterpillar faced a very challenging set of environmental forces during the last several decades. Many of Caterpillar's plants were closed by a lengthy strike in the early 1980s; a worldwide recession at the same time caused a downturn in the construction industry. This hurt companies that were Caterpillar customers. In addition, the strong dollar gave a cost advantage to foreign rivals.

Compounding Caterpillar's problems was a new competitive threat from Japan. Komatsu was the world's number-two construction equipment company and had been competing with Caterpillar in the Japanese market for years. Komatsu's products were generally acknowledged to offer a lower level of quality. The rivalry took on a new dimension after Komatsu adopted the slogan "*Maru-c*," meaning "encircle Caterpillar." Emphasizing quality and taking advantage of low labor costs and the strong dollar, Komatsu surpassed Caterpillar as number one in earthmoving equipment in Japan and made serious inroads in the United States and other markets. However, the company continued to develop new sources of competitive advantage even after it achieved world-class quality. For example, new-product development cycles were shortened and manufacturing was rationalized. Caterpillar struggled to sustain its competitive advantage because many customers found that Komatsu's combination of quality, durability, and lower price created compelling value. Yet even as recession and a strong yen put new pressure on Komatsu, the company sought new opportunities by diversifying into machine tools and robots.[14]

The Komatsu-Caterpillar saga is just one example of how more than the pursuit of generic strategies can shape global competitive battles. Many firms have gained competitive advantage by *disadvantaging* rivals through "competitive innovation." Hamel and Prahalad define *competitive innovation* as "the art of containing competitive risks within manageable proportions" and identify four successful approaches used by Japanese competitors. These are: *building layers of advantage, searching for loose bricks, changing the rules of engagement,* and *collaborating.*

Layers of Advantage

A company faces less risk in competitive encounters if it has a wide portfolio of advantages. Successful companies steadily build such portfolios by establishing layers of advantage on top of one another. Komatsu is an excellent example of this approach. Another is the TV industry in Japan. By 1970, Japan was not only the world's largest producer of black-and-white TV sets but was also well on its way to becoming the leader in producing color sets. The main competitive advantage for such companies as Matsushita at that time was low labor costs.

---

[14] Robert L. Rose and Masayoshi Kanabayashi, "Komatsu Throttles Back on Construction Equipment," *The Wall Street Journal* (May 13, 1992), p. B4.

Because they realized that their cost advantage could be temporary, the Japanese also added an additional layer of *quality and reliability* advantages by building plants large enough to serve world markets. Much of this output did not carry the manufacturer's brand name. For example, Matsushita Electric sold products to other companies such as RCA that marketed them under their own brand names. Matsushita was pursuing a simple idea: A product sold was a product sold, no matter whose label it carried.[15]

In order to build the next layer of advantage, the Japanese spent the 1970s investing heavily in marketing channels and Japanese brand names to gain recognition. This strategy added yet another layer of competitive advantage: the *global brand franchise*; that is, a global customer base. By the late 1970s, channels and brand awareness were established well enough to support the introduction of new products that could benefit from global marketing—VCRs and photocopy machines, for example. Finally, many companies have invested in *regional manufacturing* so their products can be differentiated and better adapted to customer needs in individual markets.

The process of building layers illustrates how a company can move along the value chain to strengthen competitive advantage. The Japanese began with manufacturing (an upstream value activity) and moved on to marketing (a downstream value activity) and then back upstream to basic R&D. All these sources of competitive advantage represent mutually reinforcing layers that are accumulated over time.

Loose Bricks

A second approach takes advantage of the "loose bricks" left in the defensive walls of competitors whose attention is narrowly focused on a market segment or a geographic area to the exclusion of others. For example, Caterpillar's attention was focused elsewhere when Komatsu made its first entry into the Eastern Europe market. Similarly, Taiwan's Acer prospered by following founder Stan Shih's strategy of approaching the world computer market from the periphery. Shih's inspiration was the Asian board game Go, in which the winning player successfully surrounds opponents. Shih gained experience and built market share in countries overlooked by competitors such as IBM and Compaq. By the time Acer was ready to target the United States in earnest, it was already the number one PC brand in key countries in Latin America, Southeast Asia, and the Middle East.[16] Intel's loose brick was its narrow focus on complex microprocessors for PCs. Even as it built its core business to a commanding 90 percent share of the market, markets for non-PC consumer electronics products were exploding. The new products, which include set-top boxes for televisions, digital cameras, and so-called smart cards, require chips that are far cheaper than those produced by Intel. Competitors such as NEC and LSI Logic recognized the opportunity and beat Intel into an important new market.[17]

Changing the Rules

A third approach involves changing the so-called "rules of engagement" and refusing to play by the rules set by industry leaders. For example, in the copier market, IBM and Kodak imitated the marketing strategies used by market leader Xerox. Meanwhile Canon, a Japanese challenger, wrote a new rulebook.

While Xerox built a wide range of copiers, Canon built standardized machines and components, reducing manufacturing costs. While Xerox employed a huge direct sales force, Canon chose to distribute through office-product dealers. Canon also designed serviceability, as well as reliability, into its products so that it could

[15] James Lardner, *Fast Forward: Hollywood, The Japanese, and the VCR Wars* (New York: New American Library, 1987) p. 135.

[16] Dan Shapiro, "Ronald McDonald, Meet Stan Shih," *Sales & Marketing Management* (November 1995), p. 86.

[17] Dean Takahashi, "Hand-Held Combat: How the Competition Got Ahead of Intel in Making Cheap Chips," *The Wall Street Journal* (February 12, 1998), pp. A1, A10.

rely on dealers for service rather than incurring the expense required to create a national service network. Canon further decided to sell rather than lease its machines, freeing the company from the burden of financing the lease base. In another major departure, Canon targeted its copiers at secretaries and department managers rather than at the heads of corporate duplicating operations.[18]

Canon introduced the first full-color copiers and the first copiers with "connectivity"— the ability to print images from such sources as video camcorders and computers. The Canon example shows how an innovative marketing strategy— with fresh approaches to the product, pricing, distribution, and selling—can lead to overall competitive advantage in the marketplace. Canon is not invulnerable, however; in 1991 Tektronix, a U.S. company, leapfrogged past Canon in the color copier market by introducing a plain-paper color copier that offered sharper copies at a much lower price.[19]

Collaborating

A final source of competitive advantage is using know-how developed by other companies. Such *collaboration* may take the form of licensing agreements, joint ventures, or partnerships. History has shown that the Japanese have excelled at using the collaborating strategy to achieve industry leadership. As noted in Chapter 9, one of the legendary licensing agreements of modern business history is Sony's licensing of transistor technology from AT&T's Western Electric subsidiary in the 1950s for $25,000. This agreement gave Sony access to the transistor and allowed the company to become a world leader. Building on its initial successes in the manufacturing and marketing of portable radios, Sony has grown into a superb global marketer whose name is synonymous with a wide assortment of high-quality consumer electronics products.

More recent examples of Japanese collaboration are found in the aircraft industry. Today, Mitsubishi Heavy Industries Ltd. and other Japanese companies manufacture airplanes under license to U.S. firms and also work as subcontractors for aircraft parts and systems. Many observers fear that the future of the American aircraft industry may be jeopardized as the Japanese gain technological expertise. The next section discusses various examples of "collaborative advantage."[20]

GLOBAL COMPETITION AND NATIONAL COMPETITIVE ADVANTAGE[21]

An inevitable consequence of the expansion of global marketing activity is the growth of competition on a global basis. In industry after industry, global competition is a critical factor affecting success. As Yoshino and Rangan have explained,

---

[18] Gary Hamel and C.K. Prahalad, "Strategic Intent," *Harvard Business Review* 67, no. 3 (May–June 1989), p. 69.

[19] G. Pascal Zachary, "Color Printer Gives Tektronix Jump on Canon," *The Wall Street Journal* (June 14, 1991), p. B1.

[20] Hamel and Prahalad have continued to refine and develop the concept of strategic intent since it was first introduced in their groundbreaking 1989 article. During the 1990s, the authors outlined five broad categories of resource leverage that managers can use to achieve their aspirations: Concentrating resources on strategic goals via convergence and focus; accumulating resources more efficiently via extracting and borrowing; complementing one resource with another by blending and balancing; conserving resources by recycling, co-opting, and shielding; and rapid recovery of resources in the marketplace. Gary Hamel and C. K. Prahalad, "Strategy as Stretch and Leverage," *Harvard Business Review* 71, no. 2 (March–April 1993) pp. 75–84.

[21] This section draws heavily on Chapter 3, "Determinants of National Competitive Advantage," and Chapter 4, "The Dynamics of National Advantage," in Porter 1990. For an extended country analysis based on Porter's framework, see Michael Enright, Antonio Francés, and Edith Scott Assavedra, *Venezuela: The Challenge of Competitiveness* (New York: St. Martin's Press, 1996).

global competition occurs when a firm takes a global view of competition and sets about maximizing profits worldwide, rather than on a country-by-country basis. If, when expanding abroad, a company encounters the same rival in market after market, then it is engaged in global competition.[22] In some industries, global companies have virtually excluded all other companies from their markets. An example is the detergent industry, in which three companies—Colgate, Unilever, and Procter & Gamble—dominate an increasing number of detergent markets in Latin America and the Pacific Rim. Many companies can make a quality detergent, but brand-name muscle and the skills required for quality packaging overwhelm local competition in market after market.[23]

The automobile industry has also become fiercely competitive on a global basis. Part of the reason for the initial success of foreign automakers in the United States was the reluctance—or inability—of U.S. manufacturers to design and manufacture high-quality, inexpensive small cars. The resistance of U.S. manufacturers was based on the economics of car production: the bigger the car, the higher the list price. Under this formula, small cars meant smaller unit profits. Therefore, U.S. manufacturers resisted the increasing preference in the U.S. market for smaller cars, a classic case of ethnocentrism and management myopia. European and Japanese manufacturers' product lines have always included cars smaller than those made in the United States. In Europe and Japan, market conditions were much different: less space, high taxes on engine displacement and on fuel, and greater market interest in functional design and engineering innovations. First Volkswagen, then Japanese automakers such as Nissan and Toyota discovered a growing demand for their cars in the U.S. market. It is noteworthy that many significant innovations and technical advances—including radial tires, antilock brakes, and fuel injection—also came from Europe and Japan. Airbags are a notable exception.

The effect of global competition has been highly beneficial to consumers around the world. In the two examples cited, detergents and automobiles, consumers have benefited. In Central America, detergent prices have fallen as a result of global competition. In the United States, foreign companies have provided consumers with the automobile products, performance, and price characteristics they wanted. If smaller, lower-priced imported cars had not been available, it is unlikely that Detroit manufacturers would have provided a comparable product as quickly. What is true for automobiles in the United States is true for every product class around the world. Global competition expands the range of products and increases the likelihood that consumers will get what they want.

The downside of global competition is its impact on the producers of goods and services. Global competition creates value for consumers, but it also has the potential to destroy jobs and profits. When a company offers consumers in other countries a better product at a lower price, this company takes customers away from domestic suppliers. Unless the domestic supplier can create new values and find new customers, the jobs and livelihoods of the domestic supplier's employees are threatened.

This section addresses the following issue: Why is a particular nation a good home base for specific industries? Why, for example, is the United States the home base for the leading competitors in PCs, software, credit cards, and movies? Why is Germany the home of so many world leaders in printing presses, chemicals, and luxury cars? Why are so many leading pharmaceutical, chocolate/confectionery, and trading companies located in Switzerland? Why are the world leaders in consumer electronics based in Japan?

---

[22] Michael Y. Yoshino and U. Srinivasa Rangan, *Strategic Alliances: An Entrepreneurial Approach to Globalization* (Boston: Harvard Business School Press, 1995), p. 56.

[23] See Joseph Kahn, "Cleaning Up: P&G Viewed China as a National Market and Is Conquering It," *The Wall Street Journal* (September 12, 1995), pp. A1, A6.

Figure 15-2

National Diamond

Source: Reprinted with permission of Business Review. Table from Michael E. Porter, "The Competitive Advantage of Nations," Business Review, 90, no. 2 (March–April 1990), p. 77. Copyright © 2004 by Business School Publishing Corporation; All rights reserved.

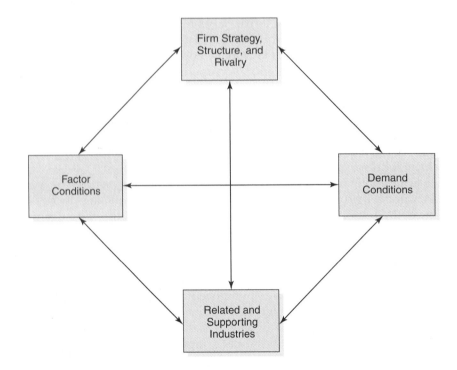

Harvard professor Michael E. Porter addressed these issues in his landmark 1990 book *The Competitive Advantage of Nations*. Many observers hailed the book as a groundbreaking guide for shaping national policies on competitiveness. According to Porter, the presence or absence of particular attributes in individual countries influences industry development, not just the ability of individual firms to create core competences and competitive advantage.[24] Porter describes these attributes— factor conditions, demand conditions, related and supporting industries, and firm strategy, structure, and rivalry—in terms of a national "diamond" that creates **national advantage**. (Figure 15-2). The diamond shapes the environment in which firms compete. Activity in any one of the four points of the diamond impacts all the others and vice versa.

Factor Conditions

The phrase **factor conditions** refers to a country's endowment with resources. Factor resources may have been created or inherited. *Basic factors* may be inherited or created without much difficulty; because they can be replicated in other nations, they are not sustainable sources of national advantage. Specialized factors, by contrast, are more advanced and provide a more sustainable source for advantage. Porter describes five categories of factor conditions: human, physical, knowledge, capital, and infrastructure.

Human Resources The quantity of workers available, the skills possessed by these workers, the wage levels, and the overall work ethic of the workforce together constitute a nation's human resources factor. Countries with a plentiful supply of low-wage workers have an obvious advantage in the production of labor-intensive products. On the other hand, such countries may be at a *disadvantage* when it comes to the production of sophisticated products requiring highly skilled workers capable of working without extensive supervision.

---

24 Michael E. Porter, *The Competitive Advantage of Nations* (New York: Free Press, 1990).

Physical Resources The availability, quantity, quality, and cost of land, water, minerals, and other natural resources determine a country's physical resources. A country's size and location are also included in this category because proximity to markets and sources of supply, as well as transportation costs, are strategic considerations. These factors are important advantages or disadvantages to industries dependent on natural resources.

Knowledge Resources The availability within a nation of a significant population having scientific, technical, and market-related knowledge means that the nation is endowed with knowledge resources. The presence of this factor is usually a function of the number of research facilities and universities—both government and private—operating in the country. This factor is important to success in sophisticated products and services, and to doing business in sophisticated markets. This factor relates directly to Germany's leadership in chemicals; for some 160 years, Germany has been home to top university chemistry programs, advanced scientific journals, and apprenticeship programs.

Capital Resources Countries vary in the availability, amount, cost, and types of capital available to the country's industries. The nation's savings rate, interest rates, tax laws, and government deficit all affect the availability of this factor. The advantage enjoyed by industries in countries with low capital costs versus those located in nations with relatively high capital costs is sometimes decisive. Firms paying high capital costs are frequently unable to stay in a market where the competition comes from a nation with low capital costs. The firms with the low cost of capital can keep their prices low and force the firms paying high costs to either accept low returns on investment or leave the industry.

Infrastructure Resources Infrastructure includes a nation's banking system, health-care system, transportation system, communications system, as well as the availability and cost of using these systems. More sophisticated industries are more dependent on advanced infrastructures for success.

Competitive advantage accrues to a nation's industry if the mix of factors available to the industry is such that it facilitates pursuit of a generic strategy (i.e., low-cost production or the production of a highly differentiated product or service). Nations that have selective factor *disadvantages* may also indirectly create competitive advantage. For example, the absence of suitable labor may force firms to develop forms of mechanization or automation that give the nation an advantage. High transportation costs may motivate firms to develop new materials that are less expensive to transport.

Demand Conditions

The nature of home demand conditions for the firm's or industry's products and services is important because it determines the rate and nature of improvement and innovation by the firms in the nation. **Demand conditions** are the factors that either train firms for world-class competition or that fail to adequately prepare them to compete in the global marketplace. Three characteristics of home demand are particularly important to the creation of competitive advantage: the composition of home demand, the size and pattern of growth of home demand, rapid home market growth, and the means by which a nation's home demand pulls the nation's products and services into foreign markets.

Composition of Home Demand This demand element determines how firms perceive, interpret, and respond to buyer needs. Competitive advantage can be achieved when the home demand sets the quality standard and gives local firms a better picture of buyer needs, at an earlier time, than is available to foreign rivals. This advantage is enhanced when home buyers pressure the nation's firms to innovate quickly and frequently. The basis for advantage is the fact that the nation's firms can stay ahead of the market when firms are more sensitive to and more responsive to home demand and when that demand, in turn, reflects or anticipates world demand.

Size and Pattern of Growth of Home Demand These are important only if the composition of the home demand is sophisticated and anticipates foreign demand. Large home markets offer opportunities to achieve economies of scale and learning while dealing with familiar, comfortable markets. There is less apprehension about investing in large-scale production facilities and expensive R&D programs when the home market is sufficient to absorb the increased capacity. If the home demand accurately reflects or anticipates foreign demand, and if the firms do not become content with serving the home market, the existence of large-scale facilities and programs will be an advantage in global competition.

Rapid Home Market Growth This is yet another incentive to invest in and adopt new technologies faster, and to build large, efficient facilities. The best example of this is in Japan, where rapid home market growth provided the incentive for Japanese firms to invest heavily in modern automated facilities. *Early home demand*, especially if it anticipates international demand, gives local firms the advantage of getting established in an industry sooner than foreign rivals. Equally important is *early market saturation*, which puts pressure on a company to expand into international markets and innovate. Market saturation is especially important if it coincides with rapid growth in foreign markets.

Means by Which a Nation's Products and Services Are Pushed or Pulled into Foreign Countries The issue here is whether a nation's people and businesses go abroad and then demand the nation's products and services in those second countries. For example, when the U.S. auto companies set up operations in foreign countries, the auto parts industry followed. The same is true for the Japanese auto industry. Similarly, when overseas demand for the services of U.S. engineering firms skyrocketed after World War II, those firms, in turn, established demand for U.S. heavy construction equipment. This provided an impetus for Caterpillar to establish foreign operations.

A related issue is that of a nation's people going abroad for training, pleasure, business, or research. After returning home, they are likely to demand the products and services with which they became familiar while abroad. Similar effects can result from professional, scientific, and political relationships between nations. Those involved in the relationships begin to demand the products and services of the recognized leaders.

It is the interplay of demand conditions that produces competitive advantage. Of special importance are those conditions that lead to initial and continuing incentives to invest and innovate, and to continuing competition in increasingly sophisticated markets.

Related and Supporting Industries

A nation has an advantage when it is home to globally competitive companies in business sectors that are **related and supporting industries**. Globally competitive supplier industries provide inputs to downstream industries. The latter, in turn, are likely to be globally competitive in terms of price and quality and, thus, gain competitive advantage from this situation. Downstream industries will have easier access to these inputs and the technology that produced them, and to the managerial and organizational structures that have made them competitive. Access is a function of proximity both in terms of physical distance and cultural similarity. It is not the inputs in themselves that give advantage. It is the *contact* and *coordination* with the suppliers, the opportunity to structure the value chain so that linkages with suppliers are optimized. These opportunities may not be available to foreign firms.

Similar advantages are present when there are globally competitive, related industries in a nation. Opportunities are available for coordinating and sharing value chain activities. Consider, for example, the opportunities for sharing between computer hardware manufacturers and software developers. Related industries also create "pull through" opportunities as described previously. For example, non-U.S. sales of PCs from Compaq, Dell, IBM, Acer, and others have bolstered demand for software from Microsoft and other U.S. companies. Porter notes that the development of the Swiss pharmaceuticals industry can be attributed in part to Switzerland's large synthetic dye industry; the discovery of the therapeutic effects of dyes, in turn, led to the development of pharmaceutical companies.[25]

Firm Strategy, Structure, and Rivalry

The **nature of firm strategy, structure, and rivalry** is the final determinant of a nation's diamond. Domestic rivalry in a single national market is a powerful influence on competitive advantage. The PC industry in the United States is a good example of how a strong domestic rivalry keeps an industry dynamic and creates continual pressure to improve and innovate. The rivalry between Dell, Hewlett-Packard, Gateway, Compaq, Apple, and others forces all the players to develop new products, improve existing ones, lower costs and prices, develop new technologies, and continually improve quality and service to keep customers happy. Rivalry with foreign firms may lack this intensity. Domestic rivals have to fight each other not just for market share, but also for employee talent, R&D breakthroughs, and prestige in the home market. Eventually, strong domestic rivalry will push firms to seek international markets to support expansions in scale and R&D investments, as Japan amply demonstrates. The absence of significant domestic rivalry can lead to complacency in the home firms and eventually cause them to become noncompetitive in the world markets.

It is not the number of domestic rivals that is important; rather, it is the intensity of the competition and the quality of the competitors that make the difference. It is also important that there be a fairly high rate of new business formations to create new competitors and safeguard against the older companies becoming comfortable with their market positions and products and services. As noted earlier in the discussion of the five forces model, new industry entrants bring new perspectives and new methods. They frequently define and serve new market segments that established companies have failed to recognize.

Differences in management styles, organizational skills, and strategic perspectives also create advantages and disadvantages for firms competing in different types of industries, as do differences in the intensity of domestic rivalry. In Germany, for example, company structure and management style tends to be hierarchical. Managers tend to come from technical backgrounds and to be most successful when dealing with industries that demand highly disciplined structures, like chemicals and precision machinery. Italian firms, on the other hand, tend to look like, and be run like, small family businesses that stress customized over standardized products, niche markets, and substantial flexibility in meeting market demands.

Capital markets and attitudes toward investments are important components of the national environments. For example, U.S. laws prohibit banks from taking an equity stake in companies to which they extend loans. This drives a short-term focus on quarterly and annual gains and losses. This focus is carried into equity

---

[25] Michael E. Porter, *The Competitive Advantage of Nations* (New York: Free Press, 1990), p. 324.

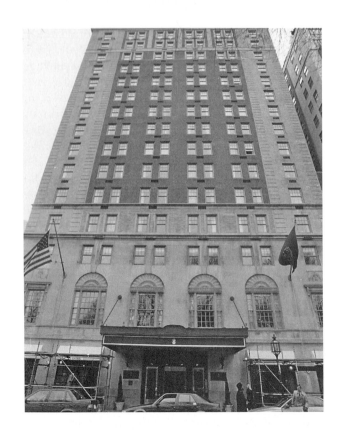

Well-known and highly esteemed in its own country, India's Tata Group participates in a variety of industries, including heavy vehicles, cars, department stores, and tea. Now the group's management team is hoping to maintain that brand image as it implements an international strategy. Historically, Tata Group's competitive advantage was based on scouring the globe to find the lowest cost, highest quality production inputs—be they raw materials or skilled labor—and then selling them in the global marketplace at a substantial profit. Now Tata is expanding by acquiring businesses in various parts of the world. For example, in 2006, the Group's Indian Hotels Company subsidiary announced plans to buy the Ritz-Carlton Hotel in Boston.

markets where low profits produce low share prices and the threat of a takeover. As a result, U.S. firms tend to do well in new-growth industries and other rapidly expanding markets. They do not do well in more mature industries where return on investment is lower and patient searching for innovations is required. Many other countries have an opposite orientation. Banks are allowed to take equity stakes in the customer companies to which they loan, which, therefore, take a long-term view and are less concerned about short-term results.

There are two final external variables to consider in the evaluation of national competitive advantage—chance and government.

Chance

Chance events play a role in shaping the competitive environment. Chance events are occurrences that are beyond the control of firms, industries, and usually governments. Included in this category are such things as wars and their aftermaths, major technological breakthroughs, sudden dramatic shifts in factor or input cost, like an oil crisis, dramatic swings in exchange rates, and so on.

Chance events are important because they create major discontinuities in technologies that allow nations and firms that were not competitive to leapfrog over old competitors and become competitive, even leaders, in the changed industry. For example, the development of microelectronics allowed many Japanese firms to overtake U.S. and German firms in industries that had been based on electromechanical technologies—areas traditionally dominated by the Americans and Germans.

From a systemic perspective, the role of chance events lies in the fact that they alter conditions in the diamond. The nation with the most favorable "diamond," however, will be the one most likely to take advantage of these events and convert them into competitive advantage. For example, Canadian researchers were the first to isolate insulin, but they could not convert this breakthrough into a globally competitive product. Firms in the United States and Denmark were able to do that because of their respective national "diamonds."

Government

Although it is often argued that government is a major determinant of national competitive advantage, government is not a determinant but rather an influence on determinants. Government influences determinants by virtue of its role as a buyer of products and services, and by its role as a maker of policies on labor, education, capital formation, natural resources, and product standards. It also influences determinants by its role as a regulator of commerce—for example, by telling banks and telephone companies what they can and cannot do.

By reinforcing determinants in industries where a nation has competitive advantage, government improves the competitive position of the nation's firms. Governments devise legal systems that influence competitive advantage by means of tariffs and nontariff barriers and laws requiring local content and labor. In the United States, for example, the dollar's decline over the past decade has been due in part to a deliberate policy to enhance U.S. export flows and stem imports. In other words, government can improve or lessen competitive advantage, but it cannot create it.

CURRENT ISSUES IN COMPETITIVE ADVANTAGE

Porter's work on national competitive advantage has stimulated a great deal of further research. The Geneva-based World Economic Forum issues an annual report ranking countries in terms of their competitiveness. A decade ago, Morgan Stanley used the Porter framework to identify 238 companies with a sustainable competitive advantage worldwide. "National advantage" was then assessed by analyzing how many of these companies were headquartered in a particular country. The United States ranked first, with 125 companies identified as world leaders (see Table 15-1). Among the world's automakers, Morgan Stanley's analysts considered only BMW, Toyota, and Honda to have worldwide competitive advantage.[26]

Hypercompetitive Industries

In a book published in the mid-1990s, Dartmouth College professor Richard D'Aveni suggests that the Porter strategy frameworks fail to adequately address the dynamics of competition in the 1990s and the new millennium.[27] D'Aveni takes a different approach. He notes that, in today's business environment, short product life cycles, short product design cycles, new technologies,

Country	Number of Companies
1. United States	125
2. United Kingdom	21
3. Japan	19
4. France	12
5. Germany	10
6. Netherlands	7
7. Canada	6
8. Switzerland	6
9. Sweden	3
10. Finland	3

Table 15-1

Location of Companies with Global Competitive Advantage

---

[26] Tony Jackson, "Global Competitiveness Observed from an Unfamiliar Angle," *Financial Times* (November 21, 1996), p. 18.

[27] Richard D'Aveni, *Hypercompetition: Managing the Dynamics of Strategic Maneuvering* (New York: Free Press, 1994).

and globalization undermine market stability. The result is an escalation and acceleration of competitive forces. In light of these changes, D'Aveni believes the goal of strategy has shifted from sustaining to disrupting advantages. The limitation of the Porter models, D'Aveni argues, is that they are static; that is, they provide a snapshot of competition at a given point in time. Acknowledging that Hamel and Prahalad broke new ground in recognizing that few advantages are sustainable, D'Aveni aims to build upon their work in order to shape "a truly dynamic approach to the creation and destruction of traditional advantages." D'Aveni uses the term **hypercompetition** to describe a dynamic competitive world in which no action or advantage can be sustained for long. In such a world, D'Aveni argues, "everything changes" because of the dynamic maneuvering and strategic interactions by hypercompetitive firms such as Microsoft and Gillette.

According to D'Aveni's model, competition unfolds in a series of dynamic strategic interactions in four arenas: cost/quality, timing and know-how, entry barriers, and deep pockets. Each of these arenas is "continuously destroyed and recreated by the dynamic maneuvering of hypercompetitive firms." According to D'Aveni, the only source of a truly sustainable competitive advantage is a company's ability to manage its dynamic strategic interactions with competitors by means of frequent movements and countermovements that maintain a relative position of strength in each of the four arenas (see Table 15-2).

Table 15-2	Arena	Dynamic Strategic Interaction
Dynamic Strategic Interactions in Hypercompetitive Industries	1. Cost/Quality	1. Price wars
		2. Quality and price positioning
		3. "The middle path"
		4. "Cover all niches"
		5. Outflanking and niching
		6. The move toward an ultimate value marketplace
		7. Escaping from the ultimate value marketplace by restarting the cycle
	2. Timing and know-how	1. Capturing first-moving advantages
		2. Imitation and improvement by follows
		3. Creating impediments to imitation
		4. Overcoming the impediments
		5. Transformation or leapfrogging
		6. Downstream vertical integration
	3. Entry barriers	1. Building a geographic stronghold by creating and reinforcing entry barriers
		2. Targeting the product market strongholds of competitors in other countries
		3. Incumbents make short-term counterresponses to guerrilla attacks
		4. Incumbents realize they must respond fully to the invaders by making strategic responses to create new hurdles.
		5. Competitors react to new hurdles
		6. Long run counter-responses via defensive or offensive moves
		7. Competition between the incumbent and entrant is exported to entrant's home turf
		8. An unstable standoff between the competitors is established
	4. Deep pockets	

Cost/Quality

Competition in the first arena, cost/quality, occurs via seven dynamic strategic interactions: price wars, quality and price positioning, "the middle path," "cover all niches," outflanking and niching, the move toward an ultimate value marketplace, and escaping from the ultimate value marketplace by restarting the cycle. D'Aveni cites the global watch industry as an example of hypercompetitive behavior in the cost/quality arena. In the 1970s, the center of the industry shifted from Switzerland to Japan as the Japanese created high-quality quartz watches that could be sold cheaply. In the early 1980s, the merger of two Swiss companies into Société Suisse Microelectronique et d'Horlogerie SA (SMH) was followed by a highly automated manufacturing innovation that allowed a quartz movement to be integrated into a stylish plastic case. As a result of this innovation and a strong marketing effort in support of the Swatch brand, the center of the watch industry shifted back to Switzerland. Today, the Swatch Group is the world's second largest watch maker; the watch industry continues to be highly segmented, with prestige brands competing on reputation and exclusivity; as with many other luxury goods, higher prices are associated with higher perceived quality. In the low-cost segment, brands compete on price and value.

Swatch Group is providing sports timing systems and services worth nearly $40 million for the 2008 Beijing Olympics. As Swatch Group CEO Georges Nicolas Hayek, Jr., noted, "We will ship 500 tons of equipment and 300 professional engineers from Switzerland to different competition venues in Beijing to measure and transmit results and scores." Hayek, the son of Swatch founder Nicolas Hayek, expects that the company's annual sales in China will reach five to six million watches by 2008. Swatch products will be available at several hundred Chinese stores and sales counters; the majority will be in Shanghai.

Timing and Know-How

The second arena for hypercompetition is based on organizational advantages derived from timing and know-how. As described by D'Aveni, a firm that has the skills to be a "first mover" and arrive first in a market has achieved a *timing advantage*. A *know-how advantage* is the technological knowledge—or other knowledge of a new method of doing business—that allows the firm to create an entirely new product or market.[28] D'Aveni identifies six dynamic strategic interactions that drive competition in this arena: capturing first-mover advantages; imitation and improvement by followers; creating impediments to imitation; overcoming the impediments; transformation or leapfrogging; and downstream vertical integration. As the consumer electronics industry has globalized, Sony and its competitors have exhibited hypercompetitive behavior in this second arena. Sony has an enviable history of first-mover achievements based on its know-how in audio technology: first pocket-sized transistor radio, first consumer VCR, first portable personal stereo, and first compact disc player. Although each of these innovations literally created an entirely new market, Sony has fallen victim to the risks associated with being a first mover. The second dynamic strategic interaction—imitation and improvement by followers—can be seen in the successful efforts of JVC and Matsushita to enter the home VCR market a few months after Sony's Betamax launch. VHS technology offered longer recording times and became the dominant consumer format worldwide until advent of the DVD era. More recently, Sony has found technological leaps harder to achieve, as evidenced by the slow market acceptance of its MiniDisc digital recording/playback units. Sony has also shown a willingness to be a follower; the company only entered the video game industry in 1994, but its 64-bit PlayStation outsold a competitive product from Sega. After Sony launched the PlayStation 2 in 2000, Sega halted production of its Dreamcast game player; the company is now concentrating on developing game software.

After years of moves and countermoves between Sony and its imitators, Sony progressed to downstream vertical integration with the 1988 purchase of CBS Records for $2 billion and then, later, the purchase of Columbia Pictures. The acquisitions, which represent the sixth dynamic strategic interaction, were intended to complement Sony's core "hardware" businesses (e.g., TVs, VCRs, and hi-fi equipment) with "software" (e.g., videocassettes and CDs). However, Matsushita quickly imitated Sony by paying $6 billion for MCA. Initially, neither Sony nor Matsushita proved successful at managing the acquisitions. Sony took a $2.7 billion pretax write-off in 1995 for losses relating to its motion picture group; Matsushita sold 80 percent of its MCA stake to Seagram. More recently, Sony Pictures Entertainment has enjoyed huge success with the *Spider-Man* movies and *Casino Royale*, the latest James Bond film. Meanwhile, Sony faced a more fundamental challenge: PCs and the Internet dramatically changed the consumer electronics industry. The digital revolution rendered Sony's core competences in analog audio technology obsolete. Sony executives must develop new know-how resources if the company is to continue to lead in the information age.

Barriers to Entry

Industries in which barriers to entry have been built up comprise the third arena in which hypercompetitive behavior is exhibited. As described earlier in the chapter, these barriers include economies of scale, product differentiation, capital investments, switching costs, access to distribution channels, cost advantages other than scale, and government policies. D'Aveni describes how aggressive competitors

---

[28] Richard D'Aveni, *Hypercompetition: Managing the Dynamics of Strategic Maneuvering* (New York: Free Press, 1994), p. 71.

erode these traditional entry barriers via eight strategic interactions. For example, a cornerstone of Dell's global success in the PC industry is a direct-sales approach that bypasses dealers and other distribution channels. Similarly, in the long distance industry, ring-back services based in the United States and elsewhere enabled persons making long-distance calls from Europe to sidestep exorbitant rates charged by government-owned telecoms.

The first dynamic strategic interaction comes as a company builds a geographic "stronghold" by creating and reinforcing barriers. After securing a market—especially the home-country market—competitors begin to seek markets outside the stronghold. Thus, the second dynamic strategic interaction takes place when companies target the product market strongholds of competitors in other countries. Honda's geographic expansion outside Japan with motorcycles and automobiles —a series of forays utilizing guerrilla tactics—is a case in point. The third dynamic strategic interaction comes when incumbents make short-term counterresponses to the guerrilla attacks. Strong incumbents may try to turn back the invader with price wars, factory investment, or product introductions, or they may adopt a wait-and-see attitude before responding. In the case of both Harley-Davidson and the Detroit-based U.S. auto industry, management originally underestimated and rationalized away the full potential of the threat from Honda and other Japanese companies. Realizing that their company was a weak incumbent, Harley-Davidson management had little choice but to appeal for government protection. The resulting "breathing room" allowed Harley to put its house in order. Similarly, the U.S. government heeded Detroit's pleas for relief and imposed tariffs and quotas on Japanese auto imports. This gave the Big Three time to develop higher-quality, fuel-efficient models to offer U.S. consumers.

The fourth dynamic strategic interaction occurs when the incumbent realizes it must respond fully to the invader by making strategic responses to create new hurdles. U.S. automakers, for example, waged a PR campaign urging U.S. citizens to "Buy American." The fifth dynamic strategic interaction takes place when competitors react to these new hurdles. In an effort to circumvent import quotas as well as co-opt the "Buy American" campaign, the Japanese automakers built plants in the United States. The sixth dynamic strategic interaction consists of long-run counterresponses to the attack via defensive moves or offensive moves. GM's 1990 introduction of Saturn is a good illustration of a well-formulated and executed defensive move. As the first decade of the twenty-first century continues, GM is launching another defensive move; in an effort to defend its Cadillac nameplate from Lexus, Acura, and Infiniti, GM is developing a global strategy for Cadillac. Competition in the third arena continues to escalate; in the seventh dynamic strategic interaction, competition between the incumbent and entrant is exported to the entrant's home turf. President Clinton's threat of trade sanctions against Japanese automakers in 1995 was intended to send a message that Japan needed to open its auto market. In 1997, GM intensified its assault on Japan with the introduction of Saturn. The eighth and final dynamic strategic interaction in this arena consists of an unstable standoff between the competitors. Over time, the stronghold erodes as entry barriers are overcome, leading competitors to the fourth arena.

As the preceding discussion shows, the irony and paradox of the hypercompetition framework is that, in order to achieve a sustainable advantage, companies must seek a series of *unsustainable* advantages! D'Aveni is in agreement with the late Peter Drucker, who long counseled that the role of marketing is innovation and the creation of new markets. Innovation begins with abandonment of the old and obsolete. Sumantra Ghoshal and Christopher Bartlett make a similar point in *The Individualized Corporation*:

> Managers are forced to refocus their attention from a preoccupation with defining defensible product-market positions to a newly awakened interest in how to

develop the organizational capability to sense and respond rapidly and flexibly to change. . . . Managers worldwide have begun to focus less on the task of forecasting and planning for the future and more on the challenge of being highly sensitive to emerging changes. Their broad objective is to create an organization that is constantly experimenting with appropriate responses, then is able to quickly diffuse the information and knowledge gained so it can be leveraged by the entire organization. The age of strategic planning is fast evolving into the era or organizational learning.[29]

Likewise, D'Aveni urges managers to reconsider and reevaluate the use of what he believes are old strategic tools and maxims. He warns of the dangers of commitment to a given strategy or course of action. The flexible, unpredictable player may have an advantage over the inflexible, committed opponent. D'Aveni notes that, in hypercompetition, pursuit of generic strategies results in short-term advantage at best. The winning companies are the ones that successfully move up the ladder of escalating competition, not the ones that lock into a fixed position. D'Aveni is also critical of the five forces model. The best entry barrier, he argues, is maintaining the initiative, not mounting a defensive attempt to exclude new entrants.

Additional Research on Comparative Advantage

Other researchers have challenged Porter's thesis that a firm's home-base country is the main source of core competencies and innovation. For example, Indiana University Professor Alan Rugman argues that the success of companies based in small economies such as Canada and New Zealand stems from the "diamonds" found in a particular set or combination of home and related countries. For example, a company based in an EU nation may rely on the national "diamond" of one of the 26 other EU members. Similarly, one impact of NAFTA on Canadian firms is to make the U.S. "diamond" relevant to competency creation. Rugman argues that, in such cases, the distinction between the home nation and the host nation becomes blurred. He proposes that Canadian managers must look to a "double diamond" and assess the attributes of both Canada and the United States when formulating corporate strategy.[30] In other words, he argues that, for smaller countries, the nation is not the relevant unit of analysis in formulating strategy. Rather, corporate strategists must look beyond the nation to the region or to sets of closely linked countries. Other critics have argued that Porter generalized inappropriately from the American experience, while confusing industry-level competition with trade at the national level. In the *Journal of Management Studies*, Howard Davies and Paul Ellis assert that nations can achieve sustained prosperity without becoming innovation driven; the authors also note the absence of strong diamonds in the home bases of many global industries.[31]

As for Michael Porter, his views on corporate strategy and competitive advantage evolved during the last quarter century. In a recent interview, he emphasized the difference between operational efficiency and strategy. The former, in Porter's view, concerns improvement via time-based competition or total quality management; the latter entails "making choices." Porter explains, "'Choice' arises from doing things differently from the rival. And strategy is about trade-offs, where you decide to do this and not that. Strategy is the deliberate choice not to respond to some customers, or choosing which customer

---

[29] Sumantra Ghoshal and Christopher Bartlett, *The Individualized Corporation* (New York: HarperBusiness, 1997), p. 71.
[30] Alan M. Rugman and Lain Verbeke, "Foreign Subsidiaries and Multinational Strategic Management: An Extension and Correction of Porter's Single Diamond Framework," *Management International Review* 3, no. 2 (1993), pp. 71–84.
[31] Howard Davies and Paul Ellis, "Porter's Competitive Advantage of Nations: Time for the Final Judgment?" *Journal of Management Studies* 37 no. 8 (December 2000) pp. 1189–1213.

needs you are going to respond to." Porter is not convinced of the validity of competitive advantage models based on core competency or hypercompetitive industries. As for core competencies, Porter notes:

> Any individual thing that a company does can usually be imitated. The whole notion that you should rest your success on a few core competencies is an idea that invites destructive competition. Successful companies don't compete that way. They fit together the things they do in a way that is very hard to replicate. [Competitors] have to match everything, or they've basically matched nothing.

On the subject of hypercompetition, Porter says:

> I don't think we're moving towards a hypercompetitive world in which there are no tradeoffs. We're probably moving in the other direction. There are more customer segments than ever before, more technological options, more distribution channels. That ought to create lots of opportunities for unique positions.[32]

---

[32] Tony Jackson, "Why Being Different Pays," *Financial Times* (June 23, 1997), p. 14.

In this chapter we focus on factors that help industries and countries achieve **competitive advantage**. According to Porter's **five forces model**, industry competition is a function of the threat of new entrants, the threat of substitutes, the bargaining power of suppliers and buyers, and rivalry among existing competitors. Managers can use Porter's **generic strategies** model to conceptualize possible sources of competitive advantage. A company can pursue broad market strategies of **cost leadership** and **differentiation** or the more targeted approaches of **cost focus** and **focused differentiation**. Rugman and D'Cruz have developed a framework known as the **flagship model** to explain how networked business systems have achieved success in global industries. Hamel and Prahalad have proposed an alternative framework for pursuing competitive advantage, growing out of a firm's **strategic intent** and use of competitive innovation. A firm can build layers of advantage, search for loose bricks in a competitor's defensive walls, change the rules of engagement, or collaborate with competitors and utilize their technology and know-how.

Today, many companies are discovering that industry competition is changing from a purely domestic to a global phenomenon. Thus, competitive analysis must also be carried out on a global scale. Global marketers must also have an understanding of national sources of competitive advantage. Porter has described four determinants of **national advantage**. **Factor conditions** include human, physical, knowledge, capital, and infrastructure resources. **Demand conditions** include the composition, size, and growth pattern of home demand. The rate of home market growth and the means by which a nation's products are pulled into foreign markets also affect demand conditions. The final two determinants are the presence of **related and supporting industries** and the **nature of firm strategy, structure, and rivalry**. Porter notes that chance and government also influence a nation's competitive advantage. Porter's work has been the catalyst for promising new research into strategy issues, including D'Aveni's work on **hypercompetition** and Rugman's recent **double-diamond framework** for national competitive advantage.

1. How can a company measure its competitive advantage? How does a firm know if it is gaining or losing competitive advantage? Cite a global company and its source of competitive advantage.

2. Outline Porter's five forces model of industry competition. How are the various barriers to entry relevant to global marketing?

3. How does the five partners, or flagship model, developed by Rugman and D'Aveni differ from Porter's five forces model?

4. Give an example of a company that illustrates each of the four generic strategies that can lead to competitive advantage: overall cost leadership, cost focus, differentiation, and differentiation focus.

5. Briefly describe Hamel and Prahalad's framework for competitive advantage.

6. How can a nation achieve competitive advantage?

7. According to current research on competitive advantage, what are some of the shortcomings of Porter's models?

8. What is the connection, if any, between *national* competitive advantage and *company* competitive advantage? Explain and discuss.

Case 15-1

Kodak in the Twenty-First Century: The Search for New Sources of Competitive Advantage

Eastman Kodak Company is at a crossroads. After inventing the famous Brownie camera in 1900, Kodak reigned as the undisputed leader in the silver-halide chemical processes that formed the basis of the photography industry throughout the twentieth century. Kodak's yellow boxes of film were iconic symbols of the brand. Once, the company's color film business was a classic cash cow, accounting for as much as 70 percent of Kodak's revenues. However, the company's long-entrenched conservative corporate culture, bureaucratic organizational structure, and go-slow approach to innovation resulted in sluggish, ill-fated responses to changes in the photography market. Although management understood that the digital revolution was changing the way consumers take, store, and access photos, the speed of the changeover from film-based photography to digital came as a shock. In the late 1990s, Kodak invested $1 billion in an alternative film-based format known as Advanced Photo System. It flopped. Meanwhile, the company maintained a premium pricing strategy, allowing competitors such as Fuji to undercut it and gain market share.

Now, management is attempting to remake the company's business model in fundamental ways. After being named president and CEO in 2000, Daniel Carp replaced most of Kodak's executive team with newcomers who had worked at technology-oriented companies such as Hewlett-Packard, Lexmark International, and General Electric. To shore up its core film business, Kodak will make private-label film for sale outside the United States. Kodak has also vowed to fight more aggressively for market share with its branded film by cutting prices. Perhaps the most dramatic move is the decision to stop selling film-based cameras for the consumer market in the United States, Canada, and Europe. The only exception is a popular line of disposable single-use cameras. The company will continue to develop and market film cameras in China, India, Eastern Europe, and Latin America,

where management believes the traditional photography format still has potential for growth.

"The trick is to get the cost structure of the traditional consumer business down. We are a business in transition."

Daniel Carp, former CEO, Eastman Kodak

By 2005, the year Carp retired and Antonio Perez was named Chairman and CEO, the digital camera market in the United States had become a key battleground. Canon ranked number one in digital camera sales; led by the PowerShot A520, Canon had 7 of the 10 top-selling models on Amazon.com. Although Canon's cameras are designed and manufactured in Japan, company engineers regularly visit the United States to absorb insights about consumer needs. One analyst noted, "Canon has built on its camera heritage and has been able to get people to believe in them as a digital company." The same analyst was also impressed by Kodak. Although the company's traditional sources of competitive advantage were in film and processing, "In a short period of time they've transitioned into a strong hardware company. They've done an amazing job," he said.

Managing the transition away from film will also require Kodak to redefine relationships with key business partners. For example, Kodak was for many years the exclusive supplier of traditional photo processing services for the Walgreens drugstore chain; the relationship, which includes one-hour services, generates about $500 million in annual revenue for Kodak. Archrival Fuji has a close partnership with Wal-Mart. Now, Fuji is making inroads at Walgreens as well. The minilabs supplied by Kodak were subject to frequent breakdowns; despite the fact that Walgreens was bound by long-term leases; the retailer began installing Fuji minilabs at a cost of $115,000 per unit. Presently, about one-third of Walgreen's 4,290 stores now use Fuji's one-hour minilab equipment. Walgreen's photo processing Web site also uses Fuji to process prints. Not to be outdone, at the 2006 Photo Marketing Association trade show, Kodak unveiled the DSP900, a modular replacement for the minilab that can produce 900 prints per hour at half the price of previous models.

Kodak currently has installed about 60,000 self-service photo kiosks in the United States that allow customers to print photos from their digital cameras. Fuji also supplies in-store kiosks bearing the Aladdin brand name. Now, Hewlett-Packard has entered the retail photo services market as well; it has begun installing $15,000 PhotoStudio kiosks at stores in the Long's Drugs chain. As Matt Troy, an analyst with Citigroup Investment Research, noted, "Kodak has been very successful in cultivating an ecosystem in the digital world. H-P's motivation is to sell more ink. The kiosks are a few more straws to drink from the ink well." Concludes Troy, "H-P is trying to be the next Kodak."

Discussion Questions

1. Assess Kodak's situation in terms of Porter's five forces model and generic strategies. Which forces are driving competition in the photo industry? What has happened to Kodak's traditional sources of competitive advantage?

2. Do you think the digital photography revolution will spread to China and India more quickly than Kodak's management expects?

3. For decades, Kodak has been known as the world's largest consumer photography company. Today, the company's strategy calls for a shift towards b-to-b marketing with an emphasis on such products as medical imaging systems and digital printing systems. What risks does this change in strategic direction present?

Sources: Francesco Guerrera, "Kodak Refocuses on Digital Age," *Financial Times* (November 29, 2006), p. 11; William M. Bulkeley, "Kodak Revamps Wal-Mart Kiosks," *The Wall Street Journal* (September 6, 2006), p. B2; Damon Darlin, "Hewlett-Packard Decides Store Photo Printing Is Its Turf," *The New York Times* (February 23, 2006), pp. C1, C17; Jefferson Graham, "Canon, Kodak Face Off in Digital Arena," *USA Today* (February 23, 2006), p. 3B; James Bandler, "Losing Focus: As Kodak Eyes, Digital Future, A Big Partner Starts to Fade," *The Wall Street Journal* (January 23, 2004), pp. A1, A8; Bandler, "Ending Era, Kodak Will Stop Selling Most Film Cameras," *The Wall Street Journal* (January 14, 2004), p. B1, B4; Bandler, "Kodak Shifts Focus from Film, Betting Future on Digital Lines," *The Wall Street Journal* (September 29, 2003), pp. A1, A12.

Case 15-2
LEGO

The LEGO Company is a $1.6 billion global business built out of the humblest of materials: interlocking plastic toy bricks. From its base in Denmark, the family-owned LEGO empire extends around the world and came to include theme parks, clothing, and computer-controlled toys. Each year, the company produces about 14 billion plastic blocks as well as tiny human figures to populate towns and operate gizmos that spring from the imaginations of young people. LEGO products, which are especially popular with boys, are available in more than 130 countries; in the key North American market, the company's overall share of the construction-toy market has been as high as 80 percent. Kjeld Kirk Kristiansen, the grandson of the company's founder as well as the main shareholder, served as CEO from 1979 until 2004. Kristiansen says that LEGO products stand for "exuberance, spontaneity, self-expression, concern for others, and innovation." (The company's name comes from the Danish phrase *leg godt*, which means "play well.") Kristiansen also attributes his company's success to the esteem the brand enjoys among parents. "Parents consider LEGO not as just a toy company but as providing products that help learning and developing new skills," he says.

For the past several years, however, some of those parents have been switching loyalties. Mega Bloks, a rival company in Montreal, Canada, has been aggressively gaining market share with its own colorful plastic blocks. Some are compatible with LEGO products, and all generally cost less than comparable LEGO products. LEGO executives believe that LEGO's proprietary mix of resin results in a higher quality toy. By contrast, Mega Bloks holds costs down by using commodity-grade resin. While LEGO dominates the 7- to 12-year-old segment, Mega Bloks is the number one player in the preschool market. Because the bricks in Mega Bloks's original line are larger and softer than LEGO, some parents believe they are easier for very young children to use. LEGO responded by introducing a Duplo line of oversized blocks made of the same material as the company's core brick line. In recent years, Mega Bloks has introduced a midsized line as well as a line called Micro for the elementary school set. Micro bricks can be used interchangeably with LEGOs. LEGO filed a lawsuit alleging that the Micro line copied the "look" of the knobs on LEGO bricks and, thus, violated Canadian trademark law. Canada's Federal Court of Appeal dismissed the claim in 2003, concluding that the bricks' design is functional and entitled to trademark protection. In 2004, Canada's Supreme Court announced that it would hear LEGO's appeal.

"For many people, the biggest part of the brand equity is the brick—which is why we must ensure a significant proportion of the business stays in the brick arena."

Francesco Ciccolella, Senior Vice President for Corporate Development, LEGO Company

In short, Mega Bloks has prospered at LEGO's expense. Mega Bloks' sales doubled between 2000 and 2003; by contrast, the Danish company reported its first loss ever—$44 million—in 1988. Meanwhile, Hasbro and other competitors are also targeting the $600 million market for construction toys. In the 1990s, LEGO's strategy called for new sources of growth beyond the core block category. The company developed its own line of original robot action figures. Known as Bionicles, the figures can be integrated with the traditional construction materials. Currently, the Bionicle line is LEGO's best seller; in 2003, a direct-to-DVD animated feature, *Bionicle—Mask of Light*, was released by Miramax. Another new product, Mybots, was a $70 toy set that included blocks with computer chips embedded to provide lights and sound. A $200 Mindstorms Robotics Invention System allowed users to build computer-controlled creatures. To further leverage the LEGO brand, the company also formed alliances with Walt Disney Company and Lucasfilm, creator of the popular *Star Wars* series. For several years, sales of licensed merchandise relating to the popular Harry Potter and Star Wars movie franchises sold extremely well.

More recently, however, although the Harry Potter movie series continued to enjoy great success, interest in the Potter-themed play sets was waning. After a disappointing Christmas 2003 season, LEGO was left with millions of dollars of unsold goods. The difficult retail situation was compounded by the dollar's weakness relative to the Danish krone; LEGO posted a record loss of $166 million for 2003. The company unveiled a number of new initiatives aimed at restoring profitability. Its new Quattro line of large, soft bricks is targeted directly at the preschool market. Clikits is a line for pastel-colored bricks targeted at young girls who want to create jewelry.

In 2004, after several years of losses, Jørgen Vig Knudstorp succeeded Kristiansen as LEGO's chief executive. Acknowledging that the company's forays into theme parts, children's clothing, and software games had been the wrong strategy, Knudstorp launched a restructuring initiative. Production was outsourced to a Singapore company with production facilities in Mexico and the Czech Republic; in the past few years, more than 2,000 jobs have been eliminated. In 2006, LEGO launched a new generation of programmable robots in the Mindstorms line. As Knudstorp noted, "Mindstorms is as close to the core as you can come other than a bucket of bricks, which is the core of the core."

Discussion Questions

1. Jørgen Vig Knudstorp became CEO in 2004. Assess the key strategic decisions he has made, including outsourcing, divesting the theme parks, and launching new toys in the Mindstorms line.

2. In 2004, LEGO continued its entertainment promotional and product tie-ins with new Harry Potter and Spiderman movies. Do you think this is the right strategy?

3. Using Porter's generic strategies framework, compare and contrast LEGO and Mega Bloks in terms of their respective pursuit of competitive advantage.

Sources: John Tagliabue, "Taking Their Blocks and Playing Toymaker Elsewhere," *The New York Times* (November 20, 2006), p. A4; Lauren Foster and David Ibison, "Spike the Robot Helps LEGO Rebuild Strategy," *Financial Times* (June 22, 2006), p. 18; Ian Austen, "Building a Legal Case, Block by Block," *The New York Times* (February 2, 2005), p. C6; Joseph Pereira and Christopher J. Chipello, "Battle of the Block Makers," *The Wall Street Journal* (February 4, 2004), pp. B1, B4; Clare MacCarthy, "Deputy Chief Sacked as LEGO Tries to Rebuild," *Financial Times* (January 9, 2004), p. 19; Majken Schultz and Mary Jo Hatch, "The Cycles of Corporate Branding: The Case of the LEGO Company," *California Management Review* 46, no. 1 (Fall 2003), pp. 6–26; Meg Carter, "Building Blocks of Success," *Financial Times* (October 30, 2003), p. 8; Peter Marsh, "LEGO Builds Its Future," *Financial Times* (March 16–17, 1996), p. 9.

Sony Corporation is a legend in the global consumer electronics industry. Its reputation for innovation and engineering has made it the envy of rivals. For decades, quality-conscious consumers paid premium prices for the company's Trinitron color televisions. Sony was a key player in the development of the VCR and virtually invented the personal stereo with its Walkman product line. Sony was a codeveloper of the compact disc music format. The various PlayStation models enjoy a commanding 70 percent market share of the video game console market. By the first years of the twenty-first century, however, Sony's vaunted innovation and marketing machine appeared to be faltering. The company had not anticipated the rapid consumer acceptance of flat-panel, widescreen LCD and plasma TV sets, and the Walkman was eclipsed by Apple's iPod and iTunes Music Store. In 2005, a tumbling stock price resulted in the resignation of chairman and CEO Nobuyuki Idei. Sir Howard Stringer, a Welsh-born American who had been knighted in 2000, was named as Idei's replacement. Although Stringer had been in charge of Sony's U.S. operations, his appointment to the top position came as a surprise to some observers: He is neither Japanese nor an engineer. One of his first priorities will be to bridge the divide between Sony's media businesses, which include music, games, and motion pictures, and its hardware businesses. As Sir Howard himself declared, "We've got to get the relationship between content and devices seamlessly managed."

This chapter focuses on the integration of each element of the marketing mix into a total plan that addresses opportunities and threats in the global marketing environment. Howard Stringer's appointment to the top job at Sony illustrates some of the challenges facing business leaders in the twenty-first century: They must be capable of articulating a coherent global vision and strategy that integrates global efficiency, local responsiveness, and leverage. The leader is also the architect of an organization design that is appropriate for the company's strategy. Finally, the leader must ensure that the organization takes a proactive approach to corporate social responsibility.

When Sir Howard Stringer was named chairman and chief executive of Sony in 2005, he became the first non-Japanese executive in the consumer electronics giant's history. Sir Howard's predecessor, Nobuyuki Idei (L) is credited with engineering Sony's turnaround in the late 1990s. Now Sir Howard faces new challenges. He has praise for Nintendo's latest videogame console, the Wii, calling it, "a very good business model." However, Sir Howard is also confident that Sony's PS3 is on track to post solid sales gains, especially when the price is cut and more game titles become available. On the subject of executive compensation, Sir Howard believes that, by American standards, "Japanese executives are astonishingly underpaid." But, he added in a recent interview, "Most executives in Japan don't work for money, pure and simple. They are motivated by something else."[1]

LEADERSHIP

Global marketing demands exceptional leadership. As noted throughout this book, the hallmark of a global company is the capacity to formulate and implement global strategies that leverage worldwide learning, respond fully to local needs and wants, and draw on the talent and energy of every member of the organization. This heroic task requires global vision and sensitivity to local needs. Overall, the leader's challenge is to direct the efforts and creativity of everyone in the company toward a global effort that best uses organizational resources to exploit global opportunities. As Carly Fiorina, former CEO of Hewlett-Packard, said in her 2002 commencement address at the Massachusetts Institute of Technology:

> Leadership is not about hierarchy or title or status: It is about having influence and mastering change. Leadership is not about bragging rights or battles or even the accumulation of wealth; it's about connecting and engaging at multiple levels. It's about challenging minds and capturing hearts. Leadership in this new era is about empowering others to decide for themselves. Leadership is about empowering others to reach their full potential. Leaders can no longer view strategy and execution as abstract concepts, but must realize that both elements are ultimately about people.[2]

An important leadership task is articulating beliefs, values, policies, and the intended geographic scope of a company's activities. Using the mission statement or similar document as a reference and guide, members of each operating unit must address their immediate responsibilities and at the same time cooperate with functional, product, and country experts in different locations. However, it is one thing to spell out the vision and another thing entirely to secure

[1] Aline van Duyn, "View from the Top: Sir Howard Stringer," *Financial Times* (June 15, 2007), p. 10.
[2] Carleton "Carly" S. Fiorina, Commencement Address, Massachusetts Institute of Technology, Cambridge, MA, June 2, 2000. See also "It's Death if You Stop Trying New Things," *Financial Times* (November 20, 2003), p. 8.

commitment to it throughout the organization. As noted in Chapter 1, global marketing entails engaging in significant business activities outside the home country. This means exposure to different languages and cultures. In addition, global marketing involves skillful application of specific concepts, considerations, and strategies. Such endeavors may represent substantial change, especially in U.S. companies with a long tradition of domestic focus. When the "go global" initiative is greeted with skepticism, the CEO must be a change agent who prepares and motivates employees.

As former Whirlpool CEO David Whitwam described his own efforts in this regard in the early 1990s:

> When we announced the Philips acquisition, I traveled to every location in the company, talked with our people, explained why it was so important. Most opposed the move. They thought, "We're spending a billion dollars on a company that has been losing money for 10 years? We're going to take resources we could use right here and ship them across the Atlantic because we think this is becoming a 'global' industry? What the hell does that mean?"[3]

Jack Welch encountered similar resistance at GE. "The lower you are in the organization, the less clear it is that globalization is a great idea," he said. As Paolo Fresco, a former GE vice chairman, explained:

> To certain people, globalization is a threat without rewards. You look at the engineer for X-ray in Milwaukee and there is no upside on this one for him. He runs the risk of losing his job, he runs the risk of losing authority—he might find his boss is a guy who does not even know how to speak his language.[4]

In addition to "selling" their visions, top management at both Whirlpool and GE face the formidable task of building a cadre of globally oriented managers. Similar challenges are facing corporate leaders in other parts of the world. For example, Uichiro Niwa, former president of ITOCHU Corporation, took steps to ensure that more of the trading company's $115 billion in annual transactions are conducted online.[5] He also radically changed the way he communicated with employees. He relied more on e-mail, a practice that until recently was virtually unknown in Japan. He also convened face-to-face meetings and conferences with employees to solicit suggestions and to hear complaints. This too represented a dramatic change in the way Japanese companies are being led; traditionally, low-level employees were expected to accept the edicts of top management without questioning them.

Top Management Nationality

Many globally minded companies realize that the best person for a top management job or board position is not necessarily someone born in the home country. Speaking of U.S. companies, Christopher Bartlett of the Harvard Business School has noted:

> Companies are realizing that they have a portfolio of human resources worldwide, that their brightest technical person might come from Germany, or their best financial manager from England. They are starting to tap their worldwide human resources. And as they do, it will not be surprising to see non-Americans rise to the top.[6]

---

3 William C. Taylor and Alan M. Webber, *Going Global: Four Entrepreneurs Map the New World Marketplace* (New York: Penguin Books USA, 1996), p. 12.
4 Noel M. Tichy and Stratford Sherman, *Control Your Destiny or Someone Else Will* (New York: HarperBusiness, 1994), p. 227.
5 Robert Guth, "Facing a Web Revolution, a Mighty Japanese Trader Reinvents Itself," *The Wall Street Journal* (March 27, 2000), p. B1.
6 Kerry Peckter, "The Foreigners Are Coming," *International Business* (September 1993), p. 53.

The ability to speak foreign languages is one difference between managers born and raised in the United States and those born and raised elsewhere. For example, the U.S. Department of Education recently reported that 200 million Chinese children are studying English; by contrast, only 24,000 American children are studying Chinese! Roberto Goizueta, the Cuban-born CEO of Coca-Cola who died in 1997, spoke English, Spanish, and Portuguese; Ford's former chief executive, Alexander Trotman, was born in England and speaks English, French, and German. Sigismundus W. W. Lubsen, the former president and CEO of Quaker Chemical Corporation, is a good example of today's cosmopolitan executive. Born in the Netherlands and educated in Rotterdam as well as New York, Lubsen, who speaks Dutch, English, French, and German, says, "I was lucky to be born in a place where if you drove for an hour in any direction, you were in a different country, speaking a different language. It made me very comfortable traveling in different cultures."[7] Table 16-1 shows additional examples of corporate leaders who are not native to the headquarters country.

As noted in the chapter introduction, Howard Stringer is the chief executive at Sony. Generally speaking, however, Japanese companies have been reluctant to place non-Japanese nationals in top positions. For years, only Sony, Mazda, and Mitsubishi had foreigners on their boards. In March 1999, however, after Renault SA bought a 36.8 percent stake in Nissan Motor, the French company installed a Brazilian, Carlos Ghosn, as president. An outsider, Ghosn was required to move aggressively to cut costs and make drastic changes in Nissan's structure. He also introduced two new words into Nissan's lexicon: *speed* and *commitment*. Ghosn's turnaround effort was so successful that his life story and exploits have been celebrated in *Big Comic Story*, a comic that is popular with Japan's salarymen.[9]

"In the end it does not matter whether the CEO is Japanese or not. Mitsubishi is a Japanese company."[10]

Rolf Eckrodt, CEO, Mitsubishi Motors

global MARKETING Q&A

Wall Street Journal: "A lot of your management team is Nokia born and bred. What do you do to encourage global, international thinking?"

Jorma Ollila, Chairman, Nokia: "The fact is that we are global, truly global, so that we are present in all major markets. And 1 percent of our sales is in our home market, where 65 percent of R&D happens and the senior management team sits. It really is an issue.

"You have to have had good international exposure, hopefully working abroad so you have really hit some hard international challenges. Then we rotate a lot, so there are a lot of Finnish expats outside. And one-third of our expats are non-Finns—Americans in Thailand and Canadians in China. It is a modus operandi. But it is a tough issue."[8]

Source: The Wall Street Journal (Western Edition) by David Pringle and Raju Narisetti. Copyright 2003 by Dow Jones & Company, Inc. Reproduced with permission of Dow Jones & Company, Inc. in the format Textbook via Copyright Clearance Center.

---

[7] Peckter, p. 58.
[8] David Pringle and Raju Narisetti, "Guiding Nokia in Technology's Rough Seas," *The Wall Street Journal* (November 24, 2003), pp. B1, B2.
[9] Norihiko Shirouzu, "U-Turn: A Revival at Nissan Shows There's Hope for Ailing Japan Inc.," *The Wall Street Journal* (November 16, 2000), pp. A1, A10. See also Todd Zaun, "Look! Up in the Sky! It's Nissan's Chief Executive!" *The Wall Street Journal* (December 27, 2001), p. B1.
[10] Todd Zaun, "Now at the Helm, Eckrodt Must Produce Results at Mitsubishi," *The Wall Street Journal* (March 29, 2002), p. A11.

Table 16-1

Who's in Charge? Executives of 2006

Company (Headquarters Country)	Executive (Nationality)	Position
Cadbury Schweppes PLC (Great Britain)	Todd Stitzer (United States)	CEO
Carrefour (France)	José-Luis Duran (Spain)	Chairman, Management Board
Coca-Cola Company	E. Neville Isdell (Northern Ireland)	Chairman and CEO
Eastman Kodak (United States)	Antonio Perez (Spain)	Chairman, President, and CEO
Ford Motor Company (United States)	Nick Scheele (Great Britain)	President and COO
L'Oréal SA (France)	Lindsay Owen-Jones (Great Britain)	Chairman
Mitsubishi Motors (Japan)	Rolf Eckrodt (Germany)	CEO
Nissan Motor (Japan)	Carlos Ghosn (Brazil)	Co-Chairman, President, and CEO; President and CEO, Nissan North America
Pearson PLC (Great Britain)	Marjorie Scardino (United States)	CEO
PepsiCo (United States)	Indra K. Nooyi (India)	CEO
Reuters Group PLC (Great Britain)	Tom Glocer (United States)	CEO
Samsung Electronics (Korea)	David Steel (Great Britain)	Vice President of Business Development
Schering-Plough (United States)	Fred Hassan (Pakistan)	Chairman, President, and CEO
Sony (Japan)	Howard Stringer (Wales)	Chairman and CEO
Sual (Russia)	Chris Norval (South Africa)	CEO
Wolters Kluwer NV (Netherlands)	Nancy McKinstry (United States)	Chairman and CEO

Leadership and Core Competence

Core competence, a concept developed by global strategy experts C. K. Prahalad and Gary Hamel, was introduced in Chapter 15. In the 1980s, many business executives were assessed on their ability to reorganize their corporations. In the 1990s, Prahalad and Hamel believed executives were judged on their ability to identify, nurture, and exploit the core competencies that make growth possible. Simply put, **core competence** is something that an organization can do better than competitors. Prahalad and Hamel note that a core competence has three characteristics:

- It provides potential access to a wide variety of markets.
- It makes a significant contribution to perceived customer benefits.
- It is difficult for competitors to imitate.

Table 16-2

Responsibility for Global Marketing

Company (Headquarters Country)	Executive	Position/Title
adidas-Solomon (Germany)	Erich Stamminger	Senior Vice President of Global Marketing
Apple Computer (United States)	Greg Joswiak	Vice President of Worldwide iPod Product Marketing
Calvin Klein (United States)	Kim Vernon	Senior Vice President, Global Advertising, Marketing and Communications
Coca-Cola (United States)	Mary Minnick	President of Global Marketing, Strategy, and Innovation
DaimlerChrysler (United States/Germany)	George Murphy	Senior Vice President for Global Marketing
Kraft Foods (United States)	Betsy D. Holden	President, Global Marketing and Category Development
McDonald's (United States)	Larry Light	Global Chief Marketing Officer
Procter & Gamble (United States)	Jim Stengel	Global Marketing Officer
Reebok International (United States)	Muktesh Pant	Vice President of Global Brand Marketing
Warner Music (United States)	John Reid	Executive Vice President, Warner Music International

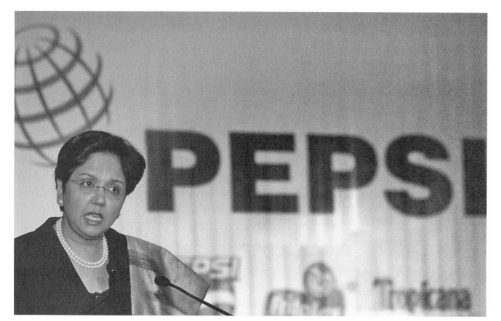

Indra Nooyi, chairman and chief executive of PepsiCo, is faced with rising prices for raw materials and weak demand for carbonated soft drinks in the United States. Despite these threats, Nooyi believes the snack-and-beverage giant's current strategy is on track. In recent quarters, the strongest results have come from PepsiCo's fast-growing international division. Snack sales are particularly strong in Mexico and Russia; international sales volume for beverage brands is also increasing, particularly in the Middle East, Argentina, China, and Brazil.

Few companies are likely to build world leadership in more than five or six fundamental competencies. In the long run, an organization will derive its global competitiveness from its ability to bring high-quality, low-cost products to market faster than its competitors. To do this, an organization must be viewed as a portfolio of competencies rather than a portfolio of businesses. In some instances, a company has the technical resources to build competencies, but key executives lack the vision to do so. As Jorma Ollila, chairman of Finland's Nokia, noted, "Design is a fundamental building block of the [Nokia] brand. It is central to our product creation and is a core competence integrated into the entire company."[11] Ollila's comment underscores the fact that today's executives must rethink the concept of the corporation if they wish to operationalize the concept of core competencies. In addition, the task of management must be viewed as building both competencies and the administrative means for assembling resources spread across multiple businesses.[12] Table 16-2 lists some of the individuals responsible for global marketing at select companies.

ORGANIZING FOR GLOBAL MARKETING

The goal in **organizing** for global marketing is to find a structure that enables the company to respond to relevant market environment differences while ensuring the diffusion of corporate knowledge and experience from national markets throughout the entire corporate system. The pull between the value of centralized knowledge and coordination and the need for individualized response to the local situation creates a constant tension in the global marketing organization. A key issue in global organization is how to achieve balance between autonomy and integration. Subsidiaries need autonomy to adapt to

---

[11] Neil McCartney, "Squaring Up to Usability at Nokia," *Financial Times—IT Review Telecom World* (October 13, 2003), p. 4.

[12] C. K. Prahalad and Gary Hamel, "The Core Competence of the Corporation," *Harvard Business Review* 68, no. 3 (May–June 1990), pp. 79–86.

their local environment, but the business as a whole needs integration to implement global strategy.[13]

When management at a domestic company decides to pursue international expansion, the issue of how to organize arises immediately. Who should be responsible for this expansion? Should product divisions operate directly or should an international division be established? Should individual country subsidiaries report directly to the company president or should a special corporate officer be appointed to take full-time responsibility for international activities? After the decision of how to organize initial international operations has been reached, a growing company is faced with a number of reappraisal points during the development of its international business activities. Should a company abandon its international division, and, if so, what alternative structure should it adopt? Should it form an area or regional headquarters? What should be the relationship of staff executives at corporate, regional, and subsidiary offices? Specifically, how should it organize the marketing function? To what extent should regional and corporate marketing executives become involved in subsidiary marketing management?

Even companies with years of experience competing around the globe find it necessary to adjust their organizational designs in response to environmental change. It is perhaps not surprising that, during his tenure at Quaker Chemical, Sigismundus Lubsen favored a global approach to organizational design over a domestic/international approach. He advised Peter A. Benoliel, his predecessor CEO, to have units in Holland, France, Italy, Spain, and England report to a regional vice president in Europe. "I saw that it would not be a big deal to put all of the European units under one common denominator," Lubsen recalled.[14]

As markets globalize and as Japan opens its own market to more competition from overseas, more Japanese companies are likely to break from traditional organization patterns. Many of the Japanese companies discussed in this text qualify as global or transnational companies because they serve world markets, source globally, or do both. Typically, however, knowledge is created at headquarters in Japan and then transferred to other country units. For example, Canon enjoys a high reputation for world-class, innovative imaging products such as bubble-jet printers and laser printers. In recent years, Canon has shifted more control to subsidiaries, hired more non-Japanese staff and management personnel, and assimilated more innovations that were not developed in Japan. In 1996, R&D responsibility for software was shifted from Tokyo to the United States, responsibility for telecommunication products to France, and computer language translation to Great Britain. As Canon President Fujio Mitarai explained, "The Tokyo headquarters cannot know everything. Its job should be to provide low-cost capital, to move top management between regions, and come up with investment initiatives. Beyond that, the local subsidiaries must assume total responsibility for management. We are not there yet, but we are moving step by step in that direction." Toru Takahashi, director of R&D, shares this view. "We used to think that we should keep research and development in Japan, but that has changed," he said. Despite these changes, Canon's board of directors includes only Japanese nationals.[15]

---

[13] George S. Yip, *Total Global Strategy* (Upper Saddle River, NJ: Prentice Hall, 1992), p. 179.

[14] Kerry Peckter, "The Foreigners Are Coming," *International Business* (September 1993), p. 58.

[15] William Dawkins, "Time to Pull Back the Screen," *Financial Times* (November 18, 1996), p. 12. See also Sumantra Ghoshal and Christopher A. Bartlett, *The Individualized Corporation* (New York: Harper Perennial, 1999), pp. 179–181.

No single correct organizational structure exists for global marketing. Even within a particular industry, worldwide companies have developed different strategic and organizational responses to changes in their environments.[16] Still, it is possible to make some generalizations. Leading-edge global competitors share one key organizational design characteristic: Their corporate structure is flat and simple, rather than tall and complex. The message is clear: The world is complicated enough so there is no need to add to the confusion with a complex internal structuring. Simple structures increase the speed and clarity of communication and allow the concentration of organizational energy and valuable resources on learning, rather than on controlling, monitoring, and reporting.[17] According to David Whitwam, former CEO of Whirlpool, "You must create an organization whose people are adept at exchanging ideas, processes, and systems across borders, people who are absolutely free of the 'not-invented-here' syndrome, people who are constantly working together to identify the best global opportunities and the biggest global problems facing the organization."[18]

A geographically dispersed company cannot limit its knowledge to product, function, and the home territory. Company personnel must acquire knowledge of the complex set of social, political, economic, and institutional arrangements that exist within each international market. Many companies start with ad hoc arrangements such as having all foreign subsidiaries report to a designated vice president or to the president. Eventually, such companies establish an international division to manage their geographically dispersed new businesses. It is clear, however, that the international division in the multiproduct company is an unstable organizational arrangement. As a company grows, this initial organizational structure frequently gives way to various alternative structures.

In the fast-changing competitive global environment of the twenty-first century, corporations will have to find new, more creative ways to organize. New forms of flexibility, efficiency, and responsiveness are required to meet the demands of globalizing markets. The need to be cost effective, to be customer driven, to deliver the best quality, and to deliver that quality quickly are some of today's global realities. Recently, several authors have described new organization designs that represent responses to today's competitive environment. These designs acknowledge the need to find more responsive and flexible structures, to flatten the organization, and to employ teams. There is the recognition of the need to develop networks, to develop stronger relationships among participants, and to exploit technology. These designs also reflect an evolution in approaches to organizational effectiveness. At the turn of the twentieth century, Frederick Taylor claimed that all managers had to see the world the same way. Then came the contingency theorists who said that effective organizations design themselves to match their conditions. These two basic theories are reflected in today's popular management writings. As Henry Mintzberg has observed, "To Michael Porter, effectiveness resides in strategy, while to Tom Peters it is the operations that count—executing any strategy with excellence."[19]

[16] Christopher Bartlett and Sumantra Ghoshal, *Managing Across Borders: The Transnational Solution* (Boston: Harvard Business School Press, 1989), p. 3.

[17] Vladimir Pucik, "Globalization and Human Resource Management," in V. Pucik, N. Tichy, and C. Barnett (eds.), *Globalizing Management: Creating and Leading the Competitive Organization* (New York: J. Wiley & Sons, 1992), p. 70.

[18] Regina Fazio Maruca, "The Right Way to Go Global: An Interview with Whirlpool CEO David Whitwam," *Harvard Business Review* 72, no. 2 (March–April 1994), p. 137.

[19] Henry Mintzberg, "The Effective Organization: Forces and Forms," *Sloan Management Review* 32, no. 2 (Winter 1991), pp. 54–55.

Kenichi Ohmae has written extensively on the implications of globalization on organization design. He recommends a type of "global superstructure" at the highest level that provides a view of the world as a single unit. The staff members of this unit are responsible for ensuring that work is performed in the best location and coordinating efficient movement of information and products across borders. Below this level, Ohmae envisions organizational units assigned to regions "governed by economies of service and economies of scale in information." In Ohmae's view of the world, there are 30 regions with populations ranging from 5 million to 20 million people. For example, China would be viewed as several distinct regions; the same is true of the United States. The first task of the CEO in such an organization is to become oriented to the single unit that is the borderless business sphere, much as an astronaut might view the earth from space. Then, zooming in, the CEO attempts to identify differences. As Ohmae explains,

> A CEO has to look at the entire global economy and then put the company's resources where they will capture the biggest market share of the most attractive regions. Perhaps as you draw closer from outer space you see a region around the Pacific Northwest, near Puget Sound, that is vibrant and prosperous. Then you recognize the region stretching from New York to Boston that is still doing awful. You might see a booming concentration of computer companies and software publishers around Denver, and similar concentrations around Dallas-Fort Worth.

the rest of the story

An American Takes the Helm at Sony

Management writers often use terms like *silos*, *stovepipes*, or *chimneys* to describe an organization in which autonomous business units operate with their own agendas and a minimum of horizontal interdependence. This was the situation at Sony, where the internal rivalries between different engineering units—the PC and Walkman groups, for example—were ingrained in the corporate culture and regarded as healthy.

The intracorporate rivalries were especially evident as Sony ramped up for the 2004 launch of Connect, an online paid music service to compete with Apple's iTunes. Sony's personal computer group developed the software; it was to be played on a new generation of Walkman devices that were created by the company's portable audio unit. Meanwhile, management at the company's music division—Sony is home to the Columbia, Epic, and RCA labels and its artist roster includes Aerosmith and Outkast— insisted on strict copy-protection measures because of concerns about piracy. As head of Sony's U.S. operations, Sir Howard had been a supporter of the service; however, he was not able to compel Sony's different divisions to work together. Given its somewhat disjointed development history, it is not surprising that consumers gave Connect a lukewarm reception.

Because Sony's consumer electronics business accounts for more than two-thirds of Sony's worldwide sales, breathing new life into the unit is important. To do this, Sir Howard developed a restructuring plan that called for cutting 10,000 jobs, reducing the number of manufacturing sites from 65 to 54, and eliminating some unprofitable products. In an effort to improve horizontal communication, he also merged some of the electronics business's units

Cost cutting is only part of the story. Boosting revenues with new products is also crucial to Sony's recovery. Sir Howard believes that Sony's TV business will recover, thanks in part to the new Bravia line of HDTVs. The company has also launched an e-book. Although Sir Howard had high hopes for the launch of the PlayStation 3 game console in mid-2006, production issues delayed the introduction until November. By the time the crucial Christmas shopping season was over, industry observers were pronouncing Nintendo's Wii the victor in the videogame console wars.

Will Sir Howard succeed in effecting a turnaround at Sony? While some consider him to be an outsider, he is known for his nonconfrontational style. Because of Sony's complexity, Sir Howard will be heavily reliant on the skills of his Japanese managers. Speaking of his management team, Sir Howard explains, "I had to do two things: develop those relationships and convince them that the kind of changes I had in mind would be worthwhile." William Ouchi, author of *Theory Z*, says, "Sony is going through the major repositioning that Intel has gone through and AOL is going through. From hardware to software to communications to content, every segment of these industries is being turned topsy-turvy."

Sixty Minutes, the CBS news magazine, recently aired a profile of Sir Howard. A DVD of the program is widely available, and it makes an excellent companion to the text discussion.

Sources: Yukari Iwatani Kane, "Sony Expects to Trim PS3 Losses, Plans More Games, Online Features," The Wall Street Journal (May 18, 2007), p. B4; Phred Dvorak, "Sony Aims to Cut Costs, Workers to Revive Its Electronics Business," The Wall Street Journal (September 23, 2005), p. A5; Dvorak, "Out of Tune: At Sony, Rivalries Were Encouraged; Then Came iPod," The Wall Street Journal (June 29, 2005), pp. A1, A6; Lorne Manly and Andrew Ross Sorkin, "Choice of Stringer Aims to Prevent Further Setbacks," The New York Times (March 8, 2005), pp. C1, C8; Dvorak and Merissa Marr, "Shock Treatment: Sony, Lagging Behind Rivals, Hands Reins to a Foreigner," The Wall Street Journal (March 7, 2005), pp. A1, A8.

Along the coast of California and in parts of New England you will see regions that are strong centers for health care and biotechnology. As a CEO, that's where you put your resources and shift your emphasis.[20]

Successful companies, the real global winners, must have both good strategies and good execution.

Patterns of International Organizational Development

Organizations vary in terms of the size and potential of targeted global markets and local management competence in different country markets. Conflicting pressures may arise from the need for product and technical knowledge; functional expertise in marketing, finance, and operations; and area and country knowledge. Because the constellation of pressures that shape organizations is never exactly the same, no two organizations pass through organizational stages in exactly the same way, nor do they arrive at precisely the same organizational pattern. Nevertheless, some general patterns hold.

A company engaging in limited export activities often has a small in-house export department as a separate functional area. Most domestically oriented companies undertake initial foreign expansion by means of foreign sales offices or subsidiaries that report directly to the company president or other designated company officer. This person carries out his or her responsibilities without assistance from a headquarters staff group. This is a typical initial arrangement for companies getting started in international marketing operations.

International Division Structure

As a company's international business grows, the complexity of coordinating and directing this activity extends beyond the scope of a single person. Pressure is created to assemble a staff that will take responsibility for coordination and direction of the growing international activities of the organization. Eventually, this pressure leads to the creation of the international division, as illustrated in Figure 16-1. Wal-Mart, Levi Strauss, Anheuser-Busch, Best Buy, Walt Disney Company, and Hershey are some examples of companies whose structures include international divisions. When Hershey announced the creation of its international division in 2005, J. P. Bilbrey, the division's senior vice president, noted that Hershey will no longer utilize the extension strategy of exporting its chocolate products from the United States. Instead, the company will tailor products to local markets and also manufacture locally. As Bilbrey explained, "We're changing our business model in Asia. The product was not locally relevant and it also got there at an unattractive cost."[21]

Four factors contribute to the establishment of an international division. First, top management's commitment to global operations has increased enough to justify an organizational unit headed by a senior manager. Second, the complexity of international operations requires a single organizational unit whose management has sufficient authority to make its own determination on important issues such as which market entry strategy to employ. Third, an international division is frequently formed when the firm has recognized the need for internal specialists to deal with the special demands of global operations. A fourth contributing factor is management's recognition of the importance of strategically scanning the global horizon for opportunities and

---

[20] William C. Taylor and Alan M. Webber, *Going Global: Four Entrepreneurs Map the New World Marketplace* (New York: Penguin, 1996), pp. 48–58.
[21] Jeremy Grant, "Hershey Chews Over Growth Strategy," *Financial Times* (December 14, 2005), p. 23.

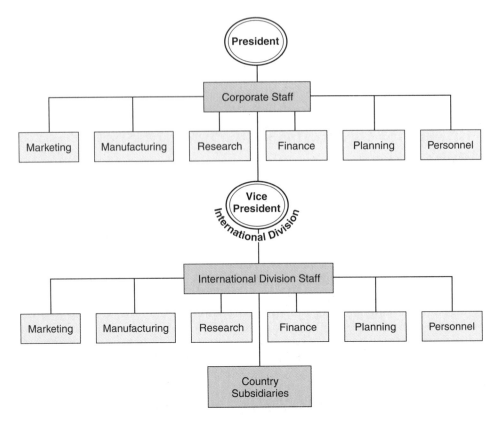

Figure 16-1

Functional Corporate Structure, Domestic Corporate Staff Orientation, International Division

aligning them with company resources rather than simply responding on an ad hoc basis to situations as they arise.

Regional Management Centers

When business is conducted in a single region that is characterized by similarities in economic, social, geographical, and political conditions, there is both justification and need for a management center. Thus, another stage of organizational evolution is the emergence of an area or regional headquarters as a management layer between the country organization and the international division headquarters. The increasing importance of the EU as a regional market has prompted a number of companies to change their organizational structures by setting up regional headquarters there. In the mid-1990s, Quaker Oats established its European headquarters in Brussels; Electrolux, the Swedish home appliance company, has also regionalized its European operations.[22] A regional center typically coordinates decisions on pricing, sourcing, and other matters. Executives at the regional center also participate in the planning and control of each country's operations with an eye toward applying company knowledge on a regional basis and optimally utilizing corporate resources on a regional basis. This organizational design is illustrated in Figure 16-2.

Regional management can offer a company several advantages. First, many regional managers agree that an on-the-scene regional management unit makes sense where there is a real need for coordinated, pan-regional decision making. Coordinated regional planning and control are becoming necessary as the national subsidiary continues to lose its relevance as an independent operating unit. Regional management can probably achieve the best balance of geographical, product, and functional considerations required to implement corporate

---

[22] " . . . And Other Ways to Peel the Onion," *Economist* (January 7, 1995), pp. 52–53.

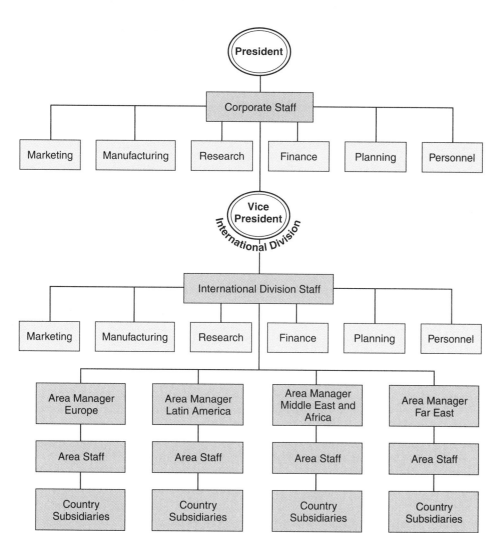

Figure 16-2

Functional Corporate Structure, Domestic Corporate Staff Orientation, International Division, Area Divisions

objectives effectively. By shifting operations and decision making to the region, the company is better able to maintain an insider advantage.[23]

A major disadvantage of a regional center is its cost. The cost of a two-person office could exceed $600,000 per year. The scale of regional management must be in line with the scale of operations in a region. A regional headquarters is inappropriate if the size of the operations it manages is inadequate to cover the costs of the additional layer of management. The basic issue with regard to the regional headquarters is "Does it contribute enough to organizational effectiveness to justify its cost and the complexity of another layer of management?"

Geographical and Product Division Structures

As a company becomes more global, management frequently faces the dilemma of whether to organize by geography or by product lines. The geographical structure involves the assignment of operational responsibility for geographic areas of the world to line managers. The corporate headquarters retains responsibility for worldwide planning and control, and each area of the world—including the "home" or base market—is organizationally equal. For the company with French origins, France is simply another geographic market under this organizational arrangement. This structure is most common in companies with closely related product lines that

---

[23] Allen J. Morrison, David A. Ricks, and Kendall Roth, "Globalization Versus Regionalization: Which Way for the Multinational?" *Organizational Dynamics* (Winter 1991), pp. 17–29.

Figure 16-3

Geographic Corporate Structure, World Corporate Staff Orientation, Area Divisions Worldwide

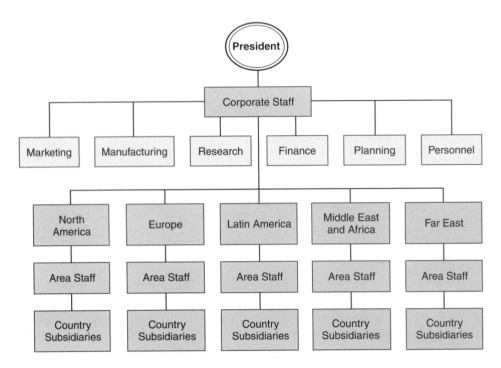

are sold in similar end-use markets around the world. For example, the major international oil companies utilize the geographical structure, which is illustrated in Figure 16-3. McDonald's organizational design integrates the international division and geographical structures. McDonald's U.S. is organized into five geographical operating divisions and McDonald's International has four.

When an organization assigns regional or worldwide product responsibility to its product divisions, manufacturing standardization can result in significant economies. For example, Whirlpool recently reorganized its European operations, switching from a geographic or country orientation to one based on product lines. One potential disadvantage of the product approach is that local input from individual country managers may be ignored with the result that products will not be sufficiently tailored to local markets. The essence of the Ford 2000 reorganization initiated in 1995 was to integrate North American and European operations. Over a three-year period, the company saved $5 billion in development costs. However, by 2000, Ford's European market share had slipped nearly 5 percent. In a shift back toward the geographic model, then-CEO Jacques Nasser returned to regional executives some of the authority they had lost.[24]

The challenges associated with devising the structure that is best suited to improving global sales can be seen in Procter & Gamble's ambitious Organization 2005 plan. Initiated by CEO Durk Jager in 1999, this reorganization entailed replacing separate country organizations with five global business units for key product categories such as paper products and feminine hygiene. A number of executives were reassigned; in Europe alone, 1,000 staff members were transferred to Geneva. Many managers, upset about the transfers and news that P&G intended to cut 15,000 jobs worldwide, quit the company; the resulting upheaval cost CEO Jager his job. To appease middle managers, new CEO A. G. Lafley restored some of the previous geographic focus.[25]

24 Joann S. Lublin, "Division Problem: Place vs. Product: It's Tough to Choose a Management Model," *The Wall Street Journal* (June 27, 2001), pp. A1, A4.
25 Emily Nelson, " Rallying the Troops at P&G: New CEO Lafley Aims to End Upheaval by Revamping Program of Globalization," *The Wall Street Journal* (August 31, 2000), pp. B1, B4.

The Matrix Design

In the fully developed large-scale global company, product or business, function, area, and customer know-how are simultaneously focused on the organization's worldwide marketing objectives. This type of total competence is a **matrix organization**. Management's task in the matrix organization is to achieve an organizational balance that brings together different perspectives and skills to accomplish the organization's objectives. In 1998, both Gillette and Ericsson announced plans to reorganize into matrix organizations. Ericsson's matrix is focused on three customer segments: network operators, private consumers, and commercial enterprises.[26] Gillette's new structure separates product-line management from geographical sales and marketing responsibility.[27] Likewise, Boeing has reorganized its commercial transport design and manufacturing engineers into a matrix organization built around five platform or aircraft model-specific groups. Previously, Boeing was organized along functional lines; the new design is expected to lower costs and quicken updates and problem solving. It will also unite essential design, engineering, and manufacturing processes between Boeing's commercial transport factories and component plants, enhancing product consistency.[28] Why are executives at these and other companies implementing matrix designs? The matrix form of organization is well-suited to global companies because it can be used to establish a multiple-command structure that gives equal emphasis to functional and geographical departments.

Professor John Hunt of the London Business School suggests four considerations regarding the matrix organizational design. First, the matrix is appropriate when the market is demanding and dynamic. Second, employees must accept higher levels of ambiguity and understand that policy manuals cannot cover every eventuality. Third, in country markets where the command-and-control model persists, it is best to overlay matrices on only small portions of the workforce. Finally, management must be able to clearly state what each axis of the matrix can and cannot do. However, this must be accomplished without creating a bureaucracy.[29]

Having established that the matrix is appropriate, management can expect the matrix to integrate four basic competencies on a worldwide basis:

1. *Geographic knowledge.* An understanding of the basic economic, social, cultural, political, and governmental market and competitive dimensions of a country is essential. The country subsidiary is the major structural device employed today to enable the corporation to acquire geographical knowledge.

2. *Product knowledge and know-how.* Product managers with a worldwide responsibility can achieve this level of competence on a global basis. Another way of achieving global product competence is simply to duplicate product management organizations in domestic and international divisions, achieving high competence in both organizational units.

3. *Functional competence in such fields as finance, production, and, especially, marketing.* Corporate functional staff with worldwide responsibility contributes toward the development of functional competence on a global basis. In a handful of companies, the corporate functional manager, who is responsible for the development of his or her functional activity on a global basis, reviews the appointment of country subsidiary functional managers.

---

[26] "Ericsson to Simplify Business Structure," *Financial Times* (September 29, 1998), p. 21.

[27] Mark Maremont, "Gillette to Shut 14 of Its Plants, Lay Off 4,700," *The Wall Street Journal* (September 29, 1998), pp. A3, A15.

[28] Paul Proctor, "Boeing Shifts to 'Platform Teams,'" *Aviation Week & Space Technology* (May 17, 1999) pp. 63–64.

[29] John W. Hunt, "Is Matrix Management a Recipe for Chaos?" *Financial Times* (January 12, 1998), p. 10.

Wall Street Journal: "By going to a global structure where you have functional leaders located in one place as opposed to dispersal of responsibility in regional centers as you've had in the past, don't you risk losing the ability to tailor products, marketing, information technology systems, whatever, to the needs of these very different regional markets?"

Rick Wagoner, Chairman and Chief Executive Officer, General Motors: "Ask the flip side of your question. Why would you be convinced that doing everything locally would give you better answers? My point is simply, this isn't 'either/or.' And trying to force it in an either/or box is a problem for me. What people have a hard time accepting is that the global auto industry is going to be played out as a matrix. People really have trouble because they want to know who's in charge. And the answer is going to be, increasingly, 'it depends.'"

Source: The Wall Street Journal (Western Edition) by Lee Hawkins, Jr. and Joseph B. White. Copyright 2005 by Dow Jones & Company, Inc. Reproduced with permission of Dow Jones & Company, Inc. in the format Other book via Copyright Clearance Center.

4. *A knowledge of the customer or industry and its needs.* Certain large and extremely sophisticated global companies have staff with a responsibility for serving industries on a global basis to assist the line managers in the country organizations in their efforts to penetrate specific customer markets.

Under this arrangement, instead of designating national organizations or product divisions as profit centers, both are responsible for profitability—the national organization for country profits and the product divisions for national and worldwide product profitability. Figure 16-4 illustrates the matrix organization. This organization chart starts with a bottom section that represents a single-country responsibility level, moves to representing the area or international level, and finally moves to representing global responsibility from the product divisions to the corporate staff, to the chief executive at the top of the structure.

At Whirlpool, North American operations are organized in matrix form. While serving as CEO, David Whitwam expected to extend this structure into Europe and other regional markets. Whirlpool managers from traditional functions such as operations, marketing, and finance also work in teams devoted to specific products, such as dishwashers or ovens. To encourage interdependence

STRATEGIC DECISION-MAKING *in global marketing*

ABB Experiments with the Matrix Design

Some companies are moving away from the matrix in response to changing competitive conditions. Heineken is one example; ABB is another. For nearly a decade, ABB was a matrix organized along regional lines. Local business units—factories that make motors or power generators, for example—reported both to a country manager and to a business area manager who set strategy for the whole world. This structure allowed ABB to execute global strategies while still thriving in local markets. However, in 1998, new chairman Göran Lindahl dissolved the matrix. As the chairman explained in a press release, "This is an aggressive move aimed at greater speed and efficiency by further focusing and flattening the organization. This step is

possible now thanks to our strong, decentralized presence in all local and global markets around the world." In January 2001, Lindahl stepped down and his successor, Jorgen Centerman, revamped the organizational structure yet again. The new design was intended to improve the focus on industries and large corporate customers; Centerman wanted to ensure that all of ABB's products were designed to the same systems standards. However, in 2002, with the chief executive under pressure to sell assets, ABB's board replaced Centerman with Jürgen Dorman.

Sources: David Woodruff, "New ABB Chairman Unveils Overhaul, Reacting to Rival GE," The Wall Street Journal (January 12, 2001), p. A16. A detailed discussion of ABB's matrix structure is found in Ghoshal and Bartlett (1999), pp. 183–190.

Figure 16-4

The Matrix Structure

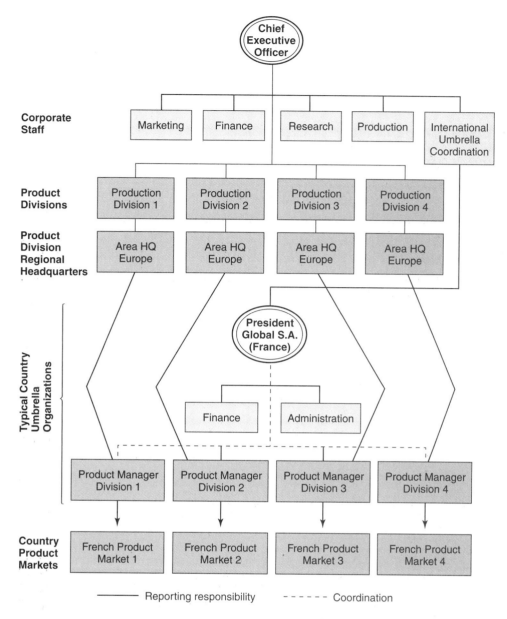

and integration, the cross-functional teams are headed by "brand czars" such as the brand chief for Whirlpool or Kenmore. As Whitwam explains, "The Whirlpool-brand czar still worries about the Whirlpool name. But he also worries about all the refrigerator brands that we make because he heads that product team. It takes a different mind-set."[30]

The key to successful matrix management is ensuring that managers are able to resolve conflicts and achieve integration of organization programs and plans. The mere adoption of a matrix design or structure does not create a matrix organization. The matrix organization requires a fundamental change in management behavior, organizational culture, and technical systems. In a matrix, influence is based on technical competence and interpersonal sensitivity, not on formal authority. In a matrix culture, managers recognize the absolute

---

[30] William C. Taylor and Alan M. Webber, *Going Global: Four Entrepreneurs Map the New World Marketplace* (New York: Penguin USA, 1996), p. 25.

Wall Street Journal: "The Sony BMG merger reduced the number of major record labels to four from five. How many majors does the industry need?"

Gunter Thielen, Chief Executive Officer, Bertelsmann AG: "I think the four majors that now exist can survive quite well. The independents as well, as long as they find good niches. Maybe there will be three at some point. In the music industry, size is really an asset because you can run your national affiliates more efficiently. At Sony BMG, we're combining operations in every country and are going to save a lot of money."

Wall Street Journal: "If you look beyond music at the rest of the media industry, what do you think the dominant trend in the media world in the coming years will be?"

Gunter Thielen: "The entire business is becoming more international. Up until now, the big U.S. majors—the world's three biggest media companies—have concentrated their business in the U.S. I think the process of globalization will mean that these companies will become much more active abroad."

Wall Street Journal: "What about Bertelsmann?"

Gunter Thielen: "For us, this is nothing new. We've been operating outside of Germany for 40 years because Germany is much smaller than the U.S. We reached the limits of our home market decades ago. That led us first into other European markets and then to the U.S. Now, we're in the midst of expanding into the third major global region—Asia. I think the big American companies are also doing this. In any case, I always run into people from Viacom, TimeWarner and so forth on my trips to Asia. They're exploring just like we are."

Wall Street Journal: "Thomas Middelhoff, your predecessor, once described himself as an American with a German passport. What are you?"

Gunter Thielen: "I feel more European. Not as much German as European."

Source: The Wall Street Journal (Western Edition) by Matthew Karnitsching. Copyright 2005 by Dow Jones & Company, Inc. Reproduced with permission of Dow Jones & Company, Inc. in the format Other book via Copyright Clearance Center.

2006 was a turbulent year for Bernd Pischetsrieder. After five years as the chief executive of Volkswagen, he lost a boardroom battle with Chairman Ferdinand Piech concerning the German automaker's ongoing efforts to cut costs and remain competitive in the face of increased competition from Asian nameplates. At the beginning of 2007, another Volkswagen executive resigned. Wolfgang Bernhard, chairman of the Volkswagen brand group, had focused on cost cutting; both Germany's powerful labor union and Chairman Piech were opposed to some of his actions.

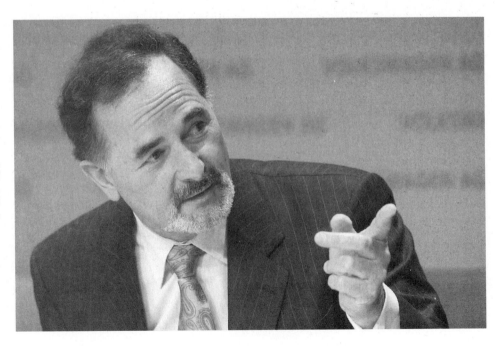

need to resolve issues and choices at the lowest possible level and do not rely on higher authority.

In the twenty-first century, an important task of top management is to eliminate a one-dimensional approach to decisions and encourage the development of multiple management perspectives and an organization that will sense and respond to a complex and fast-changing world. By thinking in terms of changing behavior rather than changing structural design, company management can free itself from the limitations of the structural chart and focus instead on achieving the best possible results with available resources.

LEAN PRODUCTION: ORGANIZING THE JAPANESE WAY

In the automobile industry, a comparison of early craft production processes, mass production, and modern "lean" production provides an interesting case study of the effectiveness of new organizational structures in the twentieth century.[31] Dramatic productivity differences existed between craft and mass producers in the first part of the twentieth century. The mass producers—most notably Ford Motor Company—gained their substantial advantage by changing their value chains so that each worker was able to do far more work each day than the craft producers. The innovation that made this possible was the moving assembly line, which required the originators to conceptualize the production process in a totally new way. The assembly line also required a new approach to organizing people, production machinery, and supplies. By rearranging their value chain activities, the mass producers were able to achieve reductions in effort ranging from 62 percent to 88 percent over the craft producers. These productivity improvements provided an obvious competitive advantage.

The advantage of the mass producers lasted until the Japanese auto companies further revised the value chain and created **lean production**, thereby gaining for themselves the kinds of dramatic competitive advantages that mass producers had previously gained over craft producers. For example, the Toyota Production System (TPS), as the Japanese company's manufacturing methods are known, achieves efficiencies of about 50 percent over typical mass production systems. Even with the reduced assembly time, the lean producer's vehicles have significantly fewer defects than the mass-produced vehicles. The lean producer is also using about 40 percent less factory space and maintaining only a fraction of the inventory stored by the mass producer. Again, the competitive advantages are obvious. Whether the strategy is based on differentiation or low cost, the lean producer has the advantage.

To achieve these gains at Toyota, production gurus Taiichi Ohno and Shigeo Shingo challenged several assumptions traditionally associated with automobile manufacturing. They made changes to operations within the auto company itself such as reducing setup times for machinery. The changes also applied to operations within supplier firms and the interfaces between Toyota and its suppliers and to the interfaces with distributors and dealers. Ohno and Shingo's innovations have been widely embraced in the industry; as a result, individual producers' value chains have been modified, and interfaces between producers and suppliers have been optimized to create more effective and efficient value systems (see Table 16-3).

---

[31] This section is adapted from the following sources: James P. Womack, Daniel T. Jones, and Daniel Roos, *The Machine that Changed the World: The Story of Lean Production* (New York: HarperCollins, 1990); Ranganath Nayak and John M. Ketteringham, *Breakthroughs!* (San Diego, CA: Pfeiffer, 1994), Chapter 9; and Michael Williams, "Back to the Past: Some Plants Tear Out Long Assembly Lines, Switch to Craft Work," *The Wall Street Journal* (October 24, 1994), pp. A1, A4.

Table 16-3

Five Assumptions About Mass Production Versus Toyota Production System

Traditional Assumptions	Ohno and Shingo's Insights
1. Maximize machine utilization	Labor is more costly than machines
2. Fixed setup times	Can reduce setup time
3. Build to inventory to reduce unit cost	Minimize inventory to cut costs, waste
4. Inspect at end of process	Inspect to prevent defective production
5. Maximize backwards integration	Outsource from supplier specialists

Source: Adapted from Adrian Slywotzky, *Value Migration* (Cambridge, MA: Harvard Business School Press, 1996), pp. 31–33.

Assembler Value Chains

Employee ability is emphasized in a lean production environment. Before being hired, people seeking jobs with Toyota participate in the Day of Work, a 12-hour assessment test to determine who has the right mix of physical dexterity, team attitudes, and problem-solving ability. Once hired, workers receive considerable training to enable them to perform any job in their section of the assembly line or area of the plant, and they are assigned to teams in which all members must be able to perform the functions of all other team members. Workers are also empowered to make suggestions and to take actions aimed at improving quality and productivity. Quality control is achieved through *kaizen,* a devotion to continuous improvement that ensures that every flaw is isolated, examined in detail to determine the ultimate cause, and then corrected. Mechanization, and particularly flexible mechanization, is increased within the lean production firm. For example, the same assembly line in Georgetown, Kentucky, that produces Toyota's Camry models also produces the Sienna minivan. The Sienna and Camry share the same basic chassis and 50 percent of their parts. There are 300 different stations on the assembly line, and Sienna models require different parts at only 26 stations. Toyota expects to build one Sienna for every three Camrys that come off the assembly line.[32]

In contrast to the lean producers, U.S. mass producers typically maintain operations with greater direct labor content, less mechanization, and much less flexible mechanization. They also divide their employees into a large number of discrete specialties with no overlap. Employee initiative and teamwork are not encouraged. Quality control is expressed as an acceptable number of defects per vehicle.

Even when the comparisons are based on industry averages, the Japanese lean producers continue to enjoy substantial productivity and quality advantages. Again, these advantages put the lean producers in a better position to exploit low cost or differentiation strategies. They are getting better productivity out of their workers and machines, and they are making better use of their factory floor space. The relatively small size of the repair area reflects the higher quality of their products. A high number of "suggestions per employee" provides some insight into why lean producers outperform mass producers. First, they invest a great deal more in the training of their workers. They also rotate all workers through all jobs for which their teams are responsible. Finally, all workers are encouraged to make suggestions, and management acts on those suggestions. These changes to the value chain translate into major improvements in the value of their products.

It should come as no surprise that many of the world's automakers are studying lean production methods and introducing them in both existing and new plants throughout the world. In 1999, for example, GM announced plans to spend nearly $500 million to overhaul its Adam Opel plant in Germany. Pressure for change came from several sources, including increasing intense rivalry in

---

32 Micheline Maynard, "Camry Assembly Line Delivers New Minivan," *USA Today* (August 11, 1997), p. 3B.

The Toyota Production System (TPS) is based on two concepts. First is jidoka, which involves visualizing potential problems. Jidoka also means that quality is built into the company's vehicles during the manufacturing process. "Just-in-time," the second pillar of the TPS, means that Toyota only produces what is needed, when it is needed, in the amount that is needed. Toyota's training programs ensure that all employees understand the Toyota Way. Future factory workers attend the Toyota Technical Skills Academy in Toyota City, Japan. Executive training takes place at the Toyota Institute.

Source: Ko Sasaki/The New York Times.

Europe's car market, worldwide overcapacity, and a realization that price transparency in the euro zone will exert downward pressure on prices. GM's goal was to transform the plant into a state-of-the-art lean production facility with a 40 percent workforce reduction. As GM Europe President Michael J. Burns said, "Pricing is more difficult today. . . . You have to work on product costs, structural costs. . . . everything."[33]

Downstream Value Chains

The differences between lean producers and U.S. mass producers in the way they deal with their respective dealers, distributors, and customers are as dramatic as the differences in the way they deal with their suppliers. U.S. mass producers follow the basic industry model and maintain an "arm's-length" relationship with dealers that is often characterized by a lack of cooperation and even open hostility. There is often no sharing of information because there is no incentive to do so. The manufacturer is often trying to force on the dealer models the dealer knows will not sell. The dealer, in turn, is often trying to pressure the customer into buying models he or she does not want. All parties are trying to keep information about what they really want from the others. This does little to ensure that the industry is responsive to market needs.

The problem starts with the market research, which is often in error. It is compounded by a lack of feedback from dealers regarding real customer desires. It continues to worsen when the product planning divisions make changes to the models without consulting the marketing divisions or the dealers. This process invariably results in the production of models that are unpopular and almost impossible to sell. The manufacturer uses incentives and other schemes to persuade the dealers to accept the unpopular models, such as making a dealer accept one unpopular model for every five hot-selling models it orders. The dealer then has the problem of persuading customers to buy the unpopular models.

Within the mass assembler's value chain, the linkage between the marketing elements and the product planners is broken. The external linkage between

---

[33] Joseph B. White, "GM Plans to Invest $445 Million, Cut Staff," *The Wall Street Journal* (May 27, 1999), p. A23.

the sales divisions and the dealers is also broken. The production process portion of the value chain is also broken in that it relies on the production of thousands of unsold models that then sit on dealer lots, at enormous cost, while the dealer works to find customers. Within the dealerships, there are even more problems. The relationship between the salesperson and the customer is based on sparring and trying to outsmart each other on price. When the salesperson gets the upper hand, the customer gets stung. It is very much like the relationship between the dealer and the manufacturer. Each is withholding information from the other in the hope of outsmarting the other. Too often, salespeople do not investigate customers' real needs and try to find the best product to satisfy those needs. Rather, they provide only as much information as is needed to close the deal. Once the deal is closed, the salesperson has virtually no further contact with the customer. No attempt is made to optimize the linkage between dealers and manufacturers or the linkage between dealers and customers.

The contrast with the lean producer is again striking. In Japan, the dealer's employees are true product specialists. They know their products and deal with all aspects of the product, including financing, service, maintenance, insurance, registration and inspection, and delivery. A customer deals with one person in the dealership, and that person takes care of everything from the initial contact through eventual trade-in and replacement and all the problems in between. Dealer representatives are included on the manufacturer's product development teams and provide continuous input regarding customer desires. The linkages between dealers, marketing divisions, and product development teams are totally optimized.

The stress caused by large inventories of finished cars is also absent. A car is not built until there is a customer order for it. Each dealer has only a stock of models for the customer to view. Once the customer has decided on the car he or she wants, the order is sent to the factory and in a matter of a couple of weeks the salesperson delivers the car to the customer's house.

Once a Japanese dealership gets a customer, it is absolutely determined to hang on to that customer for life. It is also determined to acquire all the customer's family members as customers. A joke among the Japanese says that the only way to escape from the salesperson who sold a person a car is to leave the country. Japanese dealers maintain extensive databases on actual and potential customers. These databases deal with demographic data and preference data. Customers are encouraged to help keep the information in the database current, and they cooperate in this. This elaborate store of data becomes an integral part of the market research effort and helps ensure that products match customer desires. The fact that there are no inventories of unpopular models because every car is custom ordered for each customer and the fact that the dealer has elaborate data on the needs and desires of its customers change the whole nature of the interaction between the customer and the dealer. The customer literally builds the car she or he wants and can afford. There is no need to try to outsmart each other.

The differences between U.S. mass producers and the Japanese lean producers reflect their fundamental differences in business objectives. The U.S. producers focus on short-term income and return on investment. Today's sale is a discrete event that is not connected to upstream activities in the value chain and has no value in tomorrow's activities. Efforts are made to reduce the cost of the sales activities. The Japanese see the process in terms of the long-term perspective. There are two major goals of the sales process. The first is to maximize the income stream from each customer over time. The second is to use the linkage with the production processes to reduce production and inventory costs and to maximize quality and therefore differentiation.

ETHICS, CORPORATE SOCIAL RESPONSIBILITY, AND SOCIAL RESPONSIVENESS IN THE GLOBALIZATION ERA

Today's chief executive must be a proactive steward of the reputation of the company he or she is leading. This entails, in part, understanding and responding to the concerns and interests of a variety of stakeholders. A **stakeholder** is any group or individual that is affected by, or takes an interest in, the policies and practices adopted by an organization.[34] Top management, employees, customers, persons or institutions that own the company's stock, and suppliers constitute a company's primary shareholders. *Secondary shareholders* include the media, the general business community, local community groups, and **nongovernmental organizations (NGOs)**. The latter include Oxfam, Greenpeace, and Amnesty International. **Stakeholder analysis** is the process of formulating a "win-win" outcome for all stakeholders.[35]

As noted in Chapter 1, one of the forces restraining the growth of global business and global marketing is resistance to globalization. The antiglobalization movement takes a variety of forms and finds expression in various ways. In developed countries, the movement's concerns and agenda include cultural imperialism (e.g., the French backlash against McDonald's), the loss of jobs due to offshoring and outsourcing (e.g., the furniture industry in the United States), and a distrust of global institutions (e.g., anti-WTO protesters in Hong Kong). In developing countries, globalization's opponents accuse companies of undermining local cultures, placing intellectual property rights ahead of human rights, promoting unhealthy diets and unsafe food technologies, and pursuing unsustainable consumption.[36] Environmental degradation and labor exploitation are also key issues.

---

[34] The English term *stakeholder* is sometimes hard to convey in different languages, especially in developing countries. See Neil King Jr. and Jason Dean, "Untranslatable Word in U.S. Aide's Speech Leaves Beijing Baffled," *The Wall Street Journal* (December 7, 2005), pp. A1, A8.

[35] Archie B. Carroll and Ann K. Buchholtz, *Business and Society: Ethics and Stakeholder Management 5/e* (Cincinnati: Southwester, 2003).

[36] Terrence H. Witkowski, "Antiglobal Challenges to Marketing in Developing Countries: Exploring the Ideological Divide," *Journal of Public Policy and Marketing* 24, no. 1 (Spring 2005), pp. 7–23.

In a wired world, a company's reputation can quickly be tarnished if activists target its policies and practices. Thus, the leaders of global companies must practice **corporate social responsibility (CSR)**, which can be defined as a company's obligation to pursue goals and policies that are in society's best interests. In a socially responsible firm, employees conduct business in an ethical manner. In other words, they are guided by moral principles that enable them to distinguish between right and wrong. At many companies, a formal statement or **code of ethics** summarizes core ideologies, corporate values, and expectations. GE, Boeing, and United Technologies Corporation are some of the American companies offering training programs that specifically address ethics issues. For many years, Jack Welch, the legendary former CEO of GE, challenged his employees to take an informal "mirror test." The challenge: "Can you look in the mirror every day and feel proud of what you're doing?"[37] Today, GE uses more formal approaches to ethics and compliance; it has produced training videos, instituted an online training program, and provides employees with a guide to ethical conduct titled *Spirit and Letter* (see Table 16-4).

At Johnson & Johnson, the ethics statement is known as *Our Credo*; first introduced in 1945, the credo has been translated into dozens of languages for J&J employees around the world. Starbucks founder and CEO Howard Schultz's enlightened human resources policies have played a key part in the company's success. Partners, as the company's employees are known, who work 20 hours or more per week are offered health benefits; partners can also take advantage of an employee stock option plan known as Bean Stock. As noted on the company's Web site:

> Consumers are demanding more than "'product" from their favorite brands. Employees are choosing to work for companies with strong values. Shareholders are more inclined to invest in businesses with outstanding corporate reputations. Quite simply, being socially responsible is not only the right thing to do; it can distinguish a company from its industry peers.

For the global company with operations in multiple markets, the issue of corporate social responsibility becomes complicated. When the chief executive of a global firm in a developed country or government policy makers attempt to act in

"Perhaps we have the opportunity to be a different type of global company, a global brand that can build a different model, a company that is a global business, that makes a profit, but at the same time demonstrates a social conscience and gives back to the local market."[38]

Howard Schultz, CEO, Starbucks, in response to a question about the likelihood of antiglobalization activists targeting the company as it expands globally.

"Mr. Schultz recognized ahead of most executives that customers today vote with their dollars and will spend more money at companies with values they admire."[39]

Nancy Koehn, Professor, Harvard Business School

Table 16-4

Ethics Questions from GE

| Q: A new customer wants to place a big order with GE, provided the equipment can be shipped to them overnight. That doesn't give us enough time for the terrorist watchlist screening required of GE customers. Can I ship the equipment and check the watchlists tomorrow?

 A: No, don't ship the equipment until the screening is done. GE cannot agree to do business with a customer until the required watchlist screening has been completed. | Q: An overseas customer has been invited to travel to our training facility at GE's expense. The customer wants to add a weekend side trip to Universal Studios. Can we fund the whole trip?

 A: It depends on many factors including whether the customer is a government official, local law, the customer's policies, and your business' guidelines. Consult with GE general counsel and your manager. |

Source: The Wall Street Journal (Eastern Edition) by Kathyrn Kranhold. Copyright 2005 by Dow Jones & Company, Inc. Reproduced with permission of Dow Jones & Company, Inc. in the format Textbook via Copyright Clearance Center.

---

[37] Stratford Sherman and Noel Tichy, *Control Your Destiny or Someone Else Will* (New York: HarperBusiness, 2001), Chapter 9 "The Mirror Test."

[38] John Murray Brown and Jenny Wiggins, "Coffee Empire Expands Reach by Pressing Its Luck in Ireland," *Financial Times* (December 15, 2005), p. 21.

[39] Carol Hymowitz, "Big Companies Become Big Targets Unless They Guard Images Carefully," *The Wall Street Journal* (December 12, 2005), p. B1.

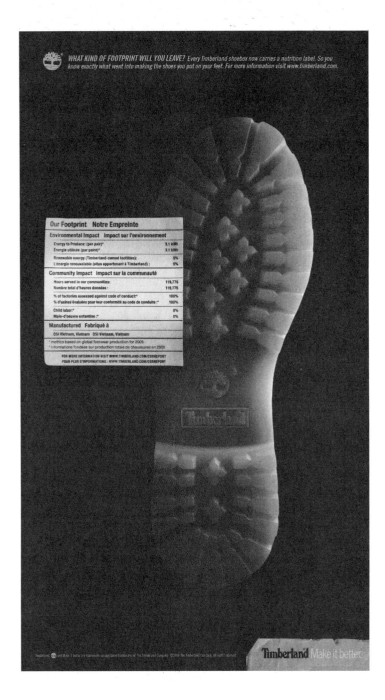

The Timberland Company, based in Stratham, New Hampshire, is best known for its popular hiking boots and work boots. Timberland is a truly global brand; each year, the company sells $1.5 billion in outdoor gear, accessories, and apparel through a network of 250 franchised and company-owned stores as well as department and sporting goods stores.

However, the company stands for more than just rugged authenticity; Timberland is a mission-centered company as well. CEO Jeff Swartz, the grandson of Timberland's founder, is deeply concerned with social justice issues. In 2006, Timberland unveiled a "nutritional label" on its footwear boxes as a means of communicating its CSR commitment to consumers.

"society's best interests," the question arises: Which society? That of the home-country market? Other developed countries? Developing countries? For example, in the late 1990s, in an effort to address the issue of child labor, the U.S. government threatened trade sanctions against the garment industry in Bangladesh. After thousands of child workers lost their jobs, their plight worsened. Whose interests were served by this turn of events? In addition, as noted in Chapter 1, companies that do business around the globe may be in different stages of evolution. Thus, a multinational firm may rely on individual country managers to address CSR issues on an ad hoc basis, while a global or transnational may create a policy at headquarters.

Consider the following:

- Nike came under fire from critics who alleged poor working conditions in the factories that make the company's athletic shoes.

- In 2005, Wal-Mart became the target of criticism for a variety of reasons. Well-publicized lawsuits put the company's compensation policies in the public spotlight. A documentary film titled *The High Cost of Low Prices* examined the social repercussions of the retailer's presence in American communities. Two separate Web sites—WakeUpWalMart.com and WalMartWatch.com—were established by organizations representing U.S. labor unions.
- As retail gasoline prices soared in the United States following the devastation of Hurricane Katrina, BP, Royal Dutch Shell, and other companies were accused of gouging. The American Petroleum Institute, the industry's trade group, launched a national TV advertising campaign aimed at explaining its business and urging conservation.[40]
- CEO pay in the United States is rising faster than average salaries and much faster than inflation. One study found that in 2004, CEOs were paid 431 times more than the average worker.

In an article in *Business Ethics Quarterly*, Arthaud-Day proposed a three-dimensional framework for analyzing the social behavior of international,

Our Credo

We believe our first responsibility is to the doctors, nurses and patients, to mothers and fathers and all others who use our products and services. In meeting their needs everything we do must be of high quality. We must constantly strive to reduce our costs in order to maintain reasonable prices. Customers' orders must be serviced promptly and accurately. Our suppliers and distributors must have an opportunity to make a fair profit.

We are responsible to our employees, the men and women who work with us throughout the world. Everyone must be considered as an individual. We must respect their dignity and recognize their merit. They must have a sense of security in their jobs. Compensation must be fair and adequate, and working conditions clean, orderly and safe. We must be mindful of ways to help our employees fulfill their family responsibilities. Employees must feel free to make suggestions and complaints. There must be equal opportunity for employment, development and advancement for those qualified. We must provide competent management, and their actions must be just and ethical.

We are responsible to the communities in which we live and work and to the world community as well. We must be good citizens – support good works and charities and bear our fair share of taxes. We must encourage civic improvements and better health and education. We must maintain in good order the property we are privileged to use, protecting the environment and natural resources.

Our final responsibility is to our stockholders. Business must make a sound profit. We must experiment with new ideas. Research must be carried on, innovative programs developed and mistakes paid for. New equipment must be purchased, new facilities provided and new products launched. Reserves must be created to provide for adverse times. When we operate according to these principles, the stockholders should realize a fair return.

Johnson & Johnson

40 Jean Halliday, "Slick: Big Oil Tries Image Makeover," *Advertising Age* (November 7, 2005), pp. 1, 56.
41 Alison Maitland, "Four Questions for Tomorrow's Leviathans," *Financial Times* (July 25, 2006), p. 7.
42 Andrew Ward, "Coke Struggles to Defend Positive Reputation," *Financial Times* (January 6, 2006), p. 15.

Company/Headquarters Country	Nature of CSR Initiative
IKEA/Sweden	IKEA's primary carpet supplier in India monitors subcontractors to ensure they do not employ children. IKEA also helps lower-caste Indian women reduce their indebtedness to moneylenders. In an effort to create a more child-friendly environment in Indian villages, IKEA sponsors "bridge schools" to increase literacy so young people—including girls and untouchables—can enroll in regular schools.*
Avon/United States	The company's Breast Cancer Awareness Crusade raised more than $250 million for cancer research. The money funds research in 50 countries.

*Edward Luce, "Ikea's Grown-Up Plan to Tackle Child Labor," *Financial Times* (September 15, 2004), p. 7.

Table 16-5

Global Marketing and Corporate Social Responsibility

multinational, global, and transnational firms.[43] The second dimension of the model includes CSR's three "content domains": human rights, labor, and the environment. These are the universal concerns for global companies established by the United Nations Global Compact. The third dimension in Arthaud-Day's framework consists of three perspectives. The *ideological dimension* of CSR pertains to the things a firm's management believes it should be doing. The *societal dimension* consists of the expectations held by the firm's external stakeholders. The *operational dimension* includes the actions and activities actually taken by the firm. As illustrated in Figure 16-5, the interaction between the dimensions can result in several conflict scenarios. Conflict may arise if there is an incongruity between those things a company's leadership believes it should be doing and the expectations of stakeholders. Conflict can also arise when there is an incongruity between those things a company's leadership believes it should be doing and the things it actually is doing. A third scenario is conflict that arises from an incongruity between society's expectations and actual corporate practices and activities.

"Every day, we strive to understand how we can best serve our community. Through our unique and diverse staff we offer excellent service and quality products while maintaining our commitment to the environment."
Patagonia Retail Mission Statement

"Our definition of quality includes a mandate for building products and working with processes that cause the least harm to the environment. We evaluate raw materials, invest in innovative technologies, rigorously police our waste and use a portion of our profits to support groups working to make a real difference. We acknowledge that the wild world we love best is disappearing. That is why those of us who work here share a strong commitment to protecting undomesticated lands and waters. We believe in using business to inspire solutions to the environmental crisis."
Patagonia Environmental Action Statement

In India's carpet belt, IKEA operationalizes the concept of corporate global responsibility by sponsoring bridge schools. The school programs are intended to reduce child labor in India's carpet industry by preparing village children to enroll in mainstream schools. To date, the bridge school program has helped an estimated 21,000 children learn to read and write.

---

[43] Marne Arthaud-Day, "Transnational Corporate Social Responsibility: A Tri-Dimensional Approach to International CSR Research," *Business Ethics Quarterly* 15, no. 1 (January 2005), pp. 1–22.

Chapter 16   Leadership, Organization, and Corporate Social Responsibility   561

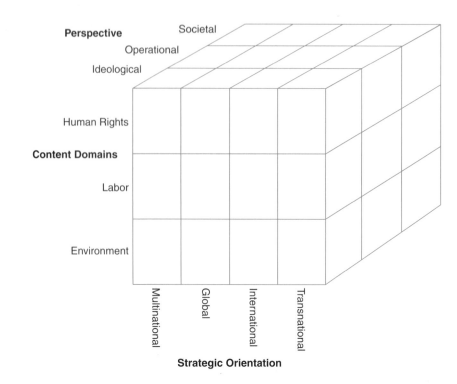

Figure 16-5

Sources of Conflict in Global CSR

Source: Business Ethics Quarterly 15 (No 1), 2005. Used with permission of Business Ethics Quarterly.

Perspective

Societal

Operational

Ideological

Human Rights

Content Domains

Labor

Environment

Multinational

Global

International

Transnational

Strategic Orientation

summary

To respond to the opportunities and threats in the global marketing environment, organizational **leaders** must develop a global vision and strategy. Leaders must also be able to communicate that vision throughout the organization and build global competencies. Global companies are increasingly realizing that the "right" person for top jobs is not necessarily a home-country national.

In **organizing** for the global marketing effort, the goal is to create a structure that enables the company to respond to significant differences in international market environments and to extend valuable corporate knowledge. Alternatives include an **international division structure**, **regional management centers**, **geographical structure**, **regional** or **worldwide product division**

structure, and the **matrix** design. Whichever form of organization is chosen, balance between autonomy and integration must be established. Many companies are adopting the organizational principle of **lean production** that was pioneered by Japanese automakers.

Many global companies are paying attention to the issue of **corporate social responsibility (CSR)**. Consumers throughout the world expect that the brands and products they buy and use are marketed by companies that conduct business in an ethical, socially responsible way. Societally conscious companies should include human rights, labor, and environmental issues in their agendas. Ideological, societal, and organizational perspectives can all be brought to bear on CSR.

1. Are top executives of global companies likely to be home-country nationals?

2. In a company involved in global marketing, which activities should be centralized at headquarters and which should be delegated to national or regional subsidiaries?

3. Identify some of the factors that lead to the establishment of an international division as an organization increases its global business activities.

4. "A matrix structure integrates four competencies on a worldwide scale." Explain.

5. In the automobile industry, how does "lean production" differ from the traditional assembly line approach?

6. Identify some of the ways the global companies discussed in this text demonstrate their commitment to CSR.

7. Identify and explain the three dimensions that provide different perspectives on CSR.

1. Several of the companies, topics, and issues discussed in this book can be assessed in terms of CSR. Examples include:

- Fair Trade Coffee (Case 4-1)[44]
- Worker exploitation (Case 8-1)
- Pricing AIDs drugs in developing countries (Chapter 11)[45]
- The Future of RFID (Case 12-2)[46]
- Porno-chic advertising in Europe (Chapter 13)
- IKEA (Chapter 15)

2. European Aeronautic Defence and Space Company (EADS), which is profiled in Case 16-1, is one of a handful of global companies with a dual management structure. As noted in the case, EADS has been forced to reevaluate the effectiveness of that structure. The same thing is happening at other companies. For example, until recently, Unilever had a tradition of two co-chairmen, one in Great Britain and one in the Netherlands. In 2005, Unilever named a single chief executive; the company still maintains separate headquarters in the two countries. Also in 2005, Royal Dutch/Shell Group abolished its dual management structure. Conduct some exploratory research to learn more about the management changes at Unilever and Shell. Should similar changes be made at EADS?

Assess each of these companies or topics in terms of corporate social responsibility.

---

44 Marion Kane, "It's Time to Wake Up to Fair Trade Coffee," *Toronto Star* (December 3, 2005).
45 For an excellent discussion, see N. Craig Smith, "Corporate Social Responsibility: 'Whether' or 'How'?" *California Management Review* 45, no. 4 (Summer 2003), pp. 52–77.
46 Andrew Bibby, "Invasion of the Privacy Snatchers," *Financial Times* (January 9, 2006), p. 7.

Case 16-1

Boeing Versus Airbus: A Battle for the Skies

What a difference a year makes! At the end of 2005, Airbus, the European aircraft manufacturer, reported that it had booked 1,055 orders for new airplanes in the preceding 12 months. By contrast, archrival Boeing Company had recorded only 1,002 orders. Moreover, for the third year in a row, Airbus delivered more airplanes to customers than Boeing. Airbus had also stolen a step in the PR arena in April with the maiden flight of its new double-decker super-jumbo jet, the 555-passenger A-380. The new jet, which was scheduled to go into service in 2006, had taken 10 years to develop at a cost of $12 billion.

The strategic decision to develop the A-380 was based on projections of large increases in air passenger traffic but a limited amount of new airport construction. The conclusion: Airlines—the industry's main customers—would need a new super jumbo to carry more passengers while reducing the number of flights between key city hubs. Airbus executives believed the A-380 would revolutionize air travel in the twenty-first century.

By mid-2006, however, production of the A-380 was running six months behind schedule and $2.5 billion over budget. Then came an announcement of an additional six months' delay due to unanticipated difficulties in wiring the giant airliner. Airbus was facing trouble on another front as well: a second new plane in the design phase, the A-350, was being criticized by Singapore Airlines and other potential customers for offering less comfort, less speed, and less operating efficiency than a rival Boeing plane, the 787 Dreamliner. As originally designed, the A-350 was essentially an upgrade of an existing model, the A-330, outfitted with new engines.

Executives at Boeing, the world's largest manufacturer of commercial aircraft, might have been forgiven if they took time to savor the reversal of fortune at Airbus. However, they were busy booking orders for the new Dreamliner. Boeing has a stellar track record with "bet the company"-type product decisions. In the 1950s, when the company was best known for military aircraft such as the B-52 bomber, Boeing single-handedly created the commercial market for jet aircraft with the introduction of the 707. In the mid-1960s, Boeing gambled that the world's airlines would be enthusiastic about a new wide-body aircraft. The gamble paid off handsomely: Since its first passenger flight in 1970, the Boeing 747 jumbo jet has generated more than $130 billion in sales. In 2001, Boeing made headlines again when it announced plans for a revolutionary new delta-wing aircraft called the Sonic Cruiser. The new jet would carry between 100 and 300 passengers and fly just below the speed of sound (Mach 1) with a range of up to 10,000 miles.

> *"We spent a great deal of time on product strategy and trying to come up with airplanes that were pleasant for customers and profitable for the airlines."*
>
> Larry Dickenson, Senior Vice President, Boeing

By 2002, Boeing was backpedaling on the Sonic Cruiser plan. The airline industry was retrenching in the wake of the September 11 terror attacks; United Airlines, a key Boeing customer, was in bankruptcy. Moreover, airline passengers appeared to be more concerned with ticket prices than with travel time. Accordingly, Boeing began assessing customer reaction to an alternative design for a more conventional aircraft. As one airline executive said in mid-2002, "The folks over at Boeing are sort of pulling their hair out right now trying to figure out which is the right avenue to take." In the past, Boeing had canceled new-product development programs such as a proposed fuel-efficient model 7J7. Alan Mulally, Boeing's top executive at its commercial airplane division, defended that record, saying that Boeing is a nimble, customer-driven company. "What a neat thing it is to look at your customers and the market and make your investments accordingly. The fact that Boeing is listening and flexible is a great thing," he said.

By the fall of 2003, the suspense was over: As some industry observers had predicted, Boeing announced it was scrapping plans for the Sonic Cruiser. Instead the company would develop a new 200-seat model, the 7E7 Dreamliner, that would offer passengers improved comfort in the air. The new aircraft features arched ceilings and "mood-enhancing lighting"; larger windows than those on the 777; and seats in economy class will be arranged 3-2-3 across rather than 2-4-2. This configuration will make it less likely that passengers will be stuck in a "bad" seat. Boeing's new baby would also represent a powerful value proposition for the airlines: The "E" stands for "efficiency." With new engines and a body comprised of carbon-enhanced plastic, the new aircraft will cost airlines 20 percent less to operate than existing aircraft.

In mid-2004, All Nippon Airlines ordered 50 7E7s valued at $6 billion; the order represented the largest product launch in Boeing's history. In January 2005, with the announcement that China had placed an order for 60 planes, Boeing officials gave the new plane the official model designation 787. The designation brought the new plane into line with Boeing's tradition of using a succession of 7–7 numberings such as 747, 767, and 777. Moreover, as Mulally noted in a press release, "Incorporating the '8' at the time of the China order is also significant because in many Asian cultures the number 8 represents good luck and prosperity." In April, Air Canada announced it would replace its entire fleet of Airbus models with the Dreamliner; in the following months, more orders poured in.

The first 787s are scheduled to go into service in 2008. Boeing's production strategy for the 787 includes dispersing design work to Russia, China, and Japan. Thanks to the Internet, engineers in these nations can collaborate in real time. Moreover, by tapping talent resources in key countries, Boeing hopes to increase the likelihood of booking orders from airlines and governments in those nations. Composite materials will not only lower the 787's operating costs, but it will also enable Boeing to reconfigure its supply chain. For

Table 16-1 *787 Suppliers*

Supplier	Percent of Project
Boeing	35
Mitsubishi Heavy Industries/Fuji Heavy Industries/Kawasaki Heavy Industries	35
Vought Aircraft Industries (Dallas, Texas)/Alenia Aeronautica (Rome)	26
Others	4

example, the wings and most of the fuselage will be manufactured in Japan and transported to Seattle in specially modified 747–400 freightliners. Previously, parts from Japan had been transported by water, rail, and, finally, truck, a journey that could take one month. Boeing expects that, by cutting transport time to one day, it can save 40 percent in shipping and inventory expenses. Companies that wish to bid on parts of the 787 will not communicate directly with Boeing headquarters. Instead, they have to deal with Boeing's new 787 Council, a group made up of top executives from several outside suppliers.

Boeing's strategy for the 787 has created some controversy. In the two years leading up to the 787 announcement, Boeing had already cut 35,000 jobs in the United States. The company had previously outsourced some aircraft production to other countries; for example, Japanese companies supply about one-fifth of the 777. One reason for outsourcing was that airlines would be more likely to buy an aircraft that had some local content. However, that strategy had not always paid off. For example, Boeing has a design center in Russia that employs more than 700 engineers. In 2002, however, Russia's largest airline, AeroFlot, ordered twice as many aircraft from Airbus than it did from Boeing. Similarly, Boeing helped establish a small plant in

South Africa to perform work that had previously been done in Seattle. In 2002, South African Airways ordered 41 jets from Airbus.

In the eyes of some critics, there is more at stake than just orders for new airplanes: The 787 project marks the first time that Being is sharing its proprietary technology for wing design and manufacture. Jennifer MacKay is president of the Society of Professional Engineering Employees in Aerospace, a union that represents Boeing engineers and other technical workers. She is deeply concerned about the long-term consequences of sharing technology with other countries. "In the end, if we teach everybody how to make the major parts, why is Boeing even needed?" she asks. Mike Blair, senior vice president of the 787, has an answer. "Figuring out what the wings look like, figuring out how to put them on the airplane, understanding whether that's something our customers will buy, understanding how to integrate that stuff, that's the magic Boeing brings to this process," he said.

Production Delays and Management Restructuring at Airbus

Meanwhile, at Airbus, the management team that had previously dismissed Boeing's claims about the 787's efficiency and downplayed customer concerns was in turmoil. In part, the problems could be traced to the complicated corporate structure of European Aeronautic Defence and Space Company (EADS), the corporate parent of Airbus. Germany's DaimlerChrysler owns 22.5 percent, Sogeade (a corporate entity owned by the French government and the Lagardère Group), holds a 30 percent stake, and Spain owns 5.4 percent through a holding company known as Sepi. (The remaining shares are listed on major European stock exchanges.) EADS, in turn, owns an 80 percent share in Airbus; BAE Systems, a British company, controls the remaining 20 percent.

Tensions were growing because of attempts by DaimlerChrysler to maintain control over the chief executive of Airbus, Noël Forgeard, who happened to be French. Observers also noted that the crisis stemmed partly from political infighting and power struggles between the French executives at EADS and their compatriots at the Airbus unit. The interpersonal dynamics had been stabilized by Jean-Luc Lagardère, the chief executive of the French company that was a key shareholder in EADS. After Lagardère died suddenly in 2003, however, the rivalries got out of hand.

The crisis was also rooted in the autonomy granted to the manufacturing locations, particularly those in France and Germany; lack of integration between those locations resulted in delays. Moreover, in an attempt to raise his profile with the EADS board, Forgeard had driven his team to deliver on-time results in the face of tight development windows. Unfortunately, this resulted in a "green-light" corporate culture that downplayed potential problems or delays. For example, the German team in Hamburg was using different computer design software than the French team in Toulouse; this led to delays in installing the complex cable system in the cabin of the A-380. In the opinion of some observers, the lack of investment in new software was the result of top management's desire to boost profits. In interviews, Forgeard asserted that he had not been alerted to the seriousness of the mounting problems. Meanwhile, Forgeard used his political connections to win a promotion to the position of co-chief executive of EADS. In June 2005, Gustav Humbert was named to replace Forgeard as Airbus CEO.

In addition to headaches with the A380 program, the Airbus management team was facing another issue: customer complaints about the new A-350. A crisis management team was assembled and given a mandate to redesign the A-350. The jet's top speed was increased slightly to .85 mach to match the 787, and the cabin was widened to allow seating nine passengers in each row instead of eight as originally planned. The redesign means that the new model will not be introduced until 2012.

In July 2006, after barely a year on the job, Humbert resigned as CEO of Airbus. Almost simultaneously, Noël Forgeard resigned as well. Christian Streiff, a Frenchman, was named as Humbert's replacement. One of Streiff's first acts was to fire Charles Champion, the head of the A380 program. He also launched a restructuring program dubbed Power8. However, Streiff himself resigned after only 100 days on the job. Louis Gallois was named chief executive of Airbus and co-CEO of EADS; a German, Thomas Enders, will share the top job at EADS.

As he settled into the job, Gallois faced a number of challenges and questions stemming from the crisis at Airbus. Would the French and German investors and management be able to set aside their differences? Should he close some of Airbus' 16 assembly plants—spread across the United Kingdom, Spain, France and Germany—and transfer production out of Europe? Would key customers such as Virgin Atlantic Airways cancel orders for the A380? Would the euro's strength relative to the dollar translate into a significant cost advantage for Boeing?

Discussion Questions

1. What key mistakes did Airbus make with its A-350 and A-380 product programs?
2. What are some of the factors contributing to the success of Boeing's 787 Dreamliner?
3. Assess Boeing's plans to subcontract out significant portions of the Dreamliner's manufacture.

Sources: J. Lynn Lunsford and Daniel Michaels, "New Course: Under Pressure, Airbus Redesigns a Troubled Plane" *The Wall Street Journal* (July 14, 2006), pp. A1, A7; Lunsford and Michaels "Rapid Descent: Bet on Huge Plane Trips up Airbus," *The Wall Street Journal* (June 15, 2006), pp. A1, A11; Roger Yu, "Airbus Sneaks Past Boeing in 11th Hour," *USA Today* (January 18, 2006), p. 6B; Lunsford, "Boeing's New Baby," *The Wall Street Journal* (November 18, 2003), pp. B1, B8; Caroline Daniel, "Airbus Takes on Boeing with More Than Banter," *Financial Times* (November 14, 2003), p. 23; Byron Acohido, "Boeing Rips a Page out of Airbus' Book," *USA Today* (October 22, 2003), p. 3B; Lunsford, "Boeing Explores Plan 'B'," *The Wall Street Journal* (June 11, 2002), p. D5; Lunsford, "Lean Times: With Airbus on Its Tail, Boeing Is Rethinking How It Builds Planes," *The Wall Street Journal* (September 5, 2001), pp. A1, A16; Lunsford, "Navigating Change: Boeing, Losing Ground to Airbus, Faces Key Choice," *The Wall Street Journal* Alan Levin, "Boeing's Sonic Cruiser: Gambling on Speed," *USA Today* (June 18, 2001), pp. 1A, 2A; Laurence Zuckerman, "Boeing Plays an Aerial Wild Card," *The New York Times* (June 17, 2001), sec. 3, pp. 1, 11; Daniel Michaels, "New Approach: Airbus Revamp Brings Sense to Consortium, Fuels Boeing Rivalry," *The Wall Street Journal* (April 3, 2001), pp. A1, A8; Jeff Cole, "Wing Commander: At Boeing, an Old Hand Provides New Tricks in Battle with Airbus," *The Wall Street Journal* (January 10, 2001), pp. A1, A12.

Johnson & Johnson Credos: Brazil, Russia, India, and China

Nosso Credo

Cremos que nossa primeira responsabilidade é para com os médicos, enfermeiras e pacientes,
para com as mães, pais e todos os demais que usam nossos produtos e serviços.
Para atender suas necessidades, tudo o que fizermos deve ser de alta qualidade.
Devemos constantemente nos esforçar para reduzir nossos custos,
a fim de manter preços razoáveis.
Os pedidos de nossos clientes devem ser pronta e corretamente atendidos.
Nossos fornecedores e distribuidores devem ter a oportunidade
de auferir um lucro justo.

Somos responsáveis por nossos empregados,
homens e mulheres que conosco trabalham em todo o mundo.
Todos devem ser considerados em sua individualidade.
Devemos respeitar sua dignidade e reconhecer o seu mérito.
Eles devem se sentir seguros em seus empregos.
A remuneração pelo seu trabalho deve ser justa e adequada
e o ambiente de trabalho limpo, ordenado e seguro.
Devemos ter em mente maneiras de ajudar nossos empregados
a atender às suas responsabilidades familiares.
Os empregados devem se sentir livres para fazer sugestões e reclamações.
Deve haver igual oportunidade de emprego, desenvolvimento
e progresso para os qualificados.
Devemos ter uma administração competente,
e suas ações devem ser justas e éticas.

Somos responsáveis perante as comunidades nas quais vivemos e trabalhamos,
bem como perante a comunidade mundial.
Devemos ser bons cidadãos – apoiar boas obras sociais e de caridade
e pagar corretamente os tributos.
Devemos encorajar o desenvolvimento do civismo e a melhoria da saúde e da educação.
Devemos manter em boa ordem
as propriedades que temos o privilégio de usar,
protegendo o meio ambiente e os recursos naturais.

Nossa responsabilidade final é para com os acionistas.
Os negócios devem proporcionar lucros adequados.
Devemos experimentar novas idéias.
Pesquisas devem ser levadas avante. Programas inovadores desenvolvidos
e os erros corrigidos.
Novos equipamentos devem ser adquiridos, novas fábricas construídas
e novos produtos lançados.
Reservas devem ser criadas para enfrentar tempos adversos.
Ao operarmos de acordo com esses princípios,
nossos acionistas devem
receber justa recompensa.

Johnson & Johnson

Наше Кредо

Наша основная ответственность – перед врачами и медицинскими сестрами,
перед пациентами, перед отцами и матерями, перед всеми,
кто пользуется нашей продукцией и услугами. В соответствии с их
потребностями мы должны обеспечивать высокие стандарты качества во всем,
что мы делаем. Мы должны постоянно стремиться к снижению затрат,
чтобы поддерживать приемлемый уровень цен. Заказы клиентов должны
выполняться точно и в срок. Наши поставщики и дистрибьюторы
должны иметь возможность получать достойную прибыль.

Мы несем ответственность перед нашими сотрудниками,
мужчинами и женщинами, которые работают у нас по всему миру.
Мы должны ценить индивидуальность в каждом из них.
Мы должны уважать их достоинство и признавать их заслуги:
нам важно поддерживать в них чувство уверенности в завтрашнем дне.
Вознаграждение должно быть справедливым и соразмерным,
а условия труда обеспечивать чистоту, порядок и безопасность.
Нам важно, чтобы сотрудники имели возможность заботиться о семье.
Сотрудники должны чувствовать, что они могут свободно
выступать с предложениями и замечаниями.
У всех квалифицированных специалистов должны быть
равные возможности для получения работы, развития и продвижения.
Мы должны обеспечивать компетентное управление,
действия руководителей должны быть справедливыми и этичными.

Мы несем ответственность перед обществом,
в котором живем и работаем, а также перед мировым сообществом.
Мы должны выполнять свой гражданский долг:
поддерживать добрые начинания и благотворительные акции,
честно платить налоги. Мы должны содействовать улучшениям
в социальной сфере, здравоохранении и образовании.
Мы должны бережно относиться к вверенной нам собственности,
сохраняя природные ресурсы и защищая окружающую среду.

И, наконец, мы несем ответственность перед нашими акционерами.
Бизнес должен приносить существенную прибыль.
Мы должны экспериментировать с новыми идеями,
вести научно-исследовательскую работу,
внедрять инновации, учиться на своих ошибках.
Мы должны приобретать новое оборудование, обеспечивать современные
условия работы и выводить на рынок новую продукцию.
Мы должны быть готовы к сложным ситуациям и иметь резервы
для их решения. Придерживаясь этих принципов,
мы обеспечим нашим акционерам достойный доход.

हमारी नीति

हम यह मानते हैं कि हमारी पहली जिम्मेदारी डाक्टरों, नर्सों, रोगीयों, माताओं, पिताओं तथा
उन सभी लोगों के प्रति है जो हमारे उत्पादनों और सेवाओं का उपयोग करते हैं।
उनकी आवश्यकताओं की पूर्ति के लिए जो कुछ भी हम करें, वह उत्तम दर्जे का हो।
हमें अपने उत्पादनों की कीमत घटाने की लगातार कोशिश करनी चाहिए
ताकि वे उचित कीमतों में उपलब्ध हों।
ग्राहकों की माँगें सही तौर पर तथा तत्परता से पूरी की जानी चाहिए।
हमारे विक्रेताओं और वितरकों को उचित लाभ मिलने का अवसर मिले।

हम अपने उन स्त्री और पुरुष कर्मचारियों के प्रति
जिम्मेदार हैं जो हमारे साथ संसार के हर देश में काम करते हैं।
हर व्यक्ति को व्यक्तिगत रूप से देखा जाय।
हमें उनकी प्रतिष्ठा और योग्यता का आदर करना चाहिए।
उन्हें अपनी नौकरी की सुरक्षा का विश्वास रहे।
उनका वेतन उचित और पर्याप्त हो।
काम करने का वातावरण स्वच्छ, सुव्यवस्थित और सुरक्षित हो।
पारिवारिक जिम्मेदारियाँ निभाने के लिए हमें अपने कर्मचारियोंको दक्षतापूर्वक मार्ग दिखाना चाहिए।
कर्मचारियों को उनके सुझाव और शिकायतें उचित ढंग से प्रस्तुत करने की स्वतंत्रता हो।
योग्य लोगों को सेवा, प्रगति और विकास का समान अवसर मिले।
हमारा व्यवस्थापन निपुण हो और प्रबंधकों की कृति उचित और न्यायपूर्ण हो।

हम जिस समाज में रहते और काम करते हैं और जिस विश्व समाज के हम भाग हैं
उस समाज के प्रति हमारी जिम्मेदारी है।
हमें अच्छा नागरिक होना चाहिए – दान, धर्म और दूसरे अच्छे कार्यों में
भाग लेना चाहिए तथा अपने हिस्से का कर बराबर देते रहना चाहिए।
हम नगर-सुधार, स्वास्थ्य और शिक्षा को प्रोत्साहित करें।
वातावरण और नैसर्गिक अलनियों को सुरक्षित रखते हुए, जिस संपत्ति का उपयोग
करने का हमें सुअवसर मिला है इसे हम अच्छी तरह संभाल कर रखें।

हमारी आखरी जिम्मेदारी भागधारकों के प्रति है।
व्यापार में पर्याप्त लाभ होना चाहिए।
हमें नये-नये विचारों को अमल में लाना चाहिए।
अनुसंधान किए जाएं, आविष्कारिक योजनाओं का विकास किया जाए और
भूलों से हुई हानि का मूल्य चुकाया जाए।
नये यंत्र खरीदे जाएं, नई सुविधाएं उपलब्ध हों और नये उत्पादनों का
निर्माण किया जाए ताकि बुरे दिनों के लिए प्रबंध हो।
यदि हम इन सिद्धान्तों के अनुसार कार्य करते हैं तो
भागधारकों को पर्याप्त लाभ मिल सकता है।

जॉन्सन अॅण्ड जॉन्सन

我们的信条

我们相信我们首先要对医生、护士和病人,
对父母亲以及所有使用我们的产品和接受我们服务的人负责.
为了满足他们的需求, 我们所做的一切都必须是高质量的.
我们必须不断地致力于降低成本, 以保持合理的价格.
客户的订货必须迅速而准确地供应.
我们的供应商和经销商应该有机会获得合理的利润.

我们要对世界各地和我们一起共事的男女同仁负责,
每一位同仁都应视为独立的个体.
我们必须维护他们的尊严, 赞赏他们的优点,
要使他们对其工作有一种安全感.
薪酬必须公平合理.
工作环境必须清洁、整齐和安全.
我们必须设法帮助员工履行他们对家庭的责任.
必须让员工在提出建议和申诉时畅所欲言.
对于合格的人必须给予平等的雇用、发展和升迁的机会.
我们必须具备称职的管理人员.
他们的行为必须公正并符合道德.

我们要对我们所生活和工作的社会, 对整个世界负责.
我们必须做好公民 – 支持好社会有益的活动和慈善事业.
做纳我们应付的税款.
我们必须鼓励全民进步, 促进健康和教育事业.
我们必须很好地维护我们所使用的财产,
保护环境和自然资源.

最后, 我们要对全体股东负责.
企业经营必须获取可靠的利润.
我们必须尝试新的构想.
必须坚持研究工作, 开发革新项目.
承担错误的代价并加以改正.
必须购置新设备, 提供新设施, 推出新产品.
必须设立储备金, 以备不时之需.
如果我们能遵这些准则进行经营,
股东们就会获得合理的回报.

Johnson & Johnson

The Digital Revolution and the Global E-Marketplace

According to a recent "digital opportunity index" published by the United Nations, South Korea leads the world in providing its citizens with access to information and communications technologies (ICT). The country's high-tech infrastructure takes a variety of forms. The availability of broadband Internet connections is one example. South Korea currently leads the world in broadband penetration (23 connections per 100 inhabitants); with 68 connections per 100 households, South Korea ranks second only to Hong Kong. By comparison, the United States leads the world in total number of broadband subscribers; however, it ranks 19th in terms of connections per 100 households. South Korea's government budgeted $50 billion in an effort to link 80 major cities and towns via broadband; moreover, South Korea's network is extremely fast, offering standard speeds of 8 megabits per second (Mbps). By comparison, much of Europe's broadband network currently operates at less than 1 Mbps. As Stephen Ward, a consultant with Deloitte, explains, "Koreans tend to be early adopters of technology and, more significantly, are fast followers. They are always conscious of the need not to get left behind by the Japanese and the young have a great desire to conform with the gadget-carrying norm of their peers."

The digital revolution is driving the creation of new companies, industries, and markets in all parts of the world; the same process is also contributing to the *destruction* of companies, industries, and markets. In short, the revolution is dramatically transforming the world in which we live. Policy makers in South Korea and other countries are hoping to be leaders, rather than followers, as the revolution gains traction and picks up speed. In this final chapter, we will begin by briefly reviewing the key innovations that served as precursors to the digital revolution. In the next two sections, convergence, the disruptive nature of Internet technology, and its effect on global companies are discussed. Next, key e-commerce issues that face global marketers are examined and a typology of Web sites categories is introduced. Next is an overview of Web site design issues as they pertain to global marketing. The final section of the chapter examines some of the new products and services made possible by the digital revolution.

South Koreans in traditional scholar robes use laptop computers at the digital version of a state examination at Sungkyunkwan University in Seoul. The event commemorates the traditional means for selecting government officers during the Chosun Dynasty, which dates back to the 14th century. Several hundred participants competed by composing Korean, Chinese, and English poems, demonstrating foreign language skills, and playing Internet games.

THE DIGITAL REVOLUTION: A BRIEF HISTORY

The **digital revolution** is a paradigm shift resulting from technological advances that allow for the digitization (i.e., conversion to binary code) of analogue sources of information, sounds, and images. The origins of the digital revolution can be traced back to the mid-twentieth century. Over a five-year period between 1937 and 1942, John Vincent Atanasoff and Clifford Berry developed the world's first electromechanical digital computer at Iowa State University. The Atanasoff-Berry Computer (ABC) incorporated several major innovations in computing including the use of binary arithmetic, regenerative memory, parallel processing, and separation of the memory and computing functions. In 1947, William Shockley and two colleagues at AT&T's Bell Laboratories invented a "solid state amplifier," or **transistor,** as it became known. This was a critical innovation because the vacuum tubes that were used in computers and electronics products at that time were large, consumed a large amount of power, and generated a great deal of heat. Shockley and collaborators John Bardeen and William Brattain were awarded the Nobel Prize in physics in 1956 for their invention.

In 1948, a Bell Labs researcher named Claude Shannon wrote a technical report titled *A Mathematical Theory of Communication* in which he proposed that all information media could be encoded in *binary digits*, or bits. Earlier, in 1940, Shannon had argued in his doctoral dissertation that the logical values "true" and "false" could be denoted by "1" and "0", respectively, and that streams of 1s and 0s could transmit media over a wire. In the mid-1950s, Sony licensed the transistor from Bell Labs; Sony engineers boosted the yield of the transistor and created the market for transistor radios. The sound was "lo-fi" but the devices were portable and stylish, which is what consumers—especially teenagers—wanted. Also during the 1950s, Robert Noyce and Jack Kilby independently invented the silicon chip (also known as the integrated circuit or IC).[1] In essence, the IC put the various parts of an electrical circuit—including resistors, diodes, and capacitors—on a single piece of material. The IC gave the transistor its modern form and allowed its power to be harnessed in a reliable, low-cost way.

The IC and the concept of binary code permitted the development of the **personal computer (PC),** a compact, affordable device whose appearance marked the next phase of the digital revolution. Many of the events and people associated with this era have become the stuff of legend. Some observers credit Alan Kay with research that permitted the development of the first PCs. During the 1970s, Kay was director of the Learning Research Group at the Xerox Palo Alto Research Center (PARC). Then, between 1981 and 1983, Kay worked at Atari, which, along with other pioneering PC companies such as Osborne and Commodore, has long since disappeared. Kay's work at Xerox PARC had a strong impact on Steve Jobs who, with partner Steve Wozniak, started Apple Computer in a garage in the late 1970s. The company's Apple II is widely regarded as the first "true" PC; the Apple II's popularity received a big boost in 1979 when a spreadsheet program known as VisiCalc was introduced. A computer **spreadsheet** is an electronic ledger that automatically calculates the effect of a change to one figure on other figures across rows and down columns; previously, these changes had to be done manually. While such powerful, time-saving functionality is taken for granted today, VisiCalc was a true milestone in the digital revolution.[2]

IBM brought its first PC to market in 1981; Bill Gates initially declined an offer to create an **operating system**—the software code that provides basic instructions—for IBM's new machine. Gates later changed his mind and developed the Microsoft Disk Operating System (MS-DOS). In 1984, Apple introduced the revolutionary Macintosh, with its user-friendly graphical interface and point-and-click mouse. A few years, later, Microsoft replaced MS-DOS with Windows. Meanwhile, component manufacturers were innovating as well; Intel began marketing the 286 microprocessor in 1982. This was followed in quick succession by the 386 and 486 versions; in 1993, Intel unveiled the Pentium.

The rise of the Internet and the World Wide Web marks the next phase of the digital revolution. The Internet's origins can be traced back to an initiative by the **Defense Advanced Research Projects Agency (DARPA)** that created a computer network that could maintain lines of communication in the event of a war. In 1969, the ARPAnet was unveiled; this was a network linking computer research centers at colleges and universities. E-mail within a computer network was made possible by the creation of a file-transfer program in 1972. There was a problem, however; it was not possible to send e-mail that was created on one network to a computer on a different network. This problem was solved the following year when Vinton Cerf and Robert Kahn created a software framework known as TCP/IP. Launched in 1973, this cross-network protocol paved the way for a " network of networks", and the **Internet** was born.

The ability to exchange e-mail messages on the Internet had a revolutionary impact on society, as technology guru Stewart Brand noted in the mid-1980s:

> Marshall McLuhan used to remark, "Gutenburg made everybody a reader. Xerox made everybody a publisher." Personal computers are making everybody an author. E-mail, word processing programs that make revising as easy as thinking, and laser printers collapse the whole writing-publishing-distributing process into

---

[1] Noyce founded Fairchild Semiconductor and later, Intel. His Intel cofounder was Gordon Moore, who is famous for formulating "Moore's Law," according to which computer power doubles every 18 months. Kilby was the founder of Texas Instruments. See Evan Ramstad, "At the End of an Era, Two Tech Pioneers are Remembered," *The Wall Street Journal* (August 15, 2005), p. B1.

[2] For more on the development of VisiCalc, see Dan Bricklin, "Natural Born Entrepreneur," *Harvard Business Review* 79, no. 8 (September 2001), pp. 53–59.

one event controlled entirely by the individual. If, as alleged, the only real freedom of the press is to own one, the fullest realization of the First Amendment is being accomplished by technology, not politics.[3]

The Internet revolution does not end with the advent of e-mail. More innovations were yet to come. In 1990, a software consultant named Tim Berners-Lee invented the **uniform resource locator (URL),** an Internet site's address on the World Wide Web; **hypertext markup language (HTML),** a format language that controls the appearance of Web pages; and **hypertext transfer protocol (http),** which enables hypertext files to be transferred across the Internet.[4] These innovations allowed Web sites to be linked and visually rich content to be posted and accessed. In short, Berners-Lee is the father of the **World Wide Web**. In the mid-1990s, a computer scientist at the University of Illinois named Marc Andreesen developed a Web browser; called Mosaic, it combined images and words together on the same screen and allowed users to search and view resources on the Web. Andreesen joined forces with Jim Clark, one of the founders of Silicon Graphics, to form Mosaic Communications. Renamed Netscape Communications, the company became one of the brightest stars in the dot-com era as commercial demand for the Netscape browser software exploded. As Thomas L. Friedman notes, "Marc Andreessen did not invent the Internet, but he did as much as any single person to bring it alive and popularize it."[5]

Within five years of the Web's debut, the number of users increased from 600,000 to 40 million. In the following decade, search engines such as Yahoo! and Google were created and encryption and security features were built into the Web. Search engines have also been dramatically improved; for example, Google's novel "page ranking" has superceded an earlier technology known as "link analysis." As the twenty-first century gets underway, Internet usage is exploding around the world; in 2005, the OECD estimated that the Internet had nearly 1 billion users.

The Internet's powerful capabilities and increasing importance have resulted in a backlash that manifests itself in various ways. For example, the Chinese government, alarmed by the free flow of information across the Internet, closely monitors the content on Web sites that its citizens access. In addition, policy makers in some countries are concerned about U.S. control of the Internet. The nonprofit Internet Corporation for Assigned Names and Numbers (Icann) is based in Marina del Ray, California. Icann maintains a database of Web addresses, approves new suffixes for Web addresses (e.g., .info and .tv) and performs other behind-the-scenes procedures that are critical for keeping the Internet functioning properly. Icann's advisory body includes international members, but the U.S. Department of Commerce retains veto power over all decisions. For example, after Icann tentatively approved the domain name .xxx for pornography sites, Commerce blocked the decision. Recently, China, India, Brazil, and the EU have taken the position that since the Internet is global, no single country should be in control. Accordingly, these nations are seeking to have the United Nations assume a role in Internet governance.[6] Privacy is another issue. As companies become more adept at using the Internet to gather, store, and access information about customers, privacy issues are becoming a focal point of concern among policy makers and the general public. In the EU, for example, a privacy protection directive was established in 1995; in 2002, the EU adopted a privacy and electronic communications directive.

"There are certain limitations that are part of the network, and we are struggling with that. We're worried that in the zeal to address localization that people will not be able to communicate any more. If someone gives you a business card with the e-mail address in Chinese, what are you to do?"[7]

Vinton G. Cerf, Internet Pioneer and Chairman, Icann

---

[3] Stewart Brand, *The Media Lab: Inventing the Future at MIT* (New York: Penguin Books, 1988), p. 253.
[4] Hypertext is any text that contains links to other documents.
[5] Thomas L. Friedman, *The World Is Flat* (New York: Farrar, Straus and Giroux, 2005), p. 58.
[6] Christopher Rhoads, "EU, Developing Nations Challenge U.S. Control of Internet," *The Wall Street Journal* (October 25, 2005), pp. B1, B2. See also "A Free Internet," *Financial Times* (November 14, 2003), p. 15.
[7] John Markoff, "Control the Internet? A Futile Pursuit, Some Say," *The New York Times* (November 24, 2005), p. C4.

CONVERGENCE

The digital revolution is causing dramatic changes in industry structure. **Convergence** is a term that refers to the coming together of previously separate industries and product categories (see Figure 17-1). New technologies affect the

the rest of the story

South Korea's Vision for a Digital Future

South Korea's digital future includes much more than simply broadband connections. For example, policy makers are aggressively pursuing applications for radio frequency identification tags (RFID; see Case 12-2); the South Korean government is spending nearly $300 million to build an RFID research center. The center will be part of an even more ambitious effort: the construction of a ubiquitous city on a 1,500-acre man-made island near the Incheon Free Economic Zone. What makes New Songdo City a "ubiquitous city" (U-city for short)? For one thing, all major information systems—commercial, residential, and government—share data, and computers are designed into all buildings. With an estimated price tag of $25 billion, New Songdo City is scheduled for completion in 2014. Complementing its high-tech features will be high-touch elements inspired by the world's major cities. These elements include a central park (inspired by New York) and a canal system similar to that in Venice.

John Kim is in charge of planning for the U-city, which he says will exemplify "U-life." Kim explains, "U-life will become its own brand, its own lifestyle." Residents will be able to communicate via videoconferencing and everyone will have access to video on demand. Smart-card house keys will also function as payment devices for subways, parking meters, movie tickets, and myriad other uses.

Korea is not alone in embracing the digital future. In France, for example, industry deregulation has resulted in vastly improved broadband service for consumers. The changes have shaken up France Telecom and other established firms and paved the way for newcomers such as Iliad, a company that offers a "triple play" service package. Carrying the brand name Free, the service includes broadband Internet service at 24 Mbps, 81 television channels, and Internet telephone service. The price? €29.95 per month—about $36. As Iliad chief executive Michaël Bouzoba says, "Entrepreneurship exists in France, but we're a rare example. I also say to French politicians, 'Stop focusing on national champions. Innovation's not coming from national champions.'" An analyst at eMarketer noted, "France's quick shift to broadband and the oncoming storm of Internet calling and digital television make it the country to watch as a model of market transformation."

Sources: Tom Braithwaite, "The Young Guns of Broadband," Financial Times (May 29, 2006), p. 8; Pamela Licalzi O'Connell, "Korea's High-Tech Utopia, Where Everything Is Observed," The New York Times (October 5, 2005), p. 6; Andrew Ward, "Where High-Speed Access Is Going Mainstream," Financial Times FT-IT Review: Next-Generation Broadband (June 9, 2004), p. 4; Jim Hopkins, "Other Nations Zip by USA in High-Speed Net Race," USA Today (January 19, 2004), pp. 1B, 2B.

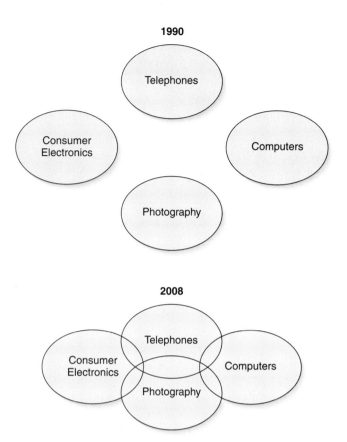

Figure 17-1

Industry Convergence

business sector(s) in which a company competes. What business is Sony in? Originally, Sony was a consumer electronics company best known for innovative products such as transistor radios, Trinitron televisions, VCRs and other stereo components, and the Walkman line of personal music players. Then, Sony entered new businesses by acquiring a record company and a motion picture studio. These acquisitions did not represent convergence because they occurred in the early days of the digital revolution. Motion pictures, recorded music, and consumer electronics were still separate industries. Today, however, Sony is in the "bits" business: Its core businesses incorporate digital technology and involve digitizing and distributing sound, images, and data. Now, Sony's competitors include Dell (computers and consumer electronics), Kodak (digital cameras), and Nokia (cell phones).

What kind of challenges does convergence present? Consider the plight of Kodak, the undisputed leader in photography-related products for more than a century. The company has been struggling to remake its business model as its sales of digital-related products grew from zero to $1 billion in five years (see Case 15-1). Because of convergence, Kodak's competitors include companies such as Gateway and Hewlett-Packard. However, competition also comes from the telecommunications industry. The cell phone camera was invented in 1997; a key benefit was the ability to download digital photos from the camera and post them on the Web or e-mail them to friends. Ironically, Motorola, a key player in the cell phone business, could have been first to market with a cell phone camera. However, management's attention was distracted by the ill-fated launch of the iridium satellite phone business (see Chapter 6). As a result, inventor Philippe Kahn took his idea to Japan where the first cell phone cameras were introduced in 1999. According to industry estimates, by 2010, annual sales of camera-equipped cell phones will reach 1 billion.[8]

---

[8] Kevin Maney, "Baby's Arrival Inspires Birth of Cellphone Camera—and Societal Evolution," *USA Today* (January 24, 2007), p. 3B.

VALUE NETWORKS AND DISRUPTIVE TECHNOLOGIES[9]

As noted at the beginning of the chapter, the digital revolution provides both opportunities and threats. IBM, Kodak, Xerox, and Motorola are examples of global companies that have struggled to remake their businesses in the face of technological innovation. IBM missed out on the minicomputer market, in part because management believed minicomputers promised lower margins and represented a smaller market. DEC, Data General, and Prime created the minicomputer market, but these companies, in turn, missed the PC revolution. This time, however, IBM's executive team demonstrated that it had learned its lesson: It set up an independent organizational unit to create the company's first PC. However, IBM subsequently was slow to recognize growing market demand for laptops; new entrants included Toshiba, Sharp, and Zenith. In an era when environmental scanning, strategic planning, and other conceptual tools of the type discussed in Chapter 15 are widely known and used, how is it that managers at many companies have failed to respond to change in a timely manner? According to Harvard professor Clayton Christensen, the problem is that executives become so committed to a current, profitable technology that they fail to provide adequate levels of investment in new, apparently riskier technologies. Ironically, companies fall into this trap by adhering to prevailing marketing orthodoxy, namely, listening to and responding to the needs of established customers. Christensen calls this situation the **innovator's dilemma**.

In every industry, companies are embedded in a **value network**. Each value network has a cost structure associated with it that dictates the margins needed to achieve profitability. The boundaries of the network are defined, in part, by the unique rank ordering of the importance of various product performance attributes. Parallel value networks, each built around a different definition of what makes a product valuable, may exist within the same broadly defined industry. Each network has its own "metrics of value" (e.g., for laptop computers, the metrics are small size, low weight and power consumption, and rugged design). For example, during the 1980s, customers who bought portable computers were willing to pay a premium for smaller size; buyers of

---

9 Much of the material in this section is adapted from Clayton Christensen, *The Innovator's Dilemma* (New York: HarperBusiness, 2003). See also Simon London, "Digital Discomfort: Companies Struggle to Deal With the 'Inevitable Surprise' of the Transition from Atoms to Bits," *Financial Times* (December 17, 2003), p. 17.

mainframe computers did not value this attribute. Conversely, mainframe buyers valued (i.e., were willing to pay more for) memory capacity as measured by megabytes; portable computer buyers placed less value on this attribute. In short, the value networks for mainframe computers and portable computers are different.

As firms gain experience within a given network, they are likely to develop capabilities, organizational structures, and cultures tailored to the distinctive requirements of their respective value networks. The industry's dominant firms—typically with reputations as "well managed" firms—lead in developing and/or adopting **sustaining technologies**, that is, incremental or radical innovations that improve product performance. According the Christensen, most new technologies developed by established companies are sustaining in nature; the vast majority of innovations are of this type. However, new entrants to an industry lead in developing **disruptive technologies** that redefine performance. The benefits associated with disruptive technologies go beyond enhancing product performance; disruptive technologies enable something to be done that was previously deemed impossible. Disruptive technologies typically enable new markets to emerge. As Christensen explains, "An innovation that is disrupting to one firm can be sustaining to another firm. The Internet was sustaining technology to Dell Computer, which already sold PCs direct by telephone. But it was disruptive technology to Compaq, whose major distribution channel was retailers."[10]

To help managers recognize the innovator's dilemma and develop appropriate responses to environmental change, Christensen has developed five principles of disruptive innovations:

1. Companies depend on customers and investors for resources. As management guru Rosabeth Moss Kanter points out, the best innovations are user-driven; paradoxically, however, if management listens to established customers, opportunities for disruptive innovation may be missed.[11]

2. Small markets don't solve the growth needs of large companies. Small organizations can most easily respond to the opportunities for growth in a small market. This fact may require large organizations to create independent units to pursue new technologies, as IBM did in developing its PC.

3. Markets that don't exist can't be analyzed. Christensen recommends that companies embrace *agnostic marketing*. This is the explicit assumption that *no one*—not company personnel, not the company's customers—can know whether, how, or in what quantities a disruptive product can or will be used before they have experienced using it.

4. An organization's capabilities define its disabilities.

5. Technology supply may not equal market demand. Some products offer a greater degree of sophistication than the market requires. For example, developers of accounting software for small businesses overshot the functionality required by the market, thus, creating an opportunity for a disruptive software technology that provided adequate, not superior, functionality and was simple and more convenient to use. This was the opportunity seized by Scott Cook, developer of Quicken and Quickbooks.

---

[10] Simon London, "Why Disruption Can Be Good For Business," *Financial Times* (October 3, 2003), p. 8.

[11] Rosabeth Moss Kanter, John Kao, and Fred Wiersema, *Innovation: Breakthrough Thinking at 3M, Dupont, GE, Pfizer, and Rubbermaid* (New York: HarperBusiness, 1997), p. 24.

GLOBAL E-COMMERCE

The term **e-commerce** refers to the general exchange of goods and services using the Internet as a marketing channel. In 2003, global e-commerce revenues stood at $1.6 trillion and growing. Consider the following:

- Every 48 hours, Yahoo! records more than 24 terabytes of data about its users' online activities. That is the equivalent of all the information contained in all the books in the Library of Congress.[12]
- Between 2003 and 2006, the number of Internet users in China increased from 68 million to 123 million. This makes China the world's second-largest e-commerce market; in Shanghai, Beijing, and Guangzhou, more than one-third of all residents use the Internet. Local companies such as Dangdang.com are proving to be formidable competitors against global rivals such as Yahoo!, Google, and eBay.[13]
- Nielsen's Netrating service estimates that Japan has about 44 million active at-home Internet users; by comparison, Germany, the United Kingdom, and France have 33 million, 24 million, and 19 million at-home users, respectively.

E-commerce activities can be divided into three broad categories: business-to-consumer (B2C or b-to-c), business-to-business (B2B or b-to-b), and consumer-to-consumer (or peer-to-peer or P2P). Many people associate e-commerce with well-known commerce service providers (CSPs) such as Amazon.com and Yahoo!. NUA Surveys projected worldwide e-commerce revenues of $2.7 trillion in 2004, with the United States accounting for more than half of the total. Forrester Research, eMarketer, Gartner Group, and Ovum are firms that track e-commerce trends; Ovum estimates that online consumer spending will increase from $90 billion in 2003 to $361 billion by 2007. However, in the United States alone, B2B transactions in 2003 totaled $700 billion. Overall, B2B commerce constitutes the biggest share of the Internet economy and will likely continue to do so for the foreseeable future. About three-fourths of 2001 B-to-C revenue was generated in North America; that figure is expected to drop to 50 percent as online sales in Europe and elsewhere increase over the next few years (see Table 17-1).

Problems can arise when a transaction site that is not designed to serve foreign customers nevertheless attracts them. Customer service can be a problem when customers are located in different time zones. For example, BlueTie is a small company based in Rochester, New York that markets e-mail and office-software applications by subscription. The company's servers continually update customer calendars and e-mail. When non-U.S. orders began to come in, BlueTie

Table 17-1

eCommerce Forecast, Select European Countries (millions)

Country	2006	2007	2008	2009	2010	2011
Italy[a]	€3,765	€5,309	€7,220	€9,444	€11,906	€14,520
Netherlands[b]	3,450	4,752	6,322	8,074	9,926	11,783
Spain[c]	3,048	4,077	5,294	6,706	8,279	10,001
Sweden[d]	2,846	3,874	5,075	6,371	7,705	9,004

[a]Forrester Research, *Italian eCommerce Forecast: 2006 To 2011* (August 28, 2006), p. 3.
[b]Forrester Research, *Dutch eCommerce Forecast: 2006 To 2011* (September 20, 2006), p. 3.
[c]Forrester Research, *Spanish eCommerce Forecast: 2006 To 2011* (August 30, 2006), p. 3.
[d]Forrester Research, *Swedish eCommerce Forecast: 2006 To 2011* (October 4, 2006), p. 3

Source: Forrester Research.

---

[12] Kevin J. Delaney, "Lab Test: Hoping to Overtake Its Rivals, Yahoo Stocks Up on Academics," *The Wall Street Journal* (August 26, 2006), p. A8.
[13] Jason Dean, "China's Web Retailers Beat U.S. Rivals at Their Own Game," *The Wall Street Journal* (August 22, 2006), p. B1.

managers found it challenging to deliver correct times and dates. Fixing the problem required spending tens of thousands of dollars and tied up precious employee time.

Web sites can be classified by purpose: **promotion sites** provide marketing communications about a company's goods or services, **content sites** provide news and entertainment and support a company's PR efforts, and **transaction sites** are cyberspace retail operations that allow customers to purchase goods and services. In many instances, Web sites combine the three functions. Web sites can also be categorized in terms of content and audience focus. When studying the categories, keep in mind that, overall, the Internet can be used as an advertising channel, as a PR tool, as a means for running a contest or sales promotion, and as support for the personal selling effort. In quadrant 1 of Figure 17-2, the focus is on providing information and service to domestic or local-country customers. Quadrant 2 companies, such as iTunes Music Store, maintain transaction-oriented e-commerce sites with a domestic focus (see Case 17-1). Companies in both quadrants 1 and 2 do attract international traffic, but the focus is still local. For example, international students at your college may have learned about your school via the Internet, even though home-country prospective students constitute the primary target audience for the Web site. Companies that initially fall into quadrants 1 and 2 can transition into quadrants 3 and 4; for example, in 2004, Apple's iTunes Music Store was rolled out in Germany, France, and the United Kingdom.

Procter & Gamble Far East Inc., the consumer products company's operation in Japan, is using the Web to build its portfolio of brands in the region. The company has launched shufufufu.com, Japan's first virtual community for women. The Web address combines *shufu* ("housewife") and *fu-fu-fu* (the sound of a woman's laughter); the P&G logo has been de-emphasized. The site was created by the digital division of Beacon Communications K.K. As Fergus Kibble, digital director at Beacon, noted, "Our research showed that Japanese housewives often feel very isolated."[15] The site's success can be attributed in part to the popularity of Harumi Kurihara, the "Japanese Martha Stewart" who writes a weekly essay on the site and provides tips on cooking, homemaking, and personal care.

Technology Forecast

Travel booked over the Internet represents the largest e-commerce category. Revenues totaled $68 billion in 2005 and are expected to reach $104 billion by 2010.[14]

Jupiter Research

Web Site Content

	Information/Support/ Service	Transactions
Domestic	**1** Simpson College *Washington Post*	**2** iTunes Music Store TiVo
Global	**3** Gucci Godin Guitars Procter & Gamble	**4** Amazon.com Dell eBay

Audience Focus

Figure 17-2

Categories of Web Sites

Source: Adapted from "The Internet and International Marketing," by John A. Quelch and Lisa R. Klein, MIT Sloan Management Review 37, no. 3 (Spring 1996), p. 65.

---

[14] Amy Yee, "Integrating New Assets the Way to Go," *Financial Times* (January 3, 2006), p. 17.

[15] Tom Boatman, "Interactive Marketing Strategies in Japan," *Japan Inc.* (June 2001).

In quadrant 3, the audience focus is global. Companies such as Federal Express and Gucci are already global in scope, and the Internet constitutes a powerful, cost-effective communication tool. Unilever PLC has begun digitizing its vast library of television commercials. Computer users can download the full-frame, full-motion videos for products, such as Salon Selectives shampoo, and watch them at any time. Although some industry observers are skeptical, Unilever's interactive marketing staff believes that the Web may represent an important new, low-cost channel for showing ads.[17] McDonald's is also putting digitized versions of its ads on the Web, but for a different purpose. The fast-food giant has established an online digital commercial archive, www.mcdcommercials.com, that allows McDonald's ad agencies anywhere in the world to review a library of 15,000 TV commercials. The agency can then request preexisting footage to incorporate into new ads.[18]

Procter & Gamble also has ambitious plans for exploiting the Internet as a global promotional and informational tool. P&G has registered a number of Internet domains based on brand names, including www.covergirl.com, www.oldspice.com, and www.sunnyd.com. Another P&G site, www.pampers.com, represents a new conceptualization of the brand. Previously, brand managers viewed Pampers as a way of keeping babies happy; the new view is that the Pampers brand is a child development aid. By mid-2006, Pampers.com was receiving 400,000 hits per month. Visitors to the site can read advice from the Pampers Parenting Institute as well as tips from mothers. Discount coupons are also available from the site.[19] P&G has also registered scores of other generic domains that relate to its various product lines, including www.cakemix.com, www.laundry.com, and www.nails.com. P&G's actions have sent a signal to other consumer packaged-goods marketers that it is striving for a first mover advantage on the Internet.

In quadrant 4, companies seek e-commerce transactions with customers on a worldwide basis. Amazon.com is perhaps the most successful example of the global audience-transaction business model. Online book shoppers can chose from more than 2.5 million titles; many titles carry discounted prices. After assessing a number of potential products in terms of their suitability for online sales, company founder Jeffrey Bezos settled on books for two reasons. First, there are too many titles for any one "brick-and-mortar" store to carry. The second reason is related to industry structure: The publishing industry is highly fragmented, with 4,200 publishers in the United States alone. That means that no single publisher has a high degree of supplier power. Bezos's instincts proved sound: Sales exploded after Amazon.com's Web site became operational in mid-1995. Within a year, orders were coming in from 66 countries.

Some products are inherently not suitable candidates for sale via the Internet: McDonald's doesn't sell hamburgers from its Web site, and Procter & Gamble does not sell shampoo. In some instances, global marketers make the strategic decision to establish a presence on the Web without offering transaction opportunities even though the product could be sold that way. Rather, such companies limit their Web activities to promotion and information in support of offline retail distribution channels. There are several reasons for this. First, many companies lack the infrastructure necessary to process orders from individual customers. Second, it can cost anywhere from $20 million to $30 million to establish a fully functioning e-commerce site. There may be other, product-specific reasons. The Web site for Godin Guitars, for example, provides a great deal of product information and a directory of the company's worldwide dealer network. Company founder Robert Godin believes that the best way for a person to select a guitar is to play one and that requires a visit to a music store.

[16] Andrew Ward, "Coke Taps into Brand New Internet Craze," *Financial Times* (August 8, 2006), p. 15.

[17] Vanessa O'Connell, "Unilever to Run Some TV Spots, Digitized, Online," *The Wall Street Journal* (March 2, 2001), pp. B1, B5.

[18] Kata MacArthur, "Fast Food Meets the Internet," *Advertising Age* (June 19, 2000), p. 28.

[19] Gary Silverman, "How May I Help You?" *Financial Times* (February 4–5, 2006), p. W2.

Likewise, visitors to Web sites for some luxury goods purveyors, including Burberry, Prada, and Gucci, are not given the opportunity to buy. Top design houses strive to create an overall retail shopping experience that enhances the brand; this objective is basically at odds with the e-commerce. As a spokesperson for Prada noted recently, "Miuccia Prada is trying to combine fashion with architecture and design. It's a 360-degree experience."[20] One notable exception is LVMH, whose www.eluxury.com Web site offers a limited selection of ready-to-wear items by Marc Jacobs and other designers. However, the site has yet to show a profit.

As the Internet has developed into a crucial global communication tool, decision makers in virtually all organizations are realizing that they must include this new medium in their communications planning. Many companies purchase banner ads on popular Web browsers such as AOL or Yahoo!; typically, the ads are linked to the company's home page or product- or brand-related sites. Although creative possibilities are limited with banner ads and **click-through rates**—the percentage of users who click on an advertisement that has been presented—are typically low, the number of companies that use the Web as a medium for global advertising is expected to increase dramatically over the next few years.

The increased importance of the Internet in global marketing can also be seen in the number and variety of alliances that advertisers are establishing with Web sites. For example, Unilever PLC sponsors the Microsoft Network (MSN) and MSN WomenCentral in the United States, France, Germany, and the United Kingdom. This type of sponsorship generally means banner ads and links to other brand-related sites are featured prominently.[21] The trend toward consolidation among media companies allows advertisers to efficiently achieve greater reach across media platforms. For example, Toyota Motors advertised its 2002 Camry on AOL Time Warner's various media properties. One of Toyota's objectives was to reposition Camry from a brand associated with older women to a brand that appeals to younger men. In fall 2001, Toyota sponsored a special issue of *Time* titled "Music Goes Global"; part of AOL's "Music Goes Global" Web site was dedicated to the Camry. Also, Toyota sponsored some music programming on CNN and TNT, which are also part of the Time Warner family.[22] An important trend is **paid search advertising,** whereby companies pay to have their ads appear when users type certain search terms. Yahoo! recently paid $1.6 billion to acquire Overture, a company specializing in paid search advertising. As a Yahoo! spokesman person noted, "Paid search is just starting to take off globally. So this acquisition wasn't just part of our strategy for search, it was important for our international strategy as well."[23]

Technology Forecast

Online music spending is forecast to increase from $800 million (7 percent of total music sales) in 2003 to $3.3 billion (26 percent of music sales) in 2008.[24]

Jupiter Research

WEB SITE DESIGN AND IMPLEMENTATION[25]

To fully exploit the Internet's potential, company executives must be willing to integrate interactive media into their marketing mixes. Web sites can be developed in-house, or an outside firm can be contracted to do the job. During the past few years, a new breed of interactive advertising agency has emerged to help companies globalize their Internet offerings (see Table 17-2). Whichever approach a company adopts, several issues must be addressed when setting up for global e-commerce.

---

20 Sally Beatty, "Fashion Tip: Get Online," *The Wall Street Journal* (October 31, 2003), pp. B1, B3.
21 Sarah Ellison, "Unilever, Microsoft in European Net Deal," *The Wall Street Journal* (February 2, 2000), p. B8.
22 Julia Angwin, "AOL Lands Toyota for Multimedia Pact," *The Wall Street Journal* (August 28, 2001), p. B7.
23 Bob Tedeschi, "E-Commerce Report," *The New York Times* (January 12, 2004), p. C6.
24 Nick Wingfield and Ethan Smith, "Microsoft Plans to Sell Music Over the Web," *The Wall Street Journal* (November 17, 2003), p. B5.
25 Much of the discussion in this section is adapted from Alexis D. Gutzman, *The E-Commerce Arsenal* (New York: AMACOM Books, 2001).

Table 17-2

Top Five Interactive Agencies by U.S. Interactive Marketing Revenue

Agency/HQ Location	Clients
Avenue A/Razorfish (New York)	AstraZeneca, Oxfam, Red Bull, Singapore Airlines
Sapient (Cambridge, MA)	Audi, Avis Europe, Deutsche Telekom, Volkswagen
Digitas (Boston)	American Express, Royal Bank of Scotland, Saab, FedEx
Agency.com (New York)	British Airways, BT, Chevron, Hewlett-Packard, T-Mobile
OgilvyInteractive (New York)	

Source: Adapted from "Top 50 Marketing Services Agencies by Discipline," *Advertising Age* (May 1, 2006), p. S-6.

This include choosing domain names, arranging payment, localizing sites, addressing privacy issues, and setting up a distribution system.

A critical first step is registering a country-specific domain name. Thus, Amazon.com has a family of different domain names, including one for each country in which it operates (see Table 17-3). Although it is certainly possible for European consumers to browse Amazon.com's U.S. site, they would likely prefer a direct link to a site with a local domain name. From both a marketing and consumer perspective, this makes sense: The Web site of choice will be one that quotes prices in euros rather than dollars, offers a product selection tailored to local tastes, and ships from local distribution points. Moreover, research suggests that visitors spend more time at sites that are in their own language; they also tend to view more pages and make more purchases. Many people will seek information about sites on local versions of well-known search engines. For example, in France, Yahoo!'s local site is fr.Yahoo.com. The same principle applies to non-U.S. companies targeting the American online consumer market. Waterford Wedgwood PLC, Harrods, and other well-known companies have acquired U.S. domain names and created sites with prices listed in dollars.[26]

While registering a ".com" domain name is a relatively straightforward procedure in the United States, requirements can vary elsewhere. In some countries, for example, a company must establish a legal entity before it can register a site with a local domain-name extension. **Cybersquatting**—the practice of registering a particular domain name for the express purpose of reselling it to the company that should rightfully use it—is also a problem. Panasonic and Avon are two companies that were victims of cybersquatting.

Payment can be another problem; in some countries, including China, credit card use is low. In such situations, e-commerce operators must arrange payment by bank check or postal money order; cash on delivery is also an option. Another issue is credit card fraud; Indonesia, Russia, Croatia, and Bosnia are among the countries where fraud is rampant. Extra identity measures may have to be taken, such as requiring buyers to fax the actual credit card they are using as well as photo IDs.[27] In Japan,

Technology Forecast

In 2004, the European online retail market was worth about €40 billion ($48 billion). By 2009, it will more than quadruple to €167 billion.

Forrester Group

Table 17-3

Amazon.com Domain Names

Domain Name	Country
amazon.co.uk	United Kingdom
amazon.de	Germany
amazon.fr	France
amazon.co.jp	Japan
amazon.at	Austria

---

26 Jessica Vascellaro, "Foreign Shopping Sites Cater to U.S. Customers," *The Wall Street Journal* (October 12, 2005), pp. D1, D14.

27 Peter Loftus, "Internet Turns Firms into Overseas Businesses," *The Wall Street Journal* (December 16, 2003), p. B4. See also Matt Richtel, "Credit Card Theft Is Thriving Online as Global Market," *The New York Times* (May 13, 2002), p. A1.

consumers pay for online purchases at convenience stores (*konbini*). After selecting an item online, the buyer goes to a nearby convenience store (e.g., a 7-Eleven) and pays cash for the item; the clerk transfers the money to the online seller's account. However, foreign companies can't participate in the *konbini* system; this means that a foreign online retailer must establish an alliance with a local company.

Ideally, each country-specific site should reflect local culture, language usage, customs, and aesthetic preferences. Logos and other elements of brand identity should be included on the site, with adjustments for color preferences and meaning differences when necessary. For example, the shopping cart icon is familiar to online shoppers in the United States and many European countries. However, online companies must determine whether that icon is appropriate in all country markets. Subtle but important language differences can occur even in English-speaking countries. For example, www.figleaves.com and www.figleaves.com/uk are, respectively, the American and British Web addresses for a U.K.-based lingerie marketer. However, the U.S. site refers to "panties" while the U.K. site has a listing for "briefs." When two or more different languages are involved, translators should be used to ensure that copy reflects current language usage. It is also important not to "reinvent the wheel" by translating the same terms over and over again. Local translators should have access to an in-house dictionary that contains preferred translations of company-specific terms. The system should be capable of identifying content that has already been translated and then reusing that content. Product descriptions may also vary from country to country; as noted in Chapter 4, American-themed merchandise is very popular in Japan. Table 17-4 compares sample product descriptions in English and Japanese.

A note of caution is in order: It is not enough to simply translate a Web site from the home-country language into other languages. Thus, another basic step is localizing a Web site in the native language and business nomenclature of the target country. From a technical point of view, Web sites designed to support English, French, German, and other languages that use the Latin alphabet only store a maximum of 256 characters in the American Standard Code for Information Interchange (ASCII) format. Even so, there are language-specific

> "Shopping on the Internet is no different than traditional sales channels. It's all about trusting the brand and having a strong relationship with one's customers."[28]
>
> Ron Fry, Internet Business Manager, Lands' End

English	Japan	Table 17-4
"New York Yankees hat with white stitching on black canvas."	"Authentic baseball hat for the New York Yankees baseball team. Just like they wear in New York City! White stitching on black canvas reflects the team's colors."	*Product Description: An English Versus Japanese Comparison*
These warm-weather cargos are made from our popular tropic-weight cotton. The 6 oz. cloth is dyed with rich pigment color that weathers gradually. Garment-washed to feel comfortably broken-in right away. Our Natural Fit offers extra room at the seat and thighs. Quarter front pockets, two flapped back pockets and roomy cargo pockets on legs. Double-needle stitching at stress seams. Fit belts up to 13/4". Imported. Machine wash and dry. (L.L.Bean)	Cargo Pants have high breathability for hot weather. This garment is made from tropic-weight cotton and dyed with rich pigment color and weathers gradually. Enjoy the way this cargo's fabric feels comfortably broken in. This fits you naturally for the way you move. Front pockets for both sides, two flapped back pockets and roomy cargo pockets on legs. Double-needle stitching at stress seams. Fit belts up to 4 cm. 100% Cotton. Washable by machine.	

Source: Alexis D. Gutzman, *The E-Commerce Arsenal* (New York: AMACOM Books, 2001), p. 165.

[28] Christopher Price, "Fashion Suits the Internet Shopper," *Financial Times* (June 24, 1998), p. 23.

needs; for example, a German language Web site requires more than double the capacity of an English language site because German copy takes more space.[29] However, languages such as Japanese and Chinese require a database that supports double-ASCII. For this reason, it is wise to start with a double-ACSII platform when designing a Web site's architecture. The site's architecture should also be flexible enough to allow different date, currency, and money formatting. For example, to someone living in the United Kingdom, "7/10/05" means October 7, 2005. To an American, it means July 10, 2005.[30]

Another critical global e-commerce issue is privacy. The EU's regulations are among the world's strictest; companies are limited in terms of how much personal information—a customer's age, marital status, and buying patterns, for example—can be gathered and how long the information can be retained. Customers have the right to view the information contained in company databases and correct errors. Moreover, the EU's standards have been adopted in other parts of the world, including Canada, Australia, and Asia. Spain's regulations are particularly stringent; taking advantage of a common language, Chile and Argentina have copied the Spanish drafts of Spain's laws. By contrast, Washington's reluctance to protect privacy is due in part to First Amendment issues as well as to national security concerns stemming from the terror attacks of September 11. To help ensure compliance with privacy laws, American companies have created a new executive-level job position: chief privacy officer.[31]

challenges in the global marketplace

Open Source Software

Global software sales have been very, very good to Microsoft. The company's Windows operating system is found in more than 90 percent of the world's PCs, and popular software programs such as Office Suite are used virtually everywhere. Because of its dominant position in the industry, Microsoft has a global pricing policy that calls for charging approximately the same amount in every world market. Today, however, Microsoft's pricing structure faces a threat from open source software that is distributed for free.

The term *open source software* is used to describe a software program for which the source code—the original program instructions—is made available so that users can make modifications. In the mid-1970s, a programmer named Richard Stallman wrote a macro editor for Unix that he called Emacs. Other programmers wanted to use Emacs, so Stallman published the GNU ("GNU's not Unix") Public License (GPL) in association with the concept of "copyleft" (a play on the notion of copyright). In essence, Stallman granted permission for others to run, copy, modify, and distribute his operating system software, with one caveat: No one could place restrictions on their modifications. In 1991, a 21-year-old Helsinki University student named Linus Torvalds developed a Unix-compatible operating system that he called Linux (a combination of Linus and Minix, a Unix clone widely used by college students). Today, numerous free versions of Linux are available, including Mandrakelinux. Worldwide, 25 percent of servers run Linux software; increasingly, Linux is being used on PCs as well.

What does the Linux phenomenon mean for Microsoft? In short, it means that the software giant's virtual monopoly on PC

operating systems may be at risk. In developing countries, such as Malaysia and Thailand, government initiatives are aimed at putting as many PCs as possible into the hands of ordinary citizens and small business owners. Government agencies are looking for the best price, making free Linux software a very attractive choice. For example, working with the Association of Thai Computer Manufacturers, the Thai government made Linux-equipped "People's PCs" available for about 10,900 baht ($260). Microsoft responded by creating a Thai-language version of Windows XP and bundling it with Microsoft Office for a price of about $36. By mid-2003, roughly one-quarter of the 134,000 PCs ordered by Thais were equipped with Windows. Similarly, in Malaysia, PCs running Linux are available at prices as low as about $263. Microsoft has responded by making a Malaysian version of Windows XP available on a PC for about $302.

Developing countries are not the only ones hoping to find cheaper alternatives to Microsoft. France, for example, needs to reduce its deficit to be in compliance with euro zone regulations. To do so, the French government is considering open source options such as OpenOffice, a version of Sun Microsystem's StarOffice, Mozilla, a Web browser, and other open source programs. In Asia, representatives from Japan and South Korea are holding meetings in an effort to set joint policies regarding information technology.

Sources: Rebecca Buckman, "Microsoft's Malaysia Policy," The Wall Street Journal (May 20, 2004), p. B1; Buckman, "Face-Off Over People's PC," The Wall Street Journal (August 14, 2003), p. B1; www.gnu.org (accessed June 2004).

---

29 Patricia Riedman, "Think Globally, Act Globally," *Advertising Age* (June 19, 2000), p. s48.
30 Alexis D. Gutzman, *The E-Commerce Arsenal* (New York: Amacom, 2001), p. 165.
31 David Scheer, "For Your Eyes Only: Europe's New High-Tech Role: Playing Privacy Cop to the World," *The Wall Street Journal* (October 10, 2003), p. A1.

A number of issues are related to physical distribution decisions. As online sales increase in a particular country or region, it may be necessary to establish local warehouse facilities to speed delivery and reduce shipping costs. In the United States, such a step has tax implications; the marketer may have to collect sales tax. To allay consumer concerns about ordering merchandise online, companies may opt to waive shipping fees and offer free returns and money-back guarantees.

NEW PRODUCTS AND SERVICES

As a result of the digital revolution, a variety of companies in all parts of the world are developing a new generation of products, services, and technologies. These include broadband networks, mobile commerce, wireless connectivity, and "smart" cell phones.

Broadband

A **broadband** communication system is one that has sufficient capacity to carry multiple voice, data, or video channels simultaneously. *Bandwidth* determines the range of frequencies that can pass over a given transmission channel. For example, traditional telephone networks offered quite limited bandwidth compared with state-of-the art digital telephone networks. As a result, a traditional telephone call sounds "lo-fi." Bandwidth is measured in bits-per-second; a full page of English text is about 16,000 bits. For example, a 56 Kbs modem connected to a conventional telephone line can move 16,000 bits in less than one second; by comparison, a broadband Internet connection that utilizes coaxial cable can move up to 10 gigabits per second. Consumer broadband service is typically available from cable TV companies or telephone companies via digital subscriber lines (DSL). In addition to faster download times and greater capacity, broadband offers other advantages. For example, it is always on (in other words, there is no need to access the Internet via phone dial-up service). Roughly one-third of American households currently have high-speed Internet access. Even so, according to figures compiled by the Organization for Economic Cooperation and Development, at the end of 2003 the United States ranked tenth in the world in terms of broadband penetration.[32]

What opportunities does broadband offer to companies outside the telecommunications industry? Broadband Internet allows users to access streaming audio, streaming video, and streaming media. **Streaming audio** allows users to listen to Internet radio stations. **Streaming video** is a sequence of moving images that are sent in compressed form over the Internet and displayed by the viewer as they arrive. **Streaming media** combines streaming video with sound. With streaming video or streaming media, a Web user does not have to wait to download a large file before seeing the video or hearing the sound. Instead, the media is sent in a continuous stream and is played as it arrives. Apple, Microsoft, RealNetworks, and MacroMedia are some of the companies that sell the software necessary to view streaming media. Streaming media represents a huge market opportunity for the video game industry, which includes electronics companies (e.g., Microsoft and Sony); game publishers (e.g., Electronic Arts); and Internet portals (e.g., Yahoo!). Yahoo! currently ranks as the top Web destination for online gaming, with more than 5.5 billion minutes of gaming hosted on its servers each month. Most of these are simple, Java-based games such as chess that are available without charge. However, in 2002, Yahoo! launched Games On Demand (GOD), a service that allows users to download and play PC games such as *Zoo Tycoon*. Another trend is online gaming: Gamers in different locations, even different countries, compete against each other using PCs, Xbox, or PlayStation consoles. These are sometimes known as massively multiplayer online games (MMOG); popular titles include *EverQuest*, *Second Life*, and *Final Fantasy IX*. As of mid-2006, Microsoft's Xbox Live service had attracted three million subscribers worldwide.[33] Next generation game consoles from Microsoft and Sony are expected to fuel consumer interest in online gaming. Broadband also permits publishers to offer full-featured games for sale online via downloads.

However, the promise of broadband goes far beyond gaming. Many industry observers and policy makers believe that broadband will be a critical economic tool in the coming decades. Broadband will provide opportunities for online education, medical diagnosis and treatment, and e-commerce. It is a key productivity tool that allows employees to save time by tapping online resources and by sharing electronic documents on desktop PCs in real time.

Singapore offers businesses grants of up to $200,000 to pay for broadband equipment and consulting services. The EU also wants to increase broadband access throughout its member nations. Several factors help explain broadband's relatively slow start in the United States. For one thing, one-quarter of the U.S. population lives in rural areas; this means that broadband is more expensive to roll out than in densely populated nations, such as South Korea. Also, U.S. telecom companies were reluctant to invest in broadband lines because of concern that the U.S. Federal Communications Commission would force them to lease the lines to rival service providers. Concerned about the lack of broadband capacity, Michigan and other states are launching their own initiatives.[35]

Technology Forecast
By 2008, 18 percent of U.S. households will be playing online PC games.[34]
Forrester Group

[32] Demetri Sevastopulo, "Rocky Road to the US's Broadband Future," *Financial Times* (December 9, 2003), p. 10.
[33] Chris Nuttall, "Everything to Play For," *Financial Times IT Review—Mobile and Online Games* (December 10, 2003), p. 4.
[34] Ben King, "Heavenly Time Playing GOD," *Financial Times IT Review—Mobile and Online Games* (December 10, 2003), p. 4.
[35] Jim Hopkins, "Other Nations Zip By USA in High-Speed Net Race," *USA Today* (January 19, 2004), pp. 1B, 2B.

Mobile Commerce and Wireless Connectivity

Mobile commerce (m-commerce) is the term for conducting commercial transactions using wireless handheld devices such as personal digital assistants (PDAs) and cell phones. Many companies are developing ways to provide Internet access without the need for a wired broadband connection. For example, **wireless fidelity (Wi-Fi)** permits laptop and PDA users to establish high-speed wireless connections to the Internet and corporate intranets via "hot spots" located in airports, cafés, or other public places. One reason for the popularity of hot spots is the need for so-called knowledge workers or "laptop warriors" to maintain high levels of productivity during business trips. As noted in the chapter opening, South Korea is home to the world's largest Wi-Fi network of more than 17,000 hot spots from local telecom company KT.

Wi-Fi networks have a limited range; an improved technology known as **World Interoperability for MicroWave Access (WiMax)** is being deployed in many parts of the world. A WiMax network can have a range of several miles, making it superior to traditional Wi-Fi. Fixed WiMax doesn't work with mobile devices; an improved technology called mobile WiMax does. Because mobile WiMax offers greater capacity and faster speeds than current mobile data networks, it is well suited for streaming music or video.[36]

A mobile communication technology known as **Bluetooth** is gaining popularity in Europe; because it consumes less power than Wi-Fi, Bluetooth is well suited to use with cell phones.[37] However, Bluetooth works over shorter distances than Wi-Fi. Each week, approximately 1 million Bluetooth-enabled devices are shipped to stores. In addition to cell phone handsets, Bluetooth has been incorporated into automobiles and home appliances such as refrigerators and microwave ovens. Currently, British Telecommunications (BT) has several thousand Bluetooth hot spots in place. In addition, BT is testing a service called Blue Phone that will allow Bluetooth users to connect to BT's phone line network from a mobile unit.[38] Bluetooth-enabled billboards can broadcast marketing information to a nearby cell phone or BlackBerry PDA. Paris-based Kameleon is a Bluetooth technology provider; Patrick Nagle, Kameleon's chairman of global marketing strategies, says, "Anything you can imagine getting off the Internet, you can get with Bluetooth." In the United Kingdom, a Bluetooth campaign for Coldplay's 2005 CD release *X&Y* enabled passengers in London's train stations to download song clips and photos. In the United States, Cingular Wireless featured Coldplay in its new Cingular Sounds program. Subscribers were offered 30-second ringtones of new songs.[39]

Wi-Fi connections require a subscription to a service provider; one problem is getting a connection in a hot spot supported by a different provider than the one to which a user subscribes.[40] In the United States, Starbucks is partnering with T-Mobile USA (the American arm of Deutsche Telekom's T-Mobile International) to offer Wi-Fi service; the strategy is to encourage patrons to stay in its coffee shops longer and, presumably, spend more money on coffee and other items. In the United States, T-Mobile also has deals with Borders bookstores, FedEx Kinko's business centers, Texaco service stations, and major airports. Current Wi-Fi technology can only handle data, not voice. However, many industry observers expect that in the near future, hot spots will allow cell phones to switch to the Internet for telephone calls.

---

[36] Sarmad Ali, "New and (Soon) Improved," *The Wall Street Journal* (November 27, 2006), p. R8.

[37] *Bluetooth* is the English translation of Harald Blatand, a Danish Viking and king who lived in the tenth century.

[38] Jonathan Moules, "Bluetooth and the Quest for a Wireless World," *Financial Times* (December 3, 2003), p. 9.

[39] "MediaMorph: Bluetooth," *Advertising Age* (November 7, 2005), p. 51.

[40] Dennis K. Berman and Jesse Drucker, "Wi-Fi Industry Bets 'Roaming' Will Lure Users," *The Wall Street Journal* (November 6, 2003), p. B1.

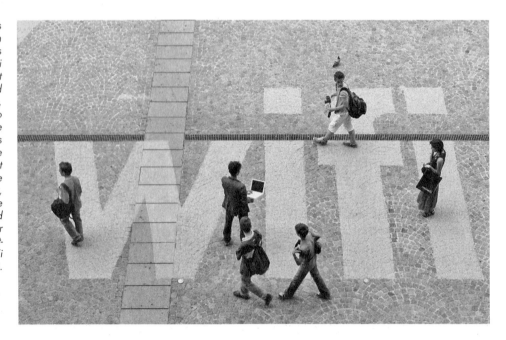

Technology Forecast

The number of MP3 players in the United States is expected to grow from 11.3 million in 2004 to 40 million in 2008.[42]

Jupiter Research

Wireless technology is being used in other ways. In the automotive world, there is a trend toward **telematics**, which is a car's ability to exchange information about the vehicle's location or mechanical performance. Cars are also being equipped with online access so passengers can send and receive e-mails. BMW Online illustrates some of telematics' potential. The system, which is available in Germany and the United Kingdom in 7 Series BMWs, provides access to a wide range of information and services, including the availability of parking spaces. The service also assists users who wish to book hotel rooms or make restaurant reservations. Mercedes-Benz is rolling out a similar service.[41]

Smart Cell Phones

Cell phones have been one of the biggest new product success stories of the digital revolution. Worldwide, 500 million cellular handsets are sold each year. The popularity of cell phones has been a boon to manufacturers such as Nokia, Motorola, Samsung, and Ericsson as well as service providers such as Deutsche Telekom, U.S. Cellular, Verizon, and others. New features such as color displays and cameras give consumers a reason to upgrade their equipment on a regular basis; a new generation of **smart phones** gives phones some of the capabilities of computers. Though smart phones only represent a small percentage of the market at present, they have the potential to boost the fortunes of the manufacturers as well as to create new sources of revenue for the service providers. The following suggest the marketing possibilities of cell phone-based e-commerce:[43]

- In Europe, France's Orange SA, Spain's Telefonica Moviles SA, Germany's T-Mobile International AG, and Britain's Vodafone Group have formed a consortium called Simpay to offer m-commerce services to 250 million cellular subscribers throughout the EU.

41   Chris Reiter, "Web-Rigged Cars Get Second Look," *The Wall Street Journal* (December 11, 2003), p. D2.
42   John Markoff, "With All Those iPods, Podcasting Is On the Air," *The New York Times* (February 25, 2005), pp. C1, C4.
43   Gren Manuel, "Dialing for Dollars," *The Wall Street Journal—E-Commerce* (October 20, 2003), p. R3.

- In Australia, a thirsty traveler can pay for a Coke at Central Station in Sydney by calling "Dial-a-Coke," making a beverage selection, and then collecting their selection from a vending machine. Charges for the purchase appear on the customer's cell phone bills.
- In Norway, mobile operator Telenor ASA has teamed with a finance group to offer mobile purchases of flowers, compact discs, bus tickets, and food.

While these and other new mobile services are in development, individuals are already using their cell phones for tasks other than calling. For example, text messaging has exploded in popularity; worldwide, about 10 billion peer-to-peer messages are sent each month. Now, advertisers are taking advantage of this capability by using **short message service (SMS)**, a globally accepted wireless standard for sending alphanumeric messages of up to 160 characters. SMS can be used to send *spam*, which is unsolicited "junk" e-mail sent to large numbers of people to promote products or services. (The term *spam* is borrowed from a famous Monty Python comedy routine in which the brand name of Hormel Foods Corporation's canned meat product is used so often that it crowds everything else out). A new global industry trade group, the Mobile Marketing Association, has been formed to address this and other issues (www.mmaglobal.com). Coca-Cola, Twentieth Century Fox, and other companies are using SMS for m-commerce purposes. Industry experts expect marketers to integrate SMS with communication via other digital channels such as interactive digital TV, the Internet, and e-mail.

"Wireless phone booths are the Starbucks of telephony in South America."[44]
Ralph de la Vega, BellSouth Latin America

Technology Forecast
Sales of cellphones with cameras reached 460 million units in 2006. By 2010, the number sold per year will exceed 1 billion.[45]
Gartner Group

Mobile Music: Ringtones, Ring Tunes, and Full-Track Downloads

Because of rampant illegal sharing of music files, record companies are searching for new sources of revenue. Thanks to technology convergence, a new generation of cell phones is leading to changes in the mobile music industry. **Mobile music** is music that is purchased and played on a cell phone. One opportunity is to license the rights to popular songs for use as cell phone ringtones. According to the Gartner research firm, cell phone users spent $6 billion on ringtones in 2006; sales are strongest in Europe and Japan. Currently, however, the primary beneficiaries of this growing market are music publishers and songwriters. The reason is simple: Many ringtones are rerecordings and, thus, represent instrumental "soundalike" or "cover" versions rather than the original versions by the original recording artists; therefore, a song's publisher and writer receive royalties of approximately 15 percent each time a ringtone is downloaded.

The situation is changing, however, as the record companies prepare to make original recordings available. **Ring tunes**, also known as music tones, song tunes, TruTones, and master tones, are digitized clips of original songs by the original recording artists. Licensing fees for ring tunes will be higher because they include master recording royalties of 30 percent to 50 percent. As John Rose, former executive vice president of EMI Group, notes, "This is quite an attractive market to us. We think it'll be a significant multi-billion-dollar market over the next couple of years as the new handsets roll out."[46] This attitude has some industry players concerned. For example, Simon

[44] Almar Latour, "Latin Lessons: BellSouth Finds Pocket of Growth in an Odd Place," *The Wall Street Journal* (November 20, 2003), p. A8.
[45] Kevin Maney, "Baby's Arrival Inspires Birth of Cellphone Camera—and Societal Evolution," *USA Today* (January 24, 2007), p. 3B.
[46] Bob Tedeschi, "E-Commerce Report," *The Wall Street Journal* (February 23, 2004), p. C5.

Technology Forecast

By 2008, annual cell phone music purchases in the United States could reach $1 billion.[48]

The Yankee Group

Technology Forecast

By 2011, annual worldwide mobile music purchases will total $14 billion. Asia is expected to account for 40 percent of the market.[49]

Juniper Research

Technology Forecast

By 2008, the global market for cellphone games could reach $7 million.[51]

Strategy Analytics

Buckingham is chief executive of PhoneFurniture, which does business as www.ringtones.com. He says, "Record companies are in danger of killing the golden goose before it has laid its eggs by charging excessive royalty rates, and are doing so more out of ignorance of the mobile market and value chain than greed."[47] Meanwhile, a Web-based company called Xingtones has begun offering software that allows users to create their own ring tunes from compact discs and digital music files.

Mobile Gaming

As noted previously, broadband's role in the console video game market is growing in importance. At the same time, many consumers are playing simple, inexpensive games on their cell phones. In the United States, Verizon Wireless sells games for about $4; in Europe, mm02 plc sells games for an equivalent amount. Because cell phones have small screens and limited storage space and computing power, mobile gaming appeals more to occasional users, such as commuters, rather than hard-core gamers. Industry growth may also be slow due to the large number of different technical standards incorporated into different brands of telephones. Currently, the economics of mobile gaming do not favor game developers; cell phone service providers keep 10 percent to 70 percent of the selling price of each game downloaded. Moreover, for games based on popular motion pictures, game developers are required to pay licensing fees to the film studios.[50] For this reason, some big industry players, including Electronic Arts, are not investing heavily in mobile games. Some simple multiplayer games written in the Java programming language are currently available for downloading on cell phones. However, mobile games are quickly becoming more sophisticated as phone makers add more features. For example, some phones are equipped with a **global positioning system (GPS)** that allows users to determine their exact geographic position. GPS capability will lead to location-based games in which players compete by trying to physically approach their opponents.

Internet Phone Service

For the telecommunications industry, Internet telephone service is the "next big thing." Thanks to a technology known as **voice over Internet protocol (VoIP),** the human voice can be digitized and broken into data packets that can be transmitted over the Internet and converted back into normal speech. If a call is placed to a conventional phone, it must be switched from the Internet to a traditional phone network; local telephone companies generally own the lines into residences and businesses. However, if the call is made between two subscribers to the same VoIP provider, it bypasses the traditional network altogether. The implications are clear: VoIP has the potential to render the current telecommunications infrastructure—consisting primarily of twisted copper and fiber optic cable—obsolete.

47 Yinka Adegoke, "Record Labels Bank on a Ring Tone Boom," *Financial Times* (December 16, 2003), p. 8.

48 Bob Tedeschi, "E-Commerce Report," *The Wall Street Journal* (February 23, 2004), p. C5.

49 Bob Ibison, "Deal Could Be Music to Nokia's Ears," *Financial Times* (August 14, 2006), p. 14.

50 David Pringle, "Making Games for Cellphones is No Easy Play," *The Wall Street Journal* (October 17, 2003), p. B1.

51 David Pringle, "Making Games for Cellphones is No Easy Play," *The Wall Street Journal* (October 17, 2003), p. B1.

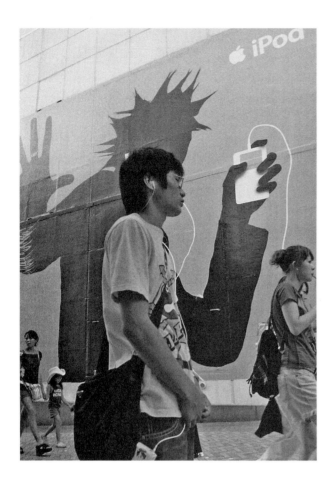

The phenomenal success of Apple's iPod digital music player has generated a backlash in different parts of the world. In Japan, the recorded music industry was unsuccessful in its 2005 attempt to persuade the government to charge a royalty fee on each iPod sold. The money generated would have been distributed to record companies, songwriters, and recording artists as partial compensation for financial losses due to illegal music file downloading.

In France, the National Assembly approved a bill that would require Apple to share the iTunes software codes with other companies so that music downloads would play on all digital music players, not just iPods.

In January 2007, Norway's consumer ombudsman ruled that iPod's lack of interoperability was illegal. In response, Apple issued a statement that the company "hopes that European governments will encourage a competitive environment that allows innovation to thrive, protects intellectual property, and allows consumers to decide which products are successful."

Currently, VoIP accounts for only 3 percent of global calling; however, the promise of a global growth market has resulted in soaring stock values for start-up companies in the United States such as SpectraLink Corporation and Verso Technologies. In Europe, Niklas Zennström, the cofounder of the KaZaA music file sharing service, has started Skyper Ltd. The company offers free peer-to-peer software for Internet calls. Revenue is generated from SkypeOut and SkypeIn, which allow users to make and receive calls from landlines and mobile phones, respectively. With 250,000 new users—many in China, India, and Sweden—joining each day, Skype has become a global phenomenon. In 2005, eBay acquired Skype for $2.6 billion.[52]

Not to be outmaneuvered, AT&T and other established phone companies are setting up their own VoIP phone services. Meanwhile, a controversy is brewing because traditional phone companies are subject to heavy regulation. By contrast, in most countries, the Internet is still unregulated; this is to encourage innovation and promote acceptance by businesses and the general public. For example, the European Commission is relying on regulators in member nations to establish rules for Internet calls. Likewise, in the United States, the Federal Communications Commission classifies VoIP as an information service. At the state level, some regulators are taking a similar "hands off" approach. In

---

[52] Jason Dean, "Everyone's Talking Skype in China," *The Wall Street Journal* (March 30, 2006), p. B3.

Yahoo! is the Internet's most visited site. The company boasts more than 140 million registered users; one of Yahoo's strengths is the number of services it offers besides search. For example, Yahoo! users can access GeoCities, My.Yahoo, Games On Demand; send instant messages; and, as shown here, compare prices with Yahoo! Shopping. The company currently has 25 global sites in 13 different languages; Yahoo! Shopping's country-specific sites include Denmark, Germany, and India.

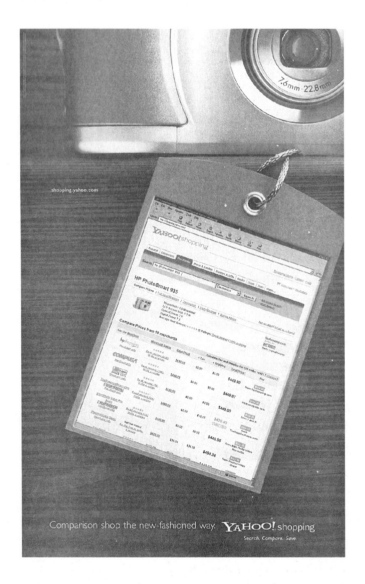

Comparison shop the new-fashioned way. YAHOO! shopping

Search. Compare. Save.

Minnesota, a district court judge ruled that Vonnage, based in Edison, New Jersey is an information service provider. As a result, Vonnage and other Internet phone service companies do not have to pay the taxes and fees that conventional telecom companies pay. This, in turn, allows them to set lower prices for their services.[53]

53 Peter Grant and Almar Latour, "Circuit Breaker: Battered Telecoms Face New Challenge: Internet Calling," *The Wall Street Journal* (October 9, 2003), pp. A1, A9. See also Anne Marie Squeo, "Internet Phone Service Threatens Industry's Giants," *The Wall Street Journal* (November 28, 2003), pp. B1, B2.

The **digital revolution** has created a global electronic marketplace. The revolution has gained momentum over the course of 70-plus years, during which time technological breakthroughs included the digital mainframe computer; the **transistor**; the **integrated circuit (IC)**; the **personal computer (PC)**; the **spreadsheet**, the PC **operating system**; **DARPAnet**; and the **Internet**. Three key innovations by Tim Berners-Lee, the **uniform resource locator (URL)**, **hypertext markup language (HTML)**, and **hypertext transfer protocol (http)**, led to the creation in the early 1990s of the **World Wide Web**.

The digital revolution has resulted in a process known as **convergence**, meaning that previously separate industries and markets are coming together. In this environment, the **innovator's dilemma** means that company management must decide whether to invest in current technologies or try to develop new technologies. Although leading firms in an industry often develop **sustaining technologies** that result in improved product performance, the revolution has also unleashed a wave of **disruptive technologies** that are creating new markets and reshaping industries and **value networks**.

E-commerce is growing in importance for both consumer and industrial goods marketers. Generally, commercial Web sites can have a domestic or global focus; in addition, they can be classified as **promotion sites**, **content sites**, and **transaction sites**. Global marketers must take care when designing Web sites. Country-specific domain names must be registered and local-language sites developed. In addition to addressing issues of technology and functionality, content must reflect local culture, customs, and aesthetic preferences.

The Internet is a powerful tool for advertisers; **click-through rates** are one measure of effectiveness. Another trend is **paid search advertising**. New products and services spawned by the digital revolution include: **broadband**, which permits transmission of **streaming media** over the Internet; **mobile commerce (m-commerce)**, which is made possible by **Wi-Fi**, **Bluetooth**, WiMax, and other forms of wireless connectivity; **telematics** and **global positioning systems (GPS)**; and **short message service (SMS)**. **Smart cell phones** are creating new markets for **mobile music** downloads, including **ringtones, ring tunes,** and complete songs; they can also be used **for mobile gaming** and Internet phone service using **VoIP**.

This is an exciting time to prepare for a career in global marketing. Until recently, one sure way to put your career at risk in many companies (especially U.S. companies) was to go overseas. There was nothing wrong with being overseas per se, but management did not always recognize the value of global experience and turned to executives who were close at hand for promotions.

Today, global experience counts. We are in a global market with global competition and those with global experience have a definite advantage.

How do you establish a career in global marketing? There are two broad paths:

1. Get directly into a job outside your home country or into a multicountry headquarters job in a global company.

2. Get company experience in an industry that prepares you for promotion to a job with multicountry responsibility or to an assignment outside your home country.

For many, the second choice is better than the first. There is no substitute for solid industry experience, and your best opportunity to get it may be in your home country. You speak the language, understand the culture, and are trained in business and marketing. You are ready to learn. An option is to get this basic experience in another country. The advantage of this move is that you will learn a new culture and language and broaden your international experience while you learn about a company and industry. Good luck!

1. Briefly review the key innovations that culminated in the digital revolution. What is the basic technological process that made the revolution possible?

2. What is convergence? How is convergence affecting Sony? Kodak? Nokia?

3. What is the innovator's dilemma? What is the difference between sustaining technology and disruptive technology? Briefly review Christensen's five principles of disruptive innovation.

4. What key issues must be addressed by global companies that engage in e-commerce?

5. Briefly outline Web design issues as they pertain to global marketing.

6. Review the key products and services that have emerged during the digital revolution. What are some products and services that are not mentioned in the chapter?

Chris Anderson is the editor of *Wired* magazine. In his view, "The story of the Long Tail is really about the economics of abundance—what happens when the bottlenecks that stand between supply and demand in our culture start to disappear and everything becomes available to everyone." Anderson notes that "below-the radar" products (e.g., obscure books, movies, and music) are driving revenues at e-commerce merchants such as Amazon.com, Netflix, and iTunes. He says, "These millions of fringe sales are an efficient, cost-effective business. . . . For the first time in history, hits and niches are on equal economic footing."

Chris Anderson, *The Long Tail: Why the Future of Business Is Selling Less of More* (Hyperion, 2006).

Case 17-1

eBay in Asia

EBay, the company whose name is synonymous with online auctions in the United States, is one of the legendary success stories of the digital revolution. Today, the company is a cultural phenomenon, boasting 230 million registered users who can bid on 45,000 different categories of goods; at any given time, customers are engaged in 100 million auctions. The company also hosts more than 250,000 online stores. In 2006, eBay generated $5.9 billion in revenues; this represents an increase of more than 100 percent from 2003. To sustain this type of growth, eBay's executive team has set its sights on international expansion. Today, the company has successfully established a presence in several countries, including Australia, Brazil, Spain, and Switzerland.

However, one of eBay's first forays outside the United States ended in defeat. Yahoo! opened its Internet portal in Japan in April 1996, four years ahead of eBay's entry. Yahoo! Japan was a joint venture between Yahoo! Inc. and Japan's Softbank Corporation. Yahoo! Japan was modeled on its U.S. parent; a variety of free services was available, including news, chat rooms, and e-mail. As more users logged on, increasing numbers of advertisers paid to post banner ads on the site. In due course, Yahoo! founder Jerry Yang and Softbank chairman Masayoshi Son encouraged Yahoo! Japan chief Masahiro Inoue to start offering online auctions. Yang had been blindsided by eBay's U.S. success and did not want to repeat the mistake a second time. Inoue resisted, noting that the Japanese have little experience with auctions of any kind. He was also skeptical that status-conscious Japanese consumers would buy products from complete strangers. However, Yang continued to press his case, stressing that eBay was gearing up for a Japanese launch. Moreover, with advertising providing 80 percent of Yahoo!'s revenues in the United States, Yang was anxious to diversify the venture's revenue stream.

In the end, Inoue relented; his team of engineers had Yahoo! Japan's auction site operational in September 1999. EBay launched its Japanese service in February 2000. Taking its cue from eBay's early development in the United States, management stressed used collectibles. This turned out to be a mistake; Japanese users showed more interest in bidding on new goods. EBay also erred by charging a commission on each transaction; initially, Yahoo! Japan users did not pay commissions or monthly fees. By the end of 2001, between 20,000 and 25,000 items were listed on eBay's Japanese site; by contrast, Yahoo! Japan had more than 3 million items. As eBay CEO Meg Whitman noted, "We're definitely in catch-up mode." In March 2001, after barely more than a year, eBay closed down the service.

Despite the setback in Japan, eBay continues to expand in Asia. In 2003, the company paid $180 million to acquire Eachnet, a popular Chinese consumer auction site. Once again, eBay faces competition from Yahoo!, whose entry

strategy included investing in a Chinese language search development company and forming a joint venture auction site with Sina.com. In 2005, Yahoo! bought a 40 percent stake in Alibaba, a company founded by Chinese Internet entrepreneur Jack Ma that operates an auction site called

Taobao.com. Initially, Taobao.com users were not charged sales commissions or listing fees.

Ma believes that global Internet companies are prone to making three types of mistakes in approaching China: They underestimate the differences between China and the U.S. market; they incur higher costs than local companies; and they go global too quickly. In 2004, Ma summarized the situation by observing, "[EBay and Yahoo!] are the sharks in the ocean, and we are the crocodiles in the Yangtze River. When they fight in the Yangtze River, they will be in trouble. The smell of the water is different." Now that Ma has joined forces with Yahoo!, he has changed his tune slightly. "I know the Chinese user market and users better than Meg Whitman. Once we start to charge, we can be profitable in 18 months," Ma said.

Ma's words were prescient: In September 2006, Martin Wu, head of eBay China, resigned. At the end of the year, eBay announced that it had spent $40 million for a 49 percent stake in Tom Online, a Chinese Internet portal and wireless operator. EBay shut down its main Chinese Web site and announced that the new Tom-eBay service would be launched in 2007.

Discussion Questions

1. Why has eBay struggled in Japan, China, and other Asian markets?

2. EBay is making a strategic shift by giving control of its main China operation to Tom Online. What does this shift signify?

Sources: Chris Nuttal and Mure Dickie, "EBay Tries to Fix Its Strategy in China," *Financial Times* (December 20, 2006), p. 15; Moon Ihlwan and Rob Hof, "Out-eBaying eBay in Korea," *Business Week* (July 17, 2006), p. 74; Mylene Mangalindan, "Hot Bidding: In a Challenging China Market, eBay Confronts a Big New Rival," *The Wall Street Journal* (August 12, 2005), pp. A1, A6; Jason Dean and Jonathan Cheng, "Meet Jack Ma, Who Will Guide Yahoo in China," *The Wall Street Journal* (August 12, 2005), p. B1;

Mure Dickie, "China's Crocodiles Ready for a Fight," *Financial Times* (July 14, 2004), p. 18; Nick Wingfield, "EBay, Conceding Missteps, Will Close Its Site in Japan," *The Wall Street Journal* (February 27, 2002), p. B4; Ken Belson, Rob Hof, and Ben Elgin, "How Yahoo! Japan Beat eBay at its Own Game," *Business Week* (June 4, 2001), p. 58; Robert A. Guth, "Yahoo Japan Learns from Parent's Achievements and Errors," *The Wall Street Journal* (December 11, 2000), p. A28.

Case 17-2

Barry Diller and IAC/InterActiveCorp

Barry Diller has always been a man with big plans. He began his career in the mailroom at the fabled William Morris talent agency. His next stop was ABC Television, where his programming innovations included the "Movie of the Week" and the miniseries. Television proved to be a stepping-stone to Hollywood; in 1974, at the age of 34, Diller became chairman of Paramount Pictures. In 1984, having presided over such blockbuster hits as *Raiders of the Lost Ark*, he moved on to Twentieth Century Fox. Cable television was next; Diller took the top spot at QVC, the home shopping channel. After resigning from QVC in the mid-1990s, Diller began building a media company that he named USA Networks. He bought the Home Shopping Network (HSN) and a family of TV stations. During the next few years, however, the burgeoning dot-com scene caught his eye. He was intrigued by the possibilities for e-commerce, especially online retailing. In 2001, only one year after the dot-com bubble had burst, he bought a 64 percent stake in Expedia, the online travel service.

Barry Diller has been described as a no-nonsense, cut-to-the-chase kind of businessperson. Hailed by some observers as a visionary, Diller laid the groundwork for a successful e-commerce empire by investing in companies with strong business plans featuring services that are well matched to the Internet.

To raise additional money to invest, he sold USA Networks to Vivendi Universal, the French media company, for $11 billion. Diller's vision is to make his new company, IAC/InterActiveCorp, the world's largest e-commerce enterprise. Today, IAC is the world's largest provider of online travel services through its Hotels.com and Expedia.com Web sites. InterActiveCorp also owns Ticketmaster, the world's leading ticketing service, and online personals listing services Match.com and uDate.com.

The travel industry experienced a steep downturn in the aftermath of September 11. In an effort to put "heads in beds," InterContinental, Marriott, and other major hotel chains sold excess room inventory at a discount to Hotels.com and other online services. When a traveler books a room through, for example, Hotels.com, the price he or she pays is 20 percent to 30 percent more than Hotels.com's cost; thus, each transaction nets a tidy gross margin for Hotels.com. According to estimates compiled by Smith Travel Research, in the United States alone, online services redirected $1 billion in revenues away from the hotel operators. Six percent of all U.S. hotel reservations were made online in 2003; travel consultancy PhoCus Wright expects that figure to increase significantly.

Hotel operators took notice and began developing their own online services. InterContinental has been especially aggressive, launching brand-neutral sites such as Accommodations.info and DealsonHotels.com that direct users to various hotel properties run by InterContinental. The company has also launched Web sites in French, German, Spanish, and Chinese. As Eric Pearson, vice president of e-commerce at InterContinental, noted, "There's a huge demand from consumers traveling abroad. That shows proof positive that if you're a global company, you need to provide services around the world."

For the moment, hotel bookings remain an extremely lucrative source of revenue and profit for IAC/InterActiveCorp. By contrast, financial results from the Match.com and uDate.com personals services have been less stable. For example, in the fourth quarter of 2003, profits from personals were only $1.5 billion, a decline of 84 percent. Match.com logs tens of thousands of new subscribers each day; however, that figure is offset by a significant number of cancellations. As Diller explained, "We went from a few thousand subscribers to 880,000. We changed the model, thinking we could change the pricing and get people to stay subscribed for longer, which turned out to be just dumb." Still, Diller sees great potential for cross selling between the personals and his company's other services.

Recently, Diller has begun sharpening his focus on Internet search. Although it is the market leader in online travel services, Diller also spun off the Expedia.com business, which now trades separately on the NASDAQ exchange. He also acquired the Ask Jeeves search engine for $1.7 billion and renamed it Ask.com. A new advertising campaign developed for the U.S. market was keyed to the slogan "Use Tools, Feel Human." The ads were intended to position Ask.com as a faster, easier, more user-friendly service. In the United Kingdom, a separate ad campaign from the Fallon Worldwide agency used an unusual creative strategy: Reminding consumers that Google is the leading search engine. The campaign, which urged people to "stop the online information monopoly" and rebel against "the establishment [i.e. Google]," appeared to be the work of a grass-roots, underground movement. However, a publicity backlash developed when it became clear that the campaign was, in fact, advertising.

Ask.com's marketing campaign in the United Kingdom is just one indication that Diller is keenly aware of global market opportunities. Currently, about 17 percent of IAC/InterActiveCorp's revenues are generated outside the United States; Diller wants to double that figure. Some industry observers predict Diller's next move will be to acquire a British travel site such as Lastminute.com or eBookers.com. As Diller explains, "The aim is to be the largest e-commerce player with a multi-brand strategy. In some cases, we're going to set up new ventures; in some cases it's more efficient to acquire, where a brand is already established."

Discussion Questions

1. Why did Barry Diller divest Expedia.com and acquire Ask Jeeves?

2. Which search engine do you use most frequently? Why?

3. What acquisition do you think Diller will make next?

An interview with Barry Diller was recently broadcast on *60 Minutes*. The program is available on DVD and makes an excellent companion to this case.

Sources: Aaron O. Patrick, "Ask.Com's 'Revolt' Risks Costly Clicks," *The Wall Street Journal* (April 5, 2007), p. B8; Peter Grant and Sara Silver, "Diller Retools IAC to Compete with Web Stars," *The Wall Street Journal* (August 31, 2006), pp. C1, C5; Grant, "Diller's IAC, AOL to Invest in Web-TV Company," *The Wall Street Journal* (November 22, 2005), p. B4; Dennis K. Berman and Kevin J. Delaney, "Diller's IAC Nears Deal for Jeeves," *The Wall Street Journal* (March 21, 2005), p. A3; Tim Burt and Peter Thal Larsen, "The Negotiator-in-Chief," *Financial Times* (April 27, 2004), p. 11; Betty Liu and Amy Lee, "Hoteliers Try to Evict an Unwelcome Visitor," *Financial Times* (April 19, 2004), p. 6; Timothy J. Mullaney and Ronald Grover, "The Web Mogul" (Cover Story), *Business Week* (October 13, 2003), pp. 62–66+ ; Tim Burt and Peter Thal Larsen, "Inside Barry Diller's Hive of Interactivity," *Financial Times* (September 19, 2003), p. 10.

GLOSSARY

The chapter number follows the definition.

80/20 rule In behavioral market segmentation, the rule of thumb that 20 percent of a company's products or customers account for 80 percent of revenues or profits. (7)

ad valorem duty A duty that is expressed as a percentage of the value of goods. (8)

adaptation approach Management's use of highly localized marketing programs in different country markets. (1)

adopter categories In the adoption process developed by Everett Rogers, a typology of buyers at different stages of the "adoption" or product life cycle. The categories are innovators, early majority, late majority, and laggards. (4)

adoption process A model developed by Everett Rogers that describes the "adoption" or purchase decision process. The stages consist of awareness, interest, evaluation, trial, and adoption. (4)

advertising Any sponsored, paid message that is communicated through a nonpersonal channel. Advertising is one of the four variables in the promotion mix. (13)

advertising appeal The communications approach that relates to the motives of the target audience. (13)

advertising organization A corporation or holding company that includes one or more "core" advertising agencies, as well as units specializing in direct marketing, marketing services, public relations, or research. (13)

advocacy advertising A form of corporate advertising in which a company presents its point of view on a particular issue. (13)

aesthetics A shared sense within a culture of what is beautiful as opposed to ugly and what represents good taste as opposed to tastelessness. (4)

agent An intermediary who negotiates transactions between two or more parties but does not take title to the goods being purchased or sold. (12)

Andean Community A customs union comprised of Bolivia, Colombia, Ecuador, Peru, and Venezuela. (3)

antidumping duties Duties imposed on products whose prices government officials deem too low. (8)

arbitration A negotiation process between two or more parties to settle a dispute outside of the court system. (5)

art direction The visual presentation of an advertisement. (13)

art director An ad agency "creative" with general responsibility for the overall look of an advertisement. The art director chooses graphics, pictures, type styles, and other visual elements. (13)

Association of Southeast Asian Nations (ASEAN) A trade bloc comprised of Brunei, Cambodia, Indonesia, Malaysia, Laos, Myanmar, the Philippines, Singapore, Thailand, and Vietnam. (3)

attitude In culture, a learned tendency to respond in a consistent way to a given object or entity. (4)

balance of payments The record of all economic transactions between the residents of a country and the rest of the world. (2)

barter The least complex and oldest form of bilateral, nonmonetized countertrade consisting of a direct exchange of goods or services between two parties. (11)

behavioral market segmentation The process of performing market segmentation utilizing user status, usage rate, or some other measure of product consumption. (7)

belief In culture, an organized pattern or knowledge that an individual holds to be true about the world. (4)

benefit segmentation The process of segmenting markets on the basis of the benefits sought by buyers. (7)

big emerging markets (BEMs) Countries that have experienced rapid economic growth and represent significant marketing opportunities. (2)

big idea A concept that can serve as the basis for a memorable, effective advertising message. (13)

bill of exchange A written order from one party directing a second party to pay to the order of a third party. (8)

Bluetooth Technology that permits access to the Internet from a cell phone when the user is within the range of a hot spot. (17)

brand A representation of a promise by a particular company about a particular product; a complex bundle of images and experiences in the customer's mind. (10)

brand equity The reflection of the brand's value to a company as an intangible asset. (10)

brand extensions A strategy that uses an established brand name as an umbrella when entering new businesses or developing new product lines that represent new categories to the company. (10)

brand image A single, but often complex, mental image about both the physical product and the company that markets it. (10)

bribery The corrupt business practice of demanding or offering some type of consideration—typically cash payment—when negotiating a cross-border deal. (5)

broadband A digital communication system with sufficient capacity to carry multiple voice, data, or video channels simultaneously. (17)

business-to-business marketing Marketing products and services to other companies and organizations. Contrasts with business-to-consumer (b-to-c or B2C) marketing. (12)

call centers Sophisticated telephone operations that provide customer support and other services to in-bound callers from around the world. May also provide outsourcing services such as telemarketing. (8)

call option The right to buy a specified amount of foreign currency at a fixed price, up to the option's expiration date. (2)

capital account In a country's balance of payments, the record of all long-term direct investment, portfolio investment, and other short- and long-term capital flows. (2)

capital requirements Costs that can be seen as fixed capital, as in manufacturing facilities, or working capital, as in financing R&D, advertising, field sales and service, customer credit, and inventories. (15)

CARICOM (Caribbean Community and Common Market) Formed in 1973, it is a free trade area whose members include Antigua and Barbuda, Bahamas, Barbados, Belize, Dominica, Grenada, Guyana, Haiti, Jamaica, Montserrat, St. Kitts and Nevis, St. Lucia, St. Vincent and the Grenadines, and Trinidad and Tobago. (3)

cartel A group of separate companies or countries that collectively set prices, control output, or take other actions to maximize profits. (5)

category killer A store that specializes in a particular product category and offers a vast selection at low prices. (12)

Central American Integration System A customs union comprised of El Salvador, Honduras, Guatemala, Nicaragua, Costa Rica, and Panama. (3)

centrally planned capitalism An economic system characterized by command resource allocation and private resource ownership. (2)

centrally planned socialism An economic system characterized by command resource allocation and state resource ownership. (2)

CFR (cost and freight) A contract in which the seller is not responsible for risk or loss at any point outside the factory. (11)

chaebol In South Korea, a type of corporate alliance group composed of dozens of companies and centered around a central bank or holding company and dominated by a founding family. (9)

channel of distribution An organized network of agencies and institutions that, in combination, perform all the activities required to link producers with users to accomplish the marketing task. (12)

characteristics of innovations In Roger's diffusion of innovation framework, five factors that affect the rate at which buyers accept a new product: relative advantage, compatibility, complexity, divisibility, and communicability. (4)

cherry picking In distribution, a situation in which a channel intermediary such as a distributor only accepts new lines from manufacturers whose products and brands already enjoy strong demand. (12)

CIF (cost, insurance, freight) named port of destination The Incoterm for a contract requiring the seller to retain responsibility and liability for goods until they have physically passed over the rail of a ship. (11)

click-through rate The percentage of visitors to an Internet site who click on an advertisement link presented on the computer screen. (17)

cluster analysis In market research, a quantitative data analysis technique that groups variables into clusters that maximize within-group similarities and between-group differences. Can be used in psychographic segmentation. (6)

co-branding A variation of tiered branding in which two or more different company or product brands are featured prominently on product packaging or in advertising. (10)

collaborating with competitors Seeking competitive advantage by utilizing know-how developed by other companies. (15)

collaborative agreements Linkages between companies from different countries for the purpose of pursuing common goals. (9)

collectivism In Hofstede's social values typology, the extent to which group cohesiveness and harmony are emphasized in a culture. A shared concern for the well-being of all members of society is also evident. (4)

combination branding A strategy in which a corporate name is combined with a product brand name; also called tiered or umbrella branding. (10)

common agricultural policy (CAP) Legislation adopted by European countries after World War II to aid and protect the interests of farmers. (8)

common external tariff (CET) A tariff agreed upon by members of a preferential trading bloc. Implementation of a CET marks the transition from a free trade area to a customs union. (3)

common market A preferential trade agreement that builds on the foundation of economic integration provided by a free trade area and a customs union. (3)

Common Market of the South (Mercosur) A customs union comprised of Argentina, Brazil, Paraguay, Uruguay, and Chile. (3)

common-law country A country in which the legal system relies on past judicial decisions (cases) to resolve disputes. (5)

comparability The degree to which research results from different countries can be used to make valid comparisons. (6)

compensation trading (buyback) A countertrade deal typically involving the sale of plant equipment or technology licensing in which the seller or licensor agrees to take payment in the form of the products produced using the equipment or technology for a specified number of years. (11)

competitive advantage The result of a match between a firm's distinctive competencies and the factors critical for creating superior customer value in an industry. (1)

competitor response The reaction of existing competitors to a new entrant's arrival in an industry or market. (15)

concentrated global marketing The target market strategy that calls for creating a marketing mix to reach a niche segment of global consumers. (7)

confiscation Governmental seizure of a company's assets without compensation. (5)

conjoint analysis In market research, a quantitative data analysis technique that can be used to gain insights into the combination of product features that will be attractive to potential buyers. (6)

consumer panel Primary data collection using a sample of consumers or households whose behavior is tracked over time; frequently used for television audience measurement. (6)

consumer sales promotions Promotion designed to make consumers aware of a new product, to stimulate nonusers to sample an existing product, or to increase overall consumer demand. (14)

containerization In physical distribution, the practice of loading long-haul truck or ocean-going freight into steel boxes measuring 20 feet, 40 feet, or longer. (12)

continuous innovation A product that is "new and improved" but requires little R&D expenditure to develop, causes minimal disruption of existing consumption patterns, and requires the least amount of learning on the part of buyers. (10)

contract manufacturing A licensing arrangement in which a global company provides technical specifications to a subcontractor or local manufacturer. (9)

convenience stores A form of retail distribution that offers some of the same products as supermarkets, but the merchandise mix is limited to high turnover convenience products. (12)

convergence The aspect of the digital revolution that pertains to the merging, overlapping, or coming together of previously distinct industries or product categories. (17)

cooperative exporter An export organization of a manufacturing company retained by other independent manufacturers to sell their products in some or all foreign markets. (8)

copy The words that are the spoken or written communication elements in advertisements. (13)

copyright The establishment of ownership of a written, recorded, performed, or filmed creative work. (5)

copywriter An advertising agency "creative" who is responsible for developing the headlines, subheads, and body copy used in print advertising and the scripts for broadcast ads. (13)

corporate advertising Advertising that is not designed to directly stimulate demand for a specific product. Image advertising and advocacy advertising are two types of corporate advertising. (13)

cost-based pricing Pricing based on an analysis of internal costs (e.g., material, labor, etc.) and external costs. (11)

cost-based transfer pricing A transfer pricing policy that uses costs as a basis for setting prices in intracorporate transfers. (11)

cost focus In Porter's generic strategies framework, one of four options for building competitive advantage. When a firm that serves a small (niche) market has a lower cost structure than its competitors, it can offer customers the lowest prices in the industry. (15)

cost leadership advantage A broad market strategy based on a firm's position as the industry's low-cost producer. (15)

cost-plus pricing The price that results from adding the additional costs and expenses not directly related to the manufacturing cost to the full-cost price. (11)

counterfeiting The unauthorized copying and production of a product. (5)

counterpurchase A monetized countertrade deal in which the seller agrees to purchase products of equivalent value that it must then sell in order to realize revenue from the original deal. (11)

countertrade An export transaction in which a sale results in product flowing in one direction to a buyer, and a separate stream of products and services, often flowing in the opposite direction. (11)

countervailing duties (CVDs) Additional duties levied to offset subsidies granted in the exporting country. (8)

country-of-origin effect Perceptions of, or attitudes toward, products or brands on the basis of the country of origin or manufacture. (10)

coupon A sales promotion tool consisting of a printed certificate that entitles the bearer to a price reduction or some other value-enhancing consideration when purchasing a particular product or service. (14)

creative In an advertising agency, a person who is responsible for developing the appropriate advertising appeal, selling proposition, and creative execution of an advertisement. (13)

creative execution In advertising, the way an appeal or selling proposition is presented. Creative execution is the "how," and creative strategy is the "what." (13)

creative strategy A statement or concept of what a particular advertising message or campaign will say. (13)

culture A society's ways of living are transmitted from one generation to another. Culture's manifestations include attitudes, beliefs, values, aesthetics, dietary customs, and language. (4)

current account A record of all recurring trade in merchandise and services, private gifts, and public aid transactions between countries. (2)

customer relationship management (CRM) The process of storing and analyzing data collected from customer "touchpoints" for the purpose of identifying a firm's best customers and serving their needs as efficiently, effectively, and profitably as possible. (6)

customer strategy A sales representative's plan for collecting and analyzing information about the needs of each customer or prospect. (14)

customs procedures Procedures that are considered restrictive if they are administered in a way that makes compliance difficult and expensive. (8)

customs union A preferential trade bloc whose members agree to seek a greater degree of economic integration than is provided by a free trade agreement. In addition to reducing tariffs and quotas, a customs union is characterized by a common external tariff (CET). (3)

data warehouse A database, part of a company's MIS, that is used to support management decision making. (6)

delivered duty paid A type of contract in which the seller has agreed to deliver the goods to the buyer at the place he or she names in the country of import, with all costs, including duties, paid. (11)

demand conditions Conditions that determine the rate and nature of improvement and innovations by the firms in the nation. (15)

demographic segmentation The process of segmenting markets on the basis of measurable characteristics such as country income, population, age, or some other measure. (7)

department store A category of retail operations characterized by multiple sections or areas under one roof, each representing a distinct merchandise line and staffed with a limited number of salespeople. (12)

devaluation The decline in value of a currency relative to other currencies. (2)

developed countries Countries that can be assigned to the high-income category. (2)

developing countries Countries that can be assigned to the upper ranks of the low-income category, the lower-middle income category, or the upper-middle-income category. (2)

differentiated global marketing A strategy that calls for targeting two or more distinct market segments with multiple marketing mix offerings. (7)

differentiation In Porter's generic strategies framework, one of four options for building competitive advantage. Differentiation advantage is present when a firm serves a broad market and its products are perceived as unique; this allows the firm to charge premium prices compared with the competition. (15)

diffusion of innovations A framework developed by Everett Rogers to explain the way that new products are adopted by a culture over time. Framework includes the five stage innovation adoption process, characteristics of innovations, and innovation adopter categories. (4)

digital revolution The paradigm shift resulting from technological advances allowing for the digitization (i.e., conversion to binary code) of analogue sources of information, sounds, and images. (17)

direct mail A direct marketing technique that uses the postal service as a vehicle for delivering an offer to prospects targeted by the marketer. (14)

direct marketing Any communication with a consumer or business recipient that is designed to generate a response in the form of an order, a request for further information, and/or a visit to a store or other place of business. (14)

direct perception In environmental scanning, the reliance on immediate sensory input (e.g., seeing, hearing, tasting) to supplement documentary information sources. (6)

discontinuous innovation A new product that, upon its success, creates new markets and new consumption patterns. (10)

discount stores A category of retail operations that emphasizes low merchandise prices. (12)

discriminatory exchange rate policies Policies that distort trade in much the same way as selective import duties and export subsidies. (8)

discriminatory procurement policies Policies that can take the form of government rules and administrative regulations, as well as formal or informal company policies that discriminate against foreign suppliers. (8)

disruptive technology A technology that redefines product or industry performance and enables new markets to emerge. (17)

distribution One of the four Ps of the marketing mix; the physical flow of goods through channels. (12)

distribution center A facility designed to efficiently receive goods from suppliers and then fill orders for individual stores or customers. (12)

distribution channels A barrier to entry into an industry created by the need to create and establish new channels. (12)

distributor A wholesale channel intermediary that typically carries product lines or brands on a selective basis. (13)

domestic company A company that limits the geographic scope of its resource commitment and marketing activities to opportunities in the home country. (1)

domestic market A company's "home turf," generally the country or countries in which the organization's headquarters is located. (1)

double diamond model A framework for understanding national competitive advantage in terms of a "double diamond" instead of the single diamond found in Michael Porter's national advantage model. (15)

dumping The sale of a product in an export market at a price lower than that normally charged in the domestic market or country of origin. (8)

duties Rate schedule; can sometimes be thought of as a tax that punishes individuals for making choices of which their government disapproves. (8)

dynamically continuous innovation An intermediate category of newness that is less disruptive and requires less learning on the part of consumers. (10)

Economic Community of West African States (ECOWAS) An association of 16 nations that includes Benin, Burkina Faso, Cape Verde, Gambia, Ghana, Guinea, Guinea-Bissau, Ivory Coast, Liberia, Mali, Mauritania, Niger, Nigeria, Senegal, Sierra Leone, and Togo. (3)

economic union A highly evolved form of cross-border economic integration involving reduced tariffs and quotas; a common external tariff; reduced restrictions on the movement of labor and capital; and the creation of unified economic policies and institutions such as a central bank. (3)

economies of scale The decline in per-unit product costs as the absolute volume of production per period increases. In Porter's five forces model, one of the eight barriers to entry that determine the potential threat of new industry entrants. (15)

efficient consumer response (ECR) An MIS tool that enables retailers to work more closely with vendors to facilitate stock replenishment. (6)

electronic data interchange (EDI) An MIS tool that allows a company's business units to submit orders, issue invoices, and transact business electronically with other company units as well as outside companies. (6)

electronic point of sale (EPOS) Purchase data gathered by checkout scanners that help retailers identify product sales patterns and the extent to which consumer preferences vary with geography. (6)

emic analysis Global market research that analyzes a country in terms of its local system of meanings and values. (6)

emotional appeal In advertising, an appeal intended to evoke a feeling response (as opposed to an intellectual response) that will direct purchase behavior. (13)

environmental scanning Gathering information about global markets. Two modes can be used: surveillance and search. (6)

environmental sensitivity A measure of the extent to which products must be adapted to the culture-specific needs of different country markets. Generally, consumer products show a higher degree of environmental sensitivity than industrial products. (4)

EPRG framework A developmental framework for analyzing organizations in terms of four successive management orientations: ethnocentric, polycentric, regiocentric, and geocentric. (1)

equity stake Market entry strategy involving foreign direct investment for the purpose of establishing partial ownership of a business. (9)

ethnocentric orientation The first level in the EPRG framework: the conscious or unconscious belief that one's home country is superior. (1)

ethnocentric pricing The practice of extending a product's home-country price to all country markets. Also known as extension pricing policy. (11)

etic analysis Global market research that analyzes a country from an outside perspective. (6)

euro The single European currency. (3)

euro zone Austria, Belgium, Finland, Ireland, the Netherlands, France, Germany, Greece, Italy, Luxembourg, Portugal, and Spain. (3)

expanded Triad The dominant economic centers of the world: the Pacific region, North America, and Europe. (2)

expatriate An employee who is sent from his or her home country to work abroad. (14)

export broker A broker who receives a fee for bringing together the seller and the overseas buyer. (8)

export commission representative Representative assigned to all or some foreign markets by the manufacturer. (8)

export distributor An individual or organization that has the exclusive right to sell a manufacturer's products in all or some markets outside the country of origin. (8)

export management company (EMC) Term used to designate an independent export firm that acts as the export department for more than one manufacturer. (8)

export marketing Exporting using the product offered in the home market as a starting point and modifying it as needed to meet the preferences of international target markets. (8)

export merchants Merchants who seek out needs in foreign markets and make purchases in world markets to fill these needs. (8)

export selling Exporting without tailoring the product, the price, or the promotional material to suit individual country requirements. (8)

exporting Selling or marketing goods or services to buyers located outside the home country. (8)

express warranty A written guarantee that assures a buyer that he or she is getting what was paid for or provides recourse in the event that a product's performance falls short of expectations. (10)

expropriation Governmental seizure of a company's assets in exchange for compensation that is generally lower than market value. (5)

extension approach Management's use of domestic country marketing programs and strategies when entering new country markets. (1)

ex-works A type of contract in which the seller places goods at the disposal of the buyer at the time specified in the contract. (11)

factor analysis In market research, a computerized quantitative data analysis technique that is used to perform data reduction. Responses from questionnaires that contain multiple items about a product's benefits serve as input; the computer generates factor loadings that can be used to create a perceptual map. (6)

factor conditions A country's endowment with resources. (15)

FAS (free alongside ship) named port of destination The Incoterm for a contract that calls for the seller to place goods alongside, or available to, the vessel or other mode of transportation and pay all charges up to that point. (11)

femininity In Hofstede's social values framework, the extent to which the social roles of men and women overlap in a culture. (4)

first-mover advantage Orthodox marketing wisdom suggesting that the first company to enter a country market has the best chance of becoming the market leader. (7)

flagship model A model of competitive advantage developed by Alan Rugman that describes how networked business systems can create competitive advantage in global industries. (15)

FOB (free on board) The Incoterm for a contract in which the responsibility and liability of the seller do not end until the goods have actually been placed aboard a ship. (11)

focus The concentration of resources on a core business or competence. (1)

focused differentiation In Porter's generic strategies framework, one of four options for building competitive advantage. When a firm serves a small (niche) market and its products are perceived as unique, the firm can charge premium prices. (15)

focus group Primary data collection method involving a trained moderator who facilitates discussion among the members of a group at a specially equipped research facility. (6)

foreign consumer culture positioning A positioning strategy that seeks to differentiate a product, brand, or company by associating it with its country or culture of origin. (7)

Foreign Corrupt Practices Act (FCPA) A law that makes it illegal for U.S. corporations to bribe an official of a foreign government or political party to obtain or retain business. (5)

foreign direct investment The market entry strategy in which companies invest in or acquire plants, equipment, or other assets outside the home country. (9)

foreign purchasing agents Purchasing agents who operate on behalf of, and are remunerated by, an overseas customer. (8)

forward market A mechanism for buying and selling currencies at a preset price for future delivery. (2)

franchising A contract between a parent company franchisor and franchisee that allows the franchisee to operate a business developed by the franchisor in return for a fee and adherence to franchise-wide policies and practices. (9)

free trade agreement (FTA) An agreement that leads to the creation of a free trade area (also abbreviated FTA). A free trade agreement represents a relatively low level of economic integration. (3)

free trade area (FTA) A preferential trading bloc whose members have signed a free trade agreement (also abbreviated FTA) that entails reducing or eliminating tariffs and quotas. (3)

free trade zone A geographical entity that may include a manufacturing facility and a warehouse. (8)

freight forwarders Specialists in traffic operations, customs clearance, and shipping tariffs and schedules. (8)

full-service advertising agency An advertising agency that provides services such as market research, media buying, and direct marketing in addition to creative campaign development. (13)

General Agreement on Tariffs and Trade (GATT) The organization established at the end of World War II to promote free trade; also, the treaty signed by member nations. (3)

generic strategies Michael Porter's model describing four different options for achieving competitive advantage: cost leadership, differentiation, cost focus, focused differentiation. (15)

geocentric orientation The fourth level in the EPRG framework: the understanding that the company should seek market opportunities throughout the world. Management also recognizes that country markets may be characterized by both similarities and differences. (1)

geocentric pricing The practice of using both extension and adaptation pricing policies in different country markets. (11)

geographical structure A pattern of organization in which the operational responsibility for a geographical area of the world is assigned to line managers; the corporate headquarters retains responsibility for worldwide planning and control. (16)

global advertising An advertising message whose art, copy, headlines, photographs, tag lines, and other elements have been developed expressly for their worldwide suitability. (13)

global brand A brand that has the same name and a similar image and positioning throughout the world. (10)

global brand leadership The act of allocating brand-building resources globally with the goal of creating global synergies and developing a global brand strategy that coordinates and leverages country brand strategies. (10)

global company A company exhibiting a geocentric orientation that pursues marketing opportunities in all parts of the world using one of two strategies: either serving world markets by exporting goods manufactured in the home-country market or by sourcing products from a variety of different countries with the primary goal of serving the home-country market. Global operations are integrated and coordinated. (1)

global competition A success strategy in which a firm takes a global view of competition and sets about maximizing profits worldwide, rather than on a country-by-country basis. (15)

global consumer culture positioning A positioning strategy that seeks to differentiate a product, brand, or company as a symbol of, or associated with, global culture or a global market segment. (7)

global elite A global market segment comprised of well-traveled, affluent consumers who spend heavily on prestige or luxury products and brands that convey an image of exclusivity. (7)

global industry An industry in which competitive advantage can be achieved by integrating and leveraging operations on a worldwide scale. (1)

global marketing The commitment of organizational resources to pursuing global market opportunities and responding to environmental threats in the global marketplace. (1)

global marketing strategy (GMS) A firm's blueprint for pursuing global market opportunities that addresses four issues: whether a standardization approach or localization approach will be used; whether key marketing activities will be concentrated in relatively few countries or widely dispersed around the globe; guidelines for coordinating marketing activities around the globe; and the scope of global market participation. (1)

global market research The project-specific gathering and analysis of data on a global basis or in one or more markets outside the home country. (6)

global market segmentation The process of identifying specific segments of potential customers with homogeneous attributes who are likely to exhibit similar buying behavior irrespective of their country of residence. (7)

global positioning system (GPS) A digital communication system that uses satellite feeds to determine the geographic position of a mobile device. (17)

global product A product that satisfies the wants and needs of buyers in all parts of the world. (10)

global retailing Engaging in or owning retail operations in multiple national markets. (12)

global strategic partnerships (GSP) A sophisticated market entry strategy via an alliance with one or more business partners for the purpose of serving the global market. (9)

global teens A global market segment comprised of persons 12 to 19 years old whose shared interest in fashion, music, and youth lifestyle issues shapes purchase behavior. (7)

government policy A barrier to entry into an industry created by the policies instituted by the government. In Porter's five forces model, one of the eight barriers to entry that determine the potential threat of new industry entrants. (15)

gray market goods Products that are exported from one country to another without authorization from the trademark owner. (11)

greenfield investment A market entry strategy that entails foreign direct investment in a factory, retail outlet, or some other form of new operations in a target country. (9)

Group of Seven (G7) Seven nations—the United States, Japan, Germany, France, Great Britain, Canada, and Italy—whose representatives meet regularly to deal with global economic issues. (2)

Gulf Cooperation Council (GCC) An association of oil-producing states that includes Bahrain, Kuwait, Oman, Qatar, Saudi Arabia, and the United Arab Emirates. (3)

Harmonized Tariff System (HTS) A system in which importers and exporters have to determine the correct classification number for a given product or service that will cross borders. (8)

hedging An investment made to protect a company from possible financial losses due to fluctuating currency exchange rates. (2)

high-context culture A culture in which a great deal of information and meaning resides in the context of communication, including the background, associations, and basic values of the communicators. (4)

high-income country A country in which per capita GNP is $9,266 or greater. (2)

hot spot Any location that offers Wi-Fi access (e.g., hotels, airports, coffee shops, restaurants, etc.). (17)

hypercompetition A strategy framework developed by Richard D'Aveni that views competition and the quest for competitive advantage in terms of the dynamic maneuvering and strategic interactions of firms in an industry. (15)

hypermarket A category of retail operations characterized by very large scale facilities that combine elements of discount store, supermarket, and warehouse club approaches. (12)

image advertising A type of corporate advertising that informs the public about a major event, such as a name change, merger, etc. (13)

importing Purchasing goods or services from companies located outside the home country. (8)

incipient market A market in which demand will materialize if particular economic, political, or sociocultural trends continue. (6)

Incoterms Internationally accepted terms of trade that impact prices. (11)

Index of Economic Freedom A league table of country rankings based on key economic variables such as trade policy, taxation policy, government consumption, monetary policy, capital flows and foreign investment, etc. (2)

individualism In Hofstede's social values typology, the extent to which each member of society is primarily concerned with his or her interests and those of the immediate family. (4)

infomercial A form of paid television programming in which a particular product is demonstrated, explained, and offered for sale to viewers who call a toll-free number shown on the screen. (14)

information technology (IT) An organization's processes for creating, storing, exchanging, using, and managing information. (6)

innovation adopter categories In Rogers' diffusion of innovation framework, a way of classifying buyers in terms of their receptivity to new products: innovators, early adopters, early majority, late majority, laggards. (4)

innovation adoption process In Rogers' diffusion of innovation framework, a five-stage hierarchy that a person goes through when deciding to buy a new product: awareness, interest, evaluation, trial, and adoption. (4)

integrated circuit (IC) The silicon chip that gave modern form to the transistor and represented a milestone in the digital revolution. (17)

integrated marketing communications (IMC) An approach to the promotion element of the marketing mix that values coordination and integration of a company's marketing communication strategy. (13)

intellectual property protection The aspect of a country's legal environment pertaining to patent, trademark, and copyright protection. (5)

intermodal transportation The aspect of physical distribution that involves transferring shipping containers between land and water transportation modes. (12)

international brand A brand that is available throughout a particular world region. (10)

international company A company that pursues market opportunities outside the home country via an extension strategy. (1)

international division structure A pattern of organization design in which the executive in charge of the international division has a direct reporting relationship to corporate staff. (16)

Internet A network of computer networks across which e-mail and other digital files can be sent. (17)

intranet An electronic system that allows authorized company personnel or outsiders to share information electronically in a secure fashion while reducing the amount of paper generated. (6)

invention A demanding but potentially rewarding product strategy for reaching mass markets in less-developed countries. (10)

inventory management The aspect of physical distribution that seeks to ensure that sufficient quantities of goods are available to meet demand or fulfill orders without incurring the extra costs associated with high inventory levels. (12)

Islamic law A legal system used in the Middle East that is based on a comprehensive code known as the sharia. (5)

joint venture A market entry strategy in which two companies share ownership of a newly created business entity. (9)

jurisdiction The aspect of a country's legal environment that deals with a court's authority to rule on particular types of controversies arising outside of a nation's borders or exercise power over individuals or entities from different countries. (5)

keiretsu In Japan, an enterprise alliance consisting of businesses that are joined together in mutually reinforcing ways. (9)

latent market An undiscovered market segment in which demand for a product would materialize if an appropriate product were offered. (6)

law of one price A market in which all customers have access to the best product at the best price. (11)

layers of advantage A strategy for creating competitive advantage by building a wide portfolio of advantages. (15)

leader Someone whose job is to direct the efforts and creativity of everyone in the company toward a global effort that best uses organizational resources to exploit global opportunities. (16)

lean production An extremely effective, efficient, and streamlined manufacturing system such as the Toyota Production System. (16)

least-developed countries (LDCs) Terminology adopted by the United Nations to refer to the 50 countries that rank lowest in per capita GNP. (2)

legal environment A nation's system of laws, courts, attorneys, legal customs, and practices. (5)

letter of credit (L/C) A payment method in export/import in which a bank substitutes its creditworthiness for that of the buyer. (8)

leverage Some type of advantage—for example, experience transfers, leverage, or scale economies—that a company enjoys by accumulating experience in multiple country markets. (1)

licensing A contractual market entry strategy whereby one company makes an asset available to another company in exchange for royalties or some other form of compensation. (9)

line extension A variation of an existing product such as a new flavor or new design. (10)

local brand A brand that is available in a single country market. (10)

local consumer culture positioning A positioning strategy that seeks to differentiate a product, brand, or company in terms of its association with local culture, local production, or local consumption. (7)

localization (adaptation) approach The pursuit of global market opportunities using an adaptation strategy of significant marketing mix variation in different countries. (1)

logistics management The management process that integrates the activities of various suppliers and distribution intermediaries to ensure an efficient flow of goods through a firm's supply chain. (12)

long-term orientation (LTO) The fifth dimension in Hofstede's social values framework, LTO is a reflection of a society's concern with immediate gratification versus persistence and thrift over the long term. (4)

loose bricks A strategy for creating competitive advantage by taking advantage of a competitor whose attention is narrowly focused on a market segment or geographic area to the exclusion of others. (15)

low-context culture A culture in which messages and knowledge are more explicit and words carry most of the information in communication. (4)

low-income country A country with per capita GNP of less than $755. (2)

lower-middle-income country A country with GNP per capita between $756 and $2,995. (2)

Maastricht Treaty The 1991 treaty that set the stage for the transition from the European monetary system to an economic and monetary union. (3)

management information system (MIS) A system that provides managers and other decision makers with a continuous flow of information about company operations. (6)

manufacturers' export representatives Combination export management firms. (8)

maquiladora A program that allows manufacturing, assembly, or processing plants to import materials, components, and equipment duty-free; in return they use Mexican labor. (2)

marginal-cost pricing A pricing strategy that sets the selling price equal to the variable costs of producing one additional unit of output. (11)

market People or organizations with needs and wants and both the ability and willingness to buy. (2)

market-based transfer price A transfer pricing policy that sets prices for intracorporate transactions at levels that are competitive in the global market. (11)

market capitalism An economic system characterized by market allocation of resources and private resource ownership. (2)

market entry strategy The manner in which company management decides to pursue market opportunities outside the home country. (9)

market expansion strategy The particular combination of product-market and geographic alternatives that management chooses when expanding company operations outside the home country. (9)

market holding A pricing strategy that allows management to maintain market share; prices are adjusted up or down as competitive or economic conditions change. (11)

market penetration A pricing strategy that calls for setting price levels that are low enough to quickly build market share. (11)

market penetration pricing policy A pricing strategy of setting price levels that are low enough to quickly build market share. (11)

market skimming A pricing strategy designed to reach customers willing to pay a premium price for a particular brand or for a specialized product. (11)

market socialism An economic system characterized by limited market resource allocation within an overall environment of state ownership. (2)

marketing mix Product, price, place, and promotion— the four Ps. (1)

marketing model drivers Key elements or factors that must be taken into account when evaluating countries as potential target markets. (7)

marketing research The project-specific, systematic gathering of data in the search scanning mode. (6)

masculinity In Hofstede's social values framework, the extent to which a culture's male population is expected to be assertive, competitive, and concerned with material success. (4)

Maslow's needs hierarchy A classic framework for understanding how human motivation is linked to needs. (10)

matrix organization A pattern of organization design in which management's task is to achieve an organizational balance that brings together different perspectives and skills to accomplish the organization's objectives. (16)

merchandise trade surplus A figure in a country's balance of payments showing that the value of the country's exports of manufactured goods exceeds the value of its imports of manufactured goods. (2)

mixed allocation system A system containing elements of both market and command allocation systems. (2)

mobile commerce (m-commerce) Conducting commercial transactions using wireless handheld devices such as personal digital assistants (PDAs) and cell phones. (17)

most favored nation (MFN) A privileged trading status in which a GATT signatory nation agrees to apply its favorable tariff or lowest tariff rate to all nations that are also signatories to GATT. (8)

multidimensional scaling (MDS) In market research, a quantitative data analysis technique that can be used to create perceptual maps. MDS helps marketers gain insights into consumer perceptions when a large number of products or brands are available. (6)

multinational company A company that pursues market opportunities outside the home country market via an adaptation strategy (i.e., different product, price, place, and/or promotion strategy than used in the domestic market). In a typical multinational, country managers are granted considerable autonomy; there is little integration or coordination of marketing activities across different country markets. (1)

multisegment targeting A marketing strategy that entails targeting two or more distinct market segments with multiple marketing mix offerings. (7)

national advantage Strategy guru Michael E. Porter's competitive advantage framework for analysis at the nation-state level. The degree to which a nation develops competitive advantage depends on four elements: factor conditions, demand conditions, the presence of related and supporting industries, and the nature of firm strategy. (15)

nationalization Broad transfer of industry management and ownership in a particular country from the private sector to the government. (5)

negotiated transfer price A transfer pricing policy that establishes prices for intracorporate transactions on the basis of the organization's affiliations. (11)

newly industrializing economies (NIEs) Upper-middle-income countries with high rates of economic growth. (2)

niche A single segment of the global market. (7)

nontariff barriers (NTBs) Any restriction besides taxation that restricts or prevents the flow of goods across borders, ranging from "buy local" campaigns to bureaucratic obstacles that make it difficult for companies to gain access to some individual country and regional markets. (1)

normal trade relations (NTR) A trading stratus under WTO rules that entitles a country to low tariff rates. (8)

North American Free Trade Agreement (NAFTA) A free trade area encompassing Canada, the United States, and Mexico. (3)

observation A method of primary data collection using trained observers who watch and record the behavior of actual or prospective customers. (6)

offset A countertrade deal in which a government recoups hard-currency expenditures by requiring some form of cooperation by the seller, such as importing products or transferring technology. (11)

one-to-one marketing An updated framework for direct marketing that calls for treating each customer in a distinct way based on his or her previous purchase history or past interactions with the company. (14)

order processing The aspect of physical distribution that includes order entry, order handling, and order delivery. (12)

organic growth In global retailing, a market expansion strategy whereby a company uses its own resources to open a store on a greenfield site or to acquire one or more existing retail facilities or sites from another company. (12)

Organization for Economic Cooperation and Development (OECD) A group of 30 nations that work together to aid in the development of economic systems based on market capitalism and pluralistic democracy. (2)

organizing The goal of creating a structure that enables the company to respond to significant differences in international market environments and to extend valuable corporate knowledge. (16)

outlet mall A grouping of outlet stores. (12)

outlet store A category of retail operations that allows marketers of well-known consumer brands to dispose of excess inventory, out-of-date merchandise, or factory seconds. (12)

outsourcing Shifting jobs or work assignments to another company to cut costs. When the work moves abroad to a low-wage country, such as India or China, the term *offshoring* is sometimes used. (8)

ownership A market entry strategy that involves foreign direct investment for the purpose of acquiring or merging with another company. (9)

paid search advertising An Internet communication tactic in which companies pay to have their ads appear when users type certain search terms. (17)

parallel importing The act of importing goods from one country to another without authorization from the trademark owner. Parallel import schemes exploit price differentials between country markets. (11)

patent A formal legal document that gives an inventor the exclusive right to make, use, and sell an invention for a specified period of time. (5)

pattern advertising A communication strategy that calls for developing a basic panregional or global concept for which copy, artwork, or other elements can be adapted as required for individual country markets. (13)

personal interview Primary data collection via interactive communication (e.g., face-to-face, telephone, etc.) that allows interviewers to ask "why"-type questions. (6)

personal selling One of four variables in the promotion mix; face-to-face communication between a prospective buyer and a company sales representative. (14)

personal selling philosophy A sales representative's commitment to the marketing concept coupled with a willingness to adopt the role of problem solver or partner in helping customers. The first step in the Strategic/Consultative Selling Model. (14)

physical distribution All activities involved in moving finished goods from manufacturers to customers. Includes order processing, warehousing, inventory management, and transportation. (12)

piggyback marketing A distribution strategy in which one manufacturer obtains product distribution by utilizing another company's channels. (12)

platform A core product design element or component that can be quickly and cheaply adapted to various country markets. (10)

political environment The set of governmental institutions, political parties, and organizations that are the expression of the people in the nations of the world. (5)

political risk The risk of a change in political environment or government policy that would adversely affect a company's ability to operate effectively and profitably. (5)

polycentric orientation The second level in the EPRG framework: the view that each country in which a company does business is unique. In global marketing, this orientation results in high levels of marketing mix adaptation, often implemented by autonomous local managers in each country market. (1)

polycentric pricing The practice of setting different price levels for a given product in different country markets. Also known as adaptation pricing policy. (11)

positioning The act of differentiating a product or brand in the minds of customers or prospects relative to competing products or brands. (7)

positioning by benefit A positioning strategy that seeks to differentiate a company, product, or brand in terms of one or more specific benefits (e.g., reliability) offered to buyers. (7)

positioning by competition A positioning strategy that seeks to differentiate a company, product, or brand by comparing it. (7)

positioning by quality/price A positioning strategy that seeks to differentiate a product, brand, or company in terms expensiveness/exclusivity, acceptable quality/good value, etc. (7)

positioning by use or user A positioning strategy that seeks to differentiate a product by associating it with users whose expertise or accomplishments potential buyers admire. (7)

power distance In Hofstede's social values typology, the cultural dimension that reflects the extent to which it is acceptable for power to be distributed unequally in a society. (4)

preferential tariff A reduced tariff rate applied to imports from certain countries. (8)

preferential trade agreement A trade agreement between a relatively small number of signatory nations, often on a regional or subregional basis. Different levels of economic integration can characterize such trade agreements. (3)

presentation plan In personal selling, the heart of the presentation strategy. The plan has six stages: approach, presentation, demonstration, negotiation, closing, and servicing the sale. (14)

presentation strategy Setting objectives for each sales call and establishing a presentation plan to meet those objectives. (14)

price discrimination The practice of setting different prices when selling the same quantity of like-quality goods to different buyers. (11)

price escalation The increase in an imported product's price due to expenses associated with transportation, currency fluctuations, etc. (11)

price fixing Secret agreements between representatives of two or more companies to set prices. (11)

price transparency Euro-denominated prices for goods and services that enable consumers and organizational buyers to comparison shop across Europe. (11)

primary data In market research, data gathered through research pertaining to the particular problem, decision, or issue under study. (6)

private international law The body of law that applies to disputes arising from commercial transactions between companies of different nations. (5)

product One of the four Ps of the marketing mix: a good, service, or idea with tangible and/or intangible attributes that collectively create value for a buyer or user. (10)

product adaptation–communication extension strategy A strategy of extending, without change, the basic home-market communications strategy while adapting the product to local use or preference conditions. (10)

product-communication adaptation A dual-adaptation strategy that uses a combination of marketing conditions. (10)

product-communication extension A strategy for pursuing opportunities outside the home market. (10)

product differentiation A product's perceived uniqueness that can serve as a barrier to entry in an industry. In Porter's five forces model, one of the eight barriers to entry that determine the potential threat of new industry entrants. (15)

product extension–communication adaptation strategy The strategy of marketing an identical product by adapting the marketing communications program. (10)

product invention In global marketing, developing new products with the world market in mind. (10)

product market A market defined in terms of a particular product category (e.g., in the automotive industry, "the SUV market," "the sports car market," etc.). (7)

product placement A marketing communication tool that involves a company paying a fee to have one or more products and brand names appear in popular television programs, movies, and other types of performances. (14)

product saturation level The percentage of customers or households that own a product in a particular country market; a measure of market opportunity. (2)

product strategy In personal selling, a sales representative's plan for selecting and positioning products that will satisfy customer needs. The third step in the Strategic/Consultative Selling Model. (14)

product transformation When a product that has been introduced into multiple country markets via a product extension–communication adaptation strategy serves a different function or use than originally intended. (10)

pro forma invoice A document that sets an export/import transaction into motion. The pro forma specifies the amount and the means by which an exporter wants to be paid; also specifies the items to be purchased. (8)

psychographic segmentation The process of assigning people to market segments on the basis of their attitudes, interests, opinions, and lifestyles. (7)

public international law The body of international law that pertains to noncommercial disputes between nations. (5)

publicity Communication about a company or product for which the company does not pay. (13)

public relations (PR) One of four variables in the promotion mix. Within an organization, the department or function responsible for evaluating public opinion about, and attitudes toward, the organization and its products and brands. PR personnel also are responsible for fostering goodwill, understanding, and acceptance among a company's various constituents and the public. (13)

purchasing power parity (PPP) A concept that permits adjustment of national income measurements in various countries to reflect what a unit of each country's currency can actually buy. (2)

put option The right to sell a specified number of foreign currency units at a fixed price, up to the option's expiration date. (2)

quota Government-imposed limit or restriction on the number of units or the total value of a particular product or product category that can be imported. (8)

rational appeal In advertising, an appeal to the target audience's logic and intellect. (13)

reactivity The tendency of research subjects to behave differently because they are being studied. (6)

regiocentric orientation The third level in the EPRG framework: the view that similarities as well as differences characterize specific regions of the world. In global marketing, a regiocentric orientation is evident when a company develops an integrated strategy for a particular geographic area. (1)

regional management center A pattern of organization in which there is an area or regional headquarters as a management layer between the country organization and the international division headquarters. (16)

regional or worldwide product division structure A pattern of organization in which international responsibility shifts from a corporate international division to the product division international departments, which, in turn, shift to total divisional organization. (16)

regulatory environment Governmental and nongovernmental agencies and organizations that enforce laws or establish guidelines for conducting business. (5)

relationship strategy In personal selling, a sales representative's game plan for establishing and maintaining high-quality relationships with prospects and customers. The second step in the Strategic/Consultative Selling Model. (14)

restrictive administrative and technical regulations Regulations that can create barriers to trade; it may take the form of antidumping, size, or safety and health regulations. (8)

ringtone A digital sound file that is an instrumental version of a song or composition. (17)

ring tune A digital sound file of a song or composition featuring the original recording artist. (17)

rules of engagement A strategy for creating competitive advantage that involves breaking these rules and refusing to play by the rules set by industry leaders. (15)

rules of origin A system of certification that verifies the country of origin of a shipment of goods. (3)

sales agent An agent who works under contract rather than as a full-time employee. (14)

sales force automation (SFA) An information technology tool that automates lead assignment, contact follow-up, and other routine tasks associated with personal selling. (6)

sales promotion One of the four elements of the promotion mix. A paid, short-term communication program that adds tangible value to a product or brand. (14)

sampling A sales promotion technique that provides potential customers with the opportunity to try a product or service at no cost. (14)

search The environmental scanning mode characterized by a formal information-gathering activity. (6)

secondary data Existing data in personal files, published sources, and databases. (6)

self-reference criterion (SRC) The unconscious human tendency to interpret the world in terms of one's own cultural experience and values. (4)

selling proposition In advertising, the promise or claim that captures the reason for buying the product or the benefit that product ownership confers. (13)

short message service (SMS) A globally accepted wireless standard for sending alphanumeric messages of up to 160 characters. (17)

single-column tariff A schedule of duties in which the rate applies to imports from all countries on the same basis; the simplest type of tariff. (8)

social values typology A study by Dutch organizational anthropologist Geert Hofstede that classifies national cultures according to five dimensions: individualism versus collectivism, masculinity versus femininity, power distance, uncertainty avoidance, and long-term orientation versus short-term orientation. (4)

sourcing decision A strategic decision that determines whether a company makes a product itself or buys products from other manufacturers as well as where it makes or buys. (8)

Southern African Development Community (SADC) An association whose member states are Angola, Botswana, Democratic Republic of Congo, Lesotho, Malawi, Mauritius, Mozambique, Namibia, Seychelles, South Africa, Swaziland, Tanzania, Zambia, and Zimbabwe. (3)

sovereignty A country's supreme and independent political authority. (5)

spam Unsolicited "junk" e-mail received via the Internet; often sent to a large number of people to promote products or services. (17)

specialty retailer A category of retail operations characterized by a more narrow focus than a department store and offering a relatively narrow merchandise mix aimed at a particular target market. (12)

specific duty A duty expressed as a specific amount of currency per unit of weight, volume, length, or other unit of measurement. (8)

sponsorship A form of marketing communication that involves payment of a fee by a company to have its name associated with a particular event, team or athletic association, or sports facility. (14)

spreadsheet A software application in the form of an electronic ledger that automatically recalculates changes made to figures entered in rows and columns. (17)

standardized (extension) approach The pursuit of a global market opportunity using an extension strategy of minimal marketing mix variation in different countries. (1)

standardized global marketing A target market strategy that calls for creating the same marketing mix for a broad mass market of potential buyers. (7)

strategic alliance A partnership among two or more firms created to minimize risk while maximizing leverage in the marketplace. (9)

Strategic/Consultative Selling Model A five-step framework for approaching the personal selling task: personal selling philosophy, relationship strategy, product strategy, customer strategy, and presentation strategy. (14)

strategic intent A competitive advantage framework developed by strategy experts Gary Hamel and C. K. Prahalad. (15)

streaming media The transmission of combined audio and video content via a broadband network. (17)

streaming video A sequence of moving images sent in compressed form via the Internet and displayed on a computer screen. (17)

subculture Within a culture, a small group of people with their own shared subset of attitudes, beliefs, and values. (4)

supercenter A category of retail operations that combines elements of discount stores and supermarkets in a space that occupies about half the size of a hypermarket. (12)

supermarket A category of retail operations characterized by a departmentalized, single-story retail establishment that offers a variety of food and nonfood items on a self-service basis. (12)

supply chain A group of firms that perform support activities by generating raw materials, converting them into components of finished goods, and making them available to buyers. (12)

survey research Primary data collection via questionnaire-based studies designed to generate qualitative responses, quantitative responses, or both. (6)

switching costs A barrier to entry into an industry created by the need to change suppliers and products. In Porter's five forces model, one of the eight barriers to entry that determine the potential threat of new industry entrants. (15)

switch trading A transaction in which a professional switch trader, switch trading house, or bank steps into a simple barter arrangement or other countertrade arrangement in which one of the parties is not willing to accept all the goods received in the transaction. (11)

targeting The process of evaluating market segments and focusing marketing efforts on a country, region, or group of people. (7)

tariffs The rules, rate schedules (duties), and regulations of individual countries affecting goods that are imported. (8)

telematics A car's ability to exchange information about the vehicle's location or mechanical performance via a wireless Internet connection. (17)

temporary surcharge Surcharges introduced from time to time to provide additional protection for local industry and, in particular, in response to balance-of-payments deficits. (8)

tiered branding A strategy in which a corporate name is combined with a product brand name; also called combination or umbrella branding. (10)

trade deficit A negative number in the balance of payments showing that the value of a country's imports exceeds the value of its exports. (2)

trade mission A state- or federally sponsored show outside the home country organized around a product, a group of products, an industry, or an activity at which company personnel can learn about new markets as well as competitors. (8)

trade sales promotion Promotion designed to increase product availability in distribution channels. (14)

trade show A gathering of company representatives organized around a product, a group of products, or an industry, at which company personnel can meet with prospective customers and gather competitor intelligence. (8)

trade surplus A positive number in the balance of payments showing that the value of a country's exports exceeds the value of its imports. (2)

trademark A distinctive mark, motto, device, or emblem that a manufacturer affixes to a particular product or package to distinguish it from goods produced by other manufacturers. (5)

transaction exposure In global finance, the type of risk that is created when a company's sales or purchases of products or services are denominated in a foreign currency. (11)

transfer pricing The pricing of goods, services, and intangible property bought and sold by operating units or divisions of a company doing business with an affiliate in another jurisdiction. (2)

transistor A "solid state amplifier" that replaced vacuum tubes in electronics products; it was a milestone in the digital revolution. (17)

transnational company A company exhibiting a geocentric orientation that pursues marketing opportunities in all parts of the world. However, a transnational company differs from a global company by fully integrating and coordinating two strategies: both sourcing products from a variety of different countries and serving multiple country markets across most world regions. (1)

transportation The aspect of physical distribution that involves moving or transferring goods from one location to another. (12)

transportation mode In physical distribution, the particular means by which goods are shipped. The six main transportation modes are rail, water, truck, air, pipeline, and Internet. (12)

Triad The three regions of Japan, Western Europe, and the United States, which represented the dominant economic centers of the world. (2)

two-column tariff General duties plus special duties indicating reduced rates determined by tariff negotiations with other countries. (8)

uncertainty avoidance In Hofstede's social values framework, the extent to which members of a culture are uncomfortable with unclear, ambiguous, or unstructured situations. (4)

upper-middle-income country A country with GNP per capita between $2,996 and $9,266. (2)

usage rate In behavioral market segmentation, an assessment of the extent to which a person uses a product or service. (7)

user status In behavioral market segmentation, an assessment of whether a person is a present user, potential user, nonuser, former user, etc. (7)

value A customer's perception of a firm's product or service offering in terms of the ratio of benefits (product, place, promotion) relative to price. This ratio can be represented by the value equation: $V = B/P$. (1)

value chain The various activities that a company performs (e.g., research and development, manufacturing, marketing, physical distribution, and logistics) in order to create value for customers. (1)

value equation $V = B/P$, where V stands for "perceived value," B stands for "product, price, and place," and P stands for "price." (1)

value network The cost structure in a particular industry that dictates the margins needed to achieve profitability. A broadly-defined industry (e.g., computers) may have parallel value networks, each with its own metrics of value. (17)

values In culture, enduring beliefs or feelings that a specific mode of conduct is personally or socially preferable to another mode of conduct. (4)

variable import levies A system of levies applied to certain categories of imported agricultural products. (8)

warehouse club A form of retailing that offers low merchandise prices in a no-frills format. Consumers typically pay a nominal fee to join the club and gain entrance to the store. (12)

warehousing The aspect of physical distribution that involves the storage of goods. (12)

wireless connectivity Technology that allows a computer, cell phone, PDA, or other digital device to access the Internet without using a cable connection. (17)

wireless fidelity (Wi-Fi) Technology based on a low-power radio signal that permits access to the Internet from a laptop computer or PDA when the user is within range of a base station transmitter ("hot spot"). (17)

World Trade Organization (WTO) The successor to the General Agreement on Tariffs and Trade. (3)

CREDITS

CHAPTER 1

Page 3: Courtesy of China Photos/Getty Images, Inc. Page 6: Courtesy of Ryan Pyle. Page 8: Courtesy of Jordan Fischer/Greensburg Daily News. Page 12: Courtesy of HSBC Bank. Page 13: Courtesy of The Coca Cola Company. Page 25: Reprinted Courtesy of Caterpillar, Inc. Page 31: "Labor Day" Courtesy of Mike Thompson/Copley News Service. Page 35: Courtesy of AP Wide World Photos. Page 39: Courtesy of David Hartung/Getty Images, Inc.

CHAPTER 2

Page 41: Courtesy of Alexander Nemenov/AFP/Getty Images, Inc. Page 46: Courtesy of AP Wide World Photos. Page 48: Courtesy of Tim Hall/Getty Images, Inc.–Photodisc. Page 53: Courtesy of CITGO. Page 54: Courtesy of Alfredo Sosa/The Christian Science Monitor © 2006 www.csmonitor.com. All rights reserved. Page 56: Courtesy of William B. Plowman/AP Wide World Photos. Page 56: Courtesy of Scott Eells/Redux Pictures. Page 57: Courtesy of Antonio Regalado/Dow Jones & Company, Inc./Reprinted with permission of the Wall Street Journal, © 2007 Dow Jones & Company, Inc. All Rights Reserved Worldwide. Page 58: Courtesy of Dmitry Astakhove./AFP/Getty Images, Inc. Page 60: Courtesy of AP Wide World Photos. Page 71: Courtesy of the Vietnam Emabssy.

CHAPTER 3

Page 77: Courtesy of Jung Yeon-je/AFP/Getty Images, Inc. Page 88: Courtesy of Alexandre Meneghini/AP Wide World Photos. Page 95: Courtesy of Paul O'Briscoll/Bloomberg News/Landov LLC. Page 100: Courtesy of Kamran Jebreili/AP Wide World Photos. Page 108: Courtesy of AP Wide World Photos.

CHAPTER 4

Page 111: Courtesy of Kahled Desouki/Agence France Presse/Getty Images. Page 114: Courtesy of Rachel Donnan. Page 114: Courtesy of Hugo Philpott/Getty Images, Inc–Liaison. Page 115: Courtesy of Bonile Bam/Getty Images, Inc. Page 117: Courtesy of Frederic J. Brown/Getty Images, Inc. Page 120: Under permission by V&S Vin & Sprit AB (publ)". Absolut Country of Sweden Vodka & Logo, Absolut, Absolut Bottle Design and Absolut Calligraphy Are Trademarks Owned By V&S Vin & Sprit Ab (Publ). © 2007 V&S Vin & Sprit Ab (publ). Page 121: Courtesy of China Photos/Getty Images, Inc. Page 124: Courtesy of Telefonica USA, Inc. Page 126: Courtesy of Peter Menzel Photography. Page 133: Courtesy of MN Chan/Getty Images, Inc. Page 139: Courtesy of Gurinder Osan/AP Wide World Photos. Page 142: Courtesy of The Image Works. Page 142: Courtesy of Cafedirect. Page 143: Courtesy of Jerown Kramer/Getty Images, Inc.

CHAPTER 5

Page 147: Courtesy of Geert Vanden Wijngaert/AP Wide World Photos. Page 149: Courtesy of ExxonMobil Historical Collection, The Center for American History, The University of Texas at Austin. Page 154: Courtesy of U. N./Corbis/Sygma. Page 157: Courtesy of Lee Snider/The Image Works. Page 159: Courtesy of Champagne, USA. Page 160: Reprinted with permission from the World

Intellectual Property Organization, which owns the copyright. Page 161: Courtesy of AP Wide World Photos. Page 162: Courtesy of Eugene Hoshiko/AP Wide World Photos. Page 163: Courtesy of DuPont/Ogilvy & Mather/"Phase VI EVA Spacesuit Gloves created by ILC Dover to protect astronauts". Page 166: Courtesy of Thierry Roge/Reuters/Landov LLC. Page 168: Used with permission by AMD. Page 171: Courtesy of Yuri Kadobnov/AFP/Getty Images, Inc. Page 180: Courtesy of Alejandro Ernesto/Landov LLC.

CHAPTER 6
Page 185: Courtesy of Chiaki Tsukumo/AP Wide World Photos. Page 192: Courtesy of China Photos/Getty Images, Inc. Page 202: Courtesy of Odd Andersen/AFP/Getty Images, Inc. Page 217: Courtesy of Whirlpool Corporation.

CHAPTER 7
Page 221: Courtesy of AP Wide World Photos. Page 230: Courtesy of Paul Young/Reuters/Landov LLC. Page 235: Courtesy of Oleg Nikishin/Getty Images, Inc–Liaison. Page 239: Courtesy of Ng Han Guan/AP Wide World Photos. Page 246: Courtesy of Charles Pertwee/Bloomberg News/Landov LLC. Page 249: Courtesy of Seiko Corporation of America. Page 250: Courtesy of Unilever. Page 251: Courtesy of Audi of America, Inc. Page 252: Courtesy of Apple Computers, Inc. Page 255: Courtesy of American Honda Motor Co. Inc. Page 256: Courtesy of Ellen Elmendorp.

CHAPTER 8
Page 259: Courtesy of Richard Vogel/AP Wide World Photos. Page 265: Courtesy of Dean Conger/Corbis/Bettmann. Page 266: Courtesy of Oscar Sosa/AP Wide World Photos. Page 269: Courtesy of Babu/Reuters/Landov LLC. Page 275: Courtesy of Barry Johnson/Getty Images, Inc–Liaison. Page 281: Courtesy of CRASTO/Reuters/Corbis/Bettmann. Page 281: Courtesy of Cartoon Features Syndicate. Page 288: Courtesy of Bill Butcher Ltd.

CHAPTER 9
Page 293: Courtesy of Cancan Chu/Getty Images, Inc. Page 294: Courtesy of The Image Works. Page 297: Courtesy of Doctor's Association, Inc. Page 298: Courtesy of Hyundai Motor America. Page 302: Courtesy of Sony Ericsson. Page 305: Courtesy of Jason Lee/Reuters/Landov LLC. Page 305: Courtesy of Cartoon Features Syndicate. Page 309: Courtesy of Getty Images, Inc. Page 323: Courtesy of Ford Motor Company. Page 323: Courtesy of Luke MacGregor/Reuters/Landov LLC. Page 324: SABMiller PLC.

CHAPTER 10
Page 327: Courtesy of Jae C. Hong/AP Wide World Photos. Page 332: Courtesy of Stephen Cherin/Getty Images, Inc. Page 333: Courtesy of NucorCorp Steel Division. Page 336: Courtesy of Robert Nickelsberg/Getty Images, Inc. Page 339: Courtesy of David Turnley/Corbis Images.com. Page 342: Courtesy of The Embassy of the Republic of Slovenia. Page 359: Courtesy of Katsumi Kasahara/AP Wide World Photos. Page 360: Courtesy of Chitose Suzuki/AP Wide World Photos.

CHAPTER 11
Page 363: Courtesy of Stephen Shaver/Bloomberg News/Landov LLC. Page 369: Courtesy of Morton Beebe/Corbis–NY/© Morton Beebe/Corbis. All Rights Reserved. Page 372: Courtesy of TWPhoto/Corbis–NY/© (Photographer)/Corbis. All Rights Reserved. Page 378: Courtesy of Dibyangshu Sarkar/Getty

Images, Inc. Page 387: Courtesy of Stand Up for Steel. Page 394: Courtesy of Landov LLC.

CHAPTER 12

Page 399: Courtesy of Guang Niu/Getty Images, Inc. Page 402: Courtesy of Magdalena Gutierrez/ Kashmir Servicos Culturais LTDA. Page 404: Courtesy of Hufton & Crow/Alamy Images. Page 407: Courtesy of Dell/© 2007 Dell Inc. All Rights Reserved. Page 412: Courtesy of Eugene Hoshiko/AP Wide World Photos. Page 417: Courtesy of Richard Drew/AP Wide World Photos. Page 421: Courtesy of Corbis/SABA Press Photos, Inc. Page 425: Courtesy of FEDEX Corporation. Page 426: Courtesy of Carlos Barria/Reuters/Landov LLC. Page 431: Courtesy of Mark H. Milstien/Northfoto/NewsCom. Page 432: Courtesy of Rolf Vennenbernd/DPA/Landov LLC.

CHAPTER 13

Page 435: Courtesy of STR/AFP/NewsCom. Page 441: Courtesy of Pioneer Hi-Bred International. Page 456: Courtesy of Giblin & James/BASF. Page 458: Courtesy of Raveendran/AFP/Getty Images, Inc. Page 460: Courtesy of Chuck Kennedy/NewsCom. Page 466: Courtesy of EUTERS/Adidas/HO/Landov.

CHAPTER 14

Page 469: Courtesy of Feature Photo Service/AP Wide World Photos. Page 470: Courtesy of Bloomberg News/Landov LLC. Page 483: Courtesy of Bridgestone Firestone North American Tire, LLC. Firestone Agricultural Tire. Page 484: Courtesy of Harry Maynard/ZEFA/Corbis–NY/© (Photographer)/Corbis. All Rights Reserved. Page 490: Courtesy of Fabian Bimmer/AP Wide World Photos. Page 492: Courtesy of Ian Waldie/Reuters/Landov LLC. Page 493: Courtesy of Alamy Images. Page 494: Courtesy of Itsuo Inouye/AP Wide World Photos. Page 494: Courtesy of Jason Lee/ Reuters/Landov LLC. Page 496: Courtesy of Jasper Juinen/AP Wide World Photos. Page 497: Courtesy of Starstock/Photoshot/NewsCom. Page 498: Courtesy of Cartoon Features Syndicate.

CHAPTER 15

Page 503: Courtesy of Mark Antman/The Image Works. Page 506: Courtesy of Teri Stratford/Six-Cats Research Inc./ © Teri Stratford. All rights reserved. Page 510: Courtesy of Siemens Corporation. Page 511: Courtesy of Klipsch Audio Technologies. Page 512: Courtesy of Amit Bhargava/Bloomberg News/Landov LLC. Page 514: Courtesy of Chung Sung-Jun/Getty Images, Inc. Page 515: Courtesy of Marcelo del Pozo/Reuters/Corbis Images.com. Page 524: Courtesy of Kuni/AP Wide World Photos. Page 527: Courtesy of Swatch. Page 533: Courtesy of James Leynse/Corbis–NY/© James Leynse/Corbis. All Rights Reserved. Page 534: Courtesy of AP Wide World Photos.

CHAPTER 16

Page 537: Courtesy of Koji Sasahara/AP Wide World Photos. Page 541: Courtesy of Manish Swarup/AP Wide World Photos. Page 561: Courtesy of Pallava Bagla/Corbis–NY/© James Leynse/Corbis. All Rights Reserved. Page 552: Courtesy of Marcus Brandt/Getty Images, Inc. Page 559: Reprinted with the permission of The Timberland Company © 2006 The Timberland Company. Page 565: Courtesy of Francois Mori/AP Wide World Photos. Page 565: Courtesy of Lord Saatchi, "Battle for Survival Favours the Simplest," Financial Times (January 5, 1998). Page 567: Courtesy of Johnson & Johnson. Page 559: Courtesy of Johnson & Johnson.

CHAPTER 17

Page 569: Courtesy of Kim Kyang-Hoon/Reuters/Landov LLC. Page 572: Courtesy of Louisa Gouliamaki/AFP/Getty Images, Inc. Page 583: Courtesy of Paul Sakuma/AP Wide World Photos. Page 586: Courtesy of MEIDNEUX/SIPA Press. Page 589: Courtesy of Katsumi Kasahara/AP Wide World Photos. Page 590: Courtesy of Yahoo! Inc. Page 593: Courtesy of AP Wide World Photos. Page 594: Courtesy of IAC InterActive Corporation.

AUTHOR/NAME INDEX

de la Vega, Ralph, 587
de Leon, Rudy, 263
de Lome, Enrique Dupuy, 476
Dean, Jason, 39, 55, 368, 557, 576, 589, 593
Deane, Daniela, 222
Defforey, Louis, 224
DeGeorge, Gail, 182
Delaney, Kevin J., 433, 576, 595
Delkin, Jeff, 447
Dell, Michael, 406
della Cava, Marco R., 139
Deming, W. E., 515
Dengel, Birgit, 299
Deogun, Nikhil, 11
DePalma, Anthony, 300
Dholakia, Nikhilesh, 208
Di Benedetto, Anthony C., 122, 452
Dickenson, Larry, 564
Dickie, Jim, 187
Dickie, Mure, 365, 472, 593, 594
Dickson, Richard, 145
Dierks, Michael P., 169
Diller, Barry, 57, 594, 595
Dillon, Sam, 182
DiMasi, Joseph A., 26
DiMassimo, Mark, 38
Dinh, Do Duc, 72
Doanh, Le Dang, 73
Dobychin, Vyacheslav, 365
Doerken, Uwe, 281
Dolan, Kerry A., 202
Domzal, Teresa J., 250
Doney, Patricia M., 45
Donocki, Tadeusz, 398
Doorley, Thomas, 316
Dorf, Bob, 487
Dormann, Jürgen, 8
Dorrell, Beth, 371, 422
Douglas, Susan P., 9
Dovgan, Vladimir, 233
Doz, Yves L., 310, 311
Draper, Matthew, 207
Dreazen, Yochi J., 378
Drossos, Basil, 22
Drucker, Jesse, 585
Drucker, Peter F., 200, 201, 529
Duncan, Thomas R., 435
Dunne, Nancy, 151
Duplantis, David, 189
Duran, José Luis, 431
Dutta, Shantanu, 384
Dvorak, Phred, 9, 309, 330, 366, 544
Dyer, Geoff, 341

E

Eberhardt, Joe, 381
Eckrodt, Rolf, 539
Edmondson, Gail, 396
Edmonson, R. G., 280
Edmonston, Jack, 207
Edwards, Francis, 491
Edwards, Trevor, 435
Eggleton, Art, 182
Ehren, Harald, 245
Einhorn, Bruce, 39
Einstein, Albert, 113
Eisner, Michael D., 132, 133
Eizenstat, Stuart E., 182
Elgin, Ben, 594
Elinder, Eric, 439
Elkin, Tobi, 232
Elliot, Stuart, 38, 233
Ellis, Paul, 530
Ellison, Sarah, 235, 425, 432, 472, 579
Emmerson, Peter, 189
Enders, Thomas, 566
Enrico, Dottie, 451
Enright, Michael, 518
Erdem, S. Altan, 131
Erlich, Joseph, 73, 262
Ernest, Bill, 133
Everett, Stephen E., 435
Everke, Cornelius, 292

F

Fackler, Martin, 330
Fairclough, Gordon, 324, 447
Farrell, Diana, 7
Fatt, Arther C., 221
Feder, Barnaby J., 433
Feils, Dorothee J., 175
Felix, Prince, 130
Fetterman, Mindy, 15
Fettig, Jeff M., 218
Finney, Megan, 414
Finnigan, David, 145
Fiorina, Carleton "Carly" S., 537
Fischer, Jordan, 8
Fisher, George, 211, 228
Fishman, Charles, 430
FitzGerald, Niall, 191
Flagg, Michael, 412
Flask, A. Paul, 122
Fleming, Charles, 173
Fletcher, Pascal, 182
Flynn, Lauren J., 366
Ford, John B., 483, 484
Ford, Richard, 231
Forelle, Charles, 220

Forgeard, Noël, 566
Forman, Craig, 324
Fortes, Isabela, 56
Foster, George, 389
Foster, Lauren, 189, 223, 403, 535
Foulkes, Nicholas, 361
Fournier, Marcel, 224
Fowler, Geoffrey A., 196, 348, 445, 446, 447, 467, 470, 473, 493
Fram, Eugene H., 207
Francés, Antonio, 518
Frank, Robert, 122, 222
Frank, Stephen E., 450
Frankfort, Lew, 184, 185, 189
Fraone, Gina, 188
Freeman, Sholnn, 256
Freidheim, Cyrus, 319
Fresco, Paolo, 538
Freston, Tom, 257
Friedland, Jonathan, 413
Friedman, Thomas L., 6, 25, 29, 47, 457, 571
Friedman, Vanessa, 189
Friedrich, Jacqueline, 118
Frisby, Michael K., 103
Frith, Katherine Toland, 131
Fritsch, Peter, 51, 143
Fry, Ron, 581
Fryer, Bronwyn, 186
Fujimoto, Noboru, 329
Fuller, Melville, 147
Fuyuno, Ichiko, 145

G

Gallacher, Suzanne, 230
Gallo, Carlo, 171
Gallois, Louis, 566
Galloni, Alessandra, 396, 511
Gapper, John, 252, 360, 433
Garber, Don, 6
Garfield, Bob, 325
Gargan, Edward A., 73
Garrahan, Matthew, 132, 467
Gates, Bill, 570
Gatsoulis, Joyce-Ann, 446
Gelfond, Rich, 369
Gerlach, Michael L., 315
Gershman, Carl, 182
Ghazanfar, S. M., 391, 392
Ghoshal, Sumantra, 242, 341, 351, 529, 530, 542, 543
Ghosn, Carlos, 539
Ghymn, Kyung-I, 115
Gibson, Richard, 38, 117, 296, 304, 306

Gidwitz, Ronald J., 304
Gifford, Kathie Lee, 288
Gillis, Malcolm, 225
Gilly, Mary C., 452
Gilson, Ronald J., 315
Gladwell, Malcolm, 136
Gnepa, Tahi J., 267
Godin, Robert, 578
Goizueta, Roberto, 539
Golab, Jan, 145
Gold, Jack, 211
Golden, Peggy A., 45
Goldman, Kevin, 74, 467
Goldman, Marshall, 43
Goldschlager, Seth, 448
Goldsmith, Charles, 257
Gordon, Bernard, 91
Gould, Stephen J., 435, 497
Govindarajan, Vijay, 7
Grabner-Krauter, Sonja, 497
Grabowski, Henry G., 26
Graham, Jefferson, 534
Graham, John L., 123
Grant, Jeremy, 38, 245, 256,
    338, 545
Grant, Peter, 590, 595
Grasee, Michael, 491
Grassley, Charles, 74
Gray, Steven, 38, 299, 344
Green, Mark, 39
Green, Peter S., 30
Green, Robert T., 452
Greenberg, Jack M., 37
Greenberger, Robert S., 182, 227
Greenbury, Sir Richard, 416
Greene, Marilyn, 74
Greenhouse, Steven, 290
Greider, William, 16, 41, 46, 48,
    50, 392
Grein, Andreas F., 435
Gresser, Charis, 295
Griffith, Victoria, 332
Griswold, Daniel, 78
Grossman, Laurie M., 432
Grover, Ronald, 595
Grunig, Larissa A., 462
Guerrera, Francesco, 423, 534
Guido, G., 97
Gupta, Anil, 7
Gupta, Pola B., 497
Gupwell, Yvonne, 72
Gurría, José Ángel, 172
Guth, Robert A., 9, 374, 538, 594
Gutierrez, Carlos, 305
Gutzman, Alexis D., 579,
    581, 582

H

Hagenbaugh, Barbara, 284
Haider, Mahtab, 51
Hakim, Danny, 324
Halder, Dipankar, 40
Hall, Edward T., 125, 501
Hall, Emma, 440
Hallett, Andrew Hughes, 89
Halliday, Jean, 560
Hallinan, Joseph T., 294
Halpert, Julie Edelson, 320
Halstead, L. Lindsay, 323
Hamel, Gary, 309, 310, 311, 515,
    518, 540, 541
Hamilton, David P., 301
Hammond, Allen, 54
Handler, Ruth, 143
Handy, Charles, 449
Hansell, Saul, 21
Hansen, Finn, 110
Hansen, Ronald W., 26
Harding, James, 202
Hardy, Quentin, 201
Harford, Tim, 143
Harich, Katrin R., 453, 454
Harleman, Peter, 460
Harney, Alexandra, 428
Harnischfeger, Uta, 467
Harper, Lucinda, 378
Harris, Philip R., 501
Hart, Stuart L., 55
Hassan, Salah S., 221
Hatch, Mary Jo, 535
Hatfield, Joe, 192
Hauser, John R., 208
Hawes, Aubrey, 252
Hawkins, Lee, Jr., 21, 239, 550
Hawkins, Tony, 103, 105
Hayek, Georges Nicolas, Jr., 527
Hayek, Nicolas, 282, 360, 361
Healy, James R., 324
Heberger, Roy A., Jr., 123
Heenan, David A., 309, 310
Hegmann, Gerhard, 299
Hein, Kenneth, 192
Helliker, Kevin, 38, 361
Helms, Jesse, 181
Henderson, Angelo B., 314
Henderson, Bruce, 505
Henderson, David, 145
Hengst, Rainer, 488
Hennequin, Denis, 38
Herbert, Bob, 290
Herman, David, 331
Hershman, Michael, 59
Hershorn, Mark, 492

Herzegova, Eva, 451
Hewett, Kelly, 115
Higgins, Andrew, 130, 152
Hill, Jeffrey, 235
Hille, Kathrin, 330, 340
Hilsenrath, Jon E., 42, 264, 491
Hirt, Martin, 39
Hisey, Pete, 377
Hitt, Greg, 43, 425
Hof, Rob, 593, 594
Hoff, Edward J., 13
Hofstede, Geert, 111, 112, 126,
    127, 128
Hollinger, Peggy, 384, 432
Holman, Michael, 103, 105
Holness, Stewart, 188
Holt, Douglas B., 332
Holusha, John, 245, 312
Honeycutt, Earl D., Jr., 483, 484
Hood, Marlow, 118
Hooper-Greenhill, Orlando, 437
Hopkins, Jim, 572, 584
Hopp, Dietmar, 188
Horngren, Charles T., 389
Horovitz, Bruce, 38
Horovitz, Jacques, 416, 418
Houlder, Vanessa, 188
Howard, Donald G., 274
Howard, Theresa, 467, 513
Howell, Llewellyn D., 150
Hudgins, Edward L., 265
Hudson, Kris, 421
Huff, Lenard C., 476
Hughes, Owen, 257
Hulme, Virginia A., 402
Humbert, Gustav, 566
Hunt, John, 549
Hutton, Bethan, 38, 131, 186, 420
Hutzler, Charles, 374
Hwang, Suein L., 237
Hymowitz, Carol, 257, 558

I

Ibison, Bob, 588
Ibison, David, 130, 535
Ibrahim, Abala, 144
Ibrahim, Youssef M., 425
Ibuka, Masaru, 295
Iger, Robert A., 133
Ihlwan, Moon, 593
Illingworth, J. Davis, 200
Inamori, Kazuo, 406
Ingrassia, Lawrence, 81
Innocenti, Nicol Deglil, 325
Inoue, Masahiro, 593
Insana, Ron, 228, 281, 285, 369

Moyer, Kerry, 510
Mulally, Alan, 564
Mullaney, Timothy J., 595
Mullich, Joe, 461
Munk, Nina, 15
Murayama, Hiroshi, 310
Murdoch, Rupert, 362, 491
Murdock, George P., 112
Murjani, Mohan, 238
Murphy, Clarence, 405
Murphy, Michael, 473
Murray, Sarah, 296
Murray, Shailagh, 81
Mussey, Dagmar, 467
Myerson, Allen R., 290

N

Nagle, Patrick, 585
Nakamoto, Michiyo, 330,
    340, 360
Narisetti, Raju, 539, 574
Nash, Roland, 150
Naughton, Keith, 300
Nayak, Ranganath, 334, 366, 553
Nayak, Sapna, 36, 223
Neff, Jack, 433
Negroponte, Nicholas, 56
Nelson, Emily, 205, 235, 403, 548
Nelson, Mark M., 156
Nessman, Karl, 461
Ning, Susan, 385
Niwa, Uichiro, 538
Nixon, Richard, 170
Nomani, Asra Q., 290
Nonaka, Ikujiro, 212
Nooy, Indra, 541
Normann, Richard, 423
Noyce, Robert, 569
Nuttall, Chris, 330, 340, 360,
    584, 593

O

O'Connell, Pamela Licalzi, 572
O'Connell, Vanessa, 347, 440, 578
O'Donnell, Jayne, 15
O'Grady, Mary Anastasia, 49,
    182, 291
O'Malley, Gavin, 435
O'Neill, Finbarr, 345
O'Toole, John, 445, 450
Ogura, Nobumasa, 403
Ohmae, Kenichi, 11, 60, 309, 544
Ohno, Taiichi, 553
Okui, Toshifumi, 245
Olins, Rufus, 416
Ollila, Jorma, 539, 541, 574

Ono, Yumiko, 38, 120, 164, 235,
    300, 403
Oram, Roderick, 470
Ortego, Joseph, 158
Orwall, Bruce, 8, 403
Osborne, Magz, 222, 257
Oster, Patrick, 219
Ouaki, Fabien, 124
Ouchi, William, 544
Owen, David, 396

P

Palepu, Krishna G., 352, 422
Palmer, Kimberly, 349
Palmer, Maija, 360
Panke, Helmut, 9, 240, 246, 329
Pant, Muktesh, 377
Parker, Ginny, 189
Parker-Pope, Tara, 247, 405
Parkes, Christopher, 204
Parmar, Arundhati, 205
Passariello, Christina, 223, 238, 343
Paterson, James H., 245
Patitz, Tatjana, 490
Patrick, Aaron O., 492, 595
Paul, Vivek, 51
Pawle, John, 199
Pearl, Daniel, 391
Peckter, Kerry, 538, 542
Pecotich, Anthony, 73
Peers, Martin, 8
Pennar, Karen, 148
Pennefather, James, 492
Penteado, Claudia, 257
Pentz, Michelle, 492
Peppers, Don, 487
Pereira, Joseph, 360, 467, 535
Perkins, Jerry, 182
Perlmutter, Howard, 17, 309, 310
Perot, Ross, 61
Perry, Sir Michael, 356
Peterson, George, 255
Petrecca, Laura, 467
Petsch, Greg, 283
Phan, Michel, 145
Phillips, Don, 24
Phillips, Michael M., 103, 374
Phuc, Vu Tien, 72
Piech, Ferdinand, 552
Pierpoint, Stephen, 467
Piirto, Rebecca, 231
Pines, Daniel, 169, 171
Pinkston,Will, 361
Pirko, Tom, 560
Pischetsrieder, Bernd, 552
Platinin, Sergei, 233

Polegato, Mario Moretti, 161
Polgreen, Lydia, 130
Politkovskaya, Anna, 171
Pondy, Louis R., 337, 338
Pope, Kyle, 93
Popeil, Ron, 491
Porter, Eduardo, 237
Porter, Michael E., 7, 503, 504, 505,
    508, 511, 512, 520, 530, 531
Posner, Michael, 288
Potacki, Joseph, 474
Power, Stephen, 68, 361, 367
Prahalad, C. K., 54, 70, 310, 311,
    515, 518, 540, 541
Prestowitz, Clyde, 317, 318
Price, Christopher, 581
Pringle, David, 25, 325, 539,
    574, 588
Pritchard, Marc, 472
Proctor, Paul, 549
Prokesch, Steven, 324
Protzman, Ferdinand, 361
Prystay, Cris, 206, 229, 489
Pucik, Vladimir, 543
Putin, Vladimir, 40, 43, 58, 150,
    152, 171
Pynder, Richard, 163

Q

Qinghong, Zeng, 133
Quelch, John A., 13, 332, 471, 577
Quinlan, Joseph, 388
Quinlan, Michael R., 37
Quintanilla, Carl, 120, 219
Quraeshi, Zahir, 156, 457

R

Raghavan, Anita, 8, 165
Rahman, Bayan, 400
Rai, Saritha, 38, 40, 59, 223
Ramachandran, K., 229
Ramirez, Rafael, 423
Ramstad, Evan, 120, 309, 330,
    472, 570
Rangan, U. Srinivasa, 23, 307, 309,
    313, 519
Raphael, Therese, 182
Rappoport, Carla, 317, 318
Rappoport, Jon, 497
Ratliff, William, 72
Ravaud, René, 312
Rawsthorn, Alice, 97, 120,
    167, 229
Ray, Alastair, 400
Reagan, Ronald, 170
Redstone, Sumner, 257

SUBJECT/ORGANIZATION INDEX

Bangladesh, 51
Banner ads, 579
Barbie, 143–145
Bargaining power of buyers, 505–506
Bargaining power of suppliers, 507
Barter, 390–391
BASF, advertising, 456
Bath & Body Works, competition with Body Shop, 249, 419
Bayer, 167
Bayerische Motoren Werke. See BMW
Behavior segmentation, 232–234
Beliefs, 112
    aesthetics, 114–117
    dietary preferences, 117–118
    religion, 113–114
Benefit segmentation, 234–235
Benetton, "United Colors of Benetton" slogan, 250, 253, 459
BERI (Business Environment Risk Intelligence), 150
Bertelsmann AG, 552
Bethlehem Steel, 169
Big emerging markets (BEMs), 50
Big idea, 445
Big Mac Index, 66
Bill of exchange, 278
Billboards, 492–494
Blockbuster Video
    as a category killer, 417
    entry in Japan, 206
Bluetooth, 585
Blu-ray DVD players in Sony PS3, 359–360
BMW, 9
    brand strength, 329
    positioning, 248
    targeting, 240, 246
Body Shop, competition with Bath & Body Works, 249, 419
Boeing, 21, 24
    global strategic partnership with Japan, 312–314
    versus Airbus, 564–566
Bottom of the pyramid (BOP) markets, 54
BP PLC, 172
    corporate social responsibility, 560
Brand equity, 329
Brand extensions, 334
Brand image, 329

Brands, 328–329
    advertising agencies, 444
    co-branding, 333
    combination/tiered branding, 333
    country-of-origin, 341–342
    definition of, 328
    development of global brands, 335–337
    global, 331–335
    global vs. local, 337–341
    international, 331
    local, 330–331
    product/brand matrix, 335
    world's most valuable brands, 335
Brazil
    antitrust, 164
    Bridgestone Firestone Brazil, customer service, 483
    economy, 52
    Nestlé competitors, 57
    Nestlé distribution, 402
Bribery, 169–173
BRIC (Brazil, Russia, India, and China), 40
    product markets, vs. United States and EU, 352
    stages of economic development. See Stages of economic development
    supplier base and infrastructure/logistics, vs. United States and EU, 422
Bridgestone/Firestone
    customer service in Brazil, 483
    negative publicity, 458
BRL Hardy, 242
Broadband, 583–584
Budweiser, 161
Burberry, 3
Business Environment Risk Intelligence (BERI), 150
Business-to-business marketing (b-to-b or B2B), 400
Business-to-consumer marketing (b-to-c or B2C), 400
Buy American Act of 1933, 267
Byrd Amendment, 385

C

CADE (Administrative Council of Economic Defense), 164
CAF (currency adjustment factor), 372
Call centers, 280–283

Call option, 68
Campbell soups
    benefit segmentation, 234
    market research, 212
CAN (Andean Community), 86–87
Canada
    banning of MMT, 153
    Imax Corporation, 369
CAP (Common Agricultural Policy), 264
Capital account, 62
Caribbean Basin Initiative (CBI), 90
Caribbean Community and Common Market (CARICOM), 89–90
Carrefour hypermarkets, 431–432
Cartel, 167
Catalogs, 489–491
Category killers, 413, 417
Caterpillar, 13, 27
    Canada-Chile free trade area, 79
    currency fluctuation problems in 1980s, 478
CEFTA (Central European Free Trade Association), 98–99
Celebrities, and product placement, 495–496
Cell phones
    Bluetooth, 585
    cameras, 573–574
    emerging markets, 336, 339
    mobile commerce (m-commerce), 585
    mobile gaming, 588
    ringtones, 587–588
    smart phones, 586–588
    Telefónica, 124
Cemex, 192
Censorship of Rolling Stones in China, 46
Central America, Free Trade Area of the Americas (FTAA), 90, 108
Central American Integration System (SICA), 84–85
Central European Free Trade Association (CEFTA), 98–99
Centrally planned capitalism, 46–50
Centrally planned socialism, 45–46
CETs (common external tariffs), 79
CFR (cost and freight), 371
CFTA (U.S.-Canada Free Trade Agreement), 82
Chaebol, 318–319

Champagne, proposed restriction
of name usage, 159
Chance, role in competitive
environment, 524–525
Channel of distribution, 398
consumer products and services,
401–405
establishing, 407–410
industrial products, 405–406
objectives of, 399–400
terminology and structure of,
400–401
working with channel
intermediaries, 407–410
Chapter 89, Harmonized Tariff
System (HTS), 270–271
Characteristics of
innovations, 135
Chase Manhattan bank, global
consumer culture
positioning, 252
Cherry picking, 409
Chevron, 29
Chile, expropriation of copper
companies, 154
China
Antidumping and Antisubsidy
Regulations in March
1997, 385
antiglobalization sentiment
in America, 31
balance of payments, 63
centrally planned socialism,
46–47
Coca-Cola's sponsorship
of Beijing Olympics, 494
devaluation of yuan, 65
eBay, 593
economy, 52
exports, 63–64
FedEx, 425
furniture exports, 264–265
growth of exports, 262
Home Depot acquisition of
HomeWay, 305
Internet usage, 576
joint ventures, 300–301
Lenovo Group, 468–469, 472
local brands, strength of, 331
localizing ad executions, 447
marketing of Scotch whiskey,
434, 437
need for stronger PR, 463
normal trade relations
(NTR), 271
population segmentation, 228

Procter & Gamble shampoo
sampling, 473
segment size and growth
potential, 238
South African
Breweries/SABMiller in
China, 324–325
Starbucks in Forbidden
City, 293
strength of currency, 74–75
targeting of Olympics
visitors, 239
tariffs on shoe exports to
Europe, 258, 262
Tobacco advertising
regulation, 446
Wal-Mart market research, 191
Chinese Value Survey
(CVS), 128
Chrysler, 16
CIF (cost, insurance, freight)
named port, 371
Citicorp, 21
Civil-law country, 155
Click-through rates, 579
Cluster analysis, 209
Coach, 184, 189
Co-branding, 333
Coca-Cola, 10–13, 15
brands, 329–330
global product and brand, 337
India, 47
Minute Maid, 7
negative publicity, 458
packaging, 343
Singapore marketing, 205–206
sponsorship of Beijing
Olympics, 494
Vitango, 55
Code of ethics, 558
Coffee
affect of marketing on
consumption, 139
fair trade, 142–143
Colgate-Palmolive
antitrust issues in Brazil, 164
product innovation
strategy, 351
Collaboration, 518
Collaborative agreements, 307
Collectivist cultures, 127, 130
Color, associations with, 115
Combination branding, 333
Combustion Engineering, 8
Commercial Fan Moteur (CFM)
International, 312

Committee of Professional
Agriculture Organizations and
the General Confederation of
Agricultural Cooperatives
(COPA-COGECA), 81
Common Agricultural Policy
(CAP), 264
Common external tariffs (CETs), 79
Common market, 80
Common Market of the South
(Mercosur), 87, 89
Common-law country, 155–156
Communication
advertising. See Advertising
affect of improvements on global
marketing, 26
American communication
styles, 123
direct marketing, 487–493
global media decisions,
454–457
integrated marketing
communications (IMC), 434
language and, 118–122
personal selling. See Personal
selling
product placement, 495–498
public relations and publicity,
457–463
sales promotion, 469–476
Companion products, 366–367
Comparability, 213
Comparative analysis of research
data, 211–212
Compensation trading, 392
Competition
effect of competitive behavior on
pricing, 380
five forces model, 503
global competition, 518–520
hypercompetition, 526–531
influencing forces, 503–507
positioning, 249–250
potential competition and
targeting, 239–240
rivalry among competitors, 507
Competitive advantage, 6–9, 508
current issues in, 525–530
flagship firm, 512–515
global competition, 518–520
global, 525
national. See National
competitive advantage
research on, 530–531
strategic intent, 515–518
strategies for creating, 508–512

Incoterms (International Commercial Terms), 370–371
India
  auto exports, 269
  call centers, 281, 283
  Coca-Cola, 47
  Coca-Cola/PepsiCo negative publicity, 458
  economy, 51
  McDonald's, 35–36
  media environment, 456
  population segmentation, 229
  power distribution system, 56
  pricing of Reeboks, 377–378
  retail sector, 415
  segment size and growth potential, 238
  Thermax product innovation strategy, 351
  Wal-Mart, 152
Individualist cultures, 127, 130
Industrial product marketing in Latin America, 500–501
Inflation, 376–378
Infomercials, 491–492
Information revolution, affect on global marketing, 25–26
Information systems
  management information system (MIS), 185
  marketing information system as a strategic asset, 214
  subject categories for global marketing information system, 195
Information technology (IT), 185–190
  Ireland, 59
Information utility, 399
Innovation, 350
  characteristics of innovations, 135
  continuous, 354
  diffusion of innovations in Pacific Rim countries, 136–137
  discontinuous, 353
  dynamically continuous, 353
  in global retailing, 420–421
Innovator's dilemma, 574
Integrated circuit (IC), 570
Integrated marketing communications (IMC), 434
Intel, Advanced Micro Devices (AMD) antitrust suit against, 168
Intellectual property, 158–163

Interactive television (ITV), 491–492
Intermodal transportation, 427
Internal Revenue Code Section 482, 397
International Chamber of Commerce (ICC), 175
International Convention for the Protection of Industrial Property, 161
International Court of Justice (ICJ), 154
International finance, 65–66
  economic exposure, 67
  exchange rate exposure, 67–68
  purchasing power parity (PPP), 66
International law, 154–157
  common law vs. civil law, 155–156
  Islamic law, 156–157
International Monetary Fund, Balance of Payments Statistics Yearbook, 62
International products/brands, 331
International Union for the Protection of Literary and Artistic Property, 162
Internet, 570
  advertising, 579
  Ask.com, 595
  broadband, 583–584
  domain names, 580
  eBay in Asia, 593
  e-commerce, 576–579
  evolution of, 570–571
  gambling, 183
  gaming, 584
  phone service, 588–590
  privacy, 582
  types of Web sites, 577
  Web sites design and implementation, 579–583
  wireless, 585–586
Internet Corporation for Assigned Names and Numbers (Icann), 571
Internet Governance Forum (IGF), 572
Intranet, 186
Inventory management, 423
Investment, 297–306
  equity stake, 301–306
  foreign direct investment (FDI), 297
  joint ventures, 298–301

iPod, 589
Iraq war, 100
Ireland, information technology, 59
Iridium satellite telephone system, 201–202
Islamic law, 156–157
  Denmark-Middle East clash, 110, 130
IT (information technology), 185–190
ITOCHU Corporation, leadership, 538
iTunes Music Store, 577
ITV (interactive television), 491–492

J
Jaguar, acquisition by Ford, 323–324
Japan
  7-Eleven, 420–421
  American market gains by Japanese automakers in the 1980s, 5
  Barbie, 144
  Blockbuster Video, 206
  Coca-Cola brands, 330
  cooperative strategies (keiretsu), 315–318
  eBay, 593
  Fair Trade Commission, 164
  global strategic partnership with Boeing, 312–314
  Good Housekeeping magazine, 119
  Harley-Davidson, 245–246
  IKEA success, 513
  konbini, 581
  L'Oréal, 201
  lean production, 553–556
  marketing in Asia-Pacific region, 92–93
  Ministry for International Trade and Industry (MITI), 263
  transit advertising, 493
  Yahoo! Japan, 593
  yen vs. dollar, 374
JCDecaux, 493
JCPenney, international retail expansion, 415–416
Johnson & Johnson, credos, 558, 567
Joint ventures, 298–301
Jurisdiction, 157–158

K

Keiretsu, 315–318
 digital keiretsu, 319
KFC, 114
Kodak
 convergence, 573
 search for competitive
  advantage in 21st century,
  533–534
 trade dispute with Fuji Photo
  Film, 158
Konbini, 581
Kyocera, 406

L

L/C (letter of credit), 277
L'Oréal
 acquisition of Body Shop, 250
 Japan, 201
 targeting of emerging middle
  class, 220, 223
Labeling, 343–344
Language, and communication,
  118–122
 Citibank in China, 450
 e-commerce, 581
 McDonald's in China, 449
Latent market, 200
Latin America
 Barbie, 144
 Free Trade Area of the Americas
  (FTAA), 90, 108
 industrial product marketing,
  500–501
 market research, 205
 PepsiCo Numeromania
  contest, 470
 regional market, 84–90
Law of one price, 363
Laws. See Legal environment
LDCs (least-developed
  countries), 52
 marketing opportunities in,
  53–56
Leadership, 536–538
 core competence, 540–541
 nationality of top management,
  538–540
Lean production, 553–556
Least-developed countries
  (LDCs), 52
 marketing opportunities in,
  53–56
Legal environment
 antitrust, 147, 164–168
 bribery and corruption, 169–173

conflict resolution/dispute
  settlement, 173–176
European Commission ruling
  against Microsoft, 146,
  151, 166
highest lawyers per capita, 173
intellectual property, 158–163
international law, 154–157
Internet gambling, 183
jurisdiction, 157–158
licensing and trade secrets,
  167, 169
litigation, 173–176
Sun Microsystems vs. Microsoft
  lawsuit, 146, 151
LEGO Company, competitive
  advantage, 534–535
Lenovo Group, generating
  publicity through
  sponsorship, 468–469, 472
Leo Burnett Worldwide, 347
Letter of credit (L/C), 277
Leverage, 28–30
 experience transfers, 29
 global strategy, 30
 resource utilization, 30
 scale economics, 29
Levi Strauss, gender segmentation,
  230, 232
LG Electronics, 4
Licensing, 167, 169, 293–297
 contract manufacturing, 295–296
 franchising, 296–297
Line extensions, 354
Linux, 582–583
Litigation, 173–176
Local consumer culture
  positioning (LCCP), 253
Local product/brand, 330–331
 versus global, 337–341
Localized/adaptation approach to
  marketing, 21
Logistics, 421–423
Logistics management, 428
Logistics of sourcing, 284
Long-term orientation
  (LTO), 128
Loose bricks, 517
Low-context culture, 125–126
Lower-middle-income
  countries, 52
Low-income countries, 50–51
LVMH (Moët Hennessy-Louis
  Vuitton)
 Louis Vuitton counterfeits,
  162, 511

luxury goods marketing,
  394–396
operating profit from Louis
  Vuitton, 511

M

M&M'S color promotion, 470
Maastricht Treaty, 96
Madrid Protocol, 161
Major League Soccer (MLS), 6
Management
 myopia, 31
 view on outsourcing, 282
Management information system
  (MIS), 185
Management orientations, 17–23
 ethnocentric, 19–20
 geocentric, 22–23
 polycentric, 20–21
 regiocentric, 21
Manufacturer's export agent
  (MEA), 274
Market capitalism, 45
Market development strategy, 4
Market entry strategies, 292–293
 investment, 297–306
 licensing, 293–297
 strategic partnerships. See
  Global strategic
  partnerships (GSPs)
Market expansion strategy,
  320–321
Market holding strategy, 375
Market penetration pricing
  strategy, 365
Market research
 analysis of data, 208–212
 assessment of research
  value, 198
 choice of unit of analysis, 196
 data collection, 199–202
 definition of, 192
 design of research, 198–207
 examination of data availability,
  196–198
 formal market research, 192–195
 global market research, 192–193
 headquarters control of, 213–214
 identification of information
  requirement, 195
 international marketing research
  process, 194
 Latin America, 205
 marketing information system
  as a strategic asset, 214
 peoplemeter, 203–204

Multilateral trade agreements, 24
Multinational company, 21
Multisegment targeting, 246

N

NAFTA. *See* North American Free
     Trade Agreement
Napoleon's code of 1804, 157
National advantage, 520
National competitive advantage
     chance, 524–525
     demand conditions, 521–522
     factor conditions, 520–521
     firm strategy, structure, and
          rivalry, 523–524
     government, 525
     related and supporting
          industries, 522
National Football League (NFL)
     Europe, 6
Nationality of top management,
     538–540
Nationalization, 153
Nation-states, and sovereignty,
     147–148
Negotiated transfer prices, 388
Nestlé, 7
     benefit segmentation,
          234–235
     competitors in Brazil, 57
     currency exposure, 67
     direct mail in Asia, 489
     distribution in Brazil, 402
     global branding, 334
     international packaging
          teams, 343
     PowerGel, 205
     Pure Life bottled water in
          Pakistan, 55
     telephone research, 190
New products
     development, 354–355
     identifying, 353–354
     new-product departments,
          355–356
     testing of, 356
Newly industrializing economies
     (NIEs), 53
Newspaper sales in India, 456
NFL (National Football League)
     Europe, 6
NGOs (nongovernmental
     organizations), 557
Nielsen Media Research, 193
     peoplemeter, 203–204
     video gamer research, 208

Nike
     defense of labor practices and
          policies, 460–461
     factory working conditions,
          289–290
     gender segmentation, 230
     international advertising, 450
     negative publicity, 458
Nintendo, video game console
     wars, 359–360
Nokia, 574
     hypothetical market research
          scale, 208–209
     image and advocacy
          advertising, 459
     leadership, 539, 541
     psychographic segmentation,
          230–231
Nongovernmental organizations
     (NGOs), 31, 557
Nontariff barriers (NTBs), 32, 267
Normal trade relations (NTR),
     270–271
North America
     Free Trade Area of the Americas
          (FTAA), 108–109
     regional market, 80–84
North American Free Trade
     Agreement (NAFTA), 21, 24,
     82–83
     income and population of
          members, 82
     map of countries, 83
     Mexican currency crisis, 61
"Not invented here" (NIH)
     syndrome, 352
Novartis, 26
NTBs (nontariff barriers), 32, 267
NTR (normal trade relations),
     270, 271
Nucor minimills, 333

O

Observation, as data collection
     method, 203–204
OECD (Organization for Economic
     Cooperation and
     Development), 58–59
     antibribery convention, 172
Offset, 391–392
Omnicom Group, 443
One Laptop Per Child, 55, 56
One-to-one marketing, 487
Open source software, 582–583
Operating system (OS)
     software, 570

OPIC, 151
Option, 68
Order processing, 423
Organic growth, 418
Organization, 541–545
     geographical and product
          division structures, 547–548
     international division structure,
          545–546
     lean production, 553–556
     matrix design, 549–553
     regional management centers,
          546–547
Organization for Economic
     Cooperation and
     Development (OECD), 58–59
Organizing for global marketing,
     541. *See also* Organization
Outdoor advertising, 492–493
Outlet malls, 414
Outlet stores, 414
Outsourcing, 280. *See also*
     Sourcing
     management view on, 282

P

Packaging, 342–345
     aesthetics, 344–345
     labeling, 343–344
Paid search advertising, 579
Parallel importing, 383
Parallel translations, 203
Pareto's Law, 233
Paris Union, 161
Parker Pen, 31
Partnerships. *See* Global strategic
     partnerships (GSPs)
Patagonia, corporate social
     responsibility, 561
Patent Cooperation Treaty (PCT),
     The, 162
Patents, 158–163
Patterns of international
     organizational
     development, 545
     geographical and product
          division structures, 547–548
     international division structure,
          545–546
     matrix design, 549–551, 553
     regional management centers,
          546–547
PC (personal computer), 570
Peer-to-peer (p-to-p), 401
Penetration pricing, 365–366
Peoplemeter, 203–204

PepsiCo
leadership, 541
negative publicity, 458
Numeromania contest (Latin America), 470
publicity for new blue can, 460
Persian Gulf War, 100
Personal computer (PC), 570
Personal interviews, 203
Personal selling, 476–478
nationality of sales force, 483–486
Strategic/Consultative Selling Model, 478–483
Personal selling philosophy, 478
Petróleos de Venezuela S.A. (PDVSA), 53
Pharmaceutical industry, product development costs, 26–27
Phasing, 122
Philip Morris, 152
Philips Electronics, 25
Phones
cell phone cameras, 573–574
Internet phone service, 588–590
Iridium satellite telephone system, 201–202
mobile commerce (m-commerce), 585
mobile gaming, 588
Nestlé telephone research, 190
smart phones, 586–588
Physical distribution, 398, 421–423
inventory management, 423
logistics management, 428
order processing, 423
transportation, 424–428
warehousing, 424
Piggyback marketing, 405
Pirated movies, 362–363, 365
Place utility, 399
Platform, 354
Political environment, 147–154
nation-states and sovereignty, 147–148
risk, 148–154
sourcing, 284–285
Political risk, 148–154
seizure of assets, 153–154
taxes, 151–152
Polycentric orientation, 20–21
Polycentric pricing, 381
PolyGram, 8
Population, segmentation by, 225–229

Porsche
hedging, 67–68
insulation from currency fluctuations, 374
psychographic segmentation, 231
Ports
foreign management of U.S. ports, 425–426
Port of New York, 427
Positioning, 247–253
attribute or benefit, 248
competition, 249–250
foreign consumer culture positioning (FCCP), 248, 253
global consumer culture positioning (GCCP), 250–253
local consumer culture positioning (LCCP), 253
quality and price, 248
use or user, 248
Postindustrial countries, 57
Power distance, 127, 130
Prada, e-commerce, 579
Preferential tariff, 270
Preferential trade agreements, 78–80
Presentation plan, 480
Presentation strategy, 480
Price discrimination, 386
Price escalation, 372
Price fixing, 387–388
Price transparency, 375
Pricing, 362–364
adaptation/polycentric pricing, 381–382
calculating prices, 368–370
companion products, 366–367
competitive behavior, 380
cost-plus pricing, 368–370, 372–373
countertrade, 389–392
currency fluctuations, 373–376
dumping, 385–387
export price escalation, 368–369
extension/ethnocentric pricing policy, 381
financial objectives, 364–365
geocentric pricing, 382
global pricing policy alternatives, 380–383
governmental policies and regulations, 378–379
gray market goods, 383–385
inflation, 376–378

luxury goods marketing, 394–396
market skimming, 364–365
nonfinancial objectives, 365–366
penetration pricing, 365–366
sourcing as strategic pricing tool, 380
target costing, 367–368
terms of the sale, 370–373
transfer pricing, 388–389
U.S. exports to Europe, 375
Primary data, 199
Privacy, and RFID, 432–433
Private international law, 155
Pro forma invoice, 277
Procter & Gamble, 116
benefit segmentation, 235
Internet presence, 578
Organization 2005 plan, 548
shampoo sampling in China, 473
Product (RED), 557
Product adaptation-communication extension, 349
Product division structure, 547–548
Product extension-communication adaptation, 348–349
Product invention, 345
Product markets, United States and EU vs. BRIC, 352
Product placement, 495–498
Product saturation levels, 60
Product strategy, 479
Product transformation, 349
Product/brand matrix, 335
Product/market growth matrix, 4
Product-communication adaptation (dual adaptation), 349–350
Product-communication extension (dual extension), 347
Product-market, 241
Products, 327
brands, 328–329. *See also* Brands
companion products, 366–367
definition of, 327
global, 331–335
global vs. local, 337–341
international, 331
invention and innovation, 350–351
local, 330–331
new products in global marketing, 353–356
packaging, 342–345
types, 327–328
warranties, 345

diffusion theory, 134–137
impact of marketing on culture, 122–125
language and communication, 118–122
marketing implications of social environments, 137–139
religion, 113–114
Software
operating systems, 570
patents, 163
Sony
companion products, 366–367
convergence, 573
leadership, 536–537, 544
PlayStation 3 (PS3)/video game console wars, 359–360
pricing of PlayStation 2 (PS2) and PlayStation 3 (PS3), 366
segmentation, 232
transistor radios, 295, 569
Walkman, 333–334, 366
SonyEricsson, 302
Sourcing, 280–286
as strategic pricing tool, 380
call centers, 280–283
country infrastructure, 284
customer needs, 283
factor costs and conditions, 282–283
foreign exchange rates, 285–286
laptop computers, 368
logistics, 284
management vision, 282
political factors, 284–285
Sourcing decision, 280
South African
Breweries/SABMiller in China, 324–325
South America, Free Trade Area of the Americas (FTAA), 90, 108
South Korea
cooperative strategies (chaebol), 318–319
digital future, 572
information and communications technologies (ICT) access, 568
Southern African Customs Union (SACU), 105
Southern African Development Community (SADC), 105
Sovereignty, 147–148
Soviet Union, economy of former countries, 51
Special economic zones (SEZ), 265

Specialty retailers, 412
Specific duty, 272
Sponsorship, 493–495
Lenovo Group, generating publicity through sponsorship, 468–469, 472
Spotmarket, 65
Spreadsheet, 570
SRC (self-reference criterion), 132–133
SRI International, 230
Stages of market development
high-income countries, 57–59
lower-middle-income countries, 52
low-income countries, 50–51
marketing implications of the stages of development, 60–61
marketing opportunities in LDCs and developing countries, 53–56
The Triad, 60
upper-middle-income countries, 52–53
Stakeholder, 557
Stakeholder analysis, 557
Standardized global marketing, 244–245
Standardized/extension approach to marketing, 19–20
Starbucks, 34
Beijing's Forbidden City, 293
corporate social responsibility, 558
fair trade in coffee, 142–143
sampling, 473
success and challenges, 292, 299
trademark protection in Russia, 161
Stern Pinball, pricing of exports, 375
Strategic alliances, 307. See also Global strategic partnerships (GSPs)
Strategic alternatives in global marketing, 345–347
choosing a strategy, 352
product adaptation-communication extension, 349
product extension-communication adaptation, 348–349
product invention, 350–351
product-communication adaptation (dual adaptation), 349–350

product-communication extension (dual extension), 347
Strategic decision making, 9
Strategic intent, 515–518
Strategic international alliances, 307
Strategic partnerships. See Global strategic partnerships (GSPs)
Strategic/Consultative Selling Model, 478–483
Streaming audio, 584
Streaming media, 584
Streaming video, 584
Subaru 360, 5
Subcultures, 112
Subsidies, 263
Sugar subsidies, 290–291
Sun Microsystems, Microsoft lawsuit, 146, 151
Supercenters, 413
Supermarkets, 412
Supplier bargaining power, 507
Supply chains, 421–423
Support media, 492–493
Survey research, 203
Sustaining technologies, 575
SUVs
market research, 210–211
targeting of U.S. market, 238–239
Swatchmobile, 360
Sweatshops, 288–290
Sweden, government resource ownership, 46–47
Switch trading, 392

T
Tamagotchis, 131
Target costing, 367–368
Targeting, 220, 237–243
automobile industry targeting Generation Y (Gen Y), 255
concentrated global marketing, 245
current segment size and growth potential, 238–239
development of target marketing strategies, 244–245
differentiated global marketing, 246–247
feasibility and compatibility, 240
market selection framework, 240–243
MTV, 256–257
multisegment targeting, 246
potential competition, 239–240
standardized global marketing, 244–245

Tariffs, 265, 270–273
  common external tariffs
    (CETs), 79
  countervailing duties
    (CVDs), 272
  customs duties, 272
  duping, 272
  European tariffs on Asian shoe
    imports, 258, 262
  Harmonized Tariff System
    (HTS), 266, 270, 271
  nontariff barriers (NTBs), 32, 267
  preferential tariff, 270
  single-column tariff, 270
  temporary surcharges, 273
  two-column tariff, 270
  variable import levies, 273
Taxes, 151–152
  corporate taxes and political
    risk, 152
  export tax incentives, 263
  tariffs. See Tariffs
  transfer prices, 388–389
Technology. See also Computers
  digital revolution, 569–571
  disruptive technologies, 574–575
  e-commerce, 576–579
  sustaining technologies, 575
Telefónica, 124
Telematics, 586
Telephones
  cell phone cameras, 573–574
  Internet phone service, 588–590
  Iridium satellite telephone
    system, 201–202
  mobile commerce
    (m-commerce), 585
  mobile gaming, 588
  Nestlé telephone research, 190
  smart phones, 586–588
Teleshopping, 491–492
Television
  direct marketing, 491–493
  European advertising
    regulation, 457
  flat-panel TV sets, 326, 330
  interactive television (ITV),
    491–492
  peoplemeter, 203–204
  product placement, 495–498
Temporary surcharges, 273
Terms of the sale, 370–373
Tesco, expansion of distribution,
    398–400
Testing new products, 356
Theft, video piracy, 362–363, 365

Thermax, product innovation
    strategy, 351
Tiered branding, 333
Timberland Company, The,
    corporate social
    responsibility, 559
Time drafts, 278–279
Time utility, 399
Time-series displacement, 212
Tobacco
  advertising regulation, 446
  WHO Framework Convention
    on Tobacco Controls, 495
Toyota, 14, 16, 22, 23, 28
  Toyota Production System (TPS),
    553–555
Toys "R" Us, 175, 380
Trade
  Central European Free Trade
    Association (CEFTA), 98–99
  fair trade in coffee, 142–143
  free trade agreement. See Free
    trade agreement (FTA)
  Free Trade Area of the Americas
    (FTAA), 90, 108–109
  free trade area. See Free trade
    area (FTA)
  free trade zones (FTZ), 265
  merchandise and services,
    63–65
  most-favored nation status. See
    Trade, normal trade
    relations (NTR)
  normal trade relations (NTR),
    270–271
  preferential trade agreements,
    78–80
  regional markets. See Regional
    markets
Trade and Tariff Act of 1984, 272
Trade deficit, 62
Trade mission, 260
Trade sales promotions, 469
Trade secrets, 167, 169
Trade show, 260
Trade surplus, 62
Trademarks, 158–163
Transaction sites, 577
Transaction value, 271
Transfer pricing, 388–389
Transistor, 569
  transistor radios, 295, 569
Transit advertising, 493
Transnational cyberworld, 44
Transnationality, 23
Transportation, 26, 424–428

Treaties
  Patent Cooperation Treaty
    (PCT), 162
  Treaty of Rome, 177
Triad Power, 60
Triad, The, 60
TRIPs (Agreement on Trade-Related
    Aspects of Intellectual Property
    Rights), 169
Two-column tariff, 270

U

U.S. See United States
Uncertainty avoidance, 127, 130
Uniform resource locator
    (URL), 571
Uniform Trade Secrets Act
    (UTSA), 169
Unilever
  differentiated global
    marketing, 247
  failure of Power, 356
  market research, 191
United Nations
  digital opportunity index, 568
  International Court of Justice
    (ICJ), 154
United Nations Conference on
    International Trade Law
    (UNCITRAL), 175
United States (U.S.)
  Act of State Doctrine, 154
  American Automobile Labeling
    Act, 344
  American communication
    styles, 123
  balance of payments, 62
  BRIC supplier base and
    infrastructure/logistics
    comparison, 422
  Byrd Amendment, 385
  CEO pay, 560
  coupons, 474
  Cuban Liberty and Democratic
    Solidarity Act, 180–182
  dollar vs. yen, 374
  exports, 267
  Federal Trade Commission, 164
  Foreign Corrupt Practices Act
    (FCPA), 170–171
  foreign management of U.S.
    ports, 425–426
  global automakers' targeting of
    U.S. market with SUVs,
    238–239
  import duties, 270